Street by Street

MERSEYSIDE

PLUS ASHTON-IN-MAKERFIELD, CHORLEY, ELLESMERE PORT, NESTON, ORMSKIRK, RUNCORN, SKELMERSDALE, WARRINGTON, WIDNES, WIGAN

Enlarged Areas Birkenhead, Bootle, Liverpool, St Helens, Southport

Ist edition May 2001

© Automobile Association Developments Limited 2001

This product includes map data licensed from Ordnance Survey® with the permission of the Controller of Her Majesty's Stationery Office. © Crown copyright 2000. All rights reserved. Licence No: 399221.

Published by AA Publishing (a trading name of Automobile Association Developments Limited, whose registered office is Norfolk House, Priestley Road, Basingstoke, Hampshire, RG24 9NY. Registered number 1878835).

Mapping produced by the Cartographic Department of The Automobile Association.

A CIP Catalogue record for this book is available from the British Library.

Printed by G. Canale & C. s.p.a., Torino, Italy

The contents of this atlas are believed to be correct at the time of the latest revision. However, the publishers cannot be held responsible for loss occasioned to any person acting or refraining from action as a result of any material in this atlas, nor for any errors, omissions or changes in such material. The publishers would welcome information to correct any errors or omissions and to keep this atlas up to date. Please write to Publishing, The Automobile Association, Fanum House, Basing View, Basingstoke, Hampshire, RG21 4EA.

Ref: MX048

Key to map pages	ii-iii
Key to map symbols	iv-1
Enlarged scale pages	2-21
Street by Street	22-167
Index – towns & villages	168
Index – streets	169-215
Index – featured places	215-222

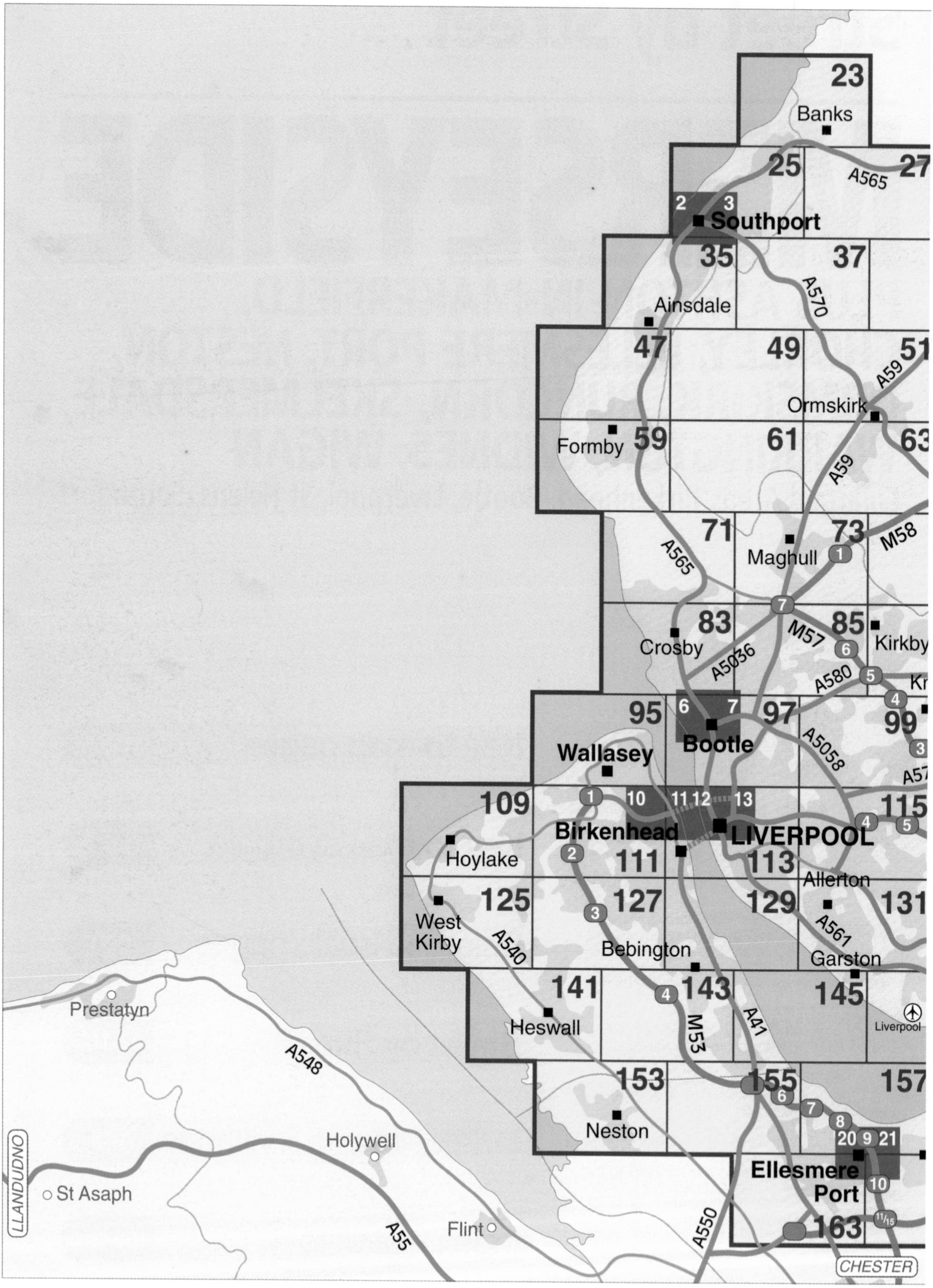

ii

23
Banks

25 A565 **27**

2 3
Southport

35 **37**
Ainsdale A570

47 **49** **51**
A59
Ormskirk

Formby **59** **61** **63**
A59

71 **73** M58
A565 Maghull 1

7

83 **85**
Crosby A5036 M57 6 Kirkby
A580 5
4 Kr

95 6 **7** **97** **99**
Wallasey **Bootle** A5058 3
A57

109 1 **10** 11 12 **13** **115**
Birkenhead **LIVERPOOL** 4
Hoylake 2 **111** **113** 5

125 3 **127** **129** Allerton **131**
West A561
Kirby A540 Bebington Garston

141 4 **143** **145**
Prestatyn Heswall M53 A41 Liverpool
A548

153 **155** **157**
Holywell 6
Neston 7
St Asaph 8
20 9 21
LLANDUDNO **Ellesmere**
Port 10
A55 Flint A550 **163** 11/15

CHESTER

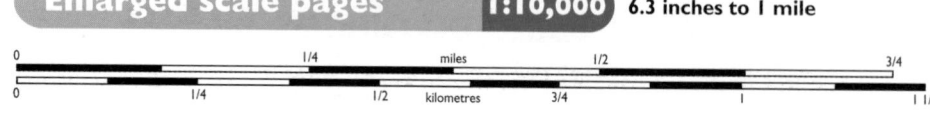

Enlarged scale pages **1:10,000** 6.3 inches to 1 mile

0   1/4   miles   1/2   3/4
0   1/4   1/2   kilometres   3/4   1   1 1/4

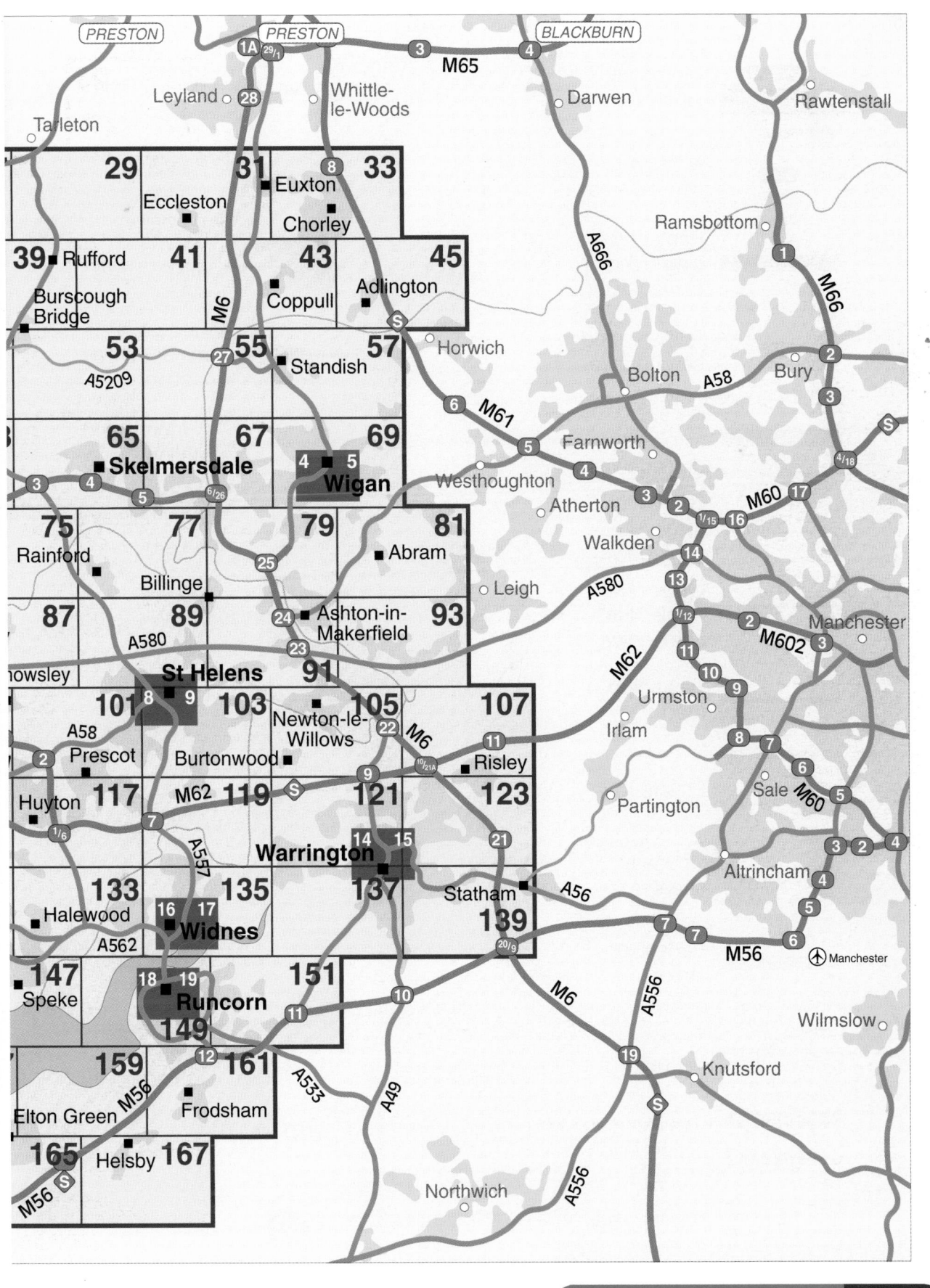

Junction 9	Motorway & junction
Services	Motorway service area
	Primary road single/dual carriageway
Services	Primary road service area
	A road single/dual carriageway
	B road single/dual carriageway
	Other road single/dual carriageway
	Restricted road
	Private road
← ←	One way street
	Pedestrian street
	Track/ footpath
	Road under construction
[- - - - -]	Road tunnel
P	Parking

P+	Park & Ride
	Bus/coach station
	Railway & main railway station
■	Railway & minor railway station
⊖	Underground station
⊖	Light railway & station
+++++++++++	Preserved private railway
LC	Level crossing
•—•—•—•—•	Tramway
--------------	Ferry route
....	Airport runway
—·—·—·—·	Boundaries- borough/ district
˅˅˅˅˅˅˅˅	Mounds
93	Page continuation 1:17,500
7	Page continuation to enlarged scale 1:10,000

	River/canal lake, pier		♿	Toilet with disabled facilities
	Aqueduct lock, weir		⛽	Petrol station
465 ▲ Winter Hill	Peak (with height in metres)		PH	Public house
	Beach		PO	Post Office
	Coniferous woodland		📖	Public library
	Broadleaved woodland		i	Tourist Information Centre
	Mixed woodland		♟	Castle
	Park		🏛	Historic house/ building
	Cemetery		Wakehurst Place NT	National Trust property
	Built-up area		Ⓜ	Museum/ art gallery
	Featured building		†	Church/chapel
	City wall		♛	Country park
A&E	Accident & Emergency hospital		🎭	Theatre/ performing arts
🚻	Toilet		🎥	Cinema

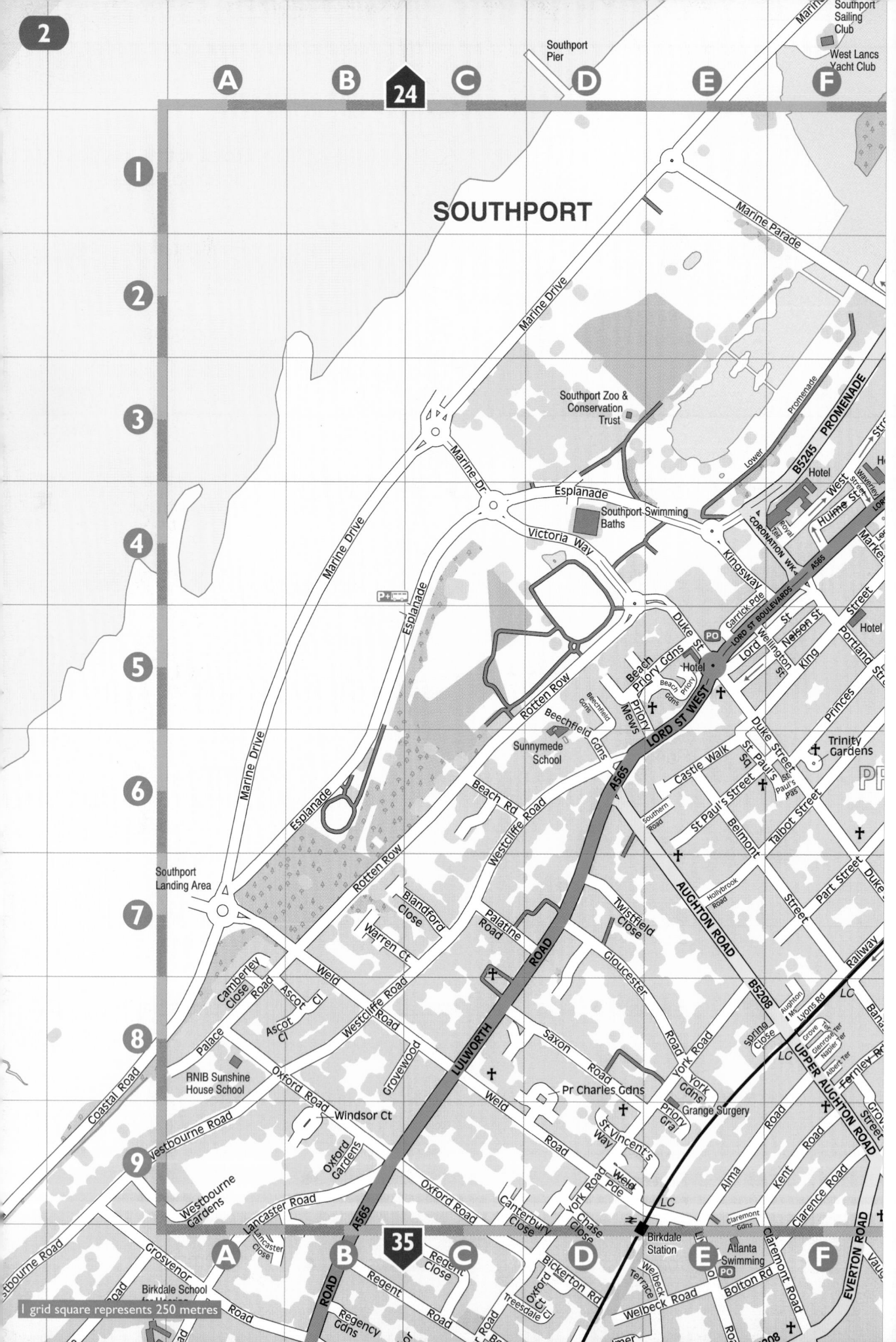

SOUTHPORT

2

24

35

1 grid square represents 250 metres

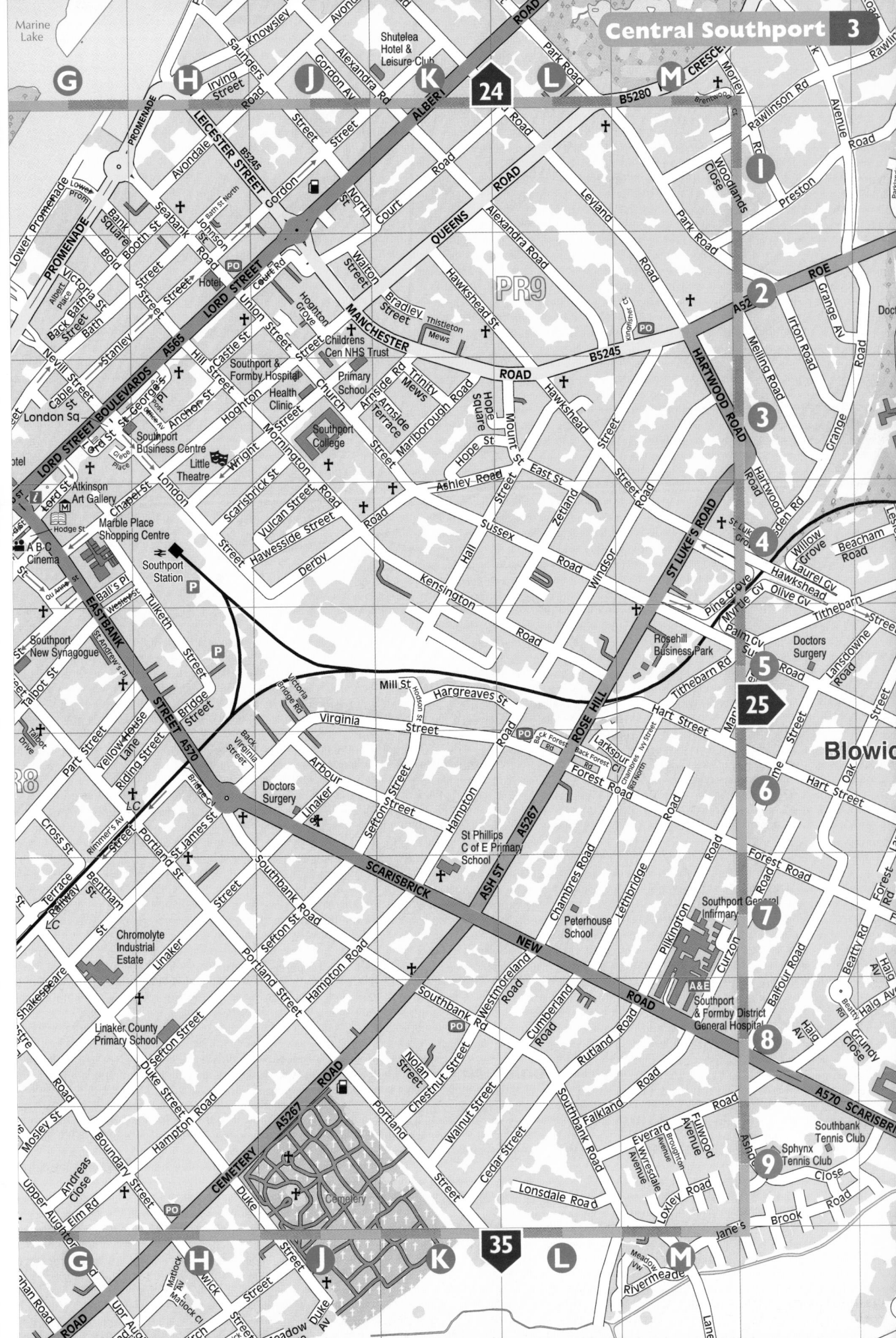

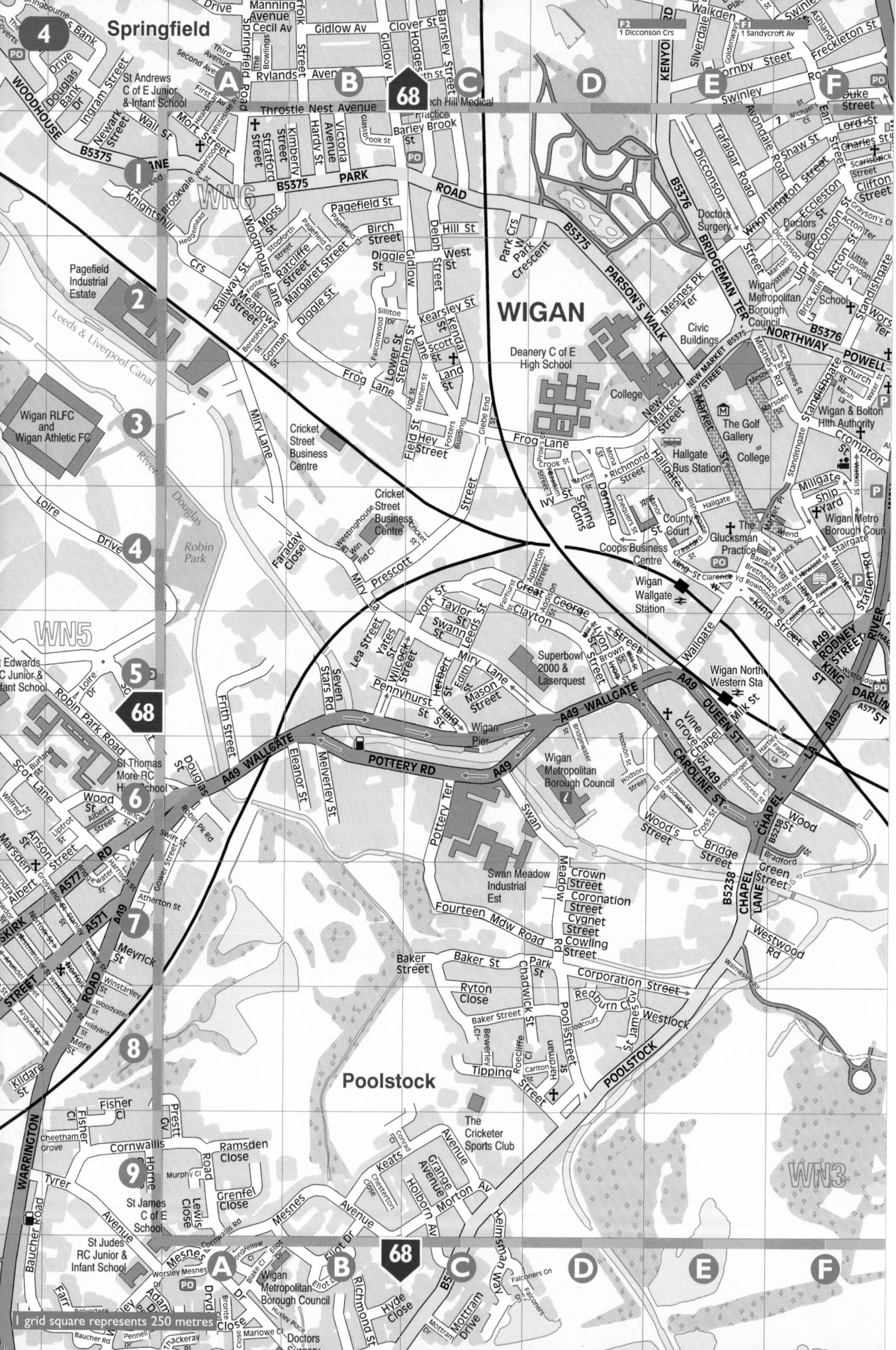

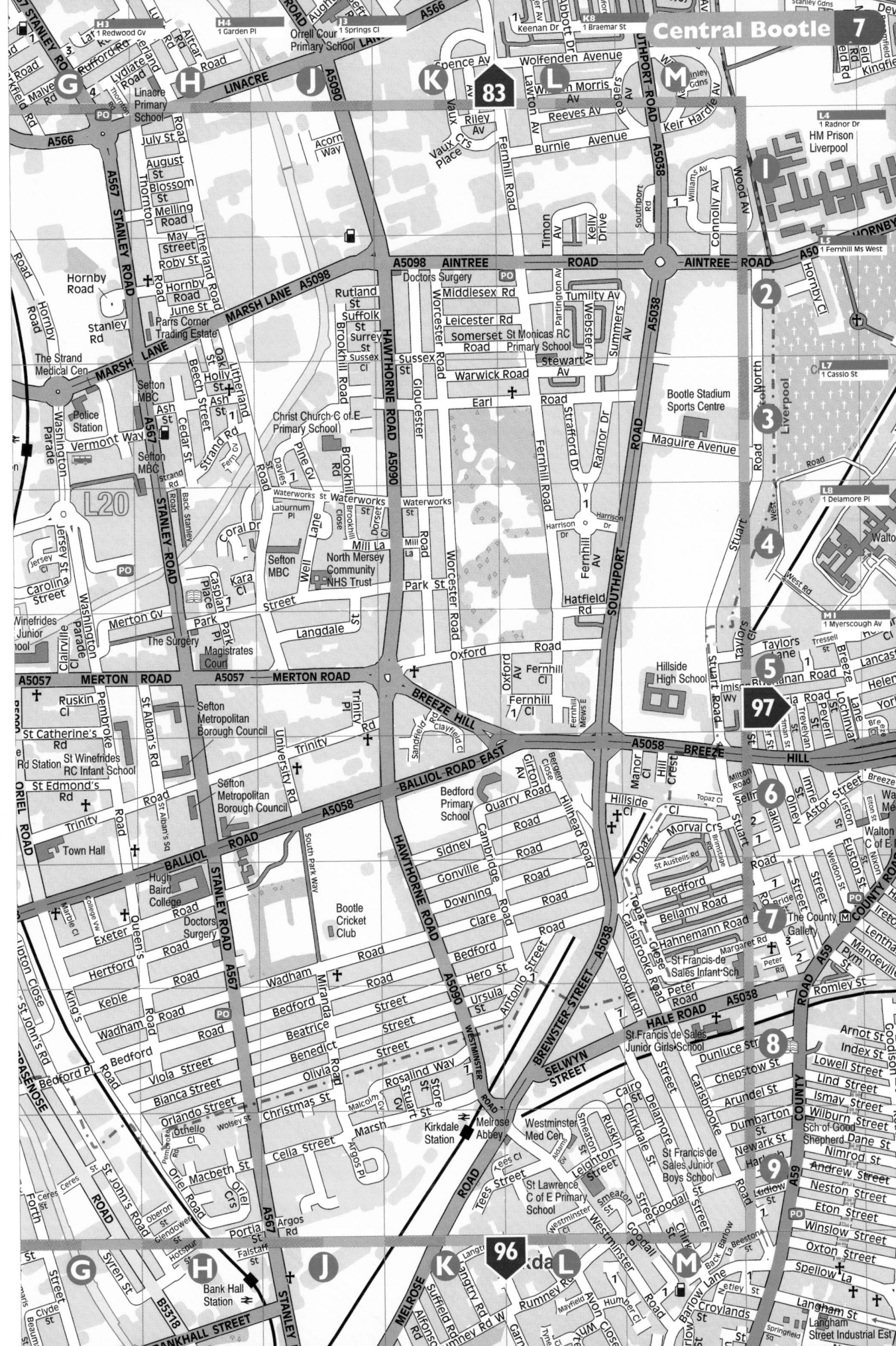

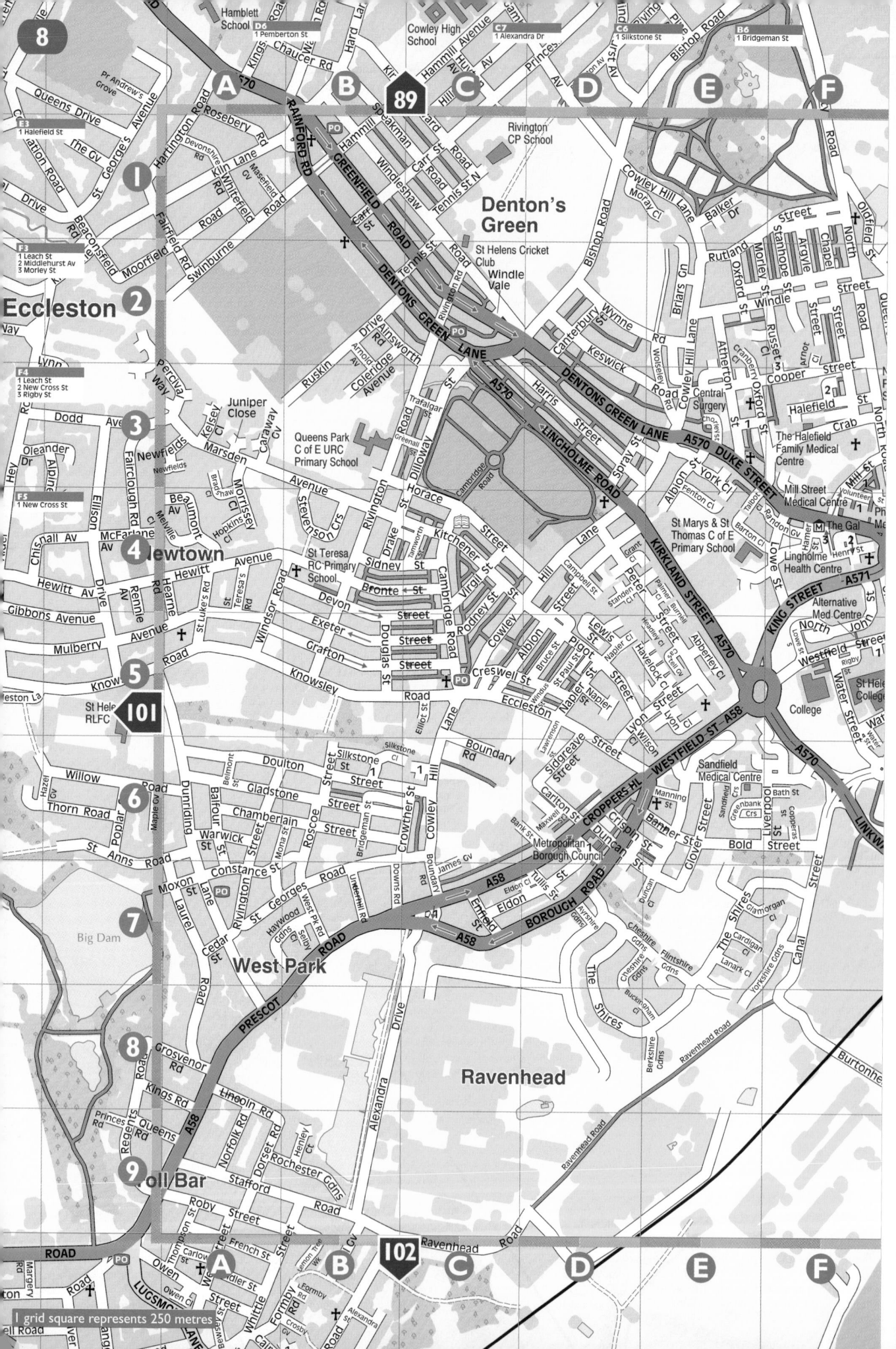

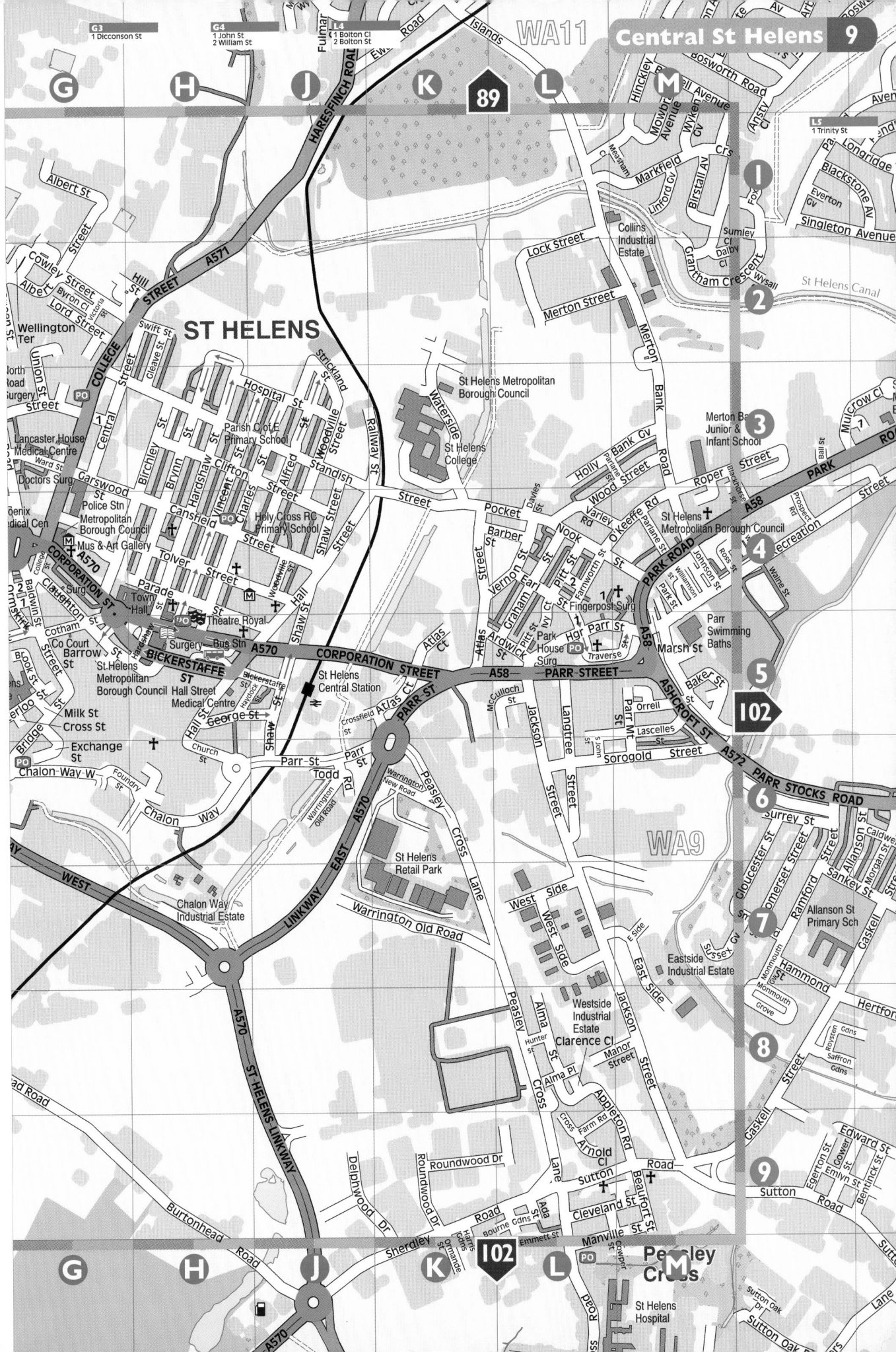

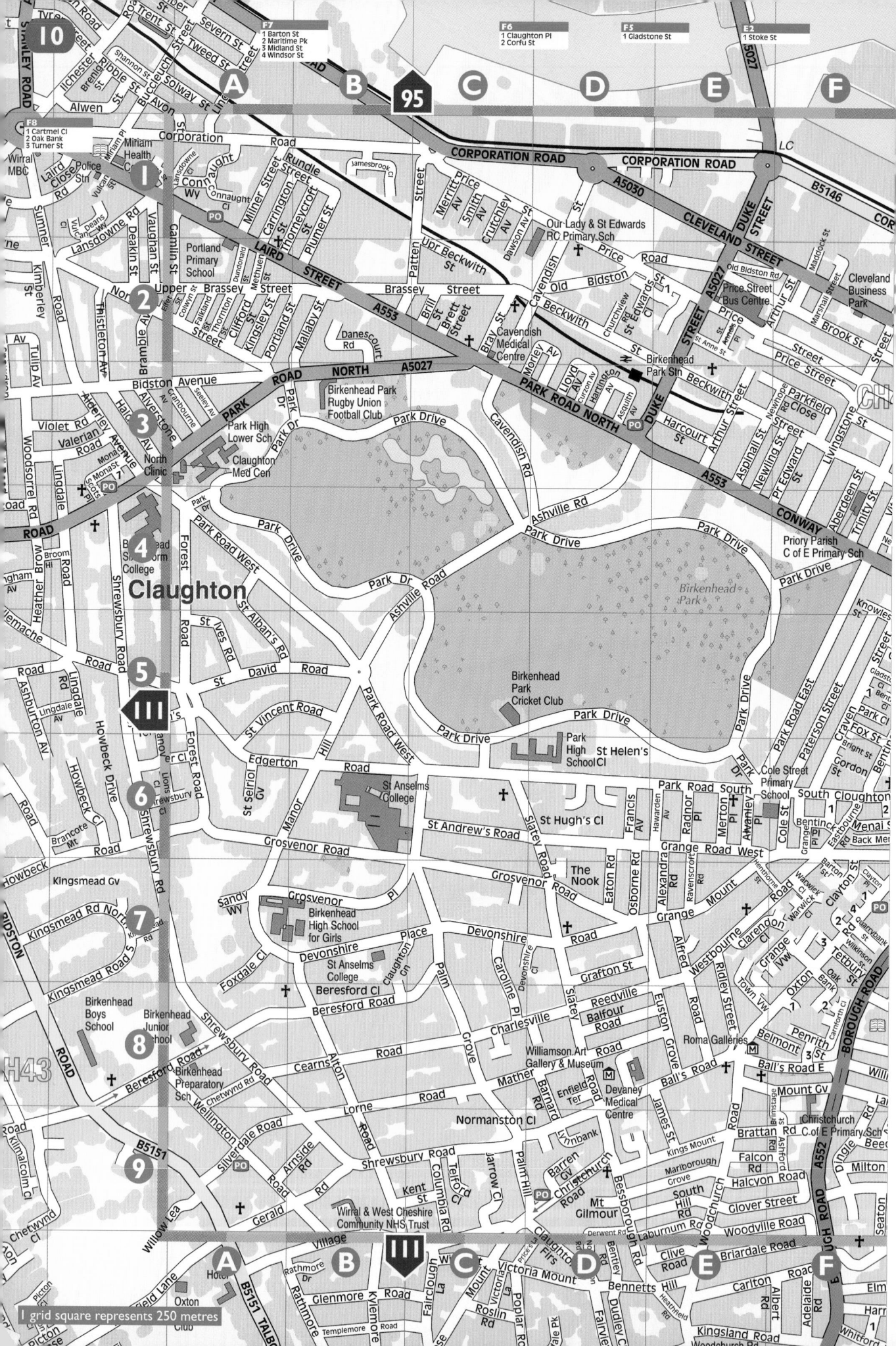

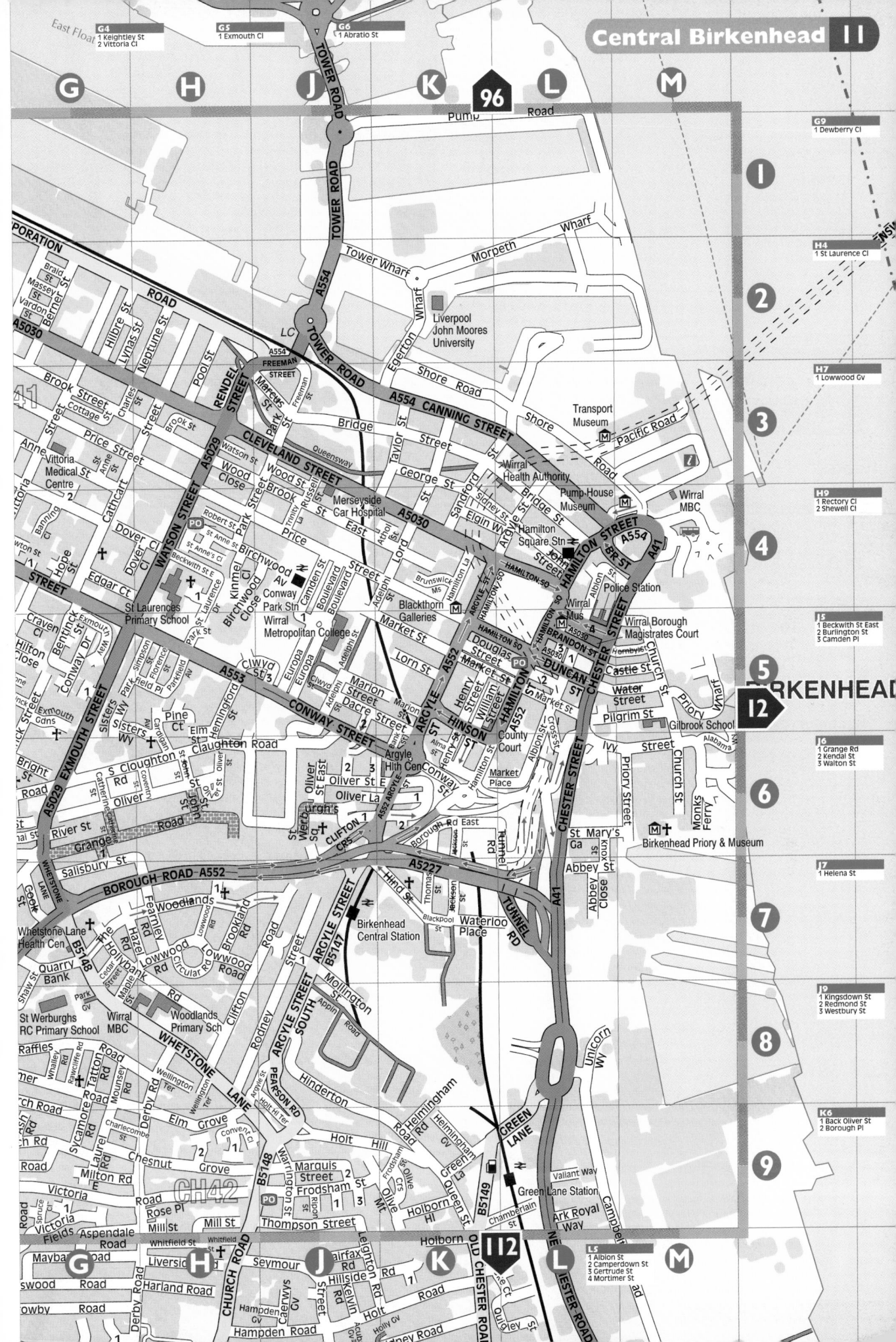

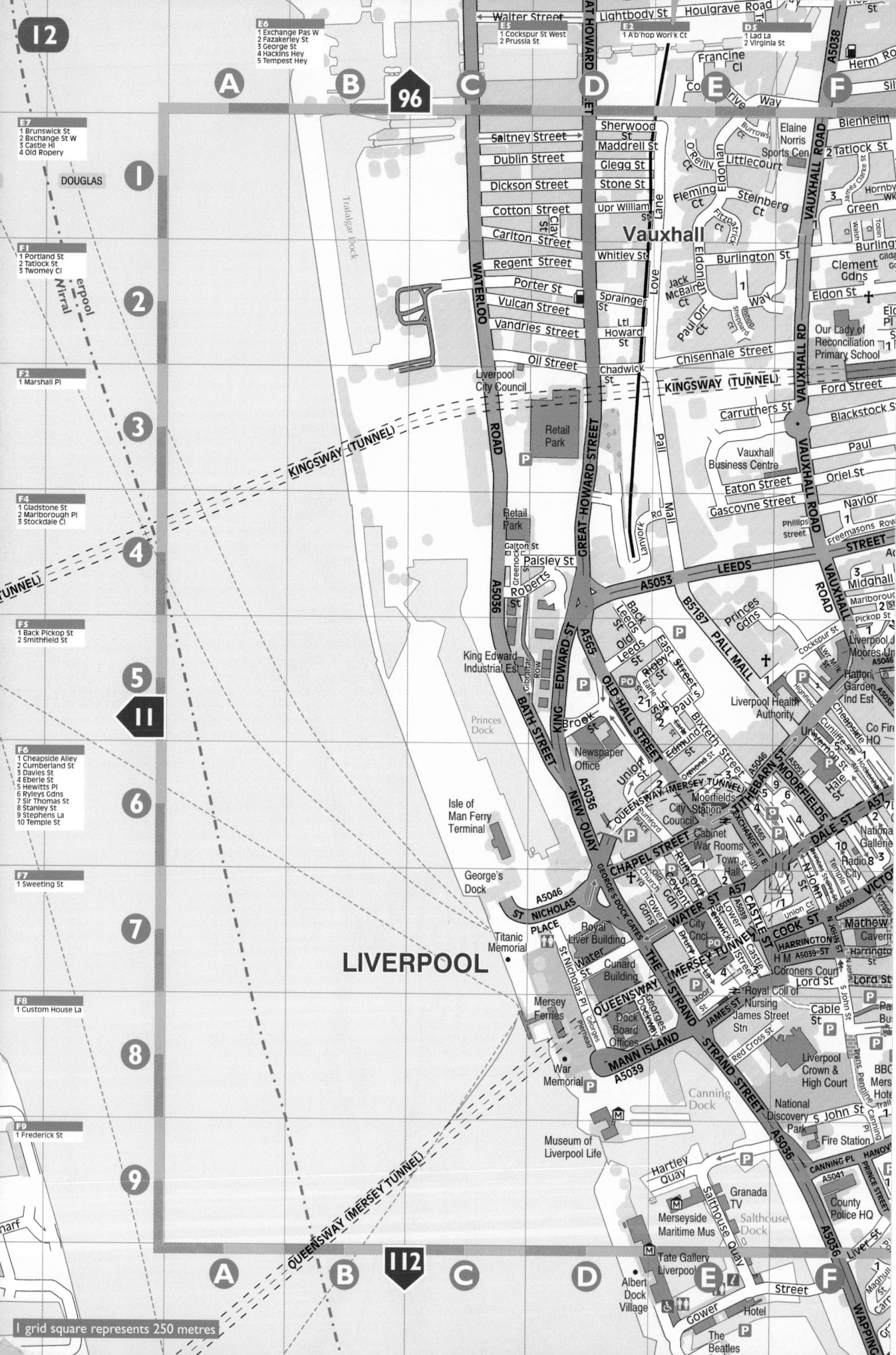

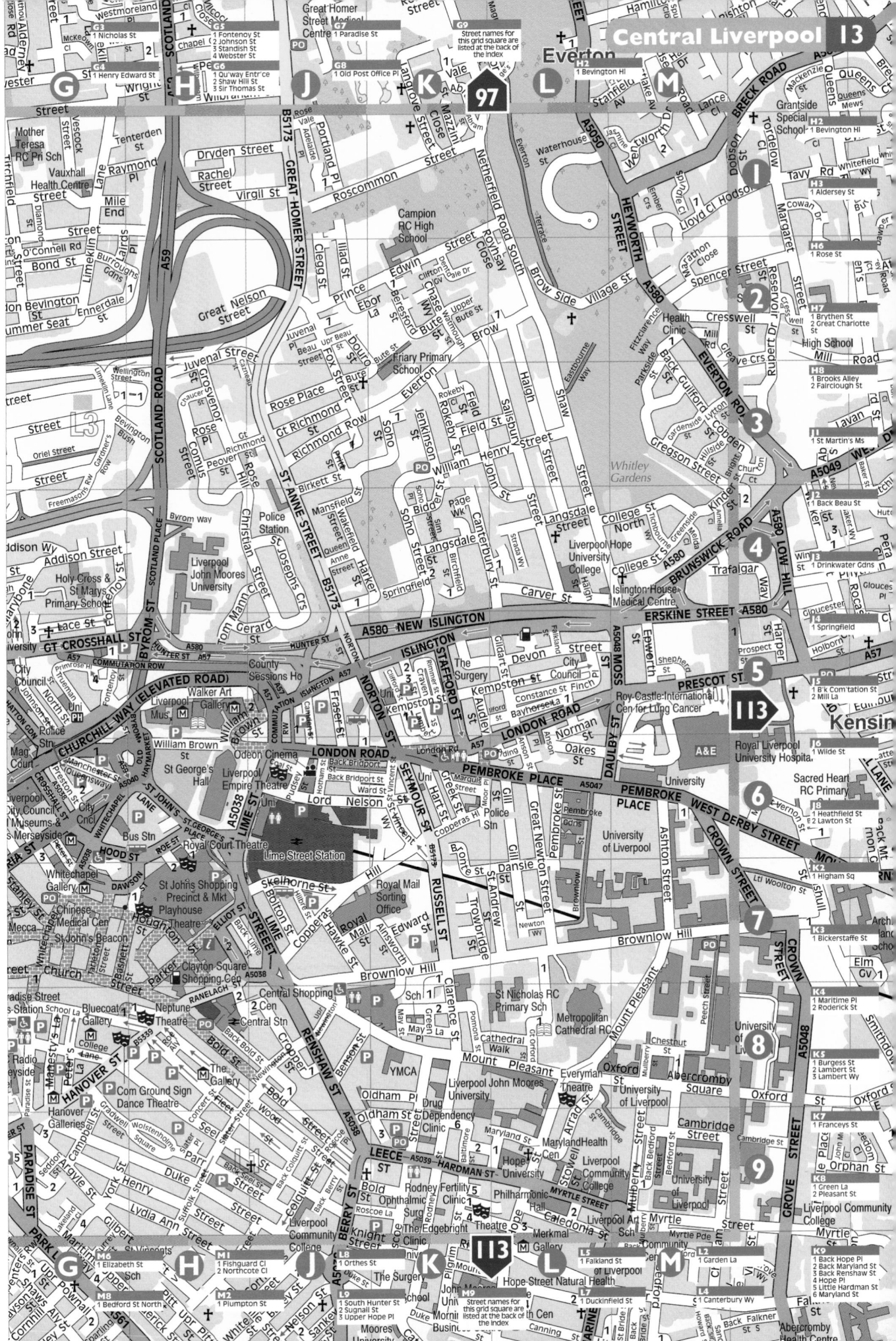

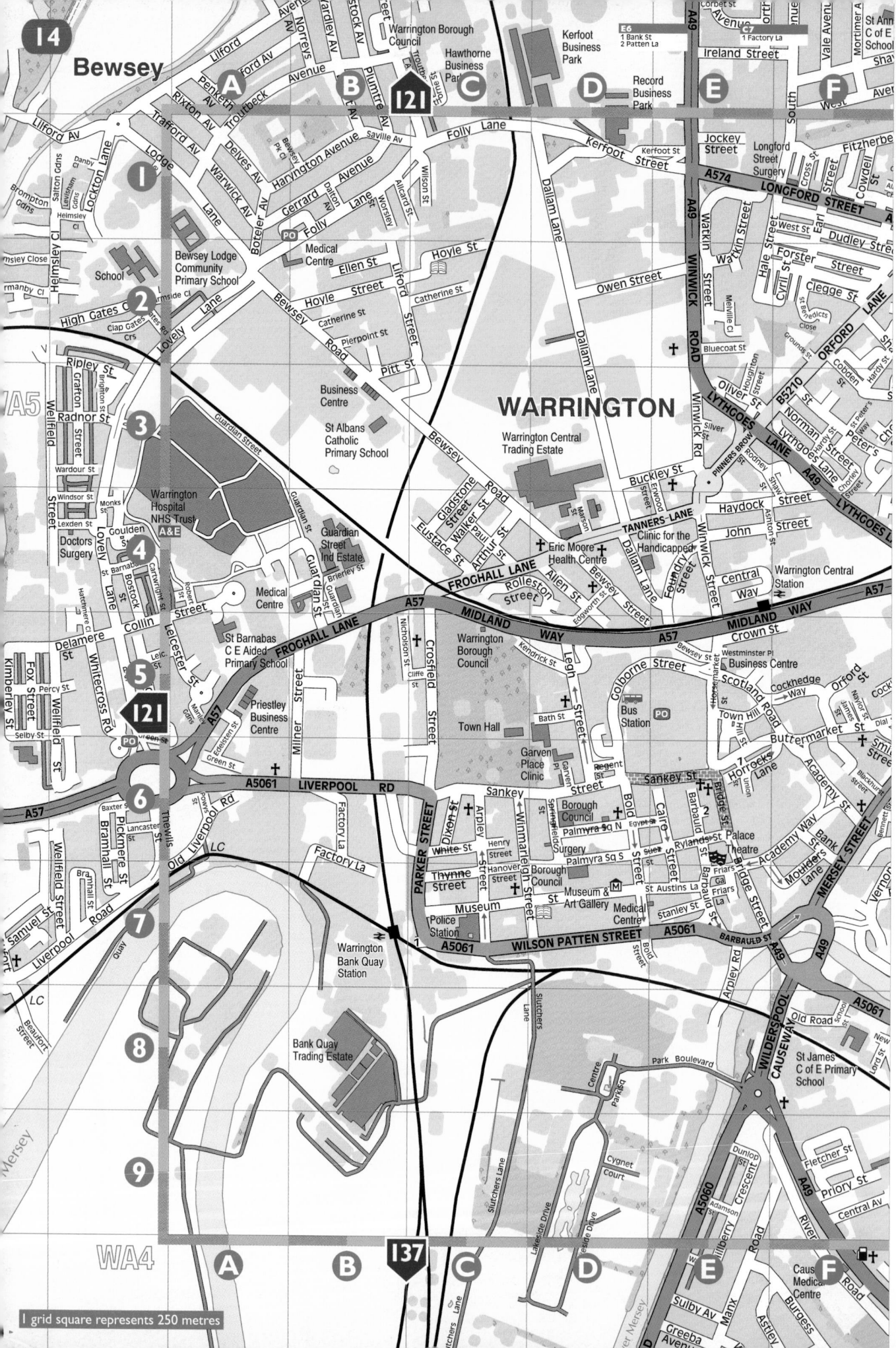

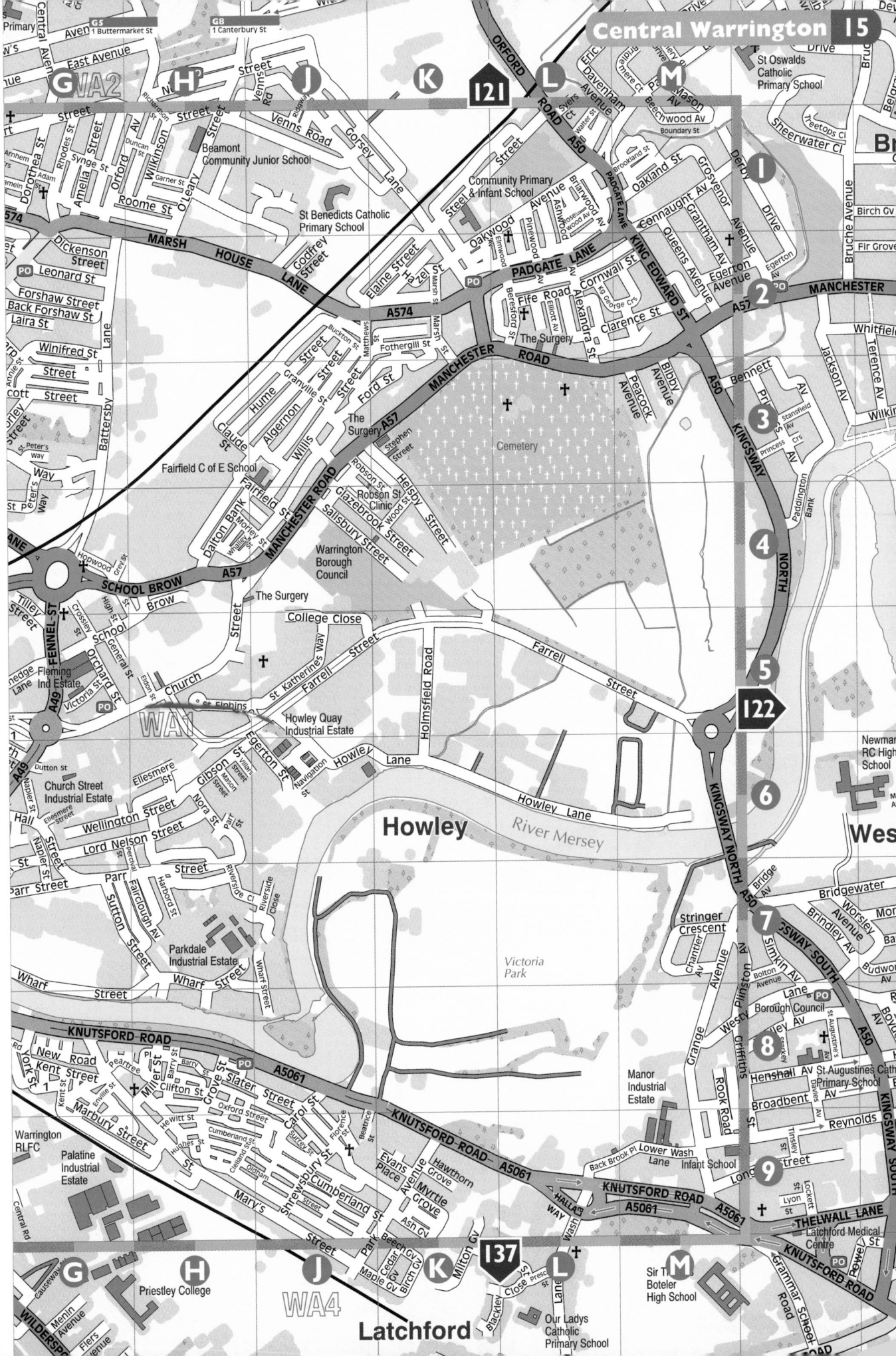

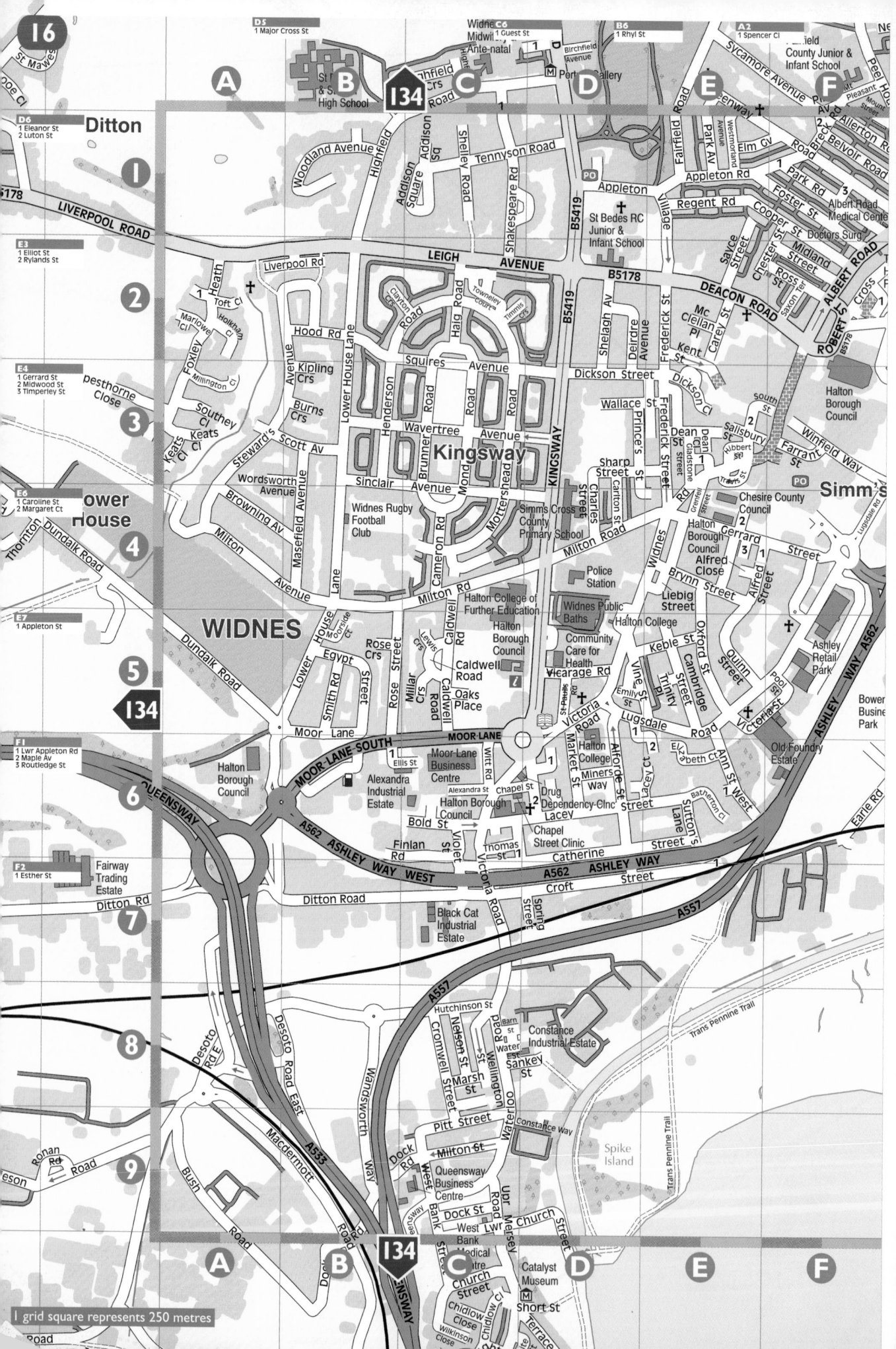

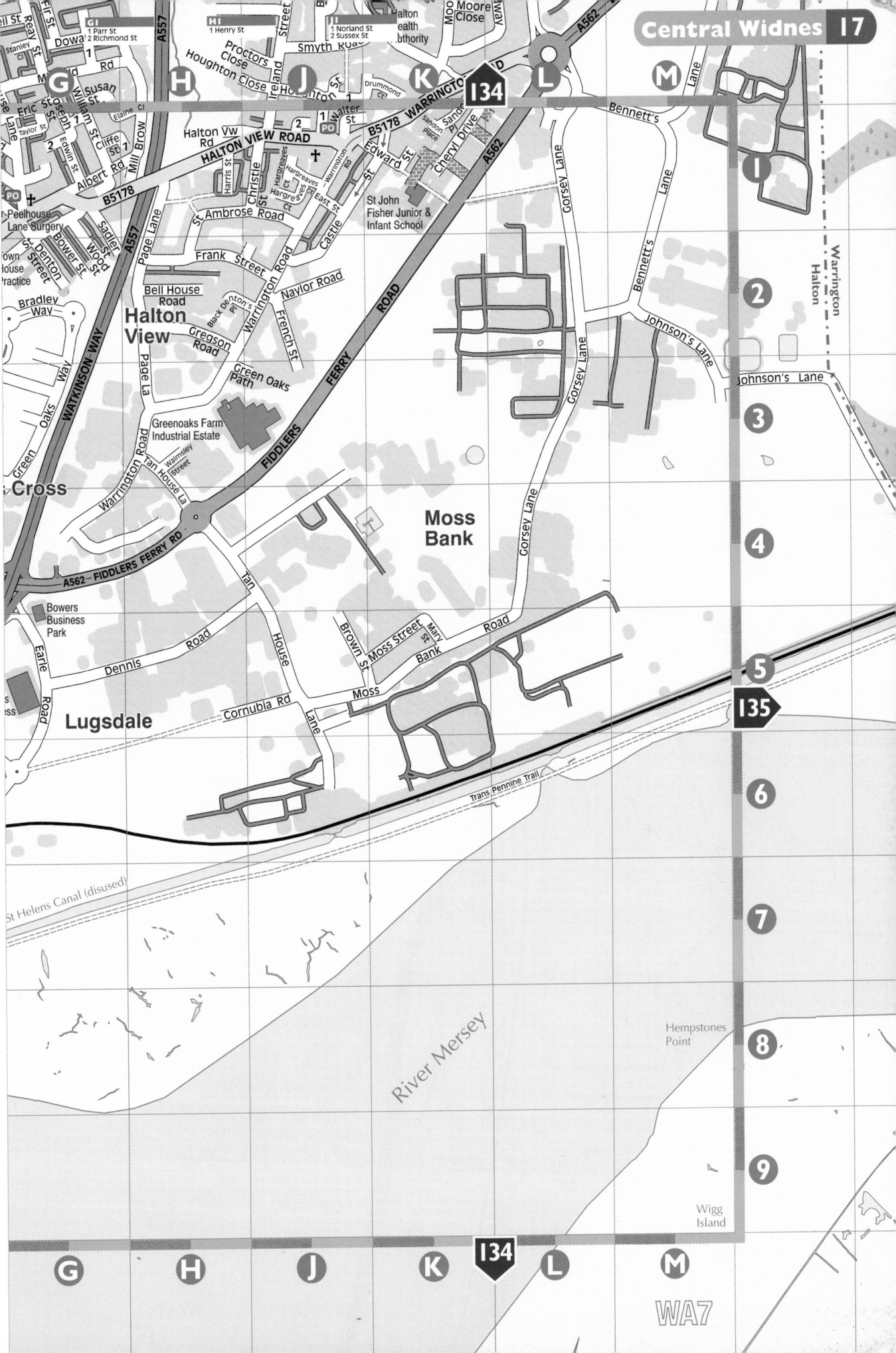

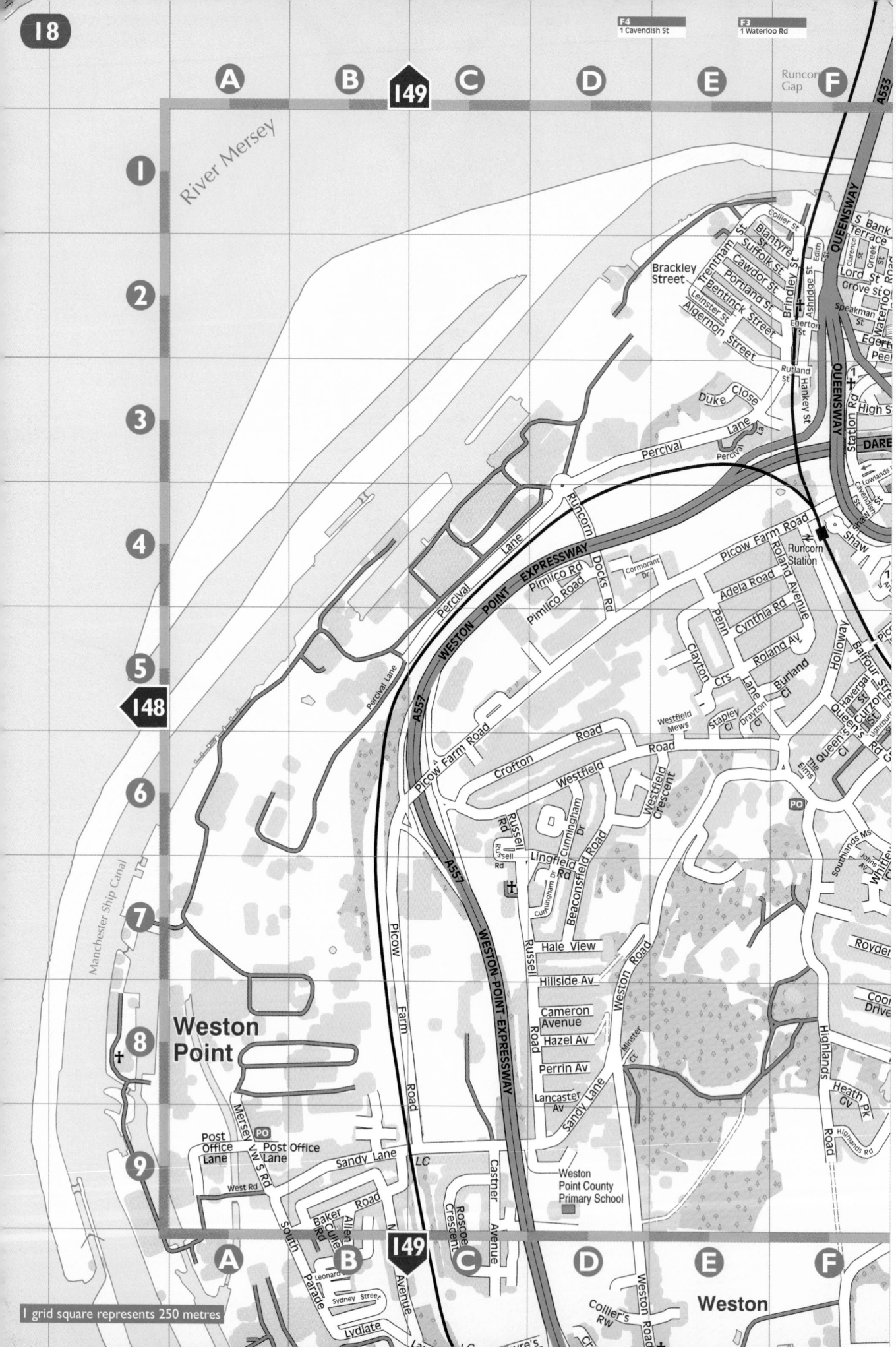

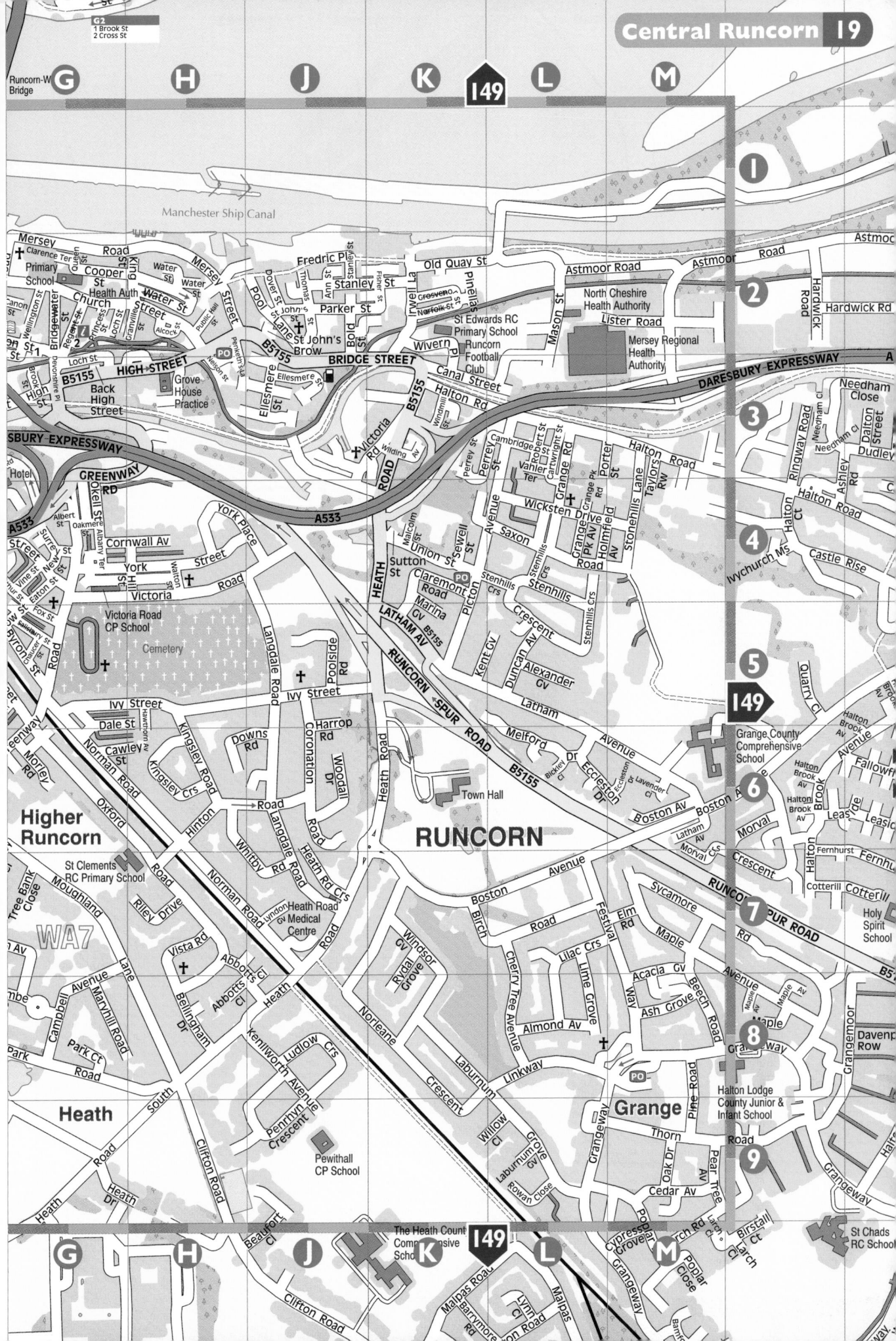

G2
1 Brook St
2 Cross St

Manchester Ship Canal

**Higher
Runcorn**

WA7

Heath

RUNCORN

Grange

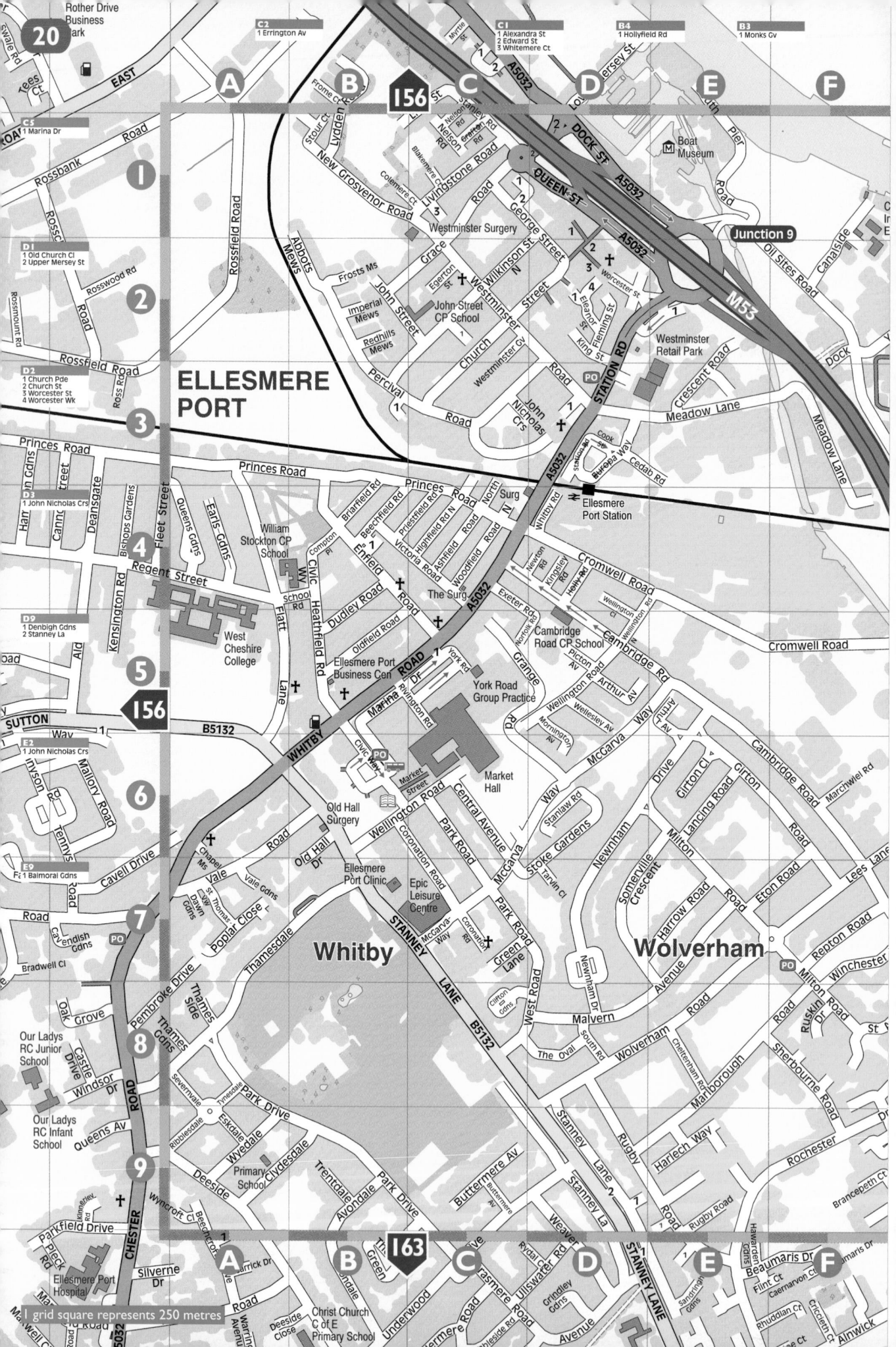

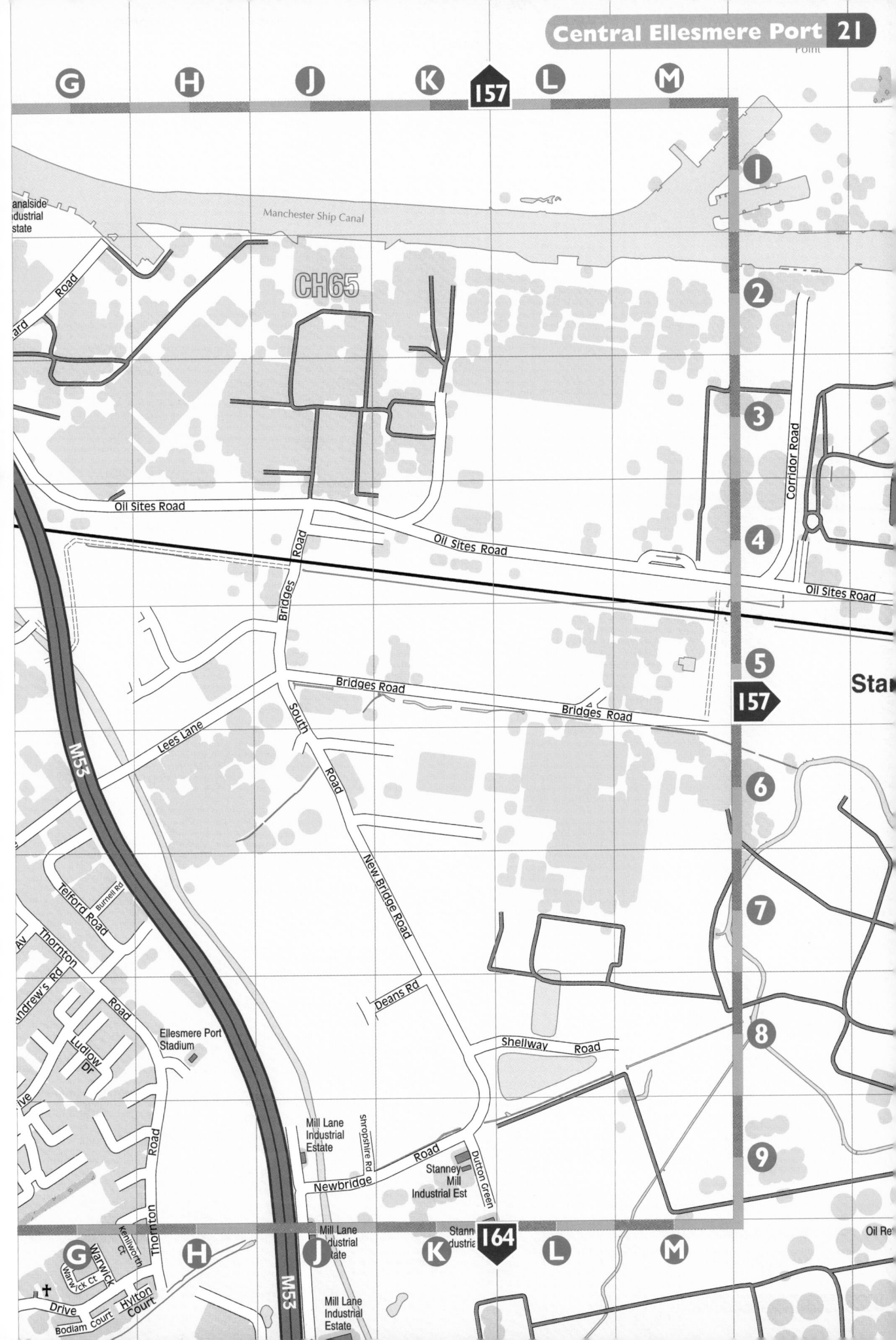

Point

G H J K L 157 L M

I

2

Manchester Ship Canal

CH65

Corridor Road

3

Oil Sites Road

4

Oil Sites Road

Oil Sites Road

Oil Sites Road

Bridges Road

5

157

Sta

Bridges Road

Bridges Road

Bridges Road

Lees Lane

South Road

6

M53

New Bridge Road

7

Telford Road

Burnell Rd

Thornton Road

8

Andrew's Rd

Deans Rd

Shellway Road

Ludlow Dr

Ellesmere Port Stadium

Shropshire Rd

Mill Lane Industrial Estate

Road

Stanney Mill Industrial Est

Dutton Green

9

Thornton Road

Newbridge

G H J K 164 L M

Warwick Ct

Warwick

Kenilworth Ct

Mill Lane Industrial Estate

Stanney dustrial

Oil Re

M53

Drive

Bodiam Court

Hylton Court

Mill Lane Industrial Estate

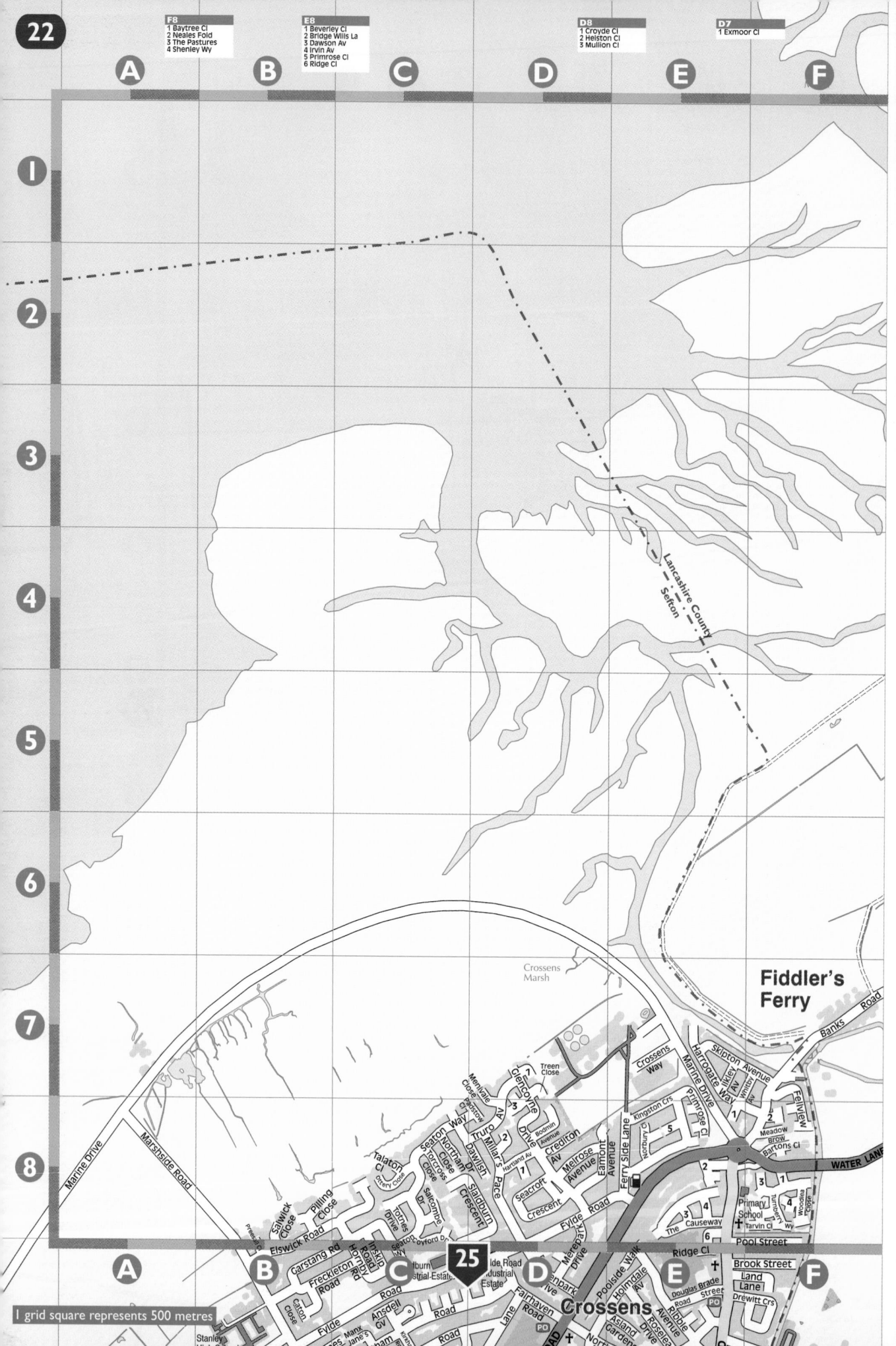

F8
1 Baytree Cl
2 Neales Fold
3 The Pastures
4 Shenley Wy

E8
1 Beverley Cl
2 Bridge Wilis La
3 Dawson Av
4 Irvin Av
5 Primrose Cl
6 Ridge Cl

D8
1 Croyde Cl
2 Helston Cl
3 Mullion Cl

D7
1 Exmoor Cl

A B C D E F

1
2
3
4
5
6
7
8

Lancashire County
Sefton

Crossens Marsh

Fiddler's Ferry

Banks Road

Marine Drive
Marshside Road

Treen Close
Crossens Way
Skipton Avenue
Ilkley Av
Winby
Wintor

Menivale Close
Clenhovne Drive
Primrose Cl
Harrogate Way
Feilview
Meadow Brow
Bartons Cl

Seaton Northam Way
Truro Av
Millat's Pace
Dawlish
Bodmin Avenue
Crediton
Av
Crossens Way
Marine Drive
Kingston Crs
Norbury
5

Talaton Cl
Ottery Close
Torcross Close
Salcombe
Seacroft Crescent
Hartland Av
Melrose Avenue
Eamont Avenue
Ferry Side Lane

WATER LANE

Pressal
Salwick Close
Pilling Close
Sladburn Crescent
Fylde Road
Crediton Av
Marepark Drive
The Causeway
Tarvin Cl
Primary School
Woodlea Close
Tarvin Wy

Elswick Road
Carstang Rd
Inskip Road
Frockleton Road
Seaton
Oyford Dr
Industrial Estate
Ide Road
Industrial Estate
Denbark
Marepark Drive
Ridge Cl
Pool Street

25

Brook Street
Land Lane
Drewitt Crs

Caton Close
Fylde Road
anes
Manx
Jane's
ntham Road
Ansdell Road
Fairhaven Road
Fairhaven Road
ROAD
Poolside Walk
Holmdale Av
Ribble Drive
Roselea Drive
Douglas Brade Road
Asland Gardens
North

Crossens

Stanley High School

PO
PO
PO

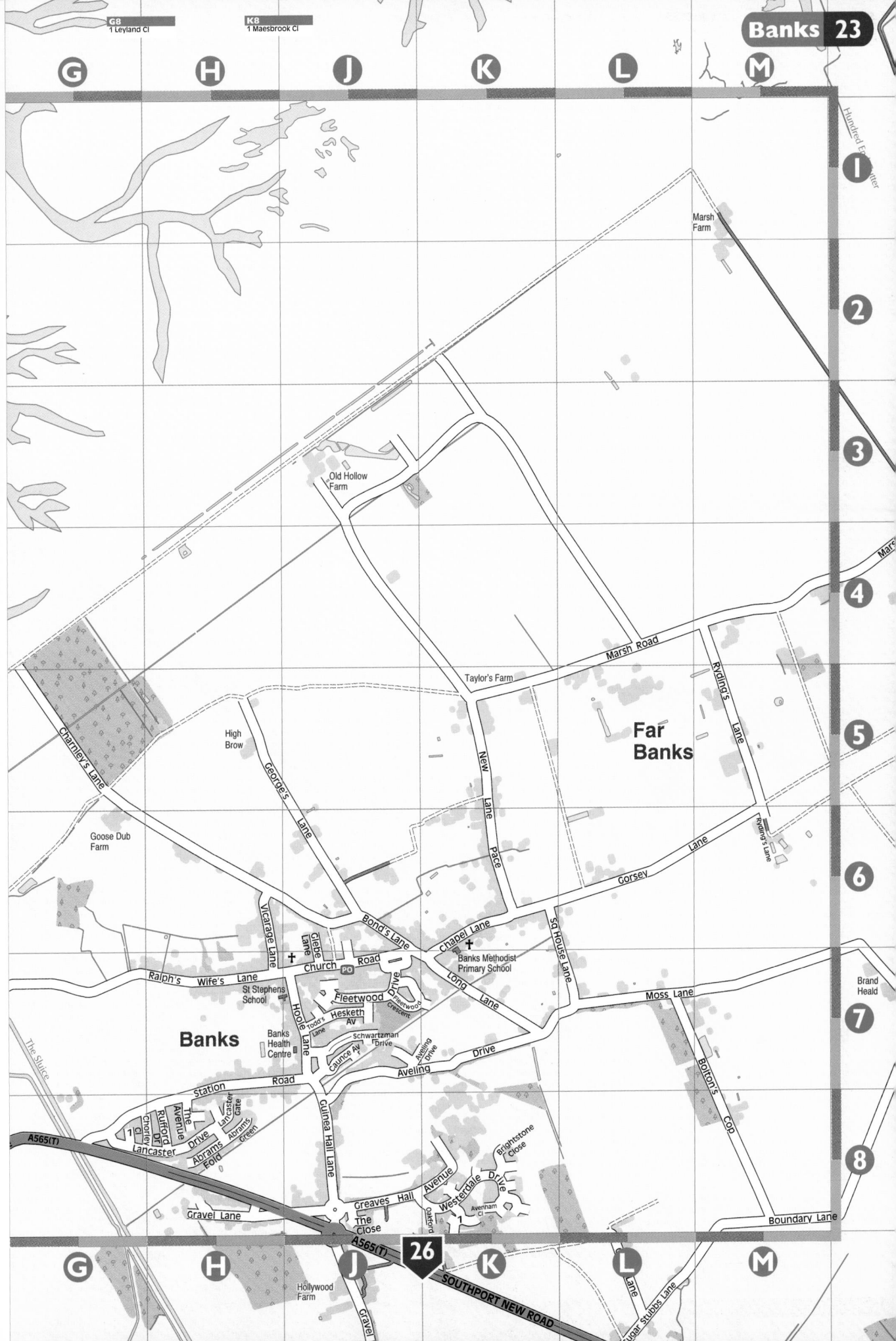

G8
1 Leyland Cl

K8
1 Maesbrook Cl

G H J K L M

I
2
3
4
5
6
7
8

Hundred End Gutter

Marsh Farm

Old Hollow Farm

Marsh Road

Taylor's Farm

Far Banks

High Brow

George's Lane

Charnley's Lane

New Lane

Ryding's Lane

Ryding's Lane

Goose Dub Farm

Pace

Gorsey Lane

Brand Heald

Vicarage Lane

Glebe Lane

Bond's Lane

Chapel Lane

Banks Methodist Primary School

Sq House Lane

The Sluice

Ralph's Wife's Lane

Church Road

PO

Fleetwood Drive

Fleetwood Crescent

Long Lane

Moss Lane

St Stephens School

Hoole Lane

Todd's Lane

Hesketh Av

Schwartzman Drive

Aveling Drive

Drive

Bolton's Cop

Banks

Banks Health Centre

Caunce Av

Aveling

Station Road

The Avenue

Lancaster Gate

Guinea Hall Lane

Rufford Dr

Chorley Cl

1

Lancaster

Abrams Fold

Abrams Green

Brightstone Close

Westerdale Drive

Avenham Cl

Avenue

Oakford

1

Gravel Lane

The Close

Greaves Hall

Boundary Lane

A565(T)

A565(T)

26

SOUTHPORT NEW ROAD

Hollywood Farm

Gravel L

Sugar Stubbs Lane

Lane

G H J K L M

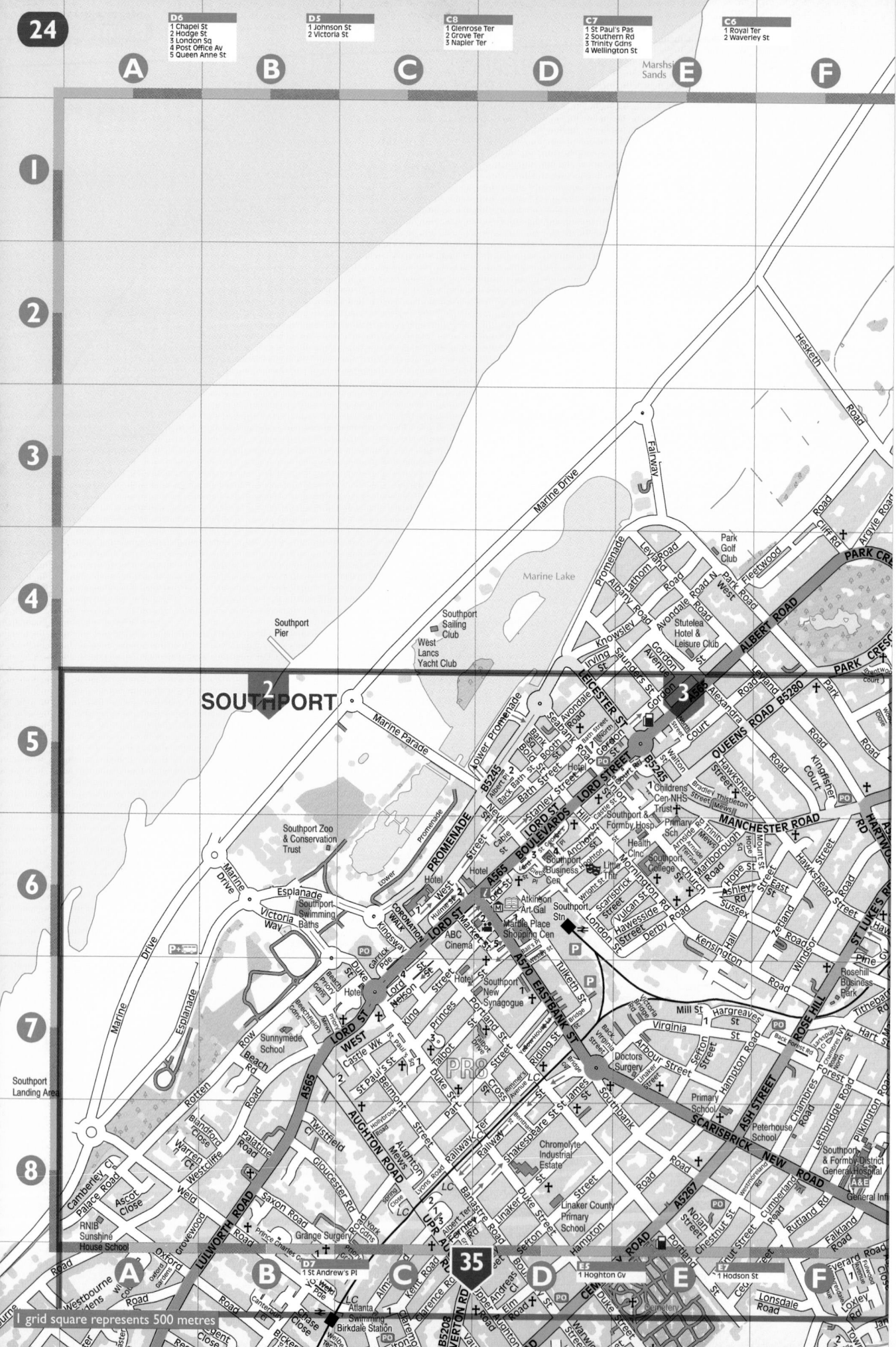

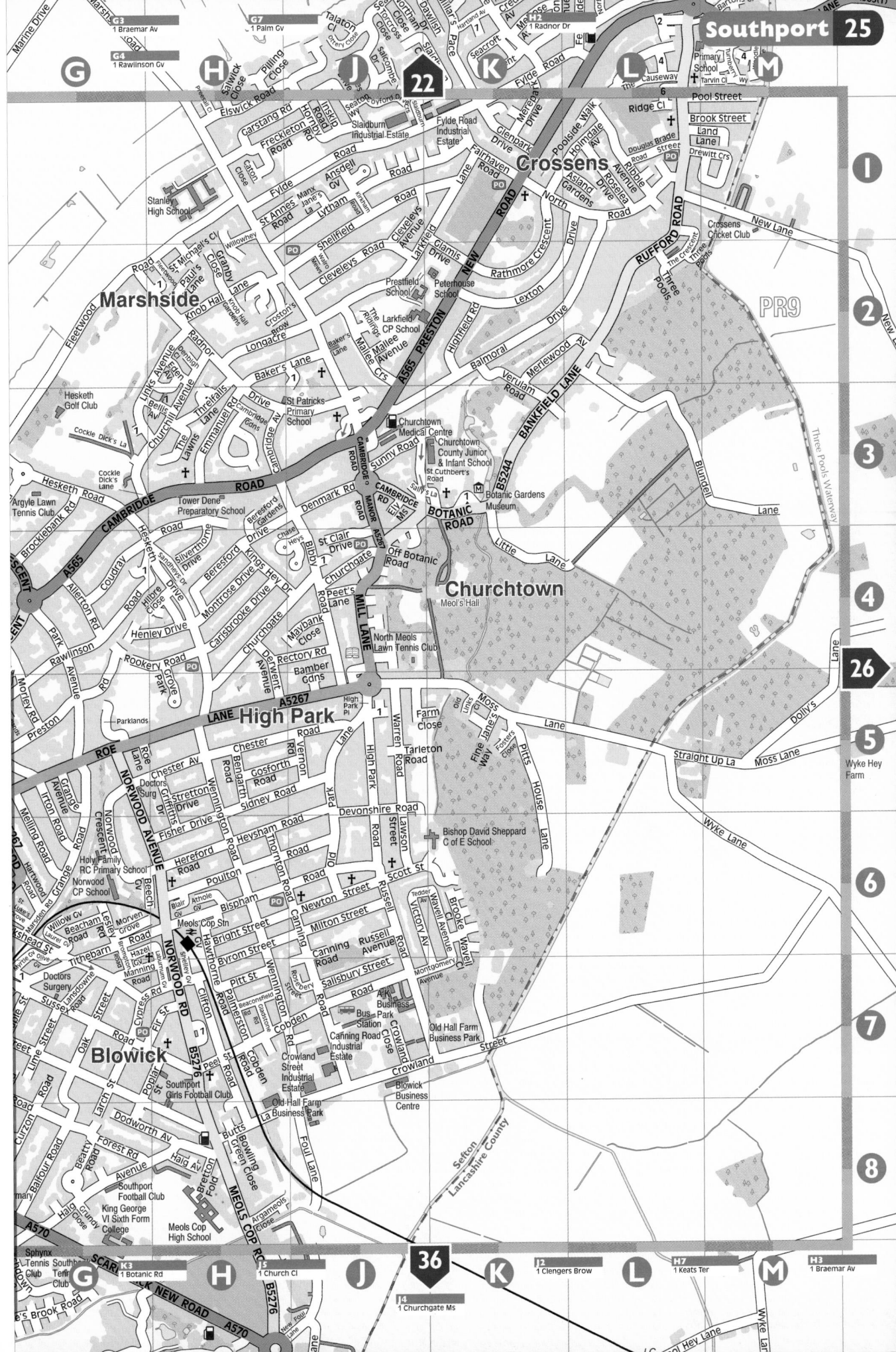

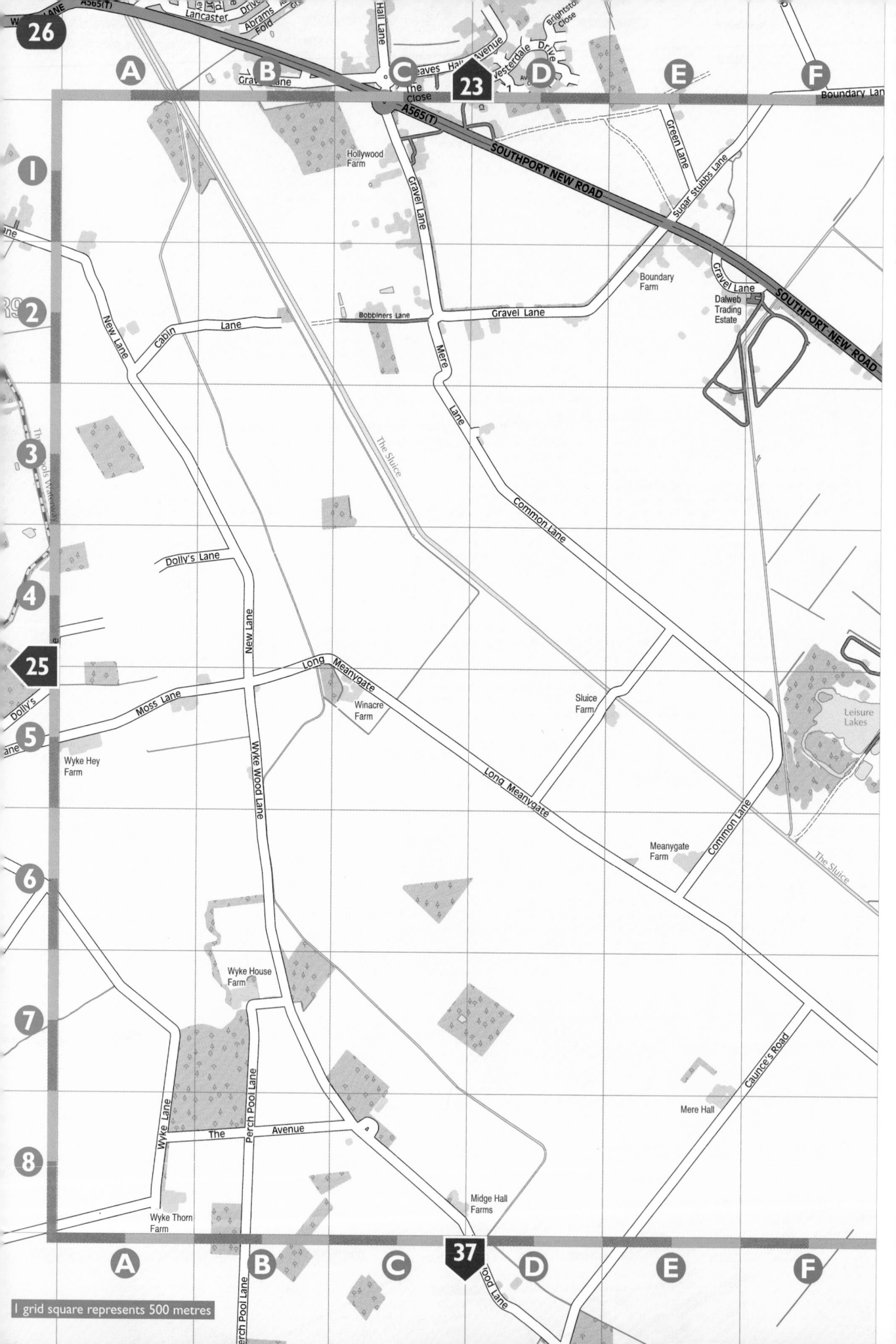

A B C 23 D E F

A565(T)
Lancaster Abrams Fold
Drive

Gravel Lane

The Close

Cleaves Hall Avenue

Yesterdale Drive

Brightstone Close

Boundary Lane

SOUTHPORT NEW ROAD

Green Lane

Sugar Stubbs Lane

SOUTHPORT NEW ROAD

1

Hollywood Farm

Gravel Lane

2

Cabin Lane

New Lane

Bobbiners Lane

Gravel Lane

Mere Lane

Boundary Farm

Gravel Lane

Dalweb Trading Estate

The Sluice

3

The Wools Waterway

Common Lane

Dolly's Lane

4

New Lane

25

Dolly's Lane

Long Meanygate

Moss Lane

Winacre Farm

Sluice Farm

Leisure Lakes

5

Wyke Hey Farm

Long Meanygate

Wyke Wood Lane

6

Meanygate Farm

Common Lane

The Sluice

Wyke House Farm

7

Caunce's Road

Mere Hall

Wyke Lane

The Avenue

Perch Pool Lane

8

Wyke Thorn Farm

Midge Hall Farms

Wood Lane

A B C 37 D E F

1 grid square represents 500 metres

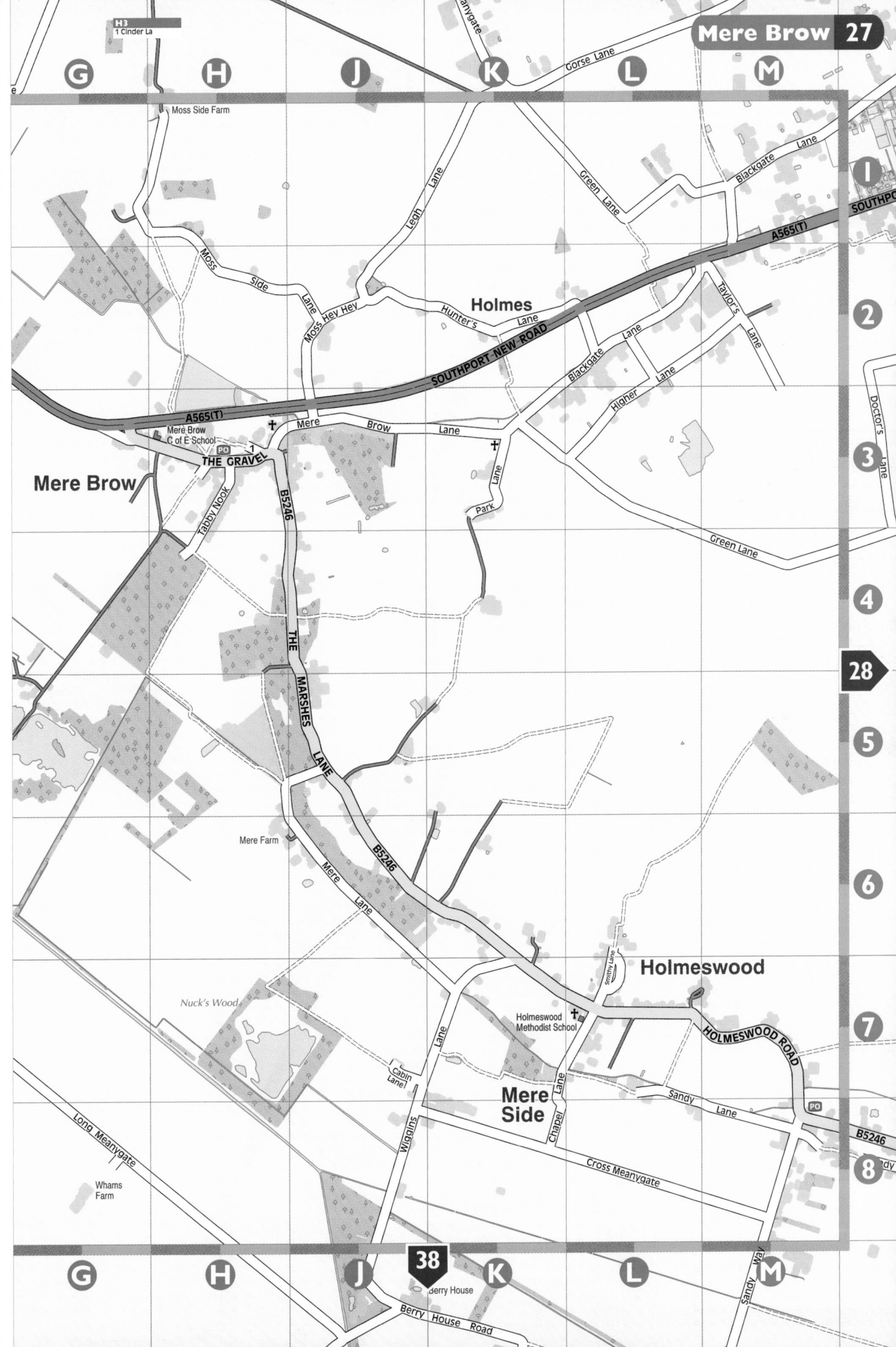

G H J K L M

H3
1 Cinder La

Moss Side Farm

SOUTHPORT

I

Gorse Lane

Blackgate Lane

A565(T)

2

Green Lane

Legh Lane

Moss Hey Hey

Taylor's Lane

Holmes

Hunter's Lane

Doctor's Lane

SOUTHPORT NEW ROAD

Moss Side Lane

Blackgate Lane

3

A565(T)

Mere Brow
C of E School

PO 1

Mere Brow Lane

Higher Lane

Green Lane

Mere Brow

THE GRAVEL

†

†

Tabby Nook

B5246

Park Lane

4

28

THE MARSHES LANE

5

Mere Farm

B5246

6

Mere Lane

Smithy Lane

Holmeswood

Nuck's Wood

Holmeswood
Methodist School

†

HOLMESWOOD ROAD

7

Cabin Lane

Wiggins Lane

**Mere
Side**

Chapel Lane

sandy Lane

PO

B5246

Long Meanygate

Whams
Farm

Cross Meanygate

Sandy Lane

8

G H J K L M

38

Berry House

Berry House Road

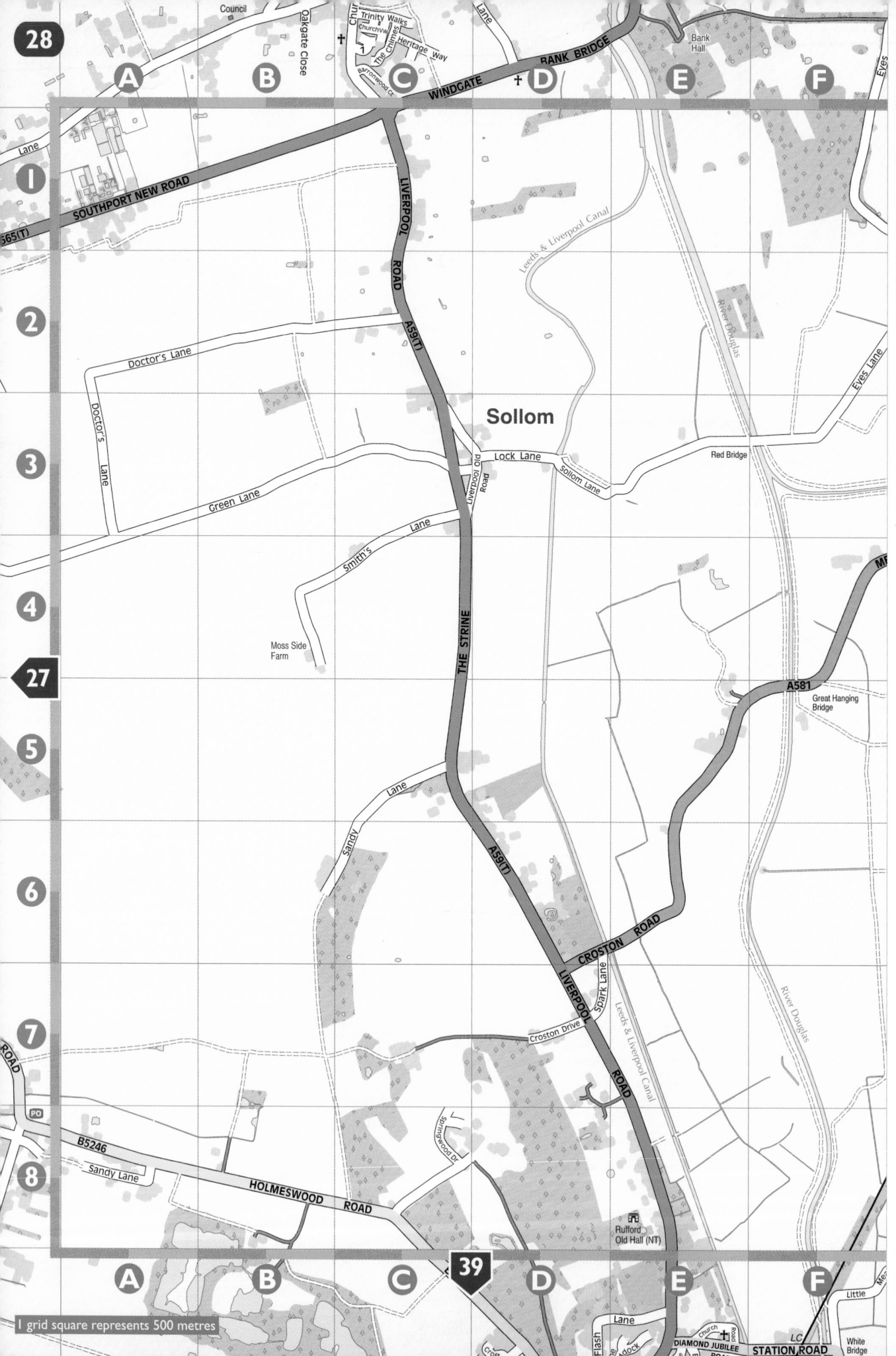

A   B   C   D   E   F

Council
Oakgate Close
Church
The Chimes
Trinity Walks
Heritage Way
Churchv...
Barronwood Ct.
1
Lane
WINDGATE
RANK BRIDGE
Bank Hall
Eyes

Lane
1
SOUTHPORT NEW ROAD
565(T)

LIVERPOOL ROAD
A59(T)
Leeds & Liverpool Canal
River Douglas

2
Doctor's Lane
Eyes Lane

3
Doctor's Lane
Green Lane
Liverpool Old Road
Lock Lane
Sollom Lane
Red Bridge

Sollom

Smith's Lane

4
Moss Side Farm
THE STRINE
A581
Great Hanging Bridge

27

5
Lane
Sandy Lane

6
A59(T)
CROSTON ROAD

7
ROAD
Croston Drive
Spark Lane
Leeds & Liverpool Canal
LIVERPOOL ROAD
River Douglas

PO
B5246

8
Sandy Lane
HOLMESWOOD ROAD
Spoo...
Rufford Old Hall (NT)

A   B   C   D   E   F

Church
Lane
DIAMOND JUBILEE
Church Road
LC
White Bridge
STATION ROAD
Flash Lane

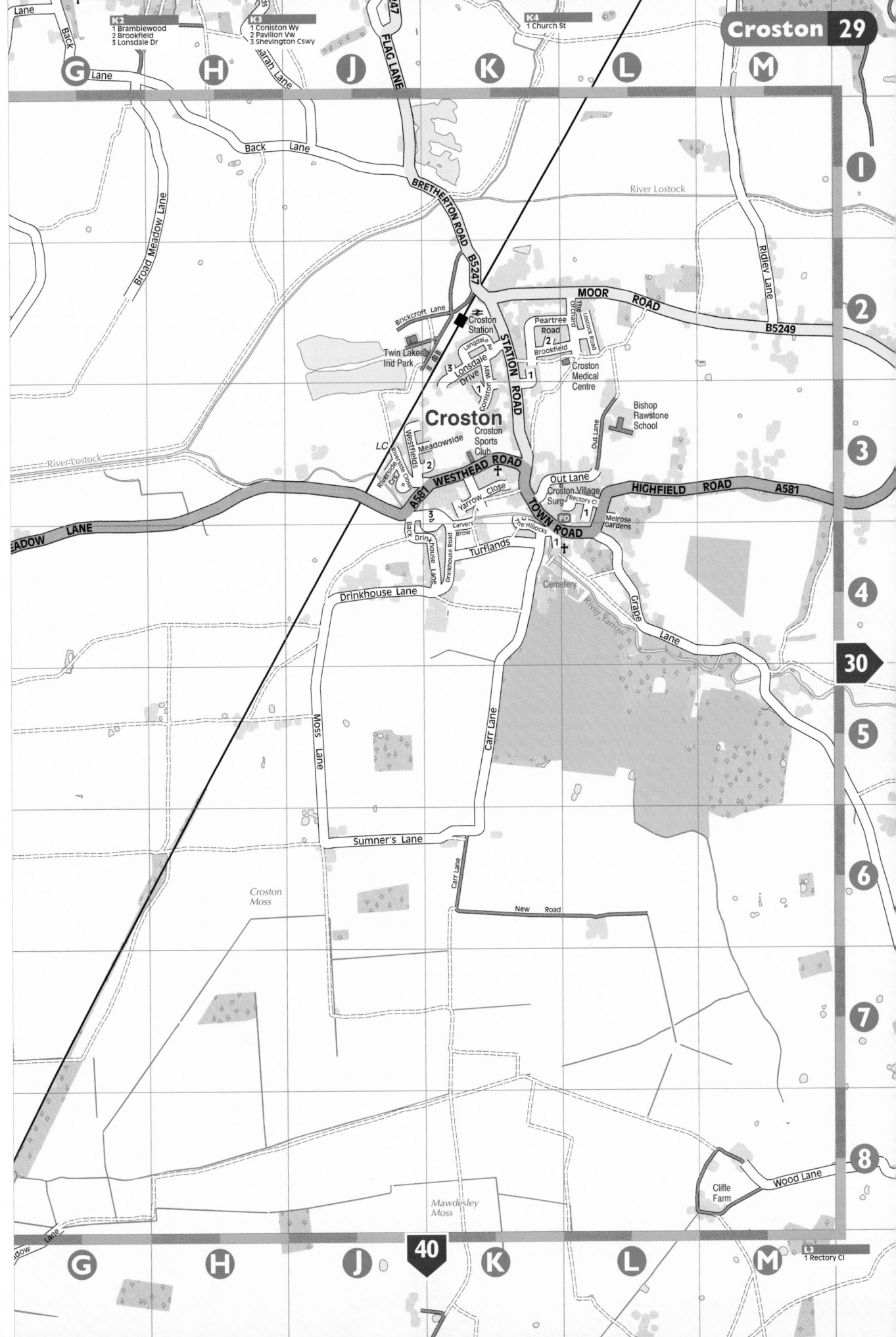

K2
1 Bramblewood
2 Brookfield
3 Lonsdale Dr

K3
1 Coniston Wy
2 Pavilion Vw
3 Shevington Cswy

K4
1 Church St

G Lane

H

J

FLAG LANE

K

L

M

I

Back Lane

River Lostock

Ridley Lane

Broad Meadow Lane

BRETHERTON ROAD

B5247

MOOR ROAD

2

B5249

Brickcroft Lane

Croston Station

Twin Lakes Ind Park

Peartree Road
2
Brookfield

The Orchard

Lostock Road

Croston Medical Centre

Langdale Av

Lonsdale Drive

Coniston Way

1

STATION ROAD

3

Croston

Croston Sports Club

Bishop Rawstone School

Out Lane

3

Westfields

LC

CES

Riverside Close

Meadowside
2

Out Lane

Croston Village Surg

Rectory Cl

Melrose Gardens

River Lostock

A581

WESTHEAD ROAD

Yarrow Close

HIGHFIELD ROAD

A581

MEADOW LANE

3

Back

Drinkhouse Lane

Carvers Brow

TOWN ROAD

PO

The Hillocks

1

Cemetery

Turflands

Drinkhouse Lane

Drinkhouse Road

River Yarrow

Grape Lane

4

30

Moss Lane

Carr Lane

5

Sumner's Lane

Croston Moss

Carr Lane

6

New Road

7

Wood Lane

8

Cliffe Farm

Mawdesley Moss

G

H

J

40

K

L

M

L3
1 Rectory Cl

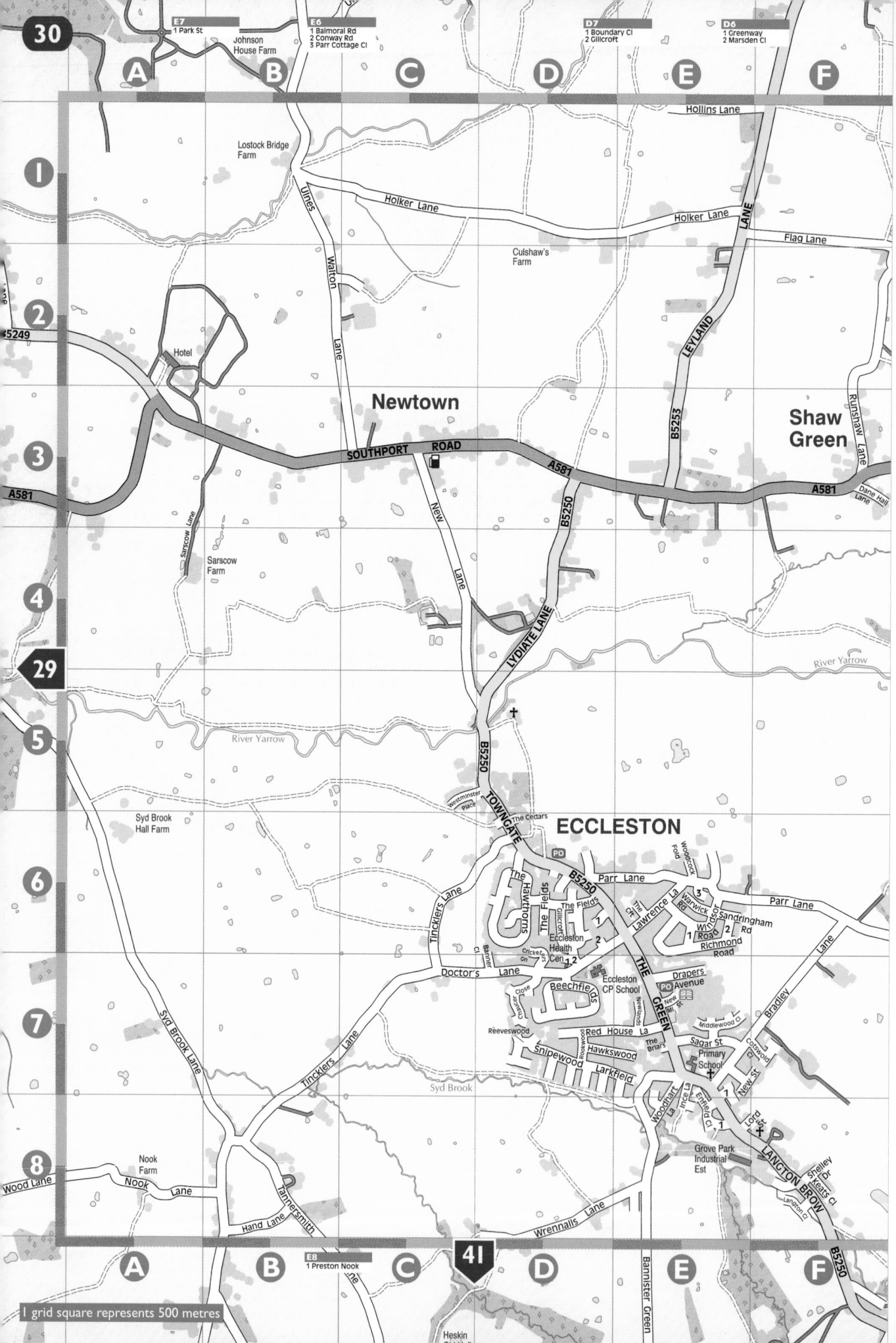

E7
1 Park St

E6
1 Balmoral Rd
2 Conway Rd
3 Parr Cottage Cl

D7
1 Boundary Cl
2 Gillcroft

D6
1 Greenway
2 Marsden Cl

A   B   C   D   E   F

1

Lostock Bridge
Farm

Hollins Lane

Holker Lane

Holker Lane

Flag Lane

Culshaw's
Farm

2

B5249

Hotel

LEYLAND LANE

B5253

Runshaw Lane

Newtown

Shaw
Green

3

A581

SOUTHPORT   ROAD

A581

B5250

A581

Dane Hall
Lane

Sarscow Lane

Sarscow
Farm

New Lane

LYDIATE LANE

River Yarrow

4

29

5

River Yarrow

Syd Brook
Hall Farm

Westminster
Place

The Cedars

TOWNGATE

B5250

ECCLESTON

6

Tincklers Lane

The Hawthorns

The Fields

The Fields

Gillcroft

1

Parr Lane

Woolcock
Fold

PO

B5250

Lawrence La

Warwick
Road

Sandringham
Rd

Parr Lane

Eccleston
Health
Cen

2

3

Richmond
Road

Doctor's
Lane

Banner Cl

Cricketers
Cl

1

2

THE GREEN

Drapers
Avenue

Bradley

7

Syd Brook Lane

Tincklers Lane

Syd Brook

Beechfields

Eccleston
CP School

PO

Newlands

Middlewood Cl

Cotswold
Cl

Reeveswood

Red House La

Hawkswood

The
Briars

Sagar St
Primary
School

Snipewood

Larkfield

New St

8

Nook
Farm

Wood Lane

Nook   Lane

Tannersmith

Hand Lane

Woodhart
La

Ince La

Enfield Cl

Lord
St

Grove Park
Industrial
Est

LANGTON BROW

Shelley
Dr

Keats Cl

Langton Cl

Wrennalls Lane

Bannister Green

B5250

A   B   C   D   E   F

Heskin
Old Hall

1 grid square represents 500 metres

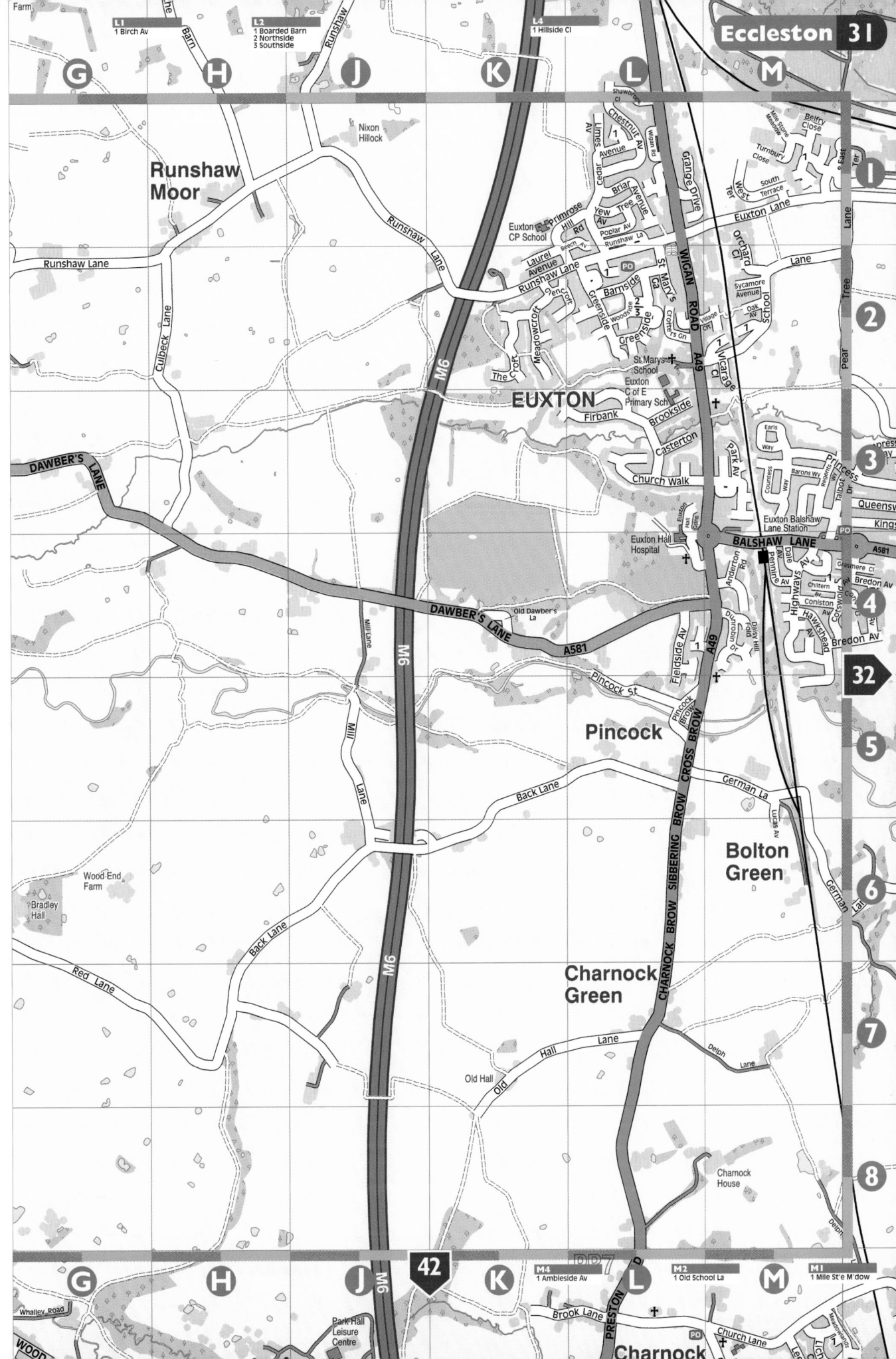

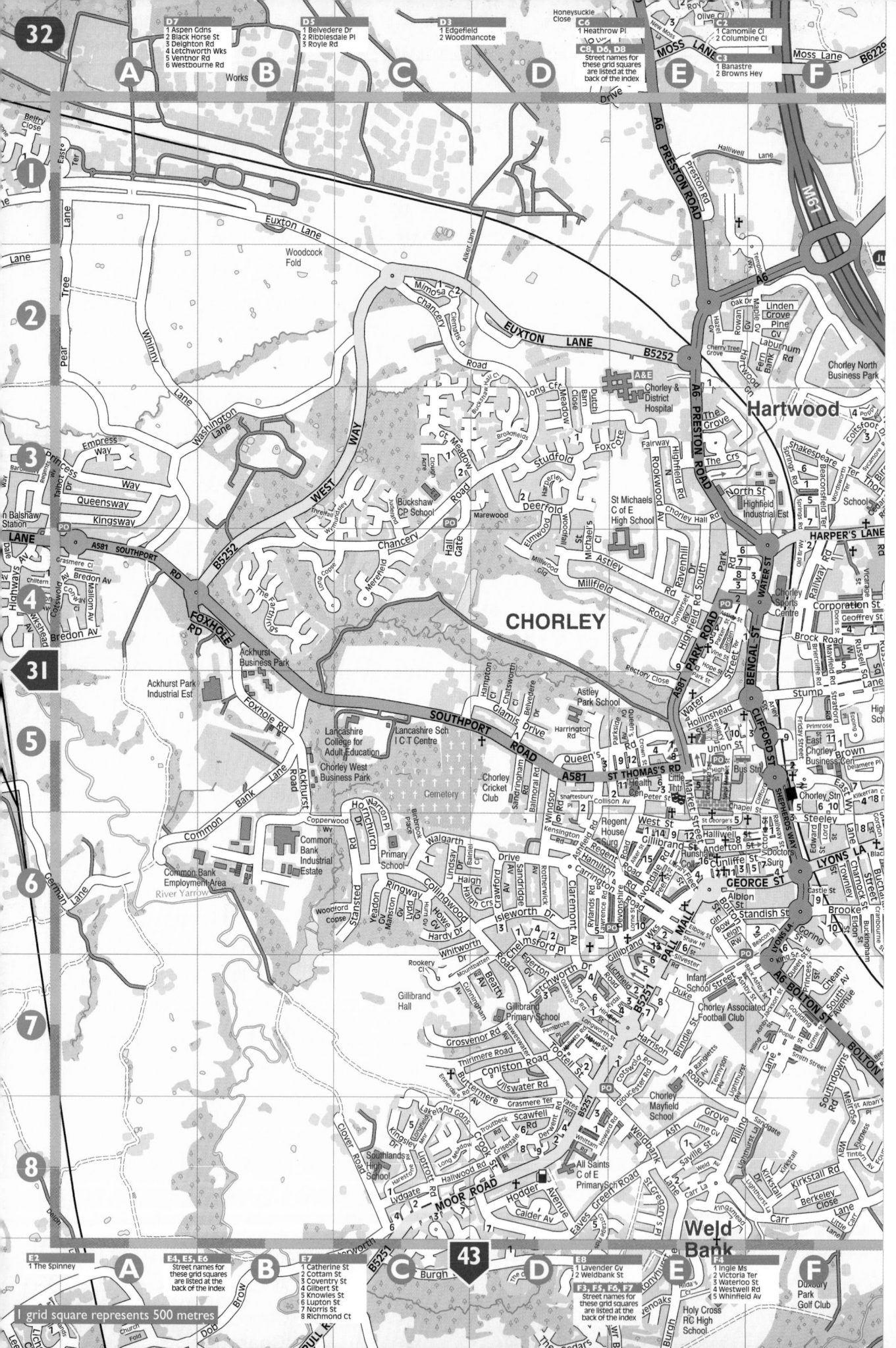

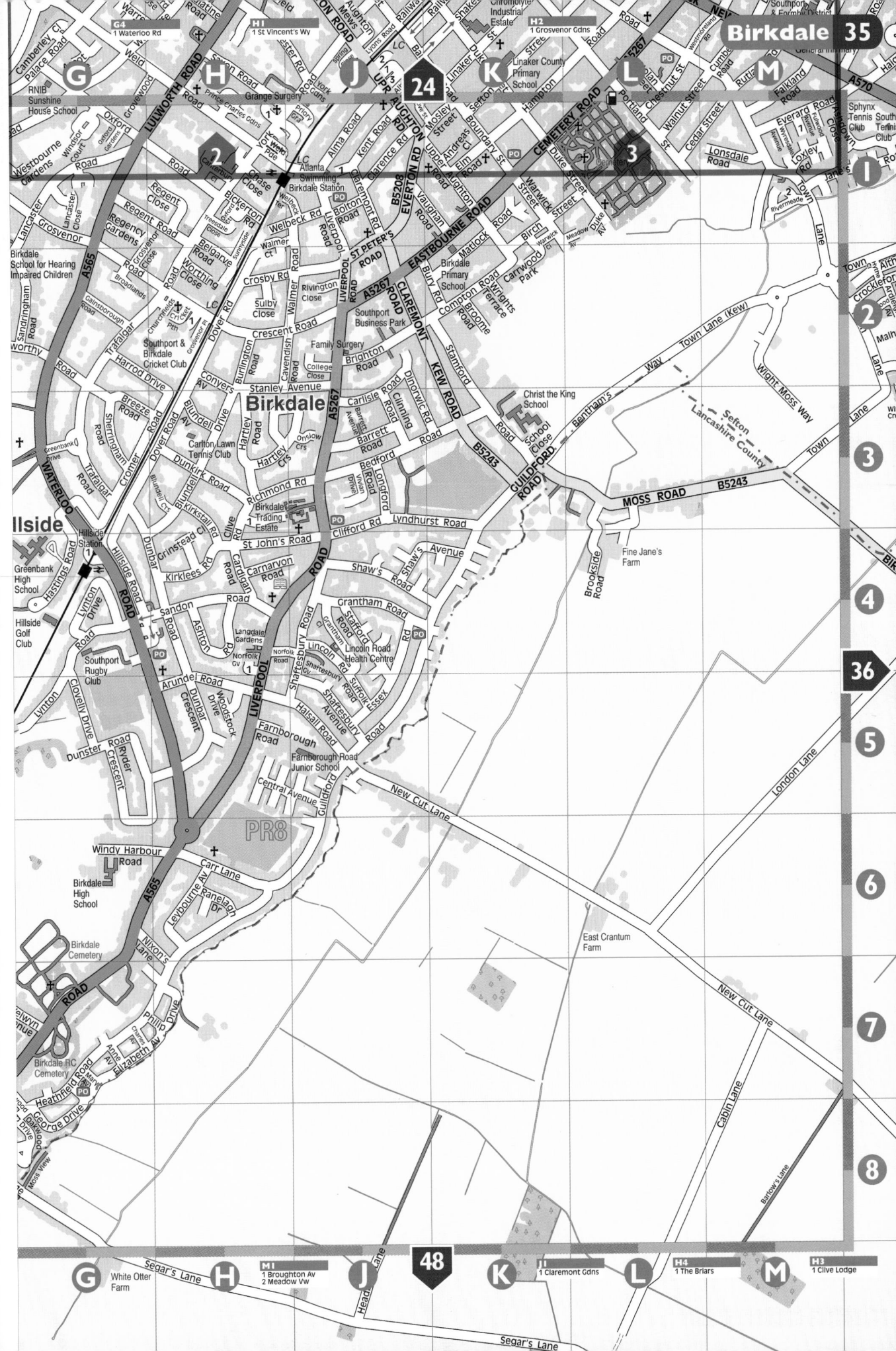

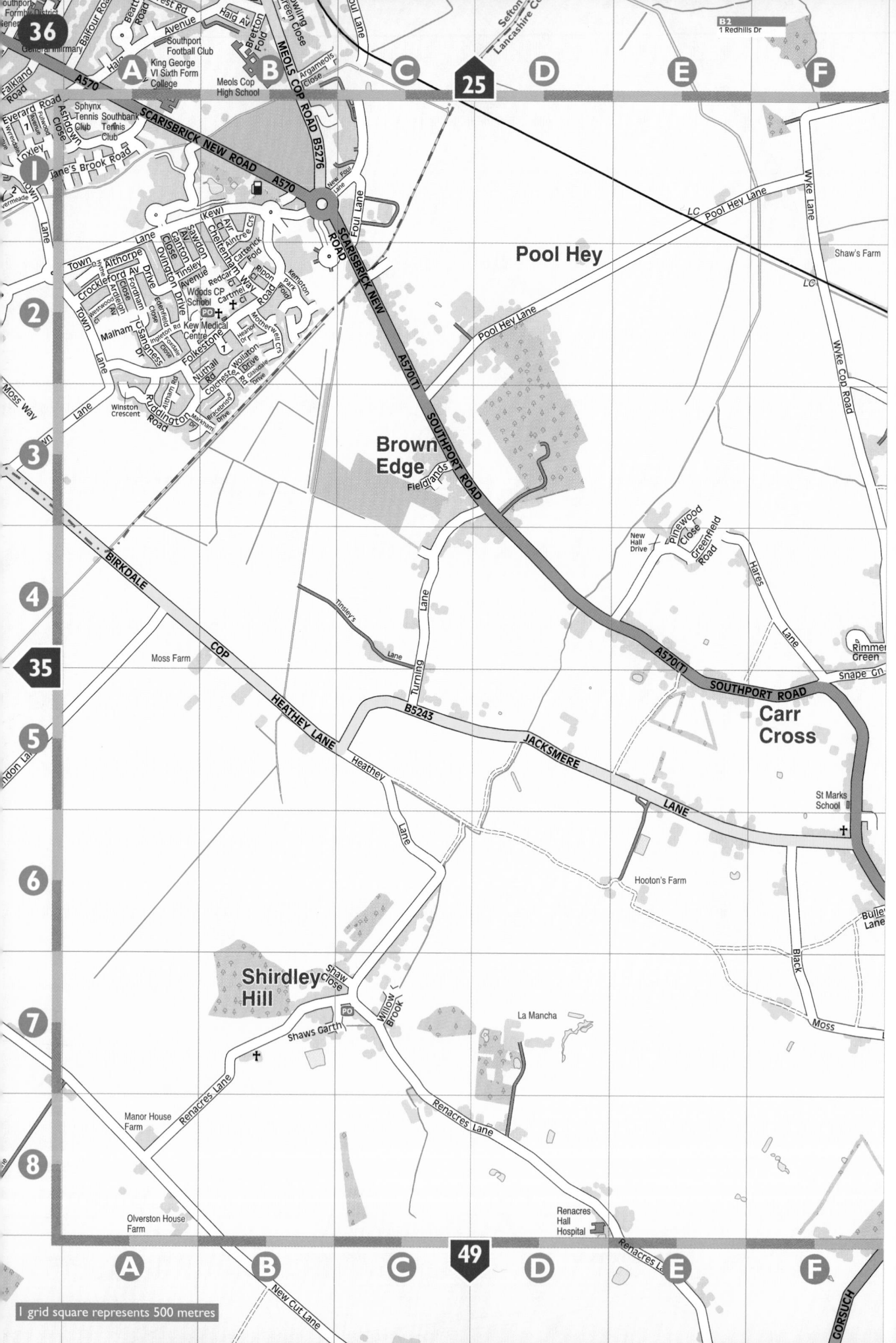

A B C **25** D E F

B2
1 Redhills Dr

1
Southport
Formby District
General Infirmary

Balfour Road
Beatty West Rd
Halg Av
Southport Football Club
King George VI Sixth Form College
Bretton Fold
Meols Cop High School

A570
Halg
Falkland Road
Everard Road
Ashdown Close
Loxley
Fulwood Av
Sphynx Tennis Club
Southbank Tennis Club

Town Lane

SCARISBRICK NEW ROAD A570

MEOLS COP ROAD B5276

Green Close
Dowling
Argameols Close

Sefton Lancashire Co

LC Pool Hey Lane

Wyke Lane

Shaw's Farm

LC

Wyke Cop Road

Pool Hey

Lane's Brook Road

(Kew)
Kew
Lane
Aintree Crs
Catterick Fold
New Foul Lane

Foul Lane

SCARISBRICK NEW ROAD

2
Crockleford Av
Althorpe
Cawdon Close
Canton Close
Ovington Drive
Tinsley Avenue
Cheltenham Av
Redcar Cl
Wollaton
Ripon Way
Cartmel Cl
Kemptor
Park
Fold

Ardagh
Fordham Close
Westwood AV
Malham Cl
Sandess Dr
Ingleton Rd
Felside
Folkestone
Heathey
Marmet Well Crs

Nuthall Rd
Colchester Drive
Wollaton Drive
Glasdale Drive
Bracemore Drive
Marsham

Kew Medical Centre
Woods CP School
7

Town Lane
Ruddington Road
Winston Crescent

Moss Way

A570(T)

SOUTHPORT ROAD

Pool Hey Lane

3
Brown Edge
Fieldlands

New Hall Drive
Pinewood Close
Greenfield Road
Hares

BIRKDALE COP

Lane

4
Moss Farm
Tinsley's
Lane

Lane
A570(T)
SOUTHPORT ROAD

Rimmer Green
Snape Gn

HEATHEY LANE

Turning
Lane
B5243
JACKSMERE

5
Heathey
Lane

LANE

Carr Cross

St Marks School

6
Hooton's Farm

Bullen Lane

7
Shirdley Hill
Shaw Close
PO
Willow Brook
Shaws Garth

La Mancha

Moss

Black

Renacres Lane

8
Manor House Farm

Renacres Lane

Olverston House Farm

Renacres Hall Hospital

Renacres La

GORSUCH

A B C **49** D E F

I grid square represents 500 metres

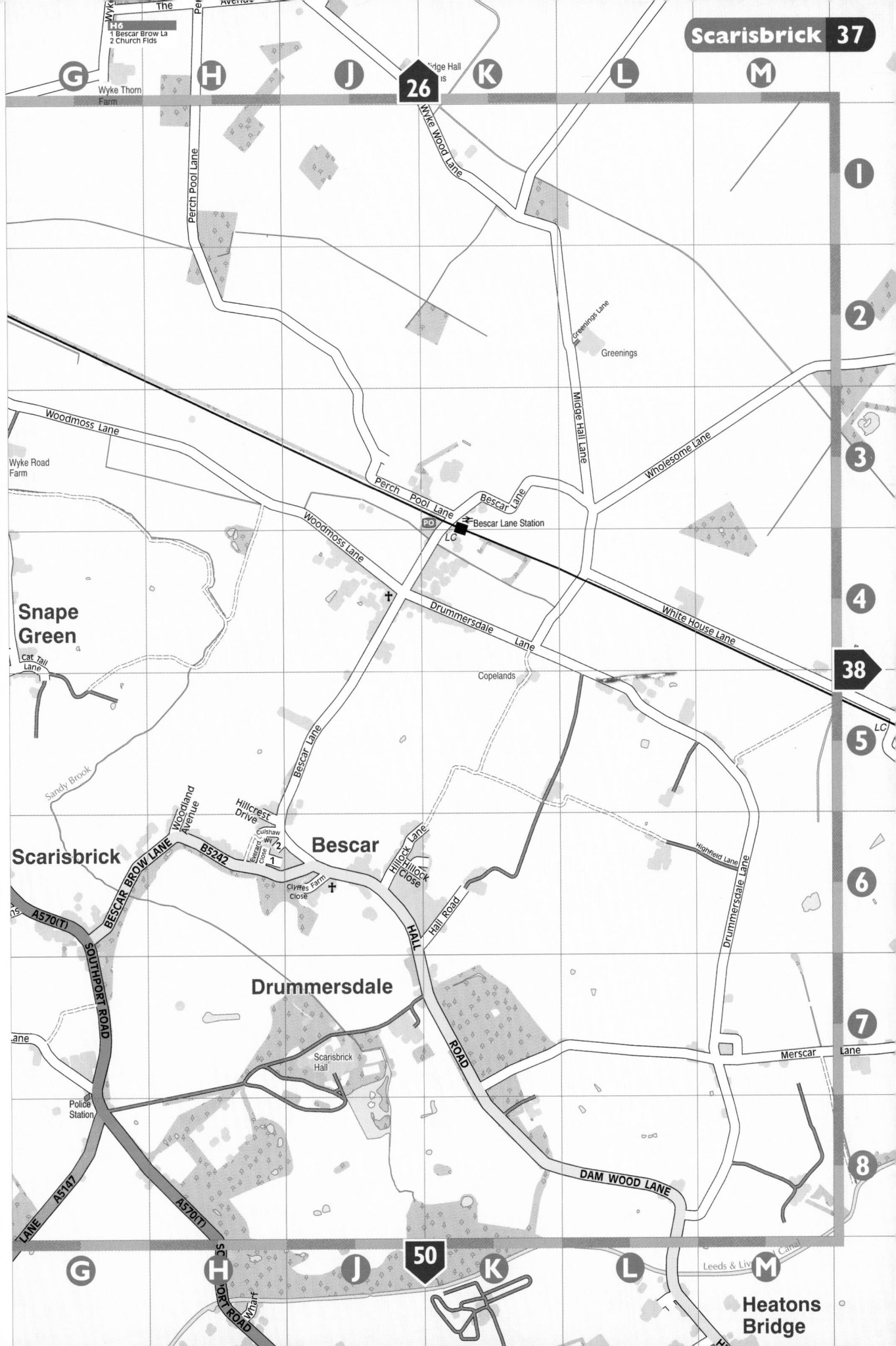

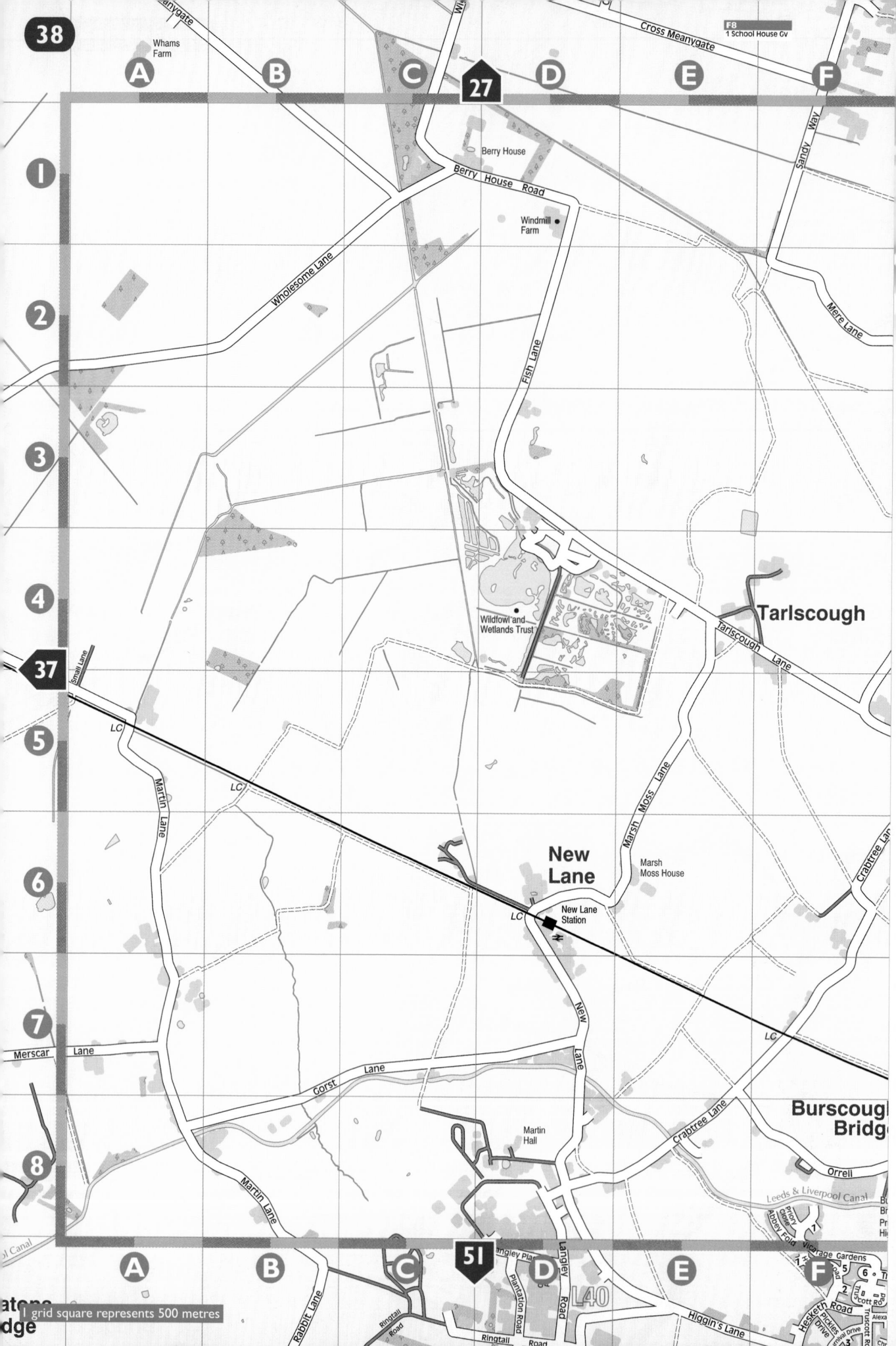

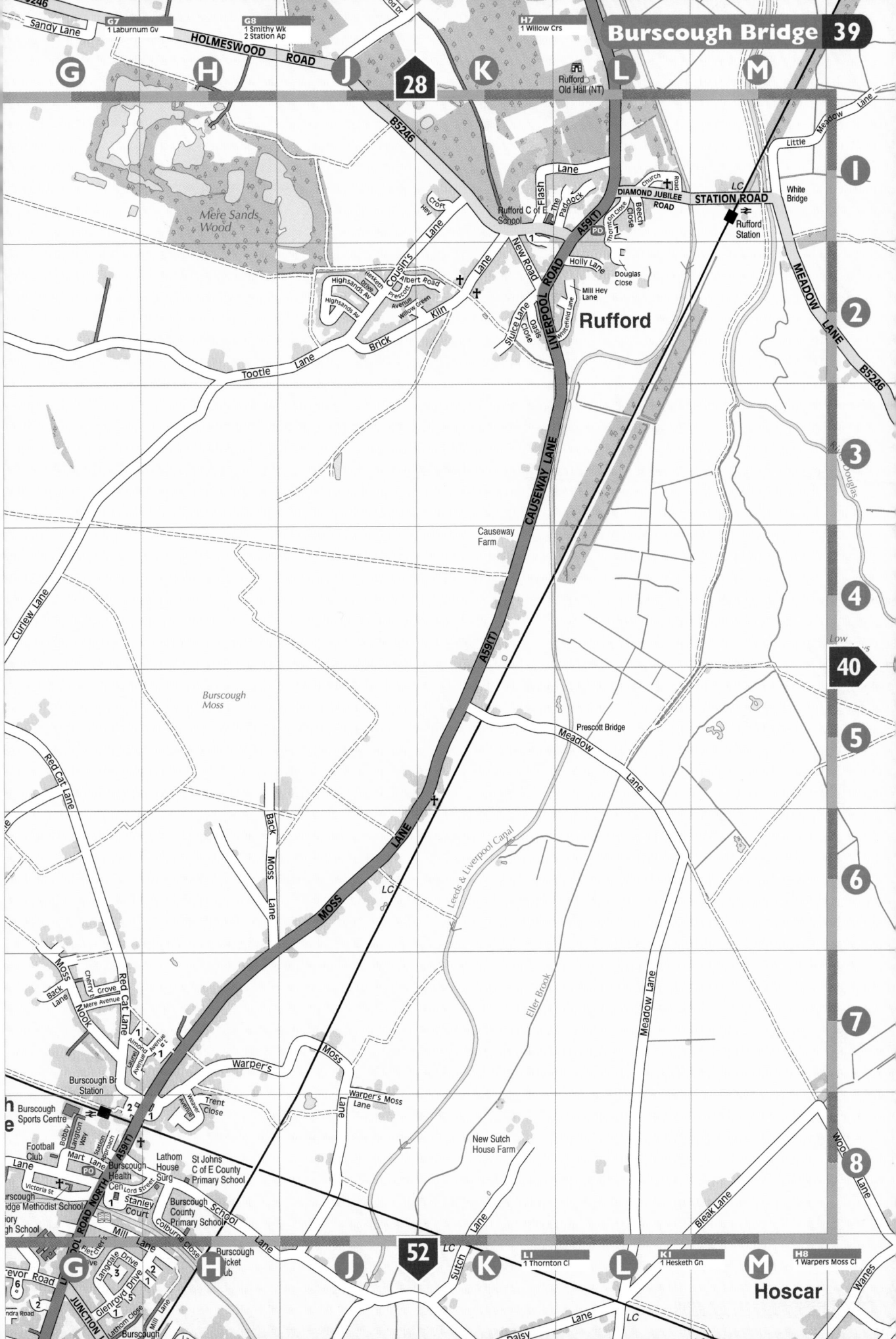

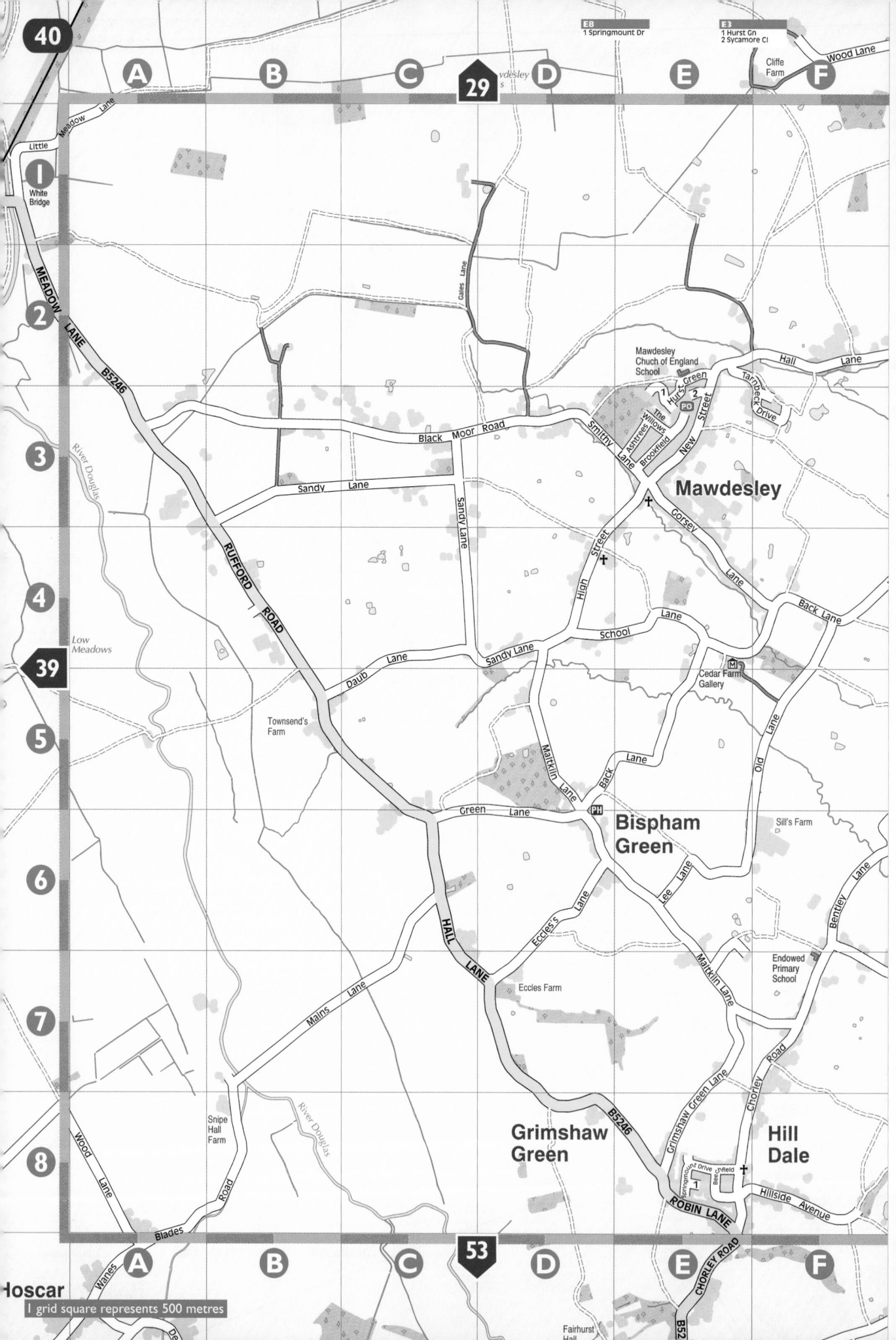

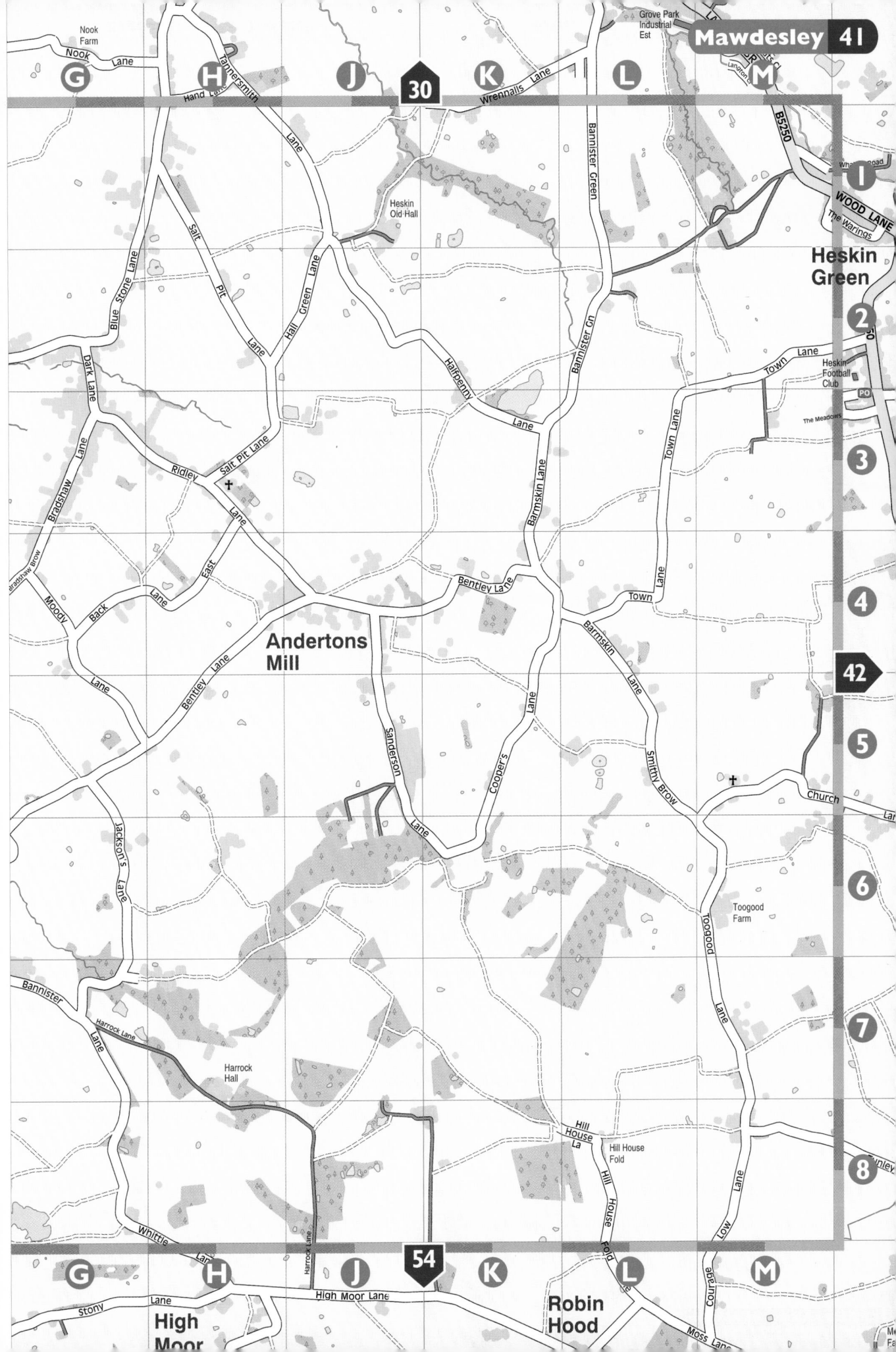

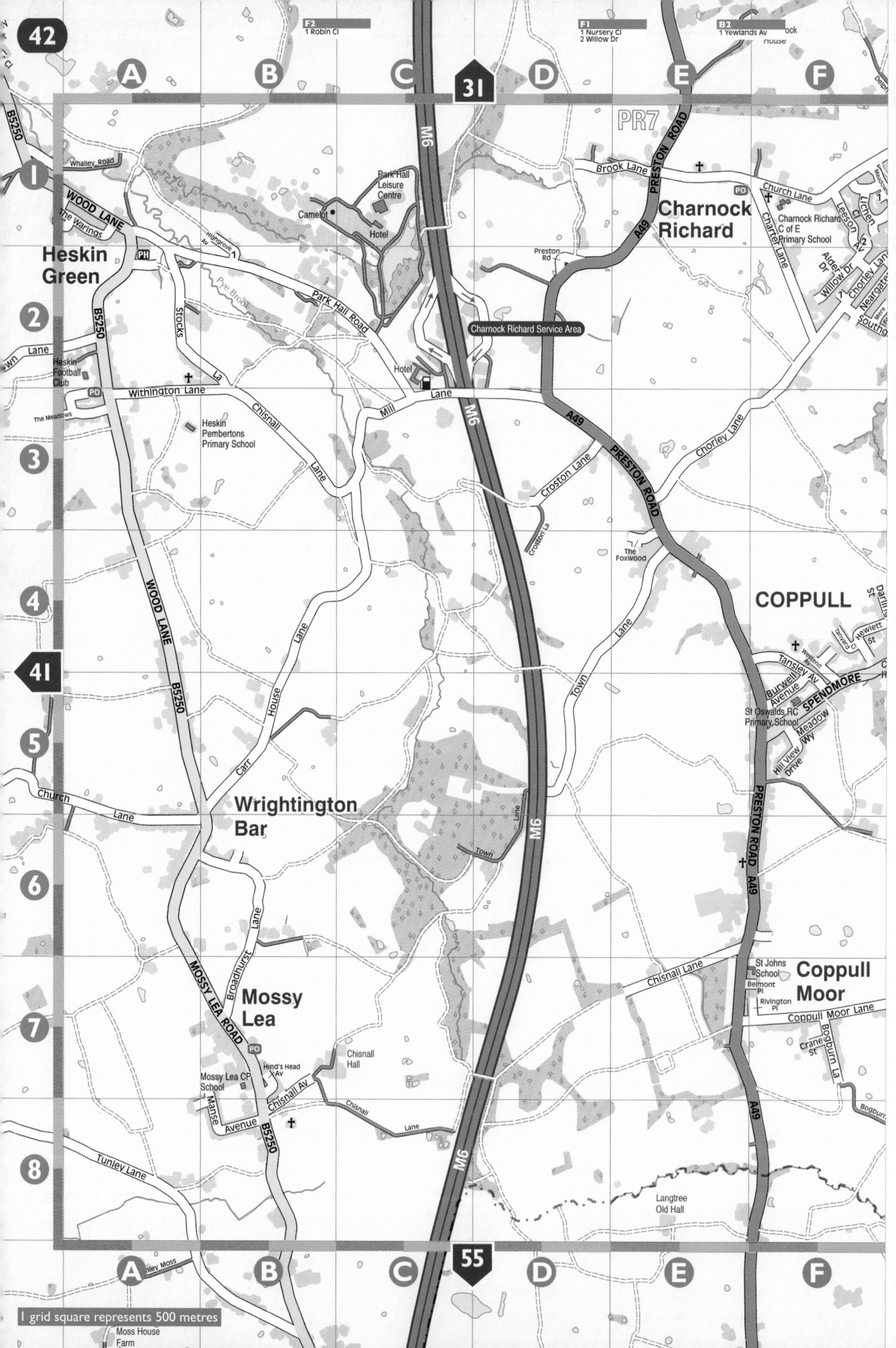

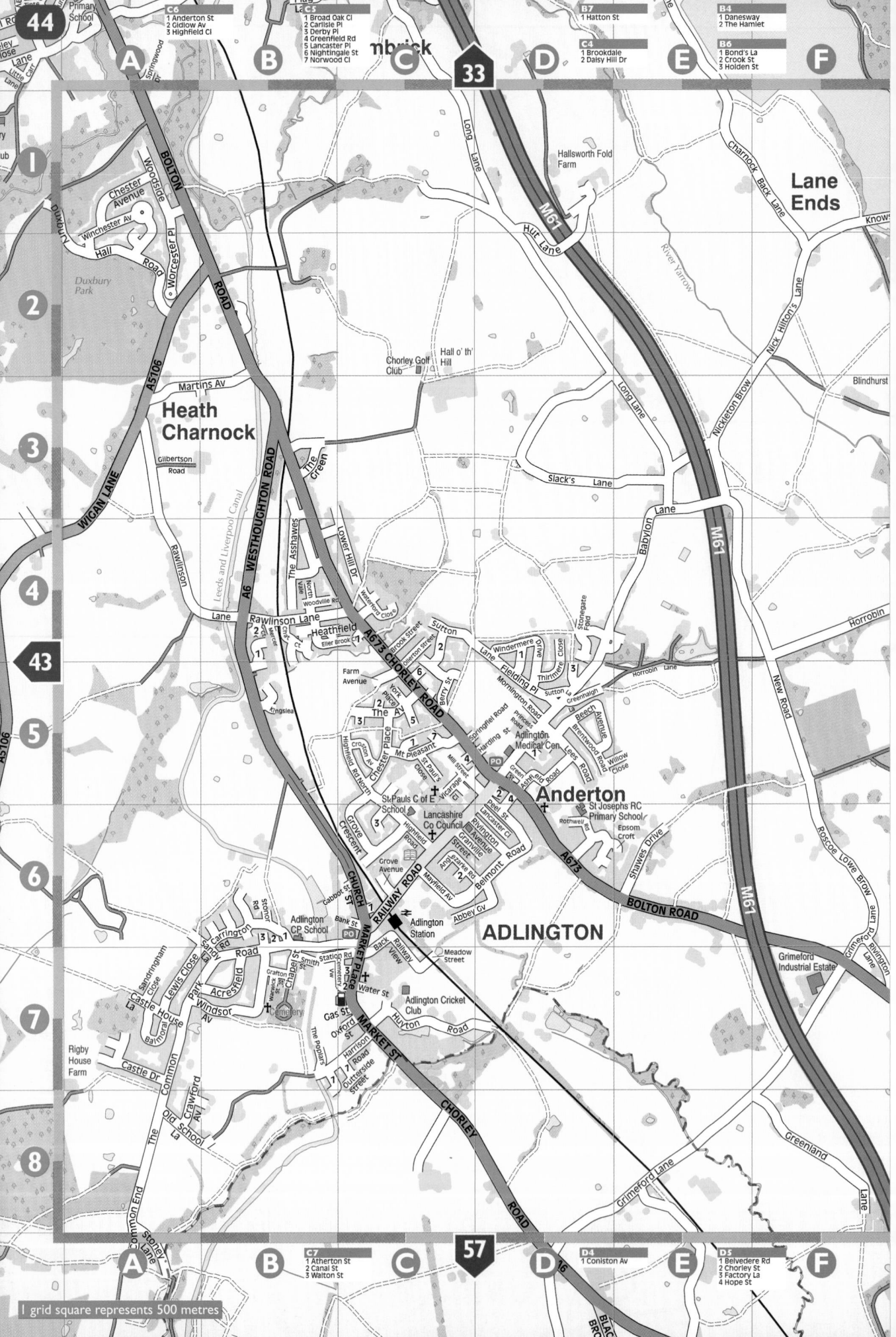

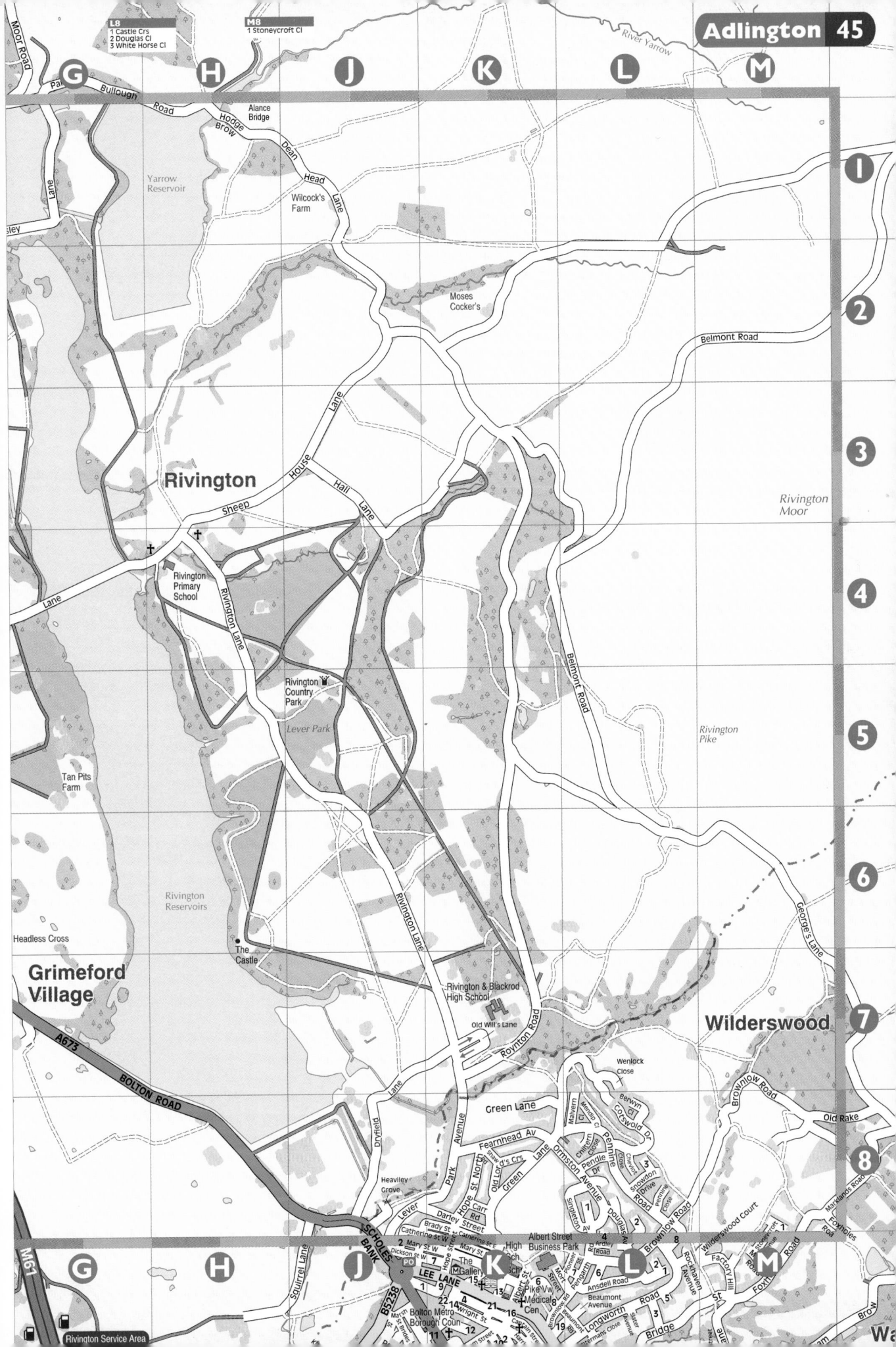

L8
1 Castle Crs
2 Douglas Cl
3 White Horse Cl

M8
1 Stoneycroft Cl

River Yarrow

G   H   J   K   L   M

Park   Bullough   Road   Hodge Brow   Alance Bridge

Moor Road

Lane

Yarrow Reservoir

Dean Head Lane

Wilcock's Farm

Moses Cocker's

Belmont Road

1

2

3

Rivington

House Lane   Hall Lane

Sheep

Rivington Lane

Rivington Primary School

Rivington Moor

4

Rivington Country Park

Lever Park

Rivington Pike

5

Tan Pits Farm

Lane

Rivington Lane

Belmont Road

Rivington Reservoirs

6

Headless Cross

George's Lane

The Castle

Grimeford Village

Rivington & Blackrod High School

Old Will's Lane

Wilderswood

7

A673

BOLTON ROAD

Roynton Road

Wenlock Close

Brownlow Road

Old Rake

Green Lane

Berwyn Cl

Cotswold

Snowdon Drive

Pennine Road

Brownlow Road

Wildeswood Court

M61

Dryfield Lane

Lever

Park Avenue

Green Lane

Fearnhead Av

Old Lodge's Crs

Ormston Avenue

Malvern

Mendip

Chiltern

Pendle Dr

Douglas Road

Rockhaven Avenue

Factory Hill

Foxtl

Marklands Road

Foxholes Road

8

Heavley Grove

Hope St North

Darley Street

Brady St

Old Carr Rd

Green Lane

Singleton Av

Ardley

Beaumont Road

Longworth Road

Ansdell Road

Bridge

G   H   J   K   L   M

SCHOLES BANK

Squirrel Lane

B5238

Rivington Service Area

Catherine St W

Dickson St

Mary St W

PO

LEE LANE

Mary St

Hope St South

The MGallery

Albert Street Business Park

High Sch

Pike Vw

Medical Cen

Wright St

Bolton Metro Borough Coun

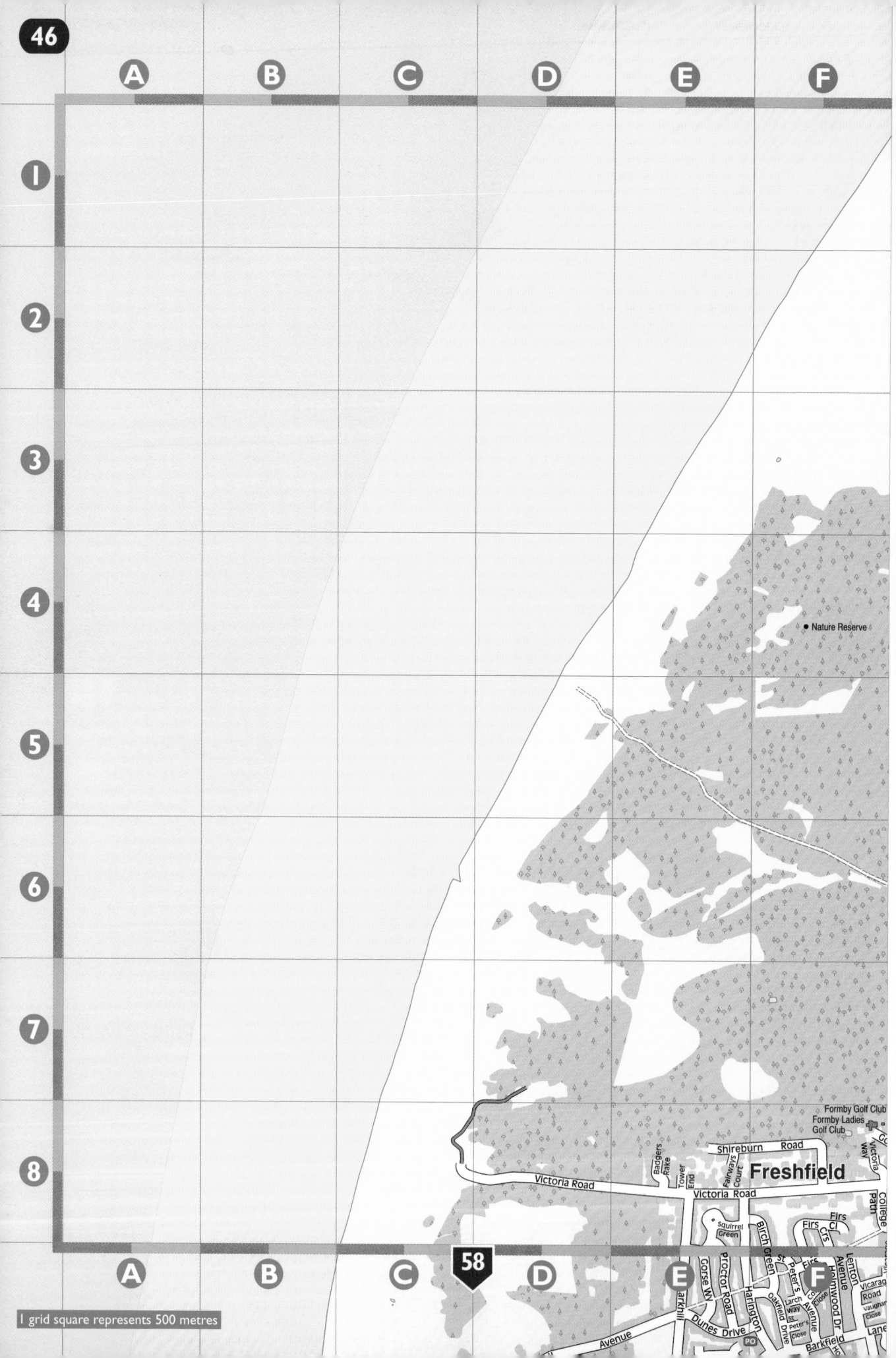

A B C D E F

1

2

3

4

• Nature Reserve

5

6

7

Formby Golf Club
Formby Ladies
Golf Club

Shireburn   Road

Badgers
Rake

Fairways
Court

Tower
End

Victoria
Way

Victoria Road

Freshfield

8

Victoria Road

Squirrel
Green

Firs
Crs

Firs
Cl

Birch green

College
Park

St Peter's
way

Larch
Drive

St Peter's
close

oakfield Drive

Lenton
Avenue

Vicarage
Road

Vaughan
close

Harnwood Dr

A B C D E F

Gorse Wy

Proctor Road

Harington

Barkhill

Dunes Drive

Avenue

Barkfield
Lane

PO

1 grid square represents 500 metres

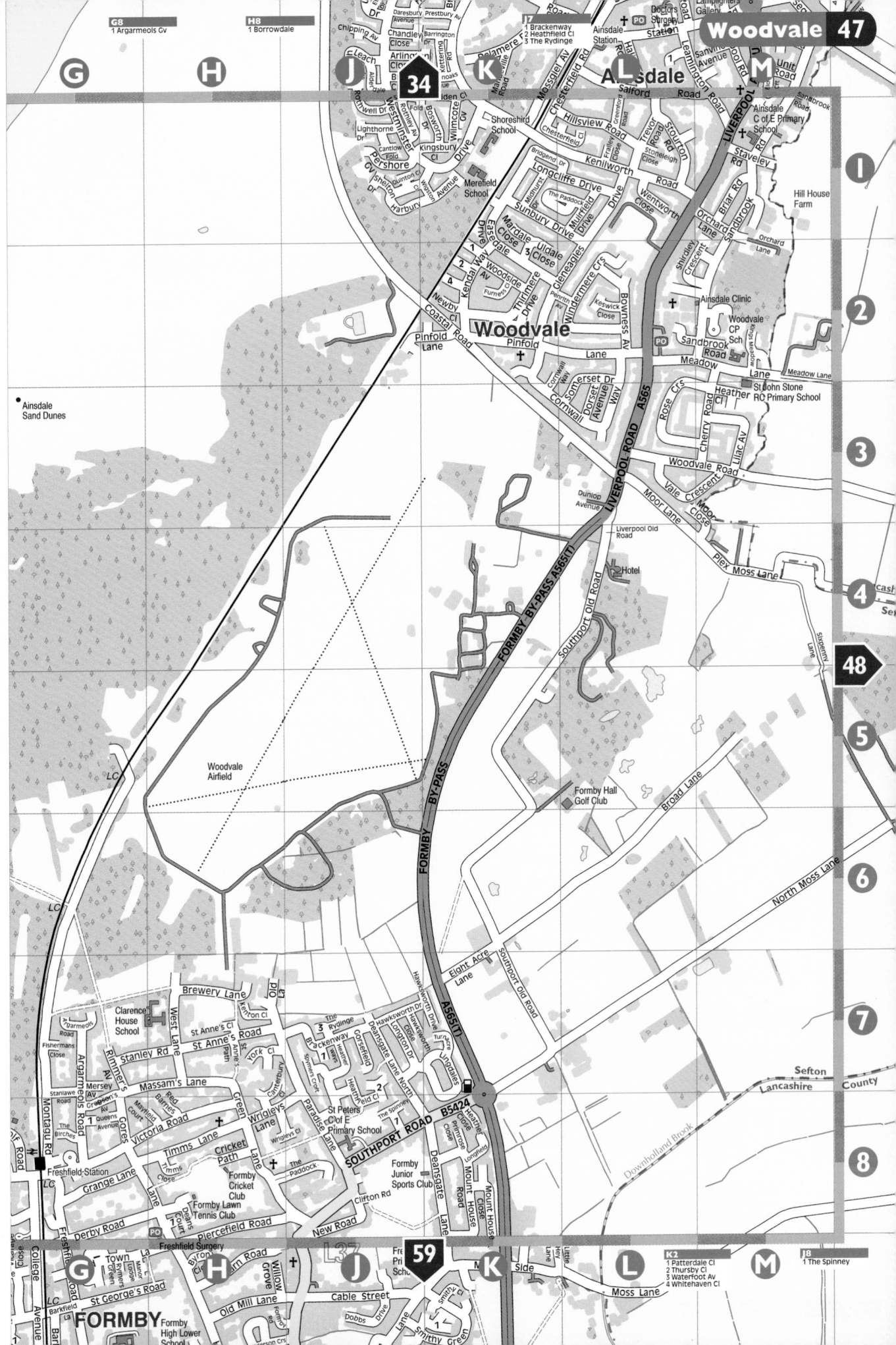

A B C 35 D E F

I

Hill House Farm

2

Meadow Lane

John Stone Primary School

3

Woodvale Road

Lancashire County
Sefton

4

47

Sefton

5

6

North ... Lane

Alder Lane

7

Sefton
Lancashire County

Cheshire Lines Path

8

White Otter Farm

Segar's Lane

Headbolt Lane

Segar's Lane

Spencer's Lane

Michael's Lane

Carr Moss Lane

Heather Farm

Plex Moss

Carr Moss Lane

Perlow's Lane

Gettern Farm

Plex Moss Lane

Plex Moss Lane

Heathy Lane

Gorsey Lane

Gorsey Lane

Moss Lane

Shaw

Old Moss Lane

A B C 60 D Downholland Moss E F

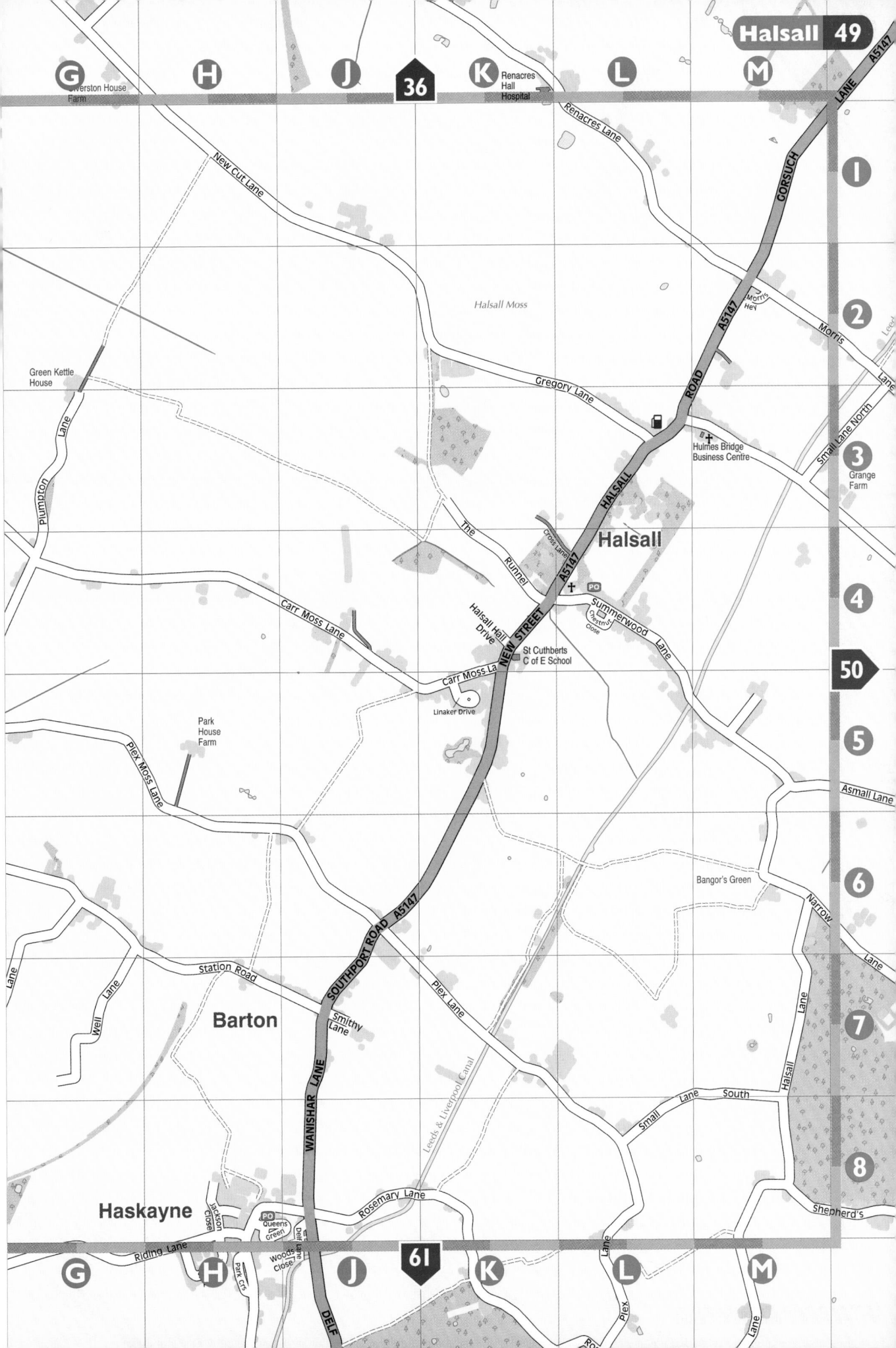

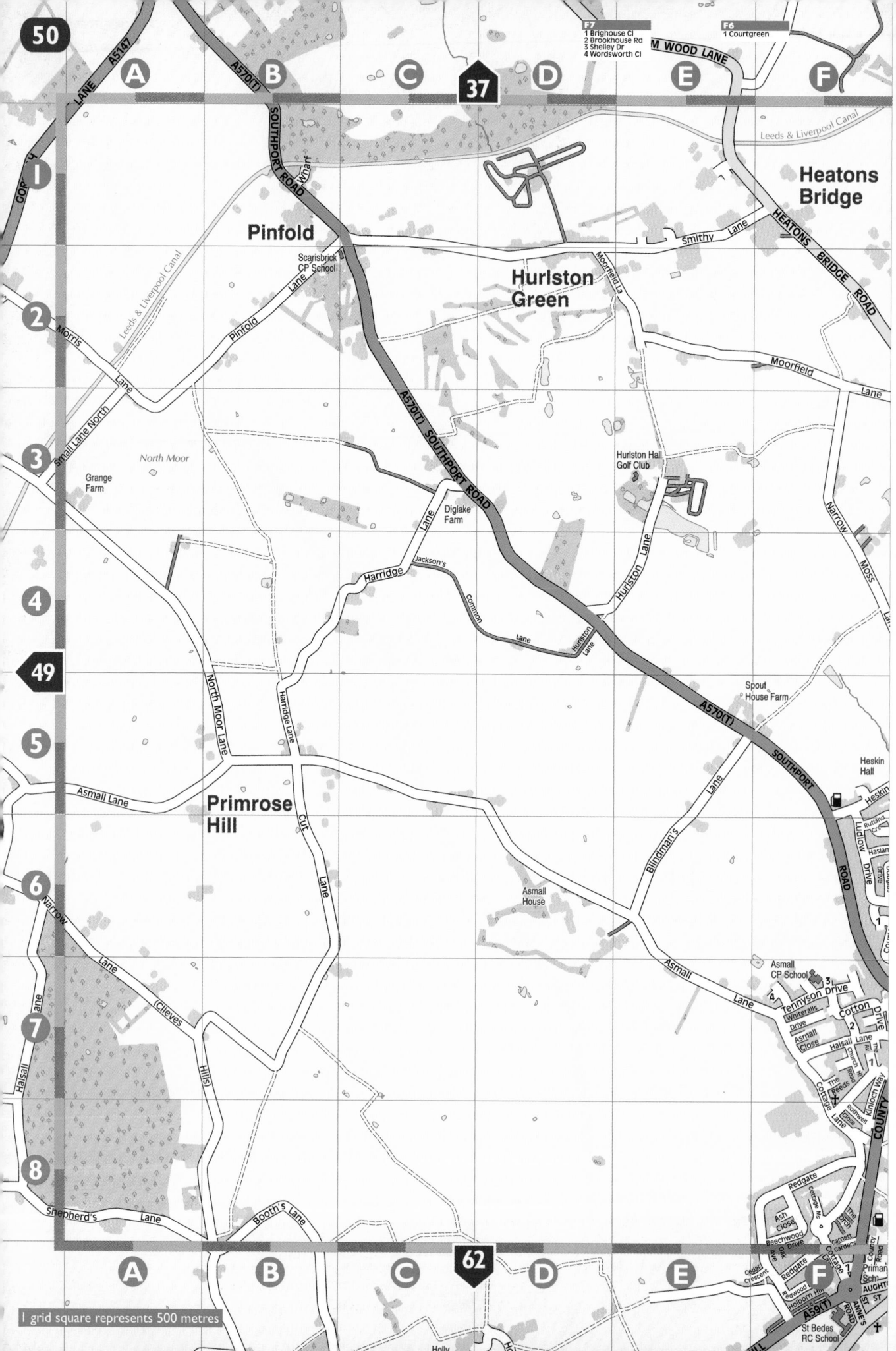

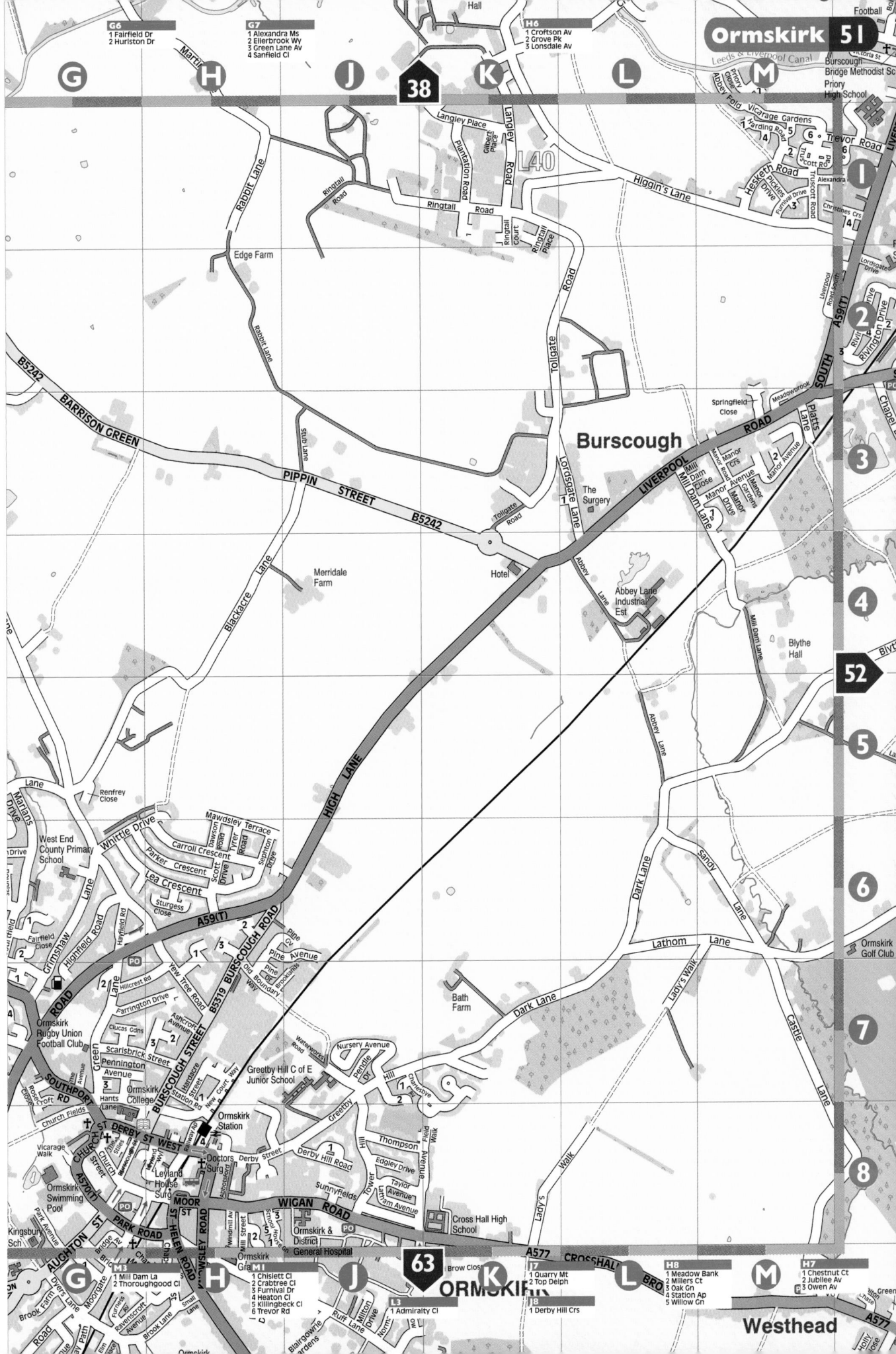

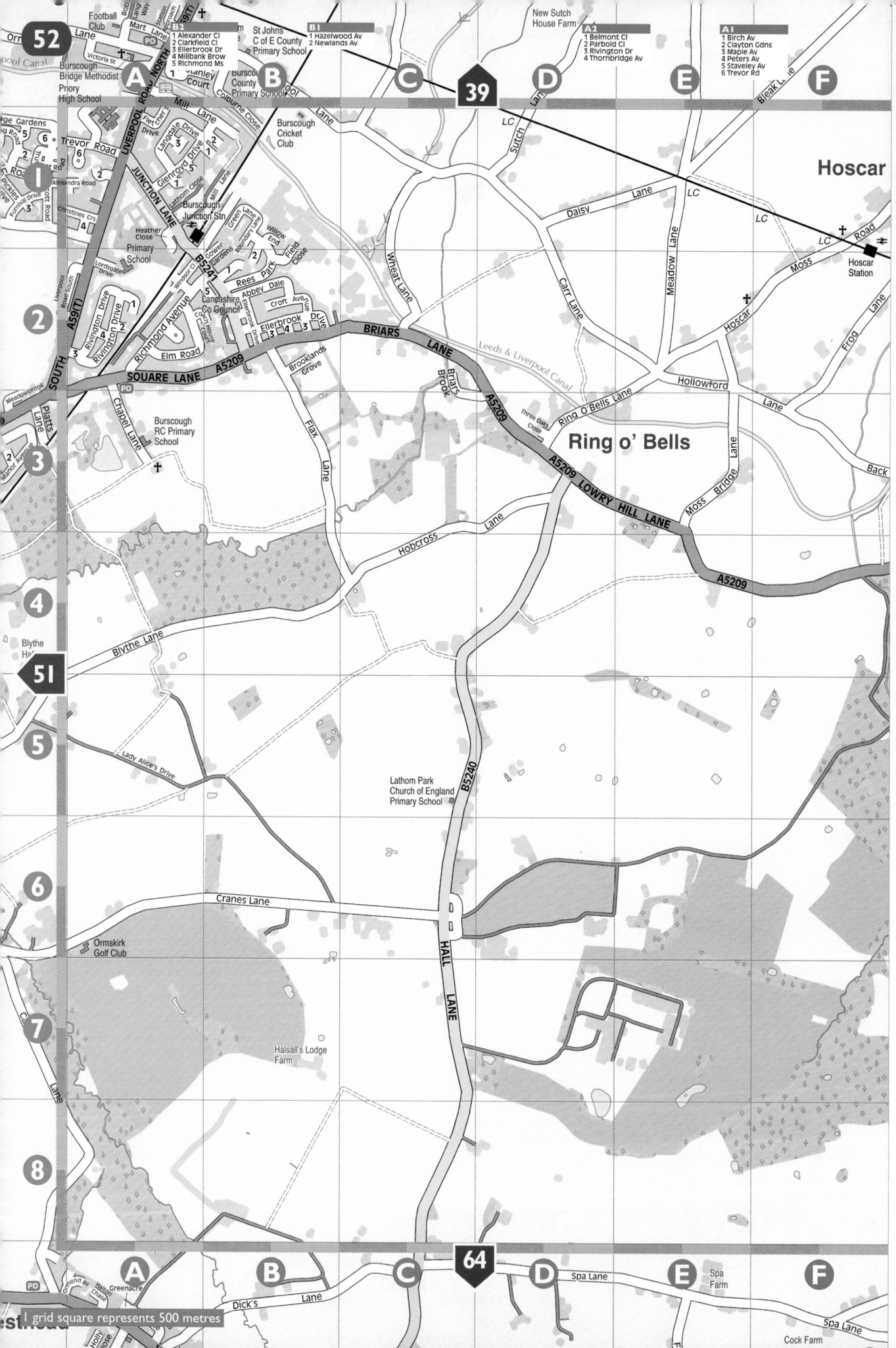

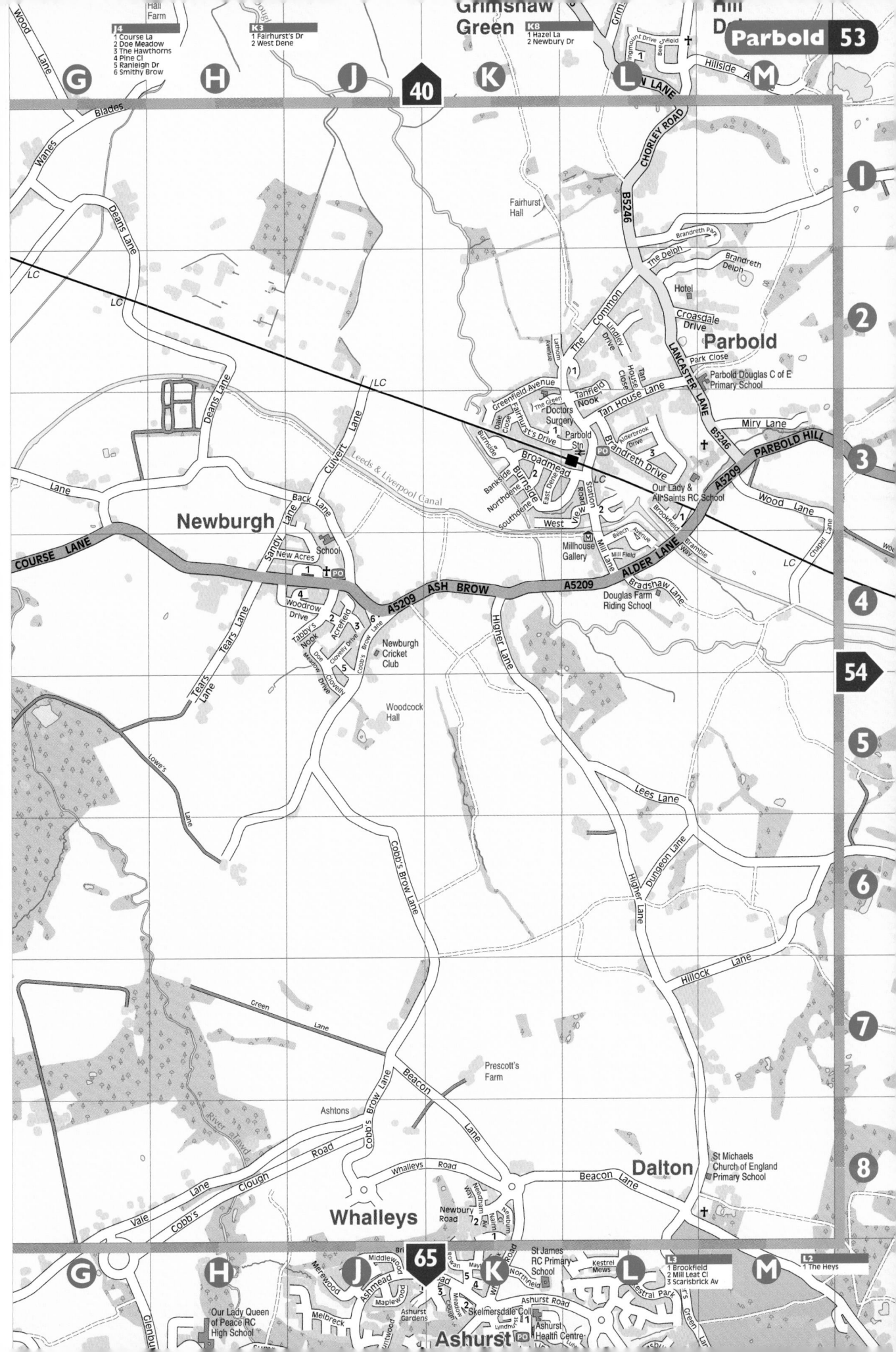

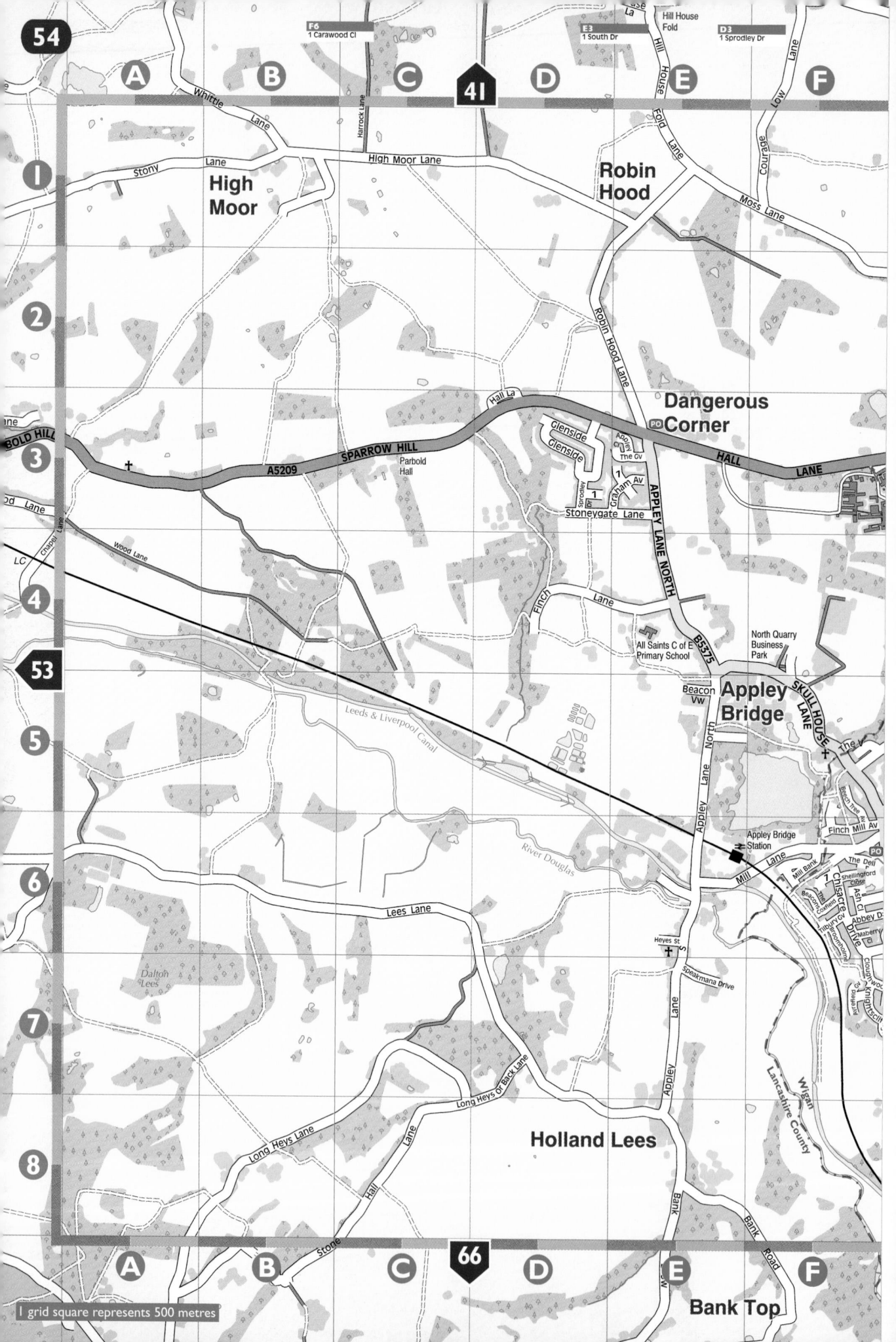

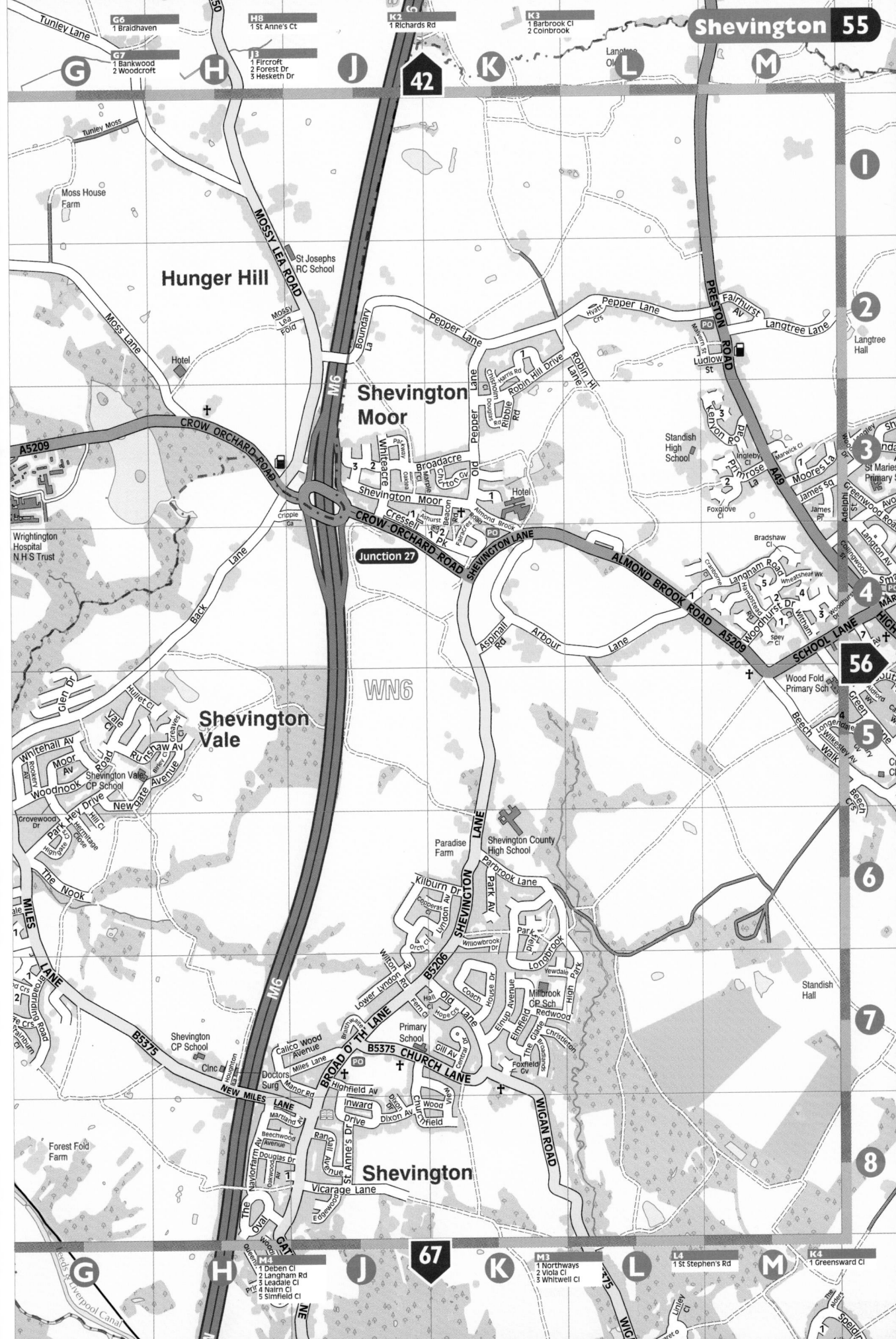

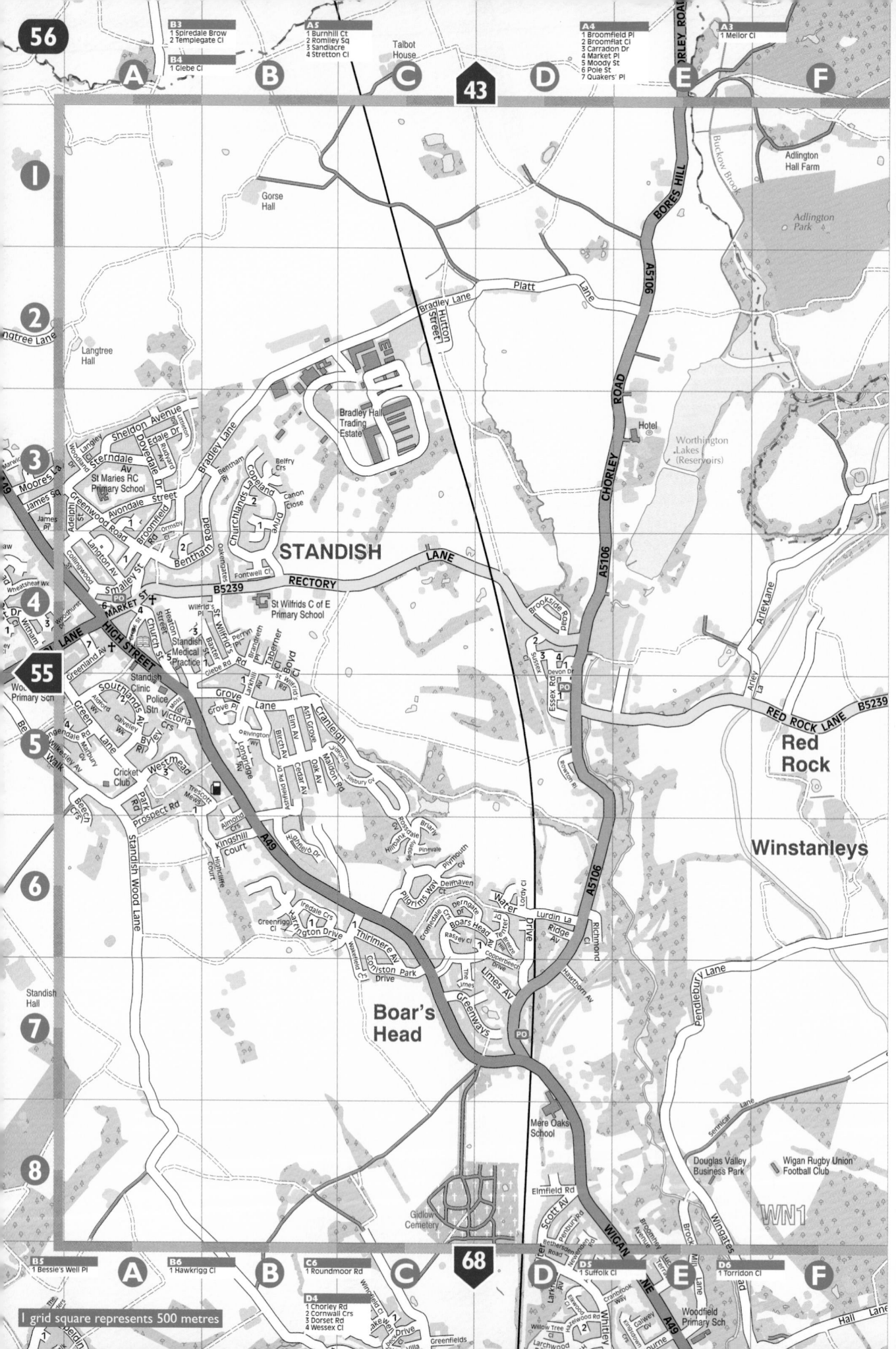

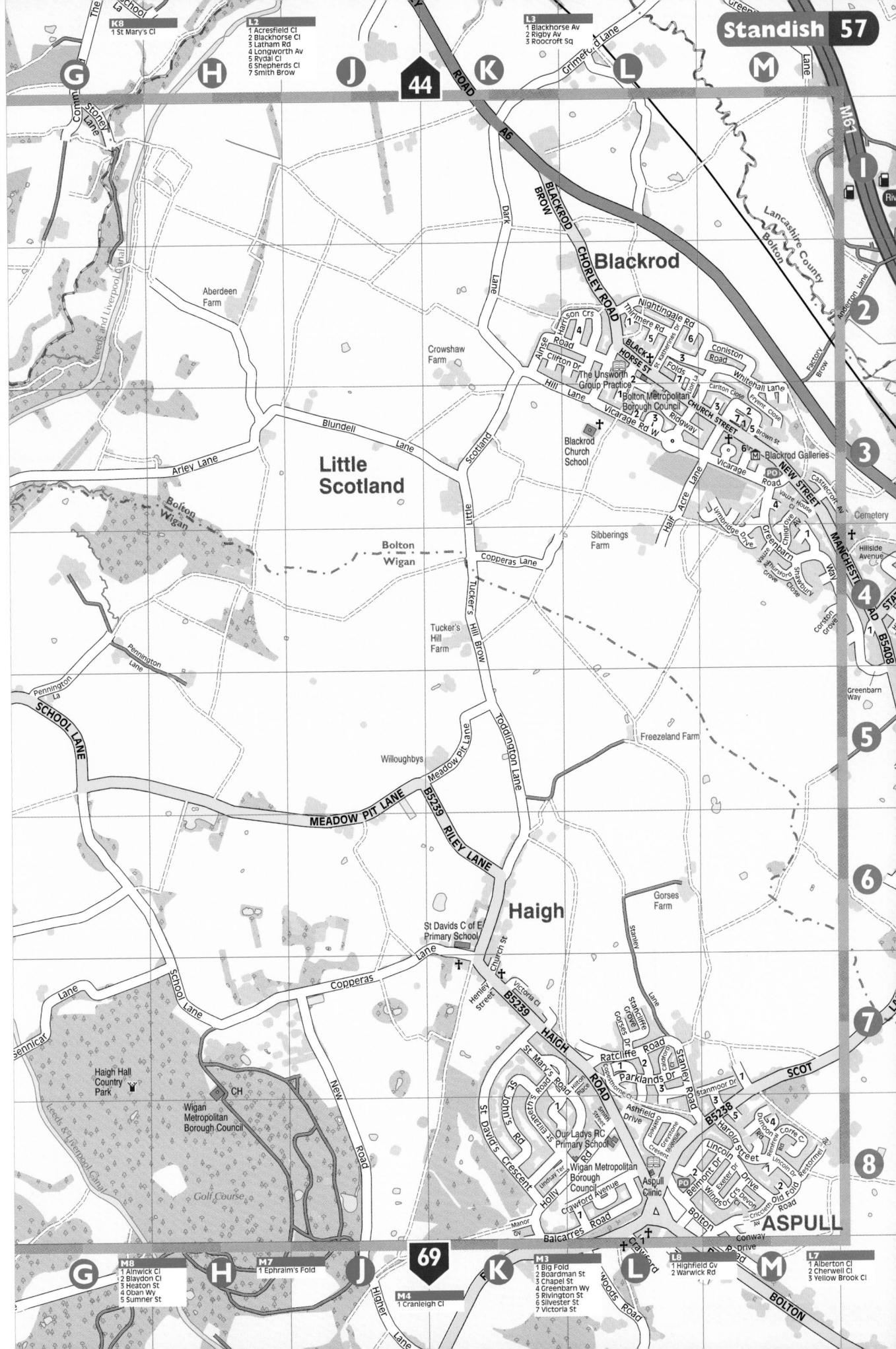

K8
1 St Mary's Cl

L2
1 Acresfield Cl
2 Blackhorse Cl
3 Latham Rd
4 Longworth Av
5 Rydal Cl
6 Shepherds Cl
7 Smith Brow

L3
1 Blackhorse Av
2 Rigby Av
3 Roocroft Sq

G H J 44 K L M I

ROAD
A6

BLACKROD BROW
CHORLEY ROAD

Blackrod

Lancashire County
Bolton

2

Aberdeen
Farm

Crowshaw
Farm

Nightingale Rd
Harrison Crs
Thirlmere Rd
Ainse Road
BLACK
HORSE ST
Clifton Dr
Hill Lane
The Unsworth
Group Practice
Bolton Metropolitan
Borough Council
Coniston
Road
Whitehall Lane
Carlton Close
Fryent Close
Brown St

Blundell
Lane
Arley Lane

**Little
Scotland**

Scotland
Little
Vicarage Rd W
Blackrod
Church
School
Vicarage Rd
Ridgway
Vicarage

Church Street
NEW STREET
Castlecroft Av
Vauze House
MANCHESTER

Blackrod Galleries
PO
Road
Cemetery
Hillside
Avenue
STATION

Bolton
Wigan

Bolton
Wigan

Copperas Lane

Sibberings
Farm

Half Acre Lane
Lymbridge Drive
Greenbarn
Way
Corston Grove

4
ROAD
B5408

Pennington
Lane
Tucker's Hill Brow
Little

Tucker's
Hill
Farm

Freezeland Farm

Greenbarn
Way

5

Pennington
La
SCHOOL LANE

Willoughbys
Meadow Pit Lane
B5239 RILEY LANE
Toddington Lane

6

MEADOW PIT LANE

Gorses
Farm
Stanley

7

Haigh

Copperas
Lane
School Lane
New Road

St Davids C of E
Primary School

Henley Street
Victoria Cl
B5239
HAIGH ROAD
Ratcliffe
Road
Parklands
Stancliffe Grove
Gorses
Road
Stanley Road
SCOT

Sennicar Lane

Haigh Hall
Country
Park
CH
Wigan
Metropolitan
Borough Council

Golf Course

Leeds & Liverpool Canal

St Mary's Road
St John's Rd
St David's Crescent
Holly
Lindsay Ter
Elizabeth St
Smith Street
Crawford Avenue
Hilton Place
Coppernose Dr
Caldecote Dr
Palatine Rd
Greystone Dr
Ashfield
Drive
Crescent
Our Ladys RC
Primary School
Wigan Metropolitan
Borough Council
Aspull
Clinic
Stanmoor Dr
B5238
Harold Street
Lincoln Drive
Belmont Dr
Winds or
Exeter Dr
St Devon
Cricceth St
Crnccoeth Av
Conway
Drive
Dunoon Rd
Lincoln Dr
Corfe Cl
Resormel
Old Fold

Manor
Gv
Balcarres Road
Bolton Road

ASPULL

G H J 69 K L M

M8
1 Alnwick Cl
2 Blaydon Cl
3 Heaton St
4 Oban Wy
5 Sumner St

M7
1 Ephraim's Fold

M4
1 Cranleigh Cl

M3
1 Big Fold
2 Boardman St
3 Chapel St
4 Greenbarn Wy
5 Rivington St
6 Silvester St
7 Victoria St

L8
1 Highfield Gv
2 Warwick Rd

L7
1 Alberton Cl
2 Cherwell Cl
3 Yellow Brook Cl

Higher Lane
Woods Road
BOLTON

shfield

Shireburn Road

Victoria Road

Victoria Rd

Victoria Road

F2
1 Buttermere Cl
2 Ennerdale Cl

E4
1 Sandhurst Cl

E3
1 Edenhurst Dr
2 Greenloon's Dr
3 Hazlehurst Cl
4 Springfield Cl

E2
1 Delph La

Badgers Rake

Squirrel Green

College Path

Firs Link

College Way

Vicarage Close

Holmwood Dr

Lemon Avenue

Birch Green

Proctor Road

St Peter's Avenue

Larch Way

Oakfield Drive

St Peter's Close

Firs Avenue

Holmwood Dr

Vaughan Close

Lane

Dunes Drive

Harington

Barkfield

Beech Dr

Holmw Close

Larkhill

Lane

PO

Wld Dr

Blundell Avenue

Wicks Green Close

Warren Gn

Wicks Crs

Wicks Grn

Ince Crs

Harington Road

Harington Close

Wicks Lane

Wicks

St Jeromes RC Primary School

Spruce Way

Woodlands Primary School

1 2 Ennerdale

Greenloon's Cl

Tarn Road

Edenhurst Dr

Foxhill

Greenloon's Drive

Derwent Avenue

Langdale Av

Rydal Cl

Eskdale

Grasmere Rdlands

Mere Rd

Eskdale Cl

Edenhurst Cl

Kirklake Way

Greenloon's Walk

Coniston Road

Langdale Close

Woodlands

Kirklake

St Luke's Drive

Church Gn

Church Way

Brooks Way

Brooks Road

Ward Av

Chindit

Bushby's Park

Lifeboat Road

Shorrocks Hill Country Club

St Luke's Church Road

Bushby's Lane

Trap Hill

Pinewood Close

Foster Rd

Sealand Cl

Que

Lime Tree Way

Maple Close

Drive

St Lukes C of E Primary School

Elson Rd

Carrs Crescent

Beechwood Drive

Cedar Grove

Chestnut Drive

Sycamore Drive

Pinewood Avenue

West

Crescent

Alexandra Road

Albert Road

Aspen Gv

Ash Grove

Milford Close

Elm Drive

Cambridge Rd

Funchal Av

Barton Hey

Mayfield Av

Heydon Close

Hadstock Avenue

Tadlow Close

Meldreth Close

Burwell Avenue

Freshlea Private Clinic

1

Orwell

Elsworth Cl

Stapleton Road

Nature Reserve

Range High School

St Luke's Church Road

F3
1 Elmdale Cl
2 Woodlands Cl

F4
1 Eccles Rd

1 grid square represents 500 metres

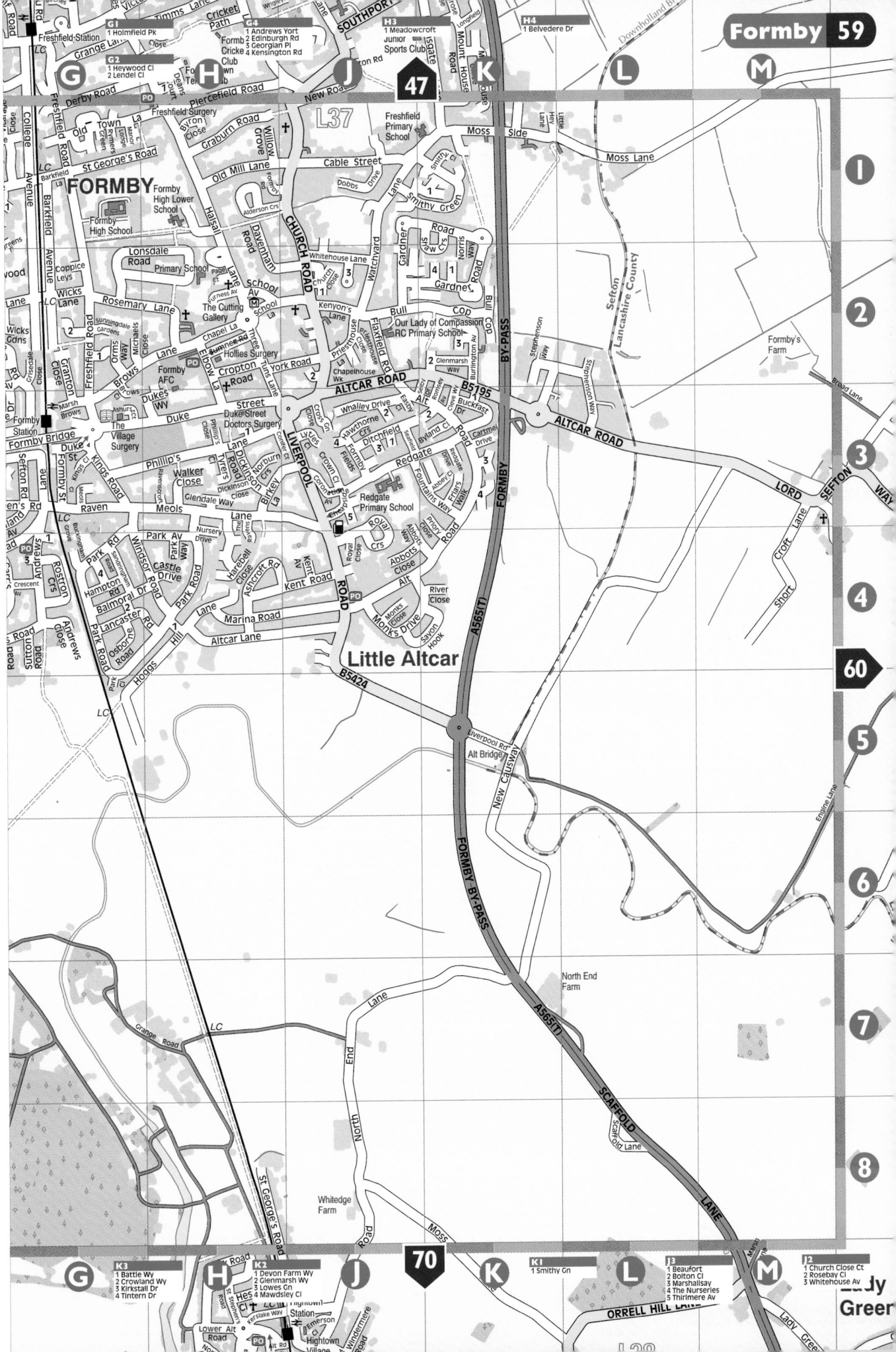

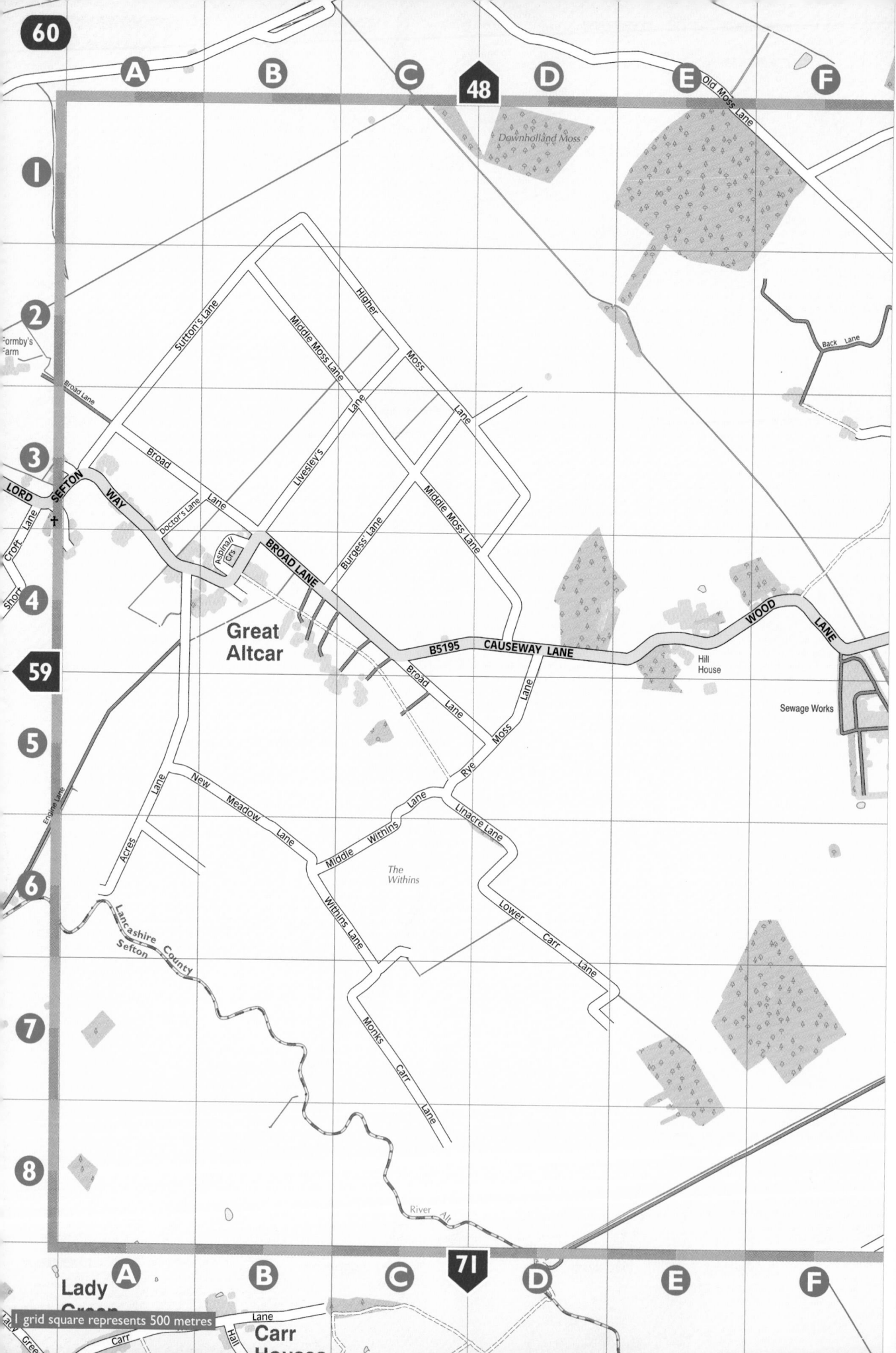

A B C **48** D E F

I

2

Formby's Farm

Broad Lane

3

LORD

SEFTON WAY

Croft Lane

Snort

4

59

5

Enshine Lane

6

Lancashire County
Sefton

7

8

Sutton's Lane

Middle Moss Lane

Higher

Moss

Lane

Broad

Lane

Doctor's Lane

Aspinall
Crs

Livesley's

Lane

Burgess Lane

Middle Moss Lane

BROAD LANE

Great
Altcar

Broad

Lane

B5195 CAUSEWAY LANE

Moss

Lane

Rye

Lane

Linacre Lane

New

Meadow

Lane

Acres

Lane

Middle

Withins

Withins Lane

The
Withins

Lower

Carr

Lane

Monks

Carr

Lane

River Alt

Downholland Moss

Back Lane

WOOD

LANE

Hill
House

Sewage Works

A **71** B C D E F

Lady
Green

Carr
Houses

Carr

Lane

Green

Hall

Lane

1 grid square represents 500 metres

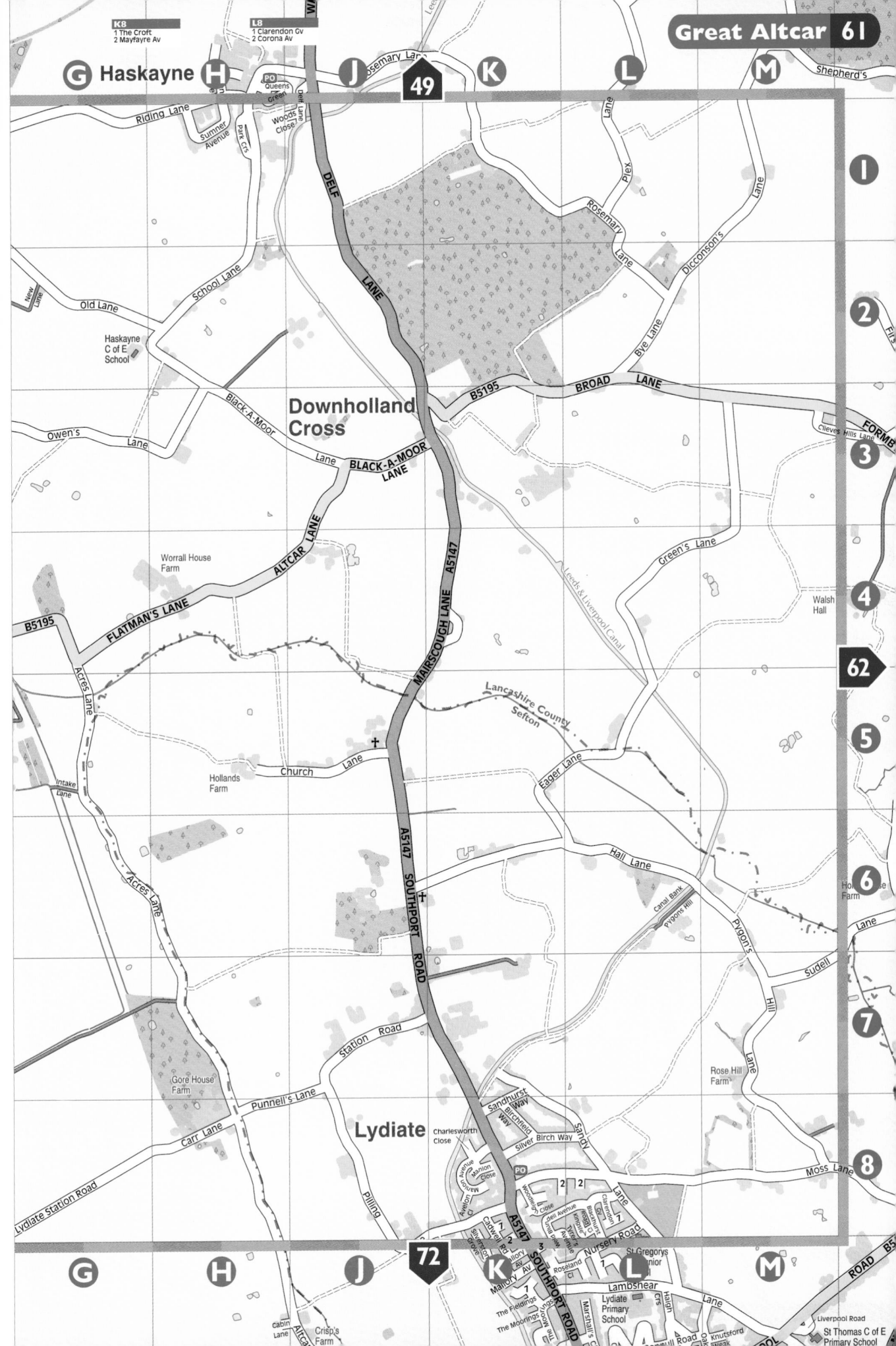

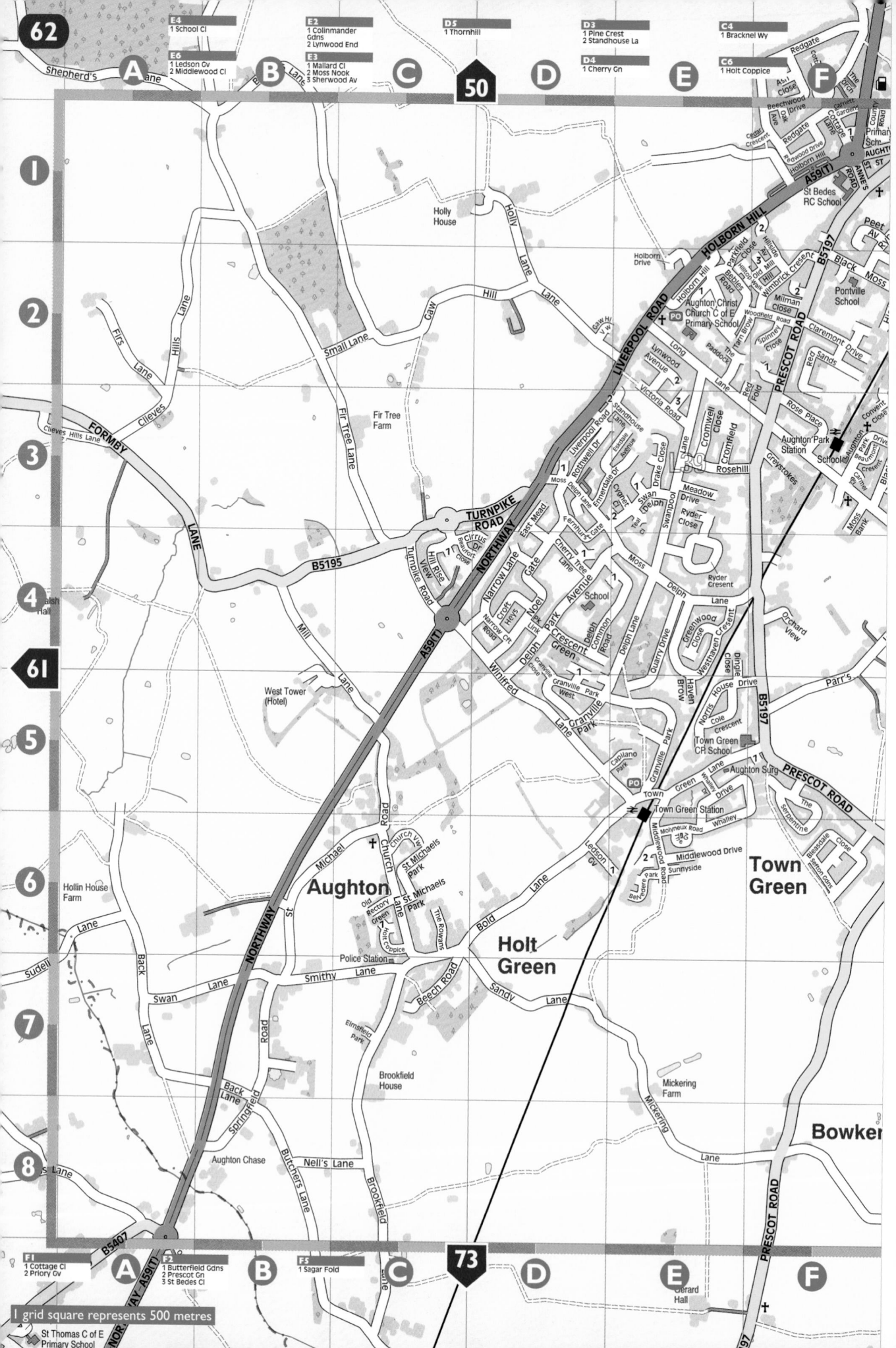

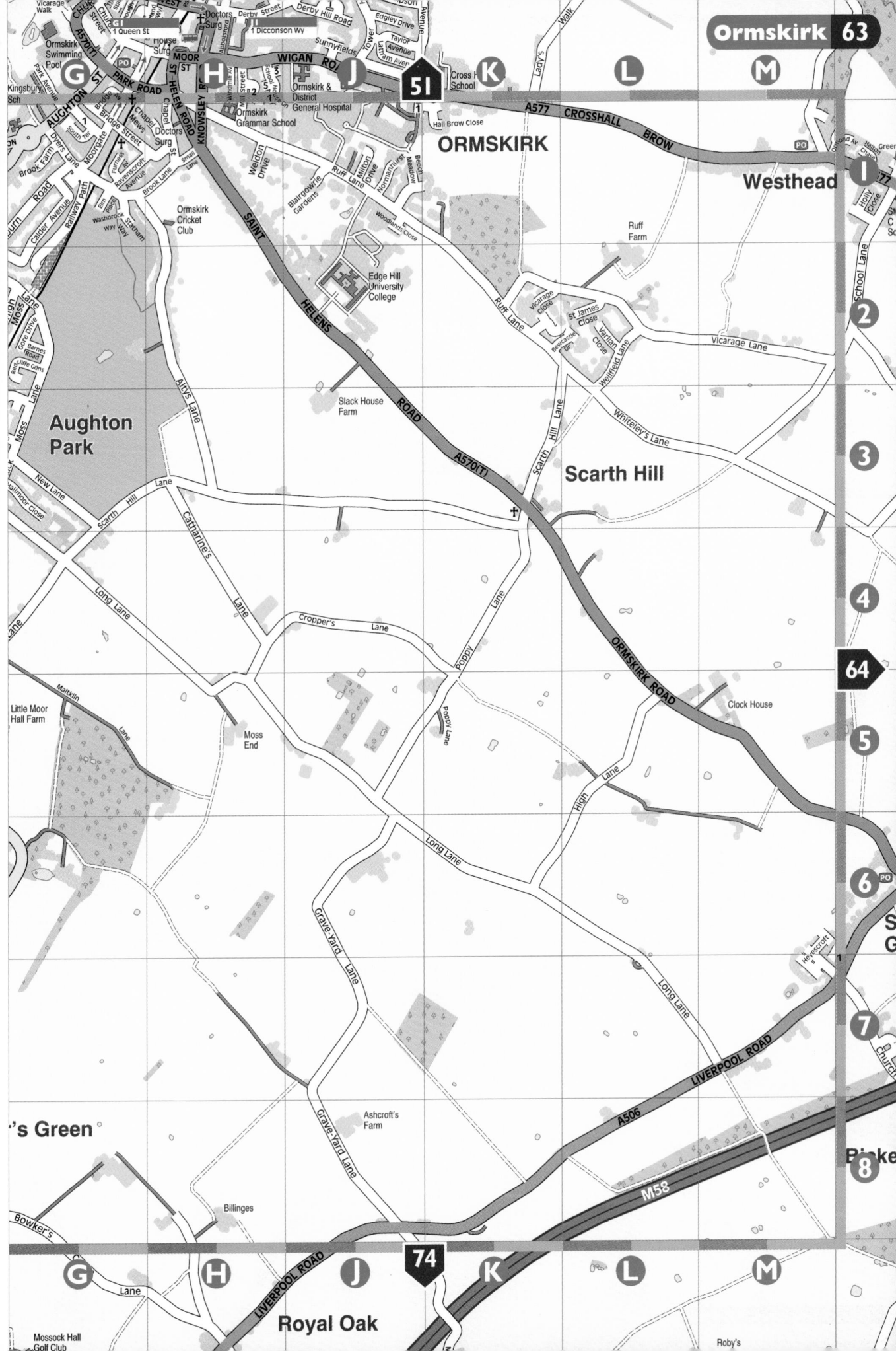

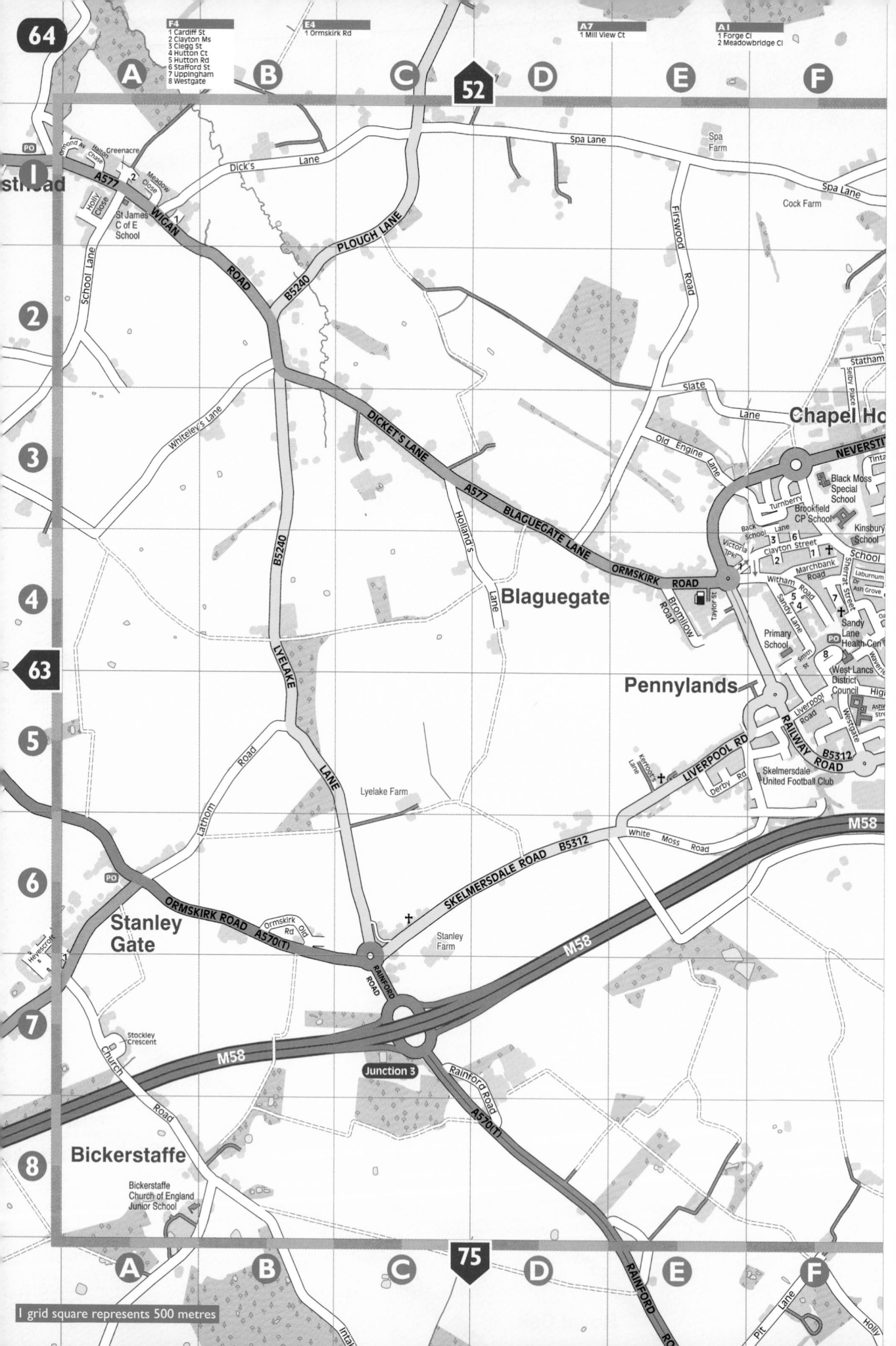

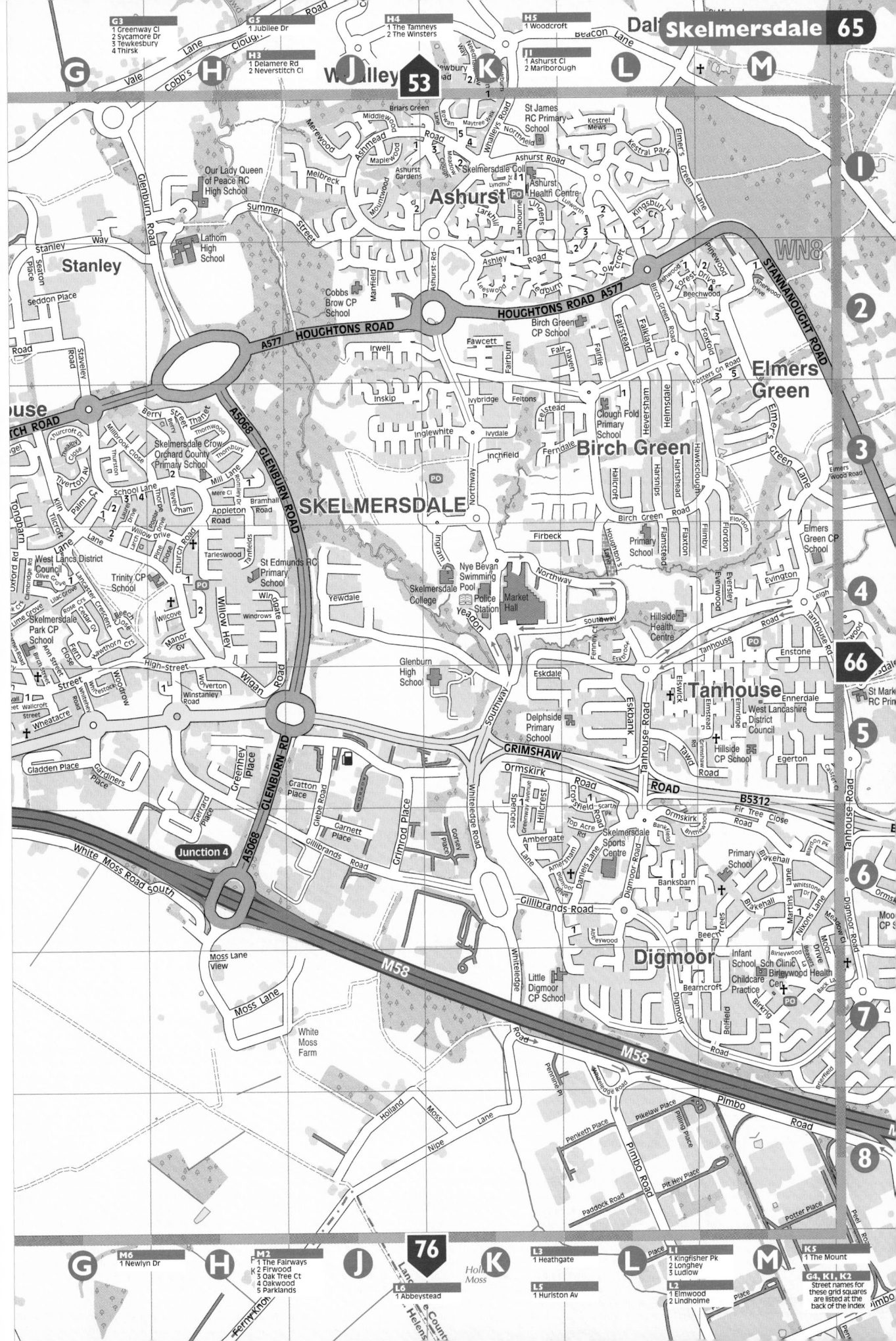

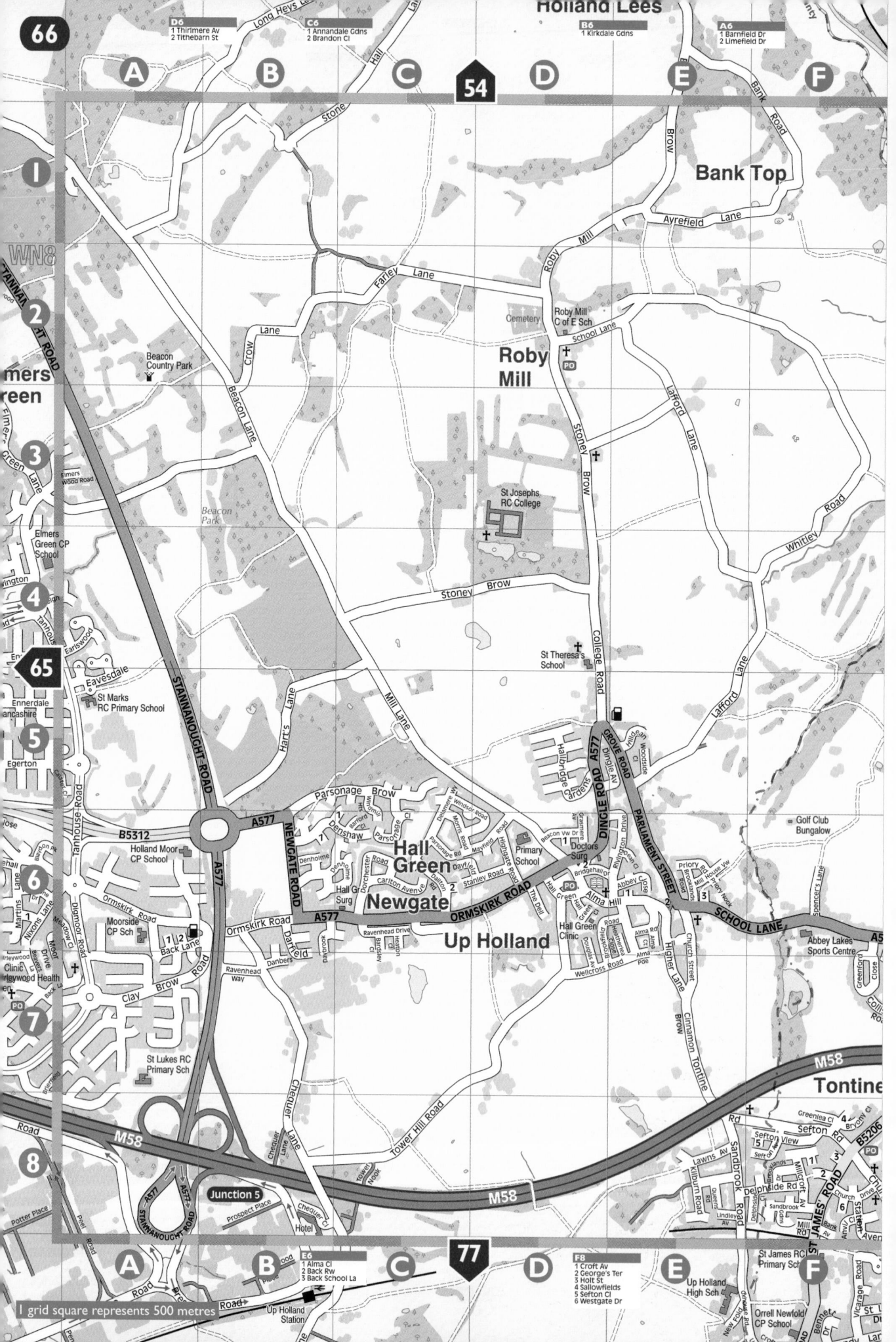

Holland Lees

Bank Top

Roby Mill

Bank Top

Ayrefield Lane

Beacon Country Park

Farley Lane

Crow Lane

Cemetery

Roby Mill C of E Sch

School Lane

Beacon Park

St Josephs RC College

Lafford Lane

Stoney Brow

Whitley Road

St Marks RC Primary School

Elmers Green CP School

Ennerdale Lancashire

Egerton

Stoney Brow

St Theresa's School

College Road

Lafford Lane

Hart's Lane

Mill Lane

Hallbridge Gardens

Dingle Road

Grove Road

Maple Cr

Woodside

Hillcrest

Parliament Street

Golf Club Bungalow

Parsonage Brow

Denshaw

Hall Green

Newgate

Primary School

Doctors Surg

Priory Brooklands

Mill House Vw

Stannought Road

B5312

Holland Moor CP School

Newgate Road

Hall Gr Surg

Carlton Avenue

Stanley Road

The Dell

Bridgehall

Abbey Rd

Alma Hill

Church Street

School Lane

Spencer's Lane

Abbey Lakes Sports Centre

Ormskirk Road

Ormskirk Road

Ravenhead Drive

Barclay

Heaton

Up Holland

Hall Green Clinic

Higher Lane

Cinnamon Tontine Brow

Moorside CP Sch

Back Lane

Darfield

Danbers

Wellcross Road

Douglas Av

Clay Brow

Ravenhead Way

Dugmoor Road

Golf Club

St Lukes RC Primary Sch

Chequer Lane

Tower Hill Road

M58

Tontine

M58

M58

Junction 5

Prospect Place

Hotel

Chequer Lane

Sefton View

Sandbrook Road

Kilburn Road

Sefton Road

B5206

Delphside Rd

St James Road

Lindley Av

St James RC Primary Sch

Up Holland Station

Up Holland High Sch

Orrell Newfold CP School

65

77

WN8

I grid square represents 500 metres

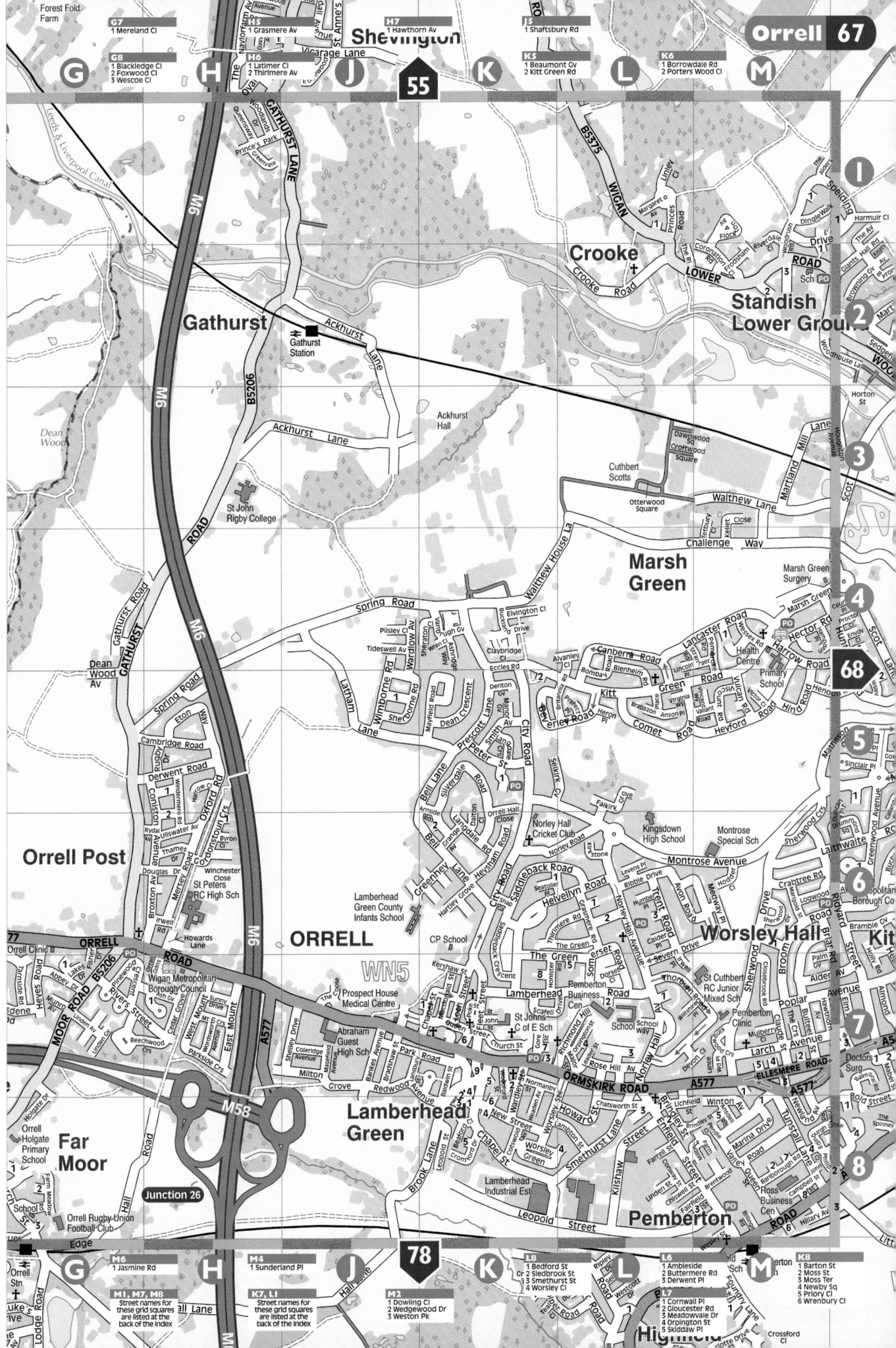

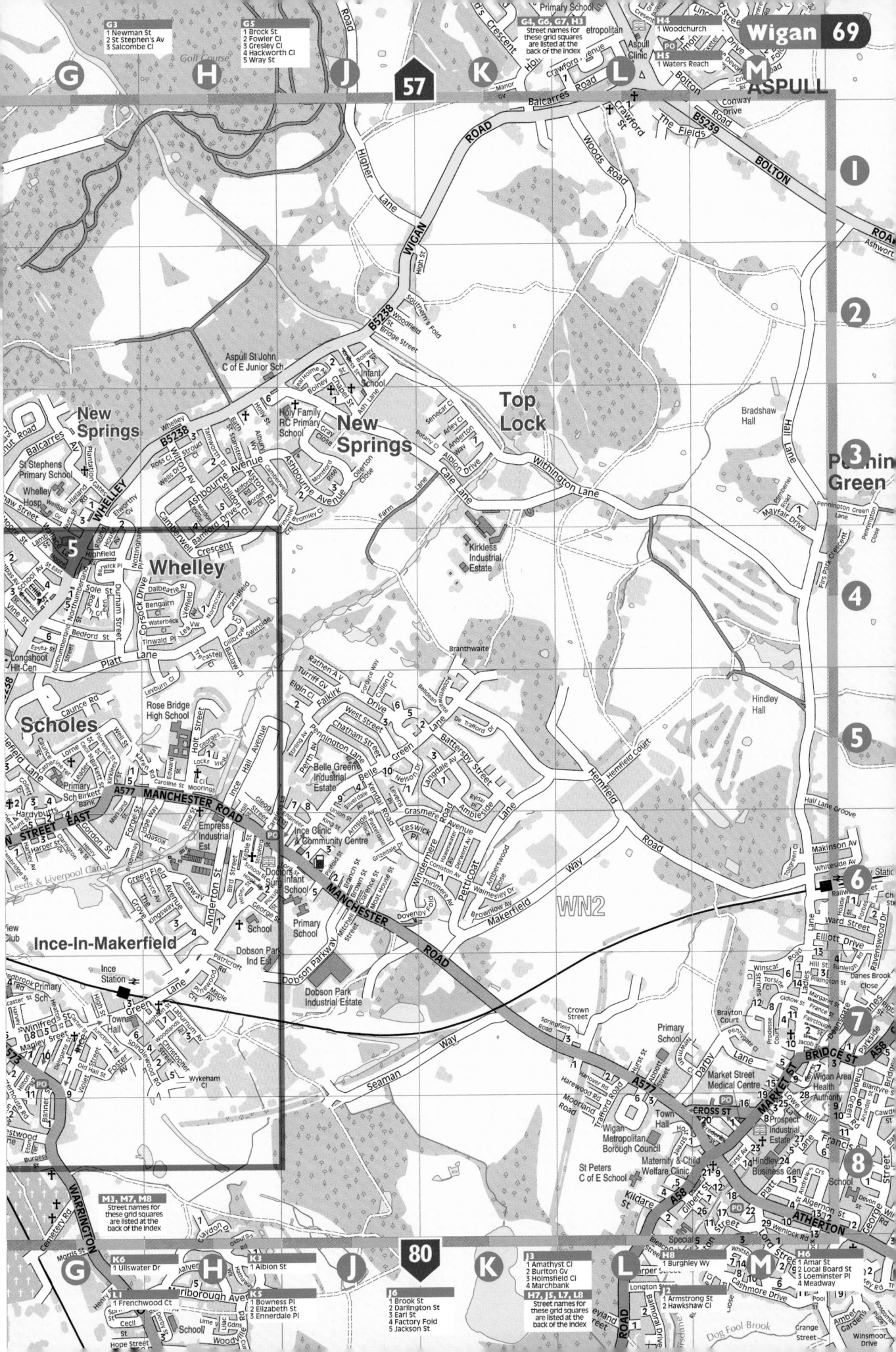

G3
1 Newman St
2 St Stephen's Av
3 Salcombe Cl

G5
1 Brock St
2 Fowler Cl
3 Gresley Cl
4 Hackworth Cl
5 Wray St

G4, G6, G7, H3
Street names for
these grid squares
are listed at the
back of the index

H4
1 Woodchurch

H5
1 Waters Reach

K6
1 Ullswater Dr

K3
1 Albion St

H8
1 Frenchwood Ct

K5
1 Bowness Pl
2 Elizabeth St
3 Ennerdale Pl

J6
1 Brook St
2 Darlington St
3 Earl St
4 Factory Fold
5 Jackson St

J3
1 Amethyst Cl
2 Buirton Gv
3 Holmsfield Cl
4 Marchbank

H7, J5, L7, L8
Street names for
these grid squares
are listed at the
back of the index

H8
1 Burghley Wy

H4
1 Amar St
2 Local Board St
3 Loeminster Pl
4 Meadway

M3, M7, M8
Street names for
these grid squares
are listed at the
back of the index

ASPULL

New Springs

New Springs

Top Lock

Pennington Green

Whelley

Scholes

Ince-In-Makerfield

WN2

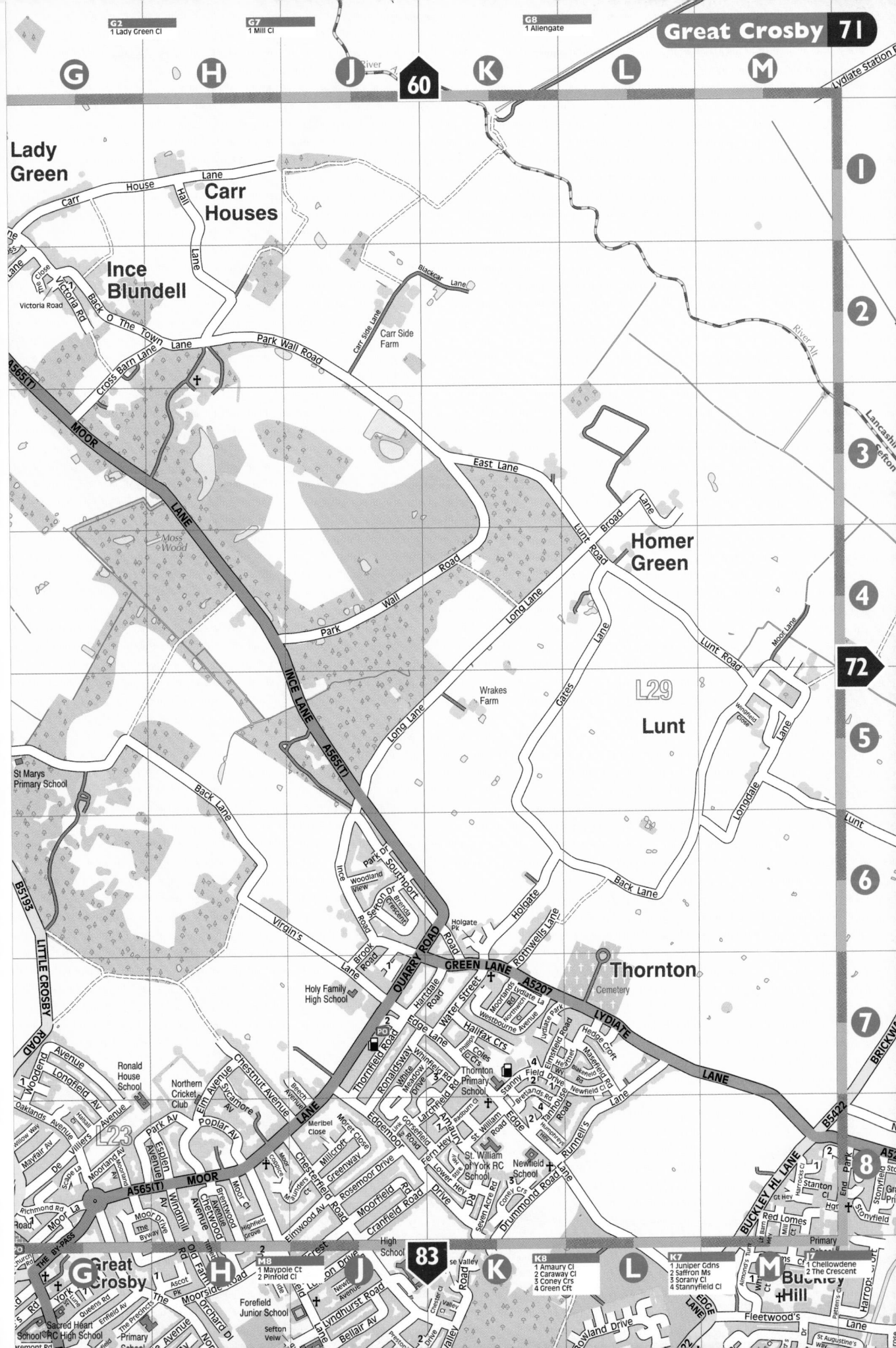

A   B   C   D   E   F

E3
1 Burgess Gdns
2 Dovedale Av
3 Hindley Beech

E4
1 Balmoral Rd
2 Green La
3 Staff'd M'ton Wy

E1
1 Huntingdon Gv

E2
1 Comer Gdns
2 Redwood Av

D5
1 Lincoln Gn

D3
1 Alregate
2 Meadow Bank
3 The Thorns
4 Wensleydale Cl

B8
1 Windsor Cl

D1
1 The Fieldings
2 Oulton Cl
3 Southport Rd

61

D4, F1
Street names for
these grid squares
are listed at the
back of the index

1
2
3
4
71
5
6
7
8

MAGHULL

Sefton

Lancashire County
Sefton

Netherton

Buckley
Hill

Junction 7

M58

M57

1 grid square represents 500 metres

A   B   C   D   E   F

E6
1 Glenholm Rd
2 The Lindens

E7
1 Pimbley Gv East
2 Pimbley Gv West
3 Whinney Gv East
4 Whinney Gv West

F2
1 Arcadia Av
2 Byron Rd
3 The Elms
4 Marlborough Av

E3
1 Central Sq
2 Howells Cl
3 Oakhill Cl

E4
1 Staff'd M'ton Wy

F6
1 Fieldway
2 Moorhey Rd

84

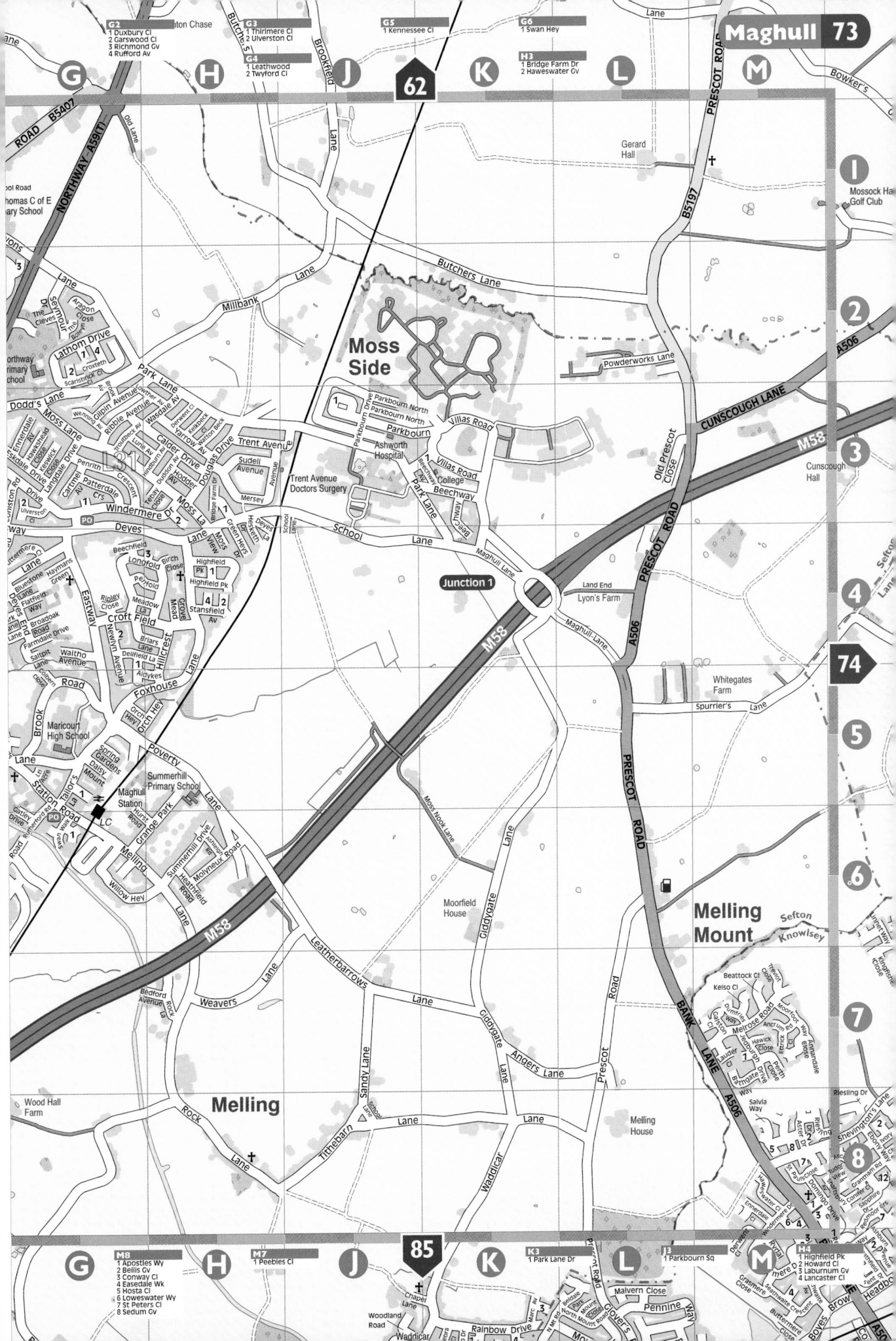

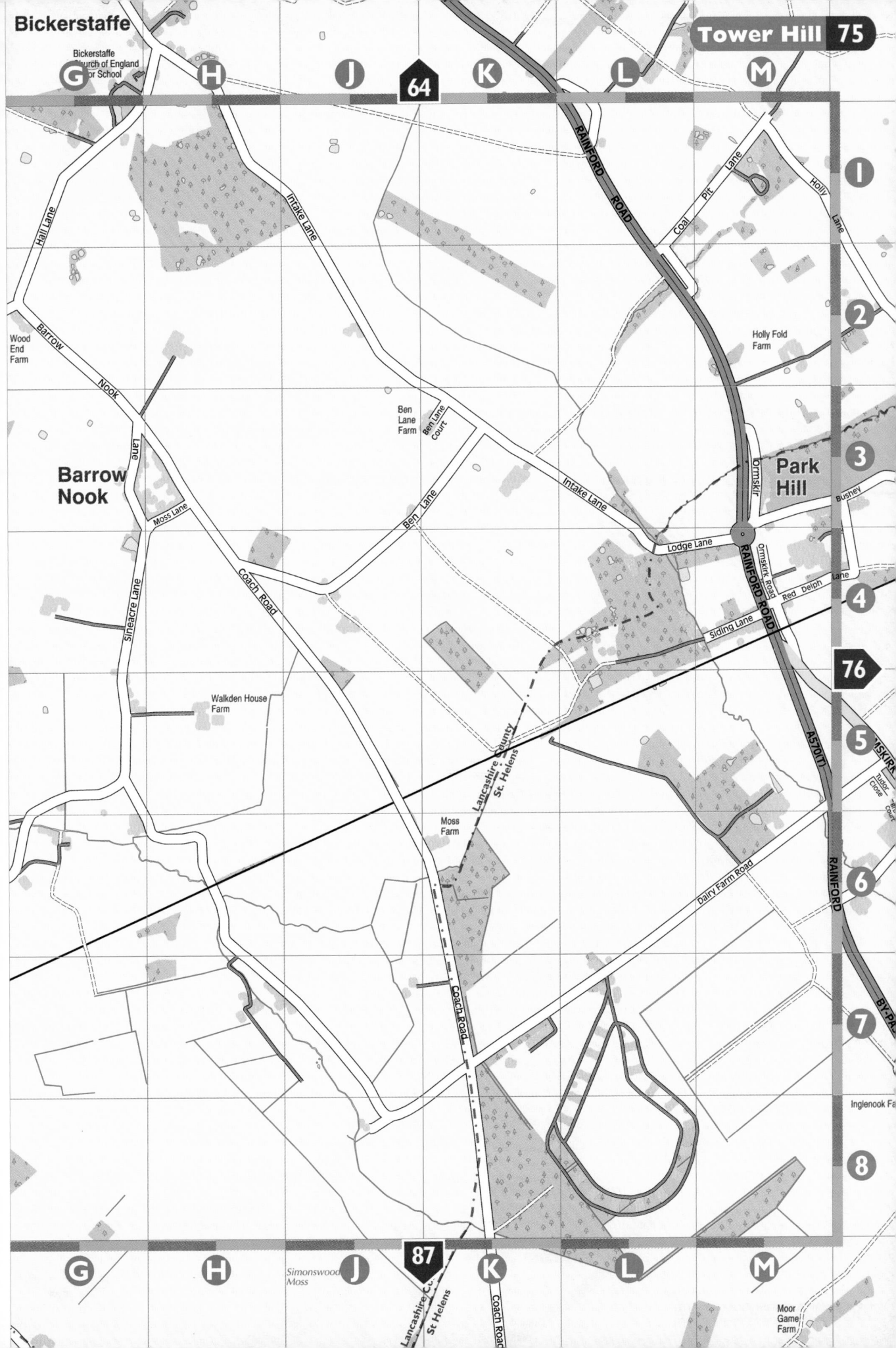

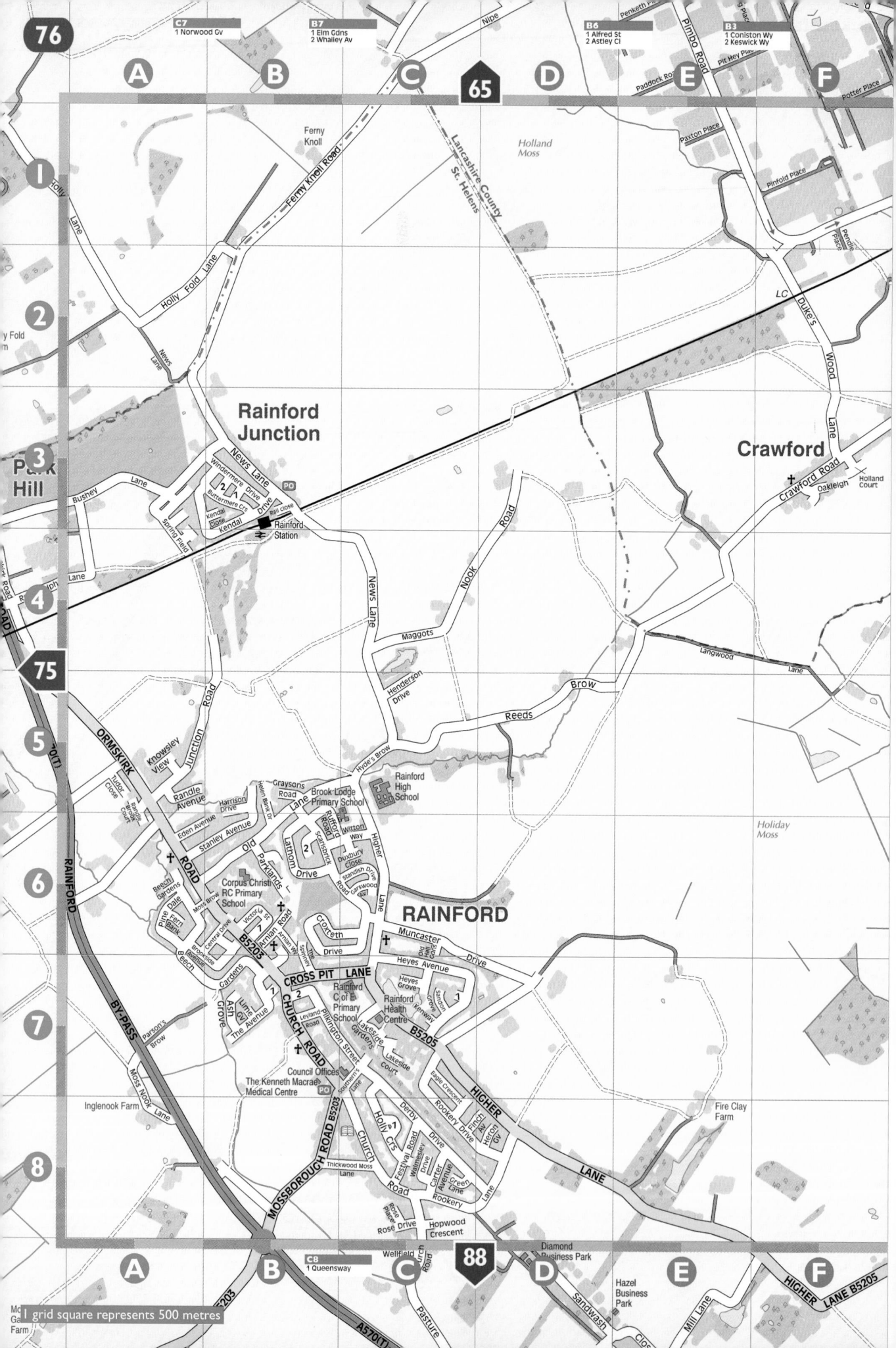

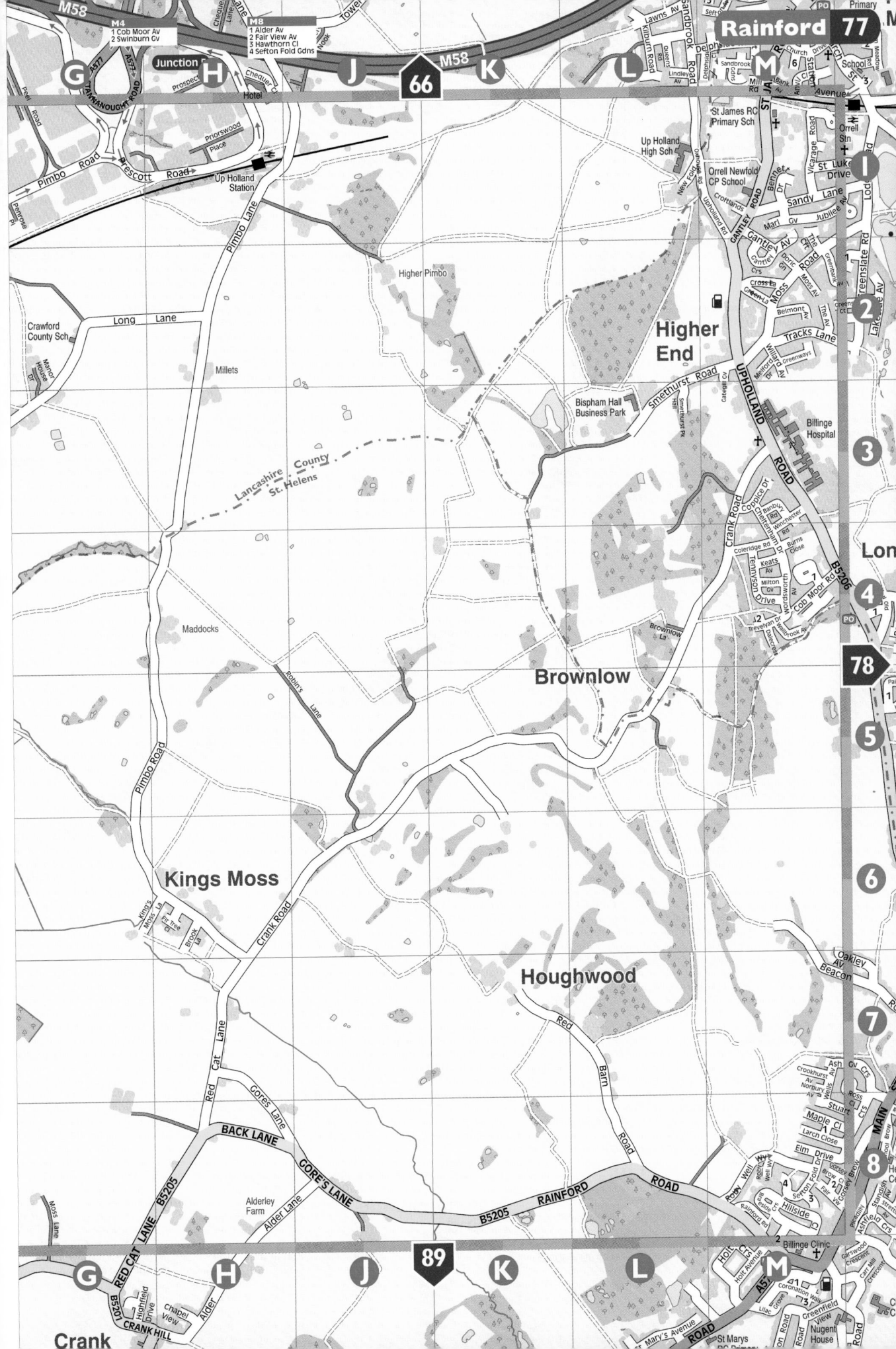

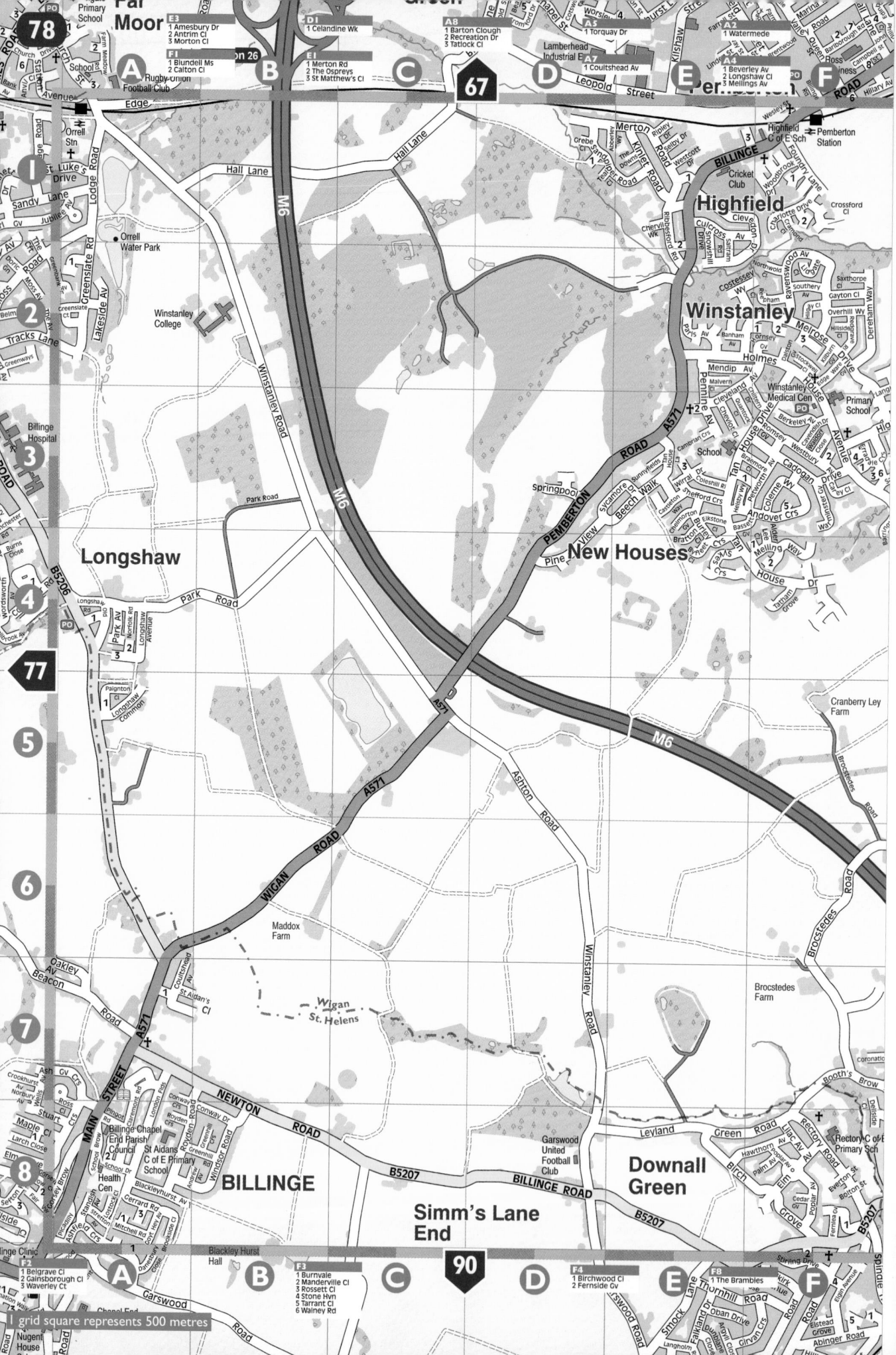

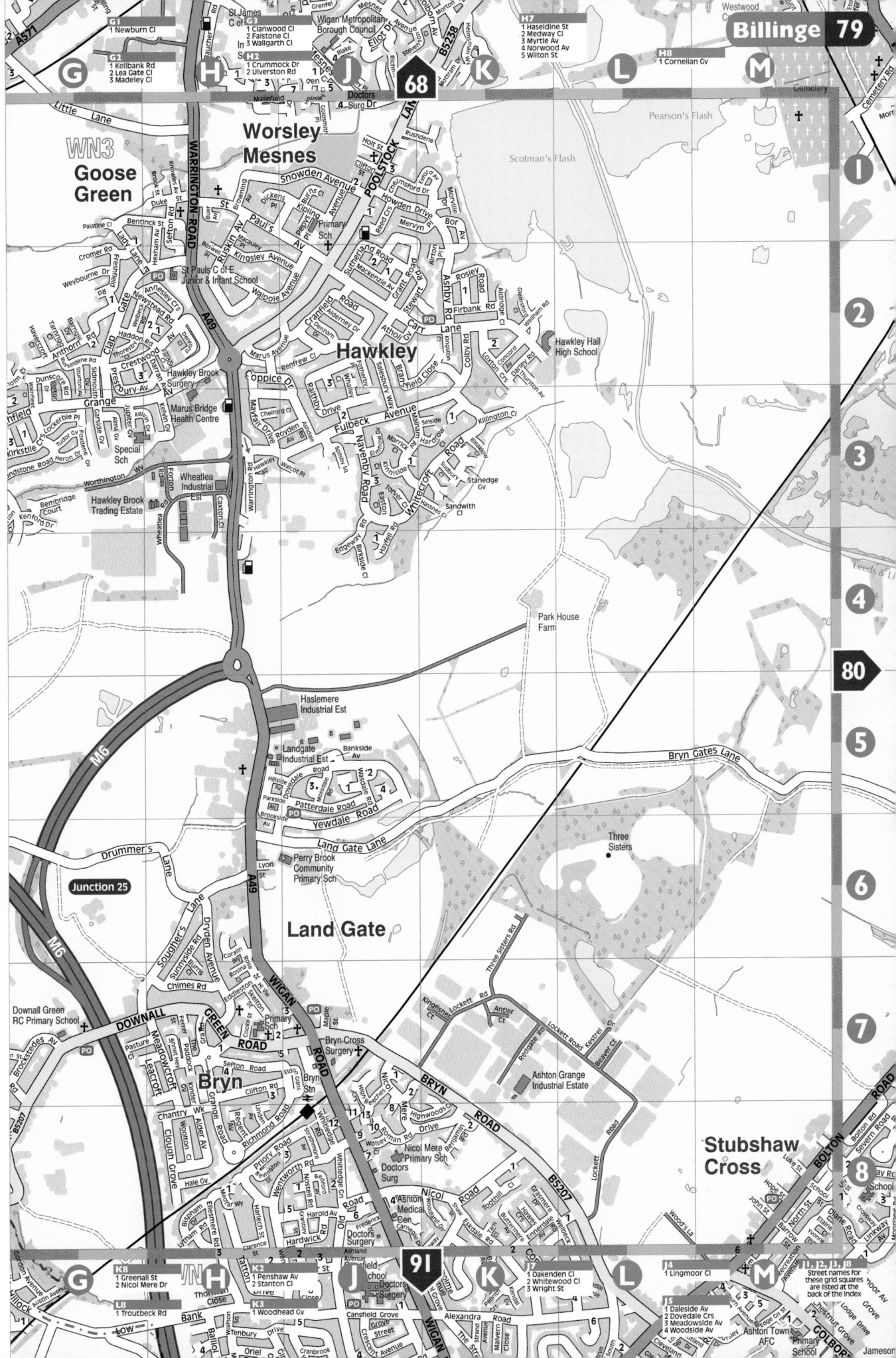

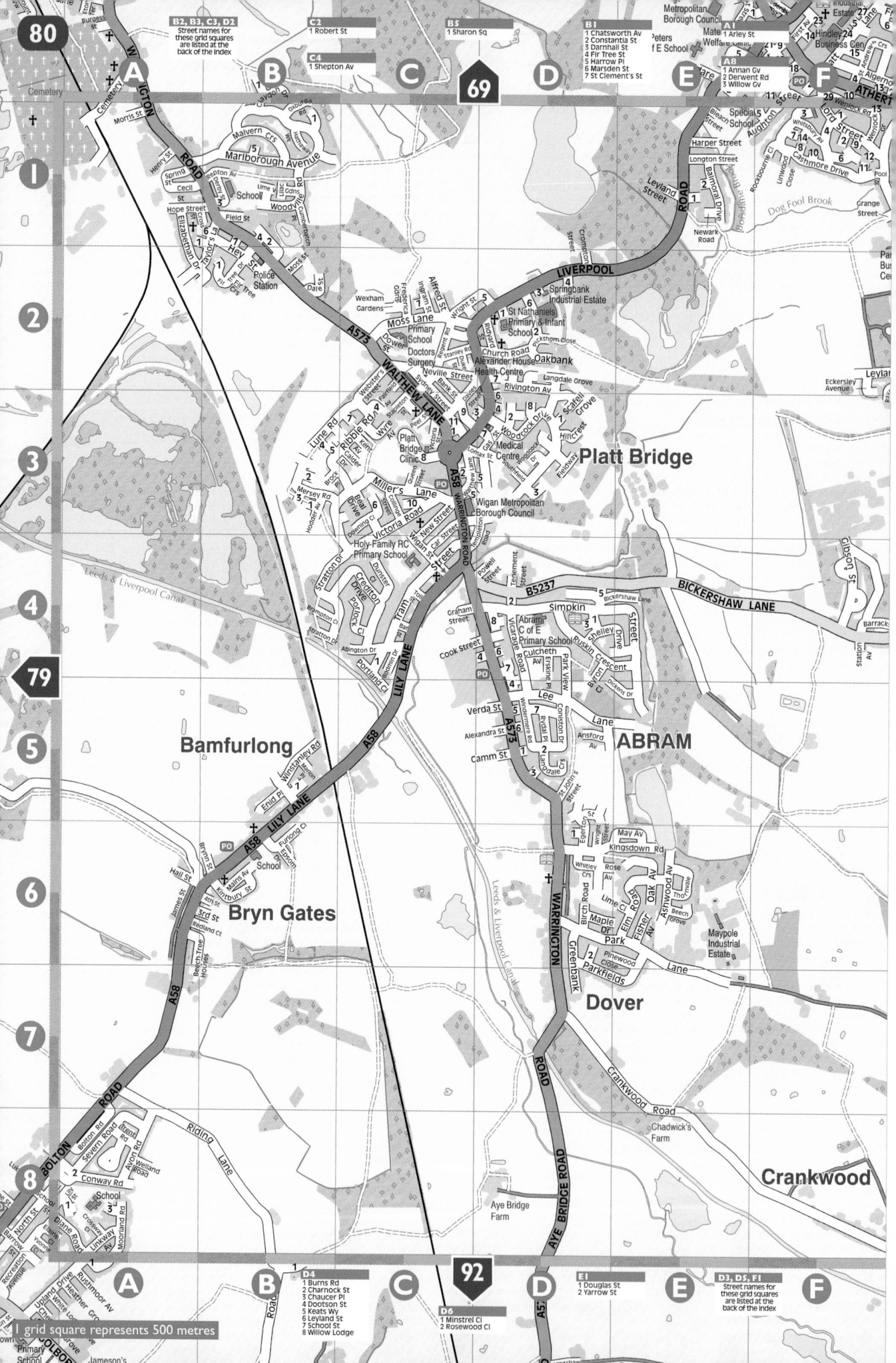

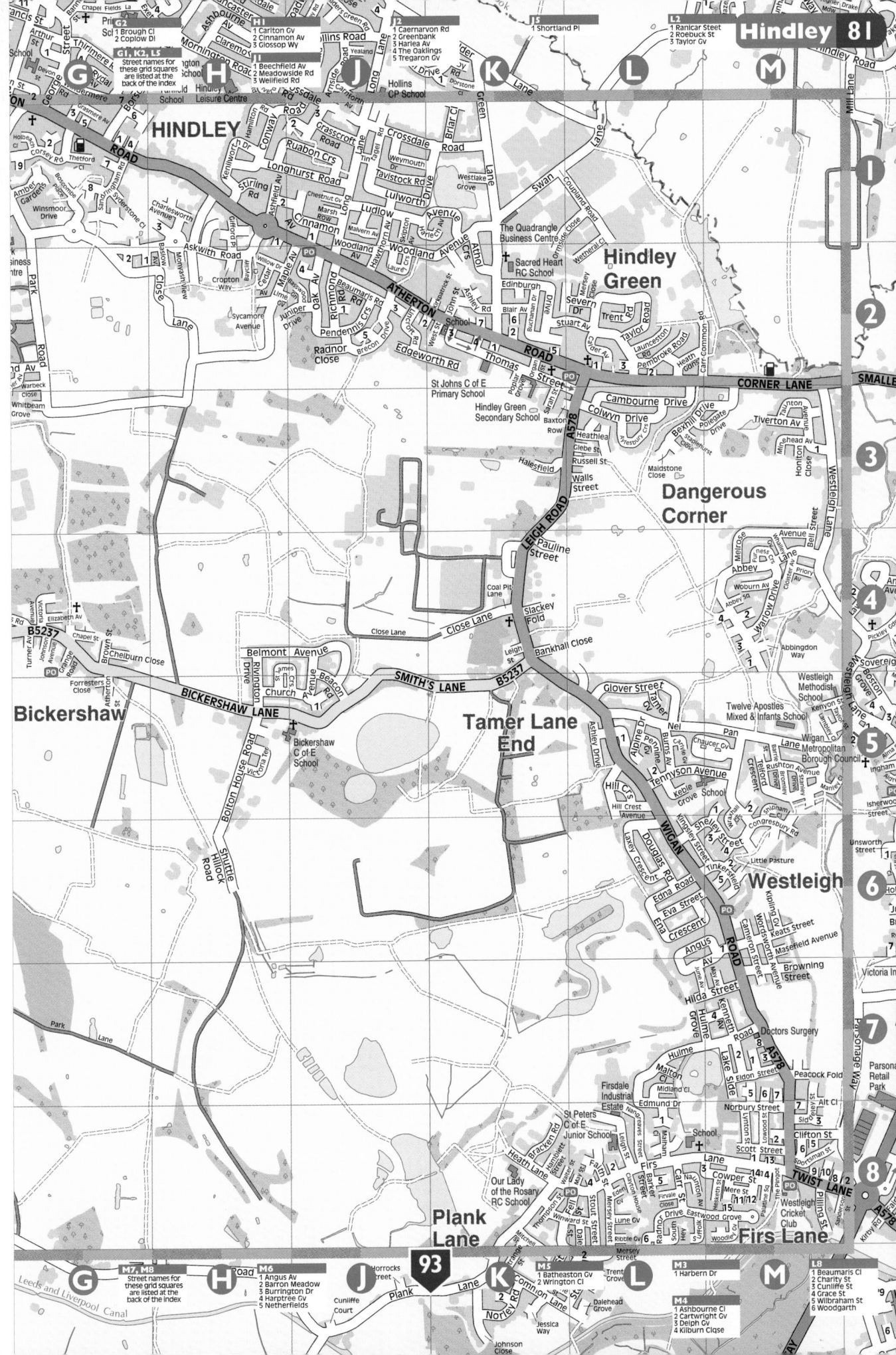

D3, F1
Street names for
these grid squares
are listed at the
back of the index

E2
1 Crossdale Rd
2 Midlothian Dr

E4
1 Lulworth Av
2 Sandheys Ter

E1
1 Blundellsands Rd
East

D2
1 Burbo Bank Rd S
2 Burbo Crs
3 Channel Reach
4 Seathwaite Cl

D1
1 Birkinshaw Av
2 Clementina Rd
3 Partridge Rd

F1
1 Valewood
Primary
School

Little Crosby
Doctors' Surg

70

A B C D E F

Blundellsands

Brighton le Sands

CROSBY

L22

Marine
Lake

Waterloo

BELFAST

DOUGLAS

F2
1 The Cloisters
2 Kimberley Av
3 The Spur

F3
1 Browning Rd

F4
1 Argo Rd
2 Back Mount St
3 Canning St
4 Corona Rd
5 Denmark St
6 Midland Ter
7 Sweden Gv

F5
1 Deacon Cl
2 Duke St

95

DUBLIN

A B C D E F

I grid square represents 500 metres

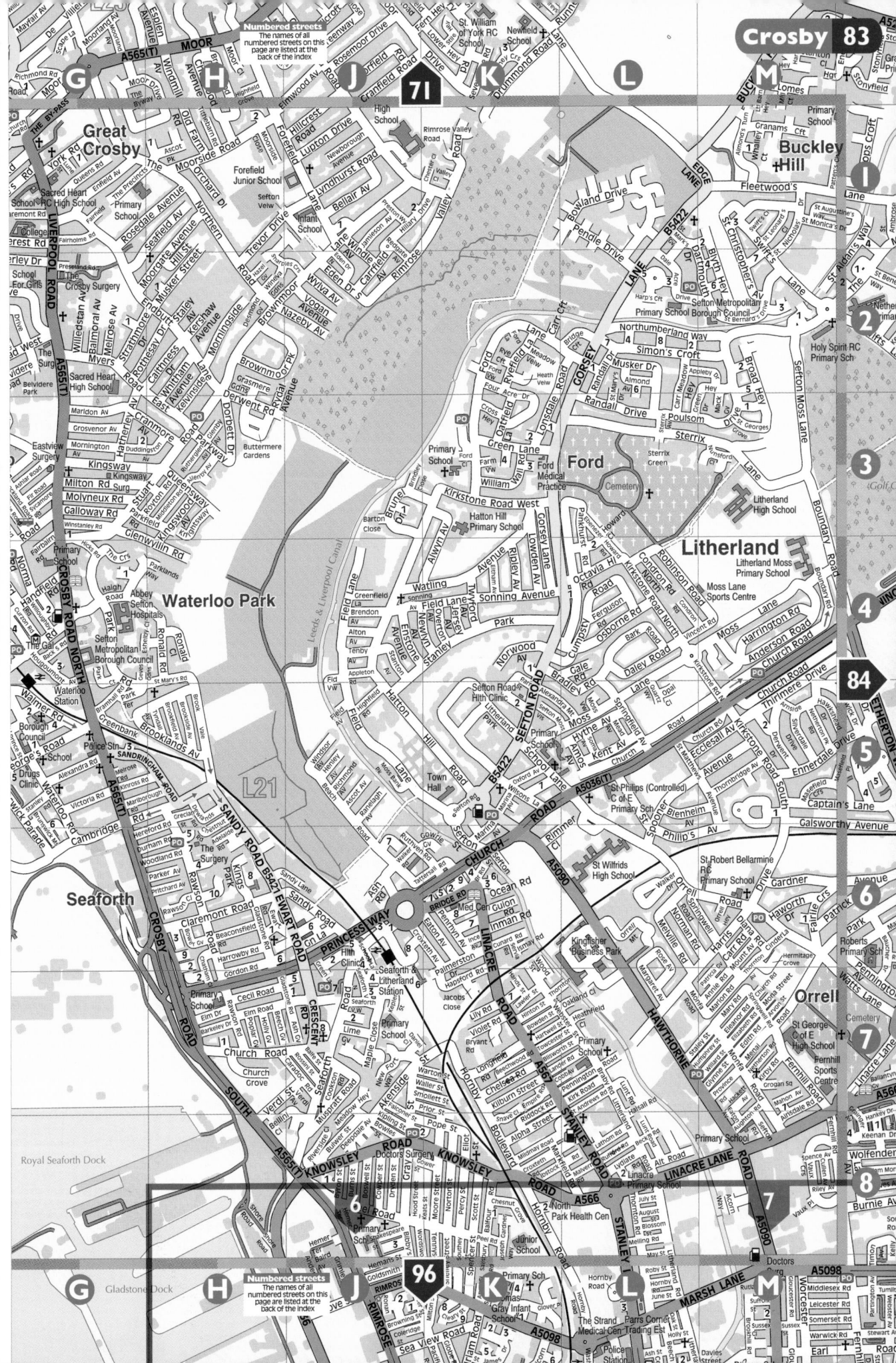

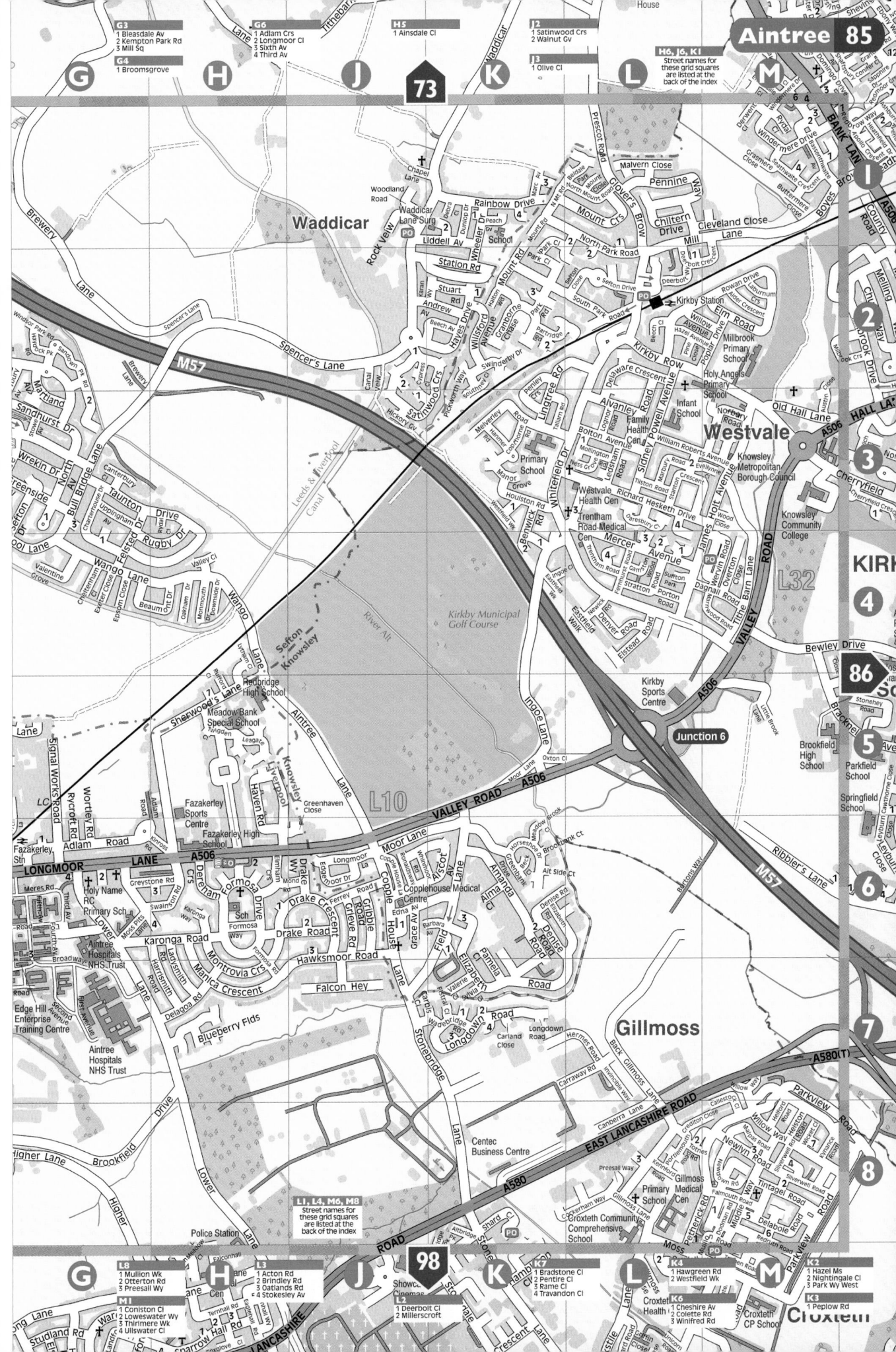

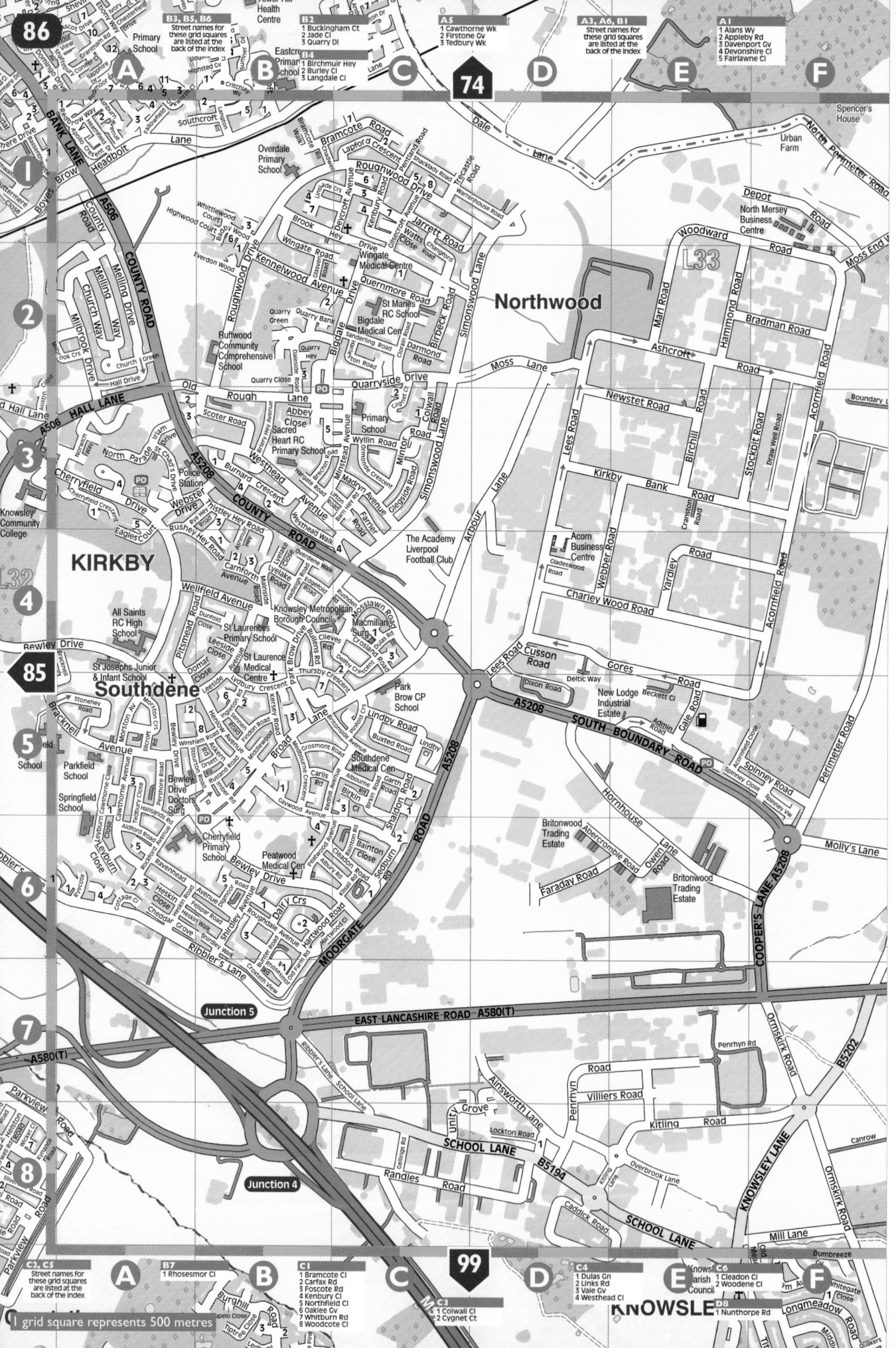

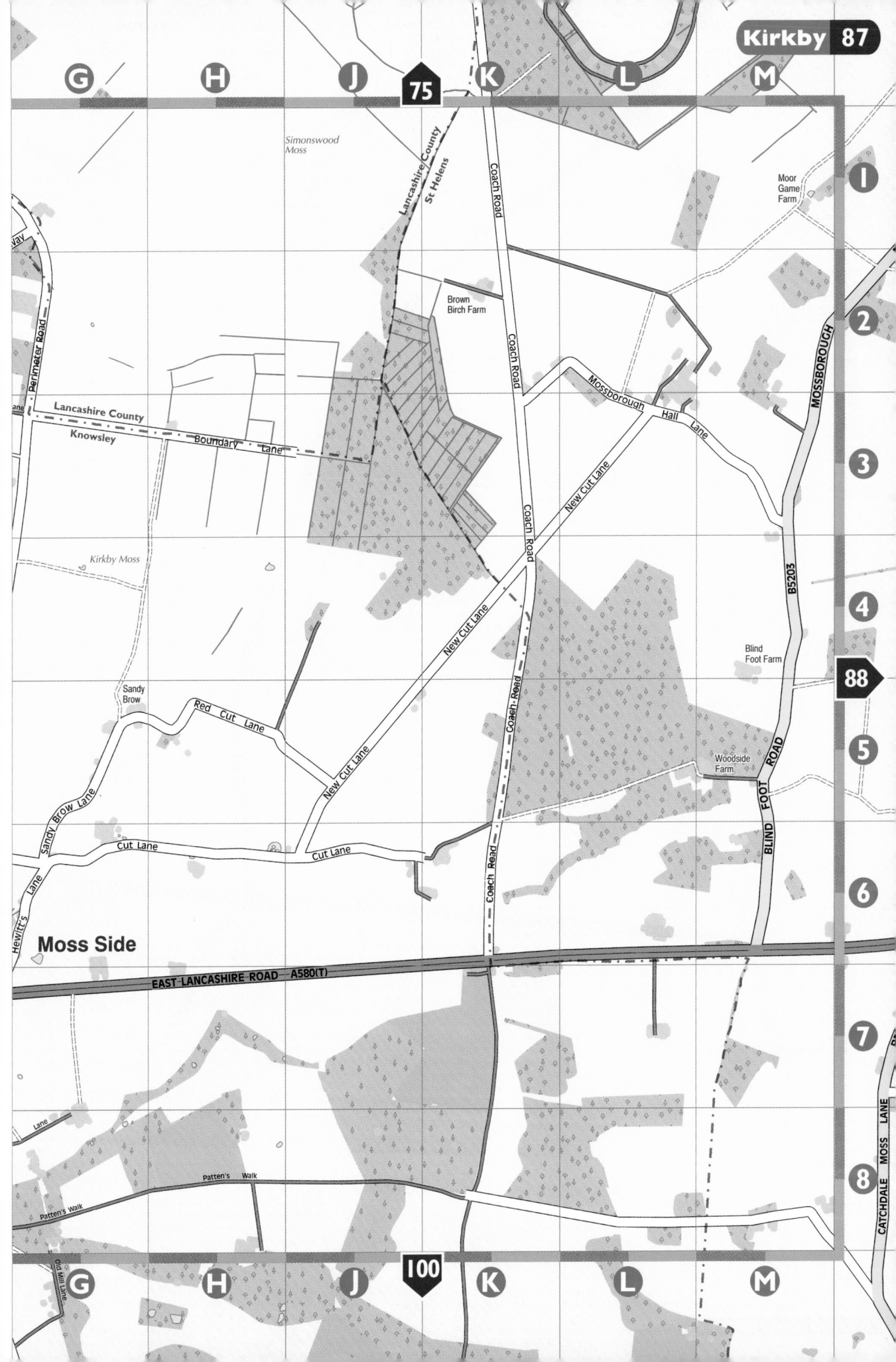

G   H   J   75   K   L   M

I

Moor Game Farm

2

3

Simonswood Moss

Lancashire County St Helens

Coach Road

Brown Birch Farm

Coach Road

Mossborough

Mossborough Hall Lane

MOSSBOROUGH

Perimeter Road

Lancashire County

Knowsley

Boundary Lane

New Cut Lane

B5203

4

Kirkby Moss

Coach Road

New Cut Lane

Blind Foot Farm

88

Sandy Brow

Red Cut Lane

New Cut Lane

Woodside Farm

5

Sandy Brow Lane

Cut Lane

Cut Lane

Coach Road

Blind Foot Road

6

Hewitt's Lane

Moss Side

EAST LANCASHIRE ROAD A580(T)

7

Lane

8

Patten's Walk

CATCHDALE MOSS LANE

Patten's Walk

G   H   J   100   K   L   M

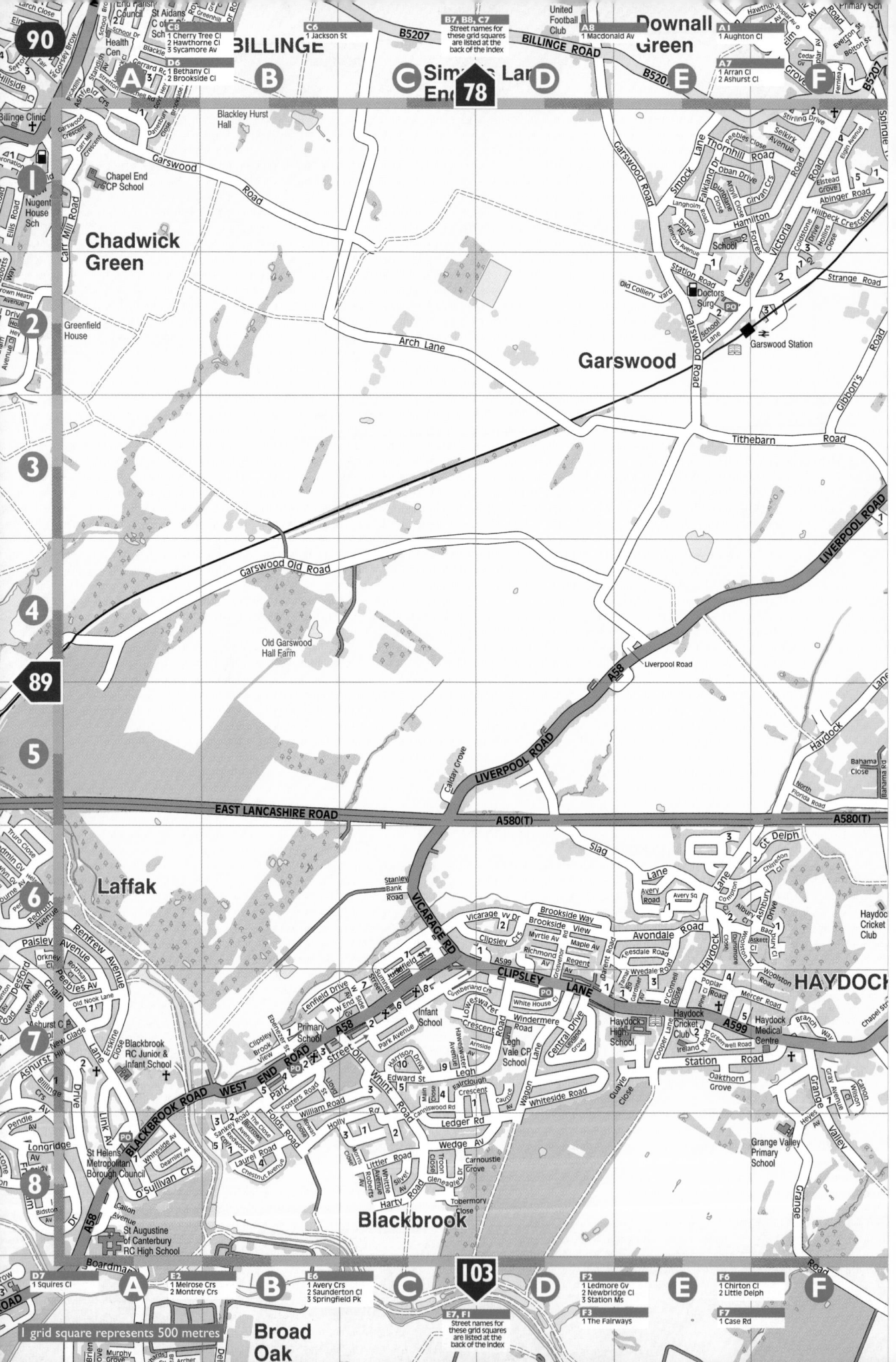

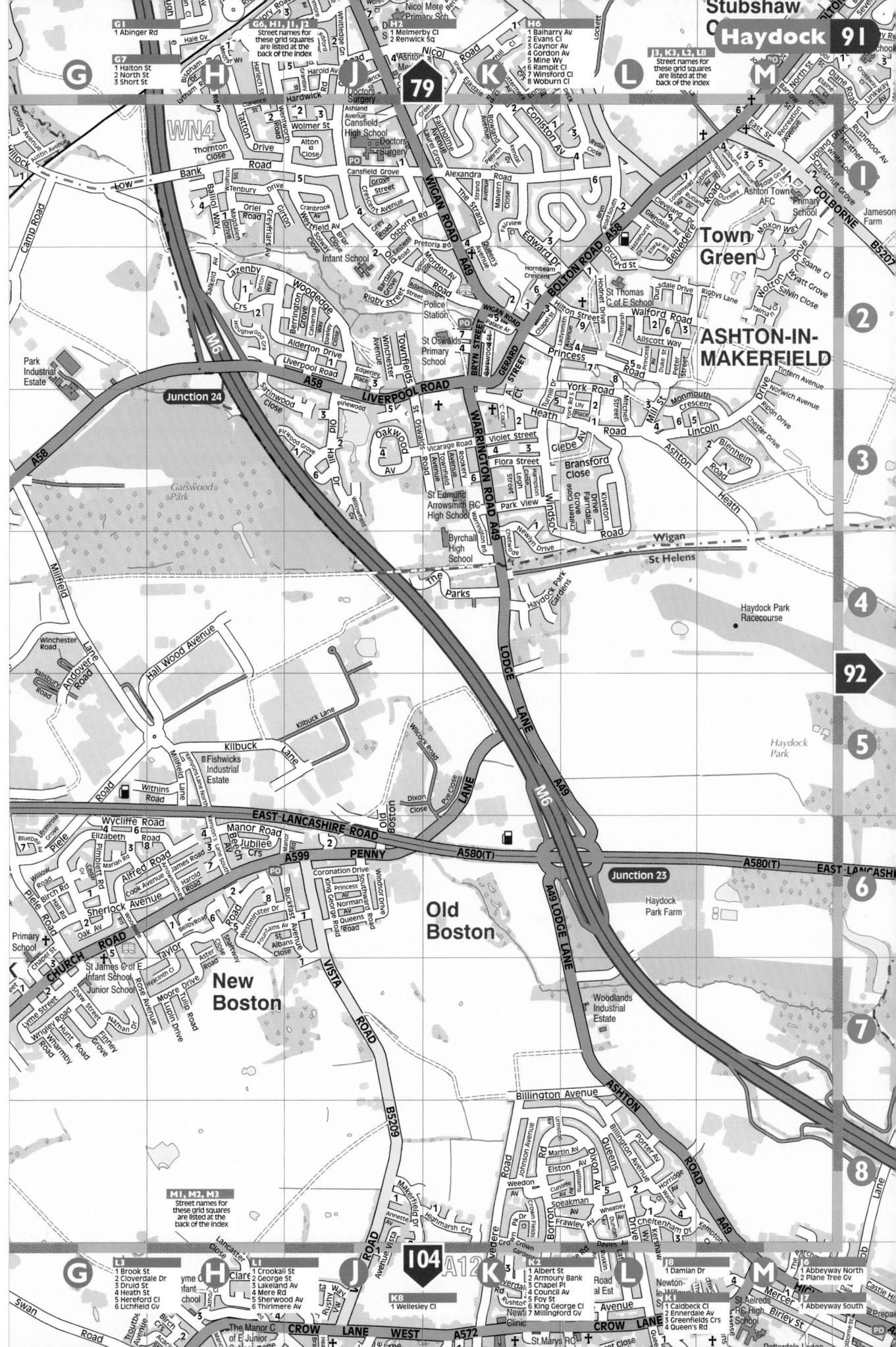

Edge
Green

GOLBORNE

Lowton

Town of
Lowton

Lowton
Heath

C4
1 Bank Pas
2 Lilac Rd
3 Prescott St
B4, C5, C6
Street names for
these grid squares
are listed at the
back of the index

B6
1 Ladybarn Av

C3
1 Hartswell Cl

B5
1 Cliftonmill Mdw
2 Highfield Av
3 Springfield Av

B3
1 Croft Av
2 Hepworth Cl
3 Prescott Av
4 Slaidburn Crs
5 Stewerton Cl

A1
1 Diane Rd

B1
1 Locker La

E4, F6
Street names for
these grid squares
are listed at the
back of the index

D5
1 Hereford Av
2 Queen St
3 Tewkesbury Rd
4 Wood St
5 Worcester Av

E5
1 Pine Gv
2 Southwell Cl
3 Thornfield Cl

E6
1 Broadley Av
2 Stone Cross La N

F4
1 Abbotsford Cl
2 Brignall Gv
3 Canterbury Av
4 Ivy House Rd

F5
1 Curlew Cl
2 Grosvenor Av
3 Lichfield Av
4 Ridgewell Av
5 St Luke's Av

1 grid square represents 500 metres

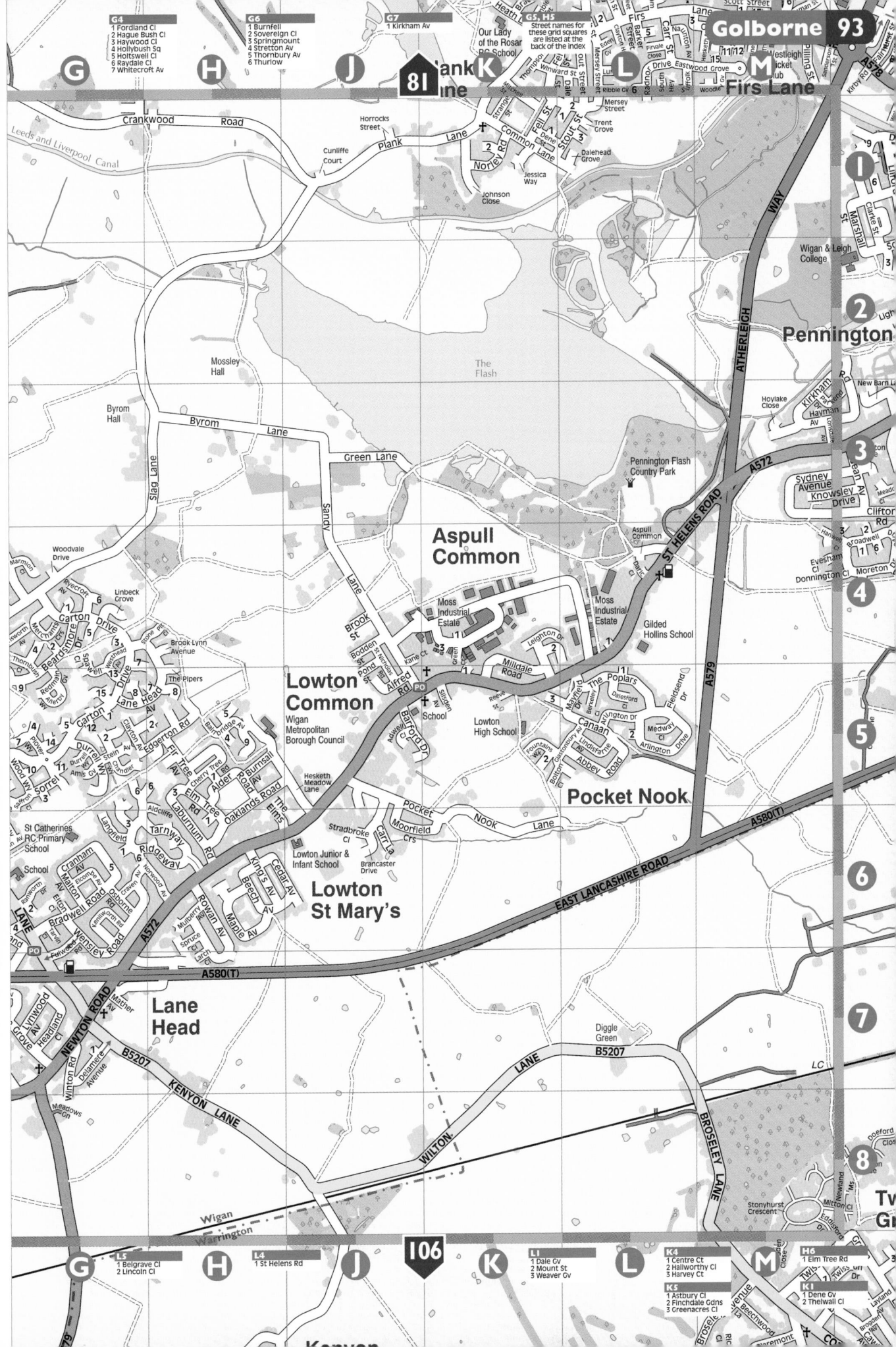

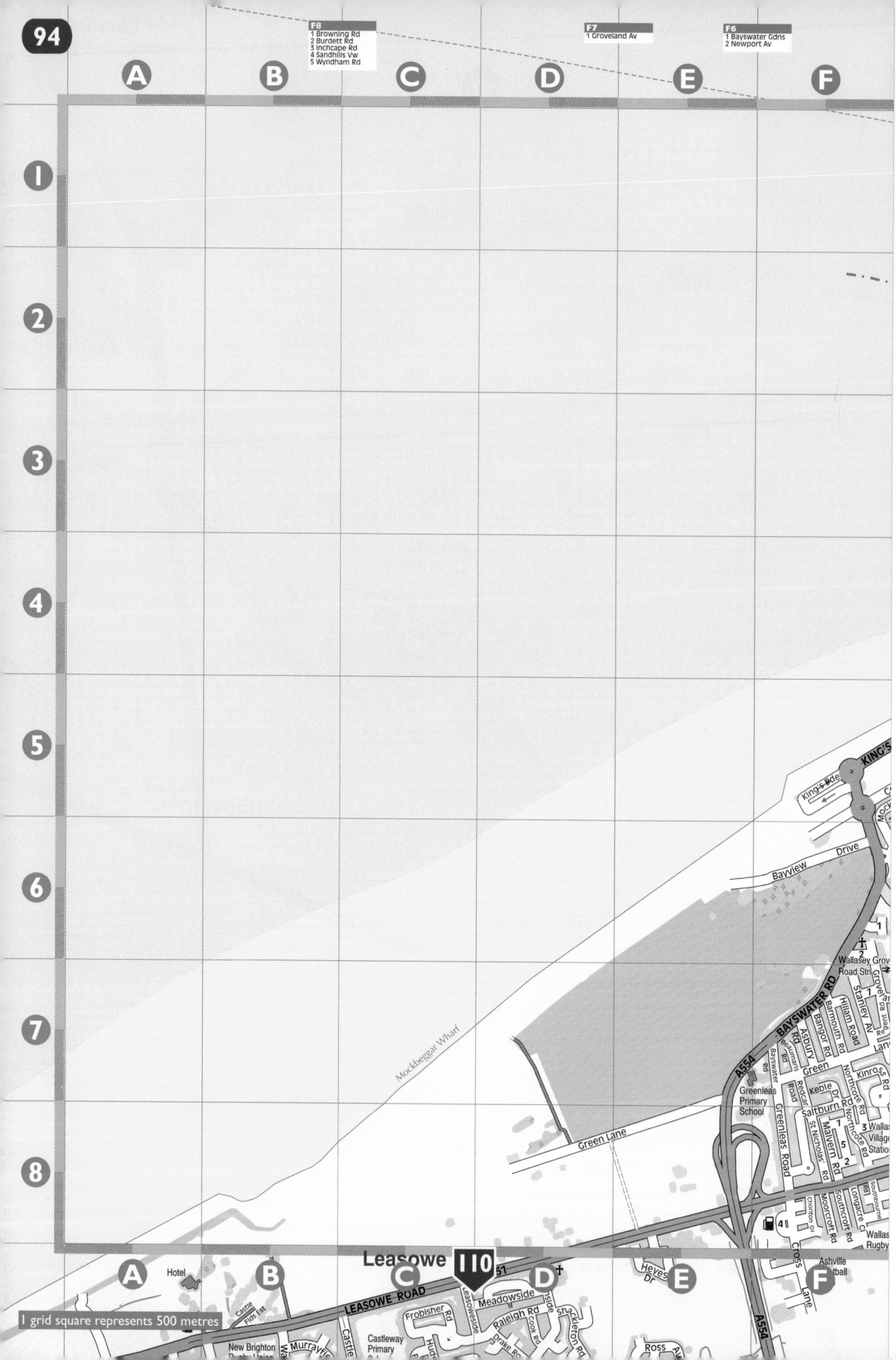

F8
1 Browning Rd
2 Burdett Rd
3 Inchcape Rd
4 Sandhills Vw
5 Wyndham Rd

F7
1 Groveland Av

F6
1 Bayswater Gdns
2 Newport Av

1
2
3
4
5
6
7
8

KING'S

King's Pde

MOCK

Bayview   Drive

Wallasey Grove
Road Stn

Mockbeggar Wharf

BAYSWATER RD

Asbury Rd
Barnmouth Rd
Bangor Rd
Hillam Road
Stanley Av
Green
Beaumaris Rd
Bayswater
Northcote Rd
Redcar Rd
Kinross Rd
Lan

Greenleas
Primary
School

Keble Dr
Saltburn Rd
St Nicholas
Malvern Rd
Greenleas Road
Wallas
Village
Station

A554

Green Lane

Southbourne
Longacre Cl
Moorcroft Rd
Wallas
Rugby

Chorlton Av
Cross Lane

Ashville
tball

Hotel

Castle
Flds Est

LEASOWE ROAD

Frobisher Rd
Meadowside
Leasoweside
Raleigh Rd
Cook Rd
Shackleton Rd
Hugh

Heyes
Dr

Ross Av

A554

Castleway
Primary

New Brighton
W Murrayfield
Castle

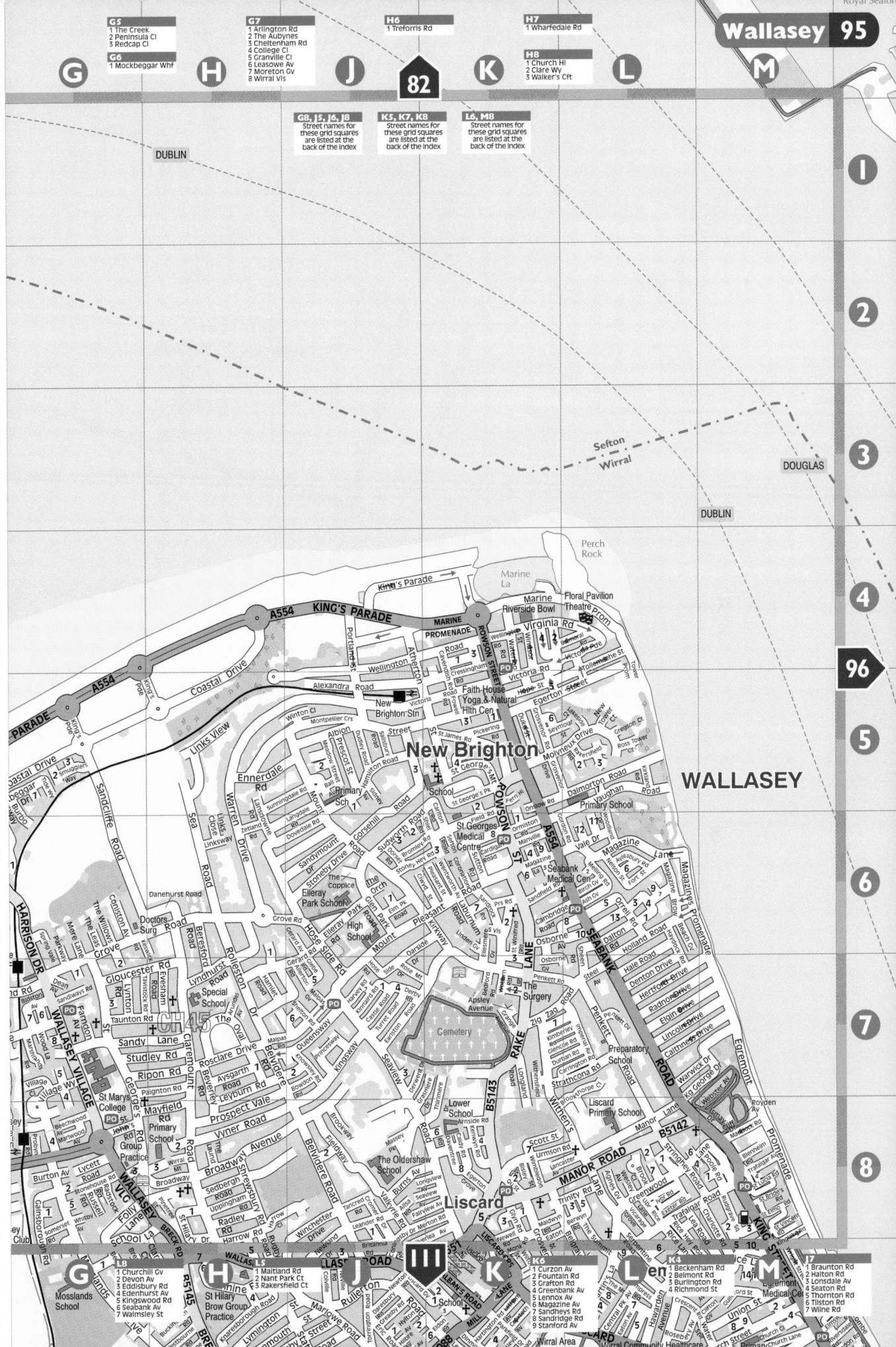

G5
1 The Creek
2 Peninsula Cl
3 Redcap Cl

G6
1 Mockbeggar Whf

G7
1 Arlington Rd
2 The Aubynes
3 Cheltenham Rd
4 College Cl
5 Granville Cl
6 Leasowe Av
7 Moreton Gv
8 Wirral Vis

H6
1 Treforris Rd

H7
1 Wharfedale Rd

H8
1 Church Hi
2 Clare Wy
3 Walker's Cft

G8, I5, J6, J8
Street names for
these grid squares
are listed at the
back of the index

K5, K7, K8
Street names for
these grid squares
are listed at the
back of the index

L6, M8
Street names for
these grid squares
are listed at the
back of the index

G   H   J   82   K   L   M

I
2
3
4
96
5
6
7
8

DUBLIN

Sefton
Wirral

DOUGLAS

DUBLIN

Perch
Rock

King's Parade

Marine
La

Floral Pavilion
Theatre

Marine
Riverside Bowl

A554   KING'S PARADE

MARINE
PROMENADE

Virginia Rd

Coastal Drive

Alexandra Road

New
Brighton Stn

New Brighton

WALLASEY

St George's Medical Centre

Links View

Ellerdale
Rd

Ellerday Park School

Ellerday Park
High School

Doctors
Surg Road

Cemetery

CH45

St Marys
College

Group
Practice

The Oldershaw
School

Liscard
Primary School

Liscard

MANOR ROAD

B5142

B5143

Wirral Area
Health Authority   Wirral Community Healthcare

G   H   J   III   K   L   M

L8
1 Churchill Gv
2 Devon Av
3 Eddisbury Rd
4 Edenhurst Av
5 Kingswood Rd
6 Seabank Av
7 Walmsley St

H6
1 Maitland Rd
2 Nantle Park Ct
3 Rakersfield Ct

K6
1 Curzon Av
2 Fountain Rd
3 Grafton Rd
4 Greenbank Av
5 Lennox Av
6 Magazine Av
7 Sandheys Rd
8 Sandridge Rd
9 Stanford Av

K4
1 Beckenham Rd
2 Belmont Rd
3 Burlington Rd
4 Richmond St

M4
1 Braunton Rd
2 Halton Rd
3 Lonsdale Av
4 Seaton Rd
5 Thornton Rd
6 Tilston Rd
7 Wilne Rd

Mosslands
School

St Hilary
Brow Group
Practice

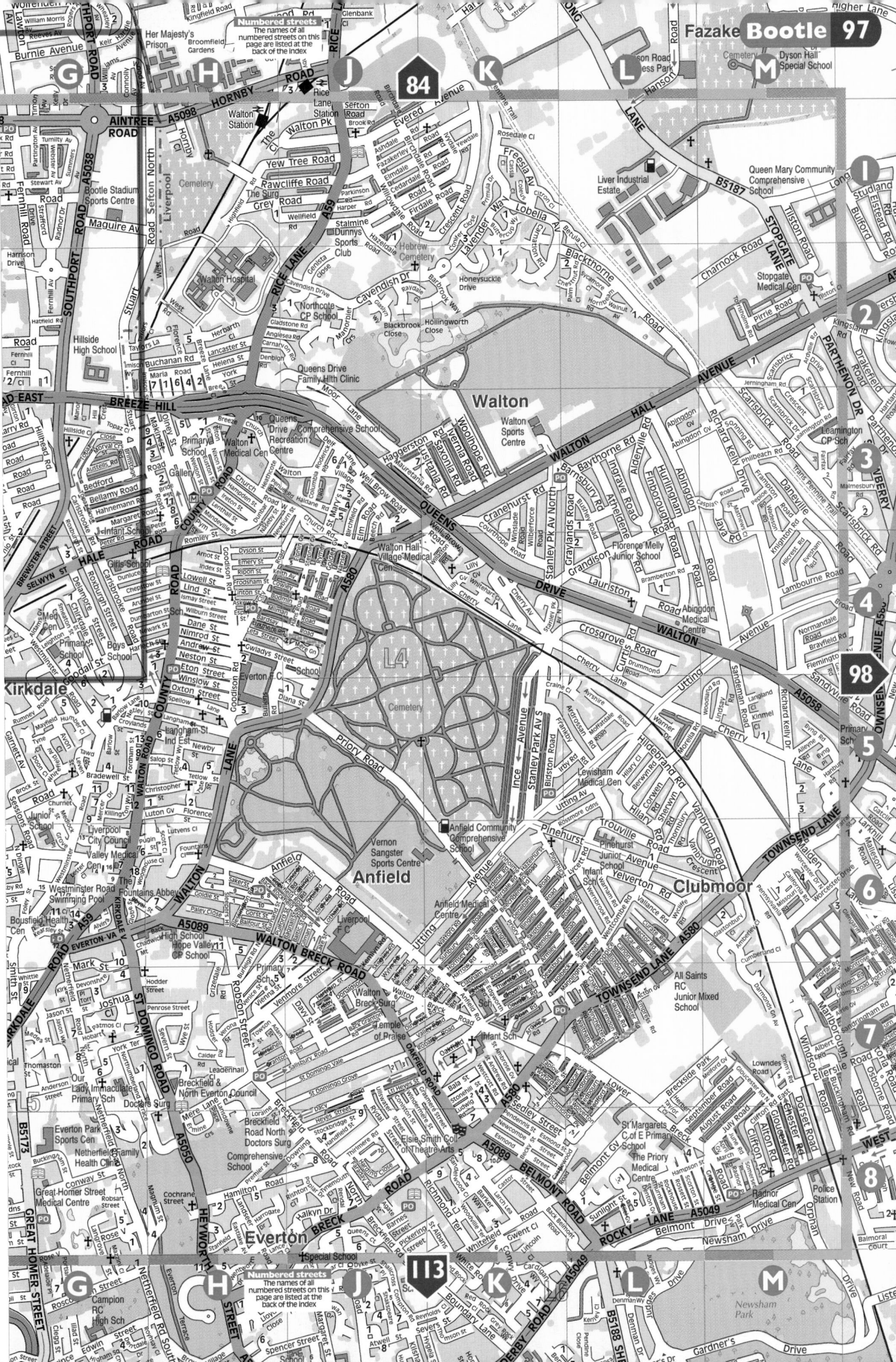

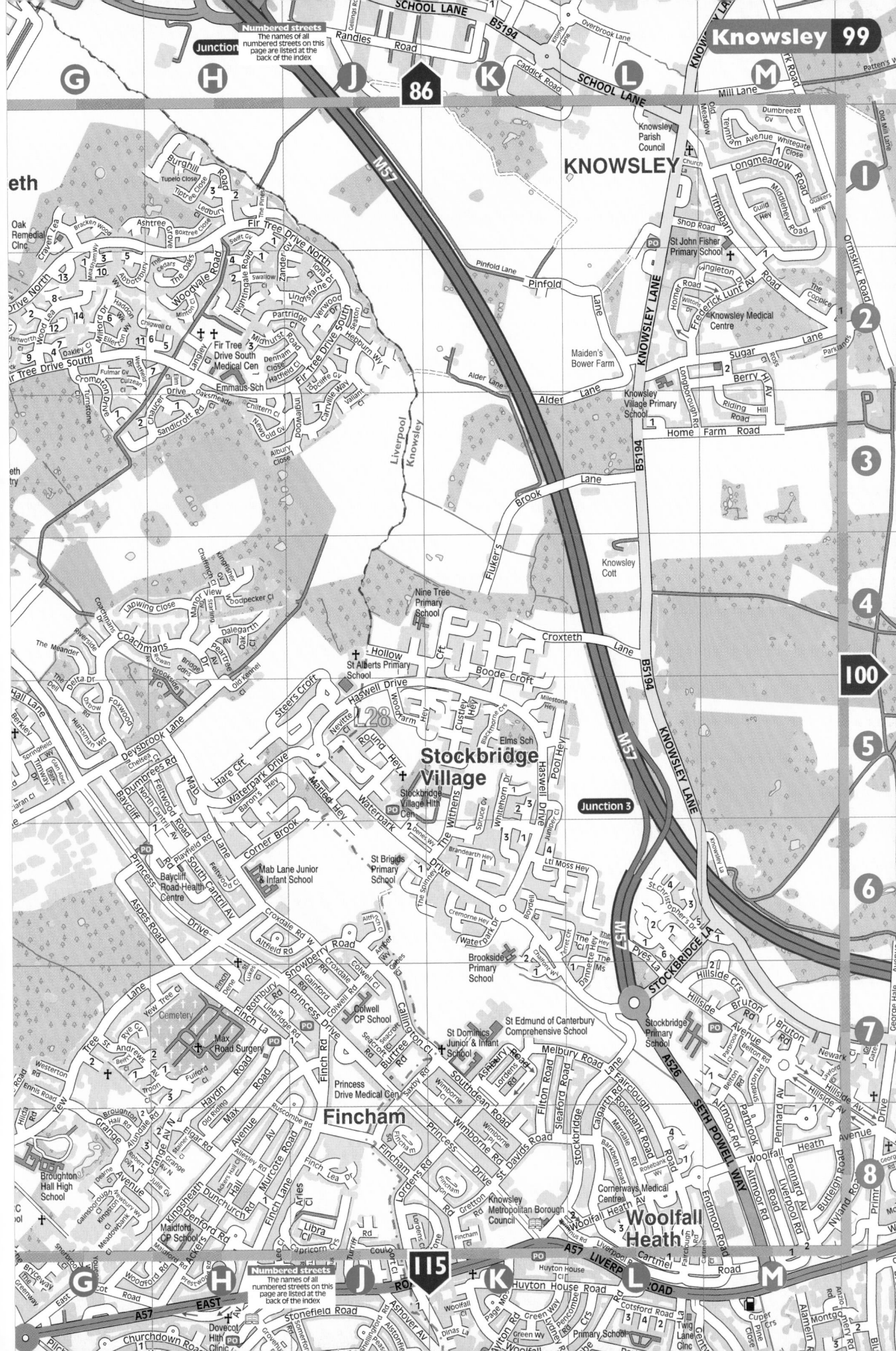

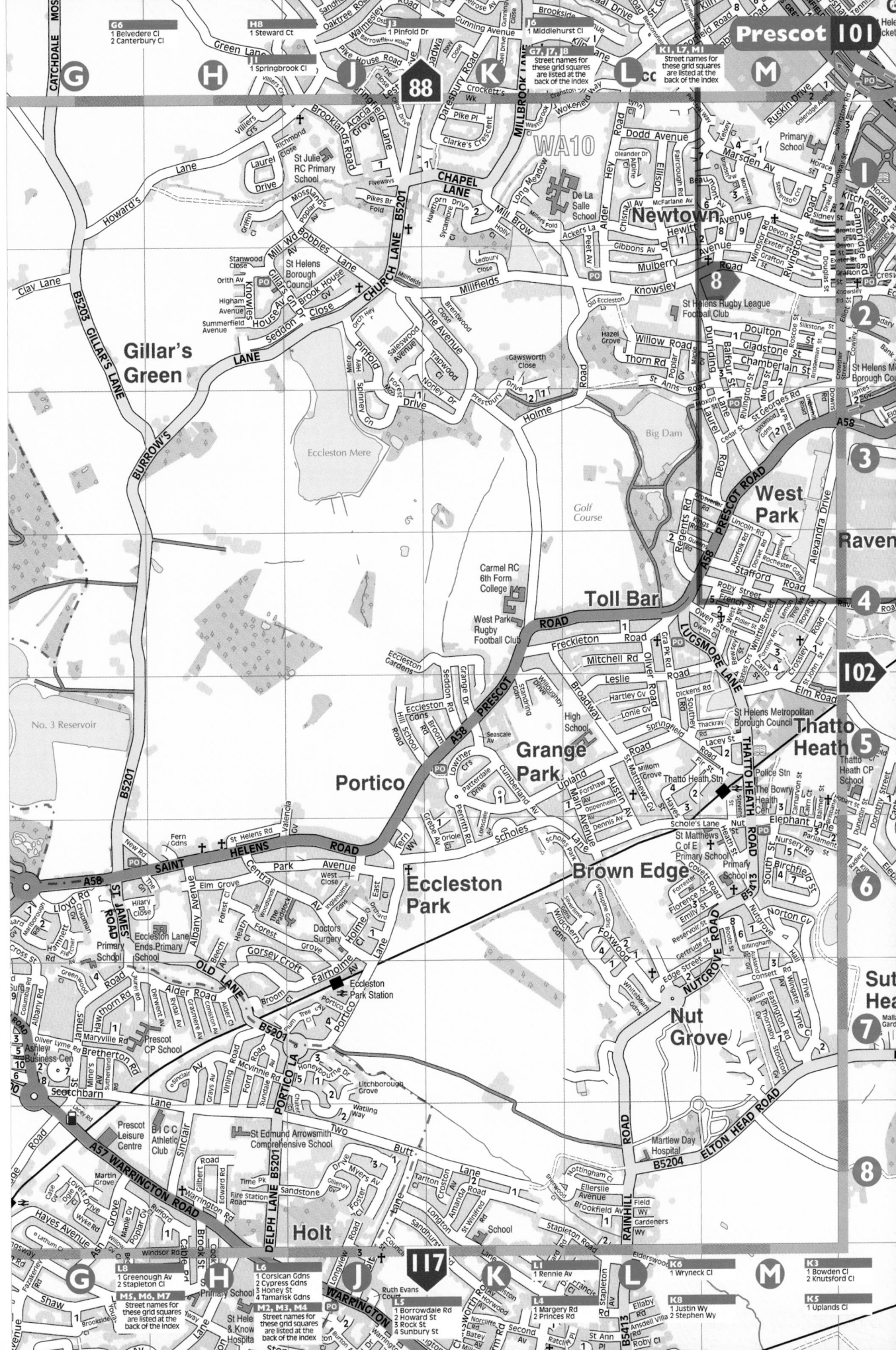

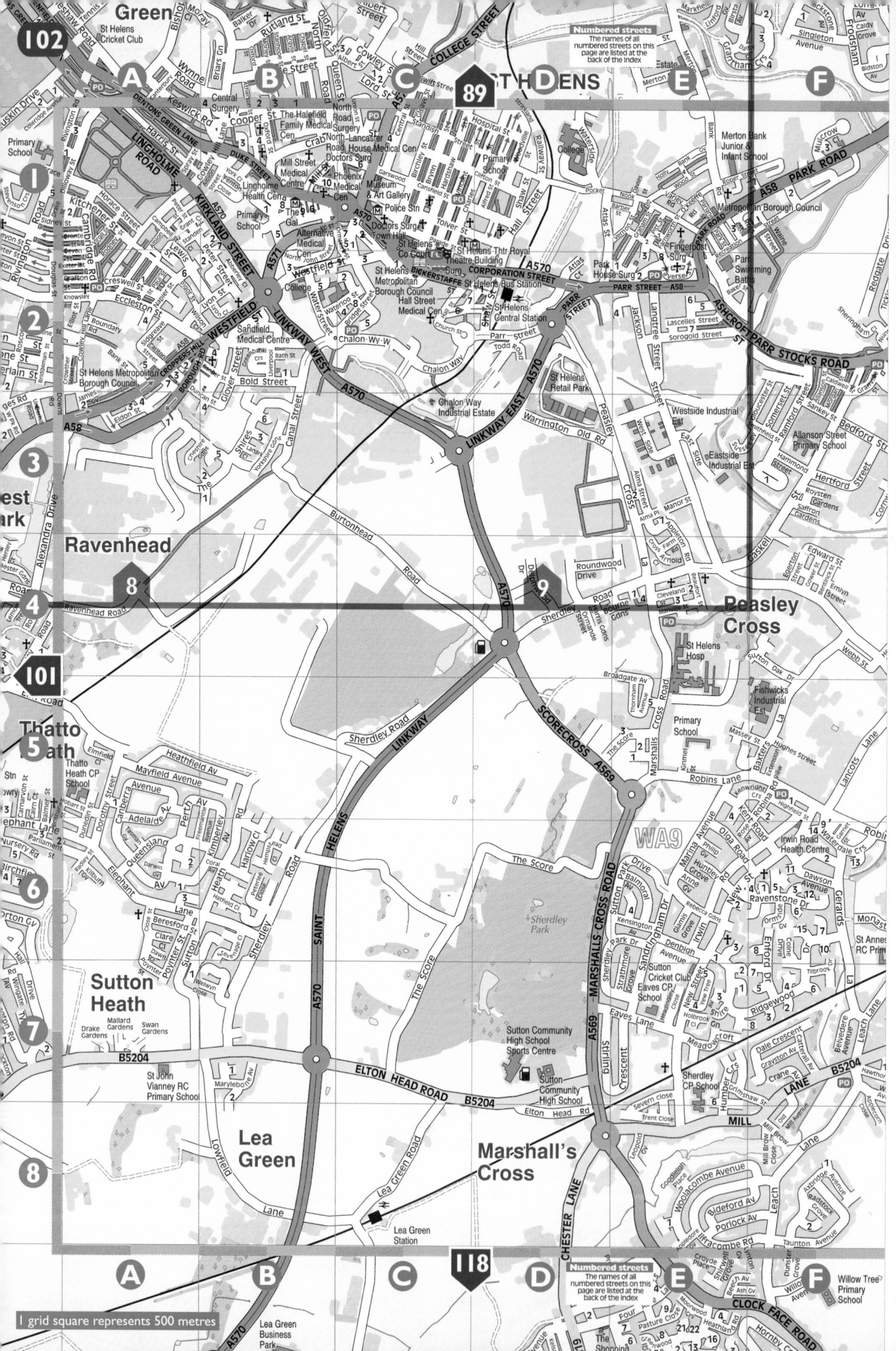

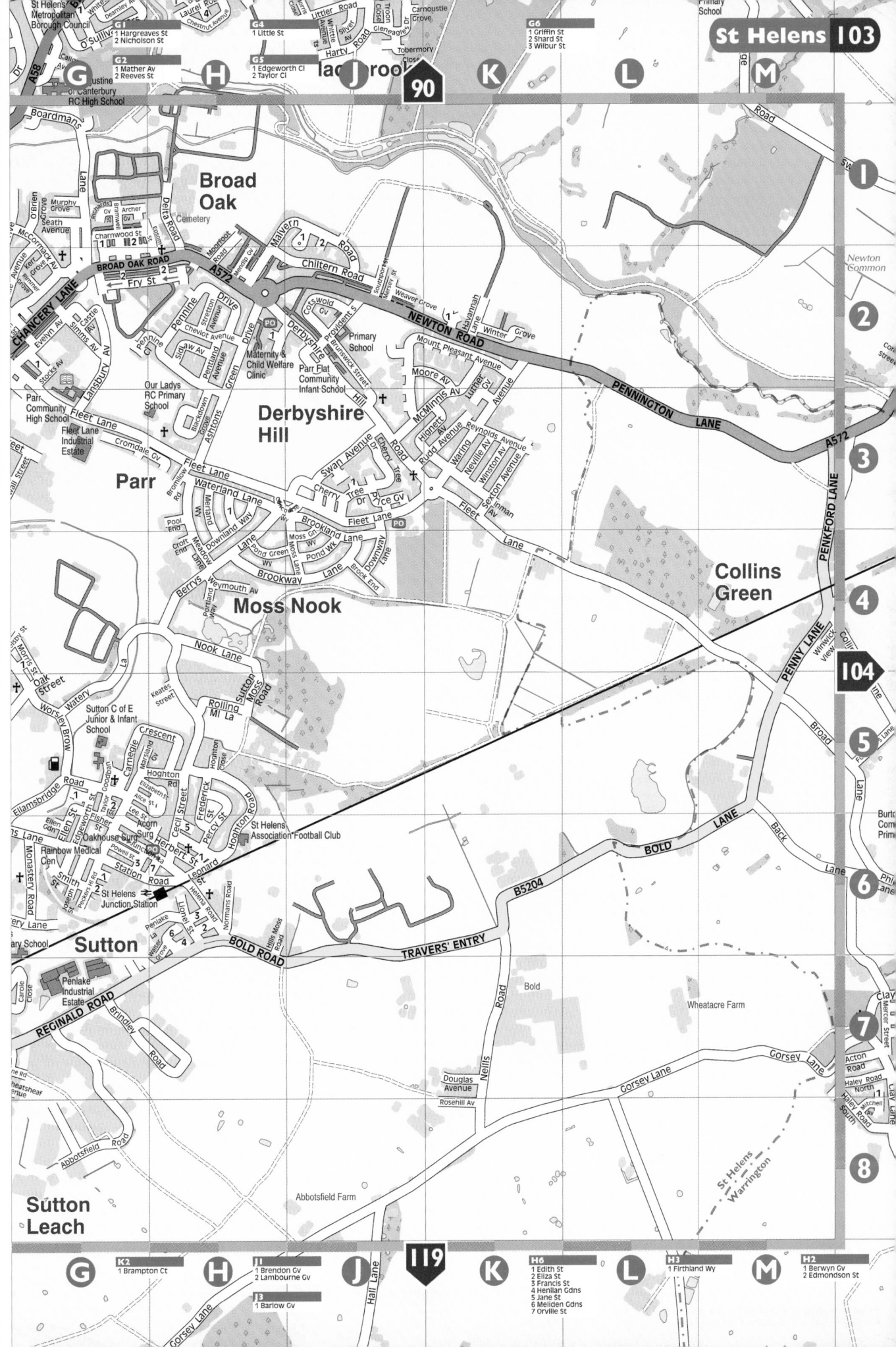

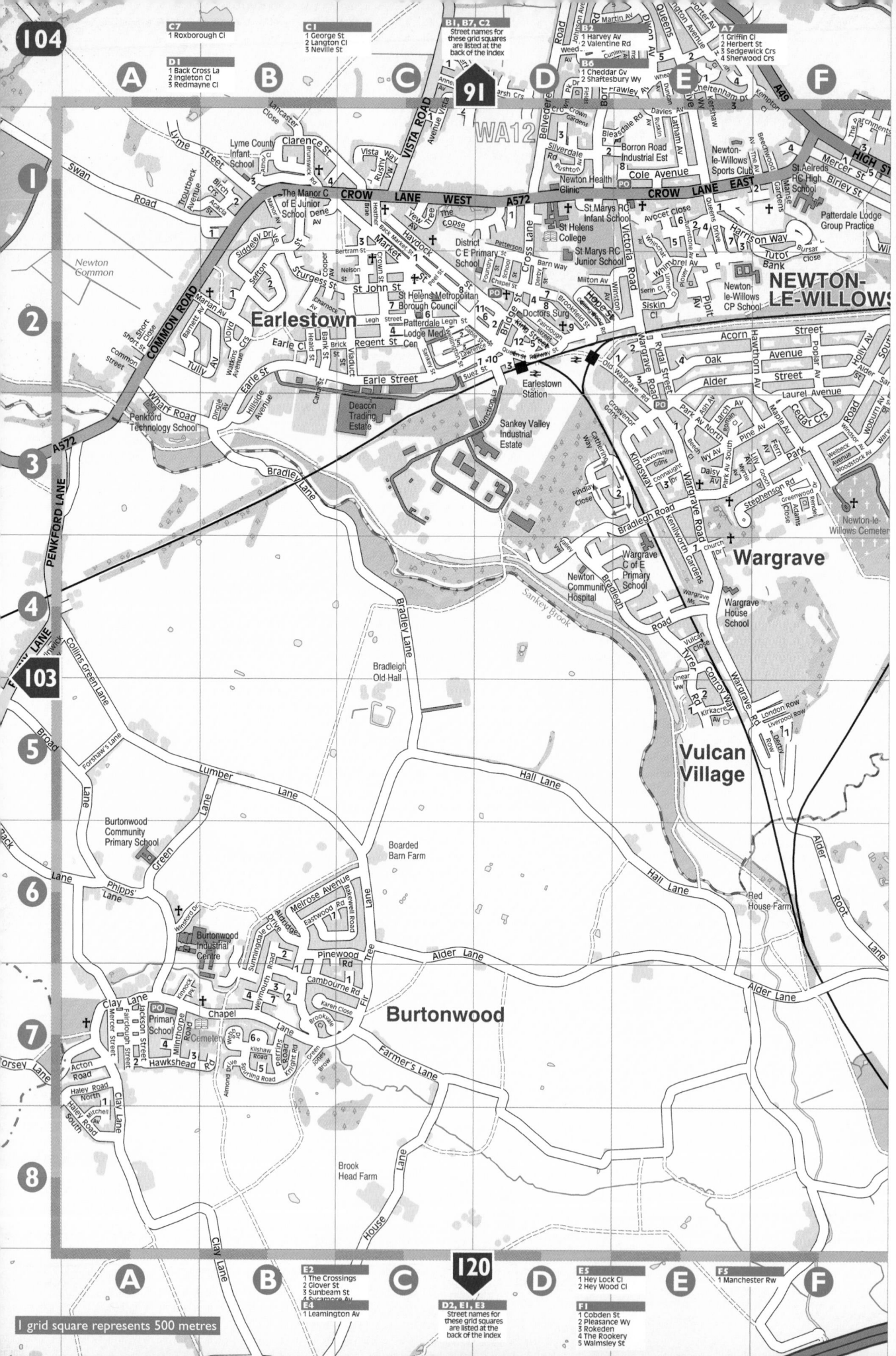

A   B   C   D   E   F

C7
1 Roxborough Cl

C1
1 George St
2 Langton Cl
3 Neville St

D1
1 Back Cross La
2 Ingleton Cl
3 Redmayne Cl

B1, B7, C2
Street names for
these grid squares
are listed at the
back of the index

B2
1 Harvey Av
2 Valentine Rd

B6
1 Cheddar Gv
2 Shaftesbury Wy

A7
1 Griffin Cl
2 Herbert St
3 Sedgewick Crs
4 Sherwood Crs

91

WA12

A49   HIGH ST

1 Swan Road

Newton Common

2 Earlestown

COMMON ROAD

Lyme Street

3 A572   PENKFORD LANE

Wharf Road

Penkford Technology School

Deacon Trading Estate

Sankey Valley Industrial Estate

Earlestown Station

NEWTON-LE-WILLOWS

Newton-le-Willows Sports Club

St Aelreds RC High School

Patterdale Lodge Group Practice

CROW LANE WEST   A572   CROW LANE EAST

Borron Road Industrial Est

Cole Avenue

Newton Health Clinic

St Helens College

St Marys RC Infant School

St Marys RC Junior School

St Helens Metropolitan Borough Council

Doctors Surg

Newton-le-Willows CP School

Acorn   Street

Oak   Avenue

Alder   Street

Laurel Avenue

Wargrave

Newton-le-Willows Cemetery

4 FERRY LANE   103

Bradley Lane

Bradleigh Old Hall

Newton Community Hospital

Sankey Brook

Wargrave C of E Primary School

Wargrave House School

5 Broad Lane

Lumber Lane

Hall Lane

Vulcan Village

6 Burtonwood Community Primary School

Phipps' Lane

Green Lane

Boarded Barn Farm

Melrose Avenue

Burtonwood Industrial Centre

Pinewood Rd

Alder Lane

Hall Lane

Red House Farm

Alder Lane

Alder Root

7 Acton Road

Haley Road North

Haley Road South

Clay Lane

Jackson Street

Mercer Street

Hawkshead

Cambourne Rd

Farmer's Lane

Burtonwood

Chapel Primary School

Cemetery

8 Brook Head Farm

House Road

A   B   C   D   E   F

120

E2
1 The Crossings
2 Glover St
3 Sunbeam St
4 Sycamore Av

E4
1 Leamington Av

D2, E1, E3
Street names for
these grid squares
are listed at the
back of the index

E5
1 Hey Lock Cl
2 Hey Wood Cl

F1
1 Cobden St
2 Pleasance Wy
3 Rokeden
4 The Rookery
5 Walmsley St

F5
1 Manchester Rw

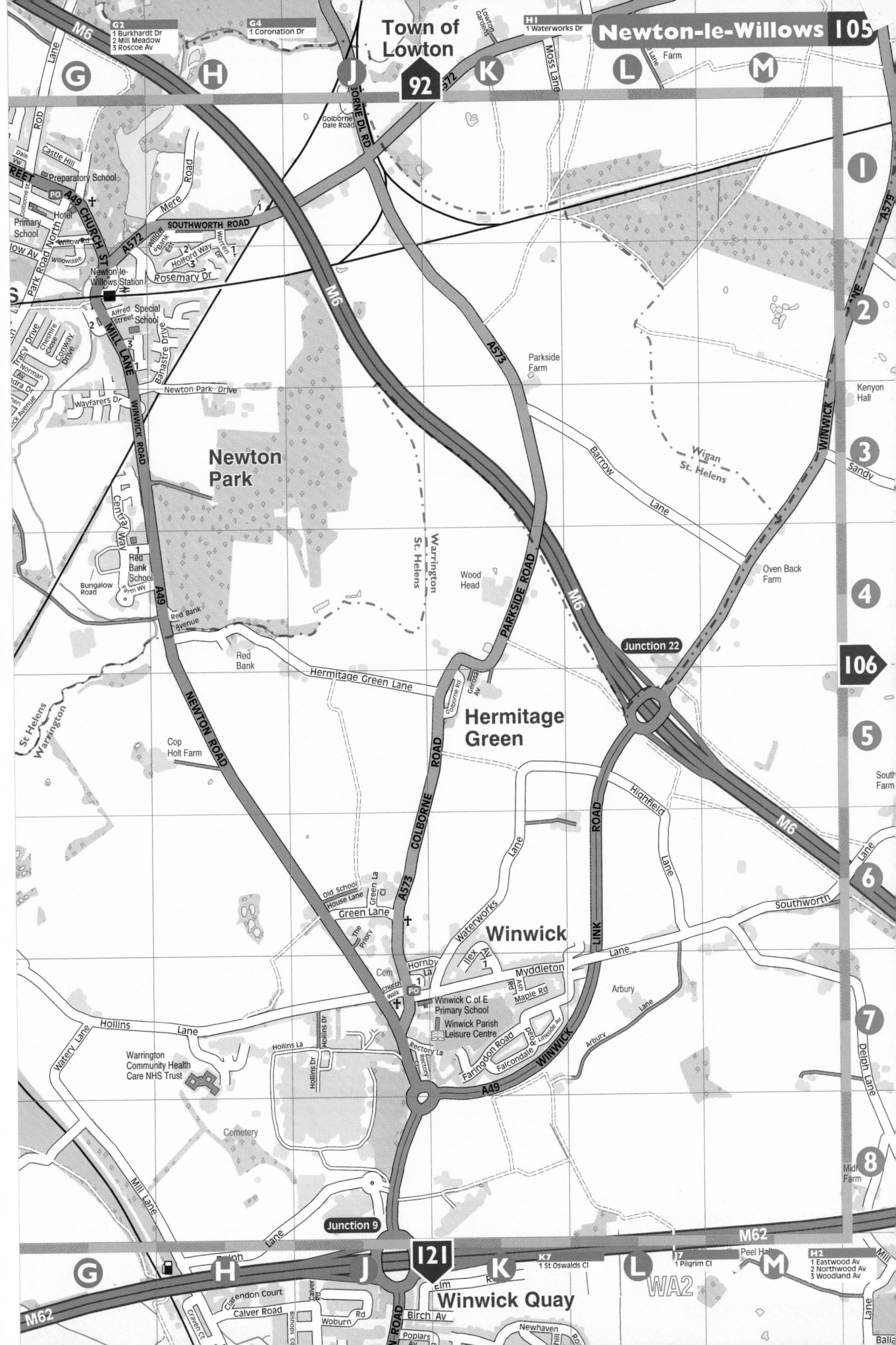

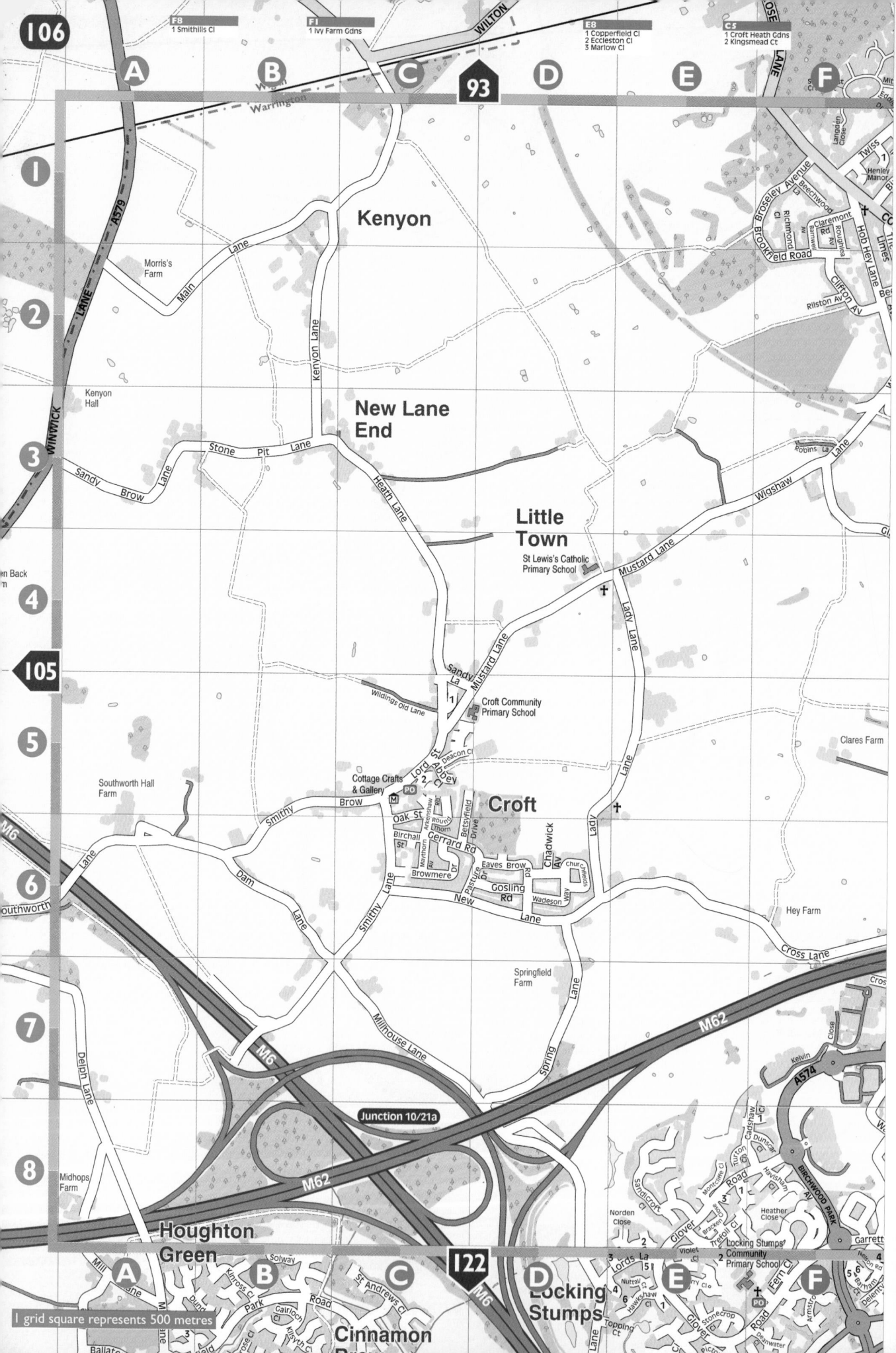

E5
1 Ethelbert Rd

D7
1 Airlie Rd
2 Albert Rd

D6
1 Back Seaview
2 Evans Rd
3 Groveland Av
4 Grove Ter
5 Melrose Av
6 Wood St

C8
1 Morpeth Rd

C6
1 Cromer Rd
2 Kings Ct

A B C D E F

1

2

3

4

5

6

7

8

Red Rocks

Golf Course

Golf Course

Barn Hey

Meols

Meols Road

Forest Close

Birkenhead Road

Kingsmead School

Manor Road Station

HOYLAKE

CH47

Hoylake Cottage Hospital

Hoylake Cottage Hospital Trust Ltd

Hoylake Business Centre

Primary School

Hoylake Rugby Football Club

Carr Lane Industrial Estate

Police Station

Hoylake Stn

MARKET STREET

A553

A540 DRIVE

Drummond Road

Eddisbury Road

Newhall Lane

Carr Lane

Stanley Road

Coronation Rd

The Royal

Beach Road

Barton Close

Pennos Road

St Margaret's Road

Courtenay Road

Curzon Road

Marine Road

Warren Road

Queen's Rd

Gable Road

Alderley Road

The King's Gap

Valentia Rd

North Parade

Trinity Road

Grove Rd

Dovedale Road

Avondale Road

Ferndale Road

Clydesdale Road

Saxon Road

Hoyle Road

Manor Road

Newton Rd

Carrton Lane

Sandringham Av

Bertram Drive

Queen's Road

Winstay Road

Ashford Rd

Fishraw Rd

Meols Parade

Deneshery Road

Egbert Road

Charles Road

Grosvenor Rd

Carr Lane

Proctor Road

Carrhorne Road

Carshborne Road

Edward Lane

Yeoman Cottages

George Road

A
E6
1 Berwyn Av
2 Elm Ter
3 Sandringham Cl

B

E7
1 Carsgoe Rd

C

124

D
F4
1 Brosters La

E

F5
1 Frankby Rd
2 Redstone Cl
3 Roman Rd
4 St John's Cl
5 Sandiway

F

1 grid square represents 500 metres

G4
1 Meadowcroft Rd
2 Mumfords La

G5
1 Dovepoint Rd
2 Mannington Cl

H6
1 Sherwood Gv

K4
1 Anstey Cl
2 Ashby Cl
3 Carnoustie Cl
4 Glenfield Cv
5 Tanworth Gv
6 Turnberry Cl

K6
1 Cambrian Cl
2 Carr Hey
3 Carrow Cl
4 Millers Cl

K5, L4, L5, L6
Street names for
these grid squares
are listed at the
back of the index

M8
1 Binsey Cl
2 Botley Cl
3 Cowley Cl
4 Glen Ronald Dr
5 Headington Rd
6 Iffley Cl
7 Littlemore Cl
8 Wellbrae Cl

M7
1 Blakenhall Wy
2 Coney Wk
3 Curlew Cl
4 Hawksmore Cl
5 Henderson Cl
6 Kestrel Av

M6
1 Childwall Cl
2 Inglewood Av
3 Oak Cl

M4
1 Berrylands Cl
2 Overgreen Gv
3 Willaston Rd

M5
1 Ambleside Av
2 Levens Hey
3 Litherland Av

L7
1 Ainsworth Av
2 Applegarth
3 Birchfield Cl
4 Poplar Farm Ct

M3
Street names for
this grid square
are listed at the
back of the index

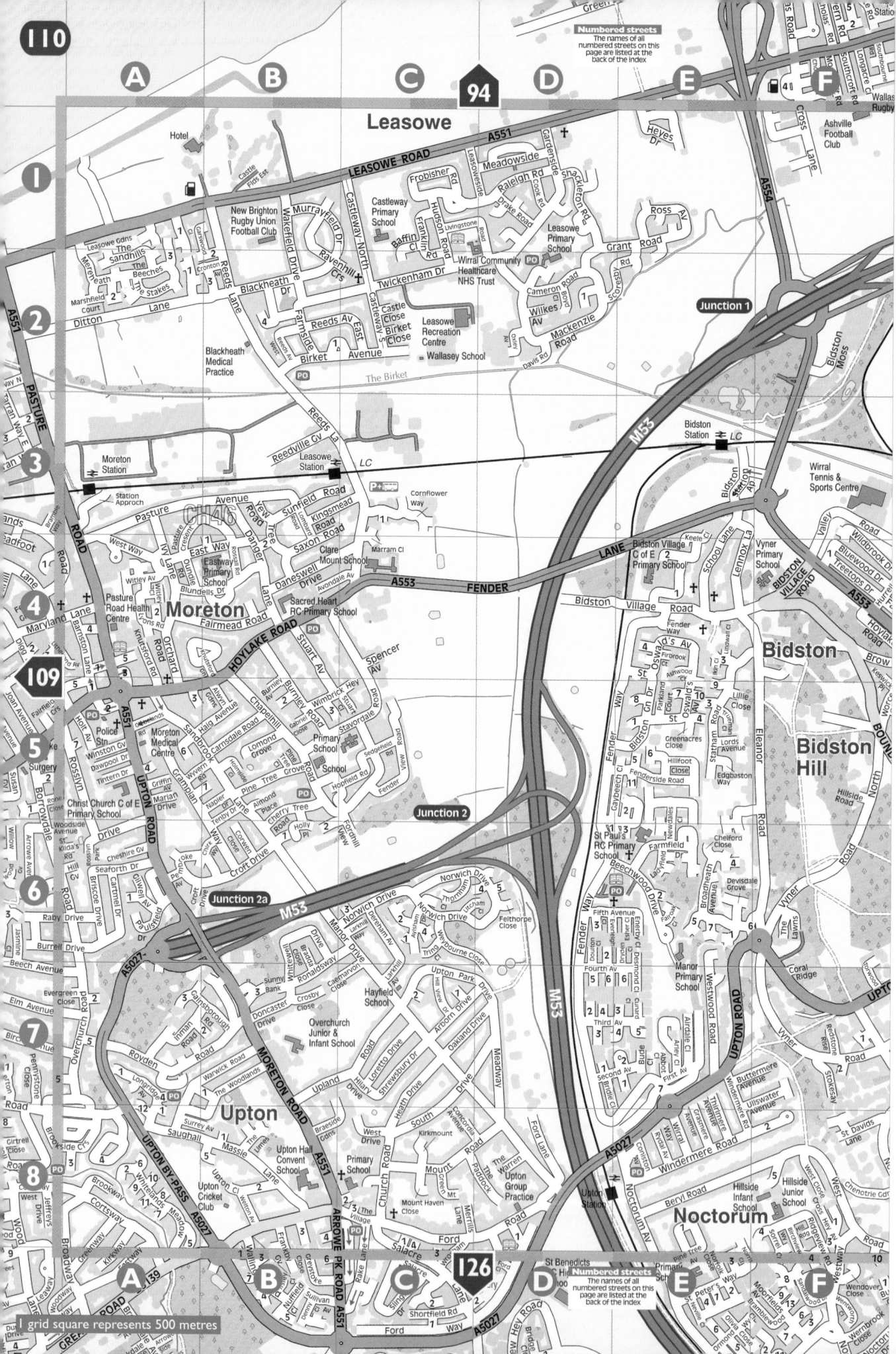

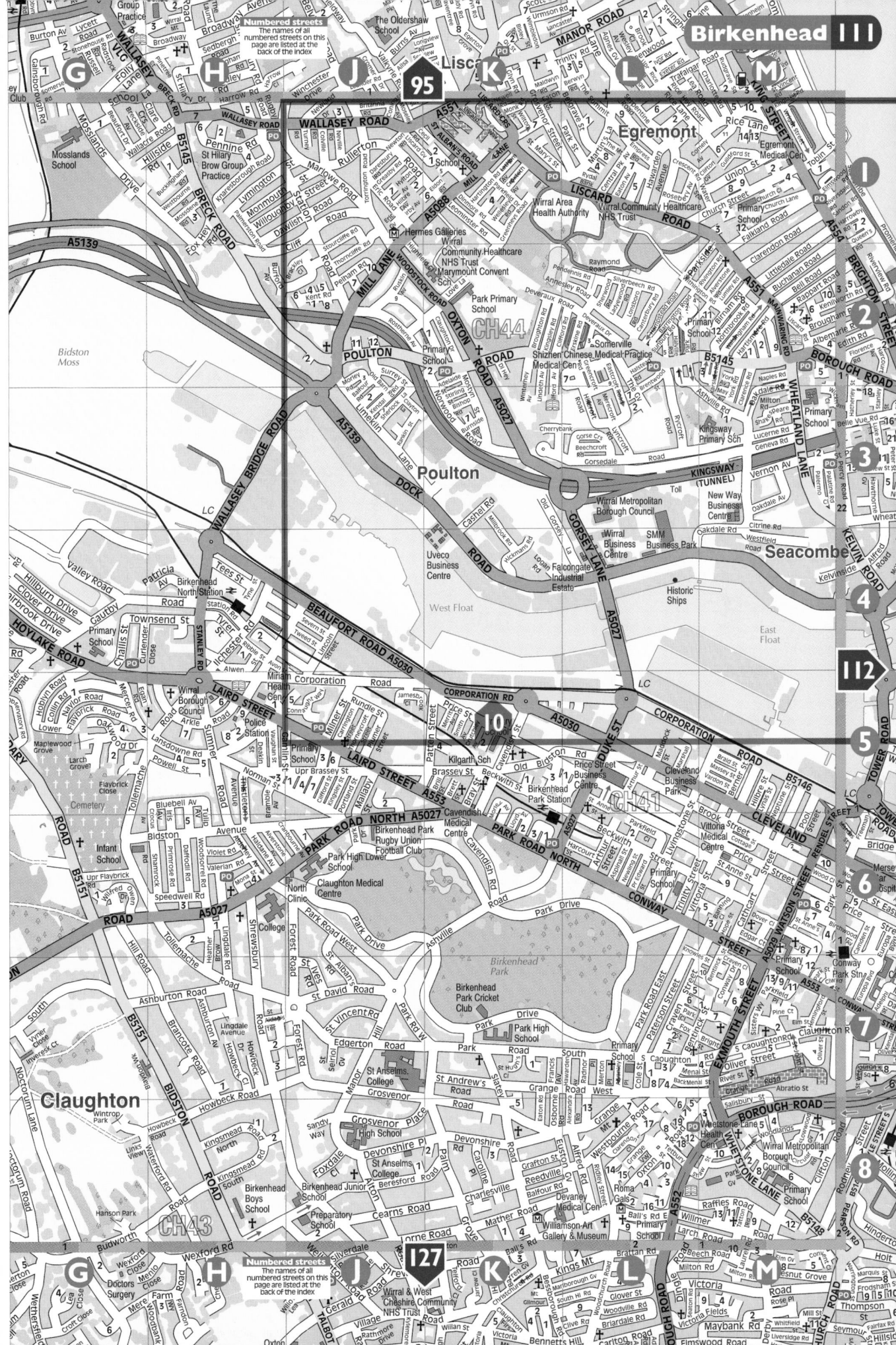

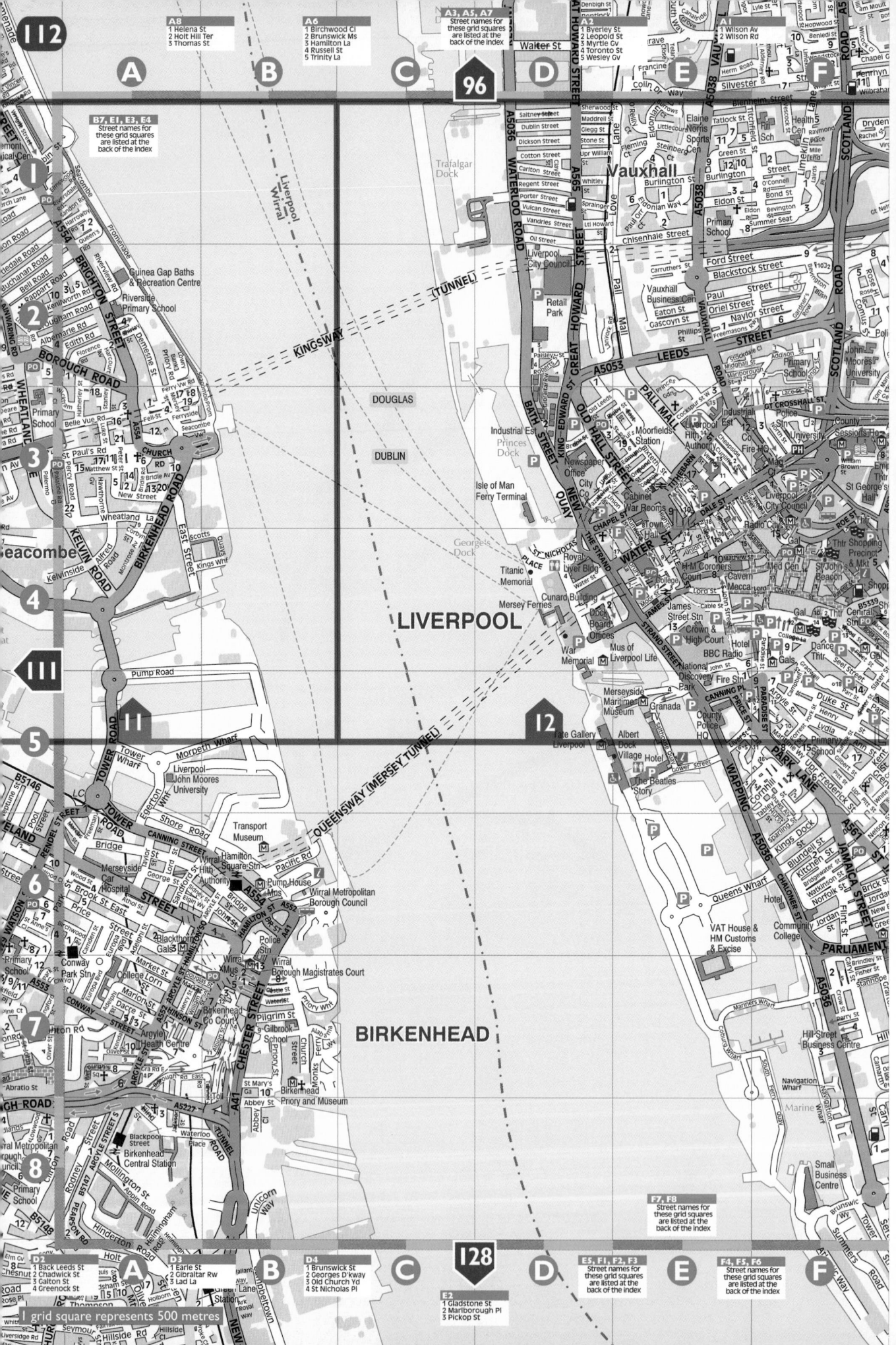

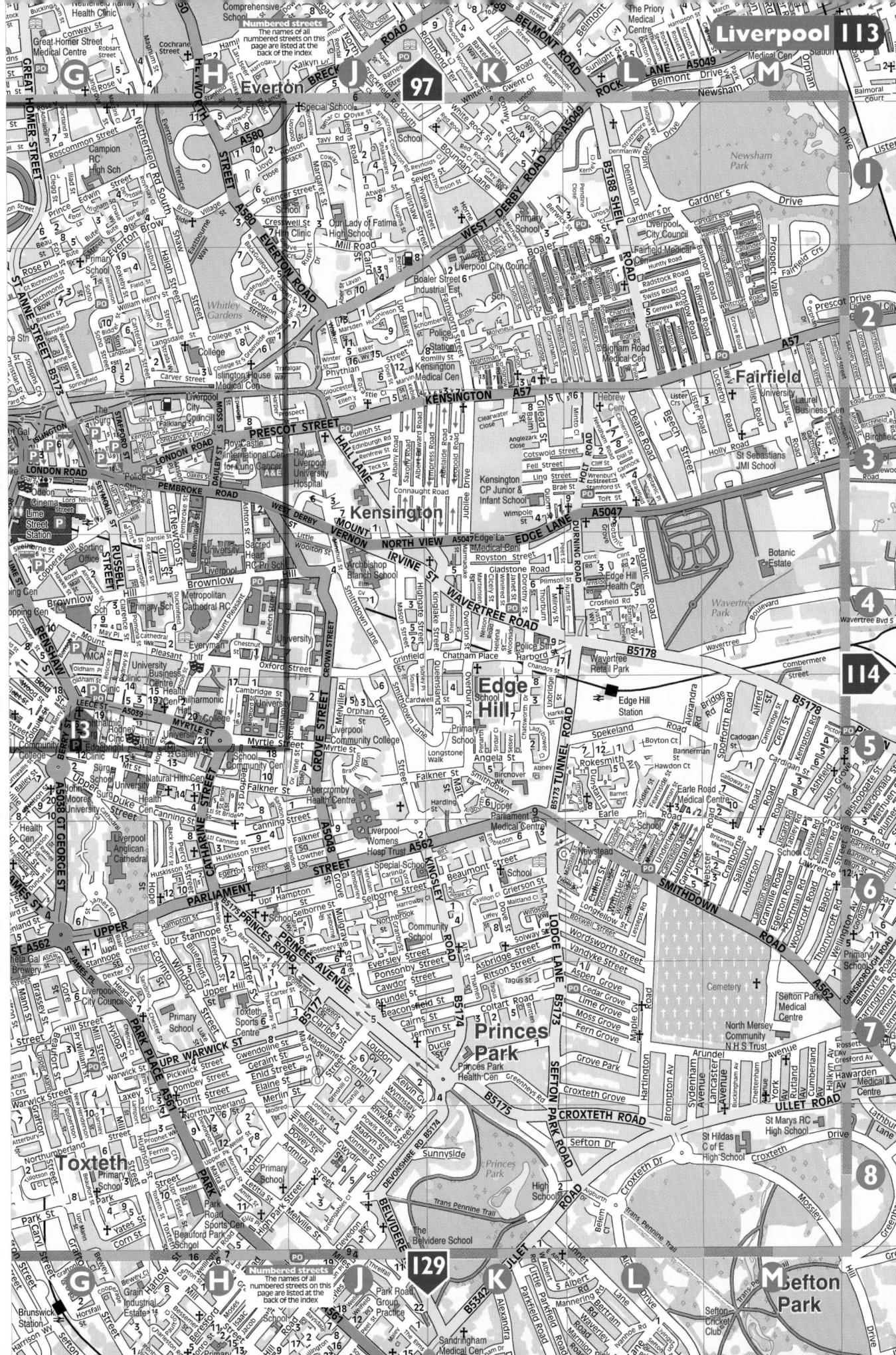

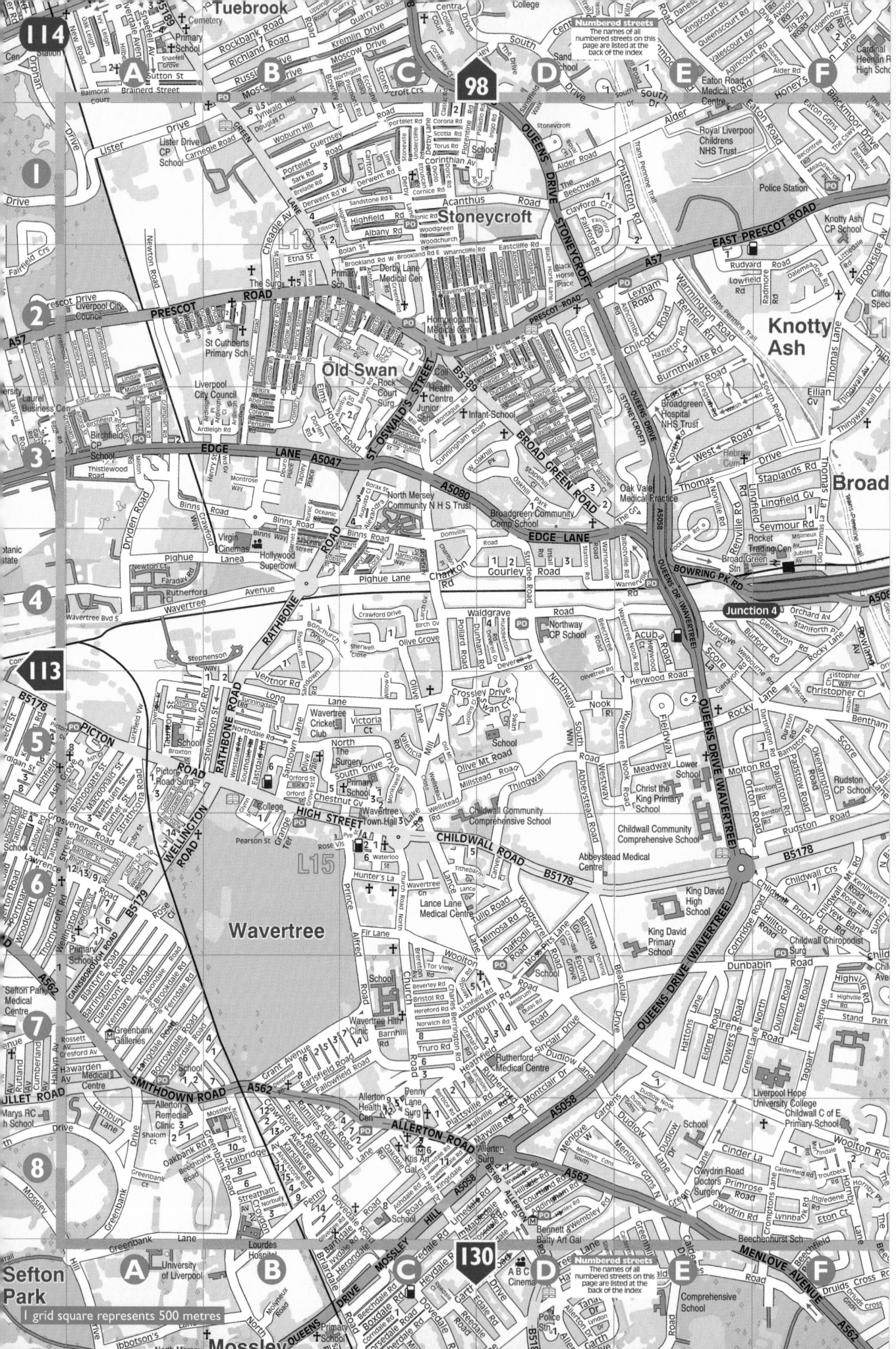

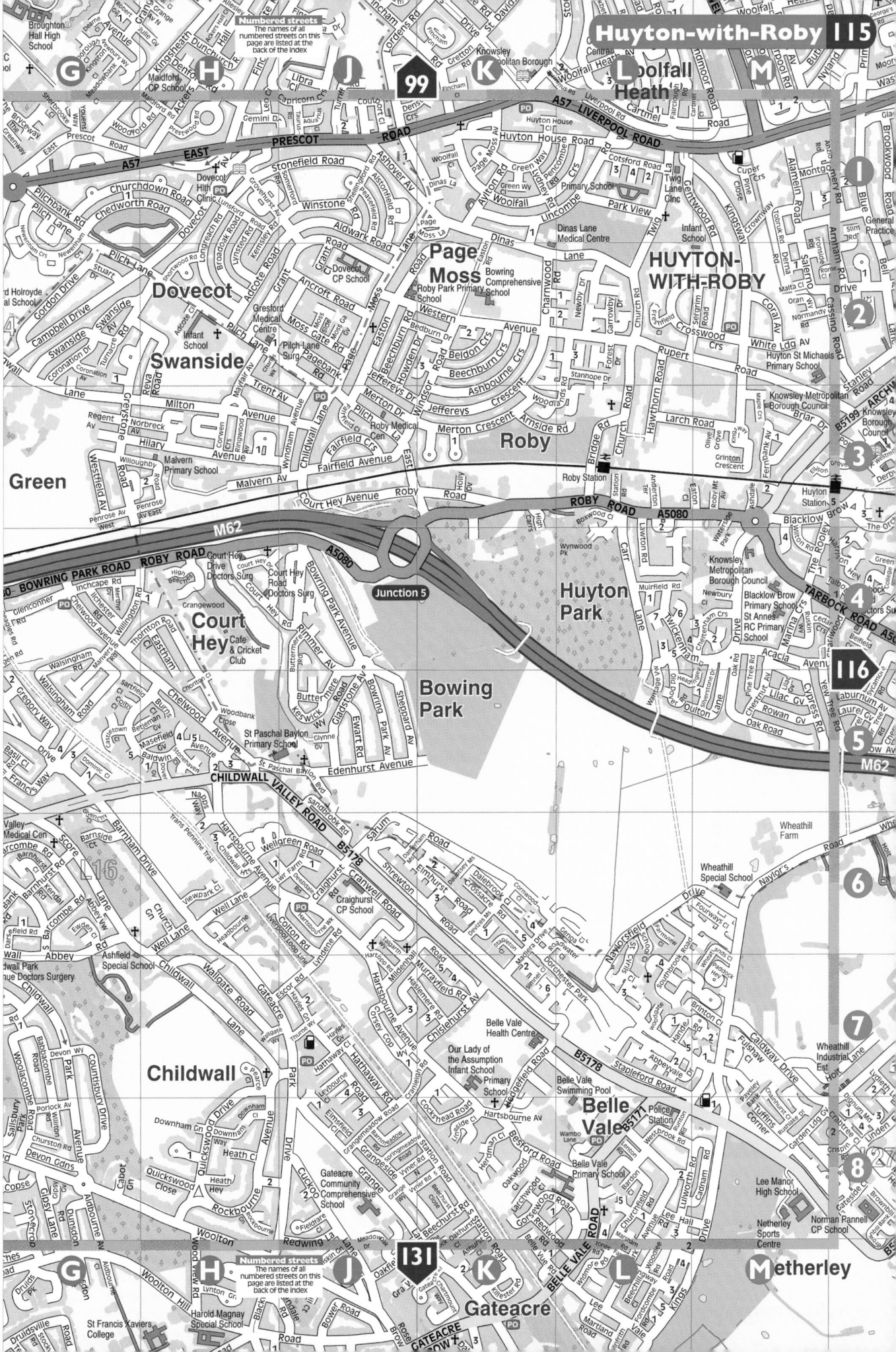

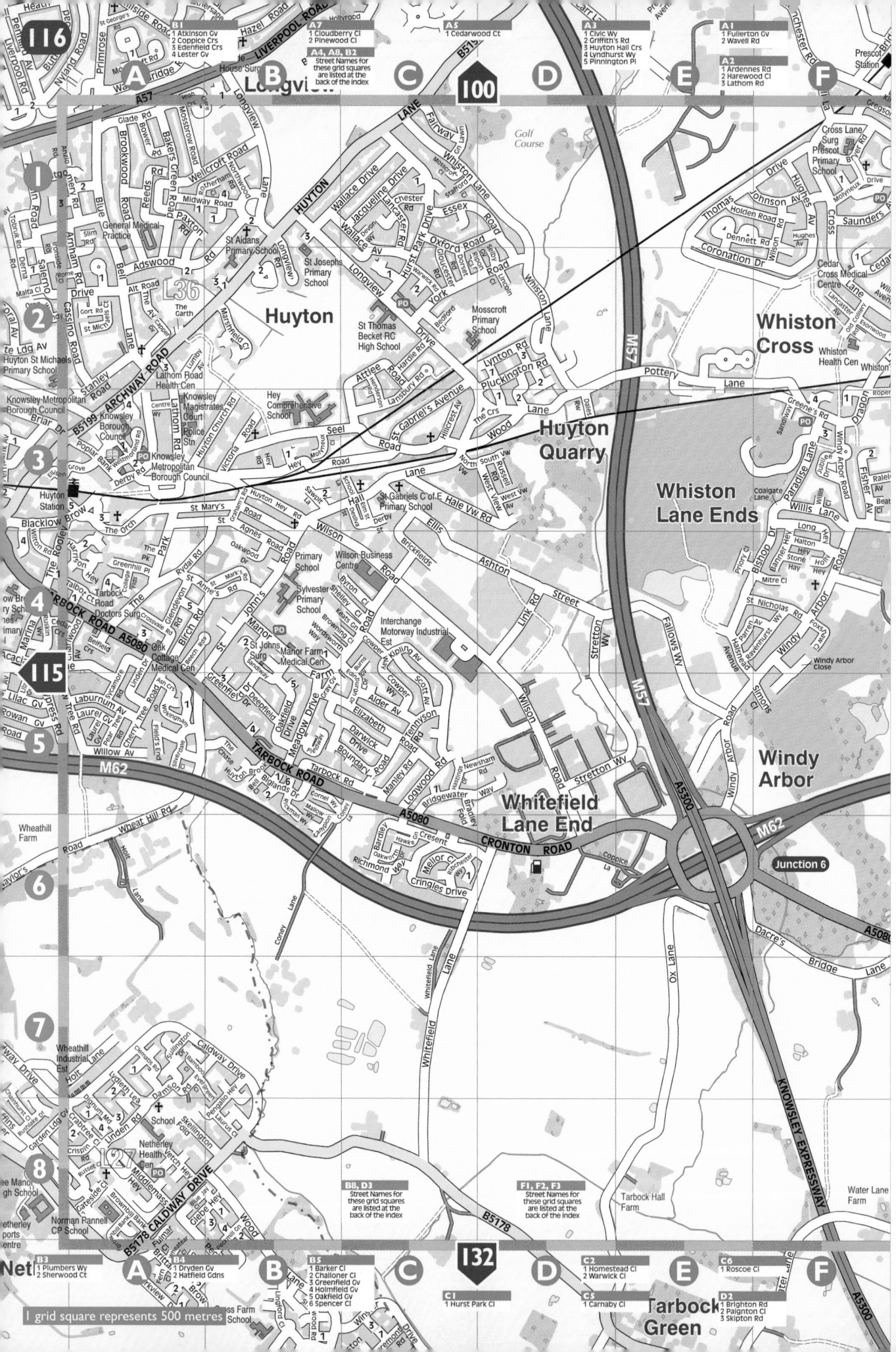

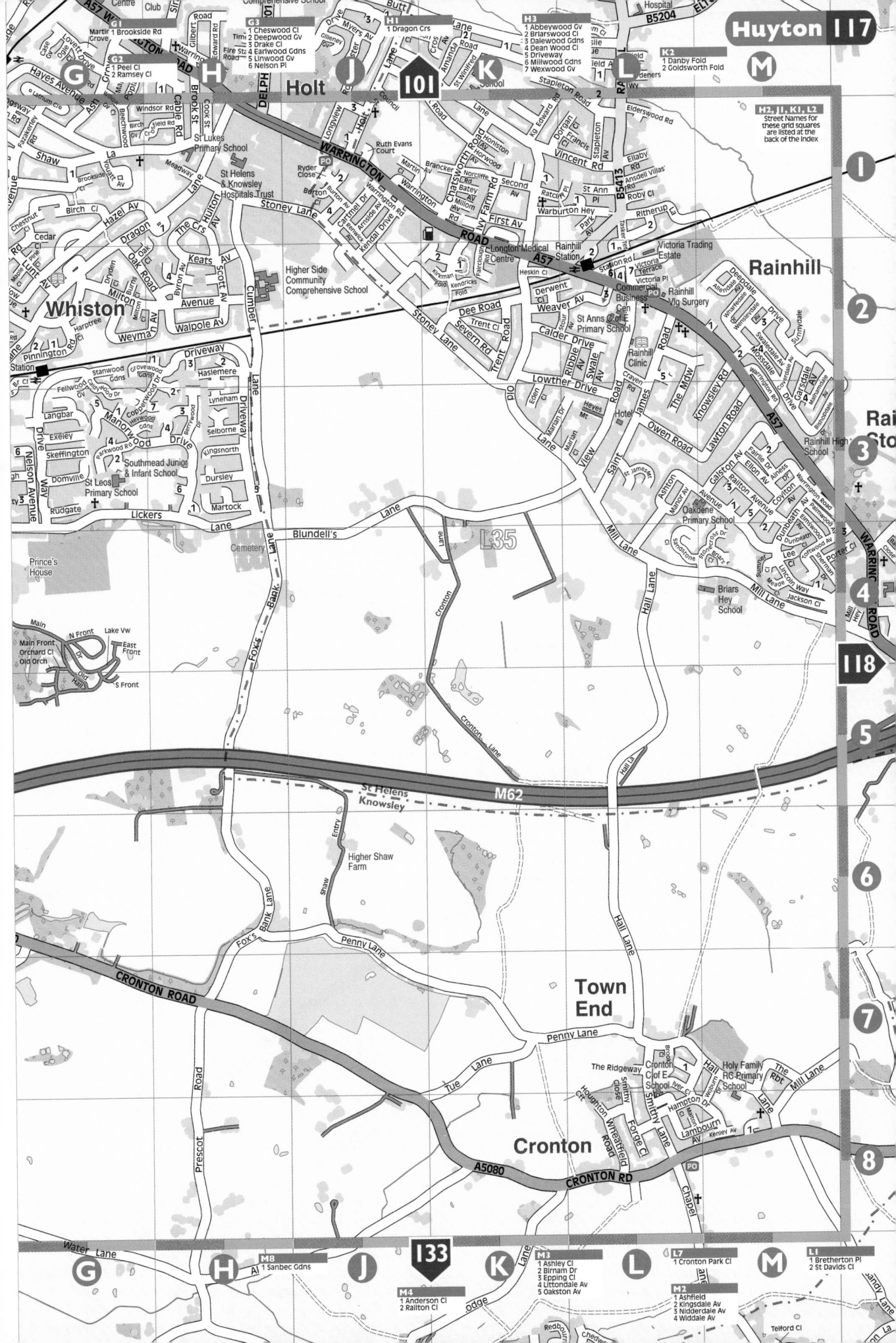

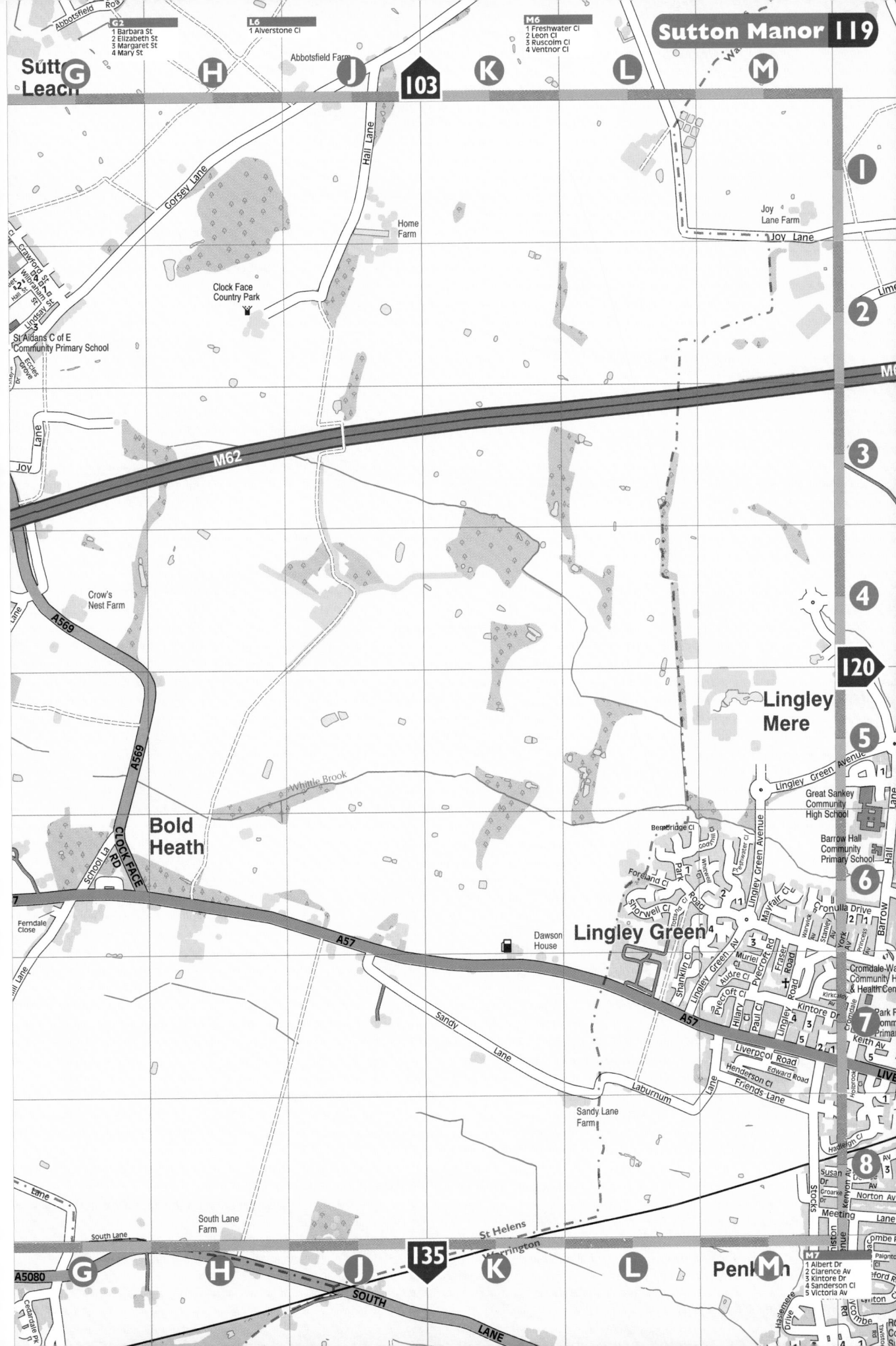

Abbotsfield Ro

G2
1 Barbara St
2 Elizabeth St
3 Margaret St
4 Mary St

L6
1 Alverstone Cl

M6
1 Freshwater Cl
2 Leon Cl
3 Ruscolm Cl
4 Ventnor Cl

Sutt
Leach

G   **H**   **J**   **103**   **K**   **L**   **M**

Abbotsfield Farm

Gorsey Lane

Hall Lane

Home Farm

Joy Lane Farm

Joy Lane

I

Clock Face Country Park

St Aidans C of E Community Primary School

Eccles Grove

Crawford St

Joy Lane

M62

2

3

Crow's Nest Farm

A569

A569

Lingley Mere

4

I20

5

Lingley Green Avenue

Great Sankey Community High School

Whittle Brook

Bold Heath

School La

CLOCK FACE RD

Ferndale Close

Bembridge Cl

Barrow Hall Community Primary School

6

Foreland Cl

Shorwell Cl

Park Road

Whitcliffe

Mayfair Cl

Lingley Green Avenue

Cronulla Drive

Barrow

Warwick

York

Stanley Cl

Princess

Dawson House

Lingley Green

A57

Sandy Lane

Shanklin Cl

Lingley Green Av

Piecroft Rd

Muriel Cl

Audre Cl

Piecroft Cl

Hilary Cl

Paul Cl

Fraser Road

Lingley

Kirkcaldy

Kintore Dr

Cromdale Wa Community H & Health Cen

Park F Comm Primar

7

Liverpool Road

Edward Road

Henderson Cl

Keith Av

Friends Lane

LIVE

Laburnum

Lane

Sandy Lane Farm

Hadleigh Cl

Susan Dr

8

Groarke Dr

Norton Av

Stocks Lane

Meeting Lane

South Lane Farm

South Lane

St Helens

Warrington

G   **H**   **J**   **135**   **K**   **L**   **Penk** **M**h

A5080

SOUTH LANE

M7
1 Albert Dr
2 Clarence Av
3 Kintore Dr
4 Sanderson Cl
5 Victoria Av

C4
1 Dovecote Gn
2 Matlock Cl

C5
1 Cheltenham Cl

B7
1 Cedar Rd
2 Conway Cl
3 Lilford Dr
4 Palin Dr
5 Southfields Av
6 Woodside Rd

B6
1 Garsdale Cl

A7
1 Barrow Hall La
2 Duncansby Crs
3 Kingston Av
4 Ramworth Rd
5 Rhona Dr
6 Sheringham Rd
7 Snowdon Cl
8 Sunnyside

A5
1 Billington Cl

A6, A8, B8
Street names for
these grid squares
are listed at the
back of the index

D7, E8, F3, F4
Street names for
these grid squares
are listed at the
back of the index

F5, F6, F7
Street names for
these grid squares
are listed at the
back of the index

Gemini

Kingswood

Callands

M62

Westbrook

119

ingley
ere

Great Sankey
Community
High School

Barrow Hall
Community
Primary School

WA5

New
Hall

Great
Sankey

Hood
Manor

Warrington
New Town
Cricket Club

St Gregorys
Catholic
High School

LIVERPOOL
ROAD

SANKEY WAY - A57

SANKEY WAY

C6
1 Wharfdale Cl

C7
1 Hale Gv
2 Orrell Cl
3 Roby Gv

C8
1 Morrison Cl
2 Parsonage Wy

D5
1 Bicknell Cl
2 Buchan Cl
3 Firman Cl
4 Hunt Cl
5 Tilman Cl

D8
1 Charminster Cl
2 Elsenhower Cl
3 Hilton Av
4 Lynham Av
5 Sgt York Loop

E7
1 Lindsworth Cl
2 Rosemary Cl
3 Wheat Cft

F
1 Cabot Cl
2 Cartier Cl

Eagle
Sports
Club

Penketh
Business Park

Sankey Bridge

1 grid square represents 500 metres

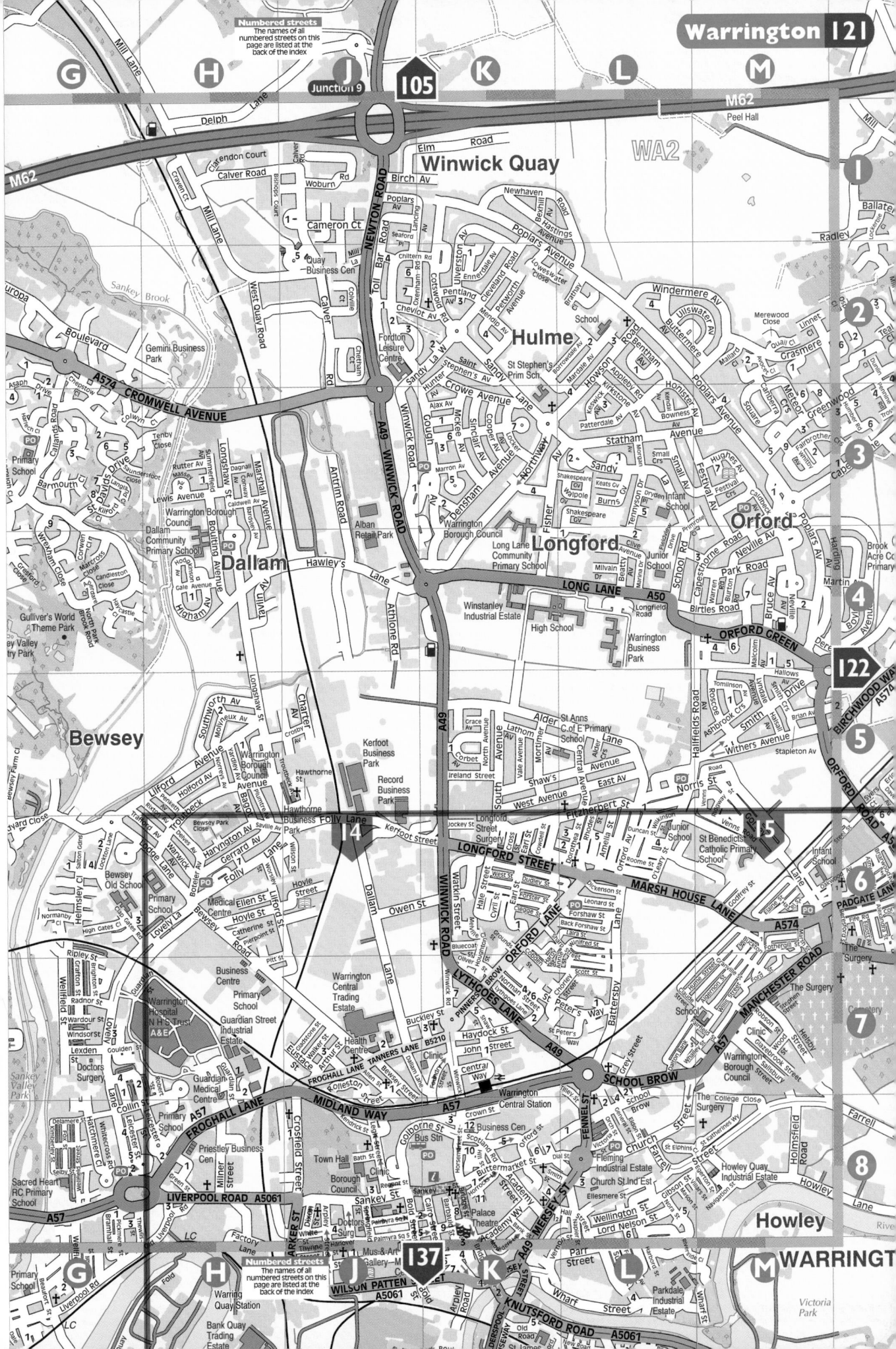

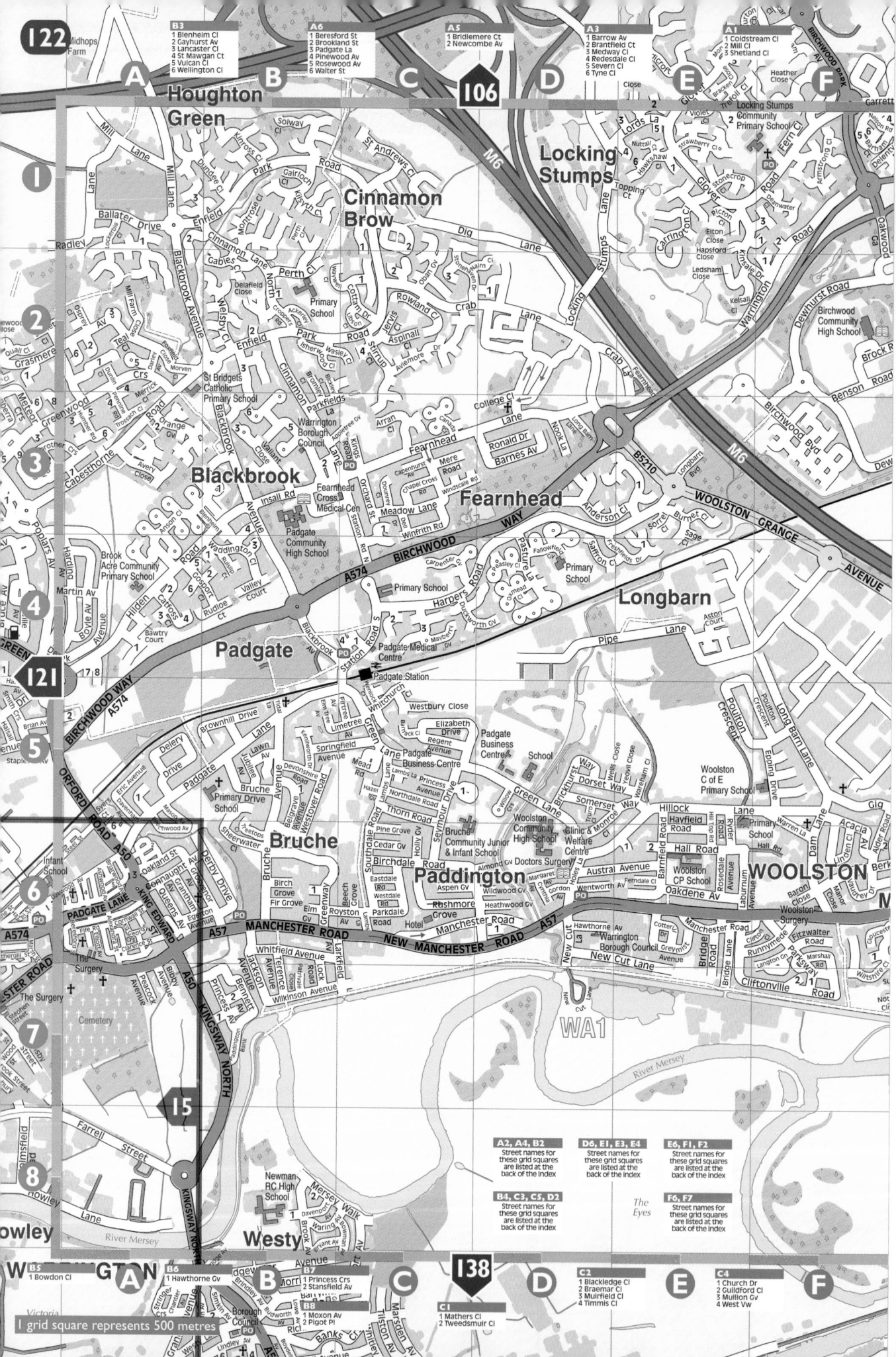

B3
1 Blenheim Cl
2 Gayhurst Av
3 Lancaster Cl
4 St Mawgan Ct
5 Vulcan Cl
6 Wellington Cl

A6
1 Beresford St
2 Brookland St
3 Padgate La
4 Pinewood Av
5 Rosewood Av
6 Walter St

A5
1 Bridlemere Ct
2 Newcombe Av

A3
1 Barrow Av
2 Brantfield Ct
3 Medway Cl
4 Redesdale Cl
5 Severn Cl
6 Tyne Cl

A1
1 Coldstream Cl
2 Mill Cl
3 Shetland Cl

Houghton Green

Cinnamon Brow

Locking Stumps

Locking Stumps Community Primary School

Birchwood Community High School

Blackbrook

Fearnhead

Longbarn

Padgate

Padgate Station

Woolston Grange

Bruche

Paddington

WOOLSTON

Manchester Road

New Manchester Road

WA1

River Mersey

The Eyes

River Mersey

Westy

A2, A4, B2
Street names for these grid squares are listed at the back of the index

D6, E1, E3, E4
Street names for these grid squares are listed at the back of the index

E6, F1, F2
Street names for these grid squares are listed at the back of the index

B4, C3, C5, D2
Street names for these grid squares are listed at the back of the index

F6, F7
Street names for these grid squares are listed at the back of the index

B5
1 Bowdon Cl

B6
1 Hawthorne Gv

B5
1 Princess Crs
2 Stansfield Av

C2
1 Blackledge Cl
2 Brearnar Cl
3 Mulrfield Cl
4 Timmis Cl

C4
1 Church Dr
2 Guildford Cl
3 Mullion Gv
4 West Vw

B5
1 Moxon Av
2 Pigot Pl

C1
1 Mathers Cl
2 Tweedsmuir Cl

1 grid square represents 500 metres

G
G1
1 Fernbank Cl
2 Goldfinch La
3 Kestrel La
4 Redpoll La

H
G2
1 Hamnett Ct
2 Patterson Cl
3 Ramsay Cl

J

107

K
G6
1 Cypress Cl
2 Durham Cl
3 Ladycroft Cl
4 Magnolia Cl
5 Mancroft Cl
6 Stirling Cl
7 Wessex Cl
8 White House Dr

L

M

Birchwood

Oakwood
Primary School

Primary School

School

Birchwood Medical Cen

Birchwood Station

Risley Moss Nature Park

Prospect Farm

Prospect Lane

Rixton Moss

Woodend Lane

Holly Bush Lane

Woolston Moss

Marshall's Farm

Green Alley Farm

M6

Nicol Av

WOOLSTON GRANGE AVENUE

Juniper Lane

Brook Lane

A57

MANCHESTER ROAD

Brookside Farm

Warrington Borough Council

Martinscroft

A57

B5210

Manchester Road

Junction 21

River Mersey

Bollin Point

Golf Course

Statham Lane

Thelwall Viaduct

139

Laskey House

Manchester Ship Canal

H6
1 Clares Farm Cl

H1
1 Fieldfare Cl
2 Keyes Gdns
3 Nightingale Cl
4 Swallow Cl
5 Wren Cl

G7
1 Berwick Cl
2 Mulberry Cl
3 Shropshire Cl

Brookside

Oldfield Road
Oldfield Rd
Whitbarrow Rd

Whitbarrow Road

1 I
2
3
4
5
6
7
8

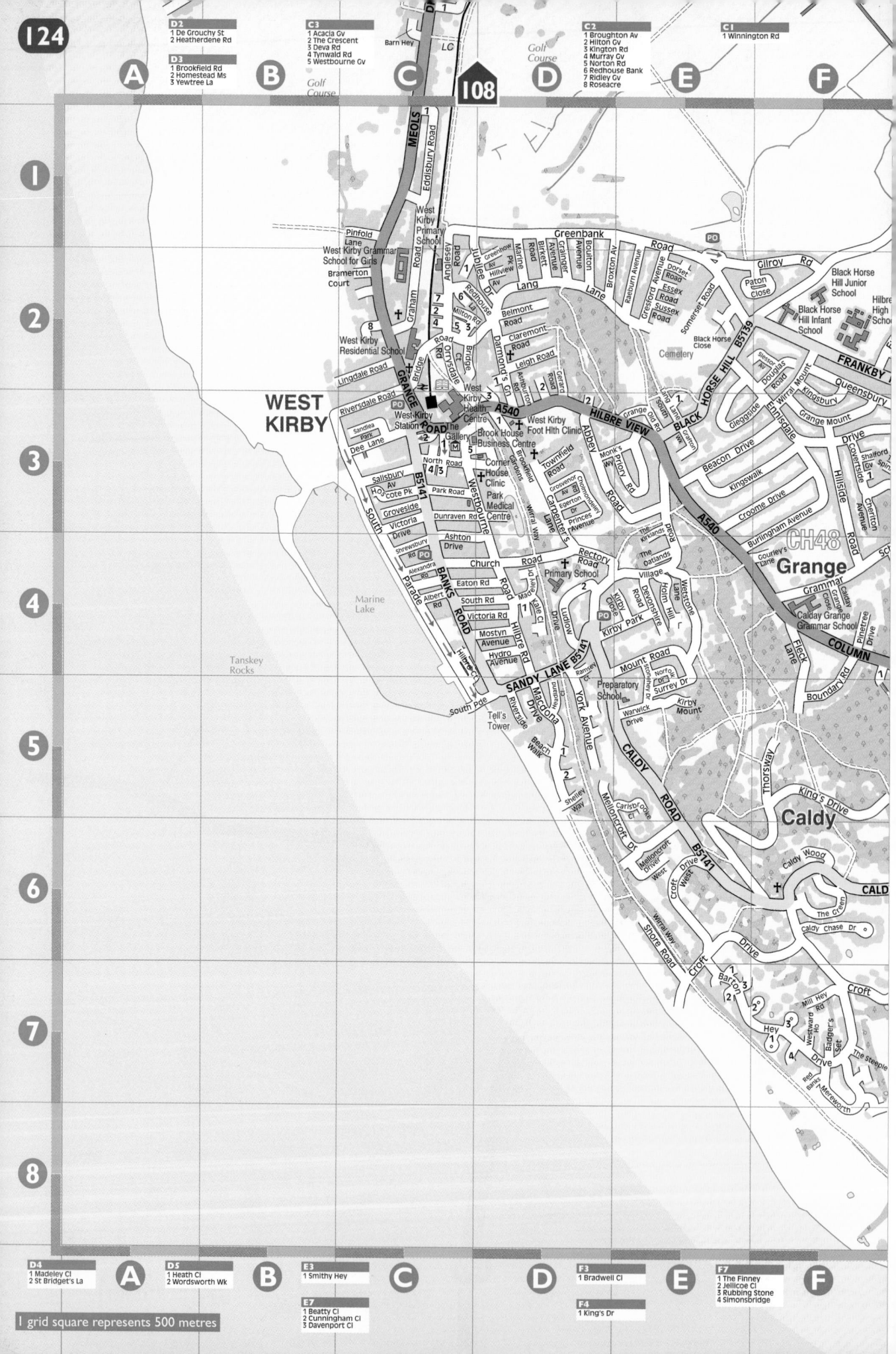

D2
1 De Grouchy St
2 Heatherdene Rd

D3
1 Brookfield Rd
2 Homestead Ms
3 Yewtree La

C3
1 Acacia Gv
2 The Crescent
3 Deva Rd
4 Tynwald Rd
5 Westbourne Gv

C2
1 Broughton Av
2 Hilton Gv
3 Kington Rd
4 Murray Gv
5 Norton Rd
6 Redhouse Bank
7 Ridley Gv
8 Roseacre

C1
1 Winnington Rd

108

A B C D E F

I

2

**WEST
KIRBY**

3

4

Marine
Lake

Tansley
Rocks

5

6

7

8

D4
1 Madeley Cl
2 St Bridget's La

D5
1 Heath Cl
2 Wordsworth Wk

E3
1 Smithy Hey

E7
1 Beatty Cl
2 Cunningham Cl
3 Davenport Cl

F3
1 Bradwell Cl

F4
1 King's Dr

F7
1 The Finney
2 Jellicoe Cl
3 Rubbing Stone
4 Simonsbridge

A B C D E F

I grid square represents 500 metres

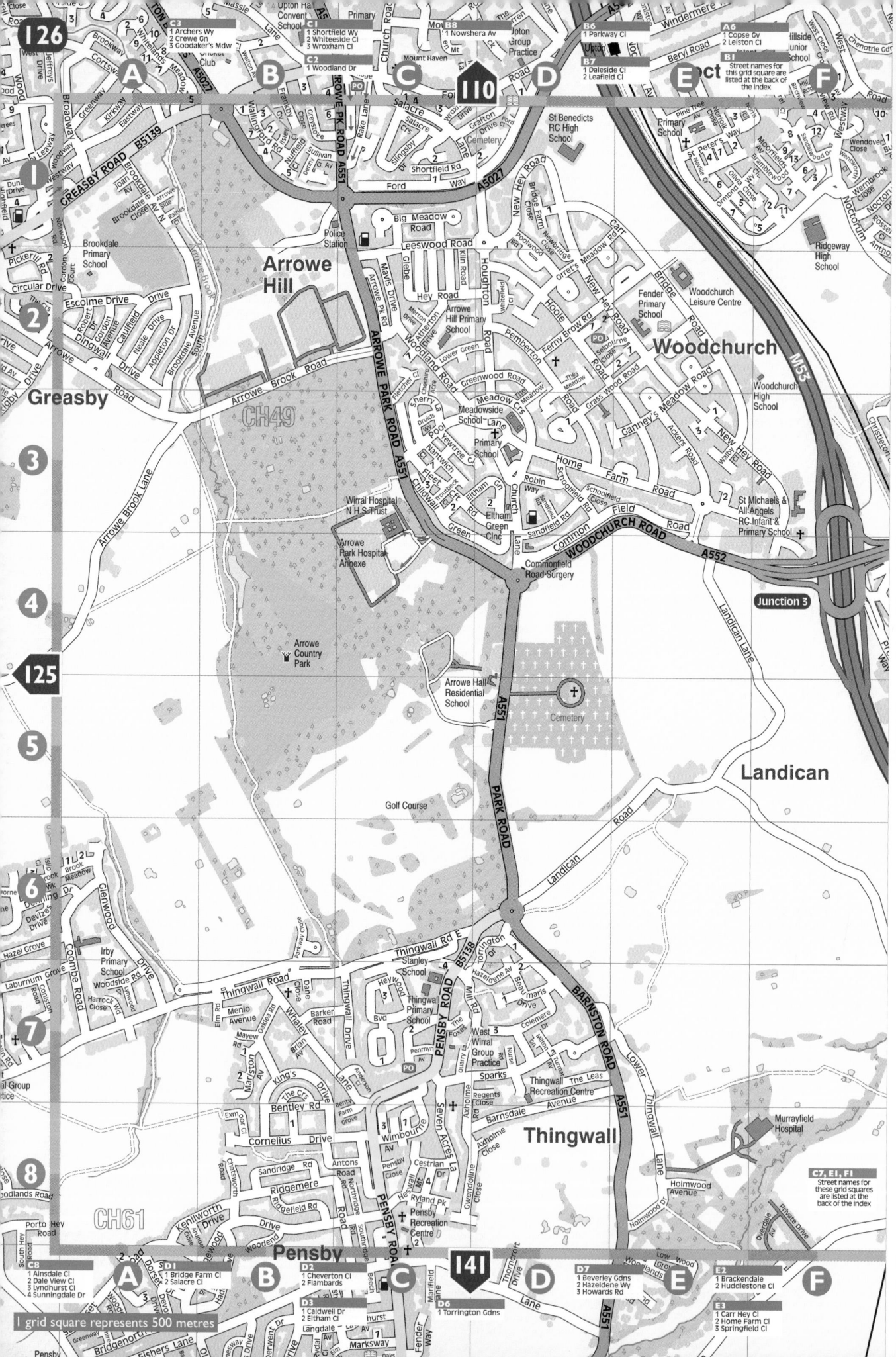

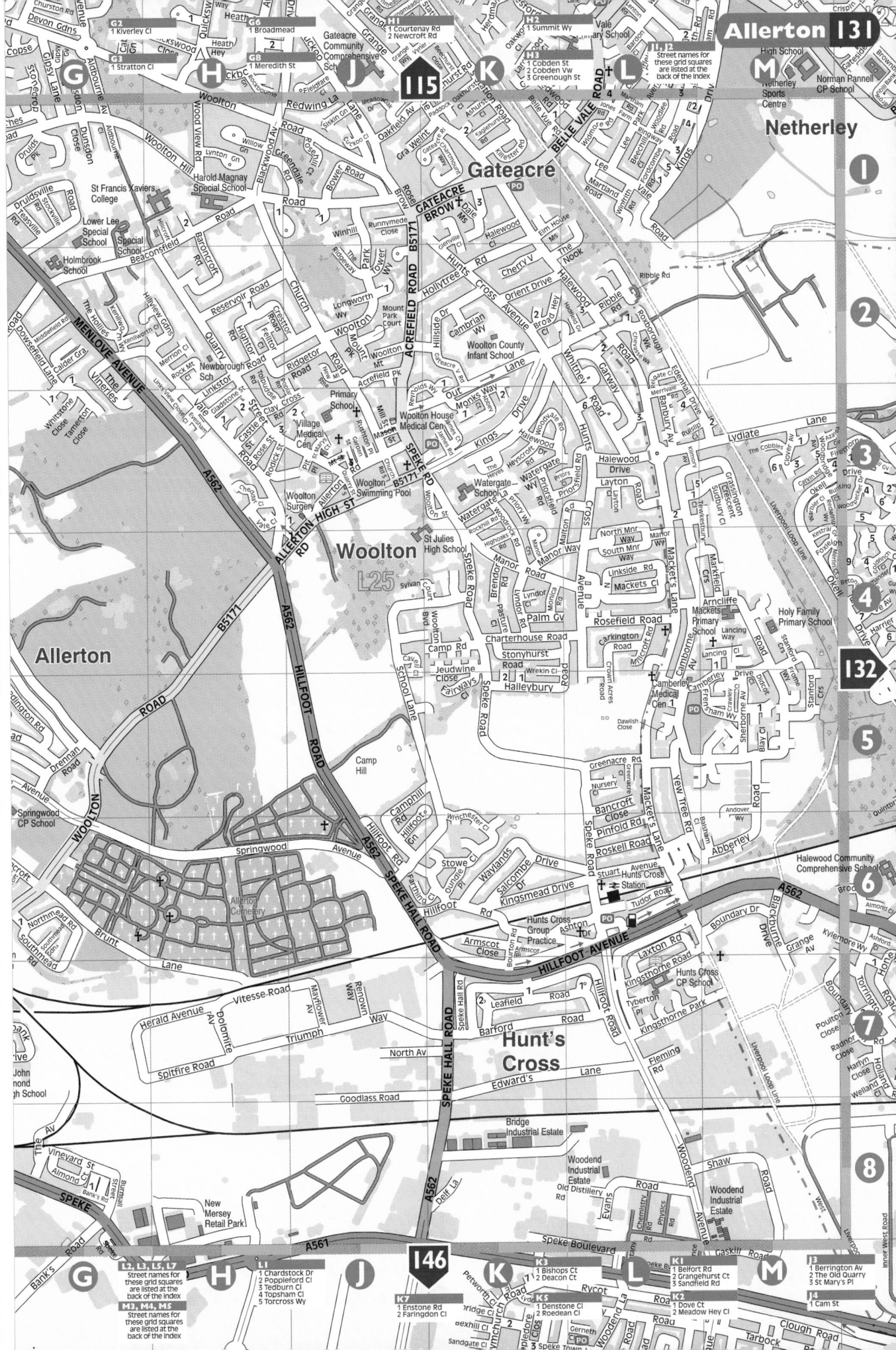

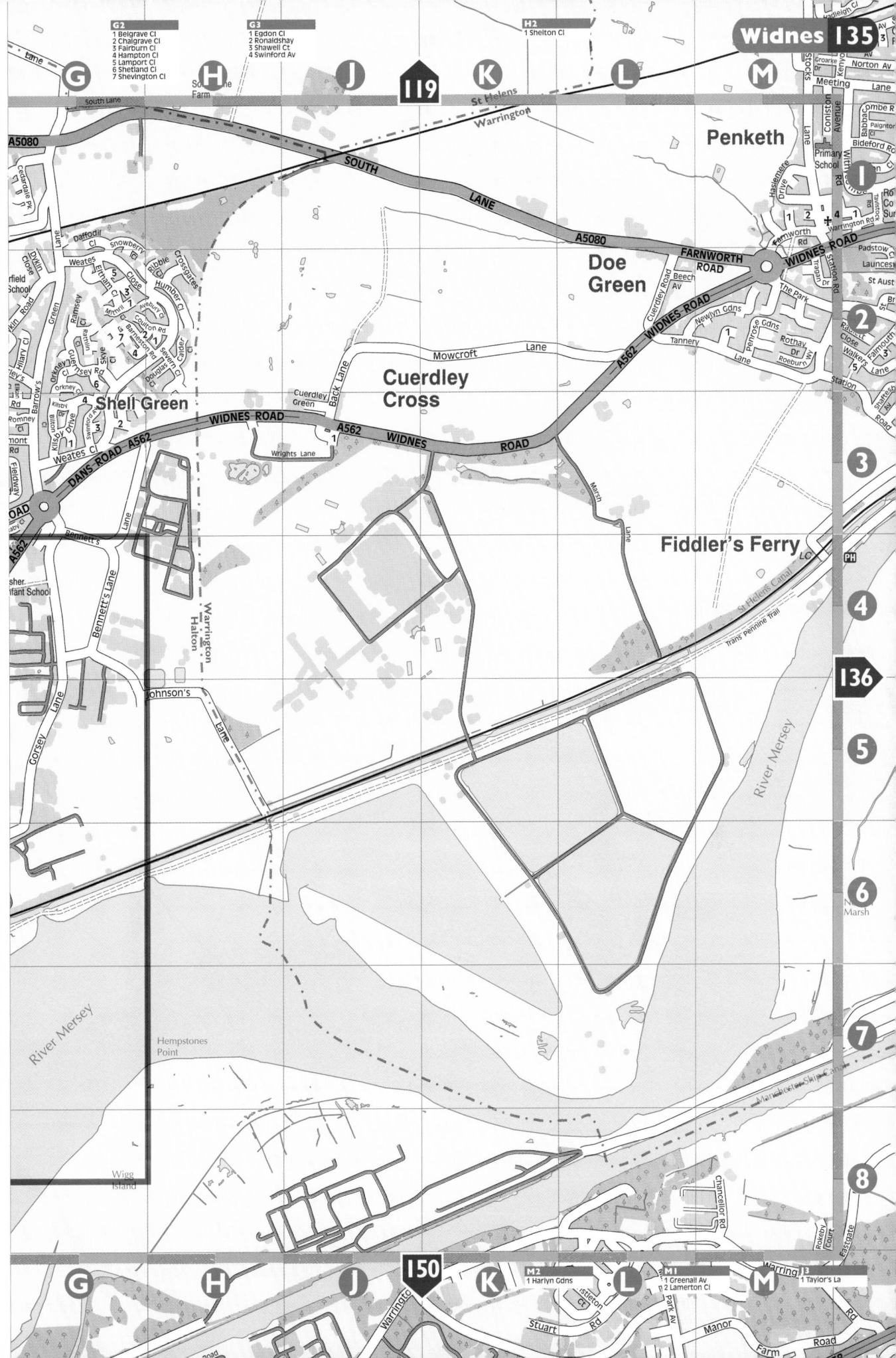

G2
1 Belgrave Cl
2 Chalgrave Cl
3 Fairburn Cl
4 Hampton Cl
5 Lamport Cl
6 Shetland Cl
7 Shevington Cl

G3
1 Egdon Cl
2 Ronaldshay
3 Shawell Ct
4 Swinford Av

H2
1 Shelton Cl

G   H   J   119   K   St Helens   L   M

Warrington

South Lane

SOUTH LANE   A5080

A5080

Penketh

Primary School

Norton Av

Meeting Lane

Hasleмere Drive

Farnworth Rd

I

Doe Green

FARNWORTH ROAD

WIDNES ROAD

The Park

2

Warrington Rd

St Aust

Cuerdley Road

Beech Av

Newlyn Gdns

Rothay

Penrose Gdns

Roeburn

Roeburn Dr

Tannery

Station

3

WIDNES ROAD

A562

Mowcroft   Lane

Cuerdley Green

Back Lane

Cuerdley Cross

Shell Green

Daffodil Cl

snowberry

Weates

Ribble

Crossgates

Humber Cl

Close

Aveyard Cl

Coulton Rd

Severn Cl

Skye

Douglas Cl

Barrow's

Ramsey

Kilsby

Swinford Cl

WIDNES ROAD   A562   WIDNES   ROAD

DANS ROAD   A562

Weates

Wrights Lane

1

Marsh Lane

Fiddler's Ferry

LC

PH

St Helens Canal

Trans Pennine Trail

4

136

River Mersey

5

Bennett's

Bennett's Lane

Warrington Halton

Johnson's Lane

6

N
Marsh

Gorsey Lane

River Mersey

Hempstones Point

Manchester Ship Canal

7

Wigg Island

8

M2
1 Harlyn Gdns

M1
1 Greenall Av
2 Lamerton Cl

1 Taylor's La

Warrington

Stuart Rd

Park Av

Manor Farm Road

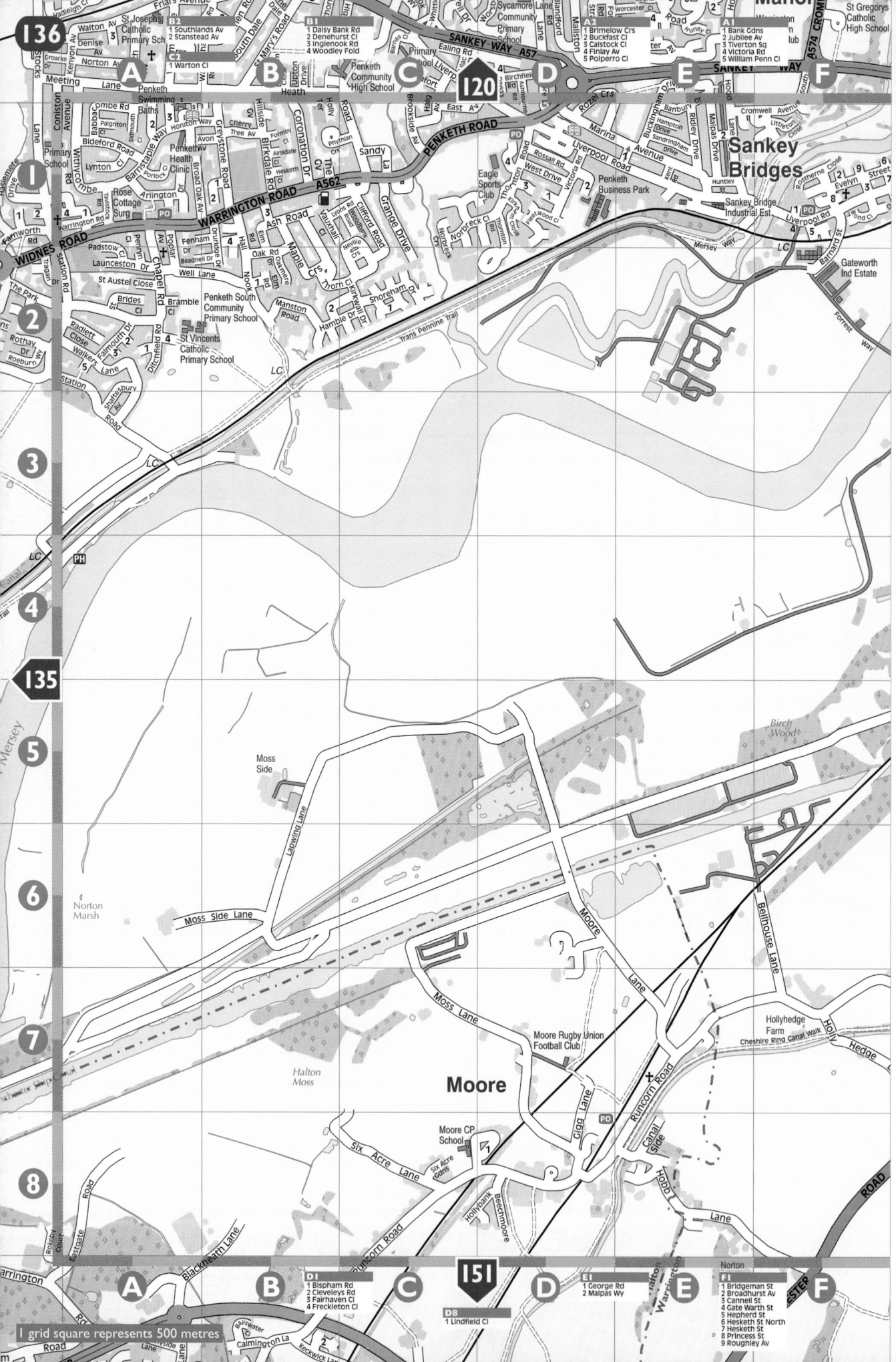

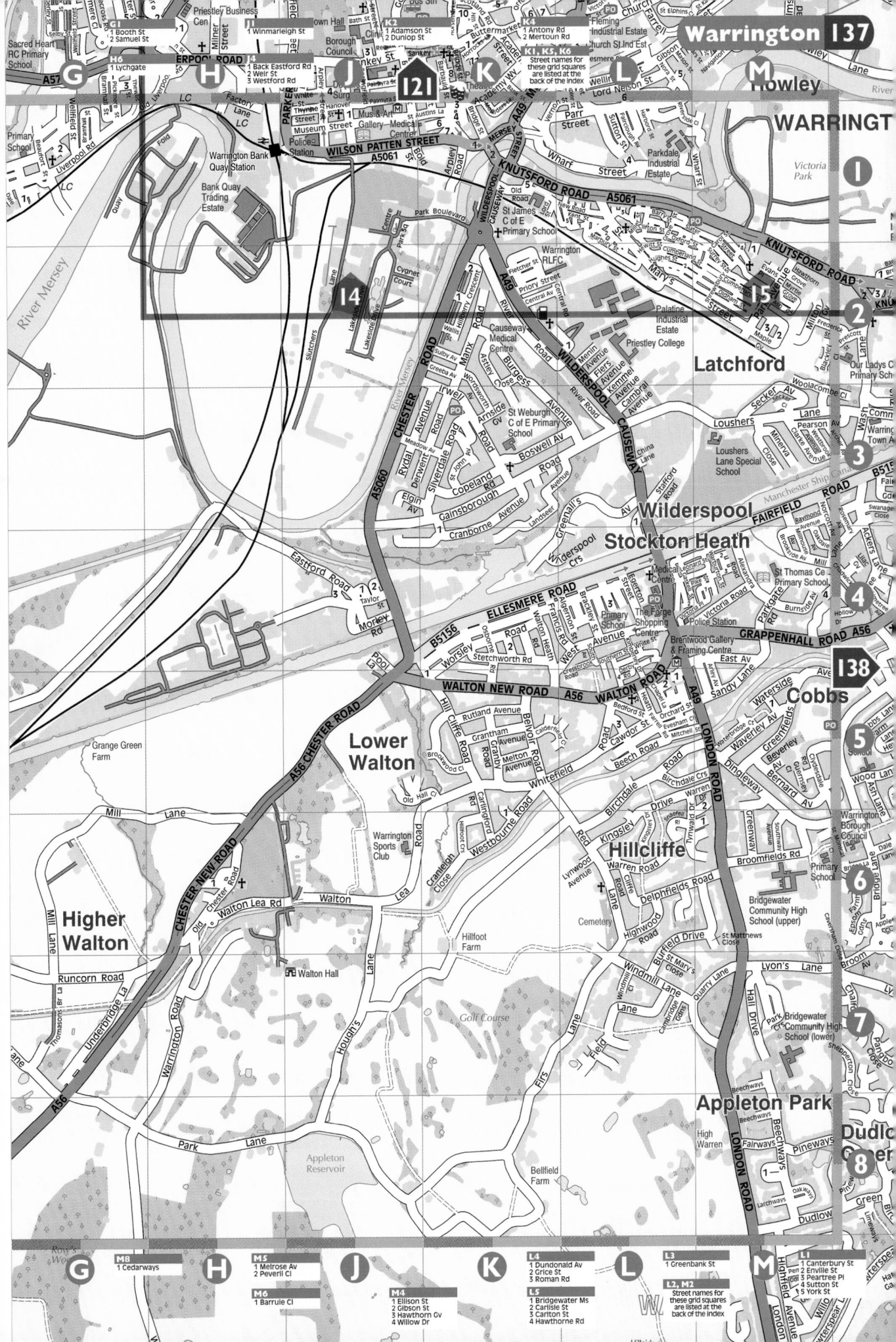

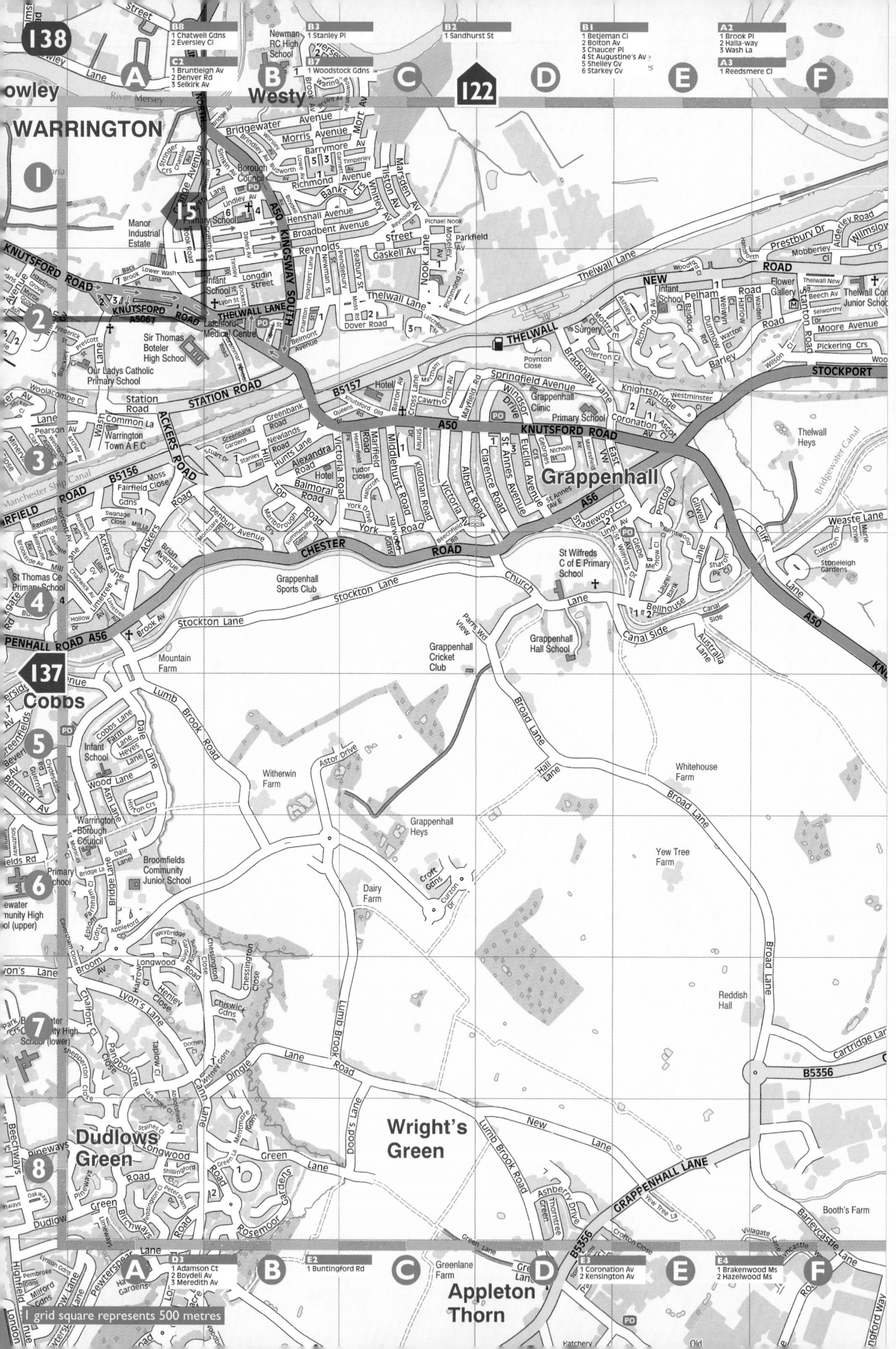

138
B8
1 Chatwell Gdns
2 Eversley Cl
C2
1 Bruntleigh Av
2 Denver Rd
3 Selkirk Av
B3
1 Stanley Pl
B7
1 Woodstock Gdns
B2
1 Sandhurst St
B1
1 Betjeman Cl
2 Bolton Av
3 Chaucer Pl
4 St Augustine's Av
5 Shelley Gv
6 Starkey Gv
A2
1 Brook Pl
2 Halla-way
3 Wash La
A3
1 Reedsmere Cl
122
A
B
C
D
E
F
1
2
3
4
5
6
7
8
Westy
WARRINGTON
River Mersey
Newman RC High School
Bridgewater Avenue
Morris Avenue
Barrymore Av
Richmond Avenue
Banks Crs
Tilston Av
Marsden Av
Whitley Av
Borough Council
Manor Industrial Estate
15
Primary School
Henshall Avenue
Broadbent Avenue
Reynolds Street
Gaskell Av
Nook Lane
Moseley Av
Parkfield Av
Pichael Nook
KNUTSFORD ROAD
A5061
Longdin Street
Infant School
Latchford Medical Centre
THELWALL LANE
A50 KINGSWAY SOUTH
Thelwall Lane
Dover Road
Sir Thomas Boteler High School
Our Ladys Catholic Primary School
Station Road
STATION ROAD
ACKERS ROAD
Warrington Town A F C
Common La
Pearson Av
B5156
Manchester Ship Canal
B5157
Hotel
Thelwall Lane
THELWALL
NEW ROAD
Infant School
Pelham Road
Surgery
Flower Gallery
Thelwall Com Junior School
Stanton Road
Moore Avenue
Pickering Crs
Prestbury Dr
Alderley Road
Wilmslow Crs
Mobberley Cl
Barley
Poynton Close
Springfield Avenue
Grappenhall Clinic
Primary School
Bradshaw Lane
Knightsbridge Av
Westminster
STOCKPORT
A50
KNUTSFORD ROAD
Coronation Av
Ascot Cl
Thelwall Heys
Bridgewater Canal
Grappenhall
A56
Victoria Road
Marfield Road
Middlehurst Road
Kildonan Road
Victoria Av
Albert Road
Clarence Road
St Annes Avenue
Euclid Avenue
Alexandra Road
Balmoral Road
York Road
Hotel
Denbury Avenue
CHESTER ROAD
Portola Cl
Gilwell Cl
Cliff Lane
Weaste Lane
Stoneleigh Gardens
Shadewood Crs
St Wilfreds C of E Primary School
Church Lane
Grappenhall Sports Club
Stockton Lane
St Thomas Ce Primary School
PENHALL ROAD A56
Brook Av
Mountain Farm
Parrs Wd View
Grappenhall Cricket Club
Grappenhall Hall School
Canal Side
Australia Lane
Bellhouse Lane
A50
137
Cobbs
Lumb Brook Road
Broad Lane
Hall Lane
Whitehouse Farm
Witherwin Farm
Astor Drive
Grappenhall Heys
Infant School
Wood Lane
Ash Lane
Dale Lane
Warrington Borough Council
Broomfields Community Junior School
Croft Gdns
Curzon Dr
Dairy Farm
Yew Tree Farm
Broad Lane
Reddish Hall
Broom Av
Longwood Road
Lyon's Lane
Henley Close
Chessington Close
Chiswick Gdns
Chalfont Cl
Pangbourne Close
Dingle Lane
Cann Lane
Lumb Brook Road
Cartridge Lane
B5356
Wright's Green
Dood's Lane
New Lane
Dudlows Green
Longwood
Green Lane
Rosemoor Gardens
Ashberry Drive
GRAPPENHALL LANE
B5356
Yew Tree La
Booth's Farm
Barleycastle Lane
Crofton Close
Green Lane
Greenlane Farm
Appleton Thorn
Pewterspear Lane
Highfield
London
D3
1 Adamson Ct
2 Boydell Av
3 Meredith Av
E2
1 Buntingford Rd
E3
1 Coronation Av
2 Kensington Av
E4
1 Brakenwood Ms
2 Hazelwood Ms
1 grid square represents 500 metres

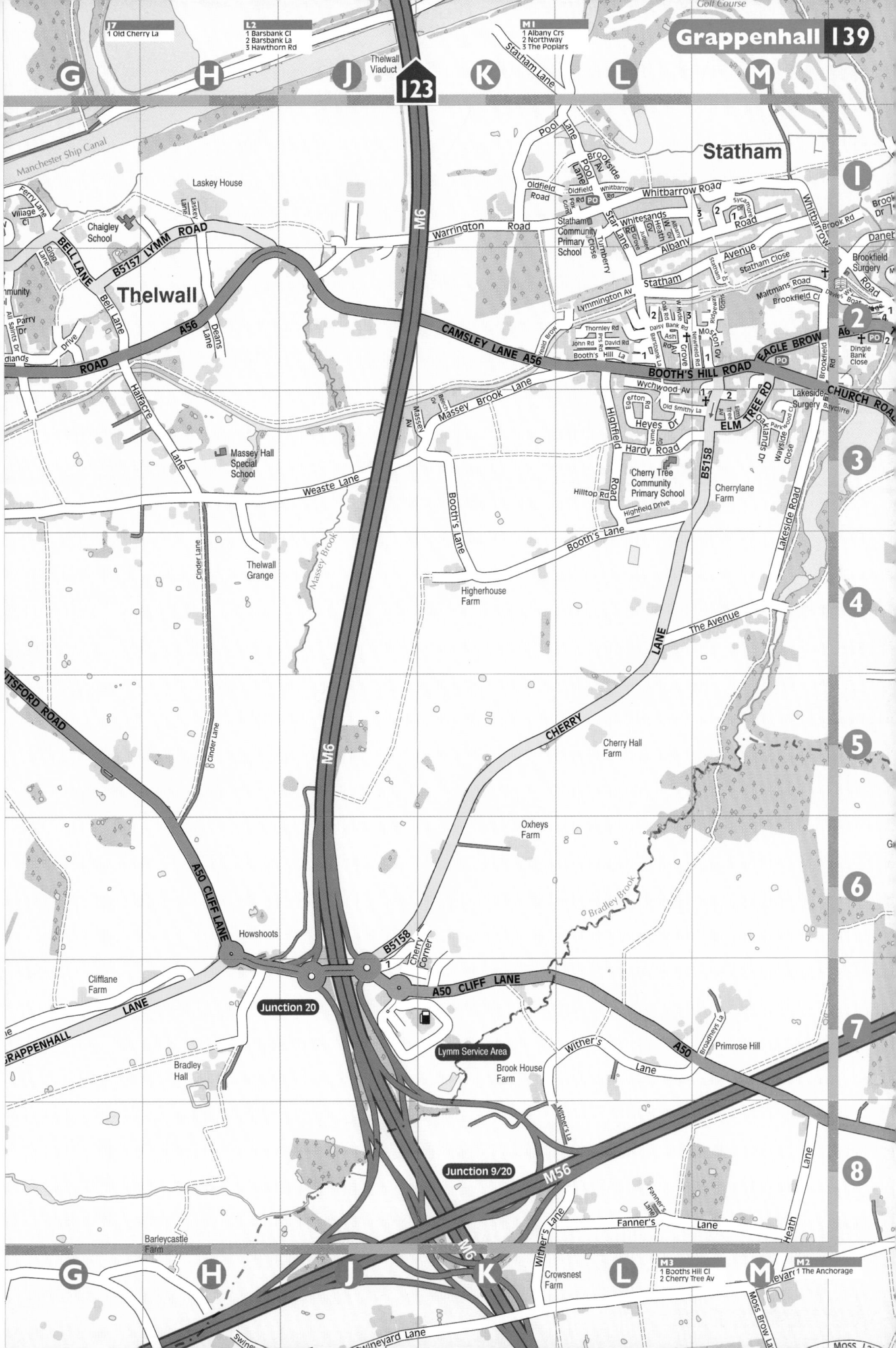

G H J K L M

123

Statham

Thelwall

I

2

3

4

5

6

7

8

G H J K L M

Manchester Ship Canal

Laskey House

Chaigley School

B5157 LYMM ROAD

Thelwall Viaduct

Pool Lane

Brookside Av

Oldfield Road

Whitbarrow Road

Statham Community Primary School

Albany Avenue

Statham Close

Maltmans Road

Brookfield Cl

Brookfield Surgery

Dingle Bank Close

CHURCH ROAD

Warrington Road

CAMSLEY LANE A56

BOOTH'S HILL ROAD

EAGLE BROW

ELM TREE RD

B5158

Lakeside Road

Massey Brook Lane

Heyes Dr

Hardy Road

Cherry Tree Community Primary School

Highfield Drive

Cherrylane Farm

Booth's Lane

Weaste Lane

Massey Hall Special School

Massey Brook

Thelwall Grange

Higherhouse Farm

Booth's Lane

CHERRY LANE

The Avenue

Cherry Hall Farm

PITTSFORD ROAD

Cinder Lane

Oxheys Farm

Bradley Brook

A50 CLIFF LANE

Howshoots

Clifflane Farm

GRAPPENHALL LANE

B5158

Cherry Corner

Junction 20

A50 CLIFF LANE

Lymm Service Area

Brook House Farm

Wither's Lane

A50

Primrose Hill

Broadleys La

Bradley Hall

Junction 9/20

M56

Witner's Lane

Barleycastle Farm

Fanner's Lane

Fanner's Lane

Crowsnest Farm

Moss Brow Lane

M6

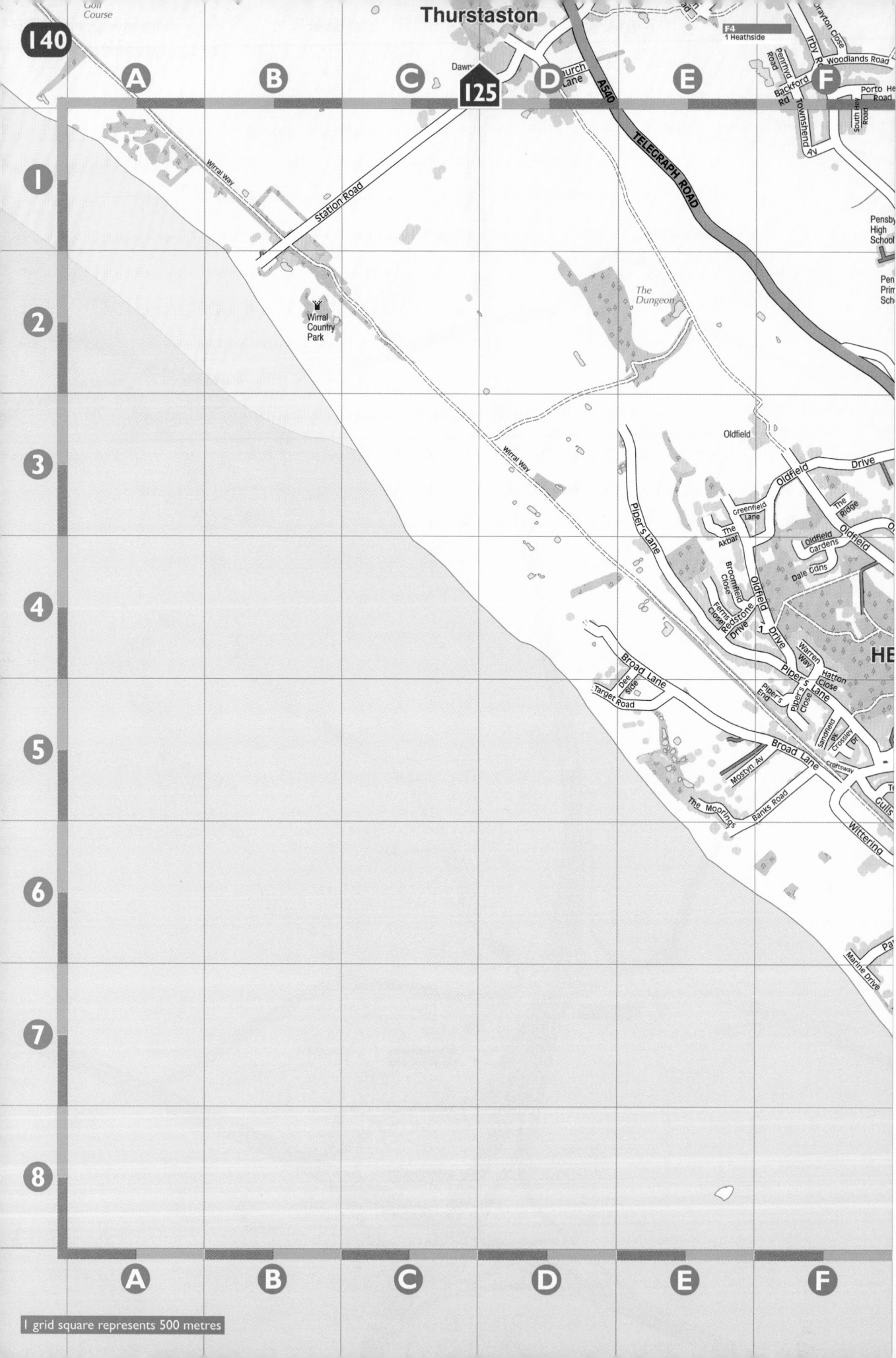

Thurstaston

A   B   C   125   D   A540   E   F4
1 Heathside   F

TELEGRAPH ROAD

Golf Course

Wirral Way

Station Road

1

Wirral Country Park

2

The Dungeon

Oldfield

3

Wirral Way

Piper's Lane

Oldfield Drive

The Ridge

Greenfield Lane

The Akbar

Oldfield Gardens

Oldfield

Dale Gdns

4

Broomfield Close

Ferns Close

Redstone Drive

Oldfield Drive

Warren Way

Hatton Close

HE

Piper's Lane

Broad Lane

Dee Side

Target Road

Piper's End

Piper's Close

Sandfield

Crossley Dr

5

Mostyn Av

Broad Lane

croftsway

Guls

The Moorings

Banks Road

Wittering

6

Marine Drive

7

8

1 grid square represents 500 metres

Pensby High School

Pen Prim Sch

Porto He Road

South He Road

Woodlands Road

Irby Rd

Townshend Av

Backford Rd

Penrhyd Road

Drayton Close

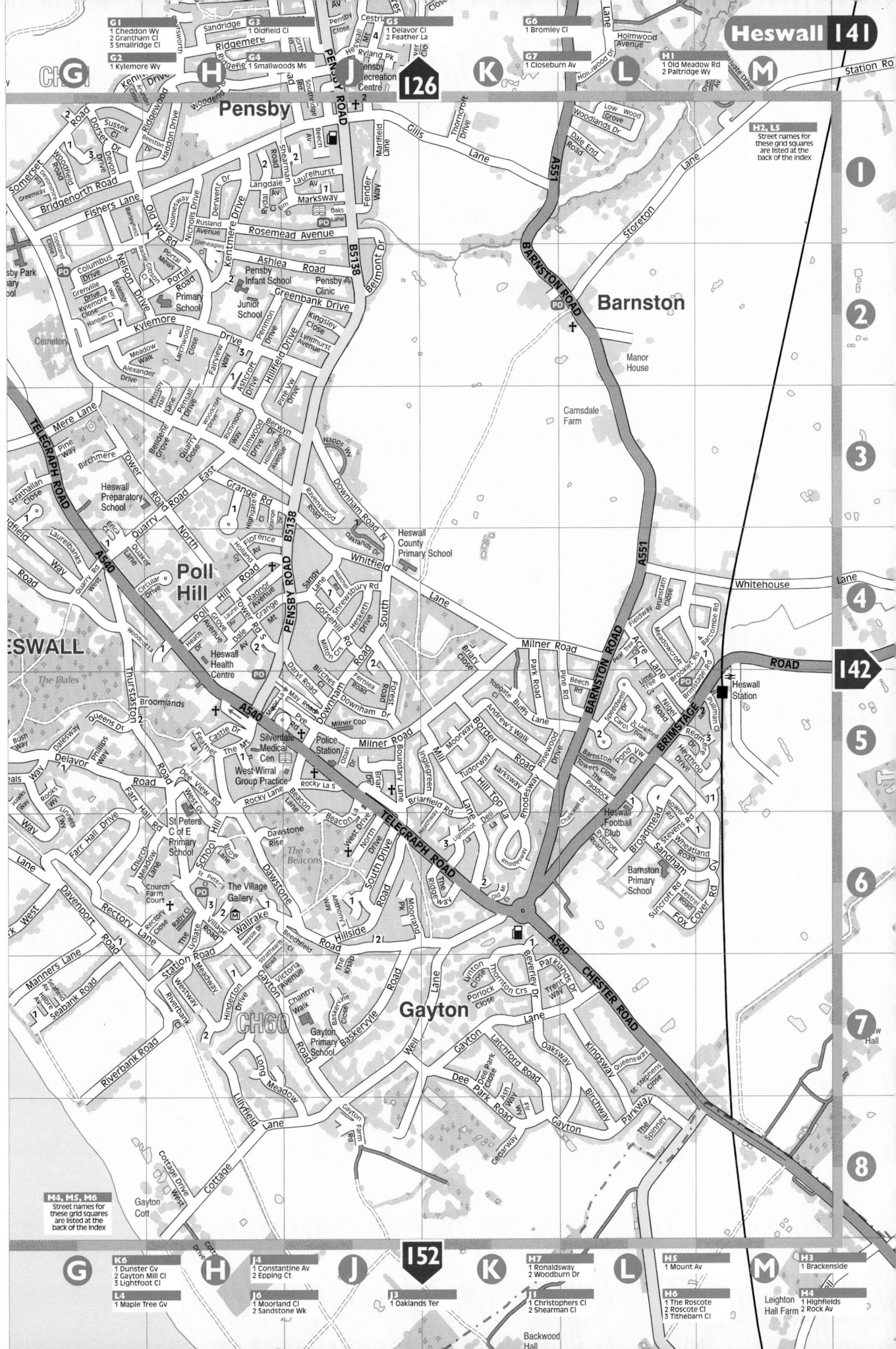

G1 1 Cheddon Wy 2 Grantham Cl 3 Smallridge Cl
G2 1 Kylemore Wy
G3 1 Oldfield Cl
G4 1 Smallwoods Ms
G5 1 Delavor Cl 2 Feather La
G6 1 Bromley Cl
G7 1 Closeburn Av
H1 1 Old Meadow Rd 2 Paltridge Wy
H2, L5 Street names for these grid squares are listed at the back of the index

M4, M5, M6 Street names for these grid squares are listed at the back of the index
G **K6** 1 Dunster Gv 2 Gayton Mill Cl 3 Lightfoot Cl
L4 1 Maple Tree Gv
H **J4** 1 Constantine Av 2 Epping Ct
J6 1 Moorland Cl 2 Sandstone Wk
J **J3** 1 Oaklands Ter
K **K1** 1 Christophers Cl 2 Shearman Cl
L **H7** 1 Ronaldsway 2 Woodburn Dr
H5 1 Mount Av
H6 1 The Roscote 2 Roscote Cl 3 Tithebarn Cl
M **H3** 1 Brackenside
H4 1 Highfields 2 Rock Av

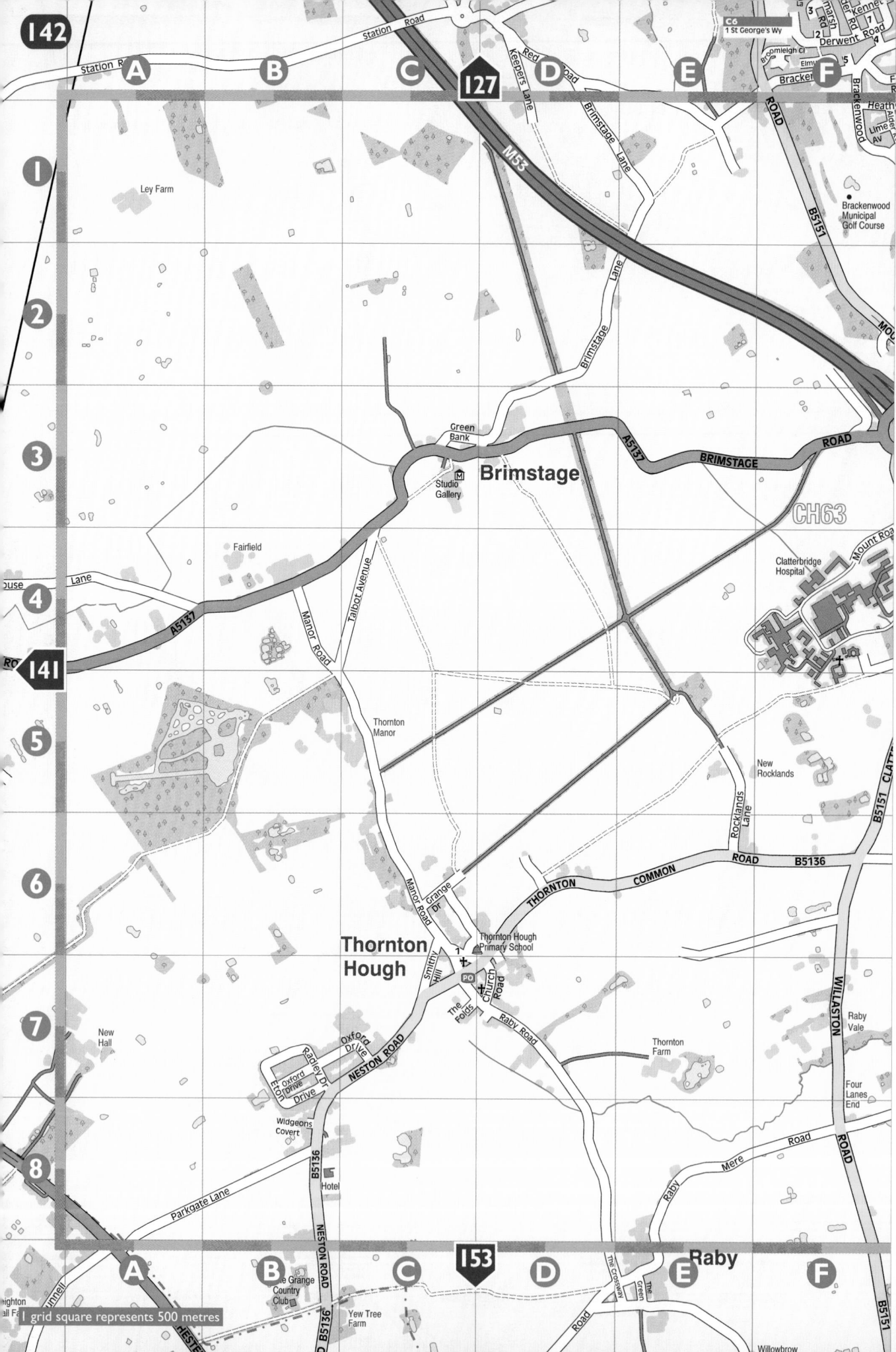

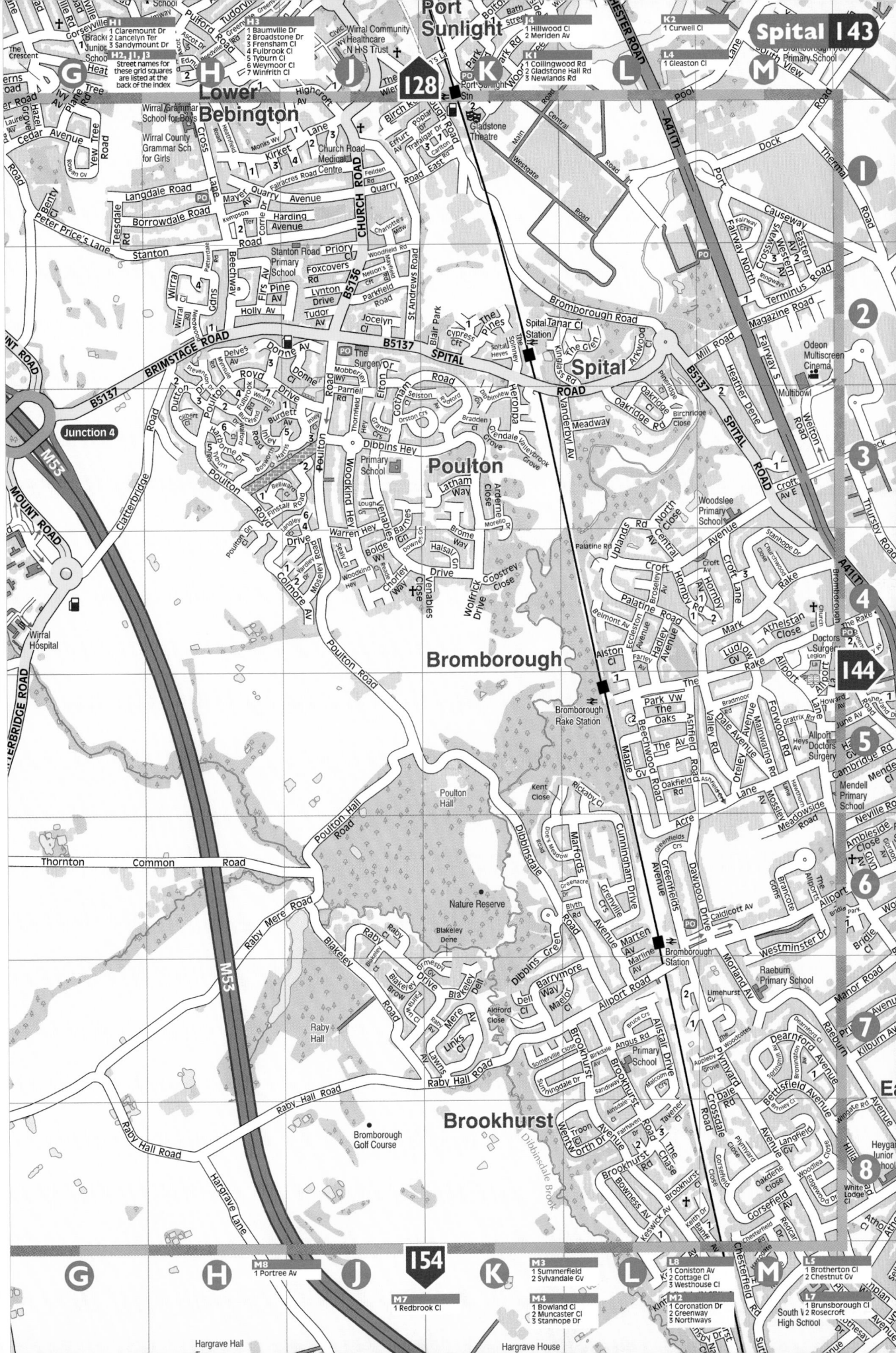

A8
1 Swaledale Cl

A6
1 Osbourne Cl

A5
1 Grassmoor Cl
2 Parkwood Cl

A4
1 Hawkeshead Rd
2 High St

A **B** **C** 129 **D** **E** **F**

Liverpool
Wirral

I

2

3

4

143

5

6

7

8

Bromborough Pool
Primary School

Causeway
Eastern
Western
Sussex
ways
mazine
Terminus Road

Thermal Road

Magazine Lane

Georgia Av

Stadium Road

Commercial Road

Odeon
Multiscreen
Cinema

Multibowl

Welton Road

Caldbeck Road

Thursby Road

Carrock Rd

Bassenthwaite Road

Mosedale Road

skiddaw Rd

Martindale Rd

Plantation
Business Park

Plantation Road

Old Hall Rd

Power Road

Riverwood Road

Job's
Ferry

Croft
Av E

Rake

Chelstan
Close

Doctors
Surgery

the Rake
PO

Church Road

Bromborough

Village

the rake
Old Hall Road

Hardknott Rd

Gridale Rd

CH62

Howard
Av

Gratrix Rd

June Av

Wrynose Rd

Eastham
Ferry

Norwood Road

Harrow
Gv

Cambridge Road

Mendell
Cl

Tebay Road

Mendell
Primary
School

Ferry Road

Meadowside
Road

Neville Road

Ambleside
Close

Primary
School

Lock Rd

Eastham
Country
Park

Brancote

Allport

Bridle
Park

Bridle
Cl

Woodyear Road

Eastham
Locks

Westminster Dr

Manor Road

Bridle Road

Cemetery

Wirral
Metropolitan
College

Mayfield
Dr

Manchester Ship Canal

burn
mary School

Raeburn Avenue

Princes Avenue

Kilburn Avenue

New Chester Road A41(T)

Park Road

St David Road

St John's
Road

Seaview Av

Ferry Road

learmo
Avenue

ntisfield Avenue

Eastham

Langfield
Gv

Heygarth
Junior
School

Hillary Avenue

Elgar Avenue

Heygarth
Road

Wingate Rd

Bridle Road

Mallowdale
Dr

Wharfedale
Dr

Millersdale

Carlett
Blvd

Handford

Eastham Village Road

Christopher
Drive

Ferry
Road

Bankfields

Athol
Athol Drive

White Lodge
Cl

Danleydale
Dr

Avondale

Esk dale
Wendale

Dovedale

Lyndale
School

St Marys C of E
Primary School

Eastham
House

Grampian
Way

Plymyard
Paisley
Glenburn
Adaston Av

Eastham Rake

Berwick

Cranford

Stanley La

Eastham Vi
New Chester Rd

Cloathwaite

35132

Bankfields Drive

A **B** C 155 **D** **E** **F**

1 Ribblesdale Cl
B8

RIVACR

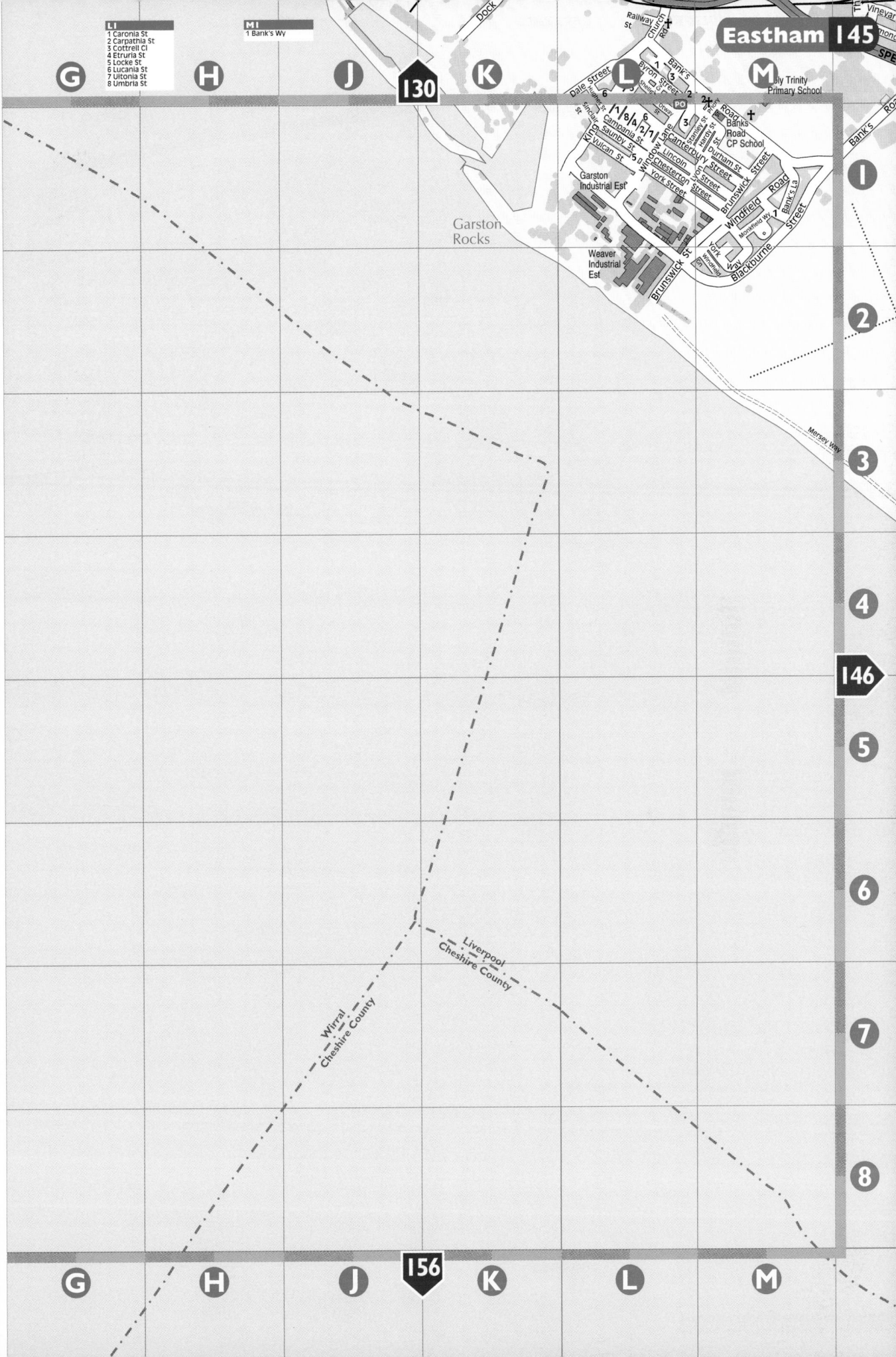

L1
1 Caronia St
2 Carpathia St
3 Cottrell Cl
4 Etruria St
5 Locke St
6 Lucania St
7 Uitonia St
8 Umbria St

M1
1 Bank's Wy

G   H   J   130   K   L   M

I

2

3

4

146

5

6

7

8

Garston
Rocks

Garston
Industrial Est

Weaver
Industrial
Est

Holy Trinity
Primary School

Banks
Road
CP School

Mersey Way

Liverpool
Cheshire County

Wirral
Cheshire County

G   H   J   156   K   L   M

I grid square represents 500 metres

G
H
J
132
K
L
M

148

I
2
3
4
5
6
7
8

132

G1
1 Eastham Gn
2 Northern Rd
3 Penketh Gn

G2
1 Prenton Gn
2 Upton Cl
3 Upton Gn

G3
1 Bramhall Cl
2 Ganworth Cl
3 Southern Rd

Speke

Austin
Rawlinson
Sports Cen

Police
Station

North Parade
Hlth Authority
Speke Family Health
Clinic
South Parade
PO

The Margaret
Thompson Medical
Cen

Millwood
Road Doctors
Surgery

Alderwood
CP School

St Ambrose
Primary
School

Brook Farm

Hale

Carlow
Cl

Morcott Lane

Police
Station

Ivy Farm
Court Doctors
Surg
School

Hale
Primary
School

PO

Liverpool
Halton

Liverpool
Cheshire County

Halton
Cheshire County

Oglet

Oglet Lane

Mersey Way

Mersey Way

Mersey Way

Burnt
Mill

G
H
M3
1 Bandon Cl
2 Greenore Dr
J
158
K
J3
1 Almeda Rd
2 Daneswell Rd
L
J2
1 Harland Gn
2 Ringsfield Rd
M
J1
1 Huttfield Rd
2 Millway Rd

A   B   C   D   E   F

Carr Lane

Burn
Mill

F6
1 Cullen Rd

A3
1 Assheton Wk
2 Wellington Ga

Baguley
Ave

Crescent

Blackburne
Avenue

Fou

1

Herriview Rd

Kenview Cl

Pickering Road

Halebank
C of E
Controlled
Primary School

133

Hale Bank

Mersey View Road

Trans Pennine Trail

1

I

Potters La

Carr Lane

2

Hale Gate Road

Garnetts

Lane

Pickerings
Pasture

River Mersey

Trans Pennine Trail

Lane

ale

3

Errwood
Cl

Town

Halegate
Farm

Callender Wy

Heskwin Road

Hoghton Rd

Lane
Police
Station

Erins

Lane

Holly Cl

1

2

Cockdale

Pepper St

Ivy Farm
Court Doctors
Surg

School

Ireland
Road

Town

PO

Street

4

Church
End

Vicarage
Close

Within Way

147

†

5

Church

Road

Lighthouse Road

6

Mersey Way

Hale
Head

Weston
Point

Picow Farm Rd

†

Post
Office

PO

Mersey Vw S Rd

West Rd

Sandy Lane

Baker Road

South Parade

Leonard St

Sydney St

Road

7

Halton
Cheshire County

8

A   B   C   D   E   F

1 grid square represents 500 metres

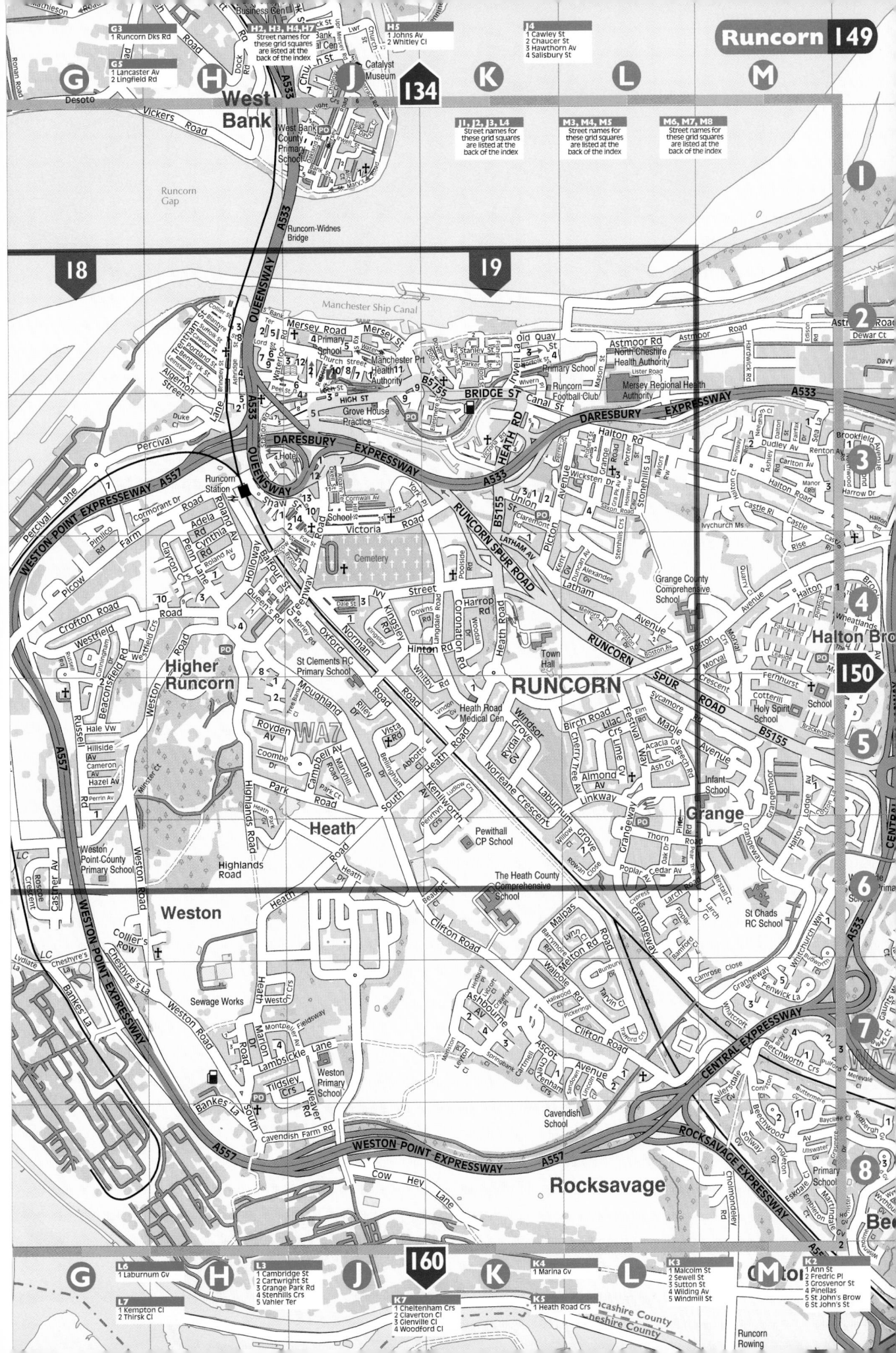

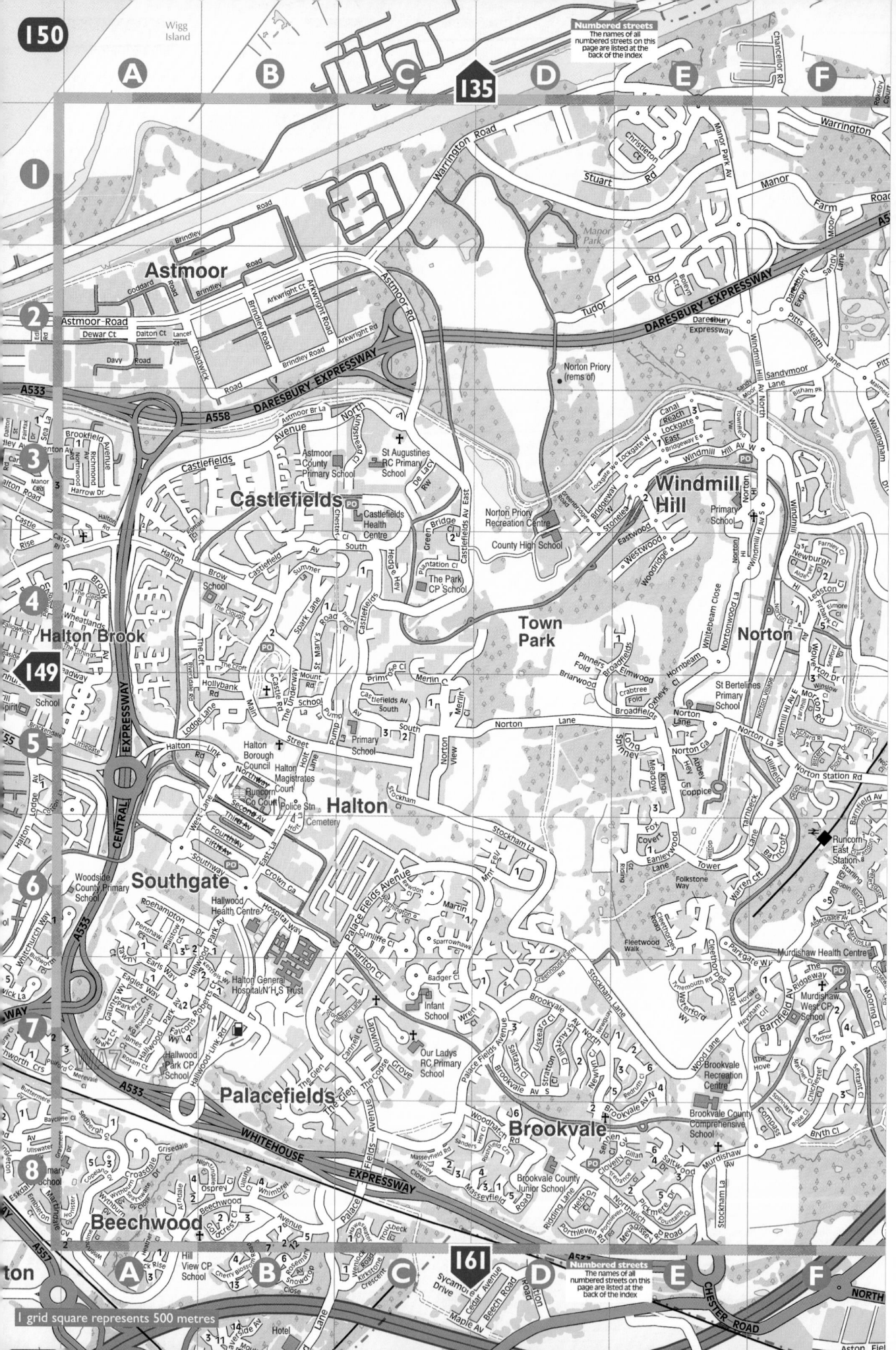

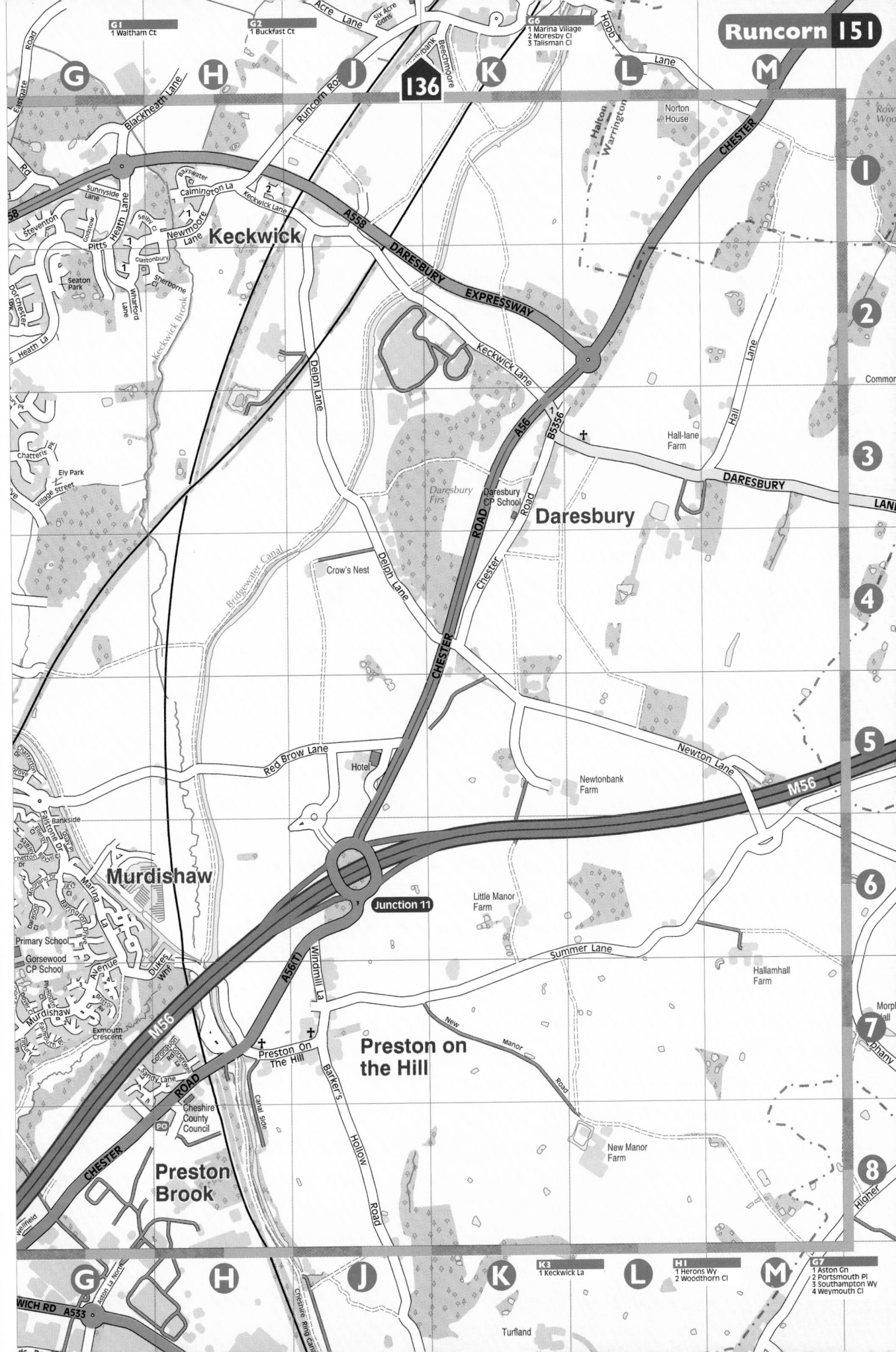

A B C D E F

1

2

3

4

5

6

7

8

Gayton
Cott

Cottage
Drive West

Cottage
Drive East

141

Backwood
Hall

Leighton
Hall Farm

Wirral Way

LANE

B5135

Leighton Road

The Runnell

North Parade

BOATHOUSE

The
Looms

Brook Hey

The Looms

Titthebarn

Tithebarn
Drive

Carlton Dr

Brook La

Wood

Paddock Dr

Pinehey

1
Leighton
Chase

B5135

THE PARADE

Bevyl Road

Moorings
Cl

School

Bowling
Green

Hawthorn Road

Moorfield
Drive

Brooklands
Road

Brooklands
Gardens

Parkgate CP
School

Parkgate

Wirral Way

Leighton
Pk

Woodlands Rd

Leighton
Pk

Earle
Crs

The
Leightons

Leighton
Lane

The
Way

The Square

Grenfell
Close

Little
7

Grenfell Pk

Springcroft

Hollwell

7

PO

Mostyn
House
School

STATION RD

PARKGATE RD

The
Earle

Spinney

Albert
Drive

B5135

The
Green

Buggen
Lane

Beechways Dr

Neston
Cricket
Club

The
Parade

Manorial Way

Hunters Way

Manorial Road

Moorside
Avenue

Moorside
Lane

Manor
Cl

Wesley
Pk

Boundary
Pk

West

The
Di

Heron
Ct

Manorial Rd South

The
Anchorage

1

Walray Pictures
Gallery

M

Moorside

NESTON

Old Quay Lane

Little
Neston

Riverside
Walk

Stratford
Rd

Quay

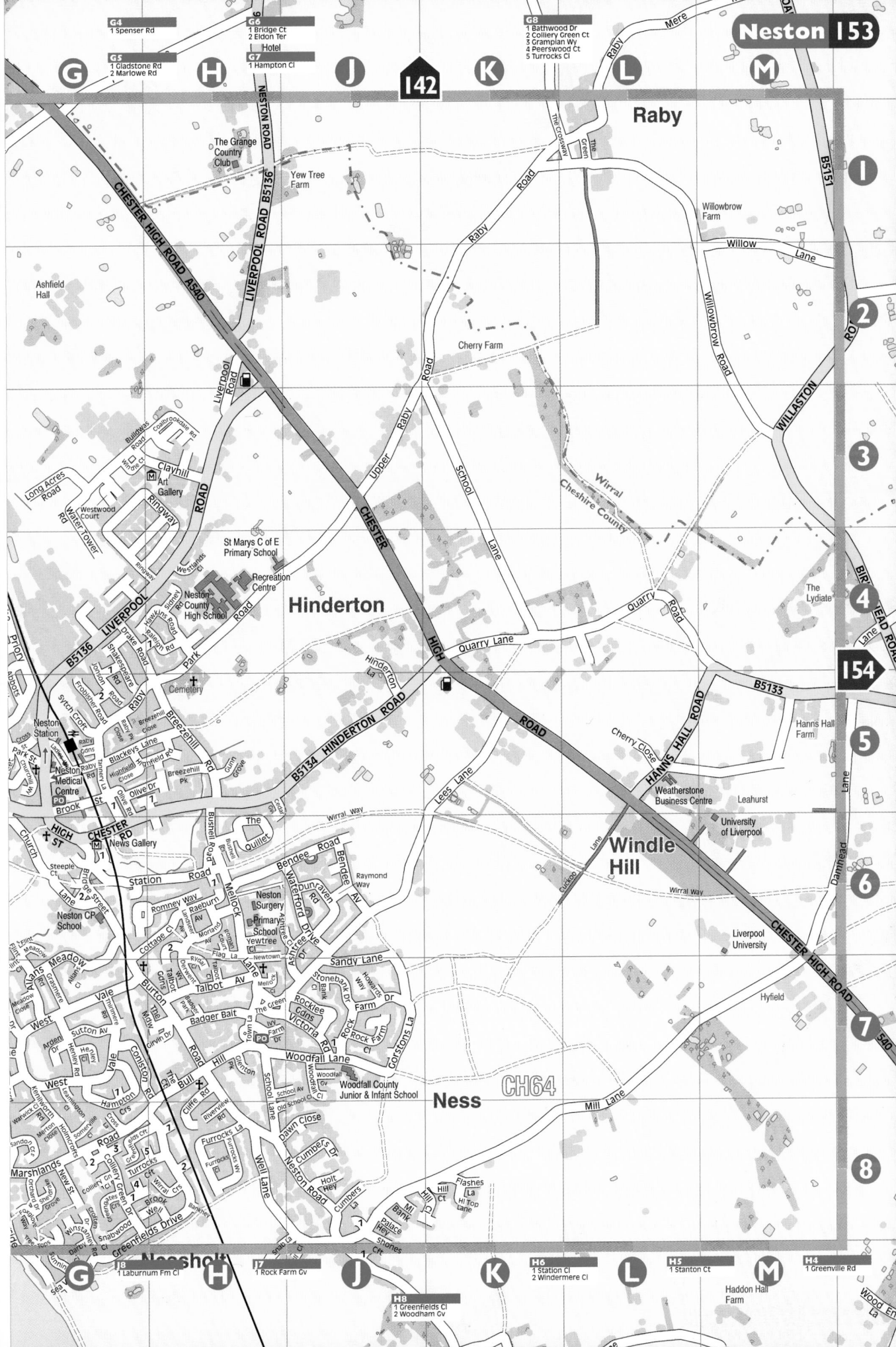

Heygarth Junior School

Heygarth Primary School

St Marys C of E Primary School

G2
1 Lowfields Cl
2 Stretton Cl

H7
1 Peebles Cl

H8
1 Coldstream Dr
2 Selkirk Cl

J1
1 Christie Cl

J7
1 Hambledon Cl
2 Ledsham Park Dr
3 Mourne Cl
4 Quantock Cl

Eastham House

Millfields Primary School

Wirral
Cheshire County

Junction 5

M53

Junction 6

B5132 RIVACRE ROAD

B5132

Rivacre Road

M53

Vernon Av

Hooton Way

Hooton Green

Hooton

HOOTON ROAD B5133

Grange Crs

Woodclose

Welsh Road

Hooton Lane

New School Lane

The Oaklands

School Lane

A41

Childer Thornton CP School

Woodland View

Childer Thornton

Cemetery

Rivacre Valley Country Park

156

B5132

5

Mossvale

Rossmore CP School

Pound Rd

Links Av

Cloverfield Gdns

6

Blackboards Lane

Heath Lane

Margaret's Lane

CHESTER ROAD A41

St Pauls Gdns

Childer Crs

Beverley Way

Granville Dr

Greentle Lane

Red Lion Lane

Station Gn

Little Sutton

Berwick Road

Snowdon Close

Sidlaw Cl

Wicklow

B5463

Heath Grove

Heathlands Road

Little Sutton Station

B5463 STATION RD

ROSSMORE ROAD WEST

7

Pius XII RC School

Hawthorn

Briardale Rd

Glenwood Road

Parklands Gdns

Parklands Road

Cambrian Close

Sutton Park

Hillcrest Drive

Berwick Gdns

Black Lion Lane

CHESTER ROAD

Dudleston Road

Dunmore Rd

School

Cedar Av

Maple Avenue

Parklands CP Infant School

Parklands

Acre

LEDSHAM

WELSH ROAD A550(T)

Roxburgh Rd

Cleveland Dr

Berwyn Dr

Armthorpe

Wetherby

Heywood Road

Brook Rd

Whetstone Hey

Valley View

Great Sutton

Sutton New Hall

CH66

162

Great Sutton Health Cen

Great Sutton Mill Lane

8

M8
1 Old Chester Rd

M6
1 Deerwood Cl

L8
1 Braeside Cl
2 Glenwood Cl
3 Chalfield Cl
4 Eden Cl
5 Innisfree Cl
6 Leas Cl

L7
1 Briardale Gdns
2 Glenwood Gdns
3 Glenwood Gdns
4 Southfield Rd

L6
1 Sheepfield Cl

M7
1 Oliver

M6

K6
1 Heyfield Park Rd

J8
1 Blackdown Cl
2 Hawick Cl

G   H   J   **146**   K   L   M

I

2

3

4

158

5

6

21

Manchester Ship Canal

Canalside Industrial Estate

rd Road

CH65

Manch

7

Stanlow Point

Corridor Road

Oil Sites Road

Oil Sites Road

8

Bridges Road

Stanlow

Stanlow & Thornton Station

G   H   J   **164**   K   L   M

Lees

South Road

New Br

Telford

Burnell

A   B   C   **147**   D   E   F

Cheshire County
Halton
Cheshire County

1

2

3

4

157

5

6

7

8

Ince
Banks

Manchester Ship Canal

Holme
Farm

Ince

Kinsey's Lane

Marsh Lane

Pool Lane

Station Road

Marsh Lane

Perimeter Road

Stanlow & Thornton
Station

Ince &
Elton Stn
Mt
Pleasant
PO
Orchards
Ince
Orchard
Park
Lane
Green
Hapsford Lane

Elton

1 grid square represents 500 metres

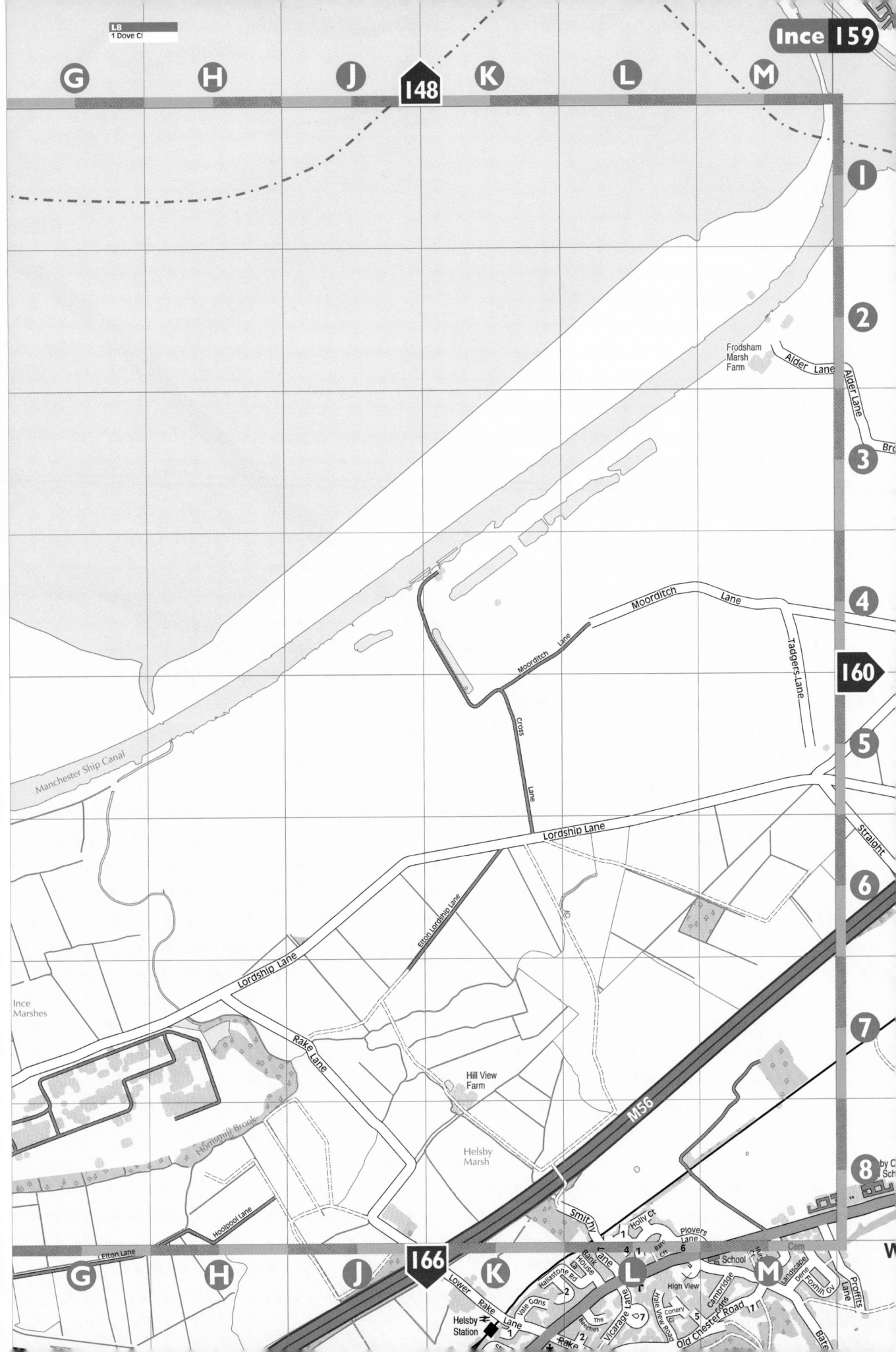

L8
1 Dove Cl

G   H   J   **148**   K   L   M

1

2

Frodsham
Marsh
Farm   Alder Lane

3   Alder Lane   Br

Moorditch   Lane   4

Moorditch   Lane   Tadgers Lane

160

5

Cross

Lane   Lordship Lane   Straight

6

Elton Lordship Lane

Lordship Lane

Ince
Marshes   Rake Lane

7

Hill View
Farm

M56

Hornsmill Brook   Helsby
Marsh   8   by C
                                                        Sch

Hoolpool Lane   Smithy   Holly Ct
                                    Lane   Plovers
                                                            Lane
Elton Lane   **166**   School

G   H   J   **166**   K   L   M   W

Lower   Vale Gdns   High View
Rake
Lane   Old Chester Road
Helsby
Station

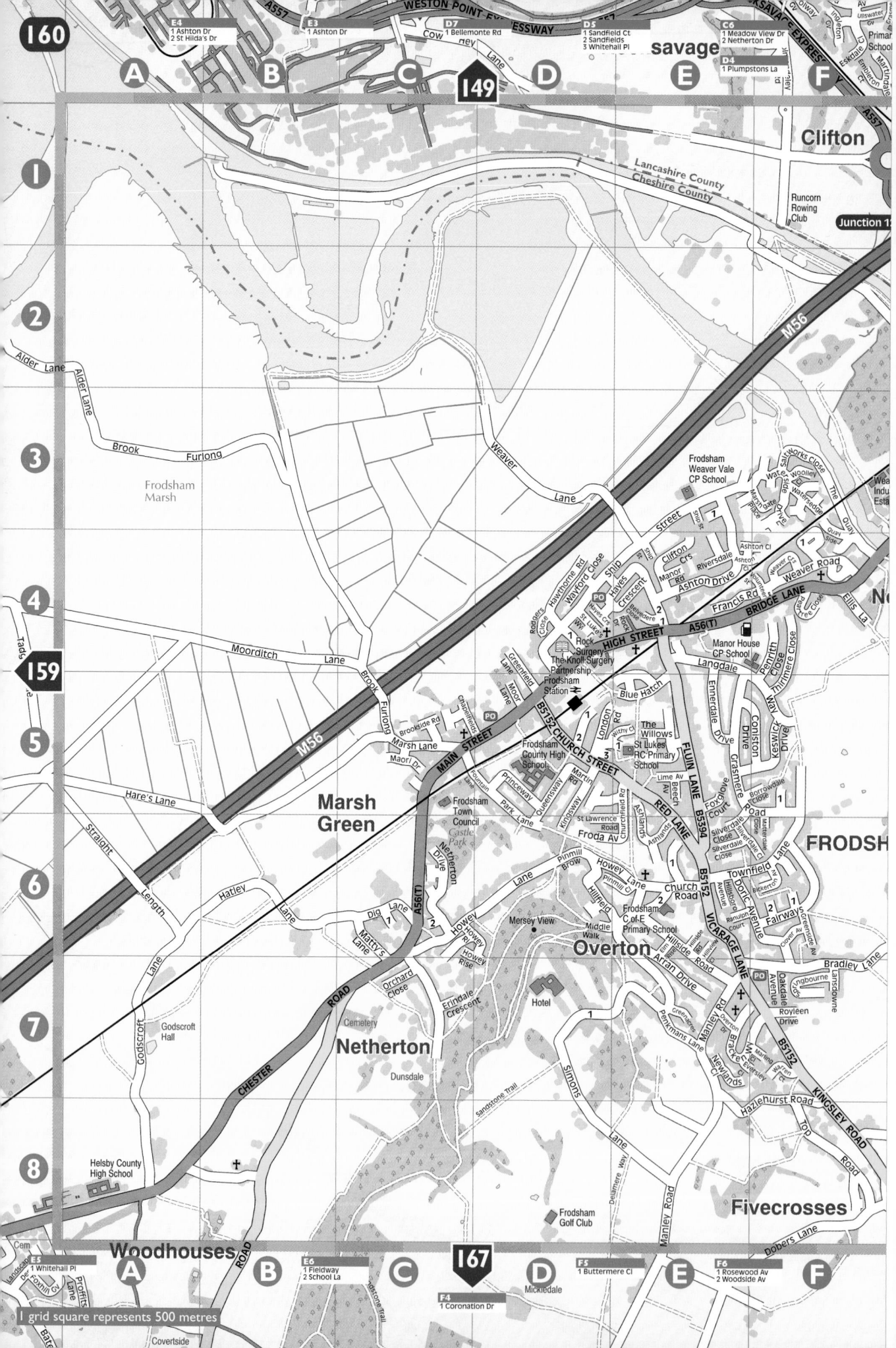

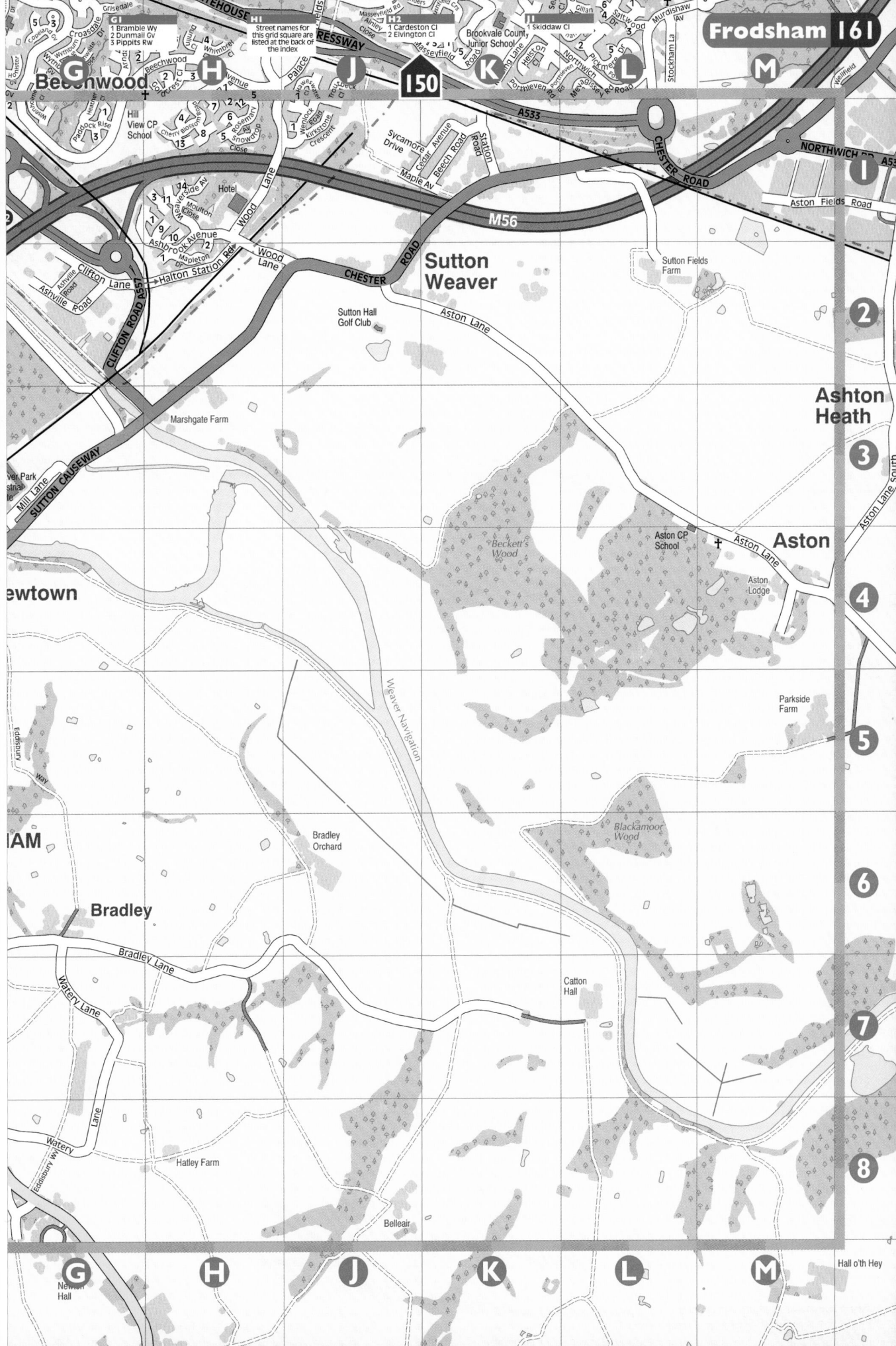

G H J 150 K L M

Beechwood

G1
1 Bramble Wy
2 Dunmail Gv
3 Pippits Rw

Street names for
this grid square are
listed at the back of
the index

H2
1 Cardeston Cl
2 Elvington Cl

J1
1 Skiddaw Cl

Brookvale County
Junior School

Grisedale

Hill
View CP
School

Padlock Rise

Cherry Blossom
Close

Beechwood
Avenue

Rosemary

Snowdrop
Close

Kirkstone
Crescent

Palace

Wenlock

Wood Lane

Sycamore
Drive

Cedar
Avenue

Beech Road

Maple Av

Station
Road

A533

M56

NORTHWICH RD A53

Aston Fields Road

CHESTER ROAD

Hotel

Weaverside Av

Ashbrook Avenue

Mapleton
Dr

Clifton Lane

Ashville
Road

Halton Station Rd

Wood
Lane

CLIFTON ROAD A57

Ashville Road

CHESTER   ROAD

Sutton
Weaver

Sutton Hall
Golf Club

Aston Lane

Sutton Fields
Farm

Ashton
Heath

Marshgate Farm

SUTTON CAUSEWAY

Mill Lane

...ver Park
...strial
...e

Beckett's
Wood

Aston CP
School

Aston Lane

Aston

Aston
Lodge

Aston Lane South

...ewtown

Weaver Navigation

Parkside
Farm

...AM

Bradley
Orchard

Blackamoor
Wood

Bradley

Bradley Lane

Watery Lane

Catton
Hall

Eddisbury
Way

Watery
Lane

Hatley Farm

Belleair

Newton
Hall

Hall o'th Hey

I A53

1

2

3

4

5

6

7

8

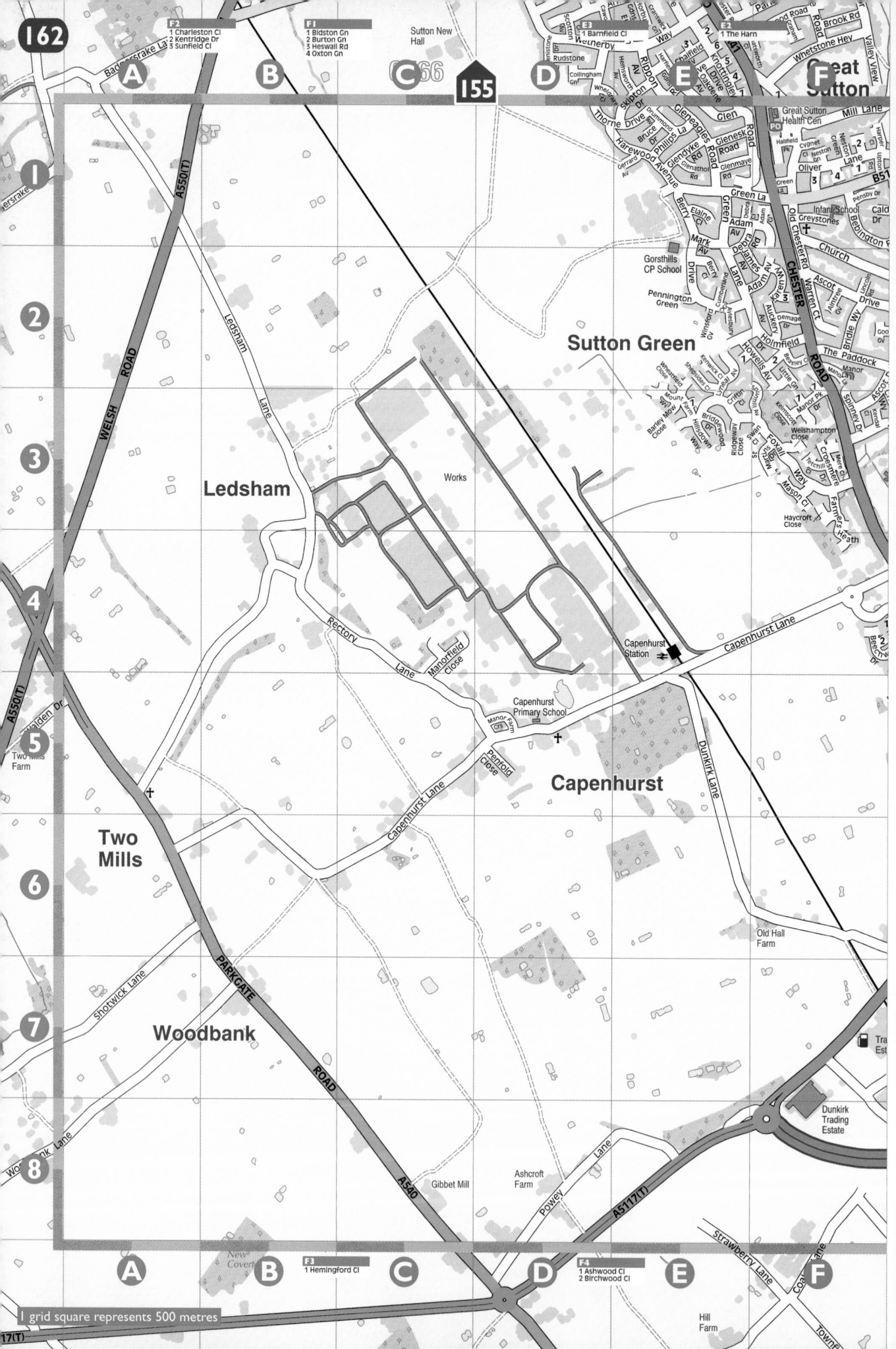

F2
1 Charleston Cl
2 Kentridge Dr
3 Sunfield Cl

F1
1 Bidston Gn
2 Burton Gn
3 Heswall Rd
4 Oxton Gn

Sutton New Hall

E3
1 Barnfield Cl

F6
1 The Harn

Wetnerby
Rudstone
Collingham

Great Sutton
Health Cen
Halifield
Pk

Gorshills
CP School

Pennington
Green

Sutton Green

Great Sutton

Infant School
Greystones

Church

Ledsham

Badgersrake La

A550(T)

WELSH ROAD

Ledsham Lane

Ledsham

Works

Capenhurst Lane

Capenhurst Station

Rectory Lane

Mannorfield Close

Capenhurst Primary School

Manor Farm

Capenhurst Lane

Pentold Close

Capenhurst

Dunkirk Lane

A550(T)

Maiden Dr

Two Mills Farm

Two Mills

Shotwick Lane

PARKGATE ROAD

Woodbank

Wood Bank Lane

Old Hall Farm

Dunkirk Trading Estate

A540

Gibbet Mill

Ashcroft Farm

Powey Lane

A5117(T)

Strawberry Lane

B3
1 Hemingford Cl

F3
1 Ashwood Cl
2 Birchwood Cl

New Covert

Hill Farm

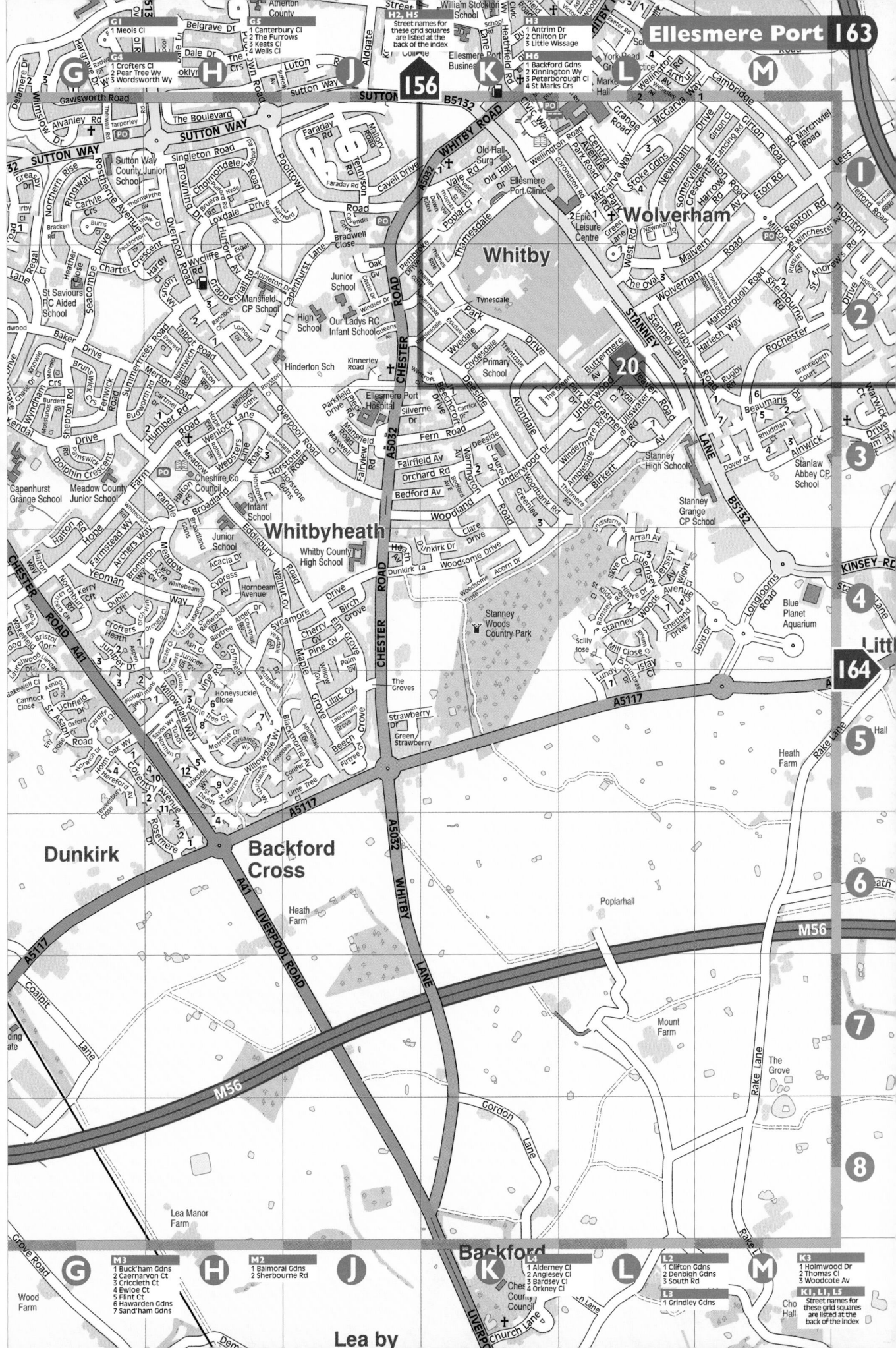

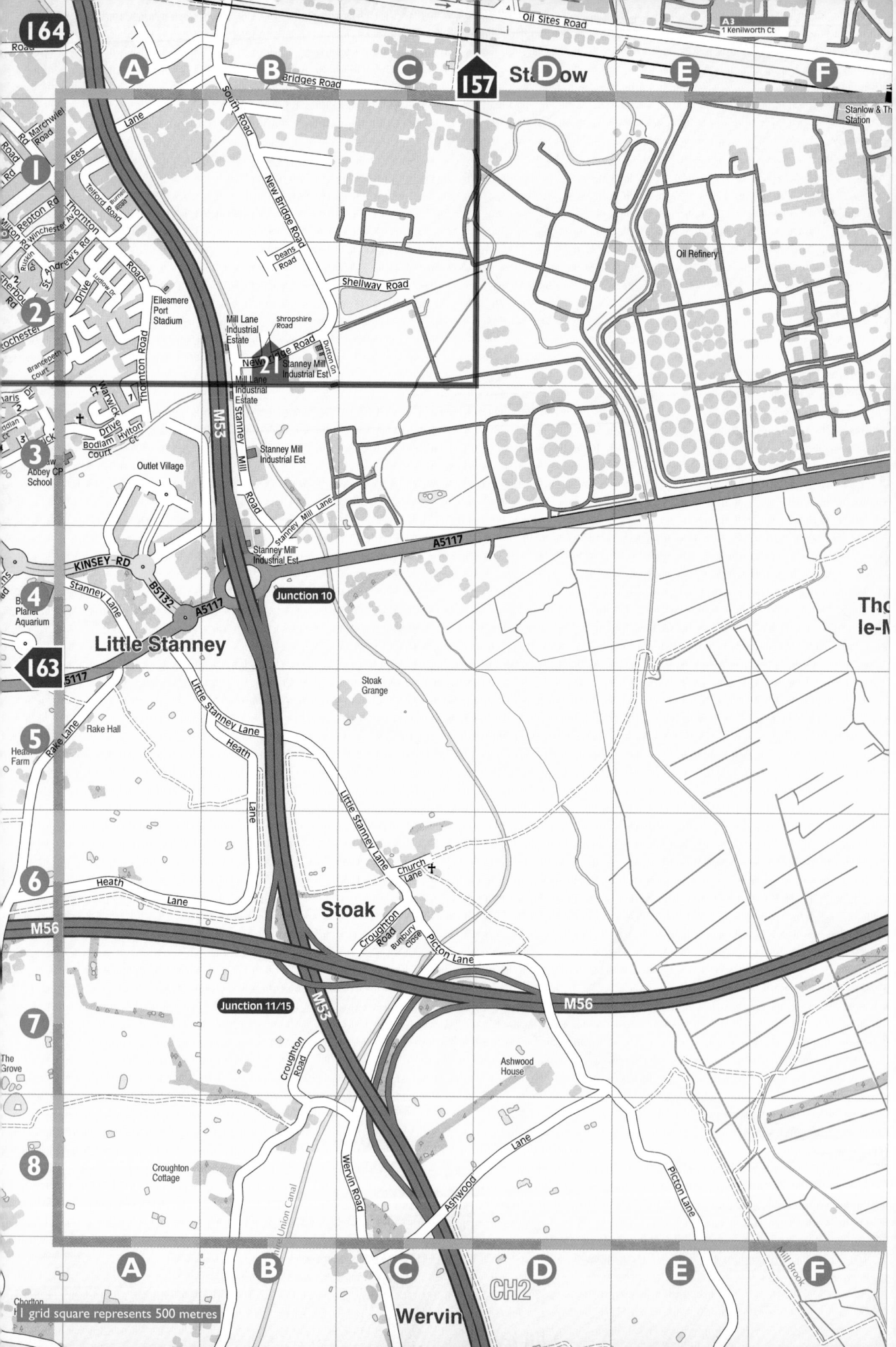

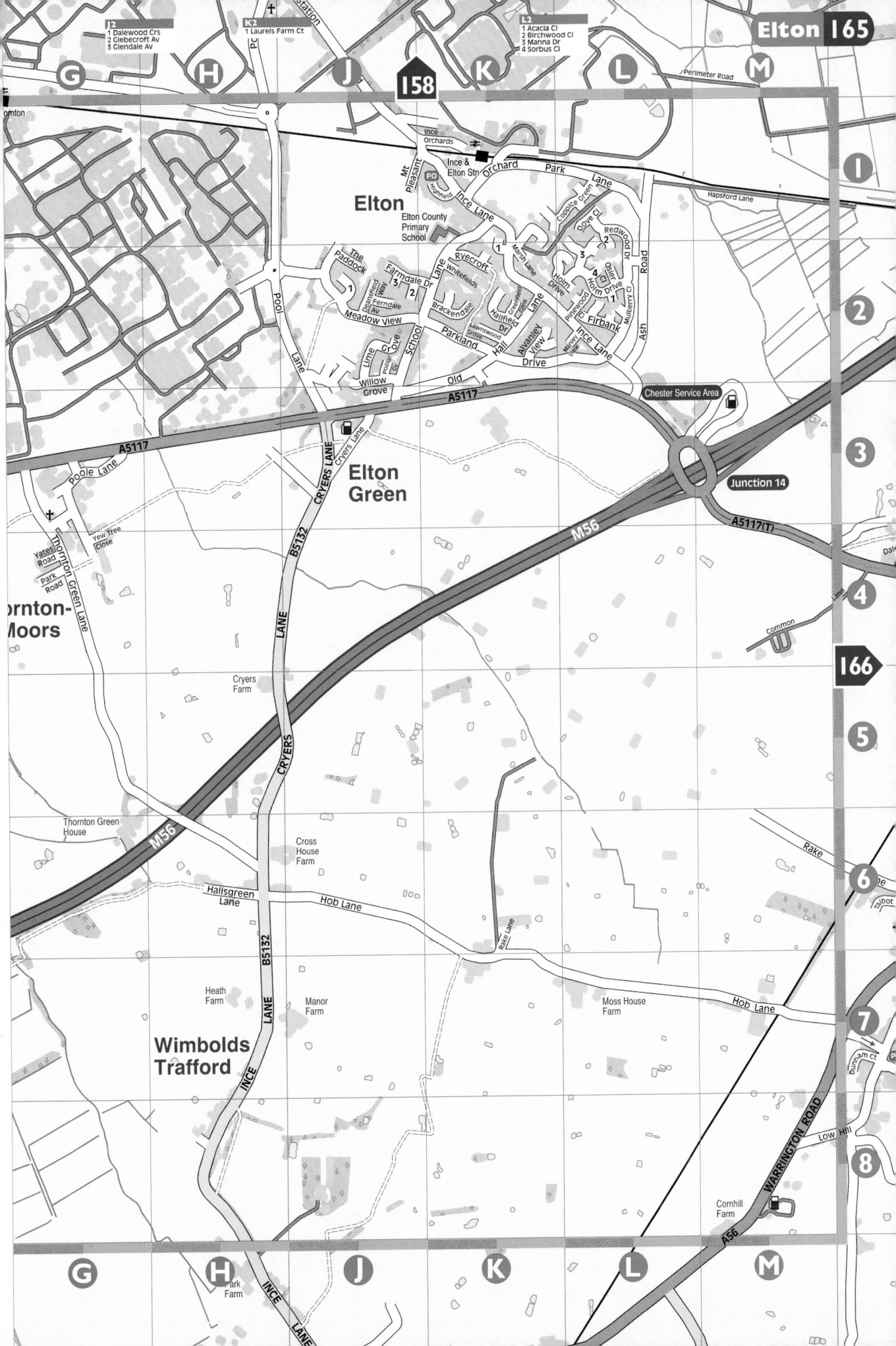

158

166

Elton

Elton Green

Thornton-Moors

Wimbolds Trafford

Junction 14

Chester Service Area

Elton County Primary School

Ince & Elton Stn

Ince Orchards

J2
1 Dalewood Crs
2 Glebecroft Av
3 Glendale Av

K2
1 Laurels Farm Ct

L2
1 Acacia Cl
2 Birchwood Cl
3 Manna Dr
4 Sorbus Cl

Perimeter Road
Hapsford Lane
Orchard Park Lane
Ince Lane
Mt Pleasant
Highfield
Coppice Green
Dove Cl
Redwood Cl
Ash Road
Marsh Lane
Holm Drive
Holm
Osier Cl
Mulberry Cl
Pinewood
Firbank
Ince Lane
Malus View
The Paddock
Ryecroft
Farmdale Dr
Whitefields
Densfield
Ferndale Av
Way
Hallfield
Greenfield Gdns
Brackendale
Lane
Alvanley View Drive
Meadow View
Lime Cl
Dove Gr
Poplar Gr
School
Willow Grove
Parkland
Hall
Old
Lawnswood Grove
A5117
A5117
Poole Lane
Cryers Lane
Cryers Lane
B5132
CRYERS LANE
Yew Tree Close
Thornton Green Lane
Yates Road
Park Road
M56
M56
A5117(T)
Cryers Farm
Thornton Green House
Cross House Farm
Hallsgreen Lane
Hob Lane
Rake
Rake Lane
Heath Farm
Manor Farm
Moss House Farm
Hob Lane
INCE LANE
B5132
Cornhill Farm
WARRINGTON ROAD
Low Hill
A56
Park Farm
Burham Ct
Talbot
Common
Lane
Dale

PO

G H J K L M
I
2
3
4
5
6
7
8
G H J K L M

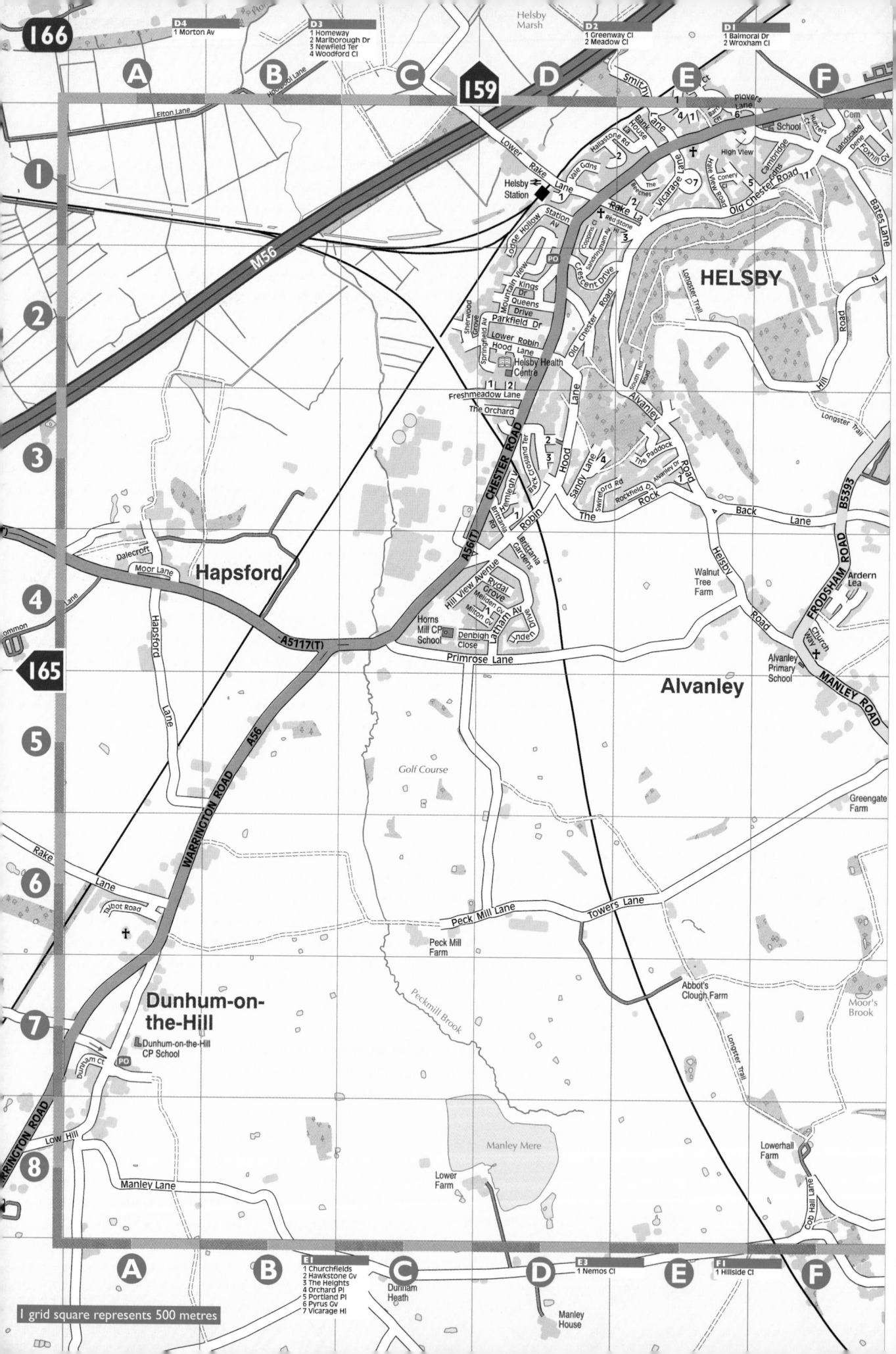

D4
1 Morton Av

D3
1 Homeway
2 Marlborough Dr
3 Newfield Ter
4 Woodford Cl

D2
1 Greenway Cl
2 Meadow Cl

D1
1 Balmoral Dr
2 Wroxham Cl

A B C **159** D E F

Helsby
Marsh

smith

Ct

plovers
Lane

Cem

I

M56

Helsby
Station

Lower Rake Lane

Vale Gdns

Hallastone Rd

Banks
House

High View

The
Beeches

School

Hunters

Landscape
Dene

Foxhill Gv

2

Lodge Hollow

Station Av

Rake La

Red stone

Copenc

Sandringham Av

Vicarage Lane

Conery

Hale View Road

Cambridge
Road

5

Old Chester Pote
Road

17

Bates Lane

HELSBY

2

Mountain View

Kings
Dr

Queens
Drive

Crescent Drive

Old Chester Road

Longster Trail

Hill
Road

3

PO

Sherwood
Grove

Parkfield Dr

Lower Robin
Hood
Lane

Springfield Av

Helsby Health
Centre

1 2

Freshmeadow Lane

The Orchard

CHESTER ROAD

Hood Lane

Alvanley Road

South Hill Road

Longster Trail

2
3

Hemleigh V

Brittania

Robin

Sandy Lane

Tye Paddock

4

Swineford Rd

Rockfield Cl

The Rock

Alvanley Dr

Back Lane

B5393

4

A56(T)

Britannia
Gardens

1

Hill View Avenue

Rydal Grove

Melden Cl

Milton Gv

Durham Av

Linden

Drive

Walnut
Tree
Farm

Helsby Road

FRODSHAM ROAD

Ardern
Lea

Hapsford

Dalecroft

Moor Lane

Hapsford Lane

A5117(T)

A56

Horns
Mill CP
School

Denbigh
Close

Primrose Lane

Alvanley

Alvanley
Primary
School

Church
Way

MANLEY ROAD

165

WARRINGTON ROAD

Rake Lane

Golf Course

Greengate
Farm

5

6

Talbot Road

Peck Mill Lane

Towers Lane

Peck Mill
Farm

Peckmill Brook

Abbot's
Clough Farm

Moor's
Brook

Longster Trail

7

**Dunhum-on-
the-Hill**

Dunhum-on-the-Hill
CP School

PO

Dunham Ct

Low Hill

Manley Mere

Lowerhall
Farm

Cob Hall Lane

8

WARRINGTON ROAD

Manley Lane

Lower
Farm

Manley House

A B C D E F

E2
1 Churchfields
2 Hawkstone Gv
3 The Heights
4 Orchard Pl
5 Portland Pl
6 Pyrus Gv
7 Vicarage Hl

Dunham
Heath

E3
1 Nemos Cl

F1
1 Hillside Cl

1 grid square represents 500 metres

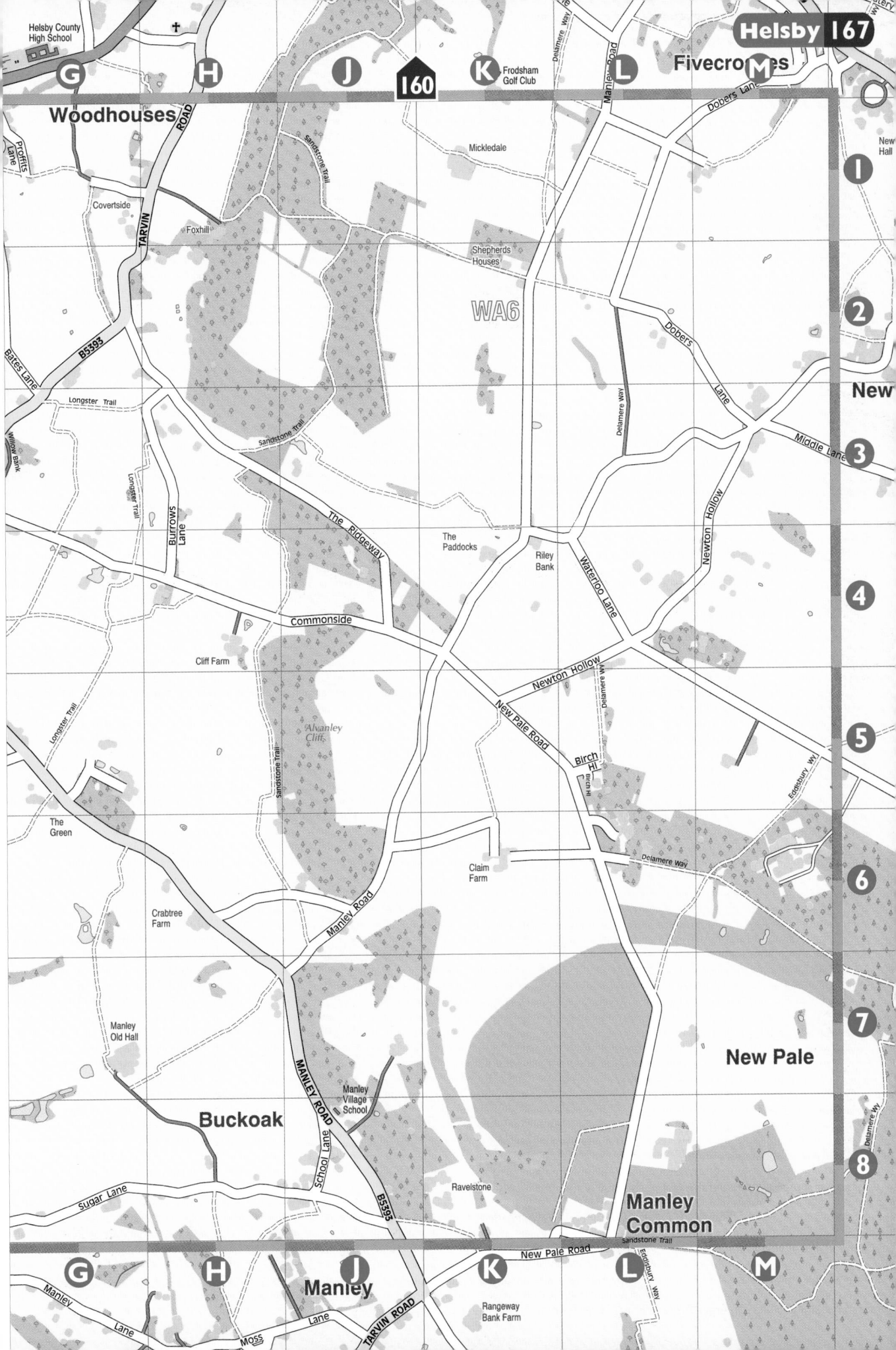

Abram 80 E5
Adlington 44 D6
Aigburth 130 B4
Ainsdale 34 E8
Ainsdale-on-Sea 34 A8
Aintree 84 F3
Allerton 131 G4
Alvanley 166 E5
Anderton 44 D5
Andertons Mill 41 H4
Anfield 97 J6
Appleton 134 D3
Appleton Park 137 M8
Appley Bridge 54 E5
Arrowe Hill 126 B2
Ashton Heath 161 M3
Ashton-in-Makerfield 91 M2
Ashurst 65 K1
Aspull 57 M8
Aspull Common 93 K4
Astmoor 150 A2
Aston 161 M4
Aughton 62 B6
Aughton Park 63 G3
Backford Cross 163 H6
Ball o' Ditton 134 A4
Bamfurlong 80 A5
Banks 23 H7
Bank Top 66 E1
Barnston 141 L2
Barrow Nook 75 G3
Barrow's Green 134 F1
Barton 49 H7
Bebington 128 A7
Beech Hill 68 B3
Beechwood 150 A8
Belle Vale 115 L8
Bescar 37 J6
Bewsey 121 G5
Bickershaw 81 G5
Bickerstaffe 64 A8
Bidston 110 F4
Bidston Hill 110 F5
Billinge 78 B8
Birch Green 65 L3
Birchwood 123 G1
Birkacre 43 J2
Birkdale 35 H3
Birkenhead 112 C7
Bispham Green 40 E6
Blackbrook 90 C8
Blackbrook 122 A3
Blackrod 57 L2
Blaguegate 64 D4
Blowick 25 G7
Blundellsands 82 B1
Boar's Head 56 C7
Bold Heath 119 G6
Bolton Green 31 M6
Bootle 6 C5
Bowing Park 115 K5
Bowker's Green 62 F8
Bradley 161 G6
Brighton le Sands 82 C2
Brimstage 142 D3
Broad Green 114 F3
Broad Oak 103 H1
Bromborough 143 K4
Bromborough Pool 128 F8
Brookhurst 143 K8
Brookvale 150 D8
Brown Edge 36 C3
Brown Edge 101 L6
Brownlow 77 K5
Bruche 122 B6
Bryn 79 H7
Bryn Gates 80 B6
Buckley Hill 83 M1
Buckoak 167 H8
Burscough 51 L3
Burscough Bridge 38 F7
Burtonwood 104 C7
Calderstones 130 E2
Caldy 124 F6
Callands 120 F3
Capenhurst 162 D5
Carr Cross 36 F5
Carr Houses 71 H1
Castlefields 150 B3
Chadwick Green 90 A1
Chapel House 64 F3
Charnock Green 31 K7
Charnock Richard 42 E1
Childer Thornton 155 K5
Childwall 115 H7
Chorley 32 D4
Churchtown 25 K4
Cinnamon Brow 122 C1
Claughton 111 G8
Clifton 160 F1
Clinkham Wood 89 L3
Clock Face 118 F2
Clubmoor 97 L6
Cobbs 137 M5
Collins Green 103 M4
Coppull 42 F4
Coppull Moor 42 F7
Court Hey 115 H4
Cowling 33 G7
Crank 89 G1
Crankwood 80 F8
Crawford 76 E3
Croft 106 D5
Cronton 117 K8
Crooke 67 L2
Crosby 82 D4
Crossens 25 K1
Croston 29 K3
Crow Wood 134 F3
Croxteth 98 F1
Cuerdley Cross 135 J2
Culcheth 107 J2
Dallam 121 H4
Dalton 53 L8
Dangerous Corner 54 E3
Dangerous Corner 81 L3
Daresbury 151 K3
Denton's Green 8 C1
Derbyshire Hill 103 H3
Digmoor 65 L7
Dingle 129 J2
Ditton 133 K6
Doe Green 135 L2
Dog & Gun 98 C2
Dovecot 115 H2
Dover 80 D7
Downall Green 78 E8
Downholland Cross 61 J3
Drummersdale 37 H7
Dudlows Green 138 A8
Dunhum-On-The-Hill 166 A7
Dunkirk 163 G6
Earlestown 104 B2
Eastham 144 A7
Eastham Ferry 144 C5
Eccleston 30 D6
Eccleston 88 E8
Eccleston Park 101 J6
Edge Green 92 B2
Edge Hill 113 K5
Egremont 111 L1
Ellesmere Port 20 A3
Elmers Green 65 M2
Elton 165 J1
Elton Green 165 J3
Euxton 31 K3
Everton 97 H8
Fairfield 113 M2
Far Banks 23 L5
Far Moor 67 G8
Farnworth 134 C2
Fazakerley 84 E8
Fearnhead 122 C3
Fiddler's Ferry 22 F7
Fiddler's Ferry 135 L4
Fincham 99 J8
Firs Lane 81 M8
Fivecrosses 160 E8
Ford 83 L3
Formby 59 G1
Frankby 125 J3
Freshfield 46 E8
Frodsham 160 F6
Garston 130 F8
Garswood 90 D2
Gateacre 131 K1
Gathurst 67 H2
Gayton 141 J7
Gemini 120 F2
Gillar's Green 101 G2
Gillmoss 85 L7
Golborne 92 D6
Goose Green 79 G1
Gorse Covert 107 K7
Grange 19 M9
Grange 124 F4
Grange Park 101 K5
Grappenhall 138 D3
Grassendale 130 C6
Greasby 125 M3
Great Altcar 60 B4
Great Crosby 83 G1
Great Sankey 120 D7
Great Sutton 155 M8
Grimeford Village 45 G7
Grimshaw Green 40 D8
Haigh 57 K6
Hale 147 M3
Hale Bank 148 D1
Halewood 132 B5
Hall Green 66 C6
Halsall 49 L4
Halton 150 B5
Halton Brook 149 M4
Halton View 17 H2
Hapsford 166 A4
Haresfinch 89 J6
Hartwood 32 E3
Haskayne 49 G8
Hawkley 79 J2
Haydock 90 F7
Heath 19 G9
Heath Charnock 44 A3
Heaton's Bridge 50 F1
Helsby 166 E1
Hermitage Green 105 K5
Heskin Green 41 M2
Heswall 140 F4
Higher Bebington 127 K6
Higher End 77 L2
Higher Runcorn 19 G6
Higher Walton 137 G6
Highfield 78 E1
High Moor 54 B1
High Park 25 H5
Hightown 70 A2
Hillcliffe 137 L6
Hill Dale 40 F8
Hillside 34 F3
Hinderton 153 J4
Hindley 81 H1
Hindley Green 81 L2
Holland Lees 54 D8
Holmes 27 K2
Holmeswood 27 L7
Holt 101 J8
Holt Green 62 D6
Homer Green 71 L4
Hood Manor 120 E8
Hooton 155 H4
Hoscar 52 F1
Hough Green 133 J4
Houghton Green 106 A8
Houghwood 77 J7
Howley 15 K6
Hoylake 108 E6
Hulme 121 K2
Hunger Hill 55 H2
Hunt's Cross 131 K7
Hurlston Green 50 D2
Huyton 116 B2
Huyton Park 115 L4
Huyton Quarry 116 D3
Huyton-With-Roby 115 L2
Ince 158 C7
Ince Blundell 71 G2
Ince-in-Makerfield 5 K6
Irby 125 M7
Keckwick 151 H1
Kensington 113 J3
Kenyon 106 C1
Kings Moss 77 H6
Kingsway 16 C3
Kingswood 120 C2
Kirkby 86 A4
Kirkdale 96 F5
Kitt Green 68 A6
Knotty Ash 114 F2
Knowsley 99 L1
Lady Green 71 G1
Laffak 90 A6
Lamberhead Green 67 J8
Land Gate 79 J6
Landican 126 E5
Lane Ends 44 F1
Lane Head 93 H7
Latchford 137 L2
Lea Green 102 B8
Leasowe 110 C1
Ledsham 162 B3
Limbrick 33 J8
Lingley Green 119 L6
Lingley Mere 119 M5
Liscard 95 K8
Litherland 83 L4
Little Altcar 59 J4
Little Crosby 70 E5
Little Neston 152 F7
Little Scotland 57 J3
Little Stanney 164 A4
Little Sutton 155 H7
Little Town 106 D3
Liverpool 12 B7
Locking Stumps 122 D1
Longbarn 122 E4
Longford 121 K4
Longshaw 78 A4
Longview 100 B8
Lower Bebington 128 B8
Lower House 134 A5
Lower Walton 137 J5
Lowton 92 F5
Lowton Common 93 J5
Lowton Heath 92 E7
Lowton St Mary's 93 J6
Lugsdale 17 G5
Lunt 71 L5
Lunts Heath 118 C8
Lydiate 61 J8
Maghull 72 F5
Manley Common 167 L8
Marshall's Cross 102 D8
Marsh Green 67 L4
Marsh Green 160 B5
Marshside 25 G2
Martinscroft 122 F6
Marylebone 68 F2
Mawdesley 40 E3
Melling 73 H8
Melling Mount 73 M6
Meols 108 F5
Mere Brow 27 G3
Mere Side 27 K8
Moore 136 C7
Moorside 152 E6
Moreton 110 A4
Moss Bank 17 K4
Moss Bank 89 K4
Mossley Hill 130 B1
Moss Nook 103 H4
Moss Side 73 J2
Moss Side 87 G6
Mossy Lea 42 B7
Ness 153 K8
Neston 152 F6
Netherley 131 M1
Netherton 72 B8
Netherton 160 B7
New Boston 91 H7
New Brighton 95 J5
Newburgh 53 H3
New Ferry 128 E6
Newgate 66 C6
New Houses 78 D4
New Lane 38 D6
New Lane End 106 C3
New Pale 167 M7
New Springs 69 G3
Newton 125 H3
Newton-Le-Willows 104 F2
Newton Park 105 H3
Newtown 30 C3
Newtown 68 A7
Newtown 101 L1
Newtown 160 F4
Noctorum 110 E8
Norris Green 98 B4
Northwood 86 D2
Norton 150 E4
Nut Grove 101 L7
Oakwood 123 H1
Oglet 146 F5
Old Boston 91 K6
Old Swan 114 B2
Orford 121 M4
Ormskirk 63 K1
Orrell 67 J6
Orrell 83 M7
Orrell Post 67 G6
Otterspool 129 M4
Overpool 156 B6
Overton 160 D6
Oxton 127 H1
Paddington 122 C6
Padgate 122 B4
Page Moss 115 K2
Palacefields 150 B8
Parbold 53 M2
Parkgate 152 E4
Park Hill 75 M3
Parr 103 G3
Peasley Cross 102 E4
Pemberton 67 L8
Penketh 135 M1
Pennington 93 M2
Pennylands 64 E5
Pensby 141 H1
Pincock 31 L5
Pinfold 50 B1
Plank Lane 81 K8
Platt Bridge 80 D3
Pocket Nook 93 L5
Poll Hill 141 H4
Pool Hey 36 D2
Poolstock 4 B8
Portico 101 J5
Port Sunlight 128 D8
Poulton 111 J3
Poulton 143 K3
Prenton 127 J4
Prescot 100 D7
Preston Brook 151 H8
Preston on the Hill 151 J7
Primrose Hill 50 B5
Princes Park 113 K7
Raby 153 L1
Rainford 76 C6
Rainford Junction 76 B3
Rainhill 117 M2
Rainhill Stoops 118 A3
Ravenhead 8 C8
Red Rock 56 F5
Ring o' Bells 52 D3
Risley 107 G7
Rivington 45 H3
Robin Hood 54 D1
Roby 115 K3
Roby Mill 66 D2
Rock Ferry 128 B3
Rocksavage 149 K8
Royal Oak 74 B1
Rufford 39 L2
Runcorn 19 K6
Runshaw Moor 31 H1
St Helens 9 H2
St Michael's Hamlet 129 K3
Sandhills 96 E5
Sankey Bridges 136 E1
Saughall Massie 109 K7
Scarisbrick 37 G6
Scarth Hill 63 L3
Scholes 5 H4
Seacombe 111 M4
Seaforth 83 G6
Sefton 72 B6
Sefton Park 129 M1
Shaw Green 30 F3
Shell Green 135 G3
Shevington 55 J8
Shevington Moor 55 J3
Shevington Vale 55 H5
Shirdley Hill 36 B7
Simm's Cross 16 F4
Simm's Lane End 78 C8
Skelmersdale 65 J3
Snape Green 37 G4
Sollom 28 D3
Southdene 86 A5
Southgate 150 A6
Southport 2 C1
Speke 147 G2
Spital 143 L2
Springfield 68 B3
Standish 56 B4
Standish Lower Ground 67 M2
Stanley 65 G2
Stanley Gate 64 A6
Stanlow 157 K8
Statham 139 M1
Stoak 164 B6
Stockbridge Village 99 J5
Stockton Heath 137 L4
Stoneycroft 114 C1
Storeton 127 K8
Stubshaw Cross 79 M8
Sutton 103 G6
Sutton Green 162 D2
Sutton Heath 102 A7
Sutton Leach 103 G8
Sutton Manor 118 C3
Sutton Weaver 161 K2
Swanside 115 H2
Tamer Lane End 81 K5
Tanhouse 65 L5
Tarbock Green 132 E1
Tarlscough 38 F4
Thatto Heath 101 M5
Thelwall 139 G2
Thingwall 126 D8
Thornton 71 L7
Thornton Hough 142 B6
Thornton-le-Moors 164 F4
Thurstaston 125 J8
Toll Bar 101 L4
Tontine 66 F7
Top Lock 69 K3
Tower Hill 74 A8
Town End 117 L7
Town Green 62 F6
Town Green 91 M1
Town of Lowton 92 C8
Town Park 150 D4
Toxteth 113 G8
Tranmere 128 A2
Tuebrook 98 B8
Two Mills 162 A6
Up Holland 66 C6
Upton 110 B8
Upton 133 K3
Upton Rocks 134 A2
Vauxhall 12 D1
Vulcan Village 104 E5
Waddicar 85 J1
Wallasey 95 L5
Walton 97 K3
Wargrave 104 E4
Warrington 14 C3
Waterloo 82 F3
Waterloo Park 83 H4
Wavertree 114 B6
Weld Bank 32 E8
West Bank 134 B8
Westbrook 120 C4
Westhead 63 M1
West Kirby 124 B3
Westleigh 81 M6
Weston 149 H7
Weston Point 18 A8
West Park 8 A7
Westvale 85 M3
Westy 122 B8
Whalleys 53 J8
Whelley 5 L1
Whiston 117 G2
Whiston Cross 116 F2
Whiston Lane Ends 116 E3
Whitby 20 B7
Whitbyheath 163 H4
White Coppice 33 M3
Whitefield Lane End 116 D5
Whitley 68 C2
Widnes 16 A5
Wigan 4 C2
Wilderspool 137 L3
Wilderswood 45 M7
Willaston 154 D5
Wimbolds Trafford 165 H7
Windle Hill 153 L6
Windmill Hill 150 E3
Windy Arbor 116 F5
Winstanley 78 E2
Winstanleys 56 E6
Winwick 105 K6
Winwick Quay 121 K1
Wirral 126 B5
Wolverham 20 D7
Woodbank 162 A7
Woodchurch 126 E2
Woodhey 128 B6
Woodhouses 167 G1
Woodvale 47 K2
Woolfall Heath 99 L8
Woolston 122 E6
Woolton 131 J4
Worsley Hall 67 M6
Worsley Mesnes 79 H1
Wrightington Bar 42 B5
Wrights Green 138 C8

USING THE STREET INDEX

Street names are listed alphabetically. Each street name is followed by its postal town or area locality, the Postcode District, the page number, and the reference to the square in which the name is found.

Example: **Abbeyfields** *WGNNW/ST* WN6 ....**68** A2 **1**

Some entries are followed by a number in a blue box. This number indicates the location of the street within the referenced grid square. The full street name is listed at the side of the map page.

GENERAL ABBREVIATIONS

ACC ACCESS
ALY ALLEY
AP APPROACH
AR ARCADE
ASS ASSOCIATION
AV AVENUE
BCH BEACH
BLDS BUILDINGS
BND BEND
BNK BANK
BR BRIDGE
BRK BROOK
BTM BOTTOM
BUS BUSINESS
BVD BOULEVARD
BY BYPASS
CATH CATHEDRAL
CEM CEMETERY
CEN CENTRE
CFT CROFT
CH CHURCH
CHA CHASE
CHYD CHURCHYARD
CIR CIRCLE
CIRC CIRCUS
CL CLOSE
CLFS CLIFFS
CMP CAMP
CNR CORNER
CO COUNTY
COLL COLLEGE
COM COMMON
COMM COMMISSION
CON CONVENT
COT COTTAGE
COTS COTTAGES
CP CAPE
CPS COPSE
CR CREEK
CREM CREMATORIUM
CRS CRESCENT
CSWY CAUSEWAY
CT COURT
CTRL CENTRAL
CTS COURTS
CTYD COURTYARD
CUTT CUTTINGS
CV COVE
CYN CANYON
DEPT DEPARTMENT
DL DALE
DM DAM
DR DRIVE
DRO DROVE
DRY DRIVEWAY
DWGS DWELLINGS
E EAST
EMB EMBANKMENT
EMBY EMBASSY
ESP ESPLANADE
EST ESTATE
EX EXCHANGE
EXPY EXPRESSWAY
EXT EXTENSION
F/O FLYOVER
FC FOOTBALL CLUB
FK FORK
FLD FIELD
FLDS FIELDS
FLS FALLS
FLS FLATS
FM FARM
FT FORT
FWY FREEWAY
FY FERRY
GA GATE
GAL GALLERY
GDN GARDEN
GDNS GARDENS
GLD GLADE
GLN GLEN
GN GREEN
GND GROUND
GRA GRANGE
GRG GARAGE
GT GREAT
GTWY GATEWAY
GV GROVE
HGR HIGHER
HL HILL
HLS HILLS
HO HOUSE
HOL HOLLOW
HOSP HOSPITAL
HRB HARBOUR
HTH HEATH
HTS HEIGHTS
HVN HAVEN
HWY HIGHWAY
IMP IMPERIAL
IN INLET
IND EST INDUSTRIAL ESTATE
INF INFIRMARY
INFO INFORMATION
INT INTERCHANGE
IS ISLAND
JCT JUNCTION
JTY JETTY
KG KING
KNL KNOLL
L LAKE
LA LANE
LDG LODGE
LGT LIGHT
LK LOCK
LKS LAKES
LNDG LANDING
LTL LITTLE
LWR LOWER
MAG MAGISTRATE
MAN MANSIONS
MD MEAD
MDW MEADOWS
MEM MEMORIAL
MKT MARKET
MKTS MARKETS
ML MALL
ML MILL
MNR MANOR
MS MEWS
MSN MISSION
MT MOUNT
MTN MOUNTAIN
MTS MOUNTAINS
MUS MUSEUM
MWY MOTORWAY
N NORTH
NE NORTH EAST
NW NORTH WEST
O/P OVERPASS
OFF OFFICE
ORCH ORCHARD
OV OVAL
PAL PALACE
PAS PASSAGE
PAV PAVILION
PDE PARADE
PH PUBLIC HOUSE
PK PARK
PKWY PARKWAY
PL PLACE
PLN PLAIN
PLNS PLAINS
PLZ PLAZA
POL POLICE STATION
PR PRINCE
PREC PRECINCT
PREP PREPARATORY
PRIM PRIMARY
PROM PROMENADE
PRS PRINCESS
PRT PORT
PT POINT
PTH PATH
PZ PIAZZA
QD QUADRANT
QU QUEEN
QY QUAY
R RIVER
RBT ROUNDABOUT
RD ROAD
RDG RIDGE
REP REPUBLIC
RES RESERVOIR
RFC RUGBY FOOTBALL CLUB
RI RISE
RP RAMP
RW ROW
S SOUTH
SCH SCHOOL
SE SOUTH EAST
SER SERVICE AREA
SH SHORE
SHOP SHOPPING
SKWY SKYWAY
SMT SUMMIT
SOC SOCIETY
SP SPUR
SPR SPRING
SQ SQUARE
ST STREET
STN STATION
STR STREAM
STRD STRAND
SW SOUTH WEST
TDG TRADING
TER TERRACE
THWY THROUGHWAY
TNL TUNNEL
TOLL TOLLWAY
TPK TURNPIKE
TR TRACK
TRL TRAIL
TWR TOWER
U/P UNDERPASS
UNI UNIVERSITY
UPR UPPER
V VALE
VA VALLEY
VIAD VIADUCT
VIL VILLA
VIS VISTA
VLG VILLAGE
VLS VILLAS
VW VIEW
W WEST
WD WOOD
WHF WHARF
WK WALK
WKS WALKS
WLS WELLS
WY WAY
YD YARD
YHA YOUTH HOSTEL

POSTCODE TOWNS AND AREA ABBREVIATIONS

AIG/SPK Aigburth/Sefton Park
AIMK Ashton-in-Makerfield
AIN/FAZ Aintree/Fazakerley
ALL/GAR Allerton/Garston
ANF/KKDL Anfield/Kirkdale
BEB Bebington
BIRK Birkenhead
BRSC Burscough
BTL Bootle
CALD/MH Calderstones/Mossley Hill
CH/BCN Chester/Blacon
CHLDW Childwall
CHLY/EC Chorley/Eccleston
CHLYE Chorley east/Adlington/Whittle-le-Woods
CHNE Chester northeast
CHTN/BK Churchtown/Banks
CL/PREN Claughton/Prenton
CLB/OSW/ST Clubmoor/Old Swan/Stoneycroft
CLVP Central Liverpool
CLVPS Central Liverpool south
CSBY/BLUN Crosby/Blundellsands
CSBY/WL Crosby/Waterloo
DV/KA/FCH Dovecot/Knotty Ash/Fincham
ECCL Eccleston
EHL/KEN Edge Hill/Kensington
EP Ellesmere Port
EV Everton
FMBY Formby
FROD/HEL Frodsham/Helsby
GOL/RIS/CUL Golborne/Risley/Culcheth
GR/UP/WCH Greasby/Upton/Woodchurch
GTS/LS Great Sutton/Little Sutton
HES Heswall
HLWD Halewood
HOR/BR Horwich/Blackrod
HOY Hoylake
HTWN Hightown
HUY Huyton
KIRK/FR/WAR Kirkham Freckleton/Warton
KKBY Kirkby
LEIGH Leigh
LEY/BBR Leyland/Bamber Bridge
LITH Litherland
LYMM Lymm
MGHL Maghull
MOR/LEA Moreton/Leasowe
NEWLW Newton-le-Willows
NG/CROX Norris Green/Croxteth
NPK/KEN Newsham Park/Kensington
NSTN Neston
NTHLY Netherley
NTHTN Netherton
NWD/KWIPK Northwood/Knowsley Industrial Park
ORM Ormskirk
PEN/TH Pensby/Thingwall
PR/KW Prescot/Knowsley
PS/BROM Port Sunlight/Bromborough
RAIN/WH Rainhill/Whiston
RF/TRAN Rock Ferry/Tranmere
RNFD/HAY Rainford/Haydock
RUNC Runcorn
SFTN Sefton
SKEL Skelmersdale
SPK/HALE Speke/Hale
STBRV Stockbridge Village
STHEL St Helens
STHP Southport
TOX Toxteth
VAUX/LVPD Vauxhall/Liverpool Docks
WAL/EG Wallasey/Egremont
WAL/NB Wallasey/New Brighton
WARR Warrington
WARRN/WOL Warrington north/Woolston
WARRS Warrington south
WARRW/BUR Warrington west/Burtonwood
WAV Wavertree
WD/CROXPK West Derby/Croxteth Park
WDN Widnes
WGN Wigan
WGNE/HIN Wigan east/Hindley
WGNNW/ST Wigan northwest/Standish
WGNS/IIMK Wigan south/Ince-in-Makerfield
WGNW/BIL/OR Wigan west/Billinge/Orrell
WHTN Westhoughton
WKBY West Kirby
WLT/FAZ Walton/Fazakerley
WLTN Woolton

Index - streets

3rd St WGNE/HIN WN2 80 A6
4th St WGNE/HIN WN2 80 B6

A

Abacus Rd CLB/OSW/ST L13 114 C1
Abberley Cl ECCL WA10 8 E5
Abberley Rd WLTN L25 131 M6
Abberley Wy WGNS/IIMK WN3 78 D1
Abbey Cl BIRK CH41 11 L7
FMBY L37 59 K3
GOL/RIS/CU WA3 106 C5
NWD/KWIPK L33 86 B3
SKEL WN8 66 E6
WDN WA8 133 L5
Abbey Ct WGNNW/ST WN6 68 A3
WLTN L25 131 K3
Abbey Dl BRSC L40 52 B2
WGNNW/ST WN6 54 F6
Abbey Dr WGNW/BIL/O WN5 67 G7
Abbeyfield Dr WD/CROXPK L12 98 F3
Abbeyfields WGNNW/ST WN6 68 A2 1
Abbey Fold BRSC L40 38 F8
Abbey Gv CHLYE PR6 44 C6
Abbey Hey RUNC WA7 150 E5
Abbey La BRSC L40 51 L5
LEIGH WN7 81 M4
Abbey Rd ECCL WA10 89 G6
GOL/RIS/CU WA3 93 L5
RNFD/HAY WA11 91 G6 1
WDN WA8 133 K5
WKBY CH48 124 D3
Abbey Sq LEIGH WN7 81 M4
Abbeystead SKEL WN8 65 L6 1
Abbeystead Av NTHTN L30 84 C4
Abbeystead Rd WAV L15 114 D5
Abbey St BIRK CH41 11 L7
Abbeyvale Dr NTHLY L27 115 L7
Abbey Vw CHLDW L16 115 G6
Abbeyway North
RNFD/HAY WA11 91 J6 1
Abbeyway South
RNFD/HAY WA11 91 J7 1
Abbeywood SKEL WN8 65 L6
Abbeywood Gv
RAIN/WH L35 117 H3 1
Abbingdon Wy LEIGH WN7 81 M4
Abbot Cl CL/PREN CH43 110 E7
Abbotsbury Wy
WD/CROXPK L12 99 G2
Abbots Cl FMBY L37 59 J4
Abbots Dr BEB CH63 143 J1 1
Abbotsfield Cl WARRS WA4 138 A7
Abbotsfield Rd STHEL WA9 103 G8
Abbotsford ORM L39 51 H8
Abbotsford Cl
GOL/RIS/CU WA3 92 F4 1
Abbotsford Gdns
CSBY/BLUN L23 82 E2
Abbotsford Rd CSBY/BLUN L23 82 E2
NG/CROX L11 98 A3
Abbotsford St WAL/EG CH44 112 A3 1
Abbots Hall Av STHEL WA9 118 F2
Abbots Ms EP CH65 20 B2
Abbots Wy FMBY L37 59 J3
NSTN CH64 152 F4
Abbott Dr BTL L20 84 A8 1
Abbotts Cl CALD/MH L18 130 D2
RUNC WA7 19 H8
Abbottshey Av CALD/MH L18 130 D2
Abbott St WGNE/HIN WN2 69 L7
Abbotts Wy WGNW/BIL/O WN5 89 M2
Abdale Rd NG/CROX L11 98 B2
Abercrombie Rd
NWD/KWIPK L33 86 D6
Abercromby Sq EHL/KEN L7 13 M8
Aberdale Rd CLB/OSW/ST L13 114 D2
Aberdare Cl WARRW/BUR WA5 121 G4
Aberdeen St BIRK CH41 10 F4
Aberford Av WAL/NB CH45 95 G8 1
Abergele Rd CLB/OSW/ST L13 114 B3
Aber St NPK/KEN L6 113 J2
Abingdon Av WARR WA1 123 G6
Abingdon Gv ANF/KKDL L4 97 L3
HLWD L26 132 C4 1
Abingdon Rd ANF/KKDL L4 97 L3
GR/UP/WCH CH49 125 K2
Abinger Rd AIMK WN4 91 G1 1
Abington Dr WGNE/HIN WN2 80 C4
Abney Cl EHL/KEN L7 113 K5
Aboyne Cl WLT/FAZ L9 97 J1 1
Abrams Fold CHTN/BK PR9 23 H8
Abrams Gn CHTN/BK PR9 23 H8
Abram St EV L5 13 K1
EV L5 97 G8 1
Abratio St BIRK CH41 11 G6 1
Abstone Cl WARR WA1 122 E6 1
Abyssinia Cl WAV L15 114 A6 1
Acacia Av HUY L36 115 M4
WARR WA1 122 F5
WDN WA8 134 D2
Acacia Cl CHNE CH2 165 L2 1
GR/UP/WCH CH49 125 L3 1
Acacia Crs WGNNW/ST WN6 68 B2
Acacia Dr GTS/LS CH66 163 H4
Acacia Gv ECCL WA10 101 J1
RUNC WA7 19 M8
WAL/EG CH44 112 A3 2
WKBY CH48 124 C3 1
WLT/FAZ L9 84 D7 1
Acacia St NEWLW WA12 104 B1
Academy St WARR WA1 14 F6
Academy Wy WARR WA1 14 E7
Acanthus Rd CLB/OSW/ST L13 114 C1
Access Rd WD/CROXPK L12 98 F6 1
Acer Leigh AIG/SPK L17 129 M4
Acheson Rd CLB/OSW/ST L13 98 A7
Achilles Av WARRN/WOL WA2 121 K3 1
Ackerley Cl WARRN/WOL WA2 122 B2
Ackers Hall Av DV/KA/FCH L14 115 H1
Ackers Hall Cl DV/KA/FCH L14 99 H8
Ackers La ECCL WA10 101 L1
HTWN L38 70 F5
WARRS WA4 138 A4
Ackers Rd GR/UP/WCH CH49 126 E3
WARRS WA4 138 A3
Ackhurst La WGNW/BIL/O WN5 67 J2
Ackhurst Rd CHLY/EC PR7 32 B5
Acland Rd WAL/EG CH44 111 K1 1
Aconbury Cl NG/CROX L11 98 B2
Aconbury Pl NG/CROX L11 98 B2
Acorn Cl BEB CH63 127 M7
STHEL WA9 118 E1 1
Acorn Dr EP CH65 163 K4
Acornfield Cl NWD/KWIPK L33 86 E5
Acornfield Rd NWD/KWIPK L33 86 F4
Acorn St NEWLW WA12 104 E2
Acorn Wy BTL L20 7 J1
A Ct AIMK WN4 91 K3
Acrefield SKEL WN8 53 J4
Acrefield Pk WLTN L25 131 J2
Acrefield Rd RF/TRAN CH42 127 K4
WDN WA8 133 K4 1
WLTN L25 131 J2
Acre Gn HLWD L26 132 C7
Acre La HES CH60 141 L4
PS/BROM CH62 143 L6
Acre Rd GTS/LS CH66 155 M8
Acresfield CHLY/EC PR7 44 B7
Acresfield Cl HOR/BR BL6 57 L2 1
Acresgate Ct WLTN L25 115 J8 1
Acres La FMBY L37 60 A6
ORM L39 61 G6
Acres Rd BEB CH63 128 B7
HOY CH47 109 G6
Acreswood Cl CHLY/EC PR7 43 G5 1
Acreville Rd BEB CH63 128 B8
Acton Cl RNFD/HAY WA11 90 E7 1
Acton Gv NPK/KEN L6 97 L7
Acton La MOR/LEA CH46 109 L6
Acton Rd KKBY L32 85 L3 1
RF/TRAN CH42 128 C4
WARRW/BUR WA5 104 A7
Acton St WGN WN1 4 F2
Acton Ter WGN WN1 4 F1
Acton Wy EHL/KEN L7 113 L5 1
Acuba Gv BIRK CH41 128 A1 1
Acuba Rd WAV L15 114 E4
Adair Pl CLB/OSW/ST L13 98 A6
Adair Rd CLB/OSW/ST L13 98 A6
Adam Av GTS/LS CH66 162 E2
Adam Cl GTS/LS CH66 162 F1
Adams Cl NEWLW WA12 104 F3
Adams Dr WGNS/IIMK WN3 68 B8
Adamson Ct WARRS WA4 138 D3 1
Adamson St AIMK WN4 91 J2
EHL/KEN L7 113 M3 1
WARRS WA4 14 E9
Adam St EV L5 97 H7
WARRN/WOL WA2 15 G1
Adaston Av PS/BROM CH62 155 H1
Ada St STHEL WA9 9 L9
Adcote Cl DV/KA/FCH L14 115 H2
Adcote Rd DV/KA/FCH L14 115 H2
Adderley St EHL/KEN L7 113 K3 1
Addingham Av WDN WA8 133 L6
Addingham Rd CALD/MH L18 114 D8
Addington St WAL/EG CH44 111 M2 1
Addison Sq WDN WA8 16 C1
Addison St BTL L20 83 J8 1
VAUX/LVPD L3 13 G4
WGNS/IIMK WN3 4 D5
Addison Wy VAUX/LVPD L3 12 F4
Adelaide Av STHEL WA9 102 A6
Adelaide Pl EV L5 13 J1
Adelaide Rd EHL/KEN L7 113 K3
LITH L21 83 H6
RF/TRAN CH42 127 L1
Adelaide St WAL/EG CH44 111 K3
Adelaide Ter CSBY/WL L22 82 E4
Adela Rd RUNC WA7 18 E4
Adele Thompson Dr TOX L8 113 J6 1
Adelphi St BIRK CH41 11 J5
WGNNW/ST WN6 56 A4
Adfalent La NSTN CH64 154 C6
Adkins St EV L5 97 J7 1
Adlam Crs WLT/FAZ L9 85 G6 1
Adlam Rd AIN/FAZ L10 85 G6
Adlington Ct
GOL/RIS/CU WA3 107 H7 1
GOL/RIS/CU WA3 107 H7 1
Adlington Rd RUNC WA7 150 F3 1
Admin Rd NWD/KWIPK L33 86 E5
Admirals Rd GOL/RIS/CU WA3 123 G2
Admiral St TOX L8 113 H8
Admiralty Cl BRSC L40 51 L3 1
Adrian's Wy KKBY L32 86 A3 1
Adshead Rd CLB/OSW/ST L13 98 A6
Adstone Rd WLTN L25 115 L8 1
Adswood Rd HUY L36 116 A2
Adwell Cl GOL/RIS/CU WA3 93 J5
Africander Rd RNFD/HAY WA11 89 J5
Afton WDN WA8 133 J3
Agar Rd NG/CROX L11 98 B6
Agate St NPK/KEN L6 97 J8
Agincourt Rd WD/CROXPK L12 98 E8
Agnes Gv WAL/EG CH44 95 L8
Agnes Rd CSBY/BLUN L23 82 E2
RF/TRAN CH42 127 M2
Agnes St STHEL WA9 118 E2
Agnes Wy EHL/KEN L7 113 K4 1
Aiden Long Gv PR/KW L34 100 A4
Aigburth Dr AIG/SPK L17 129 L1 1
Aigburth Hall Av ALL/GAR L19 130 C5
Aigburth Hall Rd ALL/GAR L19 130 C5
Aigburth Rd AIG/SPK L17 129 K2
ALL/GAR L19 130 B5
Aigburth St TOX L8 113 K5
Aigburth V AIG/SPK L17 129 M3
CALD/MH L18 130 A2
Ailsa Rd WAL/NB CH45 95 J8
Ainley Cl RUNC WA7 150 C8
Ainscough Rd GOL/RIS/CU WA3 123 G2
Ainsdale Cl AIN/FAZ L10 85 H5 1
BEB CH63 143 L8
PEN/TH CH61 126 C8 1
WARRW/BUR WA5 136 B1
Ainsdale Rd BTL L20 83 M8
Ainse Rd HOR/BR BL6 57 K2
Ainsworth Av MOR/LEA CH46 109 L7 1
Ainsworth La PR/KW L34 86 D7
Ainsworth Rd ECCL WA10 8 B2
Ainsworth St VAUX/LVPD L3 13 K7
Aintree Crs STHP PR8 36 B2
Aintree Gv GTS/LS CH66 162 F2
Aintree La AIN/FAZ L10 84 E3
Aintree Rd BTL L20 7 K2
WLT/FAZ L9 84 F7 1

Airdale Cl CL/PREN CH43 ... 110 E7
Airdale Rd WAV L15 ... 114 B7
Airdrie Cl PS/BROM CH62 ... 154 F2
Aire WDN WA8 ... 133 K3
Aire Cl EP CH65 ... 156 C6
Airedale Cl WARRW/BUR WA5 ... 120 B6
Airegate MGHL L31 ... 72 D3
Airlie Gv CLB/OSW/ST L13 ... 97 M7
Airlie Rd HOY CH47 ... 108 D7
Airton Pl WGNS/IIMK WN3 ... 79 K2
Aisthorpe Gv MGHL L31 ... 72 F6
Ajax Av WARRN/WOL WA2 ... 121 K3
The Akbar HES CH60 ... 140 E4
Akenside St BTL L20 ... 83 J7
Alabama Wy BIRK CH41 ... 11 M6
Alamein Crs WARRN/WOL WA2 ... 14 F1
Alamein Rd HUY L36 ... 115 M1
Alance Br CHLYE PR6 ... 45 H1
Alans Wy NWD/KWIPK L33 ... 86 A1
Alastair Crs CL/PREN CH43 ... 127 H4
Alban Rd CHLDW L16 ... 114 F5
Albany Av PR/KW L34 ... 101 H6
Albany Crs LYMM WA13 ... 139 M1
Albany Gdns GTS/LS CH66 ... 155 L6
Albany Gv LYMM WA13 ... 139 L1
Albany Rd CLB/OSW/ST L13 ... 114 C1
EHL/KEN L7 ... 113 J3
LYMM WA13 ... 139 L2
PR/KW L34 ... 101 G7
RF/TRAN CH42 ... 128 A3
STHP PR8 ... 24 D4
WLT/FAZ L9 ... 84 D6
Albany Ter RUNC WA7 ... 19 G4
Albemarle Rd WAL/EG CH44 ... 111 M2
Albert Dr BTL L20 ... 84 B7
NSTN CH64 ... 152 F5
WARRW/BUR WA5 ... 119 M7
Albert Edward Rd EHL/KEN L7 ... 113 J3
Albert Gv CSBY/BLUN L23 ... 82 F1
WAV L15 ... 114 C5
Alberton Cl WGNE/HIN WN2 ... 57 L7
Albert Pk AIG/SPK L17 ... 113 K8
Albert Pl STHP PR8 ... 3 G2
Albert Rd BRSC L40 ... 39 J2
CHTN/BK PR9 ... 3 K1
CLB/OSW/ST L13 ... 97 M7
CSBY/WL L22 ... 82 F4
FMBY L37 ... 58 D5
HOY CH47 ... 108 D7
RF/TRAN CH42 ... 127 L1
WARRS WA4 ... 138 C3
WDN WA8 ... 16 F2
WKBY CH48 ... 124 C4
Albert Schweitzer Av
NTHTN L30 ... 84 B2
Albert St AIMK WN4 ... 91 K2
CHLY/EC PR7 ... 32 F6
ECCL WA10 ... 9 G1
EHL/KEN L7 ... 113 J4
RUNC WA7 ... 19 G4
WGNE/HIN WN2 ... 69 M8
WGNW/BIL/O WN5 ... 68 B7
Albert Ter STHP PR8 ... 2 F8
Albion Dr WGNE/HIN WN2 ... 69 K3
Albion Pl WAL/NB CH45 ... 95 K5
Albion St BIRK CH41 ... 11 L5
CHLY/EC PR7 ... 32 E6
ECCL WA10 ... 8 D5
EV L5 ... 97 G7
WAL/NB CH45 ... 95 J5
WGNE/HIN WN2 ... 69 K3
WGNE/HIN WN2 ... 80 C3
Albourne Rd KKBY L32 ... 86 C5
Albury Cl RNFD/HAY WA11 ... 90 E6
WD/CROXPK L12 ... 99 H3
Albury Rd KKBY L32 ... 86 B6
Albury Wy WGNE/HIN WN2 ... 69 H3
Alcester Rd WD/CROXPK L12 ... 98 E7
Alcock St RUNC WA7 ... 19 H2
Aldams Gv ANF/KKDL L4 ... 7 L9
Aldbourne Av CALD/MH L18 ... 115 G8
Aldbourne Cl WLTN L25 ... 131 G1
Aldcliffe GOL/RIS/CU WA3 ... 93 H6
Alder Av AIMK WN4 ... 79 H8
HUY L36 ... 116 C5
WDN WA8 ... 134 C2
WGNW/BIL/O WN5 ... 67 M7
WGNW/BIL/O WN5 ... 77 M8
Alderbank Rd
WARRW/BUR WA5 ... 120 C7
Alderbrook Dr SKEL WN8 ... 53 L3
Alder Cl PR/KW L34 ... 101 H7
Alder Crs KKBY L32 ... 85 M2
WARRN/WOL WA2 ... 121 L5
Alderdale Av STHP PR8 ... 34 C8
Alder Dr CHLY/EC PR7 ... 42 F2
GTS/LS CH66 ... 163 H4
Alderfield Dr SPK/HALE L24 ... 147 J3
Alder Gv CHLY/EC PR7 ... 43 H4
CSBY/WL L22 ... 82 F3
Alder Hey Rd ECCL WA10 ... 101 L1
Alder La FROD/HEL WA6 ... 159 M2
ORM L39 ... 48 A5
PR/KW L34 ... 99 K3
RNFD/HAY WA11 ... 77 H8
SKEL WN8 ... 53 L4
WARRN/WOL WA2 ... 121 K5
WARRW/BUR WA5 ... 104 C6
WDN WA8 ... 133 H1
Alder Lee Cl WGNS/IIMK WN3 ... 78 F3
Alderley Av BIRK CH41 ... 111 H6
GOL/RIS/CU WA3 ... 92 F6
Alderley Rd HOY CH47 ... 108 D6
WAL/EG CH44 ... 111 K2
WARRS WA4 ... 138 F1
Alderney Cl EP CH65 ... 163 L4
Alderney Dr WGNS/IIMK WN3 ... 79 J2
Alderney Rd EV L5 ... 96 F8
Alder Rd BEB CH63 ... 142 F1
GOL/RIS/CU WA3 ... 93 H5
PR/KW L34 ... 101 H7
WARR WA1 ... 122 F6
WD/CROXPK L12 ... 114 D1
Alder Root La
WARRN/WOL WA2 ... 104 F6
Aldersey Cl RUNC WA7 ... 150 F4
Aldersey St VAUX/LVPD L3 ... 13 H3
Aldersgate RF/TRAN CH42 ... 128 B3
Aldersgate Av RUNC WA7 ... 150 F6
Aldersgate Dr HLWD L26 ... 132 C7
Alderson Crs FMBY L37 ... 59 H1
Alderson Rd WAV L15 ... 113 M6
The Alders WGNNW/ST WN6 ... 67 M1
Alder St NEWLW WA12 ... 104 E2
Alderton Dr AIMK WN4 ... 91 J2
Alderville Rd ANF/KKDL L4 ... 97 L3
Alder Wood Av SPK/HALE L24 ... 147 G2
Aldewood Cl GOL/RIS/CU WA3 ... 107 J7
Aldford Cl BEB CH63 ... 143 K7
CL/PREN CH43 ... 127 G3
Aldford Rd KKBY L32 ... 86 A6
Aldford Wy WGNNW/ST WN6 ... 56 A5
Aldgate EP CH65 ... 156 C8
Aldred St WGNE/HIN WN2 ... 80 F1
Aldridge Cl WD/CROXPK L12 ... 99 G2
WGNS/IIMK WN3 ... 79 K2
Aldridge Dr WARRW/BUR WA5 ... 104 B6
Aldrins La NTHTN L30 ... 84 B1
Aldwark Rd DV/KA/FCH L14 ... 115 J1
Aldwych Rd WD/CROXPK L12 ... 98 E7
Aldykes MGHL L31 ... 73 G5
Alexander Cl BRSC L40 ... 52 B2
Alexander Dr MGHL L31 ... 72 F2
PEN/TH CH61 ... 141 G2
WDN WA8 ... 133 M5
Alexander Fleming Av
NTHTN L30 ... 84 B1
Alexander Gv RUNC WA7 ... 19 L5
Alexandra Ct NPK/KEN L6 ... 113 K2
Alexandra Crs
WGNW/BIL/O WN5 ... 68 A7
Alexandra Dr AIG/SPK L17 ... 129 K1
BTL L20 ... 84 A7
ECCL WA10 ... 8 C7
RF/TRAN CH42 ... 128 A4
Alexandra Ms ORM L39 ... 51 G7
Alexandra Mt LITH L21 ... 83 K5
Alexandra Pk AIG/SPK L17 ... 129 K2
Alexandra Rd AIMK WN4 ... 91 K1
BRSC L40 ... 51 M1
CHTN/BK PR9 ... 3 K1
CL/PREN CH43 ... 10 E7
CLB/OSW/ST L13 ... 114 C4
CSBY/BLUN L23 ... 82 F1
CSBY/WL L22 ... 83 G5
EHL/KEN L7 ... 113 L5
FMBY L37 ... 58 D5
WAL/NB CH45 ... 95 J5
WARRS WA4 ... 138 B3
WKBY CH48 ... 124 C4
Alexandra St ECCL WA10 ... 101 M4
EP CH65 ... 20 C1
WARR WA1 ... 15 L2
WDN WA8 ... 16 C6
WGNE/HIN WN2 ... 80 C5
WGNW/BIL/O WN5 ... 68 B7
Alexandria Rd ALL/GAR L19 ... 130 E6
Alfonso Rd ANF/KKDL L4 ... 96 F5
Alford Av STHEL WA9 ... 118 D1
Alforde St WDN WA8 ... 16 D6
Alford St EHL/KEN L7 ... 114 A5
Alfred Cl WDN WA8 ... 16 E4
Alfred Rd CL/PREN CH43 ... 10 E7
GOL/RIS/CU WA3 ... 93 J5
RNFD/HAY WA11 ... 91 G6
WAL/EG CH44 ... 112 A4
Alfred St ECCL WA10 ... 9 J3
NEWLW WA12 ... 105 G2
RNFD/HAY WA11 ... 76 B6
WAV L15 ... 113 M5
WDN WA8 ... 16 E4
WGN WN1 ... 68 D3
WGNE/HIN WN2 ... 80 C2
WGNS/IIMK WN3 ... 5 H8
Alfriston Rd WD/CROXPK L12 ... 98 E7
Algernon St RUNC WA7 ... 18 E2
WARR WA1 ... 15 J3
WARRS WA4 ... 137 L4
WGNE/HIN WN2 ... 69 M8
WGNS/IIMK WN3 ... 79 J1
Alice Ct WDN WA8 ... 149 J1
Alice St STHEL WA9 ... 103 G5
Alison Av RF/TRAN CH42 ... 128 B2
Alison Pl CLB/OSW/ST L13 ... 98 A6
Alison Rd CLB/OSW/ST L13 ... 98 A6
Alistair Dr BEB CH63 ... 143 L7
Alker La CHLYE PR6 ... 32 C2
Alker St CHLY/EC PR7 ... 32 E6
WGNW/BIL/O WN5 ... 68 B7
Allangate Cl GR/UP/WCH CH49 ... 125 L3
Allangate Rd ALL/GAR L19 ... 130 D5
Allan Rd RNFD/HAY WA11 ... 89 L6
Allans Cl NSTN CH64 ... 153 G7
Allans Meadow NSTN CH64 ... 153 G7
Allanson St STHEL WA9 ... 102 F3
Allcard St WARRW/BUR WA5 ... 14 B1
Allcot Av RF/TRAN CH42 ... 127 M3
Allen Av GOL/RIS/CU WA3 ... 107 L1
Allenby Av CSBY/WL L22 ... 83 H3
Allenby Sq CLB/OSW/ST L13 ... 114 B3
Allendale RUNC WA7 ... 150 D7
Allendale Av RAIN/WH L35 ... 117 M2
WLT/FAZ L9 ... 84 D6
Allengate CSBY/BLUN L23 ... 71 G8
Allen Rd RUNC WA7 ... 18 B9
Allen St WARRN/WOL WA2 ... 14 D4
Allerby Wy GOL/RIS/CU WA3 ... 93 G5
Allerford Rd WD/CROXPK L12 ... 98 F5
Allerton Beeches CALD/MH L18 ... 130 E2
Allerton Dr CALD/MH L18 ... 130 D1
Allerton Gv RF/TRAN CH42 ... 127 M2
Allerton Rd CALD/MH L18 ... 114 D8
CHTN/BK PR9 ... 25 G4
RF/TRAN CH42 ... 127 M2
WAL/NB CH45 ... 95 J7
WDN WA8 ... 16 F1
WLTN L25 ... 131 H4
Allesley Rd DV/KA/FCH L14 ... 99 H8
Alleyne Rd ANF/KKDL L4 ... 97 M5
Alliance St WGN WN1 ... 4 F3
Allington St AIG/SPK L17 ... 129 K2
Allonby Cl CL/PREN CH43 ... 127 G1
Allport La PS/BROM CH62 ... 143 M4
Allport Rd BEB CH63 ... 143 L7
The Allports PS/BROM CH62 ... 143 M6
All Saints Cl NTHTN L30 ... 84 A2
All Saints Dr WARRS WA4 ... 139 G2
All Saints Rd SPK/HALE L24 ... 146 E2
Allscott Wy AIMK WN4 ... 91 L2
Alma Cl AIN/FAZ L10 ... 85 K6
SKEL WN8 ... 66 E6
Alma Ct SKEL WN8 ... 66 E6
Almacs Cl CSBY/BLUN L23 ... 82 D2
Alma Dr CHLY/EC PR7 ... 43 G1
Alma Gv WGNS/IIMK WN3 ... 79 G3
Alma Hl SKEL WN8 ... 66 D6
Alma Pde SKEL WN8 ... 66 E7
Alma Pl STHEL WA9 ... 9 L8
Alma Rd AIG/SPK L17 ... 130 A5
SKEL WN8 ... 66 E6
STHP PR8 ... 2 E9
Alma St BIRK CH41 ... 11 K6
NEWLW WA12 ... 104 D2
PS/BROM CH62 ... 128 C6
STHEL WA9 ... 9 L8
Alma Vale Ter BTL L20 ... 6 F5
Almeda Rd SPK/HALE L24 ... 147 J3
Almer Dr WARRW/BUR WA5 ... 120 E8
Almond Av BRSC L40 ... 39 G7
NTHTN L30 ... 83 L2
RUNC WA7 ... 19 L8
Almond Brook Rd
WGNNW/ST WN6 ... 55 K3
Almond Cl HLWD L26 ... 132 A6
RNFD/HAY WA11 ... 90 B8
Almond Ct ALL/GAR L19 ... 131 G8
Almond Crs WGNNW/ST WN6 ... 56 B6
Almond Dr WARRW/BUR WA5 ... 104 B7
Almond Gv WARR WA1 ... 122 D6
WGNW/BIL/O WN5 ... 68 A7
Almond Pl MOR/LEA CH46 ... 110 B5
Almond's Gn WD/CROXPK L12 ... 98 C5
Almond's Gv WD/CROXPK L12 ... 98 C6
Almonds Pk WD/CROXPK L12 ... 98 C5
Almond's Turn NTHTN L30 ... 83 M1
Almond Wy
GR/UP/WCH CH49 ... 125 L3
Alness Dr RAIN/WH L35 ... 117 M3
Alnwick Cl WGNE/HIN WN2 ... 57 M8
Alnwick Dr EP CH65 ... 163 M3
MOR/LEA CH46 ... 109 L5
Alpass Rd AIG/SPK L17 ... 129 K2
Alpha Dr RF/TRAN CH42 ... 128 C4
Alpha St LITH L21 ... 83 K8
Alpine Cl ECCL WA10 ... 101 L1
Alpine Dr LEIGH WN7 ... 81 L5
Alpine Rd CHLYE PR6 ... 33 G2
Alpine St NEWLW WA12 ... 104 C2
Alresford Rd ALL/GAR L19 ... 130 B5
Alroy Rd ANF/KKDL L4 ... 97 J6
Alscot Av AIN/FAZ L10 ... 85 K6
Alscot Cl MGHL L31 ... 72 F5
Alston Cl PS/BROM CH62 ... 143 L4
Alstonfield Rd DV/KA/FCH L14 ... 115 J1
Alston Rd AIG/SPK L17 ... 130 A5
WGNE/HIN WN2 ... 69 H3
Alt WDN WA8 ... 133 K3
Alt Av MGHL L31 ... 72 E6
Altbridge Pk NG/CROX L11 ... 85 K8
Alt Bridge Rd HUY L36 ... 115 M1
Altcar Av WAV L15 ... 113 M6
Altcar Dr MOR/LEA CH46 ... 109 M6
Altcar La FMBY L37 ... 59 H4
MGHL L31 ... 72 C1
ORM L39 ... 61 H4
Altcar Rd FMBY L37 ... 59 K3
Alt Cl LEIGH WN7 ... 81 M8
Altcross Rd NG/CROX L11 ... 98 E2
Altcross Wy NG/CROX L11 ... 98 E1
Altfield Rd DV/KA/FCH L14 ... 99 H6
Altfinch Cl DV/KA/FCH L14 ... 99 J6
Altham Rd NG/CROX L11 ... 98 B6
STHP PR8 ... 36 A3
Althorpe Dr STHP PR8 ... 36 A2
Althorp St TOX L8 ... 129 H2
Altmoor Rd HUY L36 ... 99 M7
Alton Av LITH L21 ... 83 J4
Alton Cl AIMK WN4 ... 91 J1
HTWN L38 ... 70 B3
Alton Rd CL/PREN CH43 ... 10 B8
NPK/KEN L6 ... 97 M8
Alt Rd BTL L20 ... 83 L8
FMBY L37 ... 59 J4
HTWN L38 ... 70 B1
HUY L36 ... 116 A2
Alt Side Ct AIN/FAZ L10 ... 85 K6
Alt St TOX L8 ... 113 K6
Altway AIN/FAZ L10 ... 84 E2
Altys La ORM L39 ... 63 H2
Alundale Rd WD/CROXPK L12 ... 99 G8
Alvanley Cl WGNW/BIL/O WN5 ... 67 K4
Alvanley Dr FROD/HEL WA6 ... 166 E3
Alvanley Pl CL/PREN CH43 ... 10 E6
Alvanley Rd FROD/HEL WA6 ... 166 E3
GTS/LS CH66 ... 163 G1
KKBY L32 ... 85 L3
WD/CROXPK L12 ... 98 E8
Alvanley Vw CHNE CH2 ... 165 K2
Alvega Cl PS/BROM CH62 ... 128 E6
Alverstone Av BIRK CH41 ... 111 H6
Alverstone Cl
WARRW/BUR WA5 ... 119 L6
Alverstone Rd CALD/MH L18 ... 114 B8
WAL/EG CH44 ... 111 M2
Alverton Cl WDN WA8 ... 133 M5
Alvina La ANF/KKDL L4 ... 97 G6
NWD/KWIPK L33 ... 74 C8
Alwain Gn SPK/HALE L24 ... 147 H3
Alwen St BIRK CH41 ... 111 H4
Alwyn Av LITH L21 ... 83 K4
Alwyn Gdns MOR/LEA CH46 ... 110 B5
Alwyn St AIG/SPK L17 ... 129 K2
WGN WN1 ... 5 H1
Alwyn Ter WGN WN1 ... 5 H1
Amanda Rd AIN/FAZ L10 ... 85 K6
RAIN/WH L35 ... 101 K8
Amanda Wy MGHL L31 ... 85 K1
Amar St WGNE/HIN WN2 ... 5 M6
Amathyst Cl WGNE/HIN WN2 ... 69 J3
Amaury Cl CSBY/BLUN L23 ... 71 K8
Amaury Rd CSBY/BLUN L23 ... 71 K8
Ambassador Dr HLWD L26 ... 132 C4
Amber Gdns WGNE/HIN WN2 ... 81 G1
Ambergate SKEL WN8 ... 65 K6
Ambergate Cl STHEL WA9 ... 102 F6
Ambergate Rd ALL/GAR L19 ... 130 D6
Amberley Av MOR/LEA CH46 ... 109 L6
Amberley Cl MOR/LEA CH46 ... 109 L6
NPK/KEN L6 ... 97 M6
WGNE/HIN WN2 ... 69 H3
Amberswood Cl WGNE/HIN WN2 ... 69 K6
Amber Wy DV/KA/FCH L14 ... 99 J6
Ambleside WGNE/HIN WN2 ... 69 K5
WGNW/BIL/O WN5 ... 67 L6
Ambleside Av CHLY/EC PR7 ... 31 M4
MOR/LEA CH46 ... 109 M5
Ambleside Cl PEN/TH CH61 ... 126 C7
PS/BROM CH62 ... 144 A6
Ambleside Crs
WARRN/WOL WA2 ... 121 L2
Ambleside Rd CALD/MH L18 ... 130 F4
EP CH65 ... 163 L3
MGHL L31 ... 72 F3
Amelia Cl NPK/KEN L6 ... 13 M4
WDN WA8 ... 134 D1
Amelia St WARRN/WOL WA2 ... 15 G1
Amersham SKEL WN8 ... 65 K6
Amersham Rd ANF/KKDL L4 ... 97 L3
Amery Gv RF/TRAN CH42 ... 127 L3
Amesbury Dr
WGNS/IIMK WN3 ... 78 E3
Amherst Rd AIG/SPK L17 ... 129 L3
Amis Gv GOL/RIS/CU WA3 ... 93 G5
Amity St TOX L8 ... 113 H8
Amos Av LITH L21 ... 83 L5
Ampleforth Cl KKBY L32 ... 85 L4
Ampthill Rd AIG/SPK L17 ... 129 L3
Ampulla Rd NG/CROX L11 ... 98 E2
Ancaster Rd AIG/SPK L17 ... 129 L3
Ancholme Cl RAIN/WH L35 ... 101 J7
The Anchorage LYMM WA13 ... 139 M2
NSTN CH64 ... 152 E6
VAUX/LVPD L3 ... 112 F7
Anchor Cl RUNC WA7 ... 150 F7
Anchor St CHTN/BK PR9 ... 3 H3
Ancient Mdw WLT/FAZ L9 ... 84 D6
Ancroft Rd DV/KA/FCH L14 ... 115 J2
Ancrum Rd NWD/KWIPK L33 ... 73 M7
Anders Dr NWD/KWIPK L33 ... 74 C8
Anderson Av BTL L20 ... 6 C2
Anderson Cl PEN/TH CH61 ... 126 C7
RAIN/WH L35 ... 117 M4
WARRN/WOL WA2 ... 122 D3
Anderson Rd LITH L21 ... 83 M4
Anderson St EV L5 ... 97 G7
Anderton Rd CHLY/EC PR7 ... 31 M4
Anderton St CHLY/EC PR7 ... 32 E6
CHLYE PR6 ... 44 C6
WGNE/HIN WN2 ... 5 L6
Anderton Ter HUY L36 ... 115 L3
Anderton Wy WGNE/HIN WN2 ... 69 K3
Andover Cl
WARRN/WOL WA2 ... 122 A4
Andover Crs WGNS/IIMK WN3 ... 78 E3
Andover Rd RNFD/HAY WA11 ... 91 G5
Andover Wy WLTN L25 ... 131 M5
Andreas Cl STHP PR8 ... 3 G9
Andrew Av MGHL L31 ... 85 J2
WGNW/BIL/O WN5 ... 78 A8
Andrew Cl WDN WA8 ... 133 L5
Andrews Cl FMBY L37 ... 59 G4
Andrews La FMBY L37 ... 59 G4
Andrew St ANF/KKDL L4 ... 97 H4
Andrew's Wk HES CH60 ... 141 K5
Andrews Yort FMBY L37 ... 59 G4
Anfield Rd ANF/KKDL L4 ... 97 H6
Angela St EHL/KEN L7 ... 113 K5
Angers La MGHL L31 ... 73 K7
Anglesea Rd WLT/FAZ L9 ... 97 H2
Anglesea Wy TOX L8 ... 129 H1
Anglesey Cl EP CH65 ... 163 L4
Anglesey Rd WAL/EG CH44 ... 95 K8
WKBY CH48 ... 124 C2
Anglezark Cl EHL/KEN L7 ... 113 K3
Anglezarke Rd CHLYE PR6 ... 44 C6
Anglo Cl WLT/FAZ L9 ... 84 E5
Angus Av LEIGH WN7 ... 81 M6
Angus Rd BEB CH63 ... 143 L7
NG/CROX L11 ... 98 B5
Aniline St CHLYE PR6 ... 33 G5
Anjou Bvd WGNW/BIL/O WN5 ... 68 A5
Annandale Cl NWD/KWIPK L33 ... 73 M7
Annandale Gdns SKEL WN8 ... 66 C6
Annan Gv AIMK WN4 ... 80 A8
Ann Cl GTS/LS CH66 ... 155 M6
Anne Av STHP PR8 ... 35 G7
Anne Gv STHEL WA9 ... 102 E6
Annerley St EHL/KEN L7 ... 113 L5
Annesley Crs WGNS/IIMK WN3 ... 79 H2
Annesley Rd AIG/SPK L17 ... 129 L3
WAL/EG CH44 ... 111 K2
Anne St STHEL WA9 ... 118 F2
Annette Av NEWLW WA12 ... 91 J8
Annie Rd BTL L20 ... 83 M7
Annie St WARRN/WOL WA2 ... 15 G3
Ann St RUNC WA7 ... 19 J2
SKEL WN8 ... 65 G4
Ann St West WDN WA8 ... 16 E6
Anscot Av BEB CH63 ... 128 B7
Ansdell Dr ECCL WA10 ... 88 D8
Ansdell Gv CHTN/BK PR9 ... 25 J1
Ansdell Rd WDN WA8 ... 134 D3
WGNW/BIL/O WN5 ... 67 M8
Ansdell Villas' Rd RAIN/WH L35 ... 117 L1
Ansford Av WGNE/HIN WN2 ... 80 D5
Anson Cl WARRN/WOL WA2 ... 122 A3
Anson Pl VAUX/LVPD L3 ... 13 L5
WGNW/BIL/O WN5 ... 67 L5
Anson St VAUX/LVPD L3 ... 13 L6
WGNW/BIL/O WN5 ... 68 B6
Anstey Cl MOR/LEA CH46 ... 109 K4
Anstey Rd CLB/OSW/ST L13 ... 114 D2
Ansty Cl RNFD/HAY WA11 ... 89 M8
Anthony's Wy HES CH60 ... 141 J6
Anthorn Cl CL/PREN CH43 ... 126 F1
Anthorn Rd WGNS/IIMK WN3 ... 79 G2
Antler Ct AIMK WN4 ... 79 K7
Antonio St BTL L20 ... 7 L8
Antons Cl HLWD L26 ... 132 B7
Antons Rd HLWD L26 ... 132 B7
PEN/TH CH61 ... 126 B8
Antony Rd WARRS WA4 ... 137 K4
Antrim Cl RNFD/HAY WA11 ... 90 E7
WGNS/IIMK WN3 ... 78 E3
Antrim Dr GTS/LS CH66 ... 163 H3
Antrim Rd WARRN/WOL WA2 ... 121 J3
Antrim St CLB/OSW/ST L13 ... 98 A6
Anvil Cl BTL L20 ... 6 E2
WGNW/BIL/O WN5 ... 66 F8
The Anzacs PS/BROM CH62 ... 128 E7
Anzio Rd HUY L36 ... 115 M1
Apollo Crs NWD/KWIPK L33 ... 86 A1
Apollo Wy NPK/KEN L6 ... 97 K8
NTHTN L30 ... 84 B1
Apostles Wy NWD/KWIPK L33 ... 73 M8
Appin Rd BIRK CH41 ... 11 J8
Appleby Cl WDN WA8 ... 133 L5
Appleby Dr NTHTN L30 ... 83 L2
Appleby Gn WD/CROXPK L12 ... 98 F7
Appleby Gv PS/BROM CH62 ... 143 L7
Appleby Rd NTHLY L27 ... 132 C1
NWD/KWIPK L33 ... 86 A1
WARRN/WOL WA2 ... 121 L2
Applecorn Cl STHEL WA9 ... 102 F7
Applecross Cl
GOL/RIS/CU WA3 ... 107 J7
Appledale Dr GTS/LS CH66 ... 163 J5
Apple Dell Av
GOL/RIS/CU WA3 ... 92 E4
Appledore Cl SPK/HALE L24 ... 146 D1
Appledore Gv STHEL WA9 ... 118 E1
Appleford Cl WARRS WA4 ... 138 A6
Applegarth MOR/LEA CH46 ... 109 L7
Applethwaite WGNE/HIN WN2 ... 69 K5
Appleton Dr EP CH65 ... 163 H2
GR/UP/WCH CH49 ... 126 A2
Appleton Rd ANF/KKDL L4 ... 97 J4
LITH L21 ... 83 J4
SKEL WN8 ... 65 H3
STHEL WA9 ... 9 L8
WDN WA8 ... 16 E1
Appleton St WDN WA8 ... 16 E7
WGNS/IIMK WN3 ... 4 D4
Appleton Village WDN WA8 ... 16 D1
Appletree Cl CALD/MH L18 ... 130 E4
Apple Tree Cl STBRV L28 ... 99 K5
Apple Tree Gv GTS/LS CH66 ... 163 H5
Appletree Gv WARRN/WOL WA2 ... 122 B3
Appley Cl WGNNW/ST WN6 ... 54 E3
Appley La North
WGNNW/ST WN6 ... 54 E6
Appley La South SKEL WN8 ... 54 E7
April Gv NPK/KEN L6 ... 97 M8
April Ri NTHTN L30 ... 84 A2
Apsley Av WAL/NB CH45 ... 95 K7
Apsley Brow MGHL L31 ... 72 D4
Apsley Gv BEB CH63 ... 128 C7
Apsley Rd PS/BROM CH62 ... 128 D5
WD/CROXPK L12 ... 98 E7
Aquarius Cl DV/KA/FCH L14 ... 115 J1
Aragon Cl MGHL L31 ... 73 G2
Aran Cl SPK/HALE L24 ... 147 M3
Arborn Dr GR/UP/WCH CH49 ... 110 C7
Arbour La NWD/KWIPK L33 ... 86 C4
WGNNW/ST WN6 ... 55 K4
Arbour St STHP PR8 ... 3 J6
Arbury Av RNFD/HAY WA11 ... 89 M7
Arbury La WARRN/WOL WA2 ... 105 L7
Arcade St WGN WN1 ... 4 F4
Arcadia Av MGHL L31 ... 72 F2
Archbishop Worlock Ct
VAUX/LVPD L3 ... 12 E2
Archer Av WARRS WA4 ... 138 A3
Archer Cl ANF/KKDL L4 ... 97 G6
Archerfield Rd CALD/MH L18 ... 130 D4
Archer Gv STHEL WA9 ... 103 G1
Archers Gn PS/BROM CH62 ... 155 G1
Archer St ANF/KKDL L4 ... 97 G6
Archers Wy
GR/UP/WCH CH49 ... 126 C3
GTS/LS CH66 ... 163 G4
Arch La AIMK WN4 ... 90 C2
Archway Rd HUY L36 ... 116 A3
Arcon Rd CHLY/EC PR7 ... 43 G4
Arctic Rd BTL L20 ... 6 D4
Arden WDN WA8 ... 133 J3
Arden Cl GOL/RIS/CU WA3 ... 107 K7
STHP PR8 ... 34 C7
Arden Dr NSTN CH64 ... 153 G7
Ardennes Rd HUY L36 ... 116 A2
Arderne Cl BEB CH63 ... 143 K3
Ardern Lea FROD/HEL WA6 ... 166 F4
Ardleigh Av STHP PR8 ... 36 A2
Ardleigh Cl CLB/OSW/ST L13 ... 114 B3
Ardleigh Gv CLB/OSW/ST L13 ... 114 B3
Ardleigh Pl CLB/OSW/ST L13 ... 114 B3
Ardleigh Rd CLB/OSW/ST L13 ... 114 A3
Ardmore Rd CALD/MH L18 ... 130 C3
Ardrossan Rd ANF/KKDL L4 ... 97 L5
Ardville Rd NG/CROX L11 ... 97 M2
Ardwick Rd SPK/HALE L24 ... 147 H2
Ardwick St STHEL WA9 ... 9 K5
Argameols Cl STHP PR8 ... 25 H8
Argarmeols Gv FMBY L37 ... 47 G8
Argarmeols Rd FMBY L37 ... 47 G7
Argo Rd CSBY/WL L22 ... 82 F4
Argos Pl BTL L20 ... 7 J9
Argos Rd BTL L20 ... 7 J9
Argyle Rd ALL/GAR L19 ... 130 E7
ANF/KKDL L4 ... 97 K7
CHTN/BK PR9 ... 24 F4
Argyle St BIRK CH41 ... 11 J7
CLVPS L1 ... 13 G9
ECCL WA10 ... 8 F1
WGNE/HIN WN2 ... 69 M8
WGNW/BIL/O WN5 ... 68 B7
Argyle Street Hamilton Sq
BIRK CH41 ... 11 K5
Argyle St South BIRK CH41 ... 11 H8
Argyll Av PS/BROM CH62 ... 154 F1
Argyll Cl AIMK WN4 ... 90 E1
Aries Cl DV/KA/FCH L14 ... 99 J8
Ariss Gv RAIN/WH L35 ... 101 J8
Arkenshaw Rd
GOL/RIS/CU WA3 ... 106 C6
Arkenstone Cl WDN WA8 ... 133 L3
Arkle Rd CL/PREN CH43 ... 111 H5
Arkles Rd ANF/KKDL L4 ... 97 J7
Arklow Dr SPK/HALE L24 ... 147 M3
Ark Royal Wy BIRK CH41 ... 11 L9

Arkwood Cl PS/BROM CH62 143 L2
Arkwright Ct RUNC WA7 150 B2
Arkwright Rd RUNC WA7 150 B2
Arlescourt Rd WD/CROXPK L12 98 E8
Arley Av WARRS WA4 137 M4
Arley Cl CL/PREN CH43 110 E7
WGNE/HIN WN2 69 K3
Arley Dr WDN WA8 133 K3
Arley La CHLY/EC PR7 57 H3
WGN WN1 56 F4
WGNE/HIN WN2 56 F5
Arley St CHLY/EC PR7 32 F5
WGNE/HIN WN2 80 A1 1
Arlington Av CALD/MH L18 114 B8 1
Arlington Cl STHP PR8 34 C8
Arlington Dr GOL/RIS/CU WA3 93 L5
LEIGH WN7 93 L5
WARRW/BUR WA5 136 A1
Arlington Rd WAL/NB CH45 95 G7 1
Armill Rd NG/CROX L11 98 E2
Armitage Gdns
CALD/MH L18 130 D4 1
Armitstead St
WGNE/HIN WN2 80 F1 2
Armley Rd ANF/KKDL L4 97 K6
Armour Av
WARRN/WOL WA2 121 K3 2
Armoury Bank AIMK WN4 91 K2 2
The Armoury
WD/CROXPK L12 98 D6 1
Armscot Cl WLTN L25 131 K6
Armscot Pl WLTN L25 131 K6
Armstrong Cl GOL/RIS/CU WA3 122 F1
Armstrong Quay
VAUX/LVPD L3 129 H2 1
Armstrong St WGNE/HIN WN2 69 J2 1
Armthorpe Dr GTS/LS CH66 155 K8
Arncliffe Dr
WARRW/BUR WA5 104 B7 1
Arncliffe Rd WLTN L25 131 M4
Arndale RUNC WA7 150 A8
Arnham Rd HUY L36 115 M1
Arnhem Crs WARRN/WOL WA2 14 F1
Arnian Rd RNFD/HAY WA11 76 B6
Arnian Wy RNFD/HAY WA11 76 B6
Arnold Av ECCL WA10 8 B2
Arnold Cl STHEL WA9 9 L9
TOX L8 113 J7 1
Arnold Gv WAV L15 114 C5 2
Arnold Pl CHLY/EC PR7 32 C8 1
WDN WA8 133 L6
Arnold St TOX L8 113 H7 1
WAL/NB CH45 95 K8 2
Arno Rd CL/PREN CH43 127 K2
Arnot Cl ECCL WA10 8 F2
Arnot St ANF/KKDL L4 97 H4
Arnot Wy BEB CH63 127 M7
Arnside LITH L21 83 M5
Arnside Av RAIN/WH L35 117 J1
RNFD/HAY WA11 90 C7
WGNE/HIN WN2 69 J6
Arnside Gv WARRS WA4 137 K3
Arnside Rd CHTN/BK PR9 3 J3
CL/PREN CH43 10 B9
EHL/KEN L7 113 L4
HUY L36 115 K3
WAL/NB CH45 95 K8
WGNW/BIL/O WN5 67 J5
Arnside Ter CHTN/BK PR9 3 K3
Arpley Rd WARR WA1 14 E8
Arpley St WARR WA1 14 C6
Arrad St EHL/KEN L7 13 L9
Arran Av EP CH65 163 L4
Arran Cl RNFD/HAY WA11 90 A7 1
WARRN/WOL WA2 122 C3
Arran Dr FROD/HEL WA6 160 E6
Arranmore Rd CALD/MH L18 130 C3
Arrowe Av MOR/LEA CH46 109 M6
Arrowe Brook La
GR/UP/WCH CH49 126 A4
Arrowe Brook Rd
GR/UP/WCH CH49 126 B3
Arrowe Park Rd
GR/UP/WCH CH49 126 C2
Arrowe Rd GR/UP/WCH CH49 125 M2
Arrowe Side GR/UP/WCH CH49 126 A1
Arrowsmith Rd RNFD/HAY WA11 91 H6
Arthur Av EP CH65 20 D5
Arthur St ALL/GAR L19 130 F8 1
BIRK CH41 10 E3
RUNC WA7 18 F4
WARRN/WOL WA2 14 C4
Arundel Av AIG/SPK L17 113 L7
WAL/NB CH45 95 H7
Arundel Cl PEN/TH CH61 126 A8
Arundel Rd STHP PR8 35 H5
Arundel St ANF/KKDL L4 7 M9
TOX L8 113 J7
WGNW/BIL/O WN5 68 B7
Arvon St BTL L20 83 M7
Asbridge St TOX L8 113 K7
Asbury Cl CALD/MH L18 130 F2
Asbury Rd WAL/NB CH45 94 F7
Ascot Av LITH L21 83 J5
RUNC WA7 149 K7
Ascot Cl STHP PR8 2 A8
WARR WA1 123 G6
WARRS WA4 138 E3
Ascot Dr BEB CH63 128 B8
GTS/LS CH66 162 F2
NWD/KWIPK L33 74 A8
Ascot Gv BEB CH63 128 B8
Ascot Pk CSBY/BLUN L23 83 H1 1
Ascroft Av WGNNW/ST WN6 68 B2
Ascroft Rd WLT/FAZ L9 84 D5 1
Ascroft St WGN WN1 5 J5
Ash Av NEWLW WA12 104 E3
Ashbank Rd NG/CROX L11 98 C3
Ashberry Dr WARRS WA4 138 D8
Ashbourne Av CSBY/BLUN L23 82 E1
NTHTN L30 84 A3
RUNC WA7 149 K7
WGNE/HIN WN2 69 H3
Ashbourne Cl GTS/LS CH66 163 G5
LEIGH WN7 81 M4 1
Ashbourne Crs HUY L36 115 K3
Ashbourne Rd AIG/SPK L17 129 L4
WARRW/BUR WA5 120 D8
Ashbrook Av RUNC WA7 161 H1 1
Ashbrook Crs
WARRN/WOL WA2 121 M5
Ashbrook Dr WLT/FAZ L9 84 E7
Ash Brow SKEL WN8 53 K4
Ashburn Av NWD/KWIPK L33 86 A1
Ashburton Av CL/PREN CH43 111 H7
Ashburton Rd CL/PREN CH43 111 G7
WAL/EG CH44 111 K1 2
WKBY CH48 124 D2
Ashbury Cl RUNC WA7 150 F3 2
Ashbury Dr RNFD/HAY WA11 90 F6
Ashbury Rd DV/KA/FCH L14 99 K7
Ashby Cl HOY CH47 109 K4 2
Ashby Gv LEIGH WN7 81 L5 1
Ashby Rd WGNS/IIMK WN3 79 K2
Ashby St CHLY/EC PR7 32 E7
Ash Cl GTS/LS CH66 163 H4
ORM L39 50 F8
WAV L15 114 A5
WGNNW/ST WN6 54 F6
Ashcombe Rd DV/KA/FCH L14 114 E2
Ash Crs HUY L36 116 A5
Ashcroft Av ORM L39 51 H7
Ashcroft Dr PEN/TH CH61 141 H3
Ashcroft Rd FMBY L37 59 H4
NWD/KWIPK L33 86 E2
Ashcroft St BTL L20 6 F5
STHEL WA9 9 M5
WGNE/HIN WN2 81 G1 1
Ashdale HUY L36 115 M3
Ashdale Cl FMBY L37 58 E3
Ashdale Pk GR/UP/WCH CH49 125 K2
Ashdale Rd CALD/MH L18 114 C8
CSBY/WL L22 82 F3
WGNS/IIMK WN3 79 J3
WLT/FAZ L9 97 J1
Ashdown Crs STHEL WA9 118 E1
Ashdown Dr GR/UP/WCH CH49 125 L3
Ashdown Gv HLWD L26 132 C4
Ashdown La GOL/RIS/CU WA3 107 J8
Ashfarm Ct DV/KA/FCH L14 115 H2 1
Ashfield RAIN/WH L35 117 M2 1
WAV L15 113 M5
Ashfield Av WGNE/HIN WN2 81 H1
Ashfield Crs PS/BROM CH62 143 M5
WGNW/BIL/O WN5 78 A8
Ashfield Dr WGNE/HIN WN2 57 L8
Ashfield Park Dr
WGNNW/ST WN6 56 B5
Ashfield Rd AIG/SPK L17 129 M3
CHLY/EC PR7 32 D6
CHLYE PR6 44 D5
PS/BROM CH62 143 L5
Ashfield Rd North EP CH65 20 C4
Ashford Cl HLWD L26 132 A6
Ashford Ri WGN WN1 68 D1
Ashford Rd BIRK CH41 10 F9
HOY CH47 108 E5
Ash Gv CHLY/EC PR7 32 E8
FMBY L37 58 E4
GTS/LS CH66 155 L7
LITH L21 83 J7
RAIN/WH L35 117 G1
RNFD/HAY WA11 76 B7
RUNC WA7 19 M8
SKEL WN8 64 F4
STHEL WA9 118 E1
WAL/NB CH45 95 L6
WARRS WA4 15 K9
WAV L15 113 M5
WGNNW/ST WN6 56 B5
WGNW/BIL/O WN5 67 H7
Ash Grove Crs
WGNW/BIL/O WN5 77 M7
Ashland Av AIMK WN4 91 J1
WGN WN1 68 E3 1
Ashlands FROD/HEL WA6 160 E6
Ash La WARRS WA4 138 A5
WDN WA8 133 H5
WGNE/HIN WN2 69 J3
Ashlar Gv AIG/SPK L17 130 A3 1
Ashlar Rd AIG/SPK L17 130 A3
CSBY/WL L22 83 G3
Ashlea Rd PEN/TH CH61 141 H2
Ashleigh Rd MGHL L31 73 H6
Ashley Av HOY CH47 109 H4
Ashley Cl NWD/KWIPK L33 74 A8 1
RAIN/WH L35 117 M3 1
WARRS WA4 138 E2
Ashley Dr LEIGH WN7 81 L5
Ashley Rd CHTN/BK PR9 3 K4
RUNC WA7 149 M3
SKEL WN8 65 K2
WGNE/HIN WN2 81 K2
Ashley St RF/TRAN CH42 128 B3 2
Ashley Wy WDN WA8 16 D7
Ashley Wy West WDN WA8 16 B6
Ashmead Rd SKEL WN8 65 J1
Ashmore Cl GOL/RIS/CU WA3 123 J2
Ashmuir Hey KKBY L32 86 B4
Ashover Av DV/KA/FCH L14 115 J1
Ash Priors WDN WA8 133 M2
Ashridge St RUNC WA7 18 F2
Ashridge Wy WGNW/BIL/O WN5 67 K4
Ash Rd BEB CH63 128 B6
CHLY/EC PR7 43 G5
CHNE CH2 165 L2
LITH L21 83 J6
LYMM WA13 139 L2
RF/TRAN CH42 11 G9
RNFD/HAY WA11 91 G6 2
WARRN/WOL WA2 105 K7
WARRW/BUR WA5 136 B1
Ash St BTL L20 7 H3
GOL/RIS/CU WA3 92 D3
STHP PR8 3 K7
Ashton Av RAIN/WH L35 117 L3
Ashton Cl FROD/HEL WA6 160 E4
PS/BROM CH62 155 G2
RUNC WA7 149 H7 1
Ashton Dr FROD/HEL WA6 160 E3 1
FROD/HEL WA6 160 E4 1
WKBY CH48 124 C4
WLTN L25 131 K6
Ashton Heath AIMK WN4 91 L3
Ashton Rd GOL/RIS/CU WA3 92 B3
NEWLW WA12 91 L7
STHP PR8 35 H4
WGNW/BIL/O WN5 78 D5
Ashtons Green Dr STHEL WA9 103 H3
Ashton St CLB/OSW/ST L13 114 C2
VAUX/LVPD L3 13 M6
WARRN/WOL WA2 14 E4
Ashtree Cl NSTN CH64 153 H6
Ashtree Cft NSTN CH64 154 C6
Ashtree Dr NSTN CH64 153 J7
Ashtree Farm Ct NSTN CH64 154 C5 1
Ashtree Gv WD/CROXPK L12 99 G1
Ashtrees BRSC L40 40 E3
Ashurst Cl RNFD/HAY WA11 90 A7 2
SKEL WN8 65 J1 1
WLTN L25 131 K1
Ashurst Ct FMBY L37 59 G3
Ashurst Dr RNFD/HAY WA11 89 M7
Ashurst Gdns SKEL WN8 65 J1
Ashurst Rd SKEL WN8 65 K1
WGNNW/ST WN6 55 J3
Ash V WAV L15 114 A5
Ashville Rd BIRK CH41 10 D4
RUNC WA7 161 G2
WAL/EG CH44 111 L3
Ashwall St SKEL WN8 64 F5
Ashwater Rd NG/CROX L11 98 E3
Ash Wy HES CH60 141 K8
Ashwell Av GOL/RIS/CU WA3 92 F4
Ashwell St TOX L8 113 G6
Ashwood SKEL WN8 65 L2
Ashwood Av AIMK WN4 91 J3 1
GOL/RIS/CU WA3 92 F5
WARR WA1 15 L1
WGNE/HIN WN2 80 E6
Ashwood Cl GTS/LS CH66 162 F4 1
NWD/KWIPK L33 74 A8 2
Ashwood Ct CL/PREN CH43 110 E4
Ashwood Dr WD/CROXPK L12 98 F2
Ashwood La CHNE CH2 164 C8
Askern Rd KKBY L32 86 B5
Askett Cl RNFD/HAY WA11 90 E6
Askew Cl WAL/EG CH44 111 M1 1
Askew St ANF/KKDL L4 97 H4
Askham Cl TOX L8 113 K6 1
Askrigg Av GTS/LS CH66 155 K8
Askwith Rd WGNE/HIN WN2 81 H2
Asland Gdns CHTN/BK PR9 25 L1
Asmall Cl ORM L39 50 F7
Asmall La ORM L39 50 A5
Aspen Cl GTS/LS CH66 163 G4
HES CH60 141 M5 1
NWD/KWIPK L33 74 B7 1
Aspendale Rd
RF/TRAN CH42 127 M1 2
Aspen Gdns CHLY/EC PR7 32 D7 1
Aspen Gv FMBY L37 58 E4
TOX L8 113 L7
WARR WA1 122 C6
Aspenwood AIMK WN4 91 J3 2
Aspes Rd WD/CROXPK L12 99 G6
Aspinall Cl WARRN/WOL WA2 122 C2
Aspinall Crs FMBY L37 60 B4
Aspinall Rd WGNNW/ST WN6 55 K4
Aspinall St BIRK CH41 10 E3
WGNE/HIN WN2 80 C3 2
Aspinal St PR/KW L34 100 F7
Aspull Cl GOL/RIS/CU WA3 122 E1 1
Aspull Common LEIGH WN7 93 L4
Asquith Av BIRK CH41 10 D3
Asser Rd NG/CROX L11 98 A5
The Asshawes CHLYE PR6 44 B4
Assheton Wk SPK/HALE L24 148 A3 1
Assissian Crs NTHTN L30 84 A1 1
Astbury Cl GOL/RIS/CU WA3 93 K5 1
Aster Crs RUNC WA7 161 H1 2
Aster Dr NWD/KWIPK L33 73 M8
Asterfield Av BEB CH63 128 A6
Aster Rd RNFD/HAY WA11 91 H7
Astley Cl RNFD/HAY WA11 76 B6 2
WARRS WA4 137 K2
WDN WA8 133 L2
Astley Rd CHLY/EC PR7 32 D4
HUY L36 100 A7
Astley St CHLY/EC PR7 32 E4
Astmoor Bridge La RUNC WA7 150 B3
Astmoor Rd RUNC WA7 19 M2
Aston Av GOL/RIS/CU WA3 107 H8 1
Aston Cl CL/PREN CH43 127 H2 1
Aston Ct WARR WA1 122 E4
Aston Fields Rd RUNC WA7 161 M1
Aston Gn RUNC WA7 151 G7 1
Aston La RUNC WA7 161 K2
Aston St ALL/GAR L19 130 F8 2
Astonwood Rd
RF/TRAN CH42 127 M2 2
Astor Dr WARRS WA4 138 B5
Astor St ANF/KKDL L4 97 H3 1
Atheldene Rd ANF/KKDL L4 97 L3
Athelstan Cl PS/BROM CH62 143 M4
Atherleigh Wy LEIGH WN7 93 M2
Atherton Cl EV L5 97 G8 2
Atherton Dr GR/UP/WCH CH49 126 C2
Atherton Rd EP CH65 156 B7
WGNE/HIN WN2 69 M8
WLT/FAZ L9 84 E7
Atherton St CHLY/EC PR7 44 C7 1
ECCL WA10 8 E2
PR/KW L34 100 F7
WAL/NB CH45 95 J4
WGNE/HIN WN2 81 G5
WGNW/BIL/O WN5 68 B7 2
Athlone Rd WARRN/WOL WA2 121 J4
Athol Cl NEWLW WA12 104 B1
PS/BROM CH62 144 A8
Athol Crs WGNE/HIN WN2 81 K1
Athol Dr PS/BROM CH62 144 A8
Athole Gv CHTN/BK PR9 25 H6
Athol Gv CHLYE PR6 33 G7
Atholl Crs AIN/FAZ L10 84 F3
Atholl Gv WGNS/IIMK WN3 78 F4
Athol St BIRK CH41 11 K4
EV L5 96 F8
Atkinson Gv HUY L36 116 B1 1
Atkinson St WGNE/HIN WN2 80 D5 1
Atlantic Rd BTL L20 6 E4
Atlantic Wy NTHTN L30 84 A5 1
VAUX/LVPD L3 128 F1
Atlas Ct STHEL WA9 9 K5
Atlas Rd BTL L20 6 D4
Atlas St STHEL WA9 9 K5
Atterbury Cl WDN WA8 133 L3
Atterbury St TOX L8 113 G8
Attlee Av GOL/RIS/CU WA3 107 K1
Attlee Rd HUY L36 116 C2
Attwood St ANF/KKDL L4 97 H6 1
Atwell St NPK/KEN L6 113 J1
Auburn Cl WDN WA8 133 L2 1
Auburn Rd CLB/OSW/ST L13 98 A8
WAL/NB CH45 95 J6 1
The Aubynes WAL/NB CH45 95 G7 2
Auckery Av GTS/LS CH66 162 F2
Audie Murphy Rd
WARRW/BUR WA5 120 D7 1
Audlem Av CL/PREN CH43 127 H2
Audlem Cl RUNC WA7 161 H1 3
Audley St VAUX/LVPD L3 13 K5
Audre Cl WARRW/BUR WA5 119 M7
Aughton Cl
WGNW/BIL/O WN5 90 A1 1
Aughton Ms STHP PR8 2 F8
Aughton Park Dr ORM L39 62 F3
Aughton Rd BTL L20 83 M8
STHP PR8 2 E7
Aughton St ORM L39 62 F1
WGNE/HIN WN2 80 E1
Augusta Cl CLB/OSW/ST L13 114 C3
August Rd NPK/KEN L6 97 L8
August St BTL L20 7 H1
Aukland Gv RAIN/WH L35 101 M6
Aukland Rd CALD/MH L18 114 C8 1
Aurorean Cl NTHLY L27 115 M7 1
Austell Cl RNFD/HAY WA11 89 M6
Austin Av AIMK WN4 91 G1
ECCL WA10 101 L5
Austin Cl KKBY L32 85 M3
Austin St LEIGH WN7 81 M8 1
WAL/EG CH44 111 J3 1
Austral Av WARR WA1 122 D6
Australia La WARRS WA4 138 E4
Autumn Gv RF/TRAN CH42 128 A5
Avebury Cl GOL/RIS/CU WA3 93 G5 1
WDN WA8 135 G2
Aveley Cl WARR WA1 122 D6 1
Aveling Dr CHTN/BK PR9 23 J7
Avelon Cl CL/PREN CH43 110 F8 1
MGHL L31 61 K8
Avenham Cl CHTN/BK PR9 23 K8
Avenham Rd CHLY/EC PR7 32 E6 1
The Avenue ALL/GAR L19 131 G8
CHLYE PR6 44 C5
CHTN/BK PR9 23 H8
CHTN/BK PR9 26 B8
ECCL WA10 101 K2
HLWD L26 132 A6
HUY L36 116 A2
LYMM WA13 139 L4
NEWLW WA12 104 E1
ORM L39 50 F7
PS/BROM CH62 143 L5
RNFD/HAY WA11 76 B7
WGN WN1 68 F3
WGNNW/ST WN6 68 A1
WGNW/BIL/O WN5 77 M2
Averham Cl AIMK WN4 91 K3 1
Avery Cl WARRN/WOL WA2 122 A3
Avery Crs RNFD/HAY WA11 90 E6 1
Avery Rd RNFD/HAY WA11 90 E6
Avery Sq RNFD/HAY WA11 90 E6
Aviemore Cl AIMK WN4 90 F1 1
Aviemore Dr WARRN/WOL WA2 122 C2
Aviemore Rd
CLB/OSW/ST L13 114 B2 1
Avocet Cl NEWLW WA12 104 E1
WARRN/WOL WA2 121 M2
Avolon Rd WD/CROXPK L12 98 F8
Avon WDN WA8 133 J3
Avon Av WARRW/BUR WA5 136 A1
Avon Cl ANF/KKDL L4 97 G5
NWD/KWIPK L33 74 B7 2
Avondale EP CH65 20 B9
Avondale Av MGHL L31 72 E5
MOR/LEA CH46 110 B4
PS/BROM CH62 144 A8
Avondale Dr WDN WA8 133 K4
Avondale Rd CHLY/EC PR7 32 E6
CHTN/BK PR9 3 H1
HOY CH47 108 D6
RNFD/HAY WA11 90 E6
WAV L15 114 A7
WGN WN1 68 E3
Avondale Rd North
CHTN/BK PR9 24 E4
Avondale St WGNNW/ST WN6 56 A3
Avonmore Av CALD/MH L18 130 C2
Avon Rd AIMK WN4 80 A8
GOL/RIS/CU WA3 107 J3
WGNW/BIL/O WN5 67 L6
WGNW/BIL/O WN5 89 M2
Avon St BIRK CH41 111 H4
NPK/KEN L6 97 K8 2
Awelon Cl WD/CROXPK L12 98 E5
Axbridge Av STHEL WA9 102 F8
Axholme Cl PEN/TH CH61 126 D8
Axholme Rd PEN/TH CH61 126 C8
Ayala Cl BTL L20 84 B6
Aycliffe Rd RAIN/WH L35 101 M7 1
Aye Bridge Rd GOL/RIS/CU WA3 80 D8
Aylesbury Av CL/PREN CH43 127 G3
Aylesbury Cl GTS/LS CH66 162 E2
Aylesbury Crs WGNE/HIN WN2 81 L3
Aylesbury Rd WAL/NB CH45 95 L6
Aylesford Rd CLB/OSW/ST L13 114 C2
Aylsham Cl WDN WA8 133 L2
Aylsham Dr GR/UP/WCH CH49 110 C6
Aylton Rd HUY L36 115 K1
Aylward Pl BTL L20 6 F2 1
Ayr Cl STHP PR8 36 B1
Ayrefield Gv WGNNW/ST WN6 54 F7
Ayrefield La SKEL WN8 66 E1
Ayrshire Gdns ECCL WA10 8 D7
Ayrshire Rd ANF/KKDL L4 97 L5
Aysgarth Av WD/CROXPK L12 98 E7
Aysgarth Rd WAL/NB CH45 95 H7
Azalea Gv HLWD L26 131 M3
RUNC WA7 161 H1 2

B

Babbacombe Rd CHLDW L16 115 G7
WARRW/BUR WA5 136 A1
Babylon La CHLYE PR6 44 E4
Back Ashby St CHLY/EC PR7 32 E7
Back Barlow La ANF/KKDL L4 97 G5 1
Back Bath St STHP PR8 3 G2
Back Beau St EV L5 13 J2 1
Back Bedford St EHL/KEN L7 13 M9
Back Belmont Rd NPK/KEN L6 97 K8
Back Berry St CLVPS L1 13 J9
Back Blackfield Ter
ANF/KKDL L4 96 F6 1
Back Bold St CLVPS L1 13 H8
Back Booth St NEWLW WA12 104 C2 2
Back Boundary St EV L5 96 F7 1
Back Bridge St
NEWLW WA12 104 D2 2
Back Bridport St VAUX/LVPD L3 13 J6
Back Brook Pl WARRS WA4 15 L9
Back Canning St TOX L8 113 H5 4
Back Catharine St TOX L8 113 H5 5
Back Chadwick Mt EV L5 97 H6
Back Chatham Pl
EHL/KEN L7 113 K4 2
Back Colquitt St CLVPS L1 13 J9
Back Commutation St
VAUX/LVPD L3 13 J5 1
Back Crosland Ter
FROD/HEL WA6 166 D3
Back Cross La NEWLW WA12 104 D1 1
Back Drinkhouse La
LEY/BBR PR5 29 J3
Back Eastford Rd
WARRS WA4 137 J4 1
Back Egerton St North
TOX L8 113 H6 1
Back Falkner St South
TOX L8 113 J5 1
Backford Cl CL/PREN CH43 127 G2
RUNC WA7 150 E8 1
Backford Gdns GTS/LS CH66 163 H6 1
Backford Rd PEN/TH CH61 125 M8
Backford Wy CL/PREN CH43 127 G2
Back Forest Rd STHP PR8 3 L6
Back Forshaw St
WARRN/WOL WA2 15 G2
Back Gibson St TOX L8 113 H6
Back Gillmoss La NG/CROX L11 85 L7
Back Granton Rd EV L5 97 J7
Back Guilford St NPK/KEN L6 13 M2
Back High St RUNC WA7 19 G3
Back Holland Pl EHL/KEN L7 113 K4 3
Back Hope Pl CLVPS L1 13 K9 1
Back Huskisson St TOX L8 113 H6 2
Back Kelvin Gv TOX L8 113 J7 2
Back Knight St CLVPS L1 113 G5 2
Back La BRSC L40 39 G7
BRSC L40 40 D5
BRSC L40 52 F3
CHLY/EC PR7 31 H6
CHLY/EC PR7 31 K5
CSBY/BLUN L23 71 H5
FROD/HEL WA6 166 E3
LEY/BBR PR5 29 H1
ORM L39 60 F2
ORM L39 62 B7
ORM L39 74 C2
RNFD/HAY WA11 77 H8
SFTN L29 71 L6
SKEL WN8 53 J3
SKEL WN8 65 M7
SKEL WN8 66 A7
WARRW/BUR WA5 103 M6
WARRW/BUR WA5 135 J3
WGNNW/ST WN6 55 H4
Back La East BRSC L40 41 G4
Back Lawrence St
NEWLW WA12 104 C2 3
Back Leeds St VAUX/LVPD L3 12 D4
Back Legh St NEWLW WA12 104 C2 2
Back Lime St CLVPS L1 13 H7
Back Little Canning St
TOX L8 113 H6 3
Back Luton Gv ANF/KKDL L4 97 H5 1
Back Market St NEWLW WA12 104 C1
WGNE/HIN WN2 69 M8 3
Back Maryland St CLVPS L1 13 K9 2
Back Mersey Vw CSBY/WL L22 82 E3
Back Mesnes St WGN WN1 4 F2
Back Moss La BRSC L40 39 H6
Back Mt CHLY/EC PR7 32 E5 1
Back Mount St CSBY/WL L22 82 F4 2
Back Mount Vernon Gn
EHL/KEN L7 113 J3 1
Back Mulberry St TOX L8 113 H5 7
Back Oliver St BIRK CH41 11 K6 1
Back Orford St WAV L15 114 B5
Back O the Town La HTWN L38 71 G2
Back Percy St TOX L8 113 H6
Back Pickop St VAUX/LVPD L3 12 F5 1
Back Railway Vw CHLY/EC PR7 44 C7
Back Renshaw St CLVPS L1 13 K9 3
Back Rockfield Rd ANF/KKDL L4 97 H6
Back Rw SKEL WN8 66 E6 2
Back St Bride St TOX L8 113 H5 8
Back Sandon St TOX L8 113 H6 3
Back Sandstone Rd
CLB/OSW/ST L13 114 B1 1
Back School La SKEL WN8 64 E3
SKEL WN8 66 E6 3
Back Seaview HOY CH47 108 D6 1
Back Seel St CLVPS L1 13 H9
Back Sir Howard St TOX L8 113 H5 9
Back South Rd CSBY/WL L22 83 G4
Back Stanley Rd BTL L20 7 H4
Back Towerlands St
EHL/KEN L7 113 K4 3
Back Virginia St STHP PR8 3 H6
Back Wellesley Rd TOX L8 129 J1 1
Back Westminster Rd
ANF/KKDL L4 97 G5 2
Back Windsor Vw TOX L8 113 K6 2
Back Winstanley Rd
CSBY/WL L22 83 G3 1

Back York Ter EV L5 97 G7 2
Baclaw Cl WGN WN1 5 M2
Badbury Cl RNFD/HAY WA11 90 F6
Badby Wd NWD/KWIPK L33 86 B1
Baden Rd CLB/OSW/ST L13 114 D2
Bader Cl PEN/TH CH61 141 G2
Badger Bait NSTN CH64 153 H7
Badger Cl RUNC WA7 150 C7
Badgers Cl GTS/LS CH66 163 H5 1
Badgers Pk NSTN CH64 153 H7
Badgers Rake FMBY L37 46 E8
Badger's Set WKBY CH48 124 F7
Badger Wy CL/PREN CH43 127 G5 1
Badminton St TOX L8 129 H2 2
Baffin Cl MOR/LEA CH46 110 C1
Bagganley La CHLYE PR6 33 G4
Bagnall Cl WARRW/BUR WA5 120 E8
Bagnall St ANF/KKDL L4 97 J6
Bagot Av WARRW/BUR WA5 121 H5
Bagot St WAV L15 113 M6
Baguley Av WDN WA8 133 J8
Bahama Cl RNFD/HAY WA11 90 F5
Bahama Rd RNFD/HAY WA11 90 F5
Bailey Av EP CH65 156 B7
Bailey Dr BTL L20 84 A7
Baileys Cl WDN WA8 118 C8
Baileys La HLWD L26 132 C5
SPK/HALE L24 147 J4
Bailey St CLVPS L1 113 G5
Bainbridge Av GOL/RIS/CU WA3 93 H5
Bainton Cl KKBY L32 86 C6
Bainton Rd KKBY L32 86 C6
Baird Av BTL L20 6 C2
Baker Dr GTS/LS CH66 163 G2
Baker Rd RUNC WA7 18 B9
Bakers Green Rd HUY L36 116 A1
Baker's La CHTN/BK PR9 25 H2
Baker St NPK/KEN L6 113 J2 1
STHEL WA9 9 M5
WGNS/IIMK WN3 4 C8
Baker Wy NPK/KEN L6 113 J2
Bakewell Cl GTS/LS CH66 163 G5
Bakewell Dr WGNNW/ST WN6 68 C1
Bakewell Gv WLT/FAZ L9 84 D6 3
Bakewell Rd WARRW/BUR WA5 104 C6
Bala Cl WARRW/BUR WA5 121 G3 1
Bala Gv WAL/EG CH44 111 J2 1
Bala St ANF/KKDL L4 97 K7
Balcarres Av CALD/MH L18 114 B8 2
WGN WN1 69 G3
Balcarres Rd CHLY/EC PR7 32 D8 1
WGNE/HIN WN2 69 K1
Baldock Cl WARRS WA4 138 E2
Baldwin Av CHLDW L16 115 H5
Baldwin St ECCL WA10 9 G4
WGN WN1 5 H3
WGNE/HIN WN2 81 K2 1
WGNS/IIMK WN3 5 H6
WGNW/BIL/O WN5 67 K8
The Bales NTHTN L30 84 C1 1
Balfe St LITH L21 83 J7
Balfour Av BTL L20 6 F1 1
Balfour Rd BTL L20 6 E1
CL/PREN CH43 10 D8
STHP PR8 25 G8
WAL/EG CH44 111 J3
Balfour St ANF/KKDL L4 97 H6
ECCL WA10 8 A6
RUNC WA7 18 F5
Balham Cl WDN WA8 134 C1
Balharry Av RNFD/HAY WA11 91 H6 1
Balker Dr ECCL WA10 8 E1
Ballantrae Rd CALD/MH L18 130 E2
Ballantyne Dr CL/PREN CH43 110 E4 1
Ballantyne Gv BTL L20 84 A7
CLB/OSW/ST L13 98 A6
Ballantyne Pl CLB/OSW/ST L13 98 A6
Ballantyne Rd CLB/OSW/ST L13 98 A7
Ballantyne Wy
GOL/RIS/CU WA3 93 G5 2
Ballard Rd WKBY CH48 125 G2
Ballater Dr WARRN/WOL WA2 122 A1
Ball Av WAL/NB CH45 95 J5
Balliol Cl CL/PREN CH43 110 E4 2
Balliol Gv CSBY/WL L22 82 D3 1
Balliol Rd BTL L20 7 H7
Balliol Rd East BTL L20 7 K6
Balliol Wy AIMK WN4 91 H1
Ball's Pl STHP PR8 3 G4
Ball's Rd CL/PREN CH43 10 E8
Ball's Rd East BIRK CH41 10 E8
Balmer St STHEL WA9 101 M6
Balmoral CHLY/EC PR7 44 A7
Balmoral Av CSBY/BLUN L23 83 G2
GOL/RIS/CU WA3 92 F4
STHEL WA9 102 E6
Balmoral Cl NWD/KWIPK L33 74 A8 3
Balmoral Ct CLB/OSW/ST L13 98 A8
Balmoral Dr CHTN/BK PR9 25 K2
FMBY L37 59 G4
FROD/HEL WA6 166 D1 1
WGNE/HIN WN2 80 E1
Balmoral Gdns EP CH65 20 E9 1
Balmoral Rd AIMK WN4 91 J1 1
CHLY/EC PR7 30 E6 1
CHLY/EC PR7 32 D5
MGHL L31 72 E4 1
NPK/KEN L6 113 L2
WAL/NB CH45 95 K4
WARRS WA4 138 B3
WDN WA8 134 C1
WGNW/BIL/O WN5 68 A7
WLT/FAZ L9 84 C7 1
Balm St EHL/KEN L7 113 K3
Balniel Cl CHLY/EC PR7 32 D6
Balniel St STHEL WA9 118 F2
Balsham Cl WLTN L25 131 L6
Balshaw La CHLY/EC PR7 31 M4
Baltic Rd BTL L20 6 E4
Baltic St ANF/KKDL L4 97 J6
Baltimore St CLVPS L1 13 K9
Bamber Gdns CHTN/BK PR9 25 J5
Bamber St CHLY/EC PR7 32 D8 2
Bamboo Cl NTHLY L27 116 A7
Bamburgh Pl AIMK WN4 79 J8 1
Bamford Cl RUNC WA7 149 L7
Bamford Dr WGNE/HIN WN2 5 L1
Bampton Av RNFD/HAY WA11 89 K4
Bampton Rd CHLDW L16 114 F5
Banastre CHLY/EC PR7 32 C3 1
Banastre Dr NEWLW WA12 105 H2
Banastre Rd STHP PR8 2 F8
Banbury Av WLTN L25 131 L3
Banbury Dr WARRW/BUR WA5 136 E1
Banbury Rd WGNW/BIL/O WN5 77 M3
Banbury Wy CL/PREN CH43 127 G3
Bancroft Cl WLTN L25 131 L6
Bancroft Rd WDN WA8 134 F3
Bandon Cl SPK/HALE L24 147 M3 1
Banff Av BEB CH63 143 L8
Bangor Cl GTS/LS CH66 163 H5 2
Bangor Rd WAL/NB CH45 94 F7
Bangor St EV L5 96 E8
Banham Av WGNS/IIMK WN3 78 E2
Bank Av WGNW/BIL/O WN5 66 F8
Bankbrook WGNNW/ST WN6 67 M1 1
Bank Brow SKEL WN8 54 E8
Bankburn Rd CLB/OSW/ST L13 98 A7
Bank Cl NSTN CH64 153 J7
Bank Dene RF/TRAN CH42 128 C5
Bankes Av WGNW/BIL/O WN5 67 J7
Bankes' La RUNC WA7 149 G7
Bankfield SKEL WN8 65 L6
Bankfield Ct CLB/OSW/ST L13 98 B8
Bankfield La CHTN/BK PR9 25 K3
Bankfield Rd CLB/OSW/ST L13 98 B8
WDN WA8 133 K4
Bankfields Dr PS/BROM CH62 144 D8
Bankfield St BTL L20 96 D5
Bank Gdns
WARRW/BUR WA5 136 A1 1
Bankhall Cl WGNE/HIN WN2 81 K4
Bankhall La BTL L20 96 E6
Bankhall St BTL L20 96 E5
Bankhey NSTN CH64 153 H8
Bank House La FROD/HEL WA6 166 E1
Bankland Rd CLB/OSW/ST L13 98 B8 1
Bank La MGHL L31 73 L7
NWD/KWIPK L33 85 M1
Bank Pas GOL/RIS/CU WA3 92 C4 1
Bank Rd BTL L20 6 F4
SKEL WN8 54 E8
Banks Av HOY CH47 108 F5
Banksbarn SKEL WN8 65 L6
Banks Ct LEIGH WN7 81 M8 2
Banks Crs WARRS WA4 138 B1
Bankside HTWN L38 70 B2
RUNC WA7 151 G6
SKEL WN8 53 K3
Bankside Av AIMK WN4 79 J5
Bankside Rd RF/TRAN CH42 128 B5
Bank's La ALL/GAR L19 145 M1
SPK/HALE L24 146 B3
Bank Sq CHTN/BK PR9 3 G1
Bank's Rd ALL/GAR L19 130 E8
CHTN/BK PR9 22 F7
HES CH60 140 E5
SPK/HALE L24 146 A1
WKBY CH48 124 C4
Bank St BIRK CH41 11 K6
CHLY/EC PR7 32 E5 2
CHLY/EC PR7 44 B6
ECCL WA10 8 C6
GOL/RIS/CU WA3 92 C4
NEWLW WA12 104 B2
WARR WA1 14 E6 1
WDN WA8 149 J1
WGNE/HIN WN2 80 C2
WGNW/BIL/O WN5 68 A7 1
Bank's Wy ALL/GAR L19 145 M1 1
Bankville Rd RF/TRAN CH42 128 A2
Bankwood WGNNW/ST WN6 55 G7 1
Banner Cl CHLY/EC PR7 30 D6
Banner Hey RAIN/WH L35 116 F4
Bannerman St EHL/KEN L7 113 L5
Bannerman Ter CHLYE PR6 32 F3 1
Banner St ECCL WA10 8 E6
WAV L15 114 A6
WGNS/IIMK WN3 5 J9
Banning Cl BIRK CH41 11 G4
Bannister Gn CHLY/EC PR7 41 L2
Bannister La BRSC L40 41 G7
Bannister St CHLY/EC PR7 32 E6 2
Banstead Gv WAV L15 114 D6
Barbara Av AIN/FAZ L10 85 J6
Barbara St STHEL WA9 119 G2 1
Barbauld St WARR WA1 14 E6
Barberry Cl MOR/LEA CH46 109 K5 1
Barberry Crs NTHTN L30 84 C1
Barber St STHEL WA9 9 K4
Barbondale Cl
WARRW/BUR WA5 120 B6
Barbour Dr BTL L20 84 A7 1
Barbrook Cl WGNNW/ST WN6 55 K3 1
Barbrook Wy WLT/FAZ L9 97 K2
Barchester Dr AIG/SPK L17 129 L4
Barclay St TOX L8 129 H1 2
Barcombe Rd HES CH60 141 M4
Bardale Gv AIMK WN4 91 J2
Bardley Crs HUY L36 116 C6
Bardney Av GOL/RIS/CU WA3 92 B3
Bardon Cl WLTN L25 115 L8
Bardsay Rd ANF/KKDL L4 97 H4
Bardsey Cl EP CH65 163 L4 3
Bardsley Av WARRW/BUR WA5 121 H3
Bardsley Cl SKEL WN8 66 C6
Barford Cl CL/PREN CH43 110 D7 1
SKEL WN8 66 C6
STHP PR8 34 C7
WARRW/BUR WA5 120 D4
Barford Dr GOL/RIS/CU WA3 93 J5
Barford Gra NSTN CH64 154 D5
Barford Rd HUY L36 100 B7
SPK/HALE L24 131 K7
Barham Ct GOL/RIS/CU WA3 122 F1
Barington Dr RUNC WA7 151 G6
Barkbeth Rd HUY L36 99 L8
Barkeley Dr LITH L21 83 H7
Barker Cl HUY L36 116 B5 1
Barker La GR/UP/WCH CH49 125 M3
Barker Rd PEN/TH CH61 126 B7
Barker's Hollow Rd
WARRS WA4 151 J7
Barker St LEIGH WN7 81 L8
Barkerville Cl
CLB/OSW/ST L13 97 M6 1
Barker Wy NPK/KEN L6 97 K8
Barkfield Av FMBY L37 59 G1
Barkfield La FMBY L37 58 F1
Barkhill Rd AIG/SPK L17 130 B4
Barkiss Cl TOX L8 113 H8 1
Bark Rd LITH L21 83 L4
Barlborough Rd
WGNW/BIL/O WN5 67 M8
Barley Brook St WGNNW/ST WN6 4 B1
Barleycastle La WARRS WA4 138 F8
Barleyfield PEN/TH CH61 141 G1
Barley Mow Cl CH/BCN CH1 162 E3
Barley Rd WARRS WA4 138 E2
Barlow Av BEB CH63 128 C6
Barlow Gv STHEL WA9 103 J3 1
Barlow La ANF/KKDL L4 97 G5
Barlows Cl WLT/FAZ L9 84 F5
Barlow's La ORM L39 35 M8
WLT/FAZ L9 84 F5
Barlow St ANF/KKDL L4 97 G5
Barmouth Cl WARRW/BUR WA5 121 G3
Barmouth Rd WAL/NB CH45 94 F7
Barmouth Wy EV L5 96 E8
Barmskin La CHLY/EC PR7 41 L4
Barnack Cl WARR WA1 122 C5
Barnacre Dr NSTN CH64 152 D3
Barnacre La WKBY CH48 109 K7
Barnard Rd CL/PREN CH43 10 D8
Barnard St WARRW/BUR WA5 136 F2
Barn Cl NTHTN L30 84 C1
Barn Cft FROD/HEL WA6 166 E1
Barncroft RUNC WA7 150 F6
Barn Croft Rd HLWD L26 132 C6
The Barncroft
GR/UP/WCH CH49 125 M1 1
Barndale Rd CALD/MH L18 130 B1
Barnes Av WARRN/WOL WA2 122 D3
Barnes Cl WARRW/BUR WA5 120 C8
WDN WA8 134 F3 1
Barnes Dr MGHL L31 72 E1
Barnes Gn BEB CH63 143 J4
Barnes Rd ORM L39 63 G2
SKEL WN8 64 F4
WDN WA8 134 E3
Barnes St NPK/KEN L6 97 J8
Barneston Rd WDN WA8 135 G2
Barnet Cl EHL/KEN L7 113 L5
Barnett Av NEWLW WA12 104 A2
Barnfield Av RUNC WA7 150 F7
Barnfield Cl GTS/LS CH66 162 E3 1
HOY CH47 109 G4
NTHTN L30 84 A3
WD/CROXPK L12 98 D7 1
Barnfield Dr SKEL WN8 66 A6 1
WD/CROXPK L12 98 D7
Barnfield Rd WARR WA1 122 E6
Barngill Gv WGNS/IIMK WN3 79 G2
Barnham Cl GOL/RIS/CU WA3 92 C5 1
SPK/HALE L24 146 D1
Barnham Dr CHLDW L16 115 G6
Barn Hey HOY CH47 108 C8
Barn Hey Crs HOY CH47 109 H6
Barn Hey Gn WD/CROXPK L12 98 D7
Barn Hey Rd NWD/KWIPK L33 86 C3
Barnhill Rd WAV L15 114 C7
Barnhurst Cl CHLDW L16 115 G6
Barnhurst Rd CHLDW L16 115 G6
Barn La GOL/RIS/CU WA3 92 B6
Barnmeadow Rd WLTN L25 115 J8
Barnsbury Rd ANF/KKDL L4 97 K3
Barnsdale Av PEN/TH CH61 126 D8
Barnside CHLY/EC PR7 31 L2
Barnside Ct CHLDW L16 115 G6
Barnsley St WGNNW/ST WN6 68 C2
Barnstaple Wy
WARRW/BUR WA5 136 A1
Barnston La MOR/LEA CH46 110 A5 1
Barnston Rd HES CH60 141 L5
PEN/TH CH61 126 D7
WLT/FAZ L9 84 C6
Barnston Towers Cl HES CH60 141 L5
Barn St WDN WA8 16 C8
Barnswood Cl WARRS WA4 138 E4
Barnton Cl GOL/RIS/CU WA3 92 F6 1
Barn Wy NEWLW WA12 104 D2
Barnwell Av GOL/RIS/CU WA3 106 F1
WAL/EG CH44 95 K8 3
Barnwood Rd HUY L36 115 K1 1
Baron Cl WARR WA1 122 F6
Baroncroft Rd WLTN L25 131 H1
Baron's Cl WDN WA8 133 L5
Baron's Hey STBRV L28 99 H5
Barons Wy CHLY/EC PR7 31 M3
Barrack Sq WGN WN1 4 F4
Barracks Rd WGNE/HIN WN2 80 F4
Barracks Yd WGN WN1 4 E4
Barren Gv CL/PREN CH43 10 D9
Barrett Av STHP PR8 35 J3
Barrett Rd STHP PR8 35 J3
Barrie St LEIGH WN7 81 M5
Barrington Cl WGNS/IIMK WN3 78 F4
Barrington Dr STHP PR8 34 D8
Barrington Rd WAL/EG CH44 111 L2
WAV L15 114 A7
Barrison Gn BRSC L40 51 G3
Barron Meadow LEIGH WN7 81 M6 2
Barrow Av WARRN/WOL WA2 122 A3 1
Barrow Cl WD/CROXPK L12 98 E4 1
Barrowdale Rd GOL/RIS/CU WA3 92 D5
Barrowfield Rd ECCL WA10 88 C8
Barrow Hall La
WARRW/BUR WA5 120 A7 1
Barrow La GOL/RIS/CU WA3 105 L3
Barrow Nook La ORM L39 75 G2
Barrow's Green La WDN WA8 135 G3
Barrow's Rw WDN WA8 134 D1 2
Barrow St AIMK WN4 79 M8
ECCL WA10 9 G5
Barrule Cl WARRS WA4 137 M6 1
Barrymore Av WARRS WA4 138 B1
Barrymore Rd
CLB/OSW/ST L13 114 B2 2
RUNC WA7 149 K6
Barrymore Wy BEB CH63 143 K7
Barry St WARRS WA4 15 H8
Barsbank Cl LYMM WA13 139 L2 1
Barsbank La LYMM WA13 139 L2 2
Barston Av EP CH65 156 B8
Bar St WGNE/HIN WN2 80 C4
Bartholomew Cl RAIN/WH L35 118 A4
Bartlegate RUNC WA7 150 D8 1
Bartlett St WAV L15 114 A6
Barton Av WARRS WA4 138 C3
WGN WN1 68 D3
Barton Cl ECCL WA10 8 E4
HOY CH47 108 B7
LITH L21 83 J3
RUNC WA7 150 F6 1
Barton Clough
WGNW/BIL/O WN5 78 A8 1
Barton Hey Dr WKBY CH48 124 E7
Barton Heys Rd FMBY L37 58 F4
Barton Rd HOY CH47 108 C7
WLT/FAZ L9 97 H1 1
Bartons Cl CHTN/BK PR9 22 F8
Barton St BIRK CH41 10 F7 1
CL/PREN CH43 10 F6
GOL/RIS/CU WA3 92 C5
WGNE/HIN WN2 80 D2 1
WGNW/BIL/O WN5 67 K8 1
Barwell Av RNFD/HAY WA11 89 L7
Basil Cl CHLDW L16 115 G5
Basildon Cl STHEL WA9 102 A7 1
Basil Rd CHLDW L16 114 F5
Basing St ALL/GAR L19 130 E7
Baskervyle Cl HES CH60 141 J7
Baskervyle Rd HES CH60 141 J7
Baslow Av WGNE/HIN WN2 81 H1
Basnett St CLVPS L1 13 G7
Bassendale Rd PS/BROM CH62 144 A3
Bassenthwaite Av
CL/PREN CH43 110 F8 2
NWD/KWIPK L33 85 M1
RNFD/HAY WA11 89 J5
Bassett Gv WGNS/IIMK WN3 78 E3
Basswood Gn WGNE/HIN WN2 81 J2
Bates Crs ECCL WA10 101 M5
Bates La FROD/HEL WA6 166 F1
Batey Av RAIN/WH L35 117 K1
Batheaston Gv LEIGH WN7 81 M5 1
Batherton Cl WDN WA8 16 E6
Bathgate Wy NWD/KWIPK L33 73 M7
Bath St CSBY/WL L22 82 F5
ECCL WA10 8 F6
PS/BROM CH62 128 D8
STHP PR8 3 G2
VAUX/LVPD L3 12 C5
WARR WA1 14 D5
WGNE/HIN WN2 69 H3
Bath St North CHTN/BK PR9 3 H1
Bathurst Rd ALL/GAR L19 130 D6
Bathwood Dr NSTN CH64 153 G8 1
Batley St CLB/OSW/ST L13 114 C2
Battenberg St EHL/KEN L7 113 J3 2
Battersby La WARRN/WOL WA2 15 G3
Battersby St WGNE/HIN WN2 69 K5
Battersea Ct WDN WA8 134 B2 1
Battery Cl AIG/SPK L17 129 L3 1
Battery La WARR WA1 123 H7
Battle Wy FMBY L37 59 K3 1
Baucher Dr BTL L20 84 A6
Baucher Rd WGNS/IIMK WN3 68 B8
Baumville Dr BEB CH63 143 H3 1
Baverstock Cl WGNS/IIMK WN3 5 H7
Bawtry Ct WARRN/WOL WA2 122 A4
Baxter Cl RUNC WA7 150 F6 2
Baxters La STHEL WA9 102 F5
Baxter's Rw WGNE/HIN WN2 81 K3
Baxter St WARRW/BUR WA5 121 G8 1
WGNNW/ST WN6 56 B4
Baycliff Cl WGNE/HIN WN2 81 H2
Baycliffe LYMM WA13 139 M3
Baycliffe Cl RUNC WA7 149 M8
Baycliff Rd WD/CROXPK L12 99 G5
Bayfield Rd ALL/GAR L19 130 C6
Bayhorse La VAUX/LVPD L3 13 L5
Baysdale Cl TOX L8 129 J1
Bayswater Cl RUNC WA7 151 H1
Bayswater Gdns
WAL/NB CH45 94 F6 1
Bayswater Rd WAL/NB CH45 94 F7
Baythorne Rd ANF/KKDL L4 97 L3
Baytree Cl CHTN/BK PR9 22 F8 1
GTS/LS CH66 163 H4
Baytree Rd RF/TRAN CH42 128 A2
WGNNW/ST WN6 68 B3
WKBY CH48 125 H3
Bayview Dr WAL/NB CH45 94 F6
Bayvil Cl RUNC WA7 151 G6
Beacham Rd STHP PR8 25 G6
Beach Bank CSBY/WL L22 82 E3
Beachcroft Rd HOY CH47 108 F4
Beach Gv WAL/NB CH45 95 L6
Beach Lawn CSBY/WL L22 82 E4
Beach Priory Gdns STHP PR8 2 E5
Beach Rd HOY CH47 108 B7
LITH L21 83 K6 1
STHP PR8 2 C6
Beach Wk WKBY CH48 124 D5
Beacon Dr WKBY CH48 124 E3
Beacon Gv RNFD/HAY WA11 89 M7 1
Beacon La BRSC L40 53 J7
EV L5 97 H7 1
HES CH60 141 J5
SKEL WN8 53 L8
SKEL WN8 66 B3
Beacon Rd WGNE/HIN WN2 81 J5
WGNNW/ST WN6 55 K4
WGNW/BIL/O WN5 77 M7
Beaconsfield Cl BIRK CH41 128 B2 2
Beaconsfield Crs WDN WA8 134 C1
Beaconsfield Gv WDN WA8 134 D1 3
Beaconsfield Rd CHTN/BK PR9 25 H7
ECCL WA10 88 E8
LITH L21 83 H6
PS/BROM CH62 128 D6 1
RUNC WA7 18 D7
WDN WA8 134 D2
WLTN L25 131 G2
Beaconsfield St TOX L8 113 J7
Beaconsfield Ter CHLYE PR6 32 F3
The Beacons WGNNW/ST WN6 54 F6
Beacon St CHLY/EC PR7 32 F6
EV L5 96 D7
Beacon Vw WGNNW/ST WN6 54 E5
Beacon View Dr SKEL WN8 66 D6
Beadnell Dr WARRW/BUR WA5 136 A2
Beaford Cl WGNW/BIL/O WN5 67 K8
Beal Dr WGNE/HIN WN2 80 C3
Beames Cl EHL/KEN L7 113 L4 1
Beamont St WDN WA8 149 J1 1
Beardsmore Dr
GOL/RIS/CU WA3 93 G5
Bearncroft SKEL WN8 65 L7
Beasley Cl GTS/LS CH66 162 F2
Beatrice Av BEB CH63 128 A6
Beatrice St BTL L20 7 J8
WARRS WA4 15 J9
Beattock Cl NWD/KWIPK L33 73 M7
Beatty Av CHLY/EC PR7 32 D7
WARRN/WOL WA2 121 L4
Beatty Cl RAIN/WH L35 116 F3
WKBY CH48 124 E7 1
Beatty Rd CLB/OSW/ST L13 114 C3
STHP PR8 25 G8
Beauclair Dr WAV L15 114 D7
Beaufort FMBY L37 59 J3 1
Beaufort Cl ORM L39 62 C4
RUNC WA7 149 K6
WARRW/BUR WA5 120 C8
WDN WA8 133 J5 1
Beaufort Dr WAL/EG CH44 111 G1
Beaufort Rd BIRK CH41 111 J4
Beaufort St STHEL WA9 9 M9
TOX L8 113 G7
WARRW/BUR WA5 137 G1
WGNE/HIN WN2 69 M8 4
WGNW/BIL/O WN5 68 A7 2
Beaumaris Cl LEIGH WN7 81 L8 1
Beaumaris Dr EP CH65 163 M3
PEN/TH CH61 126 D7
Beaumaris Rd WAL/NB CH45 94 F7
WGNE/HIN WN2 81 J2
Beaumaris St BTL L20 96 D5
Beaumont Av ECCL WA10 8 A4
Beaumont Crs ORM L39 62 F3
Beaumont Dr AIN/FAZ L10 85 G4
Beaumont Gv
WGNW/BIL/O WN5 67 K5 1
Beaumont St TOX L8 113 K6
Beau St VAUX/LVPD L3 13 J2
Beauworth Av
GR/UP/WCH CH49 125 L2 1
Beaverbrook Av
GOL/RIS/CU WA3 107 K1
Beaver Ct AIMK WN4 79 L7
Beaver Gv WLT/FAZ L9 84 C7
Beavers La SKEL WN8 65 M7
Bebington Rd GTS/LS CH66 162 F1
PS/BROM CH62 128 C7
RF/TRAN CH42 127 M3
Bebles Rd ORM L39 62 E2
Bechers WDN WA8 133 K2
Bechers Rw WLT/FAZ L9 84 B6
Beck Cl AIN/FAZ L10 85 K6
Beckenham Av
CALD/MH L18 114 B8 3
Beckenham Rd WAL/NB CH45 95 K4 1
Becket St ANF/KKDL L4 96 F6
Beckett Cl NWD/KWIPK L33 86 E5
Beckett Gv BEB CH63 127 M6 1
Beck Gv RNFD/HAY WA11 89 K5 1
Beck Rd BTL L20 83 L8
Beckwith WGNE/HIN WN2 80 D2 2
Beckwith St BIRK CH41 10 E3
Beckwith St East BIRK CH41 11 J5 1
Becky St NPK/KEN L6 97 K8
Becontree Rd WD/CROXPK L12 114 F1
Bective St EHL/KEN L7 113 L5 3
Bedburn Dr HUY L36 115 J2
Bedford Av EP CH65 163 J3
MGHL L31 73 G7
RF/TRAN CH42 128 A4
Bedford Av East EP CH65 163 K3
Bedford Cl HUY L36 116 C2
TOX L8 113 H5 10
Bedford Pl AIMK WN4 79 J8
BTL L20 6 F8 1
LITH L21 83 H6 1
RF/TRAN CH42 128 C3
Bedford Rd ANF/KKDL L4 7 M7
BTL L20 7 G8
RF/TRAN CH42 128 B3
STHP PR8 35 J3
WAL/NB CH45 95 K7
Bedford Rd East
RF/TRAN CH42 128 C3
Bedford St STHEL WA9 102 F3
WARRS WA4 137 L5
WGN WN1 5 J2
WGNW/BIL/O WN5 67 L8 1
Bedford St North
EHL/KEN L7 13 M8 1
Bedford St South EHL/KEN L7 13 M9
Beecham Cl HUY L36 115 M4 1
Beech Av AIG/SPK L17 129 K3
CHLY/EC PR7 31 K2
CHLYE PR6 44 D5
CSBY/BLUN L23 71 J7
FROD/HEL WA6 160 E5
GOL/RIS/CU WA3 93 H6
GOL/RIS/CU WA3 107 J2
GR/UP/WCH CH49 109 M7
MGHL L31 85 K2
PEN/TH CH61 141 J1
PR/KW L34 101 H7
RNFD/HAY WA11 91 H6
SKEL WN8 53 L4
STHEL WA9 118 E1
WARRS WA4 138 F2
WARRW/BUR WA5 135 L2
Beechbank Rd AIG/SPK L17 114 A8
Beechburn Crs HUY L36 115 K2
Beechburn Rd HUY L36 115 J2
Beech Cl BRSC L40 39 L1
KKBY L32 85 L2
NEWLW WA12 104 E3
SKEL WN8 65 G4
WD/CROXPK L12 98 F2 1
Beech Ct CALD/MH L18 130 F2 1
Beech Crs WGNNW/ST WN6 56 A5
Beechcroft Dr EP CH65 20 A9
Beechcroft Rd WAL/EG CH44 111 L3
Beechdale Rd CALD/MH L18 130 C1

Beechdene Rd ANF/KKDL L4 97 K6
Beech Dr FMBY L37 58 F1
The Beeches CALD/MH L18 114 F8
FROD/HEL WA6 166 E1
MOR/LEA CH46 110 A2
Beechfield MGHL L31 73 G4
SKEL WN8 40 E8
Beechfield Av WGNE/HIN WN2 81 J1 1
Beechfield Cl HES CH60 141 H6
Beechfield Gdns STHP PR8 2 D5
Beechfield Rd CALD/MH L18 130 F1
EP CH65 20 B4
WARRS WA4 138 C4
Beechfields CHLY/EC PR7 30 D7
Beech Gdns RNFD/HAY WA11 76 A6
Beech Gn WD/CROXPK L12 98 C5
Beech Gv CHTN/BK PR9 25 G6
GTS/LS CH66 163 J5
LITH L21 83 H7
LYMM WA13 139 K3
NTHTN L30 84 C3
WARR WA1 122 C6
WARRS WA4 15 K9
WGNE/HIN WN2 80 E6
WGNNW/ST WN6 68 A2
WLT/FAZ L9 84 D7 2
Beech Hall St WGNNW/ST WN6 68 C3
Beech Hey La NSTN CH64 154 D4
Beech Hill Av WGNNW/ST WN6 68 A2
Beech Hill La WGNNW/ST WN6 68 A2
Beechill Cl WLTN L25 131 L1
Beech Lawn ALL/GAR L19 130 B6 1
Beech Meadow ORM L39 63 J1
Beechmill Dr GOL/RIS/CU WA3 106 F2
Beechmoore WARRS WA4 136 D8
Beech Pk WD/CROXPK L12 98 C7
Beech Rd ANF/KKDL L4 97 J4
BEB CH63 128 B6
GOL/RIS/CU WA3 92 C4
HES CH60 141 L5
HUY L36 116 A4
ORM L39 62 C7
RF/TRAN CH42 10 F9
RUNC WA7 19 M8
RUNC WA7 161 K1
WARRS WA4 137 L5
Beech St BTL L20 7 H2
ECCL WA10 101 M5 1
EHL/KEN L7 113 L3
Beech Tree Av WGNNW/ST WN6 54 F5
Beech Tree Houses
WGNE/HIN WN2 80 A7
Beechtree Rd WAV L15 114 E5 1
Beechtrees SKEL WN8 65 L6
Beechurst Cl WLTN L25 115 K8
Beechurst Rd WLTN L25 115 K8
Beech Wk WGNNW/ST WN6 55 M5
WGNS/IIMK WN3 78 E3
The Beechwalk DV/KA/FCH L14 114 D1
Beechway BEB CH63 143 H2
MGHL L31 73 K3
Beechway Av MGHL L31 73 J3
Beechways WARRS WA4 137 M8
Beechways Dr NSTN CH64 152 F5
Beechwood SKEL WN8 65 L2
Beechwood Av AIMK WN4 91 J3 3
HLWD L26 132 A6
NEWLW WA12 104 F1
RUNC WA7 149 M8
RUNC WA7 150 B8
WAL/NB CH45 95 G8
WARR WA1 122 A5
WARRW/BUR WA5 120 B8 1
WGNNW/ST WN6 55 H8
Beechwood Cl ALL/GAR L19 130 C6 1
RAIN/WH L35 117 G1
Beechwood Crs
WGNW/BIL/O WN5 67 G7
Beechwood Dr CL/PREN CH43 110 D6
FMBY L37 58 E4
GTS/LS CH66 162 F4
ORM L39 62 F1
Beechwood Gdns
ALL/GAR L19 130 B6 2
Beechwood La
GOL/RIS/CU WA3 106 F1
Beechwood Rd ALL/GAR L19 130 B6
CHLY/EC PR7 32 F7
LITH L21 83 K7
PS/BROM CH62 143 L5
Beecroft Cl WARRW/BUR WA5 120 F4
Beesands Cl NTHLY L27 132 B1 1
Beesley Rd PR/KW L34 100 E7
Beeston Cl CL/PREN CH43 110 E7 1
GOL/RIS/CU WA3 122 F1 1
Beeston Dr PEN/TH CH61 141 G1
Beeston Gn GTS/LS CH66 156 A8 1
Beeston Gv ALL/GAR L19 130 C6
Beeston St ANF/KKDL L4 97 G5 3
Beilby Rd RNFD/HAY WA11 91 H6
Beldale Pk KKBY L32 85 L1
Beldon Crs HUY L36 115 K2
Belem Cl AIG/SPK L17 113 L8
Belfast Rd CLB/OSW/ST L13 114 D2
Belfield SKEL WN8 65 M7
Belfield Crs HUY L36 116 A4
Belfield Dr CL/PREN CH43 127 K2
Belford Dr MOR/LEA CH46 109 L5 1
Belfort Rd WLTN L25 131 K1 1
Belfry Cl CHLYE PR6 31 M1
MOR/LEA CH46 109 K4
WD/CROXPK L12 99 G7
Belfry Crs WGNNW/ST WN6 56 B3
Belgarve Rd STHP PR8 35 H1
Belgrave Av WAL/EG CH44 111 L1 1
WARR WA1 122 B6
Belgrave Cl LEIGH WN7 93 L5 1
WDN WA8 135 G2 1
WGNS/IIMK WN3 78 F2 1
Belgrave Dr EP CH65 156 B8
Belgrave Rd AIG/SPK L17 129 K2
LITH L21 83 H6 2
Belgrave St WAL/EG CH44 95 L8
Belhaven Rd CALD/MH L18 114 B8 4
Bellair Av CSBY/BLUN L23 83 J1
Bellairs Rd NG/CROX L11 98 A5
Bellamy Rd ANF/KKDL L4 7 M7
Bell Cl HUY L36 116 B5
Belldean WGNE/HIN WN2 69 J5
Belldene Gv HES CH60 141 H3
Bellefield Av WD/CROXPK L12 98 D7
Belle Green La WGNE/HIN WN2 69 J5
Bellemonte Rd
FROD/HEL WA6 160 D7 1
Belle Vale Rd WLTN L25 131 K1
Belle Vue Rd WAL/EG CH44 112 A3
WLTN L25 115 K8
Belle Vue St
WGNW/BIL/O WN5 67 M8 1
Bellew Rd NG/CROX L11 98 B6
Bellfield Crs WAL/NB CH45 95 J5 1
Bellgreen Rd NG/CROX L11 98 C3
Bellhouse La WARRS WA4 136 F6
WARRS WA4 138 E4
Bell House Rd WDN WA8 17 H2
Bellingham Av WGN WN1 68 E3
Bellingham Dr RUNC WA7 19 H8
WGN WN1 68 E3
Bellingham Mt WGN WN1 68 F2
Bellini Cl LITH L21 83 H8
Bellis Av CHTN/BK PR9 25 G3
Bellis Gv NWD/KWIPK L33 73 M8 2
Bell La RAIN/WH L35 118 C3
WARRS WA4 139 G1
WGNW/BIL/O WN5 67 K5
Bellmore St ALL/GAR L19 130 E6
Bell Rd WAL/EG CH44 111 M2
Bell's Cl MGHL L31 72 D2
Bell's La MGHL L31 72 C2
Bell St CLB/OSW/ST L13 114 C2
LEIGH WN7 81 M4
Bellward Cl BEB CH63 143 H3
Belmont BIRK CH41 10 E8
Belmont Av GOL/RIS/CU WA3 92 E4
PS/BROM CH62 143 L4
WARRS WA4 138 B2
WGNE/HIN WN2 81 H4
WGNW/BIL/O WN5 77 M2
Belmont Cl BRSC L40 52 A2 1
Belmont Crs WARRW/BUR WA5 120 B7
Belmont Dr CHLYE PR6 33 G4
NPK/KEN L6 97 L8
PEN/TH CH61 141 J2
WGNE/HIN WN2 57 L8
Belmont Gv NPK/KEN L6 97 L8
Belmont Pl CHLY/EC PR7 42 E7
Belmont Rd CHLYE PR6 44 D6
HOR/BR BL6 45 L4
NPK/KEN L6 97 K8
WAL/NB CH45 95 K4 2
WDN WA8 134 F3
WKBY CH48 124 D2
Belmont St ECCL WA10 8 A6
STHP PR8 2 E6
Beloe St TOX L8 129 H1
Belper St ALL/GAR L19 130 D7
Belston Rd CHLDW L16 114 F6
Belton Rd HUY L36 99 M7
Belvedere Av STHEL WA9 102 F7
Belvedere Cl FROD/HEL WA6 160 E4
PR/KW L34 101 G6 1
Belvedere Dr CHLY/EC PR7 32 D5 1
FMBY L37 59 H4 1
Belvedere Pk ORM L39 62 E6
Belvedere Pl WGNS/IIMK WN3 68 B8 1
Belvedere Rd AIMK WN4 91 L2
CHLYE PR6 44 D5 1
NEWLW WA12 104 D1
STHP PR8 34 E8
Belvidere Pk CSBY/BLUN L23 83 G2
Belvidere Rd CSBY/BLUN L23 82 F2
TOX L8 113 J8
WAL/NB CH45 95 H7
Belvoir Rd CALD/MH L18 130 E1
WARRS WA4 137 K5
WDN WA8 16 F1
Belvoir St WGN WN1 5 H4
Bembridge Cl
WARRW/BUR WA5 119 L6
WDN WA8 134 B1
Bembridge Ct WGNS/IIMK WN3 79 G3
Benbow Rd AIG/SPK L17 129 K3 1
Benbow St BTL L20 6 E7
Bendee Av NSTN CH64 153 J6
Bendee Rd NSTN CH64 153 H6
Benedict St BTL L20 7 J8
Bengairn Cl WGN WN1 5 K2
Bengal St CHLY/EC PR7 32 E4 1
Bengarth Rd CHTN/BK PR9 25 H5
Bengel St EHL/KEN L7 113 J3 3
Benjamin Fold AIMK WN4 79 K8
Ben La RNFD/HAY WA11 75 K3
Ben Lane Ct ORM L39 75 K3
Benledi St EV L5 96 F8
Benmore Rd CALD/MH L18 130 C3
Bennet Cl NSTN CH64 154 C5
Bennet's La HOY CH47 109 G3
Bennett Av WARR WA1 15 M3
Bennett Dr WGNW/BIL/O WN5 77 M1
Bennetts Hl CL/PREN CH43 127 K1
Bennett's La WDN WA8 17 M1
Bennett St ALL/GAR L19 130 E7
WARR WA1 14 F6
Ben Nevis Rd RF/TRAN CH42 127 M3
Bennison Dr ALL/GAR L19 130 C6 2
Benson Cl GR/UP/WCH CH49 126 B1 1
Benson Rd GOL/RIS/CU WA3 122 F3
Benson St CLVPS L1 13 J8
Bentfield AIG/SPK L17 130 B5 1
Bentfield Cl BEB CH63 127 M6
Bentfield Gdns BEB CH63 127 M6
Bentham Av WARRN/WOL WA2 121 L2
Bentham Cl CL/PREN CH43 127 G2
Bentham Dr CHLDW L16 114 F5
Bentham Pl WGNNW/ST WN6 56 B3
Bentham Rd GOL/RIS/CU WA3 107 J3
WGNNW/ST WN6 56 A4
Bentham St CHLY/EC PR7 43 G4
STHP PR8 3 G7
Bentham's Wy STHP PR8 35 L3
Bentinck Cl BIRK CH41 10 F5
Bentinck Pl BIRK CH41 10 F6
Bentinck St BIRK CH41 11 G5
EV L5 96 D8
RUNC WA7 18 E2
STHEL WA9 102 F4
WGNS/IIMK WN3 79 G1
Bent La GOL/RIS/CU WA3 107 J3
Bentley La BRSC L40 40 F6
Bentley Rd CL/PREN CH43 127 K1 1
PEN/TH CH61 126 B8
TOX L8 113 K7 1
Bentley St STHEL WA9 118 E1
Benton Cl EV L5 96 F7
Benty Cl BEB CH63 143 G1
Benty Farm Gv PEN/TH CH61 126 C8
Benty Heath La NSTN CH64 154 C2
Benwick Rd KKBY L32 85 K4
Berbice Rd WAV L15 114 C7
Beresford Av BEB CH63 128 C7
Beresford Cl CL/PREN CH43 10 B8
Beresford Dr CHTN/BK PR9 25 H4
Beresford Gdns CHTN/BK PR9 25 H3
Beresford Rd CL/PREN CH43 10 B8
TOX L8 129 H1
WAL/NB CH45 95 H6
Beresford St BTL L20 6 E8
EV L5 13 K2
STHEL WA9 102 A6
WARR WA1 15 L2
WGNNW/ST WN6 4 A2
Bergen Cl BTL L20 7 L6
Berkeley Av CL/PREN CH43 127 G4
WGNS/IIMK WN3 78 F3
Berkeley Cl CHLY/EC PR7 32 F8
LEIGH WN7 93 L5
Berkeley Dr WAL/NB CH45 95 L6 1
Berkeley Rd CSBY/BLUN L23 70 E8
Berkeswell Rd NG/CROX L11 98 C4
Berkley Av WD/CROXPK L12 98 F5
Berkley St TOX L8 113 H7 1
Berkshire Dr WARR WA1 122 F6
Berkshire Gdns ECCL WA10 8 E8
Bermuda Rd MOR/LEA CH46 109 L5
Bernard Av WAL/NB CH45 95 L6 2
WARRS WA4 137 M5
Berner's Rd ALL/GAR L19 130 D6
Berner St BIRK CH41 11 G2
Berrington Av WLTN L25 131 J3 1
Berrington Gv AIMK WN4 91 J2
Berrington's La
RNFD/HAY WA11 88 E3
Berry Cl GTS/LS CH66 162 E2
SKEL WN8 65 H3
Berry Dr GTS/LS CH66 162 E1
Berry Hill Av PR/KW L34 99 M2
Berry House Rd BRSC L40 38 C1
Berrylands Cl
MOR/LEA CH46 109 M4 1
Berrylands Rd MOR/LEA CH46 109 M3
Berry Rd WDN WA8 133 M4
Berrys La STHEL WA9 103 H4
Berry St BTL L20 6 F5
CHLYE PR6 44 C5
CLVPS L1 113 G5
SKEL WN8 65 G3
Berrywood Dr RAIN/WH L35 117 H3
Bertha St BIRK CH41 111 H5 1
Bertram Dr HOY CH47 108 E5
Bertram Dr North HOY CH47 108 F5
Bertram Rd AIG/SPK L17 129 L1
Bertram St NEWLW WA12 104 B2
Berwick Av PS/BROM CH62 155 G1
STHP PR8 34 E7
Berwick Cl CL/PREN CH43 110 E7 2
MOR/LEA CH46 109 K5
NPK/KEN L6 113 K1 1
WARR WA1 123 G7 1
Berwick Dr CSBY/BLUN L23 70 E8
Berwick Gdns GTS/LS CH66 155 K7
Berwick Gv GTS/LS CH66 155 K7
Berwick Pl WGN WN1 5 K1
Berwick Rd GTS/LS CH66 155 J7
Berwick St NPK/KEN L6 113 K1
Berwyn Av HOY CH47 108 E6 1
PEN/TH CH61 126 C7 2
Berwyn Bvd BEB CH63 128 A5
Berwyn Cl GTS/LS CH66 155 J7
HOR/BR BL6 45 L8
Berwyn Dr PEN/TH CH61 141 H3
Berwyn Gv STHEL WA9 103 H2 1
Berwyn Rd ANF/KKDL L4 97 L5
WAL/EG CH44 95 L8
Beryl Rd CL/PREN CH43 110 E8
Beryl St CLB/OSW/ST L13 114 C4
Bescar Brow La BRSC L40 37 H6 1
Bescar La BRSC L40 37 J5
Besford Rd WLTN L25 115 K8
Bessborough Rd CL/PREN CH43 10 D9
Bessbrook Rd AIG/SPK L17 130 A3 2
Bessemer St TOX L8 129 H1
Bessie's Well Pl
WGNNW/ST WN6 56 B5 1
Beta Cl PS/BROM CH62 128 C6
Betchworth Crs RUNC WA7 149 M7
Bethany Cl RNFD/HAY WA11 90 D6 1
Bethersden Rd WGN WN1 56 D8
Betjeman Cl WARRS WA4 138 B1 1
Betjeman Gv CHLDW L16 115 G5
Betony Cl HLWD L26 132 A4
Betsyfield Dr GOL/RIS/CU WA3 106 C6
Bettisfield Av PS/BROM CH62 143 M8
Betula Cl WLT/FAZ L9 97 L1
Beulah Av WGNW/BIL/O WN5 89 M1 1
Bevan Cl STHEL WA9 101 M7 2
WARRW/BUR WA5 120 F7
Bevan's La WD/CROXPK L12 98 E6
Beverley Av WARRS WA4 137 M5
WGNW/BIL/O WN5 78 A4 1
Beverley Cl CHTN/BK PR9 22 E8 1
Beverley Dr HES CH60 141 K6
Beverley Gdns PEN/TH CH61 126 D7 1
Beverley Rd PS/BROM CH62 128 D5
WAL/NB CH45 95 H7
WARRW/BUR WA5 120 E7
WAV L15 114 C7
WGNW/BIL/O WN5 67 K5
Beverley Wy GTS/LS CH66 155 K6
Beversbrook Rd NG/CROX L11 98 D3
Bevin Av GOL/RIS/CU WA3 107 K1
Bevington Bush VAUX/LVPD L3 13 G3
Bevington Hl VAUX/LVPD L3 13 H2 1
Bevington St AIMK WN4 79 H8
VAUX/LVPD L3 13 G2
Bevyl Rd NSTN CH64 152 D3
Bewcastle Dr BRSC L40 63 K2
Bewerley Cl WGNS/IIMK WN3 4 C8
Bewey Cl TOX L8 129 G1
Bewley Dr KKBY L32 85 M4
Bewsey Farm Cl
WARRW/BUR WA5 120 F6 1
Bewsey Park Cl
WARRW/BUR WA5 14 A1
Bewsey Rd WARRW/BUR WA5 14 A2
Bewsey St ECCL WA10 101 M4
WARR WA1 14 E5
WARRN/WOL WA2 14 D4
Bexhill Av WARRN/WOL WA2 121 K1
Bexhill Cl SPK/HALE L24 146 D1
Bexhill Dr WGNE/HIN WN2 81 L3
Bexley St WGNE/HIN WN2 81 K2 2
Bianca St BTL L20 7 H8
Bibby Av WARR WA1 15 M3
Bibby Rd CHTN/BK PR9 25 J4
Bibby's La BTL L20 6 D1
Bibby St CLB/OSW/ST L13 114 B2 3
Bickershaw La WGNE/HIN WN2 80 D4
Bickerstaffe St ECCL WA10 9 H5
VAUX/LVPD L3 13 K3 1
Bickerton Av BEB CH63 127 M5
FROD/HEL WA6 160 F6
Bickerton Cl
GOL/RIS/CU WA3 122 F1 2
Bickerton Rd STHP PR8 35 H1
Bickerton St AIG/SPK L17 129 L2
Bickley Cl RUNC WA7 19 L6
WARRN/WOL WA2 122 B2
Bicknell Cl WARRW/BUR WA5 120 D5 1
Bidder St VAUX/LVPD L3 13 K4
Bideford Av STHEL WA9 102 E8
Bideford Rd WARRW/BUR WA5 136 A1
Bidston Av BIRK CH41 111 H6
RNFD/HAY WA11 89 M8
WAL/NB CH45 95 G7
Bidston Gn GTS/LS CH66 162 F1 1
Bidston Green Ct
CL/PREN CH43 110 E5 1
Bidston Green Dr
CL/PREN CH43 110 E5
Bidston Moss WAL/EG CH44 110 F2
Bidston Rd ANF/KKDL L4 97 K5
CL/PREN CH43 111 H7
Bidston Station Ap
CL/PREN CH43 110 E3
Bidston Village Rd
CL/PREN CH43 110 D4
Bigdale Dr NWD/KWIPK L33 86 C2
Big Fold HOR/BR BL6 57 M3 1
Biggin Ct WARRN/WOL WA2 122 A4 2
Bigham Rd NPK/KEN L6 113 L2
Biglands Dr HUY L36 116 B5
Big Meadow Rd
GR/UP/WCH CH49 126 C1
Billinge Crs RNFD/HAY WA11 89 M7
Billinge Rd AIMK WN4 78 D8
WGNS/IIMK WN3 78 E1
WGNW/BIL/O WN5 67 M8
Billingham Rd RAIN/WH L35 101 M6
Billings Cl EV L5 96 F7 2
Billington Av NEWLW WA12 91 K7
Billington Cl
WARRW/BUR WA5 120 A5 1
Billington Rd WDN WA8 133 K1 1
Bilston Rd AIG/SPK L17 130 A5
Bilton Cl WDN WA8 135 G3
Binbrook Pl CHLY/EC PR7 32 C5
Bingley Rd ANF/KKDL L4 97 K6
Binns Rd CLB/OSW/ST L13 114 C4
Binns Wy CLB/OSW/ST L13 114 B4
Binsey Cl GR/UP/WCH CH49 109 M8 1
Birbeck Rd NWD/KWIPK L33 86 C2
Birchall Av GOL/RIS/CU WA3 106 F1
Birchall St BTL L20 96 E6
GOL/RIS/CU WA3 106 C6
Birch Av BRSC L40 52 A1 1
CHLY/EC PR7 31 L1 1
ECCL WA10 89 H7
GR/UP/WCH CH49 109 M7
WARRN/WOL WA2 121 J1
WGNNW/ST WN6 56 B5
WLT/FAZ L9 84 D7 3
Birchcliffe Rd RF/TRAN CH42 128 B3 3
Birch Cl CL/PREN CH43 127 K2
MGHL L31 73 H4
RAIN/WH L35 117 G1
Birch Crs NEWLW WA12 104 B1
Birchdale Cl
GR/UP/WCH CH49 125 M1 2
Birchdale Crs WARRS WA4 137 L5
Birchdale Rd CSBY/WL L22 82 F3
WARR WA1 122 C6
WARRS WA4 137 L6
WLT/FAZ L9 84 C8
Birchen Rd HLWD L26 132 C6
Birches Cl HES CH60 141 J4
The Birches FMBY L37 47 G8
STBRV L28 99 J6 1
WAL/EG CH44 112 A3 3
Birchfield MOR/LEA CH46 109 L6
Birchfield Av WDN WA8 134 C3 1
Birchfield Cl EHL/KEN L7 114 A3 1
MOR/LEA CH46 109 L7 3
Birchfield Rd ANF/KKDL L4 97 J4
EHL/KEN L7 114 A3
WARRW/BUR WA5 120 D8
WDN WA8 16 D1
WDN WA8 134 C2 1
Birchfield St RAIN/WH L35 101 M6
VAUX/LVPD L3 13 K4
Birchfield Wy MGHL L31 61 K8
Birch Gdns ECCL WA10 89 H7
Birch Gn FMBY L37 46 F8
Birch Green Rd SKEL WN8 65 L3
Birch Gv AIMK WN4 78 E8
GTS/LS CH66 163 J4
HUY L36 115 M3 1
RAIN/WH L35 117 G1
WAL/NB CH45 95 L6
WARR WA1 122 B6
WARRS WA4 137 M2 2
WAV L15 114 C4
Birch Heys WKBY CH48 125 J4
Birch Hl FROD/HEL WA6 167 L5
Birchill Rd NWD/KWIPK L33 86 E3
Birchley Av WGNW/BIL/O WN5 89 L2
Birchley Rd WGNW/BIL/O WN5 89 L2
Birchley St ECCL WA10 9 H3
Birchley Vw RNFD/HAY WA11 89 K3 1
Birchmere HES CH60 141 G3
Birchmuir Hey KKBY L32 86 B4 1
Birchover Wk EHL/KEN L7 113 K5
Birchridge Cl PS/BROM CH62 143 L3
Birch Rd BEB CH63 143 J1
CHLY/EC PR7 43 G4 1
CHLYE PR6 32 F3
CL/PREN CH43 127 K2
HOY CH47 109 G5
HUY L36 116 A4
RNFD/HAY WA11 91 G6
RUNC WA7 19 K7
WDN WA8 134 C2
WGNE/HIN WN2 80 D6
Birch St EV L5 96 D8
SKEL WN8 65 G4
STHP PR8 35 K1
WGNE/HIN WN2 69 M8 5
WGNNW/ST WN6 4 B1
Birch Tree Av RNFD/HAY WA11 89 H5
Birch Tree Ct WD/CROXPK L12 98 G7
Birchtree Rd AIG/SPK L17 130 A2
Birch Tree Rd
GOL/RIS/CU WA3 93 H5 1
Birchview Wy CL/PREN CH43 110 F8
Birchway HES CH60 141 L7
Birchways WARRS WA4 138 A8
Birchwood Av BIRK CH41 11 H4
Birchwood Bvd
GOL/RIS/CU WA3 122 F3
Birchwood Cl BIRK CH41 11 H5
CHNE CH2 165 L2 2
GTS/LS CH66 162 F4 2
WGNS/IIMK WN3 78 F4 1
Birchwood Dr CHLY/EC PR7 43 G2
Birchwood Park Av
GOL/RIS/CU WA3 106 F8
Birchwood Wy
GOL/RIS/CU WA3 123 H1
WARRN/WOL WA2 122 A5
Bird St EHL/KEN L7 113 L6 1
WGNE/HIN WN2 5 M6
Birdwell Dr WARRW/BUR WA5 120 C8
Birdwood Rd NG/CROX L11 98 B5
Birkacre Brow CHLY/EC PR7 43 H3
Birkacre Rd CHLY/EC PR7 43 H1
Birkdale Av BEB CH63 143 L7
Birkdale Cl HUY L36 115 L4 1
NPK/KEN L6 97 M7 1
Birkdale Cop STHP PR8 36 A4
Birkdale Rd WARRW/BUR WA5 136 B1
WDN WA8 118 D8
Birkenhead Rd HOY CH47 108 E5
NSTN CH64 154 A4
WAL/EG CH44 112 A4
Birkenshaw Av
CSBY/BLUN L23 82 D1 1
Birket Av MOR/LEA CH46 110 B2
Birket Cl MOR/LEA CH46 110 C2
Birket Sq MOR/LEA CH46 110 B2 1
Birkett Av EP CH65 163 L3
Birkett Bank WGN WN1 5 K4
Birkett Rd RF/TRAN CH42 128 A4
WKBY CH48 124 D1
Birkett St VAUX/LVPD L3 13 J4
WGN WN1 5 K4
Birkey La FMBY L37 59 H3
Birkin Cl KKBY L32 86 C5
Birkin Rd KKBY L32 86 C5
Birkrig SKEL WN8 65 M7
Birkside Cl WGNS/IIMK WN3 79 J4
Birley Cl WGNNW/ST WN6 55 H5
Birley Ct TOX L8 113 H6 5
Birley St NEWLW WA12 104 F1
Birleywood SKEL WN8 65 M7
Birnam Dr RAIN/WH L35 117 M3 2
Birnam Rd WAL/EG CH44 111 M2
Birstall Av RNFD/HAY WA11 9 M1
Birstall Ct RUNC WA7 149 M6
Birstall Rd NPK/KEN L6 113 K2
Birt Cl TOX L8 113 K6
Birtles Rd WARRN/WOL WA2 121 L4
Bisham Pk RUNC WA7 150 F3
Bishopdale Cl
WARRW/BUR WA5 120 B6
Bishopdale Dr RAIN/WH L35 117 M3
Bishop Dr RAIN/WH L35 116 F4
Bishopgate WGN WN1 4 E4
Bishopgate St WAV L15 114 A6
Bishop Reeves Rd
RNFD/HAY WA11 91 G6 3
Bishop Rd ECCL WA10 8 D2
NPK/KEN L6 97 L6
WAL/EG CH44 111 K3
Bishops Ct WARRN/WOL WA2 121 H1
WLTN L25 131 K3 1
Bishops Gdns EP CH65 156 C8
Bishop Sheppard Ct
VAUX/LVPD L3 12 E2
Bishops Wy WDN WA8 134 F2
Bisley St WAL/NB CH45 95 K8
WAV L15 114 A6 2
Bispham Dr AIMK WN4 79 H8
HOY CH47 109 G6
Bispham Rd CHTN/BK PR9 25 H6
WARRW/BUR WA5 136 D1 1
Bittern Cl RUNC WA7 150 F5
WARRN/WOL WA2 121 M2 1
Bixteth St VAUX/LVPD L3 12 E5
Blackacre La BRSC L40 51 H4
Black-a-moor La ORM L39 61 J3
Blackberry Gv HLWD L26 131 M3 1
Blackboards La GTS/LS CH66 155 J6
Blackbrook Av
WARRN/WOL WA2 122 B3
Blackbrook Cl CHLYE PR6 33 J3 1
WDN WA8 133 L2
WLT/FAZ L9 97 J2
Blackbrook Rd RNFD/HAY WA11 90 A8
Blackburn Brow CHLYE PR6 33 G3
Blackburn Cl GOL/RIS/CU WA3 93 H5 2
Blackburne Av WDN WA8 133 K8

Blackburne Cl
WARRN/WOL WA2 .... 122 E3 1
Blackburne Dr *WLTN* L25............. 131 M6
Blackburne Pl *TOX* L8 .... 113 H5 11
Blackburne St *SPK/HALE* L24 .... 145 M2
Blackburn St *CHLYE* PR6 .... 32 F6
Blackcar La *SFTN* L29.................... 71 J2
Black Denton's Pl *WDN* WA8 .... 17 H2
Blackdown Cl *GTS/LS* CH66 ...... 155 J8 1
Blackdown Gv *STHEL* WA9 .... 103 H3
Blackeys La *NSTN* CH64............... 153 G5
Blackfield St *EV* L5 .... 96 F7 3
Blackgate La *KIRK/FR/WA* PR4....... 27 L2
Blackheath Dr *MOR/LEA* CH46..... 110 B2
Blackheath La *RUNC* WA7 .... 151 G1
Blackhorse Av *HOR/BR* BL6 .... 57 L3 1
Blackhorse Cl *HOR/BR* BL6 .... 57 L2 2
Black Horse Cl *WKBY* CH48........... 124 E2
Black Horse Hl *WKBY* CH48........... 124 E3
Black Horse La
CLB/OSW/ST L13 .... 114 D2
Black Horse Pl
CLB/OSW/ST L13 .... 114 D2
Black Horse St *CHLY/EC* PR7 ..... 32 D7 2
HOR/BR BL6 .... 57 L2
Blackhorse St *STHEL* WA9 .... 9 M3
STHEL WA9 .... 102 F1 1
Blackhurst Rd *MGHL* L31................. 61 L8
Blackhurst St *WARR* WA1 .... 14 F6
Blackledge Cl
WARRN/WOL WA2 .... 122 C2 1
WGNW/BIL/O WN5 .... 67 G8 1
Blackley Cl *WARRS* WA4.............. 137 M2
Blackley Gv *NWD/KWIPK* L33 .... 74 C7 1
Blackleyhurst Av
WGNW/BIL/O WN5 .... 78 A8
Black Lion La *GTS/LS* CH66 .... 155 K7
Blacklock Hall Rd
SPK/HALE L24............................. 146 E2
Blacklow Brow *HUY* L36 .... 115 M3
Blackmoor Dr *WD/CROXPK* L12 .... 98 E7
Black Moor Rd *BRSC* L40................ 40 C3
Black Moss La *BRSC* L40 .... 36 F6
ORM L39 .... 62 F3
Blackpool St *BIRK* CH41................... 11 K7
Blackrod Av *SPK/HALE* L24 .... 146 E2
Blackrod Brow *HOR/BR* BL6.......... 57 K1
Blackshaw Dr
WARRW/BUR WA5 .... 120 D4
Blackstock St *VAUX/LVPD* L3 .... 12 F3
Blackstone Av *RNFD/HAY* WA11.... 89 M8
Blackstone Rd *CHLYE* PR6.............. 33 G4
Blackstone St *EV* L5........................ 96 D8
Blackthorn Av *WGNNW/ST* WN6 .. 8 A6 1
Blackthorn Cl
MOR/LEA CH46 .... 110 B6 1
Blackthorne Av *GTS/LS* CH66 ...... 163 J5
Blackthorne Crs *STBRV* L28 .... 99 K5
Blackthorne Rd *WLT/FAZ* L9........... 97 L2
Blackwater Rd *NG/CROX* L11 .... 98 F1
Blackwood Av *WLTN* L25................ 131 H1
Blaguegate La *SKEL* WN8 .... 64 D3
Blainscough Rd *CHLY/EC* PR7 ...... 43 G5
Blair Av *WGNE/HIN* WN2 .... 81 K2
Blair Dr *WDN* WA8......................... 133 K2
Blairgowrie Gdns *ORM* L39............ 63 J1
Blair Gv *CHTN/BK* PR9 .... 25 H6
Blair Pk *BEB* CH63 .... 143 K2
Blair St *TOX* L8.............................. 113 G6
Blaisdon Cl *NG/CROX* L11 .... 98 C4
Blakeacre Cl *HLWD* L26 .... 132 B7 1
Blakeacre Rd *HLWD* L26 .... 132 B7
Blake Cl *WGNS/IIMK* WN3 .... 68 C8
Blakefield Rd *CSBY/BLUN* L23 .... 71 M7
Blakehall *SKEL* WN8 .... 65 M6
Blakeley Brow *BEB* CH63 .... 143 J7
Blakeley Ct *BEB* CH63 .... 143 J7
Blakeley Dell *BEB* CH63................. 143 K7
Blakeley Dene *BEB* CH63 .... 143 K6
Blakeley Rd *BEB* CH63................... 143 J6
Blakemere Ct *EP* CH65 .... 20 C1
Blakeney Cl
GR/UP/WCH CH49 .... 110 C6 1
Blakenhall Wy
GR/UP/WCH CH49 .... 109 M7 1
Blaking Dr *PR/KW* L34 .... 99 M1 1
Blandford Cl *STHP* PR8 .... 2 B7
Blandford Rd
WARRW/BUR WA5...................... 120 D8
Blantyre Rd *WAV* L15 .... 114 A7
Blantyre St *RUNC* WA7................... 18 E1
Blay Cl *WLTN* L25.......................... 131 M5
Blaydon Cl *NTHTN* L30 .... 84 C4 1
WGNE/HIN WN2 .... 57 M8 2
Blaydon Gv *RAIN/WH* L35 .... 101 M6 1
Blaydon Pk *SKEL* WN8.................... 65 M6
Blaydon Wk *CL/PREN* CH43 .... 111 H7
Bleach St *WGNE/HIN* WN2............. 80 E1
Bleak Hill Cl *ECCL* WA10................. 88 E6
Bleak Hill Rd *ECCL* WA10 .... 88 E7 1
Bleak La *BRSC* L40 .... 39 M8
Bleaklow Cl *WGNS/IIMK* WN3 .... 79 K3
Bleasdale Av *AIN/FAZ* L10 .... 85 G3 1
Bleasdale Cl
GR/UP/WCH CH49 .... 110 A7 1
ORM L39.. 62 F6
Bleasdale Rd *CALD/MH* L18 .... 130 D1
NEWLW WA12............................. 104 D1
Blenheim Av *LITH* L21 .... 83 L5
Blenheim Cl
WARRN/WOL WA2 .... 122 B3 1
Blenheim Dr *HUY* L36 .... 100 B8
Blenheim Rd *AIMK* WN4 .... 91 M3
CALD/MH L18 .... 114 B8 5
STHP PR8 .... 34 D7
WAL/EG CH44.............................. 95 M8
WGNW/BIL/O WN5 .... 67 L5
Blenheim St *EV* L5 .... 12 F1
Blenheim Wy
RNFD/HAY WA11 .... 89 K7 1
SPK/HALE L24............................. 146 D2
Blessington Rd *ANF/KKDL* L4 .... 97 H6
Bletchley Av *WAL/EG* CH44 ...... 111 H1 1
Bligh St *WAV* L15......................... 114 A6
Blind Foot Rd *RNFD/HAY* WA11 ..... 87 M6
Blindman's La *ORM* L39................. 50 E6
Blissford Cl *WGNE/HIN* WN2 ...... 80 F1 1
Blisworth St *LITH* L21...................... 83 K7
Blomfield Rd *ALL/GAR* L19 .... 130 F5
Bloomsbury Wy *WDN* WA8 ...... 133 M2 1
Blossom St *BTL* L20 .... 7 H1
Blucher St *CSBY/WL* L22 .... 82 E4
Bluebell Av *BIRK* CH41.................. 111 H5
RNFD/HAY WA11 .... 91 G6
Blue Bell Av *WGNNW/ST* WN6....... 68 B1
Bluebell Cl *CSBY/WL* L22 .... 83 G4 1
Bluebell Ct *RUNC* WA7 .... 161 H1 5
Blue Bell La *HUY* L36 .... 116 A1
Blueberry Flds *AIN/FAZ* L10 .... 85 H7
Bluecoat St *WARRN/WOL* WA2 ...... 14 E2
Bluefields St *TOX* L8..................... 113 H6
Blue Hatch *FROD/HEL* WA6.......... 160 E5
Blue Jay Cl *NTHLY* L27 .... 116 A8
Blue Stone La *BRSC* L40................. 41 G2
Bluestone La *MGHL* L31.................. 73 G4
Bluewood Dr *BIRK* CH41 .... 110 F4
Blundell Av *FMBY* L37 .... 58 D1
HTWN L38....................................... 70 B2
STHP PR8 .... 35 H3
Blundell Crs *STHP* PR8................... 35 H3
Blundell Dr *STHP* PR8 .... 35 H3
Blundell Gv *HTWN* L38................... 70 B2
Blundell La *CHTN/BK* PR9 .... 25 L3
HOR/BR BL6 .... 57 J3
Blundell Ms *WGNS/IIMK* WN3 .... 78 F1 1
Blundell Rd *HTWN* L38................... 70 B3
WDN WA8.................................... 133 M5
Blundellsands Rd East
CSBY/BLUN L23 .... 82 E1 1
Blundellsands Rd West
CSBY/BLUN L23 .... 82 D2
Blundells Dr *MOR/LEA* CH46........ 110 A4
Blundell's La *RAIN/WH* L35 .... 117 J4
Blundell St *CLVPS* L1 .... 112 F6
Blyth Cl *RUNC* WA7....................... 150 F8
Blythe Av *WDN* WA8 .... 118 D8 1
Blythe La *BRSC* L40 .... 52 A4
Blythewood *SKEL* WN8 .... 65 L6
Blyth Hey *NTHTN* L30.................... 83 M2
Blyth Rd *BEB* CH63......................... 143 L6
Blythswood St *AIG/SPK* L17 .... 129 K2
Boaler St *NPK/KEN* L6 .... 113 K2
Boarded Barn *CHLY/EC* PR7 ...... 31 L2 1
Boardmans La *STHEL* WA9 .... 103 G1
Boardman St *HOR/BR* BL6 .... 57 M3 2
Boars Head Av *WGNNW/ST* WN6 .. 56 C6
Boathouse La *NSTN* CH64............ 152 D3
Bobbies La *ECCL* WA10.................. 101 J1
Bobbiners La *CHTN/BK* PR9 .... 26 C2
Bobby Langton Wy *BRSC* L40 .... 39 G8
Bodden St *GOL/RIS/CU* WA3 .... 93 J4
STHEL WA9 .... 118 F1
Bodiam Ct *EP* CH65 .... 164 A3
Bodley St *ANF/KKDL* L4 .... 97 H6 2
Bodmin Av *CHTN/BK* PR9 .... 22 D8
Bodmin Cl *RUNC* WA7 .... 150 D7 2
Bodmin Dr *WGNE/HIN* WN2 .... 80 C4
Bodmin Gv *RNFD/HAY* WA11......... 89 M6
Bodmin Rd *ANF/KKDL* L4............... 97 H4
Bodmin Wy *HLWD* L26 .... 132 A5
Bogburn La *CHLY/EC* PR7 .... 42 F8
Bognor Cl *SPK/HALE* L24 .... 146 D1 1
Bolan St *CLB/OSW/ST* L13 .... 114 C2
Bolderwood Dr
WGNE/HIN WN2 .... 80 F1 2
Bolde Wy *BEB* CH63...................... 143 J4
Bold La *ORM* L39............................ 62 D6
WARRW/BUR WA5....................... 103 L6
Bold Rd *STHEL* WA9 .... 103 H6
Bold St *CHTN/BK* PR9........................ 3 G2
CLVPS L1 .... 13 H8
ECCL WA10 .... 8 E6
RUNC WA7 .... 19 J2
WARR WA1 .... 14 D6
WDN WA8... 16 C6
WGNW/BIL/O WN5 .... 68 A8
Boleyn Ct *RUNC* WA7 .... 150 E2
The Boleyn *MGHL* L31.................... 73 G2
Bollin Cl *GOL/RIS/CU* WA3 .... 107 J3
Bollington Cl *CL/PREN* CH43 ..... 127 H2 2
Bolney St *WGNE/HIN* WN2 .... 69 J2
Bolton Av *KKBY* L32 .... 85 L3
WARRS WA4 .... 138 B1 2
Bolton Cl *FMBY* L37 .... 59 J3 2
GOL/RIS/CU WA3 .... 93 K5
STHEL WA9 .... 9 L4 1
Bolton House Rd
WGNE/HIN WN2 .... 81 H6
Bolton Rd *AIMK* WN4...................... 79 M8
CHLY/EC PR7 .... 32 F7
CHLYE PR6 .... 44 E6
PS/BROM CH62 .... 128 E7
STHP PR8 .... 35 J1
WGNE/HIN WN2............................. 57 L8
Bolton Rd East *PS/BROM* CH62 .. 128 E7
Bolton's Cop *CHTN/BK* PR9............ 23 M7
Bolton St *AIMK* WN4 .... 78 F8
CHLY/EC PR7 .... 32 E6
STHEL WA9 .... 9 L4 2
VAUX/LVPD L3 .... 13 J7
Bombay Rd *WGNW/BIL/O* WN5 .... 67 L5
Bonchurch Dr *WAV* L15................. 114 B4
Bond Cl *WARRW/BUR* WA5 .... 136 F1
Bond's La *CHLY/EC* PR7 .... 44 B6 1
CHTN/BK PR9 .... 23 J6
Bond St *PR/KW* L34 .... 100 F7 1
VAUX/LVPD L3 .... 13 G2
Bonnington Av *CSBY/BLUN* L23...... 70 E8
Bonsall Rd *WD/CROXPK* L12 .... 98 D7
Boode Cft *STBRV* L28...................... 99 K4
Booker Av *CALD/MH* L18................ 130 D4
Booth's Brow Rd *AIMK* WN4............ 78 F7
Booths Hill Cl *LYMM* WA13 ...... 139 M3 1
Booth's Hill La *LYMM* WA13 .... 139 L2
Booth's Hill Rd *LYMM* WA13 .... 139 L2
Booth's La *LYMM* WA13................... 139 K3
ORM L39.. 50 B8
Booth St *CHTN/BK* PR9 .... 3 G2
CLB/OSW/ST L13 .... 114 C2
NEWLW WA12 .... 104 C2 5
RAIN/WH L35 .... 101 M6
WARRW/BUR WA5 .... 137 G1 1
Boothwood Cl *EHL/KEN* L7 .... 113 K5 1
Bor Av *WGNS/IIMK* WN3 .... 79 K1
Borax St *CLB/OSW/ST* L13............. 114 C3
Borden Cl *WGNE/HIN* WN2 .... 69 H3
Border Rd *HES* CH60 .... 141 K5
Borella Rd *CLB/OSW/ST* L13 .... 98 B7
Bores Hl *WGN* WN1.......................... 56 E1
Borough Pl *BIRK* CH41 .... 11 K6 2
Borough Rd *BIRK* CH41 .... 11 G7
ECCL WA10 .... 8 D7
RF/TRAN CH42 .... 10 F8
WAL/EG CH44.............................. 111 M2
Borough Rd East *BIRK* CH41.......... 11 K6
WAL/EG CH44 .... 112 A3 4
Borron Rd *NEWLW* WA12............... 91 K8
Borrowdale *FMBY* L37 .... 47 H8 1
Borrowdale Av
WARRN/WOL WA2 .... 121 K2
Borrowdale Cl *FROD/HEL* WA6..... 160 F5
Borrowdale Rd *BEB* CH63 .... 143 G1
ECCL WA10 .... 101 L5 1
MOR/LEA CH46 .... 109 M5
WAV L15 .... 114 A7
WDN WA8 .... 133 L5
WGNW/BIL/O WN5 .... 67 K6 1
Borsdane Av *WGNE/HIN* WN2........ 81 G1
Boscombe Pl *WGNE/HIN* WN2 ...... 81 G1
Boscow Crs *STHEL* WA9 .... 102 F6 2
Bosnia St *TOX* L8........................... 129 J2
Bostock Gn *EP* CH65 .... 156 B8
Bostock St *EV* L5 .... 96 F8
WARRW/BUR WA5 .... 121 G7 1
Boston Av *RUNC* WA7 .... 19 K7
Boston Cl *GOL/RIS/CU* WA3.......... 107 H1
Boswell Av *WARRS* WA4............... 137 K3
Boswell Pl *WGNS/IIMK* WN3 .... 79 H1
Boswell Rd *CL/PREN* CH43 .... 127 H4
Boswell St *BTL* L20 .... 6 D1
TOX L8.. 113 L6
Bosworth Cl *BEB* CH63 .... 143 H3
Bosworth Dr *STHP* PR8 .... 47 K1
Bosworth Rd *RNFD/HAY* WA11....... 89 L7
Botanic Gv *EHL/KEN* L7 .... 113 L3
Botanic Pl *EHL/KEN* L7 .... 113 L3
Botanic Rd *CHTN/BK* PR9 .... 25 K3 1
EHL/KEN L7 .... 113 L4
Botany Brow *CHLYE* PR6................. 33 G3
Botany Cl *WGNE/HIN* WN2 .... 69 J3
Botany Rd *SPK/HALE* L24 .... 146 E1
Boteler Av *WARRW/BUR* WA5........ 14 A2
Botley Cl *GR/UP/WCH* CH49 ... 109 M8 2
The Boulevard *EP* CH65 .... 163 H1
WD/CROXPK L12 .... 98 D5
Boulting Av *WARRW/BUR* WA5.... 121 H3
Boulton Av *PS/BROM* CH62 .... 128 D5
WKBY CH48................................... 124 D1
Boundary Cl *CHLY/EC* PR7 .... 30 D7 1
Boundary Dr *CSBY/BLUN* L23.......... 70 E7
WLTN L25 .... 131 M6
Boundary Farm Rd *HLWD* L26 ..... 131 M7
Boundary La *BRSC* L40 .... 52 B2
CHTN/BK PR9 .... 23 M8
HES CH60 .... 141 J5
NPK/KEN L6 .... 113 K1
NWD/KWIPK L33 .... 86 F3
WGNNW/ST WN6............................ 55 J2
Boundary Pk *NSTN* CH64 .... 152 F5
Boundary Rd *CL/PREN* CH43 ...... 110 F5
ECCL WA10 .... 8 C6
HUY L36 .... 116 B5
LITH L21 .... 83 M4
PS/BROM CH62 .... 128 D6
WKBY CH48.................................... 124 F5
Boundary St *EV* L5 .... 96 D7
STHP PR8 .... 3 G9
WARR WA1 .... 15 M1
WGN WN1 .... 5 H6
Boundary St East *EV* L5 .... 96 F7 4
Bourne Av *GOL/RIS/CU* WA3........... 92 F5
Bourne Gdns *STHEL* WA9.............. 102 D4
Bournemouth Cl *RUNC* WA7 ..... 150 F7 1
Bourne St *NPK/KEN* L6 .... 113 K2 2
Bourton Rd *WLTN* L25 .... 131 K7
Bousfield St *ANF/KKDL* L4 .... 97 G6 3
Bowden Cl *ECCL* WA10 .... 101 K3 1
GOL/RIS/CU WA3 .... 107 H1
WD/CROXPK L12 .... 99 G3 1
Bowden Rd *ALL/GAR* L19............... 130 D7
Bowden St *LITH* L21........................ 83 K7
Bowdon Cl *WARR* WA1 .... 122 B5 1
Bowdon Rd *WAL/NB* CH45 .... 95 J7
Bowen Cl *WDN* WA8 .... 133 M1 1
Bower Gv *LITH* L21 .... 83 H6
Bower Rd *HES* CH60....................... 141 L5
HUY L36 .... 116 A1
WLTN L25 .... 131 H1
Bower St *WDN* WA8 .... 17 G1
Bowfell Cl *BEB* CH63 .... 154 F2 1
Bowfield Rd *ALL/GAR* L19 .... 130 D6
Bowgreen Cl *CL/PREN* CH43 .... 110 E6 1
Bowker's Green La *ORM* L39 .... 63 G8
Bowland Av *AIMK* WN4 .... 91 K1
CHLDW L16 .... 114 F4
CHLYE PR6 .... 32 F5 1
GOL/RIS/CU WA3 .... 92 E4 2
STHEL WA9 .... 118 C2
Bowland Cl *GOL/RIS/CU* WA3 .. 107 K8 1
PS/BROM CH62 .... 143 M4 1
RUNC WA7 .... 150 A8 1
Bowland Dr *LITH* L21 .... 83 L1
Bowles St *BTL* L20 .... 83 J8
Bowley Rd *CLB/OSW/ST* L13........... 98 B8
Bowling Green Cl *STHP* PR8 .... 25 H8
The Bowlings
WGNNW/ST WN6 .... 68 C3 1
Bowman Av *WARRS* WA4 .... 122 C8
Bowness Av *BEB* CH63 .... 143 L8
CL/PREN CH43 .... 127 J3
RNFD/HAY WA11 .... 89 K5
STHP PR8 .... 47 L2
WARRN/WOL WA2 .... 121 L3
Bowness Pl *WGNE/HIN* WN2 ..... 69 K5 1
Bowood Ct
WARRN/WOL WA2 .... 121 J1 1
Bowood St *TOX* L8 .... 129 H2 3
Bowring Cl *TOX* L8 .... 129 J1 2
Bowring Dr *NSTN* CH64 .... 152 D4
Bowring Park Av *CHLDW* L16........ 115 J5
Bowring Park Rd
DV/KA/FCH L14 .... 114 E4
Bowring St *TOX* L8 .... 129 J1 3
Bowscale Cl
GR/UP/WCH CH49 .... 110 A8 1
Bowscale Rd *NG/CROX* L11 .... 98 C4
Boxdale Rd *CALD/MH* L18............ 130 C1
Boxgrove Cl *WDN* WA8 .... 134 D2 1
Boxmoor Rd *CALD/MH* L18 ...... 130 C3 1
Boxtree Cl *WD/CROXPK* L12 .... 99 H1
Boxwood Cl *HUY* L36.................... 115 L3
Boycott St *EV* L5 .... 97 J7 2
Boyd Cl *MOR/LEA* CH46 .... 110 D2
WGNNW/ST WN6 .... 56 B5
Boydell Av *WARRS* WA4 .... 138 D3 2
Boydell Cl *STBRV* L28 .... 99 K6
Boyer Av *MGHL* L31 .... 72 F6
Boyes Brow *NWD/KWIPK* L33........ 85 M1
Boyle Av *WARRN/WOL* WA2 .... 122 A4
Boyton Ct *EHL/KEN* L7................... 113 L5
Brabant Rd *AIG/SPK* L17 .... 130 A4
Brabazon Pl *WGNW/BIL/O* WN5.... 67 L5
Braby Rd *LITH* L21 .... 83 L7
Bracebridge Dr *STHP* PR8............... 36 B3
Bracewell Cl *STHEL* WA9 .... 102 E7 1
Bracken Cl *CHLYE* PR6 .... 33 G5
GOL/RIS/CU WA3 .... 106 E8
Bracken Ct *STHEL* WA9 .... 118 E1 2
Brackendale *CHNE* CH2 .... 165 K2
GR/UP/WCH CH49 .... 126 E2 1
RUNC WA7 .... 149 M5
Brackendale Av *WLT/FAZ* L9 ..... 84 D6 4
Bracken Dr *WKBY* CH48................. 125 G3
Brackenhurst Dr
WAL/NB CH45 .... 95 L6 3
Brackenhurst Gn
NWD/KWIPK L33 .... 86 A3 2
Bracken La *BEB* CH63 .... 127 M8
Bracken Rd *GTS/LS* CH66 .... 163 G1
LEIGH WN7 .... 81 K8
Brackenside *HES* CH60 .... 141 H3 1
Brackenway *FMBY* L37 .... 47 J7 1
Bracken Wy *FROD/HEL* WA6......... 160 E7
Bracken Wd *WD/CROXPK* L12 ...... 99 G1
Brackenwood Gv
RAIN/WH L35 .... 117 H2 1
Brackenwood Rd *BEB* CH63......... 127 M8
Brackley Cl *WAL/EG* CH44 .... 111 J2
Brackley St *RUNC* WA7 .... 18 E2
WARRS WA4 .... 137 L4
Bracknell Av *KKBY* L32 .... 85 M5
Bracknell Cl *KKBY* L32 .... 86 A4
Bracknel Wy *ORM* L39 .... 62 C4 1
Bradbourne Cl
WD/CROXPK L12 .... 99 G2 2
Bradda Cl *GR/UP/WCH* CH49 ...... 110 B6
Braddan Av *CLB/OSW/ST* L13 .... 98 A8 1
Bradden Cl *BEB* CH63 .... 143 K3
Brade St *CHTN/BK* PR9 .... 25 L1
Bradewell Cl *ANF/KKDL* L4 .... 97 G5 2
Bradewell St *ANF/KKDL* L4 .... 97 G5
Bradfield Av *AIN/FAZ* L10 .... 84 E2 1
Bradfield St *EHL/KEN* L7 .... 113 L3
Bradford St *WGNS/IIMK* WN3.......... 4 E6
Bradgate Cl *HOY* CH47.................... 109 K4
Bradlegh Rd *NEWLW* WA12........... 104 E3
Bradley Bvd *WARRW/BUR* WA5 .. 120 D7
Bradley Fold *RAIN/WH* L35 .... 116 C5
Bradley La *CHLY/EC* PR7 .... 30 F7
FROD/HEL WA6 .... 160 F7
WARRW/BUR WA5 .... 104 B3
WGNNW/ST WN6............................ 56 B3
Bradley Rd *LITH* L21 .... 83 K4
Bradley St *CHTN/BK* PR9................... 3 K2
Bradley Wy *WDN* WA8 .... 17 G2
Bradman Rd *MOR/LEA* CH46 .... 109 L4
NWD/KWIPK L33 .... 86 E2
Bradmoor Rd *PS/BROM* CH62 .... 143 M5
Bradshaw Brow *BRSC* L40 .... 41 G4
Bradshaw Cl *ECCL* WA10 .... 8 A3
WGNNW/ST WN6 .... 55 M4
Bradshawgate *WGN* WN1................. 5 H4
Bradshaw La *BRSC* L40 .... 41 G3
SKEL WN8 .... 53 L4
WARRS WA4 .... 138 D2
Bradshaw's La *STHP* PR8 .... 34 F7
Bradshaw St *WDN* WA8 .... 134 C3 2
WGN WN1 .... 68 F3
WGNW/BIL/O WN5 .... 67 J7
Bradstone Cl *NG/CROX* L11 .... 85 K7 1
Bradville Rd *WLT/FAZ* L9................. 84 E6
Bradwell Cl *EP* CH65 .... 163 J1
WKBY CH48 .... 124 F3 1
Bradwell Rd *GOL/RIS/CU* WA3 .... 93 G6
Brady St *HOR/BR* BL6 .... 45 J8
Braeburn Ct *LEIGH* WN7 .... 81 M8 3
Braehaven Rd *WAL/NB* CH45 ..... 95 L6 2
Braemar Av *CHTN/BK* PR9 .... 25 G3 1
CHTN/BK PR9 .... 25 H3 1
Braemar Cl *RAIN/WH* L35 .... 117 H2 2
WARRN/WOL WA2 .... 122 C2 2
Braemar St *BTL* L20 .... 7 K8 1
Braemore Cl *WGNS/IIMK* WN3 ...... 78 E3
Braemore Rd *WAL/EG* CH44 ...... 111 H1 2
Braeside Cl *GTS/LS* CH66 .... 155 L8 1
Braeside Crs *WGNW/BIL/O* WN5 .. 77 M8
Braeside Gdns
GR/UP/WCH CH49......................... 110 B8
Brae St *EHL/KEN* L7 .... 113 K3
Brahms Cl *TOX* L8 .... 113 K7 2
Braidhaven *WGNNW/ST* WN6 .... 55 G6 1
Braid St *BIRK* CH41 .... 11 G2
Brainerd St *CLB/OSW/ST* L13 .... 98 A8
Braithwaite *WGNNW/ST* WN6 .... 55 J7
Braithwaite Cl *RAIN/WH* L35 .... 117 L2 1
RUNC WA7 .... 149 M8 1
Braithwaite Rd *GOL/RIS/CU* WA3.. 92 F4
Brakenwood Ms *WARRS* WA4 .. 138 E4 1
Bramberton Pl *ANF/KKDL* L4 ...... 97 L4 1
Bramberton Rd *ANF/KKDL* L4 .... 97 L4
Bramble Av *BIRK* CH41 .... 111 H6
Bramble Cl *WARRW/BUR* WA5 .... 136 A2
Bramble Gv *WGNW/BIL/O* WN5 .... 68 A6
The Brambles *AIMK* WN4 .... 78 F8 1
CHLY/EC PR7 .... 43 H3 1
Bramble Wy *MOR/LEA* CH46........ 109 M3
RUNC WA7 .... 161 G1 1
SKEL WN8 .... 53 L4
Bramblewood *LEY/BBR* PR5 .... 29 K2 1
Bramblewood Cl
CL/PREN CH43 .... 126 E1
NTHLY L27 .... 116 A8 1
Brambling Cl *RUNC* WA7 .... 150 A8 2
Brambling Pk *HLWD* L26 .... 132 A4
Brambling Wy
GOL/RIS/CU WA3 .... 93 G5 3
Bramcote Av *RNFD/HAY* WA11...... 89 M7
Bramcote Cl *NWD/KWIPK* L33 ... 86 C1 1
Bramcote Rd *NWD/KWIPK* L33...... 86 B1
Bramcote Wk *NWD/KWIPK* L33 .... 86 B1
Bramerton Ct *WKBY* CH48 .... 124 B2
Bramford Cl
GR/UP/WCH CH49 .... 110 A8 2
Bramhall Cl *SPK/HALE* L24 ...... 147 G3 1
Bramhall Dr *PS/BROM* CH62........ 155 H2
Bramhall Rd *CSBY/WL* L22 .... 83 G5
SKEL WN8 .... 65 H3
Bramhall St *WARRW/BUR* WA5.... 121 G8
Bramley Av *BEB* CH63 .... 128 A6
Bramley Cl *GTS/LS* CH66 .... 163 H5 3
NTHLY L27 .... 116 A8 2
The Bramleys *MGHL* L31 .... 72 E6
Brampton Cl *WGNE/HIN* WN2........ 80 B4
Brampton Ct *STHEL* WA9 .... 103 K2 1
Brampton Dr *TOX* L8 .... 113 J5
Bramshill Cl *GOL/RIS/CU* WA3...... 107 J7
Bramwell Av *CL/PREN* CH43 .... 127 J4
Bramwell St *STHEL* WA9 .... 103 G1
Brancaster Dr *GOL/RIS/CU* WA3.... 93 J6
Brancepeth Ct *EP* CH65 .... 20 F9
Branch St *WGNE/HIN* WN2 .... 69 J6
Branch Wy *RNFD/HAY* WA11........... 90 F7
Brancker Av *RAIN/WH* L35 .... 117 K1
Brancker St *CHLY/EC* PR7 .... 32 C8 2
Brancote Gdns *PS/BROM* CH62 .. 143 M6
Brancote Mt *CL/PREN* CH43 ..... 111 H7 1
Brancote Rd *CL/PREN* CH43 .... 111 H7
Brandearth Hey *STBRV* L28 .... 99 K6
Brandon *WDN* WA8 .... 133 J3
Brandon Cl *SKEL* WN8 .... 66 C6 2
Brandon St *BIRK* CH41 .... 11 L5
Brandreth Cl *RAIN/WH* L35 .... 117 L2 2
Brandreth Delph *SKEL* WN8 .... 53 M2
Brandreth Dr *SKEL* WN8 .... 53 L3
Brandreth Pk *SKEL* WN8 .... 53 L1
Brandreth Pl *WGNNW/ST* WN6....... 56 B4
Brandwood Av
WARRN/WOL WA2 .... 121 K3 3
Branfield Cl *WD/CROXPK* L12 .... 99 G2 3
Bransdale Cl *WARRW/BUR* WA5 .. 120 A6
Bransfield Cl *WGNS/IIMK* WN3 ...... 79 J2
Bransford Cl *AIMK* WN4.................. 91 L3
Branstree Av *NG/CROX* L11............ 98 B3
Brantfield Ct
WARRN/WOL WA2 .... 122 A3 3
Branthwaite *WGNE/HIN* WN2......... 69 K4
Branthwaite Cl *NG/CROX* L11 .... 98 C4 1
Branthwaite Crs *NG/CROX* L11 ...... 98 C4
Branthwaite Gv *NG/CROX* L11 .. 98 C4 2
Brasenose Rd *BTL* L20 .... 6 F8
Brassey St *BIRK* CH41 .... 10 B2
TOX L8.. 113 G7
Brathay Cl *WARRN/WOL* WA2 ...... 121 L2
Brattan Rd *RF/TRAN* CH42 .... 10 E9
Bratton Cl *WGNS/IIMK* WN3 .... 78 E4
Braunton Rd *AIG/SPK* L17 .... 130 A5
WAL/NB CH45 .... 95 J7 1
Braybrooke Rd *NG/CROX* L11.......... 98 C2
Bray Cl *RUNC* WA7 .... 149 M7
Braydon Cl *WLTN* L25 .... 131 L7 1
Brayfield Rd *ANF/KKDL* L4 .... 97 M4
Bray Rd *SPK/HALE* L24.................. 146 E1
Bray St *BIRK* CH41 .... 10 C2
Brayton Ct *WGNE/HIN* WN2 .... 69 M7
Brechin Rd *NWD/KWIPK* L33.......... 86 B3
Breckfield Pl *EV* L5 .... 97 H8 1
Breckfield Rd North *EV* L5 .... 97 H7
Breckfield Rd South
NPK/KEN L6 .... 97 J8
Breck Pl *WAL/EG* CH44 .... 111 J2 2
Breck Rd *NPK/KEN* L6 .... 97 J8
WAL/EG CH44 .... 95 H8
WDN WA8 .... 16 F1
Breckside Av *WAL/EG* CH44 .... 111 G1
Breckside Pk *NPK/KEN* L6.............. 97 L7
The Breck *GTS/LS* CH66 .... 156 A6
Brecon Av *NTHTN* L30 .... 84 B4
Brecon Cl *WGNE/HIN* WN2 .... 80 D3 1
Brecon Dr *GTS/LS* CH66 .... 163 G4
WGNE/HIN WN2 .... 81 J2
Brecon Rd *RF/TRAN* CH42 .... 127 L4
Bredon Av *CHLY/EC* PR7 .... 31 M4
Bredon Cl *GTS/LS* CH66 .... 155 J7
Breeze Cl *WLT/FAZ* L9..................... 97 H3
Breeze Hl *ANF/KKDL* L4 .... 7 M6
BTL L20 .... 7 K5 1
WGNNW/ST WN6 .... 56 D6
Breezehill Cl *NSTN* CH64 .... 153 G5
Breezehill Pk *NSTN* CH64 .... 153 H5
Breezehill Rd *NSTN* CH64 .... 153 H5
Breeze La *WLT/FAZ* L9 .... 97 H2
Breeze Rd *STHP* PR8 .... 35 G3
Brelade Rd *CLB/OSW/ST* L13 ...... 114 B1
Bremhill Rd *NG/CROX* L11.............. 98 B2
Bremner Cl *EHL/KEN* L7 .... 113 L4 2
Brenda Crs *CSBY/BLUN* L23 .... 71 J6
Brendale Av *MGHL* L31 .... 72 E5
Brendon Av *LITH* L21 .... 83 J4
WARRN/WOL WA2 .... 121 J2 2
Brendon Gv *STHEL* WA9 .... 103 J1 1
Brendor Rd *WLTN* L25 .... 131 K4
Brenig St *BIRK* CH41 .... 111 H4 1
Brenka Av *WLT/FAZ* L9................... 84 D4
Brentfield *WDN* WA8 .... 133 M3 1
Brentnall Cl
WARRW/BUR WA5 .... 120 E8 1
Brent Wy *HLWD* L26 .... 132 B7
Brentwood *WGNW/BIL/O* WN5 .... 67 M8
Brentwood Av *AIG/SPK* L17 .... 129 L2
CSBY/BLUN L23 .... 71 H8
Brentwood Cl *ECCL* WA10 .... 101 K2
HTWN L38 .... 70 B3
Brentwood Ct *CHTN/BK* PR9 .... 24 F4
Brentwood Rd *CHLYE* PR6 .... 44 D5
Brentwood St *WAL/EG* CH44 .... 111 L3
Brereton Av *BEB* CH63 .... 128 C7
WAV L15 .... 114 C6
Brereton Cl *RUNC* WA7 .... 150 C5 1
Bretherton Pl *RAIN/WH* L35 .... 117 L1 1

Bretherton Rd LEY/BBR PR5 29 J1
PR/KW L34 101 G7
Bretherton Rw WGN WN1 4 E4
Bretherton St WGNE/HIN WN2 69 L7 1
Bretlands Rd CSBY/BLUN L23 71 K8
Bretton Fold STHP PR8 25 H8
Brett St BIRK CH41 10 C2
Brewery La FMBY L37 47 H7
MGHL L31 85 G1
Brewster St ANF/KKDL L4 7 L8
Brian Av PEN/TH CH61 126 B7
WARRN/WOL WA2 121 M5
WARRS WA4 138 A4
Briar Av CHLY/EC PR7 31 L1
Briar Cl AIMK WN4 91 J1
WGNE/HIN WN2 81 K1
Briardale Gdns GTS/LS CH66 155 L7 1
Briardale Rd BEB CH63 128 B6
CALD/MH L18 130 B1
GTS/LS CH66 155 L7
NSTN CH64 154 C5
RF/TRAN CH42 127 L1
WAL/EG CH44 112 A3 3
Briar Dr HES CH60 141 J5
HUY L36 115 M3
Briarfield Av WDN WA8 133 J4
Briarfield Rd EP CH65 20 B4
HES CH60 141 J5
Briarly WGNNW/ST WN6 56 C6
Briar Rd GOL/RIS/CU WA3 92 D5
STHP PR8 47 M1
WGNW/BIL/O WN5 67 M6
Briars Brook BRSC L40 52 C2
Briars Cl RAIN/WH L35 117 M4
Briars Gn ECCL WA10 8 E2
SKEL WN8 65 J1
Briars La BRSC L40 52 C2
MGHL L31 73 G4
The Briars CHLY/EC PR7 30 E7
STHP PR8 35 H4 1
Briar St ANF/KKDL L4 96 F6
Briarswood Cl RAIN/WH L35 117 H3 2
RF/TRAN CH42 128 B5
Briarwood RUNC WA7 150 D4
Briarwood Av WARR WA1 15 L1
Briarwood Rd AIG/SPK L17 130 A2
Briary Cl HES CH60 141 K4
Briary Cl HTWN L38 70 B2
Brickcroft La LEY/BBR PR5 29 J2
Brickfields HUY L36 116 C4
Brickhurst Wy WARR WA1 122 D5
Brick Kiln La BRSC L40 39 J2
WGN WN1 4 F2
Brick St CLVPS L1 112 F6
NEWLW WA12 104 B2
Brickwall Gn SFTN L29 72 B6
Brickwall La SFTN L29 72 B6
Bride St ANF/KKDL L4 97 H3
Bridge Av ORM L39 63 G1
WARRS WA4 138 B1
Bridge Ct NSTN CH64 153 G6 1
WKBY CH48 124 C2
Bridge Cft LITH L21 83 L2
Bridgecroft Rd WAL/NB CH45 95 K7 1
Bridge Farm Cl
GR/UP/WCH CH49 126 D1 1
Bridge Farm Dr MGHL L31 73 H3 1
Bridgefield Cl WLTN L25 115 K6 1
Bridgeford Av
WD/CROXPK L12 98 C6 1
Bridge Gdns WD/CROXPK L12 99 H4
Bridge Gv STHP PR8 3 H6
Bridgehall Dr SKEL WN8 66 D6
Bridge La FROD/HEL WA6 160 E4
NTHTN L30 84 A2
WARR WA1 122 E7
WARRS WA4 138 A6
Bridgeman St ECCL WA10 8 B6 1
WARRW/BUR WA5 136 F1 1
Bridgeman Ter WGN WN1 4 E1
Bridge Meadow GTS/LS CH66 163 H3
Bridgend Cl WDN WA8 133 M2
Bridgend Dr STHP PR8 47 K1
Bridgenorth Rd PEN/TH CH61 141 G1
Bridge Rd CALD/MH L18 130 C2
CSBY/BLUN L23 82 E2
EHL/KEN L7 113 M5
HUY L36 115 L3
LITH L21 83 J6 1
MGHL L31 72 F6
PR/KW L34 100 F8
STHEL WA9 118 F3
WARR WA1 122 E6
WKBY CH48 124 C2
Bridges La SFTN L29 72 B6
Bridges Rd EP CH65 21 J5
Bridge St BIRK CH41 11 L4
BTL L20 6 F7
ECCL WA10 9 G6
GOL/RIS/CU WA3 92 C6 1
NEWLW WA12 92 C6
NEWLW WA12 104 D2
NSTN CH64 153 G6
ORM L39 63 G1
RUNC WA7 19 J3
STHP PR8 3 H5
WARR WA1 14 E6
WGNE/HIN WN2 69 J2
WGNE/HIN WN2 69 M7
WGNS/IIMK WN3 4 E6
Bridge View Cl WDN WA8 149 J1 2
Bridgeview Dr
NWD/KWIPK L33 86 B1 1
Bridgewater Av WARRS WA4 138 B1
Bridgewater Cl LITH L21 83 J3 1
Bridgewater Ms WARRS WA4 137 L5 1
Bridgewater St CLVPS L1 112 F6
RUNC WA7 19 G2
WGNS/IIMK WN3 4 D5
WGNW/BIL/O WN5 68 B7 3
Bridgewater Wy HUY L36 116 C5
Bridgeway NG/CROX L11 98 A4 1
Bridgeway East RUNC WA7 150 E3
Bridgeway West RUNC WA7 150 D3
Bridge Wills La CHTN/BK PR9 22 E8 2
Bridgewood Dr GTS/LS CH66 162 E3
Bridle Av WAL/EG CH44 112 A3
Bridle Cl CL/PREN CH43 110 D7
PS/BROM CH62 144 A6
Bridle Ct STHEL WA9 102 E5 1
Bridlemere Ct WARR WA1 122 A5 1
Bridle Pk PS/BROM CH62 143 M6
Bridle Rd NTHTN L30 84 C5
PS/BROM CH62 144 A6
WAL/EG CH44 112 A3
Bridle Wy GTS/LS CH66 162 F2
NTHTN L30 84 B5
Briercliffe Rd CHLYE PR6 32 F4
Brierfield SKEL WN8 65 M8
Brierfield Rd WAV L15 114 B7 2
Brierley Cl NTHTN L30 84 D1 1
Brierley St WARRW/BUR WA5 14 B4
Briers Cl WARRN/WOL WA2 122 B2 1
Briery Hey Av NWD/KWIPK L33 86 B3
Brighouse Cl ORM L39 50 F7 1
Brightgate Cl EHL/KEN L7 113 K5 2
Brighton Rd CSBY/WL L22 82 F4
HUY L36 116 D2 1
STHP PR8 35 J2
Brighton St CHLYE PR6 33 G5 1
WAL/EG CH44 112 A2
WARRW/BUR WA5 121 G7
Brighton V CSBY/WL L22 82 E3 1
Brightstone Cl CHTN/BK PR9 23 K8
Bright St BIRK CH41 10 F6
CHTN/BK PR9 25 H6
NPK/KEN L6 113 J2
Brightwell Cl
GR/UP/WCH CH49 126 B1 2
WARRW/BUR WA5 120 A8 1
Brignall Gv GOL/RIS/CU WA3 92 F4 2
Brill St BIRK CH41 10 C2
Brimelow Crs
WARRW/BUR WA5 136 A2 1
Brimstage Av BEB CH63 127 M5
Brimstage Cl HES CH60 141 L5 1
Brimstage Gn HES CH60 141 M5 2
Brimstage La BEB CH63 142 D1
Brimstage Rd ANF/KKDL L4 7 M6
BEB CH63 142 E3
HES CH60 141 L5
Brimstage St BIRK CH41 10 F9
Brindle St CHLY/EC PR7 32 E7
Brindley Av WARRS WA4 138 B1
Brindley Cl LITH L21 83 J3
Brindley Rd KKBY L32 85 L3 2
RUNC WA7 150 B2
STHEL WA9 103 G7
Brindley St RUNC WA7 18 F2
TOX L8 112 F7
WGNW/BIL/O WN5 67 L8
Brinklow Cl STHP PR8 34 C8
Brinley Cl PS/BROM CH62 143 M8
Brinton Cl NTHLY L27 115 L7
WDN WA8 134 A5
Brisbane Av WAL/NB CH45 95 J5 2
Brisbane St STHEL WA9 101 M6
Briscoe Dr MOR/LEA CH46 110 A6
Bristol Av RUNC WA7 151 G7
WAL/EG CH44 111 L1 2
Bristol Dr GTS/LS CH66 163 G4
Bristol Rd WAV L15 114 C7
Bristow Cl WARRW/BUR WA5 120 C5
Britannia Av EHL/KEN L7 113 M6
Britannia Crs TOX L8 129 H2
Britannia Rd WAL/NB CH45 111 J1
WGNW/BIL/O WN5 67 L5
Britonside Av KKBY L32 86 B5
Brittania Gdns FROD/HEL WA6 166 D3
Brittania Rd FROD/HEL WA6 166 D3
Brittarge Brow NTHLY L27 132 A1
Britten Cl TOX L8 113 K7
Broadacre WGNNW/ST WN6 55 J3
Broadbelt St ANF/KKDL L4 97 H3 2
Broadbent Av WARRS WA4 138 B1
Broadfield Av CL/PREN CH43 110 E5 2
Broadfield Cl CL/PREN CH43 110 D6 1
Broadfields CHLY/EC PR7 32 D3
RUNC WA7 150 E5
Broadgate Av STHEL WA9 102 D4
Broad Green Rd
CLB/OSW/ST L13 114 D3
Broadheath Av CL/PREN CH43 110 E6
Broad Hey NTHTN L30 83 M2
Broad Hey Cl WLTN L25 131 K2
Broadheys La KNUT WA16 139 M7
Broadhurst Av
GOL/RIS/CU WA3 107 H3
WARRW/BUR WA5 136 F1 2
Broadhurst La WGNNW/ST WN6 42 B7
Broadhurst St AIG/SPK L17 129 L2 1
Broadlake NSTN CH64 154 B5
Broadland Gdns GTS/LS CH66 163 H3
Broadland Rd GTS/LS CH66 163 H3
Broadlands STHP PR8 35 G2
WGNNW/ST WN6 55 K7
Broad La ANF/KKDL L4 97 M4
FMBY L37 47 L6
FMBY L37 60 A3
HES CH60 140 E4
KKBY L32 86 B5
NG/CROX L11 98 C4
ORM L39 61 L3
RNFD/HAY WA11 89 K3
SFTN L29 71 L4
WARRS WA4 138 D5
WARRW/BUR WA5 103 M5
Broadley Av GOL/RIS/CU WA3 92 E6 1
Broadmead ALL/GAR L19 131 G6 1
HES CH60 141 L6
SKEL WN8 53 K3
Broad Meadow La LEY/BBR PR5 29 G2
Broad Oak Av
RNFD/HAY WA11 90 C7 1
WARRW/BUR WA5 136 A1
Broad Oak Cl CHLYE PR6 44 C5 1
Broadoak Rd DV/KA/FCH L14 115 H2
MGHL L31 73 G4
Broad Oak Rd STHEL WA9 103 G2
Broadoaks
GR/UP/WCH CH49 110 A7 2
Broad O' Th' La WGNNW/ST WN6 55 J7
Broad Pl NG/CROX L11 98 B5
Broadriding Rd
WGNNW/ST WN6 55 G7
Broad Sq NG/CROX L11 98 B5
Broadstone Dr BEB CH63 143 H3 2
Broad Vw NG/CROX L11 98 B5
Broadway BEB CH63 127 M6
ECCL WA10 88 D8
ECCL WA10 101 L5
GR/UP/WCH CH49 109 M8
NG/CROX L11 98 A4
WAL/NB CH45 95 H8
WDN WA8 133 J4
Broadway Av WAL/NB CH45 95 H8
Broadway Cl STHP PR8 34 D8
Broadwood Av MGHL L31 72 E6
Broadwood St WAV L15 114 A6 3
Brockenhurst Rd WLT/FAZ L9 84 C8 1
Brockhall Cl RAIN/WH L35 101 J7 2
Brock Hall Cl STHEL WA9 118 E1 3
Brockholme Rd CALD/MH L18 130 C4
Brocklebank La ALL/GAR L19 130 F5
Brocklebank Rd CHTN/BK PR9 25 G4
Brock Mill La WGN WN1 56 E8
Brock Pl WGNE/HIN WN2 80 B3
Brock Rd CHLYE PR6 32 F4
GOL/RIS/CU WA3 122 F2
Brockstedes Av AIMK WN4 79 G7
Brock St ANF/KKDL L4 97 G5
WGN WN1 5 K4
Brocstedes Rd AIMK WN4 78 F6
Brodie Av ALL/GAR L19 130 D5
CALD/MH L18 130 C2
Brogden Av GOL/RIS/CU WA3 107 G1
Bromborough Rd BEB CH63 128 C8
Bromborough Village Rd
PS/BROM CH62 143 M4
Brome Wy BEB CH63 143 K3
Bromilow Rd SKEL WN8 64 E4
STHEL WA9 103 H3
Bromley Av CALD/MH L18 114 B8 3
GOL/RIS/CU WA3 92 F6
Bromley Cl HES CH60 141 G6 1
WARRN/WOL WA2 122 B2
WGNE/HIN WN2 69 J3
Bromley Dr LEIGH WN7 81 M5
Bromley Gn CHLYE PR6 33 H1 1
Bromley Rd WAL/NB CH45 95 J6
Brompton Av AIG/SPK L17 113 L8
CSBY/BLUN L23 82 E2
WAL/EG CH44 111 L1 3
Brompton Gdns
WARRW/BUR WA5 121 G6 1
Brompton Rd STHP PR8 25 G6
Brompton Wy GTS/LS CH66 163 G4
Bromsgrove Rd
GR/UP/WCH CH49 125 L1
Bromyard Cl BTL L20 6 E3 1
Bronington Av PS/BROM CH62 143 M7
Bronte Cl CSBY/BLUN L23 82 D1
WGNS/IIMK WN3 68 C8 1
Bronte St ECCL WA10 8 B4
VAUX/LVPD L3 13 K6
Brook Av MGHL L31 73 G2
WARRS WA4 122 B8
WARRS WA4 138 A4
Brookbank Ct AIN/FAZ L10 85 K6
Brookbridge Rd
CLB/OSW/ST L13 98 A7 1
Brook Cl WAL/EG CH44 95 L8
WDN WA8 117 L7
Brookdale CHLYE PR6 44 C4 1
RAIN/WH L35 133 J2
Brookdale Av North
GR/UP/WCH CH49 126 A1
Brookdale Av South
GR/UP/WCH CH49 126 A2
Brookdale Cl GR/UP/WCH CH49 126 A1
Brookdale Rd WAV L15 114 A7
Brook Dr WARRW/BUR WA5 120 C8
Brooke Cl CHTN/BK PR9 25 K6
Brook End STHEL WA9 103 J4
Brooke Rd East CSBY/WL L22 82 F3
Brooke Rd West CSBY/WL L22 82 E3
Brooke St CHLYE PR6 32 F6
Brook Farm ORM L39 63 G1
Brookfield BRSC L40 40 E3
LEY/BBR PR5 29 K2 2
SKEL WN8 53 L3 1
Brookfield Av CSBY/BLUN L23 82 F2
CSBY/WL L22 83 H5
RAIN/WH L35 101 L8
RUNC WA7 150 A3
Brookfield Cl LYMM WA13 139 M2
Brookfield Dr WLT/FAZ L9 84 E8
Brookfield Gdns WKBY CH48 124 D3
Brookfield La ORM L39 62 C8
Brookfield Pk WARRS WA4 138 C3 1
Brookfield Rd GOL/RIS/CU WA3 106 E1
LYMM WA13 139 M2
SKEL WN8 66 E7
WKBY CH48 124 D3 1
Brookfield St NEWLW WA12 104 D2
Brook Furlong FROD/HEL WA6 160 A3
Brook Hey NSTN CH64 152 D3
Brook Hey Dr NWD/KWIPK L33 86 B1
Brookhill Cl BTL L20 7 J4
Brookhill Rd BTL L20 7 J3
Brook House Gv ECCL WA10 101 J2
Brookhouse Rd ORM L39 50 F7 2
Brookhouse St WGN WN1 5 G4
Brookhouse Ter WGN WN1 5 G5
Brookhurst Av BEB CH63 143 L7
Brookhurst Cl BEB CH63 143 L8
Brookhurst Rd BEB CH63 143 L7
Brookland Av
WGNE/HIN WN2 69 M8 6
Brookland La STHEL WA9 103 J3
Brookland Rd BIRK CH41 111 J7
WGN WN1 68 D2
Brookland Rd East
CLB/OSW/ST L13 114 C2
Brookland Rd West
CLB/OSW/ST L13 114 C2
Brooklands ORM L39 51 H7
Brooklands Av AIMK WN4 91 M3 1
CSBY/WL L22 83 G5
Brooklands Dr MGHL L31 72 F5
WGNW/BIL/O WN5 66 F8
Brooklands Gdns NSTN CH64 152 E4
Brooklands Gv BRSC L40 52 B2
Brooklands Rd ECCL WA10 101 J1
NSTN CH64 152 E4
SKEL WN8 66 E6
The Brooklands HUY L36 116 A4 1
Brookland St WARR WA1 15 M1
Brook La CHLY/EC PR7 42 D1
GOL/RIS/CU WA3 123 J5
NSTN CH64 152 E3
ORM L39 63 G1
RNFD/HAY WA11 77 H6
WGNW/BIL/O WN5 67 J8
Brooklet Rd HES CH60 141 L5
Brooklyn Dr EP CH65 156 B8
Brook Lynn Av GOL/RIS/CU WA3 93 H4
Brook Meadow PEN/TH CH61 126 A6
Brook Pk MGHL L31 72 E6
Brook Rd BTL L20 6 E4
CSBY/BLUN L23 71 J7
GTS/LS CH66 155 M8
LYMM WA13 139 M1
MGHL L31 73 G5
WLT/FAZ L9 97 J1
Brooks Aly CLVPS L1 13 H8 1
Brookside CHLY/EC PR7 31 L3
CHLY/EC PR7 43 H4
Brookside Av AIMK WN4 79 H5
CSBY/WL L22 83 H5
DV/KA/FCH L14 114 F2
ECCL WA10 88 E8 1
LYMM WA13 139 L1
RNFD/HAY WA11 76 A6
WARRS WA4 137 M4
WARRW/BUR WA5 120 C8
Brookside Cl RAIN/WH L35 117 G1
RNFD/HAY WA11 90 D6 2
WD/CROXPK L12 99 H4
WGNW/BIL/O WN5 90 A1
Brookside Crs
GR/UP/WCH CH49 109 M8
Brookside Dr
GR/UP/WCH CH49 110 A8 3
Brookside Rd FROD/HEL WA6 160 C5
RAIN/WH L35 117 G1 1
STHP PR8 35 L4
WGN WN1 56 D4
Brookside Vw RNFD/HAY WA11 90 D6
Brookside Wy RNFD/HAY WA11 90 D6
Brooks Rd FMBY L37 58 F3
The Brooks RNFD/HAY WA11 89 J6
Brook St AIMK WN4 91 L3 1
BIRK CH41 10 F2
CHLYE PR6 44 C4
CHTN/BK PR9 25 L1
ECCL WA10 9 G5
GOL/RIS/CU WA3 92 C6
GOL/RIS/CU WA3 93 J4
NSTN CH64 153 G5
PS/BROM CH62 128 C7
RAIN/WH L35 101 H8
RUNC WA7 19 G2 1
VAUX/LVPD L3 12 D5
WGNE/HIN WN2 69 J6 1
WGNS/IIMK WN3 79 H1
Brook St East BIRK CH41 11 J4
Brooks Wy FMBY L37 58 F3
Brookthorpe Cl WAL/NB CH45 95 K8
Brook V CSBY/WL L22 83 H5
Brookvale Av North RUNC WA7 150 D8
Brookvale Av South RUNC WA7 150 D7
Brookvale Cl WARRW/BUR WA5 104 B7
Brookview WGNE/HIN WN2 80 F1 5
Brook Wk PEN/TH CH61 125 M6
Brookway CL/PREN CH43 127 G4
GR/UP/WCH CH49 110 A8
WAL/NB CH45 95 J8
Brook Wy WARRW/BUR WA5 120 C8
Brookway La STHEL WA9 103 H4
Brook Well NSTN CH64 153 G8
Brookwood Cl WARRS WA4 137 K5
Brookwood Rd HUY L36 116 A1
Broom Av WARRS WA4 138 A7
Broom Cl PR/KW L34 101 H7
Broome Ct RUNC WA7 150 D8 2
Broome Rd STHP PR8 35 K2
Broomfield Cl HES CH60 140 E4
Broomfield Gdns WLT/FAZ L9 84 B8
Broomfield Pl
WGNNW/ST WN6 56 A4 1
Broomfield Rd WGNNW/ST WN6 56 A4
WLT/FAZ L9 84 B8 1
WLT/FAZ L9 84 B8 1
Broomfields Rd WARRS WA4 137 M6
Broomflat Cl
WGNNW/ST WN6 56 A4 2
Broomhey Av WGN WN1 56 E8
Broomhey Ter WGNE/HIN WN2 5 K5
Broom Hl CL/PREN CH43 111 H6 1
Broomhill Cl NTHLY L27 115 L7 1
Broomholme WGNNW/ST WN6 54 F6
Broomlands HES CH60 141 G5
Broomleigh Cl BEB CH63 127 M8
Broom Rd ECCL WA10 101 K5
WGNW/BIL/O WN5 67 M7
Broomsgrove AIN/FAZ L10 85 G4 1
Broom Wy HLWD L26 131 M6
Broseley Av GOL/RIS/CU WA3 106 F1
PS/BROM CH62 143 L4
Broseley La GOL/RIS/CU WA3 93 M8
Broster Av MOR/LEA CH46 109 L5
Broster Cl MOR/LEA CH46 109 L5
Brosters La HOY CH47 108 F4 1
Brotherton Cl
PS/BROM CH62 143 L5 1
Brougham Av BIRK CH41 128 B2 3
Brougham Rd WAL/EG CH44 111 M2
Brough Cl WGNE/HIN WN2 81 G2 1
Broughton Av GOL/RIS/CU WA3 92 F6
STHP PR8 3 M9
WKBY CH48 124 C2 1
Broughton Dr ALL/GAR L19 130 C6
Broughton Hall Rd
WD/CROXPK L12 99 C8
Broughton Rd WAL/EG CH44 111 K2
Brow La HES CH60 141 H6
Browmere Dr GOL/RIS/CU WA3 106 C6
Brownbill Bank NTHLY L27 116 A8
Brown Heath Av
WGNW/BIL/O WN5 89 M2
Brownhill Dr WARR WA1 122 B5
Browning Av RF/TRAN CH42 128 B4
WDN WA8 16 A4
WGNS/IIMK WN3 79 H1
Browning Cl HUY L36 116 B4
Browning Dr EP CH65 163 H1
Browning Gv WGNNW/ST WN6 68 A2
Browning Rd CSBY/WL L22 82 F3 1
WAL/NB CH45 94 F8 1
Browning St BTL L20 6 D2
LEIGH WN7 81 M7
Brownley St CHLYE PR6 33 G6 1
Brownlow Av WGNE/HIN WN2 69 K6
Brownlow Hl VAUX/LVPD L3 13 J7
Brownlow La WGNW/BIL/O WN5 77 L4
Brownlow Rd PS/BROM CH62 128 D6
Brownlow St VAUX/LVPD L3 13 L7
Brownmere WGNNW/ST WN6 68 B3 1
Brownmoor La
CSBY/BLUN L23 83 J1 1
Brownmoor Pk CSBY/BLUN L23 83 H2
Browns Hey CHLY/EC PR7 32 C3 2
Brown's La NTHTN L30 84 C2 1
Brown St CHLYE PR6 32 F5
HOR/BR BL6 57 M3
WDN WA8 17 J5
WGNE/HIN WN2 69 J6
WGNE/HIN WN2 81 G4
WGNS/IIMK WN3 4 D5
Brownville Rd
CLB/OSW/ST L13 97 M7 2
Brow Rd CL/PREN CH43 110 F4
Brows Cl FMBY L37 59 G2
Brow Side EV L5 13 L2
Brows La FMBY L37 59 G2
Broxholme Wy MGHL L31 72 F6
Broxton Av CL/PREN CH43 127 H3
WGNW/BIL/O WN5 67 H6
WKBY CH48 124 D2
Broxton Cl WDN WA8 133 L2 2
Broxton Rd GTS/LS CH66 156 A8
Broxton St WAV L15 114 A5
Bruce Av WARRN/WOL WA2 121 M4
Bruce Crs BEB CH63 143 L7
Bruce Dr GTS/LS CH66 162 E1
Bruce St ECCL WA10 8 D5
TOX L8 129 J1 1
Bruche Av WARR WA1 122 B6
Bruche Dr WARR WA1 122 B5
Bruera Rd EP CH65 163 H1
Brunel Dr LITH L21 83 J3
Brunner Rd WDN WA8 16 C3
Brunsborough Cl
PS/BROM CH62 143 L7 1
Brunsfield Cl MOR/LEA CH46 109 L6 2
Brunstath Cl HES CH60 141 L4
Brunswick Cl ANF/KKDL L4 97 G5 5
Brunswick Crs GTS/LS CH66 163 G2
Brunswick Ms BIRK CH41 11 K4
CSBY/WL L22 83 G5
Brunswick Pde CSBY/WL L22 82 F5
Brunswick Pl BTL L20 96 D5
Brunswick Rd NEWLW WA12 104 B1
NPK/KEN L6 13 M4
Brunswick St ALL/GAR L19 145 M1
CHLY/EC PR7 32 F5 2
CLVP L2 12 E7 1
STHEL WA9 103 J2
Brunswick Wy VAUX/LVPD L3 112 F8
Brunt La ALL/GAR L19 131 G6
Bruntleigh Av WARRS WA4 138 C2 1
Bruton Rd HUY L36 99 M7
Bryanston Rd AIG/SPK L17 129 K2
RF/TRAN CH42 127 J3
Bryant Av WARRS WA4 138 B1
Bryant Rd LITH L21 83 K7
The Bryceway WD/CROXPK L12 114 F1
Brydges St EHL/KEN L7 113 J4 2
Bryer Rd RAIN/WH L35 116 F1
Bryham St WGN WN1 5 H4
Bryn Bank WAL/EG CH44 111 L1 4
Bryn Gates La AIMK WN4 79 L5
Brynmor Rd CALD/MH L18 130 C4
Brynmoss Av WAL/EG CH44 111 H1 3
Brynn St ECCL WA10 9 H3
WDN WA8 16 E4
WGNE/HIN WN2 80 A6
Bryn Rd AIMK WN4 79 J7
Bryn Rd South AIMK WN4 91 L1
Bryn St AIMK WN4 91 K2
WGNS/IIMK WN3 5 J8
Bryony Cl WGNW/BIL/O WN5 66 F8
Bryony Wy RF/TRAN CH42 128 B5
Brythen St CLVPS L1 13 H7 1
Buchanan Dr WGNE/HIN WN2 81 K2
Buchanan Rd WAL/EG CH44 111 M2
WGNW/BIL/O WN5 68 A6
WLT/FAZ L9 97 H2
Buchanan St CHLYE PR6 32 F6
Buchan Cl WARRW/BUR WA5 120 D5 2
Buckfast Av RNFD/HAY WA11 91 H6
Buckfast Cl NTHTN L30 84 B1 2
WARRW/BUR WA5 136 A2 2
Buckfast Ct RUNC WA7 151 G2 1
Buckfast Dr FMBY L37 59 K3
Buckingham Av AIG/SPK L17 113 M8
BEB CH63 128 A6
CL/PREN CH43 111 H6 2
WDN WA8 134 C1
Buckingham Cl ECCL WA10 8 D8
WGNW/BIL/O WN5 68 A8 1
Buckingham Ct
NWD/KWIPK L33 86 B2 1
Buckingham Dr
RNFD/HAY WA11 89 J6
WARRW/BUR WA5 136 E1
Buckingham Gdns EP CH65 163 M3 1
Buckingham Gv FMBY L37 59 G3
Buckingham Rd
CLB/OSW/ST L13 97 M7
MGHL L31 72 E5
WAL/EG CH44 111 H1
WLT/FAZ L9 84 C7
Buckingham St CHLYE PR6 32 F6
EV L5 97 G8
Buckland Cl WDN WA8 133 M6
Buckland Dr BEB CH63 143 H3
WGNW/BIL/O WN5 67 K4
Buckland St AIG/SPK L17 129 K2

Buckley Hill La NTHTN L30 ... 71 M8
Buckley St WARRW/WOL WA2 ... 14 D3
WGNNW/ST WN6 ... 68 C3
Buckley St West
WGNNW/ST WN6 ... 68 C3
Buckshaw Hall Cl CHLY/EC PR7 ... 32 D3
Buckthorn Cl STBRV L28 ... 99 K6 1
Buckthorn Gdns
RAIN/WH L35 ... 101 L7 1
Buckton St WARR WA1 ... 15 J2
Bude Cl CL/PREN CH43 ... 110 E7
Bude Rd WDN WA8 ... 134 A3
Budworth Av STHEL WA9 ... 118 D2
WARRS WA4 ... 138 B1
WDN WA8 ... 133 M3
Budworth Cl CL/PREN CH43 ... 127 G1 2
RUNC WA7 ... 149 M6
Budworth Dr WLTN L25 ... 131 L3 1
Budworth Rd CL/PREN CH43 ... 127 G1
GTS/LS CH66 ... 163 G3
Buer Av WGNS/IIMK WN3 ... 79 H1
Buerton Cl CL/PREN CH43 ... 126 F1
Buffs La HES CH60 ... 141 K5
Buggen La NSTN CH64 ... 152 F5
Buildwas Rd NSTN CH64 ... 153 G3
Bulford Rd WLT/FAZ L9 ... 98 A1
Bulkeley Rd WAL/EG CH44 ... 111 M2 2
Bull Bridge La AIN/FAZ L10 ... 85 G3
Bull Cop FMBY L37 ... 59 K2
Bullens La BRSC L40 ... 36 F6
Bullens Rd ANF/KKDL L4 ... 97 H5
KKBY L32 ... 86 B4
Bullfinch Ct HLWD L26 ... 132 A4 1
Bull Hl NSTN CH64 ... 153 H7
Bull La WLT/FAZ L9 ... 84 D6
The Bulrushes AIG/SPK L17 ... 129 H2 1
Bulteel St WGNW/BIL/O WN5 ... 67 M7
Bulwer St BTL L20 ... 83 J8
EV L5 ... 97 J8 1
Bunbury Cl CHNE CH2 ... 164 C6
Bunbury Dr RUNC WA7 ... 149 L7
Bundoran Rd AIG/SPK L17 ... 130 A3
Bunter Rd KKBY L32 ... 86 B4
Bunting Cl GOL/RIS/CU WA3 ... 93 G5 1
Bunting Ct HLWD L26 ... 131 M3
Buntingford Rd WARRS WA4 ... 138 E2 1
Burbo Bank Rd CSBY/BLUN L23 ... 82 C1
Burbo Bank Rd North
CSBY/BLUN L23 ... 70 B8
Burbo Bank Rd South
CSBY/BLUN L23 ... 82 D2 1
Burbo Crs CSBY/BLUN L23 ... 82 D2 2
Burbo Wy WAL/NB CH45 ... 95 G5
Burden Rd MOR/LEA CH46 ... 109 L5
Burdett Av BEB CH63 ... 143 H3
Burdett Cl BEB CH63 ... 143 J3 1
Burdett Rd CSBY/WL L22 ... 82 F4
GTS/LS CH66 ... 163 G3
WAL/NB CH45 ... 94 F8 2
Burdett St AIG/SPK L17 ... 129 L2
Burfield Dr WARRS WA4 ... 137 L7
Burford Av WAL/EG CH44 ... 111 H2
Burford Rd CHLDW L16 ... 114 E4
Burgess Av WARRS WA4 ... 137 K2
Burgess Gdns MGHL L31 ... 72 E3 1
Burgess' La FMBY L37 ... 60 C4
Burgess St VAUX/LVPD L3 ... 13 K5 1
WGNS/IIMK WN3 ... 5 J9
Burgh Hall Rd CHLY/EC PR7 ... 43 J2
Burghill Rd WD/CROXPK L12 ... 99 H1
Burgh La CHLY/EC PR7 ... 43 L1
Burgh La South CHLY/EC PR7 ... 43 K3
Burghley Wy WGNE/HIN WN2 ... 69 H8 1
Burgh Mdw CHLY/EC PR7 ... 43 K1
Burgundy Cl AIG/SPK L17 ... 129 L3 2
Burkhardt Dr NEWLW WA12 ... 105 G2 1
Burland Cl RUNC WA7 ... 18 F5
Burland St WGNW/BIL/O WN5 ... 68 B6 1
Burleigh Rd North EV L5 ... 97 H7
Burleigh Rd South EV L5 ... 97 H6 1
Burley Av GOL/RIS/CU WA3 ... 92 F4
Burley Cl KKBY L32 ... 86 B4 2
Burley Crs WGNS/IIMK WN3 ... 78 E3
Burlingham Av WKBY CH48 ... 124 E4
Burlington Av FMBY L37 ... 59 K2
Burlington Rd STHP PR8 ... 35 H2
WAL/NB CH45 ... 95 K4 1
Burlington St BIRK CH41 ... 11 J5 2
CHLY/EC PR7 ... 32 F6 2
VAUX/LVPD L3 ... 12 E2
Burlton Gv WGNE/HIN WN2 ... 69 J3 2
Burman Crs ALL/GAR L19 ... 130 E6
Burman Rd ALL/GAR L19 ... 130 F6
Burnage Av STHEL WA9 ... 118 E1
Burnage Cl SPK/HALE L24 ... 147 H3
Burnand St ANF/KKDL L4 ... 97 H6
Burnard Cl NWD/KWIPK L33 ... 86 B3 1
Burnard Crs NWD/KWIPK L33 ... 86 B3
Burnaston Gv
WGNW/BIL/O WN5 ... 67 M8 2
Burnell Cl ECCL WA10 ... 8 E4
Burnell Rd EP CH65 ... 21 G7
Burnet Cl WARRN/WOL WA2 ... 122 E3
Burnfell GOL/RIS/CU WA3 ... 93 G6 1
Burnham Cl
GOL/RIS/CU WA3 ... 107 G1 1
WARRW/BUR WA5 ... 120 B8
WDN WA8 ... 133 L2 1
Burnham Gv WGNE/HIN WN2 ... 69 H3 2
Burnham Rd CALD/MH L18 ... 130 E2
Burnhill Ct WGNNW/ST WN6 ... 56 A5 1
Burnie Av BTL L20 ... 7 L1
Burnley Av MOR/LEA CH46 ... 110 B5
Burnley Cl NPK/KEN L6 ... 113 J1 2
Burnley Rd MOR/LEA CH46 ... 110 B5
STHP PR8 ... 34 E8
Burnsall Av GOL/RIS/CU WA3 ... 93 H5
Burnsall Dr WDN WA8 ... 133 L2
Burnsall St ALL/GAR L19 ... 131 G8
Burns Av LEIGH WN7 ... 81 L5
WAL/NB CH45 ... 95 J8
Burns Cl AIMK WN4 ... 79 H7
CHLDW L16 ... 115 H5
GTS/LS CH66 ... 163 G1
RAIN/WH L35 ... 117 G2
WGNS/IIMK WN3 ... 79 J1
WGNW/BIL/O WN5 ... 77 M4
Burns Crs WDN WA8 ... 16 B3
Burns Gv HUY L36 ... 116 C4
WARRN/WOL WA2 ... 121 L3
Burnside SKEL WN8 ... 53 K3
Burnside Av WAL/EG CH44 ... 111 K3 1
WARRS WA4 ... 137 M4
Burnside Rd WAL/EG CH44 ... 111 K3
Burns Rd STHEL WA9 ... 118 C2
WGNE/HIN WN2 ... 80 D4 1
Burns St BTL L20 ... 6 C1
Burnt Ash Cl ALL/GAR L19 ... 130 B6 3
Burnthwaite Rd
DV/KA/FCH L14 ... 114 E2
Burnvale WGNS/IIMK WN3 ... 78 F3 1
Burrell Cl RF/TRAN CH42 ... 127 L4
Burrell Dr MOR/LEA CH46 ... 109 M6
Burrell Rd RF/TRAN CH42 ... 127 L4
Burrell St ANF/KKDL L4 ... 97 H5 2
Burrington Dr LEIGH WN7 ... 81 M6 3
Burrough Cl GOL/RIS/CU WA3 ... 123 H2
Burroughs Gdns VAUX/LVPD L3 ... 13 G2
Burrows Av RNFD/HAY WA11 ... 90 B8
Burrows Ct VAUX/LVPD L3 ... 12 E1
Burrow's La ECCL WA10 ... 101 G3
FROD/HEL WA6 ... 167 H4
Burrows St RNFD/HAY WA11 ... 90 C7 2
Bursar Cl NEWLW WA12 ... 104 F1
Burscough Rd ORM L39 ... 51 H7
Burscough St ORM L39 ... 51 G8
Burton Av RAIN/WH L35 ... 117 J1
WAL/NB CH45 ... 95 G8
Burton Cl CLVPS L1 ... 112 F5 2
GOL/RIS/CU WA3 ... 107 H2
RAIN/WH L35 ... 117 J1
WDN WA8 ... 134 B2 2
Burton Gn GTS/LS CH66 ... 162 F1 2
Burtonhead Rd STHEL WA9 ... 8 F8
Burton Rd NSTN CH64 ... 153 G7
WARRN/WOL WA2 ... 121 M4
Burton St EV L5 ... 96 E7 1
Burtons Wy NG/CROX L11 ... 85 L6
Burtonwood Rd
WARRW/BUR WA5 ... 120 C5
Burtree Rd DV/KA/FCH L14 ... 99 J7
Burwell Av CHLY/EC PR7 ... 42 F5
FMBY L37 ... 58 F4
Burwen Dr WLT/FAZ L9 ... 84 B7
Bury Rd STHP PR8 ... 35 J2
Busby's Cottages
WAL/NB CH45 ... 95 K5 2
Bushby's La FMBY L37 ... 58 E3
Bushby's Pk FMBY L37 ... 58 E3
Bushell Cl NSTN CH64 ... 153 H6
Bushell Rd NSTN CH64 ... 153 H5
Bushel's Dr STHEL WA9 ... 118 F3
Bushey La RNFD/HAY WA11 ... 76 A3
Bushey Rd ANF/KKDL L4 ... 97 L3
Bushley Cl BTL L20 ... 6 F3
Bush Rd WDN WA8 ... 16 A9
Bush Wy HES CH60 ... 141 G5
Butchers La ORM L39 ... 62 B8
Bute St EV L5 ... 13 K2
VAUX/LVPD L3 ... 13 J3
Butleigh Rd HUY L36 ... 99 M8
Butler Crs NPK/KEN L6 ... 113 K2
Butler St NPK/KEN L6 ... 113 K1
WGN WN1 ... 5 G4
Buttercup Cl MOR/LEA CH46 ... 110 C3 1
Buttercup Wy WLT/FAZ L9 ... 97 K1
Butterfield Gdns ORM L39 ... 62 F2 1
Butterfield St ANF/KKDL L4 ... 97 H6 2
Buttermarket St WARR WA1 ... 15 G5 1
Buttermere Av AIMK WN4 ... 79 K8
CHLY/EC PR7 ... 32 C7
CL/PREN CH43 ... 110 F7
EP CH65 ... 20 C9
RNFD/HAY WA11 ... 89 J5 1
WARRN/WOL WA2 ... 121 L2
Buttermere Cl FMBY L37 ... 58 F2 1
FROD/HEL WA6 ... 160 F5 1
MGHL L31 ... 72 F4
NWD/KWIPK L33 ... 85 M1
Buttermere Crs
RNFD/HAY WA11 ... 76 B3
Buttermere Gdns
CSBY/BLUN L23 ... 83 H3
Buttermere Gv RUNC WA7 ... 149 M7
Buttermere Rd CHLDW L16 ... 115 J5
WGNW/BIL/O WN5 ... 67 L6 2
Buttermere St TOX L8 ... 113 K6 3
Butterton Av
GR/UP/WCH CH49 ... 109 M7
Butterwick Dr
WD/CROXPK L12 ... 99 G2 4
Butterworth Brow CHLY/EC PR7 .. 43 H1
Butts La STHP PR8 ... 25 H8
Buxted Rd KKBY L32 ... 86 C5
Buxton Cl WARRW/BUR WA5 ... 120 C5
Bxchange St West CLVP L2 ... 12 E7 2
Bye La ORM L39 ... 61 L2
Byerley St WAL/EG CH44 ... 112 A2 1
Byfleet Cl WGNS/IIMK WN3 ... 78 E4
Byland Cl FMBY L37 ... 59 K3
WDN WA8 ... 118 E8
Byles St TOX L8 ... 129 J1
Byley Ri WGNNW/ST WN6 ... 56 A5
Byng Pl ANF/KKDL L4 ... 97 M5
Byng Rd ANF/KKDL L4 ... 97 M5
Byng St BTL L20 ... 6 E7
The By-pass CSBY/BLUN L23 ... 83 G1
Byrne Av RF/TRAN CH42 ... 128 B3 1
Byrom La GOL/RIS/CU WA3 ... 93 H3
Byrom St CHTN/BK PR9 ... 25 H7
VAUX/LVPD L3 ... 13 H5
Byrom Wy VAUX/LVPD L3 ... 13 H4
Byron Av RAIN/WH L35 ... 117 H2
WGNE/HIN WN2 ... 69 M8 1
Byron Cl CL/PREN CH43 ... 127 H5
ECCL WA10 ... 9 G2
FMBY L37 ... 59 H1
HUY L36 ... 116 B4
WGNE/HIN WN2 ... 80 D5
WGNNW/ST WN6 ... 68 A2
WGNW/BIL/O WN5 ... 67 H6
Byron Ct WARRN/WOL WA2 ... 121 L3 1
Byron Crs CHLY/EC PR7 ... 43 G5
Byron Rd CSBY/BLUN L23 ... 82 D1
MGHL L31 ... 72 F2 2
Byron St ALL/GAR L19 ... 130 E8
BTL L20 ... 6 C1
CHLY/EC PR7 ... 32 F5 3
RUNC WA7 ... 18 F5
The Byway CSBY/BLUN L23 ... 71 G8

C

Cabes Cl DV/KA/FCH L14 ... 99 J7
Cabin La CHTN/BK PR9 ... 26 A2
KIRK/FR/WA PR4 ... 27 J7
MGHL L31 ... 72 B1
ORM L39 ... 35 M8
Cable Rd HOY CH47 ... 108 D6
RAIN/WH L35 ... 101 H8
Cable St CLVPS L1 ... 12 F8
FMBY L37 ... 59 J1
STHP PR8 ... 3 G3
Cabot Cl WARRW/BUR WA5 ... 120 E4 1
Cabot Gn WLTN L25 ... 115 G8
Caddick Rd PR/KW L34 ... 86 D8
Cadman Gv WGNE/HIN WN2 ... 80 F1 6
Cadnam Rd WLTN L25 ... 115 M8
Cadogan Dr WGNS/IIMK WN3 ... 78 F3
Cadogan St WAV L15 ... 113 M5
Cadshaw Cl GOL/RIS/CU WA3 ... 106 F8
Cadwell Rd MGHL L31 ... 61 K8
Caernarvon Cl
GR/UP/WCH CH49 ... 110 B7
Caernarvon Ct EP CH65 ... 163 M3 2
Caernarvon Rd
WGNE/HIN WN2 ... 81 J2 1
Caerwys Gv RF/TRAN CH42 ... 128 A1
Caird St NPK/KEN L6 ... 113 J2
Cairn Ct STHEL WA9 ... 101 M6
Cairnmore Rd CALD/MH L18 ... 130 C3
Cairns St TOX L8 ... 113 J7
Cairo St ANF/KKDL L4 ... 7 L8
ECCL WA10 ... 101 M4
WARR WA1 ... 14 E6
Caister Cl SKEL WN8 ... 65 M5
Caithness Dr CSBY/BLUN L23 ... 83 H2
WAL/NB CH45 ... 95 L7
Caithness Rd CALD/MH L18 ... 130 D4
Calday Grange Cl WKBY CH48 ... 124 F4
Calday Gv RNFD/HAY WA11 ... 90 C5
Caldbeck Av
WARRN/WOL WA2 ... 121 M3 1
Caldbeck Cl AIMK WN4 ... 91 K1 1
Caldbeck Gv RNFD/HAY WA11 ... 89 L4 1
Caldbeck Rd PS/BROM CH62 ... 144 A3
Calder Av CHLY/EC PR7 ... 32 D8
CL/PREN CH43 ... 127 J3 1
ORM L39 ... 63 G1
WGNE/HIN WN2 ... 81 L2
Calderbank St
WGNW/BIL/O WN5 ... 68 A8 2
Calder Cl NWD/KWIPK L33 ... 74 B7
WDN WA8 ... 135 H2
Calder Dr CALD/MH L18 ... 114 E8
MGHL L31 ... 73 H3
RAIN/WH L35 ... 117 K2
WGNE/HIN WN2 ... 80 C3
Calderfield Cl WARRS WA4 ... 137 K5
Calderfield Rd CALD/MH L18 ... 114 F8
Calder Gra WLTN L25 ... 131 G2
Calderhurst Dr ECCL WA10 ... 88 D7
Calder Pl WGNW/BIL/O WN5 ... 67 L6
Calder Rd BEB CH63 ... 127 M8
EV L5 ... 97 H7
The Calders CALD/MH L18 ... 130 E2
Calderstones Av CALD/MH L18 ... 114 E8
Calderstones Rd CALD/MH L18 ... 130 E1
Calder Wy GTS/LS CH66 ... 155 L8 2
Caldford Cl WGNE/HIN WN2 ... 57 L7
Caldicott Av PS/BROM CH62 ... 145 M2
Caldway Dr NTHLY L27 ... 115 M7
Caldwell Av WARRW/BUR WA5 ... 121 H3
Caldwell Cl NWD/KWIPK L33 ... 74 B8 3
NWD/KWIPK L33 ... 86 B1 2
Caldwell Dr
GR/UP/WCH CH49 ... 126 D3 1
Caldwell Rd ALL/GAR L19 ... 130 F5
WDN WA8 ... 16 C5
Caldwell St STHEL WA9 ... 102 F2
Caldy Chase Dr WKBY CH48 ... 124 F6
Caldy Dr GTS/LS CH66 ... 162 F1
Caldy Gv RNFD/HAY WA11 ... 89 M8
Caldy Rd WAL/NB CH45 ... 95 K8
WKBY CH48 ... 124 F6
WLT/FAZ L9 ... 84 C6
Caldy Wd WKBY CH48 ... 124 F6
Caldywood Dr RAIN/WH L35 ... 117 G2
Caledonia St EHL/KEN L7 ... 13 L9
TOX L8 ... 113 H5 12
Cale La WGNE/HIN WN2 ... 69 K3
Calgarth Rd HUY L36 ... 99 L8
Calico Wood Av
WGNNW/ST WN6 ... 55 H7
California Cl WARRW/BUR WA5 ... 120 E5
California Rd CLB/OSW/ST L13 ... 97 M6
Callaghan Cl EV L5 ... 96 F8 1
Callander Ct WGNW/BIL/O WN5 ... 68 A6
Callander Rd NPK/KEN L6 ... 113 M2
Callands Rd WARRW/BUR WA5 ... 120 F3
Callestock Cl NG/CROX L11 ... 85 M8
Callington Cl DV/KA/FCH L14 ... 99 J7
Callon Av RNFD/HAY WA11 ... 90 A8
Callow Rd WAV L15 ... 113 M6
Calmet Cl EV L5 ... 97 G7 3
Calmington La RUNC WA7 ... 151 H1
Calne Cl PEN/TH CH61 ... 125 M6
Calstock Cl
WARRW/BUR WA5 ... 136 A2 3
Calthorpe St ALL/GAR L19 ... 130 D7
Calthorpe Wy CL/PREN CH43 ... 110 F7 1
Calton Av CALD/MH L18 ... 114 C8 2
Calton Cl WGNS/IIMK WN3 ... 78 F1 2
Calvados Cl AIG/SPK L17 ... 129 L4 1
Calveley Av PS/BROM CH62 ... 155 H1
Calveley Cl CL/PREN CH43 ... 127 G2
Calveley Wk WGNNW/ST WN6 ... 56 A5
Calverhall Wy AIMK WN4 ... 91 J2
Calverly Cl RUNC WA7 ... 150 E8 2
Calver Rd WARRN/WOL WA2 ... 121 H1
Camarthen Crs TOX L8 ... 112 F7
Camberley Cl STHP PR8 ... 2 A8
Camberley Dr WLTN L25 ... 131 L5
Camberwell Crs WGNE/HIN WN2 ... 5 M1
Camborne Av WLTN L25 ... 131 L5
Camborne Cl RUNC WA7 ... 150 E7 1
Cambourne Av RNFD/HAY WA11 ... 89 M6
Cambourne Dr WGNE/HIN WN2 ... 81 L3
Cambourne Rd
WARRW/BUR WA5 ... 104 B7
Cambrai Av WARRS WA4 ... 137 L3
Cambrian Cl GTS/LS CH66 ... 155 J7
MOR/LEA CH46 ... 109 K6 1
Cambrian Crs WGNS/IIMK WN3 ... 78 E3
Cambrian Rd MOR/LEA CH46 ... 109 L6
Cambrian Wy WLTN L25 ... 131 K2
Cambria St NPK/KEN L6 ... 113 K2
Cambridge Av CHTN/BK PR9 ... 25 H3
CSBY/BLUN L23 ... 82 F1
LITH L21 ... 83 K5 1
Cambridge Cl WARRS WA4 ... 137 K6 1
Cambridge Dr CSBY/BLUN L23 ... 70 E8
HLWD L26 ... 132 B5 1
Cambridge Gdns CHTN/BK PR9 ... 25 H3
FROD/HEL WA6 ... 166 F1
WARRS WA4 ... 137 L7
Cambridge Rd BTL L20 ... 7 K6
CHTN/BK PR9 ... 25 G4
CSBY/BLUN L23 ... 70 E8
ECCL WA10 ... 8 C4
EP CH65 ... 20 D5
FMBY L37 ... 58 F4
LITH L21 ... 83 G6
PS/BROM CH62 ... 143 M5
RF/TRAN CH42 ... 127 J3
SKEL WN8 ... 65 G4
WAL/NB CH45 ... 95 K6
WGNW/BIL/O WN5 ... 67 G5
WLT/FAZ L9 ... 84 D5 2
Cambridge St CHLY/EC PR7 ... 32 E6 3
EHL/KEN L7 ... 13 L9
EHL/KEN L7 ... 113 J5 2
PR/KW L34 ... 100 F7 1
RUNC WA7 ... 19 L3
WAV L15 ... 113 M5
WDN WA8 ... 16 E5
WGN WN1 ... 5 H5
Camdale Cl STBRV L28 ... 99 K6 2
Camden Ct RUNC WA7 ... 150 F4 1
Camden Pl BIRK CH41 ... 11 J5 2
Camden Rd EP CH65 ... 156 C8
Camden St BIRK CH41 ... 11 J4
VAUX/LVPD L3 ... 13 J5
Camelford Rd NG/CROX L11 ... 85 M8 1
Camelia Ct AIG/SPK L17 ... 129 J3
Camelot Cl NEWLW WA12 ... 104 B1 1
Cameron Av RUNC WA7 ... 18 D8
Cameron Ct WARRN/WOL WA2 ... 121 J1
Cameron Cft CHLYE PR6 ... 32 F5 1
Cameron Pl WGNW/BIL/O WN5 ... 68 A5
Cameron Rd MOR/LEA CH46 ... 110 D2
WDN WA8 ... 16 C4
Cameron St EHL/KEN L7 ... 113 L3
LEIGH WN7 ... 81 M6
Camm St WGNE/HIN WN2 ... 80 C5
Camomile Cl CHLY/EC PR7 ... 32 C2 1
Campania St ALL/GAR L19 ... 145 L1
Campbell Av RUNC WA7 ... 19 G8
Campbell Crs
WARRW/BUR WA5 ... 120 B7
Campbell Dr DV/KA/FCH L14 ... 115 G2
Campbell St BTL L20 ... 6 D5
CLVPS L1 ... 13 G9
ECCL WA10 ... 8 D4
WGNW/BIL/O WN5 ... 67 M8
Camperdown St BIRK CH41 ... 11 L5 2
Camphill Rd WLTN L25 ... 131 J6
Campion Cl GOL/RIS/CU WA3 ... 122 E1 2
RNFD/HAY WA11 ... 89 K6 1
Campion Gv AIMK WN4 ... 91 H1 1
Campion Wy HUY L36 ... 116 B6
Camp Rd AIMK WN4 ... 91 G2
WLTN L25 ... 131 K4
Campsey Ash WDN WA8 ... 134 B2
Camrose Cl RUNC WA7 ... 149 L7
Camsley La LYMM WA13 ... 139 K2
Cam St WLTN L25 ... 131 J4 1
Canaan GOL/RIS/CU WA3 ... 93 L5
Canada Cl WARRN/WOL WA2 ... 122 C3
Canal Bank Pygons Hl
MGHL L31 ... 61 L6
Canal Reach RUNC WA7 ... 150 E3
Canalside EP CH65 ... 20 F2
Canal Side WARRS WA4 ... 136 E8
WARRS WA4 ... 138 E4
WARRS WA4 ... 151 H7
Canalside Gv EV L5 ... 96 E8
Canal St BTL L20 ... 6 F6
CHLY/EC PR7 ... 44 C7 2
ECCL WA10 ... 8 F7
NEWLW WA12 ... 104 B3
RUNC WA7 ... 19 K3
WGNNW/ST WN6 ... 68 B4
Canal Vw MGHL L31 ... 85 J3
Canal Wk CHLYE PR6 ... 33 G5
Canberra Av STHEL WA9 ... 102 A6
Canberra La NG/CROX L11 ... 85 L8
Canberra Rd WGNW/BIL/O WN5 ... 67 L4
Canberra Sq WARRN/WOL WA2 ... 121 M3
Candleston Cl
WARRW/BUR WA5 ... 121 G4
Canford Cl WARRW/BUR WA5 ... 120 E7
Cannell Ct RUNC WA7 ... 150 C7
Cannell St WARRW/BUR WA5 ... 136 F1 3
Canning Pl CLVPS L1 ... 12 F8
Canning Rd CHTN/BK PR9 ... 25 J6
Canning St BIRK CH41 ... 11 K3
CLVPS L1 ... 113 H5
CSBY/WL L22 ... 82 F4 3
Canniswood Rd
RNFD/HAY WA11 ... 90 C8
Cann La WARRS WA4 ... 138 A7
Cannock Cl GTS/LS CH66 ... 163 G5
Cannock Gn MGHL L31 ... 72 D4 2
Cannon St EP CH65 ... 156 C8
STHEL WA9 ... 118 E2
Canon Cl WGNNW/ST WN6 ... 56 B3
Canon Rd NPK/KEN L6 ... 97 L6
Canons Rd WARRW/BUR WA5 ... 120 F7
Canon St RUNC WA7 ... 18 F2
Canon Wilson Cl
RNFD/HAY WA11 ... 90 F7
Canrow La PR/KW L34 ... 86 F8
Cansfield Gv AIMK WN4 ... 91 J1
Cansfield St ECCL WA10 ... 9 H4
Canterbury Av CSBY/WL L22 ... 82 F2
GOL/RIS/CU WA3 ... 92 F4 3
Canterbury Cl AIN/FAZ L10 ... 85 G3
FMBY L37 ... 47 H8
GTS/LS CH66 ... 163 G5 1
PR/KW L34 ... 101 G6 2
STHP PR8 ... 2 C9
Canterbury Pk CALD/MH L18 ... 130 E5
Canterbury Rd RF/TRAN CH42 ... 128 C4
WAL/EG CH44 ... 111 L2
WDN WA8 ... 133 L6
Canterbury St ALL/GAR L19 ... 145 L1
CHLYE PR6 ... 33 G7
ECCL WA10 ... 8 D2
VAUX/LVPD L3 ... 13 K4
WARRS WA4 ... 15 G8 1
Canterbury Wy NTHTN L30 ... 84 B1
VAUX/LVPD L3 ... 13 L4 1
Canter Cl WLT/FAZ L9 ... 84 F5 1
Cantley Cl RUNC WA7 ... 149 M7 1
Cantlow Fold STHP PR8 ... 47 J1
Cantsfield St EHL/KEN L7 ... 113 L6
Canvey Cl WAV L15 ... 114 D6
Capenhurst Av
WARRN/WOL WA2 ... 122 C3
Capenhurst La CH/BCN CH1 ... 162 C6
EP CH65 ... 163 J2
Cape Rd WLT/FAZ L9 ... 84 E7 1
Capesthorne Cl WDN WA8 ... 134 A5
Capesthorne Rd
WARRN/WOL WA2 ... 121 M4
Capilano Pk ORM L39 ... 62 E5
Capper Gv HUY L36 ... 116 A2
Capps St WGNE/HIN WN2 ... 80 D2 3
Capricorn Crs DV/KA/FCH L14 ... 99 H8
Capricorn Wy BTL L20 ... 6 F3
Captain's La AIMK WN4 ... 91 L2 1
NTHTN L30 ... 83 M5
Caradoc Rd LITH L21 ... 83 H7
Caraway Cl CSBY/BLUN L23 ... 71 K8 2
Caraway Gv ECCL WA10 ... 8 A3
Carawood Cl WGNNW/ST WN6 .. 54 F6 1
Carbis Cl AIN/FAZ L10 ... 85 J7
Carden Cl ANF/KKDL L4 ... 97 G6 4
GOL/RIS/CU WA3 ... 122 F1 3
Cardeston Cl RUNC WA7 ... 161 H2 1
Cardiff Cl GTS/LS CH66 ... 163 G5
Cardiff St SKEL WN8 ... 64 F4 1
Cardigan Av BIRK CH41 ... 11 H5
Cardigan Cl ECCL WA10 ... 8 E7
WARRW/BUR WA5 ... 120 F3
Cardigan Rd STHP PR8 ... 35 H4
WAL/NB CH45 ... 95 K6
Cardigan St WAV L15 ... 113 M5
Cardigan Wy NPK/KEN L6 ... 113 K1
NTHTN L30 ... 84 D1 2
Cardus Cl MOR/LEA CH46 ... 109 K5 2
Cardwell Rd ALL/GAR L19 ... 130 F7
Cardwell St EHL/KEN L7 ... 113 J5
Careless La WGNE/HIN WN2 ... 5 M5
Carey Av BEB CH63 ... 127 M7
Carey Cl WGNS/IIMK WN3 ... 78 F3
Carey St WDN WA8 ... 16 E2
Carfax Rd NWD/KWIPK L33 ... 86 C1 2
Cargill Gv RF/TRAN CH42 ... 128 D5
Carham Rd HOY CH47 ... 108 E7
Carisbrooke Cl WKBY CH48 ... 124 E5
Carisbrooke Dr CHTN/BK PR9 ... 25 H4
Carisbrooke Pl ANF/KKDL L4 ... 97 H4 1
Carisbrooke Rd ANF/KKDL L4 ... 7 L7
Carkington Rd WLTN L25 ... 131 L4
Carland Cl NG/CROX L11 ... 85 K7
Carlaw Rd RF/TRAN CH42 ... 127 J3
Carleen Cl AIG/SPK L17 ... 129 K3
Carleton Rd CHLYE PR6 ... 33 G1
Carlett Bvd PS/BROM CH62 ... 144 B8
Carlile Wy NWD/KWIPK L33 ... 74 B7
Carlingford Cl TOX L8 ... 113 J6
Carlingford Rd WARRS WA4 ... 137 K5
Carlisle Cl ANF/KKDL L4 ... 97 M5 1
Carlisle Pl CHLYE PR6 ... 44 C5 2
Carlisle Rd STHP PR8 ... 35 J3
Carlisle St WARRS WA4 ... 137 L5 2
WGNW/BIL/O WN5 ... 67 M7 1
Carlis Rd KKBY L32 ... 86 B5
Carlow Cl SPK/HALE L24 ... 147 L3
Carlow St ECCL WA10 ... 101 M4 2
Carl's Wy NWD/KWIPK L33 ... 74 C7
Carlton Av RUNC WA7 ... 149 M3
SKEL WN8 ... 66 C6
Carlton Cl AIMK WN4 ... 91 J1 2
HOR/BR BL6 ... 57 M3
NSTN CH64 ... 152 E3
Carlton Crs GTS/LS CH66 ... 156 A5
Carlton Gv WGNE/HIN WN2 ... 81 H1 1
Carlton La CLB/OSW/ST L13 ... 114 C1
HOY CH47 ... 108 E5
Carlton Rd BEB CH63 ... 143 K1
GOL/RIS/CU WA3 ... 92 F4
RF/TRAN CH42 ... 127 L1
STHP PR8 ... 34 F7
WAL/NB CH45 ... 95 K5
Carlton St ECCL WA10 ... 8 D6
PR/KW L34 ... 100 F7 6
VAUX/LVPD L3 ... 12 C1
WARRS WA4 ... 137 L5
WDN WA8 ... 16 D3
WGNS/IIMK WN3 ... 4 D8
Carlyle Crs GTS/LS CH66 ... 163 G1
Carlyle Gv LEIGH WN7 ... 81 L5
Carlyon Wy HLWD L26 ... 132 A5 1
Carmarthen Cl
WARRW/BUR WA5 ... 120 F3
Carmel Cl ORM L39 ... 62 F3
Carmel Ct WDN WA8 ... 134 D1 3
Carmelite Crs ECCL WA10 ... 88 C8
Carmichael Av
GR/UP/WCH CH49 ... 125 M3
Carnaby Cl HUY L36 ... 116 C5 1
Carnarvon Rd STHP PR8 ... 35 H4
WLT/FAZ L9 ... 97 H2
Carnarvon St STHEL WA9 ... 101 M6
Carnatic Rd AIG/SPK L17 ... 130 A2 1

CALD/MH L18 .... **130** A2
Carnation Rd *WLT/FAZ* L9 ..... **97** K1
Carnegie Av *CSBY/BLUN* L23..... **82** F2
Carnegie Crs *STHEL* WA9 ...... **103** G5
Carnegie Dr *AIMK* WN4 .... **79** J8
Carnforth Av *KKBY* L32 .... **86** B4
Carnforth Cl *BIRK* CH41 ...... **10** F8
WD/CROXPK L12 .... **98** E4
Carnforth Rd *CALD/MH* L18 .... **130** E3
Carno St *WAV* L15 .... **114** A5
Carnoustie Cl *MOR/LEA* CH46 ... **109** K4
WD/CROXPK L12 .... **99** H7
Carnoustie Gv *RNFD/HAY* WA11... **90** C8
Carnsdale Rd *MOR/LEA* CH46 ... **110** B5
Carol Dr *HES* CH60 .... **141** G5
Carole Cl *STHEL* WA9 .... **103** G7
Carolina St *BTL* L20 .... **7** G4
Caroline Pl *CL/PREN* CH43 .... **10** C7
Caroline Rd *WDN* WA8 .... **16** E6
WGN WN1 .... **5** L4
WGNS/IIMK WN3 .... **4** E6
Carol St *WARRS* WA4 .... **15** J9
Caronia St *ALL/GAR* L19 ...... **145** L1
Carpathia St *ALL/GAR* L19 .... **145** L1
Carpenter Gv
WARRN/WOL WA2 .... **122** C4
Carpenter's La *AIMK* CH48 .... **124** D3
Carpenters Rw *CLVPS* L1 ...... **112** F5
Carradon Dr *WGNNW/ST* WN6 .... **56** A4
Carraway Rd *NG/CROX* L11 ..... **85** K7
Carr Bridge Rd
GR/UP/WCH CH49 .... **126** D1
Carr Cl *NG/CROX* L11 .... **98** D3
Carr Common Rd
WGNE/HIN WN2 .... **81** M2
Carr Cft *LITH* L21 .... **83** K2
Carrfield Av *CSBY/BLUN* L23 .. **83** J2
Carr Ga *MOR/LEA* CH46 .... **109** K6
Carr Hey *MOR/LEA* CH46 .... **109** K6
Carr Hey Cl
GR/UP/WCH CH49 .... **126** E3
Carr House La *HTWN* L38 ...... **71** G1
MOR/LEA CH46 .... **109** G1
WGNNW/ST WN6 .... **42** B5
Carrick Dr *EP* CH65 .... **163** K3
Carrickmore Av *CALD/MH* L18 .. **130** C3
Carrington Cl *GOL/RIS/CU* WA3 . **122** E1
Carrington Rd *CHLY/EC* PR7 ... **32** D6
CHLY/EC PR7 .... **44** B6
WAL/NB CH45 .... **95** K7
Carrington St *BIRK* CH41 ..... **10** A1
Carr La *BRSC* L40 .... **29** K6
BRSC L40 .... **52** D2
CHLY/EC PR7 .... **32** F8
GOL/RIS/CU WA3 .... **93** J6
HOY CH47 .... **108** D7
HUY L36 .... **115** L4
LEY/BBR PR5 .... **29** K5
MGHL L31 .... **61** H8
NG/CROX L11 .... **98** B3
PR/KW L34 .... **100** D8
SPK/HALE L24 .... **147** M3
STHP PR8 .... **35** H6
WGNS/IIMK WN3 .... **79** J2
WKBY CH48 .... **108** F8
Carr La East *NG/CROX* L11 .... **98** D3
Carr Meadow Hey *NTHTN* L30 ... **83** L3
Carr Mill Crs *RNFD/HAY* WA11 . **90** A1
Carr Mill Rd *RNFD/HAY* WA11 .. **89** L5
WGNW/BIL/O WN5 .... **90** A2
Carr Moss La *ORM* L39 .... **48** E2
ORM L39 .... **49** K5
Carrock Rd *PS/BROM* CH62 ..... **144** A3
Carroll Crs *ORM* L39 .... **51** H6
Carrow Cl *MOR/LEA* CH46 ...... **109** K6
Carr Rd *BTL* L20 .... **83** M6
HOR/BR BL6 .... **45** K8
Carr's Crs *FMBY* L37 .... **58** F4
Carr's Crs West *FMBY* L37 .... **58** F4
Carr Side La *HTWN* L38 .... **71** J2
Carr St *CHLYE* PR6 .... **33** G4
ECCL WA10 .... **8** C1
LEIGH WN7 .... **81** L8
WGNE/HIN WN2 .... **69** M7
Carruthers St *VAUX/LVPD* L3 .. **12** E3
Carrville Wy *WD/CROXPK* L12 .. **99** J3
Carrwood Cl *RNFD/HAY* WA11 ... **90** C7
Carrwood Pk *STHP* PR8 .... **35** K2
Carsdale Rd *CALD/MH* L18 ..... **114** C8
Carsgoe Rd *HOY* CH47 .... **108** E7
Carsington Rd *NG/CROX* L11 ... **98** C3
Carstairs Rd *NPK/KEN* L6 ..... **113** L1
Carsthorne Rd *HOY* CH47 ...... **108** E7
Car St *WGNE/HIN* WN2 .... **80** C4
Cartbridge La *HLWD* L26 ...... **132** B4
Carter Av *RNFD/HAY* WA11 ..... **76** C3
The Carters
GR/UP/WCH CH49 .... **125** L1
NTHTN L30 .... **84** C7
Carter St *TOX* L8 .... **113** H7
WGNS/IIMK WN3 .... **5** J7
Carterton Rd *HOY* CH47 .... **108** E7
Cartier Cl *WARRN/BUR* WA5 .... **120** E4
Cartmel Av *ECCL* WA10 .... **89** G6
MGHL L31 .... **73** G3
WARRN/WOL WA2 .... **121** L2
WGN WN1 .... **68** D2
Cartmel Cl *BIRK* CH41 .... **10** F8
HUY L36 .... **115** M1
STHP PR8 .... **36** B2
WARRW/BUR WA5 .... **121** G3
Cartmel Dr *FMBY* L37 .... **59** K3
GTS/LS CH66 .... **163** H6
MOR/LEA CH46 .... **110** A6
RAIN/WH L35 .... **117** J1
WD/CROXPK L12 .... **98** E4
Cartmel Rd *RUNC* WA7 .... **149** K7
Cartmel Ter *HUY* L36 .... **115** M1
Cartmel Wy *HUY* L36 .... **115** L1
Cartridge La *WARRS* WA4 ...... **138** F7
Cartwright Gv *LEIGH* WN7 ..... **81** M4
WARRW/BUR WA5 .... **121** G3
Cartwright St *RUNC* WA7 ...... **19** L4
WARRW/BUR WA5 .... **121** G3

Case Gv *RAIN/WH* L35 .... **101** G8
Case Rd *RNFD/HAY* WA11 .... **90** F7
Cashel Rd *BIRK* CH41 .... **111** K3
Cashmore Dr *WGNE/HIN* WN2 .... **80** F1
Caspian Pl *BTL* L20 .... **7** H4
Caspian Rd *ANF/KKDL* L4 ...... **97** K1
Cassia St *WLT/FAZ* L9 .... **97** K1
Cassino Rd *HUY* L36 .... **115** M2
Cassio St *BTL* L20 .... **7** L7
Cassley Rd *SPK/HALE* L24 ..... **147** J2
Cassville Rd *CALD/MH* L18 .... **114** C7
Castell Gv *ECCL* WA10 .... **8** E5
Casterton *CHLY/EC* PR7 .... **31** L3
Casterton St *EHL/KEN* L7 ..... **113** L5
Castle Av *STHEL* WA9 .... **103** G2
Castle Crs *HOR/BR* BL6 .... **45** L8
Castlecroft Av *HOR/BR* BL6 ... **57** M3
Castle Dr *CHLY/EC* PR7 .... **44** A7
EP CH65 .... **163** J2
FMBY L37 .... **59** H4
HES CH60 .... **141** H5
Castlefield Av South *RUNC* WA7 . **150** B4
Castlefield Cl *WD/CROXPK* L12 . **98** C5
Castlefield Rd *WD/CROXPK* L12 . **98** C5
Castlefields Av East *RUNC* WA7 . **150** C4
Castlefields Av North
RUNC WA7 .... **150** C3
Castlefields Av South
RUNC WA7 .... **150** C5
Castle Fields Est
MOR/LEA CH46 .... **110** B1
Castleford Ri *MOR/LEA* CH46 .. **110** A2
Castleford St *WAV* L15 .... **114** C6
Castlegate Gv *WD/CROXPK* L12 . **98** C6
Castlegrange Cl
MOR/LEA CH46 .... **110** A1
Castle Gn *WARRN/BUR* WA5 ..... **120** C3
Castleheath Cl
MOR/LEA CH46 .... **110** A2
Castle Hl *CLVP* L2 .... **12** E7
NEWLW WA12 .... **105** G1
Castle House La *CHLY/EC* PR7 . **44** A7
Castle La *BRSC* L40 .... **51** M7
Castle Ri *RUNC* WA7 .... **150** B5
WAL/NB CH45 .... **95** J7
Castlesite Rd *WD/CROXPK* L12 . **98** D6
Castle St *BIRK* CH41 .... **11** L5
CHLY/EC PR7 .... **32** F6
CHTN/BK PR9 .... **23** K7
CLVP L2 .... **12** E7
WDN WA8 .... **17** J2
WLTN L25 .... **131** H3
Castleton Dr *NTHTN* L30 ...... **84** D1
Castleton Wy *WGNS/IIMK* WN3 .. **78** E3
Castletown Cl *CHLDW* L16 ..... **115** C5
Castleview Rd *WD/CROXPK* L12 . **98** D6
Castle Wk *STHP* PR8 .... **2** E6
Castleway North
MOR/LEA CH46 .... **110** C1
Castleway South
MOR/LEA CH46 .... **110** C2
Castlewood Rd *NPK/KEN* L6 .... **97** K8
Castner Av *RUNC* WA7 .... **18** C9
Castor St *NPK/KEN* L6 .... **97** K8
Catchdale Moss La *ECCL* WA10 . **88** A8
Catford Cl *WDN* WA8 .... **133** L3
Catford Gn *SPK/HALE* L24 ..... **147** H2
Catfoss Cl *WARRN/WOL* WA2 .... **122** A4
Catharine's La *ORM* L39 ...... **63** H3
Catharine St *TOX* L8 .... **113** H6
Cathcart St *BIRK* CH41 .... **11** C4
Cathedral Ga *CLVPS* L1 .... **113** C5
Cathedral Rd *NPK/KEN* L6 ..... **97** L2
Cathedral Wk *VAUX/LVPD* L3 ... **13** K8
Catherine St *BIRK* CH41 ...... **11** C6
CHLY/EC PR7 .... **32** E7
LITH L21 .... **83** K7
WARRW/BUR WA5 .... **14** B2
WDN WA8 .... **16** D7
Catherine St East *HOR/BR* BL6 . **45** K8
Catherine St West *HOR/BR* BL6 . **45** J8
Catherine Ter *WGN* WN1 .... **5** J4
Catherine Wy *NEWLW* WA12 ..... **104** D3
RNFD/HAY WA11 .... **90** B7
Catkin Rd *HLWD* L26 .... **131** M3
Caton Cl *CHTN/BK* PR9 .... **25** H1
Catonfield Rd *CALD/MH* L18 ... **114** E8
Cat Tail La *STHP* PR8 .... **37** G4
Catterall Av *STHEL* WA9 ...... **102** F7
WARRN/WOL WA2 .... **121** M3
Catterick Cl *HLWD* L26 .... **132** B5
Catterick Fold *STHP* PR8 ..... **36** B2
Caulfield Dr *GR/UP/WCH* CH49 . **126** A2
Caunce Av *CHLY/EC* PR7 .... **23** J7
GOL/RIS/CU WA3 .... **92** C6
RNFD/HAY WA11 .... **90** D7
Caunce Rd *WGN* WN1 .... **5** J3
Caunce's Rd *CHTN/BK* PR9 ..... **26** F7
Caunce St *WGN* WN1 .... **5** J3
Causeway Av *WARRS* WA4 .... **137** L2
Causeway Cl *PS/BROM* CH62 .... **128** D6
Causeway La *BRSC* L40 .... **39** K4
FMBY L37 .... **60** D4
The Causeway *CHLYE* PR6 ...... **33** G5
CHTN/BK PR9 .... **22** E8
PS/BROM CH62 .... **128** D6
WD/CROXPK L12 .... **114** F1
Cavan Rd *NG/CROX* L11 .... **98** A5
Cavell Cl *WLTN* L25 .... **131** J4
Cavell Dr *EP* CH65 .... **163** J1
Cavendish Av *GOL/RIS/CU* WA3 . **92** F6
Cavendish Cl *WARRW/BUR* WA5.. **120** F6
Cavendish Dr *RF/TRAN* CH42 ... **127** M4
WGNS/IIMK WN3 .... **78** F3
WLT/FAZ L9 .... **97** J2
Cavendish Farm Rd *RUNC* WA7 . **149** H8
Cavendish Gdns *EP* CH65 ...... **163** J1
Cavendish Rd *BIRK* CH41 ...... **10** C3
CSBY/BLUN L23 .... **82** D2
STHP PR8 .... **35** H2
WAL/NB CH45 .... **95** K4
Cavendish St *CHLYE* PR6 ...... **18** F4
RUNC WA7 .... **19** L6
Caversham Cl *WARRS* WA4 ...... **137** M6
Cawdor St *RUNC* WA7 .... **18** E2
TOX L8 .... **113** J7

WGNS/IIMK WN3 .... **4** C7
WGNW/BIL/O WN5 .... **68** J7
Cawfield Av *WDN* WA8 .... **133** M4
Cawley Av *GOL/RIS/CU* WA3 .... **107** G1
Cawley St *RUNC* WA7 .... **19** G6
Cawood Cl *GTS/LS* CH66 .... **155** K8
WARRS WA4 .... **138** C3
Cawthorne Av *KKBY* L32 .... **86** A6
Cawthorne Cl *KKBY* L32 .... **86** A5
Cawthorne Wk *KKBY* L32 .... **86** A5
Caxton Cl *CL/PREN* CH43 ...... **110** E7
WDN WA8 .... **133** L2
WGNS/IIMK WN3 .... **79** H3
Caxton Rd *RAIN/WH* L35 .... **118** A4
Cazneau St *VAUX/LVPD* L3 ..... **13** H2
C Ct *AIMK* WN4 .... **91** K3
Cearns Rd *CL/PREN* CH43 ...... **10** B8
Cecil Av *WGNNW/ST* WN6 .... **68** C3
Cecil Dr *ECCL* WA10 .... **88** C8
Cecil Rd *LITH* L21 .... **83** H7
PS/BROM CH62 .... **128** D5
RF/TRAN CH42 .... **127** K3
WAL/EG CH44 .... **111** J1
Cecil St *STHEL* WA9 .... **103** H6
WAV L15 .... **113** M5
WGN WN1 .... **5** K4
WGNE/HIN WN2 .... **80** A1
Cedab Rd *EP* CH65 .... **20** D3
Cedar Av *BEB* CH63 .... **143** G1
CHLY/EC PR7 .... **31** L1
GOL/RIS/CU WA3 .... **93** H6
GTS/LS CH66 .... **155** L7
RUNC WA7 .... **19** M9
RUNC WA7 .... **161** J1
WDN WA8 .... **134** D2
WGNE/HIN WN2 .... **81** H2
WGNNW/ST WN6 .... **56** B5
Cedar Cl *CALD/MH* L18 .... **130** F2
RAIN/WH L35 .... **117** G3
Cedar Ct *GOL/RIS/CU* WA3 ..... **107** H3
Cedar Crs *HUY* L36 .... **115** M4
NEWLW WA12 .... **104** F3
ORM L39 .... **62** E1
Cedardale Dr *GTS/LS* CH66 .... **163** H4
Cedardale Pk *WGNE/HIN* WN2 ... **135** G1
Cedardale Rd *WLT/FAZ* L9 ..... **97** J1
Cedar Dr *FMBY* L37 .... **58** E4
WGN WN1 .... **68** F3
Cedar Gv *AIMK* WN4 .... **78** F8
CSBY/WL L22 .... **82** F3
MGHL L31 .... **72** F7
NSTN CH64 .... **153** H5
RNFD/HAY WA11 .... **91** G6
SKEL WN8 .... **65** G4
TOX L8 .... **122** C6
WARR WA1 .... **137** M2
WARRS WA4 .... **137** M3
WGNW/BIL/O WN5 .... **67** H7
Cedar Rd *CHLYE* PR6 .... **32** F3
RAIN/WH L35 .... **116** F2
WARRW/BUR WA5 .... **120** B7
WLT/FAZ L9 .... **84** D7
The Cedars *CHLY/EC* PR7 ...... **30** D6
CHLY/EC PR7 .... **43** K1
MOR/LEA CH46 .... **109** L6
WD/CROXPK L12 .... **99** H2
Cedar St *BIRK* CH41 .... **11** G7
BTL L20 .... **7** H3
ECCL WA10 .... **8** A7
NEWLW WA12 .... **104** E3
STHP PR8 .... **3** K9
Cedarway *HES* CH60 .... **141** K8
Cedarways *WARRS* WA4 .... **137** M8
Cedarwood Cl
GR/UP/WCH CH49 .... **125** K1
Cedarwood Ct *HUY* L36 .... **116** A5
Celandine Wk
WGNS/IIMK WN3 .... **78** D1
Celebration Dr *NPK/KEN* L6 ... **97** L8
Celedine Cl *WAV* L15 .... **114** B5
Celia St *BTL* L20 .... **7** J9
Celtic Rd *HOY* CH47 .... **109** G4
Celtic St *TOX* L8 .... **113** J7
Celt St *NPK/KEN* L6 .... **113** L1
Cemetery Rd *STHP* PR8 .... **3** H9
WGNS/IIMK WN3 .... **80** A1
Cemetery Vw *CHLY/EC* PR7 ..... **44** B7
Central Av *EP* CH65 .... **20** C6
PR/KW L34 .... **100** E7
PR/KW L34 .... **101** H6
PS/BROM CH62 .... **143** L4
SPK/HALE L24 .... **146** F2
WARRN/WOL WA2 .... **121** L5
WARRS WA4 .... **14** F9
Central Avnue *STHP* PR8 ...... **35** H5
Central Dr *RNFD/HAY* WA11 .... **76** B6
RNFD/HAY WA11 .... **90** D7
WD/CROXPK L12 .... **98** D8
WGNNW/ST WN6 .... **55** K7
Central Expy *RUNC* WA7 .... **149** M7
Central Park Av *WAL/EG* CH44 . **111** L1
Central Park Wy *WGN* WN1 ..... **5** G1
Central Rd *PS/BROM* CH62 ..... **128** D6
WARRS WA4 .... **15** G9
Central Sq *MGHL* L31 .... **72** F3
Central St *ECCL* WA10 .... **9** G3
Central Wy *NEWLW* WA12 .... **105** G3
SPK/HALE L24 .... **147** G3
Centre Ct *LEIGH* WN7 .... **93** K4
Centre Park Sq *WARR* WA1 ..... **14** D8
Centreville Rd *CALD/MH* L18 .. **114** C7
Centre Wy *HUY* L36 .... **116** A3
Centurion Cl
GOL/RIS/CU WA3 .... **122** F1
HOY CH47 .... **109** G4
Centurion Dr *HOY* CH47 .... **7** G9
Ceres St *BTL* L20 .... **7** G4
Cestrian Dr *PEN/TH* CH61 ..... **126** C8
Chadlow Rd *KKBY* L32 .... **86** B1
Chadwell Rd *NWD/KWIPK* L33 ... **86** B1
Chadwick Pl *GOL/RIS/CU* WA3 .. **107** G8
Chadwick Rd *RNFD/HAY* WA11... **89** L6
WARRS WA4 .... **138** A4
Chadwick St *MOR/LEA* CH46 ... **110** A5
VAUX/LVPD L3 .... **12** D1

Chaffinch Cl *GOL/RIS/CU* WA3 . **123** H2
WD/CROXPK L12 .... **99** H4
Chaffinch Gld *HLWD* L26 ...... **132** A4
Chainhurst Cl *NTHLY* L27 ..... **115** M7
Chain La *RNFD/HAY* WA11 ...... **89** M7
Chalbury Rd *WGNE/HIN* WN2 ... **80** F1
Chalfield Gv *GTS/LS* CH66 .... **155** L8
Chalfield Cl *GTS/LS* CH66 .... **155** L8
Chalfont Cl *WARRS* WA4 .... **138** A7
Chalfont Rd *CALD/MH* L18 ..... **130** C4
Chalfont Wy *STBRV* L28 .... **99** L1
Chalgrave Cl *WDN* WA8 .... **135** G2
Chalkwell Dr *HES* CH60 .... **141** L6
Challenge Wy
WGNW/BIL/O WN5 .... **67** L4
Challis St *BIRK* CH41 .... **111** H2
Challoner Cl *HUY* L36 .... **116** B5
Chaloner Gv *ALL/GAR* L19 .... **130** B6
Chaloner St *VAUX/LVPD* L3 .... **112** F6
Chalon Wy *ECCL* WA10 .... **9** H6
Chalon Wy West *ECCL* WA10 ... **9** G6
Chamberlain St *BIRK* CH41 .... **11** K9
ECCL WA10 .... **8** A6
WAL/EG CH44 .... **111** J3
Chambres Rd *STHP* PR8 .... **3** L7
Chambres Rd North *STHP* PR8.. **3** M6
Chancellor Rd *RUNC* WA7 ...... **135** M4
Chancel St *ANF/KKDL* L4 ...... **97** G6
Chancery La *STHEL* WA9 .... **103** G2
Chancery Rd *CHLY/EC* PR7 ..... **32** C4
Chandler Wy *GOL/RIS/CU* WA3 . **93** G5
Chandley Cl *STHP* PR8 .... **34** C3
Chandos St *EHL/KEN* L7 .... **113** K4
Change La *NSTN* CH64 .... **154** D5
Changford Rd *NWD/KWIPK* L33.. **86** C2
Channel Rd *NPK/KEN* L6 .... **113** L2
Channel Reach
CSBY/BLUN L23 .... **82** D3
Chantler Av *WARRS* WA4 ...... **15** M7
Chantrell Rd *WKBY* CH48 ...... **125** L8
Chantry Cl *CL/PREN* CH43 ..... **110** E7
Chantry Wk *AIMK* WN4 .... **79** H8
HES CH60 .... **141** J7
Chatburn Av *GOL/RIS/CU* WA3 . **92** E4
Chatburn Ct
GOL/RIS/CU WA3 .... **107** H3
Chatburn Wk *TOX* L8 .... **129** H1
Chater Cl *RAIN/WH* L35 .... **101** J7
Chatfield Dr *GOL/RIS/CU* WA3 . **123** G2
Chatfield Rd *LITH* L21 .... **83** H6
Chatham Pl *CHLYE* PR6 .... **33** G5
EHL/KEN L7 .... **113** K4
Chatham Rd *RF/TRAN* CH42 .... **128** C3
Chatham St *WGN* WN1 .... **69** J5
WGNE/HIN WN2 .... **69** J5
Chatsworth Av
GOL/RIS/CU WA3 .... **107** H1
WAL/EG CH44 .... **111** L1
WGNE/HIN WN2 .... **80** B1
WLT/FAZ L9 .... **84** B8
Chatsworth Cl *AIMK* WN4 ...... **91** H1
CHLY/EC PR7 .... **32** D5
GTS/LS CH66 .... **155** L8
Chatsworth Ct *CHLYE* PR6 .... **44** B4
Chatsworth Dr *EHL/KEN* L7 ... **113** K5
WDN WA8 .... **133** L2
Chatsworth Rd *PEN/TH* CH61 .. **128** B8
RAIN/WH L35 .... **117** K1
RF/TRAN CH42 .... **128** C3
STHP PR8 .... **34** C7
Chatsworth St
WGNW/BIL/O WN5 .... **67** L8
Chatteris Cl *WGNE/HIN* WN2 .. **81** G1
Chatteris Pk *RUNC* WA7 ...... **151** G3
Chatterton Dr *RUNC* WA7 ..... **151** K3
Chatterton Rd *DV/KA/FCH* L14. **114** E1
Chatwell Gdns *WARRS* WA4 .... **138** B1
Chaucer Cl *CHLY/EC* PR7 ...... **30** D7
Chaucer Dr *WD/CROXPK* L12 ... **99** H3
Chaucer Gv *LEIGH* WN7 .... **81** L5
Chaucer Pl *WARRS* WA4 .... **138** B1
WGN WN1 .... **80** D4
Chaucer Rd *ECCL* WA10 .... **8** F1
Chaucer St *BTL* L20 .... **6** D2
RUNC WA7 .... **19** H3
VAUX/LVPD L3 .... **13** H3
Cheadle Av *CLB/OSW/ST* L13 .. **114** B2
Cheam Av *CHLY/EC* PR7 .... **32** F7
Cheapside *CHLY/EC* PR7 ...... **32** E6
CLVP L2 .... **12** F5
FMBY L37 .... **59** J3
Cheapside Aly *CLVP* L2 ...... **12** F6
Cheddar Cl *WLTN* L25 .... **131** H5
Cheddar Gv *KKBY* L32 .... **86** A6
WARRW/BUR WA5 .... **104** B6
Cheddon Wy *PEN/TH* CH61 ..... **141** G1
Chedworth Rd *WDN* WA8 .... **133** L1
Chedworth St *DV/KA/FCH* L14 . **115** H2
Cheetham Gv
WGNS/IIMK WN3 .... **68** B8
Chelburn Cl *WGNE/HIN* WN2 ... **81** G4
Cheldon Rd *NG/CROX* L11 ..... **98** E3
Chelford Av *NG/CROX* L11 .... **92** F6
Chelford Cl *CL/PREN* CH43 ... **110** E6
WGNS/IIMK WN3 .... **79** H3
Chellowdene *CSBY/BLUN* L23 .. **71** J7
Chelmarsh Av *AIMK* WN4 ...... **91** L2
Chelmorton Gv *WGNS/IIMK* WN3. **78** E3
Chelmsford Dr *WGNS/IIMK* WN3. **79** H1
Chelmsford Gv *CHLY/EC* PR7 .. **32** D6
Chelmsford Ms *WGN* WN1 ...... **68** C3
Chelmsford Pl *CHLY/EC* PR7 .. **32** D7
Chelsea Cl *WD/CROXPK* L12 ... **99** G5
Chelsea Rd *LITH* L21 .... **83** K7
WLT/FAZ L9 .... **113** M8
Cheltenham Av *AIG/SPK* L17 .. **113** M8
WGNS/IIMK WN3 .... **5** H8
Cheltenham Cl
WARRW/BUR WA5 .... **120** C5
WLT/FAZ L9 .... **85** G4
Cheltenham Crs *HUY* L36 ..... **149** M1
RUNC WA7 .... **149** K7
Cheltenham Dr *NEWLW* WA12 ... **91** L8
WGNW/BIL/O WN5 .... **77** M3
Cheltenham Rd *EP* CH65 ...... **20** E8
WAL/NB CH45 .... **95** G3
Cheltenham St
WGNE/HIN WN2 .... **69** H3

Cheltenham Wy STHP PR8 36 B1
Chelwood Av CHLDW L16 115 H5
Chemical St NEWLW WA12 104 D2 3
Chemistry Rd SPK/HALE L24 131 L8
Chenotrie Gdns CL/PREN CH43 110 F8
Chepstow Av WAL/EG CH44 111 L1 6
Chepstow Cl WARRW/BUR WA5 121 G2
Chepstow St ANF/KKDL L4 7 M8
Chequer Cl SKEL WN8 66 B8
Chequer La SKEL WN8 66 B7
Chequers Gdns ALL/GAR L19 130 B5
Chequers St WGN WN1 4 D4
Cheriton Av WKBY CH48 124 F3
Cheriton Cl HLWD L26 132 A5 2
Chermside Rd AIG/SPK L17 130 A4 1
Cherry Av ANF/KKDL L4 97 K4
Cherrybank WAL/EG CH44 111 K3
Cherry Blossom Rd
RUNC WA7 150 B8 1
Cherry Cl ANF/KKDL L4 97 K4 1
NEWLW WA12 104 B1 2
NSTN CH64 153 L5
Cherry Cnr LYMM WA13 139 J7
Cherrydale Rd CALD/MH L18 130 C1
Cherryfield Crs KKBY L32 86 A3
Cherryfield Dr KKBY L32 85 M3
Cherry Gn ORM L39 62 D4 1
Cherry Gv BRSC L40 39 G7
GTS/LS CH66 163 J4
WGNNW/ST WN6 68 B2
Cherry La ANF/KKDL L4 97 M5
LYMM WA13 139 K5
Cherry Rd STHP PR8 47 M3
Cherrysutton WDN WA8 133 K2
Cherry Tree Av LYMM WA13 139 M3 2
RUNC WA7 19 L7
WARRW/BUR WA5 136 B1
Cherry Tree Cl RAIN/WH L35 116 F2 1
RNFD/HAY WA11 90 C8 1
Cherry Tree Dr STHEL WA9 103 J3
Cherry Tree Gv CHLYE PR6 32 E2
LEIGH WN7 81 M7 1
Cherry Tree La ORM L39 62 D4
RNFD/HAY WA11 89 J3
Cherry Tree Rd GOL/RIS/CU WA3 93 H5
HUY L36 116 A5
MOR/LEA CH46 110 B6
Cherry V WLTN L25 131 K2
Cherry Vw NWD/KWIPK L33 74 B8
Chervil Wk WGNS/IIMK WN3 78 E1
Cherwell Cl
WARRN/WOL WA2 121 M3 3
WGNE/HIN WN2 57 L7 2
Cheryl Dr WDN WA8 17 K1
Cheshire Acre
GR/UP/WCH CH49 126 C3
Cheshire Av AIN/FAZ L10 85 K6 1
Cheshire Cl NEWLW WA12 105 G2
Cheshire Gdns ECCL WA10 8 D7
Cheshire Gv MOR/LEA CH46 110 A6
Cheshire Lines Pth FMBY L37 48 B7
Cheshire Ring Canal Wk
WARRS WA4 136 E7
Cheshyre Dr RUNC WA7 150 B4 1
Cheshyre's La RUNC WA7 149 G7
Chesnell Gv NWD/KWIPK L33 74 B8 2
Chesney Cl TOX L8 113 G7
Chesnut Gv BTL L20 6 F2
RF/TRAN CH42 11 G9
Chessington Cl WARRS WA4 138 B6
Chester Av CHLY/EC PR7 44 A1
CHTN/BK PR9 25 H5
GOL/RIS/CU WA3 92 F5
NTHTN L30 84 B4
Chester Cl CSBY/BLUN L23 83 K1
RUNC WA7 150 B3
Chester Dr AIMK WN4 91 M3
Chesterfield Cl STHP PR8 47 K1
Chesterfield Dr NWD/KWIPK L33 74 A8
Chesterfield Rd CSBY/BLUN L23 71 J8
PS/BROM CH62 154 F1
STHP PR8 47 K1
Chesterfield St TOX L8 113 G6 1
Chester High Rd NSTN CH64 153 G1
Chester La STHEL WA9 118 D1
Chester New Rd WARRS WA4 137 H6
Chester Pl CHLYE PR6 44 C5
Chester Rd CHTN/BK PR9 25 H5
EP CH65 163 J2
FROD/HEL WA6 160 B7
GTS/LS CH66 155 L8
HES CH60 141 L7
HUY L36 116 C1
NPK/KEN L6 97 M7
NSTN CH64 153 G6
RUNC WA7 151 G8
WARRS WA4 137 J3
Chester St BIRK CH41 11 L5
PR/KW L34 100 F7
TOX L8 113 G6
WAL/EG CH44 111 J2 3
WDN WA8 16 E2
Chesterton Cl WGNS/IIMK WN3 4 B9
Chesterton St ALL/GAR L19 145 L1
Chestnut Av CHLY/EC PR7 31 L1
CHLYE PR6 33 G3 1
CSBY/BLUN L23 71 H7
GTS/LS CH66 163 H4
HUY L36 115 M5
RNFD/HAY WA11 90 B8
WARRW/BUR WA5 120 B7
WDN WA8 134 D3
Chestnut Cl
GR/UP/WCH CH49 125 L3 3
ORM L39 49 L4
RAIN/WH L35 117 G1
Chestnut Ct ORM L39 51 H7 1
Chestnut Gv AIMK WN4 91 M1
GOL/RIS/CU WA3 93 H5 3
PS/BROM CH62 143 L5 2
RNFD/HAY WA11 89 M6
WAV L15 114 B5
WGNE/HIN WN2 81 J1
Chestnut Rd LITH L21 83 H6
WGN WN1 68 F3
WLT/FAZ L9 97 K2
The Chestnuts CHLY/EC PR7 43 H3
Chestnut St EHL/KEN L7 13 M8
STHP PR8 3 K9
Chestnut Wy FMBY L37 58 E4
Cheswood Cl RAIN/WH L35 117 G3 1
Chetham Ct WARRN/WOL WA2 121 J2
Chetton Dr RUNC WA7 151 G6
Chetwode Av AIMK WN4 91 K3
Chetwood Av CSBY/BLUN L23 71 H8
Chetwood Dr WDN WA8 134 B1
Chetwynd Cl CL/PREN CH43 127 H1
Chetwynd Rd CL/PREN CH43 10 A8
Chetwynd St AIG/SPK L17 129 K2
Chevasse Wk WLTN L25 131 L2
Cheverton Cl
GR/UP/WCH CH49 126 D2 1
Cheviot Av STHEL WA9 103 H2
WARRN/WOL WA2 121 J2
Cheviot Cl HOR/BR BL6 45 L8
RF/TRAN CH42 127 M4 1
WGNS/IIMK WN3 78 E3
Cheviot Rd EHL/KEN L7 114 A3
RF/TRAN CH42 127 L4
Cheviot Wy NWD/KWIPK L33 74 B7
Chevoit Cl GTS/LS CH66 155 J7
Cheyne Gdns ALL/GAR L19 130 B5
Cheyne Wk STHEL WA9 102 B7 1
Chichester Cl RUNC WA7 150 F7
WAV L15 113 M5 1
Chidden Cl GR/UP/WCH CH49 125 L2
Chidlow Cl WDN WA8 134 C8 1
Chigwell Cl WD/CROXPK L12 99 G2
Chilcott Rd CLB/OSW/ST L13 114 E2
Childer Crs GTS/LS CH66 155 K6
Childer Gdns GTS/LS CH66 155 K6
Childers St CLB/OSW/ST L13 114 C2
Childwall Abbey Rd CHLDW L16 114 F7
Childwall Av MOR/LEA CH46 109 M6
WAV L15 113 M6 2
Childwall Bank Rd
CHLDW L16 114 F6 1
Childwall Cl MOR/LEA CH46 109 M6 1
Childwall Crs CHLDW L16 114 F6
Childwall Gn GR/UP/WCH CH49 126 C3
Childwall Hts WLTN L25 115 H6
Childwall La DV/KA/FCH L14 115 J3
WLTN L25 115 H7
Childwall Mount Rd
CHLDW L16 114 F6
Childwall Park Av CHLDW L16 115 G7
Childwall Priory Rd CHLDW L16 114 F6
Childwall Rd GTS/LS CH66 156 A5
WAV L15 114 C6
Childwall Valley Rd CHLDW L16 114 F6
WLTN L25 115 H5
Chilgrove Av HOR/BR BL6 57 M4
Chilham St WGNW/BIL/O WN5 67 K7 1
Chilhem Cl TOX L8 129 H1 3
Chilington Av WDN WA8 133 M5
Chillerton Rd WD/CROXPK L12 98 F5
Chillingham St TOX L8 129 J1
Chiltern Av CHLY/EC PR7 31 M4
WARRN/WOL WA2 121 J2 2
Chiltern Cl AIMK WN4 91 L3
HOR/BR BL6 45 L8
WD/CROXPK L12 99 H3
Chiltern Crs
WARRN/WOL WA2 121 J2 3
Chiltern Dr KKBY L32 85 L1
WGNS/IIMK WN3 78 E2
Chiltern Rd GOL/RIS/CU WA3 107 G1
RF/TRAN CH42 127 L4
STHEL WA9 103 J2
STHP PR8 34 C7
WARRN/WOL WA2 121 J2
Chilton Cl MGHL L31 72 F4
Chilton Dr GTS/LS CH66 163 H3 2
Chilton Ms MGHL L31 72 F4
Chilwell Cl WDN WA8 133 M1
Chimes Rd AIMK WN4 79 H7
China Farm La WKBY CH48 125 G1
China La WARRS WA4 137 L3
Chindit Cl FMBY L37 58 F3
Chippenham Av
GR/UP/WCH CH49 125 L1
Chipping Av STHP PR8 34 C8
Chippingdall Cl
WARRW/BUR WA5 120 E8 2
Chirkdale St ANF/KKDL L4 7 L8
Chirk Wy MOR/LEA CH46 110 B6
Chirton Cl RNFD/HAY WA11 90 F6 1
Chisacre Dr WGNNW/ST WN6 54 F6
Chisenhale St VAUX/LVPD L3 12 E2
Chisholm Cl WGNNW/ST WN6 55 K2
Chisledon Cl RNFD/HAY WA11 90 F6
Chislehurst Av WLTN L25 115 K7
Chislett Cl BRSC L40 51 M1 1
Chisnall Av ECCL WA10 101 L1
WGNNW/ST WN6 42 B8
Chisnall La CHLY/EC PR7 42 C8
Chiswell St EHL/KEN L7 113 L3 1
WGNW/BIL/O WN5 67 L8
Chiswick Cl RUNC WA7 150 F6 3
Chiswick Gdns WARRS WA4 138 B7
Cholmondeley Rd EP CH65 163 H1
RUNC WA7 149 M8
WKBY CH48 124 D3
Cholmondeley St WDN WA8 149 J1 3
Cholsey Cl GR/UP/WCH CH49 126 B1 3
Chorley Cl CHTN/BK PR9 23 G8
Chorley Hall Rd CHLY/EC PR7 32 E3
Chorley La CHLY/EC PR7 42 E3
Chorley Rd CHLY/EC PR7 43 M5
CHLYE PR6 44 C4
HOR/BR BL6 57 L2
PR/KW L34 100 D7
SKEL WN8 40 F8
WGN WN1 43 L8
WGN WN1 56 D4 1
Chorley's La WDN WA8 134 F2
Chorley St CHLYE PR6 44 D5 2
ECCL WA10 8 E3
WARRN/WOL WA2 14 F3
WGNS/IIMK WN3 5 J8
Chorley Wy BEB CH63 143 J4
Chorlton Cl CHLDW L16 115 H5
RUNC WA7 150 F4 2
Chorlton Gv WAL/NB CH45 94 F8
Christchurch Rd CL/PREN CH43 10 D9
Christian St VAUX/LVPD L3 13 H4
Christie Cl GTS/LS CH66 155 J3 1
Christie St WDN WA8 17 J1
Christines Crs BRSC L40 51 M1
Christleton WGNNW/ST WN6 55 K7
Christleton Cl CL/PREN CH43 126 F3
Christleton Ct RUNC WA7 150 E1
Christleton Dr GTS/LS CH66 156 A7
Christmas St BTL L20 7 J9
Christopher Cl CHLDW L16 114 F5
Christopher Dr PS/BROM CH62 144 C8
Christophers Cl
PEN/TH CH61 141 J1 1
Christopher St ANF/KKDL L4 97 H5
WGNS/IIMK WN3 5 L8
Christopher Wy CHLDW L16 114 F5
Chris Ward Cl EHL/KEN L7 113 L4 3
Chudleigh Cl HLWD L26 132 A4 3
Chudleigh Rd CLB/OSW/ST L13 114 B2
Church Av WGNE/HIN WN2 81 H5
WLT/FAZ L9 84 D6
Church Cl CHTN/BK PR9 25 J5 1
FMBY L37 59 J2
WAL/EG CH44 111 M1 2
Church Close Ct FMBY L37 59 J2 1
Church Crs WAL/EG CH44 112 A3 6
Churchdown Gv
DV/KA/FCH L14 115 G1 1
Churchdown Rd
DV/KA/FCH L14 115 G1
Church Dr NEWLW WA12 104 E4
PS/BROM CH62 128 D7
WARRN/WOL WA2 122 C4 1
WGNW/BIL/O WN5 66 F8
Church End SPK/HALE L24 147 M4
Church Farm Ct HES CH60 141 H6
Churchfield WGNNW/ST WN6 55 J7
Churchfield Rd FROD/HEL WA6 160 E6
WLTN L25 115 L8
Churchfields FROD/HEL WA6 166 E1 1
GOL/RIS/CU WA3 106 D6
STHEL WA9 118 E1 1
STHP PR8 35 H2
WDN WA8 118 D8
Church Flds BRSC L40 37 H6 2
ORM L39 51 G8
Church Fold CHLY/EC PR7 43 G1
CHLY/EC PR7 43 H5
Church Gdns BTL L20 6 E5 1
WAL/EG CH44 111 M1 2
Churchgate CHTN/BK PR9 25 H4
Churchgate Ms CHTN/BK PR9 25 J4 1
Church Gn CHLDW L16 115 H6
FMBY L37 58 E3
KKBY L32 86 A2
Church Gv LITH L21 83 H7
Church Hl WAL/EG CH44 95 H8 1
Church Hill Rd ORM L39 50 F7
Churchill Av CHTN/BK PR9 25 H3
GOL/RIS/CU WA3 107 K1
Churchill Gv WAL/EG CH44 95 L8 1
Churchill Wy NSTN CH64 153 G5
Churchill Wy (Elevated Rd)
CLVPS L1 13 G6
Churchlands La
WGNNW/ST WN6 56 B4
Church La AIG/SPK L17 130 A4
ANF/KKDL L4 97 H3
CHLY/EC PR7 42 F1
CHNE CH2 164 C6
ECCL WA10 101 J1
GOL/RIS/CU WA3 92 F6
GOL/RIS/CU WA3 107 H2
GR/UP/WCH CH49 126 D3
GTS/LS CH66 162 F1
NSTN CH64 153 G6
ORM L39 61 H5
ORM L39 62 C6
PEN/TH CH61 125 K8
PR/KW L34 99 L1
PS/BROM CH62 143 M4
PS/BROM CH62 144 C8
PS/BROM CH62 155 H1
WAL/EG CH44 111 M1 3
WARRS WA4 138 D4
WGNNW/ST WN6 41 M5
WGNNW/ST WN6 55 J7
Churchmeadow Cl
WAL/EG CH44 111 M1 4
Church Meadow La HES CH60 141 G6
Church Meadow Wk
WDN WA8 133 K8 1
Church Mt EHL/KEN L7 113 K4 5
Church Pde EP CH65 20 D2 1
Church Rd ALL/GAR L19 130 E8
ANF/KKDL L4 97 J3
BEB CH63 142 D7
BEB CH63 143 J1
BRSC L40 39 L1
BTL L20 83 M7
CHTN/BK PR9 23 J7
CLB/OSW/ST L13 114 B2
CSBY/BLUN L23 83 G1
CSBY/WL L22 83 G5 1
FMBY L37 59 J1
FROD/HEL WA6 160 E6
GR/UP/WCH CH49 110 C8
HLWD L26 132 B4
HUY L36 115 L2
LITH L21 83 M4
LYMM WA13 139 M3
MGHL L31 72 F6
ORM L39 64 A7
RF/TRAN CH42 127 M1
RNFD/HAY WA11 76 B7
RNFD/HAY WA11 88 C1
RNFD/HAY WA11 91 G7
SKEL WN8 65 H4
SPK/HALE L24 148 A5
WAL/EG CH44 112 A3
WAV L15 114 C7
WGNE/HIN WN2 80 D2
WKBY CH48 124 C4
WLTN L25 131 J2
Church Rd North WAV L15 114 C6
Church Rd South WLTN L25 131 J3
Church Rd West ANF/KKDL L4 97 H3
Church St BIRK CH41 11 M6
BTL L20 6 D5
CHLY/EC PR7 32 E6 5
CHLYE PR6 44 C6
CHTN/BK PR9 3 J3
CLVPS L1 13 G7
ECCL WA10 9 H6
EP CH65 20 D2 2
FROD/HEL WA6 160 D5
GOL/RIS/CU WA3 92 D4 1
HOR/BR BL6 57 L3
LEY/BBR PR5 29 K4 1
NEWLW WA12 105 G1
ORM L39 51 G8
PR/KW L34 100 F7 6
RUNC WA7 19 G2
SKEL WN8 66 E6
WAL/EG CH44 111 M1
WARR WA1 15 H5
WDN WA8 134 C8
WGN WN1 4 F3
WGNE/HIN WN2 57 K7
WGNE/HIN WN2 69 M8 9
WGNNW/ST WN6 56 A4
WGNS/IIMK WN3 5 L7
WGNW/BIL/O WN5 66 F8
WGNW/BIL/O WN5 67 K7
Church Ter RF/TRAN CH42 127 M2
Church Vw BTL L20 6 F5
ORM L39 62 C6
Churchview Rd BIRK CH41 10 D2
Church Wk BTL L20 6 E5
CHLY/EC PR7 31 L3
WARRN/WOL WA2 105 J7
Church Wy FMBY L37 58 E3
FROD/HEL WA6 166 F4
KKBY L32 86 A2
Churchway Rd SPK/HALE L24 147 J3
Churchwood Cl
PS/BROM CH62 143 M4
Churnet St ANF/KKDL L4 97 G5
Churn Wy GR/UP/WCH CH49 125 M1
Churston Rd CHLDW L16 115 G8
Churton Av CL/PREN CH43 127 H2
Churton Ct NPK/KEN L6 113 J2 2
Churton Gv WGNNW/ST WN6 55 K3
Ciaran Cl WD/CROXPK L12 98 F5
Cicely St EHL/KEN L7 113 K4
Cinder La BTL L20 83 M6
CALD/MH L18 114 E8
KIRK/FR/WA PR4 27 H3 1
WARRS WA4 139 H5
Cinnamon Av WGNE/HIN WN2 81 H1 2
Cinnamon Brow SKEL WN8 66 E7
Cinnamon La WARRN/WOL WA2 122 B2
Cinnamon La North
WARRN/WOL WA2 122 B1
Circular Dr GR/UP/WCH CH49 125 M2
HES CH60 141 G4
PS/BROM CH62 128 D6
Circular Rd BIRK CH41 11 H7
Circular Rd East NG/CROX L11 98 B5
Circular Rd West NG/CROX L11 98 B4
Cirencester Av
GR/UP/WCH CH49 125 L1
Cirrus Dr ORM L39 62 C4
Citrine Rd WAL/EG CH44 111 M3
Citron Cl WLT/FAZ L9 97 K1
City Gdns ECCL WA10 89 H7
City Rd ANF/KKDL L4 97 H4
ECCL WA10 89 H7
WGNW/BIL/O WN5 67 K6
Civic Wy EP CH65 20 B4
HUY L36 116 A3 1
Clairville Cl BTL L20 7 G5
Clairville Wy CLB/OSW/ST L13 98 A8 2
Clancut La CHLY/EC PR7 43 H3
Clandon Rd CALD/MH L18 130 F4
Clanfield Av WDN WA8 133 L2
Clanfield Rd NG/CROX L11 98 D4
Clanwood Cl WGNS/IIMK WN3 79 G3 1
Clap Gate Crs WDN WA8 133 K8
Clap Gate La WGNS/IIMK WN3 79 G2
Clap Gates Rd
WARRW/BUR WA5 121 G6
Clapham Rd ANF/KKDL L4 97 K7
Clare Cl STHEL WA9 102 A6
Clare Crs WAL/EG CH44 111 G1
Clare Dr EP CH65 163 K4
Claremont Av CHLY/EC PR7 32 D6
MGHL L31 72 D5
WDN WA8 134 E1 1
Claremont Cl LITH L21 83 H6 3
Claremont Dr ORM L39 62 F2
WDN WA8 134 D1
Claremont Gdns STHP PR8 2 E9
Claremont Rd CHLY/EC PR7 32 D8 3
CSBY/BLUN L23 82 F1
GOL/RIS/CU WA3 106 F1
LITH L21 83 H6
RUNC WA7 19 K4
WAV L15 114 A7
WGNW/BIL/O WN5 78 A8
WKBY CH48 124 D2
Claremont Wy BEB CH63 127 M5
Claremount Dr BEB CH63 143 H1 1
Claremount Rd WAL/NB CH45 95 H7
Clarence Av
WARRW/BUR WA5 119 M7 2
WDN WA8 134 C1
Clarence Cl STHEL WA9 9 L8
Clarence Rd RF/TRAN CH42 127 L2 1
STHP PR8 35 J1
WAL/EG CH44 111 M3
WARRS WA4 138 D3
Clarence St AIMK WN4 91 H1
CHLY/EC PR7 32 F6 1
GOL/RIS/CU WA3 92 C4
NEWLW WA12 104 B1
RUNC WA7 18 F2
VAUX/LVPD L3 13 K7
WARR WA1 15 L2
WGNE/HIN WN2 69 J6
Clarence Ter RUNC WA7 19 G2
Clarence Yd WGN WN1 4 E4
Clarendon Cl CL/PREN CH43 10 E7
RUNC WA7 150 F6
Clarendon Ct WARRN/WOL WA2 121 H1
Clarendon Gv MGHL L31 61 L8 1
Clarendon Rd ALL/GAR L19 130 E7
LITH L21 83 H7 1
NPK/KEN L6 97 L7
WAL/EG CH44 111 M2
Clarendon St CHLYE PR6 33 G6 3
Clare Rd BTL L20 7 K7
Clares Farm Cl WARR WA1 123 H6 1
Claret Cl AIG/SPK L17 129 L4
Clare Wy WAL/NB CH45 95 H8 2
Claribel St TOX L8 113 J7
Clarington Gv WGN WN1 5 J5
Clarke Av GOL/RIS/CU WA3 107 H1
RF/TRAN CH42 128 A3
WARRS WA4 137 M3
Clarke's Crs ECCL WA10 101 K1
Clarkfield Cl BRSC L40 52 B2 2
Classic Rd CLB/OSW/ST L13 114 C1
Clatterbridge Rd BEB CH63 142 F5
Claude Rd NPK/KEN L6 97 L7
Claude St WARR WA1 15 H3
WGNW/BIL/O WN5 67 M7
Claughton Cl EHL/KEN L7 113 L4 3
Claughton Dr WAL/EG CH44 111 K2
Claughton Firs CL/PREN CH43 10 D9
Claughton Gn CL/PREN CH43 10 B8
Claughton Pl BIRK CH41 10 F6 1
Claughton Rd BIRK CH41 11 H6
Claughton St ECCL WA10 9 G4
Clavell Rd ALL/GAR L19 130 F5
Claverton Cl RUNC WA7 149 K7 2
Claybridge Cl WGNW/BIL/O WN5 67 K4
Clay Brow Rd SKEL WN8 66 A7
Clayburn Cl CHLYE PR6 32 F3 2
Clay Cross Rd WLTN L25 131 H3
Claydon Ct HLWD L26 132 C4
Claydon Dr WGNE/HIN WN2 80 B1
Clayfield Cl BTL L20 7 K5
Clayford Crs DV/KA/FCH L14 114 D1
Clayford Pl DV/KA/FCH L14 114 D1 1
Clayford Rd DV/KA/FCH L14 114 E1 1
Clayford Wy DV/KA/FCH L14 114 E1 2
Clayhill NSTN CH64 153 H3
Clayhill Gn GTS/LS CH66 155 L6
Clay La ECCL WA10 101 G2
WARRW/BUR WA5 104 A7
Claypole Cl EHL/KEN L7 113 L5 3
Clay St VAUX/LVPD L3 12 D1
Clayton Av GOL/RIS/CU WA3 93 G5
Clayton Crs RUNC WA7 18 E5
WDN WA8 16 B2
Clayton Gdns BRSC L40 52 A1 2
Claytongate CHLY/EC PR7 43 H3
Clayton House LEIGH WN7 81 L8
Clayton La WAL/EG CH44 111 J3
Clayton Ms SKEL WN8 64 F4 2
Clayton Pl CL/PREN CH43 10 F7
Clayton Rd GOL/RIS/CU WA3 107 H7
Clayton St SKEL WN8 64 F4
WGNS/IIMK WN3 4 C4
Cleadon Cl KKBY L32 86 C6 1
Cleadon Rd KKBY L32 86 B6
Clearwater Cl EHL/KEN L7 113 K3
Cleary St BTL L20 6 E2
Clee Hill Rd RF/TRAN CH42 127 L4
Cleethorpes Rd RUNC WA7 150 E6
Clegge St WARRN/WOL WA2 14 F2
Clegg St EV L5 13 J2
SKEL WN8 64 F4 3
Clelland St WARRS WA4 15 H9
Clematis Cl CHLY/EC PR7 32 C2
Clematis Rd NTHLY L27 116 A7
Clement Gdns VAUX/LVPD L3 12 F2
Clementina Rd
CSBY/BLUN L23 82 D1 2
Clemmey Dr BTL L20 84 A7
Clengers Brow CHTN/BK PR9 25 J2 1
Clent Av MGHL L31 72 E2
Clent Gdns MGHL L31 72 F2
Clent Rd MGHL L31 72 E3
Cleopas St TOX L8 129 H1 5
Clevedon Dr WGNS/IIMK WN3 78 E1
Clevedon St TOX L8 129 J1
Cleveland Av WGNS/IIMK WN3 78 E3
Cleveland Buildings CLVPS L1 13 G9 1
Cleveland Cl KKBY L32 85 L1
Cleveland Dr AIMK WN4 91 L1
GOL/RIS/CU WA3 92 F5
GTS/LS CH66 155 J7
Cleveland Rd WARRN/WOL WA2 121 K2
Cleveland Sq CLVPS L1 13 G9 2
Cleveland St BIRK CH41 10 E1
CHLY/EC PR7 32 E5
CHLY/EC PR7 43 G4 2
STHEL WA9 9 L9
Cleveley Pk CALD/MH L18 130 F4
Cleveley Rd CALD/MH L18 130 F4
HOY CH47 109 G5
Cleveleys Av CHTN/BK PR9 25 J1
WDN WA8 134 F2
Cleveleys Rd CHTN/BK PR9 25 J2
WARRW/BUR WA5 136 D1 2
The Cleves MGHL L31 73 G2
Cleve Wy FMBY L37 59 K3
Clieves Hills La ORM L39 61 M3
Clieves Rd KKBY L32 86 B4
Cliff Dr WAL/EG CH44 95 M8
Cliffe Rd NSTN CH64 153 H8
WARRS WA4 137 L6
Cliffe St WARR WA1 14 B5
WDN WA8 17 G1
Cliff La LYMM WA13 139 K7
WARRS WA4 138 F3
WARRS WA4 139 H6
Clifford Rd STHP PR8 35 J4
WAL/EG CH44 111 K2
WARRW/BUR WA5 136 C1
Clifford St CHLY/EC PR7 32 F5
VAUX/LVPD L3 13 K5
Cliff Rd CHTN/BK PR9 24 F3
WAL/EG CH44 111 J2
Cliff St EHL/KEN L7 113 L3
Clifton Av GOL/RIS/CU WA3 106 F2
HLWD L26 132 A4
PS/BROM CH62 155 G2
Clifton Cl WARR WA1 122 E6
Clifton Crs BIRK CH41 11 J6
FROD/HEL WA6 160 E4
Clifton Cresent WGN WN1 68 E3
Clifton Dr AIN/FAZ L10 84 F3

HOR/BR BL6 57 K2
Clifton Gdns EP CH65 20 C8
Clifton Gv CHLY/EC PR7 32 D6 2
EV L5 13 K2
WAL/EG CH44 111 M1
Clifton La RUNC WA7 161 G2
Cliftonmill Mdw
GOL/RIS/CU WA3 92 B5 1
Clifton Rd AIMK WN4 79 H7
BIRK CH41 11 H8
FMBY L37 47 J8
NPK/KEN L6 97 M8
RUNC WA7 19 H9
STHP PR8 25 H7
WGNW/BIL/O WN5 89 M1
Clifton Rd East NPK/KEN L6 97 M8
Clifton St ALL/GAR L19 130 E7
ECCL WA10 9 H3
LEIGH WN7 81 M8
WARRS WA4 15 H8
WGN WN1 4 F1
WGNS/IIMK WN3 79 J1
Cliftonville Rd PR/KW L34 101 G7 1
WARR WA1 122 E7
Clincton Cl WDN WA8 133 J5
Clincton Vw WDN WA8 133 J5
Clinning Rd STHP PR8 35 J3
Clinton Pl WD/CROXPK L12 98 B6
Clinton Rd WD/CROXPK L12 98 B6
Clint Rd EHL/KEN L7 113 L4
Clipper Vw PS/BROM CH62 128 D5
Clipsley Brook Vw
RNFD/HAY WA11 90 B7
Clipsley Crs RNFD/HAY WA11 90 D6
Clipsley La RNFD/HAY WA11 90 D7
Clive Av WARRN/WOL WA2 121 L4
Clive Ldg STHP PR8 35 H3 1
Clive Rd CL/PREN CH43 127 L1
STHP PR8 35 H4
Clock Face Rd STHEL WA9 118 E1
WDN WA8 119 G6
Cloister Av LEIGH WN7 81 M4
The Cloisters CSBY/BLUN L23 82 F2 1
ECCL WA10 101 K1 1
Clorain Rd NWD/KWIPK L33 86 C2
Closebrook Rd
WGNW/BIL/O WN5 67 M7
Closeburn Av HES CH60 141 G7 1
Close La WGNE/HIN WN2 81 H2
WGNE/HIN WN2 81 K4
Close St STHEL WA9 102 A6
The Close CHTN/BK PR9 23 J8
CSBY/BLUN L23 82 F2
ECCL WA10 88 C8
GR/UP/WCH CH49 125 M3
HTWN L38 71 G2
PEN/TH CH61 125 M7
RF/TRAN CH42 127 M4
RNFD/HAY WA11 90 B8
STBRV L28 99 L6
WLT/FAZ L9 97 H1
Cloudberry Cl NTHLY L27 116 A7 1
Clough Acre CHLY/EC PR7 32 C3
Clough Av WARRN/WOL WA2 121 K3 1
Clough Gv AIMK WN4 79 H8
Clough Rd SPK/HALE L24 146 F1
The Clough RUNC WA7 150 B4
Cloughwood Crs
WGNNW/ST WN6 54 F6
Clovelly Av STHEL WA9 102 F7 1
WARRW/BUR WA5 120 A6 1
Clovelly Dr SKEL WN8 53 J5
STHP PR8 35 G5
Clovelly Gv RUNC WA7 150 D8
Clovelly Rd ANF/KKDL L4 97 K7
Clover Av FROD/HEL WA6 160 F6
HLWD L26 131 M3
Clover Ct RUNC WA7 150 D8 3
Cloverdale Dr AIMK WN4 91 L3 2
Cloverdale Rd WLTN L25 115 K6 2
Clover Dr BIRK CH41 111 G4
Cloverfield RUNC WA7 150 E6 1
Cloverfield Gdns GTS/LS CH66 155 M6
Clover Hey RNFD/HAY WA11 89 K6
Clover Rd CHLY/EC PR7 32 C8
Clover St WGNNW/ST WN6 68 C3
Club St RNFD/HAY WA11 89 J4
Clucas Gdns ORM L39 51 G7
Clwyd Gv WD/CROXPK L12 98 D5 1
Clwyd St BIRK CH41 11 H5
WAL/NB CH45 95 J6
Clwyd Wy GTS/LS CH66 155 J7
Clyde Rd CLB/OSW/ST L13 114 A3 2
Clydesdale EP CH65 20 A9
Clydesdale Rd HOY CH47 108 D5
WAL/EG CH44 111 M1 5
WARRS WA4 137 M5
Clyde St BTL L20 96 E5
RF/TRAN CH42 128 B3
Clyffes Farm Cl BRSC L40 37 J6
Coach House Ct BRSC L40 52 A2
Coach House Dr
WGNNW/ST WN6 55 K7
Coachmans Dr WD/CROXPK L12 99 G4
Coach Rd ORM L39 75 H4
PR/KW L34 87 K6
Coalbrookdale Rd NSTN CH64 153 H3
Coalgate La RAIN/WH L35 116 F3
Coalpit La CH/BCN CH1 163 G7
Coal Pit La ORM L39 75 L1
WGNE/HIN WN2 81 K4
Coal St CLVPS L1 13 J6
Coalville Rd RNFD/HAY WA11 89 M7
Coastal Dr WAL/NB CH45 94 F5
Coastal Rd STHP PR8 34 C7
Coastgaurd La NSTN CH64 152 D4
Cobb Av LITH L21 83 K7
The Cobbles HLWD L26 131 M3
Cobb's Brow La SKEL WN8 53 J6
Cobb's Clough Rd BRSC L40 53 H8
Cobbs La WARRS WA4 138 A5
Cobden Av BIRK CH41 128 B2
Cobden Ct BIRK CH41 128 B2 4
Cobden Pl RF/TRAN CH42 128 B2 5
Cobden Rd CHTN/BK PR9 25 H7
Cobden St CHLYE PR6 33 G4
NEWLW WA12 104 F1 1
NPK/KEN L6 13 M3
WARRN/WOL WA2 14 F2
WLTN L25 131 H3 1
Cobden Vw WLTN L25 131 H3 2
Cob Hall La FROD/HEL WA6 166 F8
Cobham Av WLT/FAZ L9 84 B7
Cobham Rd MOR/LEA CH46 109 M5
Cob Moor Av
WGNW/BIL/O WN5 77 M4 1
Cob Moor Rd WGNW/BIL/O WN5 77 M4
Coburg Whf VAUX/LVPD L3 112 E7
Cochrane St EV L5 97 H8
Cockburn St TOX L8 129 H1
Cockerell Cl ANF/KKDL L4 97 G6 6
Cockerham Wy NG/CROX L11 85 K8
Cockhedge La WARR WA1 14 F5
Cockhedge Wy WARR WA1 14 E5
Cocklade La SPK/HALE L24 147 M4
Cock Lane Ends WDN WA8 133 K8 2
Cockle Dick's La CHTN/BK PR9 25 G3
Cockshead Rd WLTN L25 115 K8
Cockshead Wy WLTN L25 115 K7 1
Cockspur St VAUX/LVPD L3 12 F5
Cockspur St West
VAUX/LVPD L3 12 E5 1
Coerton Rd WLT/FAZ L9 84 D6
The Cokers BEB CH63 128 A5
Colbern Cl MGHL L31 73 G5
Colbrooke Rd AIG/SPK L17 129 K2
Colburn Cl WGNS/IIMK WN3 79 J3 1
Colburne Cl BRSC L40 39 H8
Colby Cl CHLDW L16 115 G5
Colby Rd WGNS/IIMK WN3 79 K2
Colchester Rd STHP PR8 36 B3
Coldstone Dr AIMK WN4 90 F1
Coldstream Cl
WARRN/WOL WA2 122 A1 1
Coldstream Dr GTS/LS CH66 155 H8 1
Cole Av NEWLW WA12 104 E1
Colebrook Cl
GOL/RIS/CU WA3 123 J1 1
Coleclough Pl GOL/RIS/CU WA3 107 H1
Cole Crs ORM L39 62 E5
Coleman Dr GR/UP/WCH CH49 125 K2
Colemere Ct EP CH65 20 B1
Colemere Dr PEN/TH CH61 126 D7
Coleridge Av ECCL WA10 8 B3
WGNW/BIL/O WN5 67 J7
Coleridge Rd WGNW/BIL/O WN5 77 M4
Coleridge St BTL L20 6 D3
NPK/KEN L6 113 K2
Colerne Wy WGNS/IIMK WN3 78 F3
Colesborne Rd NG/CROX L11 98 C3
Coles Crs CSBY/BLUN L23 71 K7
Coleshill Ri WGNS/IIMK WN3 78 E3
Coleshill Rd NG/CROX L11 98 A2
Cole St CL/PREN CH43 10 F6
Colette Rd AIN/FAZ L10 85 K6 2
Coleus Cl WLT/FAZ L9 97 K1
Colin Cl HUY L36 115 L4 2
Colindale Rd CHLDW L16 115 G6 1
Colin Dr VAUX/LVPD L3 96 E8
Colinmander Gdns ORM L39 62 E2 1
Colin St WGN WN1 5 G1
Colinton St WAV L15 114 A5 2
College Av CSBY/BLUN L23 82 F2
FMBY L37 59 G1
WGN WN1 4 F5
College Cl CL/PREN CH43 110 D7 2
FMBY L37 58 F1
STHP PR8 35 J2
WAL/NB CH45 95 G7 4
WARR WA1 15 J5
WARRN/WOL WA2 122 C3
College Ct WD/CROXPK L12 98 C8
College Dr BEB CH63 128 C6 2
College Flds HUY L36 116 A4
College La CLVPS L1 13 G6
College Pth FMBY L37 46 F8
College Rd CSBY/BLUN L23 82 F2
SKEL WN8 66 D4
College Rd North
CSBY/BLUN L23 70 E8
College St ECCL WA10 9 G4
College St North NPK/KEN L6 13 L4
College St South NPK/KEN L6 13 M4
College Vw BTL L20 7 G7
Collett Cl WGN WN1 5 J4
Collier's Rw RUNC WA7 149 G6
Collier St RUNC WA7 18 E1
WGNE/HIN WN2 69 M7 1
Colliery Green Cl NSTN CH64 153 G8
Colliery Green Ct NSTN CH64 153 G8 2
Colliery Green Dr NSTN CH64 153 G8
Collinge St WGNE/HIN WN2 80 C3
Collingham Gn GTS/LS CH66 155 K8
Collingwood Rd BEB CH63 143 K1 1
CHLY/EC PR7 32 C6
NEWLW WA12 104 D2
Collingwood St
WGNNW/ST WN6 56 A4
Collin Rd CL/PREN CH43 111 G5
Collins Cl BTL L20 83 J8 2
Collins Green La
WARRW/BUR WA5 104 A4
Collin St WARRW/BUR WA5 121 G8
Collisdene Rd
WGNW/BIL/O WN5 66 F7
Collison Av CHLY/EC PR7 32 D5
Colmore Av BEB CH63 143 H4
Colmore Rd NG/CROX L11 98 A3
Colnbrook WGNNW/ST WN6 55 K3 2
Colne Dr STHEL WA9 102 F6
Colne Rd WARRW/BUR WA5 104 B7 2
Colorado Cl WARRW/BUR WA5 120 E6
Colquitt St CLVPS L1 13 J9
Coltart Rd TOX L8 113 K7
Colton Rd WLTN L25 115 H6
Coltsfoot Dr CHLYE PR6 32 F3
Columban Cl NTHDN L30 84 A2
Columbia Rd ANF/KKDL L4 97 J3
CL/PREN CH43 10 C9
PR/KW L34 101 G7
Columbine Cl CHLY/EC PR7 32 C2 2
WDN WA8 133 K1
Columbus Dr PEN/TH CH61 141 G2
Columbus Quay VAUX/LVPD L3 129 G2
Columbus Wy LITH L21 83 K6 2
Column Rd WKBY CH48 124 F4
Colville Ct WARRN/WOL WA2 121 J2
Colville Rd WAL/EG CH44 111 J1
Colville St WAV L15 114 A5
Colwall Cl NWD/KWIPK L33 86 C3 1
Colwall Rd NWD/KWIPK L33 86 C3
Colwell Cl DV/KA/FCH L14 99 J6
Colwell Rd DV/KA/FCH L14 99 J7
Colwyn Cl WARRW/BUR WA5 121 G3
Colwyn Dr WGNE/HIN WN2 81 L3
Colwyn Rd CLB/OSW/ST L13 114 B3
Colwyn St BIRK CH41 10 A2
Colyton Av STHEL WA9 102 F8 1
Colyton Cl CHLYE PR6 33 G5 5
Colyton Rd CHLYE PR6 33 G5
Colyton Rd East CHLYE PR6 33 G5 6
Combermere St TOX L8 113 H7 5
WAV L15 113 M4
Comely Av WAL/EG CH44 111 L1
Comely Bank Rd
WAL/EG CH44 111 M1 6
Comer Gdns MGHL L31 72 E2 1
Comet Rd WGNW/BIL/O WN5 67 L5
Comfrey Gv HLWD L26 132 A3 1
Commercial Rd CHLY/EC PR7 32 E4 2
EV L5 96 E7
PS/BROM CH62 144 A2
Commodore Pl
WGNW/BIL/O WN5 68 A4 1
Common Bank La CHLY/EC PR7 32 A6
Common End CHLY/EC PR7 57 G1
Common Field Rd
GR/UP/WCH CH49 126 D4
Common La CHTN/BK PR9 26 D3
FROD/HEL WA6 165 M4
GOL/RIS/CU WA3 106 F1
LEIGH WN7 93 K1
WARRS WA4 138 A3
Common Rd NEWLW WA12 104 A2
Commonside FROD/HEL WA6 167 J4
Common St NEWLW WA12 104 A2
STHEL WA9 101 M6 2
The Common CHLY/EC PR7 44 A8
SKEL WN8 53 L2
Commutation Rw
VAUX/LVPD L3 13 G5
Company's Cl RUNC WA7 149 H7 2
Compass Cl RUNC WA7 150 F8
Compton Cl RNFD/HAY WA11 90 E6
Compton Pl EP CH65 20 B4
Compton Rd BIRK CH41 110 F4 1
NPK/KEN L6 113 J1
STHP PR8 35 K2
Compton Wy HLWD L26 132 A7
Comus St VAUX/LVPD L3 13 H3
Concert St CLVPS L1 13 H9
Concord Av WGNS/IIMK WN3 79 K2
Concorde Pl
WARRN/WOL WA2 121 M3 4
Concordia Av
GR/UP/WCH CH49 110 C8
Concourse Wy STHEL WA9 103 H3
Condor Cl ALL/GAR L19 130 F7
Condron Rd LITH L21 83 L4
Condron Rd North LITH L21 83 L4
Conery Cl FROD/HEL WA6 166 E1
Coney Crs CSBY/BLUN L23 71 K8 3
Coney Gv RUNC WA7 150 D8 4
Coney La HUY L36 116 B6
RAIN/WH L35 116 B6
Coney Wk
GR/UP/WCH CH49 109 M7 2
Congresbury Rd LEIGH WN7 81 M6
Congress St CHLY/EC PR7 32 E4 3
Conifer Cl GTS/LS CH66 163 J5
NWD/KWIPK L33 74 A8
WLT/FAZ L9 97 K2
Conifer Ct FMBY L37 59 H3
Conifer Gv WARRW/BUR WA5 120 B6
The Conifers MGHL L31 72 E2
Coningsby Dr WAL/NB CH45 111 J1
Coningsby Rd ANF/KKDL L4 97 J6
Coniston Av AIMK WN4 91 K1
BEB CH63 143 L8 1
CHLY/EC PR7 31 M4
CHLYE PR6 44 D4 1
CL/PREN CH43 110 E8
PR/KW L34 101 H7
WAL/NB CH45 95 G6
WARRW/BUR WA5 135 M1
WGN WN1 68 D2
WGNE/HIN WN2 69 K6
WGNW/BIL/O WN5 67 H5
Coniston Cl GTS/LS CH66 155 J4
NWD/KWIPK L33 85 M1 1
RUNC WA7 149 M7
WLT/FAZ L9 84 D6 5
Coniston Dr FROD/HEL WA6 160 F5
WGNE/HIN WN2 80 D5
Coniston Gv RNFD/HAY WA11 89 J6
Coniston Park Dr
WGNNW/ST WN6 56 C6
Coniston Rd CHLY/EC PR7 32 D7
FMBY L37 58 F3
HOR/BR BL6 57 M2
MGHL L31 73 G3
NSTN CH64 153 G7
PEN/TH CH61 125 M7
WGNE/HIN WN2 81 G1 5
Coniston St EV L5 97 J7
Coniston Wy LEY/BBR PR5 29 K3 1
RNFD/HAY WA11 76 B3 1
Conleach Rd SPK/HALE L24 147 G2
Connaught Av WARR WA1 15 M1
Connaught Cl BIRK CH41 10 A1
Connaught Dr NEWLW WA12 104 E3
Connaught Rd EHL/KEN L7 113 J3
Connaught Wy BIRK CH41 10 A1
Connolly Av BTL L20 7 M2
Conrad Cl WGNS/IIMK WN3 4 B9
Conroy Wy NEWLW WA12 104 E4
Consett Rd RAIN/WH L35 101 M7
Constables Cl RUNC WA7 150 C4 1
Constance St ECCL WA10 8 A7
VAUX/LVPD L3 13 L5
Constance Wy WDN WA8 16 C9
Constantia St WGNE/HIN WN2 80 B1 2
Constantine Av HES CH60 141 J4 1
Convent Cl ALL/GAR L19 130 C6 5
ORM L39 62 F3
RF/TRAN CH42 11 H9
Conville Bvd BEB CH63 128 A5
Conway Av WARRW/BUR WA5 121 H3
Conway Cl BEB CH63 127 M8
CHLY/EC PR7 32 A4
NWD/KWIPK L33 73 M8 3
WARRW/BUR WA5 120 B7 2
Conway Crs WGNW/BIL/O WN5 78 A7
Conway Dr BIRK CH41 11 G5
NEWLW WA12 105 G2
WGNE/HIN WN2 69 M1
WGNW/BIL/O WN5 78 B8
Conway Rd AIMK WN4 80 A8
CHLY/EC PR7 30 E6 2
WGNE/HIN WN2 81 H1
Conway St BIRK CH41 10 F4
EV L5 97 G8
WAL/EG CH44 111 K1 3
WGNW/BIL/O WN5 67 L8
Conwy Dr NPK/KEN L6 97 K8
Conyers Av STHP PR8 35 H2
Coogee Av
WARRW/BUR WA5 120 A6 2
Cook Av RNFD/HAY WA11 91 G6
Cooke St AIMK WN4 79 H7
Cook Rd MOR/LEA CH46 110 D1
Cookson Rd LITH L21 83 J7
Cookson St CLVPS L1 113 G6
Cook St CLVP L2 12 F7
EP CH65 20 D3
RAIN/WH L35 101 H8
WGNE/HIN WN2 80 C4
Coombe Dr RUNC WA7 18 F8
Coombe Rd PEN/TH CH61 126 A6
Cooperage Cl TOX L8 129 G1
Co-operative St LEIGH WN7 81 M8 4
Cooper Av NEWLW WA12 104 B2
WARRN/WOL WA2 121 K3
Cooper Av North CALD/MH L18 130 C4
Cooper Av South CALD/MH L18 130 C4
Cooper Cl ALL/GAR L19 130 C5
Cooper La RNFD/HAY WA11 90 E7
Coopers Gln WGNE/HIN WN2 69 J5 1
Cooper's La CHLY/EC PR7 41 K5
NWD/KWIPK L33 86 F7
Cooper St ECCL WA10 8 F3
RUNC WA7 19 G2
WDN WA8 16 E1
Coop St WGN WN1 5 H2
Copeland Cl PEN/TH CH61 141 G1
Copeland Dr WGNNW/ST WN6 56 B3
Copeland Gv RUNC WA7 150 A8
Copeland Rd WARRS WA4 137 K3
Copesthorne Cl WGNE/HIN WN2 57 L7
Coplow Dl WGNE/HIN WN2 81 G2 2
Copperas Cl WGNNW/ST WN6 55 J6
Copperas Hl VAUX/LVPD L3 13 K6
Copperas La HOR/BR BL6 57 K4
WGNE/HIN WN2 57 J7
Copperas St ECCL WA10 8 F6
Copperbeech Dr
WGNNW/ST WN6 56 D6
Copperfield WGN WN1 68 E3
Copperfield Cl
GOL/RIS/CU WA3 106 E8 1
TOX L8 113 H8 2
Copperwood Dr RAIN/WH L35 117 G3
Copperwood Wy CHLY/EC PR7 32 B6
Coppice Cl CHLYE PR6 33 G4
CL/PREN CH43 110 D7 3
Coppice Crs HUY L36 116 B1 2
Coppice Dr WGNS/IIMK WN3 79 H2
WGNW/BIL/O WN5 77 M3
Coppice Gra MOR/LEA CH46 109 L6
Coppice Gn CHNE CH2 165 L1
WARRW/BUR WA5 120 D3
Coppice Gv
GR/UP/WCH CH49 125 L3 3
Coppice La CHLYE PR6 33 L1
RAIN/WH L35 116 D6
Coppice Leys FMBY L37 59 G2
The Coppice NPK/KEN L6 97 L7
PR/KW L34 99 M2
WAL/NB CH45 95 J6
Coppins Cl FROD/HEL WA6 166 D2
The Coppins
WARRN/WOL WA2 121 L3 2
Copple House La AIN/FAZ L10 85 J6 1
Coppull Hall La CHLY/EC PR7 43 J4
Coppull La WGN WN1 68 F3
Coppull Moor La CHLY/EC PR7 42 F7
Coppull Rd CHLY/EC PR7 43 H1
MGHL L31 72 E1
Copse Gv PEN/TH CH61 126 A6 1
The Copse CALD/MH L18 114 F8
CHLY/EC PR7 43 K1
NEWLW WA12 104 C1
RUNC WA7 150 C7
WGNW/BIL/O WN5 67 J7
Copthorne Rd KKBY L32 85 K3
Copy La NTHTN L30 84 C1
Coral Av HUY L36 115 M2
STHEL WA9 102 B6
Coral Dr BTL L20 7 H4
Coralin Wy AIMK WN4 79 H6
Coral Rdg CL/PREN CH43 110 F7
Coral St CLB/OSW/ST L13 114 C4
WGNNW/ST WN6 68 C2
Corbet Av WARRN/WOL WA2 121 K5
Corbet St WARRN/WOL WA2 121 K5 1
Corbridge Rd CHLDW L16 114 E7
Corbyn St WAL/EG CH44 112 A4
Corfe Cl WGNE/HIN WN2 57 M8
Corfu St BIRK CH41 10 F6 2
Corinthian Av CLB/OSW/ST L13 114 C1
Corinthian St LITH L21 83 H6 4
RF/TRAN CH42 128 B3 5
Corinto St TOX L8 113 H6
Cormorant Dr RUNC WA7 18 D4
Corncroft Rd PR/KW L34 99 M2 1
Corndale Rd CALD/MH L18 130 C1
Cornelian Gv AIMK WN4 79 H8 1
Cornelius Dr PEN/TH CH61 126 B8
Cornel Wy HUY L36 116 B5
Corner Brook STBRV L28 99 H6
Cornerhouse La WDN WA8 133 M2
Corner La WGNE/HIN WN2 81 M3
Cornett Rd WLT/FAZ L9 84 D6
Corney St EHL/KEN L7 113 L6
Cornfield Cl GTS/LS CH66 163 H4
Cornflower Cl CHLYE PR6 32 F3 3
Cornflower Wy MOR/LEA CH46 110 C3
Cornforth Wy WDN WA8 134 B2
Cornhill CLVPS L1 112 F5
Cornice Rd CLB/OSW/ST L13 114 C1
Corniche Rd PS/BROM CH62 128 D7
Corn St LEIGH WN7 81 M8 5
TOX L8 113 G8
Cornubia Rd WDN WA8 17 H5
Cornwall Av RUNC WA7 19 G4
Cornwall Cl PS/BROM CH62 128 D5
Cornwall Crs WGN WN1 56 D4 2
Cornwall Dr CL/PREN CH43 127 J4
Cornwall Rd WGNS/IIMK WN3 68 C8 3
Cornwallis St CLVPS L1 112 F5
Cornwall Pl
WGNW/BIL/O WN5 67 L7 1
Cornwall Rd WDN WA8 134 D2
Cornwall St STHEL WA9 102 F3
WARR WA1 15 L2
Cornwall Wy STHP PR8 47 K3
Cornwood Cl HUY L36 115 K6
Corona Av MGHL L31 61 L8 2
Corona Rd CLB/OSW/ST L13 114 C1
CSBY/WL L22 82 F4 4
PS/BROM CH62 128 E7
Coronation Av DV/KA/FCH L14 115 G2
FMBY L37 59 J3
WAL/NB CH45 95 K6
WARRS WA4 138 E3 1
Coronation Dr CSBY/BLUN L23 82 F2
DV/KA/FCH L14 115 G2
FROD/HEL WA6 160 F4 1
NEWLW WA12 105 G4 1
PS/BROM CH62 143 M2 1
RAIN/WH L35 116 E2
RNFD/HAY WA11 91 J6
WARRW/BUR WA5 136 B1
WDN WA8 133 K5
Coronation Rd CSBY/BLUN L23 82 F2
ECCL WA10 88 E7
EP CH65 20 C7
HOY CH47 108 B7
MGHL L31 72 F2
RUNC WA7 19 J5
RUNC WA7 151 H7
WGNNW/ST WN6 67 M2
Coronation St AIMK WN4 78 F7
WGNS/IIMK WN3 4 D7
Coronation Wk STHP PR8 2 E4
WGNW/BIL/O WN5 89 M1
Coroner's La WDN WA8 118 C8
Coronet Rd NG/CROX L11 98 E2
Coronet Wy WDN WA8 133 K5
Corporation Rd BIRK CH41 10 C1
Corporation St CHLYE PR6 32 F4
ECCL WA10 9 G4
WGNS/IIMK WN3 4 D7
Corridor Rd EP CH65 157 K8
Corrie Dr BEB CH63 143 H1
Corsewall St EHL/KEN L7 113 M5 2
Corsey Av NTHTN L30 83 L2 1
Corsey Rd WGNE/HIN WN2 81 G1
Corsham Rd HLWD L26 132 A7
Corsican Gdns RAIN/WH L35 101 L6 1
Corsock Dr WGN WN1 5 K1
Corston Gv HOR/BR BL6 57 M4
Cortsway GR/UP/WCH CH49 110 A8
Cortsway West
GR/UP/WCH CH49 109 M8
Corwen Cl CL/PREN CH43 110 D7 4
MOR/LEA CH46 110 B6
WARRW/BUR WA5 121 G4
Corwen Crs DV/KA/FCH L14 115 H3
Corwen Dr NTHTN L30 84 C1
Corwen Rd ANF/KKDL L4 97 L5
HOY CH47 108 E6
Cosgrove Cl NPK/KEN L6 97 M6 2
Cossack Av
WARRN/WOL WA2 121 L4 1
Costain St BTL L20 96 E5
Costessey Wy WGNS/IIMK WN3 78 E2
Cote Lea Ct RUNC WA7 150 B7 1
Cotham St ECCL WA10 9 G5
Cotsford Cl HUY L36 115 L1 2
Cotsford Pl HUY L36 115 L1 3
Cotsford Rd HUY L36 115 L1
Cotsford Wy HUY L36 115 L1 4
Cotswold Av CHLY/EC PR7 31 M4
GOL/RIS/CU WA3 92 F7
WGNW/BIL/O WN5 67 K8
Cotswold Cl CHLY/EC PR7 30 E7
Cotswold Dr HOR/BR BL6 45 L8
Cotswold Gv STHEL WA9 103 J2
Cotswold Rd CHLY/EC PR7 32 E7
RF/TRAN CH42 127 L4
WARRN/WOL WA2 121 K2
Cotswolds Crs HLWD L26 132 A6 1
Cotswold St EHL/KEN L7 113 K3
Cottage Cl BEB CH63 143 L8 2
KKBY L32 86 A6
NSTN CH64 153 G6
ORM L39 62 F1 1
Cottage Dr East HES CH60 152 B1
Cottage Dr West HES CH60 141 H8
Cottage Flds CHLY/EC PR7 32 D8
Cottage La HES CH60 141 H8
ORM L39 50 F7
Cottage Ms ORM L39 50 F8
Cottage Pl STHEL WA9 118 E1 5
Cottage St BIRK CH41 11 G3
Cottam Dr WARRN/WOL WA2 122 C2
Cottam St CHLY/EC PR7 32 E7 2
Cottenham St EHL/KEN L7 113 K2 3
Cotterdale Cl STHEL WA9 102 E7 2
WARRW/BUR WA5 120 B6
Cotterill RUNC WA7 149 M5
Cotterill Dr WARR WA1 122 E6
Cottesbrook Cl NG/CROX L11 98 C2
Cottesbrook Pl NG/CROX L11 98 C2 1
Cottesbrook Rd NG/CROX L11 98 C2
Cottesmore Dr HES CH60 141 M5 3
Cottesmore Wy
GOL/RIS/CU WA3 92 D4
Cotton Dr ORM L39 50 F7

Cotton La RUNC WA7 149 M5
Cotton St LEIGH WN7 81 M8 6
VAUX/LVPD L3 12 C1
Cottonwood AIG/SPK L17 129 H2
Cottrell Cl ALL/GAR L19 145 L1 3
Coudray Rd CHTN/BK PR9 25 G4
Coulport Cl DV/KA/FCH L14 115 J1
Coulsdon Pl TOX L8 129 J1
Coulthard Rd RF/TRAN CH42 128 C5 1
Coulton Rd WDN WA8 135 G2
Coultshead Av
WGNW/BIL/O WN5 78 A7 1
Council Av AIMK WN4 91 K2 4
Council St RAIN/WH L35 101 J8
Countess Pk NG/CROX L11 98 E3
Countess Wy CHLY/EC PR7 31 M3
Countisbury Dr CHLDW L16 115 G7
County Police St WGNE/HIN WN2 5 M5
County Rd ANF/KKDL L4 97 H5
KKBY L32 86 A1
ORM L39 50 F8
Coupland Rd WGNE/HIN WN2 81 K1
Courage Low La
WGNNW/ST WN6 54 F1
Courier Pl WGNW/BIL/O WN5 68 A4
Course La BRSC L40 53 G4
SKEL WN8 53 J4 1
Court Av HLWD L26 132 C4
Courtenay Av CSBY/WL L22 82 E3
Courtenay Rd CSBY/WL L22 82 E3
HOY CH47 108 C6
WLTN L25 131 H1 1
Courtfield ORM L39 50 F6
Courtfields Cl WD/CROXPK L12 98 D8
Courtgreen ORM L39 50 F6 1
Court Hey Av DV/KA/FCH L14 115 J3
Court Hey Dr CHLDW L16 115 H4
Court Hey Rd CHLDW L16 115 H4
Courthope Rd ANF/KKDL L4 97 K3
Courtland Rd CALD/MH L18 114 D8
Courtney Av WAL/EG CH44 111 J2 4
Courtney Rd RF/TRAN CH42 128 C5 2
Court Rd CHTN/BK PR9 3 K1
The Court NSTN CH64 153 H7
Cousin's La BRSC L40 39 J2
Covent Gdn CLVP L2 12 E7
Coventry Av GTS/LS CH66 163 G5
Coventry Rd WAV L15 114 C7 3
Coventry St BIRK CH41 11 H6
CHLY/EC PR7 32 E7 3
Coverdale Av RAIN/WH L35 117 M3
Coverdale Cl WARRW/BUR WA5 120 B6
Covertside WKBY CH48 124 F3
The Coverts WGNNW/ST WN6 68 B3 2
Cowan Dr NPK/KEN L6 113 J1
Cowanway WDN WA8 118 B8
Cowburn St LEIGH WN7 81 M8 7
Cowdell St WARRN/WOL WA2 14 F1
Cowdrey Av CL/PREN CH43 110 E4 3
Cow Hey La RUNC WA7 149 J8
Cowley Cl GR/UP/WCH CH49 109 M8 3
Cowley Hill La ECCL WA10 8 D1
Cowley Rd ANF/KKDL L4 97 H4
Cowley St ECCL WA10 9 G2
Cowling Brow CHLYE PR6 33 G6
Cowling St WGNS/IIMK WN3 4 D7
Cowper Rd CLB/OSW/ST L13 114 D3
Cowper St BTL L20 6 D1
LEIGH WN7 81 M8
Cowper Wy HUY L36 116 C5
Cowslip Wy CHLYE PR6 32 F3 4
Coxfield WGNNW/ST WN6 54 F6
Coyford Dr CHTN/BK PR9 22 C8
Coylton Av RAIN/WH L35 117 M3
Crab La WARRN/WOL WA2 122 C2
Crab St ECCL WA10 8 F3
Crabtree Cl BRSC L40 51 M1 2
NTHLY L27 115 M8
Crabtree Fold RUNC WA7 150 E5
Crabtree La BRSC L40 38 E8
Crabtree Rd WGNW/BIL/O WN5 67 M6
Cradley WDN WA8 133 L3
Crag Gv RNFD/HAY WA11 89 K4
Craigburn Rd CLB/OSW/ST L13 98 A7
Craig Gdns GTS/LS CH66 156 A6
Craighurst Rd WLTN L25 115 J6
Craigleigh Gv PS/BROM CH62 155 H1
Craigmore Rd CALD/MH L18 130 C4
Craigside Av WD/CROXPK L12 98 C6 2
Craigs Rd CLB/OSW/ST L13 98 A7
Craigwood Wy HUY L36 115 K2 1
Craine Cl ANF/KKDL L4 97 K5
Cramond Av CALD/MH L18 114 C8 4
Cramond Cl WGNS/IIMK WN3 78 F1
Cranage Cl RUNC WA7 149 M6 1
Cranberry Av WGNNW/ST WN6 68 B2
Cranberry Cl ECCL WA10 8 E2
Cranborne Av HOY CH47 109 G4
WARRS WA4 137 K4
Cranborne Cl WGNNW/ST WN6 55 M4
Cranborne Rd WAV L15 113 M6
Cranbourne Av BIRK CH41 111 H6
MOR/LEA CH46 109 M6
Cranbourne Dr CHLYE PR6 33 G6
Cranbourne St CHLYE PR6 32 F6
Cranbrook Av AIMK WN4 91 J1
Cranbrook Wy WGN WN1 68 D1
Cranby St WGNE/HIN WN2 69 M8 10
Crane Av STHEL WA9 102 F7
Cranehurst Rd ANF/KKDL L4 97 K3
Cranes La BRSC L40 52 B6
Crane St CHLY/EC PR7 42 F7
Cranfield Rd CSBY/BLUN L23 71 J8
WGNS/IIMK WN3 79 J2
Cranford Cl PS/BROM CH62 155 H1
Cranford Rd ALL/GAR L19 130 D5
Cranford St WAL/EG CH44 111 L3 1
Cranham Av GOL/RIS/CU WA3 93 G6
Crank Hl RNFD/HAY WA11 89 G1
Crank Rd RNFD/HAY WA11 77 H6
RNFD/HAY WA11 88 E6
Crankwood Rd WGNE/HIN WN2 80 D7
Cranleigh WGNNW/ST WN6 56 B5
Cranleigh Cl HOR/BR BL6 57 M4 1
WARRS WA4 137 K6
Cranleigh Pl WLTN L25 115 J7 1
Cranleigh Rd WLTN L25 115 J8
Cranmer St EV L5 96 F7
Cranmore Av CSBY/BLUN L23 83 G3
Cranshaw Av STHEL WA9 118 F2
Cranshaw La WDN WA8 118 D8
Cranston Cl ECCL WA10 88 D8
Cranston Rd NWD/KWIPK L33 86 E3
Cranswick Gn GTS/LS CH66 155 L8
Crantock Cl HLWD L26 132 B5
NG/CROX L11 98 E1 2
Crantock Gv ECCL WA10 88 E7
Cranwell Av GOL/RIS/CU WA3 107 H1
Cranwell Cl AIN/FAZ L10 84 E3
Cranwell Rd GR/UP/WCH CH49 125 K2
WLTN L25 115 J6
Craven Av GOL/RIS/CU WA3 93 G6
Craven Cl BIRK CH41 11 G5
Craven Ct WARRN/WOL WA2 121 H1
Craven Lea WD/CROXPK L12 99 G2
Craven Rd RAIN/WH L35 117 L2
WD/CROXPK L12 98 E7 1
Craven St BIRK CH41 10 F6
VAUX/LVPD L3 13 K5
Cravenwood Rd HLWD L26 132 B6
Crawford Av CALD/MH L18 114 B8
CHLY/EC PR7 32 D6
CHLY/EC PR7 44 A8
MGHL L31 72 D2
WDN WA8 133 K4
WGNE/HIN WN2 57 K8
Crawford Cl STHEL WA9 118 F1
WD/CROXPK L12 98 F6
Crawford Dr WAV L15 114 C4
Crawford Pk CALD/MH L18 130 B2 1
Crawford Pl RUNC WA7 149 K7
Crawford Rd SKEL WN8 76 F3
Crawford St STHEL WA9 119 G1
WGN WN1 4 E4
WGNE/HIN WN2 69 L1
Crawford Wy CLB/OSW/ST L13 114 A3
Crawley Av
WARRN/WOL WA2 121 J2 4
Crawley Cl WLTN L25 131 M5
Crediton Av CHTN/BK PR9 22 D8
Crediton Cl NG/CROX L11 85 L8
Crediton Dr WGNE/HIN WN2 80 C4
The Creek WAL/NB CH45 95 G5 1
Cremorne Hey STBRV L28 99 K6
Crescent Av AIMK WN4 91 J1
FMBY L37 59 G4
Crescent Dr FROD/HEL WA6 166 D2
Crescent Gn ORM L39 62 D4
Crescent Rd CSBY/BLUN L23 70 D8
EP CH65 20 E3
LITH L21 83 J7
STHP PR8 35 H2
WAL/EG CH44 111 L1
WLT/FAZ L9 97 K1
The Crescent BEB CH63 128 A8
CHLY/EC PR7 32 E3
CHTN/BK PR9 25 L2
CSBY/BLUN L23 71 J7 2
CSBY/WL L22 83 G4
EP CH65 156 B8
GR/UP/WCH CH49 125 M2
HUY L36 116 C3
MGHL L31 72 E6
PEN/TH CH61 126 B7
RAIN/WH L35 117 H1
WGNW/BIL/O WN5 67 M7
WKBY CH48 124 C3 2
Cressbrook Rd WARRS WA4 137 L5
Cressell Pk WGNNW/ST WN6 55 J3
Cressingham Rd WAL/NB CH45 95 K5
Cressington Av RF/TRAN CH42 127 M4
Cressington Prom ALL/GAR L19 130 B7
Cresswell Cl NTHTN L30 84 B4
WARRW/BUR WA5 120 F3 1
Cresswell St NPK/KEN L6 13 M2
NPK/KEN L6 113 J1 3
Cresta Dr RUNC WA7 149 H7 3
Cresttor Rd WLTN L25 131 H2
Crestwood Av WGNS/IIMK WN3 79 G2
Creswell St ECCL WA10 8 C5
Cretan Rd WAV L15 113 M6
Crewe Gn GR/UP/WCH CH49 126 C3 2
Criccieth Av WGNE/HIN WN2 57 M8
Criccieth Ct EP CH65 163 M3 3
Cricketers Gn CHLY/EC PR7 30 D6
Cricket Pth FMBY L37 47 H8
STHP PR8 35 H2
Cricket St WGNNW/ST WN6 4 C4
Cricklade Cl BTL L20 6 E3 2
Criftin Cl GTS/LS CH66 162 E3
Cringles Dr RAIN/WH L35 116 C6
Cripple Ga WGNNW/ST WN6 55 H3
Crispin Rd NTHLY L27 115 M8
Crispin St ECCL WA10 8 D6
Critchley Rd SPK/HALE L24 147 J3
Critchley Wy NWD/KWIPK L33 74 B8
Croal Av WGNE/HIN WN2 80 C3 4
Croasdale Dr RUNC WA7 150 A8
SKEL WN8 53 L2
Crockett's Wk ECCL WA10 88 D8
Crockleford Av STHP PR8 36 A2
Crocus Av BIRK CH41 111 H5
Crocus St EV L5 96 F6 2
Croesmere Dr GTS/LS CH66 162 F3
Croft Av BRSC L40 52 B2
GOL/RIS/CU WA3 92 B3 1
PS/BROM CH62 143 L4
WGNW/BIL/O WN5 66 F8 1
Croft Av East PS/BROM CH62 143 M3
Croft Cl CL/PREN CH43 127 G1
Croft Dr GR/UP/WCH CH49 110 A6
MOR/LEA CH46 110 B6
WKBY CH48 124 E7
Croft Dr East WKBY CH48 124 F7
Croft Dr West WKBY CH48 124 E6
Croft Edge CL/PREN CH43 127 K2
Croft End STHEL WA9 103 H4
Croften Dr NSTN CH64 153 G8
Crofters Cl GTS/LS CH66 163 G4 1
Crofters Gn CHLY/EC PR7 31 L2
Crofters Heath GTS/LS CH66 163 G4
The Crofters GR/UP/WCH CH49 125 M1
Croft Fld MGHL L31 73 G4
Croft Gdns WARRS WA4 138 C6
Croft Heath Gdns
GOL/RIS/CU WA3 106 C5 1
Croft Hey BRSC L40 39 K1
Croft Heys ORM L39 62 D4
Croftlands WGNW/BIL/O WN5 77 M1
Croft La PS/BROM CH62 143 M4
WLT/FAZ L9 84 F6
Crofton Cl WARRS WA4 138 E8
Crofton Crs CLB/OSW/ST L13 114 D2
Crofton Gdns
GOL/RIS/CU WA3 107 G2 1
Crofton Rd CLB/OSW/ST L13 114 D2
RF/TRAN CH42 128 A2
RUNC WA7 18 C6
Croft Rd CHLYE PR6 33 G6
Croftside WARR WA1 123 H6
Croftson Av ORM L39 51 H6 1
Croft St GOL/RIS/CU WA3 92 C5 2
WDN WA8 16 D7
Croftsway HES CH60 140 F5
The Croft CHLY/EC PR7 30 E6
CHLY/EC PR7 31 K2
GR/UP/WCH CH49 125 M3
MGHL L31 61 K8 1
RUNC WA7 150 A4
WD/CROXPK L12 98 D6
WGNW/BIL/O WN5 77 M1
Croftwood Sq
WGNW/BIL/O WN5 67 L3
Cromarty Rd CLB/OSW/ST L13 114 B3
WAL/EG CH44 111 H1 4
Cromdale Gv STHEL WA9 103 G3
Cromdale Wy
WARRW/BUR WA5 120 A7
Cromedale Crs WGNNW/ST WN6 56 C6
Cromer Dr WAL/NB CH45 95 J8
Cromer Rd AIG/SPK L17 130 A4
HOY CH47 108 C6 1
STHP PR8 35 G3
WGNS/IIMK WN3 79 G2
Cromer Wy HLWD L26 132 B7
Cromfield ORM L39 62 E3
Cromford Dr WGNW/BIL/O WN5 67 K8
Cromford Rd HUY L36 100 A8 1
Crompton Dr WD/CROXPK L12 99 G2
Cromptons La CALD/MH L18 114 F8
Crompton St EV L5 96 F8
WGN WN1 4 F3
WGNE/HIN WN2 80 B2 1
Cromwell Av WARRW/BUR WA5 120 E5
Cromwell Av South
WARRW/BUR WA5 136 E1
Cromwell Cl ORM L39 62 E3
Cromwell Rd ANF/KKDL L4 97 H3 3
EP CH65 20 D4
Cromwell St WDN WA8 16 C8
Crondall Gv WAV L15 114 D6
Cronton Av MOR/LEA CH46 110 A2
Cronton La RAIN/WH L35 117 K4
WDN WA8 117 K5
Cronton Park Cl WDN WA8 117 L7 1
Cronton Rd RAIN/WH L35 116 D6
WAV L15 114 C8 5
Cronulla Dr WARRW/BUR WA5 119 M6
Crookall St AIMK WN4 91 L1 1
Crooke Rd WGNNW/ST WN6 67 L2
Crookhurst Av
WGNW/BIL/O WN5 77 M7
Crook St CHLY/EC PR7 32 D8
CHLY/EC PR7 44 B6 2
WGN WN1 4 D3
WGNE/HIN WN2 80 F1 9
Croome Dr WKBY CH48 124 E3
Croppers Hl ECCL WA10 8 D6
Cropper's La ORM L39 63 J4
Croppers Rd WARRN/WOL WA2 122 B2
Cropper St CLVPS L1 13 J8
Cropton Rd FMBY L37 59 H2
Cropton Wy WGNE/HIN WN2 81 H2
Crosby Av WARRW/BUR WA5 121 J5
Crosby Cl GR/UP/WCH CH49 110 B7
Crosby Gn WD/CROXPK L12 98 C6
Crosby Gv ECCL WA10 101 M4 3
NSTN CH64 154 D4
Crosby Rd STHP PR8 35 H2
Crosby Rd North CSBY/WL L22 83 G4
Crosby Rd South CSBY/WL L22 83 G5
LITH L21 83 H6
Crosender Rd CSBY/BLUN L23 82 E2
Crosfield Cl EHL/KEN L7 113 L4 5
Crosfield Rd EHL/KEN L7 113 L4
RAIN/WH L35 117 H1
WAL/EG CH44 111 L2 1
Crosfield St WARR WA1 14 C5
Crosgrove Rd ANF/KKDL L4 97 L4
Crosland Rd KKBY L32 86 C4
Crossacre Rd WLTN L25 115 K6
Cross Barn La HTWN L38 71 G3
Cross Brow Preston Rd
CHLY/EC PR7 31 L5
Crossdale Rd CSBY/BLUN L23 82 E2 1
PS/BROM CH62 143 M7
WGNE/HIN WN2 81 J1
Crossdale Wy RNFD/HAY WA11 89 K4
Crosse Hall La CHLYE PR6 33 G6
Crosse Hall St CHLYE PR6 33 H6
Crossens Wy CHTN/BK PR9 22 E7
Cross Farm Rd STHEL WA9 9 L9
Crossfield Av GOL/RIS/CU WA3 107 H3
Crossfield Rd SKEL WN8 65 L5
Crossfield St STHEL WA9 9 J5
Crossford Cl WGNS/IIMK WN3 78 F1
Crossgates WDN WA8 135 H2
Cross Green Cl FMBY L37 59 J3
Crosshall Brow BRSC L40 63 L1
Crosshall St CLVPS L1 13 G6
Cross Hey LITH L21 83 K3
Cross Hey Av CL/PREN CH43 110 F8
Cross Hillocks La RAIN/WH L35 133 G2
The Crossings NEWLW WA12 104 E2 1
Cross La BEB CH63 143 H1
FROD/HEL WA6 159 K5
GOL/RIS/CU WA3 106 F6
NEWLW WA12 104 D2
NSTN CH64 153 G8
ORM L39 49 K4
RAIN/WH L35 116 F1
WAL/NB CH45 94 F8
WARRS WA4 138 C3
WGNW/BIL/O WN5 77 M2
Cross La South
GOL/RIS/CU WA3 106 F7
Crossley Av GTS/LS CH66 156 A7
Crossley Dr HES CH60 140 F5
WAV L15 114 C5
Crossley Rd ECCL WA10 101 M5
Crossley St WARR WA1 15 G4
Cross Meanygate
KIRK/FR/WA PR4 27 L8
Cross Pit La RNFD/HAY WA11 76 B7
Cross St BIRK CH41 11 L5
CHLY/EC PR7 32 E4 4
CSBY/WL L22 82 F5
ECCL WA10 9 G5
GOL/RIS/CU WA3 92 C6
NSTN CH64 153 G5
PR/KW L34 100 F6
PS/BROM CH62 128 D8 1
RUNC WA7 19 G2 2
STHP PR8 3 G6
WARRN/WOL WA2 14 F1
WDN WA8 16 F2
WGNE/HIN WN2 69 M8
WGNNW/ST WN6 56 A4
WGNS/IIMK WN3 4 E6
WGNW/BIL/O WN5 67 K7 2
The Cross HTWN L38 70 F2
Crossvale Rd HUY L36 116 A4
Crossway CL/PREN CH43 111 G5 1
WDN WA8 133 M5
Crossway Cl AIMK WN4 80 A8
Crossways PS/BROM CH62 143 M2
The Crossway BEB CH63 153 K1
Crosswood Crs HUY L36 115 L2
Crosthwaite Av
PS/BROM CH62 155 H1
Croston Av CHLYE PR6 44 C5
RAIN/WH L35 101 K8
Croston Cl WDN WA8 133 L1
Croston Dr BRSC L40 28 D7
Croston La CHLY/EC PR7 42 D4
Croston Rd BRSC L40 28 D7
Croston's Brow CHTN/BK PR9 25 H2
Croston St WGNE/HIN WN2 69 L7 2
Crouch St EV L5 97 J7 3
STHEL WA9 102 F5 1
Croughton Rd CHNE CH2 164 C6
GTS/LS CH66 156 B5
Crowe Av WARRN/WOL WA2 121 K2
Crowhurst Dr WGN WN1 68 D2
Crowland Cl CHTN/BK PR9 25 J7
Crowland St CHTN/BK PR9 25 J7
Crowland Wy FMBY L37 59 K3 2
Crow La SKEL WN8 66 B2
Crow La East NEWLW WA12 104 E1
Crow La West NEWLW WA12 104 C1
Crowmarsh Cl
GR/UP/WCH CH49 126 B1 4
Crown Acres Rd WLTN L25 131 L4
Crown Av WDN WA8 133 K5
Crown Cl FMBY L37 59 J3
Crown Fields Cl NEWLW WA12 91 K8
Crown Gdns NEWLW WA12 104 D1
Crown Ga RUNC WA7 150 B6
Crown Park Dr NEWLW WA12 104 D1
Crown Rd WD/CROXPK L12 98 E6
Crown St CHLY/EC PR7 32 E5
EHL/KEN L7 13 M6
NEWLW WA12 104 C2
STHEL WA9 101 M6 3
TOX L8 113 J6 2
WARR WA1 14 E5
WGNE/HIN WN2 69 L7
WGNS/IIMK WN3 4 D7
Crownway HUY L36 115 M1
Crow Orchard Rd
WGNNW/ST WN6 55 H3
Crow St TOX L8 112 F7
Crowther St ECCL WA10 8 C6
Crow Wood La WDN WA8 134 F3
Crow Wood Pl WDN WA8 134 F2 1
Crow Wood Rd GOL/RIS/CU WA3 92 F4
Croxdale Rd DV/KA/FCH L14 99 J6
Croxdale Rd West
DV/KA/FCH L14 99 H6
Croxteth Av LITH L21 83 J6
WAL/EG CH44 111 K1
Croxteth Cl MGHL L31 73 G2
Croxteth Dr AIG/SPK L17 113 L8
RNFD/HAY WA11 76 B6
Croxteth Gv TOX L8 113 K7
Croxteth Hall La NG/CROX L11 98 E2
WD/CROXPK L12 98 E3
Croxteth La STBRV L28 99 K4
Croxteth Rd BTL L20 83 L8 1
TOX L8 113 K8
Croxteth Vw KKBY L32 86 B7
Croyde Cl CHTN/BK PR9 22 D8 1
Croyde Pl STHEL WA9 118 E1
Croyde Rd SPK/HALE L24 147 J2
Croydon Av CALD/MH L18 114 B8
Croylands St ANF/KKDL L4 97 G5
Crucian Wy WD/CROXPK L12 98 F2
Crummock Dr
WGNS/IIMK WN3 79 H2 1
Crump St CLVPS L1 113 G6 2
Crutchley Av BIRK CH41 10 C2
Cryers La CHNE CH2 165 J3
Cubbin Crs EV L5 96 F7
Cubert Rd NG/CROX L11 98 E1
Cuckoo Cl WLTN L25 131 J1
Cuckoo La NSTN CH64 153 K6
WLTN L25 115 J8
Cuerden St CHLYE PR6 33 G6 4
Cuerdley Gn WDN WA8 135 J3
Cuerdley Rd WARRW/BUR WA5 135 L2
Cuerdon Dr WARRS WA4 138 F4
Culbeck La CHLY/EC PR7 31 H2
Culbin Cl GOL/RIS/CU WA3 107 J7 2
Culcheth Av WGNE/HIN WN2 80 D4
Culcheth Hall Dr
GOL/RIS/CU WA3 107 H1
Culcross Av WGNS/IIMK WN3 78 E1
Culford Cl RUNC WA7 150 F4 3
Cullen Av BTL L20 83 M8
Cullen Cl BEB CH63 154 E1
WGNE/HIN WN2 69 J5
Cullen Rd RUNC WA7 18 B9
RUNC WA7 148 F6 1
Cullen St TOX L8 113 L6
Culme Rd WD/CROXPK L12 98 B6
Culshaw Wy BRSC L40 37 H6
Culvert La SKEL WN8 53 J3
Culvert St WGNNW/ST WN6 68 C3
Culzean Cl WD/CROXPK L12 99 G2
Cumberbatch Pl
WGNE/HIN WN2 80 B1
Cumberland Av AIG/SPK L17 113 M7
CL/PREN CH43 127 J3
ECCL WA10 101 K5
NTHTN L30 83 L2 2
Cumberland Cl NPK/KEN L6 97 M7
Cumberland Crs
RNFD/HAY WA11 90 C7
Cumberland Ga NTHTN L30 84 C2
Cumberland Gv GTS/LS CH66 162 E2
Cumberland Rd STHP PR8 3 L8
WAL/NB CH45 95 L6 5
Cumberland St CLVPS L1 12 F6 2
WARRS WA4 15 H9
WGN WN1 5 J1 1
Cumber La RAIN/WH L35 117 H2
Cumbers Dr NSTN CH64 153 J8
Cumbers La NSTN CH64 153 J8
Cumbrae Dr EP CH65 163 L4
Cumbrian Cl WGNE/HIN WN2 80 D3 2
Cumbria Wy WD/CROXPK L12 98 E4
Cummings St CLVPS L1 113 G5 7
Cumpsty Rd LITH L21 83 L4
Cunard Cl CL/PREN CH43 110 E7
Cunard Rd LITH L21 83 K6
Cunliffe Av NEWLW WA12 91 K8
Cunliffe Cl RUNC WA7 150 C6
Cunliffe Ct LEIGH WN7 93 J1
Cunliffe St CHLY/EC PR7 32 E6
CLVP L2 12 F5
LEIGH WN7 81 L8 3
Cunningham Av CHLY/EC PR7 32 C7
Cunningham Cl
WARRW/BUR WA5 120 B8 2
WKBY CH48 124 E7 2
Cunningham Dr BEB CH63 143 L6
RUNC WA7 18 D7
Cunningham Rd
CLB/OSW/ST L13 114 C3
WDN WA8 133 M5
Cunscough La MGHL L31 73 M3
Cuper Crs HUY L36 115 M1
Curate Rd NPK/KEN L6 97 L6
Curate St CHLYE PR6 32 F4
Curlender Cl BIRK CH41 111 G4
Curlender Wy SPK/HALE L24 148 A3
Curlew Av GR/UP/WCH CH49 109 M7
Curlew Cl GOL/RIS/CU WA3 92 F5 1
GR/UP/WCH CH49 109 M7 3
Curlew Ct MOR/LEA CH46 109 L4
Curlew Gv GOL/RIS/CU WA3 123 G2
Curlew La BRSC L40 39 G4
Curlew Wy MOR/LEA CH46 109 L4
Currans Rd
WARRN/WOL WA2 121 J3 1
Curtana Crs NG/CROX L11 98 E2
Curtis Rd ANF/KKDL L4 97 L4
Curtis St WGNW/BIL/O WN5 67 M7 2
Curwell Cl BEB CH63 143 K2 1
Curzon Av BIRK CH41 10 D3
WAL/NB CH45 95 K6 1
Curzon Dr WARRS WA4 138 C6
Curzon Rd CSBY/WL L22 83 G4
HOY CH47 108 C6
RF/TRAN CH42 127 K3
STHP PR8 3 M7
Curzon St RUNC WA7 18 F5
Cusson Rd NWD/KWIPK L33 86 D4
Custley Hey STBRV L28 99 K5
Custom House La CLVPS L1 12 F8 1
Cuthbert St
WGNW/BIL/O WN5 67 M7 3
Cut La BRSC L40 50 B6
NWD/KWIPK L33 87 G6
Cygnet Cl GTS/LS CH66 162 F1
ORM L39 62 E3
Cygnet Ct NWD/KWIPK L33 86 C3 2
WARR WA1 14 D9
Cygnet St WGNS/IIMK WN3 4 D7
Cynthia Av WARR WA1 122 D6
Cynthia Rd RUNC WA7 18 E5
Cypress Av GTS/LS CH66 163 H4
WDN WA8 134 D2
Cypress Cl MGHL L31 85 J2
WARR WA1 123 G6 1
Cypress Cft BEB CH63 143 K2
Cypress Gdns RAIN/WH L35 101 L6 2
Cypress Gv RUNC WA7 149 L6
Cypress Rd HUY L36 115 M5
STHP PR8 25 G7
WGNW/BIL/O WN5 68 A7
Cyprus St PR/KW L34 100 F7
Cyril Gv AIG/SPK L17 130 A3
Cyril St WARRN/WOL WA2 14 F2

D

Dacre's Bridge La RAIN/WH L35 116 F6
Dacre St BIRK CH41 11 J5
BTL L20 6 E9
Dacy Rd EV L5 97 J8
Daffodil Cl WDN WA8 135 G1
Daffodil Rd BIRK CH41 111 H6
WAV L15 114 D6
Dagnall Av WARRW/BUR WA5 121 H3
Dagnall Rd KKBY L32 85 L4
Dahlia Cl WLT/FAZ L9 97 K1 1
Dailton Rd SKEL WN8 66 C6
Dairy Farm Rd RNFD/HAY WA11 75 M6
Daisy Av NEWLW WA12 104 E3
Daisybank Cl
WGNE/HIN WN2 69 M8 11
Daisy Bank Rd LYMM WA13 139 L2
WARRW/BUR WA5 136 B1 1
Daisy Fold CHLYE PR6 33 G3
Daisy Hill Dr CHLYE PR6 44 C4 2
Daisy Hill Fold CHLY/EC PR7 31 M4
Daisy La BRSC L40 52 D1

Daisy Mill Bank Cl
GOL/RIS/CU WA3 107 G2
Daisy Mt MGHL L31 73 G5
Daisy Rd WGNW/BIL/O WN5 68 A7
Daisy St EV L5 96 F6
Dalbeattie Ri WGN WN1 5 L1
Dalby Cl GOL/RIS/CU WA3 107 K8
RNFD/HAY WA11 9 M2
Dale Acre Dr NTHTN L30 83 L2
Dale Av CHLY/EC PR7 31 M4
GTS/LS CH66 155 L7
HES CH60 141 H4
PS/BROM CH62 143 M5
Dalebrook Cl WLTN L25 115 K6
Dale Cl MGHL L31 72 E3
SKEL WN8 53 K3
WARRW/BUR WA5 136 F1
WDN WA8 133 J5
Dale Crs STHEL WA9 102 F7
Dalecrest WGNW/BIL/O WN5 77 M4
Dalecroft FROD/HEL WA6 166 A4
Dale Dr EP CH65 156 B8
Dale End Rd PEN/TH CH61 141 L1
Dale Gdns HES CH60 140 F4
Dalegarth Av WD/CROXPK L12 99 G4
Dale Gv LEIGH WN7 93 L1 1
Dalehead Gv LEIGH WN7 93 L1
Dalehead Pl RNFD/HAY WA11 89 K4 1
Dale Hey GTS/LS CH66 155 G3
WAL/EG CH44 111 K2
Dalehurst Cl WAL/EG CH44 111 M1 2
Dale La NWD/KWIPK L33 86 C1
WARRS WA4 138 A6
Dalemeadow Rd
DV/KA/FCH L14 114 F2
Dale Ms WLTN L25 131 K1
Dale Rd GOL/RIS/CU WA3 92 C6
PS/BROM CH62 143 M8
Dalesford Cl LEIGH WN7 93 L5
Daleside Av AIMK WN4 79 J5 1
Daleside Cl PEN/TH CH61 126 B7 1
Daleside Rd NWD/KWIPK L33 86 B2
Dales Rw HUY L36 116 D3
Dale St ALL/GAR L19 130 E8
CLVP L2 12 F6
CLVPS L1 12 F6
LEIGH WN7 81 L8
RUNC WA7 19 G6
WGNE/HIN WN2 80 B2
Dalesway HES CH60 141 G5
The Dale NSTN CH64 152 F7
WARRW/BUR WA5 120 B8
Dale Vw CHLY/EC PR7 43 L1
NEWLW WA12 105 G1
Dale View Cl PEN/TH CH61 126 C8 2
Dalewood WD/CROXPK L12 99 G2 6
Dalewood Crs CHNE CH2 165 J2 1
Dalewood Gdns
RAIN/WH L35 117 H3 3
Daley Pl BTL L20 84 A6
Daley Rd LITH L21 83 L4
Dallam La WARRN/WOL WA2 14 D4
Dallas Gv WLT/FAZ L9 84 C7
Dalmeny St AIG/SPK L17 129 K2
Dalmorton Rd WAL/NB CH45 95 L5
Dalry Crs KKBY L32 86 B6
Dalrymple St EV L5 96 F8
Dalston Dr RNFD/HAY WA11 89 K4
Dalston Gv WGNS/IIMK WN3 78 F2
Dalton Av WARRW/BUR WA5 14 B1
Dalton Bank WARR WA1 15 H4
Dalton Cl WD/CROXPK L12 98 E3
WGNW/BIL/O WN5 67 K6
Dalton Ct RUNC WA7 150 A2
Dalton Dr WGNS/IIMK WN3 79 G2
Dalton Gv AIMK WN4 91 J1 3
Dalton Rd WAL/NB CH45 95 L6
Dalton St GOL/RIS/CU WA3 107 G7
RUNC WA7 149 M3
Daltry Cl WD/CROXPK L12 98 C6
Dalwood Cl RUNC WA7 151 G6
Damerham Ms WLTN L25 115 J6
Damfield La MGHL L31 72 E4
Damhead La NSTN CH64 154 A6
Damian Dr NEWLW WA12 91 J8 1
Dam La GOL/RIS/CU WA3 92 B2
GOL/RIS/CU WA3 106 B6
WARR WA1 122 F6
Damson Rd NTHLY L27 116 A8
Dam Wood La BRSC L40 37 L8
Dam Wood Rd SPK/HALE L24 146 F3
Danbers SKEL WN8 66 B7
Danby Cl EV L5 97 H8 2
RUNC WA7 149 M7 2
WARRW/BUR WA5 121 G6 2
Danby Fold RAIN/WH L35 117 K2 1
Danebury Cl WGNE/HIN WN2 80 F1 10
Dane Cl GR/UP/WCH CH49 126 B7
Danefield Pl ALL/GAR L19 130 F5 1
Danefield Rd ALL/GAR L19 130 F5
GR/UP/WCH CH49 125 L3
Dane Hall La CHLY/EC PR7 30 F3
Danehurst Rd WAL/NB CH45 95 H6
WLT/FAZ L9 84 D6 6
Danesbury Cl WGNW/BIL/O WN5 90 A1
Danescourt Rd BIRK CH41 10 B2
WD/CROXPK L12 98 E8
Danescroft WDN WA8 133 K2
Dane St ANF/KKDL L4 97 H4
Danesway CHLY/EC PR7 44 B4 1
WGN WN1 68 D2
Daneswell Dr MOR/LEA CH46 110 B4
Daneswell Rd SPK/HALE L24 147 J3 2
Daneville Rd ANF/KKDL L4 97 M3
Daneway STHP PR8 34 D7
Danger La MOR/LEA CH46 110 B3
Daniel Cl GOL/RIS/CU WA3 123 J1
LITH L21 83 J7
Daniel Davies Dr TOX L8 113 J6 3
Daniels La SKEL WN8 65 L6
Dannette Hey STBRV L28 99 L7
Dansie St VAUX/LVPD L3 13 L7
Dans Rd WDN WA8 135 G3
Dante Cl WLT/FAZ L9 84 E5
Danube St TOX L8 113 L6 2
Darby Gv ALL/GAR L19 130 D7 1
Darby La WGNE/HIN WN2 69 M7
Darby Rd ALL/GAR L19 130 C5
Darent Rd RNFD/HAY WA11 90 D7
Daresbury Av STHP PR8 34 C8
Daresbury Cl KKBY L32 85 L3
Daresbury Expy RUNC WA7 18 F3
WARRS WA4 151 J2
Daresbury La WARRS WA4 151 M3
Daresbury Rd ECCL WA10 101 K1
WAL/EG CH44 111 J1
Darfield SKEL WN8 66 B6
Daric Cl LEIGH WN7 93 L4
Dark Entry PR/KW L34 100 A4
Dark La BRSC L40 41 G2
BRSC L40 51 K7
HOR/BR BL6 57 K1
MGHL L31 72 F4
Darley Av WARRN/WOL WA2 122 A2
Darley Cl WDN WA8 133 K2
Darleydale Dr PS/BROM CH62 144 B8
Darley Dr WD/CROXPK L12 98 E7
Darley Rd WGNS/IIMK WN3 79 K2
Darley St HOR/BR BL6 45 K8
Darlington Cl WAL/EG CH44 111 M1 8
Darlington St CHLY/EC PR7 42 F4
WAL/EG CH44 111 M1 9
WGN WN1 4 F5
WGNE/HIN WN2 69 J6 2
Darlington St East WGN WN1 5 H5
Darmond Rd NWD/KWIPK L33 86 C2
Darmond's Gn WKBY CH48 124 D2
Darmonds Green Av
NPK/KEN L6 97 M7
Darnaway Cl GOL/RIS/CU WA3 107 K7
Darnhall St WGNE/HIN WN2 80 B1 3
Darnley St TOX L8 113 G8
Darran Av WGNS/IIMK WN3 79 H2
Darrel Dr EHL/KEN L7 113 L6 3
Darsefield Rd CHLDW L16 115 G6
Dartington Rd CHLDW L16 114 F5
Dartmouth Av AIN/FAZ L10 84 E3
Dartmouth Dr NTHTN L30 83 L1
Darvel Av AIMK WN4 90 E1
Darwall Rd ALL/GAR L19 130 F5
Darwen St EV L5 96 D8 1
Darwick Dr HUY L36 116 C5
Darwin Gv STHEL WA9 102 A6
Daryl Rd HES CH60 141 J4
Daten Av GOL/RIS/CU WA3 107 H7
Daub La BRSC L40 40 C5
Daulby St VAUX/LVPD L3 13 M6
Dauntsey Brow WLTN L25 115 K6 3
Dauntsey Ms WLTN L25 115 K6
Davenham Av CL/PREN CH43 127 H2
WARR WA1 122 A5
Davenham Cl CL/PREN CH43 127 H3 1
Davenham Rd FMBY L37 59 H1
Davenhill Pk WLT/FAZ L9 84 E3
Davenport Av WARRS WA4 122 B8
Davenport Cl WKBY CH48 124 E7 3
Davenport Gv
NWD/KWIPK L33 86 A1 3
Davenport Rd HES CH60 141 G6
Davenport Rw RUNC WA7 149 M5 1
Daventree Rd WAL/NB CH45 95 K8
Daventry Rd AIG/SPK L17 130 A3
David Rd LYMM WA13 139 L2
David's Av WARRW/BUR WA5 120 D8
Davidson Rd
CLB/OSW/ST L13 114 B2 4
David St TOX L8 129 H1
Davids Wk WLTN L25 131 L2 1
Davies Av NEWLW WA12 104 E1
WARRS WA4 138 B1
Davies Cl WDN WA8 149 J1
Davies St BTL L20 7 J3
CLVPS L1 12 F6 3
STHEL WA9 9 L4
WGNE/HIN WN2 80 C3
Davies Wy LYMM WA13 139 M2
Davis Rd MOR/LEA CH46 110 D2
Davy Av GOL/RIS/CU WA3 107 G8
Davy Cl ECCL WA10 88 D8
Davy Rd RUNC WA7 150 A2
Davy St EV L5 97 J7
Dawber Cl NPK/KEN L6 113 J1 4
Dawber's La CHLY/EC PR7 31 G3
Dawber St AIMK WN4 91 M1 1
Dawley Cl AIMK WN4 91 J2
Dawlish Cl WLTN L25 131 L5
Dawlish Dr CHTN/BK PR9 22 C8
Dawlish Rd PEN/TH CH61 125 L8
WAL/EG CH44 111 H1
Dawn Cl NSTN CH64 153 G7
STHEL WA9 102 A6
Dawn Gdns EP CH65 20 A7
Dawnwood Sq
WGNW/BIL/O WN5 67 L3
Dawpool Dr MOR/LEA CH46 110 A5
PS/BROM CH62 143 L6
Dawson Av BIRK CH41 10 C2
CHTN/BK PR9 22 E8 3
STHEL WA9 102 F6
WGNNW/ST WN6 68 C2
Dawson Gdns MGHL L31 72 E3
Dawson Rd ORM L39 62 E6
Dawson St CLVPS L1 13 G7
Dawstone Ri HES CH60 141 H6
Dawstone Rd HES CH60 141 H6
Daybrook SKEL WN8 66 B7
Dayfield SKEL WN8 66 C6
Days Meadow
GR/UP/WCH CH49 125 L2 2
Day St CLB/OSW/ST L13 114 C2
Deacon Cl CSBY/WL L22 82 F5 1
GOL/RIS/CU WA3 106 C5
Deacon Ct CSBY/WL L22 82 F5
WLTN L25 131 K3 2
Deacon Rd WDN WA8 16 E2
Deakin St BIRK CH41 111 H5
WGNS/IIMK WN3 5 J9
Dean Av WAL/NB CH45 95 G7
Dean Cl SKEL WN8 66 E6
WDN WA8 16 E3
WGNW/BIL/O WN5 89 M2
Dean Ct GOL/RIS/CU WA3 92 C6 2
Dean Crs WARRN/WOL WA2 121 K3 5
WGNW/BIL/O WN5 67 K5
Deane Rd EHL/KEN L7 113 L3
Dean Head La CHLYE PR6 45 J1
Dean Meadow NEWLW WA12 104 E1 1
Dean Rd GOL/RIS/CU WA3 92 C6
Deansburn Rd CLB/OSW/ST L13 98 A7
Deanscales Rd NG/CROX L11 98 B3
Deans Ct FMBY L37 47 H8
Deansfield Wy CHNE CH2 165 J2
Deansgate EP CH65 156 C8
Deansgate La FMBY L37 47 K8
Deansgate La North FMBY L37 47 J7
Deans La BRSC L40 53 G1
SKEL WN8 53 H3
WARRS WA4 139 H2
Deans Rd EP CH65 21 K8
Dean St CSBY/WL L22 82 F5
WDN WA8 16 E3
Deans Wy CL/PREN CH43 111 H5 2
Deansway WDN WA8 133 L5
Deanwater Cl GOL/RIS/CU WA3 122 F1
Dean Wy STHEL WA9 118 D2
Dean Wood Av
WGNW/BIL/O WN5 67 G4
Dean Wood Cl RAIN/WH L35 117 H3 1
Dearham Av RNFD/HAY WA11 89 J6
Dearne Cl WD/CROXPK L12 99 G8
Dearnford Av PS/BROM CH62 143 M7
Dearnford Cl PS/BROM CH62 143 M7
Dearnley Av RNFD/HAY WA11 90 A8
Deauville Rd WLT/FAZ L9 84 E6
Deben Cl WGNNW/ST WN6 55 M4 1
Debra Cl GTS/LS CH66 162 E1
MGHL L31 85 K1
Debra Rd GTS/LS CH66 162 E2
Dee Cl NWD/KWIPK L33 74 B7
Dee La WKBY CH48 124 C3
Deeley Cl EHL/KEN L7 113 L4
Dee Park Cl HES CH60 141 K7
Dee Park Rd HES CH60 141 K7
Deep Dl WARRW/BUR WA5 120 B7
Deepdale WDN WA8 133 L2
Deepdale Av BTL L20 83 J8
RNFD/HAY WA11 89 L4 2
Deepdale Cl CL/PREN CH43 110 E7 6
Deepdale Dr RAIN/WH L35 117 M2
Deepdale Rd WLTN L25 115 J6
Deepfield Dr HUY L36 116 B5
Deepfield Rd WAV L15 114 B7
Deepwood Gv RAIN/WH L35 117 G3 2
Deerbarn Dr NTHTN L30 84 D2
Deerbolt Cl KKBY L32 85 L2 1
Deerbolt Crs KKBY L32 85 L2
Deerbolt Wy KKBY L32 85 L2
Deerfold CHLY/EC PR7 32 D3
Dee Rd RAIN/WH L35 117 K2
Deer Park Ct RUNC WA7 150 B7 2
Deerwood Cl GTS/LS CH66 155 M6 1
Deerwood Crs GTS/LS CH66 155 M6
Deeside EP CH65 20 A9
Dee Side HES CH60 140 E5
Deeside Cl CL/PREN CH43 110 D7 5
EP CH65 163 K3
Dee View Rd HES CH60 141 H5
De Grouchy St WKBY CH48 124 D2 1
Deighton Rd CHLY/EC PR7 32 D7 3
Deirdre Av WDN WA8 16 D2
Delabole Rd NG/CROX L11 85 M8
De Lacy Rw RUNC WA7 150 C3
Delafield Cl WARRN/WOL WA2 122 B2
Delagoa Rd AIN/FAZ L10 85 H7
Delamain Rd CLB/OSW/ST L13 98 A7
Delamere Av GOL/RIS/CU WA3 93 G7
GTS/LS CH66 156 A8 2
PS/BROM CH62 155 G1
STHEL WA9 118 C2
WDN WA8 133 L4
Delamere Cl CL/PREN CH43 110 D7 6
PS/BROM CH62 155 G1
WD/CROXPK L12 98 F2 2
Delamere Dr GTS/LS CH66 163 G1
Delamere Gv WAL/EG CH44 112 A3 2
Delamere Pl CHLYE PR6 32 F5
Delamere Rd SKEL WN8 65 H3 1
STHP PR8 34 D8
Delamere St WARRW/BUR WA5 121 G8
Delamere Wy FROD/HEL WA6 160 E8
SKEL WN8 66 C6
Delamore Pl ANF/KKDL L4 7 L8 1
Delamore's Acre NSTN CH64 154 C5
Delamore St ANF/KKDL L4 7 M8
Delavor Cl HES CH60 141 G5 1
Delavor Rd HES CH60 141 G5
Delaware Crs KKBY L32 85 L2
Delegarte St WGNS/IIMK WN3 5 J8
Delenty Dr GOL/RIS/CU WA3 122 F1
Delery Dr WARR WA1 122 A5
Delfby Crs KKBY L32 86 C4
Delfhaven Ct WGNNW/ST WN6 56 C6
Delf La ANF/KKDL L4 97 J3
ORM L39 49 J8
SPK/HALE L24 131 K8
Dell Av WGNNW/ST WN6 68 A2
Dell Cl BEB CH63 143 K7
Dell Dr WARRN/WOL WA2 122 C3
Dellfield La MGHL L31 73 G4
Dell Gv RF/TRAN CH42 128 C5
Dell La HES CH60 141 K6
Dellside Cl AIMK WN4 78 F7
Dellside Gv STHEL WA9 102 E5 2
Dell St EHL/KEN L7 113 L3 2
The Dell CHLYE PR6 33 J2
RF/TRAN CH42 128 D4
SKEL WN8 66 D6
WD/CROXPK L12 99 G4
WGNNW/ST WN6 54 F6
Delph Common Rd ORM L39 62 D4
Delphfields Rd WARRS WA4 137 L6
Delph Gv LEIGH WN7 81 M4 3
Delphfield RUNC WA7 150 F5
Delph La CHLY/EC PR7 31 M7
FMBY L37 58 E2 1
ORM L39 62 E4
RAIN/WH L35 117 H1
WARRN/WOL WA2 106 A7
WARRS WA4 151 J2
Delph Park Av ORM L39 62 D4
Delph Rd HTWN L38 70 F5
Delphside Cl WGNW/BIL/O WN5 66 F8
Delphside Rd WGNW/BIL/O WN5 66 E8
Delph St WGNNW/ST WN6 4 C1
The Delph SKEL WN8 53 L2
Delphwood Dr STHEL WA9 9 J9
Delta Dr WD/CROXPK L12 99 G5
Delta Rd LITH L21 83 K6 3
STHEL WA9 103 H1
Delta Rd East RF/TRAN CH42 128 D4 1
Delta Rd West
RF/TRAN CH42 128 D4 2
Deltic Wy NTHTN L30 84 C5
NWD/KWIPK L33 86 D5
Delves Av BEB CH63 143 H2
WARRW/BUR WA5 14 A1
Delyn Cl RF/TRAN CH42 128 A4
Demage Dr GTS/LS CH66 162 F2
Demesne St WAL/EG CH44 112 A2
Denbigh Av CHTN/BK PR9 25 H2
STHEL WA9 102 E6
Denbigh Cl FROD/HEL WA6 166 C4
Denbigh Gdns EP CH65 20 D9 1
Denbigh Rd WLT/FAZ L9 97 H2
Denbigh St EV L5 96 D8
Denbury Av WARRS WA4 138 B3
Dencourt Rd NG/CROX L11 98 D4
Dene Av NEWLW WA12 104 B1
Denebank Rd ANF/KKDL L4 97 K6
Dene Gv LEIGH WN7 93 K1 1
Denehurst Cl
WARRW/BUR WA5 136 B1 2
Deneshey Rd HOY CH47 108 E5
Dene St LEIGH WN7 93 K1
Denes Wy STBRV L28 99 J6
Denford Cl WGNS/IIMK WN3 79 H2
Denford Rd DV/KA/FCH L14 99 H8
Denham Av WARRW/BUR WA5 120 D8
Denham Cl WD/CROXPK L12 99 H2
Denham Dr WGNS/IIMK WN3 79 J2
Denholme SKEL WN8 66 B6
Denise Av WARRW/BUR WA5 120 A8
Denise Rd AIN/FAZ L10 85 K6
Denison Gv STHEL WA9 102 A6 1
Denman Dr NPK/KEN L6 113 L1
Denman Gv WAL/EG CH44 112 A3 8
Denman St EHL/KEN L7 113 K2 4
Denman Wy NPK/KEN L6 113 L1
Denmark Rd CHTN/BK PR9 25 J3
Denmark St CSBY/WL L22 82 F4 5
Dennett Cl MGHL L31 72 F6
WARR WA1 123 G7
Dennett Rd RAIN/WH L35 116 E1
Denning Dr PEN/TH CH61 125 M6
Dennis Av ECCL WA10 101 L6
Dennis Rd WDN WA8 17 G5
Denny Cl GR/UP/WCH CH49 126 B1
Densham Av WARRN/WOL WA2 121 K3
Denshaw SKEL WN8 66 B6
Denston Cl CL/PREN CH43 110 D6 2
Denstone Av AIN/FAZ L10 84 F3
Denstone Cl WLTN L25 131 K5 1
Denstone Crs DV/KA/FCH L14 115 J1
Dentdale Dr EV L5 13 K2
Denton Dr WAL/NB CH45 95 L7
Denton Gv NPK/KEN L6 97 L8
WGNW/BIL/O WN5 67 K5
Dentons Green La ECCL WA10 8 B2
Denton St TOX L8 129 H1
WDN WA8 17 G2
Dentwood St TOX L8 129 J1 5
Denver Rd KKBY L32 85 L4
WARRS WA4 138 C2 2
Depot Rd NWD/KWIPK L33 86 E1
Derby Cl NEWLW WA12 104 D2 4
Derby Dr RNFD/HAY WA11 76 C8
WARR WA1 15 M1
Derby Gv MGHL L31 72 F7
Derby Hill Crs ORM L39 51 J8 1
Derby Hill Rd ORM L39 51 J8
Derby La CLB/OSW/ST L13 114 C2 1
Derby Pl CHLYE PR6 44 C5 3
Derby Rd BTL L20 6 E6
CHTN/BK PR9 3 J4
EV L5 96 D7
FMBY L37 59 G1
GOL/RIS/CU WA3 92 E4
HUY L36 116 A3
RF/TRAN CH42 127 M1
SKEL WN8 64 E5
WAL/NB CH45 95 J7
WARRS WA4 137 L5
WDN WA8 134 F1
Derby Rw NEWLW WA12 104 F5
Derbyshire Hill Rd STHEL WA9 103 J2
Derby Sq PR/KW L34 101 G7 2
Derby St CLB/OSW/ST L13 114 B2 5
HUY L36 116 C3
NEWLW WA12 104 D2
ORM L39 51 H8
WGNE/HIN WN2 80 B1
Derby St West ORM L39 51 G8
Dereham Av GR/UP/WCH CH49 110 C6
Dereham Crs AIN/FAZ L10 85 H6
Dereham Wy WGNS/IIMK WN3 78 F2
Derek Av WARRN/WOL WA2 121 M4
Derna Rd HUY L36 115 M2
Derngate Dr WGNNW/ST WN6 56 C6
Derringstone Cl ECCL WA10 101 M4 4
Derwent Av CHTN/BK PR9 25 H4
FMBY L37 58 F3
GOL/RIS/CU WA3 92 E4 1
PR/KW L34 101 H7
WGNE/HIN WN2 69 K6
Derwent Cl BEB CH63 127 M8 1
GOL/RIS/CU WA3 107 J3 1
MGHL L31 73 H3
NWD/KWIPK L33 85 M1
RAIN/WH L35 117 K2
Derwent Dr GTS/LS CH66 155 K3
LITH L21 83 M5
PEN/TH CH61 141 H1
WAL/NB CH45 95 J7
Derwent Pl WGNW/BIL/O WN5 67 L6 3
Derwent Rd AIMK WN4 80 A8 2
BEB CH63 127 M8
CHLY/EC PR7 32 D8
CL/PREN CH43 127 K1 2
CSBY/BLUN L23 83 H3
HOY CH47 109 G5
RNFD/HAY WA11 89 K6
WARRS WA4 137 J3
WDN WA8 133 L4
WGNW/BIL/O WN5 67 H5
Derwent Rd East
CLB/OSW/ST L13 114 C1
Derwent Rd West
CLB/OSW/ST L13 114 B1
Derwent Sq
CLB/OSW/ST L13 114 C1 1
Derwent Wy NSTN CH64 153 H7
Desborough Crs
WD/CROXPK L12 98 C6 3
Desford Av RNFD/HAY WA11 89 M7
Desford Cl MOR/LEA CH46 109 K4
Desford Rd ALL/GAR L19 130 A5
Desilva St HUY L36 116 C3
Desmond Cl CL/PREN CH43 110 E6
Desmond Gv CSBY/BLUN L23 83 H2
Desoto Rd WDN WA8 134 A8
Desoto Rd East WDN WA8 16 A8
De Trafford Dr WGNE/HIN WN2 69 K5
Deva Cl NWD/KWIPK L33 74 A6
Deva Rd WKBY CH48 124 C3 3
Deveraux Dr WAL/EG CH44 111 L2
Deveraux Rd WAL/EG CH44 111 K2
Deverell Gv WAV L15 114 D4
Deverell Rd WAV L15 114 D4
Deverill Rd RF/TRAN CH42 128 A4
De Villiers Av CSBY/BLUN L23 71 G8
Devisdale Gv CL/PREN CH43 110 E6
Devizes Dr PEN/TH CH61 125 M6
Devizes Ms WLTN L25 115 K6
Devoke Av RNFD/HAY WA11 89 J4
Devon Av WAL/EG CH44 95 L8 2
Devon Cl CSBY/BLUN L23 82 C1
WGNE/HIN WN2 57 M8
WGNW/BIL/O WN5 67 L7
Devondale Rd CALD/MH L18 114 C8 3
Devon Dr PEN/TH CH61 141 G1
WGN WN1 56 D4
Devon Farm Wy FMBY L37 59 K2 1
Devonfield Rd WLT/FAZ L9 84 B8
Devon Gdns CHLDW L16 115 G8
RF/TRAN CH42 128 B4 1
Devon Pl WDN WA8 134 C2 2
Devonport St TOX L8 113 H8
Devonport Wy CHLYE PR6 33 G5
Devonshire Cl
NWD/KWIPK L33 86 A1 4
Devonshire Gdns NEWLW WA12 104 E3
Devonshire Pl CL/PREN CH43 10 B7
EV L5 97 G7 4
RUNC WA7 19 G2
Devonshire Rd CHLY/EC PR7 32 E6
CHTN/BK PR9 25 J6
CL/PREN CH43 10 C7
CSBY/WL L22 82 E3
ECCL WA10 8 A1
GR/UP/WCH CH49 110 A8 4
PEN/TH CH61 141 G1
TOX L8 113 J8
WAL/EG CH44 111 K1 4
WARR WA1 122 B5
WKBY CH48 124 E4
Devonshire Rd West TOX L8 113 J8 1
Devon St ECCL WA10 8 B4
VAUX/LVPD L3 13 L5
Devon Wy CHLDW L16 115 G7
HUY L36 116 C1
Dewar Ct RUNC WA7 150 A2
Dewar St GOL/RIS/CU WA3 107 G8
Dewberry Cl RF/TRAN CH42 11 G9 1
Dewey Av WLT/FAZ L9 84 D5
Dewhurst Rd GOL/RIS/CU WA3 122 F3
Dewlands Rd LITH L21 83 H5
Dewsbury Rd ANF/KKDL L4 97 K7
Dexter St TOX L8 113 G7
Deycroft Av NWD/KWIPK L33 86 C1
Deyes End MGHL L31 73 G4
Deyes La MGHL L31 72 F4
Deysbrook La WD/CROXPK L12 98 E7
Deysbrook Side
WD/CROXPK L12 98 E7 2
Deysbrook Wy WD/CROXPK L12 98 F5
Dial Rd RF/TRAN CH42 127 M2
Dial St EHL/KEN L7 113 L3
WARR WA1 14 F5
Diamond Jubilee Rd BRSC L40 39 L1
Diamond St EV L5 13 G1
WGNNW/ST WN6 68 C2
Diana Rd BTL L20 83 M6
Diana St ANF/KKDL L4 97 H5
Diane Rd AIMK WN4 79 M8
AIMK WN4 92 A1 1
Dibbinsdale Rd BEB CH63 143 K6
Dibbins Gn BEB CH63 143 K7
Dibbins Hey BEB CH63 143 J3
Dibbinview Gv BEB CH63 143 K3
Dibb La CSBY/BLUN L23 70 E6
Dicconson Crs WGN WN1 4 F2 1
Dicconson's La ORM L39 61 L2
Dicconson St ECCL WA10 9 G3 1
WGN WN1 4 E1
Dicconson Ter WGN WN1 4 E1
Dicconson Wy ORM L39 63 J1 1
Dickens Av CL/PREN CH43 127 H4 1
Dickens Cl CL/PREN CH43 127 H4 2
Dickens Dr WGNE/HIN WN2 80 D5
Dickenson St CLVPS L1 112 F5 6
WARRN/WOL WA2 15 G2
WGNE/HIN WN2 81 G1 4
Dickens Pl WGNS/IIMK WN3 79 H1
Dickens Rd CHLY/EC PR7 43 G5
ECCL WA10 101 L5
Dickens St TOX L8 113 H7 4
Dicket's La SKEL WN8 64 C3
Dickinson Cl FMBY L37 59 H3
RNFD/HAY WA11 90 C7 4
Dickinson Rd FMBY L37 59 H3
Dick's La BRSC L40 64 B1
Dickson Cl WDN WA8 16 E3
Dickson St VAUX/LVPD L3 12 C1
WDN WA8 16 D3
Didcot Cl WLTN L25 131 M5
Didsbury Cl NWD/KWIPK L33 86 B3 2
Didsbury Gv
WGNE/HIN WN2 69 M8 12
Digg La MOR/LEA CH46 109 M4
Diggle St WGNNW/ST WN6 4 B2

Dig La *FROD/HEL* WA6 .... 160 C6
WARRN/WOL WA2 .... 122 C1
Digmoor Dr *SKEL* WN8.................. 65 K6
Digmoor Rd *KKBY* L32 .... 86 B6
SKEL WN8 .... 65 L6
Dignum Md *NTHLY* L27 .... 116 A7
Dilloway St *ECCL* WA10 .... 8 C3
Dinas La *HUY* L36 .... 115 J1 1
Dinesen Rd *ALL/GAR* L19 .... 130 E6
Dingle Av *NEWLW* WA12 .... 104 B3
SKEL WN8 .... 66 D5
Dingle Brow *TOX* L8 .... 129 J2 1
Dingle Cl *ORM* L39 .... 62 E4
Dingle Gv *TOX* L8 .... 129 J1 2
Dingle La *TOX* L8.................. 129 J2
WARRS WA4 .... 138 B7
Dingle Mt *TOX* L8 .... 129 J2
Dingle Rd *RF/TRAN* CH42 .... 10 F9
SKEL WN8 .... 66 D6
TOX L8.................. 129 H2
The Dingle *CHLYE* PR6 .... 33 J2
Dingle V *TOX* L8 .... 129 J2
Dingle Wk *WGNNW/ST* WN6 .... 67 M1
Dingleway *WARRS* WA4.................. 137 M5
Dingley Av *WLT/FAZ* L9 .... 84 B7 1
Dingwall Dr *GR/UP/WCH* CH49 .. 126 A2
Dinmore Rd *WAL/EG* CH44 .... 111 K1
Dinorwic Rd *ANF/KKDL* L4.................. 97 J7
STHP PR8 .... 35 J2
Ditchfield *FMBY* L37.................. 59 J3
Ditchfield Pl *WDN* WA8 .... 133 K5
Ditchfield Rd
WARRW/BUR WA5 .... 136 A2
WDN WA8 .... 133 J5
Ditton La *MOR/LEA* CH46 .... 110 A2
Ditton Rd *WDN* WA8.................. 16 B7
Dixon Av *NEWLW* WA12 .... 91 L8
WGNNW/ST WN6 .... 55 J8
Dixon Cl *RNFD/HAY* WA11 .... 91 J5
Dixon Dr *WGNNW/ST* WN6 .... 55 J8
Dixon St *WARR* WA1 .... 14 C6
Dob Brow *CHLY/EC* PR7 .... 43 H1
Dobbs Dr *FMBY* L37 .... 59 J1
Dobers La *FROD/HEL* WA6.................. 167 L2
Dobson Pkwy *WGNE/HIN* WN2 .... 5 M7
Dobson St *NPK/KEN* L6 .... 113 J1
Dock Rd *ALL/GAR* L19.................. 130 D8
BIRK CH41.................. 111 J3
WDN WA8 .... 16 B9
Dock Rd North *PS/BROM* CH62 .. 128 E7
Dock Rd South *PS/BROM* CH62 .. 143 M1
Dock St *EP* CH65.................. 20 D1
WDN WA8 .... 16 C9
Dock Yard Rd *EP* CH65 .... 20 F3
Doctor's La *CHLY/EC* PR7 .... 30 C7
FMBY L37 .... 60 A4
KIRK/FR/WA PR4 .... 28 A3
Dodd Av *ECCL* WA10.................. 101 L1
GR/UP/WCH CH49.................. 125 M2
Doddridge Rd *TOX* L8 .... 113 G8 2
Dodd's La *MGHL* L31 .... 72 F3
Dodleston Cl *CL/PREN* CH43 .... 126 F1 1
Dodman Rd *NG/CROX* L11.................. 85 M8
Dodworth Av *STHP* PR8 .... 25 G8
Doel St *NPK/KEN* L6 .... 113 J2
Doe Meadow *SKEL* WN8 .... 53 J4 2
Doe's Meadow Rd *BEB* CH63 .... 143 K6
Dole La *CHLY/EC* PR7 .... 32 E5 1
Dolly's La *CHTN/BK* PR9.................. 25 M5
Dolomite Av *ALL/GAR* L19 .... 131 H7
Dolphin Crs *GTS/LS* CH66 .... 163 G3
Domar Cl *KKBY* L32.................. 86 A5
Dombey St *TOX* L8.................. 113 H7
Domingo Dr *NWD/KWIPK* L33.................. 73 M8
Dominic Cl *CHLDW* L16 .... 115 G5
Dominic Rd *CHLDW* L16 .... 115 G5 1
Dominion St *NPK/KEN* L6 .... 97 L8 2
Domville *RAIN/WH* L35 .... 117 G3
Domville Rd *CLB/OSW/ST* L13 .... 114 C4
Donaldson St *EV* L5 .... 97 J7
Donalds Wy *AIG/SPK* L17.................. 130 A4
Doncaster Dr
GR/UP/WCH CH49.................. 110 B7
Donegal Rd *CLB/OSW/ST* L13 .... 114 D2
Donne Av *BEB* CH63.................. 143 H2
Donne Cl *BEB* CH63 .... 143 J2
Donnington Cl *HUY* L36 .... 115 M5 1
LEIGH WN7 .... 93 M4
Donsby Rd *WLT/FAZ* L9 .... 84 D7
Dood's La *WARRS* WA4.................. 138 C8
Dooley Dr *NTHTN* L30 .... 84 D1
Doon Cl *ANF/KKDL* L4.................. 97 G5
Dootson St *WGNE/HIN* WN2 .... 80 D4 1
Dorbett Dr *CSBY/BLUN* L23.................. 83 H3
Dorchester Cl
GR/UP/WCH CH49 .... 126 B1 5
Dorchester Pk *RUNC* WA7.................. 150 F2
WLTN L25 .... 115 K7
Dorchester Rd *SKEL* WN8 .... 66 C6
WARRW/BUR WA5.................. 120 D8
Dorchester Wy
WARRW/BUR WA5 .... 104 B7 5
Doreen Av *MOR/LEA* CH46 .... 109 M5
Dorgan Cl *RAIN/WH* L35 .... 117 K1
Doric Av *FROD/HEL* WA6 .... 160 E6
Doric Gn *WGNW/BIL/O* WN5 .... 77 M2
Doric Rd *CLB/OSW/ST* L13.................. 114 C1
Doric St *LITH* L21 .... 83 H6 3
RF/TRAN CH42 .... 128 B3 5
Dorien Rd *CLB/OSW/ST* L13 .... 114 B3
Doris St *CHLYE* PR6.................. 32 F4
Dorking Gv *WAV* L15.................. 114 D6
Dorking Rd *CHLYE* PR6 .... 33 H1
Dorney Cl *WARRS* WA4.................. 138 A7
Dorning St *WGN* WN1 .... 4 D3
Dorothea St *WARRN/WOL* WA2 .... 15 G1
Dorothy St *EHL/KEN* L7 .... 113 K4
STHEL WA9.................. 102 A6
Dorrington Cl *RUNC* WA7 .... 150 F5 1
Dorrit St *TOX* L8 .... 113 H7
Dorset Av *STHP* PR8.................. 47 L3
WAV L15 .... 113 M6 3
Dorset Cl *BTL* L20 .... 7 K4
WGNW/BIL/O WN5 .... 67 L7
Dorset Dr *PEN/TH* CH61 .... 141 G1
Dorset Rd *ECCL* WA10.................. 8 A9
HUY L36 .... 116 C2
NPK/KEN L6 .... 97 M7
WAL/NB CH45.................. 95 J6
WGN WN1 .... 56 D4 3
WKBY CH48.................. 124 E2
Dorset Wy *WARR* WA1 .... 122 D5
Douglas Av *HOR/BR* BL6 .... 45 L8
SKEL WN8 .... 66 D6
STHEL WA9 .... 103 K7
WGNW/BIL/O WN5 .... 89 M2
Douglas Bank Dr
WGNNW/ST WN6 .... 68 B4
Douglas Cl *BRSC* L40 .... 39 L2
CLB/OSW/ST L13 .... 114 B1
HOR/BR BL6 .... 45 L8 2
WDN WA8 .... 135 H2
Douglas Dr *MGHL* L31 .... 73 H3
MOR/LEA CH46 .... 109 L5
ORM L39 .... 50 F6
WGNNW/ST WN6 .... 55 H8
WGNW/BIL/O WN5 .... 67 G6
Douglas Pl *BTL* L20.................. 6 F7
Douglas Rd *ANF/KKDL* L4 .... 97 K7
CHTN/BK PR9.................. 25 L1
LEIGH WN7.................. 81 L6
WGN WN1.................. 5 G1
WGNNW/ST WN6 .... 55 K3
WKBY CH48.................. 124 F2
Douglas St *BIRK* CH41 .... 11 K5
ECCL WA10 .... 8 B5
WGNE/HIN WN2 .... 80 E1 1
WGNW/BIL/O WN5 .... 4 A6
Douglas Wy *NWD/KWIPK* L33 .... 74 B7
Doulton Cl *CL/PREN* CH43.................. 110 D6
Doulton St *ECCL* WA10.................. 8 A6
Dounrey Cl *WARRN/WOL* WA2 .... 122 C3
Douro Pl *CLB/OSW/ST* L13 .... 114 B3
Douro St *EV* L5 .... 13 J2
Dove Cl *CHNE* CH2 .... 165 L1
EP CH65 .... 156 B6
FROD/HEL WA6 .... 159 L8 1
GOL/RIS/CU WA3 .... 123 H1
Dovecot Av *DV/KA/FCH* L14 .... 115 H1
Dovecote Gn
WARRW/BUR WA5 .... 120 C4 1
Dove Ct *WLTN* L25 .... 131 K2 1
Dovedale Av *MGHL* L31 .... 72 E3 2
PS/BROM CH62 .... 144 A8
Dovedale Cl *CL/PREN* CH43 .... 127 H3
WARRN/WOL WA2 .... 122 A2 1
Dovedale Crs *AIMK* WN4 .... 79 J5 2
Dovedale Dr *WGNNW/ST* WN6 .... 56 A3
Dovedale Rd *AIMK* WN4 .... 79 J5
CALD/MH L18 .... 114 B8
HOY CH47 .... 108 D5
WAL/NB CH45.................. 95 J6
Dovenby Fold *WGNE/HIN* WN2 .... 69 J6
Dovepoint Rd *HOY* CH47 .... 109 G5 1
Dovercliffe Rd
CLB/OSW/ST L13 .... 114 D2
Dover Cl *BIRK* CH41 .... 11 G4
RUNC WA7 .... 151 G7
Dover Dr *EP* CH65 .... 163 M3
Dover Gv *CHLDW* L16 .... 115 H5
Dover Rd *MGHL* L31 .... 72 E7
STHP PR8 .... 35 H3
WARRS WA4 .... 138 C2
WLT/FAZ L9.................. 84 B7
Dover St *RUNC* WA7 .... 19 J2
Dovesmead Rd *HES* CH60 .... 141 M6 1
Dovestone Cl *EHL/KEN* L7 .... 113 K5 5
Dove St *GOL/RIS/CU* WA3 .... 92 C3
TOX L8.................. 113 K6
Dovey St *TOX* L8 .... 113 H8
Doward St *WDN* WA8 .... 134 E3 1
Dower St *WGNE/HIN* WN2.................. 80 C2
Dowhills Dr *CSBY/BLUN* L23 .... 70 D8
Dowhills Pk *CSBY/BLUN* L23.................. 70 D7
Dowhills Rd *CSBY/BLUN* L23.................. 70 D8
Dowling Cl *WGNNW/ST* WN6 .... 67 M2 1
Downall Green Rd *AIMK* WN4.................. 79 G7
Downes Gn *BEB* CH63 .... 143 J4
Downham Av
GOL/RIS/CU WA3 .... 107 H3 2
Downham Cl *WLTN* L25 .... 115 H8
Downham Dr *HES* CH60 .... 141 J5
Downham Gn *WLTN* L25 .... 115 H8
Downham Rd *RF/TRAN* CH42.................. 128 A2
Downham Rd North
PEN/TH CH61 .... 141 J3
Downham Rd South *HES* CH60 .. 141 J5
Downham Wy *WLTN* L25.................. 115 H8
Downing Cl *CL/PREN* CH43.................. 127 K2
WGNE/HIN WN2.................. 80 C4
Downing Rd *BTL* L20.................. 7 K7
Downing St *EV* L5.................. 97 J8
Downland Wy *STHEL* WA9 .... 103 H4
Downside *WDN* WA8 .... 133 K2
Downside Cl *NTHTN* L30 .... 84 A1 2
Downside Dr *AIN/FAZ* L10.................. 85 H4
Downs Rd *ECCL* WA10 .... 8 B7
RUNC WA7 .... 19 H6
The Downs *WGNS/IIMK* WN3 .... 78 E1
Downton Av
WGNE/HIN WN2 .... 80 F1 11
Downway La *STHEL* WA9 .... 103 J4
Dowsefield La *CALD/MH* L18 .... 131 G2
Dragon Cl *NG/CROX* L11 .... 98 E1
Dragon Crs *RAIN/WH* L35 .... 117 H1 1
Dragon La *RAIN/WH* L35 .... 116 F3
Dragon Yd *WDN* WA8 .... 134 D1 1
Drake Cl *AIN/FAZ* L10 .... 85 J6 2
ORM L39.................. 62 E3
RAIN/WH L35 .... 117 G3 1
WARRW/BUR WA5 .... 120 F4 1
Drake Crs *AIN/FAZ* L10.................. 85 J6
Drakefield Rd *NG/CROX* L11 .... 98 A2
Drake Gdns *STHEL* WA9.................. 102 A7
Drake Pl *AIN/FAZ* L10 .... 85 H6 1
Drake Rd *AIN/FAZ* L10 .... 85 H6
MOR/LEA CH46 .... 110 D1
NSTN CH64 .... 153 G4
Drake St *BTL* L20.................. 6 E8
ECCL WA10 .... 8 B4
Drake Wy *AIN/FAZ* L10.................. 85 J6
Drapers Av *CHLY/EC* PR7.................. 30 E7
Draycott St *TOX* L8.................. 129 H2
Drayton Cl *PEN/TH* CH61 .... 125 M8
RUNC WA7 .... 18 E5
Drayton Crs *RNFD/HAY* WA11.................. 89 M7
Drayton Rd *ANF/KKDL* L4 .... 97 J3 1
WAL/EG CH44 .... 111 M2 3
Drennan Rd *ALL/GAR* L19 .... 131 G5
Drewell Rd *CALD/MH* L18 .... 130 B2
Drewitt Crs *CHTN/BK* PR9.................. 25 L1
Driffield Rd *PR/KW* L34 .... 100 E7
Drinkhouse La *LEY/BBR* PR5 .... 29 J4
Drinkhouse Rd *LEY/BBR* PR5 .... 29 K4
Drinkwater Gdns
VAUX/LVPD L3 .... 13 J3 1
The Drive *WD/CROXPK* L12 .... 98 D8
Drive Wy *RAIN/WH* L35 .... 117 G3
Driveway *RAIN/WH* L35.................. 117 H2
RAIN/WH L35 .... 117 H3 5
Droitwich Av
GR/UP/WCH CH49.................. 125 L1
Dromore Av *CALD/MH* L18 .... 130 C2 1
Dronfield Wy *WLTN* L25 .... 115 H6 1
Druids Cross Gdns
CALD/MH L18 .... 130 F1
Druids Cross Rd *CALD/MH* L18.................. 130 F1
Druids Pk *CALD/MH* L18 .... 131 G1
Druid St *AIMK* WN4 .... 91 L3 3
Druidsville Rd *CALD/MH* L18.................. 131 G1
Druids Wy *GR/UP/WCH* CH49 .... 126 C3
Drummersdale La *BRSC* L40.................. 37 K4
Drummer's La *AIMK* WN4 .... 79 G6
Drummond Av *GTS/LS* CH66.................. 162 E1
Drummond Ct *WDN* WA8 .... 134 F3 2
Drummond Rd *ANF/KKDL* L4 .... 97 L4
CSBY/BLUN L23 .... 71 K8
HOY CH47 .... 108 C8
Drummond Sq
WGNW/BIL/O WN5 .... 68 A6
Druridge Dr *WARRW/BUR* WA5 .. 136 B1
Drury La *CLVP* L2 .... 12 E7
Dryden Av *AIMK* WN4 .... 79 H6
Dryden Cl *CL/PREN* CH43 .... 110 E6
RAIN/WH L35 .... 117 G2
WGNS/IIMK WN3 .... 68 C8
Dryden Gv *HUY* L36 .... 116 B4 1
Dryden Pl *WARRN/WOL* WA2 .... 121 L3
Dryden Rd *EHL/KEN* L7 .... 114 A4
Dryden St *BTL* L20 .... 6 D1
EV L5 .... 13 H1
Dryebeck Gv *STHEL* WA9 .... 102 F7 2
Dryfield Cl
GR/UP/WCH CH49 .... 125 M1 3
Dryfield La *HOR/BR* BL6 .... 45 J8
Drysdale St *TOX* L8 .... 129 J1 7
Drysdale Wk *TOX* L8 .... 129 J1 8
Dublin Cft *GTS/LS* CH66 .... 163 G4
Dublin St *VAUX/LVPD* L3 .... 12 C1
Ducie St *TOX* L8.................. 113 K7
Duckinfield St *VAUX/LVPD* L3 .... 13 L7 1
Duck Pond La *RF/TRAN* CH42.................. 127 J3
Duckworth Gv
WARRN/WOL WA2 .... 122 C4
Duddingston Av
CALD/MH L18 .... 114 C8 7
CSBY/BLUN L23 .... 83 G3
Duddon Av *MGHL* L31 .... 73 H3
Duddon Cl *CL/PREN* CH43 .... 127 H2 3
Dudleston Rd *GTS/LS* CH66.................. 155 K7
Dudley Av *RUNC* WA7.................. 149 M3
Dudley Cl *CL/PREN* CH43.................. 127 K1
Dudley Crs *PS/BROM* CH62.................. 155 K2
Dudley Gv *CSBY/BLUN* L23 .... 83 G3 2
Dudley Rd *CALD/MH* L18.................. 114 B8
EP CH65 .... 20 B5
WAL/NB CH45.................. 95 J5
Dudley St *AIMK* WN4 .... 79 J8 2
WARRN/WOL WA2 .... 14 F1
Dudlow Dr *CALD/MH* L18 .... 114 E8
Dudlow Gdns *CALD/MH* L18 .... 114 E7
Dudlow Green Rd *WARRS* WA4 .. 137 M8
Dudlow La *CALD/MH* L18 .... 114 D7
Dudlow Nook Rd *CALD/MH* L18.. 114 E7
Dugdale Cl *ALL/GAR* L19 .... 130 C6 4
Duke Av *STHP* PR8 .... 35 L1
Duke Cl *RUNC* WA7 .... 18 E3
Dukes Rd *EV* L5 .... 97 G7 3
Duke St *AIMK* WN4 .... 91 L2
ALL/GAR L19.................. 130 E7
BIRK CH41.................. 10 D3
CHLY/EC PR7 .... 32 E7
CLVPS L1 .... 13 H9
CSBY/WL L22 .... 82 F5 2
ECCL WA10 .... 8 E3
FMBY L37 .... 59 G3
GOL/RIS/CU WA3 .... 92 C4
NEWLW WA12 .... 104 D2 3
PR/KW L34 .... 100 F7 7
STHP PR8 .... 2 E5
WAL/NB CH45.................. 95 K5
WGN WN1 .... 68 E3
WGNE/HIN WN2.................. 80 C2
WGNS/IIMK WN3 .... 79 H1
Duke Street La *CLVPS* L1 .... 13 G9 3
Dukes Wy *FMBY* L37 .... 59 H3
Dukes Whf *RUNC* WA7.................. 151 H7
Duke's Wood La *SKEL* WN8.................. 76 F2
Dulas Gn *KKBY* L32 .... 86 C4 1
Dulas Rd *KKBY* L32 .... 86 C4
WAV L15 .... 114 D7
Dulverton Rd *AIG/SPK* L17 .... 130 A5
Dumbarton Gn *WGNNW/ST* WN6.. 68 A3
Dumbarton St *ANF/KKDL* L4.................. 7 M9
Dumbrees Rd *WD/CROXPK* L12 .... 99 G5
Dumbreeze Gv *PR/KW* L34 .... 99 M1
Dumfries Wy *NWD/KWIPK* L33.................. 73 M7
Dunacre Wy *HLWD* L26 .... 132 B6
Dunbabin Rd *CHLDW* L16 .... 114 E7
Dunbar Cl *GTS/LS* CH66 .... 155 L8
Dunbar Crs *STHP* PR8 .... 35 H5
Dunbar Rd *STHP* PR8 .... 35 G4
Dunbar St *ANF/KKDL* L4.................. 97 H3
Dunbeath Av *RAIN/WH* L35.................. 117 M4
Dunbeath Cl *RAIN/WH* L35 .... 117 M4
Dunblane Cl *AIMK* WN4 .... 90 E1
Duncan Av *NEWLW* WA12 .... 91 L8
RUNC WA7 .... 19 L5
Duncan Cl *ECCL* WA10 .... 8 E7
Duncan Dr *GR/UP/WCH* CH49 .... 125 M1
Duncan Pl *WGNW/BIL/O* WN5 .... 68 A6
Duncansby Crs
WARRW/BUR WA5 .... 120 A7 2
Duncansby Dr *BEB* CH63.................. 154 E1
Duncan St *BIRK* CH41.................. 11 L5
CLVPS L1 .... 113 G6
ECCL WA10 .... 8 D6
WARRN/WOL WA2 .... 15 H1
Dunchurch Rd *DV/KA/FCH* L14.................. 99 H8
Duncombe Rd North
ALL/GAR L19 .... 130 D6
Duncombe Rd South
ALL/GAR L19.................. 130 D6
Duncote Cl *RAIN/WH* L35 .... 101 J8 2
Dundale Rd *CLB/OSW/ST* L13 .... 114 D2
Dundalk La *WDN* WA8 .... 133 M5
Dundalk Rd *WDN* WA8.................. 134 A5
Dundas St *BTL* L20 .... 6 E8
Dundee Cl *WARRN/WOL* WA2 .... 122 A1
Dundee Gv *WAL/EG* CH44 .... 111 J2 3
Dundonald Av *WARRS* WA4 .... 137 L4 1
Dundonald Rd *AIG/SPK* L17 .... 130 A4
Dundonald St *BIRK* CH41 .... 10 A2
Dunedin St *STHEL* WA9 .... 102 A6
Dunes Dr *FMBY* L37 .... 58 E1
Dunfold Cl *KKBY* L32 .... 86 B4
Dungeon La *SKEL* WN8 .... 53 L6
SPK/HALE L24.................. 147 H4
Dunham Av *GOL/RIS/CU* WA3 .... 92 B4 1
Dunham Cl *PS/BROM* CH62 .... 155 H1
Dunham Ct *FROD/HEL* WA6 .... 166 A7
Dunham Rd *WAV* L15 .... 114 C4
Dunkeld Cl *NPK/KEN* L6 .... 113 J2 3
Dunkeld St *NPK/KEN* L6 .... 113 J2 4
Dunkirk Dr *EP* CH65.................. 163 J4
Dunkirk La *CH/BCN* CH1 .... 162 E5
GTS/LS CH66.................. 163 J4
Dunkirk Rd *STHP* PR8 .... 35 H3
Dunley Cl *GOL/RIS/CU* WA3 .... 107 J7 3
Dunlin Av *NEWLW* WA12 .... 104 E1 2
Dunlin Cl *NTHLY* L27 .... 132 A1
RUNC WA7 .... 150 B8
WARRN/WOL WA2 .... 122 A2
Dunlop Av *STHP* PR8 .... 47 L3
Dunlop Dr *MGHL* L31 .... 85 K1
Dunlop Rd *SPK/HALE* L24 .... 146 D3
Dunlop St *WARRS* WA4.................. 14 E9
Dunluce St *ANF/KKDL* L4 .... 7 M8
Dunmail Av *RNFD/HAY* WA11 .... 89 L4
Dunmail Gv *RUNC* WA7 .... 161 G1 2
Dunmore Crs *GTS/LS* CH66 .... 155 K7
Dunmore Rd *CLB/OSW/ST* L13.................. 114 A2
GTS/LS CH66.................. 155 K7
Dunmow Rd *WARRS* WA4 .... 138 E2
Dunmow Wy *WLTN* L25 .... 131 L5 1
Dunnerdale Rd *NG/CROX* L11.................. 98 C3
Dunnett St *BTL* L20 .... 6 F9
Dunning Cl
GR/UP/WCH CH49 .... 110 A8 5
Dunnings Bridge Rd *NTHTN* L30 .... 84 A4
Dunnock Cl
WARRN/WOL WA2 .... 122 A2 2
WLTN L25 .... 115 J8 2
Dunnock Gv *GOL/RIS/CU* WA3 .... 123 G1
Dunoon Rd *WGNE/HIN* WN2.................. 57 M8
Dunraven Rd *NSTN* CH64 .... 153 J6
WKBY CH48.................. 124 C3
Dunriding La *ECCL* WA10.................. 8 A6
Dunrobin Dr *CHLY/EC* PR7 .... 31 M4
Dunscar Cl *GOL/RIS/CU* WA3.................. 106 F8
Dunscar Dr *CHLYE* PR6 .... 33 G4
Dunscore Rd *WGNS/IIMK* WN3.................. 79 G2
Dunscroft *STHEL* WA9 .... 102 F6 5
Dunsdale Dr *AIMK* WN4 .... 91 L2
Dunsdon Cl *CALD/MH* L18.................. 131 G1
Dunsdon Rd *CALD/MH* L18.................. 115 G8
Dunsford *WDN* WA8.................. 133 L2
Dunsmore Cl *RNFD/HAY* WA11 .... 90 E6
Dunsop Av *STHEL* WA9.................. 118 F1
Dunstan La *EHL/KEN* L7 .... 113 L5
Dunstan St *WAV* L15 .... 114 A5 3
Dunster Cl *WGNE/HIN* WN2.................. 80 C4
Dunster Gv *HES* CH60 .... 141 K6 1
STHEL WA9 .... 118 F1
Dunster Rd *STHP* PR8 .... 35 G5
Durban Rd *CLB/OSW/ST* L13.................. 114 D3
WAL/NB CH45.................. 95 K7
Durden St *EHL/KEN* L7.................. 113 L6
Durham Av *NTHTN* L30.................. 84 C4
Durham Cl *WARR* WA1 .... 123 G6 2
Durham Ms East *NTHTN* L30 .... 84 C4 2
Durham Ms West *NTHTN* L30 .... 84 C4 3
Durham Rd *LITH* L21 .... 83 G6
WDN WA8 .... 134 D2 2
Durham St *ALL/GAR* L19 .... 145 M1
WGN WN1.................. 5 K2
Durham Wy *NTHTN* L30.................. 84 C4
Durley Dr *CL/PREN* CH43.................. 127 G4
Durley Rd *WLT/FAZ* L9 .... 84 D7
Durlston Cl *WDN* WA8 .... 133 L3
Durning Rd *EHL/KEN* L7 .... 113 L3
Durrant Rd *NG/CROX* L11 .... 98 A5
Durrell Wy *GOL/RIS/CU* WA3.................. 93 G5
Dursley *RAIN/WH* L35.................. 117 H3
Dursley Dr *AIMK* WN4 .... 91 M1
Durston Rd *CHLDW* L16.................. 114 F5
Durweston Wk *NTHLY* L27 .... 115 L7 2
Dutch Barn Cl *CHLY/EC* PR7 .... 32 D3
Dutton Dr *BEB* CH63 .... 143 H3
Dutton Gn *EP* CH65 .... 21 K9
Dutton St *WARR* WA1.................. 15 G6
Duxbury Cl *MGHL* L31 .... 73 G2 1
RNFD/HAY WA11 .... 76 B6
Duxbury Hall Rd *CHLY/EC* PR7 .... 43 M1
Duxford Ct
WARRN/WOL WA2 .... 122 A4 5
Dwerryhouse La *NG/CROX* L11 .... 98 D3
Dwerryhouse St *TOX* L8 .... 112 F7 2
Dyers La *ORM* L39 .... 63 G1
Dyer St *GOL/RIS/CU* WA3.................. 92 B5
Dyke St *NPK/KEN* L6 .... 113 J1
Dykin Cl *WDN* WA8 .... 135 G2
Dykin Rd *WDN* WA8 .... 134 F2
Dymchurch Rd *SPK/HALE* L24 .... 146 D1
Dymoke Rd *NG/CROX* L11 .... 98 E2
Dyson Hall Dr *WLT/FAZ* L9.................. 84 F8
Dyson St *ANF/KKDL* L4.................. 97 H4

E

Eager La *MGHL* L31 .... 61 K5
Eagle Brow *LYMM* WA13.................. 139 M2
Eagle Crs *RNFD/HAY* WA11 .... 76 C7
Eaglehall Rd *WLT/FAZ* L9.................. 98 B1
Eaglehurst Rd *WLTN* L25.................. 131 K1
Eagle La *GTS/LS* CH66 .... 155 M6
Eagles Ct *KKBY* L32.................. 86 A4
Eaglesfield Cl *STHEL* WA9 .... 102 F6 4
Eagles Wy *RUNC* WA7 .... 150 A7
Ealing Gv *CHLYE* PR6 .... 33 H1
Ealing Rd *WARRW/BUR* WA5.................. 120 C8
WLT/FAZ L9.................. 84 D6
Eamont Av *CHTN/BK* PR9 .... 22 D8
Eanleywood La *RUNC* WA7.................. 150 E6
Eardisley Rd *WAV* L15 .... 114 C7
Earle Cl *NEWLW* WA12 .... 104 B2
Earle Crs *NSTN* CH64 .... 152 F4
Earle Dr *NSTN* CH64 .... 152 F5
Earle Rd *EHL/KEN* L7 .... 113 L5
WDN WA8 .... 16 F6
Earle St *NEWLW* WA12 .... 104 B3
VAUX/LVPD L3 .... 12 D5
Earl Rd *BTL* L20.................. 7 K3
Earl's Cl *CSBY/BLUN* L23 .... 82 F2
Earlsfield Rd *WAV* L15 .... 114 B7
Earls Gdns *EP* CH65 .... 20 A4
Earlston Rd *WAL/NB* CH45 .... 95 J7
Earl St *PS/BROM* CH62.................. 128 D6
STHEL WA9 .... 9 L4
WARRN/WOL WA2 .... 14 F1
WGN WN1.................. 68 E3
WGNE/HIN WN2 .... 69 J6 3
Earls Wy *CHLY/EC* PR7 .... 31 M3
RUNC WA7 .... 150 A6 1
Earlswood *SKEL* WN8.................. 66 A4
Earlswood Cl *HOY* CH47 .... 109 K5 3
Earlwood Gdns
RAIN/WH L35 .... 117 G3 4
Earp St *ALL/GAR* L19.................. 130 E7
Easby Cl *FMBY* L37 .... 59 J3
Easby Rd *ANF/KKDL* L4 .... 96 F6
Easedale Dr *STHP* PR8.................. 47 K1
Easedale Wk
NWD/KWIPK L33 .... 73 M8 4
Easenhall Cl *WDN* WA8 .... 134 D1
Easington Rd *RAIN/WH* L35 .... 101 M7
East Albert Rd *AIG/SPK* L17 .... 129 K1
East Av *GOL/RIS/CU* WA3.................. 92 E4
WARRN/WOL WA2 .... 121 L5
WARRS WA4 .... 137 M4
WARRW/BUR WA5 .... 136 C1
Eastbank St *STHP* PR8.................. 3 G4
Eastbourne Rd *CL/PREN* CH43.................. 10 F6
CSBY/WL L22 .... 82 D3 2
STHP PR8 .... 35 J2
WLT/FAZ L9.................. 84 D6
Eastbourne Wy *NPK/KEN* L6 .... 13 L3
Eastbury Cl *WDN* WA8 .... 118 E8
Eastcliffe Rd *CLB/OSW/ST* L13 .... 114 D2
East Cl *PR/KW* L34 .... 101 J6
Eastcote Rd *ALL/GAR* L19 .... 130 E5
Eastcott Cl *GR/UP/WCH* CH49 .... 125 L2
Eastcroft *NWD/KWIPK* L33 .... 74 B8
Eastcroft Rd *WAL/EG* CH44.................. 111 L2
Eastdale Rd *WARR* WA1 .... 122 C6
WAV L15 .... 114 B5
East Dam Wood Rd
SPK/HALE L24.................. 147 H3
East Dene *SKEL* WN8 .... 53 K3
Easter Ct *WARRW/BUR* WA5 .... 120 D3
Eastern Av *PS/BROM* CH62.................. 143 M1
SPK/HALE L24.................. 147 H3
Eastern Dr *ALL/GAR* L19 .... 130 C6
Eastfield Dr *AIG/SPK* L17.................. 129 L2
Eastfield Wk *KKBY* L32 .... 85 K4
Eastford Rd *WARRS* WA4.................. 137 J4
East Front *RAIN/WH* L35 .... 117 G4
Eastgarth *WGNE/HIN* WN2 .... 80 D3 3
Eastgate Rd *RUNC* WA7.................. 151 G1
Eastham Cl *CHLDW* L16 .... 115 H4
Eastham Crs *STHEL* WA9 .... 118 E1
Eastham Gn *SPK/HALE* L24 .... 147 G1 1
Eastham Ms *PS/BROM* CH62 .... 155 J1
Eastham Rake *GTS/LS* CH66 .... 154 E3
Eastham Village Rd
PS/BROM CH62 .... 144 C8
Eastlake Av *EV* L5.................. 97 H8
East Lancashire Rd *ECCL* WA10 .... 89 H6
GOL/RIS/CU WA3 .... 92 D7
NG/CROX L11 .... 85 K8
NWD/KWIPK L33 .... 86 C7
RNFD/HAY WA11 .... 89 M5
East La *RUNC* WA7 .... 150 B6
SFTN L29.................. 71 K3
East Leigh *SKEL* WN8 .... 65 M4
Eastleigh Dr *PEN/TH* CH61 .... 125 M6 1
East Mains *SPK/HALE* L24 .... 147 J2
Eastman Rd *CLB/OSW/ST* L13 .... 98 A6
East Md *ORM* L39 .... 62 D4
East Meade *MGHL* L31 .... 72 E3
East Millwood Rd
SPK/HALE L24.................. 147 J1
East Mt *WGNW/BIL/O* WN5 .... 67 H7
Easton Cl *WGNS/IIMK* WN3 .... 79 J3
Easton Rd *HUY* L36 .... 115 J2
PS/BROM CH62 .... 128 D5
East Orchard La *WLT/FAZ* L9.................. 84 F6
East Prescot Rd
DV/KA/FCH L14 .... 115 G1
East Rd *DV/KA/FCH* L14.................. 114 E3
SPK/HALE L24.................. 132 D8
East Side *STHEL* WA9 .... 9 M7
East St *AIMK* WN4.................. 91 M1
CHTN/BK PR9.................. 3 L3
CSBY/WL L22 .... 82 F4
PR/KW L34 .... 101 G7 3
VAUX/LVPD L3 .... 12 E5
WAL/EG CH44.................. 112 A3
WDN WA8 .... 17 J1
WGNE/HIN WN2 .... 81 K2 3
East Ter *CHLYE* PR6 .... 32 A1
East Vw *WARRS* WA4 .... 138 D3
Eastview Cl *CL/PREN* CH43 .... 126 F1 2
East Wy *CHLYE* PR6 .... 32 F5

Eastway GR/UP/WCH CH49 126 A1
GTS/LS CH66 155 M6
MGHL L31 72 F3
East Wy MOR/LEA CH46 110 A4
Eastway WDN WA8 133 M4
Eastwell Rd AIMK WN4 91 J2
WGNNW/ST WN6 68 B2
Eastwood AIG/SPK L17 129 J2
RUNC WA7 150 E4
Eastwood Av NEWLW WA12 105 H2 1
Eastwood Gv LEIGH WN7 81 L8
Eastwood Rd
WARRW/BUR WA5 104 B6
Eatock St WGNE/HIN WN2 80 D2 4
Eaton Av BTL L20 83 M7
LITH L21 83 K6
WAL/EG CH44 111 L1
Eaton Cl HUY L36 115 L3
WD/CROXPK L12 98 C6
Eaton Gdns WD/CROXPK L12 98 F8
Eaton Rd ALL/GAR L19 130 C7
CL/PREN CH43 10 D7
ECCL WA10 88 F7
MGHL L31 72 F7
WD/CROXPK L12 98 D6
WKBY CH48 124 C4
Eaton Rd North
WD/CROXPK L12 98 C6
Eaton St PR/KW L34 100 F7
RUNC WA7 19 G4
VAUX/LVPD L3 12 E4
WAL/EG CH44 111 K1
Eaves Brow Rd
GOL/RIS/CU WA3 106 D6
Eavesdale SKEL WN8 66 A5
Eaves Green Rd CHLY/EC PR7 32 D8
Eaves La CHLYE PR6 33 G6
STHEL WA9 102 D7
Ebenezer Howard Rd LITH L21 83 L3
Ebenezer Rd EHL/KEN L7 113 L2 1
Ebenezer St RF/TRAN CH42 128 C3
RNFD/HAY WA11 90 B7
Eberle St CLVP L2 12 F6 4
Ebony Cl MOR/LEA CH46 109 K5 4
Ebony Wy NWD/KWIPK L33 74 A8
Ebor La EV L5 13 J2
Ebrington St ALL/GAR L19 130 E7
Ecclesall Av LITH L21 83 L5
Eccles Dr WLTN L25 115 K6 4
Ecclesfield Rd ECCL WA10 88 C8
Eccles Gv STHEL WA9 119 G2
Eccleshall Rd PS/BROM CH62 128 E7
Eccleshill Rd CLB/OSW/ST L13 98 C8
Eccles Rd FMBY L37 58 F4 1
WGNW/BIL/O WN5 67 K5
Eccles's La BRSC L40 40 D6
Eccleston Av GTS/LS CH66 156 A8
PS/BROM CH62 143 L4
Eccleston Cl CL/PREN CH43 127 H2
GOL/RIS/CU WA3 106 E8 2
Eccleston Dr RUNC WA7 19 M6
Eccleston Gdns ECCL WA10 101 J4
Eccleston Rd WLT/FAZ L9 84 B7
Eccleston St ECCL WA10 8 C5
PR/KW L34 100 F7
WGN WN1 4 F1
Eckersley Av WGNE/HIN WN2 80 F2
Eckersley St WGN WN1 5 J1
Edale Cl PS/BROM CH62 144 A8
Edale Dr WGNNW/ST WN6 56 A3
Edale Rd CALD/MH L18 130 C1
Eddisbury Rd GTS/LS CH66 163 H3
WAL/EG CH44 95 L8 3
WKBY CH48 124 C1
Eddisbury Wy WD/CROXPK L12 98 C6
Eddleston St AIMK WN4 79 H7
Edelsten St WARRW/BUR WA5 14 A6
Eden Av CHTN/BK PR9 25 H2
GOL/RIS/CU WA3 107 L1
RNFD/HAY WA11 76 A6
Eden Cl GTS/LS CH66 155 L8 4
NWD/KWIPK L33 74 B7
RAIN/WH L35 117 K3
Edendale WDN WA8 133 K3
Eden Dr North CSBY/BLUN L23 83 J2
Eden Dr South CSBY/BLUN L23 83 J2
Edenfield Cl STHP PR8 36 A2
Edenfield Crs HUY L36 116 B1 3
Edenfield Rd WAV L15 114 B7 3
Eden Gv LEIGH WN7 81 L8
Edenhall Dr WLTN L25 131 M3 2
Edenhurst Av CHLDW L16 115 J5
WAL/EG CH44 95 L8 4
Edenhurst Cl FMBY L37 58 E3
Edenhurst Dr FMBY L37 58 E3 3
Edenpark Rd RF/TRAN CH42 127 L2 2
Edensor Cl WGNNW/ST WN6 68 C1 1
Eden V NTHTN L30 84 B1
Edgar Ct BIRK CH41 11 G4
LITH L21 83 K4 1
Edgars Dr WARRN/WOL WA2 122 C3 1
Edgbaston Cl HUY L36 115 L4 3
Edgbaston Wy CL/PREN CH43 110 E5
Edgefield CHLY/EC PR7 32 D3 1
Edgefield Cl CL/PREN CH43 126 F1 3
Edgefold Rd KKBY L32 86 B4
Edge Green La GOL/RIS/CU WA3 92 B3
Edge Green Rd GOL/RIS/CU WA3 92 B2
Edge Green St AIMK WN4 91 M1
Edge Gv EHL/KEN L7 113 K4
Edge Hall Rd WGNW/BIL/O WN5 78 A1
Edgehill Rd MOR/LEA CH46 109 L5
Edge La CLB/OSW/ST L13 114 A3
CSBY/BLUN L23 71 J7
EHL/KEN L7 113 K4
Edge Lane Dr CLB/OSW/ST L13 114 D4
Edgeley Gdns WLT/FAZ L9 84 B7
Edgemoor Cl CL/PREN CH43 110 D6 3
WD/CROXPK L12 98 F8 1
Edgemoor Dr AIN/FAZ L10 85 J6
CSBY/BLUN L23 71 J8
PEN/TH CH61 125 L6 1
Edgemoor Rd WD/CROXPK L12 98 F8
Edgerley Pl AIMK WN4 91 J2
Edgerton Rd GOL/RIS/CU WA3 93 G5
Edge St RAIN/WH L35 101 L7
Edge Ware Gv WGNS/IIMK WN3 78 F2
Edgeway Rd WGNS/IIMK WN3 79 J4
Edgewood WGNNW/ST WN6 55 J8
Edgewood Dr PS/BROM CH62 143 M8
Edgewood Rd
GR/UP/WCH CH49 110 B7 1
HOY CH47 108 F4
Edgeworth Cl STHEL WA9 103 G5 1
Edgeworth Rd
GOL/RIS/CU WA3 92 B4 2
WGNE/HIN WN2 81 J2
Edgeworth St STHEL WA9 103 G6
Edgley Dr ORM L39 51 J8
Edgworth Rd ANF/KKDL L4 97 K7
Edgworth St WARR WA1 14 D5
Edinburgh Cl NTHTN L30 84 B5
WGNE/HIN WN2 69 J5 2
Edinburgh Dr CL/PREN CH43 127 J4
HUY L36 116 C5
WGNE/HIN WN2 81 K2
WGNW/BIL/O WN5 67 M8
Edinburgh Rd EHL/KEN L7 113 K3 2
FMBY L37 59 G4 2
WAL/NB CH45 95 K8 4
WDN WA8 133 J5
Edington St WAV L15 114 A5 4
Edison Rd RUNC WA7 149 M2
Edith Rd ANF/KKDL L4 97 J7
BTL L20 83 M7
WAL/EG CH44 112 A2
Edith St RUNC WA7 18 F2
STHEL WA9 103 H6 1
WGNS/IIMK WN3 4 C5
Edmondson St STHEL WA9 103 H2 2
Edmonton Cl EV L5 96 F7 3
Edmund Dr LEIGH WN7 81 L8
Edmund St VAUX/LVPD L3 12 E6
Edna Av AIN/FAZ L10 85 J6
Edna Rd LEIGH WN7 81 L6
Edrich Av CL/PREN CH43 110 E5 3
Edward Dr AIMK WN4 91 K1
Edward Gdns WARR WA1 123 H7
Edward Jenner Av NTHTN L30 84 B2
Edward Rd HOY CH47 108 E7
RAIN/WH L35 101 H8
WARRW/BUR WA5 119 M7
Edward's La SPK/HALE L24 131 K7
Edward Steet WGN WN1 68 E3
Edward St CHLYE PR6 32 F6
EP CH65 20 C1 2
RNFD/HAY WA11 90 C7
STHEL WA9 102 F4
VAUX/LVPD L3 13 K7
WDN WA8 17 J1
WGN WN1 5 L4
Edwards Wy WDN WA8 133 L5
Edwin St WDN WA8 17 G1
WGN WN1 5 J4
Effingham St BTL L20 6 E8
Egan Rd CL/PREN CH43 111 G5
Egbert Rd HOY CH47 108 E5
Egdon Cl WDN WA8 135 G3 1
Egerton SKEL WN8 65 M5
Egerton Av WARR WA1 15 M2
Egerton Dr WKBY CH48 124 D3
Egerton Gdns RF/TRAN CH42 128 A4
Egerton Gv CHLY/EC PR7 32 D7
WAL/NB CH45 95 K8
Egerton Park Cl RF/TRAN CH42 128 A4
Egerton Rd LYMM WA13 139 L3
PR/KW L34 100 E7
PS/BROM CH62 128 D6
WAV L15 113 M6
Egerton St EP CH65 20 C2
RUNC WA7 18 F2
STHEL WA9 102 F4
TOX L8 113 H6
WAL/NB CH45 95 K5
WARR WA1 15 H5
WARRS WA4 137 L4
WGNE/HIN WN2 80 D6
Egerton Whf BIRK CH41 11 K3
Eglington Av RAIN/WH L35 116 F3 1
Egremont Cl NTHLY L27 132 C1 1
Egremont Prom WAL/EG CH44 95 M7
Egremont Rd NTHLY L27 132 C1
Egypt St WARR WA1 14 D6
WDN WA8 16 B5
Eight Acre La FMBY L37 47 K7
Eighth Av WLT/FAZ L9 84 F6 1
Eilian Gv DV/KA/FCH L14 114 F3
Eisenhower Cl
WARRW/BUR WA5 120 D8 2
Elaine Cl AIMK WN4 79 M8
GTS/LS CH66 162 E1
WDN WA8 17 G1
Elaine St TOX L8 113 H7
WARR WA1 15 K2
Elbow La FMBY L37 59 H2
Elbow St CHLY/EC PR7 32 E6
Elcombe Av GOL/RIS/CU WA3 93 G6
Elderberry Cl WGN WN1 68 D1 1
Elderdale Rd ANF/KKDL L4 97 K6
Elder Gdns ALL/GAR L19 130 D5
Eldersfield Rd NG/CROX L11 98 D3
Elderswood Rd RAIN/WH L35 117 L1
Elderwood Rd
RF/TRAN CH42 128 A2 1
Eldon Cl ECCL WA10 8 C7
Eldon Gdns AIMK WN4 79 J7
Eldonian Wy VAUX/LVPD L3 12 E2
Eldon Pl VAUX/LVPD L3 12 F2
Eldon Rd RF/TRAN CH42 128 B3
WAL/EG CH44 111 K1
Eldons Cft STHP PR8 34 F8
Eldon St CHLYE PR6 32 F6
ECCL WA10 8 C7
LEIGH WN7 81 M7
VAUX/LVPD L3 12 F2
WARR WA1 15 H4
Eldon Ter NSTN CH64 153 G6 2
Eldred Rd CHLDW L16 114 E7
Eleanor Rd BTL L20 83 M7
CL/PREN CH43 110 F5
MOR/LEA CH46 109 L4
Eleanor St BTL L20 6 F9
EP CH65 20 D2
WDN WA8 16 D6 1
WGNS/IIMK WN3 4 B6
Elephant La RAIN/WH L35 101 M6
STHEL WA9 102 A6
Elfet St BIRK CH41 111 H5 3
Elgar Av PS/BROM CH62 144 A8
Elgar Cl EP CH65 163 H2
Elgar Rd DV/KA/FCH L14 99 H8
Elgin Av AIMK WN4 90 F1
WARRS WA4 137 J3
Elgin Cl WGNE/HIN WN2 69 J5
Elgin Dr WAL/NB CH45 95 L7
Elgin Wy BIRK CH41 11 K4
Eliot Cl PS/BROM CH62 128 C6
Eliot Dr WGNS/IIMK WN3 68 C8
Eliot St BTL L20 83 K8
Elizabethan Dr WGNE/HIN WN2 80 A1
Elizabeth Av STHP PR8 35 G7
WGNE/HIN WN2 81 G4
Elizabeth Ct WDN WA8 16 E6
Elizabeth Dr WARR WA1 122 C5
Elizabeth Rd AIN/FAZ L10 85 K6
BTL L20 83 M7
HUY L36 116 C5
RNFD/HAY WA11 91 G6
Elizabeth St STHEL WA9 119 G2 2
VAUX/LVPD L3 13 M6 1
WGNE/HIN WN2 69 K5 2
Eliza St STHEL WA9 103 H6 2
Elkan Cl WDN WA8 135 G2
Elkan Rd WDN WA8 134 F2
Elkstone Cl WGNS/IIMK WN3 78 E3
Elkstone Rd NG/CROX L11 98 D4
Elkwood Cl WGN WN1 68 D1
Ellaby Rd RAIN/WH L35 117 L1
Ellamsbridge Rd STHEL WA9 103 G6
Elland Dr GTS/LS CH66 155 L8
Ellel Gv NPK/KEN L6 97 L8
Ellen Gdn STHEL WA9 103 G6
Ellen's Cl NPK/KEN L6 113 J3
Ellen's La BEB CH63 128 C8
Ellen St STHEL WA9 103 G6
WARRW/BUR WA5 14 B2
WGN WN1 5 G5
Elleray Park Rd WAL/NB CH45 95 J6
Eller Brook Cl CHLYE PR6 44 B4
Ellerbrook Dr BRSC L40 52 B2 3
BRSC L40 52 B2 3
Ellerbrook Wy ORM L39 51 G7 2
Ellerby Cl RUNC WA7 151 G6
Ellergreen Rd NG/CROX L11 98 B3
Ellerman Rd VAUX/LVPD L3 129 H2
Ellerslie Av RAIN/WH L35 101 L8
Ellerslie Rd CLB/OSW/ST L13 97 M7
Ellerton Av GTS/LS CH66 155 L8
Ellerton Cl WDN WA8 133 M2
Ellerton Wy WD/CROXPK L12 99 G2
Ellesmere Dr AIN/FAZ L10 84 E3
Ellesmere Gv WAL/NB CH45 95 K7
Ellesmere Rd AIMK WN4 79 H8
GOL/RIS/CU WA3 107 G1
WARRS WA4 137 K4
WGNW/BIL/O WN5 67 M7
Ellesmere St RUNC WA7 19 J3
WARR WA1 15 G6
Ellesworth Cl
WARRW/BUR WA5 120 E5
Elliot St CLVPS L1 13 H7
ECCL WA10 8 C5
WDN WA8 16 E3 1
Elliott Av GOL/RIS/CU WA3 92 D4
WARR WA1 15 L2
Elliott Dr WGNE/HIN WN2 69 M6
Ellis Ashton St HUY L36 116 C3
Ellis La FROD/HEL WA6 160 F4
Ellison Dr ECCL WA10 101 L1
Ellison Gv HUY L36 115 M3
Ellison St CLB/OSW/ST L13 114 B1
WARRS WA4 137 M4 1
Ellis Pl TOX L8 113 H8
Ellis Rd WGNW/BIL/O WN5 89 M1
Ellis St WDN WA8 16 B6
WGN WN1 5 J1
Ellon Av RAIN/WH L35 117 M3
Elloway Rd SPK/HALE L24 147 J2
Elmar Rd AIG/SPK L17 130 A3
Elm Av AIMK WN4 78 F8
CSBY/BLUN L23 71 H8
GOL/RIS/CU WA3 92 C4
GR/UP/WCH CH49 109 M7
WDN WA8 134 D3
WGNNW/ST WN6 56 B5
WGNW/BIL/O WN5 68 A7
Elmbank Rd CALD/MH L18 114 A8 1
PS/BROM CH62 128 D7 2
Elmbank St WAL/EG CH44 111 L2 2
Elm Cl PEN/TH CH61 141 H1
WD/CROXPK L12 99 H2
Elm Cft WGN WN1 68 D1
Elmcroft La HTWN L38 70 C2
Elmdale Cl FMBY L37 58 F3 1
Elmdale Rd WLT/FAZ L9 97 J1
Elmdene Ct
GR/UP/WCH CH49 125 L3 3
Elm Dr FMBY L37 58 F4
GR/UP/WCH CH49 125 L2
LITH L21 83 H7
WGNW/BIL/O WN5 77 M8
Elmer's Green La SKEL WN8 65 M3
Elmers Wood Rd SKEL WN8 65 M3
Elmfield WGNNW/ST WN6 55 K7
Elmfield Cl STHEL WA9 102 A5
Elmfield Rd WGN WN1 56 D8
WLT/FAZ L9 84 C8 2
Elm Gdns LITH L21 83 J7 1
RNFD/HAY WA11 76 B7 1
Elm Gv CHLYE PR6 33 G3
EHL/KEN L7 113 J4
GTS/LS CH66 163 G1
HOY CH47 108 D6
PR/KW L34 101 H6
RF/TRAN CH42 11 H9
SKEL WN8 65 G4 1
WARR WA1 122 B6
WDN WA8 16 E1
Elm Hall Dr CALD/MH L18 114 C8
Elmham Crs AIN/FAZ L10 85 H6
Elm House Ms WLTN L25 131 K1
Elmhow Gv WGNS/IIMK WN3 79 J3
Elmhurst Rd WLTN L25 115 J6
Elmore Cl EV L5 97 H8 3
RUNC WA7 150 F4
Elm Park Rd WAL/NB CH45 95 J6
Elm Pl ORM L39 63 G1
Elmridge SKEL WN8 65 M5
Elm Ri FROD/HEL WA6 160 E6
Elm Rd ANF/KKDL L4 97 J4
BEB CH63 128 B6
BRSC L40 52 A2
ECCL WA10 101 M5
KKBY L32 85 M2
LITH L21 83 H7
NSTN CH64 154 B5
PEN/TH CH61 126 B7
RF/TRAN CH42 127 M2
RNFD/HAY WA11 91 G6 4
RUNC WA7 19 M7
STHP PR8 3 G9
WARRN/WOL WA2 121 K1
WARRW/BUR WA5 136 B2
WGNE/HIN WN2 80 E6
Elm Rd North RF/TRAN CH42 127 K3
Elmsbury St AIMK WN4 79 J8 3
Elmsdale Rd CALD/MH L18 114 C8
Elmsett Cl WARRW/BUR WA5 120 A8
Elmsfield Cl WLTN L25 115 J8
Elmsfield Pk ORM L39 62 C7
Elmsfield Rd CSBY/BLUN L23 71 K7
Elms House Rd
CLB/OSW/ST L13 114 B2
Elmsley Rd CALD/MH L18 130 B1
Elms Rd MGHL L31 72 E7
Elmstead SKEL WN8 65 M5
The Elms GOL/RIS/CU WA3 93 H5
MGHL L31 72 F2 3
RUNC WA7 18 F6
TOX L8 129 J1
Elm St BIRK CH41 11 H5
HUY L36 116 C3
WGNE/HIN WN2 80 C3 5
Elmswood Av RAIN/WH L35 117 M3
Elmswood Gv HUY L36 115 L2 1
Elmswood Rd AIG/SPK L17 130 A3
RF/TRAN CH42 127 L1
WAL/EG CH44 111 M1
Elm Ter HOY CH47 108 E6 2
Elm Tree Av LYMM WA13 139 M3
WARR WA1 122 B5
Elmtree Cl WD/CROXPK L12 98 E6
Elmtree Gv CL/PREN CH43 111 G5 2
Elm Tree Rd GOL/RIS/CU WA3 93 H6 1
LYMM WA13 139 M3
Elmure Av BEB CH63 127 M8
Elm V NPK/KEN L6 113 M2
Elmwood CHLY/EC PR7 32 D4
RUNC WA7 150 E4
SKEL WN8 65 L2 1
Elmwood Av AIMK WN4 91 J3 4
CSBY/BLUN L23 83 H1
WARR WA1 15 L2
Elmwood Dr PEN/TH CH61 141 H3
Elnup Av WGNNW/ST WN6 55 K7
Elphin Gv ANF/KKDL L4 97 J4
Elsbeck Gv STHEL WA9 102 F7 3
Elsie Rd ANF/KKDL L4 97 K7
Elsmere Av AIG/SPK L17 129 L2
Elson Rd FMBY L37 58 F4
Elstead Gv AIMK WN4 90 F1
Elstead Rd KKBY L32 85 L4
WLT/FAZ L9 98 A1
Elston Av NEWLW WA12 91 K8
Elstow St EV L5 96 F6 3
Elstree Rd NPK/KEN L6 113 M2
Elswick SKEL WN8 65 L5
Elswick Rd CHTN/BK PR9 25 H1
Elswick St TOX L8 129 H2
Elsworth Cl FMBY L37 58 E5
Eltham Av LITH L21 83 K4
Eltham Cl AIMK WN4 91 M2 1
GR/UP/WCH CH49 126 D3 2
WDN WA8 135 G2
Eltham Gn GR/UP/WCH CH49 126 C3
Eltham St EHL/KEN L7 113 M3 2
Elton Av CSBY/BLUN L23 82 E1
NTHTN L30 84 A2
Elton Cl GOL/RIS/CU WA3 93 G6
GOL/RIS/CU WA3 122 E1
PS/BROM CH62 155 G2
Elton Dr BEB CH63 143 J3
Elton Head Rd STHEL WA9 101 M8
Elton La FROD/HEL WA6 166 A1
Elton Lordship La
FROD/HEL WA6 159 J6
Elton St ANF/KKDL L4 97 H3
Elvington Cl RUNC WA7 161 H2 2
WGNW/BIL/O WN5 67 K4
Elvington Rd HTWN L38 70 C3
Elway Rd AIMK WN4 91 L2
Elworth Av WDN WA8 118 C8
Elworthy Av HLWD L26 132 B4
Elworthy Gv WGN WN1 69 G3
Elwyn Dr HLWD L26 132 B5
Elwyn Rd HOY CH47 109 G4
Elwy St TOX L8 113 J8
Ely Av MOR/LEA CH46 109 L5
Ely Cl GTS/LS CH66 163 G5
NTHTN L30 84 B4
Ely Ms CHTN/BK PR9 25 J3
Ely Pk RUNC WA7 151 G3
Ember Crs NPK/KEN L6 13 M1
Embledon St TOX L8 113 K6
Embleton Ct RUNC WA7 149 M8
Emerald Cl NTHTN L30 84 D2
Emerald St TOX L8 129 J2 2
WGNNW/ST WN6 68 C2
Emerson Cl HTWN L38 70 C1
Emerson St TOX L8 113 H6
Emery St ANF/KKDL L4 97 H4
Emily St RAIN/WH L35 101 L6
WDN WA8 16 D5
Emlyn St STHEL WA9 102 F4
Emmanuel Rd CHTN/BK PR9 25 H3
Empire Rd LITH L21 83 K7
Empress Cl MGHL L31 72 D4
Empress Rd EHL/KEN L7 113 K3
NPK/KEN L6 97 L7
WAL/EG CH44 111 L1
Empress Wy CHLY/EC PR7 32 A3
Emslie Ct NSTN CH64 152 E5
Ena Crs LEIGH WN7 81 L6
Endborne Rd WLT/FAZ L9 84 C7
Endbutt La CSBY/BLUN L23 83 G2
Enderby Av RNFD/HAY WA11 89 L7
Endfield Pk ALL/GAR L19 130 D5
Endmoor Rd HUY L36 99 L8
Endsleigh Rd CLB/OSW/ST L13 114 A2
CSBY/WL L22 82 D3
Enerby Cl CL/PREN CH43 110 E6
Enfield Av CSBY/BLUN L23 83 G1
Enfield Cl CHLY/EC PR7 30 E7
Enfield Park Rd
WARRN/WOL WA2 122 A1
Enfield Rd CLB/OSW/ST L13 114 D3
EP CH65 20 B4
Enfield St ECCL WA10 8 C7
WGNW/BIL/O WN5 67 L8
Enfield Ter CL/PREN CH43 10 D8
Enford Dr STHEL WA9 102 F6
Engineer St WGNE/HIN WN2 69 J6
Engine La FMBY L37 59 M6
Enid Pl WGNE/HIN WN2 80 B5
Enid St TOX L8 113 H7
Ennerdale SKEL WN8 65 M5
Ennerdale Av AIMK WN4 91 K1 3
MGHL L31 73 G3
PS/BROM CH62 155 H1
RNFD/HAY WA11 89 K5
WARRN/WOL WA2 121 K2
Ennerdale Cl FMBY L37 58 F2 2
NWD/KWIPK L33 73 M8
Ennerdale Dr FROD/HEL WA6 160 E5
NTHTN L30 83 M5
ORM L39 62 D3
Ennerdale Pl WGNE/HIN WN2 69 K5 3
Ennerdale Rd CHLY/EC PR7 32 C7
CL/PREN CH43 127 G4
FMBY L37 58 F2
WAL/NB CH45 95 H5
Ennerdale St VAUX/LVPD L3 13 G2
Ennis Cl SPK/HALE L24 147 M3
Ennisdale Dr WKBY CH48 124 F3
Ennismore Rd CLB/OSW/ST L13 114 B2
CSBY/BLUN L23 70 E8
Ennis Rd WD/CROXPK L12 99 G7
Ensor St BTL L20 6 F9
Enstone SKEL WN8 65 M4
Enstone Av LITH L21 83 J4
Enstone Rd WLTN L25 131 K7 1
Ensworth Rd CALD/MH L18 114 D8 1
Enville St WARRS WA4 15 G8
Envoy Cl WGNW/BIL/O WN5 68 A4
Ephraim's Fold
WGNE/HIN WN2 57 M7 1
Epping Av STHEL WA9 118 D2
Epping Cl RAIN/WH L35 117 M3 3
Epping Ct HES CH60 141 J4 2
Epping Dr WARR WA1 122 F5
Epping Gv WAV L15 114 D7
Epping Pl CHLYE PR6 32 F5
Epsom Cl CHLYE PR6 33 H1
WLT/FAZ L9 85 G4
Epsom Cft CHLYE PR6 44 E6
Epsom Dr WGNE/HIN WN2 80 B6
Epsom Gdns WARRS WA4 138 A6
Epsom Gv NWD/KWIPK L33 74 C7 2
Epsom St STHEL WA9 103 H1
Epsom Wy EV L5 96 F8
Epworth St NPK/KEN L6 13 M5
Eremon Cl WLT/FAZ L9 84 F5 2
Erfurt Av BEB CH63 143 J1
Erica Ct HES CH60 141 G3
Eric Av WARR WA1 122 A5
Eric Gv WAL/EG CH44 111 J1
Eric Rd WAL/EG CH44 111 J1
Eric St WDN WA8 17 G1
Eridge St TOX L8 129 J1
Erin Cl TOX L8 113 G7
Erindale Crs FROD/HEL WA6 160 C7
Erl St WLT/FAZ L9 84 C7 2
Ermine Crs EV L5 97 H8
Erradale Crs WGNS/IIMK WN3 78 F3
Errington Av EP CH65 20 C2 1
Errington Ct AIG/SPK L17 130 A5
Errington St EV L5 96 D7
Errol St AIG/SPK L17 129 K2
Errwood Cl SPK/HALE L24 148 A3
Erskine Cl RNFD/HAY WA11 90 A7
Erskine Pl WGNE/HIN WN2 80 D4
Erskine Rd CHLYE PR6 33 G4
WAL/EG CH44 111 L2
Erskine St NPK/KEN L6 13 M5
Erwood St WARRN/WOL WA2 14 D3
Erylmore Rd CALD/MH L18 130 C4
Escolme Dr GR/UP/WCH CH49 126 A2
Escor Rd WLTN L25 115 H7
Eshelby Cl CSBY/WL L22 83 G4
Esher Cl CL/PREN CH43 110 E6
Eshe Rd CSBY/BLUN L23 82 E1
Eshe Rd North CSBY/BLUN L23 82 E1
Esher Rd NPK/KEN L6 113 L2
RF/TRAN CH42 128 D5 2
Eskbank SKEL WN8 65 L5
Eskbrook SKEL WN8 65 L4
Eskburn Rd CLB/OSW/ST L13 98 A7
Eskdale EP CH65 20 A9
SKEL WN8 65 K5
Eskdale Av ORM L39 62 E3
PS/BROM CH62 144 A8
RNFD/HAY WA11 89 K5
WGN WN1 68 D2
Eskdale Cl FMBY L37 58 F3
RUNC WA7 149 M8
Eskdale Dr FMBY L37 58 F3
MGHL L31 72 F3
Eskdale Rd AIMK WN4 79 K8
WLT/FAZ L9 84 C7
Esk St BTL L20 96 D5
Eslington St ALL/GAR L19 130 C6 3
Esmond St NPK/KEN L6 97 K8
Esonwood Rd RAIN/WH L35 116 F2
Espin St ANF/KKDL L4 97 H4
Esplanade STHP PR8 2 D4
Esplen Av CSBY/BLUN L23 71 H8
Essex Rd HUY L36 116 C1
STHP PR8 35 J5
WGN WN1 56 D5
WKBY CH48 124 E2

Essex St TOX L8 113 H8 3
WGN WN1 5 J2
Esther St WDN WA8 16 F2 1
Esthwaite Av RNFD/HAY WA11 89 L5
Etal Cl NG/CROX L11 98 D4
Ethelbert Rd HOY CH47 108 E5 1
Ethel Rd WAL/EG CH44 111 M2 4
Etna St CLB/OSW/ST L13 114 B2
Eton Ct CALD/MH L18 114 F8
Eton Dr AIN/FAZ L10 84 E3
BEB CH63 142 B7
Eton Hall Dr STHEL WA9 102 E6 1
Eton Rd EP CH65 20 E7
Eton St ANF/KKDL L4 97 H4
Eton Ter WGNS/IIMK WN3 5 J9
Eton Wy WGNW/BIL/O WN5 67 H5
Etruria St ALL/GAR L19 145 L1 4
Etruscan Rd CLB/OSW/ST L13 114 C1
Ettington Dr STHP PR8 34 C8
Ettington Rd ANF/KKDL L4 97 K6
Ettrick Cl NWD/KWIPK L33 73 M7
Euclid Av WARRS WA4 138 D3
Eurolink STHEL WA9 118 B1
Europa Bvd BIRK CH41 11 J4
WARRW/BUR WA5 120 D2
Europa Wy EP CH65 20 D3
Eustace St WARRN/WOL WA2 14 C4
Euston Gv CL/PREN CH43 10 E8
Euston St ANF/KKDL L4 97 H3
Euxton Hall Gdns CHLY/EC PR7 31 L3
Euxton La CHLY/EC PR7 31 M1
CHLY/EC PR7 32 D2
Evans Cl RNFD/HAY WA11 91 H6 2
Evans Pl WARRS WA4 15 K9
Evans Rd HOY CH47 108 D6 2
SPK/HALE L24 131 L8
Evans St PR/KW L34 100 F6
Eva St LEIGH WN7 81 L6
Evellynne Cl KKBY L32 85 L3
Evelyn Av PR/KW L34 101 G7 4
STHEL WA9 103 G2
Evelyn Rd WAL/EG CH44 111 L2 3
Evelyn St WARRW/BUR WA5 136 F1
Evenwood SKEL WN8 65 M4
STHEL WA9 102 E7 3
Everard Cl BRSC L40 37 H6
Everard Rd STHP PR8 3 M9
Everdon Wd NWD/KWIPK L33 86 A2
Evered Av WLT/FAZ L9 97 J1
Everest Cl GTS/LS CH66 163 H2
Everest Pl WGN WN1 68 E3 3
Everest Rd CSBY/BLUN L23 82 F1
RF/TRAN CH42 127 M3
Evergreen Cl
GR/UP/WCH CH49 109 M7
NTHLY L27 116 A7
The Evergreens FMBY L37 58 F2
Everite Rd WDN WA8 133 K6
Everleigh Cl CL/PREN CH43 110 D6
Eversleigh Dr BEB CH63 143 J1 2
Eversley SKEL WN8 65 M4
WDN WA8 133 K3
Eversley Cl FROD/HEL WA6 160 E7
WARRS WA4 138 B8 2
Eversley St TOX L8 113 J7 4
Everton Brow VAUX/LVPD L3 13 K3
Everton Gv RNFD/HAY WA11 89 M8 1
Everton Rd NPK/KEN L6 113 M2
STHP PR8 35 J1
Everton St AIMK WN4 78 F8
Everton Ter EV L5 13 L1
Everton Va ANF/KKDL L4 97 G6
Everton Vw BTL L20 6 E6
Every St NPK/KEN L6 113 K1 2
Evesham Cl LEIGH WN7 93 M4
WARRS WA4 137 L5
WLTN L25 131 H3
Evesham Rd ANF/KKDL L4 97 M4
WAL/NB CH45 95 H7
Evington SKEL WN8 65 M4
Ewanville HUY L36 116 A4 2
Ewart Rd CHLDW L16 115 J5
LITH L21 83 H6
RNFD/HAY WA11 89 K7
Ewden Cl CHLDW L16 115 G6
Ewell Cl CHLYE PR6 33 H5
Ewloe Ct EP CH65 163 M3 4
Exchange Pas West CLVP L2 12 E6 1
Exchange Pl RAIN/WH L35 117 L2 3
Exchange St ECCL WA10 9 G6
Exchange St East CLVP L2 12 E6
Exeley RAIN/WH L35 117 G3
Exeter Cl WLT/FAZ L9 85 G4
Exeter Dr WGNE/HIN WN2 57 M8
Exeter Rd BTL L20 7 G7
EP CH65 20 C4
WAL/EG CH44 95 L8
Exeter St ECCL WA10 8 B5
Exford Av WGNS/IIMK WN3 79 K1
Exford Rd WD/CROXPK L12 98 F5
Exmoor Cl CHTN/BK PR9 22 D7 1
PEN/TH CH61 126 B8
Exmouth Cl BIRK CH41 11 G5 1
Exmouth Crs RUNC WA7 151 G7
Exmouth Gdns BIRK CH41 11 G5
Exmouth St BIRK CH41 11 G6
Exmouth Wy BIRK CH41 11 G5
WARRW/BUR WA5 104 B7 4
Extension Vw STHEL WA9 102 F5
Eyes La LEY/BBR PR5 28 F2

F

Factory Brow HOR/BR BL6 57 M2
Factory Fold WGNE/HIN WN2 69 J6 4
Factory La CHLYE PR6 44 D5 3
WARR WA1 14 C7 1
WDN WA8 134 D2
Faggy La WGNS/IIMK WN3 4 F6
Fairacre Rd ALL/GAR L19 130 C6
Fairacres WGNNW/ST WN6 55 K4
Fairacres Rd BEB CH63 143 H1
Fairbairn Rd CSBY/WL L22 83 G4
Fairbank St WAV L15 114 A6
Fairbeech Ct CL/PREN CH43 110 E6 2
Fairbourne Av
WGNS/IIMK WN3 79 J1 2
Fairbourne Cl
WARRW/BUR WA5 121 G2 1
Fairbrook Dr BIRK CH41 110 F4
Fairbrother Crs
WARRN/WOL WA2 121 M3
Fairburn SKEL WN8 65 K2
Fairburn Cl WDN WA8 135 G2 3
Fairburn Rd CLB/OSW/ST L13 98 A7
Fairclough Av WARR WA1 15 G7
Fairclough Crs RNFD/HAY WA11 90 C7
Fairclough La CL/PREN CH43 127 K1
Fairclough Rd ECCL WA10 101 L1
HUY L36 99 L7
RAIN/WH L35 117 K2
Fairclough St CLVPS L1 13 H8 2
NEWLW WA12 104 D2
WARRW/BUR WA5 104 A7
WGN WN1 5 G6
WGNE/HIN WN2 69 M7
Fairfax Dr RUNC WA7 149 M3
Fairfax Pl NG/CROX L11 97 M3
Fairfax Rd NG/CROX L11 98 A3
RF/TRAN CH42 128 A1
Fairfield CSBY/BLUN L23 83 G1
Fairfield Av DV/KA/FCH L14 115 J3
EP CH65 163 J3
WGNE/HIN WN2 80 C3
WGNW/BIL/O WN5 67 M8 3
Fairfield Cl HUY L36 115 J3
ORM L39 51 G6
Fairfield Crs HUY L36 115 J3
MOR/LEA CH46 109 M5
NPK/KEN L6 113 M2
Fairfield Dr ORM L39 51 G6 1
WKBY CH48 125 G2
Fairfield Gdns RNFD/HAY WA11 89 G3
WARRS WA4 138 A3
Fairfield Rd ECCL WA10 88 E8
RF/TRAN CH42 128 A3
STHP PR8 34 E7
WARRS WA4 137 M3
WDN WA8 16 E1
Fairfield St EHL/KEN L7 114 A2
WARR WA1 15 H3
WGNW/BIL/O WN5 67 L8
Fairford Crs DV/KA/FCH L14 114 D1
Fairford Rd DV/KA/FCH L14 114 D1
Fairhaven NWD/KWIPK L33 74 A8
SKEL WN8 65 K2
Fairhaven Cl RF/TRAN CH42 128 B3 2
WARRW/BUR WA5 136 D1 3
Fairhaven Dr BEB CH63 143 L8
Fairhaven Rd CHTN/BK PR9 25 K1
WDN WA8 134 E3
Fairholme Av AIMK WN4 91 K1
NSTN CH64 152 F4 1
PR/KW L34 101 J7
Fairholme Cl WD/CROXPK L12 98 C5 1
Fairholme Rd CSBY/BLUN L23 83 G1
Fairhurst Av WGNNW/ST WN6 55 M2
Fairhurst's Dr SKEL WN8 53 K3 1
Fairhurst St WGNS/IIMK WN3 4 C4
Fairlawn Cl BEB CH63 143 J7
Fairlawne Cl NWD/KWIPK L33 74 A8 4
NWD/KWIPK L33 86 A1 3
Fairlie SKEL WN8 65 L2
Fairlie Crs BTL L20 83 M6
Fairlie Dr RAIN/WH L35 117 M3
Fairmead Rd MOR/LEA CH46 110 A4
NG/CROX L11 98 A3
Fairoak Cl CL/PREN CH43 110 E6
Fairstead SKEL WN8 65 L2
Fair Vw WGNW/BIL/O WN5 77 M8
Fairview Av WAL/NB CH45 95 J8
Fair View Av
WGNW/BIL/O WN5 77 M8 2
Fairview Cl AIMK WN4 91 K1
CL/PREN CH43 127 K2
Fair View Pl TOX L8 129 J1 2
Fairview Rd CL/PREN CH43 127 K2
GTS/LS CH66 163 J3
Fairview Wy PEN/TH CH61 141 H2
Fair Wy ECCL WA10 88 E8
Fairway CHLY/EC PR7 32 E3
CHTN/BK PR9 24 E3
HUY L36 116 C1
Fairway Crs PS/BROM CH62 143 M1
Fairway North PS/BROM CH62 143 M1
Fairways CSBY/BLUN L23 70 F8
FROD/HEL WA6 160 F6
WARRS WA4 137 M8
Fairways Cl WLTN L25 131 K5
Fairways Ct FMBY L37 46 E8
Fairways Dr GTS/LS CH66 155 M6
Fairway South PS/BROM CH62 143 M2
The Fairways AIMK WN4 90 F3 1
SKEL WN8 65 M2 2
The Fairway WD/CROXPK L12 114 F1
Faith St LEIGH WN7 81 L8
Falcondale Rd
WARRN/WOL WA2 105 K7
Falconers Gn
WARRW/BUR WA5 120 D3
WGNS/IIMK WN3 68 D8 1
Falconer St BTL L20 83 J7
Falconhall Rd WLT/FAZ L9 98 B1
Falcon Hey AIN/FAZ L10 85 J7
Falcon Rd GTS/LS CH66 163 H2
RF/TRAN CH42 10 E9
Falcons Wy RUNC WA7 150 A7
Falconwood Cl WGNNW/ST WN6 4 B2
Falkirk Dr WGNE/HIN WN2 69 J5 3
Falkirk Gv WGNW/BIL/O WN5 67 L5
Falkland SKEL WN8 65 L2
Falkland Dr AIMK WN4 78 E7
Falkland Rd STHP PR8 3 L9
WAL/EG CH44 111 M1
Falklands Ap NG/CROX L11 98 A3 1
Falkland St BIRK CH41 10 A2
VAUX/LVPD L3 13 L5 1
Falkner Sq TOX L8 113 J6
Falkner St TOX L8 113 H5 13
Fallbrook Dr WD/CROXPK L12 98 D5
Fallow Cl STHEL WA9 118 E1 6
Fallowfield NWD/KWIPK L33 74 A8 5
RUNC WA7 149 M4
Fallowfield Gv
WARRN/WOL WA2 122 D4
Fallowfield Rd WAV L15 114 B7
Fallows Wy RAIN/WH L35 116 E4
Falmouth Dr WARRW/BUR WA5 136 A2
Falmouth Pl RUNC WA7 151 G7
Falmouth Rd NG/CROX L11 85 M8
Falstaff St BTL L20 96 E5 1
Falstone Cl GOL/RIS/CU WA3 107 K7
WGNS/IIMK WN3 79 G3 2
Falstone Dr RUNC WA7 151 G5
Fanner's La KNUT WA16 139 L8
Faraday Cl WGNNW/ST WN6 4 A4
Faraday Rd CLB/OSW/ST L13 114 A4
EP CH65 163 J1
NWD/KWIPK L33 86 D6
Faraday St EV L5 97 J8
GOL/RIS/CU WA3 107 G8
Fardon Cl WGNS/IIMK WN3 79 H2
Farefield Av GOL/RIS/CU WA3 92 B3
Fareham Rd EHL/KEN L7 113 M3 2
Faringdon Cl WLTN L25 131 K7 2
Faringdon Rd
WARRN/WOL WA2 105 K7
Farley Av PS/BROM CH62 143 L4
Farley La SKEL WN8 66 C2
Farlow Rd RF/TRAN CH42 128 B4
Farm Av CHLYE PR6 44 C5
Farmbrook Rd WLTN L25 115 K7 2
Farm Cl CHTN/BK PR9 25 J5
GR/UP/WCH CH49 125 L1
Farmdale Cl CALD/MH L18 130 D3
Farmdale Dr CHNE CH2 165 J2
MGHL L31 73 G4
Far Meadow La PEN/TH CH61 125 L7
Farmer Pl BTL L20 84 A6 1
Farmers Heath GTS/LS CH66 162 F3
Farmer's La WARRW/BUR WA5 104 C7
Farmfield Dr CL/PREN CH43 110 E6
Farm La WARRS WA4 138 A5
WGNE/HIN WN2 69 J3
Farmleigh Gdns
WARRW/BUR WA5 120 E7
Farm Meadow Rd
WGNW/BIL/O WN5 67 G8
Far Moss Rd CSBY/BLUN L23 70 D7
Farm Rd STHEL WA9 118 F2
Farmside MOR/LEA CH46 110 B2
Farmside Cl
WARRW/BUR WA5 121 G6 3
Farmstead Wy GTS/LS CH66 163 G4
Farm Vw LITH L21 83 K3
Farmview Cl NTHLY L27 115 L6
Farm Wy NEWLW WA12 105 G4
Farnborough Gv HLWD L26 132 B4 1
Farnborough Rd STHP PR8 35 H5
Farndale WDN WA8 118 C8
Farndale Cl WARRW/BUR WA5 120 B6
Farndale Gv AIMK WN4 91 L3
Farndon Av STHEL WA9 118 D1
WAL/NB CH45 95 G7
Farndon Dr WKBY CH48 125 G2
Farndon Rd GTS/LS CH66 156 A7
Farndon Wy CL/PREN CH43 127 H1
Farne Cl EP CH65 163 L5 1
Farnham Cl WARRS WA4 138 A6
Farnhill Cl RUNC WA7 150 F5
Farnley Cl RUNC WA7 150 F4
Farnsfield WGN WN1 5 M2
Farnworth Av
MOR/LEA CH46 110 B2 2
Farnworth Cl WDN WA8 134 D1 6
Farnworth Gv
NWD/KWIPK L33 74 A8 6
Farnworth Rd
WARRW/BUR WA5 135 M1
Farnworth St NPK/KEN L6 113 K2
STHEL WA9 9 L4
WDN WA8 134 D1
Farrant St WDN WA8 16 F3
Farrar St CLB/OSW/ST L13 97 M6
Farr Cl WGNS/IIMK WN3 68 B8
Farrell Cl MGHL L31 85 K1 2
Farrell Rd WARRS WA4 137 L5
Farrell St WARR WA1 15 J5
WGNW/BIL/O WN5 67 L8
Farr Hall Dr HES CH60 141 G6
Farr Hall Rd HES CH60 141 G5
Farrier Rd NWD/KWIPK L33 86 C3
Farrier's Cft WGNNW/ST WN6 68 A2
Farriers Wy WKBY CH48 125 K3
Farrier Wk STHEL WA9 118 E1 7
Farringdon Cl STHEL WA9 102 B7 2
Farrington Dr ORM L39 51 G7
Farrington St CHLY/EC PR7 32 E5 1
Farthing Cl WLTN L25 131 J6
The Farthings CHLY/EC PR7 32 B4
Farthingstone Cl
RAIN/WH L35 101 J7 3
Fatherside Dr NTHTN L30 83 L2 3
Faulkner Cl STHP PR8 34 E8
Faulkner Gdns STHP PR8 34 E7 1
Faversham Rd NG/CROX L11 98 A2
Fawcett SKEL WN8 65 K2
Fawcett Rd MGHL L31 72 F2
Fawley Rd CALD/MH L18 130 E3
RAIN/WH L35 118 A4
Fazakerley Rd RAIN/WH L35 117 G1
WLT/FAZ L9 97 J1
Fazakerley St CHLY/EC PR7 32 E5 3
VAUX/LVPD L3 12 E6 2
Fearnhead Av HOR/BR BL6 45 K8
Fearnhead La
WARRN/WOL WA2 122 C3
WARRN/WOL WA2 122 E2
Fearnley Rd BIRK CH41 11 H7
Fearnside St EHL/KEN L7 113 L5
Feather La HES CH60 141 G5 2
Feeny St STHEL WA9 118 D3 1
Feilden Rd BEB CH63 143 J1
Felicity Gv MOR/LEA CH46 109 M4
Fellery St CHLY/EC PR7 32 E5
Fell Gv RNFD/HAY WA11 89 J5
Fellside WGN WN1 68 F3
Fell St EHL/KEN L7 113 K3
LEIGH WN7 81 L8
WAL/EG CH44 112 A3
Felltor Cl WLTN L25 131 H2
Fell Vw CHLYE PR6 33 G7
Fellview CHTN/BK PR9 22 F7
Fellwood Gv RAIN/WH L35 117 G3
Felmersham Gn NG/CROX L11 98 B2
Felspar Rd KKBY L32 86 A6
Felstead SKEL WN8 65 K3
Felsted Av WLTN L25 131 L3 2
Felsted Dr AIN/FAZ L10 85 G4
Felthorpe Cl GR/UP/WCH CH49 110 D6
Felton Gv CLB/OSW/ST L13 114 B1 2
Feltons SKEL WN8 65 K3
Feltwell Rd ANF/KKDL L4 97 K7
Feltwood Cl WD/CROXPK L12 99 H6
Feltwood Rd WD/CROXPK L12 99 H5
Fender La MOR/LEA CH46 110 C4
Fenderside Rd CL/PREN CH43 110 E5
Fender View Rd
MOR/LEA CH46 110 C5
Fender Wy CL/PREN CH43 110 D5
PEN/TH CH61 141 J1
Fenham Dr WARRW/BUR WA5 136 A1
Fennel St WARR WA1 15 G5
Fenney Ct SKEL WN8 65 L4
Fenton Cl ECCL WA10 8 E3
NTHTN L30 84 D5
SPK/HALE L24 146 F2 1
WDN WA8 133 L2 6
Fenton Gn SPK/HALE L24 146 F3 1
Fenwick La RUNC WA7 149 M7
Fenwick Rd GTS/LS CH66 163 G3
Fenwick St CLVP L2 12 E7
Ferguson Av GR/UP/WCH CH49 125 L2
GTS/LS CH66 156 A7
Ferguson Dr
WARRN/WOL WA2 121 M4 1
Ferguson Ri
WGNW/BIL/O WN5 68 A5 1
Ferguson Rd LITH L21 83 L4
NG/CROX L11 98 A5
Fern Av NEWLW WA12 104 F3
Fern Bank CHLYE PR6 32 F2
RNFD/HAY WA11 76 A6
Fernbank Av HUY L36 115 M3
Fernbank Cl
GOL/RIS/CU WA3 123 G1 1
Fernbank Dr NTHTN L30 84 C1
Fern Cl GOL/RIS/CU WA3 122 F1
NTHLY L27 132 A1
SKEL WN8 65 G4
WGNNW/ST WN6 55 J7
Ferndale SKEL WN8 65 K3
Ferndale Av CHNE CH2 165 J2
WAL/EG CH44 111 L1 2
WKBY CH48 125 K4
Ferndale Cl WARR WA1 122 E6
WDN WA8 119 G6
WLT/FAZ L9 84 C6
Ferndale Rd CSBY/WL L22 82 F3
HOY CH47 108 D6
WAV L15 114 A7
Fern Gdns PR/KW L34 101 H6
Fern Gv BTL L20 7 H3
CL/PREN CH43 126 F1 6
TOX L8 113 L7
Fern Hey CSBY/BLUN L23 71 J8
Fern Hl WAL/NB CH45 95 K5
Fernhill Av BTL L20 7 L4
Fernhill Cl BTL L20 7 L5
Fernhill Dr TOX L8 113 J7
Fernhill Ms East BTL L20 7 L5 2
Fernhill Ms West BTL L20 7 L5 1
Fernhill Rd BTL L20 83 M8
Fernhurst RUNC WA7 149 M5
Fernhurst Cl WGNS/IIMK WN3 5 L8
Fernhurst Ga ORM L39 62 D3
Fernhurst Rd KKBY L32 85 M5
Fernie Crs TOX L8 113 G8
Fernlea Av RAIN/WH L35 101 M6 4
Fernlea Gv AIMK WN4 78 F8
Fernlea Ms CL/PREN CH43 110 E5 4
Fernlea Rd HES CH60 141 J5
Fernleigh Rd
CLB/OSW/ST L13 114 D2 1
Fernley Rd STHP PR8 2 F8
Fern Rd EP CH65 163 J3
Ferns Cl HES CH60 140 E4
Fernside Gv WGNS/IIMK WN3 78 F4 2
Ferns Rd BEB CH63 127 M8
Fernwood Dr HLWD L26 132 B5 3
Fernwood Rd AIG/SPK L17 130 A3
Ferny Brow Rd
GR/UP/WCH CH49 126 D2
Ferny Knoll Rd RNFD/HAY WA11 76 B1
Ferrer St AIMK WN4 79 H7
Ferrey Rd AIN/FAZ L10 85 J6
Ferries Cl RF/TRAN CH42 128 C5 3
Ferry La WARRS WA4 139 G1
Ferry Rd PS/BROM CH62 144 C8
Ferryside WAL/EG CH44 112 A3
Ferry Side La CHTN/BK PR9 22 E8
Ferry View Rd WAL/EG CH44 112 A3
Festival Av WARRN/WOL WA2 121 M3
Festival Crs WARRN/WOL WA2 121 M3
Festival Rd EP CH65 156 B8
RNFD/HAY WA11 76 C8
Festival Wy RUNC WA7 19 L7
Ffrancon Dr BEB CH63 128 B6
Fiddlers Ferry Rd WDN WA8 17 J3
Fidler St ECCL WA10 101 M4
Field Av LITH L21 83 J5
Field Cl BRSC L40 52 B2
PS/BROM CH62 128 D5 3
Fielden St CHLYE PR6 33 G5
Fieldfare Cl GOL/RIS/CU WA3 92 F5
GOL/RIS/CU WA3 123 H1 1
WLTN L25 115 J8
Fieldgate WDN WA8 133 K7
Field Hey La NSTN CH64 154 D4
Fielding Pl CHLYE PR6 44 D5
The Fieldings MGHL L31 72 D1 1
Fielding St EHL/KEN L7 113 J3 4
Fieldlands STHP PR8 36 C3
Field La AIN/FAZ L10 85 K6
LITH L21 83 J4
WARRS WA4 137 L7
Field Rd STHEL WA9 118 F2
WAL/NB CH45 95 K6
Field's End HUY L36 116 A5
Fieldsend Cl NTHLY L27 132 A1 1
Fieldsend Dr LEIGH WN7 93 L5
Fieldside Av CHLY/EC PR7 31 L5
Fieldside Rd RF/TRAN CH42 128 A3
The Fields CHLY/EC PR7 30 D6
WGNE/HIN WN2 69 L1
Field St VAUX/LVPD L3 13 K3
WGNE/HIN WN2 81 G1 5
WGNNW/ST WN6 4 C3
Fieldsway RUNC WA7 149 J7
Fieldton Rd NG/CROX L11 98 D2
Field Vw LITH L21 83 J4
Fieldview Dr WARRN/WOL WA2 121 L4
Field Wk ORM L39 51 K8
Field Wy RAIN/WH L35 101 L8
Fieldway BEB CH63 127 M5
FROD/HEL WA6 160 E6 1
GTS/LS CH66 155 K6
HES CH60 141 L4
HOY CH47 109 H6
HUY L36 116 B5
MGHL L31 72 F6 1
WAL/NB CH45 95 J8
WAV L15 114 E5
WDN WA8 135 G3
WGNE/HIN WN2 80 D3
Fife Cl CHLYE PR6 33 G7
Fife Rd WARR WA1 15 L2
Fifth Av CL/PREN CH43 110 D6
RUNC WA7 150 B6
WLT/FAZ L9 84 F6 2
Filbert Cl NWD/KWIPK L33 74 B7
Fildes Cl WARRW/BUR WA5 120 E8 3
File St CHLY/EC PR7 32 E6 6
Filton Rd DV/KA/FCH L14 99 K8
Finborough Rd ANF/KKDL L4 97 L3
Fincham Cl DV/KA/FCH L14 99 K8
Fincham Gn DV/KA/FCH L14 99 K8
Fincham Rd DV/KA/FCH L14 99 J8
Fincham Sq DV/KA/FCH L14 99 J8
Finch Av RNFD/HAY WA11 76 C8
Finch Cl DV/KA/FCH L14 99 J7 1
STHEL WA9 118 F2
Finchdale Gdns
GOL/RIS/CU WA3 93 K5 2
Finchdean Cl
GR/UP/WCH CH49 125 L1 2
Finch Dene DV/KA/FCH L14 99 H7
Finch La DV/KA/FCH L14 99 H7
HLWD L26 132 D7
WGNNW/ST WN6 54 D4
Finch Lea Dr DV/KA/FCH L14 99 J8
Finchley Crs WGNE/HIN WN2 69 J3
Finchley Dr RNFD/HAY WA11 89 L6
Finchley Rd ANF/KKDL L4 97 K6
Finch Meadow Cl WLT/FAZ L9 98 B1
Finch Mill Av WGNNW/ST WN6 54 F6
Finch Pl VAUX/LVPD L3 13 L5
Finch Rd DV/KA/FCH L14 99 J7
Finch Wy DV/KA/FCH L14 99 H8 1
Findlay Cl NEWLW WA12 104 E3 2
Findley Dr MOR/LEA CH46 110 B2 3
Findon Rd KKBY L32 86 B5
Fine Jane's Wy CHTN/BK PR9 25 K5
Fingall Rd WAV L15 114 D7 1
Finger House La WDN WA8 118 F4
Fingland Rd WAV L15 114 A6 4
Finlan Rd WDN WA8 16 B6
Finlay Av WARRW/BUR WA5 136 A2 4
Finlay Ct WGNW/BIL/O WN5 68 A5
Finlay St NPK/KEN L6 113 L2
Finney Gv RNFD/HAY WA11 91 G7
The Finney WKBY CH48 124 F7 1
Finningley Ct
WARRN/WOL WA2 122 A4 4
Finsbury Pk WDN WA8 118 E8
Finstall Rd BEB CH63 143 H3
Finvoy Rd CLB/OSW/ST L13 98 A6
Fir Avenue HLWD L26 132 C5
Firbank CHLY/EC PR7 31 L3
CHNE CH2 165 L2
Firbank Cl RUNC WA7 150 F4
Firbank Rd WGNS/IIMK WN3 79 K2
Firbeck SKEL WN8 65 K4
Firbrook Ct CL/PREN CH43 110 E4
Fir Cl HLWD L26 132 C5
Fircroft WGNNW/ST WN6 55 J3 1
Firdale Rd WLT/FAZ L9 97 J1
Firdene Crs CL/PREN CH43 127 G1 3
Fire Station Rd RAIN/WH L35 101 H8
Firethorne Rd HLWD L26 131 M3
Fir Gv WARR WA1 122 B6
WGNNW/ST WN6 68 C2
WLT/FAZ L9 84 E5
Fir La WAV L15 114 C6
Firman Cl WARRW/BUR WA5 120 D5 3
Fir Rd CSBY/WL L22 83 G3
Firs Av BEB CH63 143 H2
Firs Cl FMBY L37 46 F8
Firs Crs FMBY L37 46 F8
Firshaw Rd HOY CH47 108 E4
Firs La LEIGH WN7 81 L8
ORM L39 62 A2
WARRS WA4 137 K7
Firs Link FMBY L37 58 F1
Firs Park Crs WGNE/HIN WN2 69 M4
First Av CL/PREN CH43 110 E7
CSBY/BLUN L23 82 F1 2
RAIN/WH L35 117 K1
WGNE/HIN WN2 69 M8
WGNNW/ST WN6 68 C3
WLT/FAZ L9 84 E6
Firstone Gv KKBY L32 86 A5 2
Fir St ECCL WA10 101 L5
STHP PR8 25 H7
WDN WA8 134 E3
Firswood Rd BRSC L40 64 E1
Firthland Wy STHEL WA9 103 H3 1
Fir Tree Av GOL/RIS/CU WA3 93 H5
Firtree Av WARR WA1 122 C5
Firtree Cl CHLY/EC PR7 43 L2
Fir Tree Cl RNFD/HAY WA11 77 H6
SKEL WN8 65 M6
Fir Tree Crs WGNE/HIN WN2 80 B2
Fir Tree Dr WGNE/HIN WN2 80 B2
Fir Tree Dr North
WD/CROXPK L12 98 F2

Fir Tree Dr South
WD/CROXPK L12 98 F2
Firtree Gv GTS/LS CH66 163 J5
Fir Tree La ORM L39 62 C3
WARRW/BUR WA5 104 C7
Fir Tree St WGNE/HIN WN2 80 B1 1
Firvale Cl LEIGH WN7 81 L8
Fir Wy HES CH60 141 K8
Firwood SKEL WN8 65 M2 2
Firwood Gv AIMK WN4 91 H3
Fisher Av RAIN/WH L35 116 F3
WARRN/WOL WA2 121 K4
WGNE/HIN WN2 80 E6
Fisher Cl WGNS/IIMK WN3 68 B7
Fisher Dr CHTN/BK PR9 25 H6
WGNW/BIL/O WN5 67 G7
Fisherfield Dr GOL/RIS/CU WA3 107 J7
Fishermans Cl FMBY L37 47 G7
Fisher Pl RAIN/WH L35 116 F3 2
Fishers La PEN/TH CH61 141 G1
Fisher St RUNC WA7 19 K2
STHEL WA9 103 G6
TOX L8 112 F7
Fishguard Cl NPK/KEN L6 13 M1 1
Fish La BRSC L40 38 D2
Fistral Cl AIN/FAZ L10 85 K7
Fistral Dr ECCL WA10 88 D7
Fitzadam St WGN WN1 4 D3
Fitzclarence Wy NPK/KEN L6 13 M2
Fitzgerald Rd CLB/OSW/ST L13 114 C2
Fitzherbert St WARRN/WOL WA2 14 F1
Fitzpatrick Ct VAUX/LVPD L3 12 E1
Fitzroy Wy NPK/KEN L6 113 J2 5
Fitzwalter Rd WARR WA1 122 F6
Fiveways ECCL WA10 101 J1
Flag La CHLYE PR6 33 H8
LEY/BBR PR5 30 F1
NSTN CH64 153 H6
Flail Cl GR/UP/WCH CH49 125 L1
Flambards
GR/UP/WCH CH49 126 D2 2
Flamstead SKEL WN8 65 L4
Flander Cl WDN WA8 133 L3
Flashes La NSTN CH64 153 K8
Flash La BRSC L40 39 K1
Flatfield Wy MGHL L31 73 G4
Flatman's La ORM L39 61 G4
Flatt La CL/PREN CH43 127 H2
EP CH65 20 A4
Flawn Rd NG/CROX L11 98 A5
Flaxfield Rd FMBY L37 59 J2
Flaxhill MOR/LEA CH46 109 M4
Flax La BRSC L40 52 B3
Flaxley Cl GOL/RIS/CU WA3 107 J8 1
Flaxman St EHL/KEN L7 113 L3 5
Flaxton SKEL WN8 65 L4
Flaybrick Cl CL/PREN CH43 111 G5
Fleck La WKBY CH48 124 F4
Fleet Croft Rd
GR/UP/WCH CH49 126 C3
Fleet La STHEL WA9 103 K3
Fleet St CHLY/EC PR7 32 E6
CLVPS L1 13 H8
EP CH65 156 C8
WGNW/BIL/O WN5 67 K7
Fleetwood Cl CHTN/BK PR9 25 H2
WARRW/BUR WA5 136 D1
Fleetwood Crs CHTN/BK PR9 23 J7
Fleetwood Dr CHTN/BK PR9 23 J7
Fleetwood Rd CHTN/BK PR9 24 E4
Fleetwood's La NTHTN L30 83 M1
Fleetwood Wk RUNC WA7 150 E6
Fleming Ct VAUX/LVPD L3 12 E1
Fleming Rd SPK/HALE L24 131 L7
Fleming St EP CH65 20 D2
Flemington Av ANF/KKDL L4 97 M4
Flers Av WARRS WA4 137 L2
Fletcher Av PR/KW L34 101 G6
RF/TRAN CH42 128 A3
Fletcher Cl GR/UP/WCH CH49 126 C3
Fletcher Dr ALL/GAR L19 130 C6 6
Fletcher's Dr BRSC L40 52 A1
Fletcher St WARRS WA4 14 F9
Flimby SKEL WN8 65 M4
Flint Cl NSTN CH64 152 F7
Flint Ct EP CH65 163 M3 5
Flint Dr NSTN CH64 153 G6
Flint Meadow NSTN CH64 153 G6
Flintshire Gdns ECCL WA10 8 E7
Flint St CLVPS L1 112 F6
Flockton Av WGNNW/ST WN6 67 M1
Floral Wd AIG/SPK L17 129 H3
Flora St AIMK WN4 91 K3
Flordon SKEL WN8 65 M4
Florence Av HES CH60 141 H4
Florence Cl WLT/FAZ L9 97 H2
Florence Nightingale Cl
NTHTN L30 84 B1
Florence Rd WAL/EG CH44 112 A2
Florence St ANF/KKDL L4 97 H5
BIRK CH41 11 H5
RAIN/WH L35 101 L6
WARRS WA4 15 J9
WGN WN1 5 K3
Florentine Rd CLB/OSW/ST L13 114 C1
Florida Cl WARRW/BUR WA5 120 E6
Florida Ct ALL/GAR L19 130 D5
Flowermead Cl HOY CH47 109 H4
Fluin La FROD/HEL WA6 160 E5
Fluker's Brook La PR/KW L34 99 K4
Foinavon Cl BTL L20 83 J6
Folds HOR/BR BL6 57 L2
Folds La RNFD/HAY WA11 89 J6
Folds Rd RNFD/HAY WA11 90 B7
The Folds BEB CH63 142 C7
Fold St GOL/RIS/CU WA3 92 C4
Foley St ANF/KKDL L4 97 G6
WGNE/HIN WN2 69 M8 13
Folkestone Rd STHP PR8 36 A2
Folkestone Wy RUNC WA7 150 E6
Folly La WAL/EG CH44 95 G8
WARRW/BUR WA5 14 B1
Fontenoy St CLVP L2 13 G5
VAUX/LVPD L3 13 G5 1
Fonthill Cl ANF/KKDL L4 96 F6
Fonthill Rd ANF/KKDL L4 96 F5
Fontwell Cl WGNNW/ST WN6 56 B4
Forbes Cl GOL/RIS/CU WA3 123 G1
Ford Cl BTL L20 84 A6
GR/UP/WCH CH49 126 D1
LITH L21 83 K3
Fordcombe Rd WLTN L25 131 L1
Ford Dr GR/UP/WCH CH49 110 D8 1
Fordham Cl STHP PR8 36 A2
Fordham St ANF/KKDL L4 97 G5
Fordhill Vw MOR/LEA CH46 110 C5
Fordington Rd
WARRW/BUR WA5 120 D8
Fordland Cl GOL/RIS/CU WA3 93 G4 1
Ford La GR/UP/WCH CH49 110 D8
LITH L21 83 K2
Fordlea Rd WD/CROXPK L12 98 C5
Fordlea Wy WD/CROXPK L12 98 D5
Ford Rd GR/UP/WCH CH49 110 C8
RAIN/WH L35 101 H7
Ford St VAUX/LVPD L3 12 F3
WARR WA1 15 J3
Ford Vw LITH L21 83 K2
Ford Wy GR/UP/WCH CH49 126 C1
Fordyce Wy WGNE/HIN WN2 69 J5
Forefield La CSBY/BLUN L23 83 H1
Foreland Cl WARRW/BUR WA5 119 L6
Forest Av WGNNW/ST WN6 68 A2
Forest Cl HOY CH47 108 F4
PR/KW L34 101 H6
Forest Dr HUY L36 115 L2
SKEL WN8 65 L2
WGNNW/ST WN6 55 J3 2
Forest Gn WD/CROXPK L12 98 D5
Forest Gv PR/KW L34 101 H6
Forest Lawn WD/CROXPK L12 98 D5 2
Forest Md ECCL WA10 101 J2
Forest Rd CL/PREN CH43 10 A5
GTS/LS CH66 156 A6
HES CH60 141 J5
HOY CH47 108 F4
STHEL WA9 118 C2
STHP PR8 3 L6
Forfar Rd CLB/OSW/ST L13 97 M7
Forge Cl BRSC L40 64 A1 1
WDN WA8 117 L8
Forge Cottages AIG/SPK L17 129 L1 2
Forge Rd GTS/LS CH66 155 L7
WARRW/BUR WA5 120 B8
Forge St BTL L20 96 E5
WGNE/HIN WN2 5 K5
Formby Br FMBY L37 59 G3
Formby By-pass FMBY L37 47 K4
Formby Cl WARRW/BUR WA5 136 B1
Formby Flds FMBY L37 59 J3
Formby La ORM L39 62 A3
Formby Rd ECCL WA10 101 M4
FMBY L37 59 H1
Formby St FMBY L37 59 G3
Formosa Dr AIN/FAZ L10 85 H6 2
Formosa Rd AIN/FAZ L10 85 H6
Formosa Wy AIN/FAZ L10 85 H6
Fornalls Green La HOY CH47 109 G6
Forres Gv AIMK WN4 90 E1
Forrester Av RAIN/WH L35 101 L6
Forresters Cl WGNE/HIN WN2 81 G5
Forrest St CLVPS L1 13 G9 2
Forrest Wy WARRW/BUR WA5 136 F2
Forshaw Av ECCL WA10 101 L5
Forshaw's La
WARRW/BUR WA5 104 A5
Forshaw St WARRN/WOL WA2 15 G2
Forster St GOL/RIS/CU WA3 92 C4
WARRN/WOL WA2 14 F2
Forsythia Cl WLT/FAZ L9 97 L2 2
Forthlin Rd CALD/MH L18 130 E4
Forth St BTL L20 7 G9
Forton Rd WGNS/IIMK WN3 79 H3
Fort St WAL/NB CH45 95 L6
Forwood Rd PS/BROM CH62 143 M5
Foscote Rd NWD/KWIPK L33 86 C1 5
Foster Av WGNS/IIMK WN3 5 K8
Foster Cl RAIN/WH L35 101 J8
Fosterfield Pl CHLYE PR6 33 G4 1
Foster Rd FMBY L37 58 F3
Fosters Buildings
WGNNW/ST WN6 4 C3
Fosters Cl CHTN/BK PR9 25 K5
Fosters Green Rd SKEL WN8 65 L3
Fosters Gv RNFD/HAY WA11 90 B8 2
Fosters Rd RNFD/HAY WA11 90 B7
Foster St BTL L20 96 E6
CHLYE PR6 33 G4
WDN WA8 16 F1
WGNNW/ST WN6 4 A2
Fotherby Pl WGNS/IIMK WN3 79 J2
Fothergill St WARR WA1 15 K2
Foul La STHP PR8 36 C1
Foundry La WDN WA8 133 K8
WGNS/IIMK WN3 78 F1
Foundry St CHLY/EC PR7 32 E5 6
ECCL WA10 9 G6
NEWLW WA12 104 D2
WARRN/WOL WA2 14 E4
WGNE/HIN WN2 69 M8 14
Fountain Ct CSBY/BLUN L23 70 C8 1
Fountain La FROD/HEL WA6 160 C5
Fountain Rd PR/KW L34 99 M2 2
WAL/NB CH45 95 K6 2
Fountains Av RNFD/HAY WA11 91 H6
Fountains Cl ANF/KKDL L4 97 H6
CHLY/EC PR7 32 F8
RUNC WA7 150 E8
Fountains Rd ANF/KKDL L4 97 G6 7
Fountain St RAIN/WH L35 101 L7 2
RF/TRAN CH42 127 L2
Fountains Wk GOL/RIS/CU WA3 93 K5
Fountains Wy FMBY L37 59 J3
Four Acre Dr LITH L21 83 K2
Four Acre La STHEL WA9 118 E1
Fouracres MGHL L31 72 D6
Fourteen Meadows Rd
WGNS/IIMK WN3 4 C7
Fourth Av CL/PREN CH43 110 D7
RUNC WA7 150 B6
WLT/FAZ L9 84 F6
Fourways Cl NTHLY L27 115 M6
Fowell Rd WAL/NB CH45 95 K5
Fowler Cl EHL/KEN L7 113 L4 8
WGN WN1 5 J4
Foxall Wy GTS/LS CH66 162 F3
Foxcote CHLY/EC PR7 32 D3
WDN WA8 133 K3
Fox Cover Rd HES CH60 141 L6
Foxcovers Rd BEB CH63 143 J2
Fox Covert RUNC WA7 150 E6
Foxdale Cl CL/PREN CH43 10 A8
STHP PR8 35 L3
Foxdale Rd WAV L15 114 B7 4
Foxdell Cl CLB/OSW/ST L13 114 C3 1
Foxdene Gv WGNS/IIMK WN3 79 G3
The Foxes PEN/TH CH61 126 C7
Foxfield Cl WARRN/WOL WA2 122 A2
Foxfield Gv WGNNW/ST WN6 55 K7
Foxfield Rd HOY CH47 108 F5
Foxfold SKEL WN8 65 M2
Fox Gdns LYMM WA13 139 L1
Foxglove Av HLWD L26 132 A4
Foxglove Cl WGNNW/ST WN6 55 M3
WLT/FAZ L9 98 B1
Foxglove Ct FROD/HEL WA6 160 E5
Foxglove Rd BIRK CH41 111 H6 5
Foxglove Wy NSTN CH64 153 G8
Fox Hey Rd WAL/EG CH44 111 H2
Foxhill Cl FMBY L37 58 E2
TOX L8 113 J8
Foxhill Gv FROD/HEL WA6 166 F1
Foxhill La HLWD L26 132 B3
Foxhole Rd CHLY/EC PR7 32 B5
Foxholes Rd HOR/BR BL6 45 M8
Foxhouse La MGHL L31 73 G5
Foxhunter Dr WLT/FAZ L9 84 E5
Foxleigh HLWD L26 131 M4
Foxley Heath WDN WA8 16 A3
Fox's Bank La RAIN/WH L35 117 H6
WDN WA8 117 H4
Foxshaw Cl RAIN/WH L35 116 F4
Fox St BIRK CH41 10 F5
RUNC WA7 19 G5
VAUX/LVPD L3 13 J2
WARRW/BUR WA5 121 G8
Foxton Cl HOY CH47 109 K4
RNFD/HAY WA11 89 M8 2
Foxwood RAIN/WH L35 101 L6
WD/CROXPK L12 99 G5
Foxwood Cl
WGNW/BIL/O WN5 67 G8 2
WKBY CH48 125 G2
The Foxwood CHLY/EC PR7 42 E4
Foy St AIMK WN4 91 K2 5
Frailey Cl STHP PR8 47 L1
Frampton Rd ANF/KKDL L4 97 M3
France St WGNE/HIN WN2 69 M7
WGNW/BIL/O WN5 68 B6 2
Franceys St VAUX/LVPD L3 13 K7 1
Francine Cl EV L5 96 E8
Francis Av CL/PREN CH43 10 D6
MOR/LEA CH46 109 M5
Francis Cl RAIN/WH L35 117 L1
WDN WA8 133 L5
Francis Rd FROD/HEL WA6 160 E4
WARRS WA4 137 K4
Francis St STHEL WA9 103 H6 5
WGNE/HIN WN2 69 M8
Francis Wy CHLDW L16 115 G5
Frankby Av WAL/EG CH44 111 J1 1
Frankby Cl GR/UP/WCH CH49 125 K2
Frankby Gv GR/UP/WCH CH49 110 B8
Frankby Rd ANF/KKDL L4 97 K5
GR/UP/WCH CH49 125 L2
HOY CH47 108 F5 1
WKBY CH48 124 F2
Franklin Cl WARRW/BUR WA5 120 E5
Franklin Pl NPK/KEN L6 97 K8 5
Franklin Rd MOR/LEA CH46 110 C1
Frank St WDN WA8 17 H2
Fraser Rd WARRW/BUR WA5 119 M7
WGNW/BIL/O WN5 68 A6
Fraser St VAUX/LVPD L3 13 J5
Frawley Av NEWLW WA12 91 K8
Freckleton Cl
WARRW/BUR WA5 136 D1 4
Freckleton Dr NWD/KWIPK L33 74 C8
Freckleton Rd CHTN/BK PR9 25 H1
ECCL WA10 101 K4
Freckleton St WGN WN1 68 E3
Freda Av STHEL WA9 102 E7 4
Frederica Gdns WGNE/HIN WN2 80 C2
Frederick Banting Cl
NTHTN L30 84 B1 5
Frederick Gv WAV L15 114 C5 5
Frederick Lunt Av PR/KW L34 99 L2
Frederick St AIMK WN4 79 J8
CHLYE PR6 33 G6
CLVPS L1 12 F9 1
STHEL WA9 103 H6
WARRS WA4 137 M2
WDN WA8 16 E2
WGNE/HIN WN2 69 M8
WGNS/IIMK WN3 5 H8
Fredric Pl RUNC WA7 19 J2
Freedom Cl EHL/KEN L7 113 J5 5
Freehold St EHL/KEN L7 113 M2
Freeland St ANF/KKDL L4 97 G6 8
Freeman St BIRK CH41 11 J3
EHL/KEN L7 113 L5
Freemantle Av STHEL WA9 102 B6
Freemasons Rw VAUX/LVPD L3 12 F4
Freemont Rd WD/CROXPK L12 98 C6
Freeport Gv WLT/FAZ L9 84 D6 7
Freesia Av WLT/FAZ L9 97 K1
Freme Cl NG/CROX L11 98 D2
French St WDN WA8 17 J2
Frenchwood Ct
WGNE/HIN WN2 69 L1 1
Frensham Cl BEB CH63 143 H3 5
Frensham Wy WLTN L25 131 M5
Freshfield Cl HUY L36 115 L2
Freshfield Rd FMBY L37 47 G8
WAV L15 114 B7 5
WGNS/IIMK WN3 79 G2
Freshfields Dr
WARRN/WOL WA2 122 D4
Freshford STHEL WA9 102 F7 4
Freshmeadow La
FROD/HEL WA6 166 C3
Freshwater WARRW/BUR WA5 119 M6
Freshwater Cl
WARRW/BUR WA5 119 M6 1
Friars Av WARRW/BUR WA5 120 A8
Friars Cl BEB CH63 128 B8 1
Friars Ga WARR WA1 14 E7
Friars La WARR WA1 14 E7
Friar St ECCL WA10 89 H6
EV L5 97 J8 2
Friars Wk FMBY L37 59 K3
Friday St CHLY/EC PR7 32 F5 5
CHLYE PR6 32 F5
Friends La WARRW/BUR WA5 119 M7
Frinsted Rd NG/CROX L11 98 C4
Frith St WGNNW/ST WN6 4 A5
Frobisher Ct
WARRW/BUR WA5 120 F5 1
Frobisher Rd MOR/LEA CH46 110 C1
NSTN CH64 153 G5
Froda Av FROD/HEL WA6 160 D6
Frodsham Cl WGNNW/ST WN6 67 M2
Frodsham Dr RNFD/HAY WA11 89 M8
Frodsham Rd FROD/HEL WA6 166 F4
Frodsham St ANF/KKDL L4 97 H4
BIRK CH41 11 J9
Froghall La WARR WA1 14 B4
WARRN/WOL WA2 14 C4
WARRW/BUR WA5 14 A5
Frog La BRSC L40 52 F2
WGNNW/ST WN6 4 B3
Frogmore Rd CLB/OSW/ST L13 114 A2
Frome Cl PEN/TH CH61 125 M6
Frome Ct EP CH65 156 D6
Frome Wy WLTN L25 131 M4
Froom St CHLYE PR6 33 G5
Frost Dr PEN/TH CH61 125 L6
Frosts Ms EP CH65 20 B2
Frost St EHL/KEN L7 113 L3 4
Fryent Cl HOR/BR BL6 57 M3
Fry St STHEL WA9 103 G2
Fuchsia Cl GTS/LS CH66 163 H4
Fuchsia Wk GR/UP/WCH CH49 125 L3
Fulbeck WDN WA8 133 L3
Fulbeck Av WGNS/IIMK WN3 79 J3
Fulbrook Cl BEB CH63 143 H3 4
Fulbrook Rd BEB CH63 143 H3
Fulford Cl DV/KA/FCH L14 99 H7
Fullerton Gv HUY L36 116 A1 1
Fulmar Cl NTHLY L27 132 A1
RNFD/HAY WA11 89 K7
Fulmar Gv WD/CROXPK L12 99 G2
Fulshaw Cl NTHLY L27 115 M7
Fulton Av WKBY CH48 124 F2
Fulton St EV L5 96 D7
Fulwood Av STHP PR8 3 M9
Fulwood Cl AIG/SPK L17 129 M3
Fulwood Dr AIG/SPK L17 129 L3
Fulwood Gdns GTS/LS CH66 155 L7
Fulwood Ms GTS/LS CH66 155 L7
Fulwood Pk AIG/SPK L17 129 L4
Fulwood Rd AIG/SPK L17 129 L3
GOL/RIS/CU WA3 93 G7
GTS/LS CH66 155 L7
Funchal Av FMBY L37 58 F4
Furlong Cl WGNE/HIN WN2 80 B6
WLT/FAZ L9 84 F5
Furness Av ECCL WA10 89 G6
FMBY L37 59 H2
ORM L39 63 G1
WD/CROXPK L12 98 E4 2
Furness Cl CHLY/EC PR7 32 F8
STHP PR8 47 K2
Furness Crs LEIGH WN7 81 M4
Furness St ANF/KKDL L4 97 G6 9
Furnival Dr BRSC L40 51 M1 3
Furrocks Cl NSTN CH64 153 H8
Furrocks La NSTN CH64 153 H8
Furrocks Wy NSTN CH64 153 H8
The Furrows GTS/LS CH66 163 G5 2
Fylde Rd CHTN/BK PR9 22 D8

G

Gabbot St CHLY/EC PR7 44 B6
Gable Ct NG/CROX L11 98 A2 1
Gables Cl WARRN/WOL WA2 122 B2
Gable St NEWLW WA12 104 C2
Gabriel Cl MOR/LEA CH46 110 B5
Gainford Cl WDN WA8 133 L2
Gainford Rd DV/KA/FCH L14 99 J7
Gainsborough Av MGHL L31 72 D5
Gainsborough Cl
WD/CROXPK L12 99 G8
WGNS/IIMK WN3 78 F2 2
Gainsborough Ct WDN WA8 133 K4 2
Gainsborough Rd
GR/UP/WCH CH49 110 A7
STHP PR8 35 G2
WAL/NB CH45 95 G8
WARRS WA4 137 K3
WAV L15 114 A7
Gairloch Cl WARRN/WOL WA2 122 B1
Gaisgill Ct WDN WA8 133 L4 1
Gale Av WARRW/BUR WA5 121 H4
Galemeade NG/CROX L11 98 D2 1
Gale Rd LITH L21 83 L4
NWD/KWIPK L33 86 E5
Gales La BRSC L40 40 C2
Galion Wy WDN WA8 134 B1
Galloway Rd CSBY/WL L22 83 G3
Galloway St EHL/KEN L7 113 M5
Galston Av RAIN/WH L35 117 M3
Galston Cl NWD/KWIPK L33 73 M7
Galsworthy Av NTHTN L30 83 M6
Galsworthy Pl NTHTN L30 84 A5 2
Galton St VAUX/LVPD L3 12 C4
Galtres Pk BEB CH63 128 A5
Galwey Gv WGN WN1 68 E1
Gamble Av ECCL WA10 101 K2
Gamlin St BIRK CH41 111 H5
Gamston Wd KKBY L32 85 L4
Ganney's Meadow Rd
GR/UP/WCH CH49 126 E3
Gannock St EHL/KEN L7 113 L3
Gantley Av WGNW/BIL/O WN5 77 M1
Gantley Crs WGNW/BIL/O WN5 77 M2
Gantley Rd WGNW/BIL/O WN5 77 M2
Ganton Cl STHP PR8 36 A1
WDN WA8 134 D1
Ganworth Cl SPK/HALE L24 147 G3 2
Ganworth Rd SPK/HALE L24 147 G3
Garage Rd SPK/HALE L24 132 B8 1
Gardeners Vw
NWD/KWIPK L33 74 B7 5
Gardeners Wy RAIN/WH L35 101 L8
Garden Hey Rd HOY CH47 108 E5
MOR/LEA CH46 109 K6
Gardenia Gv AIG/SPK L17 129 J3
Garden La MOR/LEA CH46 110 A4 1
VAUX/LVPD L3 13 L2 1
WLT/FAZ L9 84 F6
Garden Lodge Gv NTHLY L27 115 M8
Garden Pl BTL L20 7 H4 1
Gardenside MOR/LEA CH46 110 D1
Gardenside St NPK/KEN L6 13 M3
Gardens Rd BEB CH63 128 D8 2
Garden St WLTN L25 131 J3
Garden Ter CHLY/EC PR7 32 E4
Garden Wk PR/KW L34 100 F8
Gardiner Av RNFD/HAY WA11 90 E7
Gardiners Pl SKEL WN8 65 G5
Gardner Av BTL L20 83 M6
Gardner Rd CLB/OSW/ST L13 98 A8
FMBY L37 59 J2
Gardner's Dr NPK/KEN L6 113 L1
Gardner's Rw VAUX/LVPD L3 13 G3
Gareth Av RNFD/HAY WA11 89 K7 2
Garfield Ter CHLYE PR6 32 F3 5
GR/UP/WCH CH49 110 C8 1
Garfourth Cl ALL/GAR L19 130 F6
Garfourth Rd ALL/GAR L19 130 F6
Garmoyle Cl WAV L15 114 A6 5
Garmoyle Rd WAV L15 114 A7
Garner St WARRN/WOL WA2 15 H1
Garnet St CLB/OSW/ST L13 114 B4
STHEL WA9 102 F6
Garnett Av ANF/KKDL L4 97 G5
WARRS WA4 138 B1
Garnett Gn ORM L39 62 F1
Garnett Pl SKEL WN8 65 J6
Garnetts La WDN WA8 148 C2
Garrett Fld GOL/RIS/CU WA3 106 F8
Garrick Av MOR/LEA CH46 109 L5
Garrick Pde STHP PR8 2 E5
Garrick Rd CL/PREN CH43 127 H5
Garrick St EHL/KEN L7 113 L6
Garrigill Cl WDN WA8 118 D8
Garrowby Dr HUY L36 115 L2
Garsdale Av RAIN/WH L35 117 M3
Garsdale Cl
WARRW/BUR WA5 120 B6 1
Garsfield Rd ANF/KKDL L4 97 M4
Garside Av GOL/RIS/CU WA3 92 F6
Garside Gv WGNS/IIMK WN3 79 G3
Garstang Rd CHTN/BK PR9 25 H1
Garston Old Rd ALL/GAR L19 130 D6
Garston Wy ALL/GAR L19 130 E7
Garswood Av RNFD/HAY WA11 76 C6
Garswood Cl MGHL L31 73 G2 2
MOR/LEA CH46 110 A1
Garswood Crs
WGNW/BIL/O WN5 89 M1
Garswood Old Rd AIMK WN4 90 B4
Garswood Rd AIMK WN4 90 E2
WGNW/BIL/O WN5 90 A1
Garswood St AIMK WN4 91 K2
ECCL WA10 9 G3
TOX L8 129 H2
Garter Cl NG/CROX L11 98 E2
Garth Bvd BEB CH63 128 A5
Garthdale Rd CALD/MH L18 130 C1
Garth Dr CALD/MH L18 130 D1
Garthowen Rd EHL/KEN L7 113 M3
Garth Rd KKBY L32 86 C5
The Garth HUY L36 116 A2
Garton Dr GOL/RIS/CU WA3 93 G4
Gartons La STHEL WA9 118 E2
Garven Pl WARR WA1 14 D6
Garway WLTN L25 131 L2
Garwood Cl WARRW/BUR WA5 120 D5
Gascoyne St VAUX/LVPD L3 12 E4
Gaskell Av WARRS WA4 138 C2
Gaskell's Brow AIMK WN4 79 G8
Gaskell St CHLYE PR6 33 G5
STHEL WA9 102 F4
WARRS WA4 137 L4
Gaskill Rd SPK/HALE L24 146 F1
Gas St CHLY/EC PR7 44 B7
WGNE/HIN WN2 80 D3
Gatclif Rd CLB/OSW/ST L13 98 A5
Gateacre Brow WLTN L25 131 J1
Gateacre Park Dr WLTN L25 115 H7
Gateacre Ri WLTN L25 131 K1
Gateacre Vale Rd WLTN L25 131 K2
Gategill Gv WGNW/BIL/O WN5 77 M3
Gateside Cl NTHLY L27 116 A8
Gates La SFTN L29 71 K5
Gate Warth St
WARRW/BUR WA5 136 F1 4
Gathurst La WGNNW/ST WN6 55 H8
Gathurst Rd WGNW/BIL/O WN5 67 G4
Gatley Dr MGHL L31 73 G5
Gaunts Wy RUNC WA7 150 A7
Gautby Rd BIRK CH41 111 G4
Gavin Rd WDN WA8 133 K6
Gaw Hill La ORM L39 62 C2
Gaw Hill Vw ORM L39 62 D2
Gawsworth Cl
CL/PREN CH43 127 H2 4
ECCL WA10 101 K2
Gawsworth Rd
GOL/RIS/CU WA3 92 B4
GTS/LS CH66 163 G1
Gaybeech Cl CL/PREN CH43 110 E5
Gayhurst Av
WARRN/WOL WA2 122 B3 2
Gayhurst Crs NG/CROX L11 98 C3
Gaynor Av RNFD/HAY WA11 91 H6 3
Gayton Av BEB CH63 127 L5
WAL/NB CH45 95 K5 3
Gayton Cl WGNS/IIMK WN3 78 F2
Gayton Farm Rd HES CH60 141 J8
Gayton La HES CH60 141 K7
Gayton Mill Cl HES CH60 141 K6 2
Gayton Pkwy HES CH60 141 K8
Gayton Rd HES CH60 141 H7
Gaywood Av KKBY L32 86 B5

Gaywood Cl *CL/PREN* CH43 ..... **110** E6 5
KKBY L32 .... **86** B5 1
Gellings Rd *PR/KW* L34 .... **86** C8
Gelling St *TOX* L8 .... **113** H8 4
Gemini Cl *BTL* L20 .... **6** F3
Gemini Dr *DV/KA/FCH* L14 .... **115** H1
General St *WARR* WA1 .... **15** G5
Geneva Rd *NPK/KEN* L6 .... **113** L2
WAL/EC CH44 .... **111** M3
Genista Cl *WLT/FAZ* L9 .... **97** J2 1
Genoa Cl *WLTN* L25 .... **115** L6
Gentwood Rd *HUY* L36 .... **115** L1
Geoffrey St *CHLYE* PR6 .... **32** F4
George Dr *STHP* PR8 .... **35** G8
George Hale Av *PR/KW* L34 .... **100** A7
George Harrison Cl
NPK/KEN L6 .... **113** K2 5
George Rd *HOY* CH47 .... **108** E7
WARRW/BUR WA5 .... **136** E1 1
Georges Crs *WARRS* WA4 .... **138** D3
George's Dock Gates
VAUX/LVPD L3 .... **12** D6
Georges Dockway *VAUX/LVPD* L3 .. **12** D8
George's La *CHTN/BK* PR9 .... **23** H5
HOR/BR BL6 .... **45** M6
WGN WN1 .... **5** L4
Georges Pierhead
VAUX/LVPD L3 .... **12** D8
George's Ter
WGNW/BIL/O WN5 .... **66** F8 2
George St *AIMK* WN4 .... **91** L1 2
BIRK CH41 .... **11** K3
CHLY/EC PR7 .... **32** E6 2
ECCL WA10 .... **9** H5
EP CH65 .... **20** C1
NEWLW WA12 .... **104** C1 1
VAUX/LVPD L3 .... **12** E6 5
WGNE/HIN WN2 .... **5** M6
Georgia Av *PS/BROM* CH62 .... **144** A2
Georgian Cl *HLWD* L26 .... **132** B7 2
RAIN/WH L35 .... **101** J7 4
Georgian Pl *FMBY* L37 .... **59** G4 5
Geraint St *TOX* L8 .... **113** H7
Gerald Rd *CL/PREN* CH43 .... **127** J1
Gerard Av *WAL/NB* CH45 .... **95** J6
Gerard Rd *WAL/NB* CH45 .... **95** J7
WKBY CH48 .... **124** D2
Gerards La *STHEL* WA9 .... **102** F6
Gerard St *AIMK* WN4 .... **91** K2
VAUX/LVPD L3 .... **13** H5
Germander Cl *HLWD* L26 .... **132** A4
German La *CHLY/EC* PR7 .... **31** M5
Gerneth Cl *SPK/HALE* L24 .... **146** E1
Gerneth Rd *SPK/HALE* L24 .... **146** D2
Gerosa Av *WARRN/WOL* WA2 .... **105** K5
Gerrard Av *GTS/LS* CH66 .... **162** E1
WARRW/BUR WA5 .... **14** A1
Gerrard Cl *WGNE/HIN* WN2 .... **69** M3 1
Gerrard Pl *SKEL* WN8 .... **65** H6
Gerrard Rd *GOL/RIS/CU* WA3 .... **106** C6
WGNW/BIL/O WN5 .... **78** A8
Gerrard's La *HLWD* L26 .... **132** A3
Gerrard St *WDN* WA8 .... **16** E4 1
Gertrude Rd *ANF/KKDL* L4 .... **97** J7
Gertrude St *BIRK* CH41 .... **11** L5 5
RAIN/WH L35 .... **101** L7
Geves Gdns *CSBY/WL* L22 .... **83** G4
Ghyll Gv *RNFD/HAY* WA11 .... **89** K4
Giants Hall Rd *WGNNW/ST* WN6 .... **68** A2
Gibbons Av *ECCL* WA10 .... **101** L2
Gibbon's Rd *AIMK* WN4 .... **90** F3
Gibraltar Rw *VAUX/LVPD* L3 .... **12** D5
Gibson Cl *PEN/TH* CH61 .... **141** H2
Gibson St *TOX* L8 .... **113** H6 5
WARR WA1 .... **15** H6
WARRS WA4 .... **137** M4 2
WGNE/HIN WN2 .... **80** F3
Giddygate La *MGHL* L31 .... **73** K7
Gidlow Av *CHLYE* PR6 .... **44** C6 2
WGNNW/ST WN6 .... **68** C3
Gidlow La *WGNNW/ST* WN6 .... **4** B2
Gidlow Rd *CLB/OSW/ST* L13 .... **114** B2
Gidlow Rd South
CLB/OSW/ST L13 .... **114** B2
Gidlow St *WGNE/HIN* WN2 .... **69** J5 5
Gifford Pl *WGNE/HIN* WN2 .... **81** H1
Gigg La *WARRS* WA4 .... **136** D8
WARRS WA4 .... **139** G1
Gig La *WARR* WA1 .... **122** F5
Gilbert Cl *BEB* CH63 .... **143** H3
Gilbert Pl *BRSC* L40 .... **51** K1
Gilbert Rd *RAIN/WH* L35 .... **101** H8
Gilbertson Rd *CHLY/EC* PR7 .... **44** A3
Gilbert St *CHLY/EC* PR7 .... **32** E7 5
CLVPS L1 .... **13** G9
CLVPS L1 .... **112** F5
WGNE/HIN WN2 .... **69** L8
Gildarts Gdns *VAUX/LVPD* L3 .... **12** F2
Gildart St *VAUX/LVPD* L3 .... **13** L5
Gilderdale Cl *GOL/RIS/CU* WA3 .... **107** K8
Gilead St *EHL/KEN* L7 .... **113** K3
Gillan Cl *RUNC* WA7 .... **150** E8
Gillan Rd *WGNNW/ST* WN6 .... **68** D3
Gillars Green Dr *ECCL* WA10 .... **101** H2
Gillar's La *ECCL* WA10 .... **101** G2
Gill Av *WGNNW/ST* WN6 .... **55** K7
Gillbrow Crs *WGN* WN1 .... **5** M2
Gillcroft *CHLY/EC* PR7 .... **30** D7 2
Gilleney Gv *RAIN/WH* L35 .... **101** J8
Gillibrands Rd *SKEL* WN8 .... **65** J6
Gillibrand St *CHLY/EC* PR7 .... **32** E6
Gillibrand Wks *CHLY/EC* PR7 .... **32** E7
Gillmoss Cl *NG/CROX* L11 .... **98** E1
Gillmoss La *NG/CROX* L11 .... **85** L8
Gills La *PEN/TH* CH61 .... **141** J1
Gill St *VAUX/LVPD* L3 .... **13** L6
Gilman St *ANF/KKDL* L4 .... **97** J6
Gilpin Av *MGHL* L31 .... **73** G3
Gilpin Pl *WGNE/HIN* WN2 .... **80** B3 1
Gilroy Rd *NPK/KEN* L6 .... **113** K2
WKBY CH48 .... **124** F2
Gilroy St *WGN* WN1 .... **5** H4
Gilsecroft Av *NWD/KWIPK* L33 .... **86** C2
Giltbrook Cl *WDN* WA8 .... **134** B2 5
Gilwell Av *MOR/LEA* CH46 .... **110** A6
Gilwell Cl *MOR/LEA* CH46 .... **110** A6 1
WARRS WA4 .... **138** E3
Gin Bow *CHLY/EC* PR7 .... **32** F7 1
The Ginnel *PS/BROM* CH62 .... **128** D8
Gipsy Gv *CALD/MH* L18 .... **115** G8
Gipsy La *CALD/MH* L18 .... **115** G8
Girton Av *AIMK* WN4 .... **91** H1
BTL L20 .... **7** L6
Girton Cl *EP* CH65 .... **20** E6
Girton Rd *EP* CH65 .... **20** E6
Girtrell Cl *GR/UP/WCH* CH49 .... **109** M8
Girtrell Rd *GR/UP/WCH* CH49 .... **109** M8
Girvan Crs *AIMK* WN4 .... **90** E1
Girvin Dr *NSTN* CH64 .... **153** G7
Gisburn Av *GOL/RIS/CU* WA3 .... **92** B3
Givenchy Cl *CHLDW* L16 .... **115** G5
Gladden Pl *SKEL* WN8 .... **65** G5
Glade Rd *HUY* L36 .... **116** A1
Gladeswood Rd
NWD/KWIPK L33 .... **86** D4
The Glade *HOY* CH47 .... **108** F4
WGNNW/ST WN6 .... **55** K7
Gladeville Rd *AIG/SPK* L17 .... **130** A3
Gladstone Av *CHLDW* L16 .... **115** J5
LITH L21 .... **83** H6 5
Gladstone Hall Rd
PS/BROM CH62 .... **143** K1 2
Gladstone Rd *ALL/GAR* L19 .... **130** E7
CHTN/BK PR9 .... **25** H7
EHL/KEN L7 .... **113** K4
LITH L21 .... **83** H6
NSTN CH64 .... **153** G5 1
RF/TRAN CH42 .... **128** B2 5
WAL/EC CH44 .... **111** M2 5
WLT/FAZ L9 .... **97** H2
Gladstone St *BIRK* CH41 .... **10** F5 1
ECCL WA10 .... **8** A6
VAUX/LVPD L3 .... **12** F4 1
WARRN/WOL WA2 .... **14** C4
WDN WA8 .... **16** E3
WLTN L25 .... **131** H3
Glaisdale Cl *AIMK* WN4 .... **91** L2 2
Glaisdale Dr *STHP* PR8 .... **36** B2
Glaisher St *EV* L5 .... **97** J7 4
Glamis Dr *CHLY/EC* PR7 .... **32** D5
CHTN/BK PR9 .... **25** K2
Glamis Gv *STHEL* WA9 .... **102** E6
Glamis Rd *CLB/OSW/ST* L13 .... **97** M7
Glamorgan Cl *ECCL* WA10 .... **8** E7
Glan Aber Pk *WD/CROXPK* L12 .... **99** G5
Glasier Rd *MOR/LEA* CH46 .... **109** L4
Glaslyn Wy *WLT/FAZ* L9 .... **97** J2
Glassbrook St *WGNNW/ST* WN6 .... **4** B1
Glassonby Crs *NG/CROX* L11 .... **98** C4
Glassonby Wy *NG/CROX* L11 .... **98** C4 5
Glastonbury Av
GOL/RIS/CU WA3 .... **93** K5
Glastonbury Cl *NPK/KEN* L6 .... **97** M6
RUNC WA7 .... **151** G2
Glasven Rd *NWD/KWIPK* L33 .... **86** B2
Glazebrook St *WARR* WA1 .... **15** J4
Glaziers La *GOL/RIS/CU* WA3 .... **106** F3
Gleadmere *WDN* WA8 .... **133** L3
Gleaston Cl *PS/BROM* CH62 ..... **143** L4 1
Gleave Crs *NPK/KEN* L6 .... **13** M2
Gleave Rd *WARRW/BUR* WA5 .. **104** B7 5
Gleave St *ECCL* WA10 .... **9** H3
Glebe Av *AIMK* WN4 .... **91** K3
WARRS WA4 .... **138** E4
Glebe Cl *MGHL* L31 .... **72** D4
WGNNW/ST WN6 .... **56** B4 1
Glebecroft Av *CHNE* CH2 .... **165** J2 2
Glebe End *SFTN* L29 .... **72** A6
Glebe End St *WGNNW/ST* WN6 .... **4** C3
Glebe Hey *NTHLY* L27 .... **116** A8
Glebe Hey Rd
GR/UP/WCH CH49 .... **126** C2
Glebeland *GOL/RIS/CU* WA3 .... **107** G2
Glebelands Rd *MOR/LEA* CH46 .... **110** A5
Glebe La *CHTN/BK* PR9 .... **23** J6
WDN WA8 .... **118** C8
Glebe Pl *STHP* PR8 .... **3** G3
Glebe Rd *SKEL* WN8 .... **65** J6
WAL/NB CH45 .... **95** J7
WGNNW/ST WN6 .... **56** B5
Glebe St *WGNE/HIN* WN2 .... **81** L3
The Glebe *RUNC* WA7 .... **150** A4
Gleggside *WKBY* CH48 .... **124** E3
Glegg St *VAUX/LVPD* L3 .... **12** D1
WGNE/HIN WN2 .... **5** M4
Glegside Rd *NWD/KWIPK* L33 .... **86** C3
Glemsford Cl *WGNS/IIMK* WN3 .... **79** K2
Glenalmond Rd
WAL/EC CH44 .... **111** M1 10
Glenathol Rd *CALD/MH* L18 .... **130** E3
GTS/LS CH66 .... **162** E1
Glenavon Rd *CHLDW* L16 .... **114** E5
CL/PREN CH43 .... **127** J4
Glenbank *CSBY/WL* L22 .... **82** E3
Glenbank Cl *WLT/FAZ* L9 .... **84** C8
Glenbranter Av
WGNE/HIN WN2 .... **69** J5 5
Glenburn Av *PS/BROM* CH62 .... **155** G1
Glenburn Rd *SKEL* WN8 .... **65** G1
WAL/EC CH44 .... **111** M2 6
Glenby Av *CSBY/BLUN* L23 .... **83** H3
Glencairn Rd *CLB/OSW/ST* L13 .... **114** B3
Glencoe Rd *WAL/NB* CH45 .... **95** K7
Glenconner Rd *CHLDW* L16 .... **115** G4
Glencourse Rd *WDN* WA8 .... **118** C8 1
Glencoyne Dr *CHTN/BK* PR9 .... **22** D7
Glencroft *CHLY/EC* PR7 .... **31** K2
Glencroft Cl *HUY* L36 .... **99** L8 1
Glendale Av *AIMK* WN4 .... **91** L1
CHNE CH2 .... **165** J2 5
Glendale Cl *TOX* L8 .... **129** H2
Glendale Gv *BEB* CH63 .... **143** K3
Glendale Wy *FMBY* L37 .... **59** H3
Glendevon Cl *WGNE/HIN* WN2 ... **69** J5 5
Glendevon Rd *CHLDW* L16 .... **114** F4
HUY L36 .... **116** A4
Glendower Rd *CSBY/WL* L22 .... **83** G4 2
Glen Dr *WGNNW/ST* WN6 .... **55** G5
Glendyke Rd *CALD/MH* L18 .... **130** E3
GTS/LS CH66 .... **162** E1
Gleneagles Cl *PEN/TH* CH61 .... **141** H2
Gleneagles Dr *RNFD/HAY* WA11 .... **90** C8
STHP PR8 .... **47** K2
WDN WA8 .... **118** C8
Gleneagles Rd *CHLDW* L16 .... **114** F4
GTS/LS CH66 .... **162** E1
Glenesk Rd *GTS/LS* CH66 .... **162** E1
Glenfield Cl *CL/PREN* CH43 .... **110** E5 5
MOR/LEA CH46 .... **109** K4 4
Glenfield Rd *WAV* L15 .... **114** C7 4
Glengariff St *CLB/OSW/ST* L13 ..... **98** A6
Glenhead Rd *ALL/GAR* L19 .... **130** D5
Glenholm Rd *MGHL* L31 .... **72** E6 1
Glenluce Rd *ALL/GAR* L19 .... **130** D5
Glenmarsh Cl *BEB* CH63 .... **127** M8 2
WD/CROXPK L12 .... **98** F7 5
Glenmarsh Wy *FMBY* L37 .... **59** K2 2
Glenmaye Cl *WD/CROXPK* L12 ... **99** G3 2
Glenmaye Rd *GTS/LS* CH66 .... **162** E1
Glenmore Av *CALD/MH* L18 .... **130** C2
Glenmore Rd *CL/PREN* CH43 .... **127** J1
Glenn Pl *WDN* WA8 .... **133** M4
Glenpark Dr *CHTN/BK* PR9 .... **25** K1
Glen Park Rd *WAL/NB* CH45 .... **95** J6
Glen Rd *CLB/OSW/ST* L13 .... **114** D3
GTS/LS CH66 .... **162** E1
Glen Ronald Dr
GR/UP/WCH CH49 .... **109** M8 4
Glenrose Ter *STHP* PR8 .... **2** F8
Glenroyd Dr *BRSC* L40 .... **52** A1
Glenside *CALD/MH* L18 .... **130** E3
WGNNW/ST WN6 .... **54** D3
The Glen *CALD/MH* L18 .... **130** E2
PS/BROM CH62 .... **143** L2
RUNC WA7 .... **150** B7
Glenton Pk *NSTN* CH64 .... **153** H7
Glentrees Cl *GR/UP/WCH* CH49 .... **109** M8
Glentrees Rd *WD/CROXPK* L12 .... **98** D5
Glentworth Cl *MGHL* L31 .... **72** F5
Glenville Cl *RUNC* WA7 .... **149** K7 5
WLTN L25 .... **131** K2
Glen Vine Cl *CHLDW* L16 .... **115** H5 1
Glenway *NWD/KWIPK* L33 .... **74** B7
Glenwood Cl *GTS/LS* CH66 .... **155** L7 2
Glenwood Dr *PEN/TH* CH61 .... **126** A6
Glenwood Gdns *GTS/LS* CH66 .. **155** L7 5
Glenwood Rd *GTS/LS* CH66 .... **155** L7
Glenwyllin Rd *CSBY/WL* L22 .... **83** G3
Globe Rd *BTL* L20 .... **6** E3
Globe St *ANF/KKDL* L4 .... **97** G6
Glossop Wy *WGNE/HIN* WN2 .... **81** H1 5
Gloucester Av *GOL/RIS/CU* WA3 .... **92** C6
Gloucester Cl *GTS/LS* CH66 .... **163** H5 1
WARR WA1 .... **122** F6
Gloucester Pl *NPK/KEN* L6 .... **113** J2 5
Gloucester Rd *BTL* L20 .... **7** K3
CHLY/EC PR7 .... **32** E8
HUY L36 .... **116** C2
NPK/KEN L6 .... **97** M8
STHP PR8 .... **2** D7
WAL/NB CH45 .... **95** G7
WDN WA8 .... **134** D2
WGNW/BIL/O WN5 .... **67** L7 2
Gloucester Rd North
NPK/KEN L6 .... **97** M7
Gloucester St *STHEL* WA9 .... **102** F3
Glover Pl *BTL* L20 .... **6** F2
Glover Rd *GOL/RIS/CU* WA3 .... **106** E8
Glover's Brow *KKBY* L32 .... **85** L1
Glover's La *NTHTN* L30 .... **84** A1
Glover St *ECCL* WA10 .... **8** E7
LEIGH WN7 .... **81** L5
NEWLW WA12 .... **104** E2 2
RF/TRAN CH42 .... **10** E9
Glyn Av *PS/BROM* CH62 .... **144** A6
Glynne Gv *CHLDW* L16 .... **115** J5
Glynne St *BTL* L20 .... **83** M7
Glynn St *WAV* L15 .... **114** B6
Glyn Rd *WAL/EC* CH44 .... **95** K8
Goddard Rd *RUNC* WA7 .... **150** A2
Godetia Cl *WLT/FAZ* L9 .... **98** B1 1
Godfrey St *WARRN/WOL* WA2 .... **15** J1
Godscroft La *FROD/HEL* WA6 .... **160** A7
Godshill Cl *WARRW/BUR* WA5 .... **119** M6
Godstow *RUNC* WA7 .... **151** G1
Golborne Dale Rd *NEWLW* WA12 .. **92** C8
Golborne Rd *AIMK* WN4 .... **91** M1
GOL/RIS/CU WA3 .... **92** E5
WARRN/WOL WA2 .... **105** J6
Golborne St *NEWLW* WA12 .... **105** G1
WARR WA1 .... **14** D5
Goldcliffe Cl *WARRW/BUR* WA5 .. **120** F3
Goldcrest Cl *RUNC* WA7 .... **150** B8
WD/CROXPK L12 .... **99** H1 1
Goldcrest Ms *HLWD* L26 .... **132** A4 4
Golden Gv *ANF/KKDL* L4 .... **97** J4
Goldenways *WGN* WN1 .... **68** E3 4
Goldfinch Cl *HLWD* L26 .... **132** A4
Goldfinch Farm Rd
SPK/HALE L24 .... **146** E2
Goldfinch La
GOL/RIS/CU WA3 .... **123** G1 2
Goldie St *ANF/KKDL* L4 .... **97** H6
Goldsmith Pl *WGNS/IIMK* WN3 .... **79** J1
Goldsmith Rd *CL/PREN* CH43 .. **127** H4 5
Goldsmith St *BTL* L20 .... **6** D2
NPK/KEN L6 .... **113** K2 5
Goldsmith Wy
CL/PREN CH43 .... **127** H4 4
Goldsworth Fold
RAIN/WH L35 .... **117** K2 2
Golf Links Rd *RF/TRAN* CH42 .... **127** K4
Golf Rd *FMBY* L37 .... **46** F8
Gondover Av *WLT/FAZ* L9 .... **84** B7
Gonville Rd *BTL* L20 .... **7** K7
Gooch Dr *NEWLW* WA12 .... **104** F3
Goodacre Rd *WLT/FAZ* L9 .... **84** D6
Goodaker's Meadow
GR/UP/WCH CH49 .... **126** C3 5
Goodall Pl *ANF/KKDL* L4 .... **7** L9
ANF/KKDL L4 .... **97** G5 6
Goodall St *ANF/KKDL* L4 .... **7** M9
Goodban St *STHEL* WA9 .... **103** G5
Goodison Av *ANF/KKDL* L4 .... **97** H5 5
Goodison Pl *ANF/KKDL* L4 .... **97** H4 2
Goodison Rd *ANF/KKDL* L4 .... **97** H4
Goodlass Rd *SPK/HALE* L24 .... **131** J8
Goodleigh Pl *STHEL* WA9 .... **102** E8
Good Shepherd Cl
NG/CROX L11 .... **98** D3 1
Goodwood Cl *HUY* L36 .... **115** M4 2
Goodwood Gv *GTS/LS* CH66 .... **162** F2
Goodwood St *EV* L5 .... **96** F8
Gooseberry La *RUNC* WA7 .... **150** F4 4
Goose Green Av *CHLY/EC* PR7 .... **43** H4
Goostrey Cl *BEB* CH63 .... **143** K4
Gordale Cl *WARRW/BUR* WA5 .... **120** B6
Gordon Av *AIMK* WN4 .... **91** G1
CHTN/BK PR9 .... **24** E4
CSBY/WL L22 .... **82** E3 2
GR/UP/WCH CH49 .... **126** A2
MGHL L31 .... **72** E2
PS/BROM CH62 .... **144** A6
RNFD/HAY WA11 .... **91** H6 4
WARR WA1 .... **122** D6
Gordon Cl *WGNW/BIL/O* WN5 .... **68** A5
Gordon Ct *GR/UP/WCH* CH49 .... **126** A2
Gordon Dr *ALL/GAR* L19 .... **130** C6
DV/KA/FCH L14 .... **115** G2
Gordon La *CHNE* CH2 .... **163** K8
Gordon Rd *LITH* L21 .... **83** H7
WAL/NB CH45 .... **95** K6
Gordonstoun Crs
WGNW/BIL/O WN5 .... **67** H6
Gordon St *BIRK* CH41 .... **10** F6
CHLYE PR6 .... **32** F5
CHTN/BK PR9 .... **3** J1
WAV L15 .... **114** A6
WGN WN1 .... **5** K5
Gore Dr *ORM* L39 .... **63** G2
Gores La *FMBY* L37 .... **47** G8
RNFD/HAY WA11 .... **77** H7
RNFD/HAY WA11 .... **77** J8
Gores Rd *NWD/KWIPK* L33 .... **86** D4
Gore St *TOX* L8 .... **113** G7
WGNW/BIL/O WN5 .... **67** K7
Goring St *CHLY/EC* PR7 .... **32** F6
Gorman St *WGNNW/ST* WN6 .... **4** A3
Gorse Av *WD/CROXPK* L12 .... **98** D4
Gorsebank Rd *CALD/MH* L18 .... **114** A8 2
Gorsebank St *WAL/EC* CH44 ..... **111** L2 4
Gorseburn Rd *CLB/OSW/ST* L13 .... **98** A7
Gorse Covert Rd
GOL/RIS/CU WA3 .... **107** J8
Gorse Crs *WAL/EC* CH44 .... **111** L3
Gorsedale Pk *WAL/EC* CH44 .... **111** M3 1
Gorsedale Rd *CALD/MH* L18 .... **130** C1
WAL/EC CH44 .... **111** L3
Gorsefield *FMBY* L37 .... **47** J7
RAIN/WH L35 .... **101** M6 5
Gorsefield Av *PS/BROM* CH62 .... **143** M8
Gorsefield Cl *PS/BROM* CH62 .... **143** M8
Gorsefield Rd *CSBY/BLUN* L23 .... **71** J8
RF/TRAN CH42 .... **127** L2
Gorse Hey Ct *WD/CROXPK* L12 .... **98** C8
Gorsehill Rd *HES* CH60 .... **141** J4
WAL/NB CH45 .... **95** J6
Gorse La *WKBY* CH48 .... **125** G4
Gorse Rd *HOY* CH47 .... **108** F5
Gorses Dr *WGNE/HIN* WN2 .... **57** L7
Gorse Wy *FMBY* L37 .... **58** E1
Gorsewood Gv *WLTN* L25 .... **115** K8 1
Gorsewood Rd *RUNC* WA7 .... **150** F7
WLTN L25 .... **115** K8
Gorsey Brow *WGNW/BIL/O* WN5 .. **77** M8
Gorsey Brow Cl
WGNW/BIL/O WN5 .... **77** M8
Gorsey Cop Wy *WLTN* L25 .... **115** J7
Gorsey Cft *PR/KW* L34 .... **101** H6
Gorsey La *BRSC* L40 .... **40** E3
CHTN/BK PR9 .... **23** L6
HTWN L38 .... **70** C4
LITH L21 .... **83** L4 1
NTHTN L30 .... **83** L2
ORM L39 .... **48** C6
STHEL WA9 .... **119** H1
WAL/EC CH44 .... **111** K3
WARRN/WOL WA2 .... **15** J1
WDN WA8 .... **17** L4
Gorsey Pl *SKEL* WN8 .... **65** K6
Gorseyville Crs *BEB* CH63 .... **128** A8 1
Gorseyville Rd *BEB* CH63 .... **128** A8
Gorseywell La *RUNC* WA7 .... **151** H7
Gorst La *CHTN/BK* PR9 .... **38** B7
Gorstons La *NSTN* CH64 .... **153** J7
Gorst St *ANF/KKDL* L4 .... **97** H6
Gorsuch La *BRSC* L40 .... **49** M1
Gorton Rd *CLB/OSW/ST* L13 .... **114** D3
Gort Rd *HUY* L36 .... **116** A2
Goschen St *BIRK* CH41 .... **111** H5 5
CLB/OSW/ST L13 .... **114** B2
EV L5 .... **97** H6 5
Gosford St *TOX* L8 .... **129** H1
Gosforth Rd *CHTN/BK* PR9 .... **25** H5
Gosling Rd *GOL/RIS/CU* WA3 .... **106** D6
Gosport Cl *WARRN/WOL* WA2 .... **122** A4
Goswell St *WAV* L15 .... **114** A6
Gotham Rd *BEB* CH63 .... **143** J3
Gothic St *RF/TRAN* CH42 .... **128** B3
Gough Av *WARRN/WOL* WA2 .... **121** K3
Gough Rd *CLB/OSW/ST* L13 .... **98** A6
Goulden St *WARRW/BUR* WA5 .... **121** G7
Goulders Ct *RUNC* WA7 .... **150** D8 5
Goulding St *CHLY/EC* PR7 .... **32** F7
Gourley Rd *CLB/OSW/ST* L13 .... **114** D4
Gourley's La *WKBY* CH48 .... **124** F4
Government Rd *HOY* CH47 .... **108** D6
Govett Rd *RAIN/WH* L35 .... **101** L6
Gower Gdns *BRSC* L40 .... **52** B2
Gower St *BTL* L20 .... **83** J8
STHEL WA9 .... **102** F4
VAUX/LVPD L3 .... **112** E5
WGNW/BIL/O WN5 .... **68** B7
Gowrie Gv *LITH* L21 .... **83** J6
Goyt Hey Av *WGNW/BIL/O* WN5 .... **90** A1
Graburn Rd *FMBY* L37 .... **59** H1
Grace Av *AIN/FAZ* L10 .... **85** J6
WARRN/WOL WA2 .... **121** K5
Grace Rd *EP* CH65 .... **20** C2
WLT/FAZ L9 .... **84** C7
Grace St *LEIGH* WN7 .... **81** L8 1
TOX L8 .... **129** H1
Gradwell St *CLVPS* L1 .... **13** G8
Grafton Ct *CHLY/EC* PR7 .... **32** D8 4
Grafton Dr *GR/UP/WCH* CH49 .... **126** C1
STHP PR8 .... **34** C8
Grafton Gv *TOX* L8 .... **129** G1
Grafton Rd *EP* CH65 .... **20** C1
WAL/NB CH45 .... **95** K6 5
Grafton St *CHLY/EC* PR7 .... **44** B7
CL/PREN CH43 .... **10** D7
ECCL WA10 .... **8** B5
NEWLW WA12 .... **104** D2 6
TOX L8 .... **112** F7
TOX L8 .... **113** G7 1
WARRW/BUR WA5 .... **121** G7
Grafton Wk *WKBY* CH48 .... **124** E3
Graham Av *GTS/LS* CH66 .... **155** M8
WGNNW/ST WN6 .... **54** E3
Graham Cl *WDN* WA8 .... **133** L4 2
Graham Dr *HLWD* L26 .... **132** C5 1
Graham Rd *WDN* WA8 .... **133** L5
WKBY CH48 .... **124** C2
Graham's Rd *HUY* L36 .... **116** B3
Graham St *STHEL* WA9 .... **9** L5
WGNE/HIN WN2 .... **80** C4
Grainger Av *BTL* L20 .... **84** A7
CL/PREN CH43 .... **127** H3
WKBY CH48 .... **124** D1
Graley Cl *HLWD* L26 .... **132** B7
Grammar School La
WKBY CH48 .... **124** F4
Grammar School Rd
WARRS WA4 .... **138** B2
Grampian Av *MOR/LEA* CH46 .. **110** B5 1
Grampian Rd *EHL/KEN* L7 .... **114** A3
Grampian Wy *GOL/RIS/CU* WA3 .... **92** F4
MOR/LEA CH46 .... **110** A5
NSTN CH64 .... **153** G8 5
PS/BROM CH62 .... **155** G1
Granams Cft *NTHTN* L30 .... **83** M1
Granard Rd *WAV* L15 .... **114** C7
Granary Wy *VAUX/LVPD* L3 ..... **112** F7 5
Granborne Cha *KKBY* L32 .... **85** K2
Granby Cl *CHTN/BK* PR9 .... **25** H2
RUNC WA7 .... **150** E8 5
Granby Crs *BEB* CH63 .... **143** J3
Granby Rd *WARRS* WA4 .... **137** K5
Granby St *TOX* L8 .... **113** J6
Grandison Rd *ANF/KKDL* L4 .... **97** L4
Grange Av *CHTN/BK* PR9 .... **25** G5
WAL/NB CH45 .... **95** K7
WARRS WA4 .... **15** M8
WD/CROXPK L12 .... **99** G8
WGNS/IIMK WN3 .... **4** C9
WGNW/BIL/O WN5 .... **67** K6
WLTN L25 .... **131** M6
Grange Av North
DV/KA/FCH L14 .... **99** H8
WD/CROXPK L12 .... **99** H8
Grange Cl *GOL/RIS/CU* WA3 .... **92** E7
Grange Crs *GTS/LS* CH66 .... **155** J4
Grange Cross Cl *WKBY* CH48 .... **125** G4
Grange Cross Hey *WKBY* CH48 .... **125** G4
Grange Cross La *WKBY* CH48 .... **125** G4
Grange Dr *BEB* CH63 .... **142** C6
CHLYE PR6 .... **31** L1
ECCL WA10 .... **101** K4
HES CH60 .... **141** H4
WARRW/BUR WA5 .... **136** C1
WDN WA8 .... **133** M4
Grange Farm Crs *WKBY* CH48 .... **125** G2
Grangehurst Ct *WLTN* L25 .... **131** K1 2
Grange La *FMBY* L37 .... **47** G8
WLTN L25 .... **115** J8
Grangemeadow Rd *WLTN* L25 .... **115** J8
Grangemoor *RUNC* WA7 .... **149** M6
Grange Mt *CL/PREN* CH43 .... **10** E7
HES CH60 .... **141** H4
WKBY CH48 .... **124** F3
Grange Old Rd *WKBY* CH48 .... **124** E3
Grange Pk *MGHL* L31 .... **73** G6
Grange Park Av *RUNC* WA7 .... **19** L4
Grange Park Rd *ECCL* WA10 .... **101** L4
RUNC WA7 .... **19** L4
Grange Pl *CL/PREN* CH43 .... **10** F6
Grange Rd *AIMK* WN4 .... **79** H7
BIRK CH41 .... **11** J6 1
CHTN/BK PR9 .... **25** G6
EP CH65 .... **20** C5
HES CH60 .... **141** H3
HTWN L38 .... **59** G7
NTHTN L30 .... **84** D3
RNFD/HAY WA11 .... **90** F8
RUNC WA7 .... **19** L4
WGNE/HIN WN2 .... **81** G4
WKBY CH48 .... **124** D3
Grange Rd West *CL/PREN* CH43 .... **10** E6
Grangeside *WLTN* L25 .... **115** J8
Grange St *NPK/KEN* L6 .... **97** M8
WGNE/HIN WN2 .... **80** F1
Grange Ter *WAV* L15 .... **114** B6
The Grange *WAL/EC* CH44 .... **111** L1 5
Grange V *RF/TRAN* CH42 .... **128** C4
Grange Va *RNFD/HAY* WA11 .... **90** F7
Grange Vw *CL/PREN* CH43 .... **10** E7
Grangeway *RUNC* WA7 .... **19** L9
Grange Wy *WLTN* L25 .... **115** J8
Grange Weint *WLTN* L25 .... **131** J1
Grangewood *CHLDW* L16 .... **115** H4
Granston Cl
WARRW/BUR WA5 .... **121** G3 5
Grant Av *WAV* L15 .... **114** B7
Grant Cl *DV/KA/FCH* L14 .... **115** J2
ECCL WA10 .... **8** D4
WARRW/BUR WA5 .... **120** F4
Grantham Av *WARR* WA1 .... **15** M1
WARRS WA4 .... **137** K5
Grantham Cl *PEN/TH* CH61 .... **141** G1 2
STHP PR8 .... **35** J4
Grantham Crs *RNFD/HAY* WA11 ...... **9** M2
Grantham Gv *WGNE/HIN* WN2 .. **69** H3 4
Grantham Rd *NWD/KWIPK* L33 .... **74** A8
STHP PR8 .... **35** J4
Grantham St *NPK/KEN* L6 .... **113** K2
Grantham Wy *NTHTN* L30 .... **84** C1
Grantley Rd *WAV* L15 .... **114** D7 2
Grantley St *AIMK* WN4 .... **79** J8
Granton Cl *FMBY* L37 .... **59** G2
Granton Rd *EV* L5 .... **97** H7
Grant Rd *DV/KA/FCH* L14 .... **115** H2
MOR/LEA CH46 .... **110** D1
WARRW/BUR WA5 .... **120** D7 2
WGNS/IIMK WN3 .... **79** J2
Grantwood *AIMK* WN4 .... **79** J8 4
Granville Av *MGHL* L31 .... **72** E3
Granville Cl *ORM* L39 .... **62** D4
WAL/NB CH45 .... **95** G7 5
Granville Dr *GTS/LS* CH66 .... **155** K6
Granville Pk *ORM* L39 .... **62** D5

Granville Pk West ORM L39 62 D5
Granville Rd ALL/GAR L19 130 E7 1
CHLYE PR6 33 G4
STHP PR8 34 F2
WAV L15 113 M6
Granville St CHLYE PR6 44 C6
RUNC WA7 19 H2
STHEL WA9 102 F2
WARR WA1 15 J3
Grape La LEY/BBR PR5 29 L4
Grappenhall La WARRS WA4 138 F7
Grappenhall Rd EP CH65 163 H2
WARRS WA4 137 M4
Grappenhall Wy
CL/PREN CH43 110 E6 4
Grasmere Av CL/PREN CH43 110 E8
PR/KW L34 101 H7
RNFD/HAY WA11 89 K6
SKEL WN8 66 D5
WARRN/WOL WA2 121 M2
WGNE/HIN WN2 69 J6
WGNE/HIN WN2 81 G1
WGNW/BIL/O WN5 67 H5 1
Grasmere Cl CHLY/EC PR7 31 M4
NWD/KWIPK L33 85 M1
RNFD/HAY WA11 89 K6 2
Grasmere Ct RNFD/HAY WA11 89 K6 5
Grasmere Dr AIMK WN4 79 K8
LITH L21 84 A4
RUNC WA7 149 M8
WAL/NB CH45 95 J8
Grasmere Fold
RNFD/HAY WA11 89 K6 4
Grasmere Gdns CSBY/BLUN L23 83 H2
Grasmere Rd EP CH65 163 L3
FMBY L37 58 F2
FROD/HEL WA6 160 E5
MGHL L31 72 F3
NSTN CH64 153 G7
WGNW/BIL/O WN5 67 L6
Grasmere St EV L5 97 J7
Grasmere Ter CHLY/EC PR7 32 D8
WGNE/HIN WN2 80 D5 2
Grasscroft Rd WGNE/HIN WN2 81 J1
Grassendale La ALL/GAR L19 130 C6
Grassendale Prom
ALL/GAR L19 130 B7
Grassendale Rd ALL/GAR L19 130 C6
Grassington Crs WLTN L25 131 M3
Grassmoor Cl
PS/BROM CH62 144 A5 1
Grass Wood Rd
GR/UP/WCH CH49 126 D3
Grasville Rd RF/TRAN CH42 128 A2
Gratrix Rd PS/BROM CH62 143 M5
Gratton Pl SKEL WN8 65 J5
Gravel La CHTN/BK PR9 23 H8
CHTN/BK PR9 26 C1
The Gravel KIRK/FR/WA PR4 27 H3
Grave-yard La ORM L39 63 J6
Gray Av RNFD/HAY WA11 90 F7
Gray Cl WGNE/HIN WN2 69 J3
Gray Gv HUY L36 116 B5
Graylag Cl RUNC WA7 150 B8 2
Graylands Pl ANF/KKDL L4 97 L4 2
Graylands Rd ANF/KKDL L4 97 L4
PS/BROM CH62 128 E7
Grayling Dr WD/CROXPK L12 98 F2
Grays Av RAIN/WH L35 101 H7
Grayson's Cl WGN WN1 4 F1
Graysons Rd RNFD/HAY WA11 76 B5
Grayson St CLVPS L1 112 E5 3
Grayston Av STHEL WA9 102 F7
Gray St BTL L20 83 J8
Greasby Dr GTS/LS CH66 163 G1
Greasby Rd GR/UP/WCH CH49 125 L2
WAL/EG CH44 111 J1
Great Acre WGN WN1 5 H1
Great Ashfield WDN WA8 133 M2
Great Charlotte St CLVPS L1 13 H7 2
CLVPS L1 13 H7 3
Great Crosshall St VAUX/LVPD L3 12 F5
Great Delph RNFD/HAY WA11 90 F6
Great George Pl CLVPS L1 113 G6 3
Great George's Rd CSBY/WL L22 82 F5
Great George St CLVPS L1 113 G5 3
WGNS/IIMK WN3 4 C4
Great Hanging Br LEY/BBR PR5 28 F5
Great Hey NTHTN L30 71 M8
Great Homer St EV L5 97 G8
Great Howard St EV L5 96 D8
VAUX/LVPD L3 12 D4
Great Meadow CHLY/EC PR7 32 C3
Great Mersey St EV L5 96 F7
Great Nelson St VAUX/LVPD L3 13 H2
Great Newton St VAUX/LVPD L3 13 L6
Great Orford St VAUX/LVPD L3 13 L8
Great Richmond St
VAUX/LVPD L3 13 J3
Great Riding RUNC WA7 150 E6
Greaves Cl WGNNW/ST WN6 55 H5
Greaves Hall Av CHTN/BK PR9 23 J8
Greaves St TOX L8 129 H1 6
Grebe Av ECCL WA10 101 J5
Grebe Cl WGNS/IIMK WN3 78 D1
Grecian St LITH L21 83 H5
Grecian Ter EV L5 97 H7 2
Gredington St TOX L8 129 J1 10
Greeba Av WARRS WA4 137 K2
Greek St RUNC WA7 18 F2
VAUX/LVPD L3 13 K6
Greenacre BRSC L40 64 A1
WGN WN1 5 H1
Greenacre Cl WLTN L25 131 L5
Greenacre Dr BEB CH63 143 K6
Greenacre Rd WLTN L25 131 L5
Greenacres FROD/HEL WA6 160 E7
Greenacres Cl CL/PREN CH43 110 E5
GOL/RIS/CU WA3 93 K5 3
Greenall Av
WARRW/BUR WA5 135 M1 1
Greenall's Av WARRS WA4 137 L4
Greenall St AIMK WN4 79 K8 1
ECCL WA10 8 B3
Green Bank BEB CH63 142 C3
Greenbank CSBY/WL L22 83 G5
WGNE/HIN WN2 80 D6
WGNE/HIN WN2 81 J2 2
Greenbank Av GTS/LS CH66 155 L6
MGHL L31 72 E2
WAL/NB CH45 95 K6 4
WGNW/BIL/O WN5 77 M2
Greenbank Ct AIG/SPK L17 114 A8
Greenbank Crs ECCL WA10 8 E6
Greenbank Dr AIG/SPK L17 114 A8
AIN/FAZ L10 85 K6
PEN/TH CH61 141 H2
STHP PR8 35 G3
Greenbank Gdns WARRS WA4 138 B3
Greenbank La AIG/SPK L17 130 A1
Greenbank Rd CALD/MH L18 114 B8
RF/TRAN CH42 127 L2
WARRS WA4 138 B3
WKBY CH48 124 D1
Greenbank St WARRS WA4 137 L3 1
Greenbarn Wy HOR/BR BL6 57 M3 4
Green Bridge Cl RUNC WA7 150 C4 2
Greenbridge Rd RUNC WA7 150 D3
Greenburn Av
RNFD/HAY WA11 89 L4 3
Green Coppice RUNC WA7 150 E5
Green Ct GOL/RIS/CU WA3 93 K4
Green Cft CSBY/BLUN L23 71 K8 4
Greencroft Rd WAL/EG CH44 111 L2
Greendale Rd PS/BROM CH62 128 C7
WLTN L25 131 H1
Green End La STHEL WA9 102 E5 3
Green End Pk
WD/CROXPK L12 98 C6 4
Greene's Rd RAIN/WH L35 116 F3
Greenfield Av SKEL WN8 53 K3
WGNE/HIN WN2 5 L6
Greenfield Dr HUY L36 116 B5
Greenfield Gdns CHNE CH2 165 K2
Greenfield Gv HUY L36 116 B5 3
Greenfield La FROD/HEL WA6 160 D4
HES CH60 140 E3
LITH L21 83 J4
Greenfield Rd CHLYE PR6 33 G5 3
CHLYE PR6 44 C5 4
CLB/OSW/ST L13 114 C2
ECCL WA10 8 B1
GTS/LS CH66 155 K6
STHP PR8 36 E4
Greenfields WGNNW/ST WN6 68 C1
Greenfields Av PS/BROM CH62 143 L6
WARRS WA4 137 M5
Greenfields Cl NEWLW WA12 104 E1 3
NSTN CH64 153 H8 1
WARR WA1 122 E6 2
Greenfields Crs AIMK WN4 91 K1 3
PS/BROM CH62 143 L6
Greenfields Cft NSTN CH64 153 G8
Greenfield Vw
WGNW/BIL/O WN5 89 M1
Greenfield Wy CALD/MH L18 130 E4 1
Greenfinch Cl HLWD L26 132 A4 5
WD/CROXPK L12 99 H2 1
Greenford Cl WGNW/BIL/O WN5 66 F7
Greenford Rd STHP PR8 47 L1
Greengables Cl TOX L8 113 J8
Green Gates HUY L36 100 A7
Greengates Crs NSTN CH64 153 G8
Greenhalgh La CHLYE PR6 44 D5
Greenham Av NWD/KWIPK L33 74 B7
Greenhaven Cl AIN/FAZ L10 85 J5
Green Hayes Av WGN WN1 68 E2
Greenheath Wy
MOR/LEA CH46 110 B2 4
Greenhey WGNW/BIL/O WN5 67 J6
Green Hey Dr NTHTN L30 83 L3
Greenhey Pl SKEL WN8 65 H5
Green Heys Dr MGHL L31 73 H3
Greenheys Rd PEN/TH CH61 125 L8
TOX L8 113 K7
WAL/EG CH44 111 K1
Greenhill Av CALD/MH L18 114 E8
Greenhill Cl CALD/MH L18 130 D3
Greenhill Crs WGNW/BIL/O WN5 78 B8
Greenhill Pl HUY L36 116 A4
Greenhill Rd ALL/GAR L19 130 E5
CALD/MH L18 130 D1
WGNW/BIL/O WN5 78 A8
Greenholme Cl NG/CROX L11 98 C2 2
Greenhouse Farm Rd
RUNC WA7 150 D7
Greenhow Av WKBY CH48 124 D2
Greenings La CHTN/BK PR9 37 L2
Green Jones Brow
WARRW/BUR WA5 104 B7
Greenlake Rd CALD/MH L18 130 D3
Greenland Av WGNNW/ST WN6 56 A5
Greenland La CHLYE PR6 44 F8
Greenlands HUY L36 116 A4 3
Greenland St CLVPS L1 113 G6 4
Green La BEB CH63 128 B8
BIRK CH41 11 K9
BRSC L40 40 C6
BRSC L40 52 B1
BRSC L40 53 H7
CALD/MH L18 114 E8
CALD/MH L18 130 D1
CHLY/EC PR7 43 J6
CHTN/BK PR9 26 E1
CLB/OSW/ST L13 114 B1
CSBY/BLUN L23 71 K7
CSBY/WL L22 82 E3
ECCL WA10 88 A7
EP CH65 20 C7
FMBY L37 47 H7
GOL/RIS/CU WA3 93 J3
GTS/LS CH66 162 F1
HOR/BR BL6 45 K8
KIRK/FR/WA PR4 27 L1
LITH L21 83 J6
LITH L21 83 K3
MGHL L31 72 E4 2
ORM L39 51 G7
RNFD/HAY WA11 76 C8
VAUX/LVPD L3 13 K8 1
WAL/NB CH45 94 D8
WARR WA1 122 C5
WARRN/WOL WA2 105 J6
WARRS WA4 138 C8
WARRW/BUR WA5 104 A6
WDN WA8 134 A4
WGNNW/ST WN6 56 A5
WGNW/BIL/O WN5 77 M2
Green Lane Av ORM L39 51 G7 3
Green Lane Cl
WARRN/WOL WA2 105 J6
Green La North CHLDW L16 114 E7
Green Lawn HUY L36 116 C1
RF/TRAN CH42 128 B4
Green Lawn Gv
RF/TRAN CH42 128 B4 2
Green Lawns Dr GTS/LS CH66 163 H5 3
Green Leach Av
RNFD/HAY WA11 89 K6
Green Leach Ct
RNFD/HAY WA11 89 K6 5
Green Leach La RNFD/HAY WA11 89 K6
Greenlea Cl BEB CH63 128 B7
EP CH65 163 K3
WGNW/BIL/O WN5 66 F8
Greenleaf St TOX L8 113 L6
Greenleas Rd WAL/NB CH45 94 F7
Greenleigh Rd CALD/MH L18 130 D3
Green Link MGHL L31 72 D3
Greenloon's Dr FMBY L37 58 E3 2
Greenloon's Wk FMBY L37 58 E3
Green Mt GR/UP/WCH CH49 110 C8
Green Oaks Pth WDN WA8 17 H3
Green Oaks Wy WDN WA8 17 G3
Greenock St VAUX/LVPD L3 12 C4
Greenodd Av WD/CROXPK L12 98 E4
Greenore Dr SPK/HALE L24 147 M3 2
Greenough Av RAIN/WH L35 101 L8 1
Greenough St WGN WN1 5 H3
WLTN L25 131 H3 3
Green Pk NTHTN L30 72 B8
Green Park Dr MGHL L31 72 D4
Greenrigg Cl WGNNW/ST WN6 56 B6
Green Rd PR/KW L34 100 E7 1
Greensbridge La HLWD L26 132 D4
Greenshank Cl NEWLW WA12 104 E1 4
Greenside CHLY/EC PR7 31 L2
NPK/KEN L6 13 M4
Greenside Av AIN/FAZ L10 84 F3
FROD/HEL WA6 160 F6
WAV L15 114 C6 3
Greenside Cl NWD/KWIPK L33 74 C7 3
Green's La MGHL L31 61 L4
Greenslate Ct
WGNW/BIL/O WN5 77 M2
Greenslate Rd
WGNW/BIL/O WN5 78 A2
Green Strawberry EP CH65 163 J5
Green St CHLY/EC PR7 32 C8 3
CHLYE PR6 44 D5
EV L5 12 F1
WARRW/BUR WA5 14 A6
WARRW/BUR WA5 121 G8 2
WGNE/HIN WN2 80 D3 4
WGNS/IIMK WN3 4 E7
Greensward Cl
WGNNW/ST WN6 55 K4 1
The Green BEB CH63 153 L1
CHLY/EC PR7 30 E7
CHLYE PR6 44 B3
CLB/OSW/ST L13 114 E3
EP CH65 163 K3
NSTN CH64 152 F5
NSTN CH64 153 H7
PR/KW L34 101 G6
PS/BROM CH62 129 G8
RUNC WA7 150 B4 2
SKEL WN8 53 K3
WGNW/BIL/O WN5 67 K7
WKBY CH48 124 F6
Greenvale WGNNW/ST WN6 67 H1
Greenville Cl BEB CH63 128 B8
Greenville Dr MGHL L31 72 E4
Greenville Rd BEB CH63 128 B8
NSTN CH64 153 H4 1
Green Wk STHP PR8 34 F8 1
Green Wy HUY L36 115 K1
Greenway AIMK WN4 91 J1
CHLY/EC PR7 30 D6 1
CSBY/BLUN L23 71 J8
GR/UP/WCH CH49 126 A1
PEN/TH CH61 141 G1
PS/BROM CH62 143 M2 2
WARR WA1 122 B6
WARRS WA4 137 M6
WARRW/BUR WA5 120 A6 3
Greenway Av SKEL WN8 65 K6
Greenway Cl FROD/HEL WA6 166 D2 1
Green Way Cl HUY L36 115 K1
Greenway Cl SKEL WN8 65 G3 1
Greenway Rd RF/TRAN CH42 127 M2
RUNC WA7 18 F6
SPK/HALE L24 147 J2
WDN WA8 134 D3
Greenways WGNNW/ST WN6 56 C7
WGNW/BIL/O WN5 77 M2
The Greenway
WD/CROXPK L12 115 G1
Greenwell Rd RNFD/HAY WA11 90 E7
Greenwich Ct WLT/FAZ L9 84 D5
Greenwich Rd WLT/FAZ L9 84 D5
Greenwood Av
WGNW/BIL/O WN5 68 A6
Greenwood Cl
GOL/RIS/CU WA3 107 H3
ORM L39 62 E4
PR/KW L34 101 G7
Greenwood Ct STHEL WA9 118 E1
Greenwood Crs
WARRN/WOL WA2 121 M3 5
Greenwood Dr NEWLW WA12 104 F3
Greenwood La WAL/EG CH44 95 L8
Greenwood Rd CALD/MH L18 130 D4
GR/UP/WCH CH49 126 C2
WGNNW/ST WN6 56 A3
Greetby Hl ORM L39 51 J8
Greetham St CLVPS L1 112 F5 3
Gregory Cl CHLDW L16 115 G5 2
WARRW/BUR WA5 120 E6
Gregory La ORM L39 49 K2
Gregory St WGNE/HIN WN2 69 L7 3
Gregory Wy CHLDW L16 115 G5
Gregson Ct WAL/NB CH45 95 L5
Gregson Rd DV/KA/FCH L14 114 E2
RAIN/WH L35 100 F8
WDN WA8 17 H2
Gregson's Av FMBY L37 47 G8
Gregson St NPK/KEN L6 13 M3
Grenfell Cl WGNS/IIMK WN3 4 A9
Grenfell Cl NSTN CH64 152 E4
Grenfell Pk NSTN CH64 152 E4
Grenfell Rd CLB/OSW/ST L13 98 A5
Grenfell St WDN WA8 16 E4
The Grennan WAL/NB CH45 95 K5 4
Grenville Crs BEB CH63 143 L6
Grenville Dr PEN/TH CH61 141 G2
Grenville Rd RF/TRAN CH42 128 B2
Grenville St South CLVPS L1 112 F5
Grenville Wy RF/TRAN CH42 128 B2 7
Gresford Av AIG/SPK L17 113 M7
CL/PREN CH43 127 J3
WKBY CH48 124 E2
Gresford Cl RAIN/WH L35 117 H2 3
WARRW/BUR WA5 120 F3 2
Gresham St EHL/KEN L7 113 M3
Gresley Cl EHL/KEN L7 113 L4 7
WGN WN1 5 J4
Gressingham Rd CALD/MH L18 130 E2
Gretton Rd DV/KA/FCH L14 99 K8
Greyfriars AIMK WN4 91 H1
Greyfriars Rd STHP PR8 34 D7
Grey Heights Vw CHLYE PR6 33 G5
Greyhound Farm Rd
SPK/HALE L24 146 E2
Greymist Av WARR WA1 122 E6
Grey Rd AIMK WN4 91 J1
WLT/FAZ L9 97 H1
Grey Rock Wk NPK/KEN L6 113 K1
Greystoke Cl GR/UP/WCH CH49 126 B1
Greystokes ORM L39 62 F3
Greystone Av WGNE/HIN WN2 57 L8
Greystone Crs
DV/KA/FCH L14 115 G2 1
Greystone Pl AIN/FAZ L10 85 H6 3
Greystone Rd AIN/FAZ L10 85 G6
DV/KA/FCH L14 115 G3
WARRW/BUR WA5 136 B1
Greystones GTS/LS CH66 162 F1
Grey St TOX L8 113 H6 7
TOX L8 113 H7 3
WARR WA1 15 G4
Gribble Rd AIN/FAZ L10 85 J6
Grice St WARRS WA4 137 L4 2
Grierson St TOX L8 113 K6
Grieve Rd AIN/FAZ L10 85 J6
Griffin Av MOR/LEA CH46 110 A5
Griffin Cl ECCL WA10 101 H1
NG/CROX L11 98 E1
WARRW/BUR WA5 104 A7 1
Griffin Ms WDN WA8 134 D2 3
Griffin St STHEL WA9 103 G6 1
Griffith Av GOL/RIS/CU WA3 107 G8
Griffiths Cl GR/UP/WCH CH49 125 L2
Griffiths Dr CHTN/BK PR9 25 H5
Griffith's Rd HUY L36 116 A3 2
Griffiths St CLVPS L1 113 G5 3
WARRS WA4 15 M8
WARRS WA4 138 B1
Grimeford La CHLYE PR6 44 F7
HOR/BR BL6 44 E8
Grime St CHLY/EC PR7 32 F7
Grimley Av BTL L20 6 C2
Grimrod Pl SKEL WN8 65 J6
Grimshaw Green La SKEL WN8 40 E8
Grimshaw La ORM L39 51 G7
Grimshaw Rd SKEL WN8 65 M5
Grimshaw St BTL L20 6 E6
GOL/RIS/CU WA3 92 C4
STHEL WA9 102 E7
Grindley Gdns EP CH65 163 L3 1
Grinfield St EHL/KEN L7 113 J4
Grinshill Cl TOX L8 113 J7
Grinstead Cl STHP PR8 35 H4
Grinton Crs HUY L36 115 M3
Grisedale Av
WARRN/WOL WA2 121 K2 1
Grisedale Cl FMBY L37 59 G2
RUNC WA7 150 A8
Grisedale Pl CHLY/EC PR7 32 D8
Grisedale Rd PS/BROM CH62 144 A5
Grizedale WDN WA8 133 K3
Grizedale Av RNFD/HAY WA11 89 K5
Grizedale Dr WGNE/HIN WN2 69 J6
Grizedale Rd EV L5 97 H7
Groarke Dr WARRW/BUR WA5 119 M8
Groes Rd ALL/GAR L19 130 D6
Grogan Sq BTL L20 83 M7
Gronow Pl BTL L20 84 A7 2
Grosmont Rd KKBY L32 86 B5
Grosvenor Av CSBY/BLUN L23 83 G3
GOL/RIS/CU WA3 92 F5 2
WARR WA1 15 M1
WKBY CH48 124 D3
Grosvenor Cl STHP PR8 35 G2
WARRW/BUR WA5 120 E8 4
Grosvenor Dr WAL/NB CH45 95 K5
Grosvenor Gdns NEWLW WA12 104 D3
STHP PR8 35 H2 1
Grosvenor Pl CL/PREN CH43 10 A7
STHP PR8 35 H2
Grosvenor Rd ALL/GAR L19 130 C7
ANF/KKDL L4 97 H3 4
CHLY/EC PR7 32 C7
CL/PREN CH43 10 A6
ECCL WA10 101 L3
HOY CH47 108 D7
LEIGH WN7 81 M7 2
MGHL L31 72 E7
PR/KW L34 100 F7
RNFD/HAY WA11 90 D7
STHP PR8 35 G1
WAL/NB CH45 95 K5
WAV L15 113 M6
WDN WA8 134 D1
Grosvenor St RUNC WA7 19 K2
VAUX/LVPD L3 13 H3
WAL/EG CH44 95 K8
WGNE/HIN WN2 69 M8 15
WGNW/BIL/O WN5 68 B7 5
Grounds St WARRN/WOL WA2 14 F2
Grove Av CHLYE PR6 44 C6
HES CH60 141 H4
LYMM WA13 139 L2
Grove Crs CHLYE PR6 44 C6
Grovedale Rd CALD/MH L18 114 B8 7
Grovehurst Av DV/KA/FCH L14 115 H1
Groveland Av HOY CH47 108 D6 3
WAL/NB CH45 94 F7 1
Groveland Rd WAL/NB CH45 94 F7
Grove La WGNNW/ST WN6 56 B5
Grove Md MGHL L31 73 H4
Grovenor Cl NTHTN L30 84 B2 1
Grove Pk CHTN/BK PR9 25 H4
ORM L39 51 H6 2
TOX L8 113 L7
Grove Park Av WD/CROXPK L12 98 D5
Grove Pl ANF/KKDL L4 97 G6
HOY CH47 108 D6
WGNNW/ST WN6 56 B5
Grove Rd CH/BCN CH1 163 G8
HOY CH47 108 D6
NPK/KEN L6 113 M2
RF/TRAN CH42 128 B3
SKEL WN8 66 D5
WAL/NB CH45 95 G7
Grove Side EHL/KEN L7 113 J5
Groveside WKBY CH48 124 C3
Grove Sq PS/BROM CH62 128 C6
The Groves EP CH65 163 J5
KKBY L32 86 A6 1
Grove St AIMK WN4 91 J1
BTL L20 6 C2
PS/BROM CH62 128 D6
RUNC WA7 18 F2
STHP PR8 2 F9
TOX L8 113 J5
WARRS WA4 15 H8
WAV L15 114 B5
Grove Ter HOY CH47 108 D6 4
STHP PR8 2 F8
The Grove BEB CH63 128 C8
CHLYE PR6 32 E3
CL/PREN CH43 127 K2
CLB/OSW/ST L13 98 B8 2
ECCL WA10 88 E8
GOL/RIS/CU WA3 92 F4
ORM L39 62 E6
STBRV L28 99 L7 1
WAL/EG CH44 111 L2
WARRW/BUR WA5 136 B1
WGNE/HIN WN2 5 K6
WGNNW/ST WN6 54 E3
Grove Wy EHL/KEN L7 113 J5 4
Grovewood STHP PR8 2 B8
Grovewood Dr WGNNW/ST WN6 55 G6
Grovewood Gdns RAIN/WH L35 117 G2
Grundy Cl STHP PR8 25 G8
WDN WA8 134 B2 4
Grundy's La CHLY/EC PR7 43 L4
Grundy St EV L5 96 D7
GOL/RIS/CU WA3 92 C6
Guardian St WARRW/BUR WA5 14 B4
Guelph St EHL/KEN L7 113 J3
Guernsey Cl WARRS WA4 137 M5
Guernsey Dr EP CH65 163 L4
Guernsey Rd CLB/OSW/ST L13 114 B1
WDN WA8 135 G2
Guest St WDN WA8 16 C6 1
Guffitts Cl HOY CH47 109 G4
Guffitt's Rake HOY CH47 109 G4
Guildford Av CHLYE PR6 33 H1
Guildford Cl
WARRN/WOL WA2 122 C4 2
Guildford Crs WGNNW/ST WN6 68 B2
Guildford Rd STHP PR8 35 J5
Guildford St WAL/EG CH44 111 M1
Guildhall Rd WLT/FAZ L9 84 C7
Guild Hey PR/KW L34 99 M1
Guillemot Wy HLWD L26 132 A4
Guilsted Rd NG/CROX L11 98 C3
Guinea Hall La CHTN/BK PR9 23 J8
Guion Rd LITH L21 83 K6
Guion St NPK/KEN L6 113 K1 3
Gulls Wy HES CH60 140 F5
Gunn Gv NSTN CH64 153 H5
Gunning Av ECCL WA10 88 D8
Gunning Cl ECCL WA10 88 D8
Gurnall St ANF/KKDL L4 97 H6 3
Gutticar Rd WDN WA8 133 K5
Gwendoline Cl PEN/TH CH61 126 C8
Gwendoline St TOX L8 113 H7
Gwenfron Rd NPK/KEN L6 113 K2 7
Gwent Cl NPK/KEN L6 97 K8
Gwent St TOX L8 113 J7
Gwladys St ANF/KKDL L4 97 H4
Gwydir St TOX L8 113 J8
Gwydrin Rd CALD/MH L18 114 E8

H

Hackett Av BTL L20 83 M7
Hackins Hey CLVP L2 12 E6 4
Hackthorpe St EV L5 97 G6 10
Hackworth Cl WGN WN1 5 J4
Hadassah Gv AIG/SPK L17 129 L1
Hadden Cl RAIN/WH L35 117 J1 3
Haddock St BTL L20 6 F9
Haddon Av WLT/FAZ L9 84 B7
Haddon Dr PEN/TH CH61 141 H1
WDN WA8 133 L2
Haddon Rd GOL/RIS/CU WA3 92 F4
RF/TRAN CH42 128 C3
WGNS/IIMK WN3 79 G2
Haddon Wk WD/CROXPK L12 99 G2
Hadfield Av HOY CH47 108 D6
Hadfield Gv WLTN L25 131 L2
Hadleigh Cl WARRW/BUR WA5 119 M8
Hadleigh Rd KKBY L32 86 B4
Hadley Av PS/BROM CH62 143 L4
Hadlow La NSTN CH64 154 B6
Hadlow Rd NSTN CH64 154 B7
Hadstock Av FMBY L37 58 F4
Haggerston Rd ANF/KKDL L4 97 J3
Hague Bush Cl
GOL/RIS/CU WA3 93 G4 2
Hahnemann Rd ANF/KKDL L4 7 M7
Haig Av MOR/LEA CH46 110 A5
STHP PR8 25 G8

WARRW/BUR WA5 136 C1
Haigh Cl CHLY/EC PR7 32 C6
Haigh Crs CHLY/EC PR7 32 C6
MGHL L31 72 E1
Haigh Rd CSBY/WL L22 83 G4
WGNE/HIN WN2 57 K7
Haigh St VAUX/LVPD L3 13 L4
Haigh Vw WGN WN1 68 F3
WGNS/IIMK WN3 5 K7
Haig Rd WDN WA8 16 C2
Haig St WGNS/IIMK WN3 4 C5
Haileybury Av AIN/FAZ L10 84 F3
Haileybury Rd WLTN L25 131 K5
Hailsham Rd ALL/GAR L19 130 A5
Halby Rd WLT/FAZ L9 84 D7 4
Halcombe Rd WD/CROXPK L12 98 F5
Halcyon Rd RF/TRAN CH42 10 E9
Haldane Av BIRK CH41 111 H6
Haldane Rd ANF/KKDL L4 97 J3
Hale Bank Rd WDN WA8 133 G8
Hale Dr SPK/HALE L24 147 H3
Halefield St ECCL WA10 8 E3 1
Hale Gate Rd WDN WA8 148 B2
Hale Gv AIMK WN4 79 H8
WARRW/BUR WA5 120 C7 1
Hale Rd ANF/KKDL L4 7 M8
SPK/HALE L24 146 E2
WAL/NB CH45 95 L7
WDN WA8 133 K7
Halesfield WGNE/HIN WN2 81 K3
Hale St CLVP L2 12 F6
WARRN/WOL WA2 14 E2
Hale Vw RUNC WA7 18 D7
Hale View Rd FROD/HEL WA6 166 E1
HUY L36 116 C3
Halewood Av GOL/RIS/CU WA3 92 B4
Halewood Cl WLTN L25 131 K1
Halewood Dr WLTN L25 131 K3
Halewood Pl WLTN L25 131 L2 2
Halewood Rd WLTN L25 131 K2
Halewood Wy WLTN L25 131 L3 3
Haley Rd North
WARRW/BUR WA5 104 A7
Haley Rd South
WARRW/BUR WA5 104 A7
Half Acre La HOR/BR BL6 57 L4
Halfacre La WARRS WA4 139 G2
Halfpenny La CHLY/EC PR7 41 K2
Halidon Ct BTL L20 6 D2
Halifax Cl WARRN/WOL WA2 121 M3 6
Halifax Crs CSBY/BLUN L23 71 K7
Halifax Rd STHP PR8 34 E8
Halkirk Rd CALD/MH L18 130 E5
Halkyn Av AIG/SPK L17 113 M7
Halkyn Dr EV L5 97 J8 3
Hallastone Rd FROD/HEL WA6 166 D1
Hall Av WDN WA8 133 J4
Halla-way WARRS WA4 15 L9
Hallbridge Gdns SKEL WN8 66 D5
Hall Brow Cl BRSC L40 63 K1
Hall Cl WGNNW/ST WN6 55 J7
Hallcroft SKEL WN8 65 L3
Hallcroft Pl WARRS WA4 138 C3
Hall Dr GR/UP/WCH CH49 125 L2
KKBY L32 86 A3
WARRS WA4 137 M7
Hallfield Dr CHNE CH2 165 K2
Hallfield Pk GTS/LS CH66 162 F1
Hallfields Rd WARRN/WOL WA2 121 M5
Hall Ga CHLY/EC PR7 32 C4
Hallgate WGN WN1 4 E3
Hall Gn SKEL WN8 66 D6
Hall Green Cl SKEL WN8 66 D6
Hall Green La CHLY/EC PR7 41 J2
Halliday Cl GOL/RIS/CU WA3 123 H2
Halliwell La CHLYE PR6 32 E1
Halliwell Pl CHLY/EC PR7 32 E6 3
Halliwell St CHLY/EC PR7 32 E6
Hall La BRSC L40 40 C6
BRSC L40 40 F2
BRSC L40 52 C6
EHL/KEN L7 113 J3
HOR/BR BL6 45 J3
HTWN L38 71 H1
HUY L36 116 C3
KKBY L32 86 A3
MGHL L31 61 L6
MGHL L31 72 F5
NWD/KWIPK L33 74 B7
ORM L39 75 G1
PR/KW L34 100 F8
RAIN/WH L35 117 L4
STHEL WA9 119 J1
WARRS WA4 138 D5
WARRS WA4 151 M3
WARRW/BUR WA5 104 D5
WDN WA8 117 M7
WGN WN1 68 F1
WGNE/HIN WN2 69 M3
WGNNW/ST WN6 54 D3
WGNW/BIL/O WN5 78 B1
WLT/FAZ L9 84 D6
Hall Lane Gv WGNE/HIN WN2 69 M5
Hallmoor Cl ORM L39 62 F3
Hall Nook WARRW/BUR WA5 136 B1
Hallows Av WARRN/WOL WA2 121 M5
Hall Rd BRSC L40 37 K6
RNFD/HAY WA11 91 G6
WARR WA1 122 F6
Hall Rd East CSBY/BLUN L23 70 D7
Hall Rd West CSBY/BLUN L23 70 C7
Hallsands Rd KKBY L32 86 A5
Hallsgreen La CHNE CH2 165 H6
Hallside Cl ALL/GAR L19 130 C5
Hall St CHTN/BK PR9 3 K4
ECCL WA10 9 H5
STHEL WA9 119 G2
WARR WA1 15 G6
WGN WN1 5 G5
WGNE/HIN WN2 5 M4
Hall Ter WARRW/BUR WA5 120 A6 4
Halltine Cl CSBY/BLUN L23 70 C7 1
Hallville Rd CALD/MH L18 114 C8
Hall Wood Av RNFD/HAY WA11 91 H5
Hallwood Cl RUNC WA7 149 K7
Hallwood Link Rd RUNC WA7 150 A7
Hallwood Park Av RUNC WA7 150 A7
Hallwood Rd CHLY/EC PR7 32 C8
Hallworthy Cl LEIGH WN7 93 K4 2
Halsall Av WARRN/WOL WA2 121 M5
Halsall Cl CSBY/BLUN L23 71 G8
RUNC WA7 150 E8 4
Halsall Gn BEB CH63 143 K4
Halsall Hall Dr ORM L39 49 K4
Halsall La FMBY L37 59 H1
ORM L39 49 M7
ORM L39 50 F7
Halsall Rd BTL L20 83 L8
ORM L39 49 L3
STHP PR8 35 J5
Halsall St PR/KW L34 100 F6
Halsbury Rd NPK/KEN L6 113 L2
WAL/NB CH45 95 K7 2
Halsey Av WD/CROXPK L12 98 B6
Halsey Crs WD/CROXPK L12 98 B6
Halsnead Av RAIN/WH L35 116 E4
Halstead Rd WAL/EG CH44 111 L2
WLT/FAZ L9 84 B7
Halton Brook Av RUNC WA7 149 M4
Halton Brow RUNC WA7 150 A4
Halton Cha BRSC L40 64 A1
Halton Ct RUNC WA7 149 M3
Halton Crs GR/UP/WCH CH49 125 K2
GTS/LS CH66 163 H3
Halton Hey RAIN/WH L35 116 F4
Halton Link Rd RUNC WA7 150 A5
Halton Lodge Av RUNC WA7 149 M6
Halton Rd GTS/LS CH66 163 G4
MGHL L31 72 F2
RUNC WA7 19 K3
WAL/NB CH45 95 J7 2
WARRW/BUR WA5 120 B7
Halton Station Rd RUNC WA7 161 H2
Halton St RNFD/HAY WA11 91 G7 1
Halton View Rd WDN WA8 17 H1
Halton Wy GTS/LS CH66 163 G4
Halton Wd KKBY L32 85 K2
Halville Rd WAL/EG CH44 111 L2
Hambledon Cl GTS/LS CH66 155 J7 1
Hambledon Dr
GR/UP/WCH CH49 125 L1
Hamble Dr WARRW/BUR WA5 136 B2
Hambleton Cl NG/CROX L11 98 D1
WDN WA8 133 L2 2
Hamblett Crs RNFD/HAY WA11 89 K7
Hamblett St LEIGH WN7 81 K8
Hamer St ECCL WA10 8 F4
Hamil Cl HOY CH47 109 G4
Hamilton Cl NSTN CH64 152 D3
Hamilton La BIRK CH41 11 K4
Hamilton Rd AIMK WN4 90 E1
CHLY/EC PR7 32 D6
ECCL WA10 88 D7
EV L5 97 H8
WAL/NB CH45 95 J5
WGNE/HIN WN2 81 H1
Hamilton Sq BIRK CH41 11 L4
WGNW/BIL/O WN5 68 A5
Hamilton St BIRK CH41 11 K6
LEIGH WN7 81 M7 3
Hamlet Rd WAL/NB CH45 95 H7
The Hamlet CHLY/EC PR7 44 B4 2
Hammersley Av STHEL WA9 118 E2
Hammersley St STHEL WA9 118 E2 1
Hammill Av ECCL WA10 89 G7
Hammill St ECCL WA10 8 B1
Hammond Rd NWD/KWIPK L33 86 E2
Hammond St STHEL WA9 102 F3
Hamnett Ct GOL/RIS/CU WA3 123 G2 1
Hamnett Rd PR/KW L34 101 G6
Hampden Gv RF/TRAN CH42 128 A1 3
Hampden Pl WGNW/BIL/O WN5 67 M4
Hampden Rd RF/TRAN CH42 127 M1
Hampden St ANF/KKDL L4 97 H3
Hampshire Av NTHTN L30 83 L2 4
Hampson Av
GOL/RIS/CU WA3 107 H2 1
Hampson Cl AIMK WN4 91 K3
Hampson St NPK/KEN L6 97 L8
Hampstead Rd NPK/KEN L6 113 M1
WAL/EG CH44 111 L2
WGNNW/ST WN6 55 M4
Hampton Cl CHLY/EC PR7 32 D5
NSTN CH64 153 G7 1
WDN WA8 135 G2 4
Hampton Court Rd
WD/CROXPK L12 98 E8
Hampton Crs NSTN CH64 153 G8
Hampton Dr WARRW/BUR WA5 136 E1
WDN WA8 117 L8
Hampton Gdns EP CH65 156 C8
Hampton Pl RNFD/HAY WA11 89 K7 5
Hampton Rd FMBY L37 59 G4
STHP PR8 3 K6
Hampton St TOX L8 113 H6
Hamsterley Cl GOL/RIS/CU WA3 107 K7
Hanbury Rd ANF/KKDL L4 97 M5
Handel Rd NTHLY L27 115 M7 2
Handfield Pl EV L5 97 J8 4
Handfield Rd CSBY/WL L22 83 G4
Handfield St EV L5 97 J8
Handford Av PS/BROM CH62 144 B8
Handforth Cl WARRS WA4 138 E1
Handforth La RUNC WA7 149 M7 3
Hand La CHLY/EC PR7 30 B8
Handley Ct ALL/GAR L19 130 B5
Hands St LITH L21 83 K7
Hanford Av WLT/FAZ L9 84 B7
Hankey Dr BTL L20 84 A8
Hankey St RUNC WA7 18 F3
Hankin St EV L5 96 F8 2
Hanley Cl WDN WA8 133 L4
Hanley Rd WDN WA8 133 L4
Hanlon Av BTL L20 83 M7 1
Hanmer Rd KKBY L32 85 K3
Hanmer St WGNE/HIN WN2 69 M8 16
Hannah Cl PEN/TH CH61 141 G2
Hannan Rd NPK/KEN L6 113 L2
Hanns Hall Rd NSTN CH64 153 L5
Hanover Cl CL/PREN CH43 111 H7 2
Hanover Rd WGNE/HIN WN2 69 L7
Hanover St CLVPS L1 12 F9
WARR WA1 14 C7
Hanson Pk CL/PREN CH43 111 G8
Hanson Rd WLT/FAZ L9 84 E8
Hans Rd ANF/KKDL L4 97 J4 2
Hants La ORM L39 51 G7
Hanwell Cl LEIGH WN7 93 M4
Hanwell St NPK/KEN L6 97 K7
Hanworth Cl WD/CROXPK L12 98 F2
Hapsford Cl GOL/RIS/CU WA3 122 E1
Hapsford La CHNE CH2 165 M1
FROD/HEL WA6 166 A4
Hapsford Rd LITH L21 83 K7
Hapton St EV L5 97 G7 6
Harbern Cl WD/CROXPK L12 98 F7
Harbern Dr LEIGH WN7 81 M3 1
Harbord Rd CSBY/WL L22 82 E4
Harbord St EHL/KEN L7 113 K4
WARR WA1 15 H7
Harborne Dr BEB CH63 143 H3
Harbury Av STHP PR8 47 J1
Harbury Cl WGNNW/ST WN6 68 B3
Harcourt Av WAL/EG CH44 112 A2
Harcourt Cl GOL/RIS/CU WA3 123 G2
Harcourt St ANF/KKDL L4 96 F6
BIRK CH41 10 E3
Hardacre St ORM L39 51 H7
WGNS/IIMK WN3 5 H8
Hardie Av MOR/LEA CH46 109 L4
Hardie Cl STHEL WA9 118 C2 1
Hardie Rd HUY L36 116 C2
Harding Av BEB CH63 143 H1
WARRN/WOL WA2 121 M4
Harding Cl EV L5 97 J8
Hardinge Rd ALL/GAR L19 130 E5
Harding Rd BRSC L40 51 M1
Harding St CHLYE PR6 44 D5
TOX L8 113 K5
Hardknott Rd PS/BROM CH62 144 A4
Hard La ECCL WA10 88 F7
Hardman St CLVPS L1 13 K9
WGNS/IIMK WN3 4 D8
Hardrow Cl WGNS/IIMK WN3 79 K3
Hardshaw St ECCL WA10 9 H4
Hardwick Rd AIMK WN4 79 J8
RUNC WA7 149 M2
Hardybutts WGN WN1 5 G4
WGN WN1 5 J5
Hardy Cl GTS/LS CH66 163 H2
Hardy Dr CHLY/EC PR7 32 C6
Hardy Rd LYMM WA13 139 L3
Hardy St ALL/GAR L19 145 M1
CLVPS L1 112 F6 1
CLVPS L1 113 G5 10
WARRN/WOL WA2 14 F3
WGNNW/ST WN6 4 B1
Harebell Cl FMBY L37 59 H4
Harebell St EV L5 96 F6
Hare Cft STBRV L28 99 H5
Harefield Gn SPK/HALE L24 146 F2 2
Harefield Rd SPK/HALE L24 146 F2
Haresfinch Rd RNFD/HAY WA11 9 J1
Haresfinch Vw RNFD/HAY WA11 89 K7
Hare's La FROD/HEL WA6 160 A5
STHP PR8 36 F4
Harestone Av CHLY/EC PR7 32 C8
Harewell Rd NG/CROX L11 98 C4
Harewood Av GTS/LS CH66 162 E1
STHP PR8 34 E7
Harewood Cl HUY L36 116 A2 2
Harewood Rd WAL/NB CH45 95 J6 2
WGNE/HIN WN2 69 L7
Harewood St NPK/KEN L6 113 J1 5
Harfield Gdns GTS/LS CH66 155 L8
Hargate Rd NWD/KWIPK L33 86 B3
Hargrave Av CL/PREN CH43 127 G2
Hargrave Cl CL/PREN CH43 127 G2 1
Hargrave Dr GTS/LS CH66 156 A8
Hargrave La BEB CH63 143 H8
Hargreaves Ct WDN WA8 17 J1
Hargreaves Rd AIG/SPK L17 129 L2
Hargreaves St STHEL WA9 103 G1 1
STHP PR8 3 K5
Harington Cl FMBY L37 58 F2
Harington Gn FMBY L37 58 F2
Harington Rd FMBY L37 58 E1
Harker St VAUX/LVPD L3 13 J4
Harke St EHL/KEN L7 113 K5
Harland Dr AIMK WN4 91 L2 3
Harland Gn SPK/HALE L24 147 J2 1
Harland Rd RF/TRAN CH42 127 M1
Harlea Av WGNE/HIN WN2 81 J2 3
Harlech Av WGNE/HIN WN2 81 J1
Harlech Cl WARRW/BUR WA5 121 G3
Harlech Rd CSBY/BLUN L23 82 E2
Harlech St AIMK WN4 79 H8
WAL/EG CH44 112 A3 3
Harlech Wy EP CH65 20 E9
Harleston Rd NWD/KWIPK L33 86 C2
Harley Av BEB CH63 127 L5
Harley St WLT/FAZ L9 84 C7 3
Harlian Av MOR/LEA CH46 109 M6
Harlow Cl STHEL WA9 102 B6
WARRS WA4 138 E2
Harlow St TOX L8 129 G1
Harlyn Cl HLWD L26 132 A7
Harlyn Gdns
WARRW/BUR WA5 135 M2 1
Harmony Wy CLB/OSW/ST L13 114 C4
Harmuir Cl WGNNW/ST WN6 68 A1
The Harn GTS/LS CH66 162 E2 1
Harold Av AIMK WN4 79 J8
Harold Rd RNFD/HAY WA11 91 H6
Harold St WGNE/HIN WN2 57 M8
Harper Cl GTS/LS CH66 162 F1
Harperley CHLY/EC PR7 32 D3
Harper Rd WLT/FAZ L9 97 J1
Harper's La CHLY/EC PR7 32 F4
Harpers Rd WARRN/WOL WA2 122 C4
Harper St WGN WN1 5 J5
WGNE/HIN WN2 80 E1
Harp's Cft NTHTN L30 83 L2
Harptree Cl RAIN/WH L35 117 G2
Harptree Gv LEIGH WN7 81 M6 4
Harradon Rd WLT/FAZ L9 84 D6
Harridge La BRSC L40 50 B5
Harrier Dr HLWD L26 132 A4
Harringay Av CALD/MH L18 114 B8 3
Harrington Av HOY CH47 108 E6
Harrington Rd CHLY/EC PR7 32 D5
CSBY/BLUN L23 82 F1 1
LITH L21 83 M4
VAUX/LVPD L3 129 G1
Harrington St CLVP L2 12 F7
Harris Cl BEB CH63 143 H3
Harris Dr BTL L20 83 M6
Harris Gdns STHEL WA9 9 K9
Harrismith Rd AIN/FAZ L10 85 H6
Harrison Crs HOR/BR BL6 57 L2
Harrison Dr BTL L20 7 L4
RNFD/HAY WA11 76 B5
RNFD/HAY WA11 90 C7
WAL/NB CH45 95 G6
Harrison Hey HUY L36 115 M4
Harrison Rd CHLY/EC PR7 32 E7
Harrison St WDN WA8 133 K7
WGNE/HIN WN2 81 K2 4
WGNW/BIL/O WN5 68 B7 5
Harrison Wy NEWLW WA12 104 E1
VAUX/LVPD L3 129 G1
Harris Rd WGNNW/ST WN6 55 K3
Harris St ECCL WA10 8 D3
WDN WA8 17 H1
Harrock La BRSC L40 41 G7
WGNNW/ST WN6 54 C1
Harrocks Cl NTHTN L30 71 M8
Harrock Wood Cl PEN/TH CH61 126 A7
Harrod Dr STHP PR8 35 G2
Harrogate Cl PS/BROM CH62 154 F1
WARRW/BUR WA5 120 C5
Harrogate Dr EV L5 97 H8
Harrogate Rd PS/BROM CH62 154 F1
RF/TRAN CH42 128 C5
Harrogate St WGN WN1 4 F5
Harrogate Wy CHTN/BK PR9 22 E7
Harrop Rd RUNC WA7 19 J6
Harrops Cft NTHTN L30 84 A1
Harrowby Cl TOX L8 113 J6
Harrowby Rd LITH L21 83 H6
RF/TRAN CH42 127 L1
WAL/EG CH44 112 A1
Harrowby Rd South
RF/TRAN CH42 127 L1 5
Harrowby St TOX L8 113 J6 4
WGNW/BIL/O WN5 68 A7
Harrow Cl NTHTN L30 84 B2
WAL/EG CH44 95 H8
WARRS WA4 138 A7
WGNW/BIL/O WN5 67 H5
Harrow Dr AIN/FAZ L10 84 F3
RUNC WA7 150 A3
Harrow Gv PS/BROM CH62 144 A5
Harrow Pl WGNE/HIN WN2 80 B1 5
Harrow Rd ANF/KKDL L4 97 K7
EP CH65 20 E7
WAL/EG CH44 111 H1
WGNW/BIL/O WN5 67 M4
Harsnips SKEL WN8 65 L3
Hartdale Rd CALD/MH L18 130 C1 1
CSBY/BLUN L23 71 J7
Hartford Cl CL/PREN CH43 127 H2
Hartford Dr EP CH65 163 H1
Harthill Av CALD/MH L18 130 D1
Harthill Rd CALD/MH L18 130 E2
Hartington Av BIRK CH41 10 D3
Hartington Dr WGNNW/ST WN6 56 B6
Hartington Rd ALL/GAR L19 130 E7
ECCL WA10 88 E8
TOX L8 113 L7
WAL/EG CH44 111 K1
WD/CROXPK L12 98 E7
Hartismere Rd WAL/EG CH44 111 M2
Hartland Av CHTN/BK PR9 22 D8
Hartland Cl WDN WA8 118 C8
Hartland Rd NG/CROX L11 98 A3
Hartley Av WGN WN1 5 J5
WLT/FAZ L9 84 D8
Hartley Cl ANF/KKDL L4 97 H6 2
Hartley Crs STHP PR8 35 H3
Hartley Gv ECCL WA10 101 L5
WGNW/BIL/O WN5 67 K6
Hartley Quay VAUX/LVPD L3 12 E9
Hartley Rd STHP PR8 35 H3
Hartley St WGNW/BIL/O WN5 67 K7 3
Hartley Ter WGNS/IIMK WN3 4 E6
Hartnup St EV L5 97 H7 3
Hartopp Rd WLTN L25 115 J7
Hartsbourne Av WLTN L25 115 H6
Hartsbourne Cl WLTN L25 115 H6 2
Hartsbourne Wk WLTN L25 115 J6
Hartshead SKEL WN8 65 L3
Hart's La SKEL WN8 66 B5
Hart St STHP PR8 3 M5
VAUX/LVPD L3 13 K6
Hartswell Cl GOL/RIS/CU WA3 92 C3 1
Hartwell St LITH L21 83 K7
Hartwood Cl KKBY L32 86 B6
Hartwood Gn CHLYE PR6 32 E2
Hartwood Rd CHTN/BK PR9 3 M2
KKBY L32 86 B6
Hartwood Sq KKBY L32 86 B6 2
Harty Rd RNFD/HAY WA11 90 C8
Harvard Cl RUNC WA7 150 F3 3
Harvard Ct WARRN/WOL WA2 121 J2 5
Harvard Gv PR/KW L34 100 F6
Harvester Wy
GR/UP/WCH CH49 125 L1 3
NTHTN L30 84 C1
Harvest La MOR/LEA CH46 109 M4
Harvest Wy STHEL WA9 118 E1 5
Harvey Av GR/UP/WCH CH49 125 M2
NEWLW WA12 104 B2 1
Harvey Ct GOL/RIS/CU WA3 93 K4 3
WARRN/WOL WA2 121 K2 2
Harvey La GOL/RIS/CU WA3 92 B4
Harvey Rd WAL/NB CH45 95 J7
Harvey St WGNS/IIMK WN3 5 H7
Harvington Dr STHP PR8 34 C8
Harwich Gv CHLDW L16 115 H5 3
Harwood Gdns WARRS WA4 138 C3
Harwood Rd ALL/GAR L19 130 F7
Haryngton Av
WARRW/BUR WA5 14 A1
Haselbeech Cl NG/CROX L11 98 B2
Haselbeech Crs NG/CROX L11 98 B2
Haseldine St AIMK WN4 79 H7 1
Hasfield Rd NG/CROX L11 98 D3
Haslam Dr ORM L39 50 F6
Haslemere RAIN/WH L35 117 H2
Haslemere Dr
WARRW/BUR WA5 135 M1
Haslemere Rd WLTN L25 115 J7
Haslemere Wy WLTN L25 115 K7 5
Haslingden Cl
CLB/OSW/ST L13 114 D3 1
Haslington Gv HLWD L26 132 C7 1
Hassal Rd RF/TRAN CH42 128 C5
Hassnes Cl WGNS/IIMK WN3 79 K3
Hastings Av WARRN/WOL WA2 121 K1
Hastings Dr HUY L36 116 C5
Hastings Rd CSBY/WL L22 82 D3
STHP PR8 35 G4
Haswell Dr STBRV L28 99 J5
Hatchmere Cl CL/PREN CH43 127 H2 5
WARRW/BUR WA5 121 G8
Hatfield Cl STHEL WA9 102 B6
WD/CROXPK L12 99 H2
Hatfield Gdns HUY L36 116 B4 2
Hatfield Rd BTL L20 7 L4
STHP PR8 34 E7
Hathaway MGHL L31 72 D6
Hathaway Cl WLTN L25 115 J7
Hathaway Rd WLTN L25 115 J7
Hathaway Wk WGNE/HIN WN2 80 B1
Hatherley Av CSBY/WL L22 83 G3
Hatherley Cl TOX L8 113 J6 5
Hatherley St TOX L8 113 J6 6
WAL/EG CH44 112 A3
Hathersage Rd HUY L36 100 A8
Hatley La FROD/HEL WA6 160 B6
Hatton Av PS/BROM CH62 155 G2
Hatton Cl HES CH60 140 F4
Hatton Gdn VAUX/LVPD L3 12 F5
Hatton Hill Rd LITH L21 83 J5
Hattons La CHLDW L16 114 E7
Hatton St CHLY/EC PR7 44 B7 1
Hauxwell Gv RNFD/HAY WA11 89 L7 1
Havannah La STHEL WA9 103 K2
Havelock Cl ECCL WA10 8 D5
Haven Brow ORM L39 62 E5
Haven Rd AIN/FAZ L10 85 H5
Havenwood Rd WGN WN1 68 D1
Havercroft Cl WGNS/IIMK WN3 79 G2
Havergal St RUNC WA7 18 F5
Haverstock Rd NPK/KEN L6 113 M2 1
Haverton Wk
WD/CROXPK L12 99 G2 2
Havisham Cl GOL/RIS/CU WA3 106 F8
Hawarden Av AIG/SPK L17 113 M7
CL/PREN CH43 10 E6
WAL/EG CH44 111 L1
Hawarden Gdns EP CH65 20 E9
EP CH65 163 M3 3
Hawarden Gv LITH L21 83 J7 2
Hawdon Ct EHL/KEN L7 113 L5
Hawes Av RNFD/HAY WA11 89 L5
Hawes Crs AIMK WN4 79 K8
Hawesside St CHTN/BK PR9 3 H4
Haweswater Av CHLY/EC PR7 32 D7
RNFD/HAY WA11 90 C7
WGNE/HIN WN2 69 K6
Haweswater Cl NWD/KWIPK L33 73 M8
RUNC WA7 150 C8
Haweswater Gv MGHL L31 73 H3 2
Hawgreen Rd KKBY L32 85 K4 1
Hawick Cl GTS/LS CH66 155 J8 2
NWD/KWIPK L33 73 M7
Hawke Gn HUY L36 116 C6
Hawkeshead Rd
PS/BROM CH62 144 A4 1
Hawke St VAUX/LVPD L3 13 J7
Hawkesworth St ANF/KKDL L4 97 J7 5
Hawkhurst Cl TOX L8 129 H1 7
Hawkins Rd NSTN CH64 153 H4
Hawkins St NPK/KEN L6 113 K2
Hawkley Av WGNS/IIMK WN3 79 H3
Hawkrigg Cl WGNNW/ST WN6 56 B6 1
Hawksclough SKEL WN8 65 L3
Hawks Ct RUNC WA7 150 A7
Hawkshaw Cl GOL/RIS/CU WA3 122 E1
WGNE/HIN WN2 69 J2 2
Hawkshead Av CHLY/EC PR7 31 M4
WD/CROXPK L12 98 E4
Hawkshead Cl MGHL L31 73 G3
RUNC WA7 150 C8 1
Hawkshead Dr LITH L21 83 M5
Hawkshead Rd
WARRW/BUR WA5 104 A7
Hawkshead St CHTN/BK PR9 3 K2
Hawksmoor Cl AIN/FAZ L10 85 J6 3
Hawksmoor Rd AIN/FAZ L10 85 J7
Hawksmore Cl
GR/UP/WCH CH49 109 M7 4
Hawkstone Gv
FROD/HEL WA6 166 E1 2
Hawkstone St TOX L8 113 J8 2
TOX L8 129 J1 11
Hawks Wy HES CH60 141 G5
Hawkswood CHLY/EC PR7 30 D7
Hawksworth Cl FMBY L37 47 J7
Hawksworth Dr FMBY L37 47 J7
Hawley's La WARRN/WOL WA2 121 J4
Haworth Dr BTL L20 83 M6
Haworth St WGNE/HIN WN2 69 M7 2
Hawthorn Av AIMK WN4 78 E8
NEWLW WA12 104 E2
RUNC WA7 19 H5
WDN WA8 134 D3 1
WGN WN1 56 D7
WGNE/HIN WN2 81 J2
WGNW/BIL/O WN5 67 H7 1
Hawthorn Cl
WGNW/BIL/O WN5 77 M8 3
Hawthorn Crs SKEL WN8 65 G4
Hawthorn Dr ECCL WA10 101 K1
PEN/TH CH61 141 H2 1
WKBY CH48 125 G3
Hawthorne Av HLWD L26 132 A7
WARR WA1 122 D6
WARRW/BUR WA5 120 B7
Hawthorne Cl
RNFD/HAY WA11 90 C8 2
Hawthorne Crs FMBY L37 59 J3
Hawthorne Dr NSTN CH64 154 D4
Hawthorne Gv CHTN/BK PR9 25 H7
WAL/EG CH44 112 A3
WARR WA1 122 B6 1
Hawthorne Rd BTL L20 7 K6
FROD/HEL WA6 160 D4

LITH L21 83 K6
RF/TRAN CH42 127 M2
STHEL WA9 102 F7
WARRS WA4 137 L5 4
The Hawthornes NTHLY L27 115 L7 5
Hawthorne St
WARRW/BUR WA5 121 J5
Hawthorn Gv EHL/KEN L7 113 K4 6
WARRS WA4 15 K9
WARRS WA4 137 M4 3
Hawthorn La PS/BROM CH62 143 M5
Hawthorn Rd GTS/LS CH66 155 L7
HUY L36 115 L3
LYMM WA13 139 L2 3
NSTN CH64 152 D3
PR/KW L34 101 G7
Hawthorns Gv WD/CROXPK L12 98 D7
The Hawthorns CHLY/EC PR7 30 D6
SKEL WN8 53 J4 3
Haxted Gdns ALL/GAR L19 130 F7 1
Haycastle Cl WARRW/BUR WA5 121 G4
Haycroft Cl GTS/LS CH66 162 F3
Haydn Rd DV/KA/FCH L14 99 H8
Haydock La RNFD/HAY WA11 90 E7
Haydock Park Gdns
NEWLW WA12 91 K4
Haydock Park Rd AIN/FAZ L10 85 G2
Haydock Rd WAL/NB CH45 95 L6
Haydock St AIMK WN4 91 K3 2
ECCL WA10 9 H5
NEWLW WA12 104 C1
WARRN/WOL WA2 14 E4
Hayes Av RAIN/WH L35 101 G8
Hayes Crs FROD/HEL WA6 160 D4
Hayes Dr MGHL L31 85 K2
Hayes St ECCL WA10 101 L5
Hayfell Rd WGNS/IIMK WN3 79 J4
Hayfield Rd ORM L39 51 G6
WARR WA1 122 E5
Hayfield St ANF/KKDL L4 97 H6 3
Hayles Cl WLTN L25 115 J7 2
Hayles Gn WLTN L25 115 J7
Hayles Gv WLTN L25 115 J7
Haylock Cl TOX L8 129 H1 3
Hayman Av LEIGH WN7 93 M3
Hayman's Cl WD/CROXPK L12 98 C6 3
Haymans Gn MGHL L31 73 G4
WD/CROXPK L12 98 C6
Hayman's Gv WD/CROXPK L12 98 C6
Haywood Cl GOL/RIS/CU WA3 93 G4 3
Haywood Crs RUNC WA7 150 F3 4
Haywood Gdns ECCL WA10 8 A7
Hazel Av KKBY L32 85 L2
RAIN/WH L35 117 G1
RUNC WA7 18 D8
WGNNW/ST WN6 68 C1
Hazelborough Cl
GOL/RIS/CU WA3 107 K7
Hazel Cl GTS/LS CH66 163 H4
Hazeldale Rd WLT/FAZ L9 97 J1
Hazeldene Av PEN/TH CH61 126 C7
WAL/NB CH45 95 J8 1
Hazeldene Wy PEN/TH CH61 126 D7 2
Hazelfield Cl STHEL WA9 118 E1 1
Hazel Gv BEB CH63 143 G1
CHLYE PR6 32 E2
CSBY/BLUN L23 83 H2
ECCL WA10 101 L2
GOL/RIS/CU WA3 92 D5
PEN/TH CH61 125 M6
STHP PR8 25 G6
WARR WA1 122 C5
WLT/FAZ L9 84 D7 5
Hazelhurst Rd ANF/KKDL L4 97 K6
Hazel La SKEL WN8 53 K8 1
Hazelmere Gdns
WGNE/HIN WN2 81 G1 6
Hazel Ms MGHL L31 85 K2 1
Hazel Rd BIRK CH41 11 G7
HOY CH47 108 D6
HUY L36 100 B8
Hazelslack Rd NG/CROX L11 98 C3
The Hazels CHLY/EC PR7 43 G4 3
Hazel St WARR WA1 15 K2
Hazelwood GR/UP/WCH CH49 125 M1
Hazelwood Av BRSC L40 52 B1 1
Hazelwood Cl STHEL WA9 118 D2
Hazelwood Gv HLWD L26 131 M3 3
Hazelwood Ms WARRS WA4 138 E4 2
Hazelwood Rd WGN WN1 68 D1
Hazlehurst Cl FMBY L37 58 E3 3
Hazlehurst Gv AIMK WN4 91 L2
Hazlehurst Rd FROD/HEL WA6 160 E8
Hazleton Rd DV/KA/FCH L14 114 E2
Headbolt La NWD/KWIPK L33 74 C8
STHP PR8 48 C1
Headbourne Cl WLTN L25 115 H6
Headen Av WGNW/BIL/O WN5 67 K8
Headingley Cl HUY L36 115 L5
STHEL WA9 102 E7
Headington Rd
GR/UP/WCH CH49 109 M8 5
Headland Cl GOL/RIS/CU WA3 93 G7
WKBY CH48 124 D5
Headley Cl ECCL WA10 8 D5
Head St TOX L8 113 G7
Heald St CHLYE PR6 33 G5 6
NEWLW WA12 104 B2
Heanor Dr STHP PR8 36 B2
Heapey Fold La CHLYE PR6 33 J2
Heapey Rd CHLYE PR6 33 J2
Heardman Av WGNNW/ST WN6 4 A1
Heath Av GTS/LS CH66 163 J4
Heathbank Av PEN/TH CH61 125 L6
WAL/EG CH44 111 J2 6
Heathbank Rd RF/TRAN CH42 127 M2
Heath Cl PR/KW L34 101 H6
WKBY CH48 124 D5 1
WLTN L25 115 H8
Heathcote Cl EHL/KEN L7 113 L5 6
Heathcote Gdns BEB CH63 128 B8 2
Heathcote Rd ANF/KKDL L4 97 H3
Heath Dl BEB CH63 143 H2 1
Heath Dr GR/UP/WCH CH49 110 C8
HES CH60 141 H4
RUNC WA7 19 G9
Heather Bank BEB CH63 127 M7
Heather Brae NEWLW WA12 104 C1
Heather Brow CL/PREN CH43 111 H7
Heather Cl ANF/KKDL L4 97 H5 1
BRSC L40 52 A1
FMBY L37 47 K8
GOL/RIS/CU WA3 106 F8
GTS/LS CH66 163 G2
RUNC WA7 150 A8
STHP PR8 47 M3
Heatherdale Cl CL/PREN CH43 127 K2
Heatherdale Rd CALD/MH L18 130 C1
Heather Dene PS/BROM CH62 143 M2
Heatherdene Rd WKBY CH48 124 D2 2
Heather Gv AIMK WN4 92 A1
WGNW/BIL/O WN5 68 A6
Heatherlea Cl SKEL WN8 66 E6
Heather Rd BEB CH63 142 F1
HES CH60 141 J4
Heathers Cft NTHTN L30 84 A2
Heather Wy CSBY/BLUN L23 71 K7
Heatherways FMBY L37 47 J7
Heathey La STHP PR8 36 C5
Heathfield CHLYE PR6 44 B4
Heathfield Av STHEL WA9 102 A5
Heathfield Cl FMBY L37 47 J7 2
LITH L21 83 L7
Heathfield Dr
NWD/KWIPK L33 74 A8 7
Heathfield Pk WARRS WA4 138 C3
WDN WA8 133 M2
Heathfield Rd BEB CH63 143 H1
CL/PREN CH43 127 L1 6
CSBY/WL L22 82 E3
EP CH65 20 B4
MGHL L31 73 H6
STHP PR8 35 G8
WAV L15 114 C7
Heathfield St CLVPS L1 13 J8 1
CLVPS L1 13 J8 1
Heath Gdns WGNE/HIN WN2 81 L2
Heathgate SKEL WN8 65 L3 1
Heathgate Av SPK/HALE L24 147 J3
Heath Gv GTS/LS CH66 155 K6
Heath Hey WLTN L25 115 H8
Heathland Rd STHEL WA9 118 E1
Heathlands Rd GTS/LS CH66 155 K6
The Heathlands
MOR/LEA CH46 110 A2 3
Heath La CHNE CH2 164 A6
GOL/RIS/CU WA3 92 F7
GOL/RIS/CU WA3 106 C3
GTS/LS CH66 155 J6
LEIGH WN7 81 K8
NSTN CH64 154 E5
Heathlea WGNE/HIN WN2 81 L3
Heathmoor Av GOL/RIS/CU WA3 92 F7
Heathmoor Rd MOR/LEA CH46 109 M4
Heath Park Gv RUNC WA7 18 F8
Heath Rd AIMK WN4 91 K3
ALL/GAR L19 130 F5
BEB CH63 128 A8
HUY L36 99 L8 2
RUNC WA7 19 J8
WARRW/BUR WA5 120 B8
WDN WA8 134 A4
Heath Road Crs RUNC WA7 19 J6
Heath Rd South RUNC WA7 149 H6
Heathrow Pl CHLY/EC PR7 32 C6 1
Heathside HES CH60 140 F4 1
Heath St AIMK WN4 91 L3 3
GOL/RIS/CU WA3 92 C5
RAIN/WH L35 101 M6
WARRS WA4 137 L5
Heath Vw LITH L21 83 K2
Heathview Rd WDN WA8 148 C1
Heathwaite Crs NG/CROX L11 98 C4
Heathway HES CH60 141 K6
Heathwood WD/CROXPK L12 98 D8 1
Heathwood Gv WARR WA1 122 D6
Heathy La ORM L39 48 C5
Heatley Cl CL/PREN CH43 110 E6 5
Heaton Cl BRSC L40 51 M1 4
SKEL WN8 66 C6
SPK/HALE L24 147 H2
Heaton Ct GOL/RIS/CU WA3 107 H7
Heatons Bridge Rd BRSC L40 50 F1
Heaton St WGN WN1 68 E3
WGNE/HIN WN2 57 M8 3
WGNNW/ST WN6 56 A4
WGNS/IIMK WN3 5 J7
Heaviley Gv HOR/BR BL6 45 J8
Hebburn Wy WD/CROXPK L12 99 J2
Hebden Av GOL/RIS/CU WA3 107 K1
Hebden Rd NG/CROX L11 98 D2
Hebdon Cl AIMK WN4 79 J8 5
Heber St WGNE/HIN WN2 5 M6
Hector Rd WGNW/BIL/O WN5 67 M4
Hedgebank Cl WLT/FAZ L9 84 F5 3
Hedgecroft CSBY/BLUN L23 71 L7
Hedgefield Rd WLTN L25 115 K8
Hedge Hey RUNC WA7 150 C4
Hedgemead WGNNW/ST WN6 4 A2
Hedges Crs CLB/OSW/ST L13 98 A6
Hedingham Cl HLWD L26 132 C4
Heeley St WGN WN1 68 D3
The Heights FROD/HEL WA6 166 E1 3
Helena Rd STHEL WA9 103 H6
Helena St BIRK CH41 11 J7 1
EHL/KEN L7 113 K4
WLT/FAZ L9 97 H2
Helen Bank Dr RNFD/HAY WA11 76 B5
Helen St AIMK WN4 91 J1 4
GOL/RIS/CU WA3 92 B3
Helford Cl RAIN/WH L35 101 J7 3
Helford Rd NG/CROX L11 85 M8
Heliers Rd CLB/OSW/ST L13 114 D3
Hell Nook GOL/RIS/CU WA3 92 A4
Helmdon Cl NG/CROX L11 98 C4 4
Helmingham Gv BIRK CH41 11 K9
Helmingham Rd BIRK CH41 11 K9
Helmsdale SKEL WN8 65 L3
Helmsdale La
WARRW/BUR WA5 120 E7
Helmsley Cl WARRW/BUR WA5 121 G6
Helmsley Rd HLWD L26 132 B6
Helmsman Wy WGNS/IIMK WN3 4 C9
Helsby Av PS/BROM CH62 155 H2
Helsby Rd FROD/HEL WA6 166 E4
WLT/FAZ L9 84 D6
Helsby St EHL/KEN L7 113 J4 5
STHEL WA9 102 F4
WARR WA1 15 K3
Helsby Wy WGNS/IIMK WN3 78 E3
Helston Av HLWD L26 132 B4
RNFD/HAY WA11 89 M6
Helston Cl CHTN/BK PR9 22 D8 2
RUNC WA7 150 D8
WARRW/BUR WA5 120 A8 2
Helston Rd NG/CROX L11 85 M8
Helton Cl CL/PREN CH43 127 G2
Helvellyn Rd WGNW/BIL/O WN5 67 K6
Hemans St BTL L20 6 D2
Hemer Ter BTL L20 6 C1
Hemfield Ct WGNE/HIN WN2 69 L5
Hemfield Rd WGNE/HIN WN2 69 L5
Hemingford Cl GTS/LS CH66 162 F3 1
Hemingford St BIRK CH41 11 H6
Hemlegh Vw FROD/HEL WA6 166 D3
Hemlock Cl WD/CROXPK L12 98 F2
Hempstead Cl STHEL WA9 102 B6
Hemsworth Av GTS/LS CH66 155 L8
Henbury Pl RUNC WA7 149 K7
Henderson Cl
GR/UP/WCH CH49 109 M7 5
WARRW/BUR WA5 119 M7
Henderson Dr RNFD/HAY WA11 76 C5
Henderson Rd HUY L36 116 C2
WDN WA8 16 B3
Hendon Rd NPK/KEN L6 113 M1
WGNW/BIL/O WN5 67 M5
Hendon Wk
GR/UP/WCH CH49 125 L2 3
Henglers Cl NPK/KEN L6 113 J2 7
Henley Av LITH L21 83 J5
Henley Cl BEB CH63 143 J3 2
NSTN CH64 153 G7
WARRS WA4 138 A7
Henley Ct ECCL WA10 8 B9
RUNC WA7 149 M3 1
Henley Dr CHTN/BK PR9 25 G4
Henley Mnr GOL/RIS/CU WA3 106 F1
Henley Rd CALD/MH L18 114 D8
NSTN CH64 153 G7
Henley St WGNE/HIN WN2 57 K7
Henllan Gdns STHEL WA9 103 H6 4
Henlow Av KKBY L32 86 B5
Hennawood Cl NPK/KEN L6 97 K8 4
Henry Edward St
VAUX/LVPD L3 13 G4 1
Henry Park St WGN WN1 5 K5
Henry St BIRK CH41 11 K6
CLB/OSW/ST L13 114 B3
CLVPS L1 13 G9
ECCL WA10 8 F4
WARR WA1 14 C6
WDN WA8 17 H1 1
WGNE/HIN WN2 80 A1
Henshall Av WARRS WA4 138 B1
Henthorne Rd PS/BROM CH62 128 D5
Henthorne St CL/PREN CH43 10 E6
Hepherd St
WARRW/BUR WA5 136 F1 3
Hepworth Cl GOL/RIS/CU WA3 92 B3 3
Herald Av ALL/GAR L19 131 G7
Herald Cl NG/CROX L11 98 E2 1
Heralds Cl WDN WA8 133 K5
Heralds Gn WARRW/BUR WA5 120 C3
Herald St ALL/GAR L19 130 E7
Herbarth Cl WLT/FAZ L9 97 H2
Herbert St STHEL WA9 103 H6
WARRW/BUR WA5 104 A7 2
WGNS/IIMK WN3 4 C5
Herbert Taylor Cl NPK/KEN L6 97 L7
Herculaneum Ct TOX L8 129 H2 6
Herculaneum Rd TOX L8 129 G1 1
Herdman Cl WLTN L25 115 K8
Hereford Av GOL/RIS/CU WA3 92 D5 1
GR/UP/WCH CH49 110 B7 2
GTS/LS CH66 163 G5
Hereford Cl AIMK WN4 91 L3 5
WARR WA1 122 F6 1
Hereford Dr NTHTN L30 84 B4
Hereford Rd CHTN/BK PR9 25 H6
LITH L21 83 G6
WAV L15 114 C7
Heriot St EV L5 96 F7
Hermes Cl NTHTN L30 84 A5 3
Hermes Rd NG/CROX L11 85 L7
Hermitage Cl WGNNW/ST WN6 55 G6
Hermitage Green La
WARRN/WOL WA2 105 J5
Hermitage Gv BTL L20 83 M6
Herm Rd EV L5 96 E8
Heron Cl RUNC WA7 150 F5 2
Heron Ct HLWD L26 132 A4
NSTN CH64 152 E6
Herondale Rd CALD/MH L18 130 B1
Heron Dr WGNS/IIMK WN3 79 G3
Heron Gv RNFD/HAY WA11 76 D8
Heronhall Rd WLT/FAZ L9 98 B1 2
Heronpark Wy BEB CH63 143 K2
Heron Pl WGNW/BIL/O WN5 67 L5
Heron Rd WKBY CH48 109 J7
Herons Wy RUNC WA7 151 H1 1
Hero St BTL L20 7 K7
Herrick St CLB/OSW/ST L13 114 B2
Herschell St EV L5 97 H7
Hertford Cl HLWD L26 132 B6
WARR WA1 123 G6
Hertford Dr WAL/NB CH45 95 L7
Hertford Rd BTL L20 7 G7
Hertford St STHEL WA9 102 F3
Hesketh Av CHTN/BK PR9 23 J7
RF/TRAN CH42 127 M4
Hesketh Cl WARRW/BUR WA5 136 B1
Hesketh Dr BRSC L40 39 J2
CHTN/BK PR9 25 G3
HES CH60 141 J4
MGHL L31 73 H3
WGNNW/ST WN6 55 J3 3
Hesketh Gn BRSC L40 39 K1 1
Hesketh Meadow La
GOL/RIS/CU WA3 93 J5
Hesketh Rd BRSC L40 51 M1
CHTN/BK PR9 25 G3
SPK/HALE L24 148 A3
Hesketh St North
WARRW/BUR WA5 136 F1 6
Hesketh St AIG/SPK L17 129 L1 3
LEIGH WN7 81 M8
WARRW/BUR WA5 136 F1 7
WGNW/BIL/O WN5 68 A6
Heskin Cl KKBY L32 86 A6
MGHL L31 72 F1
RAIN/WH L35 117 K2
Heskin La ORM L39 50 F5
Heskin Rd KKBY L32 86 A6
Heskin Wk KKBY L32 86 A6
Hessle Dr HES CH60 141 H6
Hester Cl HTWN L38 70 B1
Heswall Av BEB CH63 127 L5
GOL/RIS/CU WA3 107 G2
STHEL WA9 118 D1
Heswall Mt PEN/TH CH61 126 C8
Heswall Rd GTS/LS CH66 162 F1 5
WLT/FAZ L9 84 D6
Hever Dr HLWD L26 132 C4
Heversham SKEL WN8 65 L3
Heward Av STHEL WA9 102 E7 5
Hewitson Av CLB/OSW/ST L13 98 B7
Hewitson Rd CLB/OSW/ST L13 98 B7
Hewitt Av ECCL WA10 101 L1
Hewitt's La PR/KW L34 87 G6
Hewitts Pl CLVP L2 12 F6 5
Hewitt St WARRS WA4 15 H9
Hewlett St CHLY/EC PR7 42 F4
WGN WN1 4 F4
Hexham Av WGNS/IIMK WN3 79 H2
Hexham Cl RAIN/WH L35 101 M7 5
Heyburn Rd CLB/OSW/ST L13 98 A7
Heydale Rd CALD/MH L18 130 C1
Heydean Rd CALD/MH L18 130 E4
Heydon Cl FMBY L37 58 F4
Heyes Av RNFD/HAY WA11 76 C7
RNFD/HAY WA11 90 F8
Heyescroft ORM L39 63 M7
Heyes Dr LYMM WA13 139 L3
WAL/NB CH45 110 E1
Heyes Gv RNFD/HAY WA11 76 C7
Heyes La WARRS WA4 138 A5
Heyes Mt RAIN/WH L35 117 L3
Heyes Rd WDN WA8 133 L5
WGNW/BIL/O WN5 67 G7
Heyes St EV L5 97 J8
SKEL WN8 54 E6
The Heyes WLTN L25 131 K3
Heyfield Park Rd
GTS/LS CH66 155 K6 1
Heyford Rd WGNW/BIL/O WN5 67 M5
Heygarth Dr
GR/UP/WCH CH49 125 M1 4
Heygarth Rd PS/BROM CH62 144 A8
Hey Green Rd WAV L15 114 A5
Hey Lock Cl NEWLW WA12 104 E5 1
Hey Rd HUY L36 116 B3
Heys Av PS/BROM CH62 143 M5
Heyscroft Rd WLTN L25 131 K3
Heysham Cl RUNC WA7 150 E7
Heysham Rd CHTN/BK PR9 25 H6
NTHLY L27 132 C1 2
NTHTN L30 84 C3
WGNW/BIL/O WN5 67 K6
The Heys CHLY/EC PR7 43 H3
RUNC WA7 150 A4 1
SKEL WN8 53 L2 1
Hey St WGNE/HIN WN2 80 B2
WGNNW/ST WN6 4 C3
The Hey STBRV L28 99 L6
Heythrop Dr HES CH60 141 L5
Heyville Rd BEB CH63 128 A7
Heywood Av GOL/RIS/CU WA3 92 D4
Heywood Bvd PEN/TH CH61 126 C7
Heywood Cl FMBY L37 59 G2 1
Hey Wood Cl NEWLW WA12 104 E5 2
Heywood Cl PEN/TH CH61 126 C7 3
Heywood Ct WAV L15 114 E4
Heywood Gdns RAIN/WH L35 117 G3
Heywood Rd GTS/LS CH66 155 M8
WAV L15 114 E5
Heyworth St EV L5 97 H8
NPK/KEN L6 13 M1
Hibbert St WDN WA8 16 E3
Hic-bibi La CHLY/EC PR7 43 G7
Hickmans Rd BIRK CH41 111 K4
Hickory Cl WARR WA1 123 G6
Hickory Gv MGHL L31 85 J3
Hickson Av MGHL L31 72 E2
Hicks Rd CSBY/WL L22 83 G4
LITH L21 83 J6 2
Hieland Rd WGN WN1 69 G3
Higgin's La BRSC L40 51 L1
Highacre Rd WAL/NB CH45 95 J6 5
Higham Av ECCL WA10 101 H2
WARRW/BUR WA5 121 H4
Higham Sq EV L5 13 K2 1
High Bank CHLYE PR6 33 J2
High Bank Cl CL/PREN CH43 110 F8 5
Highbank Dr ALL/GAR L19 130 F7
High Banks MGHL L31 72 E2
High Beeches CHLDW L16 115 H4
High Beeches Crs AIMK WN4 79 J7
High Carrs HUY L36 115 K3
High Clere Crs HUY L36 100 A8
Highcliffe Ct WGNNW/ST WN6 56 B6
Highcroft Av BEB CH63 128 C8
Highcroft Gn BEB CH63 128 C8 1
The Highcroft BEB CH63 128 B8
Higher Ashton WDN WA8 134 B2
Higher Bebington Rd
BEB CH63 128 A7
Higher End Pk NTHTN L30 71 M8
Higher House La CHLYE PR6 33 J2
Higher La KIRK/FR/WA PR4 27 L3
RNFD/HAY WA11 76 C6
SKEL WN8 53 L6
SKEL WN8 66 E6
WGNE/HIN WN2 69 J1
WLT/FAZ L9 84 F7
Higher Moss La FMBY L37 60 C2
Higher Parr St STHEL WA9 9 L5
Higher Rd HLWD L26 132 C7
SPK/HALE L24 132 D8
Highfield CHNE CH2 165 K1
NWD/KWIPK L33 74 B7 4
Highfield Av GOL/RIS/CU WA3 92 B5 2
WARRW/BUR WA5 120 C8
WGN WN1 5 K1
WGNNW/ST WN6 55 J7
Highfield Cl CHLYE PR6 44 C6 3
NSTN CH64 153 G5
WAL/EG CH44 111 J2
Highfield Crs RF/TRAN CH42 128 B4
WDN WA8 134 C3
Highfield Dr GR/UP/WCH CH49 125 M1
LYMM WA13 139 L3
RNFD/HAY WA11 89 G1
WGNNW/ST WN6 56 B6
Highfield Grange Av
WGNS/IIMK WN3 78 F3
Highfield Gv CSBY/BLUN L23 71 H8
RF/TRAN CH42 128 B4
WGNE/HIN WN2 57 L8 1
Highfield La BRSC L40 37 L6
GOL/RIS/CU WA3 92 E8
WARRN/WOL WA2 105 L5
Highfield Pk MGHL L31 73 H4 1
Highfield Pl PR/KW L34 100 F7 3
Highfield Rd CHLYE PR6 44 C6
CHTN/BK PR9 25 K2
CLB/OSW/ST L13 114 C1
GTS/LS CH66 155 K7
LEY/BBR PR5 29 L3
LITH L21 83 J5
LYMM WA13 139 L3
NSTN CH64 153 G5
ORM L39 51 G7
RF/TRAN CH42 128 B4
WDN WA8 16 B1
WLT/FAZ L9 97 H1
Highfield Rd North CHLY/EC PR7 32 E3
CHLYE PR6 44 C5
EP CH65 20 C4
Highfield Rd South
CHLY/EC PR7 32 E4
Highfields HES CH60 141 H4 1
PR/KW L34 100 E7 2
Highfield South RF/TRAN CH42 128 B4
Highfield St STHEL WA9 102 F5
VAUX/LVPD L3 12 F5
Highfield Vw CLB/OSW/ST L13 114 B1
Highgate Cl HES CH60 141 H4
Highgate Crs WGNNW/ST WN6 55 G6
Highgate Rd MGHL L31 72 F2
SKEL WN8 66 D6
High Gates Cl
WARRW/BUR WA5 121 G6
Highgate St EHL/KEN L7 113 J4
Highgreen Rd RF/TRAN CH42 127 L2
Highgrove Av CHLY/EC PR7 42 B1
Highgrove Pk ALL/GAR L19 130 C5
Highlands Rd RUNC WA7 18 F9
High La BRSC L40 51 J5
ORM L39 63 L5
Highmarsh Crs NEWLW WA12 91 K8
High Moor La WGNNW/ST WN6 54 C1
High Moss ORM L39 63 G2
Highoaks Rd WLTN L25 131 K4
High Pk WGNNW/ST WN6 55 L7
High Park Pl CHTN/BK PR9 25 J5
High Park Rd CHTN/BK PR9 25 J5
Highpark Rd RF/TRAN CH42 127 L2 3
High Park St TOX L8 113 H8
Highsands Av BRSC L40 39 J2
Highsted Gv NWD/KWIPK L33 74 A8
High St BRSC L40 40 D4
CHLY/EC PR7 32 E5
CLVP L2 12 E6
FROD/HEL WA6 160 D4
GOL/RIS/CU WA3 92 C5
NEWLW WA12 104 F1
NSTN CH64 153 G6
PR/KW L34 100 F7
PS/BROM CH62 144 A4 2
RUNC WA7 18 F3
SKEL WN8 64 F5
SPK/HALE L24 147 M4
WARR WA1 15 G4
WAV L15 114 B6
WGN WN1 68 F3
WGNE/HIN WN2 69 K2
WGNNW/ST WN6 56 A4
WGNS/IIMK WN3 5 K7
WLTN L25 131 J3
Hightor Rd WLTN L25 131 H2
High Vw FROD/HEL WA6 166 E1
Highville Rd CHLDW L16 114 F7
Highways Av CHLY/EC PR7 31 M4
Highwood Ct NWD/KWIPK L33 86 A1
Highwood Rd WARRS WA4 137 L6
Highwoods Cl AIMK WN4 79 J8
Hignett Av STHEL WA9 103 J3
Hilary Av DV/KA/FCH L14 115 G3
GOL/RIS/CU WA3 92 F4
Hilary Cl ANF/KKDL L4 97 L5
PR/KW L34 101 G6
WARRW/BUR WA5 119 M7
WDN WA8 135 G2
Hilary Dr GR/UP/WCH CH49 110 C7
Hilary Rd ANF/KKDL L4 97 L5
Hilberry Av CLB/OSW/ST L13 98 A8
Hilbre Av HES CH60 141 G7
WAL/EG CH44 111 J1
Hilbre Cl CHTN/BK PR9 25 G4
Hilbre Ct WKBY CH48 124 C4
Hilbre Dr EP CH65 163 L4
Hilbre Rd WKBY CH48 124 D4
Hilbre St BIRK CH41 11 G2
VAUX/LVPD L3 13 J7
Hilbre Vw WKBY CH48 124 D3
Hilcrest Rd ANF/KKDL L4 97 M4
Hilda Rd WD/CROXPK L12 99 G8
Hilda St LEIGH WN7 81 L7
Hildebrand Rd ANF/KKDL L4 97 L5
Hilden Rd WARRN/WOL WA2 122 A4
Hildyard St
WGNW/BIL/O WN5 68 B7 2
Hilgay Cl WGNS/IIMK WN3 78 F2
Hillam Rd WAL/NB CH45 94 F7
Hillary Av WGNW/BIL/O WN5 67 M8
Hillary Crs MGHL L31 72 F4
Hillary Dr CSBY/BLUN L23 83 J1
Hillary Rd PS/BROM CH62 144 A8

Hillary Wk CSBY/BLUN L23 83 J1 2
Hillbank WGNNW/ST WN6 56 C6
Hillbark Rd WKBY CH48 125 J3
Hillbeck Crs AIMK WN4 90 F1
Hillberry Crs WARRS WA4 137 K2
Hillbrae Av RNFD/HAY WA11 89 J5
Hillburn Dr BIRK CH41 111 G4
Hill Cliffe Rd WARRS WA4 137 K5 1
Hill Cl NSTN CH64 153 J8
WGNNW/ST WN6 55 G6
Hill Ct NSTN CH64 153 K8
Hill Crs LEIGH WN7 81 L5
Hill Crest ANF/KKDL L4 7 M6
Hillcrest MGHL L31 73 H5
SKEL WN8 65 K6
WGNE/HIN WN2 80 D3
Hillcrest Av HUY L36 116 C3
Hill Crest Av LEIGH WN7 81 L5
Hillcrest Dr BRSC L40 37 H5
GR/UP/WCH CH49 125 L2
GTS/LS CH66 155 J7
Hillcrest Rd CSBY/BLUN L23 83 J1
GTS/LS CH66 155 K7
ORM L39 51 G7
Hillcroft Rd WAL/EG CH44 111 L3
WLTN L25 131 H1
Hilldean SKEL WN8 66 E5
Hillerton Cl NG/CROX L11 98 E3 1
Hillfield FROD/HEL WA6 160 D6
RUNC WA7 150 F5
Hillfield Dr PEN/TH CH61 141 H2
Hillfield Rd GTS/LS CH66 155 M6
Hillfoot Av WLTN L25 131 K7
Hillfoot Cl CL/PREN CH43 110 E5
Hillfoot Crs WARRS WA4 137 K6
Hillfoot Gn WLTN L25 131 J6
Hillfoot Rd WLTN L25 131 L7
Hill Gv MOR/LEA CH46 110 A6
Hillhead Rd BTL L20 7 L6
Hill House Fold La
WGNNW/ST WN6 41 L8
Hill House La WGNNW/ST WN6 41 L8
Hillingden Av HLWD L26 132 B6
Hillingdon Av PEN/TH CH61 141 H3
Hillingdon Rd WAV L15 114 D7 3
Hill La HOR/BR BL6 57 K2
Hillock Cl BRSC L40 37 J6
Hillock La BRSC L40 37 J6
SKEL WN8 53 L7
WARR WA1 122 E5
The Hillocks LEY/BBR PR5 29 K3
Hillreed WGNNW/ST WN6 68 B4 1
Hill Rdg CL/PREN CH43 110 F8
Hill Rise Vw ORM L39 62 C4
Hill Rd CL/PREN CH43 111 G6
Hill Rd North FROD/HEL WA6 166 F2
Hillsboro Av FROD/HEL WA6 160 E6
Hill School Rd ECCL WA10 101 J5
Hillsdown Wy GTS/LS CH66 162 E3
Hillside Av AIMK WN4 79 H5
ECCL WA10 89 G7
HUY L36 99 L7
NEWLW WA12 104 B3
ORM L39 62 F1
RUNC WA7 18 D8
SKEL WN8 40 F8
Hillside Cl BIRK CH41 128 A1
BTL L20 7 L6
CHLY/EC PR7 31 L4 1
FROD/HEL WA6 166 F1 1
WGNS/IIMK WN3 78 F2
WGNW/BIL/O WN5 89 M1 2
Hillside Crs HUY L36 99 L7
Hillside Dr GTS/LS CH66 156 A6
WLTN L25 131 K2
Hillside Gv WARRW/BUR WA5 120 B8
Hillside Rd BIRK CH41 128 A1
CALD/MH L18 114 D8
CL/PREN CH43 110 F5
FROD/HEL WA6 160 E6
HES CH60 141 J6
HUY L36 100 A8
STHP PR8 35 G4
WAL/EG CH44 111 G1
WKBY CH48 124 F3
Hillside St NPK/KEN L6 13 M3
Hillside Vw CL/PREN CH43 127 J2
Hills Moss Rd STHEL WA9 103 H6
Hills Pl WAV L15 114 C6 4
Hill St CHTN/BK PR9 3 H2
CSBY/BLUN L23 83 H2
ECCL WA10 9 H2
RUNC WA7 19 H4
TOX L8 112 F7
WARR WA1 14 E5
WGNE/HIN WN2 69 M7
WGNNW/ST WN6 4 C1
Hillsview Rd STHP PR8 47 L1
Hilltop RUNC WA7 150 E6
Hill Top La HES CH60 141 K5
NSTN CH64 153 K8
Hilltop Rd CHLDW L16 114 F6
LYMM WA13 139 L3
RNFD/HAY WA11 88 D3
Hill Top Rd WARR WA1 122 E5
WARRS WA4 138 B3
Hilltop Wk ORM L39 62 E2
Hillview AIG/SPK L17 130 A3
Hill Vw WDN WA8 118 B8
Hill View Av FROD/HEL WA6 166 C4
Hillview Av WKBY CH48 124 D2
Hillview Cl FROD/HEL WA6 160 E6
Hill View Dr CHLY/EC PR7 42 F5
GR/UP/WCH CH49 110 C7
Hillview Gdns WLTN L25 131 G2
Hillview Rd PEN/TH CH61 125 L7
Hillwood Cl BEB CH63 143 J4 1
Hilton Av WARRW/BUR WA5 120 D8 1
Hilton Cl BIRK CH41 10 F5
Hilton Gv WKBY CH48 124 C2 2
Hilton Pl WGNE/HIN WN2 57 L7
Hilton St AIMK WN4 91 K2
WGN WN1 5 G2
WGNS/IIMK WN3 5 J8
Hinchley Gn MGHL L31 72 D4
Hinckley Rd RNFD/HAY WA11 89 L7
Hindburn Av MGHL L31 73 H3
Hinderton Dr HES CH60 141 H7
WKBY CH48 125 G4
Hinderton La NSTN CH64 153 J4
Hinderton Rd BIRK CH41 11 J8
NSTN CH64 153 J5
Hindle Av WARRW/BUR WA5 121 H4 1
Hindley Beech MGHL L31 72 E3 3
Hindley St CHLY/EC PR7 32 D7
Hindlip St TOX L8 129 J2 3
Hind Rd WGNW/BIL/O WN5 67 M5
Hind's Head Av WGNNW/ST WN6 42 B7
Hind St BIRK CH41 11 K7
Hinson St BIRK CH41 11 K5
Hinton Crs WARRS WA4 138 A5
Hinton Rd RUNC WA7 19 H6
Hinton St LITH L21 83 K7
NPK/KEN L6 113 L2
Hitchen's Cl RUNC WA7 150 F6 1
Hobart Dr NWD/KWIPK L33 74 A7
Hobart St EV L5 97 G7
STHEL WA9 101 M5
Hobb La WARRS WA4 136 E8
Hobby Ct RUNC WA7 150 A7 1
Hobcross La BRSC L40 52 C4
Hob Hey La GOL/RIS/CU WA3 106 F1
Hob La CHNE CH2 165 J6
Hoblyn Rd CL/PREN CH43 111 G5
Hockenhall Aly CLVP L2 12 F6
Hockenhull Cl BEB CH63 143 J3 3
Hodder Av CHLY/EC PR7 32 D8
MGHL L31 73 H3
WGNE/HIN WN2 80 B3
Hodder Cl RNFD/HAY WA11 89 K6 6
WGNW/BIL/O WN5 67 M6
Hodder Rd EV L5 97 H7
Hodder St EV L5 97 H7
Hodge Brow CHLYE PR6 45 H1
Hodges St WGNNW/ST WN6 68 C3
Hodge St STHP PR8 3 G4
Hodgkinson Av
WARRW/BUR WA5 121 H4
Hodnet Dr AIMK WN4 91 L2
Hodson Pl NPK/KEN L6 13 M1
Hodson St STHP PR8 3 K5
WGNS/IIMK WN3 4 D6
Hogarth St LITH L21 83 J7 3
Hoggs Hill La FMBY L37 59 G5
Hogg's La CHLYE PR6 33 H8
Hoghton Cl STHEL WA9 103 H5
Hoghton Gv CHTN/BK PR9 3 J2
Hoghton Rd SPK/HALE L24 148 A4
STHEL WA9 103 G5
Hoghton St CHTN/BK PR9 3 H3
Holbeach Cl WGNE/HIN WN2 81 G1
Holbeck St ANF/KKDL L4 97 K7
Holborn Av WGNS/IIMK WN3 4 C9
Holborn Ct WDN WA8 134 B2
Holborn Dr ORM L39 62 E2
Holborn Hl BIRK CH41 11 K9
ORM L39 62 E2
Holborn Sq BIRK CH41 128 A1
Holbrook Cl STHEL WA9 102 E7
WARRW/BUR WA5 120 A8
Holcombe Av GOL/RIS/CU WA3 92 E5
Holcombe Cl
GR/UP/WCH CH49 125 M1 2
Holcombe Gv CHLYE PR6 33 G4
Holcroft La GOL/RIS/CU WA3 107 L2
Holden Gv CSBY/WL L22 82 E3 3
Holden Rd CSBY/WL L22 82 D3
RAIN/WH L35 116 E1
Holden Rd East CSBY/WL L22 82 E3 4
Holden St CHLY/EC PR7 44 B6 3
Holden Ter CSBY/WL L22 82 E3 5
Holding St WGNE/HIN WN2 69 M7 3
Holdsworth St EHL/KEN L7 113 L3 5
Holes La WARR WA1 122 D6
Holford Av WARRW/BUR WA5 121 H5
Holford Wy NEWLW WA12 105 H2
Holgate CSBY/BLUN L23 71 K6
Holgate Dr WGNW/BIL/O WN5 67 G8
Holgate Pk CSBY/BLUN L23 71 K6
Holker La LEY/BBR PR5 30 C1
Holkham Cl WDN WA8 16 A2
Holland Ct SKEL WN8 76 F3
Holland Gv HES CH60 141 H4
Holland Moss SKEL WN8 65 J8
Holland Rd HLWD L26 132 A7
SPK/HALE L24 147 G3
WAL/NB CH45 95 L6
Holland's La SKEL WN8 64 C3
Holland St EHL/KEN L7 113 M2
Holland Wy HLWD L26 132 A7
Hollies Rd HLWD L26 132 B6
The Hollies WGN WN1 68 F2
WLTN L25 131 G2
Hollinbrook WGNNW/ST WN6 68 B3 3
Hollingbourne Pl
NG/CROX L11 98 C2 3
Hollingbourne Rd NG/CROX L11 98 C2
Hollingwood Cl AIMK WN4 91 J2 1
Hollingworth Cl WLT/FAZ L9 97 K2
Hollin Hey Cl WGNW/BIL/O WN5 89 M2
Hollin La CHLYE PR6 33 L3
Hollins Cl AIMK WN4 90 F1
WAV L15 114 C5
Hollins Dr WARRN/WOL WA2 105 J7
Hollinshead St CHLY/EC PR7 32 E5
Hollins La LEY/BBR PR5 30 E1
WARRN/WOL WA2 105 H7
Hollocombe Rd NG/CROX L11 98 E3
Holloway RUNC WA7 18 F5
Hollow Cft STBRV L28 99 J4
Hollow Dr WARRS WA4 138 A4
Hollowford La BRSC L40 52 E2
Holly Av BEB CH63 143 H2
NEWLW WA12 104 F2
Hollybank WARRS WA4 136 C8
Holly Bank Gv STHEL WA9 9 J3
Hollybank Rd BIRK CH41 11 G7
CALD/MH L18 114 A8 3
RUNC WA7 150 B5
Hollybrook Rd STHP PR8 2 E7
Holly Bush La GOL/RIS/CU WA3 123 L4
Hollybush Sq
GOL/RIS/CU WA3 93 G4 4
Holly Cl BRSC L40 64 A1
ECCL WA10 101 K1
SKEL WN8 65 G4 2
SPK/HALE L24 147 M4
Holly Ct FROD/HEL WA6 159 L8
Holly Crs CHLY/EC PR7 43 G2
RNFD/HAY WA11 76 C8
Hollydale Rd CALD/MH L18 114 C8 5
Holly Farm Rd ALL/GAR L19 130 E8
Hollyfield Rd EP CH65 20 B4 1
WLT/FAZ L9 84 B8
Holly Fold La RNFD/HAY WA11 76 A2
Holly Gv BIRK CH41 128 A1 4
HUY L36 115 K3
LITH L21 83 H7
WARR WA1 122 C6
Holly Heath Dr WGN WN1 68 D1 2
Holly Hedge La WARRS WA4 136 F7
Holly Hey RAIN/WH L35 116 F4
Holly La BRSC L40 39 L2
ORM L39 62 D1
SKEL WN8 75 M1
Holly Mt WD/CROXPK L12 98 C7
Holly Pl MOR/LEA CH46 110 B6
Holly Rd EHL/KEN L7 113 M3
EP CH65 20 D4
GOL/RIS/CU WA3 92 E5
RNFD/HAY WA11 90 B8
WARRW/BUR WA5 120 A8
WGNE/HIN WN2 57 K8
WGNW/BIL/O WN5 68 A6
Hollyrood PR/KW L34 100 B8
Holly St BTL L20 7 H3
WGNE/HIN WN2 69 H3
Holly Ter WARRW/BUR WA5 120 B8
Hollytree Rd WLTN L25 131 K2
Hollywood Rd AIG/SPK L17 130 A2 2
Holman Rd ALL/GAR L19 130 F7
Holm Cottages
CL/PREN CH43 127 H3 2
Holmcrofts NSTN CH64 153 G8
Holmdale Av CHTN/BK PR9 25 L1
Holm Dr CHNE CH2 165 L2
Holme Av WGN WN1 68 E3
Holme Cl PR/KW L34 101 J6
Holmefield Av ALL/GAR L19 130 C5
Holmefield Gv MGHL L31 72 E4
Holmefield Rd ALL/GAR L19 130 B4
Holme Rd ECCL WA10 101 K3
Holmes Ct GOL/RIS/CU WA3 122 E1 3
Holmes House Av
WGNS/IIMK WN3 78 E2
Holmes La LITH L21 83 J6 3
Holmes St TOX L8 113 L6
Holme St EV L5 96 D7
Holmesway PEN/TH CH61 141 H1
Holmeswood Rd
KIRK/FR/WA PR4 27 M7
Holme Ter WGN WN1 68 D2
Holmfield Av RUNC WA7 19 L4
Holmfield Dr GTS/LS CH66 162 F2
Holmfield Gv HUY L36 116 B5 4
Holmfield Pk FMBY L37 59 G1 1
Holm Hey Rd CL/PREN CH43 127 H3
Holm Hl WKBY CH48 124 E4
Holmlands Crs
CL/PREN CH43 127 G3 1
Holmlands Dr CL/PREN CH43 127 G3
Holmlands Wy
CL/PREN CH43 127 G3 2
Holm La CL/PREN CH43 127 H3
Holmleigh Rd WLTN L25 115 J7 3
Holm Oak Wy GTS/LS CH66 163 G5
Holmrook Rd NG/CROX L11 98 C3
Holmsfield Cl WGNE/HIN WN2 69 J3 3
Holmsfield Rd WARR WA1 15 K6
Holmside Cl MOR/LEA CH46 110 B5
Holmside La CL/PREN CH43 127 H3
Holm View Cl CL/PREN CH43 127 J2
Holmville Rd BEB CH63 128 A8
Holmway BEB CH63 128 B8
Holmwood Av PEN/TH CH61 126 E8
Holmwood Cl AIMK WN4 79 J8 6
FMBY L37 58 F2
Holmwood Dr EP CH65 163 K3 1
FMBY L37 58 F1
PEN/TH CH61 126 E8
Holmwood Gdns FMBY L37 58 F1
Holt Av MOR/LEA CH46 110 A5
WGNW/BIL/O WN5 89 M1
Holt Coppice ORM L39 62 C6 1
Holt Crs WGNW/BIL/O WN5 89 M1
Holt Hey NSTN CH64 153 J8
Holt Hl BIRK CH41 11 J9
Holt Hill Ter BIRK CH41 11 H8
Holt La NTHLY L27 115 M7
RAIN/WH L35 117 J1
RUNC WA7 150 B5
Holt Rd BIRK CH41 128 A1
EHL/KEN L7 113 L3
Holt St WGN WN1 5 L4
WGNE/HIN WN2 69 L8
WGNNW/ST WN6 68 B4
WGNS/IIMK WN3 79 J1
WGNW/BIL/O WN5 66 F8 5
Holtswell Cl GOL/RIS/CU WA3 93 G4 5
Holyhead Cl WARRW/BUR WA5 120 F2
Holyrood CSBY/BLUN L23 82 C1
Holyrood Av WDN WA8 134 C1
Holywell Cl NSTN CH64 152 D4
STHEL WA9 102 F7 5
Home Farm Cl
GR/UP/WCH CH49 126 E3 2
Home Farm Rd
GR/UP/WCH CH49 126 D3
PR/KW L34 99 L3
Homer Rd PR/KW L34 99 L2
Homerton Rd NPK/KEN L6 113 M2 2
Homestall Rd NG/CROX L11 98 C3
Homestead Av NTHTN L30 84 D2
RNFD/HAY WA11 91 G6 5
Homestead Cl HUY L36 116 C2 1
Homestead Ms WKBY CH48 124 D3 2
Homeway FROD/HEL WA6 166 D3 1
Honeybourne Dr RAIN/WH L35 101 J7
Honey Hall Rd HLWD L26 132 A7
Honeys Green Cl
WD/CROXPK L12 98 F8 2
Honey's Green La
WD/CROXPK L12 98 F8
Honey St RAIN/WH L35 101 L6 3
Honeysuckle Av
WGNNW/ST WN6 68 B2
Honeysuckle Cl GTS/LS CH66 163 H5
HLWD L26 131 M3 4
WDN WA8 134 D1 7
Honeysuckle Dr WLT/FAZ L9 97 K2
Honister Av RNFD/HAY WA11 89 L5
WARRN/WOL WA2 121 L3
Honister Cl NTHLY L27 132 C2
Honister Gv RUNC WA7 150 A8
Honister Rd WGNW/BIL/O WN5 67 K7
Honiston Av RAIN/WH L35 117 K1
Honiton Cl LEIGH WN7 81 M3
Honiton Rd AIG/SPK L17 130 A5
Honiton Wy WARRW/BUR WA5 136 A1
Hood La WARRW/BUR WA5 120 E8
Hood La North
WARRW/BUR WA5 120 E7
Hood Rd WDN WA8 16 B2
Hood St BTL L20 6 D1
CLVPS L1 13 G6
WAL/EG CH44 111 M2 7
Hookstone Dr GTS/LS CH66 155 L7
Hook St WGNE/HIN WN2 5 M5
Hoole La CHTN/BK PR9 23 J7
Hoole Rd GR/UP/WCH CH49 126 D2
Hoolpool La FROD/HEL WA6 159 H8
Hooton Gn GTS/LS CH66 155 J3
Hooton La GTS/LS CH66 155 K4
Hooton Rd NSTN CH64 154 D4
WLT/FAZ L9 84 D6
Hooton Wy GTS/LS CH66 155 H3
Hope Crs WGNNW/ST WN6 55 K7
Hope Cft GTS/LS CH66 163 H3
Hope Farm Rd GTS/LS CH66 163 G4
Hope Pl CLVPS L1 13 K9 4
Hope Sq CHTN/BK PR9 3 K3
Hope St AIMK WN4 79 M8
CHLY/EC PR7 32 E4
CHLYE PR6 44 D5 4
CHTN/BK PR9 3 K3
CLVPS L1 113 H6
NEWLW WA12 104 D2
PR/KW L34 100 F7
TOX L8 113 H5
WAL/NB CH45 95 K5
WGNE/HIN WN2 80 A1
Hope St North HOR/BR BL6 45 K8
Hope Wy TOX L8 113 H5 14
Hopfield Rd MOR/LEA CH46 110 B5
Hopkins Cl ECCL WA10 8 A4
Hopwood Cl GOL/RIS/CU WA3 93 H5 4
Hopwood Crs RNFD/HAY WA11 76 C8
Hopwood St EV L5 96 F8
WARR WA1 15 G4
Horace St ECCL WA10 8 C4
Horbury Gdns GTS/LS CH66 155 L8
Hornbeam Av GTS/LS CH66 163 H4
Hornbeam Cl MOR/LEA CH46 109 K5 5
RNFD/HAY WA11 90 B8 3
RUNC WA7 150 E5
Hornbeam Crs AIMK WN4 91 K2
Hornbeam Rd HLWD L26 132 C6
WLT/FAZ L9 97 L2
Hornby Av BTL L20 6 F1
PS/BROM CH62 143 M4
Hornby Bvd LITH L21 83 K7
Hornby Cha MGHL L31 72 F6
Hornby Cl WLT/FAZ L9 97 H1
Hornby Crs STHEL WA9 118 F1
Hornby La CALD/MH L18 114 F8
WARRN/WOL WA2 105 J7
Hornby Pk CALD/MH L18 114 F8
Hornby Pl WLT/FAZ L9 84 C8
Hornby Rd BTL L20 6 F1
CHLYE PR6 33 G7 1
CHTN/BK PR9 25 J1
PS/BROM CH62 143 L4
WLT/FAZ L9 97 H1
Hornby Steet WGN WN1 68 E3
Hornby St BIRK CH41 11 L5
CSBY/BLUN L23 83 G1 1
LITH L21 83 J7 4
Hornby Wk EV L5 12 F1
Horncastle Cl
GOL/RIS/CU WA3 93 H5 5
Hornchurch Dr CHLY/EC PR7 32 C5
Horne Gv WGNS/IIMK WN3 68 B8
Horne St NPK/KEN L6 113 K1
Hornhouse La NWD/KWIPK L33 86 D5
Hornsey Gv WGNS/IIMK WN3 78 F2
Hornsey Rd ANF/KKDL L4 97 K7
Hornspit La WD/CROXPK L12 98 C5
Horridge Av NEWLW WA12 91 L8
Horringford Rd ALL/GAR L19 130 B5
Horrobin La CHLYE PR6 44 E5
Horrocks Av ALL/GAR L19 130 F7
Horrocks Cl HUY L36 115 M1 1
Horrocks La WARR WA1 14 E6
Horrocks Rd HUY L36 115 M2 1
Horrocks St LEIGH WN7 93 J1
Horseman Pl WAL/EG CH44 112 A3 10
Horsemarket St WARR WA1 14 E5
Horseshoe Crs
WARRN/WOL WA2 122 A2 3
Horseshoe Dr AIN/FAZ L10 85 K6
Horsfall Gv TOX L8 129 G1 2
Horsfall St TOX L8 129 G1
Horsham Gv WGNE/HIN WN2 69 H3 5
Horstone Crs GTS/LS CH66 163 H3
Horstone Gdns GTS/LS CH66 163 H3
Horstone Rd GTS/LS CH66 163 H3
Horton St WGNNW/ST WN6 68 A3
Horwood Av RAIN/WH L35 117 K1
Horwood Cl NG/CROX L11 98 E3 2
Hoscar Moss Rd BRSC L40 52 E2
Hoscote Pk WKBY CH48 124 C3
Hose Side Rd WAL/NB CH45 95 J4
Hospital St ECCL WA10 9 H3
Hospital Wy RUNC WA7 150 B6
Hosta Cl NWD/KWIPK L33 73 M8 5
Hostock Cl RAIN/WH L35 116 F3 3
Hotel St NEWLW WA12 104 D2 7
Hotham St VAUX/LVPD L3 13 J6
Hothfield Rd WAL/EG CH44 111 M2 8
Hotspur St BTL L20 96 E5
Hough Green Rd WDN WA8 133 J3
Hough's La WARRS WA4 137 J7
Houghton Av WGNW/BIL/O WN5 68 A3
Houghton Cl NEWLW WA12 104 D2 8
WDN WA8 134 E3
Houghton Cft WDN WA8 117 L7
Houghton La WGNNW/ST WN6 55 H7
Houghton Rd
GR/UP/WCH CH49 126 D2
Houghton's La ECCL WA10 88 B6
SKEL WN8 65 L4
Houghtons Rd SKEL WN8 65 J2
Houghton St CHLYE PR6 32 F5 6
CLVPS L1 13 H7
NEWLW WA12 104 D2 9
PR/KW L34 100 F7
RAIN/WH L35 117 L2 4
WARRN/WOL WA2 14 E3
WDN WA8 134 F3
Houghwood Gra AIMK WN4 91 H2
Hougoumont Av CSBY/WL L22 83 G4
Hougoumont Gv
CSBY/WL L22 83 G4 3
Houlding St ANF/KKDL L4 97 J7 6
Houlgrave Rd EV L5 96 E8
Houlston Rd KKBY L32 85 K3
Houlton St EHL/KEN L7 113 L3 6
Housley Cl WGNS/IIMK WN3 79 J1
The Hove RUNC WA7 150 F7
Howard Av PS/BROM CH62 143 M5
Howard Cl LITH L21 83 L3
MGHL L31 73 H4 2
Howard Dr ALL/GAR L19 130 C6
Howard Florey Av NTHTN L30 84 B1
Howard Rd CHLY/EC PR7 32 D8
GOL/RIS/CU WA3 107 J3
Howard's La ECCL WA10 101 G1
WGNW/BIL/O WN5 67 H6
Howards Rd PEN/TH CH61 126 D7 3
Howard St ECCL WA10 101 L5 2
WGNW/BIL/O WN5 67 L8
Howards Wy NSTN CH64 153 J7
Howbeck Cl CL/PREN CH43 111 H7
Howbeck Dr CL/PREN CH43 111 H7
Howbeck Rd CL/PREN CH43 111 H8
Howden Dr HUY L36 115 J3
WGNS/IIMK WN3 79 J1
Howe Gv CHLY/EC PR7 32 C6
Howell Dr GR/UP/WCH CH49 125 M3
Howell Rd PS/BROM CH62 128 C6 3
Howells Av GTS/LS CH66 162 E2
Howells Cl MGHL L31 72 F3 2
Howe St BTL L20 6 E8
Howey La FROD/HEL WA6 160 C6
Howey Ri FROD/HEL WA6 160 C6
Howley La WARR WA1 15 J6
Howson Rd WARRN/WOL WA2 121 L3
Howson St RF/TRAN CH42 128 B3
Hoylake Cl LEIGH WN7 93 M3
RUNC WA7 150 E7
Hoylake Gv STHEL WA9 118 E1 10
Hoylake Rd BIRK CH41 111 G4
CL/PREN CH43 110 F4
MOR/LEA CH46 109 K6
Hoyle Rd HOY CH47 108 D5
Hoyle St WARRW/BUR WA5 14 B2
Huddlestone Cl
GR/UP/WCH CH49 126 E2 2
Huddleston Rd WAV L15 114 D4
Hudson Cl WARRW/BUR WA5 120 F5
Hudson Rd MGHL L31 72 F6
MOR/LEA CH46 110 C1
Hudswell Cl NTHTN L30 84 D4
Hughenden Rd CLB/OSW/ST L13 98 B8
Hughes Av RAIN/WH L35 116 F1
WARRN/WOL WA2 121 M3
Hughes Cl EHL/KEN L7 113 L4 9
Hughes Dr BTL L20 84 A7
Hughes La CL/PREN CH43 127 K2
Hughes Pl WARRN/WOL WA2 121 M3 7
Hughes St ALL/GAR L19 130 E8
NPK/KEN L6 113 J2 2
STHEL WA9 102 F5
WARRS WA4 15 H9
Hughestead Gv ALL/GAR L19 130 D7 2
Hughson St TOX L8 113 G8
Hullet Cl WGNNW/ST WN6 55 G5
Hulme Gv LEIGH WN7 81 L7
Hulme Rd LEIGH WN7 81 L7
Hulme St STHP PR8 2 F4
Hulmewood BEB CH63 128 C6 4
Hulton Av RAIN/WH L35 117 H1
Humber Cl ANF/KKDL L4 97 G5
WDN WA8 135 H2
Humber Crs STHEL WA9 102 E8
Humber Pl WGNW/BIL/O WN5 67 L6
Humber Rd GTS/LS CH66 163 H3
WARRN/WOL WA2 122 A3
Hume Ct HOY CH47 108 E5
Hume St WARR WA1 15 J3
Humphrey's Cl RUNC WA7 150 F6 5
Humphreys Hey CSBY/BLUN L23 71 K8
Humphrey St BTL L20 83 L7
Huncote Av RNFD/HAY WA11 89 M7
Hunslett Rd WLT/FAZ L9 84 D7
Hunstanton Cl
GR/UP/WCH CH49 110 C6 2
Hunt Cl WARRW/BUR WA5 120 D5 4
Hunter Av WARRN/WOL WA2 121 K3
Hunter Rd WGNW/BIL/O WN5 68 A4
Hunters Ct FROD/HEL WA6 166 F1
RUNC WA7 150 A7 2
Hunter's La KIRK/FR/WA PR4 27 K2
WAV L15 114 C6
Hunter St STHEL WA9 9 L8
VAUX/LVPD L3 13 H5
Hunters Wy NSTN CH64 152 E5
Huntingdon Cl
MOR/LEA CH46 109 K5 6
Huntingdon Gv MGHL L31 72 E1 1
Huntley Gv STHEL WA9 102 E6
Huntley St WARRW/BUR WA5 136 E1
Huntly Rd NPK/KEN L6 113 L2
Hunt Rd MGHL L31 72 F4
RNFD/HAY WA11 91 G7
Hunts Cross Av WLTN L25 131 K2
Hunts La WARRS WA4 138 B3
Huntsman Wd WD/CROXPK L12 99 G5
Hunt St WGN WN1 5 J5
Hurford Av EP CH65 163 H1

Hurley Cl WARRW/BUR WA5 .... 120 E8
Hurlingham Rd ANF/KKDL L4 .... 97 L3
Hurlston Av SKEL WN8 .... 65 L5 1
Hurlston Dr ORM L39 .... 51 G6 2
Hurlston La BRSC L40 .... 50 D4
Hurn Gv CHLY/EC PR7 .... 32 C6
Hurrell Rd BIRK CH41 .... 110 F4
Hursley Rd WLT/FAZ L9 .... 98 A1
Hurst Bank RF/TRAN CH42 .... 128 B5
Hurst Brook CHLY/EC PR7 .... 43 H4
Hurst Gn BRSC L40 .... 40 E3 1
Hurstlyn Rd CALD/MH L18 .... 130 E4
Hurst Park Cl HUY L36 .... 116 C1 1
Hurst Park Dr HUY L36 .... 116 C2
Hurst Rd MGHL L31 .... 73 G6
Hurst's La ORM L39 .... 74 C3
Hurst St CLVPS L1 .... 112 F5
WDN WA8 .... 149 J1 4
WGNE/HIN WN2 .... 69 L7
Huskisson St CLVPS L1 .... 113 H6
Hutchinson St NPK/KEN L6 .... 113 J2
WDN WA8 .... 16 C8
Hutchinson Wk NPK/KEN L6 .... 113 J2 8
Hut La CHLYE PR6 .... 44 D1
Huttfield Rd SPK/HALE L24 .... 147 J1 1
Hutton Ct SKEL WN8 .... 64 F4 4
Hutton Rd SKEL WN8 .... 64 F4 5
Hutton St WGN WN1 .... 56 C2
Huxley Cl MOR/LEA CH46 .... 109 K5
Huxley Pl WGNS/IIMK WN3 .... 68 C8
Huxley St CLB/OSW/ST L13 .... 98 A6 1
Huyton Av ECCL WA10 .... 89 G7
Huyton Brook HUY L36 .... 116 B5
Huyton Church Rd HUY L36 .... 116 A3
Huyton Hall Crs HUY L36 .... 116 A3 3
Huyton Hey Rd HUY L36 .... 116 B3
Huyton House Cl HUY L36 .... 115 K1
Huyton House Rd HUY L36 .... 115 K1
Huyton La HUY L36 .... 116 B2 1
Huyton Rd CHLY/EC PR7 .... 44 C7
Hyacinth Cl RNFD/HAY WA11 .... 91 H7
Hyatt Crs WGNNW/ST WN6 .... 55 L2
Hyde Cl EP CH65 .... 163 H1
RUNC WA7 .... 149 M7 4
WGNS/IIMK WN3 .... 68 C8
Hyde Rd CSBY/WL L22 .... 82 F4
Hyde's Brow RNFD/HAY WA11 .... 76 C5
Hydro Av WKBY CH48 .... 124 D4
Hygeia St NPK/KEN L6 .... 113 J1
Hylton Av WAL/EG CH44 .... 111 J1
Hylton Ct EP CH65 .... 164 A3
Hylton Rd ALL/GAR L19 .... 130 F5
Hyslop St TOX L8 .... 113 G7
Hythe Av LITH L21 .... 83 L5
Hythe Cl STHP PR8 .... 36 A2
Hythedale Cl AIG/SPK L17 .... 129 L3 3

I

Ibbotson's La AIG/SPK L17 .... 130 A1
Ibstock Rd BTL L20 .... 83 K8
Iffley Cl GR/UP/WCH CH49 .... 109 M8 6
Ikin Cl CL/PREN CH43 .... 110 E4
Ilchester Rd BIRK CH41 .... 111 H4
CHLDW L16 .... 115 G4
WAL/EG CH44 .... 111 M2 2
Ilex Av WARRN/WOL WA2 .... 105 K7
Ilford Av CSBY/BLUN L23 .... 70 F8
WAL/EG CH44 .... 111 K3
Ilford St VAUX/LVPD L3 .... 13 K5
Ilfracombe Rd STHEL WA9 .... 102 E8
Iliad St EV L5 .... 13 J2
Ilkley Av CHTN/BK PR9 .... 22 E7
Ilsley Cl GR/UP/WCH CH49 .... 126 B1
Imber Rd KKBY L32 .... 86 B5
Imison St WLT/FAZ L9 .... 97 H2
Imison Wy WLT/FAZ L9 .... 7 M5
Imperial Av WAL/NB CH45 .... 95 L7
Imperial Ms EP CH65 .... 20 B2
Imrie St ANF/KKDL L4 .... 97 H3 3
Ince Av ANF/KKDL L4 .... 97 K5
CSBY/BLUN L23 .... 70 E8
LITH L21 .... 83 K6
PS/BROM CH62 .... 155 G2
Ince Cl CL/PREN CH43 .... 127 H1 1
Ince Crs FMBY L37 .... 58 F2
Ince Green La WGNE/HIN WN2 .... 5 M6
WGNS/IIMK WN3 .... 5 K8
Ince Gv CL/PREN CH43 .... 127 H2
Ince Hall Av WGNE/HIN WN2 .... 5 M4
Ince La CHLY/EC PR7 .... 30 E8
CHNE CH2 .... 165 K1
CSBY/BLUN L23 .... 71 H4
Incemore Rd CALD/MH L18 .... 130 D4
Ince Orchards CHNE CH2 .... 165 K1
Ince Rd CSBY/BLUN L23 .... 71 J6
Inchcape Rd CHLDW L16 .... 115 G4
WAL/NB CH45 .... 94 F8 3
Inchfield SKEL WN8 .... 65 K3
Index St ANF/KKDL L4 .... 97 H4
Ingestre Rd CL/PREN CH43 .... 127 J2
Ingham Rd WDN WA8 .... 134 B1
Ingleborough Rd
RF/TRAN CH42 .... 127 M3
Ingleby Cl WGNNW/ST WN6 .... 55 M3
Ingleby Rd PS/BROM CH62 .... 128 D5
WAL/EG CH44 .... 111 J2 7
Ingledene Rd CALD/MH L18 .... 114 F8
Ingle Gn CSBY/BLUN L23 .... 70 C8
Inglegreen HES CH60 .... 141 J5
Ingleholme Gdns PR/KW L34 .... 101 J6
Ingleholme Rd CALD/MH L18 .... 130 C4
Inglemere Rd RF/TRAN CH42 .... 128 A3
Ingle Ms CHLY/EC PR7 .... 32 F4 1
Inglemoss Dr RNFD/HAY WA11 .... 88 D4
Inglenook Rd
WARRW/BUR WA5 .... 136 B1 3
Ingleton Cl
GR/UP/WCH CH49 .... 125 M1 6
NEWLW WA12 .... 104 D1 2
Ingleton Dr RNFD/HAY WA11 .... 89 K4
Ingleton Gn KKBY L32 .... 86 B5 2
Ingleton Gv RUNC WA7 .... 149 M8
Ingleton Rd CALD/MH L18 .... 114 B8 3
KKBY L32 .... 86 B5
STHP PR8 .... 36 A2
Inglewhite SKEL WN8 .... 65 J3
Inglewhite Av WGN WN1 .... 68 E3
Inglewhite Crs WGN WN1 .... 68 E3 5
Inglewood WD/CROXPK L12 .... 99 J3
Inglewood Av
MOR/LEA CH46 .... 109 M6 2
WGN WN1 .... 5 J5
Inglewood Cl
GOL/RIS/CU WA3 .... 107 K7 1
Inglewood Rd RNFD/HAY WA11 .... 88 D4
Inglis Rd WLT/FAZ L9 .... 84 D6 3
Ingoe Cl KKBY L32 .... 85 K4
Ingoe La KKBY L32 .... 85 K5
Ingram SKEL WN8 .... 65 K4
Ingram St WGNE/HIN WN2 .... 80 C2
WGNNW/ST WN6 .... 68 B4
Ingrave Rd ANF/KKDL L4 .... 97 L3
Ingrow Rd NPK/KEN L6 .... 113 K2
Inigo Rd CLB/OSW/ST L13 .... 114 D1
Inley Cl BEB CH63 .... 143 J3
Inley Rd BEB CH63 .... 143 H3
Inman Av STHEL WA9 .... 103 K3
Inman Rd GR/UP/WCH CH49 .... 110 A7
LITH L21 .... 83 K6
Inner Central Rd SPK/HALE L24 .... 132 B8
Inner Forum NG/CROX L11 .... 98 A2
Inner South Rd SPK/HALE L24 .... 147 H1
Inner West Rd SPK/HALE L24 .... 147 G1
Innisfree Cl GTS/LS CH66 .... 155 L8 5
Insall Rd CLB/OSW/ST L13 .... 114 D4
WARRN/WOL WA2 .... 122 B3
Inskip SKEL WN8 .... 65 J3
Inskip Rd CHTN/BK PR9 .... 25 J1
Intake Cl NSTN CH64 .... 154 C5 2
Intake La ORM L39 .... 61 G5
ORM L39 .... 75 J1
Inveresk Ct CL/PREN CH43 .... 111 G7
Invincible Cl NTHTN L30 .... 84 A5 4
Invincible Wy NG/CROX L11 .... 85 L7
Inward Dr WGNNW/ST WN6 .... 55 J8
Inwood Rd ALL/GAR L19 .... 130 E6
Iona Cl WD/CROXPK L12 .... 99 J2
Ionic Rd CLB/OSW/ST L13 .... 114 C1
Ionic St LITH L21 .... 83 H6 7
RF/TRAN CH42 .... 128 B3
Irby Av WAL/EG CH44 .... 111 J1
Irby Cl GTS/LS CH66 .... 163 G1
Irby Rd ANF/KKDL L4 .... 97 K5
PEN/TH CH61 .... 125 M8
Irbyside Rd WKBY CH48 .... 125 K4
Iredale Crs WGNNW/ST WN6 .... 56 B6
Ireland Rd RNFD/HAY WA11 .... 90 E7
SPK/HALE L24 .... 148 A4
Ireland St WARRN/WOL WA2 .... 121 K5
WDN WA8 .... 134 F3
Irene Av RNFD/HAY WA11 .... 89 L6
Irene Rd CHLDW L16 .... 114 E7
Ireton St ANF/KKDL L4 .... 97 H3
Iris Av BIRK CH41 .... 111 H5
Iris Cl WDN WA8 .... 133 L3
Irlam Dr KKBY L32 .... 86 A3
Irlam Pl BTL L20 .... 6 E3
Irlam Rd BTL L20 .... 6 E3
Ironbridge Vw TOX L8 .... 129 G1
Ironmonger La WGNS/IIMK WN3 .... 4 E6
Ironside Rd HUY L36 .... 115 M1
Irton Rd CHTN/BK PR9 .... 25 G5
Irvin Av CHTN/BK PR9 .... 22 E8 4
Irvine Rd RF/TRAN CH42 .... 127 M3
Irvine St EHL/KEN L7 .... 113 J4
Irving St CHTN/BK PR9 .... 24 D4
Irwell SKEL WN8 .... 65 J2
Irwell Cl AIG/SPK L17 .... 130 A2
Irwell La AIG/SPK L17 .... 130 A2
RUNC WA7 .... 19 K2
Irwell Pl WGNW/BIL/O WN5 .... 67 L7
Irwell Rd WARRS WA4 .... 137 K3
WGNW/BIL/O WN5 .... 67 H6
Irwell St WDN WA8 .... 149 J1
Irwin Rd STHEL WA9 .... 102 E6
Isaac St TOX L8 .... 129 H1
Isabel Gv CLB/OSW/ST L13 .... 98 A6
Isherwood Cl
WARRN/WOL WA2 .... 122 B2
Island Pl ALL/GAR L19 .... 130 E7 2
Island Rd ALL/GAR L19 .... 130 E7
Island Rd South ALL/GAR L19 .... 130 E7
Islands Brow RNFD/HAY WA11 .... 89 K7
Islay Cl EP CH65 .... 163 L5
Isleham Cl CALD/MH L18 .... 130 E5
Isleworth Dr CHLY/EC PR7 .... 32 D6
Islington CSBY/BLUN L23 .... 70 F8
VAUX/LVPD L3 .... 13 J5
Islip Cl PEN/TH CH61 .... 125 M6
Ismay Dr WAL/EG CH44 .... 95 M8
Ismay Rd LITH L21 .... 83 K6
Ismay St ANF/KKDL L4 .... 97 H4
Ivanhoe Av GOL/RIS/CU WA3 .... 92 F4
Ivanhoe Rd AIG/SPK L17 .... 129 L1
CSBY/BLUN L23 .... 82 E2
Ivatt Wy EHL/KEN L7 .... 113 L4
Iveagh Cl RUNC WA7 .... 150 C6 1
Iver Cl WDN WA8 .... 117 L7
Ivernia Rd ANF/KKDL L4 .... 97 K3
Ivor Rd WAL/EG CH44 .... 95 L8
Ivory Dr NWD/KWIPK L33 .... 74 A8
Ivy Av ALL/GAR L19 .... 130 C6
BEB CH63 .... 128 A8
NEWLW WA12 .... 104 E3
Ivybridge SKEL WN8 .... 65 K3
Ivychurch Ms RUNC WA7 .... 149 M3
Ivy Ct STHEL WA9 .... 9 L5
Ivydale SKEL WN8 .... 65 K3
Ivydale Rd CALD/MH L18 .... 130 B1
RF/TRAN CH42 .... 128 A2 2
WLT/FAZ L9 .... 97 K1
Ivy Farm Dr NSTN CH64 .... 153 H7
Ivy Farm Gdns
GOL/RIS/CU WA3 .... 106 F1 1
Ivy Farm Rd RAIN/WH L35 .... 117 K1
Ivy House Rd
GOL/RIS/CU WA3 .... 92 F4 4
Ivyhurst Cl ALL/GAR L19 .... 130 B5
Ivy La MOR/LEA CH46 .... 110 A4
Ivy Leigh CLB/OSW/ST L13 .... 98 A8
Ivy Rd GOL/RIS/CU WA3 .... 92 D5
WARR WA1 .... 123 G6
Ivy St BIRK CH41 .... 11 L6
RUNC WA7 .... 19 G5
STHP PR8 .... 3 M6
WGNNW/ST WN6 .... 4 D4

J

Jack Mcbain Ct VAUX/LVPD L3 .... 12 E2
Jack's Brow PR/KW L34 .... 100 A3
Jacksfield Wy ALL/GAR L19 .... 130 B6
Jacksmere La BRSC L40 .... 36 D5
Jackson Av GOL/RIS/CU WA3 .... 107 G2
WARR WA1 .... 122 B6
Jackson Cl BEB CH63 .... 128 B5
ORM L39 .... 49 H8
RAIN/WH L35 .... 117 M4
Jackson Rd CHLY/EC PR7 .... 32 C8 4
Jackson's Common La BRSC L40 .... 50 C4
Jackson's La BRSC L40 .... 41 G6
Jackson St ALL/GAR L19 .... 130 E7 3
BIRK CH41 .... 11 K7
CHLY/EC PR7 .... 32 F7
RNFD/HAY WA11 .... 90 C6 1
STHEL WA9 .... 9 L5
WARRW/BUR WA5 .... 104 A7
WGNE/HIN WN2 .... 69 J6 3
Jacobs Cl LITH L21 .... 83 K7
Jacob St TOX L8 .... 129 H1
WGNE/HIN WN2 .... 69 M7
Jacqueline Dr HUY L36 .... 116 C1
Jade Cl NWD/KWIPK L33 .... 86 B2 2
Jamaica St CLVPS L1 .... 112 F6
James Av GTS/LS CH66 .... 162 E2
Jamesbrook Cl BIRK CH41 .... 10 B1
James Clarke St EV L5 .... 12 F1
James Cl WDN WA8 .... 149 J1
James Ct WLTN L25 .... 131 K3
James Gv ECCL WA10 .... 8 C7
James Holt Av KKBY L32 .... 85 M4
James Larkin Wy
ANF/KKDL L4 .... 96 F6 4
James Pl CHLY/EC PR7 .... 43 G5
WGNNW/ST WN6 .... 55 M3
James Rd RNFD/HAY WA11 .... 91 H6
WLTN L25 .... 131 K3
James Sq WGNNW/ST WN6 .... 55 M3
James St ALL/GAR L19 .... 130 E8
CL/PREN CH43 .... 10 E8
CLVPS L1 .... 12 E8
STHEL WA9 .... 118 F2
WAL/EG CH44 .... 112 A3 11
WARR WA1 .... 14 F5
WGNE/HIN WN2 .... 80 A6
WGNS/IIMK WN3 .... 5 H7
Jamieson Av CSBY/BLUN L23 .... 83 J1
Jamieson Rd WAV L15 .... 114 A6 6
Jane's Brook Rd STHP PR8 .... 35 M1
Jane St STHEL WA9 .... 103 H6 5
Janet St EHL/KEN L7 .... 113 K4
Jarrett Rd NWD/KWIPK L33 .... 86 C1
Jarrow Cl CL/PREN CH43 .... 10 C9
Jasmine Cl EV L5 .... 13 L1
MOR/LEA CH46 .... 109 M6
Jasmine Ct HUY L36 .... 100 B8 1
Jasmine Ms AIG/SPK L17 .... 129 J2 4
Jasmine Rd
WGNW/BIL/O WN5 .... 67 M6 1
Jason St EV L5 .... 97 G7
Jason Wk EV L5 .... 97 G7
Java Rd ANF/KKDL L4 .... 97 M3
Jay Cl GOL/RIS/CU WA3 .... 123 J1
Jays Cl RUNC WA7 .... 151 G6
Jedburgh Av GTS/LS CH66 .... 155 J7
Jedburgh Dr NWD/KWIPK L33 .... 73 M7
Jeffereys Crs HUY L36 .... 115 K3
Jeffereys Dr HUY L36 .... 115 J2
Jeffreys Dr GR/UP/WCH CH49 .... 109 M8
Jeffrey St WGNE/HIN WN2 .... 69 J5 7
Jellicoe Cl WKBY CH48 .... 124 F7 2
Jenkinson St VAUX/LVPD L3 .... 13 K3
WGNE/HIN WN2 .... 69 M7 4
Jennet Hey AIMK WN4 .... 79 H7
Jericho Cl AIG/SPK L17 .... 129 M3
Jericho Farm Cl AIG/SPK L17 .... 129 M4
Jericho La AIG/SPK L17 .... 129 M4 1
Jermyn St TOX L8 .... 113 J7
Jerningham Rd NG/CROX L11 .... 97 M2
Jersey Av EP CH65 .... 163 L4
LITH L21 .... 83 K4
Jersey Cl BTL L20 .... 7 G4
Jersey St BTL L20 .... 7 G4
STHEL WA9 .... 118 E2
Jervis Cl WARRN/WOL WA2 .... 122 C2
Jesmond St WAV L15 .... 113 M5 5
Jessamine Rd RF/TRAN CH42 .... 128 A2
Jessica Wy LEIGH WN7 .... 93 K1
Jeudwine Cl WLTN L25 .... 131 K5
Joan Av GR/UP/WCH CH49 .... 126 A1
MOR/LEA CH46 .... 109 M5
Jocelyn Cl BEB CH63 .... 143 J2
Jockey St WARRN/WOL WA2 .... 14 E1
John Bagot Cl EV L5 .... 97 G8 3
John Hunter Wy NTHTN L30 .... 84 B2 2
John Lennon Dr NPK/KEN L6 .... 113 K2
John Moores Cl EHL/KEN L7 .... 113 J5 5
John Nicholas Crs EP CH65 .... 20 D3 1
EP CH65 .... 20 E2 1
John Rd LYMM WA13 .... 139 L2
Johns Av RUNC WA7 .... 18 F6
Johnson Av NEWLW WA12 .... 91 K8
RAIN/WH L35 .... 116 E1
WGNE/HIN WN2 .... 81 G4
Johnson Cl LEIGH WN7 .... 93 K1
Johnson Gv WD/CROXPK L12 .... 99 G8 1
Johnson Rd CL/PREN CH43 .... 127 H4
Johnson's La WDN WA8 .... 17 M2
Johnson St CHTN/BK PR9 .... 3 H1
STHEL WA9 .... 9 M4
VAUX/LVPD L3 .... 13 G5 2
WGNW/BIL/O WN5 .... 67 K7 3
Johnston Av BTL L20 .... 84 A7
John St AIMK WN4 .... 79 M8
BIRK CH41 .... 11 L4
CHLY/EC PR7 .... 43 G4 4
ECCL WA10 .... 9 G4 1
EP CH65 .... 20 B2
GOL/RIS/CU WA3 .... 92 C5
VAUX/LVPD L3 .... 13 K3
WARRN/WOL WA2 .... 14 E4
WGN WN1 .... 5 H4
WGNE/HIN WN2 .... 81 K2
WGNW/BIL/O WN5 .... 67 M8
Jolly Tar La CHLY/EC PR7 .... 43 J6
Jones Farm Rd WLTN L25 .... 131 L1
Jonson Rd NSTN CH64 .... 153 G4
Jonville Rd WLT/FAZ L9 .... 84 E6
Jordan St CLVPS L1 .... 112 F6
Joseph Gardner Wy BTL L20 .... 6 F2
Joseph Lister Cl NTHTN L30 .... 84 B2
Joseph St STHEL WA9 .... 103 G6
WDN WA8 .... 134 E3
Joshua Cl EV L5 .... 97 G7
Joule St GOL/RIS/CU WA3 .... 107 H8
Joy La STHEL WA9 .... 119 G3
WARRW/BUR WA5 .... 119 M1
Jubilee Av DV/KA/FCH L14 .... 114 F4
ORM L39 .... 51 H7 2
WARR WA1 .... 122 B5
WARRW/BUR WA5 .... 136 A1 2
WGNW/BIL/O WN5 .... 77 M1
Jubilee Crs PS/BROM CH62 .... 128 D8
RNFD/HAY WA11 .... 91 H6
Jubilee Dr EHL/KEN L7 .... 113 K3
NTHTN L30 .... 84 C4
RAIN/WH L35 .... 116 F3
SKEL WN8 .... 65 G5 1
WKBY CH48 .... 124 C1
Jubilee Gv LYMM WA13 .... 139 L1
Jubilee Rd CSBY/BLUN L23 .... 82 E2
FMBY L37 .... 58 F4
LITH L21 .... 83 K6 4
Jubilee Wy WDN WA8 .... 134 A4 1
Jubits La WDN WA8 .... 118 C5
Juddfield St RNFD/HAY WA11 .... 90 C7
Judeland CHLY/EC PR7 .... 32 C3
Judges Dr NPK/KEN L6 .... 113 L1
Judges Wy NPK/KEN L6 .... 113 L1
Julian Wy WDN WA8 .... 134 B1
Julie Gv WD/CROXPK L12 .... 99 G8
Juliet Av BEB CH63 .... 128 A6
July Rd NPK/KEN L6 .... 97 M8
July St BTL L20 .... 7 H1
Junction La BRSC L40 .... 52 A1
NEWLW WA12 .... 104 D2 10
STHEL WA9 .... 103 G6
Junction Rd RNFD/HAY WA11 .... 76 A5
Junction Ter WGNS/IIMK WN3 .... 5 K8
June Av LEIGH WN7 .... 81 L7
PS/BROM CH62 .... 144 A5
June Rd NPK/KEN L6 .... 97 M8
June St BTL L20 .... 7 H2
Juniper Cl ECCL WA10 .... 8 A2
GR/UP/WCH CH49 .... 125 L3
STBRV L28 .... 99 K6
Juniper Dr GTS/LS CH66 .... 163 G4
WGNE/HIN WN2 .... 81 H2
Juniper Gdns CSBY/BLUN L23 .... 71 K7 1
Juniper Gv GTS/LS CH66 .... 163 H4
Juniper La GOL/RIS/CU WA3 .... 123 J5
Juniper St BTL L20 .... 96 E6
Jupiter Gv WGNS/IIMK WN3 .... 79 G3
Jurby Ct WARRN/WOL WA2 .... 122 A4 5
WARRN/WOL WA2 .... 122 B4 1
Justin Wy RAIN/WH L35 .... 101 K8 1
Juvenal Pl VAUX/LVPD L3 .... 13 J2
Juvenal St VAUX/LVPD L3 .... 13 H3

K

Kaigh Av CSBY/BLUN L23 .... 70 F8
Kale Cl WKBY CH48 .... 124 D4
Kane Ct GOL/RIS/CU WA3 .... 93 J4
Kara Cl BTL L20 .... 7 H4
Karan Wy MGHL L31 .... 85 J2
Karen Cl WARRW/BUR WA5 .... 104 B7
Karen Rd WGN WN1 .... 5 K4
Karen Wy GTS/LS CH66 .... 162 F2
Karonga Rd AIN/FAZ L10 .... 85 G6
Karonga Wy AIN/FAZ L10 .... 85 H6
Karslake Rd CALD/MH L18 .... 114 B8
WAL/EG CH44 .... 111 M3
Kay Cl WGN WN1 .... 5 H4
Kaye Av GOL/RIS/CU WA3 .... 107 H2
Kearsley Cl ANF/KKDL L4 .... 97 G6 11
Kearsley St ANF/KKDL L4 .... 97 G6
LEIGH WN7 .... 81 M8 3
WGNNW/ST WN6 .... 4 C2
Keates St STHEL WA9 .... 103 H5
Keats Av RAIN/WH L35 .... 117 H2
WGNNW/ST WN6 .... 68 A2
WGNS/IIMK WN3 .... 4 B9
WGNW/BIL/O WN5 .... 77 M4
Keats Cl CHLY/EC PR7 .... 30 F8
GTS/LS CH66 .... 163 G5 3
WDN WA8 .... 16 A3
Keats Gn HUY L36 .... 116 B4
Keats Gv WARRN/WOL WA2 .... 121 L3
Keats St BTL L20 .... 6 E1
LEIGH WN7 .... 81 M6
Keats Ter STHP PR8 .... 25 H7 1
Keats Wy WGNE/HIN WN2 .... 80 D4 3
Keble Dr AIN/FAZ L10 .... 84 E2
WAL/NB CH45 .... 94 F7
Keble Gv LEIGH WN7 .... 81 L5
Keble Rd BTL L20 .... 7 G8
Keble St NPK/KEN L6 .... 113 J2
WDN WA8 .... 16 E5
WGNE/HIN WN2 .... 5 M5
Keckwick La RUNC WA7 .... 151 H1
WARRS WA4 .... 151 K3 1
Kedleston St TOX L8 .... 129 J1
Keegan Dr WAL/EG CH44 .... 112 A3 12
Keele Cl CL/PREN CH43 .... 110 E4
Keenan Dr BTL L20 .... 84 A8
Keepers La BEB CH63 .... 127 K8
Keighley Av WAL/EG CH44 .... 95 G8 2
Keightley St BIRK CH41 .... 11 G4 1
Keir Hardie Av BTL L20 .... 7 M1
Keith Av ANF/KKDL L4 .... 97 H4
WARRW/BUR WA5 .... 120 A7
Keith Dr BEB CH63 .... 143 L8
Kelbrook Cl STHEL WA9 .... 102 F7 6
Kelburn Ct GOL/RIS/CU WA3 .... 107 H7
Kelday Cl NWD/KWIPK L33 .... 86 A3 3
Kelkbeck Cl MGHL L31 .... 73 H3
Kellaton Cl WGNS/IIMK WN3 .... 5 J7
Kellbank Rd WGNS/IIMK WN3 .... 79 G2 1
Kellet Cl WGNW/BIL/O WN5 .... 67 M4
Kellett Rd MOR/LEA CH46 .... 110 D2 1
Kellett St CHLY/EC PR7 .... 32 E5 7
Kellitt Rd WAV L15 .... 114 A6 7
Kelly Dr BTL L20 .... 7 L2
Kelly St PR/KW L34 .... 101 G7 5
Kelmscott Cl GTS/LS CH66 .... 162 F3
Kelmscott Dr WAL/EG CH44 .... 111 G1 1
Kelsall Av PS/BROM CH62 .... 155 G2
STHEL WA9 .... 118 D1
Kelsall Cl CL/PREN CH43 .... 127 J2
GOL/RIS/CU WA3 .... 122 E2
PS/BROM CH62 .... 155 G2
WDN WA8 .... 133 M3
Kelsey Cl ECCL WA10 .... 8 A3
Kelso Cl NWD/KWIPK L33 .... 73 M7
Kelso Rd NPK/KEN L6 .... 113 L2
Kelton Gv AIG/SPK L17 .... 130 A3
Kelvin Cl AIMK WN4 .... 90 F1 2
GOL/RIS/CU WA3 .... 106 F7
Kelvin Gv TOX L8 .... 113 J7
WGNS/IIMK WN3 .... 79 H3
Kelvin Rd BIRK CH41 .... 128 A1
WAL/EG CH44 .... 112 A4
Kelvinside CSBY/BLUN L23 .... 83 H3
WAL/EG CH44 .... 111 M4
Kelvin St GOL/RIS/CU WA3 .... 107 G7
Kelway Ter WGN WN1 .... 5 H1
Kemberton Dr WDN WA8 .... 118 C8 2
Kemble St EHL/KEN L7 .... 113 K3 3
PR/KW L34 .... 101 G7 6
Kemlyn Rd ANF/KKDL L4 .... 97 J7
Kemmel Av WARRS WA4 .... 137 L3
Kempsell Wy HLWD L26 .... 132 C6
Kempsey Gv STHEL WA9 .... 102 A6 2
Kempson Ter BEB CH63 .... 143 H1
Kempston St VAUX/LVPD L3 .... 13 K5
Kempton Cl HUY L36 .... 115 M4 3
NEWLW WA12 .... 91 M8
RUNC WA7 .... 149 L7 1
Kempton Park Fold STHP PR8 .... 36 B2
Kempton Park Rd
AIN/FAZ L10 .... 85 G3 2
Kempton Rd PS/BROM CH62 .... 128 D5 6
WAV L15 .... 113 M5
Kemsley Rd DV/KA/FCH L14 .... 115 H2
Kenbury Cl NWD/KWIPK L33 .... 86 C1 1
Kenbury Rd NWD/KWIPK L33 .... 86 C1
Kendal Av WARRN/WOL WA2 .... 121 L3
Kendal Cl BEB CH63 .... 128 B7
GTS/LS CH66 .... 162 F3
RNFD/HAY WA11 .... 76 B3
Kendal Dr GTS/LS CH66 .... 162 F3
MGHL L31 .... 72 F3
RAIN/WH L35 .... 117 J2
RNFD/HAY WA11 .... 76 B4
RNFD/HAY WA11 .... 89 L5
Kendal Gv AIMK WN4 .... 91 K1
LEIGH WN7 .... 81 M8 3
Kendal Pk WD/CROXPK L12 .... 98 F7
Kendal Ri RUNC WA7 .... 149 M8 2
Kendal Rd CHLDW L16 .... 115 G6
WAL/EG CH44 .... 111 J3
WDN WA8 .... 133 L4 3
WGNE/HIN WN2 .... 69 J5
Kendal St BIRK CH41 .... 11 J6 2
WGNNW/ST WN6 .... 4 C2
Kendal Wy STHP PR8 .... 47 K2
Kendricks Fold RAIN/WH L35 .... 117 K2
Kendrick St WARR WA1 .... 14 C5
Kenford Dr WGNS/IIMK WN3 .... 79 G3
Kenilworth Av RUNC WA7 .... 19 H8
Kenilworth Cl WLTN L25 .... 131 G2
Kenilworth Ct EP CH65 .... 164 A3 1
Kenilworth Dr PEN/TH CH61 .... 126 A8
WARR WA1 .... 122 B5
WGNE/HIN WN2 .... 81 H1
Kenilworth Gdns
GR/UP/WCH CH49 .... 110 A7 3
NEWLW WA12 .... 104 E3
Kenilworth Rd CHLDW L16 .... 114 F6
CSBY/BLUN L23 .... 82 E2
GOL/RIS/CU WA3 .... 93 G6
NSTN CH64 .... 153 G7
STHP PR8 .... 47 L1
WAL/EG CH44 .... 111 M2
Kenilworth St BTL L20 .... 6 F4 1
Kenilworth Wy WLTN L25 .... 131 G2
Kenley Av WDN WA8 .... 117 M8
Kenley Cl NPK/KEN L6 .... 113 L1
Kenmare Rd WAV L15 .... 114 A7
Kenmore Gv AIMK WN4 .... 90 F1 3
Kenmore Rd CL/PREN CH43 .... 127 G4
Kennelwood Av
NWD/KWIPK L33 .... 86 B2
Kennessee Cl MGHL L31 .... 73 G5 1
Kenneth Av LEIGH WN7 .... 81 M7
Kenneth Cl NTHTN L30 .... 84 A2
Kenneth Gv LEIGH WN7 .... 81 M7 4
Kenneth Rd WDN WA8 .... 133 L5 1
Kennet Rd BEB CH63 .... 127 M8
RNFD/HAY WA11 .... 90 E7 3
Kennford Rd NG/CROX L11 .... 85 L8
Kensington EHL/KEN L7 .... 113 K3
Kensington Av STHEL WA9 .... 102 E6
WARRS WA4 .... 138 E3 2
Kensington Gdns
MOR/LEA CH46 .... 110 A5 3
Kensington Rd CHLY/EC PR7 .... 32 D6
CHTN/BK PR9 .... 3 K4
EP CH65 .... 156 C8
FMBY L37 .... 59 G4 4
WGNW/BIL/O WN5 .... 67 M8 4
Kensington St EHL/KEN L7 .... 113 J3 3
Kent Av FMBY L37 .... 59 J4
LITH L21 .... 83 L5
WGNE/HIN WN2 .... 80 C3
Kent Cl BEB CH63 .... 143 K5
Kent Gv RUNC WA7 .... 19 K5
Kentmere Av RNFD/HAY WA11 .... 89 L4
Kentmere Dr PEN/TH CH61 .... 141 H2 2
Kentmere Pl
WARRN/WOL WA2 .... 121 J2 6
Kenton Cl FMBY L37 .... 47 H7

Kenton Rd HLWD L26 132 B6
Kentridge Dr GTS/LS CH66 162 F2 2
Kent Rd FMBY L37 59 J4
STHEL WA9 102 E5
STHP PR8 2 F9
WAL/EG CH44 111 J2
WARRW/BUR WA5 136 E1
Kents Bank WD/CROXPK L12 98 E4
Kent St CL/PREN CH43 10 B9
CLVPS L1 112 F5
WARRS WA4 15 G8
WDN WA8 16 E2
WGN WN1 5 H5
Kenview Cl WDN WA8 148 C1
Kenway RNFD/HAY WA11 76 C7
Kenwick Cl GTS/LS CH66 162 E2
Kenwright Crs STHEL WA9 102 E5
Kenwyn Rd WAL/NB CH45 95 K8
Kenyon Av WARRW/BUR WA5 120 A8
Kenyon Cl NWD/KWIPK L33 74 B7 3
Kenyon La GOL/RIS/CU WA3 93 H7
GOL/RIS/CU WA3 106 B2
Kenyon Rd WAV L15 114 C8 5
WGNNW/ST WN6 55 M3
Kenyon's La FMBY L37 59 J2
MGHL L31 72 F1
Kenyons La North
RNFD/HAY WA11 91 H5
Kenyon's La South
RNFD/HAY WA11 91 H5
Kenyon St LEIGH WN7 81 M5
Kepler St LITH L21 83 J7
Keppel St BTL L20 6 E8
Kerfoot's La SKEL WN8 64 E5
Kerfoot St WARRN/WOL WA2 14 D1
Kerr Gv STHEL WA9 103 G2
Kerris Cl AIG/SPK L17 129 L3
Kerry Cft GTS/LS CH66 163 G4
Kerrysdale Cl STHEL WA9 102 F6 5
Kersey Rd KKBY L32 86 B5
Kershaw Av CSBY/BLUN L23 83 H2
Kershaw St CHLYE PR6 33 C5
WDN WA8 133 M4
WGNW/BIL/O WN5 67 K7
Kershaw Wy NEWLW WA12 91 L8
Kerslake Wy HTWN L38 70 B1
Kerswell Cl STHEL WA9 102 F7 7
Kestral Gv HLWD L26 131 M4
Kestral Pk SKEL WN8 65 L1
Kestrel Av
GR/UP/WCH CH49 109 M7 5
Kestrel Cl CHLYE PR6 33 J2 1
GR/UP/WCH CH49 109 M7
RNFD/HAY WA11 89 K7 4
Kestrel Dr AIMK WN4 79 L7
Kestrel Gv GOL/RIS/CU WA3 123 G1 5
Kestrel Ms SKEL WN8 65 L1
Kestrel Rd HES CH60 141 L6
MOR/LEA CH46 109 L5
Kestrels Wy RUNC WA7 150 B7
Keswick Av BEB CH63 143 L8
WARRN/WOL WA2 121 L3
Keswick Cl MGHL L31 73 G3
STHP PR8 47 L2
WDN WA8 133 L4
Keswick Crs
WARRN/WOL WA2 121 L3 5
Keswick Dr FROD/HEL WA6 160 F5
LITH L21 84 A5
Keswick Pl CL/PREN CH43 110 F4
WGNE/HIN WN2 69 J6
Keswick Rd CALD/MH L18 130 E3
ECCL WA10 8 D2
WAL/NB CH45 95 G6
Keswick Wy CHLDW L16 115 J5
RNFD/HAY WA11 76 B3 2
Kettering Rd STHP PR8 34 D8
Kevelioc Cl BEB CH63 143 H2 2
Kew Rd FMBY L37 58 F4
STHP PR8 35 K2
Keybank Rd WD/CROXPK L12 98 C5
Keyes Cl GOL/RIS/CU WA3 123 H1
Keyes Gdns GOL/RIS/CU WA3 123 H1 1
Kiddman St WLT/FAZ L9 97 H2 1
Kidstone Cl STHEL WA9 102 F6 6
Kilbuck La RNFD/HAY WA11 91 J5
Kilburn Av AIMK WN4 91 M1
PS/BROM CH62 144 A7
Kilburn Clqse LEIGH WN7 81 M4 4
Kilburn Dr WGNNW/ST WN6 55 J6
Kilburn Gv STHEL WA9 102 A6
WGNS/IIMK WN3 78 F2
Kilburn Rd SKEL WN8 66 E8
Kilburn St LITH L21 83 K7
Kildale Cl MGHL L31 72 E3
Kildare Cl SPK/HALE L24 147 M3
Kildare St WGNE/HIN WN2 69 L8
WGNW/BIL/O WN5 68 B7
Kildonan Rd AIG/SPK L17 129 M3
WARRS WA4 138 C3
Kilford Cl WARRW/BUR WA5 121 G3
Kilgraston Gdns AIG/SPK L17 130 B4
Kilkerran Cl CHLYE PR6 32 F5
Killarney Gv WAL/EG CH44 111 J2 2
Killarney Rd CLB/OSW/ST L13 114 C2
Killester Rd WLTN L25 131 K1
Killingbeck Cl BRSC L40 51 M1 3
Killington Cl WGNS/IIMK WN3 79 K3
Killington Wy ANF/KKDL L4 97 G5
Killingworth La
GOL/RIS/CU WA3 107 K8
Kilmalcolm Cl CL/PREN CH43 127 H1 2
Kilmore Cl WLT/FAZ L9 84 E5
Kilmory Av WLTN L25 131 L3
Kilncroft RUNC WA7 150 D8 6
Kiln Hey WD/CROXPK L12 98 E8
Kiln La ECCL WA10 88 E8
SKEL WN8 65 G3
Kiln Rd GR/UP/WCH CH49 126 C2
Kilnyard Rd CSBY/BLUN L23 82 F1
Kilrea Cl NG/CROX L11 98 B5
Kilrea Rd NG/CROX L11 98 B5
Kilsail Rd KKBY L32 86 C6
Kilsby Dr WDN WA8 135 G3
Kilshaw Rd WARRW/BUR WA5 104 B7
Kilshaw St NPK/KEN L6 113 J1
WGNW/BIL/O WN5 67 L8
Kilsyth Cl WARRN/WOL WA2 122 B1
Kimberley Av CSBY/BLUN L23 82 F2 2
STHEL WA9 102 B6
Kimberley Cl TOX L8 113 J6
Kimberley Dr CSBY/BLUN L23 82 F2
WARRS WA4 137 L4
Kimberley Pl AIMK WN4 91 L2 4
Kimberley Rd WAL/NB CH45 95 K7
Kimberley St BIRK CH41 111 H5 5
CHLY/EC PR7 43 G4
WARRW/BUR WA5 121 G8
Kimberly St WGNNW/ST WN6 4 A1
Kindale Rd CL/PREN CH43 127 G4
Kinder Gv AIMK WN4 79 H7
Kinder St NPK/KEN L6 13 M4
King Av BTL L20 84 A7
King Edward Rd ECCL WA10 88 F7
RAIN/WH L35 117 K1
King Edward's Dr
PS/BROM CH62 128 D7
King Edward St VAUX/LVPD L3 12 D5
WARR WA1 15 M2
Kingfield Rd WLT/FAZ L9 84 B8
Kingfisher Cl GOL/RIS/CU WA3 123 H1
NTHLY L27 116 B8 1
NWD/KWIPK L33 74 A7
RUNC WA7 150 B8 3
Kingfisher Ct AIMK WN4 79 K7
CHTN/BK PR9 3 M2
Kingfisher Dr RNFD/HAY WA11 89 K7
Kingfisher Gv WD/CROXPK L12 99 H4
Kingfisher Pk SKEL WN8 65 L1 1
Kingfisher Wy
GR/UP/WCH CH49 109 M7
King George Cl AIMK WN4 91 K2 6
King George Crs WARR WA1 15 L2
King George Dr WAL/NB CH45 95 L8
King George Rd
RNFD/HAY WA11 91 J6
King George's Dr
PS/BROM CH62 128 D7
Kingham Cl WLTN L25 131 L3 4
King James Ct RUNC WA7 150 A7
Kinglake Rd WAL/EG CH44 111 M1
Kinglake St EHL/KEN L7 113 K4
Kinglass Rd PS/BROM CH62 143 K2
King's Av GOL/RIS/CU WA3 93 H6
HOY CH47 108 F5
Kingsbrook Wy BEB CH63 127 M5
King's Brow BEB CH63 127 M7 1
Kingsbury WKBY CH48 124 F2
Kingsbury Cl STHP PR8 47 J1
Kingsbury Ct SKEL WN8 65 L1
Kings Cl AIG/SPK L17 129 L3
BEB CH63 127 M6
FMBY L37 59 G3
Kings Ct HOY CH47 108 C6 2
LITH L21 83 H6 3
Kingscourt Rd WD/CROXPK L12 98 E8
Kingscroft Ct WGN WN1 5 H5
Kingsdale Av RAIN/WH L35 117 M2 2
RF/TRAN CH42 127 M3 1
Kingsdale Rd CALD/MH L18 114 C8
WARRW/BUR WA5 120 B6
Kings Dock St CLVPS L1 112 F6
Kingsdown Crs WGN WN1 68 E1
Kingsdown Rd NG/CROX L11 98 C4
WGNE/HIN WN2 80 D6
Kingsdown St BIRK CH41 11 J9 1
Kings Dr FROD/HEL WA6 166 D2
PEN/TH CH61 126 B7
WKBY CH48 124 F4 1
WLTN L25 131 K3
Kingsfield Rd MGHL L31 72 E6
The King's Gap HOY CH47 108 C6
Kingshead Cl RUNC WA7 150 C3
Kingsheath Av DV/KA/FCH L14 99 H8
Kings Hey Dr CHTN/BK PR9 25 H4
Kingshill Ct WGNNW/ST WN6 56 B6
Kingsland Crs NG/CROX L11 98 A2
Kingsland Rd NG/CROX L11 97 M2
RF/TRAN CH42 127 L1 3
King's La BEB CH63 128 A6
Kingslea CHLY/EC PR7 44 B5
Kingsley Av PS/BROM CH62 155 G2
WGNS/IIMK WN3 79 H2
Kingsley Cl MGHL L31 61 L8
PEN/TH CH61 141 J2
Kingsley Crs RUNC WA7 19 H6
Kingsley Dr CHLY/EC PR7 32 C8
WARRS WA4 137 L6
Kingsley Rd ECCL WA10 88 F7
EP CH65 20 D4
FROD/HEL WA6 160 F7
RUNC WA7 19 H5
TOX L8 113 K6 4
WAL/EG CH44 111 K2
Kingsley St BIRK CH41 10 A2
LEIGH WN7 81 L6
Kingsmead CHLY/EC PR7 32 E8
Kingsmead Ct
GOL/RIS/CU WA3 106 C5 2
Kingsmead Dr WLTN L25 131 K6
Kingsmead Gv
CL/PREN CH43 111 H8 1
Kings Meadow RUNC WA7 150 E5 1
STHP PR8 47 M2
Kingsmead Rd
CL/PREN CH43 111 H8 2
MOR/LEA CH46 110 B3
Kingsmead Rd North
CL/PREN CH43 111 H8
Kingsmead Rd South
CL/PREN CH43 111 H8
Kingsmede WGN WN1 68 F2
King's Moss La RNFD/HAY WA11 77 G6
Kings Mt CL/PREN CH43 10 E9
Kingsnorth RAIN/WH L35 117 H3
Kingsoak Cl WGN WN1 5 G3
King's Pde WAL/NB CH45 94 F5
Kings Pk LITH L21 83 H6
King's Rd AIMK WN4 79 J8 7
BEB CH63 127 M6
BTL L20 7 G8
CSBY/BLUN L23 82 F1
ECCL WA10 101 L3
FMBY L37 59 G3
GOL/RIS/CU WA3 92 C6
GTS/LS CH66 155 L6
WARRN/WOL WA2 122 C3
Kingsthorne Pk SPK/HALE L24 131 L7
Kingsthorne Rd WLTN L25 131 L7
Kingston Av
WARRW/BUR WA5 120 A7 3
Kingston Cl MOR/LEA CH46 110 A5 4
RUNC WA7 150 A3 1
WD/CROXPK L12 99 G8
WGNS/IIMK WN3 79 K2
Kingston Crs CHTN/BK PR9 22 E8
King St ALL/GAR L19 145 L1
CHLY/EC PR7 32 F7
CSBY/WL L22 82 F4
ECCL WA10 8 F5
EP CH65 20 D2
NEWLW WA12 104 D2
RF/TRAN CH42 128 C4
RUNC WA7 19 H2
STHP PR8 2 F5
WAL/EG CH44 95 M8
WGN WN1 4 F5
WGNE/HIN WN2 69 M7 5
King St West WGN WN1 4 E4
Kingsville Rd BEB CH63 128 A8
Kingswalk WKBY CH48 124 E3
Kingsway CHLY/EC PR7 32 A3
CSBY/WL L22 83 G3
FROD/HEL WA6 160 D6
HES CH60 141 L7
HUY L36 115 M1
NEWLW WA12 104 E3
RAIN/WH L35 100 F8
RNFD/HAY WA11 89 J5
STHP PR8 2 E4
WAL/NB CH45 95 J7
WDN WA8 16 D3
WGN WN1 68 F3
WGNE/HIN WN2 5 L6
Kingsway North WARR WA1 15 M3
Kingsway South WARRS WA4 138 B1
Kingsway (Tunnel)
WAL/EG CH44 111 L3
Kingswell Cl EHL/KEN L7 113 K5 4
Kings Whf WAL/EG CH44 112 A4
Kingswood CHLY/EC PR7 32 D8 3
Kingswood Av CSBY/WL L22 83 H4
WLT/FAZ L9 84 D6
Kingswood Bvd BEB CH63 128 A5
Kingswood Ct
NWD/KWIPK L33 86 B1 3
Kingswood Dr CSBY/BLUN L23 82 F2
Kingswood Rd WAL/EG CH44 95 L8 5
WARRW/BUR WA5 120 C3
Kington Rd WKBY CH48 124 C2 3
Kingwood Crs
WGNW/BIL/O WN5 67 M7
Kinlet Rd WGNS/IIMK WN3 78 E1
Kinley Gdns BTL L20 84 A8 2
Kinloch Cl HLWD L26 132 C6
Kinloch Wy ORM L39 50 F8
Kinloss Rd GR/UP/WCH CH49 125 L2 4
Kinmel Cl ANF/KKDL L4 97 M5
BIRK CH41 11 H4
Kinmel St STHEL WA9 102 E5
TOX L8 113 J8
Kinnaird Rd WAL/NB CH45 95 J7
Kinnaird St TOX L8 129 J2
Kinnerley Rd EP CH65 163 J2
Kinnerton Cl MOR/LEA CH46 109 K5
Kinnington Wy GTS/LS CH66 163 H6 2
Kinniside Cl WGNS/IIMK WN3 79 J3
Kinnock Pk WARRW/BUR WA5 104 A7
Kinross Av AIMK WN4 90 E1
Kinross Cl WARRN/WOL WA2 122 B1
Kinross Rd AIN/FAZ L10 85 G6
CSBY/WL L22 83 G5
WAL/NB CH45 94 F7
Kinsale Dr GOL/RIS/CU WA3 122 E1
Kinsey Rd EP CH65 164 A4
Kinsey's La EP CH65 158 B7
Kintbury St WGNE/HIN WN2 80 B6
Kintore Cl BEB CH63 154 E1
Kintore Dr
WARRW/BUR WA5 119 M7 3
Kintore Rd ALL/GAR L19 130 D6
Kipling Av HUY L36 116 C4
RF/TRAN CH42 128 B4 3
WARRN/WOL WA2 121 L4 2
WGNS/IIMK WN3 79 J1
Kipling Crs WDN WA8 16 B3
Kipling Gv LEIGH WN7 81 M6
STHEL WA9 118 C2
Kipling St BTL L20 83 J8
Kirby Cl WKBY CH48 124 D4
Kirby Mt WKBY CH48 124 E5
Kirby Pk WKBY CH48 124 D4
Kirby Rd BTL L20 83 M7
Kirkacre Av NEWLW WA12 104 E5
Kirkbride Cl NTHLY L27 132 C1 3
Kirkburn Cl TOX L8 129 H1 3
Kirkby Bank Rd NWD/KWIPK L33 86 D3
Kirkby Rd GOL/RIS/CU WA3 107 H2
Kirkby Rw KKBY L32 85 L2
Kirkcaldy Av WARRW/BUR WA5 119 M7
Kirkdale Gdns SKEL WN8 66 B6 1
Kirkdale Rd EV L5 96 F7
Kirkdale V ANF/KKDL L4 97 G6
Kirket Cl BEB CH63 143 J1 3
Kirket La BEB CH63 143 H1
Kirkfield Gv RF/TRAN CH42 128 C4 1
Kirkham Av GOL/RIS/CU WA3 93 G7 1
Kirkham Cl WARRW/BUR WA5 136 D1
Kirkham Rd CHTN/BK PR9 25 J1
LEIGH WN7 93 M3
WDN WA8 134 E3
Kirkham St WGNE/HIN WN2 80 D5 3
Kirklake Bank FMBY L37 58 E3
Kirklake Rd FMBY L37 58 E3
Kirkland Av RF/TRAN CH42 127 M3
Kirkland Cl WLT/FAZ L9 84 B6 1
Kirkland Rd WAL/NB CH45 95 L5
The Kirklands WKBY CH48 124 E3
Kirkland St ECCL WA10 8 E4
Kirklees Rd STHP PR8 35 H4
Kirklees St WGN WN1 5 K4
Kirkless St WGNE/HIN WN2 69 J2
Kirkmaiden Rd ALL/GAR L19 130 D5
Kirkman Fold RAIN/WH L35 117 K2
Kirkmore Rd CALD/MH L18 130 C3
Kirkmount GR/UP/WCH CH49 110 C8
Kirkpatrick St WGNE/HIN WN2 81 K2
Kirk Rd BTL L20 83 L7
Kirkside Cl WD/CROXPK L12 98 F2 3
Kirkstall Cl CHLY/EC PR7 32 F8
Kirkstall Dr CHLY/EC PR7 32 F8
FMBY L37 59 K3 3
Kirkstall Rd CHLY/EC PR7 32 F8
STHP PR8 35 H3
Kirkstile Crs WGNS/IIMK WN3 79 G3
Kirkstone WGNW/BIL/O WN5 67 L6
Kirkstone Av RNFD/HAY WA11 89 L5
WARRN/WOL WA2 121 L2
Kirkstone Crs RUNC WA7 161 J1
Kirkstone Rd North LITH L21 83 L4
Kirkstone Rd South LITH L21 83 M5
Kirkstone Rd West LITH L21 83 K3
Kirk St EV L5 97 G7
Kirkwall Dr WARRW/BUR WA5 136 C2
Kirkway BEB CH63 127 M6
GR/UP/WCH CH49 110 B8 1
WAL/NB CH45 95 K6
Kitchener Dr WLT/FAZ L9 84 B7 2
Kitchener St ECCL WA10 8 C4
Kitchen St CLVPS L1 112 F6
Kitling La PR/KW L34 86 E8
Kitling Rd PR/KW L34 86 E8
Kitt Green Rd
WGNW/BIL/O WN5 67 K5 2
Kittiwake Rd CHLYE PR6 33 J2
Kiverley Cl WLTN L25 131 G2 1
Kiveton Dr AIMK WN4 91 L3
The Knap HES CH60 141 J7
Knaresborough Rd
WAL/EG CH44 111 H1
WGNE/HIN WN2 81 G1 7
Knighton Rd ANF/KKDL L4 97 M4
Knight Rd WARRW/BUR WA5 104 B7
Knightsbridge Av WARRS WA4 138 E2
Knightscliffe Crs
WGNNW/ST WN6 54 F7
Knightshill Crs WGNNW/ST WN6 68 B4
Knight St CLVPS L1 113 G5 12
Knightsway CSBY/WL L22 83 H4
Knob Hall Gdns CHTN/BK PR9 25 H2
Knob Hall La CHTN/BK PR9 25 H2
Knoclaid Rd CLB/OSW/ST L13 98 A6
The Knoll CL/PREN CH43 127 J2
Knottingley Dr GTS/LS CH66 155 L8
Knotty Ms WLTN L25 131 L2 3
The Knowe NSTN CH64 154 C5
Knowle Av STHP PR8 34 E7
Knowle Cl GTS/LS CH66 163 G2
NG/CROX L11 98 E3
Knowles Av WGNS/IIMK WN3 79 H1
Knowles House Av ECCL WA10 101 H2
Knowles St BIRK CH41 10 F4
CHLY/EC PR7 32 E7 3
WDN WA8 134 E3
WGNS/IIMK WN3 5 H8
Knowley Brow CHLYE PR6 33 G3
Knowl Hey Rd HLWD L26 132 C7
Knowsley Av GOL/RIS/CU WA3 92 D4
Knowsley Cl RF/TRAN CH42 128 C4 2
Knowsley Dr LEIGH WN7 93 M3
Knowsley Expy RAIN/WH L35 116 F7
WDN WA8 133 G5
Knowsley La CHLYE PR6 44 F1
PR/KW L34 86 E8
Knowsley Park La PR/KW L34 100 E6
Knowsley Rd ALL/GAR L19 130 C7
BTL L20 83 K8
CHTN/BK PR9 24 D4
ORM L39 63 H1
RAIN/WH L35 117 M3
RF/TRAN CH42 128 C4
WAL/NB CH45 95 J7
WGNNW/ST WN6 68 C2
Knowsley St ANF/KKDL L4 97 H3 6
LEIGH WN7 81 M8 10
Knowsley Vw RNFD/HAY WA11 76 A5
Knox Cl PS/BROM CH62 128 D7
Knox St BIRK CH41 11 L6
Knutsford Cl ECCL WA10 101 K3 2
Knutsford Gn MOR/LEA CH46 110 A4
Knutsford Old Rd WARRS WA4 138 C3
Knutsford Rd MOR/LEA CH46 110 A4
WARRS WA4 14 F8
Knutsford Wk MGHL L31 72 F1
Kremlin Dr CLB/OSW/ST L13 98 B8
WD/CROXPK L12 98 C8
Kronsbec Av GTS/LS CH66 155 M7
Kylemore Av CALD/MH L18 130 B2
Kylemore Cl PEN/TH CH61 141 G2
Kylemore Dr PEN/TH CH61 141 G2
Kylemore Rd CL/PREN CH43 127 J1
Kylemore Wy HLWD L26 131 M6
PEN/TH CH61 141 G2 1
Kynance Rd NG/CROX L11 85 M8

L

Laburnum Av HUY L36 116 A5
RNFD/HAY WA11 89 M6
WARR WA1 122 E6
WGNS/IIMK WN3 5 L7
Laburnum Crs KKBY L32 85 M2
Laburnum Dr SKEL WN8 64 F4
WGNNW/ST WN6 68 C1
Laburnum Farm Cl
NSTN CH64 153 J8 1
Laburnum Gv BRSC L40 39 G7 1
GTS/LS CH66 163 J5
MGHL L31 73 H4 3
PEN/TH CH61 125 M7
RUNC WA7 19 K8
STHP PR8 25 H6
Laburnum La
WARRW/BUR WA5 119 L7
Laburnum Pl BTL L20 7 J4
Laburnum Rd CHLYE PR6 32 F2
EHL/KEN L7 113 M2 3
GOL/RIS/CU WA3 93 H5
WAL/NB CH45 95 K6
Laburnum St AIMK WN4 91 K3 3
Lace St VAUX/LVPD L3 13 G5
Lacey Ct WDN WA8 16 E6
Lacey Rd PR/KW L34 101 G8
Lacey St ECCL WA10 101 M5
WDN WA8 16 D6
Ladies La WGNE/HIN WN2 69 M7
Ladies Wk NSTN CH64 153 G5
Lad La VAUX/LVPD L3 12 D5 1
Lady Alice's Dr BRSC L40 52 A5
Ladybarn Av GOL/RIS/CU WA3 92 B6 1
Ladybower Cl EHL/KEN L7 113 K5
Ladycroft Cl WARR WA1 123 G6 3
Ladyewood Rd WAL/EG CH44 111 L2
Ladyfield CL/PREN CH43 110 E6
Ladyfields WD/CROXPK L12 98 D8
Lady Green Cl HTWN L38 71 G2 1
Lady Green La HTWN L38 70 F1
Lady La GOL/RIS/CU WA3 106 E4
WGNS/IIMK WN3 79 G1
Ladypool SPK/HALE L24 147 L4
Ladysmith Av AIMK WN4 91 L2
Ladysmith Rd AIN/FAZ L10 85 H6
Lady's Wk BRSC L40 51 L7
Ladywood Rd
WARRW/BUR WA5 120 E4
Laffak Rd RNFD/HAY WA11 89 M5
Lafford La SKEL WN8 66 E2
Laggan St EHL/KEN L7 113 K3 4
Laira St WARRN/WOL WA2 15 G2
Laird Cl CL/PREN CH43 111 H5 6
Lairds Pl VAUX/LVPD L3 13 G2
Laird St BIRK CH41 10 A2
CL/PREN CH43 111 H5
Laithwaite Cl STHEL WA9 118 D2 1
Laithwaite Rd
WGNW/BIL/O WN5 67 M6
Lakeland Av AIMK WN4 91 L1 3
Lakeland Cl CLVPS L1 13 G9
Lakeland Gdns CHLY/EC PR7 32 C8
Lakemoor Cl STHEL WA9 102 F6 7
Lakenheath Rd HLWD L26 132 A7
Lake Pl HOY CH47 108 D6
Lake Rd HOY CH47 108 D6
WAV L15 114 C6
Lakes Dr WGNW/BIL/O WN5 67 G7
Lake Side LEIGH WN7 81 M7
Lakeside Av WGNW/BIL/O WN5 78 A2
Lakeside Cl WDN WA8 133 J6
Lakeside Ct RNFD/HAY WA11 76 C7
WAL/NB CH45 95 L5
Lakeside Dr WARR WA1 137 J2
Lakeside Gdns RNFD/HAY WA11 76 C7
Lakeside Rd LYMM WA13 139 M4
Lake St ANF/KKDL L4 97 J6
Lake Vw RAIN/WH L35 117 G4
Laleston Cl WDN WA8 134 A5
Lamberhead Rd
WGNW/BIL/O WN5 67 K7
Lambert St VAUX/LVPD L3 13 K5 2
Lambert Wy VAUX/LVPD L3 13 K5 3
Lambeth Rd EV L5 96 F6
Lambeth Wk ANF/KKDL L4 96 F6
Lambley Cl LEIGH WN7 81 M5
Lambourn Av WDN WA8 117 L8
Lambourne SKEL WN8 65 K1
Lambourne Cl GTS/LS CH66 163 H5 6
Lambourne Gv STHEL WA9 103 J1 2
Lambourne Rd ANF/KKDL L4 97 M4
Lambshear La MGHL L31 72 E1
Lambsickle Cl RUNC WA7 149 H7 4
Lambsickle La RUNC WA7 149 H7
Lambs La WARR WA1 122 C5
Lamb St WGN WN1 5 J1
Lambton Rd AIG/SPK L17 129 K2
Lambton St WGNW/BIL/O WN5 67 K8
Lamerton Cl
WARRW/BUR WA5 135 M1 2
Lammermoor Rd
CALD/MH L18 130 C3 2
Lampeter Cl
WARRW/BUR WA5 121 G3 4
Lampeter Rd NPK/KEN L6 97 L7
Lamport Cl WDN WA8 135 G2 3
Lamport St TOX L8 113 G7
Lanark Cl ECCL WA10 8 E7
Lancaster Av AIG/SPK L17 113 M8
CSBY/BLUN L23 82 F2
GOL/RIS/CU WA3 92 E5
RAIN/WH L35 116 F2
RAIN/WH L35 133 J3
RUNC WA7 18 D8
WAL/NB CH45 95 K8
Lancaster Cl CHLYE PR6 44 D6
EV L5 96 F7 6
MGHL L31 73 H4 4
NEWLW WA12 91 H8
PS/BROM CH62 128 D7 3
STHP PR8 35 G1
WARRN/WOL WA2 122 B3 3
Lancaster Crs SKEL WN8 65 G4
Lancaster Dr CHTN/BK PR9 23 G8
Lancaster Ga CHTN/BK PR9 23 H8
Lancaster La SKEL WN8 53 L2
Lancaster Pl CHLYE PR6 44 C5 5
Lancaster Rd FMBY L37 59 G4
HUY L36 116 C1
STHP PR8 35 G1
WDN WA8 134 C2
WGNW/BIL/O WN5 67 L4
Lancaster St CHLY/EC PR7 43 H4
EV L5 96 F7
WARRW/BUR WA5 121 G8 3
WGNS/IIMK WN3 5 H7
WLT/FAZ L9 97 H2
Lance Gv WAV L15 114 C6
Lance La WAV L15 114 C6
Lancelyn Ter BEB CH63 143 H1 2
Lancer Ct RUNC WA7 150 A2
Lancers Cft GTS/LS CH66 163 G4
Lance Wood Pl
WGNW/BIL/O WN5 67 M7
Lancing Av WARRN/WOL WA2 121 J1
Lancing Cl WLTN L25 131 M4
Lancing Dr AIN/FAZ L10 84 F3
Lancing Rd EP CH65 20 E6
WLTN L25 131 M4 1
Lancing Wy WLTN L25 131 M4
Lancots La STHEL WA9 102 F5

Land Cut La GOL/RIS/CU WA3 .. 122 F2 1
Land End MGHL L31 73 L4
Lander Cl WARRW/BUR WA5 120 F6
Lander Rd LITH L21 83 K7
Landford Av WLT/FAZ L9 98 A1
Landford Pl WLT/FAZ L9 98 A1
Land Gate La AIMK WN4 79 J6
Landican La BEB CH63 127 J7
GR/UP/WCH CH49 126 E4
Landican Rd GR/UP/WCH CH49 126 D6
Land La CHTN/BK PR9 25 L1
Landor Cl GOL/RIS/CU WA3 93 G5 5
Landscape Dene
FROD/HEL WA6 166 F1
Landseer Av NSTN CH64 153 H6
WARRS WA4 137 K4
Landseer Rd EV L5 97 H8
Land St WGNNW/ST WN6 4 C3
Lane Head Av GOL/RIS/CU WA3 93 G5
Lanfranc Cl CHLDW L16 115 G5 3
Lanfranc Wy CHLDW L16 115 G5 4
Langbar RAIN/WH L35 117 G3
Langcliffe Cl
GOL/RIS/CU WA3 107 G2 2
Langdale Av FMBY L37 58 F2
GOL/RIS/CU WA3 92 E4 5
LEY/BBR PR5 29 K2
PEN/TH CH61 141 H1
WGN WN1 68 D2
WGNE/HIN WN2 69 K5
Langdale Cl FMBY L37 58 F3
KKBY L32 86 B4 5
WARRN/WOL WA2 122 A2 4
WDN WA8 133 L5
Langdale Crs WGNE/HIN WN2 80 D5
WGNW/BIL/O WN5 67 K5
Langdale Dr BRSC L40 52 A1
MGHL L31 73 G3
Langdale Gdns STHP PR8 35 H4
Langdale Gv RNFD/HAY WA11 .. 89 K6 7
WGNE/HIN WN2 80 D2
Langdale Rd BEB CH63 143 G1
RUNC WA7 19 J5
WAL/NB CH45 95 J6
WAV L15 114 A7
WGNW/BIL/O WN5 67 K6
Langdale St BTL L20 7 J5
Langdale Wy FROD/HEL WA6 160 E4
Langfield GOL/RIS/CU WA3 93 G6
Langfield Gv PS/BROM CH62 143 M8
Langford SPK/HALE L24 147 L4
Langford Rd ALL/GAR L19 130 B5 2
Langham Av AIG/SPK L17 129 L2
Langham Rd
WGNNW/ST WN6 55 M4 2
Langham St ANF/KKDL L4 97 H5
Langholm Cl WGNS/IIMK WN3 78 F3
Langholm Rd AIMK WN4 90 E1
Langland Cl ANF/KKDL L4 97 M5
WARRW/BUR WA5 121 G3
Lang La WKBY CH48 124 D2
Lang La South WKBY CH48 124 E2
Langley Cl BEB CH63 143 H4
GOL/RIS/CU WA3 92 E4
HTWN L38 70 B3
WD/CROXPK L12 99 H2
WGNNW/ST WN6 56 A3
Langley Pl BRSC L40 51 K1
Langley Rd BEB CH63 143 J3 3
BRSC L40 51 K1
Langley St TOX L8 113 G7 2
WGNW/BIL/O WN5 67 M7 4
Langrove St EV L5 97 G8
Langsdale St VAUX/LVPD L3 13 L4
Langset Av WGNE/HIN WN2 69 M7 8
Langstone Av
GR/UP/WCH CH49 125 K3
Langton Av WGNNW/ST WN6 56 A4
Langton Brow CHLY/EC PR7 30 F8
Langton Cl CHLY/EC PR7 30 F8
NEWLW WA12 104 C1 2
WDN WA8 133 K2
Langton Gn WARR WA1 122 F6
Langton Rd NWD/KWIPK L33 74 B8
WAV L15 113 M6
Langtree SKEL WN8 65 K2 1
Langtree La WGNNW/ST WN6 55 M2
Langtree St STHEL WA9 9 L5
Langtry Cl ANF/KKDL L4 96 F5
Langtry Rd ANF/KKDL L4 96 F5
Langwell Cl GOL/RIS/CU WA3 107 J8
Langwood La RNFD/HAY WA11 76 E4
Lansbury Av STHEL WA9 103 G3
Lansbury Rd HUY L36 116 C3
Lansbury St WGNW/BIL/O WN5 67 J7
Lansdown WD/CROXPK L12 98 C7
Lansdowne FROD/HEL WA6 160 F7
GOL/RIS/CU WA3 107 G3
Lansdowne Cl BIRK CH41 10 A1
Lansdowne Pl
CL/PREN CH43 111 H5 7
EV L5 97 H7
Lansdowne Rd CL/PREN CH43 111 H5
STHP PR8 25 G7
WAL/NB CH45 95 H5
Lanville Rd ALL/GAR L19 130 D4
Lanyork Rd VAUX/LVPD L3 12 D4
Lapford Crs NWD/KWIPK L33 86 C1
Lapwing Cl GOL/RIS/CU WA3 92 F5
WD/CROXPK L12 99 G4
Lapwing Ct HLWD L26 132 A4 6
Lapwing Gv RUNC WA7 150 C7
Lapwing La WARRS WA4 136 B6
Lapworth Cl MOR/LEA CH46 109 K5 7
Lapworth St EV L5 96 F7
Larch Av CHLYE PR6 33 G3
NEWLW WA12 104 E3
WARRW/BUR WA5 120 A8
WDN WA8 134 D3 2
WGNW/BIL/O WN5 67 M7
Larch Cl ALL/GAR L19 130 B6
GOL/RIS/CU WA3 93 H7
RUNC WA7 19 M9
SKEL WN8 65 G4
WGNW/BIL/O WN5 77 M8
Larchdale Cl GTS/LS CH66 163 H5 8
Larchdale Gv WLT/FAZ L9 97 K1 2
Larchfield Rd CSBY/BLUN L23 71 J8
Larch Gv CL/PREN CH43 111 G5
WAV L15 114 C4
Larch Lea NPK/KEN L6 97 K8 5
Larch Rd HUY L36 115 L3
RF/TRAN CH42 10 F8
RNFD/HAY WA11 91 G6 6
RUNC WA7 149 L6
Larch St STHP PR8 25 G8
Larch Wy FMBY L37 58 F1
Larchways WARRS WA4 137 M8
Larchwood Av MGHL L31 72 E6
Larchwood Cl PEN/TH CH61 141 H2
WLTN L25 115 K8
Larchwood Dr BEB CH63 128 B6
WGN WN1 68 D1
Larcombe Av
GR/UP/WCH CH49 110 B8 2
Larkfield CHLY/EC PR7 30 D7
Larkfield Av WARR WA1 122 B6
WGN WN1 68 D1
Larkfield Cl AIG/SPK L17 129 L3 4
Larkfield Gv AIG/SPK L17 129 L3 5
Larkfield La CHTN/BK PR9 25 J2
Larkfield Rd AIG/SPK L17 129 L3
Larkfield Vw WAV L15 114 A5
Larkhill SKEL WN8 65 K1
Larkhill Av GR/UP/WCH CH49 110 C7
WGNNW/ST WN6 56 B5
Larkhill Cl CLB/OSW/ST L13 98 A6
Larkhill Gv HTWN L38 70 B2
Larkhill La CLB/OSW/ST L13 98 A6
FMBY L37 58 E1
Larkhill Pl CLB/OSW/ST L13 98 A6
Larkhill Vw CLB/OSW/ST L13 98 B6
Larkhill Wy GR/UP/WCH CH49 110 C6
Larkin Cl PS/BROM CH62 128 C6
Lark La AIG/SPK L17 129 L2
Larkspur Cl RUNC WA7 161 H1 6
STHP PR8 3 L6
Larkstoke Cl WARRS WA4 138 A7
Larksway HES CH60 141 K5
Lark Wy AIG/SPK L17 129 K2
Larton Rd WKBY CH48 124 F2
Lascelles Rd ALL/GAR L19 130 F6
Lascelles St STHEL WA9 9 M5
Laskey La WARRS WA4 139 H1
Latchford Rd HES CH60 141 K7
Latchford St WARRS WA4 138 C2
Late Moffatt Rd West
WLT/FAZ L9 84 D6 5
Latham Av FROD/HEL WA6 166 D4
NEWLW WA12 104 E1
ORM L39 51 J8
RUNC WA7 19 L5
Latham La WGNW/BIL/O WN5 67 J5
Latham Rd HOR/BR BL6 57 L2 3
Latham St EV L5 96 F7
Latham Wy BEB CH63 143 K3
Lathbury La AIG/SPK L17 114 A8
Lathom Av LITH L21 83 H7 2
SKEL WN8 53 K2
WAL/EG CH44 111 K1
WARRN/WOL WA2 121 K5
Lathom Cl BRSC L40 52 A1
Lathom Dr MGHL L31 73 G2
RNFD/HAY WA11 76 B6
Lathom La BRSC L40 51 L6
Lathom Rd BTL L20 83 L8
CHTN/BK PR9 24 E4
HUY L36 116 A2 5
ORM L39 64 B6
Lathum Cl RAIN/WH L35 101 G8
Latimer Cl WGNW/BIL/O WN5 .. 67 H6 1
Latimer St EV L5 96 F8
Latrigg Rd AIG/SPK L17 130 A3
Lauder Cl NWD/KWIPK L33 73 M7
Launceston Cl RUNC WA7 150 E7 2
Launceston Dr
WARRW/BUR WA5 136 A2
Launceston Rd WGNE/HIN WN2 .. 81 L2
The Laund WAL/NB CH45 95 H8
Laurel Av BEB CH63 143 G1
BRSC L40 39 G7
CHLY/EC PR7 31 K2
HES CH60 141 H4
NEWLW WA12 104 F3
WARR WA1 122 F6 2
Laurel Bank WARRS WA4 138 E4
WDN WA8 134 C2 3
Laurelbanks HES CH60 141 G4
Laurel Ct RNFD/HAY WA11 89 K6 8
Laurel Crs WGNE/HIN WN2 81 J2
Laurel Dr ECCL WA10 101 H1
EP CH65 163 K3
NSTN CH64 154 D4
SKEL WN8 65 G3
Laurel Gv AIMK WN4 91 K1
CHTN/BK PR9 25 G6
CSBY/WL L22 82 F3
GOL/RIS/CU WA3 92 F5
HUY L36 116 A5
Laurelhurst Av PEN/TH CH61 141 J1
Laurel Rd ECCL WA10 8 A7
EHL/KEN L7 113 M3
PR/KW L34 101 G7
RF/TRAN CH42 11 G9
RNFD/HAY WA11 90 B8
Laurels Farm Ct CHNE CH2 165 K2 1
The Laurels CHLY/EC PR7 43 H2
Laurelwood Dr GTS/LS CH66 163 G5
Lauriston Rd ANF/KKDL L4 97 L4
Laurus Cl NTHLY L27 116 B8
Lavan Cl NPK/KEN L6 113 J2 9
Lavan St NPK/KEN L6 113 J2 10
Lavender Cl RUNC WA7 19 M6
Lavender Crs PR/KW L34 101 G7 2
Lavender Gv CHLY/EC PR7 32 E8 1
Lavender Rd WGNNW/ST WN6 68 B2
Lavender Wy WLT/FAZ L9 97 K2
Lavrock Bank TOX L8 129 G1 3
Lawford Dr HES CH60 141 L5
Lawler St LITH L21 83 K7
Lawn Av WARR WA1 122 B5
Lawns Av BEB CH63 143 K7
SKEL WN8 66 E8
Lawnside Cl RF/TRAN CH42 128 B4
The Lawns CHTN/BK PR9 25 H3
CL/PREN CH43 110 F6
Lawnswood Gv CHNE CH2 165 K2
Lawnwood Av CHLY/EC PR7 32 C8 3
Lawrence Cl ALL/GAR L19 130 C6 7
Lawrence Ct WGNE/HIN WN2 80 D5 4
Lawrence Gv WAV L15 114 A6 3
Lawrence La CHLY/EC PR7 30 E6
Lawrence Rd CHLY/EC PR7 32 D6
ECCL WA10 88 E7
WAV L15 113 M6
Lawrence St NEWLW WA12 104 C2
Lawrenson St ECCL WA10 8 D6
Lawson Cl WARR WA1 123 G6
Lawson St CHLYE PR6 33 G6 5
CHTN/BK PR9 25 J6
Lawson Wk WD/CROXPK L12 98 F2
Lawton Av BTL L20 84 A8
Lawton Cl GOL/RIS/CU WA3 107 G2 3
Lawton Rd CSBY/WL L22 82 F3
HUY L36 115 L3
RAIN/WH L35 117 M3
Lawton St CLVPS L1 13 J8 2
Laxey Av WARR WA1 122 F7 1
Laxey Crs LEIGH WN7 81 L6
Laxey St TOX L8 113 G7
Laxton Cl GTS/LS CH66 163 H5 9
Laxton Rd WLTN L25 131 L7
Layford Cl HUY L36 99 M7
Layford Rd HUY L36 99 M8 1
Layland Av GOL/RIS/CU WA3 107 G1
Layton Av CL/PREN CH43 127 H3
Layton Cl GOL/RIS/CU WA3 123 G2
WGNW/BIL/O WN5 67 M8 5
WLTN L25 131 L3
Layton Rd WLTN L25 131 L3
Lazenby Crs AIMK WN4 91 H2
Leach Cft STBRV L28 99 J6 2
Leach La STHEL WA9 102 F8
Leach St ECCL WA10 8 F3 1
ECCL WA10 8 F4 1
Leach Wy PEN/TH CH61 125 L7
Lea Cl CL/PREN CH43 127 G1
Lea Crs ORM L39 51 G6
Leacroft AIMK WN4 79 G7
Leacroft Rd GOL/RIS/CU WA3 107 J7
Lea Cross Gv WDN WA8 133 L2
Leadale Cl WGNNW/ST WN6 55 M4 3
Leadenhall Cl EV L5 97 H7
Leader St WGN WN1 5 K4
WGNW/BIL/O WN5 67 L7
Leafield Cl PEN/TH CH61 126 B7 2
Leafield Rd WLTN L25 131 K7
Leagate AIN/FAZ L10 85 H5
Lea Gate Cl WGNS/IIMK WN3 79 G2 2
Lea Green Rd STHEL WA9 102 C8
Leal Holme Av WGNE/HIN WN2 69 J3
Leamington Av
NEWLW WA12 104 E4 1
Leamington Cl NSTN CH64 153 G7
WARRW/BUR WA5 120 C5
Leamington Rd NG/CROX L11 97 M3
STHP PR8 34 E8
Leander Rd WAL/NB CH45 95 J8
Lea Rd WAL/EG CH44 95 L8
Leas Cl GTS/LS CH66 155 L8 6
Leaside RUNC WA7 149 M4
Leasowe Av WAL/NB CH45 95 G7 6
Leasowe Gdns MOR/LEA CH46 110 A2
Leasowe Rd MOR/LEA CH46 110 C1
WLT/FAZ L9 84 D6
Leasoweside MOR/LEA CH46 110 C1
The Leas PEN/TH CH61 126 D7
WAL/NB CH45 95 G6
Lea St WGNS/IIMK WN3 4 B5
Leatham Cl GOL/RIS/CU WA3 123 G2
Leatherbarrows La MGHL L31 73 J6
Leather's La HLWD L26 132 B6
Leathwood MGHL L31 73 G4 1
Lea Vw WGN WN1 5 L2
Leaway GR/UP/WCH CH49 125 M1
WGNE/HIN WN2 5 L5
Leawood Gv MOR/LEA CH46 110 B5 2
Leckwith Rd NTHTN L30 84 D2
Ledburn SKEL WN8 65 K2
Ledbury Cl CL/PREN CH43 127 G3 3
ECCL WA10 101 H1
WD/CROXPK L12 99 H1
Ledger Rd RNFD/HAY WA11 90 C8
Ledmore Gv AIMK WN4 90 F2 1
Ledsham Cl CL/PREN CH43 127 G1 4
GOL/RIS/CU WA3 122 E2
Ledsham La GTS/LS CH66 162 B2
Ledsham Park Dr
GTS/LS CH66 155 J7 2
Ledsham Rd GTS/LS CH66 155 J8
KKBY L32 85 L3
Ledson Gv ORM L39 62 E6 1
Ledston Cl RUNC WA7 150 F4
Ledyard Cl WARRW/BUR WA5 120 F6
Leece St CLVPS L1 13 J9
Lee Cl RAIN/WH L35 117 M4
Leecourt Cl WD/CROXPK L12 98 F8 3
Leeds St VAUX/LVPD L3 12 E4
WGNS/IIMK WN3 4 C5
Lee Hall Rd WLTN L25 115 L8
Lee La BRSC L40 40 E6
WGNE/HIN WN2 80 D5
Leeming Cl ALL/GAR L19 130 E8 3
Lee Park Av WLTN L25 115 L8 2
Lee Rd HOY CH47 108 E6
WARRW/BUR WA5 120 D7 3
Lees Av RF/TRAN CH42 128 B3
Leeside Av KKBY L32 86 B5
Leeside Cl KKBY L32 86 B4
Lees La EP CH65 20 F7
NSTN CH64 153 K5
SKEL WN8 53 L5
SKEL WN8 54 C6
WD/CROXPK L12 98 F6
Leeson Av CHLY/EC PR7 42 F1
Lees Rd CHLYE PR6 44 D5
NWD/KWIPK L33 86 D3
Lee St STHEL WA9 103 G5
Leeswood SKEL WN8 65 K2
Leeswood Rd
GR/UP/WCH CH49 126 C2
Lee Vale Rd WLTN L25 131 L1
Legh La KIRK/FR/WA PR4 27 J1
Legh Rd PS/BROM CH62 128 D6
RNFD/HAY WA11 90 C7
Legh St AIMK WN4 91 K3
GOL/RIS/CU WA3 92 C5
NEWLW WA12 104 C2
WARR WA1 14 D5
Legion La PS/BROM CH62 143 M4
Legion Rd ECCL WA10 101 M5 2
Leicester Av CSBY/WL L22 82 F3
Leicester Rd BTL L20 7 K2
Leicester St CHTN/BK PR9 3 H1
STHEL WA9 101 M5 3
WARRW/BUR WA5 121 G8
Leigh Av WDN WA8 16 C2
Leigh Rd WGNE/HIN WN2 81 K4
WKBY CH48 124 D2
Leigh Rw CHLY/EC PR7 32 E6
Leighs Hey Crs KKBY L32 86 B3 3
Leigh St LEIGH WN7 81 L8
WGN WN1 5 H5
WGNE/HIN WN2 81 K4
Leighton Av HOY CH47 109 G5
MGHL L31 72 F3
Leighton Cha NSTN CH64 152 F4
Leighton Ct NSTN CH64 152 F5
Leighton Dr LEIGH WN7 93 K4
Leighton Pk NSTN CH64 152 F5
Leighton Rd BIRK CH41 128 A1 6
NSTN CH64 152 E2
The Leightons NSTN CH64 152 F5
Leighton St ANF/KKDL L4 7 L9
Leinster Rd CLB/OSW/ST L13 114 D2
Leinster St RUNC WA7 18 E2
Leison St ANF/KKDL L4 96 F6
Leiston Cl PEN/TH CH61 126 A6 2
Lemon Cl EHL/KEN L7 113 L4 9
Lemon St EV L5 96 F7
Lemon Tree Wk ECCL WA10 101 M4
Lendel Cl FMBY L37 59 G2 2
Lenfield Dr RNFD/HAY WA11 90 B7
Lenham Wy SPK/HALE L24 146 D1 2
Lennon St CHLY/EC PR7 32 E6 6
Lennox Av WAL/NB CH45 95 K6 5
Lennox La CL/PREN CH43 110 E4
Lenthall St ANF/KKDL L4 97 H3
Lenton Av FMBY L37 58 F1
Lenton Rd WLTN L25 115 L8
Leo Cl DV/KA/FCH L14 115 H1
Leominster Rd WAL/EG CH44 111 K1
Leonard Cheshire Dr NTHTN L30 .. 84 B2
Leonards Cl HUY L36 99 M7 1
Leonard St RUNC WA7 148 F6
STHEL WA9 103 H6
WARRN/WOL WA2 15 G2
WARRS WA4 137 L4
Leon Cl WARRW/BUR WA5 119 M6 2
Leonora St TOX L8 129 J1 12
Leopold Gv STHEL WA9 102 E8
Leopold Rd CSBY/WL L22 82 E3
EHL/KEN L7 113 K3
Leopold St WAL/EG CH44 112 A2 2
WGNW/BIL/O WN5 67 K8
Lesley Rd STHP PR8 25 G6
Leslie Av GR/UP/WCH CH49 125 M2
Leslie Rd ECCL WA10 101 L5
Lesseps Rd TOX L8 113 L6
Lessingham Av WGN WN1 68 D2
Lessingham Rd WDN WA8 134 B2
Lester Cl ANF/KKDL L4 97 G6
Lester Dr ECCL WA10 88 C8
PEN/TH CH61 125 L6
Lester Gv HUY L36 116 B1 4
Lestock St TOX L8 113 G6
Leta St ANF/KKDL L4 97 H4
Letchworth Dr CHLY/EC PR7 32 D7
Letchworth St NPK/KEN L6 97 L8 5
Letchworth Wks
CHLY/EC PR7 32 D7 4
Lethbridge Cl EV L5 96 F7 7
Lethbridge Rd STHP PR8 3 M7
Letitia St TOX L8 113 H8
Levens Hey MOR/LEA CH46 109 M5 2
Levens Pl WGNE/HIN WN2 69 J5
WGNW/BIL/O WN5 67 L6
Leven St ANF/KKDL L4 97 G5
Leven Wk EP CH65 156 C5
Lever Av WAL/EG CH44 112 A3 13
Lever Cswy BEB CH63 127 K6
Leveret Rd SPK/HALE L24 147 J2
Lever Park Av HOR/BR BL6 45 J8
Lever St STHEL WA9 118 F1
Leveson Rd CLB/OSW/ST L13 .. 114 D4 1
Levisham Gdns
WARRW/BUR WA5 121 G6 3
Lewis Av WARRW/BUR WA5 121 H3
Lewis Cl CHLY/EC PR7 44 A7
WGNS/IIMK WN3 4 A9
Lewis Crs WDN WA8 16 C5
Lewis Gv WDN WA8 133 M4
Lewisham Rd NG/CROX L11 98 C4
PS/BROM CH62 128 E7
Lewis St ECCL WA10 8 D5
Lexden St WARRW/BUR WA5 121 G7
Lexham Rd DV/KA/FCH L14 114 E2
Lexton Dr CHTN/BK PR9 25 K2
Leybourne Av STHP PR8 35 H6
Leybourne Cl WLTN L25 115 J7
Leybourne Gn WLTN L25 115 J7 4
Leybourne Gv WLTN L25 115 J8 3
Leybourne Rd WLTN L25 115 J7
Leyburn Cl KKBY L32 86 A6
WGN WN1 5 L2
Leyburn Rd WAL/NB CH45 95 H8
Ley Cl STHEL WA9 118 E1
Leyfield Cl WD/CROXPK L12 98 F7
Leyfield Rd WD/CROXPK L12 98 E7
Leyland Av WGNE/HIN WN2 80 F2
Leyland Cl CHTN/BK PR9 23 G8 1
Leyland Green Rd AIMK WN4 78 E8
Leyland Gv RNFD/HAY WA11 90 D7
Leyland La LEY/BBR PR5 30 E2
Leyland Mill La WGN WN1 68 E2
Leyland Rd CHTN/BK PR9 3 L1
RNFD/HAY WA11 76 B7
STHP PR8 24 E4
Leyland St PR/KW L34 100 F7 3
WGNE/HIN WN2 80 D4 6
Leyland Wy ORM L39 51 H8
Leyton Cl RUNC WA7 149 K7
Liberty St WAV L15 114 A6
Libra Cl DV/KA/FCH L14 99 J8
Library St CHLY/EC PR7 32 E6
WGN WN1 4 F4
Libson Cl WARRN/WOL WA2 122 C2
Lichen Cl CHLY/EC PR7 42 F1
Lichfield Av CSBY/WL L22 82 F2
GOL/RIS/CU WA3 92 F5 3
Lichfield Cl NTHTN L30 84 C4
Lichfield Dr GTS/LS CH66 163 G5
Lichfield Gv AIMK WN4 91 L3 6
Lichfield Rd CHLY/EC PR7 32 D7
HLWD L26 132 A7
WAV L15 114 C7 3
Lichfield St WAL/NB CH45 95 L6 6
WGNW/BIL/O WN5 67 L8
Lickers La RAIN/WH L35 117 G3
Liddell Av MGHL L31 85 J1
Liddell Rd WD/CROXPK L12 98 B6
Lidderdale Rd WAV L15 114 A7
Lidgate Cl NWD/KWIPK L33 74 A8
WGNS/IIMK WN3 78 F2
Liebig St WDN WA8 16 E4
Lifeboat Rd FMBY L37 58 C4
Liffey St TOX L8 113 K6
Lifton Rd NWD/KWIPK L33 86 B3
Lightbody St EV L5 96 D8
Lightburn St RUNC WA7 18 F6
Lightfoot Cl HES CH60 141 K6 3
Lightfoot La HES CH60 141 K6
Lighthorne Dr STHP PR8 47 J1
Lighthouse Rd HOY CH47 108 C7
SPK/HALE L24 148 A6
Lighthurst Av CHLY/EC PR7 32 E7
Lighthurst La CHLY/EC PR7 32 E8
Lightshaw La GOL/RIS/CU WA3 .. 92 D1
Lightwood Dr EHL/KEN L7 113 L5 7
Lightwood St EHL/KEN L7 113 L5 8
Lilac Av AIMK WN4 78 F8
STHP PR8 47 M3
WARRW/BUR WA5 120 C8
WDN WA8 134 D3
WGNNW/ST WN6 68 C2
Lilac Crs RUNC WA7 19 L7
Lilac Gdns WGNE/HIN WN2 80 B1
Lilac Gv GTS/LS CH66 163 J5
HUY L36 115 M5
RNFD/HAY WA11 90 B8 3
SKEL WN8 65 G4
WARRS WA4 138 A4
WGNW/BIL/O WN5 89 M1
Lilac Rd GOL/RIS/CU WA3 92 C4 2
Lilford Av WARRW/BUR WA5 121 H5
WLT/FAZ L9 84 B7 5
Lilford Dr WARRW/BUR WA5 120 B7 3
Lilford St WARRW/BUR WA5 14 B2
Lilian Dr WGNNW/ST WN6 68 C2
Lilley Rd EHL/KEN L7 113 M2
Lillian Rd ANF/KKDL L4 97 K7
Lillie Cl CL/PREN CH43 110 E5
Lillyfield HES CH60 141 H7
Lilly Gv ANF/KKDL L4 97 K4
Lilly V EHL/KEN L7 113 M2
Lily Av NEWLW WA12 104 E3
Lily La WGNE/HIN WN2 80 B6
Lily Pl AIMK WN4 91 L3
Lily Rd LITH L21 83 K7
Lily St AIMK WN4 80 A8
Limbrick Rd CHLYE PR6 33 G6
Lime Av BEB CH63 142 F1
FROD/HEL WA6 160 E5
WDN WA8 134 D3 5
Lime Cl CLB/OSW/ST L13 114 C1
WGNE/HIN WN2 80 D6
Limedale Rd CALD/MH L18 114 C8
Limefield Dr SKEL WN8 66 A6 2
Lime Gv CHLY/EC PR7 32 E8
CHNE CH2 165 J2
GOL/RIS/CU WA3 92 F7
LITH L21 83 J7
RNFD/HAY WA11 76 B7
RUNC WA7 19 L7
SKEL WN8 65 G4
TOX L8 113 L7
WGNE/HIN WN2 81 H2
Limehurst Gv PS/BROM CH62 143 M7
Limekiln La EV L5 96 F8
VAUX/LVPD L3 13 G3
WAL/EG CH44 111 J3
WARRW/BUR WA5 120 A2
Limes Av CHLY/EC PR7 31 L1
WGNNW/ST WN6 56 D7
The Limes GOL/RIS/CU WA3 106 F1
GR/UP/WCH CH49 110 B8
WGNNW/ST WN6 56 C7
Lime St CLVPS L1 13 H6
EP CH65 20 C1
STHP PR8 25 G7
VAUX/LVPD L3 13 J7
WGN WN1 5 G3
Limetree Av WARR WA1 122 B5
WARRS WA4 138 A4
Lime Tree Cl GTS/LS CH66 163 J5
WLT/FAZ L9 97 K2 1
Lime Tree Gv HES CH60 141 L5
Lime Tree Wy FMBY L37 58 E3
Lime V WGNE/HIN WN2 80 B1
Lime Vale Rd RNFD/HAY WA11 89 L2
Limeways WARRS WA4 138 A8
Limont Rd STHP PR8 34 F8
Linacre La BTL L20 83 L8
HTWN L38 60 C5
Linacre Rd LITH L21 83 K7
Linaker Dr ORM L39 49 K5
Linaker St STHP PR8 3 H7
Linbeck Gv GOL/RIS/CU WA3 93 G4
Linbridge Rd DV/KA/FCH L14 99 H7
Lincoln Av GOL/RIS/CU WA3 92 F4
Lincoln Cl GOL/RIS/CU WA3 93 L5 2
HUY L36 116 D2
NPK/KEN L6 113 K1
RUNC WA7 149 L7
WARR WA1 123 G7
Lincoln Crs RNFD/HAY WA11 89 K7
Lincoln Dr AIMK WN4 91 L3
AIN/FAZ L10 84 F2
WAL/NB CH45 95 L7
WGNE/HIN WN2 57 M8

Lincoln Gn MGHL L31 72 D5 1
Lincoln Pl WGNW/BIL/O WN5 67 H5 2
Lincoln Rd ECCL WA10 8 A8
GTS/LS CH66 162 F2
STHP PR8 35 J4
Lincoln Sq WDN WA8 134 D3
Lincoln St ALL/GAR L19 145 L1
BIRK CH41 10 A1
Lincoln Wy RAIN/WH L35 117 M4
Lincombe Rd HUY L36 115 K1
Lincroft Rd WGNE/HIN WN2 81 J2
Lindale Dr STHEL WA9 118 E1 11
Lindale Rd EHL/KEN L7 114 A2
Lindby Cl KKBY L32 86 C5
Lindby Rd KKBY L32 86 C5
Linden Av AIMK WN4 79 H8
CSBY/BLUN L23 82 E1
NTHTN L30 84 B3
WGNW/BIL/O WN5 67 G7
Linden Cl GTS/LS CH66 163 H5
WARR WA1 122 F6
Linden Ct WDN WA8 134 B1 1
Linden Dr CL/PREN CH43 127 G4
FROD/HEL WA6 166 D4
HUY L36 116 A5
Linden Gv CHLYE PR6 32 F2
RNFD/HAY WA11 89 L2
WAL/NB CH45 95 K6
WGNW/BIL/O WN5 67 G7
Linden Rd NTHLY L27 116 A8
Lindens SKEL WN8 65 K1
The Lindens MGHL L31 72 E6 2
Linden St WGNW/BIL/O WN5 67 L8
Linden Wy ECCL WA10 101 K1 2
WDN WA8 134 B1
Lindenwood KKBY L32 86 B5 3
Lindeth Av WAL/EG CH44 111 K3
Lindfield Cl WARRS WA4 136 D8 1
Lindholme SKEL WN8 65 L2 2
Lindi Av WARRS WA4 138 D4
Lindisfarne Av EP CH65 163 L4
GOL/RIS/CU WA3 93 L5
Lindisfarne Dr WD/CROXPK L12 89 L2
Lindley Av WARRS WA4 138 B1
WGNW/BIL/O WN5 66 E8
Lindley Cl EHL/KEN L7 113 L5 3
Lindley Dr SKEL WN8 53 L2
Lindley St EHL/KEN L7 113 L5
Lindow St LEIGH WN7 81 M7 5
Lindrick Cl RAIN/WH L35 117 J1 2
Lindsay Dr CHLY/EC PR7 32 C6
Lindsay Rd ANF/KKDL L4 97 M5
Lindsay St STHEL WA9 119 G2
Lindsay Ter WGNE/HIN WN2 57 K8
Lind St ANF/KKDL L4 97 H4
Lindsworth Cl
WARRW/BUR WA5 120 E7 1
Lindwall Cl CL/PREN CH43 110 E4
Linear Pk MOR/LEA CH46 109 L4
Linear Vw NEWLW WA12 104 E5
Lineside Cl WLTN L25 115 K8
Linford Gv RNFD/HAY WA11 9 M1
Lingdale Av CL/PREN CH43 111 H7
Lingdale Rd CL/PREN CH43 111 H6
WKBY CH48 124 C2
Lingdales FMBY L37 47 K7
Lingfield Cl HUY L36 115 L4 3
Lingfield Crs WGNNW/ST WN6 68 A2
Lingfield Gv DV/KA/FCH L14 114 F3
Lingfield Rd DV/KA/FCH L14 114 E3
RUNC WA7 18 D7
Lingford Cl NTHLY L27 132 B1
Lingham Cl MOR/LEA CH46 109 M3 1
Lingham La MOR/LEA CH46 109 L3
Lingholme Rd ECCL WA10 8 D3
Lingley Green Av
WARRW/BUR WA5 119 L7
Lingley Rd WARRW/BUR WA5 119 M7
Lingmell Av RNFD/HAY WA11 89 K4
Lingmell Rd WD/CROXPK L12 98 D5
Lingmoor Cl WGNS/IIMK WN3 79 J4 1
Ling St EHL/KEN L7 113 K3
Lingtree Rd KKBY L32 85 K3
Lingwell Av WDN WA8 133 M3 2
Lingwood Rd
WARRW/BUR WA5 120 A7
Linhope Wy AIG/SPK L17 129 L2 2
Link Av CSBY/BLUN L23 71 J8
RNFD/HAY WA11 90 A8
Link Rd HUY L36 116 D4
Links Av CHTN/BK PR9 25 G3
GTS/LS CH66 155 L6
Links Cl BEB CH63 143 K7
WAL/NB CH45 95 H5
Links Hey Rd WKBY CH48 125 G7
Linkside BEB CH63 127 M6
Linkside Av WARRN/WOL WA2 105 K7
Linkside Wy GTS/LS CH66 163 H5
Links Rd KKBY L32 86 C4 2
Linkstor Rd WLTN L25 131 H3
Links Vw CL/PREN CH43 111 G8
WAL/NB CH45 95 H5
Links View Cl WLTN L25 131 H2
Linksway WAL/NB CH45 95 H6
Linkway ECCL WA10 88 D7 1
RUNC WA7 19 L8
Linkway Av AIMK WN4 80 A8
Linkway East STHEL WA9 9 J7
Linkway West ECCL WA10 8 F6
Linley Cl WGNNW/ST WN6 67 L1
Linley Rd WGNW/BIL/O WN5 67 M8
Linner Rd SPK/HALE L24 146 F2
Linnet Cl NEWLW WA12 104 E2
WARRN/WOL WA2 121 M2
Linnet Gv GOL/RIS/CU WA3 123 G2
Linnet La AIG/SPK L17 113 K8
Linnets Wy HES CH60 141 G5
Linnet Wy NWD/KWIPK L33 74 A6
Linosa Cl NPK/KEN L6 113 L1
Linslade Cl NWD/KWIPK L33 86 B1 4
Linslade Crs NWD/KWIPK L33 86 B1
Linton Av GOL/RIS/CU WA3 92 B3
Linton St ANF/KKDL L4 97 H4
Linville Av CSBY/BLUN L23 82 D1
Linwood Cl RUNC WA7 150 E8 5
WGNE/HIN WN2 80 F1
Linwood Gv RAIN/WH L35 117 G3 5
Linwood Rd RF/TRAN CH42 128 A2
Lionel St STHEL WA9 103 H6
Lion La HOR/BR BL6 57 L3
Lipton Cl BTL L20 6 F7
Liptrot St WGNW/BIL/O WN5 68 B6 3
Liptrott Rd CHLY/EC PR7 32 C8
Lisburn La CLB/OSW/ST L13 98 A6
Lisburn Rd AIG/SPK L17 130 A3
Liscard Gv WAL/EG CH44 111 J1
Liscard Rd WAL/EG CH44 111 M2
WAV L15 113 M6
Liscard Village WAL/NB CH45 95 K8 5
Liscard Wy WAL/EG CH44 111 K1
Liskeard Cl RUNC WA7 150 D7
Lisleholme Crs WD/CROXPK L12 98 E7
Lisleholme Rd WD/CROXPK L12 98 E7
Lismore Rd CALD/MH L18 130 C4
Lister Crs EHL/KEN L7 113 L3
Lister Dr CLB/OSW/ST L13 114 A1
Lister Rd EHL/KEN L7 113 L3
RUNC WA7 19 L2
Liston St ANF/KKDL L4 97 H3 7
Litcham Cl GR/UP/WCH CH49 110 C6
Litchborough Gv RAIN/WH L35 101 J7
Litherland Av
MOR/LEA CH46 109 M5 3
Litherland Crs RNFD/HAY WA11 89 L6
Litherland Pk LITH L21 83 K5
Litherland Rd BTL L20 83 L7
Lithou Cl EV L5 96 F8
Little Acre MGHL L31 73 G5
Little Barn Hey NTHTN L30 83 M1
Little Brook La KKBY L32 85 M5
Little Canning St TOX L8 113 H6
Little Carr La CHLY/EC PR7 32 F8
Little Catharine St TOX L8 113 H6 9
Littlecote Cl STHEL WA9 118 E1 12
Littlecourt VAUX/LVPD L3 12 E1
Little Crosby Rd CSBY/BLUN L23 71 G6
Littledale Rd DV/KA/FCH L14 114 F2
WAL/EG CH44 111 M2
WARRW/BUR WA5 120 B6
Little Delph RNFD/HAY WA11 90 F6 2
Littlegate RUNC WA7 150 A5
Little Gn GTS/LS CH66 162 F2
Little Hardman St CLVPS L1 13 K9 5
Little Heath Rd SPK/HALE L24 147 G3
Little Heyes St EV L5 97 J7
Little Hey La FMBY L37 59 K1
Little Howard St VAUX/LVPD L3 12 D2
Little Huskisson St TOX L8 113 H6 5
Little La CHTN/BK PR9 25 K4
NSTN CH64 152 D4
WGNS/IIMK WN3 79 G1
Little London WGN WN1 4 F2
Little Meadow La BRSC L40 39 M1
Littlemore Cl
GR/UP/WCH CH49 109 M8 7
Little Moss Hey STBRV L28 99 K6
Little Parkfield Rd AIG/SPK L17 129 K1
Little Pasture LEIGH WN7 81 M6
Littler Rd RNFD/HAY WA11 90 C8
Little St Bride St TOX L8 113 H5
Little Scotland HOR/BR BL6 57 K3
Little Stanney La CHNE CH2 164 A5
Littlestone Cl WDN WA8 134 C1 1
Little Storeton La BEB CH63 127 J7
Little St STHEL WA9 103 G4 1
Littleton Cl CL/PREN CH43 127 G1 5
WARRW/BUR WA5 136 F1
Littleton Gv WGNNW/ST WN6 56 A3
Little Wissage GTS/LS CH66 163 H3 3
Little Woolton St EHL/KEN L7 113 J4
Littondale Av RAIN/WH L35 117 M3 4
Liverpool Av STHP PR8 47 M1
Liverpool Loop Line WLTN L25 115 H6
Liverpool Old Rd
KIRK/FR/WA PR4 28 C3
STHP PR8 47 L4
Liverpool Rd AIMK WN4 91 H2
BRSC L40 28 D7
CH/BCN CH1 163 H6
CSBY/BLUN L23 83 G1
FMBY L37 59 J3
HUY L36 99 L8
KIRK/FR/WA PR4 28 C1
MGHL L31 72 F1
NSTN CH64 153 H3
ORM L39 62 D3
PR/KW L34 100 D7
RNFD/HAY WA11 90 E4
SKEL WN8 64 F5
STHP PR8 34 F8
WARRW/BUR WA5 14 B6
WDN WA8 16 A2
WGNE/HIN WN2 69 L8
Liverpool Rd North BRSC L40 52 A1
MGHL L31 72 E3
Liverpool Rd South BRSC L40 51 M2
MGHL L31 72 E5
Liverpool Rw NEWLW WA12 104 F5
Liverpool St ECCL WA10 8 F6
Liverside Rd RF/TRAN CH42 127 M1
Liver St CLVPS L1 112 E5
Livesley's La FMBY L37 60 B3
Livingston Av AIG/SPK L17 129 L1
Livingston Dr AIG/SPK L17 129 L2
Livingston Dr North
AIG/SPK L17 129 L2
Livingston Dr South
AIG/SPK L17 129 L2
Livingstone Cl
WARRW/BUR WA5 120 F6
Livingstone Rd EP CH65 20 C1
MOR/LEA CH46 110 C1
RF/TRAN CH42 128 B2 5
Livingstone St BIRK CH41 10 F3
Llandaff Cl GTS/LS CH66 163 G4
Llanrwst Cl TOX L8 113 G8 3
Lloyd Av BIRK CH41 10 D3
Lloyd Cl NPK/KEN L6 13 M1
Lloyd Crs NEWLW WA12 104 B2
Lloyd Dr EP CH65 163 M4
GR/UP/WCH CH49 125 M2
Lloyd Rd PR/KW L34 101 G6
Lloyd St RNFD/HAY WA11 90 B7
Lobelia Av WLT/FAZ L9 97 K1
Lobelia Gv RUNC WA7 161 H1 7
Local Board St WGNE/HIN WN2 5 M6
Lochinvar Av GTS/LS CH66 155 H7
Lochinvar St WLT/FAZ L9 97 H2 2
Lochmore Rd CALD/MH L18 130 C4
Lochryan Rd ALL/GAR L19 130 D5 1
Loch St RUNC WA7 19 G2
WGNW/BIL/O WN5 67 K7
Locker Av WARRN/WOL WA2 121 K3
Lockerbie Cl WARRN/WOL WA2 122 A1
Lockerbie Pl WGNS/IIMK WN3 79 G3
Lockerby Rd EHL/KEN L7 113 M2
Locker La AIMK WN4 92 B1 1
Locker Pk GR/UP/WCH CH49 125 L1
Locke St ALL/GAR L19 145 L1 5
Lockett Rd AIMK WN4 79 L8
WDN WA8 134 C3
Lockett St WARRS WA4 138 B2
Lockgate East RUNC WA7 150 E3
Lockgate West RUNC WA7 150 E3
Locking Stumps La
WARRN/WOL WA2 122 D2
Lockington Cl TOX L8 129 J1 13
Lock La KIRK/FR/WA PR4 28 D3
Lock Rd PS/BROM CH62 144 D6
WARR WA1 122 B6
Lock St STHEL WA9 9 L2
Locks Vw WGN WN1 5 M4
Lockton La WARRW/BUR WA5 121 G6
Loddon Cl GR/UP/WCH CH49 110 D6 4
Lodge Dr GOL/RIS/CU WA3 107 H2
Lodge Hollow FROD/HEL WA6 166 D2
Lodge La NEWLW WA12 91 K4
PS/BROM CH62 128 D7
RNFD/HAY WA11 75 L4
RUNC WA7 150 A5
TOX L8 113 K6
WARRW/BUR WA5 121 G6
WDN WA8 133 K1
Lodge Rd WGNW/BIL/O WN5 78 A1
Lodwick St BTL L20 6 F9
Loeminster Pl WGNE/HIN WN2 5 L6
Lofthouse Ga WDN WA8 134 B2
Logan Rd BIRK CH41 111 K4
Lognor Rd KKBY L32 85 L3
Logwood Av WGNW/BIL/O WN5 67 M6
Logwood Pl WGNW/BIL/O WN5 68 A5
Logwood Rd HUY L36 116 C5
Loire Dr WGNW/BIL/O WN5 68 B5
Lomax St WGNE/HIN WN2 80 C3
Lombard Rd MOR/LEA CH46 110 B3
Lombardy Av
GR/UP/WCH CH49 125 K3
Lomond Gv EP CH65 163 H2
MOR/LEA CH46 110 B5
Lomond Rd EHL/KEN L7 114 A3
London Cl WGNW/BIL/O WN5 68 A5
Londonderry Rd
CLB/OSW/ST L13 97 M6 5
London Flds WGNW/BIL/O WN5 78 A8
London La STHP PR8 35 M5
London Rd FROD/HEL WA6 160 D5
VAUX/LVPD L3 13 L6
WARRS WA4 137 M5
London Rw NEWLW WA12 104 F5
London Sq STHP PR8 3 G3
London St CHTN/BK PR9 3 H3
Longacre CHTN/BK PR9 25 H2
Longacre Cl WAL/NB CH45 94 F8
Long Acres GR/UP/WCH CH49 109 M8
Long Acres Rd NSTN CH64 153 G3
Longbarn Bvd
WARRN/WOL WA2 122 E3
Long Barn La WARR WA1 122 F5
WARRN/WOL WA2 122 D3
Longborough Rd PR/KW L34 99 L2
Longbrook WGNNW/ST WN6 55 K7
Longcliffe Dr STHP PR8 47 K1
Long Copse CHLY/EC PR7 32 B4
Longcroft Av ALL/GAR L19 130 F6
Long Croft Meadow
CHLY/EC PR7 32 D3
Longcroft Sq ALL/GAR L19 130 F6
Longdale La STFN L29 71 M6
Longdin St WARRS WA4 15 M9
Longdown Rd NG/CROX L11 85 K7
Longendale Rd WGNNW/ST WN6 55 M5
Longfellow Cl
WGNS/IIMK WN3 68 C8 4
Longfellow Dr RF/TRAN CH42 128 C5
Longfellow St BTL L20 6 D1
TOX L8 113 L6
Longfield FMBY L37 47 K8
Longfield Av CHLY/EC PR7 43 G3
CSBY/BLUN L23 71 G7
Longfield Cl
GR/UP/WCH CH49 125 M1 2
Longfield Mnr CHLY/EC PR7 32 C8
Longfield Rd LITH L21 83 K7
WARRN/WOL WA2 121 L4
Longfold MGHL L31 73 G4
Longford Rd STHP PR8 35 J3
Longford St TOX L8 129 J2
WARRN/WOL WA2 14 E1
Long Hey RAIN/WH L35 116 F3
Longhey SKEL WN8 65 L1 2
Long Hey Rd WKBY CH48 125 G6
Long Heys La SKEL WN8 54 B3
Long Heys or Back La SKEL WN8 54 C8
Longhurst Rd WGNE/HIN WN2 81 H1
Longland Rd WAL/NB CH45 95 K7
Long La ALL/GAR L19 130 E6
CHLYE PR6 44 C1
CHTN/BK PR9 23 K7
ORM L39 62 E2
SFTN L29 71 J5
SKEL WN8 77 G2
WARRN/WOL WA2 121 L4
WAV L15 114 B5
WGNE/HIN WN2 81 J1
WLT/FAZ L9 84 E8
Longlooms Rd EP CH65 163 M4
Longmead Av AIMK WN4 91 L1
Long Meadow CHLY/EC PR7 32 C8
ECCL WA10 101 K1
HES CH60 141 H7
Longmeadow Rd PR/KW L34 99 M1
Long Meanygate CHTN/BK PR9 26 B5
Longmoor Cl AIN/FAZ L10 85 G6 2
Longmoor Gv WLT/FAZ L9 84 D7 6
Longmoor La AIN/FAZ L10 85 J6
WLT/FAZ L9 84 D7
Longreach Rd DV/KA/FCH L14 115 H2
Longridge Av
GR/UP/WCH CH49 110 A7
RNFD/HAY WA11 89 M8
WGNNW/ST WN6 56 B5
Longridge Wk ANF/KKDL L4 97 G5 7
Longshaw Av WGNW/BIL/O WN5 78 A4
Longshaw Cl
WGNW/BIL/O WN5 78 A4 2
Longshaw Common
WGNW/BIL/O WN5 78 A5
Longshaw Old Rd
WGNW/BIL/O WN5 78 A4
Longshaw St
WARRW/BUR WA5 121 H5
Long Spinney RUNC WA7 150 E5
Longster Trail FROD/HEL WA6 166 E2
Longstone Wk EHL/KEN L7 113 K5
Longton Av GOL/RIS/CU WA3 92 E5
Longton Dr FMBY L37 47 J7
Longton La RAIN/WH L35 101 K8
Longton St CHLYE PR6 33 G5 7
WGNE/HIN WN2 80 E1
Longview Av RAIN/WH L35 117 J1 3
WAL/NB CH45 95 J8
Longview Crs HUY L36 116 B2 2
Longview Dr HUY L36 116 C2
Longview La HUY L36 100 B8
Longview Rd HUY L36 116 B1
RAIN/WH L35 117 J1
Longville St TOX L8 113 G8 4
Longwood Cl RNFD/HAY WA11 88 D4
Longwood Rd WARRS WA4 138 A8
Longworth Av CHLY/EC PR7 43 H3
HOR/BR BL6 57 L2 4
Longworth St CHLY/EC PR7 32 D7
Longworth Wy WLTN L25 131 J2
Lonie Gv ECCL WA10 101 L5
Lonsboro Rd WAL/EG CH44 111 L2
Lonsdale Av ECCL WA10 101 K6
LEIGH WN7 93 M3
ORM L39 51 H6 3
WAL/NB CH45 95 J7 5
Lonsdale Cl LITH L21 83 K3 1
WDN WA8 133 L5
Lonsdale Dr LEY/BBR PR5 29 K2 3
Lonsdale Ms LITH L21 83 K3 2
Lonsdale Rd FMBY L37 59 G2
HLWD L26 132 A7 1
LITH L21 83 K3
STHP PR8 3 L9
Looe Cl WDN WA8 134 A3
Looe Rd NG/CROX L11 85 M8 2
The Looms NSTN CH64 152 D3
Loomsway PEN/TH CH61 125 L7
Loraine St EV L5 97 H8
Lordens Cl DV/KA/FCH L14 99 J8
Lordens Rd DV/KA/FCH L14 99 K7
Lord Nelson St CLVPS L1 13 J6
WARR WA1 15 G6
Lords Av CL/PREN CH43 110 E5
Lord Sefton Wy FMBY L37 59 M3
Lordsgate Dr BRSC L40 52 A2
Lordsgate La BRSC L40 51 K3
Lordship La FROD/HEL WA6 159 H7
Lords La GOL/RIS/CU WA3 122 E1
Lord St AIMK WN4 91 M1 2
ALL/GAR L19 130 E8 2
BIRK CH41 11 K4
BRSC L40 39 G8
CHLY/EC PR7 30 E8
CHLYE PR6 32 F6
CHTN/BK PR9 3 H2
CLVP L2 12 F7
CLVPS L1 12 F7
ECCL WA10 9 G2
GOL/RIS/CU WA3 106 C5
NEWLW WA12 104 C2 6
RUNC WA7 18 F2
STHP PR8 2 E5
WARRS WA4 14 F8
WGN WN1 4 F1
WGNE/HIN WN2 69 M8
Lord Street Boulevards
STHP PR8 2 E5
Lord St West STHP PR8 2 E6
Lordy Cl WGNNW/ST WN6 56 D6
Loreburn Rd WAV L15 114 C7
Lorenzo Dr NG/CROX L11 98 B4
Loretto Dr GR/UP/WCH CH49 110 C7
Loretto Rd WAL/EG CH44 111 H1 5
Lorne Rd CL/PREN CH43 10 B9
CSBY/WL L22 82 F4
Lorne St CHLY/EC PR7 32 E6
EHL/KEN L7 114 A2
WGN WN1 5 J4
Lorn St BIRK CH41 11 K5
Lorton Av RNFD/HAY WA11 89 J5
Lostock Av
WARRW/BUR WA5 121 H5 1
Lostock Cl WGNW/BIL/O WN5 78 A8
Lostock Rd LEY/BBR PR5 29 L2
Lothair Rd ANF/KKDL L4 97 J6
Lothian St TOX L8 113 J7
Loudon Gv TOX L8 113 J7
Lough Gn BEB CH63 143 J3
Loughlin Dr NWD/KWIPK L33 74 B8
Loughrigg Av RNFD/HAY WA11 89 K4
Louis Braille Cl NTHTN L30 84 B1
Louis Pasteur Av NTHTN L30 84 B1
Loushers La WARRS WA4 137 M3
Lovage Cl WARRN/WOL WA2 122 E4 1
Lovelace Rd ALL/GAR L19 130 D6
Love La VAUX/LVPD L3 12 E2
WAL/EG CH44 111 K2
Lovel Rd SPK/HALE L24 146 F3
Lovel Ter WDN WA8 133 K8
Lovel Wy SPK/HALE L24 146 F2
Lovely La WARRW/BUR WA5 121 G7
Lovett Dr RAIN/WH L35 101 G8
Low Bank Rd AIMK WN4 91 G1
Lowcroft SKEL WN8 65 L2
Lowden Av LITH L21 83 K3
Lowe Av WARRS WA4 138 B1
Lowell St ANF/KKDL L4 97 H4
Lowe Mill La WGNE/HIN WN2 69 M8
Lower Alt Rd HTWN L38 70 B1
Lower Appleton Rd WDN WA8 16 F1 1
Lower Bank Vw BTL L20 6 E9
Lower Breck Rd NPK/KEN L6 97 L7
Lower Burgh Wy CHLY/EC PR7 43 J1
Lower Carr La HTWN L38 60 D6
Lower Castle St CLVP L2 12 E7
Lower Church St WDN WA8 16 C9
Lower Cl HLWD L26 132 C5
Lower Farm Rd WLTN L25 115 H6
Lower Flaybrick Rd
CL/PREN CH43 111 G5 3
Lower Gn GR/UP/WCH CH49 126 C2
Lower Hey CSBY/BLUN L23 71 K8
Lower Hill Dr CHLYE PR6 44 C4
Lower House La NG/CROX L11 98 C2
WDN WA8 16 B5
Lower La WLT/FAZ L9 85 G6
Lower Longshoot WGN WN1 5 H3
Lower Lyndon Av
WGNNW/ST WN6 55 J7
Lower Mersey St EP CH65 156 E6
Lower Mersey Vw BTL L20 6 F9
Lower Milk St VAUX/LVPD L3 12 F5
Lower Prom STHP PR8 2 E3
Lower Rake La FROD/HEL WA6 166 D1
Lower Rd HLWD L26 132 D5
PS/BROM CH62 128 D7 4
Lower Robin Hood La
FROD/HEL WA6 166 D2
Lower St Stephen St
WGNNW/ST WN6 4 B3
Lowerson Crs NG/CROX L11 98 A5
Lowerson Rd NG/CROX L11 98 A5
Lower Thingwall La
PEN/TH CH61 126 E7
Lower Wash La WARRS WA4 15 M9
Lowes Gn FMBY L37 59 K2 3
Lowe's La SKEL WN8 53 G5
Lowe St ECCL WA10 8 F4
GOL/RIS/CU WA3 92 C5
Lowe St South ECCL WA10 8 F5
Loweswater Cl
WARRN/WOL WA2 121 K2
Loweswater Crs
RNFD/HAY WA11 90 C7
Loweswater Wy
NWD/KWIPK L33 73 M8 6
NWD/KWIPK L33 85 M1 2
Lowfield La STHEL WA9 102 B8
Lowfield Rd DV/KA/FCH L14 114 E2
Lowfields Av PS/BROM CH62 154 F2
Lowfields Cl PS/BROM CH62 155 G2 1
Low Hl FROD/HEL WA6 165 M8
Lowlands Rd RUNC WA7 18 F3
Lowndes Rd NPK/KEN L6 97 M7
Lowood St LEIGH WN7 81 M8
Lowry Bank WAL/EG CH44 112 A2
Lowry Cl WARRW/BUR WA5 120 F7
Lowry Hill La BRSC L40 52 D3
Lowther Av AIN/FAZ L10 84 F3
GOL/RIS/CU WA3 107 H1
MGHL L31 73 G3
Lowther Crs ECCL WA10 101 K5
Lowther Dr RAIN/WH L35 117 K2
Lowther St TOX L8 113 J6
Lowton Gdns GOL/RIS/CU WA3 92 D8
Lowton Rd GOL/RIS/CU WA3 92 D4
Lowwood Gv BIRK CH41 11 H7 1
Low Wood Gv PEN/TH CH61 141 L1
Lowwood Rd BIRK CH41 11 H7
Loxdale Cl TOX L8 129 J1 14
Loxdale Dr EP CH65 163 H1
Loxley Cl WARRW/BUR WA5 120 C5
Loxley Rd STHP PR8 3 M9
Loxton Crs WGNS/IIMK WN3 79 K2
Loyola Hey RAIN/WH L35 118 A5
Lucania St ALL/GAR L19 145 L1 6
Lucan Rd AIG/SPK L17 130 A3
Lucas Av CHLY/EC PR7 31 M5
Lucerne Rd WAL/EG CH44 111 M3
Lucerne St AIG/SPK L17 129 L2
Lucius Cl WLT/FAZ L9 84 B6 2
Lucknow St AIG/SPK L17 129 L1 4
Ludlow SKEL WN8 65 L1 3
Ludlow Av WGNE/HIN WN2 81 J1
Ludlow Crs RUNC WA7 19 J8
Ludlow Dr EP CH65 21 G8
ORM L39 50 F6
WKBY CH48 124 D4
Ludlow Gv PS/BROM CH62 143 M4
Ludlow St ANF/KKDL L4 97 H4 3
WGNNW/ST WN6 55 L2
Ludovic Ter WGN WN1 68 E1
Ludwig Rd ANF/KKDL L4 97 K8
Lugard Rd AIG/SPK L17 130 A3
Lugsdale Rd WDN WA8 16 D5
Lugsmore La ECCL WA10 101 L4
Luke St AIMK WN4 79 M8
TOX L8 113 H7
WAL/EG CH44 112 A3
Lulworth SKEL WN8 65 L1
Lulworth Av CSBY/WL L22 82 E4 1
Lulworth Dr WGNE/HIN WN2 81 J1
Lulworth Rd STHP PR8 2 C8
WLTN L25 115 L8
Lumb Brook Rd WARRS WA4 138 C7
Lumber La WARRW/BUR WA5 104 A5
Lumby Av HUY L36 116 A2
Lumley Rd WAL/EG CH44 111 M2
Lumley St ALL/GAR L19 130 D7
Lunar Dr NTHTN L30 72 B8
Lunar Rd WLT/FAZ L9 84 D7 2
Lundy Dr EP CH65 163 L5
Lune Av MGHL L31 73 G3
Lune Cl LEIGH WN7 81 L8
Lunehurst GOL/RIS/CU WA3 93 G5 6
Lune Rd WGNE/HIN WN2 80 B3
Lunesdale Av WLT/FAZ L9 84 D6 10
Lune St CSBY/BLUN L23 83 G1
Lunsford Rd DV/KA/FCH L14 115 H1
Lunt Av NTHTN L30 84 C3
RAIN/WH L35 117 G2
Lunt Rd BTL L20 83 L8
SFTN L29 72 A6
Lunt's Heath Rd WDN WA8 118 C8
Lupin Dr RNFD/HAY WA11 91 H7
Lupton Dr CSBY/BLUN L23 83 J1

Lupton St CHLY/EC PR7 32 E7 6
Lupus Wy GTS/LS CH66 163 H2
Lurdin La WGN WN1 56 D6
Luscombe Cl HLWD L26 132 C5 2
Lusitania Rd ANF/KKDL L4 97 J3
Luther Gv STHEL WA9 103 K3
Luton Gv ANF/KKDL L4 97 H5
Luton Rd EP CH65 156 C8
Luton St EV L5 96 E7
WDN WA8 16 D6 2
Lutyens Cl ANF/KKDL L4 97 H6
Luxmore Rd ANF/KKDL L4 97 J4 3
Lycett Rd ANF/KKDL L4 97 L6
WAL/EG CH44 95 G8
Lychgate WARRS WA4 137 H6 1
WGNW/BIL/O WN5 68 A8 3
Lycroft Cl RUNC WA7 149 K7
Lydbrook Cl RF/TRAN CH42 128 B2 9
Lydbury Cl WARRW/BUR WA5 120 F3
Lydbury Crs KKBY L32 86 B5
Lydd Cl SPK/HALE L24 146 D1
Lydden Rd EP CH65 20 B1
Lydd Gv CHLY/EC PR7 32 C6
Lydford Gn WGNNW/ST WN6 56 B5
Lydford Rd WD/CROXPK L12 98 D5
Lydgate CHLY/EC PR7 32 C8
Lydia Ann St CLVPS L1 13 H9
Lydiate La CHLY/EC PR7 30 D4
CSBY/BLUN L23 71 K7
NSTN CH64 154 A5
RUNC WA7 149 G6
WLTN L25 131 M3
Lydiate Pk CSBY/BLUN L23 71 K7
Lydiate Rd BTL L20 83 L8
Lydiate Station Rd MGHL L31 61 G8
The Lydiate HES CH60 141 H6
Lydieth Lea NTHLY L27 116 A7
Lydney Rd HUY L36 115 K1
Lydstep Ct
WARRW/BUR WA5 121 G3 5
Lyefield Av WGN WN1 5 L2
Lyelake Cl KKBY L32 86 B4
Lyelake La BRSC L40 64 B4
Lyelake Rd KKBY L32 86 B4
Lyle St EV L5 96 F8
Lymbridge Dr HOR/BR BL6 57 M3
Lyme Cl HUY L36 100 C7
Lyme Cross Rd HUY L36 100 B7
Lyme Gv HUY L36 100 B8
LYMM WA13 139 L3
Lyme St NEWLW WA12 104 A1
RNFD/HAY WA11 91 G7
Lymington Gv NTHTN L30 84 B2 3
Lymmington Av LYMM WA13 139 L2
Lymm Rd CL/PREN CH43 110 E6 6
WARRS WA4 139 H2
Lymn St WGNE/HIN WN2 80 D2 5
Lynas Gdns ALL/GAR L19 130 D5
Lynas St BIRK CH41 11 G2
Lyncot Rd WLT/FAZ L9 84 D5 3
Lyncroft Rd WAL/EG CH44 111 L3
Lyndale SKEL WN8 65 K1 1
Lyndale Av PS/BROM CH62 155 G1
WARRN/WOL WA2 121 M5
Lyndene Rd WLTN L25 115 J7
Lyndhurst SKEL WN8 65 K1
Lyndhurst Av CALD/MH L18 130 B2
PEN/TH CH61 141 J2
Lyndhurst Cl PEN/TH CH61 126 C8 3
Lyndhurst Rd CALD/MH L18 130 B1
CSBY/BLUN L23 83 J1
HOY CH47 109 G4
PEN/TH CH61 125 L8
STHP PR8 35 J3
WAL/NB CH45 95 H7
Lyndhurst Wy HUY L36 116 A3 4
Lyndon Av WGNNW/ST WN6 55 K6
Lyndon Dr CALD/MH L18 130 D1
Lyndon Gv RUNC WA7 19 J7
Lyndor Cl WLTN L25 131 K4
Lyndor Rd WLTN L25 131 K4
Lyneal Av GTS/LS CH66 162 E3
Lyneham RAIN/WH L35 117 H3
Lynham Av
WARRW/BUR WA5 120 D8 4
Lynholme Rd ANF/KKDL L4 97 K6
Lynmouth Cl WGNNW/ST WN6 68 C3 2
Lynmouth Rd AIG/SPK L17 130 A5
Lynnbank CL/PREN CH43 10 D9
Lynnbank Rd CALD/MH L18 114 F8
Lynn Cl ECCL WA10 101 L1
RUNC WA7 149 L6
Lynndene GTS/LS CH66 155 M6
Lynscott Pl CHLDW L16 114 F5
Lynsted Rd DV/KA/FCH L14 115 H2
Lynton Av WGNNW/ST WN6 68 C2
Lynton Cl ALL/GAR L19 130 D5
HES CH60 141 K7
WARRW/BUR WA5 136 A1
Lynton Crs WDN WA8 134 A3
Lynton Dr BEB CH63 143 J2
STHP PR8 35 G4
Lynton Gn WLTN L25 131 H1
Lynton Gv STHEL WA9 102 E8
Lynton Rd HUY L36 116 D2
STHP PR8 35 G5
WAL/NB CH45 95 G7
Lynton St LEIGH WN7 81 M8
Lynton Wy ECCL WA10 88 D7
Lynwood Av GOL/RIS/CU WA3 93 G7
ORM L39 62 E2
WAL/EG CH44 111 J2 9
WARRS WA4 137 L6
Lynwood Dr PEN/TH CH61 126 A7
Lynwood End ORM L39 62 E2 2
Lynwood Gdns WLT/FAZ L9 84 B8
Lynwood Rd WLT/FAZ L9 84 B8
The Lynxway WD/CROXPK L12 98 F8
Lyon Cl ECCL WA10 8 E5
Lyon Rd ANF/KKDL L4 97 K7 1
Lyons Cl MOR/LEA CH46 110 A4 2
Lyons La CHLY/EC PR7 32 F6
CHLYE PR6 32 F6
WARRS WA4 137 M7
Lyons Rd MOR/LEA CH46 110 A4
STHP PR8 2 F8
WARRW/BUR WA5 136 B1
Lyon St AIMK WN4 79 H6
ALL/GAR L19 145 L1
ECCL WA10 8 D5
WARRS WA4 138 B2
WGNS/IIMK WN3 4 D5
Lyra Rd CSBY/WL L22 82 F4
Lyster Cl GOL/RIS/CU WA3 123 H2
Lyster Rd BTL L20 6 D4
Lytham Cl WLT/FAZ L9 85 H4
Lytham Ct KKBY L32 85 L1 1
Lytham Rd AIMK WN4 79 H8
CHTN/BK PR9 25 J1
WDN WA8 134 D3
Lytham St CHLYE PR6 33 G6
Lytham Wy WD/CROXPK L12 99 H7 2
Lythgoes La WARRN/WOL WA2 14 F3
Lytles Cl FMBY L37 59 J3
Lyttelton Rd AIG/SPK L17 130 A3
Lytton Av RF/TRAN CH42 128 B4 4
Lytton Gv LITH L21 83 J7 5
Lytton St NPK/KEN L6 13 M3

M

Mabel St WGNW/BIL/O WN5 68 A7
Maberry Cl WGNNW/ST WN6 54 F6
Mab La WD/CROXPK L12 99 H5
Macalpine Cl
GR/UP/WCH CH49 110 C7 1
Macarthur Rd
WARRW/BUR WA5 120 D7 4
Macauley Pl WGNS/IIMK WN3 79 H1
Macbeth St BTL L20 7 H9
Macclesfield Cl
WGNE/HIN WN2 69 L8 1
Macdermott Rd WDN WA8 16 A9
Macdona Dr WKBY CH48 124 D5
Macdonald Av
RNFD/HAY WA11 90 A8 1
WGNS/IIMK WN3 79 J2 1
Macdonald Dr
GR/UP/WCH CH49 125 M2 1
Macdonald Rd MOR/LEA CH46 109 L5
Macdonald St WAV L15 114 A5
WGNW/BIL/O WN5 67 K7
Mace Rd NG/CROX L11 98 E2
Macfarren St
CLB/OSW/ST L13 114 C2 2
Mackay Cft CHLYE PR6 32 F5 7
Mackenzie Av WGNS/IIMK WN3 79 J2
Mackenzie Rd MOR/LEA CH46 110 D2
Mackenzie St NPK/KEN L6 97 J8 5
Mackenzie Cl CHLYE PR6 32 F5 8
Mackets Cl WLTN L25 131 L4
Macket's La WLTN L25 131 L4
Mack Gv NTHTN L30 83 M3
Macqueen St CLB/OSW/ST L13 114 C3
Maddock Rd WAL/EG CH44 95 M8
Maddocks St CLB/OSW/ST L13 114 C3
Maddock St BIRK CH41 10 F2
Maddrell St VAUX/LVPD L3 12 D1
Madelaine St TOX L8 113 J7
Madeley Cl WGNS/IIMK WN3 79 G2 3
WKBY CH48 124 D4 1
Madeley Dr WKBY CH48 124 D4
Madeley St NPK/KEN L6 113 L2 2
Madeline Mckenna Ct
WDN WA8 133 L2 8
Madiera Dr WLTN L25 115 K7
Madryn Av NWD/KWIPK L33 86 C3
Madryn St TOX L8 113 J8
Maelor Cl BEB CH63 143 K7
Maesbrook Cl CHTN/BK PR9 23 K8 1
Mafeking Cl WAV L15 114 B5 2
Mafeking Pl AIMK WN4 91 L2 5
Magazine Av WAL/NB CH45 95 K6 6
Magazine Brow WAL/NB CH45 95 L6
Magazine La PS/BROM CH62 144 A2
WAL/NB CH45 95 L6
Magazine Rd PS/BROM CH62 143 M2
Magazines Prom WAL/NB CH45 95 L6
Magdala St TOX L8 113 L6
Magdalen Dr AIMK WN4 91 H1
Magdalene Sq NTHTN L30 84 B1 4
Maggots Nook Rd
RNFD/HAY WA11 76 C4
Maghull La MGHL L31 73 K4
Maghull St CLVPS L1 112 E5 5
Magnolia Cl GTS/LS CH66 163 H4
HLWD L26 131 M3 5
RNFD/HAY WA11 90 B8 5
WARR WA1 123 G6 4
Magnolia Dr RUNC WA7 161 H1 8
Magnolia Wk
GR/UP/WCH CH49 125 L3
Magnum St EV L5 97 G8
Maguire Av BTL L20 7 M3
Mahon Av BTL L20 83 M7
Maiden La CLB/OSW/ST L13 97 M6
Maidford Rd DV/KA/FCH L14 99 H8
Maidstone Cl WGNE/HIN WN2 81 L3
Main Av ECCL WA10 101 L5
Main Cl RNFD/HAY WA11 90 C7
Main Dr RAIN/WH L35 117 G4
Main Front RAIN/WH L35 117 G4
Main La GOL/RIS/CU WA3 106 A2
Main Rd PS/BROM CH62 143 K1
Mains Av WGNE/HIN WN2 80 B6
Mainside Rd KKBY L32 86 B4
Mains La BRSC L40 40 B7
Main St FROD/HEL WA6 160 C5
RUNC WA7 150 B5
WGNW/BIL/O WN5 78 A8
Maintree Crs SPK/HALE L24 147 J1
Mainwaring Rd PS/BROM CH62 143 M5
WAL/EG CH44 111 M2
Mairesfield Av WARRS WA4 138 D3
Mairscough La ORM L39 61 J5
Maitland Cl TOX L8 113 K6
Maitland Rd WAL/NB CH45 95 L5 1
Maitland St TOX L8 113 K6 5
Major Cross St WDN WA8 16 D5 1
Major St EV L5 96 F7 8
WGNW/BIL/O WN5 67 L7
Makerfield Dr NEWLW WA12 91 J8
Makerfield Wy WGNE/HIN WN2 69 K6
Makinson Av WGNE/HIN WN2 69 M6
Makin St ANF/KKDL L4 97 H3
Malcolm Av WARRN/WOL WA2 121 M4
Malcolm Crs BEB CH63 143 L7
Malcolm Gv BTL L20 7 J8
Malcolm Pl WAV L15 114 B4 1
Malcolm St RUNC WA7 19 K4
Malden Rd NPK/KEN L6 113 L2
Maldon Cl HLWD L26 132 B7
WGNE/HIN WN2 69 H3
Maldon Rd WGNNW/ST WN6 56 B5
Maldwyn Rd WAL/EG CH44 95 K8
Maley Cl TOX L8 129 J1
Malham Av WGNS/IIMK WN3 79 J3
Malham Cl LEIGH WN7 81 L8
STHP PR8 36 A2
Malhamdale Av RAIN/WH L35 117 M3
Malin Cl SPK/HALE L24 147 M3
Maliston Rd WARRW/BUR WA5 120 D8
Mallaby St BIRK CH41 10 B2
Mallard Cl HLWD L26 132 A4
ORM L39 62 E3 1
RUNC WA7 150 B8 4
WARRN/WOL WA2 121 M2
WD/CROXPK L12 99 H2 2
Mallard Gdns STHEL WA9 102 A7
Mallard La GOL/RIS/CU WA3 123 H2
Mallard Wy MOR/LEA CH46 109 L4
RNFD/HAY WA11 89 K7
Mallee Av CHTN/BK PR9 25 J2
Mallee Crs CHTN/BK PR9 25 J2
Malleson Rd CLB/OSW/ST L13 98 A6
Mallins Cl TOX L8 129 J1 15
Mallom Av CHLY/EC PR7 32 A4
Mallory Av MGHL L31 72 D1
Mallory Gv RNFD/HAY WA11 89 M7
Mallory Rd EP CH65 163 J1
RF/TRAN CH42 127 M3
Mallowdale Cl PS/BROM CH62 144 A8
Mallow Rd NPK/KEN L6 113 L2
Mallow Wy HUY L36 116 B5
Malmesbury Cl
GR/UP/WCH CH49 125 L1 4
Malmesbury Pk RUNC WA7 150 F2
Malmesbury Rd NG/CROX L11 98 A3
Malpas Av CL/PREN CH43 127 J3 2
WGN WN1 5 H1
Malpas Dr BEB CH63 128 A6
WARRW/BUR WA5 136 E1
Malpas Gv WAL/NB CH45 95 J7
Malpas Rd EP CH65 163 H1
NG/CROX L11 85 M8
RUNC WA7 149 K6
WAL/NB CH45 95 H7
Malpas Wy
WARRW/BUR WA5 136 E1 2
Malta Cl HUY L36 115 M2
Malta St TOX L8 113 H8
Maltkiln La BRSC L40 40 D5
ORM L39 63 G5
Maltmans Rd LYMM WA13 139 M2
Malton Av GOL/RIS/CU WA3 93 G6
Malton Cl LEIGH WN7 81 L7
WDN WA8 117 L8
Malton Rd WLTN L25 131 L4
Malt St TOX L8 113 K5
Malvern Av DV/KA/FCH L14 115 H3
EP CH65 20 D8
WGNE/HIN WN2 81 J1
Malvern Cl AIMK WN4 91 K1
HOR/BR BL6 45 L8
KKBY L32 85 L1
WARRW/BUR WA5 120 C5
WGNS/IIMK WN3 78 E2
Malvern Crs DV/KA/FCH L14 115 H3 1
WGNE/HIN WN2 80 B1
Malvern Gv RF/TRAN CH42 127 M3
WLT/FAZ L9 84 E3
Malvern Rd BTL L20 83 L8
NPK/KEN L6 113 L2
STHEL WA9 103 H2
WAL/NB CH45 94 F8
Malvern St WGNNW/ST WN6 55 L2
Malwood St TOX L8 129 H1 10
Manchester Rd CHTN/BK PR9 3 J2
GOL/RIS/CU WA3 123 K6
HOR/BR BL6 57 M4
PR/KW L34 100 F8
WARR WA1 15 J4
WARR WA1 123 J6 1
WGN WN1 5 L4
WGNE/HIN WN2 69 J6
Manchester Rw
NEWLW WA12 104 F5 1
Manchester St (Queensway)
CLVPS L1 13 G6
Mancroft Cl WARR WA1 123 G6 5
Manderville Cl
WGNS/IIMK WN3 78 F3 2
Mandeville Rd STHP PR8 34 D8
Mandeville St ANF/KKDL L4 97 H3
Manesty's La CLVPS L1 13 G8
Manfield SKEL WN8 65 J2
Manica Crs AIN/FAZ L10 85 H7
Manion Av MGHL L31 61 K8
Manion Cl MGHL L31 61 K8
Manley Av GOL/RIS/CU WA3 92 B3
Manley Cl CL/PREN CH43 127 H2
LEIGH WN7 81 M5
Manley Gdns WARRW/BUR WA5 14 A5
Manley La FROD/HEL WA6 166 A8
Manley Pl STHEL WA9 102 A6 3
Manley Rd CSBY/WL L22 82 E3
FROD/HEL WA6 166 F5
HUY L36 116 C5
Manley St WGNS/IIMK WN3 5 J8
Manley Vw CHNE CH2 165 L2
Manna Dr CHNE CH2 165 L2 3
Mannering Rd AIG/SPK L17 129 K1
Manners La HES CH60 141 G7
Manning Av WGNNW/ST WN6 68 C3
Manningham Rd NPK/KEN L6 97 K7
Manning Rd STHP PR8 25 G7
Manning St ECCL WA10 8 E6
Mannington Cl HOY CH47 109 G5 2
Mann Island VAUX/LVPD L3 12 D8
Mann St TOX L8 113 G7
Manor Av BRSC L40 51 M3
CSBY/BLUN L23 70 F8
GOL/RIS/CU WA3 92 E5
NEWLW WA12 104 B1
RAIN/WH L35 117 L3
Manorbier Crs WLT/FAZ L9 97 J2
Manor Cl AIMK WN4 90 E2
BTL L20 7 M6
NSTN CH64 152 E6
WARR WA1 122 F6
WD/CROXPK L12 98 F2
Manor Ct GOL/RIS/CU WA3 92 E5
Manor Crs BRSC L40 51 M3
WLTN L25 131 K4
Manor Dr BRSC L40 51 M3
CSBY/BLUN L23 70 F8
GR/UP/WCH CH49 110 B6
NTHTN L30 84 D2
Manor Farm Crs CH/BCN CH1 162 D5
Manor Farm Rd HUY L36 116 B4
RUNC WA7 150 F1
Manor Fell RUNC WA7 150 D6
Manorfield Cl CH/BCN CH1 162 C5
Manor Gdns BRSC L40 51 M3
Manor Gv KKBY L32 85 K3
SKEL WN8 65 H4
WGNE/HIN WN2 57 K8
WGNW/BIL/O WN5 67 K5
Manor Hl CL/PREN CH43 10 A6
Manor House Cl MGHL L31 72 E4
RNFD/HAY WA11 89 J3
Manor House Dr SKEL WN8 77 G2
Manorial Rd NSTN CH64 152 E5
Manorial Rd South NSTN CH64 152 E5
Manor La GTS/LS CH66 162 F2
RF/TRAN CH42 128 C3
WAL/NB CH45 95 L8
Manor Ldg FMBY L37 59 G1
Manor Park Av RUNC WA7 150 E1
Manor Park Dr GTS/LS CH66 162 F3
Manor Pl PS/BROM CH62 128 F8
WGNS/IIMK WN3 5 L8
Manor Rd BEB CH63 142 B4
BRSC L40 51 M3
CHTN/BK PR9 25 J3
CSBY/BLUN L23 70 E7
FROD/HEL WA6 160 E4
HOY CH47 108 E5
PEN/TH CH61 125 M7
PS/BROM CH62 144 A7
RNFD/HAY WA11 91 J6
RUNC WA7 149 M3
WAL/EG CH44 95 K8
WDN WA8 133 K4
WGNNW/ST WN6 55 H7
WLTN L25 131 K4
Manorside Cl
GR/UP/WCH CH49 110 B7 3
Manor St GOL/RIS/CU WA3 92 D4 2
STHEL WA9 9 L8
WGN WN1 4 D4
WGNW/BIL/O WN5 68 B7
Manor Vw WD/CROXPK L12 99 H4
Manor Wy WLTN L25 131 K4
Manorwood Dr RAIN/WH L35 117 G3
Manse Av WGNNW/ST WN6 42 B7
Manse Gdns NEWLW WA12 104 F1
Mansell Cl WDN WA8 118 E8 1
Mansell Dr HLWD L26 132 A7
Mansell Rd NPK/KEN L6 113 K2
Mansfield Cl GOL/RIS/CU WA3 123 J1
Mansfield Rd EP CH65 163 J3
Mansfield St GOL/RIS/CU WA3 92 A4
VAUX/LVPD L3 13 J4
Manston Gv CHLY/EC PR7 32 C6
Manston Rd WARRW/BUR WA5 136 B2
Manton Rd NPK/KEN L6 113 L2
Manuel Perez Rd
WARRW/BUR WA5 120 D7 5
Manvers Rd CHLDW L16 115 G4
Manville Rd WAL/NB CH45 95 K6
Manville St STHEL WA9 102 E4
Manx Jane's La CHTN/BK PR9 25 J1
Manx Rd WARRS WA4 137 K2
Maori Dr FROD/HEL WA6 160 C5
Maple Av BRSC L40 52 A1 3
GOL/RIS/CU WA3 93 H6
GTS/LS CH66 155 L7
NEWLW WA12 104 F3
RNFD/HAY WA11 90 D6
RUNC WA7 19 M7
WDN WA8 16 F1 2
WGNE/HIN WN2 5 M7
Maple Cl FMBY L37 58 E4
LITH L21 83 J7
RAIN/WH L35 117 G2
WD/CROXPK L12 98 F2 4
WGNW/BIL/O WN5 77 M8
Maple Crs HUY L36 115 M3
WARRW/BUR WA5 136 B1
Mapledale Rd CALD/MH L18 114 C8
Maple Dr WGNE/HIN WN2 80 D6
Maple Gv CHLYE PR6 32 F2
ECCL WA10 101 L2
GTS/LS CH66 163 J4
PS/BROM CH62 143 L5
RAIN/WH L35 101 G8
TOX L8 113 L7
WARRS WA4 137 M2
WGNNW/ST WN6 68 C2
Maple Rd WARR WA1 123 G6
WARRN/WOL WA2 105 K7
Maple St AIMK WN4 79 J7
BIRK CH41 11 G8
STHP PR8 3 M6
Mapleton Cl CL/PREN CH43 127 G4
Mapleton Dr RUNC WA7 161 H2
Maple Tree Gv HES CH60 141 L4 1
Maplewood KKBY L32 86 B5 4
SKEL WN8 65 J1
Maplewood Cl NTHLY L27 116 A8 3
Maplewood Gv CL/PREN CH43 111 G5
Mapplewell Crs
WARRW/BUR WA5 120 C7
Marathon Cl NPK/KEN L6 13 M2
Marble Cl BTL L20 7 G7
Marbury Gdns EP CH65 156 B7
Marbury Gv WGNNW/ST WN6 56 A5
Marbury Rd KKBY L32 85 L3
Marbury St WARRS WA4 15 G8
Marc Av MGHL L31 85 K1
Marcham Wy NG/CROX L11 98 D4
Marchant Cl NTHTN L30 84 C5
Marchbank WGNE/HIN WN2 69 J3 4
Marchbank Rd SKEL WN8 64 F4
Marchfield Rd WLT/FAZ L9 84 B8
March Rd NPK/KEN L6 97 M8
Marchwiel Rd EP CH65 20 F6
Marchwood Wy WLTN L25 115 J6 1
Marcien Wy WDN WA8 134 B2
Marcot Rd NPK/KEN L6 113 M1
Marcross Cl WARRW/BUR WA5 121 G4
Marcus St BIRK CH41 11 J3
Mardale Av RNFD/HAY WA11 89 K5
WARRN/WOL WA2 121 L2
Mardale Cl NTHLY L27 132 C2 1
STHP PR8 47 K1
Mardale Rd HUY L36 99 L8
NTHLY L27 132 C2
Mareth Cl CALD/MH L18 130 C3
Marewood CHLY/EC PR7 32 D3
Marford Rd WD/CROXPK L12 98 D6
Marfords Av BEB CH63 143 L6
Margaret Av BTL L20 83 L6
STHEL WA9 102 E5 4
WARR WA1 122 D6
WGNNW/ST WN6 67 L1
Margaret Ct WDN WA8 16 E6 2
Margaret Rd ANF/KKDL L4 7 M7
CSBY/BLUN L23 70 C8
Margaret's La GTS/LS CH66 155 J6
Margaret St NPK/KEN L6 113 J1
STHEL WA9 119 G2 3
WGNE/HIN WN2 69 M7
WGNNW/ST WN6 4 B2
Margery Rd ECCL WA10 101 L4 1
Marian Av NEWLW WA12 104 A2
Marian Cl RAIN/WH L35 117 L3
The Marian Cl NTHTN L30 84 A1 3
Marian Dr MOR/LEA CH46 110 A5
RAIN/WH L35 117 K3
Marian Rd RNFD/HAY WA11 91 G6
Marians Dr ORM L39 51 G5
The Marian Sq NTHTN L30 84 A2 1
The Marian Wy NTHTN L30 84 A2
Maria Rd WLT/FAZ L9 97 H2
Marie Curie Av NTHTN L30 84 B1 5
NTHTN L30 84 B2 4
Marie Dr WARRS WA4 138 F3
Marigold St WGNW/BIL/O WN5 67 M6
Marina Av LITH L21 83 K5
STHEL WA9 102 E6
WARRW/BUR WA5 136 D1
Marina Crs HUY L36 115 M4
NTHTN L30 84 C4
Marina Dr EP CH65 20 C5 1
WARRN/WOL WA2 121 L4
WGNW/BIL/O WN5 67 M8
Marina Gv RUNC WA7 19 K4
Marina La RUNC WA7 151 G6
Marina Rd FMBY L37 59 H4
Marina Village RUNC WA7 151 G6 1
Marine Crs CSBY/WL L22 82 F4
Marine Dr CHTN/BK PR9 22 A8
HES CH60 140 F6
STHP PR8 2 C2
Marine Pde STHP PR8 2 E1
Marine Pk WKBY CH48 124 D1
Marine Prom WAL/NB CH45 95 K4
Mariner Cl RUNC WA7 150 F7
Marine Rd HOY CH47 108 C6
Mariners Rd CSBY/BLUN L23 82 D3
WAL/NB CH45 95 L6 7
Mariners Whf VAUX/LVPD L3 112 E7
Marine Ter CSBY/WL L22 82 F5
Marion Dr RUNC WA7 149 H7
Marion Gv CALD/MH L18 130 E3
Marion Pl WGNE/HIN WN2 80 B5
Marion Rd BTL L20 83 M7
Marion St BIRK CH41 11 K5
Maritime Cl NEWLW WA12 91 L8 1
Maritime Ct NTHTN L30 72 B8
Maritime Pk BIRK CH41 10 F7 2
Maritime Pl VAUX/LVPD L3 13 K4 1
Maritime Vw RF/TRAN CH42 127 M2 2
Maritime Wy CLVPS L1 13 G9
Mariton Cl CALD/MH L18 130 F3
Marius Cl ANF/KKDL L4 97 H5 5
Mark Av GTS/LS CH66 162 E1
Market Pl BIRK CH41 11 K6
CHLY/EC PR7 44 C6
PR/KW L34 100 F7 10
WGN WN1 4 E4
WGNNW/ST WN6 56 A4 4
Market St BIRK CH41 11 L5
CHLY/EC PR7 32 E5
CHLY/EC PR7 44 C7
EP CH65 20 B6
HOY CH47 108 D6
NEWLW WA12 104 C1
STHP PR8 2 F4
WDN WA8 16 D5
WGN WN1 4 E3
WGNE/HIN WN2 69 M8
WGNNW/ST WN6 56 A4
Markfield Crs RNFD/HAY WA11 9 M1
WLTN L25 131 M4
Markfield Rd BTL L20 83 K8
Markham Dr STHP PR8 36 A3
Marklands Rd HOR/BR BL6 45 M8
Markland St WGN WN1 5 K5
Mark Rake PS/BROM CH62 143 M4
Mark Rd HTWN L38 70 B1
Mark St EV L5 97 G7
Marksway PEN/TH CH61 141 J1
Marlborough SKEL WN8 65 J1 2
Marlborough Av MGHL L31 72 F2 4
NTHTN L30 84 C3
WGNE/HIN WN2 80 B1
Marlborough Crs WARRS WA4 138 B3
WDN WA8 118 C8 3
Marlborough Dr
FROD/HEL WA6 166 D3 2
Marlborough Gv CL/PREN CH43 10 E9
Marlborough Pl
VAUX/LVPD L3 12 F4 2
Marlborough Rd CHTN/BK PR9 3 K3
CLB/OSW/ST L13 97 M7

CSBY/BLUN L23 82 F2
CSBY/WL L22 83 G5
EP CH65 20 E9
PR/KW L34 101 G6
WAL/NB CH45 95 L6 5
Marlborough St CHLYE PR6 33 G4
VAUX/LVPD L3 12 F4
Marlbrook Rd WLTN L25 115 K7 4
Marldon Av CSBY/BLUN L23 83 G3
Marldon Rd WD/CROXPK L12 98 D5
Marled Hey STBRV L28 99 J5
Marley Cl RAIN/WH L35 118 A4 1
Marlfield La PEN/TH CH61 141 J1
Marlfield Rd WARRS WA4 138 C3
WD/CROXPK L12 98 D7
Marl Gv WGNW/BIL/O WN5 77 M1
Marline Av BEB CH63 143 L7
Marling Cl FROD/HEL WA6 160 F7
Marling Pk WDN WA8 133 K4
Marlow Cl GOL/RIS/CU WA3 106 E8 5
Marlowe Cl ALL/GAR L19 130 E8 5
WDN WA8 16 A2
WGNS/IIMK WN3 68 C8 5
Marlowe Dr WD/CROXPK L12 98 C5
Marlowe Rd NSTN CH64 153 G5 2
WAL/EG CH44 111 J1
Marl Rd NTHTN L30 84 D2
NWD/KWIPK L33 86 E2
Marlsford St NPK/KEN L6 113 L2 3
Marlston Av PEN/TH CH61 126 B7
Marlston Pl RUNC WA7 149 K7
Marlwood Av WAL/EG CH44 95 G8
Marmaduke St EHL/KEN L7 113 K4
Marmion Av BTL L20 84 A6
Marmion Cl GOL/RIS/CU WA3 93 G4
Marmion Rd AIG/SPK L17 129 K1
HOY CH47 108 D6
Marmonde St ANF/KKDL L4 97 G5 8
Marnwood Rd KKBY L32 85 M4
Marple Cl CL/PREN CH43 127 G2
WGNNW/ST WN6 55 J3
Marquis St BIRK CH41 11 J9
PS/BROM CH62 128 D6
VAUX/LVPD L3 13 K6
Marram Cl MOR/LEA CH46 110 C4
Marrick Cl WGNS/IIMK WN3 79 J3
Marron Av WARRN/WOL WA2 121 K3
Marsden Av ECCL WA10 8 A3
WARRS WA4 138 C1
Marsden Cl CHLY/EC PR7 30 D6 2
WAL/EG CH44 95 M8 1
Marsden Rd CHTN/BK PR9 25 G6
HLWD L26 132 B7
Marsden St NPK/KEN L6 113 J2
WGN WN1 4 E3
WGNE/HIN WN2 80 B1 6
WGNW/BIL/O WN5 68 B6
Marsden Wy NPK/KEN L6 113 J2 11
Marshall Av STHEL WA9 102 E5 5
WARRW/BUR WA5 121 H3
Marshall Pl VAUX/LVPD L3 12 F2 1
Marshall Rd WARR WA1 122 F6
Marshallsay FMBY L37 59 J3 3
Marshall's Cl MGHL L31 72 E1
Marshalls Cross Rd STHEL WA9 102 E5
Marshall St BIRK CH41 10 F2
Marsham Cl
GR/UP/WCH CH49 110 C6 3
Marsham Rd WLTN L25 115 L8
Marsh Av BTL L20 84 A7
Marsh Brows FMBY L37 59 G3
The Marshes La
KIRK/FR/WA PR4 27 J4
Marshfield Cl HUY L36 116 B2
Marshfield Ct MOR/LEA CH46 110 A2
Marshfield Rd NG/CROX L11 98 D4
Marshgate WDN WA8 133 K7
Marshgate Pl FROD/HEL WA6 160 E3
Marshgate Rd NG/CROX L11 98 D3
Marsh Gn WGNW/BIL/O WN5 67 M4
Marsh Hall Rd WDN WA8 134 D1
Marsh House La
WARRN/WOL WA2 15 H2
Marshlands Rd NSTN CH64 153 G8
WAL/NB CH45 95 G7
Marsh La BEB CH63 127 L6
BTL L20 6 E2
CHNE CH2 158 C7
CHNE CH2 165 K2
FROD/HEL WA6 160 C5
HTWN L38 70 F1
RUNC WA7 150 B2 1
WARRW/BUR WA5 135 L3
WGN WN1 4 F3
Marsh Moss La BRSC L40 38 E6
Marsh Rd CHTN/BK PR9 23 L4
Marsh Rw WGNE/HIN WN2 81 J1
Marshside Cl TOX L8 113 H8 5
Marshside Rd CHTN/BK PR9 22 A8
Marsh St BTL L20 7 J9
STHEL WA9 9 M5
WARR WA1 15 K2
WDN WA8 16 C8
Marsland Gv STHEL WA9 103 G5
Marson St WARRN/WOL WA2 14 D4
Marston Cl CL/PREN CH43 127 H3
PS/BROM CH62 155 G2
Marston Crs HTWN L38 70 C3
Marten Av BEB CH63 143 L6
Martensen St EHL/KEN L7 113 K4
Martham Cl WARRS WA4 138 C2
Martin Av ECCL WA10 89 H7
NEWLW WA12 91 K8
WARRN/WOL WA2 121 M4
Martin Cl CALD/MH L18 130 C4
PEN/TH CH61 125 L7
RAIN/WH L35 117 J1
RUNC WA7 150 C6
Martindale Crs
WGNW/BIL/O WN5 68 A7
Martindale Gv RUNC WA7 149 M8
Martindale Rd CALD/MH L18 114 F8
PS/BROM CH62 144 A4
RNFD/HAY WA11 89 K3
WGNW/BIL/O WN5 89 M1
Martine Cl MGHL L31 85 K1 3
Martin Gv RAIN/WH L35 101 G8
Martinhall Rd WLT/FAZ L9 98 B1 3
Martin La BRSC L40 38 A5
Martin Rd CALD/MH L18 130 C4
FROD/HEL WA6 160 D5
Martins Av CHLY/EC PR7 44 A3
Martins La SKEL WN8 65 M6
WAL/EG CH44 111 L1
Martland Av AIN/FAZ L10 85 G2
GOL/RIS/CU WA3 92 F6
WGNNW/ST WN6 55 H8
Martland Crs WGNNW/ST WN6 68 A2
Martland Mill La
WGNW/BIL/O WN5 67 M3
Martland Rd WLTN L25 131 L1
Mart La BRSC L40 39 G8
Martlesham Crs
GR/UP/WCH CH49 125 K2
Martlett Rd WD/CROXPK L12 98 F8
Martock RAIN/WH L35 117 H3
Marton Cl GOL/RIS/CU WA3 107 G1 1
SPK/HALE L24 146 F3 2
Marton Gn SPK/HALE L24 146 F3 3
Marton Rd HUY L36 100 A7
Marton St WGN WN1 4 E2
Marus Av WGNS/IIMK WN3 79 H2
Marvin St NPK/KEN L6 113 J2 12
Marwick Cl WGNNW/ST WN6 55 M3
Mary Av STHP PR8 35 G7
Marybone VAUX/LVPD L3 12 F5
Maryfield Cl GOL/RIS/CU WA3 92 C6 5
Maryhill Rd RUNC WA7 19 G8
Maryland La MOR/LEA CH46 109 M4
Maryland St CLVPS L1 13 K9 6
Marylebone Av STHEL WA9 102 B7
Marylebone Pl WGN WN1 68 F2
Mary Rd BTL L20 83 M7
Mary St STHEL WA9 119 G2 4
WDN WA8 17 K5
Maryton Gra CALD/MH L18 130 F3 1
Maryville Rd PR/KW L34 101 G7
Marywell Cl STHEL WA9 102 F6 6
Masefield Av LEIGH WN7 81 M6
WDN WA8 16 B4
WGNW/BIL/O WN5 67 J7
Masefield Crs NTHTN L30 83 M5
Masefield Dr WGNS/IIMK WN3 79 H1
Masefield Gv CHLDW L16 115 H5
ECCL WA10 8 A1
Masefield Pl NTHTN L30 84 A5
Masefield Rd CSBY/BLUN L23 71 L7
Maskell Rd CLB/OSW/ST L13 114 B2
Mason Av WARR WA1 122 A5
WDN WA8 134 C1
Mason Cl AIMK WN4 91 M1 3
GTS/LS CH66 162 F3
Mason St CHLYE PR6 33 G3
CSBY/WL L22 82 F4
EHL/KEN L7 113 J4
RUNC WA7 19 L2
WAL/NB CH45 95 K5 5
WARR WA1 15 H6
WGNE/HIN WN2 80 D5 5
WGNS/IIMK WN3 4 C5
WLTN L25 131 J3
Massam's La FMBY L37 47 G7
Massey Av LYMM WA13 139 J3
WARRW/BUR WA5 121 H3
Massey Brook La LYMM WA13 139 K3
Masseyfield Rd RUNC WA7 150 C8
Massey Pk WAL/NB CH45 95 J8
Massey St BIRK CH41 11 G2
STHEL WA9 102 E5
Mather Av ALL/GAR L19 130 F6
CALD/MH L18 130 D1
GOL/RIS/CU WA3 93 G7
RUNC WA7 18 B9
STHEL WA9 103 G2 1
Mathers Cl WARRN/WOL WA2 122 C1 1
Matheson Dr WGNW/BIL/O WN5 67 M5
Mathew St CLVP L2 12 F7
Mathieson Rd WDN WA8 134 A8
Matlock Av WLT/FAZ L9 84 C7 4
Matlock Cl WARRW/BUR WA5 120 C4 2
Matlock Rd STHP PR8 35 K2
Matterdale Cl FROD/HEL WA6 160 F6
Matthew Cl WAL/EG CH44 112 A3 14
Matthews St WARR WA1 15 J2
Matthew St WAL/EG CH44 112 A3
Matty's La FROD/HEL WA6 160 C6
Maud St CHLY/EC PR7 32 D7
TOX L8 113 J7
Maunders Ct CSBY/BLUN L23 71 H8
Mauretania Rd ANF/KKDL L4 97 J3
Mavis Dr CHLY/EC PR7 43 G4
GR/UP/WCH CH49 126 C2
Mawdsley Av WARR WA1 123 G6
Mawdsley Cl FMBY L37 59 K2 4
Mawdsley Ter ORM L39 51 H5
Mawson Cl WARRW/BUR WA5 120 F5
Max Rd DV/KA/FCH L14 99 H8
Maxton Rd NPK/KEN L6 113 L2
Maxwell Cl EP CH65 163 J3
GR/UP/WCH CH49 110 C7 2
Maxwell Pl CLB/OSW/ST L13 98 B7
Maxwell Rd CLB/OSW/ST L13 98 B7
Maxwell St ECCL WA10 8 D6
GOL/RIS/CU WA3 107 G7
May Av LEIGH WN7 81 M7
WAL/EG CH44 111 M3
WGNE/HIN WN2 80 E6
Maybank Cl CHTN/BK PR9 25 J4
Maybank Gv AIG/SPK L17 130 B4 1
Maybank Rd RF/TRAN CH42 127 M1
Mayberry Gv WARRN/WOL WA2 122 C4
Maybury Wy AIG/SPK L17 129 L3 3
Mayer Av BEB CH63 143 H1
Mayew Rd PEN/TH CH61 126 B7
Mayfair Av CSBY/BLUN L23 71 G8
DV/KA/FCH L14 115 H3
Mayfair Cl HTWN L38 70 B3
NPK/KEN L6 113 K1 4
WARRW/BUR WA5 119 M6
Mayfair Dr WGNE/HIN WN2 69 M3
WGNS/IIMK WN3 79 H3
Mayfair Gv WDN WA8 133 M4
Mayfayre Av MGHL L31 61 K8 2
Mayfield ANF/KKDL L4 97 G5
Mayfield Av CHLYE PR6 44 C6
FMBY L37 58 E4
STHEL WA9 102 A5
WDN WA8 133 K4
Mayfield Cl WD/CROXPK L12 98 F7 3
Mayfield Ct FMBY L37 47 G8
Mayfield Dr GOL/RIS/CU WA3 93 L5
LEIGH WN7 93 L5
PS/BROM CH62 144 D7
Mayfield Gdns ALL/GAR L19 130 B6
Mayfield Rd ALL/GAR L19 130 C6
BEB CH63 143 J2
CHLYE PR6 32 F4
SKEL WN8 66 D6
WAL/NB CH45 95 G8
WARRS WA4 138 C3
WGNW/BIL/O WN5 67 K5
Mayfields North
PS/BROM CH62 128 D6
Mayfields South
PS/BROM CH62 128 D6 2
Mayfield St AIMK WN4 91 J2 2
Mayflower Av SPK/HALE L24 131 J7
Maynard St TOX L8 113 K6 6
May Pl VAUX/LVPD L3 13 K8
Maypole Ct NTHTN L30 71 M8 1
May Rd HES CH60 141 J5
May St BTL L20 7 H2
GOL/RIS/CU WA3 92 D3
LEIGH WN7 81 L8
VAUX/LVPD L3 13 K8
Maythorn Av GOL/RIS/CU WA3 106 C6
Maytree Cl NTHLY L27 115 L7 4
May Tree Dr WGN WN1 68 D2
Maytree Wk SKEL WN8 65 K1
Mayville Rd CALD/MH L18 114 D8
Mazzini Cl EV L5 97 G8
Mcbride St ALL/GAR L19 130 E7
Mc Carthy Cl GOL/RIS/CU WA3 123 J2
Mc Clellan Pl WDN WA8 16 E2
Mccormack Av STHEL WA9 103 G1
Mccormack Dr WGN WN1 5 H4
Mcculloch St STHEL WA9 9 K5
Mcfarlane Av ECCL WA10 101 L1
Mcgarva Wy EP CH65 20 C7
Mcgough Cl STHEL WA9 118 C2 2
Mcgregor St EV L5 97 G8 4
Mckee Av WARRN/WOL WA2 121 K3
Mckeown Cl EV L5 96 F8 5
Mcminnis Av STHEL WA9 103 J3
Mcvinnie Rd RAIN/WH L35 101 H7
Mead Av LITH L21 83 L5
Meade Cl RAIN/WH L35 117 M4
Meade Rd CLB/OSW/ST L13 98 A7
Meadfoot Rd MOR/LEA CH46 109 M4
Meadow Av STHEL WA9 118 F2 2
STHP PR8 35 L1
WARRS WA4 137 J3
Meadow Bank MGHL L31 72 D3 2
ORM L39 51 H8 1
Meadowbank Cl
WD/CROXPK L12 99 G8
Meadowbridge Cl BRSC L40 64 A1 2
Meadowbrook BRSC L40 51 M3
Meadow Brook Cl AIN/FAZ L10 85 K6
Meadowbrook Rd
MOR/LEA CH46 109 M6
Meadow Brow CHTN/BK PR9 22 F8
Meadow Cl BRSC L40 64 A1
FROD/HEL WA6 166 D2 2
NSTN CH64 153 G7
NSTN CH64 154 B5 1
SKEL WN8 65 M6
WDN WA8 133 M2
Meadow Clough SKEL WN8 65 K1 2
Meadow Crs GR/UP/WCH CH49 126 D3
Meadow Cft NSTN CH64 154 A5
Meadowcroft AIMK WN4 79 H7
CHLY/EC PR7 31 K2
FMBY L37 59 H3 1
HES CH60 141 L4
SKEL WN8 65 K1 3
STHEL WA9 102 E7
Meadowcroft Pk
WD/CROXPK L12 114 F1
Meadowcroft Rd HOY CH47 109 G4 1
Meadow Dr HUY L36 116 B5
ORM L39 62 E3
Meadowfield Cl
RF/TRAN CH42 128 B3 3
Meadow Hey BTL L20 83 J8
Meadow Hey Cl WLTN L25 131 K2 2
Meadowlands CHLY/EC PR7 42 F1
Meadow La BRSC L40 39 L5
BRSC L40 52 E2
EP CH65 20 E3
LEY/BBR PR5 28 F4
MGHL L31 73 G4
NSTN CH64 154 A4
RF/TRAN CH42 128 B3
STHEL WA9 103 H4
STHP PR8 47 L2
WARRN/WOL WA2 122 C3
WD/CROXPK L12 98 D6
Meadow Oak Dr WLTN L25 131 J1
Meadow Pk RF/TRAN CH42 128 B3 5
Meadow Pit La WGNE/HIN WN2 57 K5
Meadow Rd WKBY CH48 125 H2
Meadows Cl
WGNE/HIN WN2 69 M8 17
Meadows Gn GOL/RIS/CU WA3 93 G8
Meadowside LEY/BBR PR5 29 J3
MOR/LEA CH46 110 D1
Meadowside Av AIMK WN4 79 J5 3
Meadowside Dr
NWD/KWIPK L33 74 B7
Meadowside Rd
PS/BROM CH62 143 M6
WGNE/HIN WN2 81 J1 2
Meadows St WGNNW/ST WN6 4 A2
The Meadows CHLY/EC PR7 41 M3
NSTN CH64 153 H7
RAIN/WH L35 117 L3
Meadow St CHLYE PR6 44 C7
WAL/NB CH45 95 J5
The Meadow
GR/UP/WCH CH49 126 D3
Meadowvale Dr
WGNW/BIL/O WN5 67 L7 3
Meadow Vw CHNE CH2 165 J2
LITH L21 83 K2
STHP PR8 35 M1 2
Meadow View Dr
FROD/HEL WA6 160 C6 1
Meadow Wk PEN/TH CH61 141 G2
Meadow Wy CHLY/EC PR7 42 F5
NG/CROX L11 98 D4
Mead Rd WARR WA1 122 C5
Meadway GOL/RIS/CU WA3 92 F5
GR/UP/WCH CH49 110 D7
GTS/LS CH66 155 K6
HES CH60 141 H7
MGHL L31 72 D6
NTHTN L30 84 B3
PS/BROM CH62 143 L3
RAIN/WH L35 117 H1
RUNC WA7 149 M4
WAL/NB CH45 95 J8 2
WAV L15 114 E5
WDN WA8 133 J4
WGNE/HIN WN2 5 L6
Mealhouse La CHLY/EC PR7 32 E5 3
The Meander WD/CROXPK L12 99 G4
Measham Cl RNFD/HAY WA11 9 L1
Measham Wy WD/CROXPK L12 99 G2
Medbourne Crs KKBY L32 86 B5
Medea St EV L5 97 G7
Medlar Wy AIMK WN4 79 H8
Medlock St ANF/KKDL L4 97 G5
Medlock Wy WGNE/HIN WN2 80 C3 6
Medway Cl AIMK WN4 79 H7 2
LEIGH WN7 93 L5
WARRN/WOL WA2 122 A3 3
Medway Pl WGNW/BIL/O WN5 67 M6
Medway Rd GOL/RIS/CU WA3 107 J3
RF/TRAN CH42 128 C3 1
Meeting La WARRW/BUR WA5 119 M8
Melbreck SKEL WN8 65 J1
Melbreck Rd CALD/MH L18 130 D4
Melbury Ct GOL/RIS/CU WA3 107 H7
Melbury Rd DV/KA/FCH L14 99 K7
Melda Cl NPK/KEN L6 13 M4
Meldon Cl NG/CROX L11 98 E3
Meldreth Cl FMBY L37 58 E4
Meldrum Rd WAV L15 114 D7
Melford Cl CHLYE PR6 33 G2
Melford Dr AIMK WN4 91 J1 5
CL/PREN CH43 127 G4
RUNC WA7 19 L6
WGNW/BIL/O WN5 77 M2
Melford Gv NPK/KEN L6 97 M7
Meliden Gdns STHEL WA9 103 H6 6
Meliden Gv FROD/HEL WA6 166 C4
Melksham Dr PEN/TH CH61 125 M6 2
Melling Av WLT/FAZ L9 84 D6
Melling Dr KKBY L32 86 A2
Melling La MGHL L31 73 G6
Melling Rd BTL L20 7 H1
CHTN/BK PR9 25 G5
WAL/NB CH45 95 L6
WLT/FAZ L9 84 D5
Mellings Av
WGNW/BIL/O WN5 78 A4 3
Melling St WGNW/BIL/O WN5 68 A8
Melling Wy KKBY L32 86 A2
WGNS/IIMK WN3 78 F4
Mellock Cl NSTN CH64 153 H7
Mellock La NSTN CH64 153 H6
Melloncroft Dr WKBY CH48 124 D5
Melloncroft Dr West
WKBY CH48 124 E6
Mellor Brook Dr
WGNE/HIN WN2 80 C3 7
Mellor Cl RAIN/WH L35 116 C6
RUNC WA7 150 F5 3
WGNNW/ST WN6 56 A3 1
Mellor Rd RF/TRAN CH42 127 L3
Melly Rd AIG/SPK L17 129 K2
Melmerby Cl AIMK WN4 91 H2 1
Melrose Av CHTN/BK PR9 22 D8
CSBY/BLUN L23 83 G2
ECCL WA10 88 D8
HOY CH47 108 D6 5
LEIGH WN7 81 M4
WARRS WA4 137 M5 1
WARRW/BUR WA5 104 B6
Melrose Crs AIMK WN4 90 E2 1
Melrose Dr GTS/LS CH66 163 H5
WGNS/IIMK WN3 78 F2
Melrose Gdns LEY/BBR PR5 29 L3
Melrose Rd ANF/KKDL L4 96 F5
CSBY/WL L22 83 G5
NWD/KWIPK L33 73 M7
Melrose Wy CHLY/EC PR7 32 F7
Melton Av WARRS WA4 137 K5
Melton Cl GR/UP/WCH CH49 110 A8 6
Melton Rd RUNC WA7 149 K7
Melverley Rd KKBY L32 85 K3
Melverley St WGNS/IIMK WN3 4 B6
Melville Av RF/TRAN CH42 128 C4
Melville Cl WARRN/WOL WA2 14 E2
Melville Pl EHL/KEN L7 113 J5
Melville Rd BEB CH63 128 A8
BTL L20 83 L6
Melville St TOX L8 113 H8
Melwood Dr WD/CROXPK L12 98 E6
Menai Rd BTL L20 83 M7
Menai St BIRK CH41 10 F6
Mendell Cl PS/BROM CH62 144 A5
Mendip Av WARRN/WOL WA2 121 K2
WGNS/IIMK WN3 78 E2
Mendip Cl GTS/LS CH66 163 G2
HLWD L26 132 A6 2
HOR/BR BL6 45 L8
RF/TRAN CH42 127 L4
Mendip Gv STHEL WA9 103 H2
Mendip Rd RF/TRAN CH42 127 L4
WAV L15 114 C7
Menin Av WARRS WA4 137 L2
Menivale Cl CHTN/BK PR9 22 C7
Menlo Av PEN/TH CH61 126 B7
Menlo Cl CL/PREN CH43 127 G1
Menlove Av CALD/MH L18 130 E1
Menlove Gdns North
CALD/MH L18 114 D8
Menlove Gdns South
CALD/MH L18 114 D8
Menlove Gdns West
CALD/MH L18 114 D8
Menlove Man CALD/MH L18 114 E7 1
Menlow Cl WARRS WA4 138 E4
Menstone Rd
CLB/OSW/ST L13 114 B1 3
Mentmore Crs NG/CROX L11 98 D4
Mentmore Gdns WARRS WA4 138 B8
Mentmore Rd CALD/MH L18 130 B4
Menzies St TOX L8 129 J1 16
Meols Cl FMBY L37 59 G3
GTS/LS CH66 163 G1 1
Meols Cop Rd STHP PR8 25 H8
Meols Dr HOY CH47 124 C1
Meols Pde HOY CH47 108 D5
Mercer Av KKBY L32 85 L4
Mercer Ct CHLY/EC PR7 44 B4
WD/CROXPK L12 99 G8 2
Mercer Dr ANF/KKDL L4 97 G5
Mercer Rd CL/PREN CH43 111 G5
RNFD/HAY WA11 90 E7
Mercer's La ORM L39 74 D1
Mercer St ALL/GAR L19 130 E8 4
NEWLW WA12 104 F1
WARRW/BUR WA5 104 A7
Merchants Crs GOL/RIS/CU WA3 93 G4
Mere Av BEB CH63 143 K7
BRSC L40 39 G7
LEIGH WN7 81 M8 11
Merebank CL/PREN CH43 127 G1 6
Merebrook Gv
NWD/KWIPK L33 74 B8 3
Mere Brow La KIRK/FR/WA PR4 27 J3
Mere Cl GTS/LS CH66 162 F3
SKEL WN8 65 H3
Merecroft Av WAL/EG CH44 111 L3
Meredale Rd CALD/MH L18 130 C1
Meredith Av WARRS WA4 138 D3 3
Meredith St ALL/GAR L19 131 G8 1
Mere Farm Gv
CL/PREN CH43 127 H1 3
Mere Farm Rd CL/PREN CH43 127 G1
Merefield CHLY/EC PR7 32 C4
Mere Fold CHLY/EC PR7 42 F2
Mere Gn ANF/KKDL L4 97 J4
Mere Gv RNFD/HAY WA11 89 K4
Mereheath MOR/LEA CH46 110 A2
Mere Hey ECCL WA10 101 J2
Mereland Cl
WGNW/BIL/O WN5 67 G7 1
Mere La BRSC L40 38 F2
CHTN/BK PR9 26 C2
EV L5 97 H8
HES CH60 141 G3
KIRK/FR/WA PR4 27 J6
WAL/NB CH45 95 G6
Merepark Dr CHTN/BK PR9 25 K1
Mere Park Rd
GR/UP/WCH CH49 125 L2
Mere Rd AIMK WN4 91 L1 4
FMBY L37 58 F3
NEWLW WA12 105 H1
WARRN/WOL WA2 122 C3
Mere St LEIGH WN7 81 M8
WGNW/BIL/O WN5 68 B7 8
Merevale Cl RUNC WA7 150 A7
Mereview Crs WD/CROXPK L12 98 F2
Merewood KKBY L32 86 B5 5
SKEL WN8 65 J1
Merewood Cl
WARRN/WOL WA2 121 M2
Mereworth WKBY CH48 124 F7
Meribel Cl CSBY/BLUN L23 71 J8
Meriden Av BEB CH63 143 J4 2
Meriden Cl RNFD/HAY WA11 89 M7
STHP PR8 34 D8
Meriden Rd WLTN L25 115 K7 5
Merland Wy STHEL WA9 103 H3
Merlewood Av CHTN/BK PR9 25 K2
Merlin Av GR/UP/WCH CH49 109 M7
Merlin Cl CHLYE PR6 33 J2
GR/UP/WCH CH49 109 L7
RNFD/HAY WA11 89 K7 6
RUNC WA7 150 C5
Merlin Ct HLWD L26 131 M4
Merlin St TOX L8 113 H7
Merrick Cl WARRN/WOL WA2 122 A3
Merrills La GR/UP/WCH CH49 110 C8
Merrilocks Rd CSBY/BLUN L23 82 D1
Merrilox Av MGHL L31 72 F3
Merrion Cl WLTN L25 131 H2
Merritt Av BIRK CH41 10 C1
Merrivale Rd WLTN L25 131 L3
Merscar La BRSC L40 37 M7
Mersey Av ALL/GAR L19 130 B5
FMBY L37 47 G7
MGHL L31 73 H3
Merseybank Rd
PS/BROM CH62 128 D5
Mersey Cl WGNE/HIN WN2 81 L2
Mersey La South
RF/TRAN CH42 128 C3
Mersey Mt RF/TRAN CH42 128 A2
Mersey Rd AIG/SPK L17 130 A5
CSBY/BLUN L23 82 E2
RF/TRAN CH42 128 C3
RUNC WA7 19 G2
WDN WA8 149 J1
WGNE/HIN WN2 80 B3
WGNW/BIL/O WN5 67 H6
Mersey St LEIGH WN7 81 L8
RUNC WA7 19 H2
STHEL WA9 103 J2
WAL/EG CH44 112 A3
WARR WA1 14 F7
Merseyton Rd EP CH65 156 D5
Mersey Vw ALL/GAR L19 130 E7 4
CSBY/WL L22 82 E3
Mersey View Rd WDN WA8 148 D1
Mersey View South Rd
RUNC WA7 18 A9
Mersey Wk WARRS WA4 122 B8
Mersey Wy SPK/HALE L24 145 M3
WARRW/BUR WA5 136 E1
Mersham Ct WDN WA8 134 B1 2
Merstone Cl HLWD L26 132 C6 1
Merthyr Gv CHLDW L16 115 G4
Merton Bank Rd STHEL WA9 9 M2

Merton Cl *NSTN* CH64 .... 153 G8
Merton Crs *HUY* L36 .... 115 K3
Merton Dr *GR/UP/WCH* CH49 .. 126 C2
  HUY L36 .... 115 J3
Merton Gv *BTL* L20 .... 7 G5
  CHLYE PR6 .... 33 G2
  CSBY/BLUN L23 .... 82 E2
Merton Pl *CL/PREN* CH43 .... 10 E6
Merton Rd *BTL* L20 .... 6 F5
  GTS/LS CH66 .... 163 G2
  PS/BROM CH62 .... 155 K2
  WAL/NB CH45 .... 95 J8
  WGNS/IIMK WN3 .... 78 E1 1
Merton St *STHEL* WA9 .... 9 L2
Mertoun Rd *WARRS* WA4 .... 137 K4 2
Mervyn Pl *WGNS/IIMK* WN3 .... 79 J1
Mesham Cl *GR/UP/WCH* CH49 .. 110 A8 2
Mesnes Av *WGNS/IIMK* WN3 .... 4 A9
Mesnes Park Ter *WGN* WN1 .... 4 E2
Mesnes Rd *WGN* WN1 .... 4 E2
Mesnes Ter *WGN* WN1 .... 4 E3
Meteor Crs *WARRN/WOL* WA2 .. 121 M3
Methuen St *BIRK* CH41 .... 10 A7
  WAV L15 .... 114 A6
Mevagissey Rd *RUNC* WA7 .... 150 E8
The Mews *AIG/SPK* L17 .... 130 B4
  STBRV L28 .... 99 L6
  WGNE/HIN WN2 .... 69 M8 13
Meyrick Rd *NG/CROX* L11 .... 98 A3
Meyrick St *WGNW/BIL/O* WN5 .. 68 B7
Micawber Cl *TOX* L8 .... 113 H8 6
Michaels Cl *FMBY* L37 .... 59 C2
Michael's La *ORM* L39 .... 48 E2
Mickering La *ORM* L39 .... 62 E7
Micklefield Rd *WAV* L15 .... 114 A7
Micklegate *RUNC* WA7 .... 150 F6 3
Mickleton Dr *STHP* PR8 .... 34 C8 1
Middlefield Rd *CALD/MH* L18 .. 131 G2
Middleham Cl *KKBY* L32 .... 85 L4 2
Middlehey Rd *PR/KW* L34 .... 99 M1
Middlehurst Av *ECCL* WA10 .... 8 F3 2
Middlehurst Cl *PR/KW* L34 .... 101 J6 1
Middlehurst Rd *WARRS* WA4 .. 138 C3
Middle La *FROD/HEL* WA6 .... 167 M3
Middlemass Rd *NTHLY* L27 .... 116 A4
Middle Moss La *FMBY* L37 .... 60 B2
Middle Rd *SPK/HALE* L24 .... 132 B8
Middlesex Rd *BTL* L20 .... 7 K2
Middleton Rd *CSBY/WL* L22 .... 83 H3
  EHL/KEN L7 .... 114 A3
Middle Wk *FROD/HEL* WA6 .... 160 D6
Middle Wy *NG/CROX* L11 .... 85 M8
Middle Withins La *HTWN* L38 .. 60 B6
Middlewood *GOL/RIS/CU* WA3 .. 93 H5 3
  KKBY L32 .... 86 B5
  SKEL WN8 .... 65 J1
Middlewood Cl *CHLY/EC* PR7 .. 30 E7 1
  ORM L39 .... 62 E6 2
Middlewood Dr *ORM* L39 .... 62 E6
Middlewood Rd *ORM* L39 .... 62 E6
Midge Hall La *CHTN/BK* PR9 .. 37 L3
Midghall St *VAUX/LVPD* L3 .... 12 F4
Midhurst Dr *STHP* PR8 .... 47 K1
Midhurst Rd *WD/CROXPK* L12 .. 99 H2 3
Midland Cl *LEIGH* WN7 .... 81 L7
Midland St *BIRK* CH41 .... 10 F7 1
  WDN WA8 .... 16 F2
Midland Ter *CSBY/WL* L22 .... 82 F4 3
Midland Wy *WARR* WA1 .... 14 C4
Midlothian Dr *CSBY/BLUN* L23 .. 82 E2 7
Midway Rd *HUY* L36 .... 116 A1
Midwood St *WDN* WA8 .... 16 E4 7
Milbrook Crs *KKBY* L32 .... 85 M2
Milbrook Dr *KKBY* L32 .... 86 A2
Mildenhall Rd *WLTN* L25 .... 115 J7
Mildmay Rd *BTL* L20 .... 8 K8
  NG/CROX L11 .... 98 A3 2
Mile End *EV* L5 .... 13 G1
Miles Cl *GOL/RIS/CU* WA3 .... 123 H2
  GR/UP/WCH CH49 .... 125 L3
Miles La *GR/UP/WCH* CH49 .. 125 L3
  WGNNW/ST WN6 .... 55 C6
Miles St *TOX* L8 .... 129 J1
Milestone Hey *STBRV* L28 .... 99 K5
Mile Stone Meadow
  CHLYE PR6 .... 31 M1 1
Milford Cl *FMBY* L37 .... 58 E4
Milford Dr *WD/CROXPK* L12 .. 99 G2
Milford Gv *WGNE/HIN* WN2 .... 69 H3
Milford St *EV* L5 .... 96 D7
  WGNS/IIMK WN3 .... 5 J7
  WGNS/IIMK WN3 .... 4 E5
Milland Cl *NG/CROX* L11 .... 98 E2
Millar Crs *WDN* WA8 .... 16 C5
Millar's Pace *CHTN/BK* PR9 .. 22 D8
Mill Av *WARRW/BUR* WA5 .... 120 A6
Mill Bank *CLB/OSW/ST* L13 .. 98 B7
  NSTN CH64 .... 153 J8
  WGNNW/ST WN6 .... 54 F6
Millbank Brow *BRSC* L40 .... 52 B2 2
Millbank La *MGHL* L31 .... 73 H2
Millbank Rd *WAL/EG* CH44 .. 111 J2 10
Millbeck Farm
  WGNW/BIL/O WN5 .... 67 M8
Millbeck Gv *RNFD/HAY* WA11 .. 89 K4
Millbrook La *ECCL* WA10 .... 101 K1
Millbrook Rd *BIRK* CH41 .... 111 K3
Mill Brow *BEB* CH63 .... 127 M7
  ECCL WA10 .... 101 K1
  STHEL WA9 .... 102 F8
  WDN WA8 .... 17 H1
Mill Brow Cl *STHEL* WA9 .... 102 F8
Millbutt Cl *BEB* CH63 .... 127 M7
Mill Cl *CSBY/BLUN* L23 .... 71 G7 1
  EP CH65 .... 163 L4
  WARRN/WOL WA2 .... 122 A1 2
Mill Ct *NTHTN* L30 .... 71 M8
Millcroft *CSBY/BLUN* L23 .... 71 J8 4
Millcroft Rd *WGNW/BIL/O* WN5 .. 66 F8
Millcroft Pk
  GR/UP/WCH CH49 .... 125 K2 2
Millcroft Rd *WLTN* L25 .... 131 L4
Mildale Rd *LEIGH* WN7 .... 93 K4
Mill Dam *BRSC* L40 .... 51 L3
Mill Dam La *BRSC* L40 .... 51 M3 2
Miller Av *CSBY/BLUN* L23 .... 70 F8

Miller Cl *TOX* L8 .... 129 J1 17
Miller's Br *BTL* L20 .... 6 E7
Millers Cl *MOR/LEA* CH46 .. 109 K6 4
Millers Ct *MOR/LEA* L39 .... 51 H8 3
Millerscroft *KKBY* L32 .... 85 L2
Millersdale Av *STHEL* WA9 .. 118 E1 13
Millersdale Av *WLT/FAZ* L9 .. 84 D6 11
Millersdale Cl *PS/BROM* CH62 .. 144 B8
Millersdale Gv *RUNC* WA7 .. 149 M8
Millersdale Rd *CALD/MH* L18 .. 130 C1
Millers Fold *ECCL* WA10 .... 101 K1
Miller's La *WGNE/HIN* WN2 .... 80 C3
Millers Wy *MOR/LEA* CH46 .. 109 L5 2
Mill Farm Cl *WARRN/WOL* WA2 .. 122 A2
Mill Fld *SKEL* WN8 .... 53 L4
Millfield Cl *CLB/OSW/ST* L13 .. 98 C7
Millfield La *RNFD/HAY* WA11 .. 91 H5
Millfield Rd *CHLY/EC* PR7 .... 32 C3
  WDN WA8 .... 134 E3
Millfields *ECCL* WA10 .... 101 J2
Millgate *WDN* WN1 .... 4 F4
Mill Gn *NSTN* CH64 .... 154 B5
Millgreen Cl *WD/CROXPK* L12 .. 99 G2 2
Mill Green La *WDN* WA8 .... 118 F8
Mill Hey *RAIN/WH* L35 .... 118 A4
Mill Hey La *BRSC* L40 .... 39 L2
Mill Hey Rd *WKBY* CH48 .... 124 F7
Mill Hl *CL/PREN* CH43 .... 127 J2
Mill Hill Rd *PEN/TH* CH61 .. 125 L6
Millhouse Av *WARRS* WA4 .. 137 M4
Millhouse La *HOY* CH47 .... 109 K4
Millhouse La *GOL/RIS/CU* WA3 .. 106 C7
  HOY CH47 .... 109 K4
  MOR/LEA CH46 .... 109 K5
Mill House Vw *SKEL* WN8 .... 66 E6
Millingford Av *GOL/RIS/CU* WA3 .. 92 B3
Millingford Gv *AIMK* WN4 .... 91 K2 2
Millington Cl *CL/PREN* CH43 .. 127 G4 1
  RUNC WA7 .... 161 H1 1
Mill La *BRSC* L40 .... 39 G8
  BTL L20 .... 7 J4
  CHLY/EC PR7 .... 31 J4
  CHLY/EC PR7 .... 42 C3
  CHLY/EC PR7 .... 43 C3
  CHTN/BK PR9 .... 25 J4
  CLB/OSW/ST L13 .... 114 C3
  FROD/HEL WA6 .... 161 G3
  GR/UP/WCH CH49 .... 125 L4
  GTS/LS CH66 .... 162 F1
  HES CH60 .... 141 K5
  KKBY L32 .... 85 L1
  NEWLW WA12 .... 105 G2
  NSTN CH64 .... 153 L8
  NSTN CH64 .... 154 A4
  NSTN CH64 .... 154 C5
  ORM L39 .... 62 B4
  PR/KW L34 .... 86 F8
  RAIN/WH L35 .... 117 L4
  RNFD/HAY WA11 .... 88 D2
  SKEL WN8 .... 53 L4
  SKEL WN8 .... 65 H3
  SKEL WN8 .... 66 C5
  STHEL WA9 .... 102 E8
  VAUX/LVPD L3 .... 13 J5 2
  WAL/EG CH44 .... 111 J2
  WARRN/WOL WA2 .... 105 G8
  WARRS WA4 .... 137 G6
  WAV L15 .... 114 C5
  WD/CROXPK L12 .... 98 C7
  WDN WA8 .... 117 M8
  WDN WA8 .... 118 F8 1
  WDN WA8 .... 134 E1
  WGNNW/ST WN6 .... 54 E6
Mill Leat Cl *SKEL* WN8 .... 53 L3 2
Mill Meadow *NEWLW* WA12 .. 105 G2 2
Mill Mdw *WDN* WA8 .... 1 G5
Millom Av *RAIN/WH* L35 .... 117 K1
Millom Gv *ECCL* WA10 .... 101 L5
  WD/CROXPK L12 .... 98 E4 3
Mill Park Dr *PS/BROM* CH62 .. 155 C2
Mill Rd *BEB* CH63 .... 127 M6
  NPK/KEN L6 .... 13 M2
  PEN/TH CH61 .... 126 C7
  PS/BROM CH62 .... 143 M2
  STHP PR8 .... 34 F8
  WGNW/BIL/O WN5 .... 66 F8
Millsborough Rd *NG/CROX* L11 .. 98 B5
Mill Sq *AIN/FAZ* L10 .... 85 G3 5
Mill St *AIMK* WN4 .... 91 L3
  CHLY/EC PR7 .... 43 G4
  CHLYE PR6 .... 44 C5
  ECCL WA10 .... 8 F3
  GOL/RIS/CU WA3 .... 92 C6
  NSTN CH64 .... 153 G5
  ORM L39 .... 63 H1
  PR/KW L34 .... 100 F1 11
  RF/TRAN CH42 .... 11 H9
  STHP PR8 .... 3 K5
  TOX L8 .... 113 G8
  WGNE/HIN WN2 .... 69 M8 11
  WGNS/IIMK WN3 .... 4 D5
  WLTN L25 .... 131 J3
Millthwaite Rd *WAL/EG* CH44 .. 111 H1 6
Millvale St *NPK/KEN* L6 .... 113 L1
Mill View Ct *ORM* L39 .... 64 A7 1
Mill View Dr *BEB* CH63 .... 127 L7
Millway Rd *SPK/HALE* L24 .. 147 J1 2
Millwood *BEB* CH63 .... 127 M7 2
Mill Wood Av *ECCL* WA10 .... 101 H2
Millwood Gld *CL/PREN* CH43 .. 127 L7
Millwood Gdns *RAIN/WH* L35 .. 117 H3 6
Millwood Rd *SPK/HALE* L24 .. 147 G2
Milman Cl *GR/UP/WCH* CH49 .. 126 B1 6
  ORM L39 .... 62 F2
Milman Rd *ANF/KKDL* L4 .... 97 H4
Milner Cop *HES* CH60 .... 141 J5
Milne Rd *CLB/OSW/ST* L13 .. 98 A5 1
Milner Rd *HES* CH60 .... 141 J5
Milner St *BIRK* CH41 .... 10 A1
  WARRW/BUR WA5 .... 14 B6
Milnthorpe Rd
  WARRW/BUR WA5 .... 104 A7 3
Milnthorpe St *ALL/GAR* L19 .. 130 E7 5

Milroy St *EHL/KEN* L7 .... 113 K4
Milton Av *DV/KA/FCH* L14 .. 115 H3
  NEWLW WA12 .... 104 D2
  RAIN/WH L35 .... 117 G2
  WDN WA8 .... 16 A4
Milton Cl *RAIN/WH* L35 .... 117 G2
Milton Crs *HES* CH60 .... 141 J4
Milton Dr *ORM* L39 .... 63 J1
Milton Gn *FROD/HEL* WA6 .. 166 C4
  WARRS WA4 .... 137 M2
  WGN WN1 .... 68 E2
Milton Gn *PEN/TH* CH61 .... 126 D7
Milton Rd *ANF/KKDL* L4 .... 7 M6
  CHLY/EC PR7 .... 43 G5
  CSBY/WL L22 .... 83 G3
  EHL/KEN L7 .... 114 A3
  EP CH65 .... 20 F7
  GOL/RIS/CU WA3 .... 92 F6
  RF/TRAN CH42 .... 10 F9
  WAL/EG CH44 .... 111 M3
  WDN WA8 .... 16 C4
  WKBY CH48 .... 124 C2
Milton Rd East *RF/TRAN* CH42 .. 11 G9
Milton St *BTL* L20 .... 6 E2
  CHTN/BK PR9 .... 25 J6
  STHEL WA9 .... 118 C3
  WDN WA8 .... 16 C9
Milton Ter *CHLYE* PR6 .... 32 F3 3
Milton Wy *MGHL* L31 .... 72 D4
Milvain Dr *WARRN/WOL* WA2 .. 121 L4
Milverton St *NPK/KEN* L6 .... 113 L1 2
Mimosa Cl *CHLY/EC* PR7 .... 32 C2
Mimosa Rd *WAV* L15 .... 114 C9
Minehead Av *LEIGH* WN7 .... 81 M3
Minehead Gv *STHEL* WA9 .. 102 F8 2
Minehead Rd *AIG/SPK* L17 .. 130 A4
Miners Wy *SPK/HALE* L24 .... 147 J2
  WDN WA8 .... 16 D6
Minerva Cl *WARRS* WA4 .... 137 M3
Mines Av *AIG/SPK* L17 .... 130 B6
  PR/KW L34 .... 101 G7
Mine Wy *RNFD/HAY* WA11 .... 91 H6 3
Minshull St *EHL/KEN* L7 .... 113 J4
Minstead Av *NWD/KWIPK* L33 .. 86 C3
Minstrel Cl *WGNE/HIN* WN2 .. 80 D6 1
Minto Cl *EHL/KEN* L7 .... 113 L3
Minto St *WD/CROXPK* L12 .. 99 H2
Minton Wy *WDN* WA8 .... 118 D8
Mintor Rd *NWD/KWIPK* L33 .. 86 C3
Minto St *EHL/KEN* L7 .... 113 K3 8
Minver Rd *WD/CROXPK* L12 .. 98 F6
Miranda Rd *BTL* L20 .... 7 J7
Mirfield Cl *GOL/RIS/CU* WA3 .. 92 F6
  HLWD L26 .... 132 B7
Mirfield St *NPK/KEN* L6 .... 113 K2
Miriam Rd *ANF/KKDL* L4 .... 97 J7
Miry La *SKEL* WN8 .... 53 M3
  WGNNW/ST WN6 .... 4 A3
Miskelly St *NPK/KEN* L6 .... 96 E5
Mission Wk *NPK/KEN* L6 .... 113 K2 1
Missouri Rd *CLB/OSW/ST* L13 .. 97 M6
Mistlethrush Wy
  WD/CROXPK L12 .... 99 H2 4
Misty Cl *WDN* WA8 .... 133 L3
Mitchell Av *WARRW/BUR* WA5 .. 104 A8
Mitchell Crs *LITH* L21 .... 83 K5 3
Mitchell Rd *ECCL* WA10 .... 101 L4
  PR/KW L34 .... 100 F7
  WGNW/BIL/O WN5 .... 78 A8
Mitchell St *AIMK* WN4 .... 91 L3
  GOL/RIS/CU WA3 .... 92 C6
  LEIGH WN7 .... 81 K8
  WARRS WA4 .... 137 L5
  WGNE/HIN WN2 .... 69 J6
  WGNW/BIL/O WN5 .... 68 A7
Mithril Cl *WDN* WA8 .... 134 F3
Mitre Cl *RAIN/WH* L35 .... 116 F4
Mitylene St *EV* L5 .... 97 G7
Moat House St *WGNE/HIN* WN2 .. 69 J6
Mobberley Cl *WARRS* WA4 .. 138 F2
Mobberley Wy *BEB* CH63 .. 143 J2
Mockbeggar Dr *WAL/NB* CH45 .. 94 F6
Mockbeggar Whf
  WAL/NB CH45 .... 95 G6 1
Modred St *TOX* L8 .... 113 H8
Moel Famau Vw *AIG/SPK* L17 .. 129 K3
Moffatdale Rd *ANF/KKDL* L4 .. 97 L5
Moffat St *WLT/FAZ* L9 .... 84 E6 1
Molesworth Gv *CHLDW* L16 .. 115 H4
Molineux Av *DV/KA/FCH* L14 .. 114 F4
Molland Cl *WD/CROXPK* L12 .. 98 F5
Mollington Av *NG/CROX* L11 .. 98 B3
Mollington Rd *KKBY* L32 .... 85 L3
  WAL/EG CH44 .... 111 L3
Mollington St *BIRK* CH41 .... 11 J7
Molly Pitcher Wy
  WARRW/BUR WA5 .... 120 D8
Molly's La *NWD/KWIPK* L33 .. 86 F6
Molton Rd *CHLDW* L16 .... 114 C5
Molyneux Av *WARRW/BUR* WA5 .. 121 H5
Molyneux Cl
  GR/UP/WCH CH49 .... 110 B8 3
  HUY L36 .... 116 B3
  RAIN/WH L35 .... 116 F1
Molyneux Dr *RAIN/WH* L35 .. 116 F1
  WAL/NB CH45 .... 95 K5
Molyneux St *WGN* WN1 .... 5 H3
Molyneux Wy *AIN/FAZ* L10 .. 84 E2
Monaghan Cl *WLT/FAZ* L9 .. 84 C6
Monash Rd *NG/CROX* L11 .. 98 B5
Monastery La *STHEL* WA9 .. 102 F6
Monastery Rd *NPK/KEN* L6 .. 97 L7 2
  STHEL WA9 .... 103 G6
Mona St *BIRK* CH41 .... 111 H6
  BTL L20 .... 83 J7
  ECCL WA10 .... 8 A6
  WGN WN1 .... 4 D3
Mond Rd *AIN/FAZ* L10 .... 85 H6
  WDN WA8 .... 16 C4
Monfa Rd *BTL* L20 .... 83 J7
Monica Dr *WDN* WA8 .... 118 C8

Monica Rd *WLTN* L25 .... 131 K4
Monica Ter *AIMK* WN4 .... 91 K3 6
Monkfield Wy *ALL/GAR* L19 .. 145 M1
Monk St *WAL/EG* CH44 .... 111 K1
Monks Carr La *HTWN* L38 .. 60 C7
Monks Cl *RAIN/WH* L35 .... 117 G2
Monks Crs *HES* CH60 .... 141 J4
Monks Dr *FMBY* L37 .... 59 J4
Monks Ferry *BIRK* CH41 .... 11 M6
Monksdown Rd *NG/CROX* L11 .. 98 C4
Monks Gn *FMBY* L37 .... 59 J4
Monksferry Wk *ALL/GAR* L19 .. 130 B6
Monks Gv *EP* CH65 .... 20 B3
Monks St *WARRW/BUR* WA5 .. 121 G7 8
Monk St *EV* L5 .... 97 H7 3
Monks Wy *BEB* CH63 .... 143 H1
  WKBY CH48 .... 124 D3
  WLTN L25 .... 131 K3
Monkswell Dr *WAV* L15 .... 114 C5
Monkswell St *TOX* L8 .... 129 J2 2
Monkswood Cl
  WARRW/BUR WA5 .... 121 G3 6
Monmouth Cl *WARR* WA1 .. 123 G6
Monmouth Crs *AIMK* WN4 .. 91 L3
Monmouth Dr *AIN/FAZ* L10 .. 85 H4
Monmouth Gv *STHEL* WA9 .. 102 F3 8
Monro Cl *TOX* L8 .... 129 H1 4
Monroe Cl *WARR* WA1 .... 122 D6
  WGNS/IIMK WN3 .... 79 J2 6
Monro St *TOX* L8 .... 129 H1
Montague Rd *FMBY* L37 .... 47 C8
Montagu Rd *FMBY* L37 .... 47 C8
Montclair Dr *CALD/MH* L18 .. 114 D8
Montclare Crs *WARRS* WA4 .. 138 A4
Montcliffe Cl *GOL/RIS/CU* WA3 .. 106 E8
Montcliffe Rd *CHLYE* PR6 .. 33 C4
Monterey Rd *CLB/OSW/ST* L13 .. 114 D3
Montford Ri *WGNE/HIN* WN2 .. 69 J3
Montfort Dr *ALL/GAR* L19 .. 130 C6
Montgomery Av *CHTN/BK* PR9 .. 25 J7
Montgomery Cl
  RAIN/WH L35 .... 116 F3 3
Montgomery Hl *WKBY* CH48 .. 125 J5
Montgomery Rd *HUY* L36 .. 115 M1
  WDN WA8 .... 133 M5
  WLT/FAZ L9 .... 84 C7
Montgomery Wy
  NPK/KEN L6 .... 113 K1 8
Montpelier Av *RUNC* WA7 .. 149 F1
Montpellier Crs *WAL/NB* CH45 .. 95 J5
Montrey Crs *AIMK* WN4 .... 90 F2
Montrose Av *WAL/EG* CH44 .. 112 A4
  WGNW/BIL/O WN5 .... 67 C3
  WGNW/BIL/O WN5 .... 67 G3
Montrose Cl *CHLYE* PR6 .... 33 G7 8
  WARRN/WOL WA2 .... 122 B1
Montrose Dr *CHTN/BK* PR9 .. 25 J4
Montrose Rd *CLB/OSW/ST* L13 .. 98 A7
Montrose Wy *CLB/OSW/ST* L13 .. 114 B3
Montrovia Crs *AIN/FAZ* L10 .. 85 H6
Monument Rd *WGN* WN1 .. 68 F3
Monville Rd *WLT/FAZ* L9 .. 84 E6
Monyash Vw *WGNE/HIN* WN2 .. 81 H2
Moody La *BRSC* L40 .... 41 G4
Moody St *WGNNW/ST* WN6 .. 56 A4 7
Moor Av *WGNNW/ST* WN6 .. 55 C5
Moorbridge Cl *NTHTN* L30 .. 84 C1
Moor Cl *CSBY/BLUN* L23 .. 71 G8
Moor Coppice *CSBY/BLUN* L23 .. 71 H8
Moorcroft Rd *CALD/MH* L18 .. 130 E4
  HUY L36 .... 100 A8
  WAL/NB CH45 .... 94 F8
Moor Dr *CSBY/BLUN* L23 .. 71 G8
  SKEL WN8 .... 65 M6
Moore Av *RF/TRAN* CH42 .. 128 A3
  STHEL WA9 .... 103 J2
  WARRS WA4 .... 138 C3
Moore Cl *WDN* WA8 .... 134 F3 8
Moore Dr *RNFD/HAY* WA11 .. 91 H7
Moore La *WARRS* WA4 .... 136 D6
Moores La *WGNNW/ST* WN6 .. 55 M3
Moore St *BTL* L20 .... 6 E1
  WGN WN1 .... 68 F3
Moore St East *WGN* WN1 .. 5 J1
Mooreway *RAIN/WH* L35 .... 118 A4
Moorfield *NWD/KWIPK* L33 .. 74 B8
Moorfield Crs *GOL/RIS/CU* WA3 .. 93 J6
Moorfield Dr *NSTN* CH64 .. 152 E3
Moorfield La *BRSC* L40 .... 50 D2
Moorfield Rd *CSBY/BLUN* L23 .. 71 J8
  ECCL WA10 .... 88 E8
  WDN WA8 .... 134 C3
Moorfields *CHLYE* PR6 .... 33 G4
  CLVP L2 .... 12 F6
Moorfields Av *CL/PREN* CH43 .. 126 F2
Moorfield St *WGNE/HIN* WN2 .. 80 D2 3
Moorfoot Rd *STHEL* WA9 .. 103 H2
Moorfoot Wy *NWD/KWIPK* L33 .. 73 M7
Moorgate *ORM* L39 .... 63 G1
Moorgate Av *CSBY/BLUN* L23 .. 83 G2
Moorgate Rd *NWD/KWIPK* L33 .. 86 B7
Moorgate St *EHL/KEN* L7 .. 113 K4
Moorhey Rd *MGHL* L31 .... 72 F6
Moorhouses *HTWN* L38 .... 70 B2
Mooring Cl *RUNC* WA7 .... 150 F7
Moorings Cl *NSTN* CH64 .. 152 D4
  WGN WN1 .... 5 L4
The Moorings *CHLYE* PR6 .. 33 G3 5
  HES CH60 .... 140 E5
  MGHL L31 .... 72 D1
Moorland Av *CSBY/BLUN* L23 .. 71 G8
Moorland Cl *HES* CH60 .. 141 J6 3
Moorland Dr *RUNC* WA7 .. 151 G6
Moorland Ga *CHLYE* PR6 .. 33 H7
Moorland Pk *HES* CH60 .. 140 A8
Moorland Rd *AIMK* WN4 .. 80 A8
  GTS/LS CH66 .... 156 A5
  MGHL L31 .... 73 H6
  RF/TRAN CH42 .... 128 A2
  WGNE/HIN WN2 .... 69 L8
Moorlands Rd *CSBY/BLUN* L23 .. 71 G8

  SFTN L29 .... 71 M4
  STHP PR8 .... 47 L3
  WDN WA8 .... 16 B6
Moor La South *WDN* WA8 .. 16 B6
Moor Pl *VAUX/LVPD* L3 .. 13 K6
Moor Rd *CHLY/EC* PR7 .... 32 C8 8
  LEY/BBR PR5 .... 29 L2
  WGNW/BIL/O WN5 .... 67 G7
Moorside Av *NSTN* CH64 .. 152 E5
Moorside Cl *CSBY/BLUN* L23 .. 83 H1
Moorside Ct *WDN* WA8 .. 16 B5
Moorside La *NSTN* CH64 .. 152 E6
Moorside Rd *CSBY/BLUN* L23 .. 83 H1
Moor St *CLVP* L2 .... 12 E8
  ORM L39 .... 51 H8
Moorway *HES* CH60 .... 141 K5
Moorwood Crs *STHEL* WA9 .. 118 E1
Moray Cl *STHEL* WA9 .... 118 E1
Morcott La *SPK/HALE* L24 .. 147 M3
Morden Av *AIMK* WN4 .... 91 K2
Morden St *NPK/KEN* L6 .... 113 L1
Morecambe St *NPK/KEN* L6 .. 97 L8 4
Morecroft Rd *RF/TRAN* CH42 .. 128 C3
Morella Rd *ANF/KKDL* L4 .. 97 L5
Morello Dr *BEB* CH63 .... 143 K3
Moresby Cl *LEIGH* WN7 .. 81 M3 2
  RUNC WA7 .... 151 G6 2
Moret Cl *CSBY/BLUN* L23 .. 71 J8
Moreton Av *STHEL* WA9 .. 118 E1 4
Moreton Cl *GOL/RIS/CU* WA3 .. 92 B4
Moreton Gv *WAL/NB* CH45 .. 95 C7 2
Moreton Rd *GR/UP/WCH* CH49 .. 110 B7
Morgan Av *WARRN/WOL* WA2 .. 121 L5
Morgan St *STHEL* WA9 .. 102 F3
Morland Av *NSTN* CH64 .. 153 H6
  PS/BROM CH62 .... 143 M6
Morley Av *BIRK* CH41 .... 10 C3
Morley Rd *CHTN/BK* PR9 .. 25 G5
  RUNC WA7 .... 19 G6
  WAL/EG CH44 .... 111 J2
  WARRS WA4 .... 137 J2
Morley St *ANF/KKDL* L4 .. 97 G6 2
  ECCL WA10 .... 8 F3
  WARR WA1 .... 15 H4
Morningside *CSBY/BLUN* L23 .. 83 H2
Morningside Pl *NG/CROX* L11 .. 98 B4
Morningside Rd *NG/CROX* L11 .. 98 B5
Morningside Wy
  NG/CROX L11 .... 98 B5 8
Mornington Av *CSBY/BLUN* L23 .. 83 G3
  EP CH65 .... 20 D5
Mornington Rd *CHLYE* PR6 .. 44 C5 3
  CHTN/BK PR9 .... 3 J3
  WAL/NB CH45 .... 95 K7 3
Mornington St *TOX* L8 .. 113 G8
Morpeth Cl *MOR/LEA* CH46 .. 109 K5 3
Morpeth Rd *HOY* CH47 .. 108 C8 3
Morpeth St *TOX* L8 .... 113 H6 10
Morpeth Whf *BIRK* CH41 .. 11 K2
Morris Av *WARRS* WA4 .. 138 B1
Morris Cl *RNFD/HAY* WA11 .. 90 C3
Morris Hey *ORM* L39 .... 49 M2
Morris La *ORM* L39 .... 49 M2
Morrison Cl
  WARRW/BUR WA5 .... 120 C8 6
Morrison St *CHLYE* PR6 .. 32 F3 7
Morris Rd *CHLYE* PR6 .... 33 C4 2
  SKEL WN8 .... 66 C6
Morrissey Cl *ECCL* WA10 .. 8 A3
Morris St *STHEL* WA9 .... 103 G4
  WGN WN1 .... 5 G3
  WGNE/HIN WN2 .... 69 M8 2
  WGNS/IIMK WN3 .... 80 A1
Morston Av *KKBY* L32 .... 86 A5
Morston Crs *KKBY* L32 .... 86 A5
Mort Av *WARRS* WA4 .... 138 C1
Mortimer Av *WARRN/WOL* WA2 .. 121 K5
Mortimer St *BIRK* CH41 .. 11 L5
Mortlake Cl *WDN* WA8 .. 118 D8
Morton Av *FROD/HEL* WA6 .. 166 D4 1
Morton Cl *WARRN/WOL* WA5 .. 120 E5
  WGNS/IIMK WN3 .... 78 E3
Morton Rd *RUNC* WA7 .. 150 F5
Morton St *TOX* L8 .... 113 H8 7
Morvah Cl *NG/CROX* L11 .. 98 E3
Morval Crs *ANF/KKDL* L4 .. 7 M6
  RUNC WA7 .... 19 M6
Morven Cl *WARRN/WOL* WA2 .. 122 A2
Morven Gv *STHP* PR8 .... 25 C6
Morville Dr *WGNS/IIMK* WN3 .. 79 K1
Moscow Dr *CLB/OSW/ST* L13 .. 98 B3
Mosedale Rd *RNFD/HAY* WA11 .. 89 K4
Mosedale Gv *RUNC* WA7 .. 150 A3 3
  WLT/FAZ L9 .... 84 C8
Moseley Av *WAL/NB* CH45 .. 111 J1
  WARRS WA4 .... 138 C1
Moseley Rd *BEB* CH63 .... 143 J4
Moses St *TOX* L8 .... 129 H1
Mosley St *STHP* PR8 .... 3 C9
Moss Av *WGNW/BIL/O* WN5 .. 77 M2
Moss Bank *CHLY/EC* PR7 .. 43 G4 8
  WDN WA8 .... 62 F3
Moss Bank Pk *LITH* L21 .. 83 J5
Moss Bank Rd *RNFD/HAY* WA11 .. 89 J4
  WDN WA8 .... 17 J5
Mossborough Hall La
  RNFD/HAY WA11 .... 87 L2
Mossborough Rd
  RNFD/HAY WA11 .... 76 B8
Moss Bridge La *BRSC* L40 .. 52 E3
Moss Brow *RNFD/HAY* WA11 .. 76 A6
Mossbrow Rd *HUY* L36 .. 116 A1
Moss Cl *CHLYE* PR6 .... 33 G5
  NSTN CH64 .... 154 C5
  WARRS WA4 .... 138 A3
Mosscraft Cl *HUY* L36 .... 116 C1
Mossdale Cl *WARRW/BUR* WA5 .. 120 C6
Mossdale Dr *RAIN/WH* L35 .. 117 M2
Mossdale Rd *AIMK* WN4 .. 91 K2
  NWD/KWIPK L33 .... 74 B8 2
Moss Delph La *ORM* L39 .. 62 D3
Mossend Rd *WAL/EG* CH44 .. 111 H1
Moss End Wy *NWD/KWIPK* L33 .. 86 F2
Mossfield Rd *CHLYE* PR6 .. 33 G5

WLT/FAZ L9 84 B7
Moss Ga GOL/RIS/CU WA3 107 J8
Moss Gate Gv DV/KA/FCH L14 115 J2
Moss Gate Rd DV/KA/FCH L14 115 J2
Mossgiel Av STHP PR8 47 K1
Moss Green Wy STHEL WA9 103 J4
Moss Gv RF/TRAN CH42 127 K3
TOX L8 113 L7
WGNNW/ST WN6 56 A5
Moss Hey Hey KIRK/FR/WA PR4 27 J2
Mosslands ECCL WA10 101 J1
Mosslands Cl GTS/LS CH66 163 G3
Mosslands Dr WAL/EG CH44 111 G1
Moss La BRSC L40 39 J6
BTL L20 84 A7
CHLY/EC PR7 43 G4
CHTN/BK PR9 23 L7
CHTN/BK PR9 25 K5
FMBY L37 59 L1
GOL/RIS/CU WA3 92 D8
HTWN L38 59 K8
HTWN L38 70 E3
LEY/BBR PR5 29 J5
LITH L21 83 M4
MGHL L31 61 M8
NWD/KWIPK L33 74 B5
NWD/KWIPK L33 86 D2
ORM L39 75 H3
RF/TRAN CH42 127 K3
RNFD/HAY WA11 77 G8
RNFD/HAY WA11 88 B5
SKEL WN8 65 H7
STHEL WA9 103 J4
WARRS WA4 136 C7
WGNE/HIN WN2 80 C2
WGNNW/ST WN6 54 E1
WLT/FAZ L9 84 B7
Moss Lane Vw SKEL WN8 65 H7
Mosslawn Rd KKBY L32 86 C4
Mosslea Pk CALD/MH L18 130 B1
Mossley Av CALD/MH L18 114 B8
PS/BROM CH62 143 M5
Mossley Hill Dr AIG/SPK L17 113 M8
Mossley Hill Rd CALD/MH L18 130 B3
Mossley Rd RF/TRAN CH42 128 A2
Moss Nook BRSC L40 39 G7
ORM L39 62 E3 2
Moss Nook La MGHL L31 73 K5
RNFD/HAY WA11 76 A7
Moss Pits Cl AIN/FAZ L10 85 H6 4
Moss Pits La AIN/FAZ L10 85 G6
WAV L15 114 D7
Moss Rd STHP PR8 35 L3
WARRS WA4 138 C2
WGNW/BIL/O WN5 77 M2
Moss Side DV/KA/FCH L14 115 J2
FMBY L37 59 K1
Moss Side La KIRK/FR/WA PR4 27 H2
WARRS WA4 136 A6
Moss St ALL/GAR L19 130 E7
NPK/KEN L6 13 M5
PR/KW L34 100 F6
WDN WA8 17 K5
WGNE/HIN WN2 80 B2
WGNNW/ST WN6 4 A1
WGNW/BIL/O WN5 67 K8 2
Moss Ter WGNW/BIL/O WN5 67 K8 3
Mossvale GTS/LS CH66 155 M5
Moss Vw LITH L21 83 L5
MGHL L31 73 H4
STHP PR8 35 G8
Mossville Cl CALD/MH L18 130 C3
Mossville Rd CALD/MH L18 130 D3
Moss Wy NG/CROX L11 98 E1
Mossy Bank Rd
WAL/EG CH44 111 M1 11
Mossy Lea Fold
WGNNW/ST WN6 55 H2
Mossy Lea Rd WGNNW/ST WN6 42 A7
Moston Gv LYMM WA13 139 M2
Moston Wy GTS/LS CH66 163 H2 1
Mostyn Av AIN/FAZ L10 84 E3
ALL/GAR L19 130 F5
HES CH60 140 E5
WKBY CH48 124 D4
Mostyn Cl ANF/KKDL L4 97 G6 13
Mostyn St WAL/EG CH44 111 K2
Motherwell Crs STHP PR8 36 B2
Mottershead Rd WDN WA8 16 C4
Mottram Cl NWD/KWIPK L33 86 B3 4
WARRS WA4 138 D2
Mottram Dr WGNS/IIMK WN3 68 D8
Moughland La RUNC WA7 19 G7
Moulders La WARR WA1 14 F7
Mould St EV L5 96 F8 4
Moulton Cl RUNC WA7 161 H1
Mounsey Rd RF/TRAN CH42 11 G8
Mountain Rd CHLY/EC PR7 43 G5
Mountain Vw FROD/HEL WA6 166 D2
Mount Av BEB CH63 127 M6
BTL L20 83 M7
HES CH60 141 H5 1
Mountbatten Rd CHLY/EC PR7 32 C7
Mount Cl KKBY L32 85 L1
Mount Crs KKBY L32 85 L1
WGNW/BIL/O WN5 67 H7
Mount Dr BEB CH63 127 L6
Mount Farm Wy GTS/LS CH66 162 E3
Mount Gilmour CL/PREN CH43 10 D9
Mount Gv BIRK CH41 10 F8
Mount Haven Cl
GR/UP/WCH CH49 110 C8
Mount House Cl FMBY L37 47 K8
Mount House Rd FMBY L37 47 K8
Mount Olive CL/PREN CH43 127 J2
Mount Pk BEB CH63 127 M6
WLTN L25 131 J2
Mount Park Ct WLTN L25 131 J2
Mount Pleasant CHLYE PR6 44 C5
CHNE CH2 165 J1
CL/PREN CH43 127 K2
CSBY/WL L22 82 F4
VAUX/LVPD L3 13 K8
WDN WA8 134 D3 4
Mount Pleasant Av STHEL WA9 103 J2
Mount Pleasant Rd
WAL/NB CH45 95 J6
Mount Rd BEB CH63 127 L7
GR/UP/WCH CH49 110 C8
KKBY L32 85 K2
RF/TRAN CH42 127 L4
RUNC WA7 150 B5
WAL/NB CH45 95 J5
WKBY CH48 124 E4
Mount St CHTN/BK PR9 3 L3
CLVPS L1 113 G5
CSBY/WL L22 82 F4
LEIGH WN7 93 L1 2
WLTN L25 131 J3
The Mount HES CH60 141 H5
SKEL WN8 65 K5 1
WAL/EG CH44 111 L1
Mount Vernon EHL/KEN L7 113 J3
Mount Vernon St
EHL/KEN L7 113 J3 6
Mount Vernon Vw
EHL/KEN L7 113 J3 7
Mount Vw WGNS/IIMK WN3 5 H9
Mountview Cl TOX L8 113 J8 3
Mountway BEB CH63 127 M6 2
Mountwood SKEL WN8 65 J1
Mount Wood Rd
RF/TRAN CH42 127 L5
Mourne Cl GTS/LS CH66 155 J7 3
Mowbray Av RNFD/HAY WA11 9 M1
Mowbray Gv CLB/OSW/ST L13 114 C4
Mowcroft La WARRW/BUR WA5 135 K2
Moxon Av WARRS WA4 122 B8 1
Moxon St ECCL WA10 101 L3
Moxon Wy AIMK WN4 91 M1
Moyles Cl WDN WA8 133 M3 3
Mozart Cl TOX L8 113 K7 3
Muirfield Cl
WARRN/WOL WA2 122 C2 3
WD/CROXPK L12 99 G7 1
Muirfield Dr STHP PR8 47 L1
Muirfield Rd HUY L36 115 L4
Muirhead Av CLB/OSW/ST L13 98 B5
Muirhead Av East
WD/CROXPK L12 98 C5
Mulberry Av ECCL WA10 101 L2
GOL/RIS/CU WA3 93 H6
Mulberry Cl CHNE CH2 165 L2
NWD/KWIPK L33 74 B7 6
WARR WA1 123 G7 2
WGNW/BIL/O WN5 67 M7
Mulberry Gv WAL/EG CH44 111 M2 10
Mulberry Pl EHL/KEN L7 13 M9 1
Mulberry Rd RF/TRAN CH42 128 B3
Mulberry St EHL/KEN L7 13 M9
Mulcrow Cl STHEL WA9 102 F1
Mulgrave St TOX L8 113 J6
Mullberry St EHL/KEN L7 13 M8
Mullein Cl GOL/RIS/CU WA3 92 F5
Mulliner St EHL/KEN L7 113 L6
Mullins Av NEWLW WA12 91 L8 2
Mullion Cl CHTN/BK PR9 22 D8 3
HLWD L26 132 A5
RUNC WA7 150 D7 3
Mullion Gv WARRN/WOL WA2 122 C4 3
Mullion Rd NG/CROX L11 98 F1
Mullion Wk NG/CROX L11 85 L8 1
Mulveton Rd BEB CH63 143 H2 3
Mumfords La HOY CH47 109 G4 2
Muncaster Cl
PS/BROM CH62 143 M4 2
Muncaster Dr RNFD/HAY WA11 76 C6
Munro Av WGNW/BIL/O WN5 67 G7
Munster Rd CLB/OSW/ST L13 114 D2
Murat Gv CSBY/WL L22 82 E4
Murat St CSBY/WL L22 82 E4
Murcote Rd DV/KA/FCH L14 99 H8
Murdishaw Av RUNC WA7 150 E8
Muriel Cl WARRW/BUR WA5 119 M7
Muriel St ANF/KKDL L4 97 J5 1
Murphy Cl WGNS/IIMK WN3 4 A9
Murphy Gv STHEL WA9 103 G1
Murrayfield Dr MOR/LEA CH46 110 B1
Murrayfield Rd WLTN L25 115 J7
Murray Gv WKBY CH48 124 C2 4
Museum St WARR WA1 14 C7
Musker Dr NTHTN L30 83 L2
Musker St CSBY/BLUN L23 83 H2
Muspratt Rd LITH L21 83 J8
Mustard La GOL/RIS/CU WA3 106 D5
Myddleton La
WARRN/WOL WA2 105 K7
Myers Av RAIN/WH L35 101 J8
Myerscough Av BTL L20 7 M1 1
Myers Rd East CSBY/BLUN L23 83 G2
Myers Rd West CSBY/BLUN L23 82 F2
Mynsule Rd BEB CH63 143 H2
Myrtle Av AIMK WN4 79 H7 3
NEWLW WA12 104 E3
RNFD/HAY WA11 90 D6
Myrtle Gv CHTN/BK PR9 3 M5
CSBY/WL L22 82 F3
STHP PR8 25 G7
WAL/EG CH44 112 A2 3
WARRS WA4 15 K9
WGNW/BIL/O WN5 89 M1 3
Myrtle Pde TOX L8 113 H5 18
Myrtle St EHL/KEN L7 13 L9
EP CH65 156 E6
WGN WN1 4 D3

N

Nab Rd CHLYE PR6 33 G4
Nairn Av SKEL WN8 53 K8
Nairn Cl BEB CH63 154 F1
WARRN/WOL WA2 122 C2
WGNNW/ST WN6 55 M4 4
Nangreaves St LEIGH WN7 81 L8
Nansen Cl WARRW/BUR WA5 120 F6
Nansen Gv ANF/KKDL L4 97 J4
Nant Park Ct WAL/NB CH45 95 L5 2
Nantwich Cl GR/UP/WCH CH49 126 C3
Nantwich Rd GTS/LS CH66 163 H2
Napier Cl ECCL WA10 8 D5
Napier Dr MOR/LEA CH46 110 B5
Napier Rd PS/BROM CH62 128 D5
Napier St BTL L20 6 E8
ECCL WA10 8 D5
WARR WA1 15 G6
Napier Ter STHP PR8 2 F8
Naples Rd WAL/EG CH44 111 M2
Napps Cl WLTN L25 115 H6 3
Napps Wy PEN/TH CH61 141 J3
WLTN L25 115 H5
Narborough Cl
WGNE/HIN WN2 81 G1 3
Nares Cl WARRW/BUR WA5 120 E4
Narrow Croft Rd ORM L39 62 D4
Narrow La ORM L39 62 D4
Narrow La (Clieves Hills)
ORM L39 49 M6
Narrow Moss La BRSC L40 50 F3
Naseby Cl CL/PREN CH43 126 E1 1
Naseby St ANF/KKDL L4 97 H3
Natal Rd WLT/FAZ L9 84 D7 3
Nathan Dr RNFD/HAY WA11 91 G7
Nathan Gv NWD/KWIPK L33 86 B1 5
Naunton Av LEIGH WN7 81 L8
Navenby Rd WGNS/IIMK WN3 79 J3
Navigation Cl NTHTN L30 84 C1
RUNC WA7 150 F7 2
Navigation St WARR WA1 15 J6
Navigation Whf VAUX/LVPD L3 112 F7
Naylor Av GOL/RIS/CU WA3 92 D5
Naylorfarm Av WGNNW/ST WN6 55 H8
Naylor Rd CL/PREN CH43 111 G5
WDN WA8 17 J2
Naylorsfield Dr NTHLY L27 115 L7
Naylor's Rd NTHLY L27 115 M6
WLTN L25 115 M8 1
Naylor St VAUX/LVPD L3 12 F4
WARR WA1 14 F5
Nazeby Av CSBY/BLUN L23 83 H2
Neale Dr GR/UP/WCH CH49 126 A2
Neales Fold CHTN/BK PR9 22 F8 2
Neargates CHLY/EC PR7 42 F2
Neasham Cl HLWD L26 132 B5 4
Nedens Gv MGHL L31 72 E2
Nedens La MGHL L31 72 E2
Needham Cl RUNC WA7 149 M3 2
Needham Rd EHL/KEN L7 113 L3
Needham Wy SKEL WN8 53 K8
Needwood Dr BEB CH63 143 H2
Neills Rd STHEL WA9 103 K7
Neilson Rd AIG/SPK L17 129 K2 2
Neil St WDN WA8 134 D3
Nell's La ORM L39 62 B8
Nel Pan La LEIGH WN7 81 L5
Nelson Av RAIN/WH L35 117 G3
Nelson Dr PEN/TH CH61 141 G2
WGNE/HIN WN2 69 J5
Nelson Pl RAIN/WH L35 117 G3 6
Nelson Rd CHLY/EC PR7 32 E6 10
EHL/KEN L7 113 K4
EP CH65 20 C1
GOL/RIS/CU WA3 122 F1
LITH L21 83 K6 5
RF/TRAN CH42 128 C4
Nelson's Cft BEB CH63 143 J2
Nelson St BTL L20 6 E7
CLVPS L1 113 G5
NEWLW WA12 104 C2
RUNC WA7 19 H3
STHP PR8 2 F5
WAL/NB CH45 95 L6
WAV L15 114 A6
WDN WA8 16 C8
WGNE/HIN WN2 69 M7 7
Nelville Rd WLT/FAZ L9 84 E6
Nemos Cl FROD/HEL WA6 166 E3 1
Neptune Cl RUNC WA7 150 F6 7
Neptune St BIRK CH41 11 H3
Ness Gv KKBY L32 85 L3
Neston Av STHEL WA9 118 D1 2
Neston Gn GTS/LS CH66 162 F1
Neston Rd BEB CH63 142 B8
NSTN CH64 153 H8
Neston St ANF/KKDL L4 97 H4
Netherby Rd WGNNW/ST WN6 68 C2
Netherby St TOX L8 129 H1 12
Netherfield WDN WA8 133 M5
Netherfield Cl CL/PREN CH43 126 E1 2
Netherfield Rd North EV L5 97 G6
Netherfield Rd South EV L5 13 K1
Netherfields LEIGH WN7 81 M6 5
Netherley Rd CHLY/EC PR7 43 G5
RAIN/WH L35 116 D8
Netherpool Rd GTS/LS CH66 156 B5
Netherton Dr
FROD/HEL WA6 160 C6 2
Netherton Gra NTHTN L30 84 D2
Netherton Gn NTHTN L30 72 B8
Netherton La NTHTN L30 72 A8
Netherton Park Rd LITH L21 83 M5
Netherton Rd BTL L20 83 M7
CALD/MH L18 130 C4
MOR/LEA CH46 110 A5 3
Netherton Wy NTHTN L30 84 A5
Netherwood Rd NG/CROX L11 98 A3
Netley St ANF/KKDL L4 97 G5 10
Nettlestead Rd NG/CROX L11 98 C5
Neva Av MOR/LEA CH46 109 M5
Nevada Cl WARRW/BUR WA5 120 D5
Neverstitch Cl SKEL WN8 65 H3 2
Neverstitch Rd SKEL WN8 64 F3
Neville Av STHEL WA9 103 K3
WARRN/WOL WA2 121 M4
Neville Cl CL/PREN CH43 126 E1
Neville Crs WARRW/BUR WA5 136 C2
Neville Rd CSBY/WL L22 83 G4 4
PS/BROM CH62 144 A6
WAL/EG CH44 111 J1
Neville St NEWLW WA12 104 C1 3
WGNE/HIN WN2 80 C2
Nevill St STHP PR8 3 G2
Nevin St NPK/KEN L6 113 J2 13
Nevison St EHL/KEN L7 113 K4 3
Nevitte Cl STBRV L28 99 J5
New Acres SKEL WN8 53 H4
New Acres Cl CL/PREN CH43 110 E5 6
Newark Cl CL/PREN CH43 126 E1 3
HUY L36 99 M7
Newark Rd WGNE/HIN WN2 80 E1
Newark St ANF/KKDL L4 7 M9
WGNNW/ST WN6 68 B4
New Bank Rd WDN WA8 133 K4
New Barn Av AIMK WN4 91 L2 6
New Barnet WDN WA8 134 B1 3
New Bird St CLVPS L1 112 F6
Newbold Crs WKBY CH48 125 G2
Newbold Gv WD/CROXPK L12 99 H3
Newborough Av
CALD/MH L18 114 B8 10
CSBY/BLUN L23 83 J1
Newborough Cl
WARRW/BUR WA5 120 F3
Newbridge Cl AIMK WN4 90 F2 2
GR/UP/WCH CH49 126 D1
RUNC WA7 150 E7 3
WARRW/BUR WA5 120 E3
New Bridge Rd EP CH65 21 J7
Newbridge Rd EP CH65 21 J9
Newburgh Cl RUNC WA7 150 F4
Newburn Cl SKEL WN8 53 K8
WGNS/IIMK WN3 79 G1 1
Newburns La CL/PREN CH43 127 K2
Newburn St ANF/KKDL L4 97 H4
Newbury Cl HUY L36 115 M4
WDN WA8 134 B2
Newbury Dr SKEL WN8 53 K8 2
Newbury Rd SKEL WN8 53 K8
Newbury Wy WD/CROXPK L12 99 G8
Newby Av RAIN/WH L35 117 J1 4
Newby Cl STHP PR8 47 K2
Newby Dr HUY L36 115 L2
Newby Gv WD/CROXPK L12 98 E3
Newby Sq WGNW/BIL/O WN5 67 K8 4
Newby St ANF/KKDL L4 97 H5
Newcastle Rd WAV L15 114 C7 6
New Cswy HTWN L38 59 K5
New Chester Rd BIRK CH41 128 B1
PS/BROM CH62 128 E8
RF/TRAN CH42 128 C4
Newchurch La
GOL/RIS/CU WA3 107 H3
Newcombe Av
WARRN/WOL WA2 122 A5 2
Newcombe St NPK/KEN L6 97 K8
New Court Wy ORM L39 51 H8
Newcroft Rd WLTN L25 131 H1 2
New Cross St ECCL WA10 8 F4 2
ECCL WA10 8 F5 1
PR/KW L34 100 F6 1
New Cut La NWD/KWIPK L33 87 J5
STHP PR8 35 J5
WARR WA1 122 D7
Newdales Cl CL/PREN CH43 110 E6
Newdown Rd NG/CROX L11 85 M8
Newell Rd WAL/EG CH44 111 K1
Newenden Rd WGN WN1 68 D1
Newenham Crs DV/KA/FCH L14 115 G2
New Ferry By-Pass
PS/BROM CH62 128 D6
New Ferry Rd PS/BROM CH62 128 D6
Newfield Cl CSBY/BLUN L23 71 L7
Newfield Rd LYMM WA13 139 M2
Newfield Ter FROD/HEL WA6 166 D3 3
New Fold WGNW/BIL/O WN5 77 L1
New Fort Wy BTL L20 83 J7
New Foul La STHP PR8 36 B1
Newgate Av WGNNW/ST WN6 55 G5
Newgate Rd SKEL WN8 66 B6
New Glade Hl RNFD/HAY WA11 89 M7
New Grosvenor Rd EP CH65 20 B1
New Hall Dr STHP PR8 36 E4
New Hall La GOL/RIS/CU WA3 107 J3
Newhall La HOY CH47 108 D7
New Hall La NG/CROX L11 98 A5
Newhall St CLVPS L1 113 G6 5
Newhaven Rd WAL/NB CH45 95 L6 9
WARRN/WOL WA2 121 K1
New Hedley Gv EV L5 96 E8
New Henderson St TOX L8 113 G7
New Hey WD/CROXPK L12 98 C8
New Hey La NSTN CH64 154 C6
New Hey Rd GR/UP/WCH CH49 126 D1
Newholme Cl
WD/CROXPK L12 99 G2 9
Newhope Rd BIRK CH41 10 E3
Newhouse Rd WAV L15 113 M6 4
New Hutte La HLWD L26 132 B7
Newick Rd KKBY L32 85 L4
Newington CLVPS L1 13 J8
New Islington VAUX/LVPD L3 13 K5
Newland Av WGNW/BIL/O WN5 67 M8
Newland Cl WDN WA8 133 L2 9
Newland Ct AIG/SPK L17 129 L2 3
Newland Dr WAL/EG CH44 111 J1
Newlands CHLY/EC PR7 30 E7
Newlands Av BRSC L40 52 B1 2
Newlands Cl FROD/HEL WA6 160 E7
Newlands Dr GOL/RIS/CU WA3 92 E5
Newlands Rd BEB CH63 143 K1 3
RNFD/HAY WA11 89 L6
WARRS WA4 138 B3
New La BRSC L40 38 D7
CHLY/EC PR7 30 C3
CHTN/BK PR9 25 M1
GOL/RIS/CU WA3 106 C6
ORM L39 61 G2
ORM L39 63 G3
WARRS WA4 138 D8
New Lane Pace CHTN/BK PR9 23 K5
Newling St BIRK CH41 10 E4
New Ldg WGN WN1 68 E3
Newlyn Av LITH L21 83 J4
MGHL L31 73 G4
Newlyn Cl HOY CH47 109 G3
RUNC WA7 150 D7
Newlyn Dr AIMK WN4 91 K3
SKEL WN8 65 M6 1
Newlyn Gdns
WARRW/BUR WA5 135 M2
Newlyn Gv RNFD/HAY WA11 89 M6
Newlyn Rd HOY CH47 109 G4
NG/CROX L11 85 M8
Newlyn Wk NG/CROX L11 85 M8 3
Newman Av WGNNW/ST WN6 68 C3
New Manchester Rd
WARR WA1 122 C6
Newman Cl WGNE/HIN WN2 69 L7
New Manor Rd WARRS WA4 151 K7
Newman St ANF/KKDL L4 96 F5
WARRS WA4 138 B2
WGN WN1 69 G3 1
New Market St CHLY/EC PR7 32 E5
WGN WN1 4 E3
New Meadow La FMBY L37 60 A5
New Miles La WGNNW/ST WN6 55 H7
New Mill Stile WLTN L25 131 J2
New Mill St CHLY/EC PR7 30 E7
Newmoore La RUNC WA7 151 H1
Newmorn Ct AIG/SPK L17 129 L3 7
Newnham Dr EP CH65 20 D7
New Pale Rd FROD/HEL WA6 167 K5
Newport Av WAL/NB CH45 94 F6 2
Newport Cl CL/PREN CH43 126 E1 4
Newport Ct EV L5 96 E8 1
New Quay VAUX/LVPD L3 12 D6
Newquay Cl RUNC WA7 150 D7
New Rd BRSC L40 39 K1
CHLY/EC PR7 43 H2
CHLYE PR6 44 F5
CLB/OSW/ST L13 98 A8
FMBY L37 47 J8
GTS/LS CH66 155 J5
LEY/BBR PR5 29 K6
PR/KW L34 101 G6
WARRS WA4 14 F8
WGNE/HIN WN2 57 J7
New School La GTS/LS CH66 155 K5
Newsham Cl WDN WA8 133 K1 2
Newsham Dr NPK/KEN L6 97 L8
Newsham Rd HUY L36 116 C5
Newsham St EV L5 96 F8 5
Newsholme Cl
GOL/RIS/CU WA3 107 H2 2
News La RNFD/HAY WA11 76 B3
Newstead Av CSBY/BLUN L23 82 D2
Newstead Rd TOX L8 113 L6 4
WGNS/IIMK WN3 79 G2
Newstet Rd NWD/KWIPK L33 86 D3
New St BRSC L40 40 E3
CHLY/EC PR7 30 E7
HOR/BR BL6 57 M3
NSTN CH64 153 G8
ORM L39 49 K4
RUNC WA7 19 G4
STHEL WA9 102 E7
WAL/EG CH44 112 A3
WGNE/HIN WN2 80 C4
WGNW/BIL/O WN5 67 K8
Newton Av GOL/RIS/CU WA3 107 G8 1
Newton Cl WD/CROXPK L12 98 D5 3
WGN WN1 68 F3
Newton Ct CLB/OSW/ST L13 114 A4
Newton Cross La WKBY CH48 125 G3
Newton Dr WKBY CH48 125 G3
Newton Gv
WARRN/WOL WA2 122 B2 2
Newton Hollow
FROD/HEL WA6 167 K5
Newton La NEWLW WA12 92 A7
WARRS WA4 151 L5
Newton Park Dr NEWLW WA12 105 H3
Newton Park Rd WKBY CH48 125 G3
Newton Rd CLB/OSW/ST L13 114 A1
EP CH65 20 D4
GOL/RIS/CU WA3 93 G7
HOY CH47 108 E6
STHEL WA9 103 J2
WAL/EG CH44 111 J1
WARRN/WOL WA2 105 H5
WARRN/WOL WA2 121 J2
WGNW/BIL/O WN5 78 B7
Newton St BIRK CH41 10 F4
CHTN/BK PR9 25 J6
Newton Wy
GR/UP/WCH CH49 110 B8 4
VAUX/LVPD L3 13 L7
New Tower Ct WAL/NB CH45 95 L5
Newtown NSTN CH64 153 H7
New Wy ORM L39 74 D3
Nicander Rd CALD/MH L18 114 B8
Nicholas Rd CSBY/BLUN L23 82 D1
WDN WA8 133 L5
Nicholas St VAUX/LVPD L3 13 G3 1
Nicholl Rd ECCL WA10 88 C7
Nicholls Dr PEN/TH CH61 141 H1
Nicholls St WARRS WA4 138 D3
Nicholson St STHEL WA9 103 G1 2
WARR WA1 14 B5
Nichol St CHLY/EC PR7 32 E4 5
Nick Hilton's La CHLYE PR6 44 F2
Nickleby Cl TOX L8 113 H8 3
Nickleton Brow CHLYE PR6 44 E3
Nicol Av GOL/RIS/CU WA3 123 H4
Nicol Mere Dr AIMK WN4 79 K8 2
Nicol Rd AIMK WN4 79 J8
Nidderdale Av RAIN/WH L35 117 M2 3
Nigel Rd HES CH60 141 L5
Nightingale Cl
GOL/RIS/CU WA3 123 H1 3
KKBY L32 85 K2 2
NTHLY L27 116 B8 2
RUNC WA7 150 A8
Nightingale Rd HOR/BR BL6 57 L2
WD/CROXPK L12 99 H2
Nightingale St CHLYE PR6 44 C5 6
Nimrod St ANF/KKDL L4 97 H4
Nipe La SKEL WN8 65 K8
Nithsdale Rd WAV L15 114 A7 1
Nixons La SKEL WN8 65 M6
STHP PR8 35 G6
Nixon St ANF/KKDL L4 97 H3
Noble Cl GOL/RIS/CU WA3 123 G2
Noctorum Av
GR/UP/WCH CH49 110 E8
Noctorum Dell CL/PREN CH43 126 F1
Noctorum La CL/PREN CH43 111 G7
Noctorum Rd CL/PREN CH43 110 F8
Noctorum Wy CL/PREN CH43 126 F1
Noel Ga ORM L39 62 D4
Noel St TOX L8 113 K6
Nolan St STHP PR8 3 K8
Nook La BRSC L40 30 A8
GOL/RIS/CU WA3 92 D5
STHEL WA9 103 H4
WARRN/WOL WA2 122 D3
WARRS WA4 138 C2
Nook Ri WAV L15 114 D5
The Nook CL/PREN CH43 10 D7

ECCL WA10 88 D7
WGNNW/ST WN6 55 G6
WKBY CH48 125 K3
WLTN L25 131 K2
Nora St WARR WA1 15 H6
Norbreck Av DV/KA/FCH L14 115 G3
Norbreck Cl WARRW/BUR WA5 136 C1
Norbreck Crs
WARRW/BUR WA5 136 C1
WGNNW/ST WN6 68 C3
Norburn Crs FMBY L37 59 H3
Norbury Av BEB CH63 128 A8
CALD/MH L18 114 B8
WARRN/WOL WA2 121 M5 1
WGNW/BIL/O WN5 77 M7
Norbury Cl BEB CH63 128 B8
CHTN/BK PR9 22 E8
Norbury Fold RAIN/WH L35 118 A4 2
Norbury Rd KKBY L32 85 M3
Norbury St LEIGH WN7 81 M8
Norcliffe Rd RAIN/WH L35 117 K1
Norcott Av WARRS WA4 137 M3
Norcott Dr
WARRW/BUR WA5 104 B7 6
Norden Cl GOL/RIS/CU WA3 106 E8
Norfolk Cl CL/PREN CH43 110 E8
Norfolk Dr WARRW/BUR WA5 120 A7
WKBY CH48 124 E4
Norfolk Gv STHP PR8 35 H4
Norfolk Pl LITH L21 83 J6 4
WDN WA8 133 L5
Norfolk Rd ECCL WA10 8 A9
EP CH65 20 C5
MGHL L31 72 E6
STHP PR8 35 H4
WGNW/BIL/O WN5 78 A4
Norfolk St CLVPS L1 112 F6
RUNC WA7 19 K2
WGNNW/ST WN6 68 C3
WGNW/BIL/O WN5 68 B7 5
Norgate St ANF/KKDL L4 97 H6 5
Norgrove Cl RUNC WA7 150 F5
Norland's La RAIN/WH L35 118 A5
WDN WA8 118 A6
Norland St WDN WA8 17 J1 1
Norleane Crs RUNC WA7 19 J8
Norley Av EP CH65 156 B7
PS/BROM CH62 155 G2
Norley Dr ECCL WA10 101 J2
Norley Hall Av
WGNW/BIL/O WN5 67 L7
Norley Pl HLWD L26 132 A7
Norley Rd LEIGH WN7 93 K1
WGNW/BIL/O WN5 67 K6
Norman Av NEWLW WA12 105 G2
RNFD/HAY WA11 91 J6
Normanby Cl
WARRW/BUR WA5 121 G6
Normanby St WGNW/BIL/O WN5 67 K7
Norman Cl GTS/LS CH66 163 H5
Normandale Rd ANF/KKDL L4 97 M4
Normandy Rd HUY L36 115 M2
Normanhurst ORM L39 63 J1
Norman Rd BTL L20 83 L6
CSBY/BLUN L23 82 F2
RUNC WA7 19 G6
WAL/EG CH44 112 A3 15
Normans Rd STHEL WA9 103 H6
Normanston Rd
CL/PREN CH43 127 K1 5
Norman St BIRK CH41 111 H5
VAUX/LVPD L3 13 L6
WARRN/WOL WA2 14 F3
Normanton Av AIG/SPK L17 129 L2
Normanton Cl
WGNNW/ST WN6 68 A1 1
Norma Rd CSBY/WL L22 83 G4
Norreys Av WARRW/BUR WA5 121 H5
Norris Cl CL/PREN CH43 110 E8
Norris Green Crs NG/CROX L11 98 C4
Norris Green Rd
WD/CROXPK L12 98 D7
Norris Green Wy NG/CROX L11 98 C4
Norris House Dr ORM L39 62 E5
Norris Rd PR/KW L34 100 E7
Norris St CHLY/EC PR7 32 E7 2
WARRN/WOL WA2 121 L5
Norris Wy FMBY L37 58 E3
Norseman Cl WD/CROXPK L12 98 D5
Northam Cl CHTN/BK PR9 22 C8
North Av AIN/FAZ L10 85 G3
SPK/HALE L24 131 J7
WARRN/WOL WA2 121 K5
North Barcombe Rd
CHLDW L16 114 F6
Northbrook Cl TOX L8 113 J6 7
Northbrook Rd WAL/EG CH44 111 M2
Northbrook St TOX L8 113 J6 8
Northbury Rd GTS/LS CH66 163 G4
North Cantril Av
WD/CROXPK L12 99 G5
North Cl PS/BROM CH62 143 L3
Northcote Cl EV L5 13 M1 2
Northcote Rd WAL/NB CH45 94 F7
WLT/FAZ L9 97 H2 3
Northcroft WGN WN1 5 M2
Northdale Rd WARR WA1 122 C5
WAV L15 114 B5
Northdene SKEL WN8 53 K3
North Dingle ANF/KKDL L4 96 F5
North Dr HES CH60 141 J6
WAV L15 114 B5
WD/CROXPK L12 98 D8
Northdunes HTWN L38 70 B1
Northenden Rd CHLY/EC PR7 43 G4
North End La HLWD L26 132 A2
HTWN L38 59 J8
Northern La RAIN/WH L35 133 J2
Northern Perimeter Rd
NTHTN L30 72 A8
Northern Ri GTS/LS CH66 163 G1
Northern Rd SPK/HALE L24 147 G1 2
The Northern Rd
CSBY/BLUN L23 83 G1
Northfield SKEL WN8 65 K1
Northfield Cl NWD/KWIPK L33 86 C1 5
STHEL WA9 118 F2 3
Northfield Rd BTL L20 84 A7
North Florida Rd
RNFD/HAY WA11 90 F5
North Front RAIN/WH L35 117 G4
Northgate Dr CHLYE PR6 33 G3
Northgate Rd CLB/OSW/ST L13 98 D8
North Gv CALD/MH L18 130 E4
North Hill St TOX L8 113 J7 5
North John St CLVP L2 12 F7
ECCL WA10 8 F5
North Leach Dr STHP PR8 34 C8
North Linkside Rd WLTN L25 131 L4
North Manor Wy WLTN L25 131 L4
North Meade MGHL L31 72 D3
Northmead Rd ALL/GAR L19 131 G6
North Moor La ORM L39 50 B5
North Moss La FMBY L37 47 M6
North Mossley Hill Rd
CALD/MH L18 130 B1
North Mount Rd KKBY L32 85 K1
Northolt Ct
WARRN/WOL WA2 122 A4 6
North Pde HOY CH47 108 C6
KKBY L32 86 A3
NSTN CH64 152 C3
SPK/HALE L24 147 G2
North Park Brook Rd
WARRW/BUR WA5 121 G4
North Park Rd KKBY L32 85 L1
North Perimeter Rd
NWD/KWIPK L33 86 F1
Northridge Rd PEN/TH CH61 126 C8
North Rd ALL/GAR L19 130 B7
CHTN/BK PR9 25 K1
DV/KA/FCH L14 114 E3
ECCL WA10 8 F1
EP CH65 156 A2
RF/TRAN CH42 127 L2
SPK/HALE L24 132 C8
WKBY CH48 124 C3
Northside CHLY/EC PR7 31 L2 2
North St AIMK WN4 79 M8
CHLYE PR6 32 E3
CHTN/BK PR9 3 J1
NEWLW WA12 104 B1 3
RNFD/HAY WA11 91 G7 2
VAUX/LVPD L3 13 G5
North Sudley Rd AIG/SPK L17 130 A3
Northumberland Gv TOX L8 112 F8 1
Northumberland St
CHLY/EC PR7 32 F6 5
TOX L8 113 G8
WGN WN1 5 J3
Northumberland Ter EV L5 97 G7
Northumberland Wy NTHTN L30 83 L2
North V CHLYE PR6 44 B4
North Vw EHL/KEN L7 113 J4
HUY L36 116 C3
WARRW/BUR WA5 120 A6
Northway HES CH60 141 M4 1
LYMM WA13 139 M1 2
MGHL L31 72 F3
RUNC WA7 150 B5
SKEL WN8 65 K4
WARRN/WOL WA2 121 K3
WAV L15 114 D5
WDN WA8 133 M4
WGN WN1 4 E2
Northways PS/BROM CH62 143 M2 3
WGNNW/ST WN6 55 M3 1
Northwich Cl CSBY/BLUN L23 71 K7
Northwich Rd RUNC WA7 150 E8
North William St
WAL/EG CH44 112 A3 16
Northwold Cl WGNS/IIMK WN3 78 E2
Northwood Av
NEWLW WA12 105 H2 2
Northwood Rd CL/PREN CH43 127 H3
HUY L36 116 B1
RUNC WA7 150 A3
Norton Av WARRW/BUR WA5 120 A8
Norton Dr PEN/TH CH61 125 L6
Norton Ga RUNC WA7 150 E5
Norton Gv MGHL L31 72 F7
RAIN/WH L35 101 M6
Norton Hl RUNC WA7 150 E3
Norton La RUNC WA7 150 E5
Norton Rd WKBY CH48 124 C2 5
Norton Station Rd RUNC WA7 150 F5
Norton St BTL L20 6 E1
VAUX/LVPD L3 13 J5
Norton Vw RUNC WA7 150 C5
Norton Village RUNC WA7 150 F5
Nortonwood La RUNC WA7 150 E4
Norville GTS/LS CH66 155 M6
Norville Rd DV/KA/FCH L14 114 E3
Norwich Av AIMK WN4 91 M3
GOL/RIS/CU WA3 92 F5
Norwich Dr GR/UP/WCH CH49 110 C6
GTS/LS CH66 163 G5
Norwich Rd WAV L15 114 C7
Norwich Wy KKBY L32 86 A3
Norwood Av AIMK WN4 79 H7 4
CHTN/BK PR9 25 G5
GOL/RIS/CU WA3 93 G6
LITH L21 83 K4
WGNNW/ST WN6 68 C2
Norwood Cl CHLYE PR6 44 C5 2
NPK/KEN L6 113 K1 6
Norwood Ct
GR/UP/WCH CH49 125 M2 2
Norwood Crs CHTN/BK PR9 25 G5
Norwood Gv NPK/KEN L6 113 K1 7
RNFD/HAY WA11 76 C7 1
Norwood Rd GR/UP/WCH CH49 125 M1
STHP PR8 25 H6
WAL/EG CH44 111 K3
Norwyn Rd NG/CROX L11 98 A3
Nostell Rd ANF/KKDL L4 79 J8
Nottingham Cl RAIN/WH L35 101 L8
WARR WA1 122 F7
Nottingham Pl WGN WN1 5 K1
Nottingham Rd HUY L36 115 L4 5
Nowshera Av PEN/TH CH61 126 B8 1
Nuffield Cl GR/UP/WCH CH49 126 B1
Nun Cl CL/PREN CH43 127 K1
Nunn St STHEL WA9 102 F2
Nunsford Cl LITH L21 83 M3
Nunthorpe Rd PR/KW L34 86 D8 1
The Nurseries FMBY L37 59 J3 4
Nurse Rd PEN/TH CH61 126 D7
Nursery Av ORM L39 51 J7
Nursery Cl CHLY/EC PR7 42 F1 1
CL/PREN CH43 127 K2
WDN WA8 134 F2
WLTN L25 131 L5
Nursery Dr FMBY L37 59 H3
Nursery La ALL/GAR L19 130 E6
Nursery Rd MGHL L31 72 E1
RAIN/WH L35 101 M6
Nutgrove Av RAIN/WH L35 101 M6 6
Nutgrove Hall Dr RAIN/WH L35 101 M6
Nutgrove Rd RAIN/WH L35 101 L7
Nuthall Rd STHP PR8 36 A2
Nut St RAIN/WH L35 101 M6
Nuttall Ct GOL/RIS/CU WA3 122 E1
Nuttall St EHL/KEN L7 113 L4
Nutt St WGN WN1 5 J1
Nyland Rd HUY L36 99 M8

O

Oak Av CHLY/EC PR7 31 M2
GOL/RIS/CU WA3 92 D5
GR/UP/WCH CH49 109 M7
NEWLW WA12 104 E2
ORM L39 62 F1
RNFD/HAY WA11 91 G6
WGNE/HIN WN2 80 E6
WGNE/HIN WN2 81 J2
WGNNW/ST WN6 56 B5
WLT/FAZ L9 84 D7 6
Oak Bank BIRK CH41 10 F8 2
Oakbank WGNE/HIN WN2 80 D2
Oakbank Rd AIG/SPK L17 114 A8
Oakbank St WAL/EG CH44 111 L2 6
Oakbourne Cl AIG/SPK L17 129 L3 3
Oak Cl MOR/LEA CH46 109 M6 3
RAIN/WH L35 117 G2
WD/CROXPK L12 99 H4
Oak Crs SKEL WN8 64 F4
Oakdale Av FROD/HEL WA6 160 F7
WAL/EG CH44 111 M3
WARRS WA4 137 M4
Oakdale Dr GR/UP/WCH CH49 125 L3
Oakdale Rd CALD/MH L18 114 C8
CSBY/WL L22 82 F3
WAL/EG CH44 111 M4
Oakdene Av GTS/LS CH66 155 L8
WARR WA1 122 E6
Oakdene Cl PS/BROM CH62 143 M8
Oakdene Rd ANF/KKDL L4 97 K6
RF/TRAN CH42 127 L2
Oak Dr CHLYE PR6 32 E2
RUNC WA7 19 M9
Oakenden Cl AIMK WN4 79 J7 1
Oakengates WGNNW/ST WN6 56 B4
Oakenholt Rd
MOR/LEA CH46 110 A4 3
Oakes St VAUX/LVPD L3 13 L6
Oakfield ANF/KKDL L4 97 K7
Oakfield Av GOL/RIS/CU WA3 92 B4
WLTN L25 131 J1
Oakfield Cl RAIN/WH L35 101 M6 7
Oakfield Crs WGNE/HIN WN2 57 L8
Oakfield Dr FMBY L37 58 F1
HUY L36 116 B5
WDN WA8 133 J5
Oakfield Gv HUY L36 116 B5 5
Oakfield Rd ANF/KKDL L4 97 J7
GTS/LS CH66 155 G5
HTWN L38 70 B3
PS/BROM CH62 143 L5
Oakford Cl CHTN/BK PR9 23 K8
Oak Gn ORM L39 51 H8 3
Oak Gv EP CH65 163 J2
Oakham Dr AIN/FAZ L10 85 H4
MOR/LEA CH46 109 K4
Oakham St TOX L8 112 F7
Oakhill Cl MGHL L31 72 F3 5
WD/CROXPK L12 98 F2 5
Oak Hill Cl WGN WN1 68 D2 1
Oakhill Cottage La MGHL L31 72 F1 1
Oakhill Dr MGHL L31 72 E1
Oakhill Pk CLB/OSW/ST L13 114 D3
Oakhill Rd CLB/OSW/ST L13 114 D3
MGHL L31 72 F3
Oakhurst Cl WLTN L25 131 K1
Oakland Cl LITH L21 83 L7
Oakland Dr GR/UP/WCH CH49 110 C7
Oakland Rd ALL/GAR L19 130 B5
Oaklands RAIN/WH L35 117 L2 5
Oaklands Av CSBY/BLUN L23 71 G8
Oaklands Ct STHEL WA9 118 E1 15
Oaklands Dr BEB CH63 128 C7
HES CH60 141 J4
LYMM WA13 139 M3
Oaklands Rd GOL/RIS/CU WA3 93 H6
Oaklands Ter PEN/TH CH61 141 J3 1
Oakland St WARR WA1 15 M1
WDN WA8 149 J1
Oak La WD/CROXPK L12 98 E3
Oak La North WD/CROXPK L12 98 E3
Oaklea WGNNW/ST WN6 55 J3
Oakleaf Ms CL/PREN CH43 110 F8 4
Oaklea Rd PEN/TH CH61 126 B7
Oaklee Gv NWD/KWIPK L33 86 C1 6
Oak Leigh CLB/OSW/ST L13 98 A8
Oakleigh SKEL WN8 76 F3
Oakleigh Gv BEB CH63 128 B7
Oakley Av WGNW/BIL/O WN5 77 M7
Oakley Cl WD/CROXPK L12 99 G2
The Oaklings WGNE/HIN WN2 81 J2 4
Oakmere Cl WLT/FAZ L9 84 C6 1
Oakmere Dr GR/UP/WCH CH49 125 L1
GTS/LS CH66 163 H5
WARRW/BUR WA5 136 B2
Oakmere St RUNC WA7 19 G4
Oakridge Cl PS/BROM CH62 143 L3
Oakridge Rd PS/BROM CH62 143 L3
Oak Rd BEB CH63 128 B6
GTS/LS CH66 155 G4
HUY L36 115 M5
LYMM WA13 139 L2
RAIN/WH L35 117 G2
WARRW/BUR WA5 136 B2
Oaks Cl STHEL WA9 118 F2 3
Oaks La PEN/TH CH61 141 J1
Oaksmeade Cl WD/CROXPK L12 99 H2
Oaks Pl WDN WA8 16 C5
The Oaks CHLY/EC PR7 43 K1
PS/BROM CH62 143 L5
WD/CROXPK L12 99 H2
Oakston Av RAIN/WH L35 117 M3 3
Oak St BTL L20 7 H2
EP CH65 156 E6
GOL/RIS/CU WA3 106 C6
STHEL WA9 103 C5
STHP PR8 25 G7
WGN WN1 5 J4
Oaksway HES CH60 141 K7
Oakthorn Gv RNFD/HAY WA11 90 E7
Oak Tree Cl SKEL WN8 65 M2 3
Oaktree Pl RF/TRAN CH42 128 B2
Oaktree Rd ECCL WA10 88 C8
Oak V CLB/OSW/ST L13 114 D3 2
Oak Vw SPK/HALE L24 147 J2
Oakways WARRS WA4 137 M8
Oakwood SKEL WN8 65 M2 4
Oakwood Av AIMK WN4 91 J3
STHP PR8 34 F7
WARR WA1 15 K2
WGNNW/ST WN6 55 H8
Oakwood Cl WLTN L25 115 K8
Oakwood Dr CL/PREN CH43 111 G5
HUY L36 116 B4
STHP PR8 35 G8
Oakwood Ga GOL/RIS/CU WA3 122 F1
Oakwood Rd CHLY/EC PR7 32 D7
CHLY/EC PR7 43 H3
HLWD L26 132 A6
Oakwood Vw CHLY/EC PR7 43 K1 1
Oakworth Dr HUY L36 116 C6
PS/BROM CH62 128 E6
Oarside Dr WAL/NB CH45 95 J7
Oasis Cl BRSC L40 39 K2
Oatfield La LITH L21 83 K3
Oatlands Rd KKBY L32 85 L3 3
The Oatlands WKBY CH48 124 E4
Oban Dr AIMK WN4 90 E1
HES CH60 141 J5
Oban Gv WARRN/WOL WA2 122 C2
Oban Rd ANF/KKDL L4 97 K7
Oban Wy WGNE/HIN WN2 57 M8 5
Oberon St BTL L20 7 H9
O'brien Gv STHEL WA9 103 G1
Observatory Rd CL/PREN CH43 110 F5
Oceanic Rd CLB/OSW/ST L13 114 B3
Ocean Rd LITH L21 83 K6
O'connell Cl RNFD/HAY WA11 90 E7
O'connell Rd VAUX/LVPD L3 13 G2
Octavia Hill Rd LITH L21 83 L4
Odsey St EHL/KEN L7 113 L3 7
Off Botanic Rd CHTN/BK PR9 25 J4
Ogle Cl RAIN/WH L35 101 G8
Oglet La SPK/HALE L24 146 E3
Oil Sites Rd EP CH65 20 E2
Oil St VAUX/LVPD L3 12 C2
O'keeffe Rd STHEL WA9 9 M4
Okehampton Rd CHLDW L16 114 F5
Okell Dr HLWD L26 131 M3
HLWD L26 132 A3 2
Okell Gv LEIGH WN7 81 M7 6
Okell St RUNC WA7 19 G4
Old Acre HTWN L38 70 B2
Old Barn Rd ANF/KKDL L4 97 K7 2
WAL/EG CH44 111 J2
Old Bidston Rd BIRK CH41 10 D2
Old Boston RNFD/HAY WA11 91 J6
Old Boundary Wy ORM L39 51 H7
Oldbridge Dr WGNE/HIN WN2 69 M7 3
Oldbridge Rd SPK/HALE L24 147 H2
Old Bridge Wy CHLYE PR6 32 F4
Old Cherry La LYMM WA13 139 J7 1
Old Chester Rd BEB CH63 128 B6
FROD/HEL WA6 166 D2
GTS/LS CH66 155 M8 1
RF/TRAN CH42 128 B3
WARRS WA4 137 H6
Old Church Cl EP CH65 20 D1 1
Old Church Yd CLVP L2 12 E7
Old Colliery Rd RAIN/WH L35 116 F2
Old Colliery Yd AIMK WN4 90 E2
Old Dawber's La CHLY/EC PR7 31 K4
Old Distillery Rd SPK/HALE L24 131 K8
Old Dover Rd HUY L36 115 L5
Old Eccleston La ECCL WA10 101 L2
Old Engine La SKEL WN8 64 E3
Old Farm Cl NSTN CH64 154 C5
Old Farm Rd CSBY/BLUN L23 83 H1
KKBY L32 86 B7
Oldfield Cl HES CH60 141 G3 1
Oldfield Dr HES CH60 140 E4
Oldfield Gdns HES CH60 140 F4
Oldfield La WKBY CH48 109 J8
Oldfield Rd ALL/GAR L19 130 C4
EP CH65 20 B5
HES CH60 140 F3
LYMM WA13 139 K1
Oldfield St ECCL WA10 8 F1
Oldfield Wy HES CH60 140 F3
Old Fold WGNW/BIL/O WN5 67 K7 5
Old Fold Rd WGNE/HIN WN2 57 M8
Oldgate WDN WA8 133 L7
Old Gorsey La WAL/EG CH44 111 K3
Old Hall RAIN/WH L35 117 G5
Old Hall Cl MGHL L31 72 F6
WARRS WA4 137 J5
Old Hall Dr AIMK WN4 91 J3
EP CH65 20 B7
Old Hall Gdns RNFD/HAY WA11 76 C7
Old Hall La CHLY/EC PR7 31 K7
CHNE CH2 165 K2
KKBY L32 85 M3
Old Hall Rd MGHL L31 72 F6
PS/BROM CH62 144 A4
WARRW/BUR WA5 120 F5
Old Hall St VAUX/LVPD L3 12 D5
WGNS/IIMK WN3 5 K8
Oldham Pl CLVPS L1 13 J8
Oldham St CLVPS L1 13 J9
WARRS WA4 15 H9
Old Haymarket CLVPS L1 13 H6
Old Higher Rd WDN WA8 132 F8
Old Hutte La SPK/HALE L24 132 C8
Old Kennel Cl STBRV L28 99 H5
Old La BRSC L40 40 F5
FMBY L37 47 H7
MGHL L31 73 G1
ORM L39 61 G2
PR/KW L34 101 H7
RAIN/WH L35 117 K3
RNFD/HAY WA11 76 B6
WGNNW/ST WN6 55 K7
Old Leeds St VAUX/LVPD L3 12 D5
Old Links Cl CHTN/BK PR9 25 K5
Old Liverpool Rd
WARRW/BUR WA5 14 A7
Old Lord's Crs HOR/BR BL6 45 K8
Old Maryland La
MOR/LEA CH46 110 A4 4
Old Meadow PR/KW L34 86 F8
Old Meadow Rd
PEN/TH CH61 141 H1 1
Old Mill Av STHEL WA9 102 F8
Old Mill Cl HES CH60 141 K6
Old Mill Hl ORM L39 62 F2
Old Mill La FMBY L37 59 H1
PR/KW L34 100 A1
WAV L15 114 C5
Old Moss La ORM L39 48 E8
Old Nook La RNFD/HAY WA11 90 A7
Old Orch RAIN/WH L35 117 G4
Old Park La CHTN/BK PR9 25 J6
Old Pepper La WGNNW/ST WN6 55 K3
Old Post Office Pl CLVPS L1 13 G8 1
Old Prescot Cl MGHL L31 73 L3
Old Pump La
GR/UP/WCH CH49 125 L2 5
The Old Quarry WLTN L25 131 J3 2
Old Quay Cl NSTN CH64 152 E6 1
Old Quay La NSTN CH64 152 F6
Old Quay St RUNC WA7 19 K2
Old Racecourse Rd MGHL L31 72 D5
Old Rake HOR/BR BL6 45 M8
Old Rectory Gn ORM L39 62 C6
SFTN L29 72 A6
Old Riding DV/KA/FCH L14 99 H8
Old Rd AIMK WN4 79 J8
WARRS WA4 14 F8
Old Ropery CLVP L2 12 E7 4
Old Rough La NWD/KWIPK L33 86 A3
Old School Cl NSTN CH64 153 H8
Old School House La
WARRN/WOL WA2 105 J6
Old School La CHLY/EC PR7 31 M2 1
CHLY/EC PR7 31 M2 1
CHLY/EC PR7 44 A8
Old School Pl AIMK WN4 91 J2 3
Old School Wy
CL/PREN CH43 111 G6 1
Old Smithy La LYMM WA13 139 L3
Old Thomas La DV/KA/FCH L14 114 F4
Old Town La FMBY L37 59 G1
Old Upton La WDN WA8 134 A1
Old Vicarage Rd NSTN CH64 154 C5
Old Wargrave Rd NEWLW WA12 104 D2
Old Whint Rd RNFD/HAY WA11 90 C7
Old Will's La HOR/BR BL6 45 K7
Old Wood Rd PEN/TH CH61 141 H1
Oleander Dr ECCL WA10 101 L1
O'leary St WARRN/WOL WA2 15 H1
Olga Rd STHEL WA9 102 E6
Olinda St PS/BROM CH62 128 D6
Olive Cl MGHL L31 85 J3 1
Olive Crs BIRK CH41 11 K9
Olivedale Rd CALD/MH L18 130 B1
Olive Dr NSTN CH64 153 G5
Olive Gv HUY L36 115 M3
NTHTN L30 84 C4
SKEL WN8 65 G4
STHP PR8 25 G6
WAV L15 114 C4
WGNNW/ST WN6 68 B2
Olive La WAV L15 114 C5
Olive Mt BIRK CH41 11 K9
Olive Mount Rd WAV L15 114 C5
Oliver La BIRK CH41 11 J6
GTS/LS CH66 162 F1
Oliver Lyme Rd PR/KW L34 101 G7
Olive Rd CSBY/WL L22 83 G5 2
NSTN CH64 153 G5
Oliver Rd ECCL WA10 101 L4
Oliver St BIRK CH41 11 G6
WARRN/WOL WA2 14 E3
Oliver St East BIRK CH41 11 J6
Olivetree Rd WAV L15 114 D5
Olive V WAV L15 114 B5
Olivia Cl CL/PREN CH43 126 E1
Olivia St BTL L20 7 J8
Ollerton Cl CL/PREN CH43 126 E1 5
WARRS WA4 138 D2
WGNE/HIN WN2 69 J3
Ollerton St CHLYE PR6 44 C5
Ollery Gn NTHTN L30 84 D1
Olney St ANF/KKDL L4 97 H3
Olton St WAV L15 114 A5
Olympia St NPK/KEN L6 113 J2 14
Olympic Wy WLT/FAZ L9 84 C5
O'neill St BTL L20 6 E2
Onslow Crs STHP PR8 35 J3
Onslow Rd NPK/KEN L6 113 L2
PS/BROM CH62 128 D5
WAL/NB CH45 95 K5
Opal Cl LITH L21 83 L5
Openfields Cl HLWD L26 132 A3 5
Oppenheim Av ECCL WA10 101 L5
Orange Gv TOX L8 113 L7 1
WARRN/WOL WA2 122 A3
Orange Tree Cl STBRV L28 99 K5 2
Oran Wy HUY L36 115 M2
Orb Cl NG/CROX L11 98 E2
Orchard Av CHLDW L16 114 F4
Orchard Cl CHLY/EC PR7 31 M1
FROD/HEL WA6 160 C7
GTS/LS CH66 163 H4
PR/KW L34 101 J6
RAIN/WH L35 117 G4
RNFD/HAY WA11 89 M6
WGNNW/ST WN6 55 J6
Orchard Ct BIRK CH41 128 B2 10

Orchard Dl CSBY/BLUN L23 83 H1
Orchard Dr NSTN CH64 153 G8
Orchard Gra MOR/LEA CH46 109 L6
Orchard Hvn GTS/LS CH66 163 G4
Orchard Hey ECCL WA10 101 J2
MGHL L31 73 G5
NTHTN L30 84 D2
Orchard La GTS/LS CH66 155 J5
STHP PR8 47 M1
Orchard Park La CHNE CH2 165 K1
Orchard Pl FROD/HEL WA6 166 E1 4
Orchard Rd EP CH65 163 J3
MOR/LEA CH46 110 A4
Orchard St AIMK WN4 91 L2
WARR WA1 15 G5
WARRN/WOL WA2 122 C3
WARRS WA4 137 L5
WGN WN1 5 G3
The Orchard AIG/SPK L17 130 B4 2
FROD/HEL WA6 166 C3
HUY L36 116 A4
LEY/BBR PR5 29 L2
ORM L39 50 F8
WAL/NB CH45 95 J6
Orchard Vw ORM L39 62 F4
Orchard Wy BEB CH63 127 M7
WDN WA8 133 J2 1
Orchid Gv AIG/SPK L17 129 H2 7
Orchil Cl GTS/LS CH66 155 J7
Ordnance Av GOL/RIS/CU WA3 123 H1
O'reilly Ct VAUX/LVPD L3 12 E1
Orford Av WARRN/WOL WA2 15 G1
Orford Gn WARRN/WOL WA2 121 M4
Orford La WARRN/WOL WA2 14 F2
Orford Rd WARRN/WOL WA2 121 M5
Orford St WARR WA1 14 F5
WAV L15 114 B5
Organ St WGNE/HIN WN2 81 K2
Oriel Cl AIN/FAZ L10 84 F2
Oriel Crs BTL L20 7 H9
Oriel Dr AIN/FAZ L10 84 F2
Oriel Rd AIMK WN4 91 H1
BTL L20 6 F6
RF/TRAN CH42 128 A2
Oriel St VAUX/LVPD L3 12 F3
Orient Dr WLTN L25 131 K2
Origen Rd CHLDW L16 114 F4
Oriole Cl ECCL WA10 101 K6
Orith Av ECCL WA10 101 H2
Orkney Cl EP CH65 163 L4 4
RNFD/HAY WA11 89 M6
WDN WA8 135 J2
Orlando Cl CL/PREN CH43 126 E1 6
Orlando St BTL L20 7 H9
Orleans Rd CLB/OSW/ST L13 114 C2
Ormande St STHEL WA9 102 D4
Ormesby Gv BEB CH63 143 J7
Ormiston Rd WAL/NB CH45 95 K6
Ormond Av BRSC L40 63 M1
Ormonde Av MGHL L31 72 E6
Ormonde Crs NWD/KWIPK L33 86 C3
Ormonde Dr MGHL L31 72 E5
Ormond St VAUX/LVPD L3 12 E6
WAL/NB CH45 95 K8 6
Ormond Wy CL/PREN CH43 126 E1
Ormsby Cl WGNNW/ST WN6 56 A4
Ormsby St WAV L15 114 A6 9
Ormside Cl WGNE/HIN WN2 81 K2
Ormside Gv STHEL WA9 102 F6
Ormskirk Old Rd ORM L39 64 B6
Ormskirk Rd ORM L39 63 L4
PR/KW L34 86 F8
RNFD/HAY WA11 75 M4
SKEL WN8 64 E4 1
SKEL WN8 66 C6
WGNW/BIL/O WN5 67 L7
WLT/FAZ L9 84 D3
Ormskirk St ECCL WA10 8 F4
Ormston Av HOR/BR BL6 45 K8
Orms Wy FMBY L37 59 G2
Orphan Dr NPK/KEN L6 97 M8
Orphan St EHL/KEN L7 113 J5
Orpington St
WGNW/BIL/O WN5 67 L7 4
Orrell Cl WARRW/BUR WA5 120 C7 2
Orrell Gdns WGNW/BIL/O WN5 67 H7
Orrell Hall Cl WGNW/BIL/O WN5 67 K6
Orrell Hey BTL L20 83 M6
Orrell Hill La HTWN L38 70 E1
Orrell La BRSC L40 38 F8
BTL L20 84 B6
WLT/FAZ L9 84 C7
Orrell Mt BTL L20 83 L6
Orrell Rd BTL L20 83 L6
WAL/NB CH45 95 L6
WGNW/BIL/O WN5 67 G6
Orrell St STHEL WA9 9 M5
WGN WN1 5 G6
Orret's Meadow Rd
GR/UP/WCH CH49 126 D2
Orrysdale Rd WKBY CH48 124 C2
Orry St EV L5 96 F8
Orsett Rd KKBY L32 86 B5
Orston Crs BEB CH63 143 J3
Ortega Cl PS/BROM CH62 128 E6 1
Orthes St VAUX/LVPD L3 13 L8 1
Orton Rd CHLDW L16 114 E5
Orton Wy AIMK WN4 91 H2
Orville St STHEL WA9 103 H6 7
Orwell Cl FMBY L37 58 E4
STHEL WA9 118 C2
Orwell Rd ANF/KKDL L4 96 F5
Osbert Rd CSBY/BLUN L23 82 D1
Osborne Av WAL/NB CH45 95 K6
WARRN/WOL WA2 121 M4 2
Osborne Gv WAL/NB CH45 95 K7
Osborne Rd AIMK WN4 91 J1
CL/PREN CH43 10 D7
CLB/OSW/ST L13 98 A7
ECCL WA10 88 C8
FMBY L37 59 G4
GOL/RIS/CU WA3 93 G6
LITH L21 83 L4
STHP PR8 37 H7
WAL/NB CH45 95 L6 10
WARRS WA4 137 K4
Osborne Wd AIG/SPK L17 129 M4
Osbourne Cl PS/BROM CH62 144 A6 1
Osier Cl CHNE CH2 165 L2
Osmaston Rd RF/TRAN CH42 127 J3
Osprey Cl CHLYE PR6 33 J2
NTHLY L27 116 B8 5
RUNC WA7 150 B8
WARRN/WOL WA2 122 A2
The Ospreys WGNS/IIMK WN3 78 E1 2
Ossett Cl CL/PREN CH43 126 E1 7
RUNC WA7 150 F5 4
Osterley Gdns WLT/FAZ L9 84 B7
O'sullivan Crs RNFD/HAY WA11 90 A8
Oteley Av PS/BROM CH62 143 M5
Othello Cl BTL L20 7 H9
Otterburn Cl MOR/LEA CH46 109 K5
Otterspool Dr AIG/SPK L17 129 M5
Otterspool Rd AIG/SPK L17 129 M4
Otterton Rd NG/CROX L11 85 L8 2
Otterwood Sq
WGNW/BIL/O WN5 67 L3
Ottery Cl CHTN/BK PR9 22 C8
Ottley St NPK/KEN L6 113 L2
Otway St ALL/GAR L19 145 L1
Oueenswood Av BEB CH63 128 A5
Oulton Cl CL/PREN CH43 127 G2
MGHL L31 72 D1 2
Oulton La HUY L36 115 L5
Oulton Rd CHLDW L16 114 F7
Oulton Wy CL/PREN CH43 127 G2 2
Oundle Dr AIN/FAZ L10 84 E2 2
Oundle Pl WLTN L25 131 K6
Oundle Rd MOR/LEA CH46 110 A4
Outer Central Rd SPK/HALE L24 132 A8
Outer Forum NG/CROX L11 98 A3
Out La LEY/BBR PR5 29 K3
WLTN L25 131 K3
Outlet La MGHL L31 74 A4
Outterside St CHLY/EC PR7 44 C7
The Oval EP CH65 20 D8
WAL/NB CH45 95 H7
WGNNW/ST WN6 55 H8
Overbeck Cl WGNNW/ST WN6 68 C1
Overbrook La PR/KW L34 86 E8
Overbury St EHL/KEN L7 113 K4
Overchurch Rd
GR/UP/WCH CH49 110 A7
Overdale Av PEN/TH CH61 126 F8
Overdale Rd NSTN CH64 154 C4
Overdene Wk KKBY L32 86 B4
Overgreen Gv
MOR/LEA CH46 109 M4 2
Overhill Wy WGNS/IIMK WN3 78 F2
Overpool Gdns GTS/LS CH66 163 H2 2
Overpool Rd EP CH65 156 B8
GTS/LS CH66 156 A7
Overton Av LITH L21 83 K4
Overton Cl CL/PREN CH43 127 H2
KKBY L32 85 M4
Overton Dr FROD/HEL WA6 160 E7
Overton Rd WAL/EG CH44 111 K1 5
Overton St EHL/KEN L7 113 K4
Overton Wy CL/PREN CH43 127 H2
Ovington Cl RUNC WA7 161 H1 10
Ovington Dr STHP PR8 36 A2
Ovolo Rd CLB/OSW/ST L13 114 C1
Owen Av ORM L39 51 H7 6
Owen Cl ECCL WA10 101 L4
Owen Dr SPK/HALE L24 146 D3
Owen Rd ANF/KKDL L4 96 F5
NWD/KWIPK L33 86 E6
RAIN/WH L35 117 L3
Owen's La ORM L39 61 G3
Owens St CHLYE PR6 33 G6 6
Owen St ECCL WA10 101 L4
LEIGH WN7 81 M8 13
WARRN/WOL WA2 14 D2
Oxborough Cl WDN WA8 134 B1 4
Oxbow Rd WD/CROXPK L12 99 G5
Oxburgh Rd WGNE/HIN WN2 80 B1
Oxendale Cl TOX L8 113 K6 7
Oxenham Rd WARRN/WOL WA2 121 J2
Oxenholme Crs NG/CROX L11 98 C3 1
Oxford Av BTL L20 7 L5
LITH L21 83 K5
Oxford Cl AIG/SPK L17 129 L3 9
GTS/LS CH66 163 G5
Oxford Ct STHP PR8 35 H1
WGN WN1 5 H2
Oxford Dr BEB CH63 142 B7
CSBY/WL L22 82 E4
HLWD L26 132 B5
Oxford Gdns STHP PR8 2 B9
Oxford Rd BTL L20 7 K5
CSBY/WL L22 82 E3
HUY L36 116 C1
RUNC WA7 19 G6
SKEL WN8 65 G4
STHP PR8 2 A8
WAL/EG CH44 111 L1 5
WGNW/BIL/O WN5 67 H6
WLT/FAZ L9 84 D5
Oxford St CHLY/EC PR7 32 E6 11
CHLY/EC PR7 44 B7
ECCL WA10 8 E3
EHL/KEN L7 13 L8
NEWLW WA12 104 D2 11
WARRS WA4 15 H8
WDN WA8 16 E5
Oxheys RUNC WA7 150 E5
Oxhouse Rd WGNW/BIL/O WN5 77 L1
Ox La RAIN/WH L35 116 E7
Oxley Av MOR/LEA CH46 110 D2
Oxley St STHEL WA9 102 F6 3
Oxmead Cl WARRN/WOL WA2 122 D4
Oxmoor Cl RUNC WA7 150 C8 2
Oxton Cl AIG/SPK L17 129 L3
KKBY L32 85 K5
WDN WA8 133 L1
Oxton Gn GTS/LS CH66 162 F1 4
Oxton Rd BIRK CH41 10 F8
WAL/EG CH44 111 K2
Oxton St ANF/KKDL L4 97 H5

P

Pacific Rd BIRK CH41 11 M3
BTL L20 6 E3
Packenham Rd
CLB/OSW/ST L13 98 B7 1
Paddington EHL/KEN L7 113 J4 4
Paddington Bank WARR WA1 122 B7
Paddock Cl CSBY/BLUN L23 70 D7
Paddock Dr NSTN CH64 152 F3
Paddock Gv STHEL WA9 118 F2
Paddock Hey NTHLY L27 115 M7
Paddock Ri RUNC WA7 161 G1
WGNNW/ST WN6 68 A2
Paddock Rd SKEL WN8 65 L3
The Paddock AIMK WN4 79 H7
BRSC L40 39 L1
CHNE CH2 165 J2
FMBY L37 47 J8
FROD/HEL WA6 166 E3
GR/UP/WCH CH49 110 D8
GTS/LS CH66 162 F2
HES CH60 141 L5
KKBY L32 85 M6 1
MOR/LEA CH46 109 L6
ORM L39 62 E2
PR/KW L34 101 H6
STHP PR8 47 K1
WLTN L25 131 K1
Padeswood Cl STHEL WA9 102 F7 8
Padgate La WARR WA1 15 L2
WARR WA1 122 A5
Padstow Cl CHTN/BK PR9 22 C8
HLWD L26 132 A4
WARRW/BUR WA5 136 A2
WGNW/BIL/O WN5 78 A5
Padstow Dr ECCL WA10 88 D7
Padstow Rd CHLDW L16 114 F5
GR/UP/WCH CH49 125 L3
Pagebank Rd DV/KA/FCH L14 115 J2
Page Ct FMBY L37 59 H2
Pagefield Cl WGNNW/ST WN6 4 B1
Pagefield Rd WAV L15 114 C7 7
Pagefield St WGNNW/ST WN6 4 B1
Page La WDN WA8 17 H2
Page Moss Av HUY L36 115 K1
Page Moss La HUY L36 115 J2
Page Wk VAUX/LVPD L3 13 K4
Pagewood Cl CL/PREN CH43 126 F1 5
Paignton Cl HUY L36 116 D2 2
WARRW/BUR WA5 136 A1
WGNW/BIL/O WN5 78 A5
Paignton Rd CHLDW L16 114 F5
WAL/NB CH45 95 G7
Painswick Rd GTS/LS CH66 163 G3
Paisley Av PS/BROM CH62 155 G1
RNFD/HAY WA11 89 M6
Paisley St VAUX/LVPD L3 12 C4
Palace Ar AIMK WN4 91 K2
Palace Fields Av RUNC WA7 150 C6
Palace Hey NSTN CH64 153 J8
Palace Rd STHP PR8 2 A8
WLT/FAZ L9 84 C7
Palatine Cl WGNS/IIMK WN3 79 G1
Palatine Rd PS/BROM CH62 143 L4
STHP PR8 2 C7
WAL/EG CH44 111 M3
Palatine Sq LEIGH WN7 81 M8
Palermo Cl WAL/EG CH44 111 M3
Palewood Cl WGN WN1 5 H1
Paley Cl ANF/KKDL L4 97 H6
Palin Dr WARRW/BUR WA5 120 B7 2
Palin St WGNE/HIN WN2 81 K2 5
Palladio Rd CLB/OSW/ST L13 114 D1
Palliser Cl GOL/RIS/CU WA3 123 J2
Pall Ml CHLY/EC PR7 32 E7
VAUX/LVPD L3 12 E3
Palm Av AIMK WN4 78 F8
Palm Cl WLT/FAZ L9 85 G8
Palm Ct SKEL WN8 65 G3
Palmer Cl ECCL WA10 8 E4
Palmer Crs WARRW/BUR WA5 120 F5
Palmerston Av LITH L21 83 J7 5
Palmerston Cl CALD/MH L18 130 B2
Palmerston Dr LITH L21 83 K7
Palmerston Rd ALL/GAR L19 130 E7
CALD/MH L18 130 B2
CHTN/BK PR9 25 H7
WAL/EG CH44 111 H1
Palmerston St
RF/TRAN CH42 128 B3 10
Palm Gv CHTN/BK PR9 3 M5
CL/PREN CH43 10 C7
GTS/LS CH66 163 J4
STHP PR8 25 G7 1
WGNW/BIL/O WN5 67 M7
WLTN L25 131 K4
Palm Hl CL/PREN CH43 10 C9
Palmwood Av RAIN/WH L35 117 M3
Palmwood Cl CL/PREN CH43 127 G4
Palmyra Sq North WARR WA1 14 D6
Palmyra Sq South WARR WA1 14 D7
Paltridge Wy PEN/TH CH61 141 H1 2
Pamela Cl AIN/FAZ L10 85 K6
Pampas Gv WLT/FAZ L9 97 K1 3
Pangbourne Cl WARRS WA4 138 A7
Pankhurst Rd LITH L21 83 L3
Pansy St EV L5 96 F6
Parade Crs SPK/HALE L24 147 G3
Parade St ECCL WA10 9 H4
The Parade NSTN CH64 152 D4
Paradise La FMBY L37 47 J8
RAIN/WH L35 116 F3
Paradise St CHLYE PR6 33 H2
CLVPS L1 13 G7 1
Paragon Cl WDN WA8 118 D8 2
Parbold Av RNFD/HAY WA11 89 M8
Parbold Cl BRSC L40 52 A2 2
Parbold Hl SKEL WN8 53 M3
Parbrook Cl HUY L36 99 M7
Parbrook La WGNNW/ST WN6 55 K6
Parbrook Rd HUY L36 99 M8
The Parchments NEWLW WA12 104 F1
Paris Av WGNS/IIMK WN3 78 E2
Park Av CALD/MH L18 130 A2
CHLY/EC PR7 31 M3
CHTN/BK PR9 25 G4
CSBY/BLUN L23 71 G8
FMBY L37 59 H4
GOL/RIS/CU WA3 92 B3
MGHL L31 72 F2
ORM L39 51 G8
PR/KW L34 101 H6
RAIN/WH L35 117 L1
RNFD/HAY WA11 90 C7
WAL/EG CH44 111 M2 11
WARRS WA4 137 M2
WDN WA8 16 E1
WGNNW/ST WN6 55 K6
WGNW/BIL/O WN5 78 A4
WLT/FAZ L9 84 F6
Park Av North NEWLW WA12 104 E3
Park Av South NEWLW WA12 104 E3
Park Bvd WARR WA1 14 E8
Parkbourn MGHL L31 73 J3
Parkbourn Dr MGHL L31 73 J3
Parkbourn North MGHL L31 73 J3
Parkbourn Sq MGHL L31 73 J3 1
Parkbridge Rd
RF/TRAN CH42 127 L2 4
Park Brow Dr KKBY L32 86 B5
Park Cl BIRK CH41 10 F5
FMBY L37 59 G5
KKBY L32 85 K2
SKEL WN8 53 L2
Park Ct CSBY/WL L22 83 G4
RUNC WA7 19 G8
Park Crs CHTN/BK PR9 24 F4
ORM L39 61 H1
WARRS WA4 137 M7
WGN WN1 4 C2
Park Crs West WGN WN1 4 C2
Parkdale Av WLT/FAZ L9 84 C6
Parkdale Rd WARR WA1 122 C6
Park Dr BIRK CH41 10 A3
CL/PREN CH43 10 A4
CSBY/BLUN L23 71 J6
CSBY/BLUN L23 82 C1
EP CH65 20 A8
Parkend Dr LEIGH WN7 93 M3
Parkend Rd RF/TRAN CH42 127 L2
Parker Av LITH L21 83 H6
Parker Cl NTHTN L30 84 D4
Parker Crs ORM L39 51 H6
Parkers Ct RUNC WA7 150 A7
Parker St CHLY/EC PR7 32 E4
CLVPS L1 13 H8
RUNC WA7 19 J2
WARR WA1 14 C7
Parkfield WGNNW/ST WN6 55 K6
Parkfield Av BIRK CH41 11 H5
NTHTN L30 84 C4
WARRS WA4 138 C1
Parkfield Cl BIRK CH41 10 F3
ORM L39 62 E2
Parkfield Dr EP CH65 163 J3
FROD/HEL WA6 166 D2
WAL/EG CH44 111 K1
Parkfield Gv MGHL L31 72 E4
Parkfield Pl BIRK CH41 11 G5
Parkfield Rd AIG/SPK L17 129 K1
BEB CH63 143 J2
CSBY/WL L22 83 G3
Parkfields WGNE/HIN WN2 80 D6
Parkfields La WARRN/WOL WA2 142 B2
Parkgate La NSTN CH64 142 A8
Parkgate Rd CH/BCN CH1 162 B7
NSTN CH64 152 E5
WARRS WA4 137 M4
Parkgate Wy RUNC WA7 150 E6
Park Gv BIRK CH41 11 G8
Park Hall Rd CHLY/EC PR7 42 B2
Park Hey Dr WGNNW/ST WN6 55 G6
Parkhill Rd RF/TRAN CH42 127 L2
Park Hill Rd TOX L8 129 H1
Parkhurst Rd NG/CROX L11 98 B4
RF/TRAN CH42 127 L3 3
Parkinson Rd WLT/FAZ L9 97 J1
Parkland Ct CL/PREN CH43 110 E5
Parkland Dr CHNE CH2 165 K2
Parklands CHTN/BK PR9 25 G5
GTS/LS CH66 155 M8
PR/KW L34 99 M2
RNFD/HAY WA11 76 B6
SKEL WN8 65 M2 6
WDN WA8 133 L2
Parklands Dr HES CH60 141 K7
WGNE/HIN WN2 57 L7
Parklands Gdns GTS/LS CH66 155 M7
Parklands Vw GTS/LS CH66 155 M7
Parklands Wy CSBY/WL L22 83 H4
Park La BTL L20 84 A6
CLVPS L1 13 G9
CLVPS L1 112 F5
FROD/HEL WA6 160 D5
HOY CH47 109 J3
KIRK/FR/WA PR4 27 K3
MGHL L31 73 G2
NTHTN L30 84 B3
WARRS WA4 137 H8
WGNE/HIN WN2 80 D6
WGNE/HIN WN2 81 G7
Park Lane Dr MGHL L31 73 K3 1
Park La West NTHTN L30 84 B2
Parklea GTS/LS CH66 155 M7
Park Link ORM L39 62 D4
Park Pl BTL L20 7 H5
TOX L8 113 H7
Park Rd CHLY/EC PR7 32 E4
CHLY/EC PR7 43 G4
CHLY/EC PR7 44 A7
CHNE CH2 165 G4
CSBY/WL L22 83 G4
EP CH65 20 C7
FMBY L37 59 G4
HES CH60 141 K4
HOY CH47 109 G4
KKBY L32 85 L1 2
NEWLW WA12 92 B6
NSTN CH64 154 D5
ORM L39 51 G8
PR/KW L34 100 E6
PS/BROM CH62 128 D8
PS/BROM CH62 144 B7
RF/TRAN CH42 128 A2
RUNC WA7 18 F8
STHEL WA9 9 M4
TOX L8 113 H8
TOX L8 129 J1 13
WAL/EG CH44 111 L2
WARRN/WOL WA2 121 M4
WARRW/BUR WA5 119 L6
WDN WA8 16 F1
WGNE/HIN WN2 81 G2
WGNNW/ST WN6 4 B1
WGNW/BIL/O WN5 67 J7
WGNW/BIL/O WN5 78 A4
WKBY CH48 124 C3
Park Rd East BIRK CH41 10 F6
Park Rd North BIRK CH41 10 A3
NEWLW WA12 105 G2
Park Rd South NEWLW WA12 104 F3
Park Rd West CHTN/BK PR9 24 E4
CL/PREN CH43 10 A4
Parkside WAL/EG CH44 111 L2
Parkside Av AIMK WN4 79 H5
CHLY/EC PR7 32 E5
STHEL WA9 118 D2
Parkside Cl BEB CH63 128 C7
NTHLY L27 132 A1 2
Parkside Crs WGNW/BIL/O WN5 67 H7
Parkside Dr WD/CROXPK L12 98 C5
Parkside Rd BEB CH63 128 C7
NEWLW WA12 105 K4
RF/TRAN CH42 128 A2
Parkside St NPK/KEN L6 13 M3
The Parks RNFD/HAY WA11 91 K4
Parkstile La NG/CROX L11 98 E1
Parkstone Rd RF/TRAN CH42 127 L2
Park St BIRK CH41 11 H5
BIRK CH41 11 H4
BTL L20 7 H5
CHLY/EC PR7 30 E7 1
CHLY/EC PR7 32 E5
NSTN CH64 153 G5
RNFD/HAY WA11 90 B7
STHEL WA9 9 M4
TOX L8 113 G8
WAL/EG CH44 111 L1
WGNS/IIMK WN3 4 D7
Parksway WARR WA1 122 F6
Park Ter CSBY/WL L22 83 G5
The Park HUY L36 116 A4
WARRW/BUR WA5 135 M2
Parkvale Av CL/PREN CH43 127 G5
Park Vale Rd WLT/FAZ L9 84 C7
Park Vw AIMK WN4 91 K3
CSBY/WL L22 82 F3
HUY L36 115 L1
NPK/KEN L6 97 M8
PS/BROM CH62 143 L5
WGNE/HIN WN2 80 D4
Parkview Dr NTHLY L27 132 A1
Parkview Rd NG/CROX L11 98 F1
Park Wall Rd HTWN L38 71 H2
SFTN L29 71 J4
Park Wy FMBY L37 59 H4
HOY CH47 109 G5
HUY L36 99 M6 1
TOX L8 113 H6 11
Parkway CSBY/BLUN L23 83 H3
NTHTN L30 72 A8
WAL/NB CH45 95 G6
WGNNW/ST WN6 55 J3
Parkway Cl
GR/UP/WCH CH49 126 B6 1
Park Wy West KKBY L32 85 K2 3
Park West HES CH60 140 F6
Parkwood Cl LYMM WA13 139 M3
PS/BROM CH62 144 A5 2
WGNS/IIMK WN3 5 K8
Parkwood Rd RAIN/WH L35 117 G3
WLTN L25 131 J1 1
Parlane St STHEL WA9 9 L3
Parliament Pl TOX L8 113 H6 12
Parliament St RAIN/WH L35 101 M6
SKEL WN8 66 E5
TOX L8 112 F6
WGNS/IIMK WN3 5 H7
Parliament Wy GTS/LS CH66 163 H5
Parlington Cl WDN WA8 133 L6
Parlow Rd NG/CROX L11 98 A5
Parnell Rd BEB CH63 143 J3
Parr Cottage Cl CHLY/EC PR7 30 E6 3
Parren Av RAIN/WH L35 116 E4
Parr Gv GR/UP/WCH CH49 125 L1
RNFD/HAY WA11 90 C7 5
Parr La CHLY/EC PR7 30 D6
Parr Mount St STHEL WA9 9 M5
Parr's La ORM L39 62 F5
Parrs Rd CL/PREN CH43 127 K2
Parr St CLVPS L1 13 H9
LITH L21 83 K4
STHEL WA9 9 J6
WARR WA1 14 F7
WDN WA8 17 G1 1
Parrs Wood View WARRS WA4 138 C4
Parry Dr WARRS WA4 139 G2
Parry St WAL/EG CH44 111 M3 2
Parsonage Brow SKEL WN8 66 B5
Parsonage Cl SKEL WN8 66 C6
Parsonage Rd SKEL WN8 66 C6
WDN WA8 149 J1 5
Parsonage Wy
WARRW/BUR WA5 120 C8 2
Parson's Brow CHLY/EC PR7 32 E6 12
RNFD/HAY WA11 76 A7
Parson's Wk WGN WN1 4 D2
Parthenon Dr NG/CROX L11 97 M2
Partington Av BTL L20 7 L2
Partington St
WGNW/BIL/O WN5 68 A5 2
Parton St NPK/KEN L6 113 L2
Partridge Cl GOL/RIS/CU WA3 123 G1
WD/CROXPK L12 99 H2
Partridge Rd CSBY/BLUN L23 82 D1 3
KKBY L32 85 K2
Part St STHP PR8 2 F7
Pasture Av MOR/LEA CH46 110 A3
Pasture Cl AIMK WN4 79 G7
STHEL WA9 118 E1
WLTN L25 131 K4
Pasture Crs MOR/LEA CH46 110 A4
Pasture Dr GOL/RIS/CU WA3 106 C6
Pasture La RNFD/HAY WA11 88 C1
WARRN/WOL WA2 122 D4
Pasture Rd MOR/LEA CH46 109 M2
The Pastures CHTN/BK PR9 22 F8 3
WKBY CH48 125 H3 1

Pateley Cl KKBY L32 85 L4 5
Paterson St BIRK CH41 10 F6
Patmos Cl EV L5 97 G7
Paton Cl WKBY CH48 124 E2
Patricia Av BIRK CH41 111 G4
Patricia Gv BTL L20 83 M7
Patrick Av BTL L20 83 M6
Patricroft Rd WGNE/HIN WN2 5 L6
Patrivale Cl WARR WA1 122 B6
Patten La WARR WA1 14 E6 2
Patten's Cl NTHTN L30 83 M1
Patten St BIRK CH41 10 C2
Patten's Wk PR/KW L34 87 G8
Patterdale Av
WARRN/WOL WA2 121 L3
Patterdale Cl STHP PR8 47 K2 1
Patterdale Crs MGHL L31 73 G3
Patterdale Dr ECCL WA10 101 K5
Patterdale Pl WGNE/HIN WN2 69 J6
Patterdale Rd AIMK WN4 79 J5
BEB CH63 143 H2
WAV L15 114 B7 7
Patterson Cl
GOL/RIS/CU WA3 123 G2 2
Patterson St NEWLW WA12 104 D1
Paul Cl WARRW/BUR WA5 119 M7
Pauline St WGNE/HIN WN2 81 K4
Paul MacCartney Wy
NPK/KEN L6 113 K2 9
Paul Orr Ct VAUX/LVPD L3 12 E2
Paulsfield Dr MOR/LEA CH46 110 A6
Paul's La CHTN/BK PR9 25 H2
Paul St VAUX/LVPD L3 12 F3
WARRN/WOL WA2 14 C4
Paulton Cl TOX L8 129 H1
Paveley Bank NTHLY L27 115 M8
Pavilion Cl TOX L8 113 K6
Pavilion Vw LEY/BBR PR5 29 K3 2
Paxton Pl SKEL WN8 76 E1
Paxton Rd HUY L36 116 A1
Payne Cl WARRW/BUR WA5 120 F7
Paythorne Cl
GOL/RIS/CU WA3 107 H2 3
Peacehaven Cl CHLDW L16 115 H5 3
Peach Gv MGHL L31 85 K1
RNFD/HAY WA11 91 G6 7
Peacock Av WARR WA1 15 M3
Peacock Fold LEIGH WN7 81 M7
Pearce Cl WLTN L25 115 H7
Pear Gv NPK/KEN L6 113 K2
Pearl St WGNNW/ST WN6 68 D2
Pearson Av WARRS WA4 137 M3
Pearson Dr BTL L20 84 A6
Pearson Rd BIRK CH41 11 J8
Pearson St WAV L15 114 B6
Pear Tree Av CHLY/EC PR7 43 H2
RUNC WA7 19 M9
Peartree Av WD/CROXPK L12 99 H4
Peartree Cl FROD/HEL WA6 160 F4
Pear Tree Cl HES CH60 141 L4
Pear Tree La CHLY/EC PR7 32 A2
Peartree Pl WARRS WA4 15 G8
Pear Tree Rd HUY L36 116 A5
Peartree Rd LEY/BBR PR5 29 K2
Pear Tree Wy GTS/LS CH66 163 G4 2
Peasefield Rd DV/KA/FCH L14 115 J1
Peasley Cl WARRN/WOL WA2 122 D4
Peasley Cross La STHEL WA9 9 L8
Peatwood Av KKBY L32 86 B6
Peckers Hill Rd STHEL WA9 103 G6
Peckfield Cl RUNC WA7 150 C8 3
Peckforton Cl
CLB/OSW/ST L13 98 A7 2
Peckforton Dr GTS/LS CH66 163 G2
RUNC WA7 161 H1 11
Peckmill Gn NTHLY L27 132 B1
Peck Mill La FROD/HEL WA6 166 C6
Peebles Av RNFD/HAY WA11 89 M7
Peebles Cl AIMK WN4 90 E1
GTS/LS CH66 155 H7 1
NWD/KWIPK L33 73 M7 1
Peech St EHL/KEN L7 13 M8
Peel Av BIRK CH41 128 B2
Peel Cl RAIN/WH L35 117 G2 1
WARR WA1 122 F7 2
Peel House La WDN WA8 134 D2
Peel Pl TOX L8 113 H6 13
Peel Rd BTL L20 6 C1
SKEL WN8 66 A8
Peel St CHLY/EC PR7 32 E6
CHLYE PR6 44 D5
NEWLW WA12 104 C2
RUNC WA7 18 F2
STHP PR8 25 H7
TOX L8 129 J1
WGNE/HIN WN2 80 C3
Peerswood Ct NSTN CH64 153 G8 4
Peet Av ECCL WA10 101 L1
ORM L39 62 F1
Peet's La CHTN/BK PR9 25 J4
Peet St EHL/KEN L7 113 K4
Pelham Gv AIG/SPK L17 129 L1
Pelham Rd WAL/EG CH44 111 J2
WARRS WA4 138 E2
Pemberlei Rd WGNE/HIN WN2 69 M3
Pemberton Cl NSTN CH64 154 C5
Pemberton Rd
CLB/OSW/ST L13 114 C2
GR/UP/WCH CH49 126 D2
WGNS/IIMK WN3 78 D4
Pembertons Ct PR/KW L34 101 G7 5
Pemberton St ECCL WA10 8 D6 1
Pembrey Wy WLTN L25 131 M5 1
Pembroke Av MOR/LEA CH46 110 A6
Pembroke Dr EP CH65 163 J2
Pembroke Gdns VAUX/LVPD L3 13 L6
Pembroke Pl CHLY/EC PR7 32 D7
VAUX/LVPD L3 13 K6
Pembroke Rd BTL L20 7 G5
VAUX/LVPD L3 13 L6
WGNE/HIN WN2 81 L2
WGNW/BIL/O WN5 67 M4
Pembroke St VAUX/LVPD L3 13 L6
Pembury Cl WD/CROXPK L12 99 G2 10
Penare Gorran Hvn
RUNC WA7 150 E7 4
Penarth Cl EHL/KEN L7 113 K5
Penbury Rd WGN WN1 56 D8
Pencombe Rd HUY L36 115 K1
Pendennis Crs WGNE/HIN WN2 81 J2
Pendennis Rd WAL/EG CH44 111 K2
Pendennis St NPK/KEN L6 97 K8
Pendine Cl NPK/KEN L6 113 L1
WARRW/BUR WA5 120 E3
Pendle Av RNFD/HAY WA11 89 M8
Pendlebury La WGN WN1 56 E7
Pendlebury St STHEL WA9 118 E1
WARRS WA4 138 B2
Pendle Cl GR/UP/WCH CH49 110 A7 4
WGNW/BIL/O WN5 67 M8
Pendle Dr HOR/BR BL6 45 L8
LITH L21 83 L1
ORM L39 51 J7
Pendle Gdns GOL/RIS/CU WA3 107 G2
Pendle Pl SKEL WN8 76 F1
Pendle Rd GOL/RIS/CU WA3 92 E4
Pendleton Gn HLWD L26 132 A6
Pendleton Rd ANF/KKDL L4 97 J3 2
Penfold MGHL L31 73 G4
Penfold Cl CALD/MH L18 114 F8 2
CH/BCN CH1 162 D5
Penfolds RUNC WA7 149 M4
Pengallo Hey NTHLY L27 116 B8
Pengwern Gv WAV L15 113 M5 4
Pengwern St TOX L8 113 J8 4
Penhale Cl AIG/SPK L17 129 K3
Peninsula Cl WAL/NB CH45 95 G5 2
Penistone Dr GTS/LS CH66 155 K8
Penketh Av WARRW/BUR WA5 121 H5
Penketh Gn SPK/HALE L24 147 G1 3
Penketh Pl SKEL WN8 65 L8
Penketh Rd WARRW/BUR WA5 136 C1
Penketh's La RUNC WA7 19 H2
Penketh St WGNNW/ST WN6 68 D3
Penkett Gv WAL/NB CH45 95 L7
Penkett Rd WAL/NB CH45 95 L7
Penkford La WARRW/BUR WA5 103 M4
Penkmans La FROD/HEL WA6 160 E7
Penlake La STHEL WA9 103 G6
Penley Crs KKBY L32 85 K3
Penmann Cl HLWD L26 132 B6 1
Penmann Crs HLWD L26 132 B6
Penmark Cl WARRW/BUR WA5 120 E3
Penmon Dr PEN/TH CH61 141 H2
Pennant Av WD/CROXPK L12 98 E4
Pennant Cl GOL/RIS/CU WA3 123 J2
Pennard Av HUY L36 99 M8
Pennell Dr WGNS/IIMK WN3 68 B8 5
Pennine Av CHLY/EC PR7 31 M4
WGNS/IIMK WN3 78 E2
Pennine Cl HOR/BR BL6 45 L8
STHEL WA9 103 G2
Pennine Dr STHEL WA9 103 H2
Pennine Gv LEIGH WN7 81 L5
Pennine La GOL/RIS/CU WA3 92 E4
Pennine Pl SKEL WN8 65 K7
Pennine Rd CHLYE PR6 33 G4 3
HOR/BR BL6 45 L8
RF/TRAN CH42 127 L4
WAL/EG CH44 111 H1
WARRN/WOL WA2 122 A3
Pennine Wy KKBY L32 85 L1
Pennington Av BTL L20 84 A6
ORM L39 51 G7
Pennington Gn GTS/LS CH66 162 E2
Pennington Green La
WGNE/HIN WN2 69 M3
Pennington La
WARRW/BUR WA5 103 L2
WGNE/HIN WN2 57 G5
WGNE/HIN WN2 69 J5
Pennington Rd LITH L21 83 L7
Pennington St ANF/KKDL L4 97 H3 3
WGNE/HIN WN2 69 M7 9
Penn La RUNC WA7 18 E5
Pennsylvania Rd
CLB/OSW/ST L13 97 M6
Pennygate Cl WGNE/HIN WN2 69 M7
Pennyhurst St WGNS/IIMK WN3 4 B5
Penny La CALD/MH L18 114 B8
RAIN/WH L35 117 J6
RNFD/HAY WA11 91 J6
WARRW/BUR WA5 103 M5
Pennystone Cl
GR/UP/WCH CH49 109 M7
Penrhos Rd HOY CH47 108 B7
Penrhyd Rd PEN/TH CH61 125 M8
Penrhyn Av LITH L21 83 K6
PEN/TH CH61 126 C7
Penrhyn Crs RUNC WA7 19 J9
Penrhyn Rd PR/KW L34 86 E7
Penrhyn St EV L5 96 F8
Penrith Av STHP PR8 47 K2
WARRN/WOL WA2 121 L3 4
Penrith Cl FROD/HEL WA6 160 F5
Penrith Crs AIMK WN4 91 K1
MGHL L31 73 G3
Penrith Rd ECCL WA10 101 K5
Penrith St BIRK CH41 10 F8
Penrose Av East
DV/KA/FCH L14 115 G3
Penrose Av West
DV/KA/FCH L14 115 G3
Penrose Gdns
WARRW/BUR WA5 135 M2
Penrose Pl SKEL WN8 77 G1
Penrose St EV L5 97 H7
Penryn Av RNFD/HAY WA11 89 M6
Penryn Cl WARRW/BUR WA5 136 A1
Pensall Dr PEN/TH CH61 141 H3
Pensarn Gdns
WARRW/BUR WA5 120 F3 5
Pensarn Rd CLB/OSW/ST L13 114 B3
Pensby Cl PEN/TH CH61 126 C8
Pensby Dr GTS/LS CH66 162 F1
Pensby Hall La PEN/TH CH61 141 H3
Pensby Rd HES CH60 141 J4
PEN/TH CH61 126 C7
Penshaw Av WGNS/IIMK WN3 79 K2 1
Penshaw Ct RUNC WA7 150 A6
Penson St WGN WN1 68 F3 1
Pentire Av ECCL WA10 88 D7
Pentire Cl NG/CROX L11 85 K7 2
Pentland Av ANF/KKDL L4 97 J4 3
STHEL WA9 103 H2
WARRN/WOL WA2 121 K2
Pentland Pl
WARRN/WOL WA2 121 K2 3
Pentland Rd NWD/KWIPK L33 86 C1
Penuel Rd ANF/KKDL L4 97 H3
Peover St VAUX/LVPD L3 13 H3
Peploe Rd ANF/KKDL L4 97 M3
Peplow Rd KKBY L32 85 K3 1
Pepper La WGNNW/ST WN6 55 K2
Pepper Mill La WGN WN1 5 G6
Pepper St SPK/HALE L24 147 M4
Pepys Pl WGNS/IIMK WN3 79 J1
Pera Cl NPK/KEN L6 113 J2 15
Perch Pool La CHTN/BK PR9 26 B8
Percival La RUNC WA7 18 D3
Percival Rd EP CH65 20 B3
Percival St WARR WA1 15 G6
Percival Wy ECCL WA10 8 E8
Percy Rd WAL/EG CH44 112 A3
Percy St BTL L20 6 E1
CHLY/EC PR7 32 F6 6
STHEL WA9 103 H6
TOX L8 113 H6
WARRW/BUR WA5 121 G8 4
Perimeter Rd CHNE CH2 158 E8
NWD/KWIPK L33 86 F5
Perrey St RUNC WA7 19 K3
Perriam Rd ALL/GAR L19 130 F5
Perrin Av RUNC WA7 18 D8
Perrin Rd WAL/NB CH45 95 G8 3
Perrins Rd WARRW/BUR WA5 104 B7
Perrygate Cl EHL/KEN L7 113 K5 5
Perryn Pl WGNNW/ST WN6 56 B4
Perry St TOX L8 112 F7
Pershore Gv STHP PR8 47 J1
Pershore Rd KKBY L32 84 F3
Perth Av STHEL WA9 102 A6
WGNE/HIN WN2 69 J5
Perth Cl NWD/KWIPK L33 73 M7
WARRN/WOL WA2 122 B1
Perth St NPK/KEN L6 113 J2
Peterborough Cl
GTS/LS CH66 163 H6 3
Peterborough Dr NTHTN L30 84 A1
Peterborough Rd WAV L15 114 C7 6
Peterlee Cl STHEL WA9 102 B6
Peter Mahon Wy BTL L20 6 E3
Peter Price's La BEB CH63 143 G1
Peter Rd ANF/KKDL L4 7 M8
Peter Salem Dr
WARRW/BUR WA5 120 D7
Peters Av BRSC L40 52 A1 4
Petersfield Cl NTHTN L30 84 B4
Petersfield Gdns
GOL/RIS/CU WA3 107 G1 3
Petersgate RUNC WA7 150 F6
Petersham Dr WARRS WA4 138 A8
Peter's La CLVPS L1 13 G8
Peterstone Cl
WARRW/BUR WA5 120 F3 4
Peter St AIMK WN4 91 L2
CHLY/EC PR7 32 E5
CLVPS L1 13 G6
ECCL WA10 8 D4
GOL/RIS/CU WA3 92 C5 3
WAL/EG CH44 112 A3
WGNE/HIN WN2 69 M8 21
WGNW/BIL/O WN5 67 K5
Peterwood RF/TRAN CH42 128 C4 3
Petherick Rd NG/CROX L11 98 E1
Petticoat La WGNE/HIN WN2 69 K6
Petunia Cl DV/KA/FCH L14 115 J1 2
Petworth Av WARRN/WOL WA2 121 K2
WGNS/IIMK WN3 78 F3
Petworth Cl SPK/HALE L24 146 D1
Petworth Rd STHP PR8 34 D7
Peveril Cl WARRS WA4 137 M5 2
Peveril St WLT/FAZ L9 97 H2 4
Pheasant Cl GOL/RIS/CU WA3 123 H1
Pheasant Fld SPK/HALE L24 147 L3
Pheasant Gv HLWD L26 132 A4
Philbeach Rd ANF/KKDL L4 97 M3
Philip Cl WGNW/BIL/O WN5 67 M8
Philip Dr STHP PR8 35 G7
Philip Gv STHEL WA9 102 E6
Philip Rd WDN WA8 133 K5
Philips Dr WARRW/BUR WA5 120 A7
Philips La GTS/LS CH66 162 E1
Phillimore Rd NPK/KEN L6 113 L2 4
Phillip Gv WD/CROXPK L12 99 H8 2
Phillips Cl CSBY/BLUN L23 71 K7
FMBY L37 59 H3
Phillip's La FMBY L37 59 H3
Phillips St VAUX/LVPD L3 12 F4
Phillips Wy HES CH60 141 G5
Phipps' La WARRW/BUR WA5 104 A6
Phoenix Av
WARRW/BUR WA5 121 H3 1
Physics Rd SPK/HALE L24 131 L8
Phythian Cl NPK/KEN L6 113 K2 10
Phythian Crs WARRW/BUR WA5 136 B1
Phythian St NPK/KEN L6 113 J2
RNFD/HAY WA11 90 B7 2
Picadilly WGNW/BIL/O WN5 78 A8
Pichael Nook WARRS WA4 138 C1
Pickerill Rd GR/UP/WCH CH49 125 M2
Pickering Crs WARRS WA4 138 F2
Pickering Rd WAL/NB CH45 95 K5
WDN WA8 133 K8
Pickerings Cl RUNC WA7 149 L7
Pickering St NPK/KEN L6 97 J8
Pickles Dr BRSC L40 51 M1
Pickmere Dr PS/BROM CH62 155 H2
RUNC WA7 150 E8
Pickmere St WARRW/BUR WA5 121 G8
Pickop St VAUX/LVPD L3 12 F5
Pickthorn Cl WGNE/HIN WN2 80 D2
Pickup St WGNE/HIN WN2 5 M6
Pickwick St TOX L8 113 H7
Pickworth Wy KKBY L32 85 K3
Picow Farm Rd RUNC WA7 18 B7
Picow St RUNC WA7 18 F5
Picton Av EP CH65 20 D5
RUNC WA7 19 K5
Picton Cl CL/PREN CH43 127 H1
GOL/RIS/CU WA3 122 E1
PS/BROM CH62 154 F2
Picton Crs WAV L15 114 A5 5
Picton Gv WAV L15 113 M5
Picton La CHNE CH2 164 C6
Picton Rd CSBY/WL L22 82 F4
WAV L15 114 A5
Piele Rd RNFD/HAY WA11 91 G6
Piercefield Rd FMBY L37 59 H1
Pierpoint St NEWLW WA12 92 C6
WARRW/BUR WA5 14 B2
Pighue La CLB/OSW/ST L13 114 A4
Pigot Pl WARRS WA4 122 B8 2
Pigot St ECCL WA10 8 D5
WGNW/BIL/O WN5 67 K7 6
Pike House Rd ECCL WA10 88 C8
Pikelaw Pl SKEL WN8 65 L8
Pike Pl ECCL WA10 101 K1
Pikes Bridge Fold ECCL WA10 101 J1
Pikes Hey Rd WKBY CH48 125 H6
Pike St WARRS WA4 137 L4
Pilchbank Rd DV/KA/FCH L14 115 G1
Pilch La DV/KA/FCH L14 115 G1
Pilch La East HUY L36 115 J3
Pilgrim Cl WARRN/WOL WA2 105 J7 1
Pilgrim St BIRK CH41 11 L5
CLVPS L1 113 G5 15
Pilgrims Wy WGNNW/ST WN6 56 C6
Pilkington Rd STHP PR8 3 M7
Pilkington St RNFD/HAY WA11 76 B7
WGNE/HIN WN2 69 M7
Pilling Cl CHLY/EC PR7 32 F7
CHTN/BK PR9 22 B8
Pilling La CHLY/EC PR7 32 E8
MGHL L31 61 J8
Pilling Pl SKEL WN8 65 L8
Pilling St LEIGH WN7 81 M8
Pilot Gv WAV L15 113 M5 3
Pilsley Cl WGNW/BIL/O WN5 67 J4
Pimblett Rd RNFD/HAY WA11 91 G6
Pimblett St GOL/RIS/CU WA3 92 C6 4
Pimbley Gv East MGHL L31 72 E7 1
Pimbley Gv West MGHL L31 72 E7 2
Pimbo La SKEL WN8 77 H2
Pimbo Rd RNFD/HAY WA11 77 G5
SKEL WN8 65 M8
Pimhill Cl TOX L8 113 J7 6
Pimlico Rd RUNC WA7 18 D5
Pincock Brow CHLY/EC PR7 31 L5
Pincock St CHLY/EC PR7 31 L5
Pine Av BEB CH63 143 H2
ECCL WA10 89 H7
NEWLW WA12 104 E3
ORM L39 51 H6
WDN WA8 134 D3 5
Pine Cl HUY L36 115 M1
KKBY L32 85 L2
RAIN/WH L35 117 G2
RNFD/HAY WA11 90 E7
SKEL WN8 53 J4 4
SKEL WN8 65 H4
Pine Crest ORM L39 62 D3 1
Pine Dl RNFD/HAY WA11 76 A6
Pinedale Cl CL/PREN CH43 126 F1 6
GTS/LS CH66 163 H5
Pine Dr ORM L39 51 H7
Pine Gv BTL L20 7 J3
CHLYE PR6 32 F2
CHTN/BK PR9 3 M5
CSBY/WL L22 82 F3
GOL/RIS/CU WA3 92 E5 1
GTS/LS CH66 163 J4
ORM L39 51 J6
WARR WA1 122 C6
Pinehey NSTN CH64 152 F4
Pinehurst Av ANF/KKDL L4 97 K6
CSBY/WL L22 82 E2
Pinehurst Rd ANF/KKDL L4 97 K6
Pinellas RUNC WA7 19 K2
Pine Ms CLVPS L1 113 G6 6
Pinemore Rd CALD/MH L18 130 C3
Pineridge Cl PS/BROM CH62 143 L2
Pine Rd HES CH60 141 L4
RUNC WA7 19 M9
WGNW/BIL/O WN5 68 A7
The Pines BEB CH63 143 K2
WD/CROXPK L12 99 H1
Pine Tree Av CL/PREN CH43 126 E1
Pine Tree Cl MOR/LEA CH46 110 B5
Pinetree Cl NTHTN L30 84 B2 5
Pinetree Ct WAL/EG CH44 95 H8
Pinetree Dr WKBY CH48 124 F4
Pine Tree Gv MOR/LEA CH46 110 B5
Pine Tree Rd HUY L36 115 M5
Pinevale WGNNW/ST WN6 56 C6
Pine Vw WGNS/IIMK WN3 78 D4
Pine View Dr PEN/TH CH61 141 H3
Pine Wks RF/TRAN CH42 127 K4
Pine Wy HES CH60 141 G3
Pineways WARRS WA4 137 M8
Pinewood AIMK WN4 91 J3
SKEL WN8 65 M2
Pinewood Av FMBY L37 58 F4
WARR WA1 15 L1
WD/CROXPK L12 98 F2
Pinewood Cl CHNE CH2 165 L2
FMBY L37 58 F3
NTHLY L27 116 A7 2
STHP PR8 36 E4
WGNE/HIN WN2 80 D6
Pinewood Crs WGNE/HIN WN2 5 L7
WGNW/BIL/O WN5 67 G7
Pinewood Dr HES CH60 141 K5
Pinewood Gdns
NWD/KWIPK L33 74 A8 6
Pinewood Rd
WARRW/BUR WA5 104 B6
Pinfold Cl NTHTN L30 71 M8 2
Pinfold Crs KKBY L32 86 C5
Pinfold Dr ECCL WA10 101 J3 1
Pinfold La BRSC L40 50 B2
PR/KW L34 99 K2
STHP PR8 47 J2
WKBY CH48 124 C1
Pinfold Pl SKEL WN8 76 F1
Pinfold Rd WLTN L25 131 L6
Pinfold St WGNE/HIN WN2 69 J6
Pingot Rd WGNW/BIL/O WN5 78 A8
The Pingot LEIGH WN7 81 M8
Pingwood La NWD/KWIPK L33 74 C7
Pinmill Brow FROD/HEL WA6 160 D6
Pinmill Cl FROD/HEL WA6 160 D6
Pinners Brow WARRN/WOL WA2 14 E3
Pinners Fold RUNC WA7 150 D4
Pinnington Pl HUY L36 116 A3 5
Pinnington Rd RAIN/WH L35 117 M1 2
Pintail Cl RNFD/HAY WA11 89 K7 6
Pipe La WARR WA1 122 D4
Piper's Cl HES CH60 140 F5
Piper's End HES CH60 140 F5
Piper's La HES CH60 140 E3
The Pipers GOL/RIS/CU WA3 93 H5
Pipit Av NEWLW WA12 104 E2
Pipit Cl HLWD L26 132 A3 5
Pipit La GOL/RIS/CU WA3 123 G2
Pippin St BRSC L40 51 J3
Pippits Rw RUNC WA7 161 G1 5
Pirrie Rd WLT/FAZ L9 97 M2
Pitch Cl GR/UP/WCH CH49 125 M1 5
Pit Hey Pl SKEL WN8 65 L8
Pit La WDN WA8 134 C1
Pit Pl WLTN L25 131 J3
Pitsmead Rd KKBY L32 86 A4
Pitts Heath La RUNC WA7 150 F2
Pitts House La CHTN/BK PR9 25 K5
Pitt St CHTN/BK PR9 25 H7
CLVPS L1 112 F5
STHEL WA9 9 L4
WARRW/BUR WA5 14 B3
WDN WA8 16 C9
WGNS/IIMK WN3 4 D5
Pitville Av CALD/MH L18 130 C2
Pitville Cl CALD/MH L18 130 C3
Pitville Gv CALD/MH L18 130 C2
Pitville Rd CALD/MH L18 130 C2
Plaistow Ct RUNC WA7 150 A6
Plane Av WGNW/BIL/O WN5 68 A6
Plane Cl WLT/FAZ L9 97 L2 2
Plane Tree Gv
RNFD/HAY WA11 91 J6 2
Plane Tree Rd BEB CH63 143 G1
Planetree Rd
WD/CROXPK L12 99 H6 1
Plank La LEIGH WN7 93 J1
Plantation Cl RUNC WA7 150 C4
Plantation Dr GTS/LS CH66 156 A6
Plantation Gates WGN WN1 69 G3
Plantation Rd BRSC L40 51 K1
PS/BROM CH62 144 B4
The Planters GR/UP/WCH CH49 125 L1
NTHTN L30 84 D1 3
Platt Gv RF/TRAN CH42 128 C5
Platt La WGN WN1 5 J3
WGNE/HIN WN2 69 M8
Platts La BRSC L40 51 M3
Platts St RNFD/HAY WA11 90 C7 6
Platt St WGNE/HIN WN2 80 C3
Plattsville Rd CALD/MH L18 114 C8
Playfield Rd WD/CROXPK L12 99 H6
Pleasance Wy NEWLW WA12 104 F1 2
Pleasant Hill St TOX L8 112 F7 4
Pleasant St BTL L20 6 E6
VAUX/LVPD L3 13 K8 2
WAL/NB CH45 95 K6
Pleasant Vw BTL L20 6 E6
CHLY/EC PR7 43 H3
Pleasington Cl
CL/PREN CH43 127 G1 7
Pleasington Dr CL/PREN CH43 127 G1
Pleck Rd EP CH65 163 J3
Plemont Rd CLB/OSW/ST L13 98 C8
Plex La ORM L39 49 K7
Plex Moss La ORM L39 48 C5
STHP PR8 47 M4
Plimsoll St EHL/KEN L7 113 K4
Plinston Av WARRS WA4 138 B1
Plough La BRSC L40 64 C2
Ploughmans Wy GTS/LS CH66 163 G5
Plover Cl NEWLW WA12 104 E2
Plover Dr RUNC WA7 150 F5
Plovers La FROD/HEL WA6 159 L8
Plover Wy GOL/RIS/CU WA3 93 G5
Pluckington Rd HUY L36 116 D3
Plumbers Wy HUY L36 116 B3 1
Plumer St BIRK CH41 10 B2
WAV L15 114 A6
Plumley Gdns RAIN/WH L35 133 J4
Plumpstons La
FROD/HEL WA6 160 D4 1
Plumpton La ORM L39 49 G3
Plumpton St NPK/KEN L6 13 M2 1
Plumtre Av WARRW/BUR WA5 121 H5
Plum Tree Cl RAIN/WH L35 101 H7
STBRV L28 99 K5 3
Plymouth Cl RUNC WA7 151 G7
Plymouth Gv CHLYE PR6 33 G5 3
WGNNW/ST WN6 56 C6
Plymyard Av PS/BROM CH62 143 M7
Plymyard Cl PS/BROM CH62 143 M8
Poachers' La WARRS WA4 138 B2
Pochard Ri RUNC WA7 150 F5
Pocket Nook La
GOL/RIS/CU WA3 93 J5
Pocket Nook St STHEL WA9 9 K4
Pocklington Ct
WARRN/WOL WA2 122 B4 2
Podium Rd CLB/OSW/ST L13 114 C1 2
Poets Cnr PS/BROM CH62 128 D8 3
Poke St WGNW/BIL/O WN5 67 K7
Poleacre Dr WDN WA8 133 M3
Polegate Dr WGNE/HIN WN2 81 L3
Pole St WGNNW/ST WN6 56 A4 6
Pollard Rd WAV L15 114 C4
Poll Hill Rd HES CH60 141 H4
Pollitt Crs STHEL WA9 118 E2
Pollitt Sq PS/BROM CH62 128 E5 1
Polperro Cl
WARRW/BUR WA5 136 A2 5
Pomfret St TOX L8 113 H7
Pomona St VAUX/LVPD L3 13 K8
Pond Green Wy STHEL WA9 103 H4
Pond St GOL/RIS/CU WA3 93 J5
Pond View Cl HES CH60 141 L5
Pond Wk STHEL WA9 103 J4
Ponsonby Rd WAL/EG CH44 95 G8 6
Ponsonby St TOX L8 113 J7
Pool Bank PS/BROM CH62 128 D6
Poolbank Rd
PS/BROM CH62 128 D6 3
Poole Av WARRN/WOL WA2 121 K3 6

Poole Crs *WARRN/WOL* WA2 121 K3 7
Poole Hall La *GTS/LS* CH66 156 A5
Poole Hall Rd *EP* CH65 156 B5
Poole La *CHNE* CH2 165 G3
Pool End *STHEL* WA9 103 H3
Poole Rd *WAL/EG* CH44 95 M8
Pool Hey *STBRV* L28 99 K5
Pool Hey La *STHP* PR8 36 D2
Pool La *CHNE* CH2 158 B8
GR/UP/WCH CH49 126 C3
LYMM WA13 139 L1
PS/BROM CH62 143 L1
RUNC WA7 19 J2
WARRS WA4 137 J4
Poolside Rd *RUNC* WA7 19 J5
Poolside Wk *CHTN/BK* PR9 25 K1
Poolstock *WGNS/IIMK* WN3 4 D8
Poolstock La *WGNS/IIMK* WN3 .. 79 J1 3
Pool St *BIRK* CH41 11 H3
CHTN/BK PR9 25 L1
WDN WA8 16 F5
WGNE/HIN WN2 80 F1
WGNS/IIMK WN3 4 D8
Pooltown Rd *EP* CH65 156 B7
Poolwood Rd
GR/UP/WCH CH49 126 D1
Pope St *BTL* L20 83 K8
Poplar Av *AIMK* WN4 78 F8
CHLY/EC PR7 31 L1
CSBY/BLUN L23 71 H8
ECCL WA10 101 J1
GOL/RIS/CU WA3 107 H2
GR/UP/WCH CH49 110 B8 5
NEWLW WA12 104 F2
RUNC WA7 19 M9
WARRW/BUR WA5 136 A1
WGNW/BIL/O WN5 67 M7
Poplar Bank *HUY* L36 116 A3
Poplar Cl *EP* CH65 20 A7
RUNC WA7 149 L6
Poplar Dr *BEB* CH63 143 J1
EV L5 97 J8
KKBY L32 85 M2
SKEL WN8 65 H4
Poplar Farm Cl
MOR/LEA CH46 109 L7 4
Poplar Gv *CHNE* CH2 165 J2
ECCL WA10 101 L2
LITH L21 83 H7
RAIN/WH L35 101 G8
RNFD/HAY WA11 90 E7 4
WGNE/HIN WN2 81 K3
Poplar Rd *CL/PREN* CH43 127 K1
RNFD/HAY WA11 90 E7
WLTN L25 131 H2
Poplars Av *WARRN/WOL* WA2 121 J1
The Poplars *CHLY/EC* PR7 44 B7
LEIGH WN7 93 L5
LYMM WA13 139 M1 3
Poplar St *CHLY/EC* PR7 32 F7
GOL/RIS/CU WA3 92 D4 3
STHP PR8 25 G7
Poplar Wy *ANF/KKDL* L4 96 F5 1
Poppleford Cl *WLTN* L25 131 L1 2
Poppy Av *CHLYE* PR6 32 F3
Poppy La *ORM* L39 63 K4
Porchester Rd *NG/CROX* L11 98 B4
Porlock Av *CHLDW* L16 115 G8
STHEL WA9 102 E8
Porlock Cl *HES* CH60 141 K7
WARRW/BUR WA5 136 A1
WGNE/HIN WN2 80 C4
Portal Ms *PEN/TH* CH61 141 H2
Portal Rd *PEN/TH* CH61 141 H2
Port Cswy *PS/BROM* CH62 143 M1
Portelet Rd *CLB/OSW/ST* L13 114 B1
Porter Av *NEWLW* WA12 91 L8
Porter Cl *RAIN/WH* L35 117 M4
Porter St *RUNC* WA7 19 M3
VAUX/LVPD L3 12 C2
Porters Wood Cl
WGNW/BIL/O WN5 67 K6 2
Portgate Cl *NG/CROX* L11 98 E3 4
Porthcawl Cl *WDN* WA8 133 L2
Porthleven Rd *RUNC* WA7 150 D8
Portia Av *BEB* CH63 128 A6
Portia St *BTL* L20 96 E5
Portico Av *RAIN/WH* L35 101 J7
Portico La *RAIN/WH* L35 101 J7
Portland Av *CSBY/WL* L22 82 E3 6
Portland Cl *WGNE/HIN* WN2 80 C4
Portland Pl *EV* L5 13 J1
FROD/HEL WA6 166 E1 5
Portland St *BIRK* CH41 10 A2
CHLY/EC PR7 32 F5 5
EV L5 12 F1 1
NEWLW WA12 104 B1 4
RUNC WA7 18 E2
STHP PR8 2 F5
WAL/NB CH45 95 J4
WGNW/BIL/O WN5 68 A7 3
Portland Wy *STHEL* WA9 103 H4
Portlemouth Rd *NG/CROX* L11 85 L8
Portloe Av *HLWD* L26 132 B4
Portman Rd *WAV* L15 113 M6
Porto Hey Rd *PEN/TH* CH61 125 M8
Portola Cl *WARRS* WA4 138 E3
Porton Rd *KKBY* L32 85 L4
Portreath Wy *ECCL* WA10 88 D7
Portree Av *BEB* CH63 143 M8 1
Portree Cl *WLT/FAZ* L9 84 C8 3
Portrush St *CLB/OSW/ST* L13 98 A7
Portsmouth Dr *CHLYE* PR6 33 G5
Portsmouth Pl *RUNC* WA7 151 G7 2
Portwood Cl *TOX* L8 113 K5 6
Post Office Av *CHTN/BK* PR9 3 H3
Post Office La *RUNC* WA7 18 A9
Potter Pl *SKEL* WN8 65 M8
Potters La *WDN* WA8 148 B1
Pottery Flds *PR/KW* L34 100 F7 2
Pottery La *RAIN/WH* L35 116 E2
Pottery Rd *WGNS/IIMK* WN3 4 B6
Pottery Ter *WGNS/IIMK* WN3 4 C6
Poulsom Dr *NTHTN* L30 83 L3
Poulter Rd *WLT/FAZ* L9 84 D6 12
Poulton Cl *HLWD* L26 131 M7
Poulton Crs *WARR* WA1 122 F5
Poulton Dr *AIMK* WN4 91 H1 3
WDN WA8 133 M5 2
Poulton Green Cl *BEB* CH63 143 H4
Poulton Hall Rd *BEB* CH63 143 J6
WAL/EG CH44 111 J2 11
Poulton Rd *BEB* CH63 143 J3
CHTN/BK PR9 25 H6
WAL/EG CH44 111 J2
Poulton Royd Dr *BEB* CH63 143 H3
Pound Rd *GTS/LS* CH66 155 L6
Poverty La *MGHL* L31 73 H5
Povey Rd *WARRN/WOL* WA2 .. 121 M4 3
Powderworks La *MGHL* L31 73 L2
Powell Av *GOL/RIS/CU* WA3 123 G1
Powell Dr *WGNW/BIL/O* WN5 89 M2
Powell St *BIRK* CH41 111 H5
STHEL WA9 103 G6
WARRS WA4 138 B2
WGN WN1 4 F2
WGNE/HIN WN2 80 D4
Power Rd *PS/BROM* CH62 144 B4
RF/TRAN CH42 128 C5
Powey La *CH/BCN* CH1 162 D8
Powis St *TOX* L8 113 J8
Pownall St *CLVPS* L1 12 F9
CLVPS L1 112 F5 11
Powys St *WARRW/BUR* WA5 14 A6
Poynter St *STHEL* WA9 102 A7
Poynton Cl *WARRS* WA4 138 D2
Pratt Rd *PR/KW* L34 100 E7
The Precincts *CSBY/BLUN* L23 83 G1
Preece Cl *WDN* WA8 133 M2
Preesall Cl *CHTN/BK* PR9 22 B8
Preesall Wy *NG/CROX* L11 85 L8 3
Prefect Pl *WGNW/BIL/O* WN5 67 L5
Premier St *EV* L5 97 H8
Prentice Rd *RF/TRAN* CH42 128 A4
Prenton Av *STHEL* WA9 118 D1
Prenton Dell Av *CL/PREN* CH43 .. 127 J5
Prenton Dell Rd *CL/PREN* CH43 .. 127 G4
Prenton Farm Rd
CL/PREN CH43 127 J5
Prenton Gn *SPK/HALE* L24 147 G2 1
Prenton Hall Rd *CL/PREN* CH43 .. 127 H4
Prenton La *RF/TRAN* CH42 127 K4
Prentonpark Rd *RF/TRAN* CH42 .. 127 L2
Prenton Rd East
RF/TRAN CH42 127 M3
Prenton Rd West
RF/TRAN CH42 127 L3
Prenton Village Rd
CL/PREN CH43 127 H4
Prenton Wy *CL/PREN* CH43 126 F4
Presbyterian Fold
WGNE/HIN WN2 69 M7 10
Prescot Dr *NPK/KEN* L6 113 M2
Prescot Gn *ORM* L39 62 F2 2
Prescot Rd *CLB/OSW/ST* L13 114 A2
ECCL WA10 101 K5
MGHL L31 73 L7
ORM L39 73 M1
WDN WA8 117 H8
Prescot St *EHL/KEN* L7 13 M5
WAL/NB CH45 95 J5
Prescott Av *BRSC* L40 39 J2
GOL/RIS/CU WA3 92 B3 3
Prescott Br *BRSC* L40 39 L5
Prescott La *WGNW/BIL/O* WN5 67 K5
Prescott Rd *SKEL* WN8 66 A8
Prescott St *GOL/RIS/CU* WA3 92 C4 3
WARRS WA4 138 A2
WGNE/HIN WN2 69 M8 22
WGNNW/ST WN6 4 B4
Preseland Rd *CSBY/BLUN* L23 83 G2
Prestbury Av *CL/PREN* CH43 127 G3
STHP PR8 34 D8
WGNS/IIMK WN3 79 G2
Prestbury Cl *CL/PREN* CH43 127 G3 4
Prestbury Dr *ECCL* WA10 101 K2
WARRS WA4 138 F2
Prestbury Rd *NG/CROX* L11 98 B1
Preston Av *PR/KW* L34 100 E8
Preston Gv *NPK/KEN* L6 97 L8 3
Preston New Rd *CHTN/BK* PR9 25 J2
Preston Nook *CHLY/EC* PR7 30 E8 1
Preston on the Hl *WARRS* WA4 .. 151 H7
Preston Rd *CHLY/EC* PR7 32 E3
CHLYE PR6 32 E1
CHTN/BK PR9 25 G5
Preston St *CLVPS* L1 13 G6
STHEL WA9 118 C3 1
Preston Wy *CSBY/BLUN* L23 83 J1
Prestt Gv *WGNS/IIMK* WN3 4 A8
Prestwich Av *GOL/RIS/CU* WA3 .. 107 G2
Prestwick Dr *CSBY/BLUN* L23 70 E7
Prestwood Rd *DV/KA/FCH* L14 115 H1
Pretoria Rd *AIMK* WN4 91 J1
WLT/FAZ L9 84 D7
Price Gv *STHEL* WA9 103 J5
Price's La *CL/PREN* CH43 127 K1 5
Price St *BIRK* CH41 10 C1
CLVPS L1 13 G9 5
Priestfield Rd *EP* CH65 20 B4
Priesthouse Cl *FMBY* L37 59 J2
Priesthouse La *FMBY* L37 59 J2
Primrose Cl *CHTN/BK* PR9 22 E8 5
FMBY L37 47 K8
RUNC WA7 150 C5
WARRN/WOL WA2 121 L4
WDN WA8 134 A4
Primrose Dr *HUY* L36 100 A8
Primrose Gv *RNFD/HAY* WA11 91 G6
WAL/EG CH44 112 A3 17
WGNW/BIL/O WN5 68 A6 1
Primrose Hl *PS/BROM* CH62 128 D7
VAUX/LVPD L3 13 G5
Primrose Hill Rd *CHLY/EC* PR7 31 K1
Primrose La *FROD/HEL* WA6 166 C4
WGNNW/ST WN6 55 M3
Primrose Rd *BIRK* CH41 111 H6
CALD/MH L18 114 E8
Primrose St *ANF/KKDL* L4 96 F6
CHLYE PR6 32 F5
LEIGH WN7 81 M8 14
Primrose Vw *AIMK* WN4 91 K3 5
Primula Dr *WLT/FAZ* L9 97 K1
Prince Albert Ms *CLVPS* L1 113 G6 7
Prince Alfred Rd *WAV* L15 114 C6
Prince Andrew's Gv *ECCL* WA10 88 E7
Prince Charles Gdns *STHP* PR8 2 D8
Prince Edward St *BIRK* CH41 10 F4
Prince Edwin St *EV* L5 13 J2
Princes Av *CSBY/BLUN* L23 82 F1
PS/BROM CH62 144 A7
TOX L8 113 H6
WKBY CH48 124 D3
Princes Bvd *BEB* CH63 127 M5
Princes Gdns *VAUX/LVPD* L3 12 E5
Princes Ga West *TOX* L8 113 K7 4
Prince's Pk *WGNNW/ST* WN6 67 H1
Princes Pl *WDN* WA8 134 A4
Princes Rd *ECCL* WA10 101 L4 2
EP CH65 156 B7
TOX L8 113 H6
Princess Av *AIMK* WN4 91 L2
ECCL WA10 89 G7
RNFD/HAY WA11 91 J6
WARR WA1 122 B7
WARRW/BUR WA5 120 A7
Princess Crs *WARR* WA1 122 B7 1
Princess Dr *DV/KA/FCH* L14 99 H7
WD/CROXPK L12 99 G6
Princess Rd *AIMK* WN4 91 K2
CHLYE PR6 44 D5
LYMM WA13 139 L2
WAL/NB CH45 95 K6
WGNNW/ST WN6 67 L1
Princess St *CHLY/EC* PR7 32 F7
CLVP L2 12 F7
RUNC WA7 19 G2
WARRW/BUR WA5 136 F1 5
WGNE/HIN WN2 69 L8 2
WGNS/IIMK WN3 4 E6
Princes St *BTL* L20 6 F8
CLVP L2 12 F6
NEWLW WA12 104 D2 12
STHP PR8 2 F5
WDN WA8 16 D3
Princess Wy *CHLY/EC* PR7 31 M3
LITH L21 83 J6
Prince St *AIMK* WN4 79 J8 5
CLVPS L1 12 F9
CSBY/WL L22 82 F5
Princes Wy *RNFD/HAY* WA11 89 J5 2
Princesway *WAL/NB* CH45 95 J7
Princeway *FROD/HEL* WA6 160 D5
Prince William St *TOX* L8 113 G7
Prior Farm Cl *ALL/GAR* L19 130 C6 5
Priors Cl *WLTN* L25 131 K3
Priorsfield *MOR/LEA* CH46 110 A5 5
Priorsfield Rd *WLTN* L25 131 K3
Prior St *BTL* L20 83 J7
Priorswood Pl *SKEL* WN8 77 H1
Priory Av *LEIGH* WN7 81 M4
Priory Cl *AIG/SPK* L17 129 K3
BEB CH63 143 J2
BRSC L40 38 F8
FMBY L37 59 K3
RAIN/WH L35 116 E4
RUNC WA7 150 C4
WGNW/BIL/O WN5 67 K8 5
Priory Gdns *ECCL* WA10 89 H6
Priory Gra *STHP* PR8 2 E9
Priory Gv *ORM* L39 62 F1 2
Priory Ms *STHP* PR8 2 D5
Priory Nook *SKEL* WN8 66 E6
Priory Rd *AIMK* WN4 79 H8
ANF/KKDL L4 97 J5
RUNC WA7 150 E3 1
SKEL WN8 66 E6
WAL/EG CH44 112 A2
WKBY CH48 124 D3
Priory St *ALL/GAR* L19 145 M1
BIRK CH41 11 M6
WARRS WA4 14 F9
The Priory *NSTN* CH64 152 F4
WARRN/WOL WA2 105 J6
Priory Wy *WLTN* L25 131 K3
Priory Whf *BIRK* CH41 11 M5
Pritchard Av *LITH* L21 83 H6
Pritt St *VAUX/LVPD* L3 13 J3
Private Dr *PEN/TH* CH61 126 F8
Prizett Rd *ALL/GAR* L19 130 D6 1
Probyn Rd *WAL/NB* CH45 95 G8
Procter Rd *RF/TRAN* CH42 128 C4
Proctor Cl *WGNW/BIL/O* WN5 68 A4
Proctor Rd *FMBY* L37 58 E1
HOY CH47 108 E7
Proctors Cl *WDN* WA8 134 E3
Prodesse Ct *WGNE/HIN* WN2 69 M7
Proe's Ct *WGN* WN1 4 D3
Proffits La *FROD/HEL* WA6 167 G1
Progress St *CHLYE* PR6 33 G5
WGNE/HIN WN2 69 M8 23
Promenade *STHP* PR8 2 F3
Promenade Gdns *AIG/SPK* L17 129 H3
Prophet Wk *TOX* L8 113 G8
Prospect La *GOL/RIS/CU* WA3 123 L2
Prospect Pl *SKEL* WN8 66 B8
Prospect Rd *RF/TRAN* CH42 127 K4
STHEL WA9 102 F1 2
WGNNW/ST WN6 56 A6
Prospect St *WGNE/HIN* WN2 .. 69 M8 24
Prospect V *NPK/KEN* L6 113 M1
WAL/NB CH45 95 H8
Prospect Wy *NTHTN* L30 84 D2 1
Providence Crs *TOX* L8 113 G7 3
Provident St *STHEL* WA9 103 J2
Province Rd *BTL* L20 83 M7
Prussia St *VAUX/LVPD* L3 12 E5 2
Pryce Av *WGNE/HIN* WN2 5 L5
Public Hall St *RUNC* WA7 19 H2
Pudsey St *CLVPS* L1 13 J6
Pugin St *ANF/KKDL* L4 97 G6
Pulford Av *CL/PREN* CH43 127 J3
Pulford Cl *RUNC* WA7 149 M7
Pulford Rd *BEB* CH63 128 B8
EP CH65 163 H1
Pulford St *ANF/KKDL* L4 97 H6
Pullman Cl *HES* CH60 141 M5
Pump La *RUNC* WA7 150 B5
WKBY CH48 125 K1
Pump Rd *BIRK* CH41 11 K1
Pump St *WGNE/HIN* WN2 69 M8 25
Punnell's La *MGHL* L31 61 H8
Purbeck Dr *PEN/TH* CH61 125 M6
Purdy Cl *WARRW/BUR* WA5 120 F4
Purley Gv *CALD/MH* L18 130 C3
Purley Rd *CSBY/WL* L22 82 E3 7
Purser Gv *WAV* L15 113 M5 6
Putney Ct *RUNC* WA7 150 A6 2
Pye Cl *RNFD/HAY* WA11 91 K5
Pyecroft Cl *WARRW/BUR* WA5 119 M7
Pyecroft Rd *WARRW/BUR* WA5 .. 119 M7
Pye Rd *HES* CH60 141 J5
Pyes Gdns *RNFD/HAY* WA11 89 K6 9
Pyes La *STBRV* L28 99 L6
Pye St *WAV* L15 114 C6
Pygon's Hill La *MGHL* L31 61 M6
Pyke St *WGN* WN1 5 H1
Pym St *ANF/KKDL* L4 97 H3
Pyrus Gv *FROD/HEL* WA6 166 E1 6

Q

The Quadrangle
CALD/MH L18 130 D1 1
Quadrant Cl *RUNC* WA7 150 F7 3
Quail Cl *WARRN/WOL* WA2 121 M2
Quaker La *HES* CH60 141 G4
Quakers Meadow *PR/KW* L34 99 M1
Quakers' Pl *WGNNW/ST* WN6 56 A4 7
Quantock Cl *GTS/LS* CH66 155 J7 4
WGNS/IIMK WN3 78 E3
Quarry Av *BEB* CH63 143 H1
Quarry Bank *BIRK* CH41 11 G7
NWD/KWIPK L33 86 B2
Quarrybank St *BIRK* CH41 10 F7
Quarry Cl *CLB/OSW/ST* L13 98 B8
HES CH60 141 H3
NWD/KWIPK L33 86 B2
RUNC WA7 149 M4
Quarry Dl *NWD/KWIPK* L33 86 B2 3
Quarry Dr *ORM* L39 62 E4
Quarry Gn *NWD/KWIPK* L33 86 B2
Quarry Hey *NWD/KWIPK* L33 86 B2
Quarry La *NSTN* CH64 153 K4
PEN/TH CH61 126 C7
WARRS WA4 137 M7
Quarry Mt *ORM* L39 51 J7 1
Quarry Rd *BTL* L20 7 K6
CHLYE PR6 33 G7
CLB/OSW/ST L13 98 C8
CSBY/BLUN L23 71 J7
NSTN CH64 153 L4
Quarry Rd East *BEB* CH63 143 J1
HES CH60 141 G4
Quarry Rd West *HES* CH60 141 G4
Quarryside Dr *NWD/KWIPK* L33 86 C3
Quarry St *WLTN* L25 131 H2
Quarry St South *WLTN* L25 131 J3
Quartz Wy *LITH* L21 83 L5
Quay Fold *WARRS* WA4 137 G1
Quayle Cl *RNFD/HAY* WA11 90 D7
Quay Pl *RUNC* WA7 151 G6
Quay Side *FROD/HEL* WA6 160 F3
Quayside *NSTN* CH64 152 F8
The Quay *FROD/HEL* WA6 160 F3
Queen Anne St *STHP* PR8 3 G4
VAUX/LVPD L3 13 J4
Queen Mary's Dr
PS/BROM CH62 128 D7
Queen's Av *AIMK* WN4 91 K1
EP CH65 163 J2
FMBY L37 47 G8
HOY CH47 108 F5
WARR WA1 15 M1
WDN WA8 133 K5
Queensberry St *TOX* L8 113 H8 9
Queensbury *WKBY* CH48 124 F2
Queensbury Av *PS/BROM* CH62 .. 144 A4
Queensbury Wy *WDN* WA8 133 M2
Queen's Cl *RUNC* WA7 18 F6
Queens Ct *NPK/KEN* L6 97 J8
Queenscourt Rd
WD/CROXPK L12 98 E8
Queens Crs *WARR* WA1 122 C5 1
Queens Cft *FMBY* L37 58 F3
Queensdale Rd *CALD/MH* L18 114 C8
Queens Dr *CL/PREN* CH43 127 J4
ECCL WA10 88 E7
FROD/HEL WA6 166 D2
GOL/RIS/CU WA3 92 E5
HES CH60 141 G5
NEWLW WA12 91 L8
WARRS WA4 138 B3
Queens Dr Mossley Hl
CALD/MH L18 130 B1
Queens Dr Stoneycroft
CLB/OSW/ST L13 114 D1
Queens Dr Walton *ANF/KKDL* L4 .. 97 J3
Queens Dr Wavertree
DV/KA/FCH L14 114 E4
Queens Dr West Derby
CLB/OSW/ST L13 98 A5
Queens Gdns *EP* CH65 20 A4
Queensgate *CHLY/EC* PR7 32 D6 3
Queens Gn *ORM* L39 49 H8
Queen's Gv *CHLY/EC* PR7 32 E5
Queensland Av *STHEL* WA9 102 A6
Queensland St *EHL/KEN* L7 113 K4
Queens Ms *NPK/KEN* L6 97 J8 6
Queen's Rd *AIMK* WN4 91 K1 5
BTL L20 7 G7
CHLY/EC PR7 32 D5
CHTN/BK PR9 3 K2
CSBY/BLUN L23 83 G1
ECCL WA10 101 L4
FMBY L37 58 F3
GTS/LS CH66 155 L6
HOY CH47 108 C6
NPK/KEN L6 113 J1
PR/KW L34 101 G7 9
RF/TRAN CH42 128 C4
RNFD/HAY WA11 91 J6
RUNC WA7 18 F5
WAL/EG CH44 112 A2
WGNW/BIL/O WN5 66 E8
Queen St *ALL/GAR* L19 130 E8
BIRK CH41 11 K9
CSBY/WL L22 82 F5
ECCL WA10 8 F2
EP CH65 20 D1
GOL/RIS/CU WA3 92 D5 2
NEWLW WA12 104 D2
ORM L39 63 G1 1
RUNC WA7 19 G2
WAL/NB CH45 95 K8
WGNE/HIN WN2 69 M7 11
WGNE/HIN WN2 80 C3
WGNS/IIMK WN3 4 E5
WGNW/BIL/O WN5 67 M8
Queen St East *CHLY/EC* PR7 32 F7
Queensway *CHLY/EC* PR7 32 A3
CSBY/WL L22 83 H3
FROD/HEL WA6 160 D6
HES CH60 141 L7
RNFD/HAY WA11 76 C8 1
RNFD/HAY WA11 89 J5
RUNC WA7 18 F2
WAL/NB CH45 95 J7
WDN WA8 134 A6
WGN WN1 68 D3
WGNE/HIN WN2 69 J5 5
WGNNW/ST WN6 67 H1
Queensway Entrance (Mersey Tunnel)
CLVPS L1 13 G6 1
Queensway (Mersey Tunnel)
BIRK CH41 11 J3
VAUX/LVPD L3 12 D6
Queens Whf *VAUX/LVPD* L3 112 E6
Quernmore Rd *NWD/KWIPK* L33 .. 86 C2
Quernmore Wk
NWD/KWIPK L33 86 C2 1
Quickswood Cl *WLTN* L25 115 H8
Quickswood Dr *WLTN* L25 115 H8
Quickswood Gn *WLTN* L25 115 H8 1
Quickthorn Crs *STBRV* L28 99 K6 3
Quigley Av *NTHTN* L30 84 C4
Quigley St *BIRK* CH41 128 A1
The Quillet *NSTN* CH64 153 H6
Quinesway
GR/UP/WCH CH49 110 C8 2
Quinn St *WDN* WA8 16 E5
Quintbridge Cl *HLWD* L26 132 A6
Quinton Cl *STHP* PR8 47 J1
Quorn St *EHL/KEN* L7 113 K3

R

Rabbit La *BRSC* L40 51 H1
Raby Av *BEB* CH63 143 K7
Raby Cl *BEB* CH63 143 J6
HES CH60 141 H6
WDN WA8 134 F3
Raby Dr *BEB* CH63 143 J6
MOR/LEA CH46 109 M6
Raby Gdns *NSTN* CH64 153 G5
Raby Gv *RF/TRAN* CH42 127 M5
Raby Hall Rd *BEB* CH63 143 G8
Raby Mere Rd *BEB* CH63 142 E8
Raby Park Cl *NSTN* CH64 153 G5
Raby Park Rd *NSTN* CH64 153 G5
Raby Rd *BEB* CH63 142 D7
NSTN CH64 153 G5
Rachel St *EV* L5 13 H1
Radburn Cl *CSBY/BLUN* L23 71 K8
Radcliffe Av *GOL/RIS/CU* WA3 107 G2
Radford Av *BEB* CH63 143 K3
Radford Cl *WDN* WA8 133 L6
Radlett Cl *WARRW/BUR* WA5 136 A2
Radley Dr *AIN/FAZ* L10 84 E2
BEB CH63 142 B7
Radley La *WARRN/WOL* WA2 121 M2
Radley Rd *WAL/EG* CH44 95 H8
Radley St *STHEL* WA9 102 A6
Radmore Rd *DV/KA/FCH* L14 114 F2
Radnor Av *HES* CH60 141 H4
Radnor Cl *HLWD* L26 131 M7
WGNE/HIN WN2 81 J2
Radnor Dr *BTL* L20 7 L4 1
CHTN/BK PR9 25 H2 1
LEIGH WN7 81 L8
WAL/NB CH45 95 L7
WDN WA8 133 M3
Radnor Pl *CL/PREN* CH43 10 E6
NPK/KEN L6 97 M8
Radnor St *WARRW/BUR* WA5 121 G7
Radstock Gv *STHEL* WA9 102 F8
Radstock Rd *NPK/KEN* L6 113 L2
WAL/EG CH44 95 G8
Radway Gn *GTS/LS* CH66 156 A8
Radway Rd *HUY* L36 100 B7
Raeburn Av *NSTN* CH64 153 H6
PS/BROM CH62 143 M7
WKBY CH48 124 E2
Raffles Rd *RF/TRAN* CH42 10 F8
Raffles St *CLVPS* L1 113 G6
Rafter Av *BTL* L20 84 A6 2
Raglan Ct *GOL/RIS/CU* WA3 107 H7
Rail Cl *RNFD/HAY* WA11 76 B3
Railside Ct *EV* L5 96 E8 2
Railton Av *RAIN/WH* L35 117 M3
Railton Cl *RAIN/WH* L35 117 M4 2
Railton Rd *NG/CROX* L11 98 A3
Railway Ap *ORM* L39 51 H8
Railway Pth *ORM* L39 63 G1
Railway Rd *CHLYE* PR6 32 F4
CHLYE PR6 33 G6
GOL/RIS/CU WA3 92 D4 4
RF/TRAN CH42 128 B3
SKEL WN8 64 F5
Railway St *ALL/GAR* L19 130 E8
CHLY/EC PR7 32 F6
NEWLW WA12 104 D2
STHEL WA9 9 J3
STHP PR8 3 G7
WGNNW/ST WN6 4 A2
Railway Ter *STHP* PR8 2 F7
Rainbow Cl *WDN* WA8 133 L2
Rainbow Dr *HLWD* L26 132 A5
MGHL L31 85 K1
Raines Cl *GR/UP/WCH* CH49 126 A1
Rainford Av *BTL* L20 84 A8
Rainford By-pass
RNFD/HAY WA11 75 M6
Rainford Rd *ECCL* WA10 88 E7
ORM L39 64 C7
RNFD/HAY WA11 75 M4

WGNW/BIL/O WN5 .... 77 M8
Rainham Cl *ALL/GAR* L19 .... 130 E5
Rainhill Rd *RAIN/WH* L35 .... 101 L8
Raithby Dr *WGNS/IIMK* WN3 .... 79 J3 2
Rake Hey *MOR/LEA* CH46 .... 109 K5
Rake Hey Cl *MOR/LEA* CH46 .... 109 L5
Rake La *CHNE* CH2 .... 163 M8
FROD/HEL WA6 .... 159 J7
FROD/HEL WA6 .... 165 M6
GR/UP/WCH CH49 .... 126 C1
WAL/NB CH45 .... 95 K7
Rakersfield Ct *WAL/NB* CH45 .... 95 L5 3
Rakersfield Rd *WAL/NB* CH45 .... 95 L5
The Rake *PS/BROM* CH62 .... 143 L5
Raleigh Av *RAIN/WH* L35 .... 116 F3
Raleigh Cl *WARRW/BUR* WA5 .... 120 F4
Raleigh Rd *MOR/LEA* CH46 .... 110 D1
NSTN CH64 .... 153 G4
Raleigh St *BTL* L20 .... 6 E9
Ralph's Wife's La *CHTN/BK* PR9 .... 23 H7
Rame Cl *NG/CROX* L11 .... 85 K7 3
Ramford St *STHEL* WA9 .... 102 F3
Ramilies Rd *CALD/MH* L18 .... 114 B8
Ramleh Cl *CSBY/BLUN* L23 .... 82 C2
Rampit Cl *RNFD/HAY* WA11 .... 91 H6 6
Ramsay Cl *GOL/RIS/CU* WA3 .... 123 G2 3
Ramsbrook Cl *SPK/HALE* L24 .... 146 E1 1
Ramsbrook La *SPK/HALE* L24 .... 147 L2
Ramsbrook Rd *SPK/HALE* L24 .... 146 E1
Ramsden Cl *WGNS/IIMK* WN3 .... 4 A9
Ramsey Cl *AIMK* WN4 .... 91 K3 6
ALL/GAR L19 .... 130 F5
RAIN/WH L35 .... 117 G2 2
WDN WA8 .... 135 G2
Ramsey Ct *WKBY* CH48 .... 124 D4
Ramsey Rd *ALL/GAR* L19 .... 130 F5
EP CH65 .... 163 L4
Ramsfield Rd *SPK/HALE* L24 .... 147 J1
Ramsons Cl *HLWD* L26 .... 132 A4 7
Randall Av *WGNNW/ST* WN6 .... 55 J8
Randall Dr *NTHTN* L30 .... 83 L3
Randle Av *RNFD/HAY* WA11 .... 76 A5
Randle Brook Ct
RNFD/HAY WA11 .... 76 A5
Randle Cl *BEB* CH63 .... 143 J3 5
Randle Meadow *GTS/LS* CH66 .... 163 H3
Randles Rd *PR/KW* L34 .... 86 C8
Randolph St *ANF/KKDL* L4 .... 97 H6 10
Randon Gv *ECCL* WA10 .... 8 E4
Ranelagh Av *LITH* L21 .... 83 J5
Ranelagh Dr *STHP* PR8 .... 35 H6
Ranelagh Dr North
ALL/GAR L19 .... 130 C5
Ranelagh Dr South
ALL/GAR L19 .... 130 C6
Ranelagh St *CLVPS* L1 .... 13 H8
Ranfurly Rd *ALL/GAR* L19 .... 130 D6
Rangemoor Cl
GOL/RIS/CU WA3 .... 107 J7 4
Rangemore Rd *CALD/MH* L18 .... 130 C4
Rangletts Av *CHLY/EC* PR7 .... 32 E7
Ranicar Steet *WGNE/HIN* WN2 .... 81 L2 1
Rankin St *WAL/EG* CH44 .... 111 J3
Ranleigh Dr *SKEL* WN8 .... 53 J4 5
Ranmore Av *AIMK* WN4 .... 90 F1 4
Rannoch Cl *GTS/LS* CH66 .... 163 H2
Ranulph Ct *FROD/HEL* WA6 .... 160 E6
Ranworth Cl *NG/CROX* L11 .... 98 A2 2
Ranworth Dr *GOL/RIS/CU* WA3 .... 93 G6
Ranworth Pl *NG/CROX* L11 .... 98 B2 1
Ranworth Rd
WARRW/BUR WA5 .... 120 A7 4
Ranworth Sq *NG/CROX* L11 .... 98 B2 2
Ranworth Wy *NG/CROX* L11 .... 98 B2 3
Rappart Rd *WAL/EG* CH44 .... 111 M2
Rassey Cl *WGNNW/ST* WN6 .... 56 C6
Ratcliffe Rd *WGNE/HIN* WN2 .... 57 L7
Ratcliffe St *WGNNW/ST* WN6 .... 4 A2
Ratcliff Pl *RAIN/WH* L35 .... 117 K1
Rathbone Rd *HTWN* L38 .... 70 B1 1
WAV L15 .... 114 B5
Rathen Av *WGNE/HIN* WN2 .... 69 J4
Rathlin Cl *WDN* WA8 .... 135 G2
Rathmell Cl *GOL/RIS/CU* WA3 .... 107 G2 4
Rathmore Av *CALD/MH* L18 .... 130 C2
Rathmore Cl *CL/PREN* CH43 .... 127 J2
Rathmore Crs *CHTN/BK* PR9 .... 25 K2
Rathmore Dr *CL/PREN* CH43 .... 127 J1
Rathmore Rd *CL/PREN* CH43 .... 127 J1
Raven Cl *NPK/KEN* L6 .... 113 J2 16
Ravendale Cl *CL/PREN* CH43 .... 126 F1 2
Ravenfield Cl *HLWD* L26 .... 132 A5 3
Ravenfield Dr *WDN* WA8 .... 133 L2
Ravenglass Av *MGHL* L31 .... 72 F3
Ravenhead Av *KKBY* L32 .... 86 A6
Ravenhead Dr *SKEL* WN8 .... 66 C6
Ravenhead Rd *ECCL* WA10 .... 8 D9
Ravenhead Wy *SKEL* WN8 .... 66 B7
Ravenhill Crs *MOR/LEA* CH46 .... 110 B2
Ravenhill Dr *CHLY/EC* PR7 .... 32 E4
Ravenhurst Ct
GOL/RIS/CU WA3 .... 107 H8
Ravenhurst Wy *RAIN/WH* L35 .... 116 E4
Raven Meols La *FMBY* L37 .... 59 G3
Ravenna Rd *ALL/GAR* L19 .... 130 F5
Ravenscroft *FMBY* L37 .... 59 H3
Ravenscroft Av *ORM* L39 .... 63 G1
Ravenscroft Rd *CL/PREN* CH43 .... 10 E7
Ravensdale Cl
WARRN/WOL WA2 .... 121 M2 2
The Ravens *FMBY* L37 .... 59 H3
Ravensthorpe Gn *NG/CROX* L11 .... 98 B2
Ravenstone Dr *STHEL* WA9 .... 102 F6
Ravenstone Rd *ALL/GAR* L19 .... 130 D5
Ravenswood Av *RF/TRAN* CH42 .... 128 B5
WGNS/IIMK WN3 .... 78 F2
Ravenswood Rd
CLB/OSW/ST L13 .... 114 C2
PEN/TH CH61 .... 141 J3
Rawcliffe Cl *WDN* WA8 .... 134 B1 5
Rawcliffe Rd *CHLY/EC* PR7 .... 32 E6 13
RF/TRAN CH42 .... 11 G8
WLT/FAZ L9 .... 97 H1
Rawdon Cl *RUNC* WA7 .... 150 C6
Rawlings Cl *GOL/RIS/CU* WA3 .... 123 H2
Rawlinson Crs *HLWD* L26 .... 132 D5 1
Rawlinson Gv *CHTN/BK* PR9 .... 25 G4 1
Rawlinson La *CHLY/EC* PR7 .... 44 A4
Rawlinson Rd *CHTN/BK* PR9 .... 25 G4
CLB/OSW/ST L13 .... 114 C2 3
Rawlins St *EHL/KEN* L7 .... 113 M2
Rawson Cl *LITH* L21 .... 83 H6
Rawson Rd *LITH* L21 .... 83 H7
Rawthey Pl *WGNE/HIN* WN2 .... 80 B3 2
Raydale Cl *GOL/RIS/CU* WA3 .... 93 G4 6
WLT/FAZ L9 .... 97 J2
Raymond Av *NTHTN* L30 .... 84 C4
WARRS WA4 .... 137 M3
Raymond Pl *EV* L5 .... 13 G1
Raymond Rd *WAL/EG* CH44 .... 111 L2
Raymond Wy *NSTN* CH64 .... 153 J6
Rayner Av *WGNE/HIN* WN2 .... 80 F3
Raynham Rd
CLB/OSW/ST L13 .... 114 B3 1
Reade Cl *BEB* CH63 .... 143 J4
Reading St *EV* L5 .... 96 F6
Reads Ct *WLT/FAZ* L9 .... 84 B7
Reaper Cl *WARRW/BUR* WA5 .... 120 F7
Reapers Wy *NTHTN* L30 .... 84 C1
Reay St *WDN* WA8 .... 134 E3
Rebecca Gdns *STHEL* WA9 .... 102 E6
Recreation Av *AIMK* WN4 .... 91 M1
Recreation Dr
WGNW/BIL/O WN5 .... 78 A8 2
Rector Rd *NPK/KEN* L6 .... 97 L6
Rectory Av *GOL/RIS/CU* WA3 .... 92 E5
Rectory Cl *CHLY/EC* PR7 .... 32 E4
HES CH60 .... 141 H6
LEY/BBR PR5 .... 29 L3 1
RF/TRAN CH42 .... 11 H9 1
WARRN/WOL WA2 .... 105 J7
Rectory Dr *HLWD* L26 .... 132 B4
Rectory La *CH/BCN* CH1 .... 162 B4
HES CH60 .... 141 G6
WARRN/WOL WA2 .... 105 J7
WGNNW/ST WN6 .... 56 B4
Rectory Rd *AIMK* WN4 .... 78 F8
CHTN/BK PR9 .... 25 H4
WKBY CH48 .... 124 D4
Red Bank Av *NEWLW* WA12 .... 105 H4
Red Banks *WKBY* CH48 .... 124 F7
Red Barnes *FMBY* L37 .... 47 H7
Red Barn Rd *WGNW/BIL/O* WN5 .... 77 K7
Redbourne Av *HLWD* L26 .... 132 B7
Redbourne Dr *WDN* WA8 .... 133 K1
Redbourn St *NPK/KEN* L6 .... 97 L7
Red Br *BRSC* L40 .... 28 E3
Redbrook Cl *PS/BROM* CH62 .... 143 M7 1
Redbrook Rd *WGNS/IIMK* WN3 .... 5 J7
Redbrook St *NPK/KEN* L6 .... 97 L7
Red Brow La *WARRS* WA4 .... 151 H5
Redbrow Wy *NWD/KWIPK* L33 .... 86 A1
Redburn Cl *TOX* L8 .... 129 J1 19
WGNS/IIMK WN3 .... 4 D8
Redcap Cl *WAL/NB* CH45 .... 95 C5 3
Redcar Cl *STHP* PR8 .... 36 B2
Redcar Dr *PS/BROM* CH62 .... 143 M8
Redcar Rd *WAL/NB* CH45 .... 94 F7
Redcar St *NPK/KEN* L6 .... 97 L7
Red Cat La *BRSC* L40 .... 39 G5
RNFD/HAY WA11 .... 77 H8
Redcliffe Gdns *ORM* L39 .... 63 G2
Red Cross St *CLVPS* L1 .... 12 E8
Red Cut La *NWD/KWIPK* L33 .... 87 H5
Red Delph La *RNFD/HAY* WA11 .... 75 M4
Redditch Cl
GR/UP/WCH CH49 .... 125 L1 5
Redesdale Cl
WARRN/WOL WA2 .... 122 A3 4
Redfern St *BTL* L20 .... 96 E5
Redfield Cl *WAL/EG* CH44 .... 111 M1 12
Red Fold *ORM* L39 .... 62 E3
Redford Cl *GR/UP/WCH* CH49 .... 125 L1 6
Redford St *NPK/KEN* L6 .... 97 L8
Redgate *FMBY* L37 .... 59 J3
ORM L39 .... 62 F1
Redgate Av *CSBY/BLUN* L23 .... 83 J1
Redgate Dr *FMBY* L37 .... 59 K3
STHEL WA9 .... 102 F2
Redgate Rd *AIMK* WN4 .... 79 K7
Redgrave Ri *WGNS/IIMK* WN3 .... 78 F2
Redgrave St *EHL/KEN* L7 .... 113 L3 3
Redhill Av *KKBY* L32 .... 86 B5
Redhill Gv *CHLYE* PR6 .... 33 G2
Red Hill Rd *BEB* CH63 .... 127 K8
Redhills Dr *STHP* PR8 .... 36 B2 1
Redhills Ms *EP* CH65 .... 20 B2
Red Hill Wy *WGNE/HIN* WN2 .... 69 M7 12
Redhouse Bank *WKBY* CH48 .... 124 C2 6
Red House La *CHLY/EC* PR7 .... 30 D7
Redhouse La *WKBY* CH48 .... 124 C2
Redington Rd *ALL/GAR* L19 .... 130 F5
Redland Ct *WGNE/HIN* WN2 .... 80 A6
Redland Rd *WLT/FAZ* L9 .... 84 D5
Red La *CHLY/EC* PR7 .... 31 G7
FROD/HEL WA6 .... 160 E5
WARRS WA4 .... 137 L6
Red Lion Cl *MGHL* L31 .... 72 E4
Red Lion La *GTS/LS* CH66 .... 155 L6
Red Lomes *NTHTN* L30 .... 71 M8
Redmain Gv *GOL/RIS/CU* WA3 .... 93 G5
Redmain Wy *WD/CROXPK* L12 .... 99 H3 1
Redmayne Cl *NEWLW* WA12 .... 104 D1 5
Redmere Dr *HES* CH60 .... 141 L5
Redmires Cl *EHL/KEN* L7 .... 113 K5 7
Redmond St *BIRK* CH41 .... 11 J9 2
Redmoor Crs *NWD/KWIPK* L33 .... 86 A1
Red Pike *GTS/LS* CH66 .... 155 M6
Redpoll Gv *HLWD* L26 .... 132 A3
Redpoll La *GOL/RIS/CU* WA3 .... 123 G1 4
Red Rock Cl *NPK/KEN* L6 .... 113 K1
Red Rock La *WGNE/HIN* WN2 .... 56 F5
Red Rock St *NPK/KEN* L6 .... 113 K1
Red Rum Cl *WLT/FAZ* L9 .... 84 F5
Redruth Av *RNFD/HAY* WA11 .... 89 M6
Redruth Cl *RUNC* WA7 .... 150 E7
Redruth Rd *NG/CROX* L11 .... 85 M8
Red Sands *ORM* L39 .... 62 F2
Redshank Cl *NEWLW* WA12 .... 104 E1 5
Redshank La *GOL/RIS/CU* WA3 .... 123 H1
Redstart Cl *GOL/RIS/CU* WA3 .... 93 G5 7
Redstone Cl *HOY* CH47 .... 108 F5 2
Redstone Dr *HES* CH60 .... 140 E4
Red Stone Hl *FROD/HEL* WA6 .... 166 D1
Redstone Ri *CL/PREN* CH43 .... 110 F7
Redvales Ct *GOL/RIS/CU* WA3 .... 122 E1 4
Redvers Av *GTS/LS* CH66 .... 155 J3
Redvers Dr *WLT/FAZ* L9 .... 84 B7
Redwing La *WLTN* L25 .... 131 J1
Redwing Wy *HLWD* L26 .... 131 M3
Redwood *WGNNW/ST* WN6 .... 55 K7
Redwood Av *MGHL* L31 .... 72 E2 2
WGNNW/ST WN6 .... 68 A2
WGNW/BIL/O WN5 .... 67 J7
Redwood Cl *CL/PREN* CH43 .... 127 H3 3
WARR WA1 .... 123 G7
Redwood Dr *CHNE* CH2 .... 165 L1
GTS/LS CH66 .... 163 H4
ORM L39 .... 62 F1
RNFD/HAY WA11 .... 90 B8
Redwood Gv *BTL* L20 .... 7 H3 1
Redwood Rd *WLTN* L25 .... 115 K8
Redwood Wy *NWD/KWIPK* L33 .... 74 A7
Reedale Cl *CALD/MH* L18 .... 130 C1
Reedale Rd *CALD/MH* L18 .... 130 C1
Reed Crs *WGNS/IIMK* WN3 .... 79 J1
Reeds Av East *MOR/LEA* CH46 .... 110 B2
Reeds Av West *MOR/LEA* CH46 .... 110 B2
Reeds Brow *RNFD/HAY* WA11 .... 76 D5
Reeds La *MOR/LEA* CH46 .... 110 B2
RNFD/HAY WA11 .... 88 B2
Reedsmere Cl *WARRS* WA4 .... 138 A3 1
WGNW/BIL/O WN5 .... 68 B7 10
Reeds Rd *HUY* L36 .... 116 A1
The Reeds *ORM* L39 .... 50 F7
Reedville Gv *MOR/LEA* CH46 .... 110 B3
Reedville Rd *BEB* CH63 .... 128 B8
Reepham Cl *WGNS/IIMK* WN3 .... 78 F2
Rees Pk *BRSC* L40 .... 52 B2
Reeves Av *BTL* L20 .... 7 L1
Reeves St *STHEL* WA9 .... 103 G2 2
Reeve St *GOL/RIS/CU* WA3 .... 93 K5
Reeveswood *CHLY/EC* PR7 .... 30 D7
Regal Cl *GTS/LS* CH66 .... 163 G2
Regal Dr *ECCL* WA10 .... 88 E8
Regal Rd *NG/CROX* L11 .... 98 E2
Regency Gdns *STHP* PR8 .... 35 G1
Regent Av *AIMK* WN4 .... 79 H8
DV/KA/FCH L14 .... 115 G3
NTHTN L30 .... 84 B2
RNFD/HAY WA11 .... 90 D6
WARR WA1 .... 122 C5
Regent Cl *STHP* PR8 .... 35 H1
Regent Rd *BTL* L20 .... 6 B2
CHLY/EC PR7 .... 32 D6
CSBY/BLUN L23 .... 82 F1
EV L5 .... 96 D7
STHP PR8 .... 35 G1
WAL/NB CH45 .... 94 F7
WDN WA8 .... 16 E1
WGNE/HIN WN2 .... 80 C2
Regents Cl *PEN/TH* CH61 .... 126 D7
Regents Rd *ECCL* WA10 .... 101 L4
Regent St *CHLY/EC* PR7 .... 43 G4
EP CH65 .... 156 C8
NEWLW WA12 .... 104 E1
RUNC WA7 .... 19 G2
VAUX/LVPD L3 .... 12 C2
WARR WA1 .... 14 D6
WGNE/HIN WN2 .... 69 M8 26
Regents Wy *BEB* CH63 .... 127 M6
CHLY/EC PR7 .... 31 M3
Regina Av *CSBY/WL* L22 .... 82 E3
Reginald Rd *STHEL* WA9 .... 103 G7
Regina Rd *WLT/FAZ* L9 .... 84 C7
Reid Av *WARRW/BUR* WA5 .... 121 H5 2
Reid Ct *GTS/LS* CH66 .... 155 L6
Reigate *CHLYE* PR6 .... 33 H2
Reigate Cl *WLTN* L25 .... 131 L3
Renacres La *ORM* L39 .... 36 A8
Rendal Cl *EV* L5 .... 97 J8 7
Rendcombe Gn *NG/CROX* L11 .... 98 B2
Rendel Cl *NEWLW* WA12 .... 104 F3
Rendelsham Cl
GR/UP/WCH CH49 .... 110 A8 8
Rendel St *BIRK* CH41 .... 11 H3
Rendlesham Cl
GOL/RIS/CU WA3 .... 107 K7
Renfrew Av *PS/BROM* CH62 .... 144 A8
RNFD/HAY WA11 .... 90 A6
Renfrew Cl *WGNS/IIMK* WN3 .... 79 J2
Renfrew Rd *WGNE/HIN* WN2 .... 57 M8
Renfrew St *EHL/KEN* L7 .... 113 J3
Renfrey Cl *ORM* L39 .... 51 G5
Rennell Rd *DV/KA/FCH* L14 .... 114 E2
Rennie Av *ECCL* WA10 .... 101 L1 1
Renown Cl *GOL/RIS/CU* WA3 .... 122 F1 5
Renown Wy *SPK/HALE* L24 .... 131 J7
Renshaw St *CLVPS* L1 .... 13 J8
Renton Av *RUNC* WA7 .... 149 M3
Renville Rd *DV/KA/FCH* L14 .... 114 E4
Renwick Av *RAIN/WH* L35 .... 117 J1
Renwick Sq *AIMK* WN4 .... 91 H2 2
Repton Av *WGNE/HIN* WN2 .... 80 B1
Repton Gv *WLT/FAZ* L9 .... 84 E3
Repton Rd *CHLDW* L16 .... 114 F5
EP CH65 .... 20 F7
Reservoir Rd *RF/TRAN* CH42 .... 127 K4
WLTN L25 .... 131 H2
Reservoir Rd North
RF/TRAN CH42 .... 127 K3
Reservoir St *NPK/KEN* L6 .... 113 J1 1
RAIN/WH L35 .... 101 L6
WGNE/HIN WN2 .... 69 J5 9
Rest Hill Rd *BEB* CH63 .... 127 K8
Restormel Av *WGNE/HIN* WN2 .... 57 M8
Retford Rd *NWD/KWIPK* L33 .... 86 B3 5
Reva Rd *DV/KA/FCH* L14 .... 115 H3
Revesby Cl *WDN* WA8 .... 133 M3 4
Rexmore Rd *CALD/MH* L18 .... 130 C3
Rexmore Wy *WAV* L15 .... 114 A6 10
Reynolds Av *GOL/RIS/CU* WA3 .... 107 G8
STHEL WA9 .... 103 K3
Reynolds Cl *NPK/KEN* L6 .... 113 J1
Reynolds St *WARRS* WA4 .... 138 B2
Reynolds Wy *WLTN* L25 .... 131 J3
Rhiwlas St *TOX* L8 .... 113 J8
Rhodesia Rd *WLT/FAZ* L9 .... 84 D7
Rhodes St *WARRN/WOL* WA2 .... 15 G1
Rhodesway *HES* CH60 .... 141 K6
Rhona Cl *BEB* CH63 .... 154 E1
Rhona Dr *WARRW/BUR* WA5 .... 120 A7 5
Rhosesmor Cl *KKBY* L32 .... 86 B7 1
Rhosesmor Rd *KKBY* L32 .... 86 B7
Rhuddlan Ct *EP* CH65 .... 163 M3
Rhum Cl *EP* CH65 .... 163 L4
Rhyl St *TOX* L8 .... 113 H8 10
WDN WA8 .... 16 B6 1
Ribbesford Rd *WGNS/IIMK* WN3 .... 78 E1
Ribble Av *CHTN/BK* PR9 .... 25 L1
MGHL L31 .... 73 G3
RAIN/WH L35 .... 117 L2
Ribble Cl *GOL/RIS/CU* WA3 .... 107 H3
WDN WA8 .... 135 H2
Ribble Crs *WGNW/BIL/O* WN5 .... 89 L2
Ribbledale Rd *CALD/MH* L18 .... 130 C1
Ribble Dr *WGNW/BIL/O* WN5 .... 67 L6
Ribble Gv *LEIGH* WN7 .... 81 L8
Ribble Rd *WGNE/HIN* WN2 .... 80 C3
WGNNW/ST WN6 .... 55 K3
WLTN L25 .... 131 L2
Ribbler's La *KKBY* L32 .... 85 M6
PR/KW L34 .... 86 B7
Ribblesdale *EP* CH65 .... 163 M2
Ribblesdale Av *WLT/FAZ* L9 .... 84 D6 13
Ribblesdale Cl
PS/BROM CH62 .... 144 B8 1
Ribblesdale Pl *CHLY/EC* PR7 .... 32 D5 2
Ribble St *BIRK* CH41 .... 111 H4
Ribchester Gdns
GOL/RIS/CU WA3 .... 107 J2
Ribchester Wy *RAIN/WH* L35 .... 116 C6
Rice Hey Rd *WAL/EG* CH44 .... 95 L8
Rice La *WLT/FAZ* L9 .... 97 J1
Rice St *CLVPS* L1 .... 113 G5 16
Richard Gv *WD/CROXPK* L12 .... 99 G8 3
Richard Hesketh Dr *KKBY* L32 .... 85 L3
Richard Kelly Cl *ANF/KKDL* L4 .... 97 M5 2
Richard Kelly Dr *ANF/KKDL* L4 .... 97 M3
Richard Kelly Pl *ANF/KKDL* L4 .... 97 M5 3
Richard Martin Rd *LITH* L21 .... 83 L4 2
Richard Rd *CSBY/BLUN* L23 .... 70 C7
Richards Gv *STHEL* WA9 .... 103 G1
Richardson Rd *RF/TRAN* CH42 .... 128 A4
Richardson St *EHL/KEN* L7 .... 113 L6 5
WARRN/WOL WA2 .... 121 L5 1
Richards Rd *WGNNW/ST* WN6 .... 55 K2 1
Richard St *WGNS/IIMK* WN3 .... 5 G7
Richland Rd *CLB/OSW/ST* L13 .... 98 B8
Richmond Av *BRSC* L40 .... 52 A2
LITH L21 .... 83 J5
RNFD/HAY WA11 .... 90 D6
RUNC WA7 .... 150 A3
WARRS WA4 .... 138 B1
WARRS WA4 .... 138 E2
Richmond Cl *BEB* CH63 .... 128 B7
ECCL WA10 .... 101 H1
GOL/RIS/CU WA3 .... 106 F1
HTWN L38 .... 70 B3
WGN WN1 .... 56 D6
Richmond Ct *CHLY/EC* PR7 .... 32 E7 5
LITH L21 .... 83 K6 6
Richmond Cresent *NTHTN* L30 .... 84 B2
Richmond Gdns
NEWLW WA12 .... 104 E3 3
Richmond Gv *MGHL* L31 .... 73 G2 3
Richmond Hl *WGNW/BIL/O* WN5 .... 67 L7
Richmond Ms *BRSC* L40 .... 52 B2 5
Richmond Pk *NPK/KEN* L6 .... 97 K7
Richmond Rd *AIMK* WN4 .... 79 H8
BEB CH63 .... 128 B7 1
CHLY/EC PR7 .... 30 E6
CHLYE PR6 .... 33 G7
CSBY/BLUN L23 .... 71 G8
STHP PR8 .... 35 H3
WGNE/HIN WN2 .... 81 J2
Richmond Rw *VAUX/LVPD* L3 .... 13 J3
Richmond St *WAL/NB* CH45 .... 95 K4 4
WARRS WA4 .... 138 C2
WDN WA8 .... 17 G1 2
WGN WN1 .... 4 D3
WGNS/IIMK WN3 .... 68 C8
Richmond Ter *NPK/KEN* L6 .... 97 J8
Richmond Wy *HUY* L36 .... 116 C6
PEN/TH CH61 .... 126 C7 4
PEN/TH CH61 .... 141 H3
Rickaby Cl *BEB* CH63 .... 143 L5
Rickman St *ANF/KKDL* L4 .... 96 F5
Rickman Wy *HUY* L36 .... 116 B5
Ridding La *RUNC* WA7 .... 150 D8
Riddock Rd *LITH* L21 .... 83 K8
Ridge Av *WGN* WN1 .... 56 D6
Ridgeborne Cl
WARRW/BUR WA5 .... 120 F3
Ridge Cl *CHTN/BK* PR9 .... 22 E8 6
Ridgefield Rd *PEN/TH* CH61 .... 126 B8
Ridgemere Rd *PEN/TH* CH61 .... 126 B8
Ridge Rd *CHLYE* PR6 .... 33 G6
The Ridge *HES* CH60 .... 140 F3
Ridgetor Rd *WLTN* L25 .... 131 J2
Ridgeview Rd *CL/PREN* CH43 .... 110 F8
Ridgeway *GOL/RIS/CU* WA3 .... 93 G6
Ridgeway Cl *GTS/LS* CH66 .... 162 E3
Ridgeway Dr *MGHL* L31 .... 72 F2
Ridgeway Gdns *LYMM* WA13 .... 139 M2
The Ridgeway *BEB* CH63 .... 127 M5 1
FROD/HEL WA6 .... 167 J3
HES CH60 .... 141 K6
HOY CH47 .... 109 G6
RUNC WA7 .... 150 F7
WDN WA8 .... 117 L7
WLTN L25 .... 131 J2
Ridgewell Av
GOL/RIS/CU WA3 .... 92 F5 4
Ridgewood Dr *PEN/TH* CH61 .... 141 H1
STHEL WA9 .... 102 F7
Ridgewood Wy *WLT/FAZ* L9 .... 84 C6
Ridgmont Av *NG/CROX* L11 .... 98 B3
Ridgway *HOR/BR* BL6 .... 57 L3
Ridgway St *WARRN/WOL* WA2 .... 15 J1
Riding Cl *STHEL* WA9 .... 118 E1 16
Riding Fold *HLWD* L26 .... 131 M3 6
Riding Hill Rd *PR/KW* L34 .... 99 M3
Riding La *AIMK* WN4 .... 80 A8
ORM L39 .... 61 G1
Ridings Hey *CL/PREN* CH43 .... 126 F1 3
The Ridings *CHTN/BK* PR9 .... 25 J2
CL/PREN CH43 .... 110 F8 5
Riding St *STHP* PR8 .... 3 G6
VAUX/LVPD L3 .... 13 L6
Ridley Dr *WARRW/BUR* WA5 .... 136 E1
Ridley Gv *WKBY* CH48 .... 124 C2 7
Ridley La *BRSC* L40 .... 41 H3
LEY/BBR PR5 .... 29 M2
MGHL L31 .... 72 F4
Ridley Rd *NPK/KEN* L6 .... 113 L2
Ridley St *CL/PREN* CH43 .... 10 E7
Ridyard St *WGNE/HIN* WN2 .... 80 D2
WGNW/BIL/O WN5 .... 68 A6
Riesling Dr *NWD/KWIPK* L33 .... 73 M8
Rigby Av *HOR/BR* BL6 .... 57 L3 2
Rigby Dr *GR/UP/WCH* CH49 .... 125 M3
Rigby Rd *MGHL* L31 .... 72 D2
Rigbys La *AIMK* WN4 .... 91 M2
Rigby St *AIMK* WN4 .... 91 J2
ECCL WA10 .... 8 F4 5
GOL/RIS/CU WA3 .... 92 C5 4
VAUX/LVPD L3 .... 12 D5
Riley Av *BTL* L20 .... 7 K1
Riley Dr *RUNC* WA7 .... 19 H7
Riley La *WGNE/HIN* WN2 .... 57 K6
Riley Sq *WGN* WN1 .... 5 H3
Rilston Av *GOL/RIS/CU* WA3 .... 106 F2
Rimington Av
GOL/RIS/CU WA3 .... 92 E4 6
Rimington Cl
GOL/RIS/CU WA3 .... 107 G2 5
Rimmer Av *CHLDW* L16 .... 115 J4
Rimmer Cl *LITH* L21 .... 83 K6
Rimmer Gn *STHP* PR8 .... 36 F4
Rimmer Gv *STHEL* WA9 .... 103 G2
Rimmer's Av *FMBY* L37 .... 47 G7
STHP PR8 .... 3 G6
Rimmers Ct *BIRK* CH41 .... 111 H6 4
Rimmer St *VAUX/LVPD* L3 .... 13 K5
Rimmington Rd *AIG/SPK* L17 .... 130 A3 3
Rimrose Rd *BTL* L20 .... 6 D4
Rimrose Valley Rd
CSBY/BLUN L23 .... 83 J2
Ringcroft Rd *CLB/OSW/ST* L13 .... 114 D2
Ringley Av *GOL/RIS/CU* WA3 .... 92 B4
Ring O'bells La *BRSC* L40 .... 52 D3
Ringo Starr Dr *NPK/KEN* L6 .... 113 K2 11
Ringsfield Rd *SPK/HALE* L24 .... 147 J2 2
Ringtail Ct *BRSC* L40 .... 51 K1
Ringtail Pl *BRSC* L40 .... 51 K2
Ringtail Rd *BRSC* L40 .... 51 K1
Ringway *CHLY/EC* PR7 .... 32 C6
GTS/LS CH66 .... 163 G1
NSTN CH64 .... 153 H3
Ringway Rd *RUNC* WA7 .... 149 M3
WLTN L25 .... 115 L8 3
Ringways *PS/BROM* CH62 .... 143 M2
Ringwood *CL/PREN* CH43 .... 127 J2
Ringwood Av *DV/KA/FCH* L14 .... 115 H3
Ringwood Cl *GOL/RIS/CU* WA3 .... 107 K8
Ripley Av *LITH* L21 .... 83 K4
Ripley Cl *MGHL* L31 .... 73 G4
Ripley Dr *WGNS/IIMK* WN3 .... 78 E1
Ripley St *WARRW/BUR* WA5 .... 121 G6
Ripon Av *GOL/RIS/CU* WA3 .... 92 F5
Ripon Cl *HUY* L36 .... 116 C2
NEWLW WA12 .... 91 L8 3
NTHTN L30 .... 84 B4 1
STHP PR8 .... 36 B2
Ripon Dr *AIMK* WN4 .... 91 M3
Ripon Rd *WAL/NB* CH45 .... 95 G7
Ripon St *ANF/KKDL* L4 .... 97 H4
BIRK CH41 .... 11 J9
Rippon Av *GTS/LS* CH66 .... 155 L8
Risbury Cl *NG/CROX* L11 .... 98 B3
The Rise *WGNNW/ST* WN6 .... 67 L2
Rishton Cl *EV* L5 .... 97 J8
Risley Rd *GOL/RIS/CU* WA3 .... 107 H7
Ritchie Av *WLT/FAZ* L9 .... 84 E6
Ritherup La *RAIN/WH* L35 .... 117 L1
Ritson St *TOX* L8 .... 113 K7
Rivacre Brow *GTS/LS* CH66 .... 156 A6
Rivacre Rd *EP* CH65 .... 155 L3
GTS/LS CH66 .... 156 A6
PS/BROM CH62 .... 155 J1
River Avon St *TOX* L8 .... 113 L6 6
Riverbank Cl *HES* CH60 .... 141 H7
Riverbank Rd *ALL/GAR* L19 .... 130 C6
HES CH60 .... 141 G7
River Cl *FMBY* L37 .... 59 K4
Riverdale Cl *WGNNW/ST* WN6 .... 67 M2
River Gv *PS/BROM* CH62 .... 128 D5
Rivermeade *STHP* PR8 .... 35 M1
River Rd *WARRS* WA4 .... 14 F9
Riversdale *FROD/HEL* WA6 .... 160 E4
WARR WA1 .... 123 H6
Riversdale Ct *AIG/SPK* L17 .... 130 B5
Riversdale Ms *ALL/GAR* L19 .... 130 B5 5
Riversdale Rd *ALL/GAR* L19 .... 130 B6
LITH L21 .... 83 H6 9
RUNC WA7 .... 150 A4
WAL/EG CH44 .... 111 M1
WKBY CH48 .... 124 C3
Riverside *HTWN* L38 .... 70 B1
PS/BROM CH62 .... 128 D8
WD/CROXPK L12 .... 99 G4
WKBY CH48 .... 124 D5
Riverside Av *WGN* WN1 .... 5 H1
Riverside Cl *BTL* L20 .... 83 J8
WARR WA1 .... 15 H7
Riverside Crs *LEY/BBR* PR5 .... 29 J3
Riverside Dr *AIG/SPK* L17 .... 129 J3
VAUX/LVPD L3 .... 129 H2
Riverside Gv *STHEL* WA9 .... 102 F6 10
Riverside Wk *NSTN* CH64 .... 152 F8
Riverslea Rd *CSBY/WL* L22 .... 82 D3
Rivers St *WGNW/BIL/O* WN5 .... 67 G7
River St *BIRK* CH41 .... 11 G6
River Vw *CSBY/WL* L22 .... 82 D3
Riverview Rd *NSTN* CH64 .... 153 H8
WAL/EG CH44 .... 112 A2
River Wy *WGN* WN1 .... 4 F5
Riverwood Rd *PS/BROM* CH62 .... 144 B4
Riviera Dr *RF/TRAN* CH42 .... 127 M4
Rivington Av *CHLYE* PR6 .... 44 C6
CL/PREN CH43 .... 127 G1
ECCL WA10 .... 89 G7
GOL/RIS/CU WA3 .... 92 E4
WGN WN1 .... 68 D3
WGNE/HIN WN2 .... 80 D2
Rivington Cl *STHP* PR8 .... 35 J2
Rivington Dr *BRSC* L40 .... 52 A2 3
SKEL WN8 .... 66 E6
WGNE/HIN WN2 .... 81 H4

Rivington La CHLYE PR6 44 F6
HOR/BR BL6 45 H4
Rivington Pl CHLY/EC PR7 42 F7
Rivington Rd CHLYE PR6 33 G4
ECCL WA10 8 B4
EP CH65 20 B5
WAL/EG CH44 111 M2
Rivington St ECCL WA10 8 A7
HOR/BR BL6 57 M3 5
Rivington Wy WGNNW/ST WN6 56 B5
Rixton Av WARRW/BUR WA5 121 H5
Roach Gn WGN WN1 5 K1
Roadside Ct GOL/RIS/CU WA3 92 E5
Roadwater Cl WLTN L25 115 K6
Robarts Rd ANF/KKDL L4 97 J7
Robeck Rd CLB/OSW/ST L13 114 D4 2
Robert Dr GR/UP/WCH CH49 126 A2
Robert Gv WD/CROXPK L12 99 G8
Roberts Av RNFD/HAY WA11 90 C8
Roberts Ct RUNC WA7 150 A7
Roberts Dr BTL L20 84 A7
Robertson St TOX L8 113 G8
Roberts St CHLY/EC PR7 32 E6 14
VAUX/LVPD L3 12 C4
Robert St BIRK CH41 11 H4
RUNC WA7 19 L3
WARRW/BUR WA5 14 A4
WDN WA8 16 F2
WGNE/HIN WN2 80 C2 1
Robina Rd STHEL WA9 102 F5
Robin Cl CHLY/EC PR7 42 F2 1
RUNC WA7 150 F6
Robin Hill Dr WGNNW/ST WN6 55 K3
Robin Hill La WGNNW/ST WN6 55 L2
Robin Hood La FROD/HEL WA6 166 D3
WGNNW/ST WN6 54 D2
Robin La SKEL WN8 40 E8
Robin Park Rd WGNW/BIL/O WN5 4 A6
Robins Cft GTS/LS CH66 163 H3
Robins La GOL/RIS/CU WA3 106 F3
RNFD/HAY WA11 77 H5
STHEL WA9 102 E5
Robinson Rd LITH L21 83 L4
Robin Wy GR/UP/WCH CH49 126 D3
Rob La NEWLW WA12 105 G1
Robsart St EV L5 97 G8
Robson St CLB/OSW/ST L13 114 B4
EV L5 97 H7
WARR WA1 15 J3
Roby Cl RAIN/WH L35 117 L1
Roby Gv WARRW/BUR WA5 120 C7 3
Roby Ml SKEL WN8 66 D2
Roby Mount Av HUY L36 115 M3
Roby Rd HUY L36 115 J3
Roby St BTL L20 7 H2
ECCL WA10 8 A9
WAV L15 114 A6
Roby Well Wy
WGNW/BIL/O WN5 77 M8
Rocastle Cl NPK/KEN L6 113 J2
Rochester Av NTHTN L30 84 B4
Rochester Cl GOL/RIS/CU WA3 92 C5 5
WARRW/BUR WA5 120 E8 5
Rochester Dr EP CH65 20 F9
Rochester Gdns ECCL WA10 8 A9
Rochester Rd RF/TRAN CH42 128 C3
Roch Pl WGNE/HIN WN2 80 B3 3
Rock Av HES CH60 141 H4 2
Rockbank Rd CLB/OSW/ST L13 98 B8
Rockbourne Av WLTN L25 115 H8
Rockbourne Cl WGNE/HIN WN2 80 E1
Rockbourne Gn WLTN L25 115 H8
Rockbourne Wy WLTN L25 115 H8 2
Rock Cl RF/TRAN CH42 128 B3 11
Rock Ct CLB/OSW/ST L13 114 C2
Rock Dr FROD/HEL WA6 160 E4
Rock Farm Cl NSTN CH64 153 J7
Rock Farm Dr NSTN CH64 153 J7
Rock Farm Gv NSTN CH64 153 J7 1
Rock Ferry By-pass
RF/TRAN CH42 128 C3
Rockfield Cl WDN WA8 133 M3
Rockfield Dr FROD/HEL WA6 166 E3
Rockfield Rd ANF/KKDL L4 97 H6
Rockford Av KKBY L32 86 A6
Rockford Cl KKBY L32 86 A6 2
Rockford Wk KKBY L32 86 A6 3
Rock Gv CLB/OSW/ST L13 114 C2
Rockhill Rd WLTN L25 131 K4
Rockhouse St NPK/KEN L6 97 L8
Rockingham Cl
GOL/RIS/CU WA3 107 K7
Rockingham Ct
NWD/KWIPK L33 86 B1 6
Rockland Rd CSBY/BLUN L22 82 F3
Rocklands Av RF/TRAN CH42 128 C6 5
Rocklands La BEB CH63 142 E6
Rock La MGHL L31 73 H8
WDN WA8 134 A2
Rock La East RF/TRAN CH42 128 C4
Rock La West RF/TRAN CH42 128 B4
Rocklee Gdns NSTN CH64 153 J7
Rockley St ANF/KKDL L4 97 G5 11
ANF/KKDL L4 97 G5 11
Rock Mount Cl WLTN L25 131 H2
Rockmount Rd AIG/SPK L17 130 B4 3
Rock Park Rd RF/TRAN CH42 128 D4
Rockpoint Av WAL/NB CH45 95 L6 1
Rocksavage Expy RUNC WA7 149 L8
Rockside Rd CALD/MH L18 130 C3
Rock St CLB/OSW/ST L13 114 B2
GOL/RIS/CU WA3 92 C3
STHEL WA9 101 L5 5
The Rock FROD/HEL WA6 166 D3
Rock Vw MGHL L31 85 J2
Rockville Rd DV/KA/FCH L14 114 E4
Rockville St RF/TRAN CH42 128 B3
Rockwell Rd WD/CROXPK L12 98 F5
Rockybank Rd RF/TRAN CH42 127 M2
Rocky La CHLDW L16 114 E5
HES CH60 141 H5
NPK/KEN L6 97 L8
Rocky La South HES CH60 141 J5
Roderick Rd ANF/KKDL L4 97 J3
Roderick St VAUX/LVPD L3 13 K4 2
Rodgers Cl FROD/HEL WA6 160 D4
Rodick St WLTN L25 131 H3
Rodmell Rd WLT/FAZ L9 84 D7
Rodney St BIRK CH41 11 H8
CLVPS L1 13 K9
ECCL WA10 8 C5
WARRN/WOL WA2 14 E3
WGN WN1 4 F5
Roe Aly CLVPS L1 13 H8
Roebuck St WGNE/HIN WN2 81 L2 2
Roeburn Wy WARRW/BUR WA5 135 M2
Roecliffe Cl WGNS/IIMK WN3 4 C8
Roedean Cl MGHL L31 72 F3
WLTN L25 131 K5 2
Roehampton Dr CSBY/BLUN L23 70 E7
RUNC WA7 150 A6
Roe Hey Dr CHLY/EC PR7 43 H3
Roe La CHTN/BK PR9 25 G5
Roemarsh Ct RUNC WA7 150 A7
Roe St CLVPS L1 13 H6
Rogers Av BTL L20 7 M1
Rogerson's Gn HLWD L26 132 A3 5
Rokeby Av GOL/RIS/CU WA3 92 F4
Rokeby Cl VAUX/LVPD L3 13 K3
Rokeby Ct RUNC WA7 135 M8
Rokeby St VAUX/LVPD L3 13 K3
Rokeden NEWLW WA12 104 F1 3
Roker Av WAL/EG CH44 111 J2 12
Rokesmith Av EHL/KEN L7 113 L5
Roland Av BEB CH63 127 M7
RNFD/HAY WA11 89 L6
RUNC WA7 18 E5
Roleton Cl NTHTN L30 84 D1
Rolleston Dr BEB CH63 143 J1 3
WAL/NB CH45 95 H6
Rolleston St WARRN/WOL WA2 14 C4
Rolling Mill La STHEL WA9 103 H5
Rollo St ANF/KKDL L4 96 F6
Roman Cl NEWLW WA12 104 E3
RUNC WA7 150 A4
Roman Ct NSTN CH64 153 H6
Roman Rd AIMK WN4 79 J8 10
BEB CH63 127 J7
CL/PREN CH43 127 J5
HOY CH47 108 F5 3
WARRS WA4 137 L4 3
Rome Cl HUY L36 115 M2
Romer Rd NPK/KEN L6 113 L2
Romford Wy HLWD L26 132 B7 3
Romiley Dr SKEL WN8 65 H3
Romiley Rd GTS/LS CH66 156 A7
Romiley Sq WGNNW/ST WN6 56 A5 2
Romilly St NPK/KEN L6 113 J2
Romley St ANF/KKDL L4 97 H4
Romney Cl WDN WA8 134 F3
Romney Wy NSTN CH64 153 H6
WGN WN1 68 D2
Romsey Av FMBY L37 59 K3
Romsey Gv WGNS/IIMK WN3 78 F3
Romulus St EHL/KEN L7 113 M3 3
Ronald Cl CSBY/WL L22 83 H4
Ronald Dr WARRN/WOL WA2 122 D3
Ronald Rd CSBY/WL L22 83 H4
Ronald Ross Av NTHTN L30 84 B2
Ronaldshay WDN WA8 135 G3 2
Ronald St CLB/OSW/ST L13 114 B2
Ronaldsway AIN/FAZ L10 85 J6
CSBY/BLUN L23 71 J7
GR/UP/WCH CH49 110 B7
HES CH60 141 H7 1
HLWD L26 132 C5
Ronan Cl BTL L20 6 D2
Ronan Rd WDN WA8 134 A8
Rone Cl MOR/LEA CH46 109 M5
Roocroft Sq HOR/BR BL6 57 L3 3
Rookery Av AIMK WN4 91 K3
WGNNW/ST WN6 55 G5
Rookery Cl CHLY/EC PR7 32 C7
Rookery Dr RNFD/HAY WA11 76 C8
Rookery La RNFD/HAY WA11 76 C8
Rookery Rd CHTN/BK PR9 25 G4
The Rookery NEWLW WA12 104 F1 1
Rook Rd WARRS WA4 15 M8
Rooks Wy HES CH60 141 G5
Rookwood CHLY/EC PR7 30 D7
Rookwood Av CHLY/EC PR7 32 E3
The Rooley HUY L36 115 M4
Roome St WARRN/WOL WA2 15 G1
Roosevelt Dr WLT/FAZ L9 84 D5
Ropers Bridge Cl RAIN/WH L35 116 F3
Roper St STHEL WA9 9 M3
TOX L8 113 H8 11
The Ropewalk NSTN CH64 152 E5 1
Rosalind Av BEB CH63 128 A6
Rosalind Wy BTL L20 7 K8
Rosam Ct RUNC WA7 150 A7
Rosclare Dr WAL/NB CH45 95 H7
Roscoe Av NEWLW WA12 105 G2 2
WARRN/WOL WA2 121 M5
Roscoe Cl RAIN/WH L35 116 C6 1
Roscoe Crs RUNC WA7 18 C9
Roscoe La CLVPS L1 13 J9
Roscoe Lowe Brow CHLYE PR6 44 F6
Roscoe Pl CLVPS L1 13 J9
Roscoe St ECCL WA10 8 B6
WGN WN1 5 J5
Roscommon St EV L5 13 J1
Roscote Cl HES CH60 141 H6 2
The Roscote HES CH60 141 H6 1
Roseacre WKBY CH48 124 C2 3
Rose Av BTL L20 83 L6
RNFD/HAY WA11 91 G7
STHEL WA9 102 E6
WGNE/HIN WN2 80 D6
WGNNW/ST WN6 68 B2
Rose Bank Cl WGN WN1 68 D1
Rose Bank Rd CHLDW L16 114 F6
Rosebank Rd HUY L36 99 L7
Rosebank Wy HUY L36 99 L8
Rosebay Cl FMBY L37 59 J2 2
Roseberry Rd AIMK WN4 79 J8 11
Rosebery Av CSBY/WL L22 82 E3
WAL/EG CH44 111 L1
Rosebery Gv RF/TRAN CH42 127 K3 1
Rosebery Rd ECCL WA10 88 F7
Rosebery St CHTN/BK PR9 25 J7
TOX L8 113 J6
Rosebourne Cl AIG/SPK L17 129 L3 10
Rose Brae CALD/MH L18 130 D1
Rosebridge Wy WGN WN1 5 L5
Rose Brow WLTN L25 131 J1
Rose Cl RUNC WA7 150 F8
WAV L15 114 A6
Rose Crs SKEL WN8 65 G4
STHP PR8 47 L3
WDN WA8 16 B5
Rosecroft PS/BROM CH62 143 L7 2
Rosecroft Cl ORM L39 51 G7
Rosedale Av CSBY/BLUN L23 83 G1
GOL/RIS/CU WA3 92 E6
WARR WA1 122 E6
Rosedale Cl WLT/FAZ L9 97 K1
Rosedale Rd CALD/MH L18 130 C1
RF/TRAN CH42 128 A2
Rose Dr RNFD/HAY WA11 76 C8
Rosefield Av BEB CH63 128 A6
Rosefield Rd WLTN L25 131 L4
Roseheath Dr HLWD L26 132 B7
Rose Hl STHP PR8 3 L6
VAUX/LVPD L3 13 H3
Rosehill Av STHEL WA9 103 K8
Rose Hill Av WGNW/BIL/O WN5 67 L7
Rosehill Ct WLTN L25 131 J1
Rosehill Dr ORM L39 62 E3
Rose Hill Vw AIMK WN4 79 H6
Roseland Cl MGHL L31 72 D1
Roselands Ct RF/TRAN CH42 128 A4
Rose La CALD/MH L18 130 B2
Rose Lea Cl WDN WA8 134 C1 2
Roselea Dr CHTN/BK PR9 25 L1
Rosemary Av RUNC WA7 150 B8 5
WARRS WA4 138 A3
Rosemary Cl CL/PREN CH43 111 G5 4
EHL/KEN L7 113 J5 6
WARRW/BUR WA5 120 E7 2
Rosemary Crs WGN WN1 68 F3
Rosemary Dr NEWLW WA12 105 H2
Rosemary La FMBY L37 59 G2
ORM L39 49 J8
Rosemead Av PEN/TH CH61 141 H1
Rosemere Dr GTS/LS CH66 163 H6
Rosemont Rd AIG/SPK L17 130 B3
Rosemoor Dr CSBY/BLUN L23 71 J8
Rosemoor Gdns WARRS WA4 138 B8
Rose Mt CL/PREN CH43 127 K2
Rose Mount Cl CL/PREN CH43 127 J2
Rose Mount Dr WAL/NB CH45 95 J7
Rose Pl BIRK CH41 128 B2 11
ORM L39 62 F3
RF/TRAN CH42 11 H9
RNFD/HAY WA11 76 C8
VAUX/LVPD L3 13 J3
Rose St CLVPS L1 13 H6 1
WDN WA8 16 B5
WGN WN1 5 L5
WGNE/HIN WN2 69 M8 27
WLTN L25 131 H3
Rose V EV L5 97 G8
Rose View Av WDN WA8 134 C3
Rose Vls WAV L15 114 B6
Rosewarne Cl AIG/SPK L17 129 K3 1
Rosewell Ct STBRV L28 99 K7 1
Rosewood Av
FROD/HEL WA6 160 F6 1
WARR WA1 122 E6
Rosewood Cl NTHLY L27 116 A8 4
STBRV L28 99 K6 4
WGNE/HIN WN2 80 D6 2
Rosewood Dr MOR/LEA CH46 109 K5
Rosewood Gdns
NG/CROX L11 98 D4 1
Roseworth Av WLT/FAZ L9 84 C6
Rosina Cl AIMK WN4 79 H7
Roskell Rd WLTN L25 131 L6
Rosklyn Rd CHLYE PR6 33 G6
Rosley Rd WGNS/IIMK WN3 79 K2
Roslin Rd CL/PREN CH43 127 K1
PEN/TH CH61 125 M7
Roslyn St BIRK CH41 128 B2
Rossall Av AIN/FAZ L10 84 F2
Rossall Gv GTS/LS CH66 155 M7
Rossall Rd CHLYE PR6 33 G4 4
CLB/OSW/ST L13 114 D3
MOR/LEA CH46 110 B4
WARRW/BUR WA5 136 D1
WDN WA8 134 F3
Ross Av MOR/LEA CH46 110 E1
Rossbank Rd EP CH65 156 C6
Rosscliffe Rd EP CH65 156 C6
Ross Cl PR/KW L34 99 M2
WARRW/BUR WA5 120 F5
WGNE/HIN WN2 69 H3
WGNW/BIL/O WN5 78 A8
Rossdale Gv WGNNW/ST WN6 56 C6
Ross Dr GTS/LS CH66 155 L8
Rossendale Cl CL/PREN CH43 126 F1
Rossendale Dr
GOL/RIS/CU WA3 107 J8 2
Rossett Av AIG/SPK L17 113 M7
Rossett Cl WARRW/BUR WA5 121 G3 7
WGNS/IIMK WN3 78 F3 3
Rossett Rd CSBY/BLUN L23 82 E2
Rossett St NPK/KEN L6 97 L8
Rossfield Rd EP CH65 156 C7
Rossini St LITH L21 83 J7
Rosslyn Av MGHL L31 72 D5
Rosslyn Crs MOR/LEA CH46 110 A5 7
Rosslyn Dr MOR/LEA CH46 110 A5
Rosslyn Pk MOR/LEA CH46 110 A6
Rosslyn St AIG/SPK L17 129 K2
Rossmore Gdns ANF/KKDL L4 97 K6
GTS/LS CH66 155 M7
Rossmore Rd East EP CH65 156 B6
Rossmore Rd West
GTS/LS CH66 155 M6
Rossmount Rd EP CH65 156 C7
Ross Rd EP CH65 156 C7
Ross St STHEL WA9 9 M4
WDN WA8 16 F2
Ross Tower Ct WAL/NB CH45 95 L5
Rosswood Rd EP CH65 156 C7
Rostherne Av GOL/RIS/CU WA3 92 F5
GTS/LS CH66 163 G1
WAL/EG CH44 111 J2
Rostherne Cl WARRW/BUR WA5 136 C1 1
Rostherne Crs WDN WA8 133 M3
Rosthwaite Cl
WGNS/IIMK WN3 79 J3 3
Rosthwaite Gv RNFD/HAY WA11 89 K4
Rosthwaite Rd WD/CROXPK L12 98 E7
Rostron Crs FMBY L37 59 G4
Rothay Dr WARRW/BUR WA5 135 M2
Rothbury Cl MOR/LEA CH46 109 L5
RUNC WA7 150 A7 5
Rothbury Ct STHEL WA9 118 D3 2
Rothbury Rd DV/KA/FCH L14 99 H7
Rother Dr EP CH65 156 C6
Rotherham Cl HUY L36 116 A1
Rotherwick Av CHLY/EC PR7 32 D6
Rotherwood Cl BEB CH63 127 M7 5
Rothesay Dr CSBY/BLUN L23 83 G2
PS/BROM CH62 154 F1
Rothley Av STHP PR8 47 J1
Rothsay Cl RNFD/HAY WA11 90 A6
Rothwell Cl ORM L39 50 F8
Rothwell Dr ORM L39 62 D3
STHP PR8 34 C8
Rothwell Rd CHLYE PR6 44 D6
GOL/RIS/CU WA3 92 E4
Rothwells La CSBY/BLUN L23 71 K7
Rothwell St NPK/KEN L6 113 J1 7
Rotten Rw STHP PR8 2 B7
Rotunda St EV L5 96 F8 6
Roughdale Av KKBY L32 86 B6
STHEL WA9 118 D1 3
Roughdale Cl KKBY L32 86 B6 3
Roughlea Av GOL/RIS/CU WA3 106 F1
Roughley Av
WARRW/BUR WA5 136 F1 9
Roughwood Dr NWD/KWIPK L33 86 B2
The Roundabout WDN WA8 117 M7
Round Hey STBRV L28 99 J5
Round House Av WGN WN1 5 K1
The Round Meade MGHL L31 72 D3
Roundmoor Rd
WGNNW/ST WN6 56 C6 1
Round Thorn GOL/RIS/CU WA3 106 C6
The Roundway HTWN L38 70 B2
Roundwood Dr STHEL WA9 9 K9
Routledge St WDN WA8 16 F1 3
Rowan Av GOL/RIS/CU WA3 93 H6
WD/CROXPK L12 99 H4
WGNNW/ST WN6 68 B2
Rowan Cl RNFD/HAY WA11 89 M6 1
RUNC WA7 19 L9
WARRW/BUR WA5 120 B7
Rowan Ct AIG/SPK L17 130 A3 4
GR/UP/WCH CH49 125 K3
Rowan Dr KKBY L32 85 M2
Rowan Gv BEB CH63 143 G1
CHLYE PR6 32 E2
HUY L36 115 M5
Rowanhill WGN WN1 5 H1
Rowan La SKEL WN8 65 K1
The Rowans ORM L39 62 C6
Rowan Tree Cl
GR/UP/WCH CH49 125 K2 2
Rowbottom Sq WGN WN1 4 E4
Rowena Cl CSBY/BLUN L23 83 H1 2
Rowland Cl WARRN/WOL WA2 122 C2
Rowsley Gv WLT/FAZ L9 84 D6 14
Rowson St PR/KW L34 100 F6
WAL/NB CH45 95 K5
Rowthorn Cl WDN WA8 134 A5 1
Rowton Cl CL/PREN CH43 127 H2
Rowton Ri WGN WN1 56 D5
Roxborough Cl
WARRW/BUR WA5 104 C7 1
Roxborough Wk WLTN L25 131 L2
Roxburgh Av AIG/SPK L17 129 L2
RF/TRAN CH42 127 M3
Roxburgh Rd GTS/LS CH66 155 H7
Roxburgh St ANF/KKDL L4 7 L7
Royal Av WDN WA8 133 K5
Royal Cl FMBY L37 59 J4
Royal Crs FMBY L37 59 J4
Royal Cft WD/CROXPK L12 114 D1
Royal Gv ECCL WA10 101 M4
Royal Mail St VAUX/LVPD L3 13 J7
Royal St ANF/KKDL L4 97 G6
Royal Ter STHP PR8 2 F4
The Royal HOY CH47 108 B7
Royden Av RUNC WA7 18 F7
WAL/EG CH44 95 M8
WGNS/IIMK WN3 79 H3
Royden Crs WGNW/BIL/O WN5 78 A8
Royden Rd
GR/UP/WCH CH49 110 A7 5
WGNW/BIL/O WN5 78 A8
Royden St TOX L8 129 H1 13
Royden Wy VAUX/LVPD L3 129 G2
Royhsay Cl EV L5 13 K1
Royleen Dr FROD/HEL WA6 160 F7
Royle Rd CHLY/EC PR7 32 D5 3
Roynton Rd HOR/BR BL6 45 K7
Roysten Gdns STHEL WA9 102 F3
Royston Av WAL/EG CH44 111 M1 13
WARR WA1 122 B6
Royston Cl GOL/RIS/CU WA3 93 G5 8
GTS/LS CH66 163 H3
Royston St EHL/KEN L7 113 K4
Royton Rd CSBY/WL L22 83 H3
Rozel Crs WARRW/BUR WA5 136 D1
Ruabon Crs WGNE/HIN WN2 81 H1
Rubbing Stone WKBY CH48 124 F7 3
Ruby St TOX L8 129 H2
Rudd Av STHEL WA9 103 J3
Ruddington Rd STHP PR8 36 A3
Rudd St HOY CH47 108 D6
Rudgate RAIN/WH L35 117 G3
Rudgrave Ms WAL/EG CH44 95 M8 2
Rudgrave Pl WAL/EG CH44 95 M8 3
Rudgrave Sq WAL/EG CH44 95 M8
Rudloe Ct WARRN/WOL WA2 122 B4
Rudstone Cl GTS/LS CH66 155 K8
Rudston Rd CHLDW L16 114 F6
Rudyard Av WGNNW/ST WN6 56 A3
Rudyard Cl DV/KA/FCH L14 114 E2 2
Rudyard Rd DV/KA/FCH L14 114 E2
Ruff La ORM L39 63 J1
Rufford Av MGHL L31 73 G2 4
Rufford Cl AIN/FAZ L10 85 H4
RAIN/WH L35 101 H8
WDN WA8 133 L3 1
Rufford Dr CHTN/BK PR9 23 H8
Rufford Rd BRSC L40 40 B4
BTL L20 83 L8
CHTN/BK PR9 25 L2
NPK/KEN L6 113 L2
RNFD/HAY WA11 76 B5
WAL/EG CH44 111 L2 7
Rugby Dr AIN/FAZ L10 85 G4
WGNW/BIL/O WN5 67 H5
Rugby Rd EP CH65 20 D9
WAL/EG CH44 95 H8
WLT/FAZ L9 84 D5
Ruislip Cl WLTN L25 131 L3
Ruislip Ct WARRN/WOL WA2 122 B4
Rullerton Rd WAL/EG CH44 111 J1
Rumford Pl VAUX/LVPD L3 12 D6
Rumford St CLVP L2 12 E6
Rumney Rd ANF/KKDL L4 97 G5
Rumney Rd West ANF/KKDL L4 96 F5
Runcorn Docks Rd RUNC WA7 18 D4
Runcorn Rd WARRS WA4 136 E8
Runcorn Spur Rd RUNC WA7 19 K5
Runcorn-Widnes Br RUNC WA7 149 J1
Rundle Rd AIG/SPK L17 130 A3
Rundle St BIRK CH41 10 A1
Runic St CLB/OSW/ST L13 114 B3
Runnell's La CSBY/BLUN L23 71 K8
The Runnell NSTN CH64 152 F1
The Runnel ORM L39 49 K3
Runnymede WARR WA1 122 E6
Runnymede Cl WLTN L25 131 J1
Runnymede Dr
RNFD/HAY WA11 90 C7 7
Runshaw Av WGNNW/ST WN6 55 G5
Runshaw La CHLY/EC PR7 30 F3
Runton Rd WLTN L25 115 L8
Rupert Dr NPK/KEN L6 113 J2
Rupert Rd HUY L36 115 L2
Rupert St WGN WN1 5 H4
Ruscar Cl HLWD L26 132 A3 6
Ruscolm Cl
WARRW/BUR WA5 119 M6 3
Ruscombe Rd DV/KA/FCH L14 99 H7
Rushdene WGNS/IIMK WN3 79 J1
Rushden Rd KKBY L32 86 C4
Rushey Hey Rd KKBY L32 86 A4
Rushfield Crs RUNC WA7 150 D8
Rushgreen Cl CL/PREN CH43 110 E6 7
Rushlake Dr NTHLY L27 115 M8
Rushmere Rd NG/CROX L11 98 B3
Rushmoor Av AIMK WN4 92 A1
Rushmore Gv WARR WA1 122 C6
Rusholme Cl HLWD L26 132 C7 2
Rushton Av LEIGH WN7 81 M5
NEWLW WA12 104 D1
Rushton Cl WDN WA8 134 B2
Rushton Pl WLTN L25 131 J3
Rushy Vw NEWLW WA12 104 C1
Ruskin Av NEWLW WA12 104 E1
RF/TRAN CH42 128 B4 5
WAL/EG CH44 111 J2
WARRN/WOL WA2 121 L3 5
WGNS/IIMK WN3 79 H2
Ruskin Cl BTL L20 7 G5
Ruskin Crs WGNE/HIN WN2 80 D4
Ruskin Dr ECCL WA10 8 B3
EP CH65 20 F8
Ruskin St ANF/KKDL L4 7 L9
Ruskin Wy HUY L36 115 M4
Rusland Av PEN/TH CH61 141 H1
Rusland Rd KKBY L32 86 B5
Russeldene Rd WGNS/IIMK WN3 79 G2
Russell Av CHTN/BK PR9 25 J6
Russell Rd ALL/GAR L19 130 F7
CALD/MH L18 114 B8
CHTN/BK PR9 25 J6
HUY L36 116 D3
RF/TRAN CH42 128 B2
RUNC WA7 18 C6
WAL/EG CH44 95 G8
Russell Sq CHLYE PR6 32 F4
Russell Sq West CHLYE PR6 32 F4
Russell St BIRK CH41 11 J4
VAUX/LVPD L3 13 K6
WGNE/HIN WN2 69 J5 10
WGNE/HIN WN2 81 L3
Russet Cl ECCL WA10 8 F2
NTHLY L27 116 A8
Russian Dr CLB/OSW/ST L13 98 B8
Rutherford Cl CLB/OSW/ST L13 114 A4
Rutherford Rd CALD/MH L18 114 D7
ECCL WA10 88 E7
MGHL L31 73 G6
Rutherglen Av CSBY/BLUN L23 83 H3
Ruth Evans Ct RAIN/WH L35 117 J1
Ruthin Cl WARRW/BUR WA5 121 G2 2
Ruthven Rd
CLB/OSW/ST L13 114 D4 5
LITH L21 83 J6
Rutland Av AIG/SPK L17 113 M7
GOL/RIS/CU WA3 92 F6
HLWD L26 132 B5
WARRS WA4 137 K5
Rutland Cl EV L5 97 J8 5
Rutland Crs ORM L39 50 F6
Rutland Dr AIMK WN4 91 L1
Rutland Rd STHP PR8 3 L8
Rutland St BTL L20 7 J2
ECCL WA10 8 E2
RUNC WA7 18 F3
Rutter Av WARRW/BUR WA5 121 H4
Rutter St TOX L8 113 G8 6
Ryburn Rd ORM L39 62 F1
Rycot Rd SPK/HALE L24 146 E1
Rycroft Rd AIN/FAZ L10 85 G5
HOY CH47 109 G5
WAL/EG CH44 111 L3
Rydal Av CL/PREN CH43 110 E8
CSBY/BLUN L23 83 H3
FMBY L37 58 F3
PR/KW L34 101 H7
WARRS WA4 137 J3
WGNW/BIL/O WN5 67 H6
Rydal Bank BEB CH63 128 C6
WAL/EG CH44 111 L1
Rydal Cl AIMK WN4 91 L1
AIN/FAZ L10 85 H3
EP CH65 163 L3
HOR/BR BL6 57 L2 8
NSTN CH64 153 H7
NWD/KWIPK L33 85 M1

PEN/TH CH61 .... 141 H1
Rydal Gv *FROD/HEL* WA6 .. 166 D4
RNFD/HAY WA11 .... 89 J6
RUNC WA7 .... 19 K8
Rydal Pl *CHLY/EC* PR7 .... 32 E7
WGNE/HIN WN1 .... 69 K5
WGNE/HIN WN2 .... 80 D5
Rydal Rd *HUY* L36 .... 116 A4
Rydal St *EV* L5 .... 97 J7
NEWLW WA12 .... 104 C2
Rydal Wy *WDN* WA8 ...... 133 L5
Ryder Cl *ORM* L39 .... 62 E3
RAIN/WH L35 .... 117 J1
Ryder Crs *ORM* L39 .... 62 E4
STHP PR8 .... 35 G5
Ryder Rd *WARR* WA1 ...... 122 E5
WDN WA8 .... 134 D1
Ryde St *WGNW/BIL/O* WN5 .. 68 A7
The Rydinge *FMBY* L37 ..... 47 J3
Ryding's La *CHTN/BK* PR9 .. 23 M4
Rye St *STHEL* WA9 .... 118 E1
Ryecote *KKBY* L32 .... 86 A6
Ryecroft *CHNE* CH2 .... 165 K2
Rye Cft *LITH* L21 .... 83 K2
Ryecroft Rd *HES* CH60 .... 141 L6
Ryedale Cl *TOX* L8 .... 113 K6
Ryefield La *LITH* L21 .... 83 K2
Ryeford Cl *WGNS/IIMK* WN3 .. 5 L8
Ryegate Rd *ALL/GAR* L19 .. 130 D6
Rye Gv *WD/CROXPK* L12 .... 99 C7
Rye Hey Rd *KKBY* L32 .... 86 A3
Rye Moss La *FMBY* L37 .... 60 C5
Ryland Pk *PEN/TH* CH61 .. 126 C8
Rylands Av *WGNNW/ST* WN6 .. 68 C3
Rylands Hey *CHLY/EC* PR7 .. 32 D6
Rylands Rd *CHLY/EC* PR7 ... 32 D6
Rylands St *WARR* WA1 ..... 16 E3
WDN WA8 .... 16 E3
Ryleys Gdns *CLVP* L2 .... 12 F6
Rymer Gv *ANF/KKDL* L4 ..... 97 J4
Rymers Gn *FMBY* L37 .... 59 C1
Ryton Cl *WGNS/IIMK* WN3 ... 4 C3

S

Sabden Brook Dr
WGNE/HIN WN2 .... 80 B3
Sabre Cl *RUNC* WA7 .... 150 F6
Sackville Rd *ECCL* WA10 .... 88 E7
Sackville St *CHLYE* PR6 ...... 33 G6
Saddleback Crs
WGNW/BIL/O WN5 .... 67 K6
Saddleback Rd
WGNW/BIL/O WN5 .... 67 K6
Saddle Cl *WLT/FAZ* L9 .... 84 F5
Saddlers Ri *RNFD/HAY* WA11 .. 90 A6
Sadler St *WGN* WN1 .... 17 G1
Saffron Cl *GOL/RIS/CU* WA3 .. 93 C5
WARRN WA2 .... 122 D4
Saffron Gdns *STHEL* WA9 .. 102 F3
Saffron Ms *CSBY/BLUN* L23 .. 71 K7
Sagar Fold *ORM* L39 .... 62 F5
Sagar St *CHLY/EC* PR7 .... 30 E7
Sage Cl *WARRN/WOL* WA2 .. 122 E3
St Agnes Rd *ANF/KKDL* L4 .. 96 F5
HUY L36 .... 116 B3
St Aidan's Cl *WGNW/BIL/O* WN5 .. 78 A7
St Aidan's Ter *CL/PREN* CH43 .. 111 H7
St Aidan's Gv *HUY* L36 ...... 99 L6
St Alban Rd *WARRW/BUR* WA5 .. 120 A8
St Albans *NPK/KEN* L6 .... 97 K8
St Albans Rd *RNFD/HAY* WA11 .. 91 H6
St Albans Ct *EV* L5 .... 96 E8
St Alban's Pl *CHLY/EC* PR7 .. 32 F8
St Alban's Rd *BTL* L20 .... 7 H5
CL/PREN CH43 .... 10 A4
WAL/EG CH44 .... 111 K1
St Alban's Sq *BTL* L20 .... 7 H6
St Ambrose Cft *NTHTN* L30 .. 84 A1
St Ambrose Gv *ANF/KKDL* L4 .. 97 K7
St Ambrose Rd *WDN* WA8 ... 17 H1
St Andrew Rd *ANF/KKDL* L4 .. 96 F5
St Andrews Av *WD/CROXPK* L12 .. 99 C7
St Andrews Cl
WARRN/WOL WA2 ...... 122 C1
St Andrew's Crs *WGNE/HIN* WN2 .. 69 M8
St Andrew's Dr *CSBY/BLUN* L23 .. 70 D7
PR/KW L34 .... 99 L6
WGNNW/ST WN6 .... 68 B3
St Andrew's Gv *NTHTN* L30 .. 83 L2
RNFD/HAY WA11 .... 89 K7
St Andrew's Pl *STHP* PR8 ..... 3 G5
St Andrews Rd *BEB* CH63 ... 143 J2
BTL L20 .... 83 L8
CSBY/BLUN L23 .... 70 D6
EP CH65 .... 20 F3
St Andrew St *VAUX/LVPD* L3 .. 13 K7
St Andrew's Vw
NWD/KWIPK L33 .... 74 A8
St Annes Av *WARRS* WA4 .. 138 D3
St Annes Av East *WARRS* WA4 .. 138 D3
St Anne's Cl *BIRK* CH41 ...... 11 H4
FMBY L37 .... 47 J7
St Anne's Ct *WGNNW/ST* WN6 .. 55 H8
St Annes Gdns *AIG/SPK* L17 .. 130 B4
St Annes Gv *AIG/SPK* L17 ... 130 A4
St Anne's Pth *FMBY* L37 ..... 47 H7
St Anne's Rd *AIG/SPK* L17 ... 130 A4
CHLYE PR6 .... 33 G6
CHTN/BK PR9 .... 25 H1
FMBY L37 .... 47 H7
HUY L36 .... 116 A4
ORM L39 .... 62 F1
WDN WA8 .... 134 D3
St Anne St *BIRK* CH41 .... 10 E1
BIRK CH41 .... 10 F3
VAUX/LVPD L3 .... 13 J3
St Ann Pl *RAIN/WH* L35 .... 117 L1
St Anns Rd *ECCL* WA10 ..... 101 L2
St Anthony's Cl *PR/KW* L34 .. 99 L6
St Anthony's Gv *NTHTN* L30 .. 83 M2

St Anthony's Rd *CSBY/BLUN* L23 .. 82 D1
St Asaph Dr *WARRW/BUR* WA5 .. 120 F3
St Asaph Gv *NTHTN* L30 ..... 84 A4
St Asaph Rd *GTS/LS* CH66 .. 163 G5
St Aubyn's Rd *WGN* WN1 ..... 68 E1
St Augustine's Av
WARRS WA4 .... 138 B1
St Augustine St *EV* L5 .... 96 F8
St Augustine's Wy *NTHTN* L30 .. 83 M1
St Austel Cl *WARRW/BUR* WA5 .. 136 A2
St Austell Cl *MOR/LEA* CH46 .. 109 K4
RUNC WA7 .... 150 D7
St Austells Rd *ANF/KKDL* L4 .. 7 M7
St Austin La *WARR* WA1 ..... 14 D7
St Barnabas Pl
WARRW/BUR WA5 ...... 121 G7
St Bedes Cl *ORM* L39 .... 62 F7
St Benedicts Cl
WARRN/WOL WA2 ...... 14 F2
St Benedict's Gv *PR/KW* L34 .. 99 L6
St Bernard's Cl *NTHTN* L30 .. 83 M2
St Bernard's Dr *NTHTN* L30 .. 83 M2
St Brendan's Cl *HUY* L36 .... 99 L6
St Brides Cl *WARRW/BUR* WA5 .. 136 A2
St Bride's Rd *WAL/EG* CH44 .. 95 M8
St Bride St *TOX* L8 .... 113 H5
St Bridget's Cl
WARRN/WOL WA2 ...... 122 D2
St Bridget's Gv *NTHTN* L30 .. 83 M2
St Bridget's La *WKBY* CH48 .. 124 D4
St Catherine's
RF/TRAN CH42 .... 127 M1
St Catherines Cl *HUY* L36 .. 116 A4
St Catherines Gdns
RF/TRAN CH42 .... 127 M1
St Catherine's Rd *BTL* L20 .... 7 G5
St Chad's Dr *KKBY* L32 .... 86 A4
St Christopher Ct
WGNNW/ST WN6 .... 67 L1
St Christopher's Av *NTHTN* L30 .. 83 M1
St Christopher's Dr *PR/KW* L34 .. 99 L6
St Clair Dr *CHTN/BK* PR9 .... 25 J4
St Clement's Rd *WGN* WN1 .. 68 E2
St Clement's St
WGNE/HIN WN2 .... 80 B1
St Columba's Cl
WAL/EG CH44 .... 95 M8
St Cuthbert's Cl
WD/CROXPK L12 .... 99 G7
St Cuthbert's Rd *CHTN/BK* PR9 .. 25 K3
St Cyrils Cl *NTHLY* L27 ..... 115 L6
St Damian's Cft *NTHTN* L30 .. 84 A2
St David Rd *PS/BROM* CH62 .. 144 C7
St Davids Cl *RAIN/WH* L35 .. 117 L1
St David's Crs *WGNE/HIN* WN2 .. 57 K8
St Davids Dr *GTS/LS* CH66 .. 163 H5
WARRW/BUR WA5 ...... 121 G3
St Davids Gv *NTHTN* L30 .... 83 M1
St David's La *CL/PREN* CH43 .. 110 F8
St David's Rd *ANF/KKDL* L4 .. 97 K7
DV/KA/FCH L14 .... 99 K8
St Domingo Gv *EV* L5 .... 97 J7
St Domingo Rd *EV* L5 .... 97 J7
St Domingo V *EV* L5 .... 97 J7
St Dunstan's Gv *NTHTN* L30 .. 83 M2
St Edmond's Rd *BTL* L20 ...... 7 C6
St Edmunds Rd *BEB* CH63 .. 128 B8
St Edwards Cl *BIRK* CH41 ... 10 D2
St Elizabeth's Rd
WGNE/HIN WN2 .... 57 K8
St Elmo Rd *WAL/EG* CH44 ... 95 H8
St Elphins Cl *WARR* WA1 ..... 15 H5
St Gabriel's Av *HUY* L36 .... 116 B2
St George's Av *ECCL* WA10 .. 88 E8
GTS/LS CH66 .... 163 H5
RF/TRAN CH42 .... 127 M3
St Georges Gv *NTHTN* L30 .. 83 M3
St George's Hi *HUY* L36 ...... 97 H8
St George's Mt *WAL/NB* CH45 .. 95 K5
St George's Pk *WAL/NB* CH45 .. 95 K5
St George's Pl *CHTN/BK* PR9 ... 3 C3
CLVPS L1 .... 13 H6
St Georges Rd *ECCL* WA10 .... 8 A7
FMBY L37 .... 59 G1
HTWN L38 .... 59 H8
HUY L36 .... 100 A8
WAL/NB CH45 .... 95 G7
St George's St *CHLY/EC* PR7 .. 32 E6
St George's Wy *BEB* CH63 .. 142 C6
St Gregory's Cft *NTHTN* L30 .. 84 A1
St Gregory's Pl *CHLY/EC* PR7 .. 32 E8
St Helen's Cl *BIRK* CH41 .... 10 D6
St Helens Linkway
RAIN/WH L35 .... 118 B4
STHEL WA9 .... 9 H8
St Helens Rd *LEIGH* WN7 .... 93 L4
ORM L39 .... 51 H8
PR/KW L34 .... 100 F7
PR/KW L34 .... 101 G6
PR/KW L34 .... 101 H6
RNFD/HAY WA11 .... 88 D3
St Hilary Brow *WAL/EG* CH44 .. 111 H1
St Hilary Dr *WAL/EG* CH44 ... 95 H8
St Hilda's Cl *CHLY/EC* PR7 ... 43 L1
St Hilda's Dr *FROD/HEL* WA6 .. 160 E4
St Hilda St *ANF/KKDL* L4 .... 97 G5
St Hugh's Cl *CL/PREN* CH43 .. 10 D6
St Ives Cl *CLB/OSW/ST* L13 .. 114 B2
St Ives Rd *CL/PREN* CH43 ... 10 A5
St Ives Wy *HLWD* L26 .... 132 B5
St James Cl *BRSC* L40 .... 49 K1
GR/UP/WCH CH49 .... 125 M1
WD/CROXPK L12 .... 98 C7
St James Crs *WGNE/HIN* WN2 .. 81 H5
St James Dr *BTL* L20 .... 6 F3
St James Gv *WGNS/IIMK* WN3 .. 4 D8
St James Mt *RAIN/WH* L35 .. 117 L3
St James Pl *HUY* L36 .... 113 C6
St James St *CLVPS* L1 .... 113 C6
HUY L36 .... 116 A4
PR/KW L34 .... 101 C3
RAIN/WH L35 .... 117 L3
WAL/NB CH45 .... 95 K5
WGNW/BIL/O WN5 .... 77 M1

St Jerome's Wy *NTHTN* L30 .. 84 A1
St John Av *WARRS* WA4 .... 137 K3
St John's Av *WLT/FAZ* L9 .... 84 D7
St John's Brow *RUNC* WA7 .. 19 J2
St John's Cl *HOY* CH47 ..... 108 F5
St John's La *CLVPS* L1 .... 13 H6
St John's Pl *BTL* L20 .... 6 F8
CSBY/WL L22 .... 82 F4
HUY L36 .... 116 B4
St John's Rd *RF/TRAN* CH42 .. 128 B3
STHP PR8 .... 35 J2
WAL/EG CH44 .... 111 M3
WDN WA8 .... 16 D5
St John's St *RUNC* WA7 ...... 19 J2
WGNE/HIN WN1 .... 80 D5
St John's Ter *BTL* L20 .... 6 F8
St John St *BIRK* CH41 .... 11 H6
ECCL WA10 .... 101 M5
NEWLW WA12 .... 104 C2
WGNW/BIL/O WN5 .... 67 K7
St Joseph's Cl
WARRW/BUR WA5 ...... 120 A8
St Josephs Crs *VAUX/LVPD* L3 .. 13 J4
St Jude's Cl *HUY* L36 .... 99 L6
St Katherines Dr *HOR/BR* BL6 .. 57 L2
St Katherines Wy *WARR* WA1 .. 15 J5
St Kilda Cl *EP* CH65 .... 163 L4
St Kilda's Rd *MOR/LEA* CH46 .. 109 M6
St Laurence Cl *BIRK* CH41 ... 11 H4
St Laurence Gv *KKBY* L32 ... 86 B5
St Lawrence Cl *TOX* L8 ...... 129 J1
St Lawrence Rd
FROD/HEL WA6 .... 160 D6
St Leonard's Cl *NTHTN* L30 .. 83 M1
St Lucia Rd *WAL/EG* CH44 ... 95 M8
St Luke's Av *GOL/RIS/CU* WA3 .. 92 F5
St Luke's Church Rd *RF/TRAN* CH42 .. 58 E3
St Lukes Cl *DV/KA/FCH* L14 .. 99 H7
St Luke's Crs *WDN* WA8 ..... 134 D1
St Luke's Dr *RF/TRAN* CH42 .. 58 E3
WGNW/BIL/O WN5 .... 77 M1
St Luke's Gv *CHTN/BK* PR9 .... 3 M4
NTHTN L30 .... 83 M1
St Luke's Rd *CHTN/BK* PR9 .... 3 M4
CSBY/BLUN L23 .... 82 F1
ECCL WA10 .... 8 A5
St Luke's Wy *FROD/HEL* WA6 .. 160 D4
St Malo Rd *WGN* WN1 .... 68 E2
St Margaret's Av
WARRN/WOL WA2 ...... 121 M4
St Margaret's Gv *NTHTN* L30 .. 83 L2
St Mark's Av *HOY* CH47 .... 108 C6
St Marks Crs *VAUX/LVPD* L3 .. 13 K6
St Mark's Gv *NTHTN* L30 .... 83 L1
St Mark's Rd *HUY* L36 ...... 116 B4
St Mark's St *RNFD/HAY* WA11 .. 90 C7
St Martins Dr *GTS/LS* CH66 .. 162 F3
St Martins Gv *KKBY* L32 ..... 86 B6
St Martins La *RUNC* WA7 ... 150 F6
St Martin's Ms *EV* L5 .... 13 J1
St Mary's Av *ANF/KKDL* L4 .. 97 J3
WGNW/BIL/O WN5 .... 89 J1
St Mary's Cl *WARRS* WA4 ... 137 L7
WGNE/HIN WN2 .... 57 K8
St Marys Ct *NTHTN* L30 .... 131 J3
St Mary's Dr *NTHTN* L30 .... 83 L3
St Mary's Ga *BIRK* CH41 ..... 11 L6
CHLY/EC PR7 .... 31 L2
St Mary's Pl *ANF/KKDL* L4 ... 97 J3
WLTN L25 .... 131 J3
St Mary's Rd *ALL/GAR* L19 .. 130 C7
CSBY/WL L22 .... 83 H5
HUY L36 .... 116 A3
RUNC WA7 .... 150 B4
WARRW/BUR WA5 ...... 120 B8
WDN WA8 .... 149 J1
WGNE/HIN WN2 .... 57 K7
St Mary's St *WAL/EG* CH44 .. 111 K1
WARRS WA4 .... 15 H9
St Mathews Cl *ANF/KKDL* L4 .. 97 M3
St Matthews Av *LITH* L21 .... 83 M5
St Matthew's Cl *HUY* L36 .. 116 B2
WARRS WA4 .... 137 M6
WGNS/IIMK WN3 .... 78 E1
St Matthews Gv *ECCL* WA10 .. 101 L5
St Mawes Cl *WDN* WA8 .... 134 A3
St Mawes Wy *ECCL* WA10 ... 88 D7
St Mawgan Ct
WARRN/WOL WA2 ...... 122 B3
St Michael Av *ORM* L39 ...... 62 B6
St Michael's Church Rd
AIG/SPK L17 .... 129 K3
St Michael's Cl *AIG/SPK* L17 .. 129 L3
CHLY/EC PR7 .... 32 D4
CHTN/BK PR9 .... 25 H2
WDN WA8 .... 133 L6
St Michaels Ct *HUY* L36 .... 116 A2
WGN WN1 .... 68 E3
St Michael's Gv *NPK/KEN* L6 .. 113 K1
NTHTN L30 .... 83 L2
St Michaels Pk *ORM* L39 ..... 62 C6
St Michael's Rd *AIG/SPK* L17 .. 129 K2
CSBY/BLUN L23 .... 70 D8
STHEL WA9 .... 118 C2
WDN WA8 .... 133 L6
St Monicas Cl *WARRS* WA4 .. 137 M6
St Monica's Dr *NTHTN* L30 .. 83 M1
St Nicholas' Dr *NTHTN* L30 .. 83 L2
St Nicholas Pl *VAUX/LVPD* L3 .. 12 D7
St Nicholas Rd *GOL/RIS/CU* WA3 .. 93 J4
RAIN/WH L35 .... 116 E4
STHEL WA9 .... 104 E4
St Oswald's Av *CL/PREN* CH43 .. 110 F5
St Oswalds Cl
WARRN/WOL WA2 ...... 105 K7
St Oswald's La *NTHTN* L30 .. 84 B1
St Oswald's Ms *CL/PREN* CH43 .. 110 E4
St Oswald's Rd *AIMK* WN4 .. 91 J3
St Oswald's St *CLB/OSW/ST* L13 .. 114 C3

St Paschal Baylon Bvd
CHLDW L16 .... 115 H5
St Patrick's Cl
NWD/KWIPK L33 .... 74 A8
St Patrick's Dr *NTHTN* L30 .. 83 M1
St Patricks Wy *WGN* WN1 .... 5 H4
St Patricks Wy *WGN* WN1 .... 5 H4
St Paul's Av *WGNS/IIMK* WN3 .. 79 H1
St Paul's Cl *CHLYE* PR6 .... 44 C5
NWD/KWIPK L33 .... 73 M8
RF/TRAN CH42 .... 128 A3
St Pauls Gdns *GTS/LS* CH66 .. 155 K6
St Paul's Pas *STHP* PR8 .... 2 E6
St Paul's Sq *STHP* PR8 .... 2 E6
VAUX/LVPD L3 .... 12 E5
St Paul's St *STHP* PR8 .... 2 E6
St Paul St *ECCL* WA10 .... 8 D5
St Paul's Vls *RF/TRAN* CH42 .. 128 A3
St Peter's Cl *FMBY* L37 .... 58 F1
HES CH60 .... 141 H6
NWD/KWIPK L33 .... 73 M8
St Peter's Ms *RF/TRAN* CH42 .. 128 D4
St Peter's Rd *RF/TRAN* CH42 .. 128 C4
STHP PR8 .... 35 J2
WLT/FAZ L9 .... 84 E7
St Peter's St *CHLYE* PR6 ...... 33 G4
St Peter's Wy *CL/PREN* CH43 .. 126 E1
WARRN/WOL WA2 .... 14 F3
St Philip's La *LITH* L21 .... 83 L5
St Seiriol Gv *CL/PREN* CH43 .. 10 A3
St Stephen Rd
WARRW/BUR WA5 ...... 120 B8
St Stephen's Av
WARRN/WOL WA2 ...... 121 K2
WGN WN1 .... 69 G3
St Stephens Cl *HES* CH60 .. 141 L7
WLTN L25 .... 115 L8
St Stephen's Gv *NTHTN* L30 .. 83 M2
St Stephen's Rd *HTWN* L38 ... 70 B1
RF/TRAN CH42 .... 127 K3
WGNNW/ST WN6 .... 55 L4
St Teresa's Rd *ECCL* WA10 .... 8 A4
St Thomas Cl *WDN* WA8 .... 134 A3
St Thomas's Dr *NTHTN* L30 .. 83 M2
St Thomas's Rd *CHLY/EC* PR7 .. 32 D5
St Thomas' Vw *EP* CH65 ..... 20 A7
St Vincent Rd *CL/PREN* CH43 .. 10 A6
WAL/EG CH44 .... 95 M8
WARRW/BUR WA5 ...... 120 B8
St Vincent's Cl
WD/CROXPK L12 .... 99 G7
St Vincent's Wy *STHP* PR8 .... 2 D7
St Vincent Wy *VAUX/LVPD* L3 .. 13 K6
St Werburgh's Sq *BIRK* CH41 .. 11 J6
St Wilfrid's Dr *WARRS* WA4 .. 138 C2
St Wilfrid's Rd *WGNNW/ST* WN6 .. 56 B5
St William Rd *CSBY/BLUN* L23 .. 71 K8
St Winefred Rd *RAIN/WH* L35 .. 101 K8
Saker St *ANF/KKDL* L4 .... 97 H6
Salacre Cl *GR/UP/WCH* CH49 .. 126 D1
Salacre Crs *GR/UP/WCH* CH49 .. 126 C1
Salacre La *GR/UP/WCH* CH49 .. 110 C8
Salcombe Dr *WGN* WN1 ..... 69 C3
Salcombe Dr *CHTN/BK* PR9 .. 22 C8
WLTN L25 .... 131 K6
Salem Vw *CL/PREN* CH43 ... 127 K2
Salerno Dr *HUY* L36 .... 116 D3
Salesbury Wy *WGNS/IIMK* WN3 .. 79 J2
Saleswood Av *ECCL* WA10 .. 101 J2
Salford Rd *STHP* PR8 .... 34 E8
Salisbury Av *NTHTN* L30 .... 84 C4
WKBY CH48 .... 124 C3
Salisbury Cl *GTS/LS* CH66 .. 163 H5
Salisbury Dr *PS/BROM* CH62 .. 128 D6
Salisbury Pk *CHLDW* L16 ... 115 C8
Salisbury Rd *AIMK* WN4 ...... 79 J3
ALL/GAR L19 .... 130 C7
BTL L20 .... 6 E2
EV L5 .... 97 J7
RNFD/HAY WA11 .... 91 C4
WAL/NB CH45 .... 95 J5
WAV L15 .... 113 M6
Salisbury St *BIRK* CH41 ...... 11 C7
CHLY/EC PR7 .... 32 F6
CHTN/BK PR9 .... 25 J7
GOL/RIS/CU WA3 .... 92 D2
PR/KW L34 .... 100 F7
RUNC WA7 .... 19 G5
VAUX/LVPD L3 .... 13 J3
WARR WA1 .... 15 J4
WDN WA8 .... 16 B3
Salisbury Ter *WAV* L15 ..... 114 B5
Salkeld Av *AIMK* WN4 .... 91 H2
Sallowfields
WGNW/BIL/O WN5 .... 66 F8
Sally's La *CHTN/BK* PR9 ..... 25 J3
Salop St *ANF/KKDL* L4 .... 97 H5
Saltash Cl *HLWD* L26 .... 132 A5
RUNC WA7 .... 150 D7
Saltburn Rd *WAL/NB* CH45 .. 94 F8
Saltersgate *GTS/LS* CH66 ... 163 H3
Salthouse Quay *VAUX/LVPD* L3 .. 12 E9
Saltney St *VAUX/LVPD* L3 ... 12 C1
Salton Gdns *WARRW/BUR* WA5 .. 121 G6
Salt Pit La *CHLY/EC* PR7 ..... 41 H1
Saltpit La *MGHL* L31 .... 73 C4
Saltram Rd *WGNS/IIMK* WN3 .. 78 E1
Saltwood Dr *RUNC* WA7 ... 150 E8
Saltworks Cl *FROD/HEL* WA6 .. 160 F3
Salvin Cl *AIMK* WN4 .... 91 M2
Salwick Cl *CHTN/BK* PR9 .... 22 B8
Samaria Av *PS/BROM* CH62 .. 124 C8
Sambourn Fold *STHP* PR8 ... 34 C8
Samuel St *RAIN/WH* L35 ... 101 M6
WARRW/BUR WA5 ...... 121 H3
Sanbec Gdns *WDN* WA8 ... 117 M8
Sandalwood *RUNC* WA7 ... 150 E4
Sandalwood Cl
WARRN/WOL WA2 ...... 121 M3
Sandalwood Dr *CL/PREN* CH43 .. 126 F1

WGNNW/ST WN6 .... 68 B2
Sandalwood Gdns
STHEL WA9 .... 102 E6
Sandbeck St *TOX* L8 .... 129 H2
Sandbrook Gdns
WGNW/BIL/O WN5 .... 66 F8
Sandbrook La *MOR/LEA* CH46 .. 110 A3
Sandbrook Rd *STHP* PR8 .... 34 F8
WGNW/BIL/O WN5 .... 66 F8
WLTN L25 .... 115 J5
Sandcliffe Rd *WAL/NB* CH45 .. 95 G5
Sandelwood Cl *NPK/KEN* L6 .. 97 K8
Sandeman Rd *ANF/KKDL* L4 .. 97 M4
Sanderling Rd *NWD/KWIPK* L33 .. 86 C2
Sanders Hey Cl *RUNC* WA7 .. 150 C8
Sanderson Cl
WARRW/BUR WA5 ...... 119 M7
Sanderson La *CHLY/EC* PR7 .. 41 J5
Sanderson St *LEIGH* WN7 .... 81 M8
Sandfield *BEB* CH63 .... 127 M7
Sandfield Av *HOY* CH47 .... 108 F4
GOL/RIS/CU WA3 .... 93 H5
WD/CROXPK L12 .... 98 E3
Sandfield Ct *FROD/HEL* WA6 .. 160 D5
Sandfield Cl *WD/CROXPK* L12 .. 98 E8
Sandfield Cl *WLTN* L25 .... 131 K1
Sandfield Cl *RAIN/WH* L35 .. 117 K1
Sandfield Crs *NSTN* CH64 ... 153 G8
Sandfield La *RNFD/HAY* WA11 .. 76 C7
Sandfield Pl *WDN* WA8 ...... 135 H2
Sandfield Rd *STHP* PR8 .... 35 H4
WAL/EG CH44 .... 111 M1
Sandon Cl *CSBY/WL* L22 .... 82 F4
TOX L8 .... 113 H5
Sandon Gv *EV* L5 .... 96 D7
Sandown Cl
GOL/RIS/CU WA3 .... 107 H1
RUNC WA7 .... 149 L7
Sandown La *WAV* L15 ...... 114 A4
Sandown Park Rd *AIN/FAZ* L10 .. 85 G2
Sandown Rd *WAV* L15 ...... 114 B5
WGNNW/ST WN6 .... 68 A2
Sandpiper Cl *GR/UP/WCH* CH49 .. 109 M7
NEWLW WA12 .... 104 C1
Sandpiper Gv *HLWD* L26 ... 132 A4
Sandpiper Rd *WGNS/IIMK* WN3 .. 78 D1
Sandra Dr *NEWLW* WA12 .. 104 F2
Sandridge Rd *PEN/TH* CH61 .. 126 B8
WAL/NB CH45 .... 95 K6
Sandringham Av
CSBY/WL L22 .... 83 C3
FROD/HEL WA6 .... 166 D2
HOY CH47 .... 108 F4
Sandringham Cl *CHLY/EC* PR7 .. 44 A7
HOY CH47 .... 108 E6
NWD/KWIPK L33 .... 74 A8
PS/BROM CH62 .... 128 C6
WGNW/BIL/O WN5 .... 68 A8
Sandringham Dr *STHEL* WA9 .. 95 J5
WAL/NB CH45 .... 95 J5
WARRW/BUR WA5 ...... 120 B8
Sandringham Gdns *EP* CH65 .. 163 M3
Sandringham Rd *CHLY/EC* PR7 .. 30 E6
CLB/OSW/ST L13 .... 98 A7
CSBY/WL L22 .... 83 G5
FMBY L37 .... 59 C4
MGHL L31 .... 72 E5
STHP PR8 .... 34 E8
WDN WA8 .... 134 B1

WGNE/HIN WN2 ... 81 G1
Sandrock Rd WAL/NB CH45 ... 95 K6
Sands Rd CALD/MH L18 ... 130 B1
Sandstone Cl RAIN/WH L35 ... 117 L4
Sandstone Dr RAIN/WH L35 ... 101 H8
WKBY CH48 ... 125 G3
Sandstone Rd WGNS/IIMK WN3 ... 78 F3
Sandstone Rd East
CLB/OSW/ST L13 ... 114 C1
Sandstone Rd West
CLB/OSW/ST L13 ... 114 B1 4
Sandstone Trail FROD/HEL WA6 ... 167 H3
Sandstone Wk HES CH60 ... 141 J6 2
Sandwash Cl RNFD/HAY WA11 ... 88 D1
Sandway WGNNW/ST WN6 ... 68 B3
Sandway Crs NG/CROX L11 ... 98 C3
Sandwith Cl WGNS/IIMK WN3 ... 79 K3
Sandy Brow La
GOL/RIS/CU WA3 ... 106 A3
NWD/KWIPK L33 ... 87 G6
Sandycroft Av WGN WN1 ... 4 F1 1
Sandy Gn WLT/FAZ L9 ... 84 E7
Sandy Gv CLB/OSW/ST L13 ... 98 B7
Sandy La BRSC L40 ... 28 C6
BRSC L40 ... 51 M6
CHLY/EC PR7 ... 44 A6
CLB/OSW/ST L13 ... 98 B7
FROD/HEL WA6 ... 166 D3
GOL/RIS/CU WA3 ... 93 J3
GOL/RIS/CU WA3 ... 106 C4
HES CH60 ... 141 J4
HTWN L38 ... 70 C2
KIRK/FR/WA PR4 ... 27 L7
LITH L21 ... 83 H6
MGHL L31 ... 61 L8
MGHL L31 ... 73 J8
NEWLW WA12 ... 92 B5
NSTN CH64 ... 153 J7
ORM L39 ... 62 D7
PEN/TH CH61 ... 125 L6
RNFD/HAY WA11 ... 88 F5
RUNC WA7 ... 18 B9
SKEL WN8 ... 53 H4
SKEL WN8 ... 64 F4
WAL/NB CH45 ... 95 G7
WARRN/WOL WA2 ... 121 K2
WARRS WA4 ... 137 M5
WARRW/BUR WA5 ... 136 C1
WDN WA8 ... 119 K7
WGNW/BIL/O WN5 ... 77 M1
WKBY CH48 ... 124 D5
WLT/FAZ L9 ... 84 D7
Sandy La North PEN/TH CH61 ... 125 L5
Sandy La West
WARRN/WOL WA2 ... 121 J2
Sandy Moor La RUNC WA7 ... 150 F2
Sandymoor La RUNC WA7 ... 150 F2
Sandymount Dr BEB CH63 ... 143 H1 5
WAL/NB CH45 ... 95 J6
Sandy Rd LITH L21 ... 83 J6 5
Sandyville Gv ANF/KKDL L4 ... 98 A5 2
Sandyville Rd ANF/KKDL L4 ... 97 M5
Sandy Wy BRSC L40 ... 38 F1
CL/PREN CH43 ... 10 A7
Sanfield Cl ORM L39 ... 51 G7 4
Sangness Dr STHP PR8 ... 36 A2
Sankey Rd MGHL L31 ... 72 F6
RNFD/HAY WA11 ... 90 B8
Sankey St CLVPS L1 ... 113 G5 20
GOL/RIS/CU WA3 ... 92 C5 6
NEWLW WA12 ... 104 C2
STHEL WA9 ... 102 F3
WARR WA1 ... 14 C6
WDN WA8 ... 16 C8
Sankey Wy WARRW/BUR WA5 ... 120 C8
Santon Av CLB/OSW/ST L13 ... 98 A8 3
Santon Dr GOL/RIS/CU WA3 ... 93 G5 5
Sanvino Av STHP PR8 ... 34 F8
Sapphire Dr NWD/KWIPK L33 ... 74 A8
Sapphire St CLB/OSW/ST L13 ... 114 B4
Sarah's Cft NTHTN L30 ... 84 A2
Sarah St WGNE/HIN WN2 ... 81 K3
Sark Rd CLB/OSW/ST L13 ... 114 B1
Sarscow La LEY/BBR PR5 ... 30 A4
Sarsfield Av GOL/RIS/CU WA3 ... 92 F5
Sartfield Cl CHLDW L16 ... 115 G5
Sarum Rd WLTN L25 ... 115 J6
Satinwood Cl AIMK WN4 ... 91 H2
Satinwood Crs MGHL L31 ... 85 J2 1
Saughall Massie La
GR/UP/WCH CH49 ... 110 A8
Saughall Massie Rd
GR/UP/WCH CH49 ... 109 L7
WKBY CH48 ... 125 J1
Saughall Rd MOR/LEA CH46 ... 109 L6
Saunby St ALL/GAR L19 ... 145 L1
Saunders Av RAIN/WH L35 ... 116 F1
Saundersfoot Cl
WARRW/BUR WA5 ... 121 G3
Saunders Ms CHLY/EC PR7 ... 43 L2
Saunders St CHTN/BK PR9 ... 24 D4
Saunderton Cl
RNFD/HAY WA11 ... 90 E6 2
Saville Av WARRW/BUR WA5 ... 14 B1
Saville Rd CLB/OSW/ST L13 ... 114 D3
MGHL L31 ... 72 E2
Saville St CHLY/EC PR7 ... 32 E8
Savon Hook FMBY L37 ... 59 K4
Savoylands Cl AIG/SPK L17 ... 129 L3
Sawdon Av STHP PR8 ... 36 A1
Sawley Av GOL/RIS/CU WA3 ... 92 F4
WGNNW/ST WN6 ... 68 B2
Sawley Cl GOL/RIS/CU WA3 ... 107 J3
RUNC WA7 ... 151 G6
Sawpit La HUY L36 ... 116 B3
Saxby Rd DV/KA/FCH L14 ... 99 J7
Saxon Cl NPK/KEN L6 ... 97 K8 6
Saxonia Rd ANF/KKDL L4 ... 97 K3
Saxon Rd CSBY/BLUN L23 ... 82 F2
HOY CH47 ... 108 E5
MOR/LEA CH46 ... 110 B4
RUNC WA7 ... 19 L4
STHP PR8 ... 2 D8
Saxon Ter WDN WA8 ... 16 F2
Saxon Wy GTS/LS CH66 ... 163 H5
NWD/KWIPK L33 ... 74 A7
Saxony Rd EHL/KEN L7 ... 113 J3
Saxthorpe Cl WGNS/IIMK WN3 ... 78 F2
Sayce St WDN WA8 ... 16 E2
Scafell Av WARRN/WOL WA2 ... 121 L2 5
Scafell Cl BEB CH63 ... 154 F2 2
NTHLY L27 ... 132 C2
Scafell Dr WGNW/BIL/O WN5 ... 67 K7
Scafell Gv WGNE/HIN WN2 ... 80 D3
Scafell Rd ECCL WA10 ... 89 J6
Scaffold La HTWN L38 ... 59 L8
Scape La CSBY/BLUN L23 ... 71 G8
Scargreen Av NG/CROX L11 ... 98 B2
Scarisbrick Av LITH L21 ... 83 K6 7
SKEL WN8 ... 53 L3 3
Scarisbrick Cl MGHL L31 ... 73 G2
Scarisbrick Crs NG/CROX L11 ... 97 M2
Scarisbrick Dr NG/CROX L11 ... 97 M2
Scarisbrick New Rd STHP PR8 ... 3 J7
Scarisbrick Pl NG/CROX L11 ... 97 M3 1
Scarisbrick Rd NG/CROX L11 ... 97 M3 2
RNFD/HAY WA11 ... 76 B6
Scarisbrick St CHTN/BK PR9 ... 3 H4
ORM L39 ... 51 G7
WGN WN1 ... 4 F1
Scarlet St CHLYE PR6 ... 33 G6 5
Scarsdale Rd NG/CROX L11 ... 98 B4
Scarth Hill La BRSC L40 ... 63 K3
ORM L39 ... 63 G3
Scarth Pk SKEL WN8 ... 65 L6
Scawfell Rd CHLY/EC PR7 ... 32 D8 5
Sceptre Cl NEWLW WA12 ... 104 C2 7
Sceptre Rd NG/CROX L11 ... 98 E2
Sceptre Wk NG/CROX L11 ... 98 E2 2
Scholar St EHL/KEN L7 ... 113 L6
Scholefield La WGN WN1 ... 5 H3
Scholes WGN WN1 ... 5 H3
Scholes Bank HOR/BR BL6 ... 45 J8
Scholes La ECCL WA10 ... 101 K6
RAIN/WH L35 ... 101 L6
Scholes Pk ECCL WA10 ... 101 K6
Schomberg St NPK/KEN L6 ... 113 J2
School Av FMBY L37 ... 59 H2
NSTN CH64 ... 153 H7
WGN WN1 ... 5 J1
School Brow WARR WA1 ... 15 G5
WGNW/BIL/O WN5 ... 78 A8
School Cl MOR/LEA CH46 ... 110 B4 1
NTHLY L27 ... 115 L6
ORM L39 ... 62 E4 1
STHP PR8 ... 35 K3
School Dr WGNW/BIL/O WN5 ... 78 A8
Schoolfield Cl
GR/UP/WCH CH49 ... 126 D3
Schoolfield Rd
GR/UP/WCH CH49 ... 126 D3
School Hl HES CH60 ... 141 H6
School House Gn ORM L39 ... 51 H8
School House Gv BRSC L40 ... 38 F8 1
School La AIMK WN4 ... 90 E2
AIN/FAZ L10 ... 84 F4
BEB CH63 ... 127 M8
BRSC L40 ... 39 H8
BRSC L40 ... 40 D4
BRSC L40 ... 64 A2
CHLY/EC PR7 ... 31 M2
CHNE CH2 ... 165 J2
CL/PREN CH43 ... 110 E4
CLVPS L1 ... 13 G8
FMBY L37 ... 59 H2
FROD/HEL WA6 ... 160 E6 2
FROD/HEL WA6 ... 167 J8
GOL/RIS/CU WA3 ... 107 L8
GTS/LS CH66 ... 155 J5
HOY CH47 ... 108 D6
HOY CH47 ... 108 E6
HUY L36 ... 116 C3
LITH L21 ... 83 K5
MGHL L31 ... 73 J4
MGHL L31 ... 73 J8
NSTN CH64 ... 152 D4
NSTN CH64 ... 153 H7
NSTN CH64 ... 153 K3
ORM L39 ... 61 H2
PEN/TH CH61 ... 125 K7
PR/KW L34 ... 86 C7
PS/BROM CH62 ... 128 D6
RAIN/WH L35 ... 118 B4
RUNC WA7 ... 150 B5
SKEL WN8 ... 64 F4
SKEL WN8 ... 66 D2
SKEL WN8 ... 66 E6
WAL/EG CH44 ... 111 G1
WDN WA8 ... 119 G6
WGN WN1 ... 5 G3
WGNE/HIN WN2 ... 57 G5
WGNE/HIN WN2 ... 57 H7
WGNNW/ST WN6 ... 55 M4
WLTN L25 ... 131 J4
School Rd EP CH65 ... 20 A4
HTWN L38 ... 70 B1
WARRN/WOL WA2 ... 121 L4
School St AIMK WN4 ... 79 M8
GOL/RIS/CU WA3 ... 92 C5
NEWLW WA12 ... 104 D2
RNFD/HAY WA11 ... 90 B7 3
WARRS WA4 ... 14 F8
WGN WN1 ... 5 G3
WGNE/HIN WN2 ... 5 M5
WGNE/HIN WN2 ... 80 D4 7
School Wy SPK/HALE L24 ... 146 D2
WDN WA8 ... 134 F2
WGNW/BIL/O WN5 ... 67 L7
Schooner Cl RUNC WA7 ... 150 F7 4
Schwartzman Dr CHTN/BK PR9 ... 23 J7
Science Rd SPK/HALE L24 ... 146 E1
Scilly Cl EP CH65 ... 163 L4
Scone Cl NG/CROX L11 ... 98 E2 3
Scorecross STHEL WA9 ... 102 D5
Score La CHLDW L16 ... 114 F5
Scoresby Rd MOR/LEA CH46 ... 110 D2
The Score STHEL WA9 ... 102 C7
Scorton St NPK/KEN L6 ... 97 L8
Scotchbarn La PR/KW L34 ... 101 G7
Scoter Rd NWD/KWIPK L33 ... 86 B3
Scotia Av PS/BROM CH62 ... 128 E6
Scotia Rd CLB/OSW/ST L13 ... 114 C1
Scotland Pl VAUX/LVPD L3 ... 13 H4
Scotland Rd EV L5 ... 96 F8
VAUX/LVPD L3 ... 13 H3
WARR WA1 ... 14 E5
Scot La WGNE/HIN WN2 ... 57 M7
WGNW/BIL/O WN5 ... 68 A3
Scott Av HUY L36 ... 116 C5
RAIN/WH L35 ... 117 H2
WDN WA8 ... 16 A3
Scott Cl ANF/KKDL L4 ... 97 H6
MGHL L31 ... 72 F4
Scott Dr ORM L39 ... 51 H6
Scotton Av GTS/LS CH66 ... 155 K8
Scott Rd GOL/RIS/CU WA3 ... 92 F4
Scotts Av STHEL WA9 ... 118 C2
Scotts Quays WAL/EG CH44 ... 112 A4
Scott St BTL L20 ... 6 E1
CHTN/BK PR9 ... 25 J6
LEIGH WN7 ... 81 M8
WAL/NB CH45 ... 95 K8
WARRN/WOL WA2 ... 14 F3
WGNNW/ST WN6 ... 4 C2
Scow Croft La CHLYE PR6 ... 33 L1
The Scythes GR/UP/WCH CH49 ... 125 L1
NTHTN L30 ... 84 D1 4
Scythia Cl PS/BROM CH62 ... 128 E5
Seabank Av WAL/EG CH44 ... 95 L8 6
Seabank Rd CHTN/BK PR9 ... 3 H1
HES CH60 ... 141 G7
WAL/NB CH45 ... 95 L6
Seabury St WARRS WA4 ... 138 C2
Seacombe Dr GTS/LS CH66 ... 163 G2
Seacombe Prom WAL/EG CH44 ... 112 A2
Seacombe Vw WAL/EG CH44 ... 112 A3
Seacroft Cl DV/KA/FCH L14 ... 99 J7
Seacroft Crs CHTN/BK PR9 ... 22 D8
Seacroft Rd DV/KA/FCH L14 ... 99 J7
Seafield FMBY L37 ... 59 J3
Seafield Av CSBY/BLUN L23 ... 83 H1
HES CH60 ... 141 G7
Seafield Rd BTL L20 ... 6 E2 1
PS/BROM CH62 ... 128 D5
STHP PR8 ... 34 E7
Seaford Cl RUNC WA7 ... 150 F4
Seaford Pl WARRN/WOL WA2 ... 121 J1
Seafore Cl MGHL L31 ... 72 D1
Seaforth Dr MOR/LEA CH46 ... 110 A6
Seaforth Rd LITH L21 ... 83 J7 7
Seaforth V North LITH L21 ... 83 J6
Seaforth V West LITH L21 ... 83 J7
Seagram Cl WLT/FAZ L9 ... 84 E5
Sealand Av FMBY L37 ... 58 F3
Sealand Cl FMBY L37 ... 58 F3
WARRN/WOL WA2 ... 122 A4 7
Sea La RUNC WA7 ... 149 M3
Sealy Cl BEB CH63 ... 143 J4
Seaman Rd WAV L15 ... 114 A6 11
Seaman Wy WGNE/HIN WN2 ... 69 J7
Sea Rd WAL/NB CH45 ... 95 H5
Seascale Av ECCL WA10 ... 101 K5
Seascale Crs WGN WN1 ... 68 E2 2
Seath Av STHEL WA9 ... 103 G1
Seathwaite Cl CSBY/BLUN L23 ... 82 D2 4
Seathwaite Crs NWD/KWIPK L33 ... 85 M1
Seathwaite Grove Cl
RUNC WA7 ... 150 A8
Seatoller Pl WGNW/BIL/O WN5 ... 67 K6
Seaton Cl WD/CROXPK L12 ... 99 J2
Seaton Gv RAIN/WH L35 ... 101 M7
Seaton Pk RUNC WA7 ... 151 G2
Seaton Pl SKEL WN8 ... 65 G2
Seaton Rd RF/TRAN CH42 ... 10 F9
WAL/NB CH45 ... 95 J7 4
Seaton Wy CHTN/BK PR9 ... 22 C8
Sea Vw HOY CH47 ... 108 D6
Seaview Av PEN/TH CH61 ... 125 M7
PS/BROM CH62 ... 144 D7
WAL/NB CH45 ... 95 J8
Sea View La PEN/TH CH61 ... 125 M7
Sea View Rd BTL L20 ... 6 D3
Seaview Rd WAL/NB CH45 ... 95 J7
Seawood Gv MOR/LEA CH46 ... 109 M6
Secker Av WARRS WA4 ... 137 M3
Secker Cl WARRS WA4 ... 137 M3
Second Av CL/PREN CH43 ... 110 D7
CSBY/BLUN L23 ... 82 F1 4
RAIN/WH L35 ... 117 K1
RUNC WA7 ... 150 B5
WGNNW/ST WN6 ... 68 C3
WLT/FAZ L9 ... 84 E6
Sedbergh Av AIN/FAZ L10 ... 84 E2
Sedbergh Gv RUNC WA7 ... 150 A8
Sedbergh Rd WAL/EG CH44 ... 95 H8
Sedburgh Gv HUY L36 ... 115 L2 2
Sedburn Rd KKBY L32 ... 86 C6
Seddon Cl ECCL WA10 ... 101 H2
Seddon House Dr
WGNNW/ST WN6 ... 68 A2
Seddon Pl SKEL WN8 ... 65 G2
Seddon Rd ALL/GAR L19 ... 130 E7
ECCL WA10 ... 101 K4
Seddons Ct PR/KW L34 ... 100 F7 1
Seddon St CLVPS L1 ... 13 G9
ECCL WA10 ... 89 H6
Sedgefield Dr WGNNW/ST WN6 ... 68 A2
Sedgefield Rd MOR/LEA CH46 ... 110 C5
Sedgely WGNNW/ST WN6 ... 56 C6
Sedgemoor Rd NG/CROX L11 ... 98 A2
Sedgewick Crs
WARRW/BUR WA5 ... 104 A7 3
Sedley St NPK/KEN L6 ... 97 K7
Sedum Gv NWD/KWIPK L33 ... 73 M8 3
Sedwyn St WGN WN1 ... 5 J1
Seeds La WLT/FAZ L9 ... 84 E6
Seeley Av BIRK CH41 ... 10 A3
Seel Rd HUY L36 ... 116 B3
Seel St CLVPS L1 ... 13 H9
Sefton Av LITH L21 ... 83 K6 8
WDN WA8 ... 134 C2 4
WGNW/BIL/O WN5 ... 66 F8
Sefton Cl KKBY L32 ... 85 L2
WGNW/BIL/O WN5 ... 66 F8 5
Sefton Coastal Footpath
CSBY/WL L22 ... 82 D3
HTWN L38 ... 70 B7
Sefton Dr AIN/FAZ L10 ... 85 G3
CSBY/BLUN L23 ... 71 J6
KKBY L32 ... 85 L2
MGHL L31 ... 72 C5
TOX L8 ... 113 L8
Sefton Fold Dr
WGNW/BIL/O WN5 ... 77 M8
Sefton Fold Gdns
WGNW/BIL/O WN5 ... 77 M8 4
Sefton Gdns ORM L39 ... 62 F6
Sefton Gv AIG/SPK L17 ... 129 L1
Sefton La MGHL L31 ... 72 D5
Sefton Mill La SFTN L29 ... 72 B6
Sefton Moss La NTHTN L30 ... 83 M2
Sefton Moss Vls LITH L21 ... 83 K5
Sefton Park Rd TOX L8 ... 113 K7
Sefton Rd AIMK WN4 ... 79 H7
BTL L20 ... 83 M8
FMBY L37 ... 59 G3
LITH L21 ... 83 K5
RF/TRAN CH42 ... 128 C4
WAL/NB CH45 ... 95 K6
WGNS/IIMK WN3 ... 79 H1
WGNW/BIL/O WN5 ... 66 F8
WLT/FAZ L9 ... 97 J1
Sefton St LITH L21 ... 83 K6
NEWLW WA12 ... 104 B2
STHP PR8 ... 3 J6
VAUX/LVPD L3 ... 112 F8
Sefton Vw CSBY/BLUN L23 ... 83 H1
WGNW/BIL/O WN5 ... 66 F8
Segar's La STHP PR8 ... 34 F8
Selborne RAIN/WH L35 ... 117 H3
Selborne Cl TOX L8 ... 113 J6
Selborne St TOX L8 ... 113 J6
Selbourne Cl GR/UP/WCH CH49 ... 126 D2
Selby Cl ECCL WA10 ... 8 B7
RUNC WA7 ... 151 G1
Selby Dr FMBY L37 ... 59 K3
WGNS/IIMK WN3 ... 78 E1
Selby Gn GTS/LS CH66 ... 155 K8
Selby Gv HUY L36 ... 116 D1
Selby Pl SKEL WN8 ... 64 F2
Selby Rd WLT/FAZ L9 ... 84 C7
Selby St WAL/NB CH45 ... 95 K8 7
WARRW/BUR WA5 ... 121 G8 5
Seldon St EHL/KEN L7 ... 113 K3 6
Selina Rd ANF/KKDL L4 ... 7 M6
ANF/KKDL L4 ... 97 H3 9
Selkirk Av AIMK WN4 ... 90 F1
PS/BROM CH62 ... 144 A8
WARRS WA4 ... 138 C2 8
Selkirk Cl GTS/LS CH66 ... 155 H8 2
Selkirk Dr ECCL WA10 ... 88 D8
Selkirk Gv WGNW/BIL/O WN5 ... 67 K5
Selkirk Rd CLB/OSW/ST L13 ... 114 B3
Sellar St ANF/KKDL L4 ... 97 G6 15
Selsdon Rd CSBY/WL L22 ... 82 E3
Selsey Cl EHL/KEN L7 ... 113 K5
Selside WGNS/IIMK WN3 ... 79 K3
Selside Rd NTHLY L27 ... 132 C2
Selston Cl BEB CH63 ... 143 J3
Selworthy Dr WARRS WA4 ... 138 F2
Selworthy Gn CHLDW L16 ... 115 G7 1
Selworthy Rd STHP PR8 ... 34 F2
Selwyn Cl WDN WA8 ... 134 F2 2
Selwyn St ANF/KKDL L4 ... 7 L8
Senecar Cl WGNE/HIN WN2 ... 69 K3
Seneschal Ct RUNC WA7 ... 150 A7 4
Sennen Cl RUNC WA7 ... 150 D8
Sennen Rd KKBY L32 ... 86 B5
Sennicar La WGN WN1 ... 56 E8
Sentinel Wy NTHTN L30 ... 84 D5
Sephton Av GOL/RIS/CU WA3 ... 107 G2
Sephton Dr ORM L39 ... 51 H6
Sephton St WGNS/IIMK WN3 ... 5 L7
September Rd NPK/KEN L6 ... 97 L8
Serenade Rd NWD/KWIPK L33 ... 74 B7
Sergeant York Loop
WARRW/BUR WA5 ... 120 D8 5
Sergrim Rd HUY L36 ... 115 M2
Serin Cl NEWLW WA12 ... 104 E2
Serpentine Rd WAL/EG CH44 ... 95 L8
The Serpentine South
CSBY/BLUN L23 ... 82 C1
The Serpentine ALL/GAR L19 ... 130 C5
CSBY/BLUN L23 ... 82 C1
ORM L39 ... 62 F5
Servia Rd LITH L21 ... 83 K6
Servite Cl CSBY/WL L22 ... 82 E3 9
EP CH65 ... 156 B7
Sessions Rd ANF/KKDL L4 ... 97 G5
Seth Powell Wy HUY L36 ... 99 L7
Settrington Rd NG/CROX L11 ... 98 B4
Seven Acre Rd CSBY/BLUN L23 ... 71 K8
Seven Acres La PEN/TH CH61 ... 126 C7
Sevenoaks CHLY/EC PR7 ... 43 L1
Sevenoaks Av STHP PR8 ... 34 D8
Sevenoaks Cl EV L5 ... 97 G8 5
Seven Stars Rd WGNS/IIMK WN3 ... 4 B5
Seventh Av WLT/FAZ L9 ... 84 F6 5
Severn Cl STHEL WA9 ... 102 E8
WARRN/WOL WA2 ... 122 A3 5
WDN WA8 ... 135 H2
WGNW/BIL/O WN5 ... 89 M1
Severn Dr WGNE/HIN WN2 ... 81 L2
WGNW/BIL/O WN5 ... 67 L7
Severn Rd AIMK WN4 ... 80 A8
GOL/RIS/CU WA3 ... 107 H3
NWD/KWIPK L33 ... 74 B7
RAIN/WH L35 ... 117 K2
Severn St BIRK CH41 ... 111 J4
EV L5 ... 97 H7
Severnvale EP CH65 ... 20 A8
Severs St NPK/KEN L6 ... 113 J1
Sewell St PR/KW L34 ... 100 F7
RUNC WA7 ... 19 K4
Sextant Cl RUNC WA7 ... 150 F7
Sexton Av STHEL WA9 ... 103 K3
Sexton Wy DV/KA/FCH L14 ... 115 H3 2
Seymour Dr GTS/LS CH66 ... 156 A7
MGHL L31 ... 73 G2
WARR WA1 ... 122 C6
Seymour Pl West
WAL/NB CH45 ... 95 K5 6
Seymour Rd DV/KA/FCH L14 ... 114 F4
LITH L21 ... 83 K6 9
Seymour St BTL L20 ... 6 E7
CHLYE PR6 ... 32 F6
RF/TRAN CH42 ... 127 M1
VAUX/LVPD L3 ... 13 K6
WAL/NB CH45 ... 95 K5
Sgt York Loop
WARRW/BUR WA5 ... 120 D7
Shacklady Rd NWD/KWIPK L33 ... 86 C1
Shackleton Cl
WARRW/BUR WA5 ... 120 F5
Shackleton Rd MOR/LEA CH46 ... 110 D1
Shadewood Crs WARRS WA4 ... 138 D3
Shadwell Cl EV L5 ... 96 E8 3
Shadwell Gv LEIGH WN7 ... 81 L5 2
Shadwell St EV L5 ... 96 D8
Shaftesbury Av STHP PR8 ... 35 J5
WARRW/BUR WA5 ... 136 A3
Shaftesbury Gv STHP PR8 ... 35 J4
Shaftesbury Pl CHLY/EC PR7 ... 32 D5
Shaftesbury Rd
CSBY/BLUN L23 ... 82 F1 5
STHP PR8 ... 35 J5
Shaftesbury St TOX L8 ... 113 G7 4
Shaftesbury Ter
CLB/OSW/ST L13 ... 114 C2 4
Shaftesbury Wy
WARRW/BUR WA5 ... 104 B6 2
Shaftsbury Av NWD/KWIPK L33 ... 73 M8
Shaftsbury Rd
WGNW/BIL/O WN5 ... 67 J5 1
Shaftsbury St WGNNW/ST WN6 ... 68 B2
Shaftway Cl RNFD/HAY WA11 ... 91 H6
Shakespeare Av RF/TRAN CH42 ... 128 B4
Shakespeare Gv
WARRN/WOL WA2 ... 121 K3
WGNS/IIMK WN3 ... 79 J1 4
Shakespeare Rd NPK/KEN L6 ... 113 J1 3
NSTN CH64 ... 153 G4
STHEL WA9 ... 118 C3
WAL/EG CH44 ... 111 M3
WDN WA8 ... 16 C2
Shakespeare St ALL/GAR L19 ... 130 E8 5
BTL L20 ... 6 D1
STHP PR8 ... 3 G8
Shakespeare Ter CHLYE PR6 ... 32 F3
Shakspeare Cl NPK/KEN L6 ... 113 J1
Shalcombe Cl HLWD L26 ... 132 C6
Shaldon Cl KKBY L32 ... 86 C5 1
Shaldon Gv KKBY L32 ... 86 C5 2
Shaldon Rd KKBY L32 ... 86 C6
Shalford Gv WKBY CH48 ... 124 F3
Shallacres EP CH65 ... 156 B6
Shallcross Pl NPK/KEN L6 ... 113 J1
Shallmarsh Cl BEB CH63 ... 127 M8 3
Shallmarsh Rd BEB CH63 ... 127 M8
Shalom Ct AIG/SPK L17 ... 114 A8
Shamrock Rd BIRK CH41 ... 111 H6
Shanklin Cl WARRW/BUR WA5 ... 119 L7
Shanklin Rd WAV L15 ... 114 B4
Shannon St BIRK CH41 ... 111 H4 2
Shap Ga WGNW/BIL/O WN5 ... 67 K6
Shard Cl NG/CROX L11 ... 85 K8
Shard St STHEL WA9 ... 103 G6 2
Shared St WGN WN1 ... 5 H5
Sharon Park Cl WARRS WA4 ... 138 E4
Sharon Sq WGNE/HIN WN2 ... 80 B5 1
Sharpeville Cl ANF/KKDL L4 ... 96 F6
Sharples Crs CSBY/BLUN L23 ... 83 H2
Sharp St WARRN/WOL WA2 ... 14 F2
WDN WA8 ... 16 D3
WGNS/IIMK WN3 ... 5 J8
Sharratts Pth CHLY/EC PR7 ... 43 H1
Sharwood Rd NTHLY L27 ... 132 B1
Shavington Av CL/PREN CH43 ... 127 H2
Shawbury Av BEB CH63 ... 127 M6
Shawbury Cl HOR/BR BL6 ... 57 M4
Shaw Cl GTS/LS CH66 ... 163 G1
ORM L39 ... 36 B7
Shaw Crs FMBY L37 ... 59 K1
Shawell Ct WDN WA8 ... 135 G3 3
Shaw Entry WDN WA8 ... 117 J6
Shawes Dr CHLYE PR6 ... 44 E6
Shaw Hill St CHLY/EC PR7 ... 32 E6
CLVPS L1 ... 13 G6 2
Shaw La GR/UP/WCH CH49 ... 125 L3
ORM L39 ... 48 F7
RAIN/WH L35 ... 117 G1
Shaw Rd HOR/BR BL6 ... 45 K8
SPK/HALE L24 ... 131 M8
Shaws Aly CLVPS L1 ... 112 E5 6
Shaw's Av STHP PR8 ... 35 J4
WARRN/WOL WA2 ... 121 K5
Shaws Dr HOY CH47 ... 108 F5
Shaws Garth ORM L39 ... 36 B7
Shaw's Rd STHP PR8 ... 35 J4
Shaw St AIMK WN4 ... 79 K8
BIRK CH41 ... 11 G8
ECCL WA10 ... 9 J4
GOL/RIS/CU WA3 ... 107 J2
HOY CH47 ... 108 D6
NPK/KEN L6 ... 13 L3
RNFD/HAY WA11 ... 91 G7
RUNC WA7 ... 18 F4
STHEL WA9 ... 9 J6
WARRN/WOL WA2 ... 14 E3
WGN WN1 ... 4 F1
Shawton Rd CHLDW L16 ... 114 F5 1
Shearman Cl PEN/TH CH61 ... 141 J1 2
Shearman Rd PEN/TH CH61 ... 141 H1
Sheen Rd WAL/NB CH45 ... 95 L6
Sheepfield Cl GTS/LS CH66 ... 155 L6 1
Sheep House La HOR/BR BL6 ... 45 H3
Sheerwater Cl WARR WA1 ... 122 B6
Sheffield Cl
WARRW/BUR WA5 ... 120 E8 6
Shefford Crs WGNS/IIMK WN3 ... 78 E3
The Sheilings
GOL/RIS/CU WA3 ... 93 H5 3
Sheil Rd NPK/KEN L6 ... 113 L2 5
Shelagh Av WDN WA8 ... 16 D2
Sheldon Av WGNNW/ST WN6 ... 56 A3
Sheldon Cl BEB CH63 ... 143 J3 6
Sheldon Rd WD/CROXPK L12 ... 98 F5
Sheldrake Gv NSTN CH64 ... 153 G8
Shelley Cl CHLY/EC PR7 ... 43 H5
HUY L36 ... 116 B4
Shelley Dr CHLY/EC PR7 ... 30 F8
ORM L39 ... 50 F7 5
WGNE/HIN WN2 ... 80 D4
WGNW/BIL/O WN5 ... 67 J7
Shelley Gv ALL/GAR L19 ... 130 E8
STHP PR8 ... 25 H6
WARRS WA4 ... 138 B1 5
Shelley Pl RAIN/WH L35 ... 117 H2 4
Shelley Rd WDN WA8 ... 16 C1
Shelley St BTL L20 ... 6 E2

LEIGH WN7 ... 81 L6
STHEL WA9 ... 118 D3
Shelley Wy WKBY CH48 ... 124 D5
Shellfield Rd CHTN/BK PR9 ... 25 J2
Shellingford Cl WGNNW/ST WN6 .. 54 F6
Shellingford Rd
DV/KA/FCH L14 ... 115 J1
Shellway Rd EP CH65 ... 21 L8
Shelmore Dr TOX L8 ... 129 H1 14
Shelton Cl CLB/OSW/ST L13 ... 114 C3 2
WDN WA8 ... 135 H2 1
Shelton Dr STHP PR8 ... 47 J1
Shelton Rd WAL/NB CH45 ... 95 J7
Shenley Cl BEB CH63 ... 128 B7
Shenley Rd WAV L15 ... 114 E5 2
Shenley Wy CHTN/BK PR9 ... 22 F8 4
Shenstone St EHL/KEN L7 ... 113 K4
Shenton Av RNFD/HAY WA11 ... 89 M7
Shepherd Cl
GR/UP/WCH CH49 ... 125 L1 7
Shepherds Cl HOR/BR BL6 ... 57 L2 3
Shepherd's La ORM L39 ... 49 M8
Shepherd St NPK/KEN L6 ... 13 M5
Shepherds Wy CHLY/EC PR7 ... 32 F5
Sheppard Av CHLDW L16 ... 115 J5
Shepperton Cl WARRS WA4 ... 137 M7
Shepsides Cl GTS/LS CH66 ... 162 E2
Shepston Av ANF/KKDL L4 ... 97 J4 3
Shepton Av WGNE/HIN WN2 ... 80 C4 1
Shepton Rd GTS/LS CH66 ... 163 G3
HUY L36 ... 99 M7
Sheraton Cl WGNW/BIL/O WN5 ... 67 K4
Sherborne Av WLTN L25 ... 131 M5
Sherborne Cl RUNC WA7 ... 151 H2
Sherborne Rd
WGNW/BIL/O WN5 ... 67 J5
Sherbourne Pl WGNS/IIMK WN3 ... 5 J9
Sherbourne Rd EP CH65 ... 20 F8
Sherbourne St CHLYE PR6 ... 32 F6 3
Sherbourne Wy
WARRW/BUR WA5 ... 104 B7 7
Sherbrooke Cl WD/CROXPK L12 ... 99 G8
Sherburn Cl WLT/FAZ L9 ... 84 F5
Sherdley Park Dr STHEL WA9 ... 102 D7
Sherdley Rd STHEL WA9 ... 102 C5
Sheridan Av GOL/RIS/CU WA3 ... 92 F6 2
Sheri Dr NEWLW WA12 ... 104 F3
Sheringham Cl
GR/UP/WCH CH49 ... 110 C6 4
STHEL WA9 ... 102 F2
Sheringham Rd
WARRW/BUR WA5 ... 120 A7 3
Sherlock Av RNFD/HAY WA11 ... 91 G6
Sherlock La WAL/EG CH44 ... 111 K2 2
Sherman Dr RAIN/WH L35 ... 117 M4
Sherrat St SKEL WN8 ... 64 F4
Sherringham Rd STHP PR8 ... 35 G3
Sherry La GR/UP/WCH CH49 ... 126 C3
Sherwell Cl WAV L15 ... 114 C4
Sherwood Av AIMK WN4 ... 91 L1 5
CSBY/BLUN L23 ... 70 F8
ORM L39 ... 62 E3 3
PEN/TH CH61 ... 125 L6
Sherwood Cl RAIN/WH L35 ... 101 K8
WDN WA8 ... 133 L4 4
Sherwood Ct HUY L36 ... 116 B3 2
WD/CROXPK L12 ... 99 H2 5
Sherwood Crs
WARRW/BUR WA5 ... 104 A7 4
WGNE/HIN WN2 ... 80 C3 3
WGNW/BIL/O WN5 ... 67 M6
Sherwood Dr BEB CH63 ... 128 A6
SKEL WN8 ... 65 M2
WGNW/BIL/O WN5 ... 67 M7
Sherwood Gv FROD/HEL WA6 ... 166 C2
HOY CH47 ... 109 H6 1
WGNW/BIL/O WN5 ... 67 M6
Sherwood Pl CHLYE PR6 ... 32 F5 11
Sherwood Rd CSBY/BLUN L23 ... 70 E8
HOY CH47 ... 109 H5
WAL/EG CH44 ... 111 L2
Sherwood's La AIN/FAZ L10 ... 85 H5
Sherwood St VAUX/LVPD L3 ... 12 D1
Sherwyn Rd ANF/KKDL L4 ... 97 L6
Shetland Cl
WARRN/WOL WA2 ... 122 A1 3
WDN WA8 ... 135 G2 3
Shetland Dr EP CH65 ... 163 L4
PS/BROM CH62 ... 144 A5
Shevington Cswy
LEY/BBR PR5 ... 29 K3 3
Shevington Cl STHEL WA9 ... 102 E6 3
WDN WA8 ... 135 G2 7
Shevington La WGNNW/ST WN6 .. 55 K6
Shevington Moor
WGNNW/ST WN6 ... 55 J3
Shevington's La NWD/KWIPK L33 .. 74 A8
Shewell Cl RF/TRAN CH42 ... 11 H9 2
Shiel Rd WAL/NB CH45 ... 95 J6
Shiggins Cl WARRW/BUR WA5 .. 120 F7 1
Shildon Cl WGNE/HIN WN2 ... 69 H3
Shillingford Cl WARRS WA4 ... 138 A8
Shimmin St EHL/KEN L7 ... 113 J4 5
Shipham Cl LEIGH WN7 ... 81 M5
Ship St FROD/HEL WA6 ... 160 E3
Shipton Cl ALL/GAR L19 ... 130 D5
CL/PREN CH43 ... 127 G4 2
WARRW/BUR WA5 ... 120 D5
WDN WA8 ... 133 M2 2
Ship Yd WGN WN1 ... 4 F4
Shirdley Av KKBY L32 ... 86 B6
Shirdley Crs STHP PR8 ... 47 L2
Shirdley Wk KKBY L32 ... 86 B6
Shirebourne Av
RNFD/HAY WA11 ... 89 K6
Shireburn Rd FMBY L37 ... 48 E5
Shire Gn STHEL WA9 ... 102 E7
The Shires ECCL WA10 ... 8 D7
Shirley Dr WARRS WA4 ... 138 C3
Shirley Rd ALL/GAR L19 ... 130 E5
Shirley St WAL/EG CH44 ... 112 A2
Shirwell Gv STHEL WA9 ... 118 E1
Shobdon Cl WD/CROXPK L12 ... 99 H1 2
Shones Cft NSTN CH64 ... 153 J8
Shop La MGHL L31 ... 72 E4
Shop Rd PR/KW L34 ... 99 L1
Shore Bank PS/BROM CH62 ... 128 E5
Shore Dr PS/BROM CH62 ... 128 E7
Shorefields PS/BROM CH62 ... 128 D5
Shorefields Village TOX L8 ... 129 H2
Shoreham Dr
WARRW/BUR WA5 ... 136 C2
Shore Rd BIRK CH41 ... 11 L3
BTL L20 ... 6 B1
LITH L21 ... 6 B1
STHP PR8 ... 34 C7
WKBY CH48 ... 124 E6
Short Cl NEWLW WA12 ... 104 A2
Short Croft La FMBY L37 ... 59 M4
Shortfield Rd
GR/UP/WCH CH49 ... 126 C1
Shortfield Wy
GR/UP/WCH CH49 ... 126 C1 1
Shortland Pl WGNE/HIN WN2 ... 81 J5 1
Short St GOL/RIS/CU WA3 ... 92 D4 5
NEWLW WA12 ... 104 A2
RNFD/HAY WA11 ... 91 G7 3
WDN WA8 ... 134 C8 5
WGNW/BIL/O WN5 ... 67 K7 7
Shortwood Rd DV/KA/FCH L14 ... 115 H2
Shorwell Cl WARRW/BUR WA5 ... 119 L6
Shotwick La CH/BCN CH1 ... 162 A7
Shrewsbury Av AIN/FAZ L10 ... 84 E2
CSBY/WL L22 ... 82 F2
Shrewsbury Cl
CL/PREN CH43 ... 111 H7 3
Shrewsbury Dr
GR/UP/WCH CH49 ... 110 C7
Shrewsbury Rd ALL/GAR L19 ... 130 E7
CL/PREN CH43 ... 10 B9
HES CH60 ... 141 J4
WAL/NB CH45 ... 95 H8
WKBY CH48 ... 124 C4
Shrewsbury St WARRS WA4 ... 15 J9
Shrewton Rd WLTN L25 ... 115 J6
Shropshire Cl NTHTN L30 ... 84 C1 3
WARR WA1 ... 123 G7 3
Shropshire Rd EP CH65 ... 21 J9
Shuttle Hillock Rd
WGNE/HIN WN2 ... 81 H6
Sibbering Brow Preston Rd
CHLY/EC PR7 ... 31 L6
Sibford Rd WD/CROXPK L12 ... 98 F8
Sibley Av AIMK WN4 ... 91 M1
Sidbrook St WGNE/HIN WN2 ... 69 L8 3
Siddall St ECCL WA10 ... 89 H6 1
Siddeley Dr NEWLW WA12 ... 104 B2
Siddeley St AIG/SPK L17 ... 129 L2
LEIGH WN7 ... 81 M8
Sidgreave St ECCL WA10 ... 8 D6
Siding La RNFD/HAY WA11 ... 75 M4
The Sidings RF/TRAN CH42 ... 128 B3 12
Sidlaw Av STHEL WA9 ... 103 H2
Sidlaw Cl GTS/LS CH66 ... 155 J7
Sidmouth Cl WARRW/BUR WA5 .. 136 A1
Sidmouth Gv WGNS/IIMK WN3 ... 79 G2
Sidney Av WAL/NB CH45 ... 95 J5
Sidney Pl EHL/KEN L7 ... 113 J4
Sidney Powell Av KKBY L32 ... 85 L3
Sidney Rd BIRK CH41 ... 128 A1
BTL L20 ... 7 K6
CHTN/BK PR9 ... 25 H5
NSTN CH64 ... 153 H4
Sidney St BIRK CH41 ... 11 K4
ECCL WA10 ... 8 B4
Sidwell St ALL/GAR L19 ... 130 E8
Signal Works Rd WLT/FAZ L9 ... 85 G5
Silcock St GOL/RIS/CU WA3 ... 92 C5
Silcroft Rd KKBY L32 ... 86 A5
Silkstone Cl ECCL WA10 ... 8 B6
EHL/KEN L7 ... 113 K5 3
Silkstone Crs RUNC WA7 ... 150 D6 1
Silkstone St ECCL WA10 ... 8 C6 1
Sillitoe Dr WGNNW/ST WN6 ... 4 B2
Silsbury Gv WGNNW/ST WN6 ... 56 C5
Silsden Av GOL/RIS/CU WA3 ... 93 K5
Silver Av RNFD/HAY WA11 ... 90 C8
Silverbeech Av CALD/MH L18 ... 130 D1
Silverbeech Rd WAL/EG CH44 ... 111 L2
Silver Birch Gv AIMK WN4 ... 79 J8 13
Silverbirch Wy GTS/LS CH66 ... 163 H5
Silver Birch Wy MGHL L31 ... 61 K8
Silverburn Av
MOR/LEA CH46 ... 110 A4 5
Silverdale WGN WN1 ... 68 E3 7
Silverdale Av CLB/OSW/ST L13 ... 98 A8
WGNE/HIN WN2 ... 69 J5
Silverdale Cl FROD/HEL WA6 ... 160 E6
HUY L36 ... 116 A5
Silverdale Dr LITH L21 ... 83 M5
Silverdale Gv RNFD/HAY WA11 .. 89 J5 3
Silverdale Rd BEB CH63 ... 128 B6
CHLYE PR6 ... 33 G6 10
CL/PREN CH43 ... 10 A9
NEWLW WA12 ... 104 D1
WARRS WA4 ... 137 K3
WGNW/BIL/O WN5 ... 67 K5
Silver La GOL/RIS/CU WA3 ... 107 L6
Silverlea Av WAL/NB CH45 ... 111 J1
Silver Leigh AIG/SPK L17 ... 129 M4
Silverlime Gdns RAIN/WH L35 ... 101 L6
Silverne Dr EP CH65 ... 163 J3
Silverstone Dr HUY L36 ... 115 M5
Silverstone Gv MGHL L31 ... 61 K8
Silver St WARRN/WOL WA2 ... 14 E3
WGNE/HIN WN2 ... 80 D3 3
Silverthorne Dr CHTN/BK PR9 ... 25 H4
Silverton Rd AIG/SPK L17 ... 130 A5
Silverwell Rd NG/CROX L11 ... 85 M8 4
Silvester Rd CHLY/EC PR7 ... 32 E7
Silvester St EV L5 ... 96 F8 3
HOR/BR BL6 ... 57 M3 6
Simfield Cl WGNNW/ST WN6 ... 55 M4 3
Simkin Av WARRS WA4 ... 138 B1
Simms Av STHEL WA9 ... 103 G2
Simm's Rd NPK/KEN L6 ... 97 M7
Simnel Cl WLTN L25 ... 115 K7
Simonsbridge WKBY CH48 ... 124 F7 4
Simons Cl RAIN/WH L35 ... 116 E5
Simon's Cft NTHTN L30 ... 83 L2
Simonside WDN WA8 ... 133 L3
Simons La FROD/HEL WA6 ... 160 D7
Simonstone Gv STHEL WA9 ... 102 F6 12
Simonswood La
NWD/KWIPK L33 ... 86 C3
ORM L39 ... 74 B2
Simpkin St WGNE/HIN WN2 ... 80 D4
Simpson St BIRK CH41 ... 11 H5
CLVPS L1 ... 112 F6 2
Sim St VAUX/LVPD L3 ... 13 K4
Sinclair Av RAIN/WH L35 ... 101 H8
WARRN/WOL WA2 ... 121 K3
WDN WA8 ... 16 B3
Sinclair Cl RAIN/WH L35 ... 101 H7
Sinclair Dr CALD/MH L18 ... 114 D7
Sinclair Pl WGNW/BIL/O WN5 ... 68 A5
Sinclair St ALL/GAR L19 ... 130 E8
Sineacre La ORM L39 ... 75 G4
Singleton Av HOR/BR BL6 ... 45 L8
RF/TRAN CH42 ... 127 L2
RNFD/HAY WA11 ... 89 M8
Singleton Dr PR/KW L34 ... 99 M2
Singleton Rd EP CH65 ... 163 H1
Sirdar Cl EHL/KEN L7 ... 113 K5
Sir Thomas St CLVPS L1 ... 12 F6 7
CLVPS L1 ... 13 G6 3
Siskin Cl NEWLW WA12 ... 104 E2
Siskin Gn WLTN L25 ... 131 J1
Sisters Wy BIRK CH41 ... 11 G5
Sittingbourne Rd WGN WN1 ... 68 E1
Six Acre Gdns WARRS WA4 ... 136 C8
Six Acre La RUNC WA7 ... 136 C8
Sixth Av WLT/FAZ L9 ... 84 F6 4
WLT/FAZ L9 ... 85 G6 3
Skeffington RAIN/WH L35 ... 117 G3
Skelhorne St VAUX/LVPD L3 ... 13 J7
Skellington Fold NTHLY L27 ... 116 A8
Skelmersdale Rd ORM L39 ... 64 C6
Skelton Cl RNFD/HAY WA11 ... 89 J6
Skelton St AIMK WN4 ... 79 H7
Skerries Rd ANF/KKDL L4 ... 97 J7
Skiddaw Cl RUNC WA7 ... 161 J1 1
Skiddaw Pl WGNW/BIL/O WN5 .. 67 L7 5
Skiddaw Rd PS/BROM CH62 ... 144 A3
Skipton Av CHTN/BK PR9 ... 22 E7
WGNE/HIN WN2 ... 81 J1
Skipton Dr GTS/LS CH66 ... 162 E1
Skipton Rd ANF/KKDL L4 ... 97 K6
HUY L36 ... 116 D2 3
Skirving Pl EV L5 ... 96 F7
Skirving St EV L5 ... 96 F7
Skull House La WGNNW/ST WN6 .. 54 F5
Skye Cl EP CH65 ... 163 L4
WDN WA8 ... 135 G2
Slackey Fold WGNE/HIN WN2 ... 81 K4
Slack's La CHLYE PR6 ... 44 D3
Slag La GOL/RIS/CU WA3 ... 93 H3
RNFD/HAY WA11 ... 90 D6
Slaidburn Cl WGNS/IIMK WN3 ... 79 J2 3
Slaidburn Crs CHTN/BK PR9 ... 22 C8
GOL/RIS/CU WA3 ... 92 B3 4
Slate La SKEL WN8 ... 64 E2
Slater Pl CLVPS L1 ... 13 H9
Slater St CLVPS L1 ... 13 H9
WARRS WA4 ... 15 H8
Slater St North LEIGH WN7 ... 81 M7 7
Slatey Rd CL/PREN CH43 ... 10 C6
Sleaford Rd DV/KA/FCH L14 ... 99 K8
Sledbrook St
WGNW/BIL/O WN5 ... 67 L8 2
Sleepers Hl ANF/KKDL L4 ... 97 H6
Slenna Cl NTHLY L27 ... 115 L7 5
Slessor Av WKBY CH48 ... 124 F2
Slim Rd HUY L36 ... 116 A1
Slingsby Dr GR/UP/WCH CH49 ... 126 C1
Sluice La BRSC L40 ... 39 K2
Slutchers La WARR WA1 ... 14 D8
Small Av WARRN/WOL WA2 ... 121 L3
Small Crs WARRN/WOL WA2 ... 121 L3
Smalley St WGNNW/ST WN6 ... 56 A4
Small La BRSC L40 ... 38 A5
ORM L39 ... 62 B2
ORM L39 ... 63 H1
Small La North ORM L39 ... 49 M3
Small La South ORM L39 ... 49 L8
Smallridge Cl PEN/TH CH61 ... 141 G1 3
Smallshaw Cl AIMK WN4 ... 91 J3 5
Smallwoods Ms HES CH60 ... 141 G4 1
Smeaton St ANF/KKDL L4 ... 7 L9
Smethurst La
WGNW/BIL/O WN5 ... 67 L8
Smethurst Park Hall
WGNW/BIL/O WN5 ... 77 L3
Smethurst Rd
WGNW/BIL/O WN5 ... 77 L3
Smethurst St
WGNW/BIL/O WN5 ... 67 L8 3
Smilie Av MOR/LEA CH46 ... 109 L4
Smith Av BIRK CH41 ... 10 C1
WGNW/BIL/O WN5 ... 67 K5
Smith Brow HOR/BR BL6 ... 57 L2 7
Smith Crs WARRN/WOL WA2 ... 121 M5
Smithdown La EHL/KEN L7 ... 113 J5
TOX L8 ... 113 K5
Smithdown Pl
CALD/MH L18 ... 114 C8 10
Smithdown Rd AIG/SPK L17 ... 114 A7
EHL/KEN L7 ... 113 L6
WAV L15 ... 114 B7
Smith Dr BTL L20 ... 84 A8
WARRN/WOL WA2 ... 121 M5
Smithfield St CLVP L2 ... 12 F5 2
Smithills Cl CHLYE PR6 ... 33 G4
GOL/RIS/CU WA3 ... 106 F8 1
Smith Rd WDN WA8 ... 16 B5
Smith's La KIRK/FR/WA PR4 ... 28 C4
WGNE/HIN WN2 ... 81 J5
Smith St CHLY/EC PR7 ... 32 F7
CHLY/EC PR7 ... 44 B7
EV L5 ... 97 G6
PR/KW L34 ... 101 G7 10
SKEL WN8 ... 64 F4
STHEL WA9 ... 103 G6
WARR WA1 ... 14 F6
WGNE/HIN WN2 ... 57 L8
Smithy Brow GOL/RIS/CU WA3 ... 106 B6
SKEL WN8 ... 53 J4 3
WGNNW/ST WN6 ... 41 L5
Smithy Cl FMBY L37 ... 59 K1
WDN WA8 ... 117 L7
Smithy Gn FMBY L37 ... 59 K1 1
Smithy Hey WKBY CH48 ... 124 E3 1
Smithy Hl BEB CH63 ... 142 C7
Smithy La BRSC L40 ... 40 D3
BRSC L40 ... 50 E1
FROD/HEL WA6 ... 159 L8
GOL/RIS/CU WA3 ... 106 C6
GTS/LS CH66 ... 155 L7
KIRK/FR/WA PR4 ... 27 L7
NSTN CH64 ... 154 C5
ORM L39 ... 49 J7
ORM L39 ... 62 B7
WDN WA8 ... 117 L8
Smithy Wk BRSC L40 ... 39 G8 1
Smock La AIMK WN4 ... 90 E1
Smollett St BTL L20 ... 83 J7
EHL/KEN L7 ... 113 K3 7
Smugglers Wy WAL/NB CH45 ... 95 G5
Smyth Rd WDN WA8 ... 134 F3
Snabwood Cl NSTN CH64 ... 153 G8
Snaefell Av CLB/OSW/ST L13 ... 98 A8
Snaefell Gv CLB/OSW/ST L13 ... 98 A8
Snaefell Ri WARRS WA4 ... 137 L6
Snape Gn STHP PR8 ... 36 F5
Snave Cl LITH L21 ... 83 K8
Snipewood CHLY/EC PR7 ... 30 D7
Snottesbrook Gn NG/CROX L11 ... 98 B2
Snowberry Cl WDN WA8 ... 135 G1
Snowberry Rd DV/KA/FCH L14 ... 99 H7
Snowden Av WGNS/IIMK WN3 ... 79 J1
Snowden Rd MOR/LEA CH46 ... 109 L5 3
Snowdon Cl GTS/LS CH66 ... 155 J7
WARRW/BUR WA5 ... 120 A7 7
Snowdon Dr HOR/BR BL6 ... 45 L8
Snowdon Gv STHEL WA9 ... 102 E6 3
Snowdon La EV L5 ... 96 E8
Snowdon Rd RF/TRAN CH42 ... 127 M3
Snowdrop Av BIRK CH41 ... 111 H6 5
Snowdrop Cl RUNC WA7 ... 161 H1
Snowdrop St EV L5 ... 96 F6 5
Snowshill Dr WGNS/IIMK WN3 ... 78 E1
Soane Cl AIMK WN4 ... 91 M2
Soham Cl WGNE/HIN WN2 ... 81 G1 3
Soho Pl VAUX/LVPD L3 ... 13 K3
Soho St VAUX/LVPD L3 ... 13 K3
WGNW/BIL/O WN5 ... 68 B6
Solar Rd WLT/FAZ L9 ... 84 D7
Sole St WGN WN1 ... 5 K1
Sollom La BRSC L40 ... 28 D3
Solly Av RF/TRAN CH42 ... 128 A3
Solomon St EHL/KEN L7 ... 113 K3 3
Solway Cl AIMK WN4 ... 91 J1
WARRN/WOL WA2 ... 122 B1
Solway Gv RUNC WA7 ... 149 M8
Solway St TOX L8 ... 113 K6
Soma Av LITH L21 ... 83 L5
Somerford Rd DV/KA/FCH L14 ... 115 J1
Somerset Av CHLY/EC PR7 ... 32 E4
Somerset Dr STHP PR8 ... 47 L3
Somerset Pl NPK/KEN L6 ... 97 M8
Somerset Rd BTL L20 ... 7 K2
CSBY/WL L22 ... 82 E3
PEN/TH CH61 ... 141 G1
WAL/NB CH45 ... 95 G8
WGNW/BIL/O WN5 ... 67 L7
WKBY CH48 ... 124 E2
Somerset St STHEL WA9 ... 102 F3
Somerset Wy WARR WA1 ... 122 D5
Somerton St WAV L15 ... 114 A5 5
Somerville Cl BEB CH63 ... 143 K7
NSTN CH64 ... 153 G8
Somerville Crs EP CH65 ... 20 D7
Somerville Gv CSBY/WL L22 ... 82 F3
Somerville Rd CSBY/WL L22 ... 82 F3
WDN WA8 ... 133 M5
WGN WN1 ... 68 E1
Sommer Av WD/CROXPK L12 ... 98 C6 3
Sonning Av LITH L21 ... 83 K4
Sonning Rd ANF/KKDL L4 ... 97 M3
Sorany Cl CSBY/BLUN L23 ... 71 K7 3
Sorbus Cl CHNE CH2 ... 165 L2 4
Sorogold St STHEL WA9 ... 9 L6
Sorrel Cl CL/PREN CH43 ... 110 F8
WARRN/WOL WA2 ... 122 E3
Sougher's La AIMK WN4 ... 79 H7
South Albert Rd AIG/SPK L17 ... 129 K1
Southampton Wy
RUNC WA7 ... 151 G7 3
South Av CHLY/EC PR7 ... 32 F7
PR/KW L34 ... 100 E8
WARRN/WOL WA2 ... 14 F1
WARRS WA4 ... 137 L4
South Bank CL/PREN CH43 ... 127 K2
South Bank Rd ALL/GAR L19 ... 130 D6
EHL/KEN L7 ... 113 M3
Southbank Rd STHP PR8 ... 3 H7
South Bank Ter RUNC WA7 ... 18 F1
South Barcombe Rd
CHLDW L16 ... 115 G6
South Boundary Rd
NWD/KWIPK L33 ... 86 D5
Southbourne Rd WAL/NB CH45 ... 94 F8
Southbrook Rd NTHLY L27 ... 115 L7
South Cantril Av
WD/CROXPK L12 ... 99 H6
South Chester St TOX L8 ... 113 G7
South Cloughton Rd BIRK CH41 .. 10 F6
Southcroft NWD/KWIPK L33 ... 86 A1
Southcroft Rd WAL/NB CH45 ... 94 F8
South Dl WARRW/BUR WA5 ... 120 B8
Southdale Rd RF/TRAN CH42 ... 128 A3
WARR WA1 ... 122 C3
WAV L15 ... 114 B5
Southdean Rd DV/KA/FCH L14 ... 99 K7
Southdene SKEL WN8 ... 53 K3
Southdowns Rd CHLY/EC PR7 ... 32 F8
South Dr GR/UP/WCH CH49 ... 110 C8
HES CH60 ... 141 J6
PEN/TH CH61 ... 125 L8
WAV L15 ... 114 B5
WD/CROXPK L12 ... 98 D8
WGNNW/ST WN6 ... 54 E3 1
Southern Crs TOX L8 ... 113 G8 7
Southern Rd SPK/HALE L24 ... 147 G3 3
STHP PR8 ... 2 E6
Southern's Fold WGNE/HIN WN2 .. 69 J2
Southern's La RNFD/HAY WA11 ... 76 C7
Southern St WARRS WA4 ... 137 L4
WGNW/BIL/O WN5 ... 67 M8 6
Southery Av WGNS/IIMK WN3 ... 78 F2
Southey Cl WDN WA8 ... 16 A3
Southey Gv MGHL L31 ... 72 F7
Southey Rd ECCL WA10 ... 101 L5
Southey St BTL L20 ... 6 E2
WAV L15 ... 114 A6 12
South Ferry Quay
VAUX/LVPD L3 ... 112 F7
Southfield WGNE/HIN WN2 ... 80 D3
Southfield Rd GTS/LS CH66 ... 155 L7 4
WLT/FAZ L9 ... 84 B7
Southfields Av
WARRW/BUR WA5 ... 120 B7 5
South Front RAIN/WH L35 ... 117 G5
Southgate Cl
WD/CROXPK L12 ... 99 G2 12
Southgate Rd CLB/OSW/ST L13 .. 114 D2
Southgates CHLY/EC PR7 ... 42 F2
South Gv CALD/MH L18 ... 130 E4
TOX L8 ... 129 J1
South Hey LEIGH WN7 ... 81 L8
South Hey Rd PEN/TH CH61 ... 140 F1
South Highville Rd CHLDW L16 .. 114 F7
South Hill Rd CL/PREN CH43 ... 10 E9
FROD/HEL WA6 ... 166 E2
TOX L8 ... 129 H2
South Hunter St CLVPS L1 ... 13 L9 1
South John St CLVPS L1 ... 12 F7
STHEL WA9 ... 9 L5
Southlands Av
WARRW/BUR WA5 ... 136 B2 1
WGNNW/ST WN6 ... 56 A5
Southlands Ms RUNC WA7 ... 18 F7
South La WDN WA8 ... 119 G8
South Manor Wy WLTN L25 ... 131 L4
South Meade MGHL L31 ... 72 D4
Southmead Gdns ALL/GAR L19 .. 131 G6
Southmead Rd ALL/GAR L19 ... 131 G6
South Mossley Hill Rd
ALL/GAR L19 ... 130 C4
Southney Cl KKBY L32 ... 85 K3
South Pde KKBY L32 ... 86 A3 4
RUNC WA7 ... 18 A9
SPK/HALE L24 ... 147 G3
WKBY CH48 ... 124 C5
South Park Rd KKBY L32 ... 85 L2
South Parkside Dr
WD/CROXPK L12 ... 98 E6
South Park Wy BTL L20 ... 7 J6
South Pier Rd EP CH65 ... 156 F6
Southport New Rd
CHTN/BK PR9 ... 26 D1
KIRK/FR/WA PR4 ... 28 A1
Southport Old Rd FMBY L37 ... 47 K6
Southport Rd BTL L20 ... 7 M1
CHLY/EC PR7 ... 32 C5
CSBY/BLUN L23 ... 71 J6
FMBY L37 ... 47 J8
LEY/BBR PR5 ... 30 C3
MGHL L31 ... 61 J6
MGHL L31 ... 72 D1 3
ORM L39 ... 49 J7
STHP PR8 ... 36 C3
Southport St STHEL WA9 ... 103 J2
Southport Ter CHLYE PR6 ... 33 G6 11
Southridge Rd PEN/TH CH61 ... 126 C8
South Rd ALL/GAR L19 ... 130 B7
CHLY/EC PR7 ... 43 G4
CSBY/WL L22 ... 82 F5
DV/KA/FCH L14 ... 114 F2
EP CH65 ... 20 D8
RF/TRAN CH42 ... 127 L3
SPK/HALE L24 ... 147 J1
WKBY CH48 ... 124 C4
Southside CHLY/EC PR7 ... 31 L2 3
South Station Rd WLTN L25 ... 115 K8
South St RAIN/WH L35 ... 101 M6
TOX L8 ... 113 J8
WDN WA8 ... 16 E3
South Sudley Rd ALL/GAR L19 ... 130 B4
South Ter CHLYE PR6 ... 31 M1
ORM L39 ... 63 G1
South Vw CSBY/WL L22 ... 83 G5 4
HUY L36 ... 116 D3
PS/BROM CH62 ... 128 F8
South Vls WAL/NB CH45 ... 95 K6
Southward Rd RNFD/HAY WA11 .. 91 J6
South Wy WAV L15 ... 114 D5
Southway RUNC WA7 ... 150 A6
SKEL WN8 ... 65 L4
WDN WA8 ... 133 M5
Southway Av WARRS WA4 ... 137 M6
Southwell Cl GOL/RIS/CU WA3 .. 92 E5 2
Southwick Rd
RF/TRAN CH42 ... 128 A2 3
Southwood Av RUNC WA7 ... 150 E3 2
Southwood Cl KKBY L32 ... 86 C5 3
Southwood Rd AIG/SPK L17 ... 129 K2
Southworth Av
WARRW/BUR WA5 ... 121 H5
Southworth La
WARRN/WOL WA2 ... 105 M6
Southworth Rd NEWLW WA12 ... 105 H1
Sovereign Cl GOL/RIS/CU WA3 ... 93 G6 2
RUNC WA7 ... 150 F6 9
Sovereign Ct
GOL/RIS/CU WA3 ... 122 E1 5
Sovereign Rd NG/CROX L11 ... 98 E2
WGN WN1 ... 5 G5
Sovereign Wy NG/CROX L11 ... 98 E2
Spa La BRSC L40 ... 64 D1
Spark La BRSC L40 ... 28 D7
RUNC WA7 ... 150 B4
Sparks La PEN/TH CH61 ... 126 D7
Sparrow Hall Cl WLT/FAZ L9 ... 98 B1 1
Sparrow Hall Rd WLT/FAZ L9 ... 98 B1
Sparrowhawk Cl HLWD L26 ... 132 A4 5
RUNC WA7 ... 150 C6
Sparrow Hl SKEL WN8 ... 54 C3
Spawell Cl GOL/RIS/CU WA3 ... 93 G4
Speakmana Dr WGNNW/ST WN6 .. 54 E7
Speakman Av NEWLW WA12 ... 91 K8
Speakman Rd ECCL WA10 ... 88 F7
Speakman St RUNC WA7 ... 18 F2
Speedwell Cl
GOL/RIS/CU WA3 ... 93 G5 10
HES CH60 ... 141 L5 2
Speedwell Dr HES CH60 ... 141 L5
Speedwell Rd BIRK CH41 ... 111 H6
Speke Bvd SPK/HALE L24 ... 131 K8

Speke Church Rd
SPK/HALE L24 146 D2
Speke Hall Av SPK/HALE L24 146 D1
Speke Hall Rd SPK/HALE L24 131 K8
WLTN L25 131 K7
Spekeland Rd EHL/KEN L7 113 L5
Speke Rd ALL/GAR L19 130 F8
HLWD L26 132 D7
SPK/HALE L24 131 G8
WDN WA8 133 K7
WLTN L25 131 K4
Speke Town La SPK/HALE L24 146 D1
Spelding Dr WGNNW/ST WN6 67 M2
Spellow La ANF/KKDL L4 97 H5
Spence Av BTL L20 83 M8
Spencer Av MOR/LEA CH46 110 C4
Spencer Cl HUY L36 116 B5 6
WDN WA8 16 A2 1
Spencer Gdns STHEL WA9 102 F5 2
Spencer Pl BTL L20 83 M6 1
Spencer Rd WGN WN1 68 D2
Spencer Rd West
WGNNW/ST WN6 68 C2
Spencer's La MGHL L31 85 H2
ORM L39 48 D2
SKEL WN8 65 K5
WGNW/BIL/O WN5 66 F6
Spencer St BTL L20 6 E2 2
NPK/KEN L6 13 M2
Spendmore La CHLY/EC PR7 42 F5
Spennymoor Ct RUNC WA7 150 A6 3
Spenser Av RF/TRAN CH42 128 B4
Spenser Rd NSTN CH64 153 G4 1
Spey Cl WGNNW/ST WN6 55 M4
Spicer Gv KKBY L32 86 A3 5
Spice St WLT/FAZ L9 84 D8
Spilsby Sq WGNS/IIMK WN3 79 J3
Spindle Cl NPK/KEN L6 13 M1
Spindle Hillock AIMK WN4 90 F1
Spindlewood Rd
WGNS/IIMK WN3 5 K8
Spindus Rd SPK/HALE L24 146 C2
Spinnaker Cl RUNC WA7 150 F7
Spinney Av WDN WA8 133 J4
Spinney Cl NWD/KWIPK L33 86 E5
ORM L39 62 F2
STHEL WA9 118 E1 18
Spinney Crs CSBY/BLUN L23 70 D7
Spinney Dr GTS/LS CH66 162 F3
Spinney Gn ECCL WA10 101 J2
Spinney Rd NWD/KWIPK L33 86 E5
The Spinney BEB CH63 143 K2
CHLYE PR6 32 E2 1
FMBY L37 47 J8 1
HES CH60 141 L8
NSTN CH64 152 F5
PR/KW L34 100 E6
RNFD/HAY WA11 76 B6
STBRV L28 99 J6
WGNW/BIL/O WN5 68 A8
WKBY CH48 124 F3
Spinney Vw NWD/KWIPK L33 86 F5
Spion Kop AIMK WN4 91 J2
Spiredale Brow
WGNNW/ST WN6 56 B3 1
Spital Heyes BEB CH63 143 K2
Spital Rd BEB CH63 143 K2
PS/BROM CH62 143 M3
Spitfire Rd ALL/GAR L19 131 H7
Spofforth Rd WAV L15 113 M5
Spooner Av LITH L21 83 L6
Sportsman St LEIGH WN7 81 M8
Sprainger St VAUX/LVPD L3 12 D2
Sprakeling Pl BTL L20 84 A6 3
Spray St ECCL WA10 8 D3
Spreyton Cl NG/CROX L11 98 E3 5
Sprig Cl WLT/FAZ L9 84 F5
Spring Av GTS/LS CH66 155 L7
Springbank Cl RUNC WA7 149 K7
Spring Bank Rd ANF/KKDL L4 97 K8 7
Springbourne FROD/HEL WA6 160 F7
WGNNW/ST WN6 68 B3 4
Springbourne Rd
AIG/SPK L17 129 K3 2
Springbrook Cl ECCL WA10 101 J1 1
Spring Cl NWD/KWIPK L33 74 C8 1
STHP PR8 2 E8
Springcroft NSTN CH64 152 E4
Springdale Cl
WD/CROXPK L12 98 E6 1
Spring Fld RNFD/HAY WA11 76 A3
Springfield VAUX/LVPD L3 13 J4 1
Springfield Av FROD/HEL WA6 166 D2
GOL/RIS/CU WA3 92 B5 3
LITH L21 83 L5
WARR WA1 122 B5
WARRS WA4 138 D2
WKBY CH48 125 G2
Springfield Cl BRSC L40 51 M3
FMBY L37 58 E3 4
GR/UP/WCH CH49 126 E3 3
Springfield La ECCL WA10 88 C8
Springfield Pk
RNFD/HAY WA11 90 E6 3
Springfield Rd CHLY/EC PR7 32 E5 9
CHLY/EC PR7 43 G5
CHLYE PR6 44 C5
ECCL WA10 101 L5
ORM L39 62 B8
WDN WA8 133 J5
WGNE/HIN WN2 69 K7
WGNNW/ST WN6 68 B3
Springfield Rd North
CHLY/EC PR7 43 G5 2
Springfield Sq ANF/KKDL L4 97 H5 6
Springfield St WARR WA1 14 D6
WGN WN1 68 E3
Springfield Wy WD/CROXPK L12 99 G5
Spring Gdns GTS/LS CH66 155 L7
MGHL L31 73 G5
WGN WN1 4 D4
Spring Gv WD/CROXPK L12 98 E7
WGN WN1 5 H5
Springhill Av PS/BROM CH62 143 M7
Spring La GOL/RIS/CU WA3 106 D7
Springmeadow Rd WLTN L25 115 J8
Springmount
GOL/RIS/CU WA3 93 G6 3
Springmount Dr SKEL WN8 40 E8 1
Springpool STHEL WA9 102 F6 13
WGNS/IIMK WN3 78 D3
Spring Rd WGNW/BIL/O WN5 67 H5
Springs Cl BTL L20 7 J3 1
Springs Rd CHLYE PR6 32 F3
Spring St RF/TRAN CH42 128 B2
WDN WA8 16 D7
WGN WN1 5 H5
WGNE/HIN WN2 80 A1
Spring V WAL/NB CH45 95 G6
Springville Rd WLT/FAZ L9 84 E6 2
Springwell Rd BTL L20 83 M7
Springwood Av ALL/GAR L19 130 F5
WLTN L25 131 H6
Springwood Dr BRSC L40 28 C8
CHLYE PR6 33 G8
Springwood Gv KKBY L32 86 B6 5
Springwood Wy RF/TRAN CH42 128 C5
Sprodley Dr WGNNW/ST WN6 54 D3 1
Spruce Cl GOL/RIS/CU WA3 93 H6
RF/TRAN CH42 11 G9
WARR WA1 123 G6
Spruce Gv STBRV L28 99 K6
Spruce Rd WGNNW/ST WN6 68 A2
Spruce Wy FMBY L37 58 E2
Sprucewood Cl NPK/KEN L6 97 K8 8
Spunhill Av GTS/LS CH66 162 E2
Spur Cl NG/CROX L11 98 E2
Spurgeon Cl EV L5 97 H8 5
Spurling Rd WARRW/BUR WA5 104 B7
Spurrier's La MGHL L31 73 M5
Spurstow Cl CL/PREN CH43 127 H2 6
The Spur CSBY/BLUN L23 82 F2 3
Spymers Cft FMBY L37 47 J7
Square House La CHTN/BK PR9 23 K6
Square La BRSC L40 52 A2
The Square NSTN CH64 152 D4
Squires Av WDN WA8 16 C3
Squires Cl RNFD/HAY WA11 90 D7 1
Squire St EHL/KEN L7 113 J4
Squirrel Gn FMBY L37 46 E8
Stable Cl GR/UP/WCH CH49 125 L1
The Stackfield WKBY CH48 125 G2
Stadium Rd PS/BROM CH62 144 A2
Stadium Wy WGNW/BIL/O WN5 68 A4
Stafford Cl HUY L36 116 C1
Stafford Moreton Wy
MGHL L31 72 E4 3
MGHL L31 72 F4 1
Stafford Rd ECCL WA10 8 A9
STHP PR8 35 J4
WARRS WA4 137 L3
Stafford St SKEL WN8 64 F4 6
VAUX/LVPD L3 13 K5
WGNE/HIN WN2 69 L8 4
Stainburn Av NG/CROX L11 98 B2
Stainburn Cl WGNNW/ST WN6 54 F7
Stainer Cl DV/KA/FCH L14 99 H8
Staines Cl WARRS WA4 138 A8
Stainmore Cl GOL/RIS/CU WA3 107 K7
Stainton Cl HLWD L26 132 A5 4
RNFD/HAY WA11 89 K5
Stairgate WGN WN1 4 F4
Stairhaven Rd ALL/GAR L19 130 D4
The Stakes MOR/LEA CH46 110 A2
Stalbridge Av CALD/MH L18 114 B8
Staley Av CSBY/BLUN L23 83 H2
Staley St BTL L20 83 L7
Stalisfield Av NG/CROX L11 98 C3
Stalisfield Gv NG/CROX L11 98 C3
Stalisfield Pl NG/CROX L11 98 C3 2
Stalmine Rd WLT/FAZ L9 97 J1
Stamfordham Dr ALL/GAR L19 130 E5
Stamfordham Gv ALL/GAR L19 130 F6
Stamfordham Pl
ALL/GAR L19 130 F6 1
Stamford Rd STHP PR8 35 K2
Stamford St EHL/KEN L7 113 L3
EP CH65 156 C8
Stanbury Av BEB CH63 128 C7
Stancliffe Gv WGNE/HIN WN2 57 L7
Standale Rd WAV L15 114 B5 4
Standard Pl RF/TRAN CH42 128 B2 12
Standard Rd NG/CROX L11 98 E1
Standen Cl ECCL WA10 8 D4
Stand Farm Rd
WD/CROXPK L12 99 H2 6
Standhouse La ORM L39 62 D3 2
Standish Av WGNW/BIL/O WN5 78 A8
Standish Dr RNFD/HAY WA11 76 C6
Standishgate WGN WN1 4 F3
Standish St CHLY/EC PR7 32 E6
ECCL WA10 9 J3
VAUX/LVPD L3 13 G5 3
Standish Wood La
WGNNW/ST WN6 56 A6
Stand Park Av NTHTN L30 84 B3 1
Stand Park Cl NTHTN L30 84 B3 2
Stand Park Rd CHLDW L16 114 F7
Stand Pkwy NTHTN L30 84 A3
Standring Gdn ECCL WA10 101 K5
Stanedge Gv WGNS/IIMK WN3 79 K3
Stanfield Av EV L5 97 H8
Stanfield Dr BEB CH63 143 H2 4
Stanford Av WAL/NB CH45 95 K6 9
Stanford Crs WLTN L25 131 M5
Stangate MGHL L31 72 D3
Stanhope Dr HUY L36 115 L2
PS/BROM CH62 143 M4 3
Stanhope St ECCL WA10 8 F1
LEIGH WN7 81 M7 8
TOX L8 112 F7
Stanier Wy EHL/KEN L7 113 L4
Staniforth Pl CHLDW L16 114 F4
Stanlawe Rd FMBY L37 47 G7
Stanlaw Rd EP CH65 20 D6
Stanley Av BEB CH63 127 L5
RNFD/HAY WA11 76 A6
STHP PR8 35 H3
WAL/NB CH45 94 F7
WARRS WA4 138 B3
WARRW/BUR WA5 119 M6
Stanley Bank Rd
RNFD/HAY WA11 90 C6
Stanley Cl ANF/KKDL L4 96 F6 6
WAL/EG CH44 112 A3 18
WDN WA8 134 E3 2
Stanley Ct BRSC L40 39 G8
RF/TRAN CH42 128 B2 13
Stanley Crs PR/KW L34 100 E7
Stanley Dr LEIGH WN7 81 M5
Stanley Gdns WLT/FAZ L9 84 B8
Stanley La PS/BROM CH62 144 B8
WGNE/HIN WN2 57 L6
Stanley Pk LITH L21 83 K4
Stanley Park Av North
ANF/KKDL L4 97 K4
Stanley Park Av South
ANF/KKDL L4 97 K5
Stanley Pl CHLY/EC PR7 32 E5 10
WARRS WA4 138 B3 1
Stanley Rd BIRK CH41 111 H4
BTL L20 7 G1
CSBY/WL L22 83 G5
EP CH65 156 D6
FMBY L37 47 G7
HOY CH47 108 C7
HUY L36 116 A3
LITH L21 83 K7
MGHL L31 72 E7
RF/TRAN CH42 128 C5
SKEL WN8 66 C6
WGNE/HIN WN2 57 L7
WGNE/HIN WN2 80 C2
Stanley St ALL/GAR L19 145 L1
CHTN/BK PR9 3 G3
CLVP L2 12 F7
CLVPS L1 12 F6 8
EHL/KEN L7 114 A2
NEWLW WA12 104 C2 8
RUNC WA7 19 J2
WAL/EG CH44 112 A3
WARR WA1 14 E7
WGNW/BIL/O WN5 68 B7 11
Stanley Wy SKEL WN8 65 G2
Stanlowe Vw ALL/GAR L19 130 B7
Stanmoor Dr WGNE/HIN WN2 57 L8
Stanmore Pk
GR/UP/WCH CH49 125 K2
Stanmore Rd WAV L15 114 D7 4
Stannanought Rd SKEL WN8 65 M2
Stanner Cl WARRW/BUR WA5 120 F3 5
Stanney Cl PS/BROM CH62 155 G2
Stanney La EP CH65 20 B7
EP CH65 20 D9 2
Stanney Mill La CHNE CH2 164 B4
Stanney Mill Rd EP CH65 164 B3
Stanney Woods Av EP CH65 163 L4
Stannyfield Cl CSBY/BLUN L23 71 K7 4
Stanny Field Dr CSBY/BLUN L23 71 K7
Stansfield Av MGHL L31 73 H4
WARR WA1 122 B7 2
Stanstead Av
WARRW/BUR WA5 136 B2 2
Stanstead Cl WGNE/HIN WN2 69 H3
Stansted Rd CHLY/EC PR7 32 C6
Stanton Av LITH L21 83 J4
Stanton Cl NTHTN L30 71 M8
RNFD/HAY WA11 90 E7 5
WGNS/IIMK WN3 79 K2 2
Stanton Ct NSTN CH64 153 H5 1
Stanton Crs KKBY L32 85 L3
Stanton Rd BEB CH63 143 G2
CALD/MH L18 114 B8 11
WARRS WA4 138 F2
Stanwood Cl ECCL WA10 101 H2
Stanwood Gdns RAIN/WH L35 117 G2
Stapehill Cl CLB/OSW/ST L13 114 D3
Stapeley Gdns HLWD L26 132 C7 3
Staplands Rd DV/KA/FCH L14 114 F3
Stapleford Rd WLTN L25 115 L7
Staplehurst Cl
WD/CROXPK L12 99 G2 13
WGNE/HIN WN2 81 L3
Stapleton Av
GR/UP/WCH CH49 125 M1
RAIN/WH L35 117 L1
SPK/HALE L24 146 F2
WARRN/WOL WA2 121 M5
Stapleton Cl RAIN/WH L35 101 L8 2
WLTN L25 115 K6
Stapleton Rd FMBY L37 58 F5
RAIN/WH L35 101 K8
Stapleton St WGNE/HIN WN2 80 C3
Stapley Cl RUNC WA7 18 E5
Starbeck Dr GTS/LS CH66 155 K7
Starkey Gv WARRS WA4 138 B1 6
Star La LYMM WA13 139 L1
Starling Cl RUNC WA7 150 F6
Starling Gv WD/CROXPK L12 99 H4
Star St TOX L8 113 G7 5
Startham Av WGNW/BIL/O WN5 89 M2
Starworth Dr PS/BROM CH62 128 E6
Statham Av LYMM WA13 139 L2
WARRN/WOL WA2 121 L3
Statham Cl LYMM WA13 139 M2
Statham Dr LYMM WA13 139 M2
Statham La LYMM WA13 123 K8
Statham Rd CL/PREN CH43 110 E5
SKEL WN8 64 F2
Statham Wy ORM L39 63 G1
Station Ap BRSC L40 39 G8 2
HOY CH47 109 G5
MOR/LEA CH46 110 A3
ORM L39 51 H8 4
Station Av FROD/HEL WA6 166 D1
GTS/LS CH66 155 L6
WGNE/HIN WN2 80 F4
WGNW/BIL/O WN5 66 F8
Station Cl NSTN CH64 153 H6 1
Station Gn GTS/LS CH66 155 L6
Station Ms AIMK WN4 90 F2 3
Station Rd AIMK WN4 90 E2
BEB CH63 127 J8
BIRK CH41 111 H4
BRSC L40 39 M1
CHLY/EC PR7 43 H4
CHLY/EC PR7 44 B7
CHNE CH2 158 C8
CHTN/BK PR9 23 H8
EP CH65 20 D3
GTS/LS CH66 155 L7
HES CH60 141 H7
HOY CH47 108 D7
HUY L36 115 L3
LEY/BBR PR5 29 K2
MGHL L31 61 J7
MGHL L31 73 G5
MGHL L31 85 K2
NSTN CH64 152 E5
NSTN CH64 153 G6
ORM L39 49 H7
ORM L39 51 H7
PEN/TH CH61 127 G8
PR/KW L34 100 F7
RAIN/WH L35 117 L2
RNFD/HAY WA11 90 E7
RUNC WA7 18 F3
SKEL WN8 53 L3
STHEL WA9 103 G6
STHP PR8 34 E8
WAL/EG CH44 111 J1
WARRS WA4 138 A3
WARRW/BUR WA5 120 B8
WARRW/BUR WA5 135 M2
WLTN L25 115 K8
Station Rd North
WARRN/WOL WA2 122 C3
Station Rd South
WARRN/WOL WA2 122 C4
Station St RAIN/WH L35 117 L2 6
Statton Rd CLB/OSW/ST L13 114 D4
Staveley Av BRSC L40 52 A1 5
Staveley Rd ALL/GAR L19 130 D5 2
SKEL WN8 65 G2
STHP PR8 47 M1
Stavert Cl NG/CROX L11 98 D2
Staverton Rd KKBY L32 85 L4 4
Stavordale Rd MOR/LEA CH46 110 C5
Steble St TOX L8 113 H8
Steel Av WAL/NB CH45 95 L7
Steel Ct EV L5 96 E8
Steeley La CHLYE PR6 32 F6
Steel St WARR WA1 15 K1
Steeplechase Cl WLT/FAZ L9 84 E5 1
Steeple Ct NSTN CH64 153 G6
The Steeple WKBY CH48 124 F7
Steeple Vw NWD/KWIPK L33 74 A8
Steers Cft STBRV L28 99 H5
Stein Av GOL/RIS/CU WA3 93 G5
Steinberg Ct VAUX/LVPD L3 12 E1
Stenhills Crs RUNC WA7 19 K4
Stephens La CLVP L2 12 F6 9
Stephenson Rd
CLB/OSW/ST L13 114 C3 3
NEWLW WA12 104 E3
Stephenson St CHLYE PR6 33 G6 12
WGNE/HIN WN2 80 D5 6
Stephenson Wy FMBY L37 59 L2
WAV L15 114 A4
Stephens Ter GTS/LS CH66 155 K7
Stephen St WARR WA1 15 K3
WGNE/HIN WN2 80 C3 9
Stephen Wy RAIN/WH L35 101 K8 2
Stepney Gv ANF/KKDL L4 97 J4
Sterling Wy EV L5 96 F7
Sterndale Av WGNNW/ST WN6 56 A3
Sterrix Av LITH L21 83 L3
Sterrix Gn LITH L21 83 L3
Sterrix La LITH L21 83 L3
Stetchworth Rd WARRS WA4 137 K4
Stevenage Cl STHEL WA9 102 B6
Stevenson Cl WGNS/IIMK WN3 68 C8
Stevenson Crs ECCL WA10 8 B4
Stevenson Dr BEB CH63 143 H2
Stevenson St WAV L15 114 B5
Stevens Rd HES CH60 141 L6
Stevens St STHEL WA9 101 M5
Steventon RUNC WA7 151 G1
Steward Ct RAIN/WH L35 101 H8 1
Steward's Av WDN WA8 16 A3
Stewart Av BTL L20 7 L3
Stewart Cl PEN/TH CH61 141 H2 3
Stewart Rd WGNS/IIMK WN3 79 J2
Stewerton Cl
GOL/RIS/CU WA3 92 B3 5
Stile Hey CSBY/BLUN L23 71 K8
Stiles Rd NWD/KWIPK L33 74 B7
The Stiles ORM L39 51 G8
Stillington Rd TOX L8 129 J1
Stirling Av CSBY/BLUN L23 83 G2 1
WGNE/HIN WN2 69 J5
Stirling Cl CHLYE PR6 33 G6 13
WARR WA1 123 G6 6
Stirling Crs STHEL WA9 102 D7
Stirling Dr AIMK WN4 90 F1
Stirling Rd SPK/HALE L24 146 D2
WGNE/HIN WN2 81 H1
Stirling St WAL/EG CH44 111 K3
WGN WN1 68 D3
Stirrup Cl WARRN/WOL WA2 122 C2
Stockbridge La HUY L36 99 L7
Stockbridge Pl EV L5 97 J8 9
Stockbridge St EV L5 97 J8
Stockdale Cl VAUX/LVPD L3 12 F4 3
Stockham Cl RUNC WA7 150 C5
Stockham La RUNC WA7 150 E8
Stockley Crs ORM L39 64 A7
Stockmoor Rd NG/CROX L11 98 B2
Stockpit Rd NWD/KWIPK L33 86 F3
Stockport Rd WARRS WA4 138 F2
Stocks Av STHEL WA9 103 G2
Stocks La CHLY/EC PR7 42 A2
WARRW/BUR WA5 119 M8
Stockswell Rd RAIN/WH L35 133 H1
Stockton Gv RAIN/WH L35 101 M7
Stockton La WARRS WA4 138 A4
Stockton Wood Rd
SPK/HALE L24 146 E2
Stockville Rd CALD/MH L18 131 G1
Stockwell Cl WGNS/IIMK WN3 78 F2
Stoddart Rd ANF/KKDL L4 97 J3 6
Stoke Cl PS/BROM CH62 155 G2
Stoke Gdns EP CH65 20 D7
Stokesay CL/PREN CH43 110 F7
Stokesley Av KKBY L32 85 L3 4
Stokes St GOL/RIS/CU WA3 107 G8
Stoke St BIRK CH41 10 E2 1
Stonebank Dr NSTN CH64 153 J7
Stonebarn Dr MGHL L31 72 E2
Stone Barn La RUNC WA7 150 B7
Stonebridge La AIN/FAZ L10 85 J7
NG/CROX L11 85 K8
Stoneby Dr WAL/NB CH45 95 J6
Stonechat Cl
GOL/RIS/CU WA3 93 G5 11
NTHLY L27 132 A1 3
RUNC WA7 150 A8 4
Stonecroop CALD/MH L18 115 G8
Stonecrop Cl GOL/RIS/CU WA3 122 E1
RUNC WA7 161 H1 12
Stonecross Dr RAIN/WH L35 117 M4
Stone Cross La North
GOL/RIS/CU WA3 92 E6 2
Stone Cross La South
GOL/RIS/CU WA3 92 E7
Stonedale Crs NG/CROX L11 98 D1
Stonefield Rd DV/KA/FCH L14 115 H1
Stonegate Dr TOX L8 129 H1
Stonegate Fold CHLYE PR6 44 D4
Stone Hall La SKEL WN8 66 B1
Stone Hvn WGNS/IIMK WN3 78 F3 4
Stonehaven Cl CHLDW L16 115 H5
Stonehaven Dr
WARRN/WOL WA2 122 C2
Stone Hay RAIN/WH L35 116 F4
Stonehey Dr WKBY CH48 124 E4
Stonehey Rd KKBY L32 86 A5
Stonehill Av ANF/KKDL L4 97 K7 4
BEB CH63 128 C7
Stonehills La RUNC WA7 19 M4
Stonehill St ANF/KKDL L4 97 K7
Stonehouse Ms CALD/MH L18 130 F2
Stonehouse Rd WAL/EG CH44 95 G8
Stonelea RUNC WA7 150 D3
Stoneleigh Cl STHP PR8 47 L1
Stoneleigh Gdns WARRS WA4 138 F4
Stoneleigh Gv
RF/TRAN CH42 128 B5 1
Stone Pit Cl GOL/RIS/CU WA3 93 G4
Stone Pit La GOL/RIS/CU WA3 106 B3
Stoneridge Ct CL/PREN CH43 110 E5 7
Stone Sq BTL L20 84 A8
Stone St VAUX/LVPD L3 12 D1
Stoneville Rd CLB/OSW/ST L13 114 C1
Stoney Brow SKEL WN8 66 D3
Stoneycroft WD/CROXPK L12 114 D1
Stoneycroft Cl CLB/OSW/ST L13 98 C8
HOR/BR BL6 45 M8 1
Stoneycroft Crs
CLB/OSW/ST L13 98 C8
Stoneygate La WGNNW/ST WN6 54 D3
Stoney Hey Rd WAL/NB CH45 95 J6
Stoney Holt RUNC WA7 150 E5 3
Stoneyhurst Av AIN/FAZ L10 84 E2 3
Stoney La CHLY/EC PR7 57 G1
RAIN/WH L35 117 H1
Stonham Cl
GR/UP/WCH CH49 110 A8 9
Stonor Rd CHLY/EC PR7 44 B6
Stonyfield NTHTN L30 72 A8
Stonyhurst CHLY/EC PR7 43 L1
Stonyhurst Av WGNS/IIMK WN3 5 H8
Stonyhurst Cl
RNFD/HAY WA11 89 K6 10
Stonyhurst Rd WLTN L25 131 K4
Stony La SKEL WN8 54 A1
Stopford St TOX L8 129 H1
WGNE/HIN WN2 5 M5
Stopforth St WGNNW/ST WN6 4 A2
Stopgate La NWD/KWIPK L33 74 C7
WLT/FAZ L9 97 M1
Store St BTL L20 7 K8
Storeton Cl CL/PREN CH43 127 J2
Storeton La PEN/TH CH61 141 L1
Storeton Rd RF/TRAN CH42 127 L4
Stormont Rd ALL/GAR L19 130 D6
Storrington Av NG/CROX L11 98 C2
Storrington Heys NG/CROX L11 98 D2
Storrsdale Rd CALD/MH L18 130 D3
Stour Av RAIN/WH L35 117 L2
Stourcliffe Rd WAL/EG CH44 111 J2
Stour Ct EP CH65 20 B1
Stourport Cl
GR/UP/WCH CH49 125 L1 8
Stourton Rd KKBY L32 86 A5
STHP PR8 47 L1
Stourton St WAL/EG CH44 111 L3 2
Stourvale Rd HLWD L26 132 B6 2
Stout St LEIGH WN7 81 L8
Stowe Av AIN/FAZ L10 85 G3
Stowe Cl WLTN L25 131 K6
Stowell St EHL/KEN L7 13 L9
Stowford Cl NG/CROX L11 98 E3
Strada Wy VAUX/LVPD L3 13 L4
Stradbroke Cl GOL/RIS/CU WA3 93 J6
Strafford Dr BTL L20 7 L3
Straight Length
FROD/HEL WA6 160 A6
Straight Up La CHTN/BK PR9 25 L5
Straker Av EP CH65 156 B7
Strand Av AIMK WN4 91 K1
Strand Rd BTL L20 7 H3
HOY CH47 108 D6
Strand St CLVPS L1 12 E8
The Strand AIMK WN4 91 K1
VAUX/LVPD L3 12 D7
Strange Rd AIMK WN4 90 F2
Strange St LEIGH WN7 93 K1
Stranraer Rd WGNW/BIL/O WN5 67 L4
Stratford Cl STHP PR8 34 C7
Stratford Rd ALL/GAR L19 130 B5
CHLYE PR6 32 F5
NSTN CH64 152 F7
Stratford St WGNNW/ST WN6 4 A1
Strathallan Cl HES CH60 141 G3
Strathcona Rd WAL/NB CH45 95 K7
WAV L15 114 A6
Strathearn Rd HES CH60 141 H7
Strathlorne Cl
RF/TRAN CH42 128 B2 14
Strathmore Av AIMK WN4 79 J8
Strathmore Dr CSBY/BLUN L23 83 G2
Strathmore Gv CHLY/EC PR7 32 D6 4
STHEL WA9 102 E7
Strathmore Rd NPK/KEN L6 113 L1
Stratton Cl RUNC WA7 150 D7
WLTN L25 131 G3 1
Stratton Dr WGNE/HIN WN2 80 B4
Stratton Pk WDN WA8 118 B8
Stratton Rd KKBY L32 85 L4

WARRW/BUR WA5 ... 120 D8
Strauss Cl TOX L8 ... 113 K7 5
Strawberry Cl GOL/RIS/CU WA3 .. 122 E1
Strawberry Dr EP CH65 ... 163 J5
Strawberry La CH/BCN CH1 ... 162 E8
Strawberry Rd NG/CROX L11 ... 98 A3
Streatham Av CALD/MH L18 ... 114 B8
Street Hey La NSTN CH64 ... 154 D3
Stretford Cl NWD/KWIPK L33 ... 74 A8
Stretton Av GOL/RIS/CU WA3 ... 93 G6 4
STHEL WA9 ... 103 H2
WAL/EG CH44 ... 111 J1 2
WGNW/BIL/O WN5 ... 78 A8
Stretton Cl CL/PREN CH43 ... 127 G2
PS/BROM CH62 ... 155 G2 2
WD/CROXPK L12 ... 99 J2 1
WGNNW/ST WN6 ... 56 A5 4
Stretton Dr CHTN/BK PR9 ... 25 H5
Stretton Wy RAIN/WH L35 ... 116 D5
Strickland St ECCL WA10 ... 9 J2
Strines Cl WGNE/HIN WN2 ... 69 M7
The Strine BRSC L40 ... 28 C4
Stringer Crs WARRS WA4 ... 15 M7
Stringhey Rd WAL/EG CH44 ... 95 L8
Stroma Rd CALD/MH L18 ... 130 D4
Stromness Cl
WARRN/WOL WA2 ... 122 D2 1
Stroud Cl GR/UP/WCH CH49 ... 125 L2
WGNE/HIN WN2 ... 69 H3
Stuart Av MOR/LEA CH46 ... 110 B4
WGNE/HIN WN2 ... 81 K2
WLTN L25 ... 131 L6
Stuart Cl MOR/LEA CH46 ... 110 C5
Stuart Crs WGNW/BIL/O WN5 ... 77 M8
Stuart Dr DV/KA/FCH L14 ... 115 G2
WARRS WA4 ... 138 B3
Stuart Gv BTL L20 ... 7 K8
Stuart Rd ANF/KKDL L4 ... 7 M6
BTL L20 ... 7 M5
CSBY/WL L22 ... 83 G3
ECCL WA10 ... 88 E7
MGHL L31 ... 85 K2
RF/TRAN CH42 ... 127 M2
RUNC WA7 ... 150 D1
Stuart Rd North BTL L20 ... 7 M4
Stub La BRSC L40 ... 51 J3
Studfold CHLY/EC PR7 ... 32 D3
Studholme St BTL L20 ... 96 E6
Studland Rd WLT/FAZ L9 ... 98 A1
Studley Rd WAL/NB CH45 ... 95 G7
Stump La CHLYE PR6 ... 32 F5
Sturdee Rd CLB/OSW/ST L13 ... 114 D4
Sturgess Cl ORM L39 ... 51 H6
Sturgess St NEWLW WA12 ... 104 B2
Sturton Av WGNS/IIMK WN3 ... 79 G2
Suburban Rd NPK/KEN L6 ... 97 L7
Sudbrook Cl
GOL/RIS/CU WA3 ... 93 G5 12
Sudbury Cl WGNS/IIMK WN3 ... 79 K3
WLTN L25 ... 131 M3
Sudbury Rd CSBY/WL L22 ... 82 D3
Sudbury Wy SPK/HALE L24 ... 146 D1 3
Sudell Av MGHL L31 ... 73 H3
Sudell La MGHL L31 ... 61 M7
Sudley Gra AIG/SPK L17 ... 130 A4
Sudworth Rd WAL/NB CH45 ... 95 J6
Suez St NEWLW WA12 ... 104 C2
WARR WA1 ... 14 D6
Suffield Rd ANF/KKDL L4 ... 96 F5
Suffolk Av EP CH65 ... 156 B8
Suffolk Cl WARR WA1 ... 122 F7
WGN WN1 ... 56 D5 1
Suffolk Gv LEIGH WN7 ... 81 L8
Suffolk Pl WDN WA8 ... 133 L6
Suffolk Rd STHP PR8 ... 35 J5
Suffolk St BTL L20 ... 7 J2
CLVPS L1 ... 13 H9
CLVPS L1 ... 112 F5
RUNC WA7 ... 18 E2
Suffton Pk KKBY L32 ... 85 L4
Sugar La FROD/HEL WA6 ... 167 G8
PR/KW L34 ... 99 M2
Sugar Stubbs La CHTN/BK PR9 ... 26 E1
Sugnall St EHL/KEN L7 ... 13 L9 2
Sulby Av CLB/OSW/ST L13 ... 98 A8 4
WARRS WA4 ... 137 K2
Sulby Cl STHP PR8 ... 35 H2
Sulgrave Cl CHLDW L16 ... 114 E4
Sullington Dr NTHLY L27 ... 116 A7
Sullivan Av GR/UP/WCH CH49 ... 126 B1
Sullivan Wy WGN WN1 ... 5 H2
Sumley Cl RNFD/HAY WA11 ... 9 M1
RNFD/HAY WA11 ... 89 M8 3
Summerfield
PS/BROM CH62 ... 143 M3 1
Summerfield Av ECCL WA10 ... 101 H2
WARRW/BUR WA5 ... 121 H3
Summerfields CHLY/EC PR7 ... 43 H6 1
Summerhill Dr MGHL L31 ... 73 H6
Summer La RUNC WA7 ... 150 B4
WARRS WA4 ... 151 K7
Summers Av BTL L20 ... 7 L2
Summer Seat BTL L20 ... 6 D5
VAUX/LVPD L3 ... 12 F2
Summers Rd VAUX/LVPD L3 ... 112 F8
Summer St SKEL WN8 ... 65 H1
Summertrees Av
GR/UP/WCH CH49 ... 125 M1
Summertrees Cl
GR/UP/WCH CH49 ... 125 M1
Summertrees Rd GTS/LS CH66 ... 163 G3
Summerville Gdns WARRS WA4 .. 138 B4
Summerwood PEN/TH CH61 .. 125 M6 3
Summerwood La ORM L39 ... 49 L4
The Summit WAL/EG CH44 ... 95 L8
Summit Wy WLTN L25 ... 131 H2 1
Sumner Av ORM L39 ... 61 H1
Sumner Cl EV L5 ... 96 E8 4
RAIN/WH L35 ... 117 M4
Sumner Gv NWD/KWIPK L33 ... 74 B8
Sumner Rd CL/PREN CH43 ... 111 H5
FMBY L37 ... 59 H2
Sumner's La BRSC L40 ... 29 J6
Sumner St RNFD/HAY WA11 ... 90 C7
WGNE/HIN WN2 ... 57 M8 5
Sunbeam Rd CLB/OSW/ST L13 ... 114 C2
Sunbeam St NEWLW WA12 ... 104 E2 3
Sunbourne Rd AIG/SPK L17 ... 129 K3 3
Sunbury Dr STHP PR8 ... 47 K1
Sunbury Gdns WARRS WA4 ... 138 A6
Sunbury Rd ANF/KKDL L4 ... 97 K6
WAL/EG CH44 ... 111 L2
Sunbury St ECCL WA10 ... 101 L5 4
Suncroft Cl WARR WA1 ... 123 G6
Suncroft Rd HES CH60 ... 141 L6
Sundale Av RAIN/WH L35 ... 101 H8
Sunderland Pl
WGNW/BIL/O WN5 ... 67 M4 1
Sundew Cl BTL L20 ... 84 B6
Sundridge St TOX L8 ... 129 J1 21
Sunfield Cl GTS/LS CH66 ... 162 F2 3
Sunfield Rd MOR/LEA CH46 ... 110 B3
Sunlight St NPK/KEN L6 ... 97 L8
Sunloch Cl WLT/FAZ L9 ... 84 F5 5
Sunningdale Av WDN WA8 ... 133 K4
Sunningdale Cl HUY L36 ... 115 L4 3
WARRW/BUR WA5 ... 104 B7
Sunningdale Dr BEB CH63 ... 143 K7
CSBY/BLUN L23 ... 70 E7
PEN/TH CH61 ... 126 C8 4
Sunningdale Gdns FMBY L37 ... 59 G2
Sunningdale Rd WAL/NB CH45 ... 95 H5
WAV L15 ... 114 B5
Sunny Bank BEB CH63 ... 127 M7
GR/UP/WCH CH49 ... 110 B7
Sunnybank Av
CL/PREN CH43 ... 126 F1 9
Sunnybank Cl NEWLW WA12 ... 104 E1 7
Sunny Bank Rd CHLDW L16 ... 114 F6
Sunny Brow CHLY/EC PR7 ... 43 J3
Sunnydale RAIN/WH L35 ... 117 M2
Sunny Dr WGNW/BIL/O WN5 ... 67 H7
Sunnyfields ORM L39 ... 51 J8
WGNS/IIMK WN3 ... 78 E3
Sunnygate Rd ALL/GAR L19 ... 130 D5 3
Sunnymede Dr MGHL L31 ... 72 F2
Sunny Rd CHTN/BK PR9 ... 25 J3
Sunnyside ORM L39 ... 62 E6
STHP PR8 ... 35 H2
TOX L8 ... 113 J8
WARRW/BUR WA5 ... 120 A7 8
Sunnyside La RUNC WA7 ... 151 G1
Sunnyside Rd AIMK WN4 ... 79 H7
CSBY/WL L22 ... 82 E2
Sunsdale Rd CALD/MH L18 ... 114 C8 11
Surby Cl CHLDW L16 ... 115 G5 5
Surrey Av GR/UP/WCH CH49 ... 110 A8
Surrey Dr WKBY CH48 ... 124 E5
Surrey St BTL L20 ... 7 J2
CLVPS L1 ... 112 F5 13
RUNC WA7 ... 19 G4
WAL/EG CH44 ... 111 J2
WARRS WA4 ... 15 J9
Susan Dr WARRW/BUR WA5 ... 119 M8
Susan Gv MOR/LEA CH46 ... 109 M5
Susan St WDN WA8 ... 134 E3 5
Sussex Cl BTL L20 ... 7 J2
PEN/TH CH61 ... 141 G1
WGN WN1 ... 56 D4
Sussex Gv STHEL WA9 ... 9 M7
Sussex Rd CHTN/BK PR9 ... 3 K4
MGHL L31 ... 72 F6
STHP PR8 ... 25 G7
WKBY CH48 ... 124 E2
Sussex St BTL L20 ... 7 K3
CSBY/WL L22 ... 82 E3 10
WDN WA8 ... 17 J1 2
Sutch La BRSC L40 ... 52 D1
Sutcliffe St CHLY/EC PR7 ... 32 F6 9
NPK/KEN L6 ... 113 K2 12
Sutherland Dr PS/BROM CH62 ... 154 F1
Sutherland Rd PR/KW L34 ... 101 G7
WGNS/IIMK WN3 ... 79 J2
Sutherland St WGNE/HIN WN2 .. 69 L8 5
WGNW/BIL/O WN5 ... 68 B7 12
Sutton Av GOL/RIS/CU WA3 ... 107 G1
NSTN CH64 ... 153 G7
Sutton Cswy FROD/HEL WA6 ... 161 G3
Sutton Cl PS/BROM CH62 ... 155 G2
Sutton Gv CHLYE PR6 ... 33 H1
Sutton Hall Dr GTS/LS CH66 ... 155 J7
Sutton Hall Gdns GTS/LS CH66 ... 155 J7
Sutton Heath Rd STHEL WA9 ... 102 A7
Sutton La CHLYE PR6 ... 44 D5
Sutton Moss Rd STHEL WA9 ... 103 H5
Sutton Oak Dr STHEL WA9 ... 102 E4
Sutton Park Dr STHEL WA9 ... 102 E6
Sutton Rd FMBY L37 ... 59 G4
STHEL WA9 ... 9 L9
WAL/NB CH45 ... 95 K6
Sutton's La FMBY L37 ... 60 A2
WDN WA8 ... 16 E6
Sutton St CLB/OSW/ST L13 ... 98 A8
RUNC WA7 ... 19 K4
WARR WA1 ... 15 G7
Sutton Wy EP CH65 ... 156 C8
GTS/LS CH66 ... 163 G1
Sutton Wood Rd SPK/HALE L24 .. 146 E2
Swainson Rd AIN/FAZ L10 ... 85 G6
Swale Av RAIN/WH L35 ... 117 L2
Swaledale Av RAIN/WH L35 ... 117 M2
Swaledale Cl PS/BROM CH62 .. 144 A8 1
WARRW/BUR WA5 ... 120 B6
Swalegate MGHL L31 ... 72 E3
Swale Rd EP CH65 ... 156 C6
Swallow Cl GOL/RIS/CU WA3 ... 123 H1 5
NTHLY L27 ... 116 B8 4
NWD/KWIPK L33 ... 74 A6
WD/CROXPK L12 ... 99 H2
Swallow Flds WLT/FAZ L9 ... 98 B1
Swallowhurst Crs NG/CROX L11 .. 98 C3
Swanage Cl WARRS WA4 ... 138 A3
Swan Av STHEL WA9 ... 103 J3
Swan Cl GTS/LS CH66 ... 162 E3
Swan Crs WAV L15 ... 114 D5
Swan Delph ORM L39 ... 62 E3
Swan Gdns STHEL WA9 ... 102 A7
Swan Hey MGHL L31 ... 73 G6 1
Swan La ORM L39 ... 62 A7
WGNE/HIN WN2 ... 81 K1
Swan Meadow Rd
WGNS/IIMK WN3 ... 4 C6
Swann St WGNS/IIMK WN3 ... 4 C5
Swanpool La ORM L39 ... 62 E3
Swan Rd NEWLW WA12 ... 104 A1
Swanside Av DV/KA/FCH L14 ... 115 G2
Swanside Rd DV/KA/FCH L14 ... 115 G2
Swanston Av ANF/KKDL L4 ... 97 J4 6
Swan St CLB/OSW/ST L13 ... 114 B2
Swan Wk MGHL L31 ... 73 G6
Sweden Gv CSBY/WL L22 ... 82 F4 7
Sweetfield Gdns GTS/LS CH66 ... 155 M6
Sweetfield Rd GTS/LS CH66 ... 155 M6
Sweeting St CLVP L2 ... 12 F7 1
Swift Cl WARRN/WOL WA2 ... 122 A2 6
Swift Gv WD/CROXPK L12 ... 99 H1
Swift's Cl NTHTN L30 ... 83 M1
Swift's La NTHTN L30 ... 83 M1
NTHTN L30 ... 84 A2
Swift St ECCL WA10 ... 9 H2
Swinbrook Gn NG/CROX L11 ... 98 B3
Swinburne Cl CHLDW L16 ... 115 H5 4
Swinburne Rd ECCL WA10 ... 8 A2
Swinburn Gv
WGNW/BIL/O WN5 ... 77 M4 2
Swindale Av
WARRN/WOL WA2 ... 121 K2 6
Swindale Cl TOX L8 ... 113 K6 5
Swinden Cl RUNC WA7 ... 150 F3 5
Swinderby Dr KKBY L32 ... 85 K2
Swindon Cl EV L5 ... 96 F6 7
GR/UP/WCH CH49 ... 125 L1 9
Swindon St EV L5 ... 96 F6
Swinford Av WDN WA8 ... 135 G3 4
Swinley La WGN WN1 ... 68 E3
Swinley St WGN WN1 ... 68 E3
Swinside WGN WN1 ... 5 M2
Swireford Rd FROD/HEL WA6 ... 166 D3
Swisspine Gdns RAIN/WH L35 ... 101 L6
Swiss Rd NPK/KEN L6 ... 113 L2
Swords Cross Cl CHLY/EC PR7 ... 32 C8 7
Sword Wk NG/CROX L11 ... 98 E2
Swynnerton Wy WDN WA8 ... 118 D8 3
Sybil Rd ANF/KKDL L4 ... 97 J6
Sycamore Av CHLY/EC PR7 ... 31 M2
CSBY/BLUN L23 ... 71 H7
GOL/RIS/CU WA3 ... 92 C4
GR/UP/WCH CH49 ... 109 M7
HLWD L26 ... 132 A7
NEWLW WA12 ... 104 E2 4
RNFD/HAY WA11 ... 90 C8 3
WDN WA8 ... 134 D3
WGNE/HIN WN2 ... 81 H2
WGNNW/ST WN6 ... 68 B2 5
Sycamore Cl BRSC L40 ... 40 E3 2
ECCL WA10 ... 101 K1
GR/UP/WCH CH49 ... 109 M6
WLT/FAZ L9 ... 97 L2
Sycamore Ct CHLY/EC PR7 ... 32 D8 7
Sycamore Dr GTS/LS CH66 ... 163 H4
LYMM WA13 ... 139 M1
RUNC WA7 ... 161 J1
SKEL WN8 ... 65 G3 2
WGNS/IIMK WN3 ... 78 D3
Sycamore Gdns ECCL WA10 ... 89 G7 1
Sycamore Gv FMBY L37 ... 58 E4
Sycamore La
WARRW/BUR WA5 ... 120 D7 5
Sycamore Pk CALD/MH L18 ... 130 F3 2
Sycamore Ri GR/UP/WCH CH49 .. 125 L3
Sycamore Rd CHLYE PR6 ... 32 F3
CSBY/WL L22 ... 83 G3
HUY L36 ... 116 A5
RF/TRAN CH42 ... 11 G9
RUNC WA7 ... 19 M7
Syd Brook La BRSC L40 ... 30 A7
Sydenham Av AIG/SPK L17 ... 113 L8
Syderstone Cl WGNE/HIN WN2 ... 81 G1
Sydney Av LEIGH WN7 ... 93 M3
Sydney St RUNC WA7 ... 148 F6
WGNE/HIN WN2 ... 80 C2
WLT/FAZ L9 ... 84 C7
Syers Ct WARR WA1 ... 15 L1
Sykes Crs WGNS/IIMK WN3 ... 78 E4
Sylvan Ct WLTN L25 ... 131 J4
Sylvandale Gv
PS/BROM CH62 ... 143 M3 2
Sylvania Rd ANF/KKDL L4 ... 97 J3 7
Sylvia Cl NG/CROX L11 ... 85 K7
Sylvia Crs WARRN/WOL WA2 ... 121 M4 5
Synge St WARRN/WOL WA2 ... 15 G1
Syren St BTL L20 ... 96 E5
Syresham St WGNE/HIN WN2 ... 80 D3 6
Syston Av RNFD/HAY WA11 ... 89 L7
Sytch Cft NSTN CH64 ... 153 G5

T

Tabby Nook KIRK/FR/WA PR4 ... 27 H4
Tabby's Nook SKEL WN8 ... 53 J4
Taberner Cl WGNNW/ST WN6 ... 56 B4
Taberner St WGNE/HIN WN2 ... 80 D3 7
Tabley Av WDN WA8 ... 133 M3
Tabley Cl CL/PREN CH43 ... 127 H2
Tabley Rd WAV L15 ... 113 M6
Tadgers La FROD/HEL WA6 ... 159 M4
Tadlow Cl FMBY L37 ... 58 E4
Taggart Av CHLDW L16 ... 114 F7
Tagus Cl TOX L8 ... 113 K7
Tagus St TOX L8 ... 113 K7
Tailor's La MGHL L31 ... 73 G5
Talaton Cl CHTN/BK PR9 ... 22 C8
Talbot Av BEB CH63 ... 142 C4
NSTN CH64 ... 153 H7
Talbot Cl ECCL WA10 ... 8 E4
GOL/RIS/CU WA3 ... 123 G2
NSTN CH64 ... 153 H7
Talbot Ct HUY L36 ... 115 M4
Talbot Dr CHLY/EC PR7 ... 31 M3
STHP PR8 ... 3 G5
Talbot Gdns NSTN CH64 ... 153 H7
Talbot Rd CL/PREN CH43 ... 127 J1
FROD/HEL WA6 ... 166 A6
GTS/LS CH66 ... 163 H2
Talbot St AIMK WN4 ... 91 M1 3
CHLYE PR6 ... 33 G4 5
GOL/RIS/CU WA3 ... 92 C5
STHP PR8 ... 2 F6
Talbotville Rd CLB/OSW/ST L13 .. 114 E4
Talgarth Wy WLTN L25 ... 115 J6
Taliesin St EV L5 ... 96 F8
Talisman Cl RUNC WA7 ... 151 G6 3
Talisman Wy BTL L20 ... 6 D2
Talland Cl HLWD L26 ... 132 A4
Tallarn Rd KKBY L32 ... 85 K3
Talman Gv AIMK WN4 ... 91 M2
Talton Rd WAV L15 ... 113 M6
Tamar Cl NPK/KEN L6 ... 113 J1
Tamarisk Gdns RAIN/WH L35 ... 101 L6 4
Tamar Rd RNFD/HAY WA11 ... 90 E7
Tamer Gv LEIGH WN7 ... 81 L5
Tamerton Cl WLTN L25 ... 131 G3
The Tamneys SKEL WN8 ... 65 H4 1
Tamworth Dr WGNE/HIN WN2 ... 69 H3
Tamworth St ECCL WA10 ... 8 C4
TOX L8 ... 113 G8 3
Tanar Cl PS/BROM CH62 ... 143 K2
Tanat Dr CALD/MH L18 ... 130 D1
Tancred Rd ANF/KKDL L4 ... 97 J6
WAL/NB CH45 ... 95 J8
Tanfield Nook SKEL WN8 ... 53 L3
Tanfields SKEL WN8 ... 65 H4
Tan House Cl SKEL WN8 ... 53 L2
Tan House Dr WGNS/IIMK WN3 ... 78 E4
Tan House La SKEL WN8 ... 53 L3
WARRW/BUR WA5 ... 120 C1
WDN WA8 ... 17 H3
WGNS/IIMK WN3 ... 78 E3
Tanhouse Rd CSBY/BLUN L23 ... 71 K8
SKEL WN8 ... 65 M4
Tankersley Gv
WARRW/BUR WA5 ... 120 C8
Tanner's La GOL/RIS/CU WA3 ... 92 D5
WARRN/WOL WA2 ... 14 D4
Tannersmith La CHLY/EC PR7 ... 30 B8
Tannery La NSTN CH64 ... 153 G5
WARRW/BUR WA5 ... 135 L2
Tansley Av CHLY/EC PR7 ... 42 F4
Tansley Cl WKBY CH48 ... 125 G3
Tansley Sq WGNW/BIL/O WN5 .. 67 M8 7
Tanworth Gv HOY CH47 ... 109 K4 5
MOR/LEA CH46 ... 109 K5 9
Tanyard Cl CHLY/EC PR7 ... 42 F4
Tapley Pl CLB/OSW/ST L13 ... 114 B3
Taplow Cl WARRS WA4 ... 138 A7
Taplow St NPK/KEN L6 ... 97 K7
Tarbock Rd HUY L36 ... 115 M4 4
SPK/HALE L24 ... 146 F1
Tarbot Hey MOR/LEA CH46 ... 109 L5
Target Rd HES CH60 ... 140 D5
Tariff St EV L5 ... 96 F8
Tarleswood SKEL WN8 ... 65 H4
Tarleton Cl HLWD L26 ... 132 A5 5
Tarleton Rd CHTN/BK PR9 ... 25 J5
Tarleton St CLVPS L1 ... 13 G7
Tarlscough La BRSC L40 ... 38 E4
Tarlton Cl RAIN/WH L35 ... 101 J8
Tarnbeck RUNC WA7 ... 150 E6
Tarnbeck Dr BRSC L40 ... 40 E2
Tarn Brow ORM L39 ... 62 E2
Tarn Cl AIMK WN4 ... 79 K8
Tarn Ct WARR WA1 ... 123 H6
Tarn Gv RNFD/HAY WA11 ... 89 K5
Tarn Hows Cl CHLY/EC PR7 ... 32 D8 9
Tarnrigg Cl WGNS/IIMK WN3 ... 79 G2
Tarn Rd FMBY L37 ... 58 F2
Tarnside Rd WGNW/BIL/O WN5 ... 67 G7
Tarnway GOL/RIS/CU WA3 ... 93 H6
Tarporley Cl CL/PREN CH43 ... 127 H2
Tarporley Rd GTS/LS CH66 ... 163 G1
Tarran Dr MOR/LEA CH46 ... 109 M3 2
Tarran Rd MOR/LEA CH46 ... 109 M3 3
Tarrant Cl WGNS/IIMK WN3 ... 78 F3 5
Tarran Wy East
MOR/LEA CH46 ... 109 M3
Tarran Wy North
MOR/LEA CH46 ... 109 M3
Tarran Wy South
MOR/LEA CH46 ... 109 M3
Tarran Wy West
MOR/LEA CH46 ... 109 M2
Tarvin Cl CHTN/BK PR9 ... 22 F8
EP CH65 ... 20 D7
GOL/RIS/CU WA3 ... 93 G6
RUNC WA7 ... 149 L7
STHEL WA9 ... 118 D1
Tarvin Rd FROD/HEL WA6 ... 166 F3
PS/BROM CH62 ... 155 H1
Tasker Ter RAIN/WH L35 ... 117 L1
Tasman Cl WARRW/BUR WA5 ... 120 E5
Tasman Gv STHEL WA9 ... 102 A6
Tate Cl WDN WA8 ... 133 M3 5
Tate St ANF/KKDL L4 ... 97 H5
Tatham Gv WGNS/IIMK WN3 ... 78 F4
Tatlock Cl WGNW/BIL/O WN5 ... 78 A8 3
Tatlock St EV L5 ... 12 F1 2
Tattersall Rd LITH L21 ... 83 J6
Tatton Dr AIMK WN4 ... 91 H1
Tatton Rd RF/TRAN CH42 ... 11 G8
WLT/FAZ L9 ... 84 C7
Taunton Av LEIGH WN7 ... 81 M3
STHEL WA9 ... 102 F8
Taunton Dr AIN/FAZ L10 ... 85 G3
Taunton Rd HUY L36 ... 116 D3 1
WAL/NB CH45 ... 95 G7
Taunton St WAV L15 ... 114 A5
Taurus Rd DV/KA/FCH L14 ... 115 J1
Tavener Cl BEB CH63 ... 143 L8
Tavistock Dr STHP PR8 ... 34 D7
Tavistock Rd WAL/NB CH45 ... 95 G7
WARRW/BUR WA5 ... 136 A1
WGNE/HIN WN2 ... 81 J1
Tavlin Av WARRW/BUR WA5 ... 121 H4
Tavy Rd NPK/KEN L6 ... 113 J1
Tawd Rd SKEL WN8 ... 65 L5
Tawd St ANF/KKDL L4 ... 97 G5
Tawny Ct RUNC WA7 ... 150 A6
Taylor Av ORM L39 ... 51 J8
Taylor Cl STHEL WA9 ... 103 G5 2
Taylor Gv WGNE/HIN WN2 ... 81 L2 5
Taylor Rd RNFD/HAY WA11 ... 91 H7
WGNE/HIN WN2 ... 81 L2
Taylors Cl WLT/FAZ L9 ... 97 H2
Taylor's La KIRK/FR/WA PR4 ... 27 M2
WARRW/BUR WA5 ... 135 J3 1
WGNE/HIN WN2 ... 80 B2
Taylors Rw RUNC WA7 ... 19 M4
Taylor St BIRK CH41 ... 11 K3
CHLY/EC PR7 ... 32 D8 9
EV L5 ... 96 F8
LEIGH WN7 ... 81 M5
SKEL WN8 ... 64 E4
STHEL WA9 ... 103 G5
WARRS WA4 ... 137 J4
WDN WA8 ... 17 G1
WGNS/IIMK WN3 ... 4 C4
Teakwood Cl NPK/KEN L6 ... 97 K8 9
Teal Cl ORM L39 ... 62 E3
RNFD/HAY WA11 ... 89 K7
WARRN/WOL WA2 ... 122 A2
WGNS/IIMK WN3 ... 78 D1
Teal Gv GOL/RIS/CU WA3 ... 123 H2
HLWD L26 ... 132 A4
Teals Wy HES CH60 ... 140 F5
Tears La SKEL WN8 ... 53 H5
Teasville Rd CALD/MH L18 ... 131 G1
Tebay Cl MGHL L31 ... 73 H3
Tebay Rd PS/BROM CH62 ... 144 A5
Teck St EHL/KEN L7 ... 113 J3
Tedburn Cl WLTN L25 ... 131 L1 3
Tedbury Cl KKBY L32 ... 86 A6
Tedbury Wk KKBY L32 ... 86 A5 3
Tedder Av CHTN/BK PR9 ... 25 J6
Tedder Sq WDN WA8 ... 133 M5
Teddington Cl WARRS WA4 ... 138 A8
Teehey Cl BEB CH63 ... 127 M7
Teehey Gdns BEB CH63 ... 127 M7
Teehey La BEB CH63 ... 127 M7
Tees Cl ANF/KKDL L4 ... 7 K9
Tees Ct EP CH65 ... 156 C6 1
Teesdale Rd BEB CH63 ... 143 G1
RNFD/HAY WA11 ... 90 E6
Tees St ANF/KKDL L4 ... 7 K9
BIRK CH41 ... 111 H4
Teilo St TOX L8 ... 113 J8
Telary Cl EV L5 ... 96 E8
Telegraph Rd WKBY CH48 ... 125 J7
Telford Cl CL/PREN CH43 ... 10 C9
WDN WA8 ... 133 M1
Telford Crs LEIGH WN7 ... 81 M5
Telford Rd EP CH65 ... 21 G7
Temperance St CHLYE PR6 ... 33 G5 10
Tempest Hey CLVP L2 ... 12 E6 5
Temple Ct CLVP L2 ... 12 F7
GOL/RIS/CU WA3 ... 107 G7
Templegate Cl
WGNNW/ST WN6 ... 56 B3 2
Temple La CLVP L2 ... 12 F6
Templemore Av CALD/MH L18 ... 130 C2
Templemore Rd CL/PREN CH43 .. 127 J1
Temple Rd RF/TRAN CH42 ... 127 L3
Temple St CLVP L2 ... 12 F6 10
Templeton Crs WD/CROXPK L12 .. 98 D4
Templeton Rd WGNE/HIN WN2 ... 80 C4
Temple Wy CHLYE PR6 ... 32 F2
Tenbury Dr AIMK WN4 ... 91 H1
Tenby Av LITH L21 ... 83 J4
Tenby Cl WARRW/BUR WA5 ... 121 H3
Tenby Dr MOR/LEA CH46 ... 110 B6
RUNC WA7 ... 149 M3 3
Tenby St EV L5 ... 97 J7
Tenement St WGNE/HIN WN2 ... 80 D4
Tennis St ECCL WA10 ... 8 B2
Tennis St North ECCL WA10 ... 8 C1
Tennyson Av CHLY/EC PR7 ... 32 E7
LEIGH WN7 ... 81 L5
RF/TRAN CH42 ... 128 B4 6
Tennyson Dr ORM L39 ... 50 F7
WARRN/WOL WA2 ... 121 L3
WGN WN1 ... 68 E2
WGNW/BIL/O WN5 ... 77 M4
Tennyson Rd EP CH65 ... 163 J1
HUY L36 ... 116 C5
WDN WA8 ... 16 C1
Tennyson St BTL L20 ... 6 E1
STHEL WA9 ... 118 C3
Tensing Cl WARRW/BUR WA5 ... 120 D5
Tensing Rd MGHL L31 ... 72 F4
Tenterden St EV L5 ... 13 G1
Tenter Dr WGNNW/ST WN6 ... 56 D6
Terence Av WARR WA1 ... 122 B6
Terence Rd CHLDW L16 ... 114 F7
Terminus Rd HUY L36 ... 99 K8
PS/BROM CH62 ... 143 M2
Tern Cl NWD/KWIPK L33 ... 74 A6
WDN WA8 ... 134 D1 3
Ternhall Rd WLT/FAZ L9 ... 98 B1
Ternhall Wy WLT/FAZ L9 ... 98 B1
Tern Wy MOR/LEA CH46 ... 109 K4
PR/KW L34 ... 101 J6
Terrace Rd WDN WA8 ... 134 C8
Terret Cft STBRV L28 ... 99 K6
Tetbury Cl WGNW/BIL/O WN5 ... 67 M4
Tetbury St BIRK CH41 ... 10 F7
Tetchill Cl GTS/LS CH66 ... 162 F3
RUNC WA7 ... 150 F5
Tetlow St ANF/KKDL L4 ... 97 H5
Tetlow Wy ANF/KKDL L4 ... 97 H5
Teversham SKEL WN8 ... 65 H3
Tewit Hall Cl SPK/HALE L24 ... 146 E2
Tewit Hall Rd SPK/HALE L24 ... 146 E2
Tewkesbury SKEL WN8 ... 65 G3 3
Tewkesbury Cl GTS/LS CH66 ... 163 G6
WD/CROXPK L12 ... 99 H1 3
WLTN L25 ... 131 L3
Tewkesbury Rd
GOL/RIS/CU WA3 ... 92 D5 3
Teynham Av PR/KW L34 ... 99 M1
Teynham Crs NG/CROX L11 ... 98 B3
Thackeray Gdns NTHTN L30 ... 83 M5 1
Thackeray Pl
WGNS/IIMK WN3 ... 68 C8 7
Thackeray Sq TOX L8 ... 113 H7 3
Thackeray St TOX L8 ... 113 H7
Thackray Rd ECCL WA10 ... 101 L5
Thamesdale EP CH65 ... 20 A7
Thames Dr WGNW/BIL/O WN5 ... 67 H6
Thames Gdns EP CH65 ... 163 J2
Thames Rd GOL/RIS/CU WA3 ... 107 H3
STHEL WA9 ... 102 E7 6
Thames Side EP CH65 ... 20 A8
Thames St TOX L8 ... 113 K7
Thanet SKEL WN8 ... 65 H3
Thatto Heath Rd ECCL WA10 ... 101 M5
Thealby Cl SKEL WN8 ... 65 G3
Thelwall Cl LEIGH WN7 ... 93 K1 2
Thelwall La WARRS WA4 ... 138 C2
Thelwall New Rd WARRS WA4 ... 138 D2

Thelwall Rd GTS/LS CH66 163 G1
Thermal Rd PS/BROM CH62 143 M1
Thetford Cl WGNE/HIN WN2 81 G1
Thetford Rd WARRW/BUR WA5 120 A7
Thewlis St WARRW/BUR WA5 121 G8
Thicknesse Av WGNNW/ST WN6 68 B2
Thickwood Moss La
RNFD/HAY WA11 76 B8
Thingwall Av DV/KA/FCH L14 114 F3
Thingwall Dr PEN/TH CH61 126 C7
Thingwall Hall Dr
DV/KA/FCH L14 114 F3
Thingwall La DV/KA/FCH L14 114 F2
Thingwall Rd PEN/TH CH61 125 M8
WAV L15 114 D5
Thingwall Rd East
PEN/TH CH61 126 C7
Third Av CL/PREN CH43 110 D7
CSBY/BLUN L23 82 F1 6
RUNC WA7 150 B6
WGNNW/ST WN6 68 C3
WLT/FAZ L9 85 G6 4
Thirlmere Av AIMK WN4 91 L1 6
CL/PREN CH43 110 E7
FMBY L37 59 J3 5
LITH L21 83 M5 2
RNFD/HAY WA11 89 K5
SKEL WN8 66 D6 1
WARRN/WOL WA2 121 L2 4
WGNE/HIN WN2 69 K6
WGNE/HIN WN2 80 D5 7
WGNNW/ST WN6 56 C6
WGNW/BIL/O WN5 67 H6 2
Thirlmere Cl CHLYE PR6 44 D5
FROD/HEL WA6 160 F5
MGHL L31 73 G3 1
Thirlmere Dr LITH L21 83 M5
STHP PR8 47 K2
WAL/NB CH45 95 K8
Thirlmere Gn EV L5 97 J8 10
Thirlmere Rd CHLY/EC PR7 32 C7
EP CH65 163 L3
EV L5 97 J8
GOL/RIS/CU WA3 92 E4 7
HOR/BR BL6 57 L2
HTWN L38 70 C1
NSTN CH64 153 G7
WGNW/BIL/O WN5 67 K6
Thirlmere Wk
NWD/KWIPK L33 85 M1 3
Thirlstane St AIG/SPK L17 129 K2
Thirsk SKEL WN8 65 G3 4
Thirsk Cl RUNC WA7 149 L7 2
Thistle Cl CHLYE PR6 33 G5
Thistledown Cl AIG/SPK L17 129 J2 6
WGNNW/ST WN6 68 C3
Thistleton Av BIRK CH41 111 H5
Thistleton Ms CHTN/BK PR9 3 K2
Thistlewood Rd EHL/KEN L7 114 A3
Thistley Hey Rd KKBY L32 86 B3
Thomas Cl ALL/GAR L19 130 E8 6
EP CH65 163 K3 2
Thomas Ct RUNC WA7 150 B6 1
Thomas Dr DV/KA/FCH L14 114 E3
RAIN/WH L35 116 E1
Thomas La DV/KA/FCH L14 114 F2
Thomasons Bridge La
WARRS WA4 137 G7
Thomas St BIRK CH41 11 K7
GOL/RIS/CU WA3 92 C5 7
RUNC WA7 19 J2
WDN WA8 16 C6
WGNE/HIN WN2 81 K2
Thomaston St EV L5 97 G7 5
Thompson Av GOL/RIS/CU WA3 107 G2
ORM L39 51 J8
Thompson St AIMK WN4 91 M1
BIRK CH41 11 J9
ECCL WA10 101 M4 5
GOL/RIS/CU WA3 107 G8
LEIGH WN7 81 K8
WGN WN1 5 J1
Thomson Rd LITH L21 83 J6 6
Thomson St NPK/KEN L6 113 K1
Thorburn Cl RF/TRAN CH42 128 D5 5
Thorburn Crs
PS/BROM CH62 128 D5 6
Thorburn Rd PS/BROM CH62 128 D5
WGNW/BIL/O WN5 67 L7
Thorburn St EHL/KEN L7 113 K4
Thoresby Cl WGNS/IIMK WN3 79 G2
Thoriby Rd GOL/RIS/CU WA3 107 H2
Thorley Cl WAV L15 114 C4 1
Thornaby Gv RAIN/WH L35 101 M7
Thornbeck Av HTWN L38 70 B2 2
Thornbeck Ct
WD/CROXPK L12 99 H2 7
Thornbridge Av BRSC L40 52 A2 4
LITH L21 83 M5
Thornbury SKEL WN8 65 H3
Thornbury Av
GOL/RIS/CU WA3 93 G6 5
Thornbury Rd ANF/KKDL L4 97 L6
Thornbush Cl GOL/RIS/CU WA3 93 G4
Thorncliffe Rd WAL/EG CH44 111 J2
Thorn Cl WARRW/BUR WA5 136 B2
Thorncroft Dr PEN/TH CH61 141 K1
Thorndale Rd CSBY/WL L22 82 F3
Thorndyke Cl RAIN/WH L35 118 A4
Thorne Dr GTS/LS CH66 162 D1
Thornes Rd NPK/KEN L6 113 K2 13
Thorness Cl
GR/UP/WCH CH49 125 L3 6
Thorneycroft St BIRK CH41 10 A2
Thornfield Cl GOL/RIS/CU WA3 92 E5 5
Thornfield Hey BEB CH63 143 J3
Thornfield Rd CSBY/BLUN L23 71 J7
WLT/FAZ L9 84 B8 2
Thornham Av STHEL WA9 102 E5
Thornham Cl
GR/UP/WCH CH49 110 C6
Thornhead La WD/CROXPK L12 98 F7
Thornhill ORM L39 62 D5 1
Thornhill Rd AIMK WN4 90 E1
CHLYE PR6 32 F3
WAV L15 114 C6 5
Thornholme Crs NG/CROX L11 98 C4
Thornhurst KKBY L32 86 A6 4
Thornleigh Av PS/BROM CH62 155 H2
Thornleigh Dr GTS/LS CH66 156 A7
Thornley Rd LYMM WA13 139 L2
MOR/LEA CH46 109 K6
Thorn Rd ECCL WA10 101 L2
RUNC WA7 19 M9
WARR WA1 122 C5
Thorns Dr GR/UP/WCH CH49 125 L3
The Thorns MGHL L31 72 D3 3
Thorn St WGNE/HIN WN2 80 F1 12
Thornton WDN WA8 134 A5 2
Thornton Av BEB CH63 127 M5
BTL L20 83 M7
Thornton Cl AIMK WN4 91 H1
BRSC L40 39 L1 1
Thornton Common Rd
BEB CH63 142 D6
Thornton Crs HES CH60 141 K7
Thorntondale Dr
WARRW/BUR WA5 120 B6
Thornton Green La CHNE CH2 165 G4
Thornton Gv BEB CH63 127 L5
Thornton Rd BEB CH63 127 M5
BTL L20 83 L8 2
CHLDW L16 115 G4
CHTN/BK PR9 25 H6
EP CH65 21 G7
WAL/NB CH45 95 J7 5
WARRW/BUR WA5 136 D1
Thornton St BIRK CH41 10 A2
LITH L21 83 K7
Thorntree Cl AIG/SPK L17 129 J2 7
Thorntree Gn WARRS WA4 138 D8
Thornvale WGNE/HIN WN2 80 E6
Thornwood SKEL WN8 65 H3
Thornwood Cl NPK/KEN L6 97 K8 10
Thornwythe Gv GTS/LS CH66 163 G1
Thornycroft Rd WAV L15 113 M7
Thoroughgood Cl BRSC L40 51 M3 2
Thorpe SKEL WN8 65 H3
Thorpe Bank RF/TRAN CH42 128 B5
Thorstone Dr PEN/TH CH61 125 L6
Thorsway RF/TRAN CH42 128 B3
WKBY CH48 124 F5
Three Butt La WD/CROXPK L12 98 B7
Three Oaks Cl BRSC L40 52 D3
Three Pools CHTN/BK PR9 25 L2
Three Sisters Rd AIMK WN4 79 K7
Three Tuns La FMBY L37 59 H2
Threlfall CHLY/EC PR7 32 B3
Threlfalls La CHTN/BK PR9 25 H3
Threlfall St TOX L8 129 J1
Thresher Av
GR/UP/WCH CH49 125 L1 10
The Threshers NTHTN L30 84 D1 5
Throne Rd NG/CROX L11 98 E2
Throstle Nest Av
WGNNW/ST WN6 4 A1
Thurcroft Dr SKEL WN8 65 G3
Thurlby Cl AIMK WN4 91 M1 5
Thurlow GOL/RIS/CU WA3 93 G6 6
Thurne Wy WLTN L25 115 J7
Thurnham St NPK/KEN L6 97 L8
Thursby Cl KKBY L32 86 B5 7
STHP PR8 47 K2 2
Thursby Crs KKBY L32 86 B5
Thursby Rd PS/BROM CH62 144 A3
Thursford Gv HOR/BR BL6 57 M4
Thurstaston Rd HES CH60 141 G4
PEN/TH CH61 125 K7
Thurston SKEL WN8 65 G3
Thurston Av WGNS/IIMK WN3 79 K2
Thurston Cl WARRW/BUR WA5 120 F7
Thurston Rd ANF/KKDL L4 97 K7
Thynne St WARR WA1 14 C7
Tibbs Cross La WDN WA8 118 F4
Tichbourne Wy NPK/KEN L6 13 M4
Tickle Av STHEL WA9 102 F2
Tidal La WARRN/WOL WA2 122 B5
Tideswell Av WGNW/BIL/O WN5 67 J4
Tide Wy WAL/NB CH45 95 G5
Tilbrook Dr STHEL WA9 102 F7
Tilbury Gv WGNNW/ST WN6 54 F6
Tilbury Pl RUNC WA7 151 G7
Tilcroft SKEL WN8 65 G3
Tildsley Crs RUNC WA7 149 H7
Tilley St WARR WA1 15 G4
Tillotson Cl TOX L8 113 G8
Tilman Cl WARRW/BUR WA5 120 D5 5
Tilney St WLT/FAZ L9 84 C7 5
Tilstock Av PS/BROM CH62 128 D5
Tilstock Crs CL/PREN CH43 127 H4
Tilston Av WARRS WA4 138 C1
Tilston Cl WLT/FAZ L9 97 M2
Tilston Rd KKBY L32 85 L3
WAL/NB CH45 95 J7 6
WLT/FAZ L9 97 M1
Timberscombe Gdns
WARR WA1 123 G7
Time Pk RAIN/WH L35 101 H8
Timmis Cl WARRN/WOL WA2 122 C2 4
Timmis Crs WDN WA8 16 C2
Timms Cl FMBY L37 47 H8
Timms La FMBY L37 47 H8
Timon Av BTL L20 7 L2
Timor Av STHEL WA9 102 A5 1
Timperley Av WARRS WA4 138 C1
Timperley St WDN WA8 16 E4 3
Timpron St EHL/KEN L7 113 L5
Timway Dr WD/CROXPK L12 99 G5
Tinas Wy GR/UP/WCH CH49 110 C8 5
Tincklers La BRSC L40 30 B7
Tinkersfield LEIGH WN7 81 M6
Tinsley Av STHP PR8 36 A2
Tinsley's La STHP PR8 36 B4
Tinsley St ANF/KKDL L4 97 J6 1
WARRS WA4 138 B2
Tintagel SKEL WN8 64 F3
Tintagel Cl RUNC WA7 150 E7 5
Tintagel Rd NG/CROX L11 85 M8
WGNE/HIN WN2 81 J1
Tintern Av AIMK WN4 91 M2
CHLY/EC PR7 32 F8
Tintern Cl WARRW/BUR WA5 121 G3 3
Tintern Dr FMBY L37 59 K3 4
MOR/LEA CH46 110 A5
Tinwald Pl WGN WN1 5 L2
Tipping St WGNS/IIMK WN3 4 C8
Tiptree Cl WD/CROXPK L12 99 H1
Titchfield St EV L5 12 F1
Tithebarn Cl HES CH60 141 H6 3
Tithebarn Dr NSTN CH64 152 D3
Tithebarn Gv WAV L15 114 C6
Tithe Barn La CHLYE PR6 33 J1
KKBY L32 85 M4
Tithebarn La MGHL L31 73 J8
Tithebarn Rd AIMK WN4 90 E3
CSBY/BLUN L23 71 H8
PR/KW L34 99 M1
STHP PR8 3 M5
Tithebarn St CLVP L2 12 E6
SKEL WN8 66 D6 2
The Tithings RUNC WA7 150 A4
Tiverton Av LEIGH WN7 81 M3
SKEL WN8 65 G3
WAL/EG CH44 111 K1 6
Tiverton Cl HUY L36 116 D3 2
WDN WA8 133 L2
Tiverton Rd HLWD L26 132 A7 2
Tiverton Sq
WARRW/BUR WA5 136 A1 3
Tiverton St WAV L15 114 A5
Tobermory Cl RNFD/HAY WA11 90 C8
Tobin Cl EV L5 12 F1
Tobin St WAL/EG CH44 111 M1
Tobruk Rd HUY L36 115 M1
Toddington La WGNE/HIN WN2 57 K5
Todd Rd STHEL WA9 9 J6
Todd's La CHTN/BK PR9 23 J7
Toft Cl WDN WA8 16 A2
Toft St EHL/KEN L7 113 L3
Toftwood Av RAIN/WH L35 118 A4 5
Toll Bar Rd WARRN/WOL WA2 121 J2
Tollemache Rd BIRK CH41 111 G5
CL/PREN CH43 111 H6
Tollemache St WAL/NB CH45 95 L5
Tollerton Rd WD/CROXPK L12 98 B7
Tollgate Rd BRSC L40 51 K2
Tollgreen Cl WGNE/HIN WN2 69 M6
Toll St WGNE/HIN WN2 80 C4
Tolpuddle Rd WLTN L25 131 H2
Tolpuddle Wy ANF/KKDL L4 96 F5 2
Tolver St ECCL WA10 9 H4
Tomlinson Av
WARRN/WOL WA2 121 M5
Tom Mann Cl VAUX/LVPD L3 13 H5
Tonbridge Cl SPK/HALE L24 146 D1
Tonbridge Dr AIN/FAZ L10 84 F2
Tongbarn SKEL WN8 65 G3
Tontine Rd SKEL WN8 66 E7
Toogood La WGNNW/ST WN6 41 M6
Tootell St CHLY/EC PR7 32 D7
Toothill Cl AIMK WN4 79 K8
Tootle La BRSC L40 39 H2
Top Acre Rd SKEL WN8 65 L6
Topaz Cl ANF/KKDL L4 7 M6
Topcliffe Gv WD/CROXPK L12 99 J2
Top Delph ORM L39 51 J7 2
Topgate Cl HES CH60 141 K5
Topping Ct GOL/RIS/CU WA3 122 D1
Top Rd FROD/HEL WA6 160 F8
Topsham Cl WLTN L25 131 L1 1
Torcross Cl CHTN/BK PR9 22 C8
Torcross Wy HLWD L26 132 A5
WLTN L25 131 L1 5
Tordelow Cl NPK/KEN L6 113 J1
Tormore Cl CHLYE PR6 33 J3
Toronto Cl HUY L36 99 M7 2
Toronto St WAL/EG CH44 112 A2 4
Torquay Dr
WGNW/BIL/O WN5 78 A5 1
Torridon Cl WGNNW/ST WN6 56 D6 1
Torridon Gv GTS/LS CH66 163 H2 5
Torrington Dr HLWD L26 132 A7
PEN/TH CH61 126 D7
Torrington Gdns
PEN/TH CH61 126 D6 1
Torrington Rd ALL/GAR L19 130 D6
WAL/EG CH44 111 J1
Torrisholme Rd WLT/FAZ L9 97 M2
Torr St EV L5 97 G7
Torside Cl WGNE/HIN WN2 69 M7
Torus Rd CLB/OSW/ST L13 114 C1
Torver Cl WGNS/IIMK WN3 79 J3
Tor Vw Rd WAV L15 114 C7
Torwood CL/PREN CH43 110 F6
Tothale Turn NTHLY L27 132 B1
Totland Cl WARRW/BUR WA5 119 L6
Totnes Av HLWD L26 132 B4
Totnes Dr CHTN/BK PR9 22 C8
Totnes Rd NG/CROX L11 85 L8
Tourney Gn WARRW/BUR WA5 120 C3
Towcester St LITH L21 83 K7
Tower End FMBY L37 46 E8
Tower Gdns VAUX/LVPD L3 12 D7
Tower Hl ORM L39 51 J8
RF/TRAN CH42 127 M2
Tower Hill Rd SKEL WN8 66 C8
Tower La RUNC WA7 150 E6
Tower Nook SKEL WN8 66 C8
Tower Prom WAL/NB CH45 95 L4
Tower Rd BIRK CH41 11 J2
RF/TRAN CH42 127 M2 3
Tower Rd North HES CH60 141 G3
Tower Rd South HES CH60 141 H4
Towers Av MGHL L31 72 E3
Towers La FROD/HEL WA6 166 D6
Towers Rd CHLDW L16 114 E7
Tower St VAUX/LVPD L3 112 F8
Tower Wy WLTN L25 131 J2
Tower Whf BIRK CH41 11 J2
Towneley Ct WDN WA8 16 C2
Townfield Av AIMK WN4 91 K3
Townfield Cl CL/PREN CH43 127 G2 3
Townfield Gdns BEB CH63 128 B6 1
Townfield La BEB CH63 128 B6
CL/PREN CH43 127 H2
FROD/HEL WA6 160 E6
Townfield Rd RUNC WA7 150 E3 5
WKBY CH48 124 D3
Townfields AIMK WN4 91 J2
Townfield Vw RUNC WA7 150 E3
Towngate CHLY/EC PR7 30 D5
Town Green La ORM L39 62 E5
Town Hl WARR WA1 14 E5
Town La BEB CH63 128 A7
CHLY/EC PR7 41 L4
NSTN CH64 153 H7
SPK/HALE L24 147 M4
STHP PR8 35 M1
Town La (Kew) STHP PR8 36 A2
Townley St CHLYE PR6 32 F6
Town Meadow La
MOR/LEA CH46 109 K5 10
Town Rd LEY/BBR PR5 29 K3
RF/TRAN CH42 127 M2
Town Rw WD/CROXPK L12 98 D6
Townsend Av NG/CROX L11 98 A3
Townsend La CLB/OSW/ST L13 97 M6
NPK/KEN L6 97 L6
Townsend St BIRK CH41 111 G4
EV L5 96 D7
Townsend Vw LITH L21 83 K3 3
NG/CROX L11 98 A2
Townshend Av PEN/TH CH61 125 M8
Town Vw CL/PREN CH43 10 E7
Towson St EV L5 97 H7
Toxteth Gv TOX L8 129 J1
Toxteth St TOX L8 113 H8
Tracks La WGNW/BIL/O WN5 77 M2
Tracy Dr NEWLW WA12 105 G2
Trafalgar Av WAL/EG CH44 95 M8
Trafalgar Dr BEB CH63 143 J1
Trafalgar Rd STHP PR8 35 G2
WAL/EG CH44 95 L8
WGN WN1 4 E1
WGNE/HIN WN2 69 M8 28
Trafalgar St CHLY/EC PR7 32 E4 6
ECCL WA10 8 C3
Trafalgar Wy NPK/KEN L6 13 M4
Trafford Av WARRW/BUR WA5 121 G5
Trafford Crs RUNC WA7 149 L7
Trafford Rd WGNE/HIN WN2 69 L8
Tragan Dr WARRW/BUR WA5 135 M2
Tram St WGNE/HIN WN2 80 C4
Tramway Rd AIG/SPK L17 129 L2
Trans Pennine Trail CHLDW L16 115 H6
CLVPS L1 12 F8
NTHTN L30 72 D7
NTHTN L30 84 D2
TOX L8 113 K8
WARRW/BUR WA5 135 M4
WD/CROXPK L12 114 E1
WDN WA8 134 C8
WLT/FAZ L9 84 D8
Trap Hl FMBY L37 58 E4
Trapwood Cl ECCL WA10 101 K2
Travandon Cl NG/CROX L11 85 K7 4
Travers' Entry STHEL WA9 103 J7
Traverse St STHEL WA9 9 L5
Travis St WDN WA8 16 E3
Treborth St TOX L8 113 J8 5
Trecastell Cl WGN WN1 5 L2
Trecastle Rd NWD/KWIPK L33 86 C1
Tree Bank Cl RUNC WA7 19 G7
Treen Cl CHTN/BK PR9 22 D7
Treesdale Cl STHP PR8 35 H1
Tree Tops NSTN CH64 153 G8
Treetops Cl WARR WA1 122 B6
Treetops Dr BIRK CH41 110 F4
Trefoil Cl GOL/RIS/CU WA3 106 E8
Treforris Rd WAL/NB CH45 95 H6 1
Trefula Pk WD/CROXPK L12 98 C7
Tregaron Gv WGNE/HIN WN2 81 J2 5
Trelawney Cl WLTN L25 115 K7 6
Tremore Cl NG/CROX L11 98 E4 4
Trenance Cl RUNC WA7 150 D8
Trendeal Rd NG/CROX L11 85 M8 5
Trent Av DV/KA/FCH L14 115 H2
MGHL L31 73 H3
Trent Cl BRSC L40 39 H8
RAIN/WH L35 117 K2
STHEL WA9 102 E8
WD/CROXPK L12 98 F2
WDN WA8 134 D1
Trentdale EP CH65 20 B9
Trent Gv LEIGH WN7 93 L1
Trentham Av CALD/MH L18 114 B8 12
Trentham Cl WDN WA8 134 D1 5
Trentham Rd KKBY L32 85 L4
WAL/EG CH44 111 L2 5
Trentham St RUNC WA7 18 E2
Trent Rd AIMK WN4 80 A8
RAIN/WH L35 117 K2
WGNE/HIN WN2 81 L2
WGNW/BIL/O WN5 67 L6
WGNW/BIL/O WN5 89 L1
Trent St EV L5 96 F7 2
Trent Wy HES CH60 141 K7
Trescott Ms WGNNW/ST WN6 56 A5
Tressel Dr STHEL WA9 118 C2
Tressell St WLT/FAZ L9 97 H2 5
Trevelyan Dr WGNW/BIL/O WN5 78 M7
Trevelyan St WLT/FAZ L9 97 H2 6
Treviot Cl NWD/KWIPK L33 73 M7
Trevor Dr CSBY/BLUN L23 83 H2
Trevor Rd BRSC L40 51 M1 6
BRSC L40 52 A1 6
STHP PR8 47 L1
WLT/FAZ L9 84 C7
Trimley Cl
GR/UP/WCH CH49 110 A8 10
Tring Cl GR/UP/WCH CH49 110 C6
Trinity Ct GOL/RIS/CU WA3 107 H8
Trinity Gdns AIMK WN4 91 H1 4
STHP PR8 2 F6
Trinity Gv CSBY/BLUN L23 82 D3 5
Trinity La BIRK CH41 11 J4
Trinity Ms CHTN/BK PR9 3 K3
Trinity Pl BTL L20 7 J5
WDN WA8 16 E5
Trinity Rd BTL L20 7 G6
CHLY/EC PR7 32 D6 5
HOY CH47 108 D6
WAL/EG CH44 95 K8
Trinity St BIRK CH41 10 F4
STHEL WA9 9 L5 1
Trispen Cl HLWD L26 132 A5
Trispen Rd NG/CROX L11 98 F1
Triumph Wy SPK/HALE L24 131 H7
Triam Rd BTL L20 6 E3
Troon Cl BEB CH63 143 L8
RNFD/HAY WA11 90 C8
WD/CROXPK L12 99 G7
Trossach Cl WARRN/WOL WA2 122 A3
Trotwood Cl WLT/FAZ L9 84 F5 6
Troutbeck Av MGHL L31 73 G3
NEWLW WA12 104 A1
WARRW/BUR WA5 14 A1
Troutbeck Cl GR/UP/WCH CH49 126 C3
RUNC WA7 150 C8
Troutbeck Gv RNFD/HAY WA11 89 K3
Troutbeck Ri
WGNW/BIL/O WN5 67 K7 8
Troutbeck Rd AIMK WN4 79 L8 1
CALD/MH L18 114 F8
CHLY/EC PR7 32 D8
Trouville Rd ANF/KKDL L4 97 L6
Trowbridge St VAUX/LVPD L3 13 K7
Trueman Cl CL/PREN CH43 110 E5
Trueman St VAUX/LVPD L3 13 G5
Trumans La GTS/LS CH66 155 L6
Truro Av CHTN/BK PR9 22 D8
NTHTN L30 84 B1
Truro Cl GTS/LS CH66 163 H5 11
RNFD/HAY WA11 89 M6
RUNC WA7 150 E7 6
WARR WA1 122 D5
Truro Rd WAV L15 114 C7
Truscott Rd BRSC L40 51 M1
Tucker's Hill Brow
WGNE/HIN WN2 57 K4
Tudor Av BEB CH63 143 J2
WAL/EG CH44 112 A3 19
Tudor Cl GTS/LS CH66 163 H5
RNFD/HAY WA11 76 A5
WARRS WA4 138 C3
Tudor Gra GR/UP/WCH CH49 125 M2 3
Tudor Gv WGNS/IIMK WN3 79 G3
Tudor Rd CSBY/BLUN L23 82 F2
RF/TRAN CH42 128 A2
RUNC WA7 150 D2
STHP PR8 34 D7
WLTN L25 131 L6
Tudor St NPK/KEN L6 113 K2
Tudor Vw NWD/KWIPK L33 74 A8
Tudorville Rd BEB CH63 128 B8
Tudorway HES CH60 141 K5
Tue La WDN WA8 117 K7
Tuffins Cnr NTHLY L27 115 M8
Tulip Av BIRK CH41 111 H5
Tulip Dr WGNNW/ST WN6 68 B2
Tulip Rd RNFD/HAY WA11 91 H7
WAV L15 114 C6
Tulketh St STHP PR8 3 H4
Tullimore Rd CALD/MH L18 130 C4
Tullis St ECCL WA10 8 D7
Tulloch St NPK/KEN L6 113 K2
Tully Av NEWLW WA12 104 A2
Tumilty Av BTL L20 7 L2
Tunbridge Cl WARRW/BUR WA5 120 C5
Tunley La WGNNW/ST WN6 42 A8
Tunley Moss WGNNW/ST WN6 55 G1
Tunnel Rd BIRK CH41 11 L6
EHL/KEN L7 113 K5
Tunstall Cl
GR/UP/WCH CH49 110 A8 11
Tunstall La WGNW/BIL/O WN5 67 M8
Tunstall St EHL/KEN L7 113 L6
Tunstall's Wy STHEL WA9 118 F1 1
Tupelo Cl WD/CROXPK L12 99 H1
Tupman St TOX L8 113 H8 12
Turflands LEY/BBR PR5 29 K4
Turmar Av PEN/TH CH61 126 D7
Turnacre DV/KA/FCH L14 115 G2
FMBY L37 47 K7
Turnall Rd WDN WA8 133 K6
Turnberry SKEL WN8 64 F3
Turnberry Cl HUY L36 115 L4 7
LYMM WA13 139 L1
MOR/LEA CH46 109 K4 6
WD/CROXPK L12 99 H7 5
Turnberry Wy CHTN/BK PR9 22 F8
Turnbridge Rd MGHL L31 72 E2
Turnbury Cl CHLYE PR6 31 M1
Turnditch Cl WGNNW/ST WN6 68 C1
Turner Av BTL L20 84 A7
WGNE/HIN WN2 81 G4
Turner Cl WDN WA8 133 M2 3
Turner St BIRK CH41 10 F8 3
WGN WN1 5 G3
WGNE/HIN WN2 69 M7 13
Turney Rd WAL/EG CH44 111 J1
Turnill Dr AIMK WN4 91 K3
Turning La STHP PR8 36 C5
Turnpike Rd ORM L39 62 C4
Turnstone Av NEWLW WA12 104 E1
Turnstone Cl WD/CROXPK L12 99 G2
Turnstone Dr HLWD L26 132 A4
Turret Hall Dr
GOL/RIS/CU WA3 93 G5 13
Turret Rd WAL/NB CH45 95 J7
Turriff Dr BEB CH63 154 E1
Turriff Gv WGNE/HIN WN2 69 J4
Turriff Rd DV/KA/FCH L14 115 J1
Turrocks Cl NSTN CH64 153 G8 5
Turrocks Cft NSTN CH64 153 G8
Turton Cl GOL/RIS/CU WA3 106 E8
Turton Dr CHLYE PR6 33 G4 6
Turton St EV L5 96 F7 9
GOL/RIS/CU WA3 92 C5
Tuscan Cl WDN WA8 118 D8
Tuson Dr WDN WA8 134 B1
Tutor Bank NEWLW WA12 104 F2
Tweed Cl NPK/KEN L6 113 L1 5
Tweedsmuir Cl
WARRN/WOL WA2 122 C1 2
Tweed St BIRK CH41 111 J4
Twenty Acre Rd
WARRW/BUR WA5 120 E5
Twickenham Dr HUY L36 115 L4
MOR/LEA CH46 110 C2
Twigden Cl AIN/FAZ L10 85 H5
Twig La HUY L36 115 L1
MGHL L31 72 F4
Twiss Green Dr
GOL/RIS/CU WA3 107 G1
Twiss Green La
GOL/RIS/CU WA3 106 F1
Twist Av GOL/RIS/CU WA3 92 E5
Twistfield Cl STHP PR8 2 D7
Twist La LEIGH WN7 81 M8

Two Acre Gv GTS/LS CH66 ... 163 H4
Two Butt La RAIN/WH L35 ... 101 J8
Twomey Cl EV L5 ... 12 F1 5
Twyford Av LITH L21 ... 83 K4
Twyford Cl MGHL L31 ... 73 G4 2
WDN WA8 ... 134 D1
Twyford La WDN WA8 ... 118 F7
Twyford St NPK/KEN L6 ... 97 K7
Tyberton Pl SPK/HALE L24 ... 131 L7
Tyburn Cl BEB CH63 ... 143 H3 5
Tyburn Rd BEB CH63 ... 143 H3
Tyndall Av CSBY/WL L22 ... 83 H5
Tyne Cl ANF/KKDL L4 ... 97 J6
RAIN/WH L35 ... 101 M7
WARRN/WOL WA2 ... 122 A3 6
Tynemouth Cl EV L5 ... 97 J8
Tynemouth Rd RUNC WA7 ... 150 E7
Tynesdale EP CH65 ... 20 A9
Tyne St BIRK CH41 ... 111 H4
Tynron Gv CL/PREN CH43 ... 126 F1 10
Tynville Rd WLT/FAZ L9 ... 84 E6
Tynwald Cl CLB/OSW/ST L13 ... 114 B1 5
Tynwald Crs WDN WA8 ... 118 B8
Tynwald Dr WARRS WA4 ... 137 L6
Tynwald Hl CLB/OSW/ST L13 ... 114 B1
Tynwald Pl CLB/OSW/ST L13 ... 114 B1 6
Tynwald Rd WKBY CH48 ... 124 C3 4
Tyrer Av WGNS/IIMK WN3 ... 68 B8
Tyrer Rd NEWLW WA12 ... 104 E4
ORM L39 ... 51 H6
Tyrer's Av MGHL L31 ... 61 L8
Tyrers Cl FMBY L37 ... 59 H3
Tyrer St BIRK CH41 ... 111 H4

U

Uldale Cl NG/CROX L11 ... 98 C3
STHP PR8 ... 47 K2
Uldale Wy NG/CROX L11 ... 98 C3
Ullapool Cl GTS/LS CH66 ... 155 H7
Ullet Rd AIG/SPK L17 ... 113 M8
Ullswater Av CL/PREN CH43 ... 110 E7
RNFD/HAY WA11 ... 89 J5
WARRN/WOL WA2 ... 121 L2
WGNW/BIL/O WN5 ... 67 H6
Ullswater Cl NWD/KWIPK L33 ... 85 M1 4
Ullswater Dr WGNE/HIN WN2 ... 69 K6 1
Ullswater Gv RUNC WA7 ... 149 M8
Ullswater Rd CHLY/EC PR7 ... 32 D7
EP CH65 ... 163 L3
GOL/RIS/CU WA3 ... 92 E4
Ullswater St EV L5 ... 97 J7
Ulnes Walton La LEY/BBR PR5 ... 30 B1
Ulster Rd CLB/OSW/ST L13 ... 114 D2
Ultonia St ALL/GAR L19 ... 145 L1 7
Ulverston Av WARRN/WOL WA2 ... 121 K2
Ulverston Cl MGHL L31 ... 73 G3 2
RNFD/HAY WA11 ... 90 C7 9
Ulverston Lawn NTHLY L27 ... 132 B1
Ulverston Rd
WGNS/IIMK WN3 ... 79 H2 2
Umbria St ALL/GAR L19 ... 145 L1 8
Underbridge La WARRS WA4 ... 137 G7
Undercliffe Rd
CLB/OSW/ST L13 ... 114 C1
Underhill Rd ECCL WA10 ... 8 B7
Underley St EHL/KEN L7 ... 113 L6
The Underway RUNC WA7 ... 150 B5
Underwood Dr EP CH65 ... 163 K3
Unicorn Rd NG/CROX L11 ... 98 E1
Unicorn Wy BIRK CH41 ... 11 L8
Union Bank La WDN WA8 ... 118 D4
Union Ct CLVP L2 ... 12 F7
Union St BIRK CH41 ... 128 B2
CHLY/EC PR7 ... 32 E5
CHTN/BK PR9 ... 3 H2
ECCL WA10 ... 9 G2
RUNC WA7 ... 19 K4
VAUX/LVPD L3 ... 12 D6
WAL/EG CH44 ... 111 M1
WARR WA1 ... 14 E6
WGNE/HIN WN2 ... 69 J5
Unit Rd STHP PR8 ... 34 F8
Unity Gv PR/KW L34 ... 86 C8
University Rd BTL L20 ... 7 J5
Unsworth Av GOL/RIS/CU WA3 ... 92 F4
Unsworth Ct
WARRN/WOL WA2 ... 122 B4 5
Upavon Av
GR/UP/WCH CH49 ... 125 K2 5
Upholland Rd
WGNW/BIL/O WN5 ... 77 M1
Upland Dr AIMK WN4 ... 91 M1
Upland Rd ECCL WA10 ... 101 K5
GR/UP/WCH CH49 ... 110 B7
Uplands Cl ECCL WA10 ... 101 K5 1
Uplands Rd PS/BROM CH62 ... 143 L4
Upper Aughton Rd STHP PR8 ... 2 F8
Upper Baker St NPK/KEN L6 ... 113 J2
Upper Beau St VAUX/LVPD L3 ... 13 J2
Upper Beckwith St BIRK CH41 ... 10 C2
Upper Bute St EV L5 ... 13 K2
Upper Dicconson St WGN WN1 ... 4 F2
Upper Duke St CLVPS L1 ... 113 G5
Upper Essex St TOX L8 ... 113 H8
Upper Flaybrick Rd
CL/PREN CH43 ... 111 G6
Upper Frederick St CLVPS L1 ... 112 F5
Upper Hampton St TOX L8 ... 113 H6
Upper Harrington St TOX L8 ... 113 G7 6
Upper Hill St TOX L8 ... 113 G7 7
TOX L8 ... 113 H7 7
Upper Hope Pl TOX L8 ... 13 L9 3
TOX L8 ... 113 H5 22
Upper Huskisson St TOX L8 ... 113 J6
Upper Mann St TOX L8 ... 113 G8
Upper Mersey Rd WDN WA8 ... 16 C9
Upper Mersey St EP CH65 ... 20 D1 2
EP CH65 ... 20 D1 2
Upper Newington CLVPS L1 ... 13 J8
Upper Park St TOX L8 ... 113 H8
Upper Parliament St TOX L8 ... 113 K5 9
Upper Pitt St CLVPS L1 ... 112 F5
Upper Pownall St CLVPS L1 ... 112 F5 16
Upper Raby Rd NSTN CH64 ... 153 J3
Upper Rice La WAL/EG CH44 ... 95 L8
Upper St Stephen St
WGNNW/ST WN6 ... 4 C3
Upper Stanhope St TOX L8 ... 113 G6
Upper Warwick St TOX L8 ... 113 H7
Upper William St VAUX/LVPD L3 .. 12 D1
Uppingham SKEL WN8 ... 64 F4 7
Uppingham Av AIN/FAZ L10 ... 85 G3
Uppingham Rd CLB/OSW/ST L13 .. 98 B8
WAL/EG CH44 ... 95 H8
Upton Av STHP PR8 ... 34 D7
Upton Barn MGHL L31 ... 72 E3
Upton Bridle Pth WDN WA8 ... 134 B1 6
Upton By-Pass
GR/UP/WCH CH49 ... 110 A8
Upton Cl GOL/RIS/CU WA3 ... 92 F5
GR/UP/WCH CH49 ... 110 B8
SPK/HALE L24 ... 147 G2 2
Upton Dr WARRW/BUR WA5 ... 120 B8
Upton Gra WDN WA8 ... 133 M1
Upton Gn SPK/HALE L24 ... 147 G2 3
Upton La WDN WA8 ... 134 B1
Upton Park Dr
GR/UP/WCH CH49 ... 110 C7
Upton Rd CL/PREN CH43 ... 110 E7
GTS/LS CH66 ... 162 F1
Upwood Rd GOL/RIS/CU WA3 ... 92 F6
Ure Ct EP CH65 ... 156 C6 2
Urmson Rd WAL/NB CH45 ... 95 K8
Urmston Av NEWLW WA12 ... 91 K8
Urmston St LEIGH WN7 ... 81 M8 15
Ursula St BTL L20 ... 7 K8
Utkinton Cl CL/PREN CH43 ... 127 H2
Utting Av ANF/KKDL L4 ... 97 K5
Utting Av East NG/CROX L11 ... 98 A4
Uxbridge St EHL/KEN L7 ... 113 K4 9

V

Vahler Ter RUNC WA7 ... 19 L3
Vale Av WARRN/WOL WA2 ... 121 K5
Vale Cl WGNNW/ST WN6 ... 55 G5
WLTN L25 ... 131 H3
Vale Crs STHP PR8 ... 47 L3
Vale Dr WAL/NB CH45 ... 95 L6
Vale Gdns EP CH65 ... 20 A7
FROD/HEL WA6 ... 166 D1
Vale Gv KKBY L32 ... 86 C4 5
Vale La BRSC L40 ... 53 G8
Valencia Gv PR/KW L34 ... 101 J6
Valencia Rd WAV L15 ... 114 C5
Valentia Rd HOY CH47 ... 108 C7
Valentine Gv AIN/FAZ L10 ... 85 G4
Valentine Rd NEWLW WA12 ... 104 B2 2
Vale Owen Rd
WARRN/WOL WA2 ... 121 M4 6
Valerian Rd BIRK CH41 ... 111 H6
Valerie Cl AIN/FAZ L10 ... 85 K7
Vale Rd CSBY/BLUN L23 ... 82 F1
EP CH65 ... 20 A7
WLTN L25 ... 131 H3
Valescourt Rd WD/CROXPK L12 ... 98 E8
The Vale WGNNW/ST WN6 ... 54 F5
Valiant Cl WARRN/WOL WA2 ... 122 B3
WD/CROXPK L12 ... 99 J3
Valiant Rd WGNW/BIL/O WN5 ... 67 M5
Valiant Wy BIRK CH41 ... 11 L9
Valkyrie Rd WAL/NB CH45 ... 95 J8
Vallance Rd ANF/KKDL L4 ... 97 L6
Valleybrook Gv BEB CH63 ... 143 K3
Valley Cl AIN/FAZ L10 ... 85 H4
CSBY/BLUN L23 ... 83 K1
Valley Ct WARRN/WOL WA2 ... 122 B4
Valley Dr GTS/LS CH66 ... 155 M8
Valley Rd AIN/FAZ L10 ... 85 K6
ANF/KKDL L4 ... 97 J7
BIRK CH41 ... 110 F3
KKBY L32 ... 85 M4
PS/BROM CH62 ... 143 M5
WGNW/BIL/O WN5 ... 67 M8
Valley Vw CHLYE PR6 ... 33 G6
GTS/LS CH66 ... 155 M8
NEWLW WA12 ... 104 D4
Vanbrugh Crs ANF/KKDL L4 ... 97 L6
Vanbrugh Gv WGNW/BIL/O WN5 .. 67 K4
Vanbrugh Rd ANF/KKDL L4 ... 97 L5
Vanderbilt Av WLT/FAZ L9 ... 84 D5
Vanderbyl Av PS/BROM CH62 ... 143 K3
Vandries St VAUX/LVPD L3 ... 12 C2
Vandyke St TOX L8 ... 113 L6
Vanguard Ct
GOL/RIS/CU WA3 ... 122 F1 6
Vanguard St EV L5 ... 97 H7 5
Vardon St BIRK CH41 ... 11 G2
Varley Rd ALL/GAR L19 ... 130 C4
STHEL WA9 ... 9 L4
Varlian Cl BRSC L40 ... 63 L2
Varthen St EV L5 ... 97 J6 2
Vaudrey Dr WARR WA1 ... 122 F6
Vaughan Cl FMBY L37 ... 58 F1
Vaughan Rd STHP PR8 ... 35 J1
WAL/NB CH45 ... 95 L5
Vaughan St BIRK CH41 ... 111 H5
Vaux Crs BTL L20 ... 83 M8
Vauxhall Cl WARRW/BUR WA5 ... 136 B1
Vauxhall Rd EV L5 ... 96 E8
VAUX/LVPD L3 ... 12 F4
WGN WN1 ... 5 H4
Vaux Pl BTL L20 ... 7 K1
Vauze Av HOR/BR BL6 ... 57 M4
Vauze House Cl HOR/BR BL6 ... 57 M3
Venables Cl BEB CH63 ... 143 K4
Venables Dr BEB CH63 ... 143 J3
Venice St EV L5 ... 97 H7
Venmore St EV L5 ... 97 H7
Venns Rd WARRN/WOL WA2 ... 15 J1
Ventnor Cl
WARRW/BUR WA5 ... 119 M6 4
Ventnor Rd CHLY/EC PR7 ... 32 D7 5
WAV L15 ... 114 B5
Verbena Cl RUNC WA7 ... 161 H1 13
Verda St WGNE/HIN WN2 ... 80 C5
Verdi Av LITH L21 ... 83 J7
Verdi St LITH L21 ... 83 H8
Vere St TOX L8 ... 113 G8 9
Vermont Av CSBY/BLUN L23 ... 82 F1
Vermont Cl WARRW/BUR WA5 ... 120 E6
Vermont Rd CSBY/BLUN L23 ... 82 F1
Vermont Wy BTL L20 ... 7 G3
Verney Crs ALL/GAR L19 ... 130 E5
Verney Crs South ALL/GAR L19 .. 130 E5
Vernon Av GTS/LS CH66 ... 155 J3
WAL/EG CH44 ... 111 M3
Vernon Rd CHTN/BK PR9 ... 25 J5
Vernon St CLVP L2 ... 12 F5
STHEL WA9 ... 9 L4
WARR WA1 ... 14 F7
Verona St EV L5 ... 97 H7
Veronica Wy GTS/LS CH66 ... 155 M6
Verulam Cl TOX L8 ... 113 J6
Verulam Rd CHTN/BK PR9 ... 25 K2
Verwood Cl PEN/TH CH61 ... 125 M6 4
Verwood Dr WD/CROXPK L12 ... 99 J2
Veryan Cl HLWD L26 ... 132 B4
Vetch Hey NTHLY L27 ... 116 A8
Viaduct St NEWLW WA12 ... 104 C2
Vicarage Cl CALD/MH L18 ... 130 D3
CHLY/EC PR7 ... 31 M2
CHLYE PR6 ... 44 C5
FMBY L37 ... 59 G1
ORM L39 ... 63 K2
RF/TRAN CH42 ... 127 K4
SPK/HALE L24 ... 148 A4
WGNE/HIN WN2 ... 80 C3 10
Vicarage Dr RNFD/HAY WA11 ... 90 C6
Vicarage Gdns BRSC L40 ... 51 M1
Vicarage Gv WAL/EG CH44 ... 95 L8
Vicarage Hl FROD/HEL WA6 ... 166 E1 7
Vicarage La BRSC L40 ... 63 M2
CHTN/BK PR9 ... 23 H6
FROD/HEL WA6 ... 160 E6
FROD/HEL WA6 ... 166 E1
WGNNW/ST WN6 ... 55 J8
Vicarage Lawn WLTN L25 ... 115 L8 5
Vicarage Pl PR/KW L34 ... 100 E7 3
Vicarage Rd AIMK WN4 ... 91 K3
FMBY L37 ... 58 F1
HOR/BR BL6 ... 57 M3
RNFD/HAY WA11 ... 90 D6
WDN WA8 ... 16 D5
WGNE/HIN WN2 ... 80 D4
WGNW/BIL/O WN5 ... 77 M1
Vicarage Rd West HOR/BR BL6 ... 57 L3
Vicarage St CHLYE PR6 ... 32 F4
Vicarage Wk ORM L39 ... 51 G8
Vicar Rd NPK/KEN L6 ... 97 L6
Viceroy St EV L5 ... 97 H7 6
Vickers Rd WDN WA8 ... 149 G1
Victor Cl WGNW/BIL/O WN5 ... 67 M5
Victoria Av CSBY/BLUN L23 ... 82 E1
DV/KA/FCH L14 ... 114 F3 1
HES CH60 ... 141 H7
RNFD/HAY WA11 ... 89 J5
WARRS WA4 ... 138 C3
WARRW/BUR WA5 ... 119 M7 5
WAV L15 ... 114 B5 5
WDN WA8 ... 134 C3
WGNE/HIN WN2 ... 81 G4
WGNNW/ST WN6 ... 4 B1
Victoria Bridge Rd STHP PR8 ... 3 J5
Victoria Cl AIG/SPK L17 ... 130 A2
WGNE/HIN WN2 ... 57 K7
Victoria Ct WAV L15 ... 114 C5
Victoria Crs WGNNW/ST WN6 ... 56 A5
Victoria Dr RF/TRAN CH42 ... 128 C4
WKBY CH48 ... 124 C3
WLT/FAZ L9 ... 84 B7
Victoria Flds RF/TRAN CH42 ... 127 L1
Victoria Gv WDN WA8 ... 134 C2 5
Victoria La CL/PREN CH43 ... 127 K1
Victoria Mt CL/PREN CH43 ... 127 K1
Victoria Pde WAL/NB CH45 ... 95 L4
Victoria Pk SKEL WN8 ... 64 E4
Victoria Park Rd
RF/TRAN CH42 ... 127 M3
Victoria Pl CLB/OSW/ST L13 ... 114 C2 5
RAIN/WH L35 ... 117 L2
WARRS WA4 ... 137 L4
Victoria Rd AIG/SPK L17 ... 130 A3
AIMK WN4 ... 90 F2
BEB CH63 ... 127 M7 5
CLB/OSW/ST L13 ... 98 A7
CSBY/BLUN L23 ... 82 F1
CSBY/WL L22 ... 83 G5
EP CH65 ... 20 B4
FMBY L37 ... 46 D8
HTWN L38 ... 71 G2
HUY L36 ... 116 B3
NEWLW WA12 ... 104 E1
NSTN CH64 ... 153 J7
ORM L39 ... 62 E2
RF/TRAN CH42 ... 11 G9
RUNC WA7 ... 19 H4
WAL/NB CH45 ... 95 J5
WARRS WA4 ... 137 M4
WARRW/BUR WA5 ... 136 A1 4
WDN WA8 ... 16 D5
WGNE/HIN WN2 ... 80 C4
WKBY CH48 ... 124 C4
Victoria St BRSC L40 ... 39 G8
CHLY/EC PR7 ... 32 F6
CLVP L2 ... 12 F7
ECCL WA10 ... 9 G2
HOR/BR BL6 ... 57 M3 7
PS/BROM CH62 ... 128 D8 4
RAIN/WH L35 ... 117 L2 7
RNFD/HAY WA11 ... 76 B6
STHP PR8 ... 3 G2
WARR WA1 ... 15 G5
WDN WA8 ... 16 E5
WGNE/HIN WN2 ... 80 C3
WGNW/BIL/O WN5 ... 68 A7
Victoria Ter CHLYE PR6 ... 32 F4 2
RAIN/WH L35 ... 117 K2
WGNE/HIN WN2 ... 81 H5
Victoria Wy FMBY L37 ... 46 F8
STHP PR8 ... 2 D4
Victor St WAV L15 ... 113 M5 8
Victory Av CHTN/BK PR9 ... 25 J6
Victory Cl NTHTN L30 ... 84 A5 5
Vienna St EV L5 ... 97 H7
Viennese Rd WLTN L25 ... 115 K6 5
Viewpark Cl CHLDW L16 ... 115 H6
View Rd RAIN/WH L35 ... 117 L3
Vigo St WGNE/HIN WN2 ... 69 H3 6
Viking Cl LITH L21 ... 83 J6 7
Villa Av WGNNW/ST WN6 ... 68 C1
Village Cl RUNC WA7 ... 150 C5 5
WAL/NB CH45 ... 95 G7
WARRS WA4 ... 139 G1
Village Ct AIG/SPK L17 ... 129 L3
Village Cft CHLY/EC PR7 ... 31 L2
Village Green Ct
CL/PREN CH43 ... 110 E5 8
Village Rd BEB CH63 ... 127 M7
CL/PREN CH43 ... 127 J1
HES CH60 ... 141 H6
WKBY CH48 ... 124 E4
Village St NPK/KEN L6 ... 13 L2
RUNC WA7 ... 151 G3
The Village BEB CH63 ... 128 C8
GR/UP/WCH CH49 ... 110 C8
Village Wy HTWN L38 ... 70 B1
WAL/NB CH45 ... 95 G8
Villa Gloria Cl ALL/GAR L19 ... 130 C5
Villars St WARR WA1 ... 15 H6
Villas Rd MGHL L31 ... 73 K3
Villiers Crs ECCL WA10 ... 88 B8
Villiers Rd PR/KW L34 ... 86 D7
Vincent Cl WARRW/BUR WA5 ... 120 D5
Vincent Ct CLVPS L1 ... 112 F5 17
Vincent Rd LITH L21 ... 83 L4
RAIN/WH L35 ... 117 K1
Vincent St CLB/OSW/ST L13 ... 114 B4
ECCL WA10 ... 9 H4
Vincent Wy WGNW/BIL/O WN5 ... 67 M5
Vine Crs WARRW/BUR WA5 ... 120 A7
Vine Gv WGNS/IIMK WN3 ... 4 E5
The Vineries WLTN L25 ... 131 G2
Vine Rd GTS/LS CH66 ... 163 H5
Vineside Rd WD/CROXPK L12 ... 98 F8
Vine St CHLY/EC PR7 ... 32 E4
EHL/KEN L7 ... 113 J5
RUNC WA7 ... 19 G4
WDN WA8 ... 16 D5
WGN WN1 ... 5 H1
WGNE/HIN WN2 ... 69 M7 14
Vineyard St ALL/GAR L19 ... 131 G8
Vining Rd RAIN/WH L35 ... 101 H7
Vining St TOX L8 ... 113 H7 8
Viola Cl WGNNW/ST WN6 ... 55 M3 2
Viola St BTL L20 ... 7 H8
Violet Cl GOL/RIS/CU WA3 ... 122 E1
Violet Rd BIRK CH41 ... 111 H6
LITH L21 ... 83 K7
Violet St AIMK WN4 ... 91 K3
WDN WA8 ... 16 C6
WGNS/IIMK WN3 ... 5 K8
Virgil St ECCL WA10 ... 8 C4
EV L5 ... 13 H1
Virginia Av MGHL L31 ... 72 E2
Virginia Gv MGHL L31 ... 72 F2
Virginia Rd WAL/NB CH45 ... 95 K4
Virginia St STHP PR8 ... 3 J5
VAUX/LVPD L3 ... 12 D5 2
Virginia Wy WGNW/BIL/O WN5 ... 67 L5
Virgin's La CSBY/BLUN L23 ... 71 H6
Viscount Rd WGNW/BIL/O WN5 ... 67 M5
Vista Av NEWLW WA12 ... 104 C1
Vista Rd NEWLW WA12 ... 104 C1
RUNC WA7 ... 19 H7
Vista Wy NEWLW WA12 ... 104 C1
Vitesse Rd ALL/GAR L19 ... 131 H7
Vittoria Cl BIRK CH41 ... 11 G4 2
Vittoria St BIRK CH41 ... 10 F4
Vivian Av WAL/EG CH44 ... 112 A3 20
Vivian Dr STHP PR8 ... 35 J3
Voelas St TOX L8 ... 113 J8 6
Vogan Av CSBY/BLUN L23 ... 83 J2
Volunteer St ECCL WA10 ... 8 F3
FROD/HEL WA6 ... 160 E4
Vose Cl WARRW/BUR WA5 ... 120 F7
Vronhill Cl TOX L8 ... 113 J7 7
Vulcan Cl CL/PREN CH43 ... 111 H5 8
NEWLW WA12 ... 104 E4
WARRN/WOL WA2 ... 122 B3 5
Vulcan Dr WGN WN1 ... 5 H5
Vulcan Rd WGNW/BIL/O WN5 ... 67 M5
Vulcan St ALL/GAR L19 ... 145 L1
BTL L20 ... 6 D3
CHTN/BK PR9 ... 3 J4
CL/PREN CH43 ... 111 H5 9
VAUX/LVPD L3 ... 12 C2
Vyner Cl CL/PREN CH43 ... 111 G7
Vyner Rd WAL/NB CH45 ... 95 H8
Vyner Rd North CL/PREN CH43 .. 110 F6
WLTN L25 ... 115 J8
Vyner Rd South CL/PREN CH43 .. 110 F7
WLTN L25 ... 115 J8
Vyrnwy St EV L5 ... 97 J7 7

W

Waddicar La MGHL L31 ... 73 K8
Waddington Cl
GOL/RIS/CU WA3 ... 93 H5 9
WARRN/WOL WA2 ... 122 B4
Wadebridge Rd NG/CROX L11 ... 85 J7
Wadeson Rd ANF/KKDL L4 ... 97 M3
Wadeson Wy GOL/RIS/CU WA3 .. 106 D6
Wadham Rd BTL L20 ... 7 G8
Wagon La RNFD/HAY WA11 ... 90 D7
Waine Gv RAIN/WH L35 ... 101 J8 3
Waine St RNFD/HAY WA11 ... 90 B7 4
STHEL WA9 ... 102 F1
Wainfleet Cl WGNS/IIMK WN3 ... 79 G2
Wainwright Cl EHL/KEN L7 ... 113 L5 10
Wainwright Gv ALL/GAR L19 ... 130 E7
Wakefield Crs WGNNW/ST WN6 ... 56 C6
Wakefield Dr MOR/LEA CH46 ... 110 B1
Wakefield Rd GTS/LS CH66 ... 163 G4
NTHTN L30 ... 84 D2
Wakefield St GOL/RIS/CU WA3 .. 92 C6 5
VAUX/LVPD L3 ... 13 J4
Walby Cl GR/UP/WCH CH49 ... 126 E3
Walcot Pl WGNS/IIMK WN3 ... 79 J3
Walden Cl WARRS WA4 ... 138 F2
Walden Rd DV/KA/FCH L14 ... 114 E2 2
Waldgrave Pl WAV L15 ... 114 D4 4
Waldgrave Rd WAV L15 ... 114 C4
Waldorf Cl WGNS/IIMK WN3 ... 78 F3
Walford Cl BEB CH63 ... 143 H3
Walford Rd AIMK WN4 ... 91 L2
Walgarth Dr CHLY/EC PR7 ... 32 C6
Walkden Av WGN WN1 ... 68 D3
Walkden Av East WGN WN1 ... 68 E3
Walker Av STHEL WA9 ... 118 D2
Walker Cl FMBY L37 ... 59 H3
Walker Dr BTL L20 ... 83 L6
Walker Pl RF/TRAN CH42 ... 127 M2
Walker Rd LITH L21 ... 83 J6
Walker's Cft WAL/NB CH45 ... 95 H8 3
Walkers La GTS/LS CH66 ... 155 L7
STHEL WA9 ... 118 C2
WARRW/BUR WA5 ... 136 A2
Walker St HOY CH47 ... 108 D6
NPK/KEN L6 ... 113 J2
PS/BROM CH62 ... 128 D7 5
RF/TRAN CH42 ... 127 M2
WARRN/WOL WA2 ... 14 C4
Walker Wy WLT/FAZ L9 ... 84 B7
The Walk SPK/HALE L24 ... 146 C3
Wallace Av HUY L36 ... 116 B1
Wallace Dr HUY L36 ... 116 B1
Wallace La WGN WN1 ... 5 J1
Wallace St WDN WA8 ... 16 D3
WLT/FAZ L9 ... 84 C7 6
Wallacre Rd WAL/EG CH44 ... 111 G1
Wallasey Bridge Rd BIRK CH41 .. 111 H4
Wallasey Rd WAL/EG CH44 ... 111 H1
Wallasey Village WAL/EG CH44 .... 95 G8
WAL/NB CH45 ... 95 G7
Wallbrook Av WGNW/BIL/O WN5 .. 77 M4
Wallcroft NSTN CH64 ... 154 C6
Wallcroft St SKEL WN8 ... 65 G5
Waller Cl ANF/KKDL L4 ... 97 G6 16
Waller St BTL L20 ... 83 J7
Walletts Rd CHLY/EC PR7 ... 32 D7
Wallgarth Cl WGNS/IIMK WN3 ... 79 G3 3
Wallgate WGNS/IIMK WN3 ... 4 D5
WGNW/BIL/O WN5 ... 4 A6
Wallgate Rd WLTN L25 ... 115 H7
Wallgate Wy WLTN L25 ... 115 H7
Wallingford Rd
GR/UP/WCH CH49 ... 110 B8
Wallis St WARRS WA4 ... 137 K2
Wallrake HES CH60 ... 141 H6
Wallsend Ct WDN WA8 ... 134 B2
Walls St WGNE/HIN WN2 ... 81 L3
Wall St WGNNW/ST WN6 ... 68 B4
Walmer Ct STHP PR8 ... 35 H2
Walmer Rd CSBY/WL L22 ... 83 G5
STHP PR8 ... 35 J2
Walmesley Av WGNS/IIMK WN3 ... 4 E7
Walmesley Dr RNFD/HAY WA11 ... 76 C8
WGNE/HIN WN2 ... 69 K6
Walmesley Rd ECCL WA10 ... 88 C8
Walmesley St WGN WN1 ... 5 G5
Walmsley St EV L5 ... 96 E8
NEWLW WA12 ... 104 F1 5
WAL/EG CH44 ... 95 L8 7
WDN WA8 ... 17 H3
Walney Rd WD/CROXPK L12 ... 98 C5
WGNS/IIMK WN3 ... 78 F3 6
Walnut Av WGN WN1 ... 68 F3
WLT/FAZ L9 ... 97 L2
Walnut Cl WARR WA1 ... 123 G6
Walnut Gv GTS/LS CH66 ... 163 H4
MGHL L31 ... 85 J2 2
Walnut St STHP PR8 ... 3 K9
Walpole Av RAIN/WH L35 ... 117 H2
WGNS/IIMK WN3 ... 79 H2
Walpole Gv WARRN/WOL WA2 ... 121 L3
Walpole Rd RUNC WA7 ... 149 K7
Walro Ms CHTN/BK PR9 ... 25 J2
Walsh Cl EV L5 ... 12 F1
NEWLW WA12 ... 91 L8
Walsh Rd DV/KA/FCH L14 ... 114 E3
Walsingham Dr RUNC WA7 ... 150 F3
Walsingham Rd CHLDW L16 ... 115 G5
WAL/EG CH44 ... 111 M2
WARRW/BUR WA5 ... 120 B8
Walter Gv STHEL WA9 ... 103 H6
Walter Scott Av WGN WN1 ... 68 D1
Walters Green Crs
GOL/RIS/CU WA3 ... 92 C3
Walter St AIMK WN4 ... 91 M1 6
LEIGH WN7 ... 81 K8
VAUX/LVPD L3 ... 96 D8
WARR WA1 ... 15 L1
WDN WA8 ... 17 J1
WGNW/BIL/O WN5 ... 67 M7 5
Waltham Av WGNNW/ST WN6 ... 68 B2
Waltham Ct RUNC WA7 ... 151 G1 1
Waltham Rd NPK/KEN L6 ... 97 L7
Walthew House La
WGNW/BIL/O WN5 ... 67 K4
Walthew La WGNE/HIN WN2 ... 80 C3 11
WGNW/BIL/O WN5 ... 67 M3
Waltho Av MGHL L31 ... 73 G4
Walton Av WARRW/BUR WA5 ... 120 A8
Walton Breck Rd ANF/KKDL L4 ... 97 J7
Walton Hall Av ANF/KKDL L4 ... 97 K3
NG/CROX L11 ... 97 M2 1
Walton Heath Rd WARRS WA4 ... 137 K4
Walton La ANF/KKDL L4 ... 97 H6
Walton Lea Rd WARRS WA4 ... 137 H6
Walton New Rd WARRS WA4 ... 137 K5
Walton Pk WLT/FAZ L9 ... 97 J1
Walton Rd ANF/KKDL L4 ... 97 G5
ECCL WA10 ... 88 F7
GOL/RIS/CU WA3 ... 107 H2
WARRS WA4 ... 137 L5
Walton St BIRK CH41 ... 11 J6 3
CHLY/EC PR7 ... 44 C7 3
CHTN/BK PR9 ... 3 J2
RUNC WA7 ... 19 H4
Walton V WLT/FAZ L9 ... 84 C7
Walton Village ANF/KKDL L4 ... 97 H3 10
Wambo La WLTN L25 ... 115 L8
Wandsworth Rd NG/CROX L11 ... 98 B4
Wandsworth Wy WDN WA8 ... 16 B8
Wanes Blades Rd BRSC L40 ... 53 G1
Wango La AIN/FAZ L10 ... 85 G4
Wanishar La ORM L39 ... 49 J8
Wansfell Pl
WARRN/WOL WA2 ... 121 J2 7
Wantage Vw HUY L36 ... 115 L5
Wapping VAUX/LVPD L3 ... 112 E5

Wapshare Rd NG/CROX L11 98 A4
Warbeck Cl WGNE/HIN WN2 81 G2
Warbler Cl HLWD L26 131 M3
Warbreck Av WLT/FAZ L9 84 C7
Warbreck Moor WLT/FAZ L9 84 D6
Warbreck Rd WLT/FAZ L9 84 C7
Warburton Hey RAIN/WH L35 117 K1
Warburton St WARRS WA4 137 M4
Ward Av FMBY L37 58 F3
Ward Cl WARRW/BUR WA5 120 D4
Warden St ANF/KKDL L4 97 G5 13
Wardgate Av
WD/CROXPK L12 99 G2 14
Ward Gv RF/TRAN CH42 128 B4 7
Wardley St WGNW/BIL/O WN5 67 K8
Wardlow Av WGNW/BIL/O WN5 67 J5
Wardour St WARRW/BUR WA5 121 G7
Ward Rd CSBY/BLUN L23 70 C7
Ward St CHLYE PR6 33 G6
ECCL WA10 9 G3
PR/KW L34 100 F6
VAUX/LVPD L3 13 J6
WGNE/HIN WN2 69 M6
Wareham Cl WARR WA1 122 E5
Wareing Rd WLT/FAZ L9 84 E7
Waresley Crs WLT/FAZ L9 98 A1
Wargrave Ms NEWLW WA12 104 E4
Wargrave Rd NEWLW WA12 104 E2
Warham Rd ANF/KKDL L4 97 L6
Waring Av RF/TRAN CH42 127 M3
STHEL WA9 103 K3
WARRS WA4 122 B8
The Warings CHLY/EC PR7 41 M1
Warkworth Cl WDN WA8 133 L2 10
Warlow Dr LEIGH WN7 81 M4
Warmington Rd
DV/KA/FCH L14 114 E2
Warminster Gv WGNS/IIMK WN3 78 F3
Warncliffe St
WGNW/BIL/O WN5 67 M8 8
Warner Dr ANF/KKDL L4 97 L5
Warnerville Rd CLB/OSW/ST L13 114 D4
Warnford St WGN WN1 68 E3 5
Warnley Cl WDN WA8 133 M2 4
Warpers Moss Cl BRSC L40 39 H8 1
Warper's Moss La BRSC L40 39 J8
Warren Ct FROD/HEL WA6 160 F7
GTS/LS CH66 162 F2
STHP PR8 2 B7
Warren Cft RUNC WA7 150 E6
Warren Dr CL/PREN CH43 110 E7 7
GTS/LS CH66 156 A6
NEWLW WA12 105 H1
WAL/NB CH45 95 H5
WARRS WA4 137 L5
Warren Gn FMBY L37 58 F1
Warren Hey BEB CH63 143 J4
Warren House Rd CSBY/WL L22 82 D3
Warrenhouse Rd
NWD/KWIPK L33 86 C1
Warren La WARR WA1 122 F5
Warren Rd CHTN/BK PR9 25 J5
CSBY/BLUN L23 70 C8
HOY CH47 108 C6
WARRN/WOL WA2 121 M4
WARRS WA4 137 L6
The Warren GR/UP/WCH CH49 110 D8
Warren Wy HES CH60 140 F4
Warrington Av EP CH65 163 K3
Warrington La WGN WN1 5 G4
Warrington New Rd STHEL WA9 9 K6
Warrington Old Rd STHEL WA9 9 J7
Warrington Rd AIMK WN4 91 K3
GOL/RIS/CU WA3 105 K2
GOL/RIS/CU WA3 107 H2 4
LYMM WA13 139 K1
NEWLW WA12 92 C7
RAIN/WH L35 101 G8
RUNC WA7 150 A3 2
WARRS WA4 137 H7
WARRW/BUR WA5 135 M1
WDN WA8 17 G4
WGNE/HIN WN2 80 C3
WGNS/IIMK WN3 5 H8
Warrington St BIRK CH41 11 J9
Warton Cl WARRW/BUR WA5 136 C2 1
WLTN L25 131 L3 5
Warton Pl CHLY/EC PR7 32 C5
Warton St BTL L20 83 J7
Warwick Av AIMK WN4 91 M3 2
CSBY/BLUN L23 82 F2
NEWLW WA12 104 F3
WARRW/BUR WA5 14 A1
Warwick Cl CL/PREN CH43 10 F7
HUY L36 116 C2 2
NSTN CH64 153 G8
STHP PR8 35 K2
Warwick Dr WAL/NB CH45 95 L7
WKBY CH48 124 E5
Warwick Rd BTL L20 7 K3
CHLY/EC PR7 30 E6
GR/UP/WCH CH49 110 B7
HUY L36 116 C2
WGNE/HIN WN2 57 L8 2
Warwick St CHLY/EC PR7 44 B7
ECCL WA10 8 A6
STHP PR8 35 K1
TOX L8 113 G8
Wasdale Av MGHL L31 73 H3
RNFD/HAY WA11 89 K5
Wasdale Rd AIMK WN4 79 J5
WLT/FAZ L9 84 C8
Washbrook Av
CL/PREN CH43 110 E5 9
Washbrook Cl ECCL WA10 101 K1
Washbrook Wy ORM L39 63 G1
Washington Dr
WARRW/BUR WA5 120 D7
Washington La CHLY/EC PR7 32 A3
Washington Pde BTL L20 7 G3
Wash La WARRS WA4 138 A3
Washway La ECCL WA10 89 J6
Wasley Cl WARRN/WOL WA2 122 B2
Wastdale Ct MOR/LEA CH46 109 L4 1
Wastdale Dr MOR/LEA CH46 109 L4
Wastdale Ms MOR/LEA CH46 109 L4 2
Wastle Bridge Rd HUY L36 100 A8
Watchyard La FMBY L37 59 J2
Waterbeck Cl WGN WN1 5 L2
Waterbridge Ct WARRS WA4 137 M5
Waterdale Crs STHEL WA9 102 F6
Waterdale Pl STHEL WA9 102 F6 14
Water Dr WGNNW/ST WN6 56 D6
Waterfield Cl BEB CH63 127 M8
Waterfoot Av STHP PR8 47 K2 3
Waterford Cl CHLYE PR6 44 C4
Waterford Dr NSTN CH64 153 J6
Waterford Rd CL/PREN CH43 111 G8
Waterford Wy RUNC WA7 150 E7
Watergate La WLTN L25 131 K3
Watergate Wy WLTN L25 131 K3
Waterhouse Cl NPK/KEN L6 97 K7 5
Waterhouse St EV L5 13 L1
Waterland La STHEL WA9 103 H3
Water La CHTN/BK PR9 22 F8
RAIN/WH L35 132 F1
Waterloo Cl CSBY/WL L22 83 G5 5
Waterloo La FROD/HEL WA6 167 L4
Waterloo Pl BIRK CH41 11 K7
Waterloo Rd CSBY/WL L22 83 G5
RUNC WA7 18 F3 1
STHP PR8 35 G4 1
VAUX/LVPD L3 12 C2
WAL/NB CH45 95 K4
WDN WA8 16 C9
Waterloo St CHLY/EC PR7 32 E4 7
CHLY/EC PR7 32 F4 3
ECCL WA10 8 F5
WAV L15 114 C6
WGNNW/ST WN6 4 A1
Watermede
WGNW/BIL/O WN5 78 A2 1
Waterpark Cl CL/PREN CH43 127 H4 5
Waterpark Dr STBRV L28 99 H5
Waterpark Rd CL/PREN CH43 127 J4
Watersedge FROD/HEL WA6 160 F3
Waterside NTHTN L30 72 A8
STHEL WA9 9 K3
WARRS WA4 137 M5
Waterside Dr FROD/HEL WA6 160 F3
Waterside Pk HUY L36 115 M4
Waters Reach WGN WN1 5 L4
Water St BIRK CH41 11 L5
CHLY/EC PR7 32 E5
CHLY/EC PR7 44 C7
CLVP L2 12 E7
CSBY/BLUN L23 71 K7
CSBY/WL L22 83 G5 6
ECCL WA10 8 F5
NEWLW WA12 104 E1 8
PS/BROM CH62 128 D7
RUNC WA7 19 H2
VAUX/LVPD L3 12 D7
WAL/EG CH44 111 M1
WDN WA8 16 C8
WGN WN1 4 F3
Water Tower Rd NSTN CH64 153 G3
Waterway Av NTHTN L30 84 D2
Waterways WARRW/BUR WA5 120 F7
Waterworks Dr
NEWLW WA12 105 H1 1
Waterworks La GTS/LS CH66 155 G4
WARRN/WOL WA2 105 K6
Waterworks Rd ORM L39 51 J7
Waterworks St BTL L20 7 J4
Watery La FROD/HEL WA6 161 G8
STHEL WA9 103 G5
WARRN/WOL WA2 105 G7
Watford Rd ANF/KKDL L4 97 K6
Watkin Cl NTHTN L30 84 D4
Watkins Av NEWLW WA12 104 B2
Watkinson St CLVPS L1 112 F6
Watkinson Wy WDN WA8 17 G3
Watkin St WARRN/WOL WA2 14 E1
WGN WN1 4 F3
Watling Av LITH L21 83 J4
Watling Wy RAIN/WH L35 101 J8
Watmough St EV L5 13 K2
Watson Av AIMK WN4 91 L2 7
GOL/RIS/CU WA3 92 B4
Watson St BIRK CH41 11 H3
Watton Beck Cl MGHL L31 73 H3
Watton Cl WARRS WA4 138 E2
WD/CROXPK L12 99 J3 1
Watts Cl NWD/KWIPK L33 86 C1
Watts La BTL L20 84 A7
Wauchope St WAV L15 114 A5
Wavell Av CHTN/BK PR9 25 K6
WDN WA8 133 L5
Wavell Cl CHTN/BK PR9 25 K6
Wavell Rd HUY L36 116 A1 2
Waverley SKEL WN8 64 F4
Waverley Av WARRS WA4 137 M5
Waverley Ct WGNS/IIMK WN3 78 F2 3
Waverley Gv RF/TRAN CH42 127 L3 3
Waverley Rd AIG/SPK L17 129 L1
CSBY/BLUN L23 82 E2
GOL/RIS/CU WA3 92 F4
HOY CH47 108 E6
WGNE/HIN WN2 69 L8 6
Waverley St BTL L20 6 F4
STHP PR8 2 F3
Waverton Av CL/PREN CH43 127 G3
Waverton Rd GTS/LS CH66 156 A8
Wavertree Av CLB/OSW/ST L13 114 A4
WDN WA8 16 C3
Wavertree Bvd EHL/KEN L7 113 M4
Wavertree Bvd South
EHL/KEN L7 114 A4
Wavertree Gn WAV L15 114 C6
Wavertree Nook Rd WAV L15 114 E5
Wavertree Rd EHL/KEN L7 113 K4
Wavertree V WAV L15 113 M5 9
Wayfarers Dr NEWLW WA12 105 G3
Wayford Cl FROD/HEL WA6 160 D4
Waylands Dr WLTN L25 131 K6
Wayside Cl LYMM WA13 139 M3
Wayville Cl CALD/MH L18 130 D3
Waywell Cl WARRN/WOL WA2 122 B2
Weald Dr GTS/LS CH66 155 J7
Weardale Rd WAV L15 114 A7 2
Wearhead Cl GOL/RIS/CU WA3 92 C6 6
Weasdale Cl STHEL WA9 102 F6 15
Weaste La WARRS WA4 138 F3
Weates Cl WDN WA8 135 G2
Weaver Av BRSC L40 39 H8
NWD/KWIPK L33 74 B7
RAIN/WH L35 117 K2
Weaver Crs FROD/HEL WA6 160 F4
Weaver Gv LEIGH WN7 93 L1 3
STHEL WA9 103 J2
Weaver La FROD/HEL WA6 160 D3
Weaver Rd EP CH65 20 D9
FROD/HEL WA6 160 F4
GOL/RIS/CU WA3 107 J3 2
RUNC WA7 149 J7
Weaver's Brow CHLYE PR6 33 H7
Weaverside Av RUNC WA7 161 H1 14
Weavers La MGHL L31 73 H7
Weaver St WLT/FAZ L9 97 H2 7
Webb Cl EHL/KEN L7 113 L4 10
Webb Dr WARRW/BUR WA5 104 B7
Webber Rd NWD/KWIPK L33 86 D4
Webb St EHL/KEN L7 113 L6
STHEL WA9 102 F4
Webster Av BTL L20 7 L2
WAL/EG CH44 95 M8
Webster Dr KKBY L32 86 A3
Webster Rd WAV L15 113 M6
Websters La GTS/LS CH66 163 H3
Webster's St WGNE/HIN WN2 80 C3
Webster St LITH L21 83 K7
VAUX/LVPD L3 13 G5 4
Weddell Cl WARRW/BUR WA5 120 F6
Wedge Av RNFD/HAY WA11 90 C8
Wedgewood Dr
WGNNW/ST WN6 67 M2 2
Wedgewood St EHL/KEN L7 113 L3 9
Wedgwood Dr WDN WA8 134 D1
Wednesbury Dr
WARRW/BUR WA5 120 B7
Weedon Av NEWLW WA12 91 K8
Weightman Gv WLT/FAZ L9 84 C7 7
Weir La WARR WA1 123 G7
Weir St WARRS WA4 137 J4 2
Welbeck Av CALD/MH L18 114 B8 13
NEWLW WA12 104 F3
Welbeck Rd AIMK WN4 79 K8
STHP PR8 35 H1
WGNS/IIMK WN3 79 G2
Welbeck Ter STHP PR8 35 H1
Welbourne Rd CHLDW L16 114 E4
Weld Av CHLY/EC PR7 32 E8
Weldbank La CHLY/EC PR7 32 E8
Weldbank St CHLY/EC PR7 32 E8 2
Weld Blundell Av MGHL L31 72 D1
Weld Dr FMBY L37 58 F1
Weldon Dr ORM L39 63 H1
Weldon Gv WGN WN1 69 G3
Weldon St ANF/KKDL L4 97 H3
Weld Pde STHP PR8 2 D9
Weld Rd CSBY/BLUN L23 82 E2
STHP PR8 2 B7
Welfield Pl TOX L8 129 J1
Welford Av CL/PREN CH43 127 H3
GOL/RIS/CU WA3 92 E6
Welland Cl HLWD L26 132 A8
Welland Rd AIMK WN4 80 A8
BEB CH63 127 M8 4
Wellbank Dr HLWD L26 132 C4 5
Wellbrae Cl
GR/UP/WCH CH49 109 M8 8
Wellbrook Cl RUNC WA7 150 E8 6
SPK/HALE L24 146 F1 1
Wellbrooke Cl AIMK WN4 91 L2 8
Wellbrook Gn SPK/HALE L24 146 F2 3
Well Brow Rd ANF/KKDL L4 97 K3
Wellcroft Rd HUY L36 116 A1
Wellcross Rd SKEL WN8 66 D7
Weller St TOX L8 113 H8
Weller Wy TOX L8 129 J1
Wellesbourne Pl
NG/CROX L11 98 C3 3
Wellesbourne Rd NG/CROX L11 98 C2
Wellesley Av EP CH65 20 D5
Wellesley Cl NEWLW WA12 91 K8 1
WGNW/BIL/O WN5 68 A5
Wellesley Gv BEB CH63 128 C7 2
Wellesley Rd TOX L8 129 J1 22
WAL/EG CH44 111 K1
Wellfield RNFD/HAY WA11 88 C1
RUNC WA7 151 G8
WDN WA8 134 C1
Wellfield Av KKBY L32 86 A4
Wellfield La BRSC L40 63 L3
Wellfield Rd GOL/RIS/CU WA3 107 G1
WGNE/HIN WN2 81 J1 3
WGNNW/ST WN6 68 B1
WLT/FAZ L9 97 J1
Wellfield St WARRW/BUR WA5 121 G8
Wellgreen Rd WLTN L25 115 H6
Wellham Rd WGNS/IIMK WN3 79 K2
Wellington Av WAV L15 113 M6
Wellington Cl AIN/FAZ L10 84 E2 4
EP CH65 20 D4
WARRN/WOL WA2 122 B3 6
Wellington Flds WAV L15 113 M7 1
Wellington Ga SPK/HALE L24 148 A3 2
Wellington Gv WAV L15 114 A5 7
WGNS/IIMK WN3 5 H9
Wellington Rd BEB CH63 128 C7
CL/PREN CH43 10 A8
EP CH65 20 B6
LITH L21 83 J6 2
TOX L8 129 H1
WAL/NB CH45 95 K4
WAV L15 114 A6
Wellington Rd North EP CH65 20 D5
Wellington St ALL/GAR L19 130 E8
CHLY/EC PR7 32 E4 8
CSBY/WL L22 82 F4
NEWLW WA12 104 C2
RUNC WA7 19 G2
STHP PR8 2 E5
VAUX/LVPD L3 13 G3
WARR WA1 15 G6
WDN WA8 16 C8
WGN WN1 5 H4
Wellington Ter BIRK CH41 11 H8
ECCL WA10 9 G1
RF/TRAN CH42 11 H9
TOX L8 113 J8 7
Well La BEB CH63 127 M7
BTL L20 7 J4
GR/UP/WCH CH49 125 L2
HES CH60 141 J7
NSTN CH64 153 H8
ORM L39 49 G7
RF/TRAN CH42 128 A3
WARRW/BUR WA5 136 A2
WLTN L25 115 H6
Wells Av WGNW/BIL/O WN5 77 M8
Wells Cl GTS/LS CH66 163 G5 4
WARR WA1 122 D5
Wells Dr WGNE/HIN WN2 69 H3
Wells St WAV L15 114 B6 1
Wellstead Cl WAV L15 114 C5
Wellstead Rd WAV L15 114 C5
Well St WGN WN1 5 K3
Wellswood Rd GTS/LS CH66 156 A6
Welsby Cl WARRN/WOL WA2 122 B2
Welshampton Cl GTS/LS CH66 162 F3
Welshpool Cl
WARRW/BUR WA5 120 F2
Welsh Rd GTS/LS CH66 155 J4
Welton Av GR/UP/WCH CH49 110 B8
Welton Cl SPK/HALE L24 146 F2 4
Welton Gn SPK/HALE L24 146 F2 5
Welton Rd PS/BROM CH62 143 M3
Welwyn Av STHP PR8 34 F7
Welwyn Cl STHEL WA9 102 A7
WARRS WA4 138 E2
Wembley Gdns WLT/FAZ L9 84 B7
Wembley Rd CALD/MH L18 114 D8
CSBY/BLUN L23 83 H2 1
Wendell St TOX L8 113 L6
Wendover Av AIG/SPK L17 129 L2
Wendover Cl CL/PREN CH43 126 F1
Wendron Rd NG/CROX L11 85 M8 6
Wenger Rd WDN WA8 118 D8
Wenlock Cl HOR/BR BL6 45 L7
WARR WA1 122 C5
Wenlock Dr HLWD L26 132 A6
Wenlock Gdns GTS/LS CH66 163 H3
Wenlock Gv WGNE/HIN WN2 80 F1
Wenlock La GTS/LS CH66 163 H3
Wenlock Rd ANF/KKDL L4 97 K6
RUNC WA7 161 J1
WGNE/HIN WN2 69 M8
Wenlock St WGNE/HIN WN2 80 F1 13
Wenning Av MGHL L31 73 G3
Wennington Rd CHTN/BK PR9 25 H5
Wensley Av HLWD L26 132 A6
Wensleydale WLT/FAZ L9 84 C6 2
Wensleydale Av
PS/BROM CH62 144 A8
RAIN/WH L35 117 M2
Wensleydale Cl MGHL L31 72 D3 4
WARRW/BUR WA5 120 B5
Wensley Rd GOL/RIS/CU WA3 93 G6
WLT/FAZ L9 84 C6
Wentworth Av WAL/NB CH45 95 K6
WARR WA1 122 D6
Wentworth Cl CL/PREN CH43 126 F1
STHP PR8 47 L1
WDN WA8 118 C8 4
Wentworth Dr BEB CH63 143 K8
EV L5 13 M1
Wentworth Gv HUY L36 115 K3 1
Wentworth Rd AIMK WN4 79 H8
Wernbrook Cl CL/PREN CH43 126 F1
Wernbrook Rd ANF/KKDL L4 97 L6
Wervin Cl CL/PREN CH43 127 G3
Wervin Rd CL/PREN CH43 127 G3
KKBY L32 85 M4
Wescoe Cl WGNW/BIL/O WN5 67 G8 3
Wesley Av RNFD/HAY WA11 91 G6 8
WAL/EG CH44 95 L8
Wesley Cl NSTN CH64 152 F6
Wesley Gv WAL/EG CH44 112 A2 5
Wesley St CSBY/WL L22 82 F5
STHP PR8 3 G5
WGNW/BIL/O WN5 78 F1
Wessex Cl WARR WA1 123 G6 7
WGN WN1 56 D4 4
Wessex Rd WGNW/BIL/O WN5 67 M4
West Albert Rd AIG/SPK L17 129 K1
West Av GOL/RIS/CU WA3 92 D4
WARRN/WOL WA2 121 K5
WARRS WA4 137 L4
West Bank CHLY/EC PR7 32 E5 11
Westbank Av WAL/NB CH45 95 L6 12
West Bank Rd EHL/KEN L7 114 A3
Westbank Rd RF/TRAN CH42 127 L2
West Bank St WDN WA8 16 C9
Westbourne Av CSBY/BLUN L23 71 K7
Westbourne Gdns STHP PR8 2 A9
Westbourne Gv WKBY CH48 124 C3 5
Westbourne Rd CHLY/EC PR7 32 D7 6
CL/PREN CH43 10 E7
STHP PR8 34 F1
WAL/EG CH44 111 H1
WARRS WA4 137 K6
WKBY CH48 124 C3
Westbridge Ms WGN WN1 4 F5
Westbrook Av PR/KW L34 100 D7
WARRS WA4 137 M3
Westbrook Centre
WARRW/BUR WA5 120 E4
Westbrook Crs
WARRW/BUR WA5 120 D4
Westbrook Rd MOR/LEA CH46 109 L6
WLTN L25 115 L8
Westbrook Wy
WARRW/BUR WA5 120 C4
Westbury Av WGNS/IIMK WN3 78 F3
Westbury Cl AIG/SPK L17 129 L4
WARR WA1 122 C5
Westbury St BIRK CH41 11 J9 3
Westcliffe Rd STHP PR8 2 B8
WD/CROXPK L12 98 C6
West Cl CL/PREN CH43 110 F8
PR/KW L34 101 J6
Westcombe Rd ANF/KKDL L4 97 L6 1
NPK/KEN L6 97 L6
Westcott Dr WGNS/IIMK WN3 78 E1
Westcott Rd ANF/KKDL L4 97 K7
Westcott Wy
CL/PREN CH43 126 F1 11
Westdale Rd RF/TRAN CH42 128 A3
WARR WA1 122 C6
WAV L15 114 B5
Westdale Vw WAV L15 114 B5 6
West Dene SKEL WN8 53 K3 2
West Derby Rd CLB/OSW/ST L13 98 A7
NPK/KEN L6 113 K1
West Derby St VAUX/LVPD L3 13 M6
West Derby Village
WD/CROXPK L12 98 D6
West Dr GR/UP/WCH CH49 110 C8
HES CH60 141 J6
NSTN CH64 152 F7
WARRW/BUR WA5 136 D1
Westend Av CHLY/EC PR7 42 F4
West End Gv RNFD/HAY WA11 90 B7
West End Rd RNFD/HAY WA11 90 B7
Westenra Av EP CH65 156 B7
Westerdale Dr CHTN/BK PR9 23 K8
Western Av HUY L36 115 K2
PS/BROM CH62 143 M1
SPK/HALE L24 146 E2
Western Dr ALL/GAR L19 130 C6
Westerton Rd WD/CROXPK L12 99 G7
Westfield Av AIMK WN4 91 J1
DV/KA/FCH L14 115 G3
Westfield Crs RUNC WA7 18 E6
Westfield Dr WD/CROXPK L12 99 G2
Westfield Gv WGN WN1 68 D2
Westfield Ms RUNC WA7 18 E5
Westfield Rd RUNC WA7 18 D6
WAL/EG CH44 111 M4
WLT/FAZ L9 84 A7
Westfields LEY/BBR PR5 29 J3
Westfield St ECCL WA10 8 F5
Westfield Wk KKBY L32 85 K4 2
Westford Rd WARRS WA4 137 J4 3
Westgate SKEL WN8 64 F4 8
Westgate Dr
WGNW/BIL/O WN5 66 F8 6
Westgate Rd PS/BROM CH62 143 K1
WAV L15 114 C8 12
West Gv HES CH60 141 H5
Westhaven Crs ORM L39 62 E5
Westhay Crs
GOL/RIS/CU WA3 107 J8 3
Westhead Av GOL/RIS/CU WA3 93 G5
NWD/KWIPK L33 86 B3
Westhead Cl NWD/KWIPK L33 86 C4 1
Westhead Rd LEY/BBR PR5 29 K3
Westhead Wk NWD/KWIPK L33 86 B3
West Heath Gv LYMM WA13 139 L1
Westhoughton Rd CHLY/EC PR7 44 B4
Westhouse Cl BEB CH63 143 L8 3
West Hyde LYMM WA13 139 L2
Westinghouse Cl
WGNNW/ST WN6 4 B4
West Kirby Rd MOR/LEA CH46 109 L8
Westlake Gv WGNE/HIN WN2 81 K1
Westlands Cl NSTN CH64 153 H4
West La FMBY L37 47 H7
RUNC WA7 150 A6
Westleigh La LEIGH WN7 81 M3
Westleigh Pl STHEL WA9 102 E8 1
Westlock WGNS/IIMK WN3 4 D8
West Mains SPK/HALE L24 147 J2
Westmead WGNNW/ST WN6 56 A5
West Meade MGHL L31 72 D3
Westminster Av NTHTN L30 84 A1
Westminster Cl WARRS WA4 138 E3
WDN WA8 133 K5 1
Westminster Dr
PS/BROM CH62 143 M7
RNFD/HAY WA11 91 H6
STHP PR8 34 C8
Westminster Gv EP CH65 20 C3
PR/KW L34 100 C8 1
Westminster Pl CHLY/EC PR7 30 C5
WARR WA1 14 E5
Westminster Rd ANF/KKDL L4 97 G6
BTL L20 7 K8
CHLY/EC PR7 32 E6 15
EP CH65 20 C2
WAL/EG CH44 111 K1 7
Westminster St
WGNW/BIL/O WN5 68 B7 13
Westmoorland St WGN WN1 5 J2
Westmoreland Pl EV L5 96 F8 9
Westmoreland Rd STHP PR8 3 K8
WAL/NB CH45 95 L6 13
Westmorland Av NTHTN L30 83 L2 8
WDN WA8 16 E1
Westmorland Rd HUY L36 116 A3
West Mt WGN WN1 68 F3
WGNW/BIL/O WN5 67 H7
West Oakhill Pk
CLB/OSW/ST L13 114 C3
Weston Crs RUNC WA7 149 H7
Weston Gv MGHL L31 72 F7
Weston Pk WGNNW/ST WN6 67 M2 3
Weston Point Expy RUNC WA7 18 C5
West Orchard La WLT/FAZ L9 84 F5
Westover Rd MGHL L31 72 E4
WARR WA1 122 B6
West Park Dr GTS/LS CH66 163 H5 12
West Park Rd ECCL WA10 8 B7
West Quay Rd
WARRN/WOL WA2 121 H2
West Rd CL/PREN CH43 110 F8
DV/KA/FCH L14 114 E3
EP CH65 20 D8
RUNC WA7 18 A9
SPK/HALE L24 131 M8
Westry Cl MOR/LEA CH46 109 K5
West Side STHEL WA9 9 L7
West Side Av RNFD/HAY WA11 90 C7
West St CHLY/EC PR7 32 E6
ECCL WA10 101 M4
PR/KW L34 100 E7
STHP PR8 2 F4
WAL/NB CH45 95 K8 8
WARRN/WOL WA2 14 F1
WGNE/HIN WN2 69 J5
WGNE/HIN WN2 81 K2
WGNNW/ST WN6 4 C2
West Ter CHLYE PR6 31 M1
West V NSTN CH64 153 G7
West Vw HUY L36 116 D3
SKEL WN8 53 K3
WARRN/WOL WA2 122 C4 4
West View Av HUY L36 116 D3

Westview Cl CL/PREN CH43 .. 126 F1 12
Westward Ho WKBY CH48 .... 124 F7
Westward Vw AIG/SPK L17 .... 129 J2
CSBY/WL L22 .... 82 D3 4
West Wy CHLY/EC PR7 .... 32 C3
MOR/LEA CH46 .... 110 A4
Westway CL/PREN CH43 .... 126 F1
GR/UP/WCH CH49 .... 125 M1
HES CH60 .... 141 H7
HTWN L38 .... 70 B1
MGHL L31 .... 72 E3
WAV L15 .... 114 D5
Westwell Rd CHLYE PR6 .... 32 F4 4
Westwick Pl HUY L36 .... 115 K2 2
Westwood RUNC WA7 .... 150 E4
Westwood Cl STHP PR8 .... 36 A2
Westwood Ct NSTN CH64 .... 153 G3
Westwood Gv WAL/EG CH44 .... 111 J1 5
Westwood La WGNS/IIMK WN3 .... 5 G9
Westwood Rd CALD/MH L18 .... 130 E5
CL/PREN CH43 .... 110 E7
WGNS/IIMK WN3 .... 4 E7
Westy La WARRS WA4 .... 15 M8
Wetheral Cl WGNE/HIN WN2 .... 81 L2
Wetherby Av WAL/EG CH44 .... 95 G8 5
Wetherby Cl NEWLW WA12 .... 91 L8 4
Wetherby Ct HUY L36 .... 99 L8 3
Wetherby Wy GTS/LS CH66 .... 155 K8
Wethersfield Rd CL/PREN CH43 .. 127 G1
Wetstone La WKBY CH48 .... 124 E4
Wexford Av SPK/HALE L24 .... 147 M3
Wexford Cl CL/PREN CH43 .... 127 G1
Wexford Rd CL/PREN CH43 .... 127 H1
Wexham Gdns WGNE/HIN WN2 .... 80 C2
Wexwood Gv RAIN/WH L35 .... 117 H3 7
Weybourne Cl
GR/UP/WCH CH49 .... 110 C6
Weybourne Dr WGNS/IIMK WN3 .. 79 G2
Weybridge Cl WARRS WA4 .... 138 A6
Weyman Av RAIN/WH L35 .... 117 G2
Weymoor Cl BEB CH63 .... 143 H3 6
Weymouth Av STHEL WA9 .... 103 H4
Weymouth Cl CHLDW L16 .... 115 H5 5
RUNC WA7 .... 151 G7 4
Weymouth Dr WGNE/HIN WN2 .... 81 J1
Weymouth Rd
WARRW/BUR WA5 .... 104 B7
Whaley La PEN/TH CH61 .... 126 B7
Whalley Av ECCL WA10 .... 89 G6
RNFD/HAY WA11 .... 76 B7 2
Whalley Cl WGNS/IIMK WN3 .... 79 J2
Whalley Ct NTHTN L30 .... 83 M1
Whalley Dr FMBY L37 .... 59 J3
ORM L39 .... 62 E5
Whalley Gv LEIGH WN7 .... 81 M4
WDN WA8 .... 134 F2
Whalley Rd CHLY/EC PR7 .... 42 A1
RF/TRAN CH42 .... 11 G8
Whalleys Rd SKEL WN8 .... 53 J8
Whalley St CHLY/EC PR7 .... 32 E6 16
TOX L8 .... 129 H1 15
WARR WA1 .... 15 H4
Wharf BRSC L40 .... 50 B1
Wharfdale Cl
WARRW/BUR WA5 .... 120 C6 1
Wharfedale RUNC WA7 .... 150 D7 4
Wharfedale Av RF/TRAN CH42 .... 127 K3
Wharfedale Dr PS/BROM CH62 .. 144 B8
RAIN/WH L35 .... 117 M2
Wharfedale Rd WAL/NB CH45 .... 95 H7 1
Wharfe La EP CH65 .... 156 C6
Wharford La RUNC WA7 .... 151 G2
Wharf Rd NEWLW WA12 .... 104 A3
Wharf St PS/BROM CH62 .... 128 D8
WARR WA1 .... 15 H7
Wharmby Rd RNFD/HAY WA11 .... 91 G7
Wharncliffe Rd
CLB/OSW/ST L13 .... 114 C2
Wharncliffe St
WGNE/HIN WN2 .... 69 M8 29
Wharton Cl GR/UP/WCH CH49 .... 109 M7
Whatcroft Cl RUNC WA7 .... 149 M7
Wheatacre SKEL WN8 .... 65 G5
Wheat Cft WARRW/BUR WA5 .. 120 E7 5
Wheatcroft Rd CALD/MH L18 .... 130 E3
Wheatear Cl NTHLY L27 .... 132 A1
Wheatfield Cl GTS/LS CH66 .... 162 E2
MOR/LEA CH46 .... 110 B6 2
NTHTN L30 .... 84 D2 2
Wheatfield Rd WDN WA8 .... 117 L8
Wheatfield Vw LITH L21 .... 83 K3 4
Wheat Hill Rd NTHLY L27 .... 116 A6
Wheatland Cl STHEL WA9 .... 118 E1 19
Wheatland Rd HES CH60 .... 141 L6
Wheatlands RUNC WA7 .... 150 A4
Wheatlands Cl NTHLY L27 .... 115 M7
Wheat La BRSC L40 .... 52 C2
Wheatlea Rd WGNS/IIMK WN3 .... 79 H4
Wheatley Av BTL L20 .... 84 A8
NEWLW WA12 .... 91 L8
Wheatsheaf Av STHEL WA9 .... 102 F7
Wheatsheaf Wk
WGNNW/ST WN6 .... 55 M4
Wheeler Dr MGHL L31 .... 85 K2
Wheldrake Cl GTS/LS CH66 .... 155 K8
Whelley WGN WN1 .... 69 G3
WGNE/HIN WN2 .... 69 H3
Whernside WDN WA8 .... 133 L3
Whetstone Hey GTS/LS CH66 .... 155 M8
Whetstone La BIRK CH41 .... 11 H8
RF/TRAN CH42 .... 127 M3
Whickham Cl WDN WA8 .... 134 B2 5
Whimberry Cl CHLYE PR6 .... 33 G5 11
Whimbrel Av NEWLW WA12 .... 104 E2
Whimbrel Cl RUNC WA7 .... 150 B8
Whimbrel Pk HLWD L26 .... 132 A4
Whinbury Ct STHEL WA9 .... 118 E1 20
Whinchat Av NEWLW WA12 .... 104 E1
Whinchat Dr GOL/RIS/CU WA3 .... 123 H2
Whinfell Gv RUNC WA7 .... 150 A8 5
Whinfell Rd WD/CROXPK L12 .... 98 E8
Whinfield Av CHLYE PR6 .... 32 F4 5
Whinfield Rd CSBY/BLUN L23 .... 71 J7
WLT/FAZ L9 .... 84 B7
Whinhowe Rd NG/CROX L11 .... 98 D3
Whinmoor Cl CL/PREN CH43 .... 110 F7 2
Whinmoor Rd AIN/FAZ L10 .... 85 J6
WD/CROXPK L12 .... 98 E8
Whinney Gv East MGHL L31 .... 72 E7 3
Whinney Gv West MGHL L31 .... 72 E7 4
Whinny La CHLY/EC PR7 .... 32 A2
Whistlecroft Ct WGNS/IIMK WN3 .... 5 L8
Whistley St WGNE/HIN WN2 .... 80 D2 7
Whiston La HUY L36 .... 116 C1
Whitbarrow Rd LYMM WA13 .... 139 L1
Whitbeam Gv WGNE/HIN WN2 .... 81 G3
Whitburn Cl AIMK WN4 .... 90 F1 5
Whitburn Rd NWD/KWIPK L33 .. 86 C1 7
Whitby Av CHTN/BK PR9 .... 22 E7
WAL/NB CH45 .... 95 G8
WARRN/WOL WA2 .... 121 M3
Whitby La CH/BCN CH1 .... 163 J6
Whitby Rd EP CH65 .... 20 D4
RUNC WA7 .... 19 H6
Whitby St NPK/KEN L6 .... 97 M7 3
Whitchurch Cl WARR WA1 .... 122 C5
Whitchurch Wy RUNC WA7 .... 149 M7 5
Whitcroft Rd NPK/KEN L6 .... 113 M2
Whiteacre WGNNW/ST WN6 .... 55 J3
Whitebeam GTS/LS CH66 .... 163 H4
Whitebeam Cl NWD/KWIPK L33 .... 74 B7
RUNC WA7 .... 150 E4
Whitebeam Dr
WD/CROXPK L12 .... 98 F2 6
Whitebeam Gdns RAIN/WH L35 .. 101 L7
Whitebeam Wk
GR/UP/WCH CH49 .... 125 K3
White Br BRSC L40 .... 39 M1
Whitechapel CLVPS L1 .... 13 G7
Whitecroft Av
GOL/RIS/CU WA3 .... 93 G4 7
Whitecroft Rd GTS/LS CH66 .... 163 G3
WGNS/IIMK WN3 .... 79 J3
Whitecross Rd
WARRW/BUR WA5 .... 121 G8
Whiteeside Cl
GR/UP/WCH CH49 .... 126 C1 2
Whitefield Av ANF/KKDL L4 .... 97 G5
Whitefield Cl
GR/UP/WCH CH49 .... 126 D2
HTWN L38 .... 70 B3 1
Whitefield Dr KKBY L32 .... 85 K3
Whitefield La BRSC L40 .... 39 L2
RAIN/WH L35 .... 116 C7
Whitefield Rd ECCL WA10 .... 8 A1
NPK/KEN L6 .... 113 K1
WARRS WA4 .... 137 K5
WLT/FAZ L9 .... 84 C8
Whitefields CHNE CH2 .... 165 K2
Whitefield Wy NPK/KEN L6 .... 113 J1 5
Whitegate Av GOL/RIS/CU WA3 .. 107 H3
Whitegate Cl PR/KW L34 .... 99 M1
White Gate Fold CHLY/EC PR7 .... 43 G2
Whitegates Cl NSTN CH64 .... 154 A4
Whitegates Crs NSTN CH64 .... 154 A5
Whitehall Av WGNNW/ST WN6 .... 55 G5
Whitehall La HOR/BR BL6 .... 57 M2
Whitehall Pl FROD/HEL WA6 .... 160 D5 3
FROD/HEL WA6 .... 160 E5 1
Whitehall St WGNS/IIMK WN3 .... 5 J7
Whitehart Cl ANF/KKDL L4 .... 97 K4
Whitehaven Cl STHP PR8 .... 47 K2 4
Whitehedge Rd ALL/GAR L19 .... 130 D6
Whitehey Rd SKEL WN8 .... 65 G5
Whitehorn Dr STBRV L28 .... 99 K6
White Horse Cl HOR/BR BL6 .... 45 L8 3
Whitehouse Av FMBY L37 .... 59 J2 3
White House Cl RNFD/HAY WA11 .. 90 D7
White House Dr WARR WA1 .... 123 G6 3
Whitehouse Expy RUNC WA7 .... 150 B8
White House La BRSC L40 .... 37 L4
Whitehouse La FMBY L37 .... 59 J2
HES CH60 .... 141 M4
Whitehouse Rd
CLB/OSW/ST L13 .... 114 D3 3
Whitelands Meadow
GR/UP/WCH CH49 .... 110 A8
Whiteledge Rd SKEL WN8 .... 65 K5
Whiteley's La BRSC L40 .... 63 L3
White Lodge Av HUY L36 .... 115 M2
White Lodge Cl PS/BROM CH62 .. 144 A8
White Lodge Dr AIMK WN4 .... 91 M1
Whitely Gv NWD/KWIPK L33 .... 74 C7 4
White Meadow Dr
CSBY/BLUN L23 .... 71 J7
Whitemere Ct EP CH65 .... 20 C1 3
White Moss Rd SKEL WN8 .... 64 E6
White Moss Rd South SKEL WN8 .. 65 G6
Whiterails Dr ORM L39 .... 50 F7
White Rock St NPK/KEN L6 .... 113 K1 8
Whitesands Rd LYMM WA13 .... 139 L1
Whiteside Av RNFD/HAY WA11 .... 90 A8
WGNE/HIN WN2 .... 69 M6
WGNNW/ST WN6 .... 4 A1
Whiteside Cl EV L5 .... 96 F8 10
Whiteside Rd RNFD/HAY WA11 .... 90 D7
Whitestock SKEL WN8 .... 65 G5
Whitestone Cl PR/KW L34 .... 99 L3 1
White St CLVPS L1 .... 112 F5
WARR WA1 .... 14 C6
WARRS WA4 .... 137 L4
WDN WA8 .... 134 C8 6
WGNW/BIL/O WN5 .... 67 K7 5
Whitethorn Av
WARRW/BUR WA5 .... 120 B8
Whitewell Dr
GR/UP/WCH CH49 .... 110 B7
Whitewood Cl AIMK WN4 .... 79 J7 2
Whitewood Pk WLT/FAZ L9 .... 84 F7
Whitfield Av WARR WA1 .... 122 B6
Whitfield Gv
RNFD/HAY WA11 .... 90 C7 10
Whitfield La HES CH60 .... 141 J4
Whitfield St RF/TRAN CH42 .... 127 M1 11
Whitford Rd RF/TRAN CH42 .... 127 L1
Whitham Av CSBY/BLUN L23 .... 83 H3
Whithorn St EHL/KEN L7 .... 113 M5 10
Whitland Rd NPK/KEN L6 .... 113 M2
Whitledge Gn AIMK WN4 .... 79 J8
Whitledge Rd AIMK WN4 .... 79 J8
Whitley Av WARRS WA4 .... 138 C1
Whitley Cl RUNC WA7 .... 18 F7
Whitley Crs WGN WN1 .... 68 D1
WGNE/HIN WN2 .... 80 D6
Whitley Rd SKEL WN8 .... 66 F4
Whitley St VAUX/LVPD L3 .... 12 D2
Whitlow Av GOL/RIS/CU WA3 .... 92 B4
Whitman St WAV L15 .... 114 A6
Whitmoor Cl RAIN/WH L35 .... 118 A4 4
Whitney Pl WLTN L25 .... 131 L3 6
Whitney Rd WLTN L25 .... 131 L2
Whitsbury Av WGNE/HIN WN2 .... 80 F1
Whitstable Pk WDN WA8 .... 134 A1
Whitstone Cl WLTN L25 .... 131 G3
Whitstone Dr SKEL WN8 .... 65 M6
Whittaker Av
WARRN/WOL WA2 .... 121 M3 9
Whittaker Cl
CLB/OSW/ST L13 .... 114 B4 2
Whittam Rd CHLY/EC PR7 .... 32 D8
Whittier St TOX L8 .... 113 L6
Whittle Av RNFD/HAY WA11 .... 90 C8
WARRW/BUR WA5 .... 120 C6
Whittle Cl EV L5 .... 97 G7 9
Whittle Dr ORM L39 .... 51 G6
Whittle Hall La
WARRW/BUR WA5 .... 120 B7
Whittle La WGNNW/ST WN6 .... 41 G8
Whittle St ECCL WA10 .... 101 M4
EV L5 .... 97 G7
Whittlewood Cl
GOL/RIS/CU WA3 .... 107 J8 4
Whittlewood Ct
NWD/KWIPK L33 .... 86 B1
Whitwell Cl WARRW/BUR WA5 .... 119 M6
WGNNW/ST WN6 .... 55 M3 8
Whitworth Cl GOL/RIS/CU WA3 .. 123 G2
Whitworth Dr CHLY/EC PR7 .... 32 C7
Wholesome La CHTN/BK PR9 .... 37 L3
Wicket Cl NG/CROX L11 .... 85 M8 7
Wickham Cl WAL/EG CH44 .... 111 M3
Wicklow Cl GTS/LS CH66 .... 155 J7
Wicks Crs FMBY L37 .... 58 E1
Wicks Gdns FMBY L37 .... 59 G2
Wicks Gn FMBY L37 .... 58 E2
Wicks Green Cl FMBY L37 .... 58 E1
Wicks La FMBY L37 .... 58 E2
Wicksten Dr RUNC WA7 .... 19 L4
Widdale Av RAIN/WH L35 .... 117 M2 4
Widdale Cl WARRW/BUR WA5 .... 120 B6
Widdrington Rd WGN WN1 .... 68 F3
Widgeons Covert BEB CH63 .... 142 B8
Widmore Rd WLTN L25 .... 131 L1
Widnes Rd WARRW/BUR WA5 .... 135 J3
WDN WA8 .... 16 E4
Wiend WGN WN1 .... 4 F4
The Wiend BEB CH63 .... 128 C8
RF/TRAN CH42 .... 127 M4
Wigan La CHLY/EC PR7 .... 43 M6
WGN WN1 .... 4 F1
Wigan Lower Rd
WGNNW/ST WN6 .... 67 L1
Wigan Rd AIMK WN4 .... 91 K1
CHLY/EC PR7 .... 31 L1
GOL/RIS/CU WA3 .... 92 D2
LEIGH WN7 .... 81 L6
ORM L39 .... 51 H8
SKEL WN8 .... 65 H5
WGNE/HIN WN2 .... 69 J2
WGNNW/ST WN6 .... 55 K8
WGNW/BIL/O WN5 .... 78 B6
Wigan St WGNE/HIN WN2 .... 80 C3
Wiggins La BRSC L40 .... 27 J8
Wight Cl EP CH65 .... 163 L4
Wightman Av NEWLW WA12 .... 91 L8 5
Wightman St NPK/KEN L6 .... 113 K2 14
Wight Moss Wy STHP PR8 .... 35 M2
Wigmore Cl GOL/RIS/CU WA3 .. 107 J8 3
Wignall Cl KKBY L32 .... 86 A6 5
Wignalls Meadow HTWN L38 .... 70 B2 3
Wigshaw La GOL/RIS/CU WA3 .... 106 F3
Wigston Cl STHP PR8 .... 47 K1
Wilberforce Rd ANF/KKDL L4 .... 97 K4
Wilbraham Pl EV L5 .... 96 F8 11
Wilbraham St EV L5 .... 96 F8
LEIGH WN7 .... 81 L8 5
STHEL WA9 .... 119 G2
Wilburn St ANF/KKDL L4 .... 97 H4
Wilbur St STHEL WA9 .... 103 G6 3
Wilcock Cl EV L5 .... 96 F8
Wilcock Rd RNFD/HAY WA11 .... 91 J5
Wilcock St WGNS/IIMK WN3 .... 4 B5
Wilcote Cl WDN WA8 .... 134 E1
Wilcove SKEL WN8 .... 65 H4
Wild Arum Cl
GOL/RIS/CU WA3 .... 93 G5 14
Wildbrook Dr BIRK CH41 .... 110 F3
Wildcherry Gdns RAIN/WH L35 .. 101 K6
Wilderspool Cswy WARRS WA4 .... 14 E8
Wilderspool Crs WARRS WA4 .... 137 K4
Wilde St VAUX/LVPD L3 .... 13 J6 1
Wilding Av RUNC WA7 .... 19 K3
Wildings Old La
GOL/RIS/CU WA3 .... 106 C5
Wilding St WGNS/IIMK WN3 .... 5 J8
Wild Pl BTL L20 .... 84 A6
Wildwood Gv WARR WA1 .... 122 D6
Wilfer Cl EHL/KEN L7 .... 113 L5 11
Wilfred Owen Dr
CL/PREN CH43 .... 111 G6
Wilfred St WGNW/BIL/O WN5 .... 68 B6
Wilfrid's Pl WGNNW/ST WN6 .... 56 A4
Wilkes Av MOR/LEA CH46 .... 110 D2
Wilkesley Av WGNNW/ST WN6 .... 55 M5
Wilkie St WAV L15 .... 114 A6 13
Wilkinson Av WARR WA1 .... 122 B7
Wilkinson Cl WDN WA8 .... 134 C8 7
Wilkinson St BIRK CH41 .... 10 F7
WARRN/WOL WA2 .... 15 H1
Wilkinson St North EP CH65 .... 20 C2
Wilkin St ANF/KKDL L4 .... 97 G6 17
Willan St CL/PREN CH43 .... 127 K1
Willard Av WGNW/BIL/O WN5 .... 77 M2
Willard St BTL L20 .... 83 M7
Willaston Dr HLWD L26 .... 132 C7
Willaston Rd ANF/KKDL L4 .... 97 K4
BEB CH63 .... 142 F7
MOR/LEA CH46 .... 109 M4 3
NSTN CH64 .... 153 M3
Willedstan Av CSBY/BLUN L23 .... 83 G2
William Brown St CLVPS L1 .... 13 H6
William Harvey Cl NTHTN L30 .... 84 B2
William Henry St BTL L20 .... 6 F7
VAUX/LVPD L3 .... 13 K3
William Morris Av BTL L20 .... 84 A8
William Moult St EV L5 .... 96 F8
William Penn Cl
WARRW/BUR WA5 .... 136 A1 5
William Rd RNFD/HAY WA11 .... 90 B8
William Roberts Av KKBY L32 .... 85 L3
Williams Av BTL L20 .... 7 M1
NEWLW WA12 .... 91 L8
Williamson St STHEL WA9 .... 9 M4
Williams St PR/KW L34 .... 100 F7
William St BIRK CH41 .... 11 K5
ECCL WA10 .... 9 G4 2
WAL/EG CH44 .... 112 A3 21
WDN WA8 .... 134 E3
WGNS/IIMK WN3 .... 5 H8
William Wall Rd LITH L21 .... 83 K3
Willingdon Rd CHLDW L16 .... 115 G4
Willington Av PS/BROM CH62 .... 155 G2
Willink Rd RNFD/HAY WA11 .... 89 L6 1
Willis Cl RAIN/WH L35 .... 116 F3
Willis La RAIN/WH L35 .... 116 F3
Willis St WARR WA1 .... 15 J3
Williton Rd CHLDW L16 .... 115 G8
Willmer Rd ANF/KKDL L4 .... 97 K6
RF/TRAN CH42 .... 10 F8
Willoughby Cl
WARRW/BUR WA5 .... 120 E4
Willoughby Dr ECCL WA10 .... 101 K5
Willoughby Rd CSBY/WL L22 .... 83 G4
DV/KA/FCH L14 .... 115 G3
Willow Av HUY L36 .... 116 A5
KKBY L32 .... 85 L2
NEWLW WA12 .... 104 F1
RAIN/WH L35 .... 116 F2
WDN WA8 .... 134 D3
Willow Bank FROD/HEL WA6 .... 167 G3
Willowbank Cl HUY L36 .... 99 L8 4
Willow Bank Est NEWLW WA12 .. 105 H2
Willowbank Rd
PS/BROM CH62 .... 128 D7 6
RF/TRAN CH42 .... 127 M2
Willow Brook ORM L39 .... 36 C7
Willowbrook Dr
WGNNW/ST WN6 .... 55 K6
Willowbrow Rd BEB CH63 .... 153 M2
Willow Cl CHLYE PR6 .... 44 D5
RUNC WA7 .... 19 K9
Willow Crs BRSC L40 .... 39 H7 1
WARR WA1 .... 122 D5
Willowcroft Rd WAL/EG CH44 . 111 L2 9
Willowdale NEWLW WA12 .... 105 G2
Willowdale Rd
CALD/MH L18 .... 114 B8 14
WLT/FAZ L9 .... 97 J1
Willowdale Wy GTS/LS CH66 .... 163 H5
Willow Dr CHLY/EC PR7 .... 42 F1 2
SKEL WN8 .... 65 G4
WARRS WA4 .... 137 M4 4
WGNE/HIN WN2 .... 81 H2
Willow End BRSC L40 .... 52 B1
Willowfield Gv AIMK WN4 .... 91 J3
Willow Gn BRSC L40 .... 39 J2
ORM L39 .... 51 H8 5
WLTN L25 .... 131 H1
Willow Gv AIMK WN4 .... 80 A8 3
CHNE CH2 .... 165 J3
CHTN/BK PR9 .... 25 G6
FMBY L37 .... 59 H1
GOL/RIS/CU WA3 .... 92 C4
GTS/LS CH66 .... 163 J4
MOR/LEA CH46 .... 109 M6
RAIN/WH L35 .... 101 G8
WAV L15 .... 114 C5
Willowhey CHTN/BK PR9 .... 25 H2
Willow Hey MGHL L31 .... 73 G6
SKEL WN8 .... 65 H4
Willow La BEB CH63 .... 153 M2
Willow Lea CL/PREN CH43 .... 127 H1
Willow Ldg WGNE/HIN WN2 .... 80 D4 8
Willow Pk GR/UP/WCH CH49 .... 125 L1
Willow Rd CHLYE PR6 .... 33 G3
ECCL WA10 .... 101 L2
NEWLW WA12 .... 105 G1
RNFD/HAY WA11 .... 91 G6
WAV L15 .... 114 A5 8
WGNNW/ST WN6 .... 68 B1
The Willows BRSC L40 .... 40 E3
FROD/HEL WA6 .... 160 E6
STHEL WA9 .... 118 E1 21
WAL/NB CH45 .... 95 G6
Willow Tree Av STHEL WA9 .... 118 F1
Willow Tree Cl WGN WN1 .... 68 D1
Willow Wk SKEL WN8 .... 65 K1 4
Willow Wy CSBY/BLUN L23 .... 71 G8
NG/CROX L11 .... 85 M7
Wills Av MGHL L31 .... 72 E3
Willsford Av KKBY L32 .... 85 K2
Wilmcote Gv STHP PR8 .... 47 K1
Wilmere La WDN WA8 .... 118 C7
Wilmot Av WARRW/BUR WA5 .... 120 B7
Wilmot Dr GOL/RIS/CU WA3 .... 92 B6
Wilmslow Av GTS/LS CH66 .... 156 A8 3
Wilmslow Crs WARRS WA4 .... 138 F1
Wilmslow Dr GTS/LS CH66 .... 156 A8
Wilne Rd WAL/NB CH45 .... 95 J7 7
Wilsden Rd WDN WA8 .... 133 K4 3
Wilsford Cl GOL/RIS/CU WA3 .... 92 D4 6
Wilson Av WAL/EG CH44 .... 112 A1 1
WGNNW/ST WN6 .... 68 D3
Wilson Cl ECCL WA10 .... 8 D5
WARRS WA4 .... 138 F2
Wilson Gv ALL/GAR L19 .... 130 E7 5
Wilson La GOL/RIS/CU WA3 .... 107 G8
Wilson Patten St WARR WA1 .... 14 C7
Wilson Rd HUY L36 .... 116 D5
RAIN/WH L35 .... 116 F2
WAL/EG CH44 .... 112 A1 2
Wilsons La LITH L21 .... 83 K5
Wilson St TOX L8 .... 129 J1 23
WARRW/BUR WA5 .... 14 C1
Wilstan Av BEB CH63 .... 127 M8 5
Wilton Av WGNE/HIN WN2 .... 69 H3
Wilton Gv CLB/OSW/ST L13 .... 114 C3 4
Wilton La GOL/RIS/CU WA3 .... 93 J8
Wilton Rd HUY L36 .... 115 M3
RF/TRAN CH42 .... 128 C4
WGNNW/ST WN6 .... 55 J6
Wiltons Dr PR/KW L34 .... 99 L2
Wilton St AIMK WN4 .... 79 H7 5
WAL/EG CH44 .... 111 K1
WGN WN1 .... 5 G6
Wiltshire Cl WARR WA1 .... 122 F7
Wiltshire Pl WGNW/BIL/O WN5 .... 67 L7
Wimbledon St WAL/NB CH45 .... 95 K8
WAV L15 .... 114 A6 14
Wimborne Cl DV/KA/FCH L14 .... 99 K7
Wimborne Pl DV/KA/FCH L14 .... 99 K8
Wimborne Rd DV/KA/FCH L14 .... 99 K8
WGNW/BIL/O WN5 .... 67 J5
Wimborne Wy PEN/TH CH61 .... 125 M6
Wimbourne Av PEN/TH CH61 .... 126 C8
Wimbrick Cl MOR/LEA CH46 .... 110 B5 3
Wimbrick Crs ORM L39 .... 62 F2
Wimbrick Hey MOR/LEA CH46 .... 110 B5
Wimpole St EHL/KEN L7 .... 113 K3
Winchester Av AIMK WN4 .... 91 J2
AIN/FAZ L10 .... 84 F2
CHLY/EC PR7 .... 44 A2
CSBY/WL L22 .... 82 E3
EP CH65 .... 20 F7
WARRW/BUR WA5 .... 120 E8
Winchester Cl
WGNW/BIL/O WN5 .... 67 H6
WLTN L25 .... 131 K6
Winchester Gv WGNS/IIMK WN3 .... 5 H8
Winchester Pl WDN WA8 .... 133 L5 2
Winchester Rd NPK/KEN L6 .... 97 L7
RNFD/HAY WA11 .... 91 G4
WGNW/BIL/O WN5 .... 77 M4
Winchfield Rd WAV L15 .... 114 B7 8
Windbourne Rd AIG/SPK L17 .. 129 K3 4
Windermere Av
RNFD/HAY WA11 .... 89 J5
WARRN/WOL WA2 .... 121 L2
WDN WA8 .... 134 D1 10
Windermere Cl NSTN CH64 .... 153 H6 2
Windermere Crs STHP PR8 .... 47 L2
Windermere Dr CHLYE PR6 .... 44 D4
MGHL L31 .... 73 G3
NWD/KWIPK L33 .... 85 M1
RNFD/HAY WA11 .... 76 B3
WD/CROXPK L12 .... 98 E4
Windermere Rd CHLYE PR6 .... 33 G6 14
CL/PREN CH43 .... 110 E7
EP CH65 .... 163 L3
HTWN L38 .... 70 C1
RNFD/HAY WA11 .... 90 D7
WGNE/HIN WN2 .... 69 J6
WGNE/HIN WN2 .... 80 D5
WGNW/BIL/O WN5 .... 67 H5
Windermere St EV L5 .... 97 J7
WDN WA8 .... 134 D1
WGN WN1 .... 5 J2
Windermere Ter TOX L8 .... 113 K8 2
Windfield Cl NWD/KWIPK L33 .... 74 C7 5
Windfield Gdns GTS/LS CH66 .... 155 M6
Windfield Gn ALL/GAR L19 .... 145 M2
Windfield Rd ALL/GAR L19 .... 145 M1
Windgate SKEL WN8 .... 65 H4
Windle Ash MGHL L31 .... 72 E3
Windle Av CSBY/BLUN L23 .... 83 J1
Windlebrook Crs ECCL WA10 .... 88 D7
Windle City ECCL WA10 .... 89 H7
Windle Ct GOL/RIS/CU WA3 .... 122 E1 6
NSTN CH64 .... 153 G3
Windle Gv ECCL WA10 .... 88 E7
Windle Hall Dr ECCL WA10 .... 89 G6
Windlehurst Av ECCL WA10 .... 89 G7
Windleshaw Rd ECCL WA10 .... 8 B1
Windleshaw St WGNS/IIMK WN3 .... 5 J8
Windle St ECCL WA10 .... 8 E2
Windle V ECCL WA10 .... 8 C2
Windmill Av CSBY/BLUN L23 .... 71 H8
ORM L39 .... 51 H8
Windmill Cl NWD/KWIPK L33 .... 74 A8 12
WARRS WA4 .... 137 L7
WGN WN1 .... 5 H3
Windmill Gdns STHEL WA9 .... 102 F1 3
Windmill Hts SKEL WN8 .... 66 C5
Windmill Hill Av RUNC WA7 .... 150 F3
Windmill Hill Av East
RUNC WA7 .... 150 F5
Windmill Hill Av North
RUNC WA7 .... 150 E2
Windmill Hill Av South
RUNC WA7 .... 150 F4
Windmill Hill Av West
RUNC WA7 .... 150 E3
Windmill La WARRS WA4 .... 137 L7
WARRS WA4 .... 151 J6
WARRW/BUR WA5 .... 120 A8
Windmill Rd SKEL WN8 .... 66 B6
Windmill St RUNC WA7 .... 19 K3
Window La ALL/GAR L19 .... 145 L1
Windrows SKEL WN8 .... 65 H4
Windscale Rd
WARRN/WOL WA2 .... 122 C3
Windsor Av CHLY/EC PR7 .... 44 A7
LITH L21 .... 83 J5
NEWLW WA12 .... 104 F3
Windsor Cl BRSC L40 .... 52 A2
CHLY/EC PR7 .... 32 D6 6
GR/UP/WCH CH49 .... 125 M2 4
NTHTN L30 .... 72 B8 1
PS/BROM CH62 .... 128 C6
Windsor Ct STHP PR8 .... 2 B9
Windsor Crs WGNE/HIN WN2 .... 57 M8
Windsor Dr EP CH65 .... 163 J2
RNFD/HAY WA11 .... 91 J6
WARRS WA4 .... 138 D2
Windsor Gv RUNC WA7 .... 19 K7
WGNE/HIN WN2 .... 81 K2 6
Windsor Park Rd AIN/FAZ L10 .... 85 G2
Windsor Rd AIMK WN4 .... 91 K3
BTL L20 .... 84 A8 4
CHLY/EC PR7 .... 30 E6
CHLY/EC PR7 .... 32 D6
CHTN/BK PR9 .... 3 L4
CLB/OSW/ST L13 .... 97 M7
ECCL WA10 .... 8 A5
FMBY L37 .... 59 G4
GOL/RIS/CU WA3 .... 92 E5
HUY L36 .... 115 K2 5
MGHL L31 .... 72 E5
RAIN/WH L35 .... 117 G1
SKEL WN8 .... 66 C5

WDN WA8 134 C1
WGNW/BIL/O WN5 78 B8
WLT/FAZ L9 84 C7 8
Windsor St BIRK CH41 10 F7 4
TOX L8 113 H6
WAL/NB CH45 95 K4
WARRW/BUR WA5 121 G7
WGN WN1 5 H2
Windsor Vw TOX L8 113 K6
Windus St ECCL WA10 8 D5
Windways GTS/LS CH66 155 M6
Windy Arbor Cl RAIN/WH L35 116 F4
Windy Arbor Rd RAIN/WH L35 116 E5
Windy Bank PS/BROM CH62 128 C7 3
Windy Bank Av
GOL/RIS/CU WA3 93 G5 8
Windy Harbour Rd STHP PR8 35 G6
Wineva Gdns CSBY/BLUN L23 83 H2
Win Field Cl WGNNW/ST WN6 4 B4
Winfield Wy WDN WA8 16 F3
Winford St WAL/EG CH44 111 M2 12
Winfrith Cl BEB CH63 143 H3 7
Winfrith Dr BEB CH63 143 H3
Winfrith Rd WARRN/WOL WA2 122 C4
WLTN L25 131 L1
Wingate Av RAIN/WH L35 101 M7
Wingate Cl CL/PREN CH43 127 G1 8
Wingate Rd AIG/SPK L17 130 A3
NWD/KWIPK L33 86 B1
PS/BROM CH62 144 A8
Wingates Rd WGN WN1 56 E8
Wingfield Cl SFTN L29 71 M5
WGNNW/ST WN6 68 C1
Wingrave Wy NG/CROX L11 98 D4
Winhill WLTN L25 131 J1
Winifred La ORM L39 62 D4
Winifred Rd AIN/FAZ L10 85 K6 3
Winifred St EHL/KEN L7 113 K4
WARRN/WOL WA2 15 G2
WGNS/IIMK WN3 5 J7
Winkle St TOX L8 113 H8 13
Winmarleigh St WARR WA1 14 C6
Winmoss Dr NWD/KWIPK L33 74 B8
Winnington Rd HOY CH47 124 C1 1
The Winnows RUNC WA7 149 M4 1
Winscar Rd WGNE/HIN WN2 69 M7
Winsford Cl RNFD/HAY WA11 91 H6 7
Winsford Dr WARRW/BUR WA5 104 A6
Winsford Gv GTS/LS CH66 162 E2
Winsford Rd CLB/OSW/ST L13 98 B7 2
Winsham Cl KKBY L32 86 B5 8
Winsham Rd KKBY L32 86 A5
Winskill Rd NG/CROX L11 98 C4
Winslade Rd ANF/KKDL L4 97 K4
Winslow Cl RUNC WA7 150 F5
Winslow St ANF/KKDL L4 97 H5
Winsmoor Dr WGNE/HIN WN2 81 G1
Winstanley Cl
WARRW/BUR WA5 120 E8 7
Winstanley Pl WGNS/IIMK WN3 5 J8
Winstanley Rd AIMK WN4 78 D6
CSBY/WL L22 83 G3
NSTN CH64 153 G8
PS/BROM CH62 128 D6
SKEL WN8 65 H5
WGNE/HIN WN2 80 B5
WGNW/BIL/O WN5 78 B2
Winstanley St
WGNW/BIL/O WN5 68 B7 14
Winster Dr NTHLY L27 132 C2
WGNE/HIN WN2 80 B3 5
The Winsters SKEL WN8 65 H4 2
Winston Av NEWLW WA12 104 D2
STHEL WA9 103 K3
Winston Crs STHP PR8 36 A3
Winston Dr CL/PREN CH43 110 E8 1
Winstone Rd DV/KA/FCH L14 115 J1
Winston Gv MOR/LEA CH46 110 A5
Winterburn Crs WD/CROXPK L12 98 F6
Winterely Dr HLWD L26 132 C7
Winter Gv STHEL WA9 103 K2
Winterhey Av WAL/EG CH44 111 K3
Winter St NPK/KEN L6 113 J2
Winthrop Pk CL/PREN CH43 111 G8
Winton Av WGNW/BIL/O WN5 67 M8
Winton Cl WAL/NB CH45 95 J5
Winton Gv RUNC WA7 150 F4 5
Winton Rd GOL/RIS/CU WA3 93 G8
Winward St LEIGH WN7 81 K8
Winwick La GOL/RIS/CU WA3 105 M3
Winwick Link Rd
WARRN/WOL WA2 105 K7
Winwick Rd NEWLW WA12 105 G3
WARRN/WOL WA2 14 E3
Winwick St WARRN/WOL WA2 14 E4
Winwick Vw WARRW/BUR WA5 103 M4
Wirral Cl BEB CH63 143 H2
GOL/RIS/CU WA3 107 G2
Wirral Crs NSTN CH64 153 H8
Wirral Dr WGNS/IIMK WN3 78 E3
Wirral Gdns BEB CH63 143 H2
Wirral Mt WAL/NB CH45 95 H8
WKBY CH48 124 F3
Wirral Vw ALL/GAR L19 130 B7
Wirral Vls WAL/NB CH45 95 G7 8
Wirral Wy CL/PREN CH43 110 E8
NSTN CH64 152 C2
WKBY CH48 124 D3
Wisenholme Cl RUNC WA7 161 G1
Witham Cl NTHTN L30 84 C1
WGNNW/ST WN6 55 M4
Witham Rd SKEL WN8 64 F4
Withburn Cl
GR/UP/WCH CH49 110 A8 12
Withensfield WAL/NB CH45 95 K7
Withen's La WAL/NB CH45 95 K8
Withens Rd MGHL L31 72 F2
The Withens STBRV L28 99 K6
Withers Av WARRN/WOL WA2 121 M5
Wither's La KNUT WA16 139 L8
Withert Av BEB CH63 127 M5
Withington Av
GOL/RIS/CU WA3 107 J1
Withington La CHLY/EC PR7 42 A3
WGNE/HIN WN2 69 K3
Withington Rd SPK/HALE L24 147 H2
WAL/EG CH44 111 L2
Withins Fld HTWN L38 70 B2
Withins La HTWN L38 60 B6
Withins Rd GOL/RIS/CU WA3 107 H2
RNFD/HAY WA11 91 G5
Within Wy SPK/HALE L24 148 A4
Withnell Cl CLB/OSW/ST L13 114 D3
Withnell Gv CHLYE PR6 33 G4
Withnell Rd CLB/OSW/ST L13 114 D3
Withy Cl FROD/HEL WA6 160 E5
Withycombe Rd
WARRW/BUR WA5 136 A1
Witley Av MOR/LEA CH46 110 A4
Witley Cl MOR/LEA CH46 110 A4
Witney Cl GR/UP/WCH CH49 125 L2 6
Witney Gdns WARRS WA4 138 B7
Wittenham Cl
GR/UP/WCH CH49 126 B1 7
Wittering La HES CH60 140 F6
Wittlon Rd CLB/OSW/ST L13 97 M7
Witton Wy RNFD/HAY WA11 76 C6
Witt Rd WDN WA8 16 C6
Wivern Pl RUNC WA7 19 K2
Woburn Av LEIGH WN7 81 M4
NEWLW WA12 104 F3
Woburn Cl CLB/OSW/ST L13 114 B1 7
RNFD/HAY WA11 91 H6 8
Woburn Dr WDN WA8 117 M8
Woburn Hl CLB/OSW/ST L13 114 B1
Woburn Pl RF/TRAN CH42 128 B3 13
Woburn Rd WAL/NB CH45 95 K7
WARRN/WOL WA2 121 J1
Wokefield Wy ECCL WA10 101 K1
Wokingham Gv HUY L36 116 A5
The Wold CHLYE PR6 33 J2
Wolfenden Av BTL L20 84 A8
Wolferton Cl
GR/UP/WCH CH49 110 D6 5
Wolfe St TOX L8 113 G8 10
Wolfrick Dr BEB CH63 143 K4
Wolfson Sq AIMK WN4 91 H1
Wollaton Dr STHP PR8 36 B2
Wolmer St AIMK WN4 91 J1
Wolseley Rd ECCL WA10 8 E2
Wolsey Cl AIMK WN4 79 J8
Wolsey St BTL L20 7 H9
Wolstenholme Sq CLVPS L1 13 H9
Wolverham Rd EP CH65 20 D8
Wolverton SKEL WN8 65 H5
Wolverton Dr RUNC WA7 150 F4
Wolverton St NPK/KEN L6 97 L7
Woodacre Rd GTS/LS CH66 156 B5
Woodale Cl WARRW/BUR WA5 120 D4
Woodall Dr RUNC WA7 19 J6
Wood Av BTL L20 7 M1
Woodbank Cl CHLDW L16 115 H5
Woodbank Pk CL/PREN CH43 127 G1
Woodbank Rd EP CH65 163 K3
WARRW/BUR WA5 136 C1
Woodberry Cl
CL/PREN CH43 126 F1 13
NWD/KWIPK L33 74 B7 7
Woodbine St EV L5 96 F6
Woodbourne Rd
DV/KA/FCH L14 114 F1 1
Woodbridge Av HLWD L26 131 M3
Woodbrook Av WLT/FAZ L9 84 B7
Woodbrook Dr WGNS/IIMK WN3 78 F1
Woodburn Bvd BEB CH63 128 A5
Woodburn Dr HES CH60 141 H7 2
Woodchurch WGN WN1 5 L1
Woodchurch La GTS/LS CH66 156 A8
RF/TRAN CH42 127 K3
Woodchurch Rd CL/PREN CH43 127 G4
CLB/OSW/ST L13 114 C1
GR/UP/WCH CH49 126 D4
RF/TRAN CH42 127 L2
Wood Cl BIRK CH41 11 H3
Woodclose GTS/LS CH66 155 J4
Wood Cl KKBY L32 85 M3
Woodcock Dr
WGNE/HIN WN2 80 D3 8
Woodcock Fold CHLY/EC PR7 30 E6
Woodcote Av EP CH65 163 K3 8
Woodcote Bank RF/TRAN CH42 128 B6
Woodcote Cl NWD/KWIPK L33 86 C1 8
WARRN/WOL WA2 121 M4 7
The Woodcotes
PS/BROM CH62 143 M7
Woodcot La HES CH60 141 G4
Woodcourt WGNS/IIMK WN3 4 D8
Woodcroft SKEL WN8 65 H5 1
WGNNW/ST WN6 55 G7 2
Woodcroft Dr PEN/TH CH61 141 H3
Woodcroft La BEB CH63 128 B5 2
Woodcroft Rd WAV L15 113 M6
Woodcroft Wy STHEL WA9 118 E1 22
Woodedge AIMK WN4 91 J2
Woodend PEN/TH CH61 141 H1
Woodend Av CSBY/BLUN L23 71 G7
MGHL L31 72 E6
SPK/HALE L24 131 L8
Woodend La GOL/RIS/CU WA3 123 M3
SPK/HALE L24 146 E1
Woodend Rd EP CH65 156 B7
Woodene Cl KKBY L32 86 C6 2
Woodfall CHLY/EC PR7 32 D3
Woodfall Cl NSTN CH64 153 J7
Woodfall Gv NSTN CH64 153 J7
Woodfall La NSTN CH64 153 H7
Woodfarm Hey STBRV L28 99 J5
Woodfield Av BEB CH63 128 A5 1
Woodfield Crs AIMK WN4 91 J3 6
Woodfield Rd BEB CH63 143 J2
CHLY/EC PR7 32 E4 9
ORM L39 62 E2
PEN/TH CH61 141 G1
WLT/FAZ L9 84 B8 3
Woodfield Rd North EP CH65 20 C4
Woodfield St WGNE/HIN WN2 69 J2
Woodford Av GOL/RIS/CU WA3 92 F6
Woodford Cl FROD/HEL WA6 166 D3 4
RUNC WA7 149 K7 4
WARRS WA4 138 E2
Woodford Copse CHLY/EC PR7 32 B6
Woodford Rd DV/KA/FCH L14 115 G1
ECCL WA10 88 E7 2
PS/BROM CH62 128 D5
Woodford St WGNW/BIL/O WN5 67 K7
Woodgarth LEIGH WN7 81 L8 6
Woodgate NTHLY L27 115 L7
Woodger St ALL/GAR L19 130 E8 7
Wood Gn CL/PREN CH43 110 E5 10
PR/KW L34 100 E7
Woodgreen Cl
WGNE/HIN WN2 80 F1 14
Woodgreen Rd
CLB/OSW/ST L13 114 C1
Wood Gv CLB/OSW/ST L13 114 B3
Woodhall Av WAL/EG CH44 111 M1 14
Woodhall Cl WARRW/BUR WA5 120 C5
Woodhall Rd CLB/OSW/ST L13 114 C2
Woodham Gv NSTN CH64 153 H8 13
Woodhart La CHLY/EC PR7 30 E8
Woodhatch Rd RUNC WA7 150 C8
Woodhead Gv
WGNS/IIMK WN3 79 K3 1
Woodhead Rd PS/BROM CH62 128 E7
Woodhead St
PS/BROM CH62 128 D6 4
Woodhey Gv BEB CH63 128 B6 2
Woodhey Rd ALL/GAR L19 130 C6 9
BEB CH63 128 B6
Woodhouse Cl ANF/KKDL L4 97 G6 18
GOL/RIS/CU WA3 123 H2
Woodhouse Dr WGNNW/ST WN6 68 A2
Woodhouse La WGNNW/ST WN6 4 A1
Woodhurst Dr WGNNW/ST WN6 55 M4
Woodin Rd RF/TRAN CH42 128 C5
Woodkind Hey BEB CH63 143 J3
Woodland Av BRSC L40 37 H6
HOY CH47 108 F4
NEWLW WA12 105 H2 3
WDN WA8 16 B1
WGNE/HIN WN2 81 J2
Woodland Dr AIMK WN4 79 K8
GR/UP/WCH CH49 126 C2 1
WAL/NB CH45 95 L6
WGNNW/ST WN6 56 A3
Woodland Gv RF/TRAN CH42 128 B5
WGN WN1 68 F3
Woodland Rd ANF/KKDL L4 97 M5
EP CH65 163 K3
GR/UP/WCH CH49 126 C2
HLWD L26 132 A6
LITH L21 83 G6
MGHL L31 85 J1
RF/TRAN CH42 128 B5
WKBY CH48 125 G3
Woodlands Av WGNS/IIMK WN3 5 L8
Woodlands Cl CHTN/BK PR9 3 M1
FMBY L37 58 F3 2
NSTN CH64 152 F5
ORM L39 63 J1
Woodlands Dr PEN/TH CH61 141 L1
WARRS WA4 138 F2
WGNNW/ST WN6 67 H1
Woodlands Meadow
CHLY/EC PR7 43 L2
Woodlands Pk WD/CROXPK L12 98 C8
Woodlands Rd AIG/SPK L17 130 A3
FMBY L37 58 F3
HUY L36 115 L2 3
NSTN CH64 152 F5
PEN/TH CH61 125 M8
RNFD/HAY WA11 89 L6
The Woodlands BIRK CH41 11 G7
GR/UP/WCH CH49 110 B7
PR/KW L34 101 H6
STHP PR8 34 E8 1
WGN WN1 68 F2
Woodland Vw CSBY/BLUN L23 71 J6
GTS/LS CH66 155 K5
Wood La BRSC L40 29 M8
BRSC L40 40 A8
CHLY/EC PR7 42 A1
FMBY L37 60 E4
GR/UP/WCH CH49 109 M8
HUY L36 116 D3
NSTN CH64 152 E3
NTHLY L27 116 B8
PR/KW L34 100 D7
RUNC WA7 150 E7
RUNC WA7 161 H2
SKEL WN8 53 M3
WAL/NB CH45 95 G7
WARRS WA4 138 A5
Wood Lea WD/CROXPK L12 99 G2
Woodlea Cl CHTN/BK PR9 22 F8
PS/BROM CH62 143 M8
Woodlee Rd WLTN L25 131 L1
Woodleigh Cl MGHL L31 61 K8
Woodley Fold
WARRW/BUR WA5 136 B1 4
Woodley Gv LEIGH WN7 81 M8
Woodley Park Rd SKEL WN8 65 K1 5
Woodley Rd MGHL L31 72 E7
Woodmancote CHLY/EC PR7 32 D3 2
Woodmoss La STHP PR8 37 G3
Woodnook Rd WGNNW/ST WN6 55 G5
Woodpecker Cl
GOL/RIS/CU WA3 123 H1
GR/UP/WCH CH49 109 M8
WD/CROXPK L12 99 H4
Woodpecker Dr HLWD L26 132 A3
Woodridge RUNC WA7 150 E4
Wood Rd HLWD L26 132 A6
Woodrock Rd WLTN L25 131 K3
Woodrow SKEL WN8 65 G5
Woodrow Dr SKEL WN8 53 H4
Woodruff St TOX L8 129 H1 16
Woodrush Rd WGNNW/ST WN6 67 M2
Woods Cl ORM L39 61 H1
Woodside CHLY/EC PR7 31 L2
CHLY/EC PR7 44 A1
Woodside Av AIMK WN4 79 J5 3
FROD/HEL WA6 160 F6 2
MOR/LEA CH46 109 M6
RNFD/HAY WA11 89 H5
STHP PR8 47 K2
Woodside Cl SKEL WN8 66 E5
WD/CROXPK L12 98 D5
Woodside Rd PEN/TH CH61 126 A7
RNFD/HAY WA11 91 G6
WARRW/BUR WA5 120 B7 6
Woodside St EHL/KEN L7 113 K4
Woodside Wy
NWD/KWIPK L33 74 B8 5
Wood's La AIMK WN4 79 L8
Woodsome Cl EP CH65 163 K4
Woodsome Dr EP CH65 163 K4
Woodsorrel Rd BIRK CH41 111 H6
WAV L15 114 D6
Wood Sorrel Wy
GOL/RIS/CU WA3 93 G5
Woods Rd WGNE/HIN WN2 69 L1
Wood's St WGNS/IIMK WN3 4 D6
Woodstock Av NEWLW WA12 104 F3
Woodstock Dr STHP PR8 35 H5
Woodstock Gdns
WARRS WA4 138 B7 1
Woodstock Gv WDN WA8 133 M3
Woodstock Rd WAL/EG CH44 111 J2
Woodstock St EV L5 96 F8
Wood St ALL/GAR L19 130 E7
BIRK CH41 11 J3
CLVPS L1 13 J8
GOL/RIS/CU WA3 92 D5 4
HOY CH47 108 D6 6
LITH L21 83 K6
PR/KW L34 100 F7 15
PS/BROM CH62 128 D8
STHEL WA9 9 L4
WARR WA1 15 K4
WDN WA8 17 G2
WGNE/HIN WN2 81 K2 7
WGNS/IIMK WN3 4 F6
WGNW/BIL/O WN5 68 B6
Woodthorn Cl RUNC WA7 151 H1 2
Woodvale Cl CL/PREN CH43 110 E5 11
WARRN/WOL WA2 122 A4 8
Woodvale Dr GOL/RIS/CU WA3 93 G4
Woodvale Rd GTS/LS CH66 155 M7
STHP PR8 47 L3
WD/CROXPK L12 99 H2
WLTN L25 131 K3
Woodview PR/KW L34 100 A2 1
Wood Vw WGNNW/ST WN6 55 J8
Woodview Av
WAL/EG CH44 112 A3 22
Woodview Crs WDN WA8 133 J5 2
Woodview Rd WDN WA8 133 J5
Wood View Rd WLTN L25 115 H8
Woodville Av CSBY/BLUN L23 82 F2
Woodville Pl WDN WA8 133 M4
Woodville Rd CHLY/EC PR7 32 E5 12
CHLYE PR6 44 B4
RF/TRAN CH42 127 L1
WGNE/HIN WN2 80 B1
Woodville St ECCL WA10 9 J4
Woodville Ter NPK/KEN L6 97 K8
Woodward Rd NWD/KWIPK L33 86 E1
RF/TRAN CH42 128 C5
Woodway GR/UP/WCH CH49 125 M1
Woodyates St
WGNW/BIL/O WN5 68 B7 15
Woodyear Rd PS/BROM CH62 144 A6
Woolacombe Av STHEL WA9 102 E8
Woolacombe Cl WARRS WA4 137 M2
Woolacombe Rd CHLDW L16 115 G7
Woolden St
WGNW/BIL/O WN5 68 B7 16
Wooler Cl MOR/LEA CH46 109 L5
Woolfall Cl HUY L36 115 K1
Woolfall Crs HUY L36 115 K1
Woolfall Heath Av HUY L36 99 L8
Woolfall Ter LITH L21 83 J7 8
Woolhope Rd WLT/FAZ L9 97 K3
Woolley Cl FROD/HEL WA6 160 F3
Woolmer Cl GOL/RIS/CU WA3 107 K7
Woolston Grange Av
WARR WA1 123 G5
WARRN/WOL WA2 122 E3
Woolston Rd RNFD/HAY WA11 90 E6
Woolton Bvd WLTN L25 131 K4
Woolton Cl AIMK WN4 79 H8
Woolton Hill Rd WLTN L25 131 G1
Woolton Mt WLTN L25 131 J2
Woolton Pk WLTN L25 131 J3
Woolton Park Cl WLTN L25 131 J2 1
Woolton Rd ALL/GAR L19 130 E7
CHLDW L16 114 F8
WAV L15 114 C6
WLTN L25 115 H8
Woolton St WLTN L25 131 K3
Worcester Av
CLB/OSW/ST L13 97 M6 4
CSBY/WL L22 82 E3
GOL/RIS/CU WA3 92 D5 5
Worcester Cl WARRW/BUR WA5 120 D8
Worcester Dr CLB/OSW/ST L13 97 M6
Worcester Dr North
CLB/OSW/ST L13 97 M6
Worcester Pl CHLY/EC PR7 44 A2
Worcester Rd BTL L20 7 K2
CL/PREN CH43 110 F5
Worcester St EP CH65 20 D2 3
Worcester Wk EP CH65 20 D2 4
Wordsworth Av LEIGH WN7 81 M6
RF/TRAN CH42 128 B4 8
STHEL WA9 118 C2 3
WARRS WA4 137 K2
WDN WA8 16 A3
WGN WN1 68 E2
WGNW/BIL/O WN5 67 H7
WGNW/BIL/O WN5 77 M4
Wordsworth Cl ORM L39 50 F7 4
Wordsworth St BTL L20 6 D1
TOX L8 113 L6
Wordsworth Ter CHLYE PR6 32 F3
Wordsworth Wk WKBY CH48 124 D5 2
Wordsworth Wy
GTS/LS CH66 163 G4 3
HUY L36 116 B4
Worrow Cl NG/CROX L11 98 D2
Worrow Rd NG/CROX L11 98 D2
Worsborough Av
WARRW/BUR WA5 120 D8
Worsley Av WARRS WA4 138 B1
Worsley Brow STHEL WA9 103 G5
Worsley Cl WGNW/BIL/O WN5 67 L8 4
Worsley Gn WGNW/BIL/O WN5 67 K8
Worsley Mesnes Dr
WGNS/IIMK WN3 68 C8 8
Worsley Rd WARRS WA4 137 K4
Worsley St GOL/RIS/CU WA3 92 C5
RNFD/HAY WA11 90 B7 5
WARRW/BUR WA5 14 B1
WGNW/BIL/O WN5 67 K8
Worsley Ter WGN WN1 4 F2
Worthing Cl STHP PR8 35 H2
Worthing St CSBY/WL L22 82 E3 11
Worthington Cl RUNC WA7 150 C6
Worthington St TOX L8 112 F7 5
WGNE/HIN WN2 69 M7 15
Worthington Wy
WGNS/IIMK WN3 79 G3
Worthy St CHLYE PR6 33 G6
Wortley Rd AIN/FAZ L10 85 G5
Wotton Dr AIMK WN4 91 M2
Wraxhall Crs LEIGH WN7 81 M6
Wray Av STHEL WA9 118 F1
Wrayburn Cl EHL/KEN L7 113 L5 12
Wray St WGN WN1 5 K4
Wrekin Cl WLTN L25 131 K5
Wrekin Dr AIN/FAZ L10 85 G3
Wrenbury Cl CL/PREN CH43 127 H3 4
WGNW/BIL/O WN5 67 K8 6
Wrenbury St EHL/KEN L7 113 L3
Wren Cl GOL/RIS/CU WA3 123 H1 5
RUNC WA7 150 C7
WGNW/BIL/O WN5 67 K4
Wrenfield Gv AIG/SPK L17 129 L3 2
Wren Gv HLWD L26 132 A4 10
Wrennalls La CHLY/EC PR7 30 D8
Wrexham Cl
WARRW/BUR WA5 121 G3 9
Wright Crs WDN WA8 149 J1
Wrightington St WGN WN1 4 E1
Wright's La WARRW/BUR WA5 120 A2
WDN WA8 135 H3
Wrights Ter STHP PR8 35 K2
WAV L15 114 C6 6
Wright St AIMK WN4 79 J7 3
CHLYE PR6 33 G5
CHTN/BK PR9 3 H3
EV L5 96 F8
WAL/EG CH44 111 M1
WGN WN1 5 J2
WGNE/HIN WN2 80 C2
WGNE/HIN WN2 80 D6
Wrigley Rd RNFD/HAY WA11 91 G7
Wrigleys Cl FMBY L37 47 H8
Wrigleys La FMBY L37 47 H8
Wrington Cl LEIGH WN7 81 M5 2
Wroxham Cl FROD/HEL WA6 166 D1 2
GR/UP/WCH CH49 126 C1 3
Wroxham Dr GR/UP/WCH CH49 126 C1
Wroxham Rd
WARRW/BUR WA5 120 A7
Wroxham Wy
GR/UP/WCH CH49 110 C8 4
Wryneck Cl ECCL WA10 101 K6 1
Wrynose Rd PS/BROM CH62 144 A5
Wulstan St ANF/KKDL L4 96 F6 8
Wyatt Gv AIMK WN4 91 M2
Wycherley Rd RF/TRAN CH42 127 M2
Wycherley St PR/KW L34 100 F7 16
Wychwood Av LYMM WA13 139 L2
Wycliffe Rd ANF/KKDL L4 97 L6
GTS/LS CH66 163 H2
RNFD/HAY WA11 91 G6
Wycliffe St RF/TRAN CH42 128 B3 14
Wye Cl RF/TRAN CH42 128 B2 15
Wyedale EP CH65 20 A9
Wyedale Rd RNFD/HAY WA11 90 E7
Wye St EV L5 97 H7
Wyke Cop Rd STHP PR8 36 F2
Wykeham Cl WGNS/IIMK WN3 5 L8
Wykeham St ANF/KKDL L4 96 F6
Wyke La CHTN/BK PR9 25 L6
Wyken Gv RNFD/HAY WA11 9 M1
Wyke Rd RAIN/WH L35 101 G8
Wyke Wood La CHTN/BK PR9 26 B5
Wyllin Rd NWD/KWIPK L33 86 C3
Wylva Av CSBY/BLUN L23 83 J2
Wylva Rd ANF/KKDL L4 97 J7
Wymundsley CHLY/EC PR7 32 B4
Wynard Av WGN WN1 5 H2
Wyncroft Cl EP CH65 163 J2
WDN WA8 133 L6
Wyncroft Rd WDN WA8 133 L6
Wyncroft St TOX L8 129 J1 24
Wyndale Cl CALD/MH L18 130 D2
Wyndcote Rd CALD/MH L18 114 D8
Wyndham Av DV/KA/FCH L14 115 J3
Wyndham Crs GTS/LS CH66 163 G3
Wyndham Rd WAL/NB CH45 94 F8 5
Wyndham St ANF/KKDL L4 97 H3 11
Wynne Rd ECCL WA10 8 D2
Wynnstay Av MGHL L31 72 F2
Wynnstay St TOX L8 113 J7
Wynstay Rd HOY CH47 108 E5
Wynwood Pk HUY L36 115 L4
Wyre Av WGNE/HIN WN2 80 C3
Wyre Rd EV L5 97 H6 11
Wyrescourt Rd WD/CROXPK L12 98 F8
Wyresdale Av ECCL WA10 89 G6
STHP PR8 3 M9
Wyresdale Rd WLT/FAZ L9 84 D6
Wyrevale Gv AIMK WN4 91 L2 9
Wysall Cl RNFD/HAY WA11 89 M8 4
Wyswall Cl HLWD L26 132 A4
Wythburn Crs RNFD/HAY WA11 89 K5
Wythburn Gv RUNC WA7 150 A8
Wyvern Rd MOR/LEA CH46 110 A5

Y

Yanwath St TOX L8 113 K6 9
Yarcombe Cl HLWD L26 132 B4 2
Yardley Av WARRW/BUR WA5 121 H5
Yardley Dr BEB CH63 143 J4
Yardley Rd NWD/KWIPK L33 86 E4
Yarmouth Rd
WARRW/BUR WA5 120 A7
Yarrow Av MGHL L31 73 H3
Yarrow Cl LEY/BBR PR5 29 K3
Yarrow Ga CHLY/EC PR7 33 G7
Yarrow Rd CHLYE PR6 33 G7
Yarrow St WGNE/HIN WN2 80 E1 2
Yates Cl WARRW/BUR WA5 120 E8 8

Yates' Ct PR/KW L34 100 F8 1
Yates Gv WGNNW/ST WN6 68 B1
Yates Rd CHLY/EC PR7 32 D8
CHNE CH2 165 G4
Yates St TOX L8 113 G8
WGNS/IIMK WN3 4 B5
Yeadon SKEL WN8 65 K4
Yeadon Gv CHLY/EC PR7 32 C6
Yeald Brow LYMM WA13 139 K2
Yellow Brook Cl
WGNE/HIN WN2 57 L7 3
Yellow House La STHP PR8 3 G6
Yelverton Cl HLWD L26 132 B4
Yelverton Rd ANF/KKDL L4 97 L6
RF/TRAN CH42 127 M2
Yeoman Cottages HOY CH47 108 E7
Yeoman Wy GTS/LS CH66 163 G4
Yeovil Cl WARR WA1 122 E5
Yew Bank Rd CHLDW L16 114 F6
Yewdale SKEL WN8 65 J4
WGNNW/ST WN6 55 K7
Yewdale Av RNFD/HAY WA11 89 K4
Yewdale Crs WGN WN1 68 D2 2
Yewdale Dr GTS/LS CH66 163 H4
Yewdale Pk CL/PREN CH43 127 K2
Yewdale Rd AIMK WN4 79 J6
WLT/FAZ L9 97 K1
Yew Gv WGNNW/ST WN6 68 B2
Yewlands Av CHLY/EC PR7 42 B2 1
Yew Tree Av CHLY/EC PR7 31 L1
NEWLW WA12 104 C1
STHEL WA9 102 E7
Yew Tree Cl CHNE CH2 165 G4
WD/CROXPK L12 99 G7
Yewtree Cl CHLY/EC PR7 43 K2 1
GR/UP/WCH CH49 126 C3
NSTN CH64 153 H6
Yew Tree Gn MGHL L31 85 K1 4
Yew Tree La WARRS WA4 138 E8
WD/CROXPK L12 99 G8
Yewtree La WKBY CH48 124 D3 3
Yew Tree Rd BEB CH63 143 G1
HUY L36 115 M5
MOR/LEA CH46 110 B3
ORM L39 51 H7
WLT/FAZ L9 97 H1
WLTN L25 131 L5
Yewtree Rd CALD/MH L18 130 F2
Yew Tree Wy GOL/RIS/CU WA3 92 D6
Yew Wy MOR/LEA CH46 110 B4 2
Yorkaster Rd CALD/MH L18 130 E4
York Av AIG/SPK L17 113 M7
CSBY/BLUN L23 82 F1
GOL/RIS/CU WA3 107 H3
WAL/EG CH44 111 M2
WARRW/BUR WA5 120 A6
WKBY CH48 124 D5
York Cl ECCL WA10 8 E3
FMBY L37 47 H7
NTHTN L30 72 B8
York Dr WARRS WA4 138 C3
York Gdns STHP PR8 2 E8
York Pl CHLYE PR6 44 C5
RUNC WA7 19 H4
York Rd AIMK WN4 91 L3
CSBY/BLUN L23 83 G1
EP CH65 20 C5
FMBY L37 59 H2
HUY L36 116 C2
MGHL L31 72 F7
STHP PR8 2 D9
WAL/EG CH44 111 M3
WARRS WA4 138 C3
WDN WA8 133 L5
York Rd South AIMK WN4 91 L3
Yorkshire Gdns ECCL WA10 8 E8
York St ALL/GAR L19 145 L1
CHLY/EC PR7 32 F6 10
CLVPS L1 13 G9
CSBY/WL L22 82 F5
GOL/RIS/CU WA3 92 C4
PS/BROM CH62 128 F8
RUNC WA7 19 G4
WARRS WA4 15 G8
WGNS/IIMK WN3 4 C5
WLT/FAZ L9 97 H2
York Ter EV L5 97 G7
York Wy ALL/GAR L19 145 M1
Youatt Av RAIN/WH L35 117 G1
Youens Wy DV/KA/FCH L14 115 G1
Yvonne Cl AIMK WN4 79 M8

Z

Zander Gv WD/CROXPK L12 99 J2
Zetland Rd CALD/MH L18 114 B8 15
WAL/NB CH45 95 H6
Zetland St CHTN/BK PR9 3 L4
Zig Zag Rd WAL/NB CH45 95 K7
WD/CROXPK L12 98 F8

Index - featured places

Abbey Lakes Sports Centre
WGNW/BIL/O WN5 66 F6
Abbey Lane Industrial Estate
BRSC L40 51 L4
Abbey Sefton Hospitals
CSBY/WL L22 83 G4
Abbeystead Medical Centre
WAV L15 114 D6
Abbots Lea Special School
WLTN L25 131 G1
A B C Cinema
CALD/MH L18 130 D1
A B C Cinema
STHP PR8 3 G4
Abercromby Health Centre
TOX L8 113 J5
Abingdon Medical Centre
ANF/KKDL L4 97 L4
Abraham Guest High School
WGNW/BIL/O WN5 67 J7
Abram C of E Primary School
WGNE/HIN WN2 80 D4
The Academy Liverpool Football Club
NWD/KWIPK L33 86 C4
Ackhurst Business Park
CHLY/EC PR7 32 B4
Ackhurst Park Industrial Estate
CHLY/EC PR7 32 A5
Acorn Business Centre
NWD/KWIPK L33 86 D4
Acorn Surgery
STHEL WA9 103 G6
Adlington CP School
CHLY/EC PR7 44 B6
Adlington Cricket Club
CHLY/EC PR7 44 C7
Adlington Medical Centre
CHLYE PR6 44 D5
Ainsdale CE Primary School
STHP PR8 47 M1
Ainsdale Clinic
STHP PR8 47 M2
Ainsdale High School
STHP PR8 34 E7
Aintree Hospitals NHS Trust
WLT/FAZ L9 84 F6
Aintree Hospitals NHS Trust
WLT/FAZ L9 85 G6
Aintree Osteopathic Clinic
WLT/FAZ L9 84 E6
Aintree Park Group Practice
WLT/FAZ L9 84 B7
A K Business Park
CHTN/BK PR9 25 J7
Alban Retail Park
WARRN/WOL WA2 121 J3
Albany High School
CHLYE PR6 33 G8
Albert Road Medical Centre
WDN WA8 16 F1
Albion Street Doctors Surgery
EV L5 97 G7
Alder Hey Hospital Trust
CALD/MH L18 130 C2
Alderwood CP School
SPK/HALE L24 147 G2
Alexander House Health Centre
WGNE/HIN WN2 80 C2
Alexandra Industrial Estate
WDN WA8 16 B6
Allanson Street Primary School
STHEL WA9 102 F3
Allerton Health Centre
WAV L15 114 C8
Allerton Remedial Clinic
AIG/SPK L17 114 A8
Allerton Surgery
CALD/MH L18 114 D8
Allport Doctors Surgery
PS/BROM CH62 143 M5
All Saints C of E Junior School
WDN WA8 133 K2
All Saints C of E Primary School
CHLY/EC PR7 32 D8
All Saints C of E Primary School
WGNNW/ST WN6 54 E4
All Saints RC High School
KKBY L32 86 A4
All Saints RC Infant School
ANF/KKDL L4 97 K7
All Saints RC Junior Mixed School
NPK/KEN L6 97 L7
Alsop High Community Comprehensive School
ANF/KKDL L4 97 J3
Alternative Medical Centre
ECCL WA10 8 F4
Alvanley Primary School
FROD/HEL WA6 166 F4
Anfield Community Comprehensive School
ANF/KKDL L4 97 K6
Anfield CP School
ANF/KKDL L4 97 K7
Anfield Medical Centre
ANF/KKDL L4 97 K6
Archbishop Beck RC High School
WLT/FAZ L9 84 D7
Archbishop Blanch School
EHL/KEN L7 113 J4
Argyle Health Centre
BIRK CH41 11 K6
Argyle Lawn Tennis Club
CHTN/BK PR9 25 G3
Arrowe Hall Residential School
GR/UP/WCH CH49 126 C5
Arrowe Hill Primary School
GR/UP/WCH CH49 126 C2
Arrowe Park Hospital Annexe
GR/UP/WCH CH49 126 C4
Art Gallery
NSTN CH64 153 H3
Ashfield Special School
CHLDW L16 115 G7
Ashley Business Centre
PR/KW L34 100 F7
Ashley Retail Park
WDN WA8 16 F5
Ashley School
WDN WA8 133 M4
Ash Surgery
AIG/SPK L17 129 M3
Ashton Grange Industrial Estate
AIMK WN4 79 K7
Ashton Medical Centre
AIMK WN4 79 J8
Ashton Town Associated Football Club
AIMK WN4 91 M1
Ashurst C P School
RNFD/HAY WA11 89 M7
Ashurst Health Centre
SKEL WN8 65 K1
Ashville Football Club
WAL/NB CH45 110 F1
Ashworth Hospital
MGHL L31 73 J3
Asmall CP School
ORM L39 50 F7
Aspull Clinic
WGNE/HIN WN2 57 L8
Aspull New Springs County Infant School
WGNE/HIN WN2 69 J2
Aspull St John C of E Junior School
WGNE/HIN WN2 69 H2
Astley Park School
CHLY/EC PR7 32 D5
Astmoor County Primary School
RUNC WA7 150 B3
Aston CP School
RUNC WA7 161 L4
Atherton County Infant School
EP CH65 156 B8
Atherton House School
CSBY/BLUN L23 82 F1
Atkinson Art Gallery
STHP PR8 3 G4
Aughton Christ Church C of E Primary School
ORM L39 62 E2
Aughton St Michaels C of E School
ORM L39 62 D4
Aughton Surgery
ORM L39 62 E5
Austin Rawlinson Sports Centre
SPK/HALE L24 147 G2
Avalon Preparatory School
WKBY CH48 124 D5
Bankfield High School
WDN WA8 133 L4
Bank Quay Trading Estate
WARRW/BUR WA5 14 B8
Banks Health Centre
CHTN/BK PR9 23 H7
Banks Methodist Primary School
CHTN/BK PR9 23 K7
Banks Road CP School
ALL/GAR L19 145 M1
Barlows CP School
WLT/FAZ L9 84 F6
Barnston Primary School
HES CH60 141 L6
Barrow Hall Community Primary School
WARRW/BUR WA5 119 M6
Baycliff Road Health Centre
WD/CROXPK L12 99 H6
Bbc Radio Merseyside
CLVPS L1 12 F8
Beamont Community Junior School
WARRN/WOL WA2 15 H1
Beauford Park School
TOX L8 113 H8
Beauford Park School
TOX L8 129 H1
Bebington High School
BEB CH63 128 B8
Bedford Drive Primary School
RF/TRAN CH42 127 M4
Bedford Primary School
BTL L20 7 K6
Beechenhurst School
CALD/MH L18 130 E1
Beech Hill Medical Practice
WGNNW/ST WN6 68 C3
Beech Hill Primary & Infant School
WGNNW/ST WN6 68 C2
Beechwood County Primary School
RUNC WA7 149 M8
Belle Green Industrial Estate
WGNE/HIN WN2 69 J5
Belle Vale Health Centre
WLTN L25 115 K7
Belle Vale Primary School
WLTN L25 115 L8
Belle Vale Swimming Pool
WLTN L25 115 L7
The Belvidere School
TOX L8 113 J8
Bennett & Batty Art Gallery
CALD/MH L18 114 D8
Bewley Drive Doctors Surgery
KKBY L32 86 A5
Bewsey Lodge Community Primary School
WARRW/BUR WA5 14 A2
Bewsey Old School
WARRW/BUR WA5 121 G6
B I C C Athletic Club
RAIN/WH L35 101 H8
Bickershaw C of E School
WGNE/HIN WN2 81 J5
Bickerstaffe C of E Junior School
ORM L39 64 A8
Bidston Avenue Junior & Infant School
CL/PREN CH43 111 G6
Bidston Village C of E Primary School
CL/PREN CH43 110 E4
Bigdale Medical Centre
NWD/KWIPK L33 86 C2
Bigham Road Medical Centre
NPK/KEN L6 113 L2
Billinge Chapel End Parish Council
WGNW/BIL/O WN5 78 A8
Billinge Clinic
WGNW/BIL/O WN5 89 M1
Billinge Hospital
WGNW/BIL/O WN5 77 M3
Birchfield CP School
EHL/KEN L7 114 A3
Birch Green CP School
SKEL WN8 65 K2
Birchwood C of E Primary School
GOL/RIS/CU WA3 123 H2
Birchwood Community High School
GOL/RIS/CU WA3 122 F2
Birchwood Medical Centre
GOL/RIS/CU WA3 123 G2
Birkdale High School
STHP PR8 35 G6
Birkdale Primary School
STHP PR8 35 K2
Birkdale School for Hearing Impaired Children
STHP PR8 35 G2
Birkdale Trading Estate
STHP PR8 35 H3
Birkenhead Boys School
CL/PREN CH43 111 H8
Birkenhead County Court
BIRK CH41 11 L6
Birkenhead High School for Girls
CL/PREN CH43 10 B7
Birkenhead Park Cricket Club
BIRK CH41 10 C5
Birkenhead Park Rugby Union Football Club
BIRK CH41 10 B3
Birkenhead Preparatory School
CL/PREN CH43 10 A8
Birkenhead Priory and Museum
BIRK CH41 11 M6
Birkenhead Sixth Form College
CL/PREN CH43 111 H6
Birleywood Health Centre
SKEL WN8 65 M7
Bishop David Sheppard C of E School
CHTN/BK PR9 25 K6
Bishop Martin C of E Primary School
WLTN L25 131 J3
Bishop Martins Junior & Infant School
SKEL WN8 65 M7
Bishop Rawstone School
LEY/BBR PR5 29 L3
Bispham Hall Business Park
WGNW/BIL/O WN5 77 L3
Blackbrook RC Junior & Infant School
RNFD/HAY WA11 90 A7
Black Cat Industrial Estate
WDN WA8 16 C7
Blackheath Medical Practice
MOR/LEA CH46 110 B2
Black Horse Hill Infant School
WKBY CH48 124 F2
Black Horse Hill Junior School
WKBY CH48 124 F2
Blacklow Brow Primary School
HUY L36 115 M4
Blackmoor Park Infant School
WD/CROXPK L12 98 F7
Blackmoor Park Junior School
WD/CROXPK L12 98 F8
Black Moss Special School
SKEL WN8 64 F3
Blackrod Church School
HOR/BR BL6 57 L3
Blackrod Galleries
HOR/BR BL6 57 M3
Blackthorn Galleries
BIRK CH41 11 K4
Bleak Hill Primary School
ECCL WA10 88 D8
Blessed Sacrament Infant School
WLT/FAZ L9 84 F6
Blessed Sacrament RC Primary School
WLT/FAZ L9 84 D7
Blowick Business Centre
CHTN/BK PR9 25 J7
Bluecoat Gallery
CLVPS L1 13 G8
The Blue Coat School
WAV L15 114 C7
Blue Planet Aquarium
EP CH65 163 M4
Boaler Street Industrial Estate
NPK/KEN L6 113 J2
Boat Museum
EP CH65 20 E1
Bold Industrial Estate
WDN WA8 118 E8
Bold Street Medical Centre
WARR WA1 14 D7
Bolton County Junior & Infant School
WARRS WA4 15 M9
Bolton County Junior & Infant School
WARRS WA4 138 B2
Bolton Metropolitan Borough Council
HOR/BR BL6 57 L3
Booker Avenue Infant & Junior School
CALD/MH L18 130 D3
Bootle Cricket Club
BTL L20 7 J7
Bootle High School
NTHTN L30 84 C1
Bootle Stadium Sports Centre
BTL L20 7 M3
Borron Road Industrial Estate
NEWLW WA12 104 E1
Borsdane Brook Special School
WGNE/HIN WN2 80 E1
Botanic Estate
EHL/KEN L7 113 M4
Botanic Gardens Museum
CHTN/BK PR9 25 K3
Bousfield Health Centre
ANF/KKDL L4 97 G6
Bowers Business Park
WDN WA8 16 F5
Bowers Business Park
WDN WA8 17 G4
Bowring Comprehensive School
HUY L36 115 K2
The Bowry Health Centre
STHEL WA9 101 M5
The Boydell Galleries
CSBY/BLUN L23 70 D8
Brackenwood Infant School
BEB CH63 128 B8
Brackenwood Junior School
BEB CH63 128 A8
Bradley Hall Trading Estate
WGNNW/ST WN6 56 C3
Bradshaw Community Primary School
WARRS WA4 138 D3
Breckfield Community Comprehensive School
EV L5 97 H8
Breckfield & North Everton Council
EV L5 97 H7
Breckfield Primary School
EV L5 97 H7
Breckfield Road North Doctors Surgery
EV L5 97 H8
Brentwood Gallery & Framing Centre
WARRS WA4 137 L4
Brewery
TOX L8 113 G7
Briars Hey School
RAIN/WH L35 117 M4
Bridgehouse Clinic
BEB CH63 127 M7
Bridge Industrial Estate
SPK/HALE L24 131 K8
Bridgewater Community High School (Lower)
WARRS WA4 137 M7
Bridgewater Community High School (Upper)
WARRS WA4 137 M6
Britannia Bridge Primary School
WGNS/IIMK WN3 5 J7
Britonwood Trading Estate
NWD/KWIPK L33 86 D6
Broadgreen Community Comprehensive School
CLB/OSW/ST L13 114 D3
Broadgreen Hospital NHS Trust
DV/KA/FCH L14 114 E3
Broad Green Junior & Infant School
CLB/OSW/ST L13 114 C3
Broad Oak Community Primary School
STHEL WA9 103 J2
Broad Square CP School
NG/CROX L11 98 B5
Broadway Community High School
ECCL WA10 101 L5
Bromborough Pool Primary School
PS/BROM CH62 128 F8
Brook Acre Community Primary School
WARRN/WOL WA2 122 A4
Brookdale Primary School
GR/UP/WCH CH49 126 A2
Brookfield CP School
SKEL WN8 64 F3
Brookfield High School
KKBY L32 85 M5
The Brookfield School
WDN WA8 134 F3
Brook House Business Centre
WKBY CH48 124 D3
Brookhurst Primary School
BEB CH63 143 L7
Brook Lodge Primary School
RNFD/HAY WA11 76 B5
Brookside Infant School
GTS/LS CH66 162 F1
Brookside Primary School
STBRV L28 99 K6

Brookvale County Comprehensive School *RUNC* WA7 150 E8
Brookvale County Junior School *RUNC* WA7 150 D8
Brookvale Recreation Centre *RUNC* WA7 150 E7
Broomfields Community Junior School *WARRS* WA4 138 A6
Broughton Hall High School *WD/CROXPK* L12 99 G8
Brow CP School *RUNC* WA7 150 B4
Bruche Community Junior & Infant School *WARR* WA1 122 C6
Bryn Cross Surgery *AIMK* WN4 79 J7
Bryn Gates CP School *WGNE/HIN* WN2 80 B6
Buckshaw CP School *CHLY/EC* PR7 32 C3
Burscough Bridge Methodist School *BRSC* L40 38 F8
Burscough County Primary School *BRSC* L40 39 H8
Burscough Cricket Club *BRSC* L40 52 B1
Burscough Health Centre *BRSC* L40 39 G8
Burscough Priory High School *BRSC* L40 38 F8
Burscough RC Primary School *BRSC* L40 52 A3
Burscough Sports Centre *BRSC* L40 39 G8
Burtonwood Community Primary School *WARRW/BUR* WA5 104 A6
Burtonwood Industrial Centre *WARRW/BUR* WA5 104 A6
Business Centre *WARR* WA1 14 E5
Business Centre *WARRW/BUR* WA5 14 B3
Bychall High School *AIMK* WN4 91 K4
Byrne Avenue Recreation Centre *RF/TRAN* CH42 128 B4
Cabinet War Rooms *CLVP* L2 12 E6
Cafe & Cricket Club *CHLDW* L16 115 H4
Calday Grange Grammar School *WKBY* CH48 124 F4
Calderstones Community Comprehensive School *CALD/MH* L18 130 E1
Callands Community Primary School *WARRW/BUR* WA5 121 G3
Camberley Medical Centre *WLTN* L25 131 L5
Cambridge Road CP School *EP* CH65 20 D5
Cammell Laird's Sports Club *RF/TRAN* CH42 128 C4
Campion RC High School *EV* L5 13 K1
Canalside Industrial Estate *EP* CH65 20 F1
Canning Road Industrial Estate *CHTN/BK* PR9 25 J7
Cansfield High School *AIMK* WN4 91 J1
Capenhurst Grange School *GTS/LS* CH66 163 G3
Capenhurst Primary School *CH/BCN* CH1 162 D5
Cardinal Heenan RC High School *WD/CROXPK* L12 98 F8
Carleton House Preparatory School *CALD/MH* L18 130 B2
Carlton Lawn Tennis Club *STHP* PR8 35 H3
Carmel RC 6th Form College *ECCL* WA10 101 K4
Carr Lane Industrial Estate *HOY* CH47 108 D6
Carr Mill Infant School *RNFD/HAY* WA11 89 K5
Castlefields Health Centre *RUNC* WA7 150 C3
Castle View CP School *RUNC* WA7 149 M5
Castleway Primary School *MOR/LEA* CH46 110 C1
Catalyst Museum *WDN* WA8 134 C8
Causeway Medical Centre *WARRS* WA4 137 K2
Cavendish Medical Centre *BIRK* CH41 10 C2
Cavendish School *RUNC* WA7 149 K8
Cavern Mecca *CLVP* L2 12 F7
Cedar Cross Medical Centre *RAIN/WH* L35 116 F2
Cedar Farm Gallery *BRSC* L40 40 E5
Centec Business Centre *NG/CROX* L11 85 K8
Central Shopping Centre *CLVPS* L1 13 J8
Central Surgery *ECCL* WA10 8 E3
Chaigley School *WARRS* WA4 139 G1
Chalon Way Industrial Estate *STHEL* WA9 9 H7
Chapel End CP School *WGNW/BIL/O* WN5 90 A1
Chapelfield Clinic *WDN* WA8 133 K4
Chapel Lane Business Park *CHLY/EC* PR7 43 H5
Chapel Street Clinic *WDN* WA8 16 D6
Charnock Richard C of E Primary School *CHLY/EC* PR7 42 F1
Chatfield Community Primary School *GOL/RIS/CU* WA3 123 G2
Cherryfield Primary School *KKBY* L32 86 B6
Cherry Tree Community Primary School *LYMM* WA13 139 L3
Cheshire County Council *GTS/LS* CH66 163 H3
Cheshire County Council *RUNC* WA7 151 H8
Chesire County Council *WDN* WA8 16 E4
Chesnut Lodge Special School *WDN* WA8 134 A4
Chesterfield High School *CSBY/BLUN* L23 83 J1
Childcare Practice *SKEL* WN8 65 M7
Childer Thornton CP School *GTS/LS* CH66 155 K5
Childrens Centre Nhs Trust *CHTN/BK* PR9 3 J2
Childwall Chiropodist Surgery *CHLDW* L16 114 F6
Childwall C of E Primary School *CHLDW* L16 114 F8
Childwall Community Comprehensive School *WAV* L15 114 E6
Childwall Community Comprehensive School *WAV* L15 114 C6
Childwall Park Avenue Doctors Surgery *CHLDW* L16 114 F7
Chorley Associated Football Club *CHLY/EC* PR7 32 E7
Chorley Cricket Club *CHLY/EC* PR7 32 D5
Chorley & District Hospital *CHLY/EC* PR7 32 E3
Chorley Golf Club *CHLYE* PR6 44 C2
Chorley Mayfield School *CHLY/EC* PR7 32 E8
Chorley North Business Park *CHLYE* PR6 32 F2
Chorley & South Ribble Health Authority *CHLY/EC* PR7 42 F4
Chorley Sports Centre *CHLY/EC* PR7 32 F4
Chorley West Business Park *CHLY/EC* PR7 32 B5
Christchurch C of E Primary School *BIRK* CH41 10 F9
Christ Church C of E Primary School *BTL* L20 7 J3
Christ Church C of E Primary School *MOR/LEA* CH46 110 A5
Christian Fellowship School *EHL/KEN* L7 113 K5
Christ the King Primary School *WAV* L15 114 E5
Christ the King RC Primary School *PS/BROM* CH62 144 A6
Christ the King School *STHP* PR8 35 K3
Chromolyte Industrial Estate *STHP* PR8 3 G7
Church Drive Primary School *PS/BROM* CH62 128 D7
Churchill Industrial Estate *WLT/FAZ* L9 84 E5
Church Road Medical Centre *BEB* CH63 143 J1
Church Street Industrial Estate *WARR* WA1 15 G6
Churchtown County Junior & Infant School *CHTN/BK* PR9 25 K3
Churchtown Medical Centre *CHTN/BK* PR9 25 J3
Cinnamon Brow C of E Primary School *WARRN/WOL* WA2 122 B2
Civic Buildings *WGN* WN1 4 E2
Claremont Medical Centre *MGHL* L31 72 D5
Claremont Special School *WAL/NB* CH45 95 H7
Clare Mount School *MOR/LEA* CH46 110 B4
Clarence House School *FMBY* L37 47 G7
Claughton Medical Centre *BIRK* CH41 10 A3
Clayton Square Shopping Centre *CLVPS* L1 13 H7
Cleveland Business Park *BIRK* CH41 10 F2
Clifford Holroyde Special School *DV/KA/FCH* L14 114 F2
Clinic for the Handicapped *WARRN/WOL* WA2 14 D4
Clinic & Welfare Centre *WARR* WA1 122 D6
Clough Fold Primary School *SKEL* WN8 65 L3
Cobbs Brow CP School *SKEL* WN8 65 J2
The Cobbs Community Infant School *WARRS* WA4 138 A5
Cole Street Primary School *BIRK* CH41 10 E6
Collins Industrial Estate *STHEL* WA9 9 M1
Colwell CP School *DV/KA/FCH* L14 99 J7
Commercial Business Centre *RAIN/WH* L35 117 L2
Common Bank Employment Area *CHLY/EC* PR7 32 A6
Common Bank Industrial Estate *CHLY/EC* PR7 32 B6
Commonfield Road Surgery *GR/UP/WCH* CH49 126 D4
Common Ground Sign Dance Theatre *CLVPS* L1 13 G8
Community Care for Health *WDN* WA8 16 D5
Community Centre *TOX* L8 113 H5
Constance Industrial Estate *WDN* WA8 16 D8
Coops Business Centre *WGN* WN1 4 D4
Copplehouse Medical Centre *AIN/FAZ* L10 85 J6
Coppull CP School *CHLY/EC* PR7 43 G4
Coppull Medical Practice *CHLY/EC* PR7 43 G5
Coppull Parish Church School *CHLY/EC* PR7 43 H4
Corinthian CP School *CLB/OSW/ST* L13 114 C1
Corner House Clinic *WKBY* CH48 124 D3
Cornerways Medical Centre *HUY* L36 99 L8
Corpus Christi RC Primary School *RNFD/HAY* WA11 76 B6
Cottage Crafts & Gallery *GOL/RIS/CU* WA3 106 C5
Council Offices *RNFD/HAY* WA11 76 B7
County Fire HQ *CLVP* L2 12 F5
The County Gallery *ANF/KKDL* L4 97 H3
County Police Hq *CLVPS* L1 12 F9
County Sessions House *VAUX/LVPD* L3 13 J5
Court Hey Drive Doctors Surgery *CHLDW* L16 115 H4
Court Hey Road Doctors Surgery *CHLDW* L16 115 H4
Cowley High School *ECCL* WA10 89 G7
Cowling Brow Industrial Estate *CHLYE* PR6 33 G7
Craighurst CP School *WLTN* L25 115 J6
Crawford County School *SKEL* WN8 77 G2
The Cricketer Sports Club *WGNS/IIMK* WN3 4 C9
Cricket Street Business Centre *WGNNW/ST* WN6 4 B3
Croft Community Primary School *GOL/RIS/CU* WA3 106 D5
Cromdale Way Community Hall & Health Centre *WARRW/BUR* WA5 120 A7
Cronton C of E School *WDN* WA8 117 L7
Crosby Baths *CSBY/BLUN* L23 82 D3
Crosby Road North Primary School *CSBY/WL* L22 83 G4
The Crosby Surgery *CSBY/BLUN* L23 83 G2
Crossens C of E Primary School *CHTN/BK* PR9 22 E8
Crossens Cricket Club *CHTN/BK* PR9 25 M1
Cross Farm CP School *NTHLY* L27 132 B1
Cross Hall High School *BRSC* L40 51 K8
Cross Lane Surgery *RAIN/WH* L35 116 F1
Croston Medical Centre *LEY/BBR* PR5 29 L2
Croston Sports Club *LEY/BBR* PR5 29 K3
Croston Village Surgery *LEY/BBR* PR5 29 K3
Crowland Street Industrial Estate *CHTN/BK* PR9 25 H7
Croxteth Community Comprehensive School *NG/CROX* L11 85 L8
Croxteth CP School *NG/CROX* L11 98 F1
Croxteth Family Health Centre *NG/CROX* L11 98 E1
Croxteth Sports Centre *NG/CROX* L11 98 E1
Culcheth Clinic *GOL/RIS/CU* WA3 107 G2
Culcheth Community Primary School *GOL/RIS/CU* WA3 107 J1
Culcheth High School *GOL/RIS/CU* WA3 107 J2
Culcheth Sports Club *GOL/RIS/CU* WA3 107 H2
Cunard Building *VAUX/LVPD* L3 12 D7
The Curtain Gallery *PR/KW* L34 100 E7
The Cutting Gallery *FMBY* L37 59 H2
Daleacre Primary School *NTHTN* L30 83 L2
Dallam Community Primary School *WARRW/BUR* WA5 121 H4
Dalweb Trading Estate *CHTN/BK* PR9 26 E2
Daresbury CP School *WARRS* WA4 151 K3
Davenhill CP School *AIN/FAZ* L10 84 F3
Dawpool C of E Primary School *PEN/TH* CH61 125 K7
Deacon Trading Estate *NEWLW* WA12 104 C3
Deanery C of E High School *WGN* WN1 4 C2
De La Salle RC High School *NG/CROX* L11 98 D3
De La Salle School *ECCL* WA10 101 L1
The Dell Primary School *RF/TRAN* CH42 128 D4
Delphside Primary School *SKEL* WN8 65 K5
Derby Lane Medical Centre *CLB/OSW/ST* L13 114 C2
Devaney Medical Centre *CL/PREN* CH43 10 D8
Devonshire Park Primary School *RF/TRAN* CH42 127 L3
Deyes High School *MGHL* L31 72 F4
Deysbrook Medical Centre *WD/CROXPK* L12 98 F6
Diamond Business Park *RNFD/HAY* WA11 88 D1
Dinas Lane Medical Centre *HUY* L36 115 L1
District C E Primary School *NEWLW* WA12 104 C1
Ditton C of E Primary School *WDN* WA8 133 J4
Ditton CP School *WDN* WA8 133 M4
Ditton Hall St Michaels RC Primary School *WDN* WA8 133 L6
Ditton Medical Centre *WDN* WA8 133 L4
Dobson Park Industrial Estate *WGNE/HIN* WN2 69 J7
Dock Board Offices *VAUX/LVPD* L3 12 D8
Douglas Farm Riding School *SKEL* WN8 53 L4
Douglas Valley Business Park *WGN* WN1 56 E8
Dovecot CP School *DV/KA/FCH* L14 115 J2
Dovecot Health Clinic *DV/KA/FCH* L14 115 H1
Dovedale CP School *CALD/MH* L18 114 C8
Downall Green RC Primary School *AIMK* WN4 79 G7
Drug Dependency Clinic *CLVPS* L1 13 K8
Drug Dependency Clinic *WDN* WA8 16 D6
Drugs Clinic *CSBY/WL* L22 83 G5
Duke Street County Infant School *CHLY/EC* PR7 32 E7
Duke Street Doctors Surgery *FMBY* L37 59 H3
Dunham on Hill CP School *FROD/HEL* WA6 166 A7
Dunkirk Trading Estate *CH/BCN* CH1 162 F7
Dunnys Sports Club *WLT/FAZ* L9 97 J1
Duxbury Park Golf Club *CHLY/EC* PR7 43 M1
Dyson Hall Special School *WLT/FAZ* L9 84 F8
Eagle Sports Club *WARRW/BUR* WA5 136 D1
Earle Primary School *EHL/KEN* L7 113 L5
Earle Road Medical Centre *EHL/KEN* L7 113 L5
East Chorley Business Centre *CHLYE* PR6 32 F5
Eastcroft Park Primary School *NWD/KWIPK* L33 74 B8
Eastside Industrial Estate *STHEL* WA9 9 M7
EasTView Surgery *CSBY/BLUN* L23 83 G3
Eastway Primary School *MOR/LEA* CH46 110 B4
Eaton Road Medical Centre *WD/CROXPK* L12 98 E8
Eaves CP School *STHEL* WA9 102 E7
Eccleston CP School *CHLY/EC* PR7 30 D7
Eccleston Health Centre *CHLY/EC* PR7 30 D6
Eccleston Lane Ends Primary School *PR/KW* L34 101 G6
Eccleston Medical Centre *ECCL* WA10 88 D8
The Edgebright Clinic *CLVPS* L1 13 K9
Edge Hill Enterprise Training Centre *WLT/FAZ* L9 85 G7
Edge Hill Health Centre *EHL/KEN* L7 113 L4
Edge Hill University College *ORM* L39 63 J2
Edge Lane Medical Centre *EHL/KEN* L7 113 K4
Egremont Medical Centre *WAL/EG* CH44 111 M1
Egremont Primary School *WAL/EG* CH44 111 M1
Elaine Norris Sports Centre *VAUX/LVPD* L3 12 F1
Elimu Study School *TOX* L8 113 K6
Elleray Park School *WAL/NB* CH45 95 J6
Ellesmere Port Business Centre *EP* CH65 20 B5
Ellesmere Port Catholic High School *EP* CH65 163 J2
Ellesmere Port Clinic *EP* CH65 20 B7
Ellesmere Port Hospital *EP* CH65 163 J3
Ellesmere Port Stadium *EP* CH65 21 H8
Elliott Clarke School *CLVPS* L1 113 G5
Elmers Green CP School *SKEL* WN8 65 M4
Elms School *STBRV* L28 99 K5
Elsie Smith College of Theatre Arts *EV* L5 97 J8
Eltham Green Clinic *GR/UP/WCH* CH49 126 D3
Elton County Primary School *CHNE* CH2 165 J1
Emmaus School *WD/CROXPK* L12 99 H2
Empress Industrial Estate *WGNE/HIN* WN2 5 L5
Endowed Primary School *BRSC* L40 40 F7
English Martyrs RC Primary School *LITH* L21 83 K5
English Martyrs RC Primary School *RNFD/HAY* WA11 91 G6
Epic Leisure Centre *EP* CH65 20 C7
Eric Moore Health Centre *WARRN/WOL* WA2 14 D4
Ernest Cookson Special School *WD/CROXPK* L12 98 D7
Euxton C of E Primary School *CHLY/EC* PR7 31 L2
Euxton CP School *CHLY/EC* PR7 31 K1
Euxton Hall Hospital *CHLY/EC* PR7 31 L4
Evelyn Primary School *PR/KW* L34 101 G6
Evelyn Street Community Primary School *WARRW/BUR* WA5 137 G1
Everite Road Industrial Estate *WDN* WA8 133 K6
Everton Football Club Co *ANF/KKDL* L4 97 H5
Everton Park Sports Centre *EV* L5 97 G8
Everton Road Health Clinic *NPK/KEN* L6 13 M2
Everyman Theatre *VAUX/LVPD* L3 13 L8
Express Industrial Estate *WDN* WA8 133 J6
Fairfield C of E School *WARR* WA1 15 H3
Fairfield County High School *WDN* WA8 134 E2
Fairfield County Junior & Infant School *WDN* WA8 134 D3
Fairfield Hospital *RNFD/HAY* WA11 89 G3
Fairfield Medical Centre *NPK/KEN* L6 113 L2
Fairfield R F Football Club *RF/TRAN* CH42 128 B3
Fairway Trading Estate *WDN* WA8 134 A6
Faith House Yoga & Natural Health Centre *WAL/NB* CH45 95 K5
Falcongate Industrial Estate *BIRK* CH41 111 K4
Family Health Centre *KKBY* L32 85 L3
Family Surgery *STHP* PR8 35 J2
Farnborough Road Junior School *STHP* PR8 35 J5
Farnworth C of E Junior & Infant School *WDN* WA8 134 C1
Fazakerley CP School *AIN/FAZ* L10 85 H6
Fazakerley High School *AIN/FAZ* L10 85 H6
Fazakerley Sports Centre *AIN/FAZ* L10 85 H5
Fearnhead Cross Medical Centre *WARRN/WOL* WA2 122 B3

Fender Primary School GR/UP/WCH CH49 126 E2
Fernhill Sports Centre BTL L20 83 M7
Ferries Industrial Estate RF/TRAN CH42 128 B2
Fingerpost Surgery STHEL WA9 9 L4
Fire Station CLVPS L1 12 F9
Firsdale Industrial Estate LEIGH WN7 81 L7
Fir Tree Drive South Medical Centre WD/CROXPK L12 99 H2
Fishwicks Industrial Estate RNFD/HAY WA11 91 H5
Fishwicks Industrial Estate STHEL WA9 102 F5
Fleet Lane Industrial Estate STHEL WA9 103 G3
Fleming Industrial Estate WARR WA1 15 G5
Floral Pavilion Theatre WAL/NB CH45 95 L4
Florence Melly Junior School ANF/KKDL L4 97 L4
Flower Gallery WARRS WA4 138 F2
Ford Medical Practice LITH L21 83 K3
Fordton Leisure Centre WARRN/WOL WA2 121 J2
Forefield Infant School CSBY/BLUN L23 83 J1
Forefield Junior School CSBY/BLUN L23 83 H1
The Forge Shopping Centre WARRS WA4 137 L4
Formby Associated Football Club FMBY L37 59 H2
Formby Cricket Club FMBY L37 47 H8
Formby Golf Club FMBY L37 46 F8
Formby Hall Golf Club FMBY L37 47 L5
Formby High Lower School FMBY L37 59 H1
Formby High School FMBY L37 59 G1
Formby Junior Sports Club FMBY L37 47 J8
Formby Ladies Golf Club FMBY L37 46 F8
Formby Lawn Tennis Club FMBY L37 47 H8
The Fountains Abbey ANF/KKDL L4 97 G6
Four Acre Health Centre STHEL WA9 118 D1
Foxfield School MOR/LEA CH46 109 M5
Freshfield Primary School FMBY L37 59 J1
Freshfield Surgery FMBY L37 59 H1
Freshlea Private Clinic FMBY L37 58 F4
Friary Primary School EV L5 13 K2
Friends of St Helens College ECCL WA10 8 F5
Frodsham C of E Primary School FROD/HEL WA6 160 E6
Frodsham County High School FROD/HEL WA6 160 D5
Frodsham Golf Club FROD/HEL WA6 160 D8
Frodsham Town Council FROD/HEL WA6 160 C5
Frodsham Weaver Vale CP School FROD/HEL WA6 160 E3
Fylde Road Industrial Estate CHTN/BK PR9 25 K1
The Gallery AIG/SPK L17 129 K1
The Gallery CLVPS L1 13 H8
The Gallery ECCL WA10 8 F4
The Gallery WKBY CH48 124 C3
Garston Industrial Estate ALL/GAR L19 145 L1
Garston Leisure Centre ALL/GAR L19 130 E7
Garston RC Primary School ALL/GAR L19 130 E7
Garston Sports Centre ALL/GAR L19 130 E6
Garswood CP School AIMK WN4 90 E1
Garswood Football Club AIMK WN4 78 D8
Garven Place Clinic WARR WA1 14 C6
Gateacre Community Comprehensive School WLTN L25 115 J8
Gateworth Industrial Estate WARRW/BUR WA5 136 F2
Gayton Primary School HES CH60 141 J7
Gemini Business Park WARRW/BUR WA5 121 H2
General Medical Practice HUY L36 116 A1
George's Dock VAUX/LVPD L3 12 C7
Gilbrook School BIRK CH41 11 M5
Gilded Hollins School LEIGH WN7 93 L4
Gillibrand Primary School CHLY/EC PR7 32 D7
Gillmoss Medical Centre NG/CROX L11 85 L8
Gilmour Infant School ALL/GAR L19 130 D6
Gilmour Junior School ALL/GAR L19 130 D6
Gladstone Theatre PS/BROM CH62 143 K1
Glenburn High School SKEL WN8 65 J4
Glenda Jackson Theatre RF/TRAN CH42 127 L2
Glovers Lane Practice NTHTN L30 84 B2
The Glucksman Practice WGN WN1 4 E4
Golborne All Saints RC School GOL/RIS/CU WA3 92 D5
Golborne Clinic GOL/RIS/CU WA3 92 D4
Golborne CP School GOL/RIS/CU WA3 92 C5
Golborne High School GOL/RIS/CU WA3 92 E4
Golden Triangle I ndustrial Estate WDN WA8 133 L7
Golf Club Bungalow WGNW/BIL/O WN5 66 F6
The Golf Gallery WGN WN1 4 E3
Gorse Covert Primary School GOL/RIS/CU WA3 107 K7
Gorsewood CP School RUNC WA7 151 G6
Gorsthills CP School GTS/LS CH66 162 E2
Grain Industrial Estate TOX L8 129 G1
Granada TV VAUX/LVPD L3 12 E9
The Grange Country Club NSTN CH64 153 H1
Grange Primary School NTHTN L30 72 A8
Grange Surgery STHP PR8 2 E9
Grange Valley Primary School RNFD/HAY WA11 90 F8
Grantside Special School NPK/KEN L6 113 J1
Grappenhall Clinic WARRS WA4 138 D3
Grappenhall Cricket Club WARRS WA4 138 C4
Grappenhall Hall School WARRS WA4 138 D4
Grappenhall Sports Club WARRS WA4 138 B4
Grassendale Medical Practice ALL/GAR L19 130 C5
Greasby Health Centre GR/UP/WCH CH49 125 M2
Greasby Infant School GR/UP/WCH CH49 125 L3
Greasby Junior School GR/UP/WCH CH49 125 L4
Great Crosby RC Primary School CSBY/BLUN L23 83 G1
Great Homer Street Medical Centre EV L5 97 G8
Great Meols Primary School HOY CH47 109 G4
Great Sankey Community High School WARRW/BUR WA5 119 M5
Great Sankey Community Primary School WARRW/BUR WA5 120 C8
Great Sutton Health Centre GTS/LS CH66 162 F1
Greenbank Galleries WAV L15 114 A7
Greenbank High School STHP PR8 35 G4
Greenbank Surgery NSTN CH64 154 B5
Green Lane Medical Centre CLB/OSW/ST L13 98 A8
Green Lane School WARR WA1 122 D5
Greenleas Primary School WAL/NB CH45 94 E7
Greenoaks Farm Industrial Estate WDN WA8 17 H3
Green Park Primary School MGHL L31 72 D3
Greenways Special School ALL/GAR L19 130 B6
Greetby Hill C of E Junior School ORM L39 51 H7
Gresford Medical Centre DV/KA/FCH L14 115 H2
Grimeford Industrial Estate CHLYE PR6 44 F7
Group Practice WAL/NB CH45 95 G8
Grove House Practice RUNC WA7 19 H3
Grove Park Industrial Estate CHLY/EC PR7 30 E8
Grove Street Community Primary School PS/BROM CH62 128 C6
Guardian Medical Centre WARRW/BUR WA5 14 A4
Guardian Street Industrial Estate WARRW/BUR WA5 14 B4
Guinea Gap Baths & Recreation Centre WAL/EG CH44 112 A2
Gwladys Street CP School ANF/KKDL L4 97 J4
Gwydrin Road Doctors Surgery CALD/MH L18 114 E8
Halebank C of E Controlled Primary School WDN WA8 148 C1
Hale C of E School SPK/HALE L24 148 A4
The Halefield Family Medical Centre ECCL WA10 8 F3
Hale Primary School SPK/HALE L24 147 M4
Halewood C of E Primary School HLWD L26 132 C4
Halewood Community Comprehensive School WLTN L25 131 M6
Halewood Health Centre HLWD L26 132 B6
Halewood Sports Centre HLWD L26 132 C6
Hall Green Clinic SKEL WN8 66 D6
Hall Green Surgery SKEL WN8 66 C6
Hall Street Medical Centre ECCL WA10 9 H5
Hallwood Health Centre RUNC WA7 150 B6
Hallwood Park CP School RUNC WA7 150 A7
Halton Borough Council RUNC WA7 150 B5
Halton Borough Council WDN WA8 16 E4
Halton Borough Council WDN WA8 16 C5
Halton Borough Council WDN WA8 16 F3
Halton Borough Council WDN WA8 16 A6
Halton Borough Council WDN WA8 133 K5
Halton College WDN WA8 16 D5
Halton College of Further Education WDN WA8 16 C4
Halton General Hospital NHS Trust RUNC WA7 150 B7
Halton Health Authority WDN WA8 134 F3
Halton Lodge County Junior & Infant School RUNC WA7 19 M8
Halton Magistrates Court RUNC WA7 150 B5
Halton St Marys C of E Primary School RUNC WA7 150 C5
Hamblett School ECCL WA10 88 F7
Hanover Galleries CLVPS L1 13 G9
Hanson Road Business Park WLT/FAZ L9 84 E8
Harold Magnay Special School WLTN L25 131 H1
Hartley Trading Estate WLT/FAZ L9 84 D8
Haskayne C of E School ORM L39 61 G2
Haslemere Industrial Estate AIMK WN4 79 J5
Hatton Garden Industrial Estate CLVP L2 12 F5
Hatton Hill Primary School LITH L21 83 K3
Hawkley Brook Surgery WGNS/IIMK WN3 79 H2
Hawkley Brook Trading Estate WGNS/IIMK WN3 79 G3
Hawkley Hall High School WGNS/IIMK WN3 79 L2
Hawthorne Business Park WARRW/BUR WA5 121 J5
Haydock Cricket Club RNFD/HAY WA11 90 F6
Haydock Cricket Club RNFD/HAY WA11 90 E7
Haydock High School RNFD/HAY WA11 90 D7
Haydock Medical Centre RNFD/HAY WA11 90 F7
Hayfield School GR/UP/WCH CH49 110 C7
Hazel Business Park RNFD/HAY WA11 88 E1
Health Authority SPK/HALE L24 147 G2
The Health Centre Surgery HLWD L26 132 B6
Heath Road Medical Centre RUNC WA7 19 J7
Helsby County High School FROD/HEL WA6 160 A8
Helsby Health Centre FROD/HEL WA6 166 D2
Her Majesty's Prison WLT/FAZ L9 84 B8
Hermes Galleries WAL/EG CH44 111 J1
Hesketh Golf Club CHTN/BK PR9 25 G3
Heskin Football Club CHLY/EC PR7 41 M2
Heskin Pembertons Primary School CHLY/EC PR7 42 B3
Heswall County Primary School PEN/TH CH61 141 J4
Heswall Football Club HES CH60 141 L6
Heswall Health Centre HES CH60 141 H4
Heswall Preparatory School HES CH60 141 G3
Hey Comprehensive School HUY L36 116 B3
Heygarth Junior School PS/BROM CH62 144 A8
Hey Green Jmi School WAV L15 114 A5
Higher Bebington Junior School BEB CH63 127 L7
Higher Side Community Comprehensive School RAIN/WH L35 117 J2
Highfield C of E School WGNS/IIMK WN3 78 F1
Highfield CP School CHLYE PR6 32 F5
Highfield Cricket Club WGNS/IIMK WN3 78 E1
Highfield Industrial Estate CHLYE PR6 32 E3
Highfield School HLWD L26 132 C6
High Pastures Surgery MGHL L31 72 E3
Hightown Village Surgery HTWN L38 70 C1
Hilbre High School WKBY CH48 124 F2
Hillside CP School FROD/HEL WA6 166 F1
Hillside CP School SKEL WN8 65 M5
Hillside Golf Club STHP PR8 35 G4
Hillside Health Centre SKEL WN8 65 L4
Hillside High School BTL L20 7 M5
Hillside House Surgery HUY L36 100 B8
Hillside Infant School CL/PREN CH43 110 E8
Hillside Junior School CL/PREN CH43 110 F8
Hillside Road Doctors Surgery HUY L36 100 A8
Hill Street Business Centre VAUX/LVPD L3 112 F7
Hill View CP School RUNC WA7 161 G1
Hinderton School EP CH65 163 J2
Hindley Business Centre WGNE/HIN WN2 69 M8
Hindley CP School WGNE/HIN WN2 69 M8
Hindley Green C of E School WGNE/HIN WN2 81 K2
HM Coroners Court CLVP L2 12 F7
HM Remand Centre GOL/RIS/CU WA3 107 G5
Holcroft Clinic GOL/RIS/CU WA3 107 G2
Holgate CP School WGNW/BIL/O WN5 67 G8
Holland Moor CP School SKEL WN8 66 A6
Hollies Surgery FMBY L37 59 H2
Holly Lodge Comprehensive School WD/CROXPK L12 98 C7
Hollywood Superbowl CLB/OSW/ST L13 114 B4
Holmbrook School WLTN L25 131 G2
Holmeswood Methodist School KIRK/FR/WA PR4 27 K7
Holy Angels Infant School KKBY L32 85 L3
Holy Angels Primary School KKBY L32 85 M2
Holy Cross RC High School CHLY/EC PR7 43 L1
Holy Cross RC Primary School BIRK CH41 111 G4
Holy Cross RC Primary School ECCL WA10 9 J4
Holy Cross & St Marys Primary School VAUX/LVPD L3 13 G4
Holy Family High School CSBY/BLUN L23 71 J7
Holy Family Primary School WLTN L25 131 M4
Holy Family RC Primary School CHTN/BK PR9 25 G6
Holy Family RC Primary School WDN WA8 117 M7
Holy Family RC Primary School WGNE/HIN WN2 69 J3
Holy Family RC Primary School WGNE/HIN WN2 80 C4
Holy Name RC Primary School WLT/FAZ L9 85 G6
Holy Rosary RC Primary School AIN/FAZ L10 84 E2
Holy Spirit RC Primary School NTHTN L30 83 M2
Holy Spirit School RUNC WA7 149 M5
Holy Trinity C of E Primary School CHTN/BK PR9 3 J3
Holy Trinity C of E Primary School FMBY L37 59 H2
Holy Trinity C of E Primary School HOY CH47 108 E6
Holy Trinity Primary School ALL/GAR L19 130 F8
Homoeopathic Medical Centre CLB/OSW/ST L13 114 C2
Hood Manor Community Primary School WARRW/BUR WA5 120 E7
Hood Manor Medical Centre WARRW/BUR WA5 120 E8
Hope Special School WGNS/IIMK WN3 79 G3
Hope Street Natural Health Centre CLVPS L1 113 G5
Hope Valley CP School EV L5 97 H6
Horns Mill CP School FROD/HEL WA6 166 C4
Hornspit Medical Centre NG/CROX L11 98 C5
Howley Quay Industrial Estate WARR WA1 15 J5
Hoylake Business Centre HOY CH47 108 E5
Hoylake Cottage Hospital HOY CH47 108 E5
Hoylake Cottage Hospital Trust HOY CH47 108 E5
Hoylake Road Surgery MOR/LEA CH46 109 M5
Hoylake Rugby Football Club HOY CH47 108 D6
Hudson Primary School MGHL L31 72 F6
Hugh Baird College BTL L20 7 H7
Hulmes Bridge Business Centre ORM L39 49 M3
Hunts Cross CP School WLTN L25 131 L7
Hunts Cross Group Practice WLTN L25 131 K6
Hurlston Hall Golf Club BRSC L40 50 E3
Hurst Special School ECCL WA10 89 G7
Huyton St Michaels Primary School HUY L36 115 M2
Ince Clinic & Community Centre WGNE/HIN WN2 69 J6
Ince C of E Primary School WGNE/HIN WN2 5 M6
Ince In Makerfield C of E Junior & Infant School WGNE/HIN WN2 69 J6
Ince Spring View Cs School WGNE/HIN WN2 80 B1
Interchange Motorway Industrial Estate HUY L36 116 C4
Irby Cricket Club PEN/TH CH61 125 M5
Irby Primary School PEN/TH CH61 126 A6
Irwin Road Health Centre STHEL WA9 102 F6
Isle of Man Ferry Terminal VAUX/LVPD L3 12 C6
Islington House Medical Centre NPK/KEN L6 13 M4
Ivy Farm Court Doctors Surgery SPK/HALE L24 147 M4
John Moores University CLVPS L1 113 G5
John Street CP School EP CH65 20 C2
John Street Medical Centre GOL/RIS/CU WA3 92 C5
Jubilee Medical Centre NG/CROX L11 98 E2
The Kenneth Macrae Medical Centre RNFD/HAY WA11 76 B7
Kensington CP Junior & Infant School EHL/KEN L7 113 K3
Kensington Medical Centre NPK/KEN L6 113 J2
Kerfoot Business Park WARRN/WOL WA2 121 J5
Kew Medical Centre STHP PR8 36 A2
Kew Woods CP School STHP PR8 36 A2
King David High School WAV L15 114 E6
King David Primary School WAV L15 114 E6
King Edward Industrial Estate VAUX/LVPD L3 12 C5
Kingfisher Business Park BTL L20 83 L6
King George Vi Sixth Form College STHP PR8 25 G8
Kingsbury School ORM L39 51 G8
Kings Business Park PR/KW L34 100 C8
Kingsdown High School WGNW/BIL/O WN5 67 L6
Kingsley Community School TOX L8 113 J6
Kingsmead School HOY CH47 108 E5
Kingsway Christian School WGN WN1 4 F2
Kingsway Primary School WAL/EG CH44 111 L3
Kingsway Surgery CSBY/WL L22 83 G3
Kinsbury School SKEL WN8 64 F3
Kirkby Industrial Estate Post Office NWD/KWIPK L33 86 E5
Kirkby Sports Centre KKBY L32 85 L5
Kirkdale CP School ANF/KKDL L4 96 F5
Kirkless Industrial Estate WGNE/HIN WN2 69 K4
The Knoll Surgery Partnership FROD/HEL WA6 160 D4

Knotty Ash CP School *DV/KA/FCH* L14 114 F1
Knowsley Borough Council *HUY* L36 116 A3
Knowsley Community College *KKBY* L32 85 M3
Knowsley Community College *PR/KW* L34 100 A2
Knowsley Industrial Park *NWD/KWIPK* L33 86 E3
Knowsley Magistrates Court *HUY* L36 116 A3
Knowsley Medical Centre *PR/KW* L34 99 M2
Knowsley Metropolitan Borough Council *DV/KA/FCH* L14 99 K8
Knowsley Metropolitan Borough Council *HLWD* L26 132 B6
Knowsley Metropolitan Borough Council *HUY* L36 115 M3
Knowsley Metropolitan Borough Council *HUY* L36 116 A3
Knowsley Metropolitan Borough Council *KKBY* L32 85 M3
Knowsley Metropolitan Borough Council *KKBY* L32 86 B4
Knowsley Metropolitan Borough Council *PR/KW* L34 100 E7
Knowsley Parish Council *PR/KW* L34 99 L1
Knowsley Village Primary School *PR/KW* L34 99 L3
Ktis Art Gallery *CALD/MH* L18 114 C8
Lady Lever Art Gallery *PS/BROM* CH62 128 D7
Ladymount RC Primary School *PEN/TH* CH61 141 H2
Lakeside Surgery *LYMM* WA13 139 M3
Lamberhead Green County Infants School *WGNW/BIL/O* WN5 67 J6
Lamberhead Green CP School *WGNW/BIL/O* WN5 67 K6
Lamberhead Industrial Estate *WGNW/BIL/O* WN5 67 K8
The Lamplighters Gallery *STHP* PR8 34 F8
Lancashire College for Adult Education *CHLY/EC* PR7 32 B5
Lancashire County Council *BRSC* L40 52 A2
Lancashire County Council *CHLYE* PR6 44 C6
Lancashire Schools I C T Centre *CHLY/EC* PR7 32 C5
Lancaster House Medical Centre *ECCL* WA10 9 G3
Lance Lane Medical Centre *WAV* L15 114 C6
Lander Road Primary School *LITH* L21 83 L7
Landgate Industrial Estate *AIMK* WN4 79 J5
Langbank Medical Centre *NG/CROX* L11 98 B4
Langham Street Industrial Estate *ANF/KKDL* L4 97 H5
Larkfield CP School *CHTN/BK* PR9 25 J2
Latchford Medical Centre *WARRS* WA4 138 A2
Lathom High School *SKEL* WN8 65 H1
Lathom House Surgery *BRSC* L40 39 H8
Lathom Park C of E Primary School *BRSC* L40 52 C5
Lathom Road Health Centre *HUY* L36 116 A2
Laurel Business Centre *EHL/KEN* L7 113 M3
Lawrence CP School *WAV* L15 113 M6
Lea Green Business Park *STHEL* WA9 118 B1
Leamington CP School *NG/CROX* L11 97 M3
Leasowe Primary School *MOR/LEA* CH46 110 D1
Leasowe Recreation Centre *MOR/LEA* CH46 110 C2
Lee Manor High School *NTHLY* L27 115 M8
Legh Vale CP School *RNFD/HAY* WA11 90 D7
Lewisham Medical Centre *ANF/KKDL* L4 97 L5
Leyland House Surgery *ORM* L39 51 H8
Lidderdale CP School *WAV* L15 114 A7
Linacre Primary School *BTL* L20 83 L8
Linaker County Primary School *STHP* PR8 3 G8
Lincoln Road Health Centre *STHP* PR8 35 J4
Lingham CP School *MOR/LEA* CH46 109 M4
Lingholme Health Centre *ECCL* WA10 8 F4
Liscard Primary School *WAL/NB* CH45 95 L8
Lister Drive CP School *CLB/OSW/ST* L13 114 A1
Litherland High School *LITH* L21 83 M3
Litherland Moss Primary School *LITH* L21 83 M4
Little Crosby Road Doctors Surgery *CSBY/BLUN* L23 70 F8
Little Digmoor CP School *SKEL* WN8 65 K7
Little Theatre *CHLY/EC* PR7 32 E5
Little Theatre *CHTN/BK* PR9 3 H3
Liver Industrial Estate *WLT/FAZ* L9 97 L1
Liverpool Airport *SPK/HALE* L24 146 E3
Liverpool Anglican Cathedral *CLVPS* L1 113 G6
Liverpool Art School *EHL/KEN* L7 13 L9
Liverpool Art School *TOX* L8 113 H5
Liverpool Chinese Medical Centre *CLVPS* L1 13 G7
Liverpool City Council *AIG/SPK* L17 129 M3
Liverpool City Council *ANF/KKDL* L4 97 G6
Liverpool City Council *CALD/MH* L18 130 F1
Liverpool City Council *CLB/OSW/ST* L13 114 A3
Liverpool City Council *CLVP* L2 12 E7
Liverpool City Council *CLVPS* L1 12 F6
Liverpool City Council *CLVPS* L1 13 G6
Liverpool City Council *NPK/KEN* L6 113 L1
Liverpool City Council *NPK/KEN* L6 114 A2
Liverpool City Council *TOX* L8 113 G7
Liverpool City Council *VAUX/LVPD* L3 12 C3
Liverpool City Council *VAUX/LVPD* L3 12 E6
Liverpool City Council *VAUX/LVPD* L3 13 L5
Liverpool City Council *WLT/FAZ* L9 84 E7
Liverpool Community College *AIG/SPK* L17 130 A6
Liverpool Community College *CLB/OSW/ST* L13 98 B7
Liverpool Community College *CLVPS* L1 13 J9
Liverpool Community College *EHL/KEN* L7 13 L9
Liverpool Community College *EHL/KEN* L7 113 J5
Liverpool Community College *EV* L5 96 F7
Liverpool Community College *VAUX/LVPD* L3 112 F6
Liverpool Cricket Club *ALL/GAR* L19 130 B5
Liverpool Crown & High Court *CLVPS* L1 12 F8
Liverpool Empire Theatre *CLVPS* L1 13 H6
Liverpool Football Club *BTL* L20 6 E2
Liverpool Football Club *WD/CROXPK* L12 98 E6
Liverpool Football Club *ANF/KKDL* L4 97 J6
Liverpool Health Authority *VAUX/LVPD* L3 12 E5
Liverpool Hope University *CLVPS* L1 13 L9
Liverpool Hope University College *CHLDW* L16 114 F7
Liverpool Hope University College *VAUX/LVPD* L3 13 L4
Liverpool John Moores University *AIG/SPK* L17 130 B4
Liverpool John Moores University *BIRK* CH41 11 K2
Liverpool John Moores University *CALD/MH* L18 130 A2
Liverpool John Moores University *CLVPS* L1 13 K8
Liverpool John Moores University *VAUX/LVPD* L3 12 F5
Liverpool John Moores University *VAUX/LVPD* L3 13 H4
Liverpool John Moores University *VAUX/LVPD* L3 13 G5
Liverpool Magistrates Court *CLVP* L2 13 G6
Liverpool Museum *VAUX/LVPD* L3 13 H5
Liverpool Playhouse Theatre *CLVPS* L1 13 H7
Liverpool St Helens Rugby Union Football Club *RNFD/HAY* WA11 88 C6
Liverpool Theatre School *AIG/SPK* L17 129 K1
Liverpool Theatre School *AIG/SPK* L17 130 B4
Liverpool University *NSTN* CH64 153 M6
Liverpool Womens Hospital Trust *TOX* L8 113 J6
Locking Stumps Community Primary School *GOL/RIS/CU* WA3 106 E8
Longbarn Community Primary School *WARRN/WOL* WA2 122 D4
Longford Street Surgery *WARRN/WOL* WA2 14 E1
Long Lane Community Primary School *WARRN/WOL* WA2 121 K4
Long Lane Doctors Surgery *ALL/GAR* L19 130 F6
Long Lane Medical Centre *WLT/FAZ* L9 98 B1
Longshoot Health Centre *WGN* WN1 5 J2
Longton Lane CP School *RAIN/WH* L35 101 K8
Longton Medical Centre *RAIN/WH* L35 117 K2
Longview Primary School *HUY* L36 100 A7
Lordsgate Township C of E Primary School *BRSC* L40 52 A2
Lourdes Hospital *CALD/MH* L18 130 B1
Loushers Lane Special School *WARRS* WA4 137 M3
Lower Lee Special School *WLTN* L25 131 G1
Low Hall County Primary School *WGNE/HIN* WN2 80 C2
Lowton High School *GOL/RIS/CU* WA3 93 K5
Lowton Junior & Infant School *GOL/RIS/CU* WA3 93 J6
Lowton St Marys C of E School *GOL/RIS/CU* WA3 93 K5
Lowton West Primary School *GOL/RIS/CU* WA3 92 E5
Lunts Heath CP School *WDN* WA8 118 D8
Lydiate Primary School *MGHL* L31 72 E1
Lyme County Infant School *NEWLW* WA12 104 B1
Lyndale School *PS/BROM* CH62 144 B8
Mab Lane Junior & Infant School *STBRV* L28 99 H6
Mabs Cross Primary School *WGN* WN1 5 G1
Mackets Primary School *WLTN* L25 131 L4
Macmillan Surgery *KKBY* L32 86 C4
Maghull Health Centre *MGHL* L31 72 F4
Maghull High School *MGHL* L31 72 D6
Maghull Primary School *MGHL* L31 72 D6
Maidford CP School *DV/KA/FCH* L14 99 H8
Malvern Primary School *DV/KA/FCH* L14 115 H3
Manchester Port Health Authority *RUNC* WA7 19 G2
Manley Village School *FROD/HEL* WA6 167 J7
The Manor C of E Junior School *NEWLW* WA12 104 B1
Manor Farm Medical Centre *HUY* L36 116 B4
Manor High School *CSBY/BLUN* L23 70 E7
Manor House CP School *FROD/HEL* WA6 160 E4
Manor Industrial Estate *WARRS* WA4 15 M8
Manor Primary School *CL/PREN* CH43 110 E7
Mansfield CP School *EP* CH65 163 H2
Marble Place Shopping Centre *STHP* PR8 3 G4
Margaret Beavan Special School *WD/CROXPK* L12 98 C6
The Margaret Thompson Medical Centre *SPK/HALE* L24 147 J1
Maricourt High School *MGHL* L31 73 G5
Marine Football Club *CSBY/BLUN* L23 82 F2
Market Hall *EP* CH65 20 C6
Market Hall *SKEL* WN8 65 K4
Market Street Medical Centre *WGNE/HIN* WN2 69 M7
Marsh Green Health Centre *WGNW/BIL/O* WN5 67 M4
Marsh Green Primary School *WGNW/BIL/O* WN5 67 M5
Marsh Green Surgery *WGNW/BIL/O* WN5 67 M4
Martlew Day Hospital *RAIN/WH* L35 101 L8
Marus Bridge Health Centre *WGNS/IIMK* WN3 79 H3
Maryland Health Centre *CLVPS* L1 13 L9
Marymount Convent School *WAL/EG* CH44 111 K2
Massey Hall Special School *WARRS* WA4 139 H3
Maternity & Child Welfare Clinic *STHEL* WA9 103 H2
Maternity & Child Welfare Clinic *WGNE/HIN* WN2 69 L8
Mather Avenue Doctors Surgery *CALD/MH* L18 130 E4
Matthew Arnold School *TOX* L8 129 J2
Mawdesley C of E School *BRSC* L40 40 E2
Max Road Surgery *DV/KA/FCH* L14 99 H7
Maypole Industrial Estate *WGNE/HIN* WN2 80 E6
Meadow Bank Special School *AIN/FAZ* L10 85 H5
Meadow County Junior School *GTS/LS* CH66 163 G3
Meadowside School *GR/UP/WCH* CH49 126 C3
Megabowl *NTHTN* L30 84 C2
Melling CP School *MGHL* L31 85 K1
Melrose Abbey *ANF/KKDL* L4 7 K9
Mendell Primary School *PS/BROM* CH62 144 A5
Meols Cop High School *STHP* PR8 25 H8
Merchant Taylors School *CSBY/BLUN* L23 83 G1
Merchant Taylors School for Girls *CSBY/BLUN* L23 83 G2
Mere Brow C of E School *KIRK/FR/WA* PR4 27 H3
Merefield School *STHP* PR8 47 K1
Mere Oaks School *WGN* WN1 56 D8
Merkmal Gallery *TOX* L8 113 H5
Mersey Ferries *VAUX/LVPD* L3 12 D8
Mersey Park Primary School *RF/TRAN* CH42 127 M2
Mersey Regional Health Authority *RUNC* WA7 19 M2
Merseyside Car Hospital *BIRK* CH41 11 J4
Merseyside Maritime Museum *VAUX/LVPD* L3 12 E9
Mersey View School *AIG/SPK* L17 130 A4
Merton Bank Junior & Infant School *STHEL* WA9 9 M3
Metropolitan Borough Council *ECCL* WA10 9 G4
Metropolitan Cathedral Rc *VAUX/LVPD* L3 13 L8
Millbrook CP School *WGNNW/ST* WN6 55 K7
Millbrook Primary School *KKBY* L32 85 M2
Millfields Primary School *PS/BROM* CH62 155 G1
Mill Green Special School *NEWLW* WA12 105 G2
Millhouse Gallery *SKEL* WN8 53 L4
Millingford Industrial Estate *GOL/RIS/CU* WA3 92 D5
Mill Lane Industrial Estate *EP* CH65 21 J9
Millstead Special Schools *WAV* L15 114 D5
Mill Street Medical Centre *ECCL* WA10 8 F4
Millwood CP School *SPK/HALE* L24 147 H3
Millwood Road Doctors Surgery *SPK/HALE* L24 147 H1
Miriam Health Centre *BIRK* CH41 111 H5
Monksdown CP School *NG/CROX* L11 98 C4
Montrose Special School *WGNW/BIL/O* WN5 67 M6
Moore CP School *WARRS* WA4 136 C8
Moore Rugby Union Football Club *WARRS* WA4 136 D7
Moorfield CP School *WDN* WA8 134 F2
Moor Lane Business Centre *WDN* WA8 16 C6
Moorside CP School *SKEL* WN8 66 A6
Moreton Medical Centre *MOR/LEA* CH46 110 A5
Mosscroft Primary School *HUY* L36 116 C2
Moss Industrial Estate *LEIGH* WN7 93 K4
Mosslands School *WAL/EG* CH44 111 G1
Moss Lane Sports Centre *LITH* L21 83 M4
Mossock Hall Golf Club *ORM* L39 74 A1
Moss Pits CP School *WAV* L15 114 D7
Mossy Lea CP School *WGNNW/ST* WN6 42 A7
Mostyn House School *NSTN* CH64 152 E5
Mother Teresa RC Primary School *EV* L5 13 G1
Mount Carmel School *ORM* L39 62 F3
Mount Primary School *WAL/NB* CH45 95 J5
Multibowl *PS/BROM* CH62 143 M3
Murdishaw Health Centre *RUNC* WA7 150 F6
Murdishaw West CP School *RUNC* WA7 150 F7
Murrayfield Hospital *PEN/TH* CH61 126 F8
Museum & Art Gallery *WARR* WA1 14 D7
Museum of Liverpool Life *VAUX/LVPD* L3 12 D9
National Discovery Park *CLVPS* L1 12 F8
National Museums & Galleries Merseyside *CLVPS* L1 12 F6
National Museums & Galleries on Merseyside 6 D4
Natural Health Clinic *PR/KW* L34 100 F7
Neptune Theatre *CLVPS* L1 13 H8
Neston County High School *NSTN* CH64 153 H4
Neston CP School *NSTN* CH64 153 G6
Neston Cricket Club *NSTN* CH64 152 E5
Neston Medical Centre *NSTN* CH64 153 G5
Neston Recreation Centre *NSTN* CH64 153 H4
Neston St Marys C of E Primary School *NSTN* CH64 153 H4
Neston Surgery *NSTN* CH64 153 H6
Netherfield Family Health Clinic *EV* L5 97 G8
Netherley Health Centre *NTHLY* L27 116 A8
Netherley Sports Centre *NTHLY* L27 115 M8
Netherpool County Infant School *GTS/LS* CH66 156 A6
Netherton Moss Primary School *NTHTN* L30 84 A2
Netherton Park Primary School *NTHTN* L30 84 B4
Newborough School *WLTN* L25 131 H2
New Brighton Primary School *WAL/NB* CH45 95 L5
New Brighton Rugby Union Football Club *MOR/LEA* CH46 110 B1
Newburgh C of E School *SKEL* WN8 53 J4
Newburgh Cricket Club *SKEL* WN8 53 J4
Newchurch Community Primary School *GOL/RIS/CU* WA3 107 G3
Newfield School *CSBY/BLUN* L23 71 K8
New Heys Community Comprehensive School *CALD/MH* L18 130 F4
New Hutte Junior School *HLWD* L26 132 A7
New Lodge Industrial Estate *NWD/KWIPK* L33 86 D5
Newman RC High School *WARRS* WA4 122 B8
New Mersey Retail Park *SPK/HALE* L24 131 H8
New Park School Butler Wing *NPK/KEN* L6 113 K2
New Park School Newsham Wing *NPK/KEN* L6 113 L1
News Gallery *NSTN* CH64 153 G6
Newspaper Office *VAUX/LVPD* L3 12 D6
Newstead Abbey *TOX* L8 113 L6
Newton Bank Preparatory School *NEWLW* WA12 105 G1
Newton Community Hospital *NEWLW* WA12 104 D4
Newton Health Clinic *NEWLW* WA12 104 D1
Newton Le Willows CP School *NEWLW* WA12 104 E2
Newton-le-willows Sports Club *NEWLW* WA12 104 E1
Newton West Park CP School *LEIGH* WN7 81 L5
New Way Business Centre *WAL/EG* CH44 111 M3
Nicol Mere Primary School *AIMK* WN4 79 J8
Nine Tree Primary School *STBRV* L28 99 J4
Norley Hall Cricket Club *WGNW/BIL/O* WN5 67 K6
Norman Pannell CP School *NTHLY* L27 115 M8
Norris Green Family Health Clinic *NG/CROX* L11 98 A4
North Cheshire Health Authority *RUNC* WA7 19 L2
Northcote CP School *WLT/FAZ* L9 97 J2
Northern Cricket Club *CSBY/BLUN* L23 71 H7
North Meols Lawn Tennis Club *CHTN/BK* PR9 25 J4
North Mersey Business Centre *NWD/KWIPK* L33 86 E1

North Mersey Community NHS Trust *BTL* L20 .... 7 J4
North Mersey Community NHS Trust *CALD/MH* L18 .... 130 A1
North Mersey Community NHS Trust *CLB/OSW/ST* L13 .... 114 C3
North Mersey Community NHS Trust *NTHTN* L30 .... 84 A1
North Mersey Community NHS Trust *TOX* L8 .... 113 M7
North Mersey Community NHS Trust *WLT/FAZ* L9 .... 84 F7
North Park Health Centre *BTL* L20 .... 6 F1
North Quarry Business Park *WGNNW/ST* WN6 .... 54 F4
North Road Doctors Surgery *ECCL* WA10 .... 9 G3
North Road Surgery *ECCL* WA10 .... 8 F3
Northway CP School *WAV* L15 .... 114 D4
Northway Primary School *MGHL* L31 .... 72 F2
Norton Priory County High School *RUNC* WA7 .... 150 D4
Norton Priory Recreation Centre *RUNC* WA7 .... 150 D3
Norwood CP School *CHTN/BK* PR9 .... 25 G6
Notre Dame High School *EV* L5 .... 97 H6
Nugent House School *WGNW/BIL/O* WN5 .... 89 M1
Nutgrove Methodist Primary School *RAIN/WH* L35 .... 101 M6
Nye Bevan Swimming Pool *SKEL* WN8 .... 65 K4
Oak Cottage Medical Centre *HUY* L36 .... 116 A4
Oakdene Primary School *RAIN/WH* L35 .... 117 L3
Oakfield County Junior & Infant School *WDN* WA8 .... 133 J5
Oakhouse Surgery *STHEL* WA9 .... 103 G6
Oak Remedial Clinic *WD/CROXPK* L12 .... 99 G1
Oak Vale Medical Practice *CLB/OSW/ST* L13 .... 114 E3
Oakwood Avenue Community Primary & Infant School *WARR* WA1 .... 15 K1
Odeon Cinema *CLVPS* L1 .... 13 H6
Odeon Cinema *NTHTN* L30 .... 84 C2
Odeon Multiscreen Cinema *PS/BROM* CH62 .... 143 M2
The Oldershaw Lower School *WAL/NB* CH45 .... 95 K8
The Oldershaw School *WAL/NB* CH45 .... 95 J8
Old Foundry Estate *WDN* WA8 .... 16 F6
Old Hall Community Primary School *WARRW/BUR* WA5 .... 120 F5
Old Hall Farm Business Park *CHTN/BK* PR9 .... 25 H8
Old Hall Farm Business Park *CHTN/BK* PR9 .... 25 K7
Old Hall Surgery *EP* CH65 .... 20 B6
Old Parkonians Rugby Club *CL/PREN* CH43 .... 127 H2
Old Rockerrians Rugby Club *CL/PREN* CH43 .... 127 H5
Old Swan Health Centre *CLB/OSW/ST* L13 .... 114 C3
Ophthalmic Surgery *CLVPS* L1 .... 13 K9
Ormskirk College *ORM* L39 .... 51 G7
Ormskirk Cricket Club *ORM* L39 .... 63 H1
Ormskirk & District General Hospital *ORM* L39 .... 51 J8
Ormskirk Golf Club *BRSC* L40 .... 52 A6
Ormskirk Grammar School *ORM* L39 .... 63 H1
Ormskirk Rugby Union Football Club *ORM* L39 .... 51 G7
Ormskirk Swimming Pool *ORM* L39 .... 51 G8
Orrell Clinic *WGNW/BIL/O* WN5 .... 67 G6
Orrell County Primary School *BTL* L20 .... 83 L8
Orrell Holgate Primary School *WGNW/BIL/O* WN5 .... 67 G8
Orrell Lane Doctors Surgery *WLT/FAZ* L9 .... 84 C7
Orrell Newfold CP School *WGNW/BIL/O* WN5 .... 77 M1
Orrell Rugby Union Football Club *WGNW/BIL/O* WN5 .... 67 G8
Orrets Meadow School *MOR/LEA* CH46 .... 110 B5
Our Lady & All Saints RC School *SKEL* WN8 .... 53 L3
Our Lady Immaculate Primary School *EV* L5 .... 97 G7
Our Lady of Compassion RC Primary School *FMBY* L37 .... 59 J2
Our Lady of Fatima High School *NPK/KEN* L6 .... 113 J1
Our Lady of Good Help Primary School *WAV* L15 .... 114 C5
Our Lady of Mount Carmel Primary School *TOX* L8 .... 113 H8
Our Lady of Perpetual Succour Junior School *WDN* WA8 .... 133 H5
Our Lady of Perpetual Succour RC Infant School *WDN* WA8 .... 133 K4
Our Lady of Pity RC Prim School *GR/UP/WCH* CH49 .... 125 M3
Our Lady of Reconciliation Primary School *VAUX/LVPD* L3 .... 12 F2
Our Lady of the Assumption Infant School *WLTN* L25 .... 115 K7
Our Lady of the Assumption Primary School *WLTN* L25 .... 115 K7
Our Lady of the Rosary RC School *LEIGH* WN7 .... 81 K8
Our Lady of Walsingham RC Infant School *NTHTN* L30 .... 84 B3
Our Lady of Walsingham RC Primary School *NTHTN* L30 .... 84 A3
Our Lady Queen of Peace RC High School *SKEL* WN8 .... 65 H1
Our Lady Queen of Peace RC Primary School *LITH* L21 .... 83 K3
Our Lady & St Edwards RC Primary School *BIRK* CH41 .... 10 D1
Our Lady & St Philomenas R C Primary School *WLT/FAZ* L9 .... 98 B1
Our Lady & St Swithens Primary School *NG/CROX* L11 .... 85 L8
Our Ladys Bishop Eton School *CALD/MH* L18 .... 114 E8
Our Ladys Catholic Primary School *WARRS* WA4 .... 138 A2
Our Ladys Primary School *PR/KW* L34 .... 100 F6
Our Ladys RC Infant School *EP* CH65 .... 163 J2
Our Ladys RC Junior School *EP* CH65 .... 163 J2
Our Ladys RC Primary School *RUNC* WA7 .... 150 C7
Our Ladys RC Primary School *STHEL* WA9 .... 103 G2
Our Ladys RC Primary School *WGNE/HIN* WN2 .... 57 K8
Our Lady Star of the Sea RC Primary School *LITH* L21 .... 83 J7
Outlet Village *EP* CH65 .... 164 A3
The Oval Sports Centre *BEB* CH63 .... 128 C6
Overchurch Junior & Infant School *GR/UP/WCH* CH49 .... 110 B7
Overdale Primary School *NWD/KWIPK* L33 .... 86 B1
Oxton Cricket Club *CL/PREN* CH43 .... 127 H1
Oxton St Saviours C of E Primary School *CL/PREN* CH43 .... 127 J2
Padgate Business Centre *WARR* WA1 .... 122 D5
Padgate Business Centre *WARR* WA1 .... 122 C5
Padgate C of E Primary School *WARRN/WOL* WA2 .... 122 C4
Padgate Community High School *WARRN/WOL* WA2 .... 122 B3
Padgate Medical Centre *WARRN/WOL* WA2 .... 122 C4
Pagefield Industrial Estate *WGNNW/ST* WN6 .... 68 B4
Palacefields County Infant School *RUNC* WA7 .... 150 C7
Palace Theatre *WARR* WA1 .... 14 E6
Palatine Industrial Estate *WARRS* WA4 .... 15 G9
Parbold Douglas C of E Primary School *SKEL* WN8 .... 53 M2
Parish C of E Primary School *ECCL* WA10 .... 9 H3
Park Brow CP School *KKBY* L32 .... 86 C5
Park Business Centre *WGNE/HIN* WN2 .... 80 F2
The Park CP School *RUNC* WA7 .... 150 C4
Parkdale Industrial Estate *WARR* WA1 .... 15 H7
Parkfield Medical Centre *PS/BROM* CH62 .... 128 D5
Parkfield School *KKBY* L32 .... 86 A5
Parkgate CP School *NSTN* CH64 .... 152 E4
Park Golf Club *CHTN/BK* PR9 .... 24 E4
Park Hall Leisure Centre *CHLY/EC* PR7 .... 42 C1
Park High Lower School *BIRK* CH41 .... 10 A3
Park High School *BIRK* CH41 .... 10 D6
Park House Medical Centre *PR/KW* L34 .... 100 F7
Park House Surgery *STHEL* WA9 .... 9 L5
Park Industrial Estate *AIMK* WN4 .... 91 G2
Parklands CP Infant School *GTS/LS* CH66 .... 155 L7
Park Medical Centre *WKBY* CH48 .... 124 D3
Park Primary School *WAL/EG* CH44 .... 111 K2
Park Road Community Primary School *WARRW/BUR* WA5 .... 120 A7
Park Road Group Practice *TOX* L8 .... 129 J1
Park Road Sports Centre *TOX* L8 .... 113 H8
Park View Primary School *HUY* L36 .... 115 L1
Parr Community High School *STHEL* WA9 .... 103 G3
Parr Flat Community Infant School *STHEL* WA9 .... 103 J2
Parrs Corner Trading Estate *BTL* L20 .... 7 H2
Parr Swimming Baths *STHEL* WA9 .... 9 M5
Pasture Road Health Centre *MOR/LEA* CH46 .... 110 A4
Patterdale Lodge Group Practice *NEWLW* WA12 .... 104 F1
Patterdale Lodge Medical Centre *NEWLW* WA12 .... 104 C2
Peatwood Medical Centre *KKBY* L32 .... 86 B6
Peelhouse Lane Surgery *WDN* WA8 .... 17 G1
Pemberton Business Centre *WGNW/BIL/O* WN5 .... 67 L7
Pemberton Clinic *WGNW/BIL/O* WN5 .... 67 M7
Pemberton CP School *WGNW/BIL/O* WN5 .... 67 L7
Penketh Business Park *WARRW/BUR* WA5 .... 136 D1
Penketh Community High School *WARRW/BUR* WA5 .... 120 C8
Penketh Community Primary School *WARRW/BUR* WA5 .... 135 M1
Penketh Health Clinic *WARRW/BUR* WA5 .... 136 A1
Penketh South Community Primary School *WARRW/BUR* WA5 .... 136 B2
Penketh Swimming Baths *WARRW/BUR* WA5 .... 120 A8
Penkford Technology School *NEWLW* WA12 .... 104 A3
Penlake Industrial Estate *STHEL* WA9 .... 103 G7
Penny Lane Surgery *WAV* L15 .... 114 C7
Pensby Clinic *PEN/TH* CH61 .... 141 J2
Pensby High School *PEN/TH* CH61 .... 140 F1
Pensby Infant School *PEN/TH* CH61 .... 141 H2
Pensby Junior School *PEN/TH* CH61 .... 141 H2
Pensby Park Primary School *PEN/TH* CH61 .... 140 F2
Pensby Recreation Centre *PEN/TH* CH61 .... 126 C8
Pepper Mill Business Park *WGN* WN1 .... 5 G5
Perry Brook Community Primary School *AIMK* WN4 .... 79 J6
Pershore House School *RF/TRAN* CH42 .... 127 K4
Peterhouse School *CHTN/BK* PR9 .... 25 K2
Peterhouse School *STHP* PR8 .... 3 L7
Peter Lloyd Leisure Centre *CLB/OSW/ST* L13 .... 98 B8
Pewithall CP School *RUNC* WA7 .... 19 J9
Philharmonic Hall *CLVPS* L1 .... 13 L9
Phoenix Medical Centre *ECCL* WA10 .... 8 F4
Picton Road Surgery *WAV* L15 .... 114 A5
Pilch Lane Surgery *DV/KA/FCH* L14 .... 115 J2
Pinehurst Junior School *ANF/KKDL* L4 .... 97 L6
Pinehurst Road County Infant School *ANF/KKDL* L4 .... 97 L6
Pink Museum *AIG/SPK* L17 .... 129 L1
Pioneer Industrial Estate *WGNW/BIL/O* WN5 .... 68 A7
Pius XII RC School *GTS/LS* CH66 .... 155 M7
Plantation Business Park *PS/BROM* CH62 .... 144 B3
Plantation Primary School *HLWD* L26 .... 132 B5
Platt Bridge Clinic *WGNE/HIN* WN2 .... 80 C3
Pleasant Street CP School *VAUX/LVPD* L3 .... 13 K8
Plessington RC High School *BEB* CH63 .... 128 C6
Pontville School *ORM* L39 .... 62 F2
Pooltown CP School *EP* CH65 .... 156 B8
Portland Primary School *BIRK* CH41 .... 10 A2
Portrait Gallery *WDN* WA8 .... 134 C3
Poulter Road Medical Centre *WLT/FAZ* L9 .... 84 D6
Poulton Lancelyn Primary School *BEB* CH63 .... 143 J3
Poulton Primary School *WAL/EG* CH44 .... 111 J2
Prenton High School for Girls *RF/TRAN* CH42 .... 127 M4
Prenton Infant & Junior School *CL/PREN* CH43 .... 127 J4
Prenton Preparatory School *CL/PREN* CH43 .... 127 K2
Prescot Associated Football Club *PR/KW* L34 .... 100 E6
Prescot CP School *PR/KW* L34 .... 101 G7
Prescot Leisure Centre *RAIN/WH* L35 .... 101 G8
Prescot Medical Centre *PR/KW* L34 .... 100 F7
Prescot Museum *PR/KW* L34 .... 100 E7
Prescot Primary School *RAIN/WH* L35 .... 116 F1
Prescot School *PR/KW* L34 .... 100 E6
Prestfield School *CHTN/BK* PR9 .... 25 J2
Price Street Business Centre *BIRK* CH41 .... 10 E2
Priestley Business Centre *WARRW/BUR* WA5 .... 14 A5
Priestley College *WARRS* WA4 .... 137 L2
Princes Park Health Centre *TOX* L8 .... 113 K7
Princess Drive Medical Centre *DV/KA/FCH* L14 .... 99 J7
Princes Special School *TOX* L8 .... 113 J6
The Priory Medical Centre *NPK/KEN* L6 .... 97 L8
Priory Parish C of E Primary School *BIRK* CH41 .... 10 F4
Prospect House Medical Centre *WGNW/BIL/O* WN5 .... 67 J7
Prospect Industrial Estate *WGNE/HIN* WN2 .... 69 M8
Pump House Museum *BIRK* CH41 .... 11 L4
The Quadrangle Business Centre *WGNE/HIN* WN2 .... 81 K1
Quay Business Centre *WARRN/WOL* WA2 .... 121 J2
Queen Mary Community Comprehensive School *WLT/FAZ* L9 .... 97 M1
Queens Drive Family Health Clinic *WLT/FAZ* L9 .... 97 J2
Queens Drive Recreation Centre *ANF/KKDL* L4 .... 97 H3
Queens Park C of E U RC Primary School *ECCL* WA10 .... 8 B3
Queensway Business Centre *WDN* WA8 .... 16 C9
Racecourse Retail Park *WLT/FAZ* L9 .... 84 D3
Radio City *CLVP* L2 .... 12 F6
Radnor Medical Centre *NPK/KEN* L6 .... 97 M8
Raeburn Primary School *PS/BROM* CH62 .... 143 M7
Rainbow Medical Centre *STHEL* WA9 .... 103 G6
Rainford C of E Primary School *RNFD/HAY* WA11 .... 76 B7
Rainford Health Centre *RNFD/HAY* WA11 .... 76 C7
Rainford High School *RNFD/HAY* WA11 .... 76 C5
Rainhill Clinic *RAIN/WH* L35 .... 117 L2
Rainhill High School *RAIN/WH* L35 .... 117 M3
Rainhill Parish Council *NTHTN* L30 .... 84 C4
Rainhill Village Surgery *RAIN/WH* L35 .... 117 L2
Range High School *FMBY* L37 .... 58 E5
Ranworth Square Jmi School *NG/CROX* L11 .... 98 B2
Ravenscroft Primary School *NWD/KWIPK* L33 .... 74 A8
Rawson Road Primary School *LITH* L21 .... 83 H7
Record Business Park *WARRN/WOL* WA2 .... 121 J5
Rectory C of E Primary School *AIMK* WN4 .... 78 F8
Red Bank School *NEWLW* WA12 .... 105 G4
Redbridge High School *AIN/FAZ* L10 .... 85 H5
Redgate Primary School *FMBY* L37 .... 59 J3
Regent House Surgery *CHLY/EC* PR7 .... 32 D6
Regional College of Art *WAV* L15 .... 114 B5
Renacres Hall Hospital *ORM* L39 .... 36 D8
Retail Park *VAUX/LVPD* L3 .... 12 D3
Rice Lane County Junior School *WLT/FAZ* L9 .... 84 C8
Richard Evans County Infant School *RNFD/HAY* WA11 .... 90 C7
Richard Evans Primary School *RNFD/HAY* WA11 .... 90 B7
Ridgeway High School *CL/PREN* CH43 .... 126 F1
Rimrose Business Park *BTL* L20 .... 6 D3
Rivacre Valley CP School *GTS/LS* CH66 .... 156 A6
Riverside Bowl *WAL/NB* CH45 .... 95 K4
Riverside Primary School *WAL/EG* CH44 .... 112 A2
Riverside Surgery *RF/TRAN* CH42 .... 128 C3
Rivington & Blackrod High School *HOR/BR* BL6 .... 45 K7
Rivington CP School *ECCL* WA10 .... 8 C1
Rivington Primary School *HOR/BR* BL6 .... 45 H4
R L Hughes County Junior & Infant School *AIMK* WN4 .... 91 J2
R N I B Sunshine House School *STHP* PR8 .... 2 A8
Roberts Primary School *BTL* L20 .... 84 A6
Robins Lane Community Primary School *STHEL* WA9 .... 102 E5
Robson Street Clinic *WARR* WA1 .... 15 J4
Roby Medical Centre *HUY* L36 .... 115 J3
Roby Mill C of E School *SKEL* WN8 .... 66 D2
Roby Park Primary School *HUY* L36 .... 115 J2
Rock Court Surgery *CLB/OSW/ST* L13 .... 114 C2
Rocket Trading Centre *DV/KA/FCH* L14 .... 114 E4
Rock Ferry High School *RF/TRAN* CH42 .... 128 B5
Rock Ferry Medical Centre *RF/TRAN* CH42 .... 128 B2
Rock Ferry Primary School *RF/TRAN* CH42 .... 128 B3
Rock Surgery *FROD/HEL* WA6 .... 160 D4
Rodney Fertility Clinic *CLVPS* L1 .... 13 K9
Roma Galleries *CL/PREN* CH43 .... 10 E8
Ronald House School *CSBY/BLUN* L23 .... 71 G7
Roscoe CP School *CLB/OSW/ST* L13 .... 98 A6
Rose Bridge High School *WGN* WN1 .... 5 L3
Rose Cottage Surgery *WARRW/BUR* WA5 .... 136 A1
Roseheath Primary School *HLWD* L26 .... 132 B6
Rosehill Business Park *CHTN/BK* PR9 .... 3 M5
Rose Hill School *AIMK* WN4 .... 80 A8
Ross Business Centre *WGNW/BIL/O* WN5 .... 67 M8
Rossmore CP School *GTS/LS* CH66 .... 155 L6
Rother Drive Business Park *EP* CH65 .... 156 C6
Royal Albert Edward Infirmary *WGN* WN1 .... 68 E3
The Royal Birkdale Golf Club *STHP* PR8 .... 34 E5
Royal College of Nursing *CLVP* L2 .... 12 E7
Royal College of Nursing *MGHL* L31 .... 73 K3
Royal Court Theatre *CLVPS* L1 .... 13 H6
Royal Liver Building *VAUX/LVPD* L3 .... 12 D7
Royal Liverpool Childrens NHS Trust *WD/CROXPK* L12 .... 114 E1
Royal Liverpool University Hospital *EHL/KEN* L7 .... 113 J3
Royal Mail Sorting Office *VAUX/LVPD* L3 .... 13 K7
Roy Castle International Centre for Lung Cancer *EHL/KEN* L7 .... 13 M5
Rudston CP School *CHLDW* L16 .... 114 F5
Rufford C of E School *BRSC* L40 .... 39 K1
Ruffwood Community Comprehensive School *NWD/KWIPK* L33 .... 86 B2
Runcorn All Saints C of E Primary School *RUNC* WA7 .... 19 G2
Runcorn County Court *RUNC* WA7 .... 150 B5
Runcorn Football Club *RUNC* WA7 .... 19 K2
Runcorn Rowing Club *RUNC* WA7 .... 160 F1

Runshaw College CHLY/EC PR7 32 E6
Rutherford Medical Centre CALD/MH L18 114 D7
Sacred Heart High School CSBY/BLUN L23 83 G2
Sacred Heart RC High School CSBY/BLUN L23 83 G1
Sacred Heart RC Primary School CHLYE PR6 33 G6
Sacred Heart RC Primary School MOR/LEA CH46 110 B4
Sacred Heart RC Primary School NWD/KWIPK L33 86 B3
Sacred Heart RC Primary School WARRW/BUR WA5 121 G8
Sacred Heart RC School WGNE/HIN WN2 81 K2
Sacred Heart RC School WGNNW/ST WN6 68 B3
St Aelreds RC High School NEWLW WA12 104 F1
St Agnes Primary School HUY L36 116 B4
St Aidans C of E Community Primary School STHEL WA9 119 G2
St Aidans C of E Primary School WGNW/BIL/O WN5 78 A8
St Aidans Primary School HUY L36 116 B1
St Aidans RC Primary School WGNS/IIMK WN3 78 F3
St Albans Catholic Primary School WARRW/BUR WA5 14 B3
St Albans RC Primary School WAL/EG CH44 111 J1
St Alberts Primary School STBRV L28 99 J4
St Aloysius RC Junior & Infant School HUY L36 115 L1
St Ambrose Barlow RC High School NTHTN L30 72 C8
St Ambrose Primary School SPK/HALE L24 147 J2
St Andrews Ce Primary School WARRN/WOL WA2 121 L2
St Andrews C of E Junior & Infant School WGNNW/ST WN6 68 B3
St Andrews C of E Primary School BEB CH63 128 B7
St Andrews Maghull C of E Primary School MGHL L31 72 F4
St Annes C of E Primary School CLB/OSW/ST L13 114 B2
St Annes RC Junior School RF/TRAN CH42 128 B5
St Annes RC Primary School EHL/KEN L7 113 K5
St Annes RC Primary School HUY L36 115 M4
St Annes RC Primary School ORM L39 62 F1
St Annes RC Primary School STHEL WA9 102 F6
St Anns C of E Primary School RAIN/WH L35 117 L2
St Anns C of E Primary School WARRN/WOL WA2 121 L5
St Anselms College CL/PREN CH43 10 B7
St Anthony of Padua Primary School CALD/MH L18 130 B1
St Augustine of Canterbury RC High School RNFD/HAY WA11 90 A8
St Augustines RC Primary School RUNC WA7 150 C3
St Austins Primary School ALL/GAR L19 130 D6
St Barnabas C E Aided Primary School WARRW/BUR WA5 14 A5
St Bartholomews RC Primary School RAIN/WH L35 118 A4
St Basils RC Primary School RAIN/WH L35 133 J3
St Bedes RC Junior & Infant School WDN WA8 16 D1
St Bedes RC School ORM L39 62 F1
St Benedicts Catholic Primary School WARRN/WOL WA2 15 J1
St Benedicts RC High School GR/UP/WCH CH49 126 D1
St Benedicts RC Primary School WGNE/HIN WN2 69 L7
St Bernadettes RC Primary School WGNNW/ST WN6 55 J7
St Bertelines Primary School RUNC WA7 150 E5
St Bridgets Catholic Primary School WARRN/WOL WA2 122 B2
St Bridgets C of E Primary School WKBY CH48 124 D4
St Brigids Primary School STBRV L28 99 J6
St Catherines C of E Primary School WGN WN1 5 J4
St Catherines RC Primary School GOL/RIS/CU WA3 93 G6
St Cecilias Primary School CLB/OSW/ST L13 98 A8
St Chads RC School RUNC WA7 149 M6
St Charles Primary School AIG/SPK L17 129 L3
St Christophers Infant School SPK/HALE L24 146 F1
St Christophers Junior School SPK/HALE L24 146 F1
St Clares Primary School WAV L15 114 A6
St Clements RC Primary School RUNC WA7 19 G7
St Cleopas C of E Primary School TOX L8 129 H1
St Columbas Primary School HUY L36 100 A8
St Cuthbert RC Junior Mixed School WGNW/BIL/O WN5 67 M7
St Cuthberts C of E School ORM L39 49 K4
St Cuthberts Primary School CLB/OSW/ST L13 114 B2
St Davids Ce Primary School WGNE/HIN WN2 57 J6
St Dominics Junior & Infant School DV/KA/FCH L14 99 K7
St Edmund Arrowsmith Comprehensive School RAIN/WH L35 101 H8
St Edmund Arrowsmith RC High School AIMK WN4 91 K3
St Edmund of Canterbury Comprehensive School DV/KA/FCH L14 99 K7
St Edmunds RC Primary School CSBY/WL L22 82 F4
St Edmunds RC Primary School SKEL WN8 65 H4
St Edwards College WD/CROXPK L12 98 D8
St Edwards RC Junior & Infant School WGNW/BIL/O WN5 68 B6
St Edwards RC Primary School RUNC WA7 19 K2
St Francis de Sales Infant School ANF/KKDL L4 7 M7
St Francis de Sales Junior Boys School ANF/KKDL L4 7 M9
St Francis de Sales Junior Girls School ANF/KKDL L4 7 M8
St Francis Xavier Lower School WAV L15 114 E5
St Francis Xaviers College WLTN L25 131 G1
St Gabriels C of E Primary School HUY L36 116 C3
St George of England High School BTL L20 83 M7
St George's Hall CLVPS L1 13 H6
St Georges Medical Centre WAL/NB CH45 95 K6
St Georges Primary School CHLY/EC PR7 33 G8
St Georges Primary School WAL/NB CH45 95 H8
St Georges RC Primary School MGHL L31 72 F6
St Gerards RC School EV L5 96 F7
St Gregorys Catholic High School WARRW/BUR WA5 120 F8
St Gregorys RC Jmi School NTHLY L27 116 A8
St Gregorys RC Junior School MGHL L31 72 E1
St Helens Associated Football Club STHEL WA9 103 H6
St Helens Borough Council ECCL WA10 9 G5
St Helens Borough Council ECCL WA10 101 J2
St Helens College ECCL WA10 8 F5
St Helens College NEWLW WA12 104 D1
St Helens College STHEL WA9 9 K3
St Helens County Court ECCL WA10 9 G5
St Helens Cricket Club ECCL WA10 8 C2
St Helens Hospital STHEL WA9 102 E4
St Helens & Knowsley Hospitals Trust RAIN/WH L35 117 H1
St Helens Metropolitan Borough Council ECCL WA10 8 D6
St Helens Metropolitan Borough Council ECCL WA10 101 M5
St Helens Metropolitan Borough Council NEWLW WA12 104 C2
St Helens Metropolitan Borough Council RNFD/HAY WA11 89 L5
St Helens Metropolitan Borough Council RNFD/HAY WA11 90 A8
St Helens Metropolitan Borough Council STHEL WA9 9 K3
St Helens Metropolitan Borough Council STHEL WA9 9 M4
St Helens Museum & Art Gallery ECCL WA10 9 G4
St Helens Retail Park STHEL WA9 9 K6
St Helens Rugby League Football Club ECCL WA10 101 L2
St Helens Theatre Royal ECCL WA10 9 H5
St Hilary Brow Group Practice WAL/EG CH44 111 H1
St Hildas C of E High School AIG/SPK L17 113 L8
St James C of E Infant School RNFD/HAY WA11 91 G7
St James C of E Junior School RNFD/HAY WA11 91 G7
St James C of E Primary School WARRS WA4 14 F8
St James C of E School BRSC L40 64 A1
St James C of E School CHLYE PR6 33 G6
St James C of E School WGNS/IIMK WN3 68 B8
St James RC Primary School BTL L20 6 F2
St James RC Primary School SKEL WN8 65 K1
St James RC Primary School WGNW/BIL/O WN5 77 M1
St Jeromes RC Primary School FMBY L37 58 E2
St Joan of Arc RC Primary School BTL L20 6 C1
St John Almond High School ALL/GAR L19 130 F7
St John Bosco High School NG/CROX L11 98 D2
St John Bosco RC Primary School MGHL L31 72 D3
St John Fisher Junior & Infant School WDN WA8 17 K1
St John Fisher Primary School PR/KW L34 99 L1
St John Fisher RC High School WGNNW/ST WN6 68 B2
St John Rigby College WGNW/BIL/O WN5 67 H3
St Johns Catholic Infant School BEB CH63 128 B6
St Johns C of E County Primary School BRSC L40 39 H8
St Johns C of E Primary School CSBY/WL L22 82 F3
St Johns C of E Primary School WGNE/HIN WN2 81 K2
St Johns C of E School WGNW/BIL/O WN5 67 K7
St Johns Junior School ANF/KKDL L4 97 G5
St John Southworth RC Primary School AIMK WN4 91 M1
St Johns RC Primary School SKEL WN8 65 L4
St Johns School CHLY/EC PR7 42 F7
St Johns Shopping Precinct & Market CLVPS L1 13 H7
St Johns Surgery HUY L36 116 B4
St John Stone RC Primary School STHP PR8 47 M3
St John Vianney RC Primary School STHEL WA9 102 A7
St Josephs Catholic Primary School WARRW/BUR WA5 120 A8
St Josephs Junior & Infant School KKBY L32 86 A4
St Josephs Primary School HUY L36 116 B2
St Josephs RC College SKEL WN8 66 D3
St Josephs RC Primary School CHLYE PR6 44 D6
St Josephs RC Primary School CL/PREN CH43 127 K3
St Josephs RC Primary School GR/UP/WCH CH49 110 C8
St Josephs RC Primary School WAL/EG CH44 111 M3
St Josephs RC School CHLYE PR6 32 F3
St Josephs RC School WGNNW/ST WN6 55 J2
St Judes RC Junior & Infant School WGNS/IIMK WN3 68 B8
St Julie RC Primary School ECCL WA10 101 J1
St Julies High School WLTN L25 131 K4
St Laurence Medical Centre KKBY L32 86 B4
St Laurences Primary School BIRK CH41 11 G4
St Laurences Primary School KKBY L32 86 B4
St Lawrence C of E Primary School ANF/KKDL L4 7 L9
St Leos Primary School RAIN/WH L35 117 G3
St Lewis's Catholic Primary School GOL/RIS/CU WA3 106 D4
St Lukes C E Primary School FMBY L37 58 F4
St Lukes C of E School GOL/RIS/CU WA3 93 G6
St Lukes Halsall C of E Primary School CSBY/BLUN L23 70 F8
St Lukes Primary School RAIN/WH L35 117 H1
St Lukes RC Primary School FROD/HEL WA6 160 E5
St Lukes RC Primary School SKEL WN8 66 A7
St Malachys RC Primary School TOX L8 113 G8
St Margaret Marys Junior & Infant School DV/KA/FCH L14 115 H2
St Margarets Ce Junior School WARRN/WOL WA2 121 L4
St Margarets C of E Controlled Infant School WARRN/WOL WA2 121 L3
St Margarets C of E High School AIG/SPK L17 130 A4
St Margarets C of E Jmi School TOX L8 113 H6
St Margarets C of E Primary School NPK/KEN L6 97 L8
St Maries RC Primary School WGNNW/ST WN6 56 A3
St Maries RC School NWD/KWIPK L33 86 C2
St Marks C of E Junior School WGNW/BIL/O WN5 68 B6
St Marks R C Primary School HLWD L26 132 C5
St Marks RC Primary School SKEL WN8 66 A5
St Marks School BRSC L40 36 F5
St Martins RC Primary School RUNC WA7 151 G6
St Mary & St. John RC Primary School WGN WN1 5 G2
St Marys C of E Primary School CHLY/EC PR7 30 E7
St Marys C of E Primary School PS/BROM CH62 144 C8
St Marys C of E School BTL L20 6 F5
St Marys College CSBY/BLUN L23 83 G1
St Marys College WAL/NB CH45 95 G7
St Marys Primary School CSBY/BLUN L23 71 G5
St Marys RC High School AIG/SPK L17 113 M8
St Marys RC High School Bellerive TOX L8 113 K8
St Marys RC Infant School NEWLW WA12 104 D1
St Marys RC Junior School NEWLW WA12 104 D2
St Marys RC Primary School CHLY/EC PR7 32 C6
St Marys RC Primary School WGNW/BIL/O WN5 89 M1
St Marys & St. Thomas C of E Primary School ECCL WA10 8 E4
St Marys School CHLY/EC PR7 31 L2
St Marys West Derby C of E Primary School WD/CROXPK L12 98 D6
St Matthews C of E Primary School RAIN/WH L35 101 L6
St Matthews Primary School ANF/KKDL L4 98 A5
St Matthews RC Primary School SKEL WN8 65 M6
St Michael In the Hamlet Infant School AIG/SPK L17 129 K2
St Michaels & All Angels RC Infant School GR/UP/WCH CH49 126 E3
St Michaels C of E High School CHLY/EC PR7 32 E3
St Michaels C of E Primary School SKEL WN8 53 M8
St Michaels Primary School NPK/KEN L6 113 K1
St Monicas Catholic Primary School WARRS WA4 137 M6
St Monicas RC Primary School BTL L20 7 L2
St Nathaniels Primary & Infant School WGNE/HIN WN2 80 D2
St Nicholas C of E Primary School CSBY/BLUN L23 82 D2
St Nicholas RC Primary School VAUX/LVPD L3 13 L8
St Oswalds Catholic Primary School WARR WA1 122 B5
St Oswalds C of E Primary School NTHTN L30 84 B2
St Oswalds Junior School CLB/OSW/ST L13 114 C3
St Oswalds Primary School AIMK WN4 91 J2
St Oswalds RC Primary School CHLY/EC PR7 42 E5
St Paschal Baylon Primary School CHLDW L16 115 H5
St Patricks Junior School WGN WN1 5 H4
St Patricks Primary School CHTN/BK PR9 25 J3
St Patricks Primary School TOX L8 113 H7
St Patricks Primary School WGN WN1 5 H5
St Paul of the Cross Catholic Primary School WARRW/BUR WA5 104 A7
St Pauls C of E Junior & Infant School WGNS/IIMK WN3 79 H2
St Pauls C of E School CHLYE PR6 44 C5
St Pauls Junior School WD/CROXPK L12 98 E7
St Paul's RC Primary School CL/PREN CH43 110 D6
St Pauls & St. Timothys Infant School WD/CROXPK L12 98 E6
St Peter & St. Paul High School WDN WA8 134 B3
St Peter & St. Paul RC Primary School RNFD/HAY WA11 89 K6
St Peter & St. Paul RC School WAL/NB CH45 95 K5
St Peter & St. Pauls Primary School NWD/KWIPK L33 74 B8
St Peters Catholic Primary School WARR WA1 122 E6
St Peters C of E Junior School CHLYE PR6 33 G3
St Peters C of E Junior School LEIGH WN7 81 K8
St Peters C of E Primary School FMBY L37 47 J8
St Peters C of E Primary School HES CH60 141 H6
St Peters C of E Primary School NEWLW WA12 104 F1
St Peters C of E School WGNE/HIN WN2 69 L8
St Peters Infants Mixed School LEIGH WN7 81 L8
St Peters Primary School AIMK WN4 79 H7
St Peters RC High School WGNW/BIL/O WN5 67 H6
St Peters RC Primary School CL/PREN CH43 126 E1
St Philips Church & Community Primary School WARRW/BUR WA5 120 D4
St Philips (Controlled) C of E Primary School LITH L21 83 L5
St Phillips C of E Primary School STHP PR8 3 K6
St Raymonds RC Primary School NTHTN L30 83 M1
St Richards RC Primary School SKEL WN8 64 F4
St Robert Bellarmine RC Primary School BTL L20 83 M6
St Saviours RC Aided School GTS/LS CH66 163 G2
St Sebastians JMI School EHL/KEN L7 113 M3
St Stephen's Primary School WARRN/WOL WA2 121 K2
St Stephens Primary School WGN WN1 69 G3
St Stephens School CHTN/BK PR9 23 H7
St Teresa RC Primary School ECCL WA10 8 B4
St Teresas Infant School NG/CROX L11 98 B3
St Teresas Junior School NG/CROX L11 98 B3
St Theresas RC Primary School STHEL WA9 118 E2
St Theresa's School SKEL WN8 66 D4
St Thomas Becket RC High School HUY L36 116 C2
St Thomas Ce Primary School WARRS WA4 137 M4
St Thomas C of E Junior & Infant School GOL/RIS/CU WA3 92 C4
St Thomas C of E Primary School MGHL L31 72 F1
St Thomas C of E School AIMK WN4 91 L2
St Thomas More RC High School WGNW/BIL/O WN5 68 B6
St Thomas of Canterbury RC School CSBY/WL L22 83 G5
St Thomas the Martyr C of E Primary School SKEL WN8 66 D6
St Vincents Catholic Primary School WARRW/BUR WA5 136 A2
St Vincents Primary School CLVPS L1 112 F5
St Weburgh C of E Primary School WARRS WA4 137 K3
St Werburghs RC Primary School BIRK CH41 11 G8
St Wilfreds C of E Primary School WARRS WA4 138 D4

St Wilfrids C of E Primary School *WGNNW/ST* WN6 56 B4
St Wilfrids High School *LITH* L21 83 L6
St William of York RC Primary School *CSBY/BLUN* L23 71 K8
St Williams RC School *WGNE/HIN* WN2 5 M6
St Winefrides R C Aided Primary School *NSTN* CH64 153 H6
St Winefrides RC Infant School *BTL* L20 7 G6
St Winefrides RC Junior School *BTL* L20 6 F5
Salisbury Road Doctors Surgery *ALL/GAR* L19 130 C7
Sandbrook Primary School *MOR/LEA* CH46 110 B5
Sandfield Medical Centre *ECCL* WA10 8 E6
Sandfield Park School *WD/CROXPK* L12 98 D8
Sandhills Business Park *EV* L5 96 E7
Sandon Industrial Estate *VAUX/LVPD* L3 96 D7
Sandringham Medical Centre *TOX* L8 129 K1
Sandy Lane Health Centre *SKEL* WN8 64 F4
Sankey Bridge Industrial Estate *WARRW/BUR* WA5 136 E1
Sankey Medical Centre *WARRW/BUR* WA5 120 A6
Sankey Valley Industrial Estate *NEWLW* WA12 104 D3
Savio RC High School *NTHTN* L30 84 A4
Scarisbrick CP School *BRSC* L40 50 B2
School Clinic *SKEL* WN8 65 M7
School of Good Shepherd *ANF/KKDL* L4 97 H4
Scot Lane Junior & Infant School *WGNW/BIL/O* WN5 68 B6
Seabank Medical Centre *WAL/NB* CH45 95 K6
Seaforth Health Clinic *LITH* L21 83 J6
Sefton Cricket Club *AIG/SPK* L17 129 M1
Sefton Metropolitan Borough Council *BTL* L20 7 H5
Sefton Metropolitan Borough Council *BTL* L20 7 H3
Sefton Metropolitan Borough Council *BTL* L20 7 J4
Sefton Metropolitan Borough Council *CSBY/WL* L22 83 G5
Sefton Metropolitan Borough Council *MGHL* L31 72 E4
Sefton Metropolitan Borough Council *NTHTN* L30 83 L2
Sefton Metropolitan Borough Council *NTHTN* L30 84 B1
Sefton Park Medical Centre *WAV* L15 113 M7
Sefton Road Health Clinic *LITH* L21 83 K5
Sewage Works *HTWN* L38 60 F5
Sherdley CP School *STHEL* WA9 102 E7
Shevington County High School *WGNNW/ST* WN6 55 K6
Shevington CP School *WGNNW/ST* WN6 55 H7
Shevington Vale CP School *WGNNW/ST* WN6 55 G5
Shizhen Chinese Medical Centre *WAL/EG* CH44 111 K2
The Shopping Centre *STHEL* WA9 118 D1
Shorefields Community Comprehensive School *AIG/SPK* L17 129 K1
Shorefiels Comm Comp School *TOX* L8 129 J2
Shoreshird School *STHP* PR8 47 K1
Shorrocks Hill Country Club *FMBY* L37 58 D4
Showcase Cinemas *NG/CROX* L11 98 C1
Silverdale Medical Centre *HES* CH60 141 H5
Simms Cross County Primary School *WDN* WA8 16 C4
Simonswood County Primary School *NWD/KWIPK* L33 86 C3
Sir Alfred Jones Memorial Hospital *ALL/GAR* L19 130 E7
Sir Thomas Boteler High School *WARRS* WA4 138 A2
Skelmersdale College *SKEL* WN8 65 J4
Skelmersdale Crow Orchard County Primary School *SKEL* WN8 65 H3
Skelmersdale Park CP School *SKEL* WN8 65 G4
Skelmersdale Sports Centre *SKEL* WN8 65 L6
Skelmersdale United Football Club *SKEL* WN8 64 F5
Slaidburn Industrial Estate *CHTN/BK* PR9 25 J1
Small Business Centre *VAUX/LVPD* L3 112 F8
Smm Business Park *WAL/EG* CH44 111 L4
Snaefell Avenue Doctors Surgery *CLB/OSW/ST* L13 98 A8
Somerville Medical Practice *WAL/EG* CH44 111 L2
Somerville Primary School *WAL/EG* CH44 111 L2
Southbank Tennis Club *STHP* PR8 36 A1
Southdene Medical Centre *KKBY* L32 86 C5
Southlands High School *CHLY/EC* PR7 32 C8
Southmead Junior & Infant School *RAIN/WH* L35 117 G3
Southport & Ainsdale Golf Club *STHP* PR8 34 F7
Southport & Birkdale Cricket Club *STHP* PR8 35 G2
Southport Business Centre *CHTN/BK* PR9 3 H3
Southport Business Park *STHP* PR8 35 J2
Southport College *CHTN/BK* PR9 3 J3
Southport Football Club *STHP* PR8 25 G8
Southport & Formby District General Hospital *STHP* PR8 3 M8
Southport & Formby Hospital *CHTN/BK* PR9 3 H3
Southport General Infirmary *STHP* PR8 3 M7
Southport Girls Football Club *STHP* PR8 25 H7
Southport New Synagogue *STHP* PR8 3 G5
Southport Pier *STHP* PR8 24 B4
Southport Rugby Club *STHP* PR8 35 G4
Southport Sailing Club *STHP* PR8 24 C4
Southport Swimming Baths *STHP* PR8 2 D4
Southport Zoo & Conservation Trust *STHP* PR8 2 D3
South Sefton Business Centre *BTL* L20 6 F6
South Wirral High School *PS/BROM* CH62 154 F1
Sovereign Business Park *WGN* WN1 5 G5
Speke Community Comprehensive School *SPK/HALE* L24 146 F3
Speke Comprehensive School *SPK/HALE* L24 146 F2
Speke Family Health Clinic *SPK/HALE* L24 147 G2
Sphynx Tennis Club *STHP* PR8 36 A1
Springbank Industrial Estate *WGNE/HIN* WN2 80 D2
Springfield School *KKBY* L32 86 A5
Spring View Cricket Club *WGNE/HIN* WN2 5 H6
Springwood CP School *ALL/GAR* L19 131 G5
Standish Clinic *WGNNW/ST* WN6 56 A4
Standish Cricket Club *WGNNW/ST* WN6 56 A5
Standish High School *WGNNW/ST* WN6 55 L3
Standish Lower Ground C of E School *WGNNW/ST* WN6 67 M2
Standish Medical Practice *WGNNW/ST* WN6 56 A4
Stanlaw Abbey CP School *EP* CH65 163 M3
Stanley High School *CHTN/BK* PR9 25 H1
Stanley Medical Centre *EV* L5 96 F7
Stanley School *PEN/TH* CH61 126 C7
Stanney Grange CP School *EP* CH65 163 L3
Stanney High School *EP* CH65 163 L3
Stanney Mill Industrial Estate *CHNE* CH2 164 B4
Stanney Mill Industrial Estate *EP* CH65 21 K9
Stanton Road Primary School *BEB* CH63 143 H2
Statham Community Primary School *LYMM* WA13 139 L1
Stockbridge Primary School *HUY* L36 99 L7
Stockbridge Village Health Centre *STBRV* L28 99 J5
Stockton Heath Community Primary School *WARRS* WA4 137 L4
Stockton Heath Medical Centre *WARRS* WA4 137 L4
Stockton Wood Jmi School *SPK/HALE* L24 146 E2
Stopgate Medical Centre *WLT/FAZ* L9 97 M2
Storrsdale Medical Centre *CALD/MH* L18 130 D2
The Strand Medical Centre *BTL* L20 7 G2
Streatham House School *CSBY/BLUN* L23 82 F1
Studio Gallery *BEB* CH63 142 C3
Stutelea Hotel & Leisure Club *CHTN/BK* PR9 24 E4
Sudley Art Gallery *AIG/SPK* L17 130 B3
Sudley Infant School *AIG/SPK* L17 130 A3
Sudley Junior School *AIG/SPK* L17 130 A4
Sullivan Way Surgery *WGN* WN1 5 G2
Summerhill Primary School *MGHL* L31 73 H5
Sunnymede School *STHP* PR8 2 C6
Superbowl 2000 & Laserquest *WGNS/IIMK* WN3 4 D5
Sutton C of E Junior & I nfant School *STHEL* WA9 103 G5
Sutton C of E Primary School *STHEL* WA9 103 G5
Sutton Community High School *STHEL* WA9 102 D7
Sutton Community High School Sports Centre *STHEL* WA9 102 D7
Sutton County High School *GTS/LS* CH66 156 A8
Sutton Cricket Club *STHEL* WA9 102 E7
Sutton Green CP School *GTS/LS* CH66 155 K8
Sutton Hall Golf Club *RUNC* WA7 161 J2
Sutton Manor Community Primary School *STHEL* WA9 118 C3
Sutton Way County Junior School *GTS/LS* CH66 163 G1
Swan Meadow Industrial Estate *WGNS/IIMK* WN3 4 C7
Sycamore Lane Community Primary School *WARRW/BUR* WA5 120 D8
Sylvester Primary School *HUY* L36 116 B4
Tarbock Road Doctors Surgery *HUY* L36 116 A4
Temple of Praise *EV* L5 97 J7
Thatto Heath CP School *STHEL* WA9 102 A5
Theatre Building Surgery *ECCL* WA10 9 H5
Thelwall Community Infant School *WARRS* WA4 138 E2
Thelwall Community Junior School *WARRS* WA4 138 F2
Thelwall New Road Surgery *WARRS* WA4 138 D2
Theta Gallery *TOX* L8 112 F6
Thingwall Primary School *PEN/TH* CH61 126 C7
Thingwall Recreation Centre *PEN/TH* CH61 126 D7
Thomas Gray Infant School *BTL* L20 6 E2
Thomas Gray Junior School *BTL* L20 6 F1
Thornton Hough Primary School *BEB* CH63 142 D6
Thornton Primary School *CSBY/BLUN* L23 71 K7
Titanic Memorial *VAUX/LVPD* L3 12 C7
Tower Dene Preparatory School *CHTN/BK* PR9 25 H3
Tower Hill Health Centre *NWD/KWIPK* L33 74 B8
Townfield Primary School *CL/PREN* CH43 127 G2
Town Green CP School *ORM* L39 62 E5
Town House Practice *WDN* WA8 16 F2
Town Lane Infant School *BEB* CH63 128 A7
Toxteth Sports Centre *TOX* L8 113 H7
Tranmere Rovers Football Club *RF/TRAN* CH42 127 L3
Transport Museum *BIRK* CH41 11 L3
Trent Avenue Doctors Surgery *MGHL* L31 73 J3
Trentham Road Medical Centre *KKBY* L32 85 L3
Trident Industrial Estate *GOL/RIS/CU* WA3 107 G7
Trinity CP School *SKEL* WN8 65 G4
Twelve Apostles Mixed & Infants School *LEIGH* WN7 81 M5
Twig Lane Clinic *HUY* L36 115 L1
Twin Lakes Industrial Park *LEY/BBR* PR5 29 J2
Twiss Green Community Primary School *GOL/RIS/CU* WA3 107 G1
Unity Theatre *CLVPS* L1 13 K9
University of Liverpool *AIG/SPK* L17 130 A1
University of Liverpool *AIG/SPK* L17 130 B3
University of Liverpool *EHL/KEN* L7 13 M8
University of Liverpool *NSTN* CH64 153 M6
University of Liverpool *VAUX/LVPD* L3 13 L6
University of Liverpool *VAUX/LVPD* L3 13 M6
University Propagation Centre *AIG/SPK* L17 130 B2
The Unsworth Group Practice *HOR/BR* BL6 57 L2
Upholland High School *WGNW/BIL/O* WN5 77 L1
Upper Parliament Medical Centre *EHL/KEN* L7 113 K5
Upton County Infants School *WDN* WA8 133 K2
Upton Cricket Club *GR/UP/WCH* CH49 110 A8
Upton Group Practice *GR/UP/WCH* CH49 110 D8
Upton Hall Convent School *GR/UP/WCH* CH49 110 B8
Upton Medical Centre *WDN* WA8 133 K2
Ursuline RC Primary School *CSBY/BLUN* L23 82 D2
Uveco Business Centre *BIRK* CH41 111 K4
Valewood Primary School *CSBY/BLUN* L23 70 F8
Valley Medical Centre *ANF/KKDL* L4 97 G6
Valley Medical Centre *CHLDW* L16 115 G6
VAT House & HM Customs & Excise *VAUX/LVPD* L3 112 E6
Vauxhall Business Centre *VAUX/LVPD* L3 12 E3
Vauxhall Health Centre *EV* L5 13 G1
Vernon Sangster Sports Centre *ANF/KKDL* L4 97 J6
Victoria Road CP School *RUNC* WA7 19 G5
Victoria Trading Estate *RAIN/WH* L35 117 L2
The Village Gallery *HES* CH60 141 H6
Village Medical Centre *WLTN* L25 131 J3
The Village Surgery *FMBY* L37 59 G3
Villa Medical Centre *CL/PREN* CH43 127 J5
Virgin Cinemas *CLB/OSW/ST* L13 114 B4
Virgin Cinemas *WGNW/BIL/O* WN5 68 B5
Vittoria Medical Centre *BIRK* CH41 11 G3
Vyner Primary School *CL/PREN* CH43 110 F4
Waddicar Lane Surgery *MGHL* L31 85 J1
Wade Deacon High School *WDN* WA8 134 B3
Walker Art Gallery *VAUX/LVPD* L3 13 H5
Wallasey Rugby Club *WAL/NB* CH45 94 F8
Wallasey School *MOR/LEA* CH46 110 C2
Walray Pictures Gallery *NSTN* CH64 152 E6
Walton Breck Surgery *EV* L5 97 J7
Walton Hall *WARRS* WA4 137 J7
Walton Hall Medical Centre *ANF/KKDL* L4 97 J4
Walton Hospital *WLT/FAZ* L9 97 H2
Walton Medical Centre *ANF/KKDL* L4 97 H3
Walton St Mary C of E Primary School *ANF/KKDL* L4 97 H3
Walton Sports Centre *WLT/FAZ* L9 97 K3
Walton Village Medical Centre *ANF/KKDL* L4 97 J4
Wargrave C of E Primary School *NEWLW* WA12 104 E4
Wargrave House School *NEWLW* WA12 104 E4
Warren Road Doctors Surgery *CSBY/BLUN* L23 82 D2
Warrington Borough Council *GOL/RIS/CU* WA3 107 H2
Warrington Borough Council *WARR* WA1 14 C5
Warrington Borough Council *WARR* WA1 15 J4
Warrington Borough Council *WARR* WA1 122 D6
Warrington Borough Council *WARR* WA1 123 H6
Warrington Borough Council *WARRN/WOL* WA2 121 K3
Warrington Borough Council *WARRN/WOL* WA2 122 B3
Warrington Borough Council *WARRS* WA4 138 A6
Warrington Borough Council *WARRS* WA4 138 B1
Warrington Borough Council *WARRW/BUR* WA5 121 H5
Warrington Borough Council *WARRW/BUR* WA5 121 H3
Warrington Business Park *WARRN/WOL* WA2 121 L4
Warrington Central Trading Estate *WARRN/WOL* WA2 14 C3
Warrington Community Health Care NHS Trust *WARRN/WOL* WA2 105 H7
Warrington New Town Cricket Club *WARRW/BUR* WA5 120 F8
Warrington Rugby League Football Club *WARRS* WA4 15 G9
Warrington Sports Club *WARRS* WA4 137 J6
Warrington Town A F C *WARRS* WA4 138 A3
Watergate School *WLTN* L25 131 K3
Waterloo Football Club *CSBY/BLUN* L23 70 D8
Wavertree Cricket Club *WAV* L15 114 B5
Wavertree Health Clinic *WAV* L15 114 C7
Wavertree Retail Park *EHL/KEN* L7 113 L4
Wavertree Town Hall *WAV* L15 114 C6
Weatherhead High School *WAL/NB* CH45 95 J6
Weatherstone Business Centre *NSTN* CH64 153 L5
Weaver Industrial Estate *ALL/GAR* L19 145 L2
Weaver Park Industrial Estate *FROD/HEL* WA6 160 F3
Wellesbourne County Primary School *NG/CROX* L11 98 B3
West Bank County Primary School *WDN* WA8 149 H1
West Bank Medical Centre *WDN* WA8 16 C9
West Bank Medical Centre *WDN* WA8 134 C8
Westbourne Preparatory School *WAL/NB* CH45 95 L7
Westbrook Medical Centre *WARRW/BUR* WA5 120 D4
West Cheshire College *EP* CH65 20 A5
West Cheshire College *EP* CH65 156 C8
West Derby Comprehensive School *CLB/OSW/ST* L13 98 B7
West End County Primary School *ORM* L39 51 G6
West Kirby Foot Health Clinic *WKBY* CH48 124 D3
West Kirby Grammar School for Girls *WKBY* CH48 124 B2
West Kirby Health Centre *WKBY* CH48 124 C2
West Kirby Primary School *WKBY* CH48 124 C1
West Kirby Residential School *WKBY* CH48 124 C2
West Lancashire District Council *SKEL* WN8 65 M5
West Lancs District Council *SKEL* WN8 64 F4
West Lancs Yacht Club *STHP* PR8 24 C4
Westleigh Cricket Club *LEIGH* WN7 81 M8
Westleigh Methodist School *LEIGH* WN7 81 M5
Westminster Industrial Park *EP* CH65 156 B7
Westminster Medical Centre *ANF/KKDL* L4 7 L9
Westminster Road Swimming Pool *ANF/KKDL* L4 97 G6
Westminster Surgery *EP* CH65 20 C1
Weston Point County Primary School *RUNC* WA7 18 D9
Weston Primary School *RUNC* WA7 149 J7
West Park Rugby Football Club *ECCL* WA10 101 K4
Westside Industrial Estate *STHEL* WA9 9 L8
WestVale Health Centre *KKBY* L32 85 L3
WestVale Primary School *KKBY* L32 85 K3
West Wirral Group Practice *HES* CH60 141 H5
West Wirral Group Practice *PEN/TH* CH61 125 M7
West Wirral Group Practice *PEN/TH* CH61 126 C7
Wheathill Industrial Estate *NTHLY* L27 115 M7
Wheathill Special School *HUY* L36 115 M6
Wheatlea Industrial Estate *WGNS/IIMK* WN3 79 H3
Whelley Hospital *WGN* WN1 69 G3
Whetstone Lane Health Centre *BIRK* CH41 11 G7
Whiston Health Centre *RAIN/WH* L35 116 F2
Whitby County High School *GTS/LS* CH66 163 J4

Whitby Heath County
Primary School
EP CH65 .... **20** A9

Whitechapel Gallery
CLVPS L1 .... **13** G7

Whitefield JMI School
NPK/KEN L6 .... **113** J1

Widnes Community
Midwifery & Ante Natal
WDN WA8 .... **134** B3

Widnes Cricket Club
WDN WA8 .... **134** D1

Widnes Public Baths
WDN WA8 .... **16** D4

Widnes Rugby Football Club
WDN WA8 .... **16** B4

Widnes Sixth Form College
WDN WA8 .... **118** A8

Wigan Area Health Authority
WGNE/HIN WN2 .... **69** M7

Wigan & Bolton
Health Authority
WGN WN1 .... **4** F3

Wigan & Leigh College
LEIGH WN7 .... **93** M2

Wigan & Leigh College
WGN WN1 .... **4** E3

Wigan & Leigh Technical College
WGN WN1 .... **4** D3

Wigan Little Theatre
WGN WN1 .... **5** G3

Wigan Magistrates Court
WGN WN1 .... **5** C5

Wigan Metro Borough Coun
WGN WN1 .... **4** F4

Wigan Metropolitan
Borough Council
GOL/RIS/CU WA3 .... **92** D5

Wigan Metropolitan
Borough Council
GOL/RIS/CU WA3 .... **93** J5

Wigan Metropolitan
Borough Council
LEIGH WN7 .... **81** M5

Wigan Metropolitan
Borough Council
WGN WN1 .... **4** E2

Wigan Metropolitan
Borough Council
WGNE/HIN WN2 .... **57** H8

Wigan Metropolitan
Borough Council
WGNE/HIN WN2 .... **57** L8

Wigan Metropolitan
Borough Council
WGNE/HIN WN2 .... **69** L8

Wigan Metropolitan
Borough Council
WGNE/HIN WN2 .... **80** C3

Wigan Metropolitan
Borough Council
WGNS/IIMK WN3 .... **4** D6

Wigan Metropolitan
Borough Council
WGNS/IIMK WN3 .... **5** G6

Wigan Metropolitan
Borough Council
WGNW/BIL/O WN5 .... **67** H7

Wigan Metropolitan
Borough Council
WGNW/BIL/O WN5 .... **68** A6

Wigan Rugby Union
Football Club
WGN WN1 .... **56** F8

Willaston C of E
Primary School
NSTN CH64 .... **154** B5

William Beaumont
Community High School
WARRN/WOL WA2 .... **121** K4

Williamson Art Gallery &
Museum
CL/PREN CH43 .... **10** C8

William Stockton CP School
EP CH65 .... **20** A4

Willow Tree Primary School
STHEL WA9 .... **118** F1

Wilson Business Centre
HUY L36 .... **116** B4

Windmill Hill County
Primary School
RUNC WA7 .... **150** E3

Wingate Medical Centre
NWD/KWIPK L33 .... **86** C2

Winstanley College
WGNW/BIL/O WN5 .... **78** A2

Winstanley CP School
WGNS/IIMK WN3 .... **78** E3

Winstanley Industrial Estate
WARRN/WOL WA2 .... **121** K4

Winstanley Medical Centre
WGNS/IIMK WN3 .... **78** F2

Winwick C of E Primary School
WARRN/WOL WA2 .... **105** K7

Winwick Parish Leisure Centre
WARRN/WOL WA2 .... **105** K7

Wirral Area Health Authority
WAL/EG CH44 .... **111** K1

Wirral Borough Council
CL/PREN CH43 .... **111** H5

Wirral Borough
Magistrates Court
BIRK CH41 .... **11** M5

Wirral Business Centre
WAL/EG CH44 .... **111** L4

Wirral Community
Healthcare N H S Trust
BEB CH63 .... **128** C8

Wirral Community
Healthcare Nhs Trust
MOR/LEA CH46 .... **110** C2

Wirral Community
Healthcare N H S Trust
RF/TRAN CH42 .... **127** M2

Wirral Community
Healthcare N H S Trust
WAL/EG CH44 .... **111** K2

Wirral Community
Healthcare N H S Trust
WAL/EG CH44 .... **111** L1

Wirral County Grammar
School for Girls
BEB CH63 .... **143** G1

Wirral Grammar School
for Boys
BEB CH63 .... **143** G1

Wirral Health Authority
BIRK CH41 .... **11** L3

Wirral Health Authority
RF/TRAN CH42 .... **128** A3

Wirral Hospital
BEB CH63 .... **143** G4

Wirral Hospital NHS Trust
GR/UP/WCH CH49 .... **126** B3

Wirral Metropolitan Borough Council
BIRK CH41 .... **11** M4

Wirral Metropolitan Borough Council
BIRK CH41 .... **11** G8

Wirral Metropolitan Borough Council
WAL/EG CH44 .... **111** L3

Wirral Metropolitan College
BIRK CH41 .... **11** J5

Wirral Metropolitan College
PS/BROM CH62 .... **144** C7

Wirral Metropolitan College
RF/TRAN CH42 .... **127** L1

Wirral Museum
BIRK CH41 .... **11** L4

Wirral Stroke & Head Injury Clinic
CL/PREN CH43 .... **127** H4

Wirral Tennis & Sports Centre
BIRK CH41 .... **110** F3

Wirral & West Cheshire Community
NHS Trust
CL/PREN CH43 .... **10** B9

Woodchurch C of E Primary School
GR/UP/WCH CH49 .... **126** C3

Woodchurch High School
GR/UP/WCH CH49 .... **126** F2

Woodchurch Leisure Centre
GR/UP/WCH CH49 .... **126** E2

Woodchurch Road Primary School
RF/TRAN CH42 .... **127** L1

Woodend Industrial Estate
SPK/HALE L24 .... **131** M8

Woodfall County Junior & Infant
School
NSTN CH64 .... **153** J7

Woodfield Primary School
WGN WN1 .... **68** E1

Wood Fold Primary School
WGNNW/ST WN6 .... **55** M5

Woodlands County Infant School
GTS/LS CH66 .... **163** H3

Woodlands County Junior School
GTS/LS CH66 .... **163** H4

Woodlands Industrial Estate
NEWLW WA12 .... **91** L7

Woodlands Primary School
BIRK CH41 .... **11** H8

Woodlands Primary School
FMBY L37 .... **58** F2

Woodside County Primary School
RUNC WA7 .... **150** A6

Woodslee Primary School
PS/BROM CH62 .... **143** M3

Woodvale CP School
STHP PR8 .... **47** M2

Woolston C of E Primary School
WARR WA1 .... **122** E5

Woolston Community High School
WARR WA1 .... **122** D5

Woolston Community Primary School
WARR WA1 .... **122** E6

Woolston Surgery
WARR WA1 .... **122** F6

Woolton County Infant School
WLTN L25 .... **131** K2

Woolton House Medical Centre
WLTN L25 .... **131** J3

Woolton Surgery
WLTN L25 .... **131** J3

Woolton Swimming Pool
WLTN L25 .... **131** J3

Worsley Mesnes County Primary
School
WGNS/IIMK WN3 .... **79** J1

Wrightington Hospital NHS Trust
WGNNW/ST WN6 .... **55** G4

YMCA
CLVPS L1 .... **13** K8

York Road Group Practice
EP CH65 .... **20** C5

Page 13
G9
1 Cleveland Buildings
2 Cleveland Sq
3 Duke Street La
4 Forrest St
5 Price St
M9
1 Mulberry Pl

Page 32
C8
1 Arnold Pl
2 Brancker St
3 Green St
4 Jackson Rd
5 Lawnwood Av
6 Moor Rd
7 Swords Cross Cl
D6
2 Clifton Gv
3 Queensgate
4 Strathmore Gv
5 Trinity Rd
6 Windsor Ct
D8
1 Balcarres Rd
2 Bamber St
3 Claremont Rd
4 Grafton Ct
5 Kingswood
6 Scawfell Rd
7 Sycamore Ct
8 Tarn Hows Cl
9 Taylor St
E4
1 Bengal St
2 Commercial Rd
3 Congress St
4 Cross St
5 Nichol St
6 Trafalgar St
7 Waterloo St
8 Wellington St
9 Woodfield Rd
E5
1 Back Mt
2 Bank St
3 Dole La
4 Farrington St
5 Fazakerley St
6 Foundry St
7 Kellett St
8 Mealhouse La
9 Springfield Rd
10 Stanley Pl
11 West Bank
12 Woodville Rd
E6
1 Avenham Rd
2 Bannister St
3 Cambridge St
4 Cheapside
5 Church St
6 File St
7 George St
8 Halliwell Pl
9 Lennon St
10 Nelson Rd
11 Oxford St
12 Parson's Brow
13 Rawcliffe Rd
14 Roberts St
15 Westminster Rd
16 Whalley St
F3
1 Bannerman Ter
2 Clayburn Cl
3 Cornflower Cl
4 Cowslip Wy
5 Garfield Ter
6 Milton Ter
7 Morrison St
F5
1 Bowland Av
2 Brunswick St
3 Byron St
4 Cameron Cft
5 Friday St
6 Houghton St
7 Mackay Cft
8 Mackenzie Cl
9 Portland St
10 Sandham St
11 Sherwood Pl
F6
1 Albert St
2 Burlington St
3 Chapel St
4 Clarence St
5 Northumberland St
6 Percy St
7 Salisbury St
8 Sherbourne St
9 Sutcliffe St
10 York St
F7
1 Gin Bow

Page 33
G5
1 Brighton St
2 Chatham Pl
3 Colyton Cl
4 Colyton Rd East
5 Greenfield Rd
6 Heald St
7 Longton St
8 The Moorings
9 Plymouth Gv
10 Temperance St
11 Whimberry Cl
G6
1 Brownley St
2 Cavendish St
3 Clarendon St
4 Cuerden St
5 Lawson St
6 Owens St
7 Saint Annes Rd
8 Saint James's Pl
9 Scarlet St
10 Silverdale Rd
11 Southport Ter
12 Stephenson St
13 Stirling Cl
14 Windermere Rd

Page 65
G4
1 Elm Gv
2 Holly Cl
K1
1 Lyndale
2 Meadow Clough
3 Meadowcroft
4 Willow Wk
5 Woodley Park Rd
K2
1 Langtree

Page 67
K7
1 Chilham St
2 Cross St
3 Hartley St
4 Johnson St
5 Old Fold
6 Pigot St
7 Short St
8 Troutbeck Rl
9 White St
L1
1 St Christopher Ct
M1
1 Bankbrook
M7
1 Carlisle St
2 Curtis St
3 Cuthbert St
4 Langley St
5 Walter St
M8
1 Belle Vue St
2 Burnaston Gv
3 Fairfield Av
4 Kensington Rd
5 Layton Cl
6 Southern St
7 Tansley Sq
8 Warncliffe St

Page 68
A1
1 Normanton Cl
A2
1 Abbeyfields
2 Sandown Rd
A4
1 Commodore Pl
A5
1 Ferguson Rl
2 Partington St
A6
1 Primrose Gv
A7
1 Bank St
2 Beaufort St
3 Portland St
4 Ryde St
A8
1 Buckingham Cl
2 Calderbank St
3 Lychgate
4 Sandringham Cl
B3
1 Brownmere
2 The Coverts
3 Hollinbrook
4 Springbourne
B4
1 Hillreed
B6
1 Burland St
2 France St
3 Liptrot St
B7
1 Alexandra St
2 Atherton St
3 Bridgewater St
4 Cawdor St
5 Grosvenor St
6 Harrison St
7 Hildyard St
8 Mere St
9 Norfolk St
10 Reedsmere Cl
11 Stanley St
12 Sutherland St
13 Westminster St
14 Winstanley St
15 Woodyates St
16 Woolden St
B8
1 Belvedere Pl
2 Cheetham Gv
3 Pennell Dr
C1
1 Edensor Cl
C3
1 The Bowlings
2 Lynmouth Cl
C4
1 Brookvale
2 Foster St
3 Heardman Av
4 Hedgemead
5 Pagefield Cl
6 Waterloo St
7 Whiteside Av
C5
1 Westinghouse Cl
C6
1 Swift St
C8
1 Bronte Cl
2 Chesterton Cl
3 Cornwallis Rd
4 Longfellow Cl
5 Marlowe Cl
6 Murphy Cl
7 Thackeray Pl
8 Worsley Mesnes Dr
D1
1 Elderberry Cl
2 Holly Heath Dr
D2
1 Oak Hill Cl
2 Yewdale Crs
D5
1 Appleton St
2 Chequers St
3 Crook St
4 Fairhurst St
5 Fitzadam St
6 Fosters Buildings
7 Mona St
8 Myrtle St
9 Proe's Ct
10 Richmond St
11 Upper St Stephen St
D6
1 Addison St
2 Bridgewater St
3 Leeds St
4 Lyon St
5 Mill St
D7
1 Bewerley Cl
2 Carlton St
3 Roecliffe Cl
4 Westlock
5 Woodcourt
D8
1 Falconers Gn
E1
1 St Aubyn's Rd
E2
1 St Malo Rd
2 Seascale Crs
E3
1 Ashland Av
2 Chelmsford Ms
3 Everest Pl
4 Goldenways
5 Inglewhite Crs
6 St Michael's Ct
7 Silverdale
8 Warnford St
E4
1 Acton Ter
2 Back Mesnes St
3 Brick Kiln La
4 Little London
5 Sandycroft Av
6 Upper Dicconson St
E5
1 Barrack Sq
2 Barracks Yd
3 Bishopgate
4 Bretherton Rw
5 Church St
6 Clarence Yd
7 Crompton St
8 Manor St
9 Market Pl
10 Market St
11 Marsden St
12 Marsh La
13 Mesnes Rd
14 Mesnes Ter
15 Rowbottom Sq
16 Stairgate
17 Standishgate
18 Station Rd
19 Water St
20 Watkin St
21 Wiend
E6
1 Hartley Ter
2 Ironmonger La
3 Milk St
4 St Thomas St
5 Westbridge Ms
6 Wood St
E7
1 Walmesley Av
F3
1 Penson St
F4
1 Oxford Ct
F5
1 Alliance St
2 Baldwin St
3 Belvoir St
4 Bradshawgate
5 Bryham St
6 Gilroy St
7 Kingsoak Cl
8 Molyneux St
9 St Patrick St
F6
1 Boundary St
2 Brookhouse St
3 Brookhouse Ter
4 Ellen St
5 Fairclough St
6 Kingscroft Ct
7 Mill Meadow
8 Spring Gv
9 Vulcan Dr
10 Walmesley St
F7
1 Baverstock Cl
2 Bridge St
3 Chapel Cl
4 Frederick St
5 Hardacre St
6 Knowles St
7 Parliament St
8 Pitt St
9 Winchester Gv

Page 69
G4
1 Cumberland St
2 Palewood Cl
3 Sedwyn St
4 Thompson St
5 Westmoorland St
6 Windermere St
7 Wright St
G6
1 Ascroft St
2 Edwin St
3 Inglewood Av
4 Oak St
5 Roscoe St
G7
1 Bryn St
2 Chorley St
3 Haigh Vw
4 Kellaton Cl
5 Milford St
6 Parkwood Cl
7 Sharp St
8 Whitehall St
9 Wilding St
10 Windleshaw St
11 Winstanley Pl
H3
1 Amberley Cl
2 Burnham Gv
3 Cheltenham St
4 Grantham Gv
5 Horsham Gv
6 Vigo St
H7
1 Church St
2 Fernhurst Cl
3 Manor Pl
4 Ryeford Cl
5 Whistlecroft Ct
J5
1 Coopers Gln
2 Edinburgh Cl
3 Falkirk Dr
4 Gidlow St
5 Glenbranter Av
6 Glendevon Cl
7 Jeffrey St
8 Queensway
9 Reservoir St
10 Russell St
L7
1 Bretherton St
2 Croston St
3 Gregory St
L8
1 Macclesfield Cl
2 Princess St
3 Sidbrook St
4 Stafford St
5 Sutherland St
6 Waverley Rd
M3
1 Gerrard Cl
M7
1 Collier St
2 Haworth St
3 Holding St
4 Jenkinson St
5 King St
6 Langset Av
7 Nelson St
8 Oldbridge Dr
9 Pennington St
10 Presbyterian Fold
11 Queen St
12 Red Hill Wy
13 Turner St
14 Vine St
15 Worthington St
M8
1 Albert St
2 Argyle St
3 Back Market St
4 Beaufort St
5 Birch St
6 Brookland Av
7 Byron Av
8 Chapel St
9 Church St
10 Cranby St
11 Daisybank Cl
12 Didsbury Gv
13 Foley St
14 Foundry St
15 Grosvenor St
16 Hanmer St
17 Meadows Cl
18 The Mews
19 Mill St
20 Morris St
21 Peter St
22 Prescott St
23 Progress St
24 Prospect St
25 Pump St
26 Regent St
27 Rose St
28 Trafalgar Rd
29 Wharncliffe St

Page 72
D4
1 Apsley Brow
2 Cannock Gn
F1
1 Oakhill Cottage La

Page 74
A8
1 Ashley Cl
2 Ashwood Cl
3 Balmoral Cl
4 Fairlawne Cl
5 Fallowfield
6 Farnworth Gv
7 Heathfield Dr
8 Pinewood Gdns
9 St Andrew's Vw
10 St Patrick's Cl
11 Sandringham Cl
12 Windmill Cl

Page 79
J1
1 Algernon St
2 Fairbourne Av
3 Poolstock La
4 Shakespeare Gv
J2
1 Macdonald Av
2 Monroe Cl
3 Slaidburn Cl
J3
1 Colburn Cl
2 Raithby Dr
3 Rosthwaite Cl
J8
1 Bamburgh Pl
2 Dudley St
3 Elmsbury St
4 Grantwood
5 Hebdon Cl
6 Holmwood Cl
7 King's Rd
8 Millwood Cl
9 Prince St
10 Roman Rd
11 Roseberry Rd
12 Salisbury Rd
13 Silver Birch Gv

Page 80
B2
1 Crompton St
B3
1 Gilpin Pl
2 Rawthey Pl
3 Roch Pl
4 Sabden Brook Dr
5 Winster Dr
C3
1 Albion St
2 Aspinall St
3 Chapel St
4 Croal Av
5 Elm St
6 Medlock Wy
7 Mellor Brook Dr
8 Sherwood Crs
9 Stephen St
10 Vicarage Cl
11 Walthew La
D2
1 Barton St
2 Beckwith
3 Capps St
4 Eatock St
5 Lynn St
6 Moorfield St
7 Whistley St
D3
1 Brecon Cl
2 Cumbrian Cl
3 Eastgarth
4 Green St
5 Silver St
6 Syresham St
7 Taberner St
8 Woodcock Dr
D5
1 Atkinson St
2 Grasmere Ter
3 Kirkham St
4 Lawrence Ct
5 Mason St
6 Stephenson St
7 Thirlmere Av
F1
1 Aldred St
2 Armitstead St
3 Bisford Cl
4 Bolderwood Dr
5 Brookview
6 Cadman Gv
7 Cashmore Dr
8 Chalbury Cl
9 Crook St
10 Danebury Cl
11 Downton Av
12 Thorn St
13 Wenlock St
14 Woodgreen Cl

Page 81
G1
1 Ashcroft St
2 Chatteris Cl
3 Coniston Rd
4 Dickenson St
5 Field St
6 Hazelmere Gdns
7 Knaresborough Rd
8 Narborough Cl
9 Soham Cl
K2
1 Baldwin St
2 Bexley St
3 East St
4 Harrison St
5 Palin St
6 Windsor Gv
7 Wood St
L5
1 Ashby Gv
2 Shadwell Gv
M7
1 Cherry Tree Gv
2 Grosvenor Rd
3 Hamilton St
4 Kenneth Gv
5 Lindow St
6 Okell Gv
7 Slater St North
8 Stanhope St
M8
1 Austin St
2 Banks Ct
3 Braeburn Ct
4 Co-operative St
5 Corn St
6 Cotton St
7 Cowburn St
8 Kearsley St
9 Kendal Gv
10 Knowsley St
11 Mere Av
12 Moresby Cl
13 Owen St
14 Primrose St
15 Urmston St

Page 82
D3
1 Balliol Gv
2 Eastbourne Rd
3 Trinity Gv
4 Westward Vw
F1
2 First Av
3 Harrington Rd
4 Second Av
5 Shaftesbury Rd
6 Third Av

Page 83
G4
1 Bluebell Cl
2 Glendower Rd
3 Hougoumont Gv
4 Neville Rd
G5
1 Church Rd
2 Olive Rd
3 Sandringham Av
4 South Vw
5 Waterloo Cl
6 Water St
H6
1 Bedford Pl
2 Belgrave Rd
3 Claremont Cl
4 Corinthian St
5 Doric St
6 Gladstone Av
7 Ionic St
8 Kings Ct
9 Riversdale Rd
10 Sandhurst Cl
J7
1 Elm Gdns
2 Hawarden Gv
3 Hogarth St
4 Hornby St
5 Lytton Gv
6 Palmerston Av
7 Seaforth Rd
8 Woolfall Ter
K6
1 Beach Rd
2 Columbus Wy
3 Delta Rd
4 Jubilee Rd
5 Nelson Rd
6 Richmond Ct
7 Scarisbrick Av
8 Sefton Av
9 Seymour Rd
L2
1 Corsey Av
2 Cumberland Av
3 Fatherside Dr
4 Hampshire Av
5 St Andrew's Gv
6 St Margaret's Gv
7 St Michael's Gv
8 Westmorland Av
L4
1 Corsey La
2 Richard Martin Rd
L8
1 Croxteth Rd
2 Thornton Rd
M1
1 Almond's Turn
2 St Luke's Gv
3 St Patrick's Dr
M2
1 Morgan Ms
2 St Anthony's Gv
3 St Bernard's Cl
4 St Bridget's Gv
5 St Dunstan's Gv
6 St Stephen's Gv
7 St Thomas's Dr
M3
1 St Davids Gv
M5
1 Thackeray Gdns
2 Thirlmere Av
M6
1 Spencer Pl
M7
1 Hanlon Av

Page 84
A1
1 Assissian Crs
2 Downside Cl
3 The Marian Cl
4 St Gregory's Cft
5 St Jerome's Wy
A2
1 The Marian Sq
2 St Damian's Cft
A5
1 Atlantic Wy
2 Calsworthy Pl
3 Hermes Cl
4 Invincible Cl
5 Victory Cl
A6
1 Farmer Pl
2 Rafter Av
3 Sprakeling Pl
A7
1 Barbour Dr
2 Gronow Pl
A8
1 Abbott Dr
2 Kinley Gdns
3 Myerscough Av
4 Windsor Rd
B1
1 Alexander Fleming Av
2 Buckfast Cl
3 Frederick Banting Cl
4 Magdalene Sq
5 Marie Curie Av
B2
1 Grovenor Cl
2 John Hunter Wy
3 Lymington Gv
4 Marie Curie Av
5 Pinetree Cl
6 St Oswalds Ct
B3
1 Stand Park Av
2 Stand Park Cl
B4
1 Ripon Cl
B6
1 Kirkland Cl
2 Lucius Cl
B7
1 Dingley Av
2 Kitchener Dr
3 Lilford Av
B8
1 Broomfield Rd
2 Thornfield Rd
3 Woodfield Rd
C1
1 The Bales
2 The Carters
3 Shropshire Cl
C2
1 Brown's La
C4
1 Blaydon Cl
2 Durham Ms East
3 Durham Ms West
C6
1 Oakmere Cl
2 Wensleydale
C7
1 Balmoral Rd
2 Erl St
3 Harley St
4 Matlock Av
5 Tilney St
6 Wallace St
7 Weightman Gv
8 Windsor Rd
C8
1 Brockenhurst Rd
2 Elmfield Rd
3 Portree Cl
D1
1 Brierley Cl
2 Cardigan Wy
3 The Planters
4 The Scythes
5 The Threshers
D2
1 Prospect Wy
2 Wheatfield Cl
D5
1 Ascroft Rd
2 Cambridge Rd
3 Lyncot Rd
D6
1 Allendale Av
2 Ancient Mdw
3 Bakewell Gv
4 Brackendale Av
5 Coniston Cl
6 Danehurst Rd
7 Freeport Gv
8 Inglis Rd
9 Late Moffatt Rd West
10 Lunesdale Av
11 Millersdale Av
12 Poulter Rd
13 Ribblesdale Av
14 Rowsley Gv
D7
1 Acacia Gv
2 Beech Gv
3 Birch Av
4 Halby Rd
5 Hazel Gv
6 Longmoor Gv
7 Lunar Rd
8 Natal Rd
9 Oak Av
E2
1 Bradfield Av
2 Oundle Dr
3 Stoneyhurst Av
4 Wellington Cl
E5
1 Steeplechase Cl
E6
1 Moffat Rd
2 Springville Rd
E7
1 Cape Rd
2 St Peter's Rd
F5
1 Canter Cl
2 Fremon Cl
3 Hedgebank Cl
4 Saddle Cl
5 Sunloch Cl
6 Trotwood Cl
F6
1 Eighth Av
2 Fifth Av
3 Seventh Av
4 Sixth Av
F7
1 Aintree Rd

Page 85
H6
1 Drake Pl
2 Formosa Dr
3 Greystone Pl
4 Moss Pits Cl
J6
1 Copple House La
2 Drake Cl
3 Hawksmoor Cl
K1
1 Amanda Wy
2 Farrell Cl
3 Martine Cl
4 Yew Tree Gn
L1
1 Lytham Ct
2 Park Rd
L4
1 Ampleforth Cl
2 Middleham Cl
3 Pateley Cl
4 Staverton Rd
M6
1 The Paddock
M8
1 Camelford Rd
2 Looe Rd
3 Newlyn Wk
4 Silverwell Rd
5 Trendeal Rd
6 Wendron Rd
7 Wicket Cl

Page 86
A3
1 Adrian's Wy
2 Brackenhurst Gn
3 Kelday Cl
4 South Pde
5 Spicer Gv
A6
1 The Groves
2 Rockford Cl
3 Rockford Wk
4 Thornhurst
5 Wignall Cl
B1
1 Bridgeview Dr
2 Caldwell Cl
3 Kingswood Ct
4 Linslade Cl
5 Nathan Gv
6 Rockingham Ct
7 Sandlewood Gv
B3
1 Burnard Cl
2 Didsbury Cl
3 Leighs Hey Crs
4 Mottram Cl
5 Retford Rd
B5
1 Gaywood Cl
2 Ingleton Gn
3 Lindenwood
4 Maplewood
5 Merewood
6 St Laurence Gv
7 Thursby Cl
8 Winsham Cl
B6
1 Chadlow Rd
2 Hartwood Sq
3 Roughdale Cl
4 St Martins Gv
5 Springwood Gv
C2
1 Quernmore Wk
C5
1 Shaldon Cl
2 Shaldon Gv
3 Southwood Cl

Page 89
J5
1 Buttermere Av
2 Princes Wy
3 Silverdale Gv
K5
1 Beck Gv
K6
1 Campion Cl
2 Grasmere Cl
3 Grasmere Ct
4 Grasmere Fold
5 Green Leach Ct
6 Hodder Cl
7 Langdale Gv
8 Laurel Ct
9 Pyes Gdns
10 Stonyhurst Cl
L4
1 Caldbeck Gv
2 Deepdale Av
3 Greenburn Av

Page 90
B7
1 Catherine Wy
2 Phythian St
3 School St
4 Waine St
5 Worsley St
B8
1 Almond Cl
2 Fosters Gv
3 Hornbeam Cl
4 Lilac Gv
5 Magnolia Cl
C7
1 Broad Oak Av
2 Burrows St
3 Carrwood Cl
4 Dickinson Cl
5 Parr Gv
6 Platts St
7 Runnymede Dr
8 St Mark's St
9 Ulverston Cl
10 Whitfield Gv
E7
1 Acton Cl
2 Antrim Cl
3 Kennet Rd
4 Poplar Gv
5 Stanton Cl
F1
1 Aviemore Cl
2 Kelvin Cl
3 Kenmore Gv
4 Ranmore Av
5 Whitburn Cl

Page 91
G6
1 Abbey Rd
2 Ash Rd
3 Bishop Reeves Rd
4 Elm Rd
5 Homestead Av
6 Larch Rd
7 Peach Gv
8 Wesley Av
H1
1 Campion Gv
2 Chatsworth Cl
3 Poulton Dr
4 Trinity Gdns
J1
1 Balmoral Rd
2 Carlton Cl
3 Dalton Gv
4 Helen St
5 Melford Dr
J2
1 Hollingwood Cl
2 Mayfield St
3 Old School Pl
J3
1 Ashwood Av
2 Aspenwood
3 Beechwood Av
4 Elmwood Av
5 Smallshaw Cl
6 Woodfield Crs
K3
1 Averham Cl
2 Haydock St
3 Laburnum St
4 Monica Ter
5 Primrose Vw
6 Ramsey Cl
L2
1 Captain's La
2 Claisdale Cl
3 Harland Dr
4 Kimberley Pl
5 Mafeking Pl
6 New Barn Av
7 Watson Av
8 Wellbrooke Cl
9 Wyrevale Gv
L8
1 Maritime Cl
2 Mullins Av
3 Ripon Cl
4 Wetherby Cl
5 Wightman Av
M1
1 Dawber St
2 Lord St
3 Mason Cl
4 Talbot St
5 Thurlby Cl
6 Walter St
M2
1 Eltham Cl
M3
1 Brooklands Av
2 Warwick Av

Page 92
B4
1 Dunham Av
2 Edgeworth Rd
C5
1 Barnham Cl
2 Croft St
3 Peter St
4 Rigby St
5 Rochester Cl
6 Sankey St
7 Thomas St
C6
1 Bridge St
2 Dean Ct
3 Maryfield Cl
4 Plimblett St
5 Wakefield St
6 Wearhead Cl
E4
1 Apple Dell Av
2 Bowland Av
3 Chatburn Av
4 Derwent Av
5 Langdale Av
6 Rimington Av
7 Thirlmere Rd
F6
1 Barnton Cl
2 Sheridan Av

Page 93
G5
1 Avebury Cl
2 Ballantyne Wy
3 Brambling Wy
4 Bunting Cl
5 Landor Cl
6 Lunehurst
7 Redstart Cl
8 Royston Cl
9 Santon Dr
10 Speedwell Cl
11 Stonechat Cl
12 Sudbrook Cl
13 Turret Hall Dr
14 Wild Arum Cl
15 Windy Bank Av
H5
1 Birch Tree Rd
2 Blackburn Cl
3 Chestnut Gv
4 Hopwood Cl
5 Horncastle Cl
6 Middlewood
7 Sandfield Cl
8 The Shellings
9 Waddington Cl

Page 95
G8
1 Aberford Av
2 Keighley Av
3 Perrin Rd
4 Ponsonby Rd
5 Wetherby Av
J5
1 Bellfield Crs
2 Brisbane Av
3 Sandringham Dr
J6
1 Auburn Rd
2 Harewood Rd
3 Highacre Rd
J8
1 Hazeldene Av
2 Meadway
K5
1 Albion Pl
2 Busby's Cottages
3 Gayton Av
4 The Grennan
5 Mason St
6 Seymour Pl West
K7
1 Bridgecroft Rd
2 Halsbury Rd
3 Mornington Rd
K8
1 Anglesey Rd
2 Arnold St
3 Barnwell Av
4 Edinburgh Rd
5 Liscard Village
6 Ormond St
7 Selby St
8 West St
L6
1 Berkeley Dr
2 Bernard Av
3 Brackenhurst Dr
4 Braehaven Rd
5 Cumberland Rd
6 Lichfield St
7 Mariners Rd
8 Marlborough Rd
9 Newhaven Rd
10 Osborne Rd
11 Rockpoint Av
12 Westbank Av
13 Westmoreland Rd
M8
1 Marsden Cl
2 Rudgrave Ms
3 Rudgrave Pl
4 St Columba's Cl

Page 96
D1
1 Aylward Pl
2 Bromyard Cl
3 Bushley Cl
4 Chesnut Gv
5 Cricklade Cl
6 Gemini Cl
7 Irlam Pl
8 O'neill St
9 Seafield Rd
E4
1 Glendower St
2 Othello Cl
3 Pembroke Rd
4 Wolsey St
F1
1 Springs Cl
2 Surrey St
F6
1 Back Blackfield Ter
2 Crocus St
3 Elstow St
4 James Larkin Wy
5 Snowdrop St
6 Stanley Cl
7 Swindon Cl
8 Wulstan St
F7
1 Back Boundary St
2 Billings Cl
3 Blackfield St
4 Boundary St East
5 Edmonton Cl
6 Lancaster Cl
7 Lethbridge Cl
8 Major St
9 Turton St
F8
1 Callaghan Cl
2 Hankin St
3 Mckeown Cl
4 Mould St
5 Newsham St
6 Rotunda St
7 St Augustine St
8 Silvester St
9 Westmoreland Pl
10 Whiteside Cl
11 Wilbraham Pl

Page 97
G2
1 Fernhill Ms East
2 Fernhill Ms West
G3
1 Bergen Cl
2 Cassio St
G4
1 Cairo St
2 Chirkdale St
3 Delamore Pl
4 Smeaton St
G5
1 Back Barlow La
2 Back Westminster Rd
3 Beeston St
4 Bradewell Cl
5 Brunswick Cl
6 Goodall Pl
7 Longridge Wk
8 Marmonde St
9 Milnthorpe Cl
10 Netley St
11 Rockley St
12 St Hilda St
13 Warden St
G6
1 Archer Cl
2 Archer St
3 Bousfield St
4 Carden Cl
5 Chancel St
6 Cockerell Cl
7 Fountains Rd
8 Freeland St
9 Furness St
10 Hackthorpe St
11 Kearsley Cl
12 Morley St
13 Mostyn Cl
14 Sandheys Cl
15 Sellar St
16 Waller Cl
17 Wilkin St
18 Woodhouse Cl
G7
1 Albion St
2 Back York Ter
3 Calmet Cl
4 Devonshire Pl
5 Dukes Rd
6 Hapton St
7 Mitylene St
8 Thomaston St
9 Whittle Cl
G8
1 Abram St
2 Atherton Cl
3 John Bagot Cl
4 Mcgregor St
5 Sevenoaks Cl
H1
1 Barton Rd
H2
1 Kiddman St
2 Lochinvar St
3 Northcote Rd
4 Peveril St
5 Tressell St
6 Trevelyan St
7 Weaver St
H3
1 Astor St
2 Broadbelt St
3 Cromwell Rd
4 Grosvenor Rd
5 Imrie St
6 Knowsley St
7 Liston St
8 Pennington St
9 Selina Rd
10 Walton Village
11 Wyndham St
H4
1 Carisbrooke Pl
2 Goodison Pl
3 Ludlow St
H5
1 Back Luton Gv
2 Burrell St
3 Goodison Av
4 Heather Cl
5 Marius Cl
6 Springfield Sq
H6
1 Attwood St
2 Bodley St
3 Burleigh Rd South
4 Butterfield St
5 Goschen St
6 Gurnall St
7 Hartley Cl
8 Hayfield St
9 Norgate St
10 Randolph St
11 Wyre Rd
H7
1 Beacon La
2 Grecian Ter
3 Hartnup St
4 Monk St
5 Vanguard St
6 Viceroy St
H8
1 Breckfield Pl
2 Danby Cl
3 Elmore Cl
4 St George's Hl
5 Spurgeon Cl
J1
1 Aboyne Cl
J2
1 Genista Cl
J3
1 Drayton Rd
2 Pendleton Rd
3 St Mary's Av
4 St Mary's Gv
5 St Mary's Pl
6 Stoddart Rd
7 Sylvania Rd
J4
1 Appleton Rd
2 Hans Rd
3 Luxmore Rd
4 Pentland Av
5 Shepston Av
6 Swanston Av
J5
1 Muriel St
J6
1 Tinsley St
2 Varthen St
J7
1 Adkins St
2 Boycott St
3 Crouch St
4 Glaisher St
5 Hawkesworth St
6 Houlding St
7 Vyrnwy St
J8
1 Bulwer St
2 Friar St
3 Halkyn Dr
4 Handfield Pl
5 Mackenzie St
6 Queens Ms
7 Rendal Cl
8 Rutland Cl
9 Stockbridge Pl
10 Thirlmere Gn
K1
1 Dahlia Cl
2 Larchdale Gv
3 Pampas Gv
K2
1 Lime Tree Cl
K4
1 Cherry Cl
K7
1 Lyon Rd
2 Old Barn Rd
3 St David's Rd
4 Stonehill Av
5 Waterhouse Cl
K8
1 Apollo Wy
2 Avon St
3 Franklin Pl
4 Hennawood Cl
5 Larch Lea
6 Saxon Cl
7 Spring Bank Rd
8 Sprucewood Cl
9 Teakwood Cl
10 Thornwood Cl
L2
1 Forsythia Cl
2 Plane Cl
L3
1 Amersham Rd
L4
1 Bramberton Pl
2 Graylands Pl
L6
1 Westcombe Rd
L7
1 Cathedral Rd
2 Monastery Rd
L8
1 Celebration Dr
2 Dominion St
3 Letchworth St
4 Morecambe St
5 Preston Gv
M2
1 Walton Hall Av
M3
1 Scarisbrick Pl
2 Scarisbrick Rd
M5
1 Carlisle Cl
2 Richard Kelly Dr
3 Richard Kelly Pl
M6
1 Barkerville Cl
2 Cosgrove Cl
3 Londonderry Rd
4 Worcester Av
M7
1 Birkdale Cl
2 Brownville Rd
3 Whitby St

Page 98
A2
1 Gable Ct
2 Ranworth Cl
A3
1 Falklands Ap
2 Mildmay Rd
A4
1 Bridgeway
A5
1 Milne Rd
2 Sandyville Gv
A6
1 Huxley St
A7
1 Brookbridge Rd
2 Peckforton Cl
A8
1 Braddan Av
2 Clairville Wy
3 Santon Av
4 Sulby Av
B1
1 Godetia Cl
2 Heronhall Rd
3 Martinhall Rd
4 Sparrow Hall Cl
B2
1 Ranworth Pl
2 Ranworth Sq
3 Ranworth Wy
B5
1 Morningside Wy
B7
1 Packenham Rd
2 Winsford Rd
B8
1 Bankland Rd
2 The Grove
C2
1 Cottesbrook Pl
2 Greenholme Cl
3 Hollingbourne Pl
C3
1 Oxenholme Crs
2 Stallsfield Pl
3 Wellesbourne Pl
C4
1 Branthwaite Cl
2 Branthwaite Gv
3 Glassonby Wy
4 Helmdon Cl
C5
1 Fairholme Cl
C6
1 Bridgeford Av
2 Craigside Av
3 Desborough Crs
4 Green End Pk
5 Hayman's Cl
6 Sommer Av
D2
1 Galemeade
D3
1 Good Shepherd Cl
D4
1 Rosewood Gdns
D5
1 Clwyd Gv
2 Forest Lawn
3 Newton Cl
D6
1 The Armoury
D7
1 Barnfield Cl
D8
1 Heathwood
E1
1 Altcross Wy
2 Crantock Cl
E2
1 Herald Cl
2 Sceptre Wk
3 Scone Cl
E3
1 Hillerton Cl
2 Horwood Cl
3 Morvah Cl
4 Portgate Cl
5 Spreyton Cl
E4
1 Barrow Cl
2 Furness Av
3 Millom Gv
4 Tremore Cl
E6
1 Springdale Cl
E7
1 Craven Rd
2 Deysbrook Side
3 Glenmarsh Cl
4 Mayfield Cl
E8
1 Sandfield Cl
F2
1 Beech Cl
2 Delamere Cl
3 Kirkside Cl
4 Maple Cl
5 Oakhill Cl
6 Whitebeam Dr
F5
1 Molland Cl
F6
1 Access Rd
F8
1 Edgemoor Cl
2 Honeys Green Cl
3 Leecourt Cl

Page 99
G2
1 Aldridge Cl
2 Bradbourne Cl
3 Branfield Cl
4 Butterwick Dr
5 Charmouth Cl
6 Dalewood
7 Haverton Wk
8 Millgreen Cl
9 Newholme Cl
10 Pembury Cl
11 St Cuthbert's Cl
12 Southgate Cl
13 Staplehurst Cl
14 Wardgate Av
G3
1 Bowden Cl
2 Glenmaye Cl
G7
1 Muirfield Cl
2 St Vincent's Cl
G8
1 Johnson Gv
2 Mercer Ct
3 Richard Gv
H1
1 Goldcrest Cl
2 Shobdon Cl
3 Tewkesbury Cl
H2
1 Greenfinch Cl
2 Mallard Cl
3 Midhurst Rd
4 Mistlethrush Wy
5 Sherwood Cl
6 Stand Farm Rd
7 Thornbeck Cl
H3
1 Redmain Wy
H6
1 Planetree Rd
H7
1 Carnoustie Cl
2 Lytham Wy
3 Turnberry Cl
H8
1 Finch Wy
2 Phillip Gv
J2
1 Stretton Cl
J3
1 Watton Cl
J6
1 The Birches
2 Leach Cft
J7
1 Finch Cl
K5
1 Apple Tree Cl
2 Orange Tree Cl
3 Plum Tree Cl
K6
1 Buckthorn Cl
2 Camdale Cl
3 Quickthorn Crs
4 Rosewood Cl
K7
1 Rosewell Ct
L3
1 Whitestone Cl
L6
1 St Aiden's Gv
2 St Andrew's Dr
3 St Anthony's Cl
4 St Benedict's Gv
5 St Brendan's Cl
6 St Jude's Cl
7 St Luke's Wy
L7
1 The Grove
L8
1 Glencroft Cl
2 Heath Rd
3 Wetherby Ct
4 Willowbank Cl
M1
1 Blaking Dr
M2
1 Corncroft Rd
2 Fountain Rd
M6
1 Park Wy
M7
1 Leonards Cl
2 Toronto Cl
M8
1 Layford Rd

Page 100

F7
1 Atherton St
2 Bond St
3 Cambridge St
4 Carlton St
5 Chapel St
6 Church St
7 Duke St
8 Highfield Pl
9 Leyland St
10 Market Pl
11 Mill St
12 Pottery Flds
13 Salisbury St
14 Seddons Ct
15 Wood St
16 Wycherley St

Page 101

G7
1 Cliftonville Rd
2 Derby Sq
3 East St
4 Evelyn Av
5 Kelly St
6 Kemble St
7 Lavender Crs
8 Pembertons Ct
9 Queens Rd
10 Smith St

J7
1 Ancholme Cl
2 Brockhall Cl
3 Farthingstone Cl
4 Georgian Cl
5 Helford Cl

J8
1 Ariss Gv
2 Duncote Cl
3 Waine Gv

K1
1 The Cloisters
2 Linden Wy

L7
1 Buckthorn Gdns
2 Fountain St

M1
1 Caraway Gv
2 Hearne Rd
3 Hopkins Cl
4 Juniper Cl
5 Kitchener St
6 Melville Cl
7 Newfields
8 St Luke's Rd
9 St Teresa's Rd

M2
1 Belmont St
2 Roscoe St
3 Warwick St

M3
1 Constance St
2 Selby Cl

M4
1 Alexandra St
2 Carlow St
3 Crosby Gv
4 Derringstone Cl
5 Thompson St

M5
1 Beech St
2 Legion Rd
3 Leicester St

M6
1 Blaydon Gv
2 Common St
3 Crown St
4 Fernlea Av
5 Gorsefield
6 Nutgrove Av
7 Oakfield Cl
8 Samuel St

M7
1 Aycliffe Rd
2 Bevan Cl
3 Hexham Cl

Page 102

A1
1 Greenall St
2 Tamworth St
3 Trafalgar St

A2
1 Bruce St
2 Crispin St
3 Duncan St
4 Lawrenson St
5 Maxwell St
6 Napier Cl
7 Pemberton St
8 Windus St

A3
1 Ayrshire Gdns
2 Boundary Rd
3 Eldon Cl
4 Tullis St

A5
1 Timor Av

A6
1 Denison Gv
2 Kempsey Gv
3 Manley Pl

A7
1 Basildon Cl

B1
1 Barton Cl
2 Burnell Cl
3 Chorley St
4 Halefield St
5 Lowe St
6 New Cross St
7 Palmer Cl
8 Randon Gv
9 Rigby St
10 Volunteer St

B2
1 Copperas St
2 Headley Cl
3 Lowe St South
4 Manning St
5 Rigby St

B3
1 Berkshire Gdns
2 Buckingham Cl
3 Cardigan Cl
4 Duncan Cl
5 Flintshire Gdns
6 Glamorgan Cl

B7
1 Cheyne Wk
2 Farringdon Cl

C1
1 Baldwin St
2 Claughton St
3 College St
4 Dicconson St
5 John St
6 Ward St
7 William St

C2
1 Barrow St
2 Brook St
3 Cotham St
4 Cross St
5 Exchange St
6 George St
7 Haydock St
8 Milk St

D2
1 Bickerstaffe St

E1
1 Bolton St
2 Earl St
3 Johnson St
4 Parlane St

E2
1 Ardwick St
2 Higher Parr St
3 Ivy Ct
4 Mcculloch St
5 Orrell St
6 Parr Mount St
7 South John St
8 Trinity St

E3
1 Clarence Cl
2 Hunter St

E4
1 Ada St
2 Cleveland St
3 Cowper St
4 Emmett St

E5
1 Bridle Ct
2 Dellside Gv
3 Green End La
4 Margaret Av
5 Marshall Av

E6
1 Eton Hall Dr
2 Sandalwood Gdns
3 Shevington Cl
4 Snowdon Gv

E7
1 Bracewell Cl
2 Cotterdale Cl
3 Evenwood
4 Freda Av
5 Heward Av
6 Thames Rd

E8
1 Westleigh Pl

F1
1 Blackhorse St
2 Prospect Rd
3 Windmill Gdns

F3
1 Monmouth Gv

F5
1 Crouch St
2 Spencer Gdns

F6
1 Ambergate Cl
2 Boscow Crs
3 Dunscroft
4 Eaglesfield Cl
5 Kerrysdale Cl
6 Kidstone Cl
7 Lakemoor Cl
8 Marywell Cl
9 Oxley St
10 Riverside Gv
11 St Nicholas Gv
12 Simonstone Gv
13 Springpool
14 Waterdale Pl
15 Weasdale Cl

F7
1 Clovelly Av
2 Drybeck Gv
3 Elsbeck Gv
4 Freshford
5 Holywell Cl
6 Kelbrook Cl
7 Kerswell Cl
8 Padeswood Cl

F8
1 Colyton Av
2 Minehead Gv

Page 104

B1
1 Camelot Cl
2 Cherry Cl
3 North St
4 Portland St

B7
1 Arncliffe Dr
2 Colne Rd
3 Dorchester Wy
4 Exmouth Wy
5 Gleave Rd
6 Norcott Dr
7 Sherbourne Wy

C2
1 Alpine St
2 Back Booth St
3 Back Lawrence St
4 Back Legh St
5 Booth St
6 Lord St
7 Sceptre Cl
8 Stanley St

D2
1 Alma St
2 Back Bridge St
3 Chemical St
4 Derby Cl
5 Duke St
6 Grafton St
7 Hotel St
8 Houghton Cl
9 Houghton St
10 Junction La
11 Oxford St
12 Princes St

E1
1 Dean Meadow
2 Dunlin Av
3 Greenfields Cl
4 Greenshank Cl
5 Redshank Cl
6 Sandpiper Cl
7 Sunnybank Cl
8 Water St

E3
1 Cedar St
2 Findlay Cl
3 Richmond Gdns

Page 107

G2
1 Crofton Gdns
2 Langcliffe Cl
3 Lawton Cl
4 Rathmell Cl
5 Rimington Cl

Page 109

K5
1 Barberry Cl
2 Cardus Cl
3 Earlswood Cl
4 Ebony Cl
5 Hornbeam Cl
6 Huntingdon Cl
7 Lapworth Cl
8 Morpeth Cl
9 Tanworth Gv
10 Town Meadow La

L4
1 Wastdale Ct
2 Wastdale Ms

L5
1 Belford Dr
2 Millers Wy
3 Snowden Rd

L6
1 Amberley Cl
2 Brunsfield Cl

M3
1 Lingham Cl
2 Tarran Dr
3 Tarran Rd

Page 110

A1
1 Castlegrange Cl

A2
1 Castleford Ri
2 Castleheath Cl
3 The Heathlands

A4
1 Garden La
2 Lyons Cl
3 Oakenholt Rd
4 Old Maryland La
5 Silverburn Av

A5
1 Barnston La
2 Chadwick St
3 Kensington Gdns
4 Kingston Cl
5 Netherton Rd
6 Priorsfield
7 Rosslyn Crs

A6
1 Gilwell Cl

A7
1 Bleasdale Cl
2 Broadoaks
3 Kenilworth Gdns
4 Pendle Cl
5 Royden Rd

A8
1 Bowscale Cl
2 Bramford Cl
3 Brookside Dr
4 Devonshire Rd
5 Dunning Cl
6 Melton Cl
7 Mesham Cl
8 Rendelsham Cl
9 Stonham Cl
10 Trimley Cl
11 Tunstall Cl
12 Withburn Cl

B2
1 Birket Sq
2 Farnworth Av
3 Findley Dr
4 Greenheath Wy

B4
1 School Cl
2 Yew Wy

B6
1 Grampian Av
2 Leawood Gv
3 Wimbrick Cl

B6
1 Blackthorn Cl
2 Wheatfield Cl

B7
1 Edgewood Rd
2 Hereford Av
3 Manorside Cl

B8
1 Kirkway
2 Larcombe Av
3 Molyneux Cl
4 Newton Wy
5 Poplar Av

C3
1 Buttercup Cl

C6
1 Blakeney Cl
2 Hunstanton Cl
3 Marsham Cl
4 Sheringham Cl

C7
1 Macalpine Cl
2 Maxwell Cl

C8
1 Garfield Ter
2 Quineway
3 Tinas Wy
4 Wroxham Wy

D2
1 Kellett Rd

D6
1 Broadfield Cl
2 Denston Cl
3 Edgemoor Cl
4 Loddon Cl
5 Wolferton Cl

D7
1 Barford Cl
2 College Cl
3 Coppice Cl
4 Corwen Cl
5 Deeside Cl
6 Delamere Cl

D8
1 Ford Dr

E4
1 Ballantyne Dr
2 Balliol Cl
3 Cowdrey Av
4 St Oswald's Ms

E5
1 Bidston Green Ct
2 Broadfield Av
3 Edrich Av
4 Fernlea Ms
5 Glenfield Cl
6 New Acres Cl
7 Stoneridge Ct
8 Village Green Ct
9 Washbrook Av
10 Wood Gn
11 Woodvale Cl

E6
1 Bowgreen Cl
2 Fairbeech Ct
3 Gaywood Cl
4 Grappenhall Wy
5 Heatley Cl
6 Lymm Rd
7 Rushgreen Cl

E7
1 Beeston Cl
2 Berwick Cl
3 Caxton Cl
4 Chantry Cl
5 Charlwood Cl
6 Deepdale Cl
7 Warren Dr

E8
1 Winston Dr

F4
1 Compton Rd

F7
1 Calthorpe Wy
2 Whinmoor Cl

F8
1 Avelon Cl
2 Bassenthwaite Av
3 High Bank Cl
4 Oakleaf Ms
5 The Ridings

Page 111

G1
1 Kelmscott Dr

G5
1 Crossway
2 Elmtree Gv
3 Lower Flaybrick Rd
4 Rosemary Cl

G6
1 Old School Wy

H1
1 Bletchley Av
2 Braemore Rd
3 Brynmoss Av
4 Cromarty Rd
5 Loretto Rd
6 Millthwaite Rd
7 St Hilary Brow

H4
1 Brenig St
2 Shannon St

H5
1 Bertha St
2 Deans Wy
3 Elfet St
4 Goschen St
5 Kimberley St
6 Laird Cl
7 Lansdowne Pl
8 Vulcan Cl
9 Vulcan St

H6
1 Broom Hl
2 Buckingham Av
3 Foxglove Rd
4 Rimmers Ct
5 Snowdrop Av

H7
1 Brancote Mt
2 Hanover Cl
3 Shrewsbury Cl

H8
1 Kingsmead Gv
2 Kingsmead Rd

J1
1 Frankby Av
2 Stretton Av
3 Westwood Gv

J2
1 Baia Gv
2 Breck Pl
3 Chester St
4 Courtney Av
5 Dundee Gv
6 Heathbank Av
7 Ingleby Rd
8 Killarney Gv
9 Lynwood Av
10 Millbank Rd
11 Poulton Hall Rd
12 Roker Av

J3
1 Austin St
2 Chamberlain St

J5
1 Colwyn St
2 Danescourt Rd
3 Dundonald St
4 Falkland St
5 Lansdowne Cl
6 Methuen St
7 Thornton St

J6
1 Seeley Av

J8
1 Beresford Ct
2 Chetwynd Rd

K1
1 Acland Rd
2 Ashburton Rd
3 Conway St
4 Devonshire Rd
5 Overton Rd
6 Tiverton Av
7 Westminster Rd

K2
1 Alderley Rd
2 Sherlock La

K3
1 Burnside Av

K5
1 Churchview Rd
2 Dawson Av
3 St Edwards Cl
4 Upper Beckwith St

K6
1 Asquith Av
2 Curzon Av
3 Hartington Av

K7
1 St Helen's Cl

K8
1 Barnard Rd
2 Claughton Gn
3 Devonshire Cl
4 Enfield Ter
5 The Nook

L1
1 Belgrave Av
2 Bristol Av
3 Brompton Av
4 Bryn Bank
5 Chatsworth Av
6 Chepstow Av
7 Ferndale Av
8 The Grange
9 Oxford Rd

L2
1 Crosfield Rd
2 Elmbank St
3 Evelyn Rd
4 Gorsebank St
5 Mollington Rd
6 Oakbank St
7 Rufford Rd
8 Trentham Rd
9 Willowcroft Rd

L3
1 Cranford St
2 Stourton St

L5
1 Stoke St

L6
1 Aberdeen St
2 Newcombe Rd

L7
1 Bentinck Pl
2 Bright St
3 Claughton Pl
4 Eastbourne Rd
5 Gladstone Cl
6 Gladstone St
7 Gordon St
8 Grange Pl

L8
1 Barton St
2 Belmont
3 Carnforth Cl
4 Cartmel Cl
5 Clayton Pl
6 Clayton St
7 Henthorne St
8 Maritime Pk
9 Mount Gv
10 Oak Bank
11 Penrith St
12 Quarrybank St
13 Ravenscroft Rd
14 Town Vw
15 Town View Ms
16 Turner St
17 Warwick Cl
18 Wilkinson St
19 Windsor St

M1
1 Askew Cl
2 Church Gdns
3 Church La
4 Churchmeadow Cl
5 Clydesdale Rd
6 Comely Bank Rd
7 Dalehurst Cl
8 Darlington Cl
9 Darlington St
10 Glenalmond Rd
11 Mossy Bank Rd
12 Redfield Cl
13 Royston Av
14 Woodhall Av

M2
1 Addington St
2 Bulkeley Rd
3 Drayton Rd
4 Ethel Rd
5 Gladstone Rd
6 Glenburn Rd
7 Hood St
8 Hothfield Rd
9 Ilchester Rd
10 Mulberry Gv
11 Park Av
12 Winford St

M3
1 Gorsedale Pk
2 Parry St

M6
1 Beckwith St East
2 Brook St
3 Keightley St
4 Kinmel Cl
5 Newton St
6 Robert St
7 St Anne St
8 St Laurence Dr
9 Vittoria Cl
10 Watson St

M7
1 Bentinck Cl
2 Cardigan Av
3 Catherine St
4 Corfu St
5 Coventry St
6 Exmouth Cl
7 Exmouth Gdns
8 Exmouth Wy
9 Florence St
10 Hilton Cl
11 Parkfield Av
12 St Laurence Cl
13 Simpson St

M8
1 Brookland Rd
2 Cedar St
3 Cook St
4 Fearnley Rd
5 Hazel Rd
6 Hollybank Rd
7 Lowwood Rd
8 Maple St
9 Mounsey Rd
10 Quarry Bank
11 Rawcliffe Rd
12 Wellington Ter
13 Whalley Rd

Page 112

A3
1 Abbotsford St
2 Acacia Gv
3 The Birches
4 Borough Rd East
5 Briardale Rd
6 Church Crs
7 Delamere Gv
8 Denman Gv
9 Harlech St
10 Horseman Pl
11 James St
12 Keegan Dr
13 Lever Av
14 Matthew Cl
15 Norman Rd
16 North William St
17 Primrose Gv
18 Stanley Cl
19 Tudor Av
20 Vivian Av
21 William St
22 Woodview Av

A5
1 Freeman St

A7
1 Alma St
2 Back Oliver St
3 Bank St
4 Borough Pl
5 Burlington St
6 Clifton Crs
7 Conway St
8 Grange Rd
9 Oliver La
10 Walton St

B7
1 Albion St
2 Brandon St
3 Camperdown St
4 Cross St
5 Duncan St
6 Gertrude St
7 Hamilton St
8 Hornby St
9 Ivy St
10 Knox St
11 Market Pl
12 Market St
13 Mortimer St

E1
1 Archbishop Worlock Ct
2 Bishop Sheppard Ct
3 Clement Gdns
4 Fitzpatrick Ct
5 Hornby Wk
6 Jack Mcbain Ct
7 James Clarke St
8 Marshall Pl
9 Portland St
10 Tobin Cl
11 Twomey Cl
12 Walsh Cl

E3
1 Back Pickop St
2 Cheapside Alley
3 Cockspur St
4 Cumberland St
5 Davies St
6 Earle St
7 Eberle St
8 Exchange Pas West
9 Exchange St East
10 Hackins Hey
11 Hale St
12 Hatton Gdn
13 Hewitts Pl
14 Highfield St
15 Lower Milk St
16 Marybone
17 Moorfields
18 Princes St
19 Prussia St
20 Ryleys Gdns
21 Stanley St
22 Stephens La
23 Tempest Hey

E4
1 Brunswick St
2 Exchange St West
3 Castle Hl
4 Cook St
5 Covent Gdn
6 Custom House La
7 Fenwick St
8 Harrington St
9 Lower Castle St
10 North John St
11 Old Ropery
12 Princess St
13 Red Cross St
14 Sweeting St
15 Temple Ct
16 Temple La
17 Tower Gdns

E5
1 Canning Pl
2 Frederick St
3 Grayson St
4 Hartley Quay
5 Maghull St
6 Shaws Alley

F1
1 Burroughs Gdns
2 Diamond St
3 Ennerdale St
4 Gildarts Gdns
5 Tenterden St

F2
1 Addison Wy
2 Aldersey St
3 Byrom Wy
4 Cazneau St
5 Chaucer St
6 Freemasons Rw
7 Henry Edward St
8 Juvenal St
9 Limekiln La
10 Nicholas St
11 Peover St

F3
1 Crosshall St
2 Fontenoy St
3 Johnson St
4 Preston St
5 Shaw Hill St
6 Standish St
7 Trueman St
8 William Brown St

F4
1 Basnett St
2 Brooks Alley
3 Brythen St
4 Concert St
5 Elliot St
6 Fairclough St
7 Great Charlotte St
8 Houghton St
9 Manesty's La
10 Old Post Office Pl
11 Paradise St
12 Peter's La
13 Roe Alley
14 School La
15 Sir Thomas St
16 Tarleton St
17 Whitechapel

F5
1 Back Seel St
2 Burton Cl
3 Carpenters Rw
4 Cleveland Buildings
5 Cleveland Sq
6 Dickenson St
7 Duke Street La
8 Greetham St
9 Hanover St
10 Lakeland Cl
11 Pownall St
12 Price St
13 Seddon St
14 Slater Pl
15 Surrey St
16 Upper Pownall St
17 Vincent Ct
18 Wolstenholme Sq

F6
1 Hardy St
2 Simpson St

F7
1 The Anchorage
2 Dwerryhouse St
3 Granary Wy
4 Pleasant Hill St
5 Worthington St

F8
1 Northumberland Gv

Page 113

G1
1 Abram St
2 Back Beau St
3 Beresford St
4 Clifton Gv
5 Douro St
6 Juvenal Pl
7 St Martin's Ms
8 Upper Beau St
9 Watmough St

G2
1 Bickerstaffe St
2 Birchfield St
3 Drinkwater Gdns
4 Field St
5 Maritime Pl
6 Page Wk
7 Pritt St
8 Roderick St
9 Rokeby Cl
10 Soho Pl

G3
1 Back Bridport St
2 Burgess St
3 Camden St
4 Clifford St
5 Craven St
6 Fraser St
7 Hotham St
8 Kempston St
9 Lambert St
10 London Rd
11 Marquis St
12 Pudsey St
13 Rimmer St
14 St Vincent St
15 St Vincent Wy
16 Ward St
17 Wilde St

G4
1 Bolton St
2 Edward St
3 Franceys St
4 Green La
5 Heathfield St
6 Hilbre St
7 May St
8 Newington
9 Pleasant St
10 Upper Newington

G5
1 Back Colquitt St
2 Back Knight St
3 Back Maryland St
4 Back Renshaw St
5 Baltimore St
6 Bold St
7 Cummings St
8 Great George St
9 Griffiths St
10 Hardy St
11 Hope Pl
12 Knight St
13 Little Hardman St
14 Maryland St
15 Pilgrim St
16 Rice St
17 Roscoe La
18 Roscoe Pl
19 Roscoe St
20 Sankey St

G6
1 Chesterfield St
2 Crump St
3 Great George Pl
4 Greenland St
5 Newhall St
6 Pine Ms
7 Prince Albert Ms

G7
1 Grafton St
2 Langley St
3 Providence Crs
4 Shaftesbury St
5 Stanhope St
6 Upper Harrington St
7 Upper Hill St

G8
1 Chapman Cl
2 Doddridge Rd
3 Llanrwst Cl
4 Longville St
5 Mornington St
6 Rutter St
7 Southern Crs
8 Tamworth St
9 Vere St
10 Wolfe St

H1
1 Ember Crs
2 Fishguard Cl
3 Fitzclarence Wy
4 Garden La
5 Jasmine Cl
6 Marathon Cl
7 Mill Rd
8 Northcote Cl
9 Plumpton St
10 Spindle Cl
11 Waterhouse St

H2
1 Amelia Cl
2 Canterbury Wy
3 Haigh St
4 Hillside St
5 Lytton St
6 Melda Cl
7 Parkside St
8 Tichbourne Wy

H3
1 Bayhorse La
2 Elizabeth St
3 Falkland St
4 Gildart St
5 Ilford St
6 Norman St
7 Riding St
8 Shepherd St

H4
1 Bedford St North
2 Great Orford St
3 Newton Wy
4 Orthes St

H5
1 Abercromby Sq
2 Arrad St
3 Back Bedford St
4 Back Canning St
5 Back Catharine St
6 Back Hope Pl
7 Back Mulberry St
8 Back Sir Howard St
9 Back St Bride St
10 Bedford Cl
11 Blackburne Pl
12 Caledonia St
13 Falkner St
14 Hope Wy
15 Maryland St
16 Mulberry Pl
17 Mulberry St
18 Myrtle Pde
19 South Hunter St
20 Stowell St
21 Sugnall St
22 Upper Hope Pl

H6
1 Back Egerton St North
2 Back Huskisson St
3 Back Little Canning St
4 Back Sandon St
5 Birley Ct
6 Gibson St
7 Grey St
8 Little Catharine St
9 Little Huskisson St
10 Morpeth St
11 Park Wy
12 Parliament Pl
13 Peel Pl

H7
1 Arnold St
2 Berkley St
3 Combermere St
4 Dickens St
5 Grey St
6 Thackeray Sq
7 Upper Hill St
8 Vining St

H8
1 Barkiss Cl
2 Copperfield Cl
3 Essex St
4 Gelling St
5 Marshside Cl
6 Micawber Cl
7 Morton St
8 Nickleby Cl
9 Queensberry St
10 Rhyl St
11 Roper St
12 Tupman St
13 Winkle St

J1
1 Aubrey Ct
2 Burnley Cl
3 Cresswell St
4 Dawber Cl
5 Harewood St
6 Reservoir St
7 Rothwell St
8 Shakespeare Rd
9 Whitefield Wy

J2
1 Baker St
2 Churton Ct
3 Dunkeld Cl
4 Dunkeld St
5 Fitzroy Wy
6 Gloucester Pl
7 Hengler's Cl
8 Hughes St
9 Hutchinson Wk
10 Lavan St
11 Marsden Wy
12 Marvin St
13 Nevin St
14 Olympia St
15 Pera Cl
16 Raven Cl

J3
1 Back Mount Vernon Gn
2 Battenberg St
3 Bengel St
4 Fielding St
5 Kensington St
6 Mount Vernon St
7 Mount Vernon Vw

J4
1 Albert St
2 Brydges St
3 Helsby St
4 Paddington
5 Shimmin St

J5
1 Back Falkner St South
2 Cambridge St
3 Freedom Cl
4 Grove Wy
5 John Moores Cl
6 Rosemary Cl

J6
1 Adele Thompson Dr
2 Crown St
3 Daniel Davies Dr
4 Harrowby St
5 Hatherley Cl
6 Hatherley St
7 Northbrook Cl
8 Northbrook St
9 Upper Huskisson St

J7
1 Arnold Cl
2 Back Kelvin Gv
3 Celtic St
4 Eversley St
5 North Hill St
6 Pimhill Cl
7 Vronhill Cl

J8
1 Devonshire Rd West
2 Hawkstone St
3 Mountview Cl
4 Pengwern St
5 Treborth St
6 Voelas St
7 Wellington Ter

K1
1 Berwick Cl
2 Every St
3 Guion St
4 Mayfair Cl
5 Montgomery Wy
6 Norwood Cl
7 Norwood Gv
8 White Rock St

K2
1 Alexandra Ct
2 Bourne St
3 Cottenham St
4 Denman St
5 George Harrison Cl
6 Goldsmith St
7 Gwenfron Rd
8 Mission Wk
9 Paul Maccartney Wy
10 Phythian Cl
11 Ringo Starr Dr
12 Sutcliffe St
13 Thornes Rd
14 Wightman St

K3
1 Adderley St
2 Edinburgh Rd
3 Kemble St
4 Laggan St
5 Minto St
6 Seldon St
7 Smollett St
8 Solomon St

K4
1 Agnes Wy
2 Back Chatham Pl
3 Back Holland Pl
4 Back Towerlands St
5 Church Mt
6 Hawthorn Gv
7 Moorgate St
8 Nevison St
9 Uxbridge St

K5
1 Boothwood Cl
2 Brightgate Cl
3 Dovestone Cl
4 Kingswell Cl
5 Perrygate Cl
6 Portwood Cl
7 Redmires Cl
8 Silkstone Cl
9 Upper Parliament St

K6
1 Askham Cl
2 Back Windsor Vw
3 Buttermere St
4 Kingsley Rd
5 Maitland St
6 Maynard St
7 Oxendale Cl
8 Swindale Cl
9 Yanwath St

K7
1 Bentley Rd
2 Brahms Cl
3 Mozart Cl
4 Princes Ga West
5 Strauss Cl

K8
1 Albert Pk
2 Windermere Ter

L1
1 Celt St
2 Milverton St
3 Tweed Cl

L2
1 Ebenezer Rd
2 Madeley St
3 Marlsford St
4 Phillimore Rd
5 Shell Rd

L3
1 Chiswell St
2 Dell St
3 Flaxman St
4 Frost St
5 Holdsworth St
6 Houlton St
7 Odsey St
8 Redgrave St
9 Wedgewood St

L4
1 Beames Cl
2 Bremner Cl
3 Chris Ward Cl
4 Claughton Cl
5 Crosfield Cl
6 Fowler Cl
7 Cresley Cl
8 Hughes Cl
9 Lemon Cl
10 Webb Cl

L5
1 Acton Wy
2 Annerley St
3 Bective St
4 Casterton St
5 Claypole Cl
6 Heathcote Cl
7 Lightwood Dr
8 Lightwood St
9 Lindley Cl
10 Wainwright Cl
11 Wilfer Cl
12 Wrayburn Cl

L6
1 Bird St
2 Danube St
3 Darrel Dr
4 Newstead Rd
5 Richardson St
6 River Avon St

L7
1 Orange Gv

M2
1 Haverstock Rd
2 Homerton Rd
3 Laburnum Rd

M3
1 Adamson St
2 Eltham St
3 Fareham Rd
4 Romulus St

M5
1 Chichester Cl
2 Corsewall St
3 Jesmond St
4 Pengwern Gv
5 Pilot Gv
6 Purser Gv
7 Sandhead St
8 Victor St
9 Wavertree V
10 Whithorn St

M6
1 Altcar Av
2 Childwall Av
3 Dorset Av
4 Newhouse Rd

M7
1 Wellington Flds

Page 114

A3
1 Birchfield Cl
2 Clyde Rd

A5
1 Carno St
2 Colinton St
3 Dunstan St
4 Edington St
5 Picton Crs
6 Somerton St
7 Wellington Gv
8 Willow Rd

A6
1 Abyssinia Cl
2 Bisley St
3 Broadwood St
4 Fingland Rd
5 Garmoyle Cl
6 Jamieson Rd
7 Kellitt Rd
8 Lawrence Gv
9 Ormsby St
10 Rexmore Wy
11 Seaman Rd
12 Southey St
13 Wilkie St
14 Wimbledon St

A7
1 Nithsdale Rd
2 Weardale Rd

A8
1 Elmbank Rd
2 Gorsebank Rd
3 Hollybank Rd

B1
1 Back Sandstone Rd
2 Felton Gv
3 Menstone Rd
4 Sandstone Rd West
5 Tynwald Cl
6 Tynwald Pl
7 Woburn Cl

B2
1 Aviemore Rd
2 Barrymore Rd
3 Bibby St
4 Davidson Rd
5 Derby St

B3
1 Raynham Rd

B4
1 Malcolm Pl
2 Whittaker Cl

B5
1 Celedine Cl
2 Mafeking Cl
3 Salisbury Ter
4 Standale Rd
5 Victoria Av
6 Westdale Vw

B6
1 Wells St

B7
1 Airdale Rd
2 Brierfield Rd
3 Edenfield Rd
4 Foxdale Rd
5 Freshfield Rd
6 Micklefield Rd
7 Patterdale Rd
8 Winchfield Rd

B8
1 Arlington Av
2 Balcarres Av
3 Beckenham Av
4 Belhaven Rd
5 Blenheim Rd
6 Bromley Av
7 Grovedale Rd
8 Harringay Av
9 Ingleton Rd
10 Newborough Av
11 Stanton Rd
12 Trentham Av
13 Welbeck Av
14 Willowdale Rd
15 Zetland Rd

C1
1 Derwent Sq
2 Podium Rd

C2
1 Derby La
2 Macfarren St
3 Rawlinson Rd
4 Shaftesbury Ter
5 Victoria Pl

C3
1 Foxdell Cl
2 Shelton Cl
3 Stephenson Rd
4 Wilton Gv

C4
1 Thorley Cl

C5
1 Albert Gv
2 Arnold Gv
3 Frederick Gv

C6
1 Castleford St
2 Chapel Yd
3 Greenside Av
4 Hills Pl
5 Thornhill Rd
6 Wrights Ter

C7
1 Cassville Rd
2 Centreville Rd
3 Coventry Rd
4 Glenfield Rd
5 Lichfield Rd
6 Newcastle Rd
7 Pagefield Rd
8 Peterborough Rd

C8
1 Aukland Rd
2 Calton Av
3 Carsdale Rd
4 Cramond Av
5 Cronton Rd
6 Devondale Rd
7 Duddingston Av
8 Hollydale Rd
9 Kenyon Rd
10 Smithdown Pl
11 Sunsdale Rd
12 Westgate Rd

D1
1 Clayford Pl

D2
1 Fernleigh Rd

D3
1 Haslingden Cl
2 Oak V
3 Whitehouse Rd

D4
1 Leveson Rd
2 Robeck Rd
3 Ruthven Rd
4 Waldgrave Pl

D7
1 Fingall Rd
2 Grantley Rd
3 Hillingdon Rd
4 Stanmore Rd

D8
1 Ensworth Rd

E1
1 Clayford Rd
2 Clayford Wy

E2
1 Rudyard Cl
2 Walden Rd

E5
1 Beechtree Rd
2 Shenley Rd

E7
1 Menlove Mansions

F1
1 Woodbourne Rd

F3
1 Victoria Av

F5
1 Shawton Rd

F6
1 Childwall Bank Rd

F8
1 Catonfield Rd
2 Penfold Cl

Page 115

G1
1 Churchdown Gv

G2
1 Greystone Crs

G5
1 Dominic Rd
2 Gregory Cl
3 Lanfranc Cl
4 Lanfranc Wy
5 Surby Cl

G6
1 Colindale Rd

G7
1 Selworthy Gn

H2
1 Ashfarm Ct

H3
1 Malvern Crs
2 Sexton Wy

H4
1 Molesworth Gv

H5
1 Glen Vine Cl
2 Harwich Gv
3 Peacehaven Cl
4 Swinburne Cl
5 Weymouth Cl

H6
1 Dronfield Wy
2 Hartsbourne Cl
3 Napps Cl

H8
1 Quickswood Gn
2 Rockbourne Wy

J1
1 Dinas La
2 Petunia Cl

J6
1 Marchwood Wy

J7
1 Cranleigh Pl
2 Hayles Cl
3 Holmleigh Rd
4 Leybourne Gn

J8
1 Acresgate Ct
2 Dunnock Cl
3 Leybourne Gv

K1
1 Barnwood Rd

K2
1 Craigwood Wy
2 Westwick Pl
3 Windsor Rd

K3
1 Wentworth Gv

K6
1 Bridgefield Cl
2 Cloverdale Rd
3 Dauntsey Brow
4 Eccles Dr
5 Viennese Rd

K7
1 Cockshead Wy
2 Farmbrook Rd
3 Haslemere Wy
4 Marlbrook Rd
5 Meriden Rd
6 Trelawney Cl

K8
1 Corsewood Gv

L1
1 Cartmel Wy
2 Cotsford Cl
3 Cotsford Pl
4 Cotsford Wy

L2
1 Elmswood Gv
2 Sedburgh Gv
3 Woodlands Rd

L4
1 Birkdale Cl
2 Colin Cl
3 Edgbaston Cl
4 Lingfield Cl
5 Nottingham Rd
6 Sunningdale Cl
7 Turnberry Cl

L7
1 Broomhill Cl
2 Durweston Wk
3 The Hawthornes
4 Maytree Cl
5 Sienna Cl

L8
1 Adstone Rd
2 Lee Park Av
3 Ringway Rd
4 St Stephens Cl
5 Vicarage Lawn

M1
1 Alt Bridge Rd
2 Cartmel Rd
3 Horrocks Cl

M2
1 Horrocks Rd

M3
1 Birch Gv
2 Sandfield

M4
1 Beecham Cl
2 Goodwood Cl
3 Kempton Cl
4 Tarbock Rd

M5
1 Donnington Cl

M7
1 Aurorean Cl
2 Handel Rd

M8
1 Naylor's Rd

Page 116

A4
1 The Brooklands
2 Ewanville
3 Greenlands
4 St Catherines Cl
5 St James' Rd

A8
1 Bramblewood Cl
2 Bramley Cl
3 Maplewood Cl
4 Rosewood Cl

B2
1 Huyton La
2 Longview Crs
3 St Matthew's Cl

B8
1 Kingfisher Cl
2 Nightingale Cl
3 Osprey Cl
4 Swallow Cl

D3
1 Taunton Rd
2 Tiverton Cl

F1
1 Molyneux Cl

F2
1 Cherry Tree Cl

F3
1 Eglington Av
2 Fisher Pl
3 Hostock Cl
4 Montgomery Cl

Page 117

H2
1 Brackenwood Gv
2 Braemar Cl
3 Gresford Cl
4 Shelley Pl

J1
1 Hadden Cl
2 Lindrick Cl
3 Longview Av
4 Newby Av

K1
1 Sandon Cl

L2
1 Braithwaite Cl
2 Brandreth Cl
3 Exchange Pl
4 Houghton St
5 Oaklands
6 Station St
7 Victoria St

Page 118

E1
1 Acorn Cl
2 Bracken Ct
3 Brock Hall Cl
4 Churchfields
5 Cottage Pl
6 Fallow Cl
7 Farrier Wk
8 Harvest Wy
9 Hazelfield Ct
10 Hoylake Gv
11 Lindale Dr
12 Littlecote Cl
13 Millersdale
14 Moreton Av
15 Oaklands Ct
16 Riding Cl
17 Rye Cl
18 Spinney Cl
19 Wheatland Cl
20 Whinbury Ct
21 The Willows
22 Woodcroft Wy

Page 120

A6
1 Clovelly Av
2 Coogee Av
3 Greenway
4 Hall Ter

A8
1 Brightwell Cl
2 Helston Cl
3 St Joseph's Cl

B8
1 Beechwood Av
2 Cunningham Cl
3 St Vincent Rd

D7
1 Audie Murphy Rd
2 Grant Rd
3 Lee Rd
4 Macarthur Rd
5 Manuel Perez Rd
6 Sycamore La

E8
1 Brentnall Cl
2 Chippingdall Cl
3 Fildes Cl
4 Crosvenor Cl
5 Rochester Cl
6 Sheffield Cl
7 Winstanley Cl
8 Yates Cl

F3
1 Cresswell Cl
2 Gresford Cl
3 Pensarn Gdns
4 Peterstone Cl
5 Stanner Cl

F4
1 Drake Cl

F5
1 Frobisher Ct

F6
1 Bewsey Farm Cl

F7
1 Shiggins Cl

Page 121

G3
1 Bala Cl
2 Cartmel Cl
3 Granston Cl
4 Lampeter Cl
5 Lydstep Ct
6 Monkswood Cl
7 Rossett Cl
8 Tintern Cl
9 Wrexham Cl

G7
1 Bostock St
2 Cartwright St
3 Monks St
4 St Barnabas Pl

G8
1 Baxter St
2 Green St
3 Lancaster St
4 Percy St
5 Selby St

J2
1 Brendon Av
2 Chiltern Av
3 Chiltern Crs
4 Crawley Av
5 Harvard Ct
6 Kentmere Pl
7 Wansfell Pl

K3
1 Achilles Av
2 Armour Av
3 Brandwood Av
4 Clough Av
5 Dean Crs
6 Poole Av
7 Poole Crs

K7
1 Ashton St
2 Chorley St
3 Erwood St
4 Hardy St
5 Rodney St
6 St Peter's Wy
7 Silver St

K8
1 Bank St
2 Bennett St
3 Bewsey St
4 Blackhurst St
5 Cockhedge Wy
6 James St
7 Naylor St
8 Patten La
9 Rylands St
10 Town Hl
11 Union St
12 Westminster Pl

L2
1 Ambleside Crs
2 Cartmel Av
3 Scafell Av
4 Thirlmere Av

L3
1 Byron Ct
2 The Coppins
3 Keswick Crs
4 Penrith Av
5 Ruskin Av

L4
1 Cossack Av
2 Kipling Av

L5
1 Richardson St

L6
1 Adam St
2 Alamein Crs
3 Arnhem Crs
4 Garner St
5 Synge St

L7
1 Chester St
2 Hopwood St
3 Morley St

L8
1 Cockhedge La
2 Crossley St
3 Dutton St
4 High St
5 Parr St
6 Percival St

M2
1 Bittern Cl
2 Ravensdale Cl

M3
1 Caldbeck Av
2 Catterall Av
3 Cherwell Cl
4 Concorde Pl
5 Greenwood Crs
6 Halifax Cl
7 Hughes Pl
8 Sandalwood Cl
9 Whittaker Av

M4
1 Ferguson Dr
2 Osborne Av
3 Povey Rd
4 St Margaret's Av
5 Sylvia Crs
6 Vale Owen Rd
7 Woodcote Cl

M5
1 Norbury Av

M6
1 Matthews St

Page 122

A2
1 Dovedale Cl
2 Dunnock Cl
3 Horseshoe Crs
4 Langdale Cl
5 Morven Cl
6 Swift Cl

A4
1 Andover Cl
2 Biggin Ct
3 Duxford Ct
4 Finningley Ct
5 Jurby Ct
6 Northolt Ct
7 Sealand Cl
8 Woodvale Cl

B2
1 Briers Cl
2 Newton Gv
3 St Bridget's Cl

B4
1 Jurby Ct
2 Pocklington Ct
3 Unsworth Ct

C3
1 Edgars Dr

C5
1 Queens Crs

D2
1 Stromness Cl

D6
1 Aveley Cl

E1
1 Aspull Cl
2 Campion Cl
3 Holmes Ct
4 Redvales Ct
5 Sovereign Ct
6 Windle Ct

E3
1 Blackburne Cl

E4
1 Lovage Cl

E6
1 Abstone Cl
2 Greenfields Cl

F1
1 Beeston Cl
2 Bickerton Cl
3 Carden Cl
4 Centurion Cl
5 Renown Cl
6 Vanguard Ct

F2
1 Land Cut La

F6
1 Hereford Cl
2 Laurel Av

F7
1 Laxey Av
2 Peel Cl

Page 124

C2
1 Broughton Av
2 Hilton Gv
3 Kington Rd
4 Murray Gv
5 Norton Rd
6 Redhouse Bank
7 Ridley Gv
8 Roseacre

D2
1 De Grouchy St
2 Heatherdene Rd

Page 125

L1
1 The Carters
2 Finchdean Cl
3 Harvester Wy
4 Malmesbury Cl
5 Redditch Cl
6 Redford Cl
7 Shepherd Cl
8 Stourport Cl
9 Swindon Cl
10 Thresher Av

M1
1 The Barncroft
2 Birchdale Cl
3 Dryfield Cl
4 Heygarth Dr
5 Holcombe Cl
6 Ingleton Cl
7 Longfield Cl
8 Pitch Cl
9 St James Cl

Page 126

B1
1 Benson Cl
2 Brightwell Cl
3 Cholsey Cl
4 Crowmarsh Cl
5 Dorchester Cl
6 Milman Cl
7 Wittenham Cl

C7
1 Ambleside Cl
2 Berwyn Av
3 Heywood Cl
4 Richmond Wy

E1
1 Naseby Cl
2 Netherfield Cl
3 Newark Cl
4 Newport Cl
5 Ollerton Cl
6 Orlando Cl
7 Ossett Cl

F1
1 Dodleston Cl
2 Eastview Cl
3 Edgefield Cl
4 Fern Gv
5 Pagewood Cl
6 Pinedale Cl
7 Ravendale Cl
8 Ridings Hey
9 Sunnybank Av
10 Tynron Gv
11 Westcott Wy
12 Westview Cl
13 Woodberry Cl

Page 127

G2
1 Hargrave Cl
2 Oulton Wy
3 Townfield Cl

G4
1 Millington Cl
2 Shipton Cl

H1
1 Ince Cl
2 Kilmalcolm Cl
3 Mere Farm Gv

H2
1 Aston Cl
2 Bollington Cl
3 Duddon Cl
4 Gawsworth Cl
5 Hatchmere Cl
6 Spurstow Cl

H3
1 Davenham Cl
2 Holm Cottages
3 Redwood Cl
4 Wrenbury Cl

H4
1 Dickens Av
2 Dickens Cl
3 Goldsmith Rd
4 Goldsmith Wy
5 Waterpark Cl

L1
1 Ashford Rd
2 Brimstage St
3 Falcon Rd
4 Halcyon Rd
5 Harrowby Rd South
6 Heathfield Rd
7 James St
8 Kingsland Rd
9 Laburnum Rd

M1
1 Ash Rd
2 Aspendale Rd
3 Charlecombe St
4 Dewberry Cl
5 Rectory Cl
6 St Catherine's
7 St Catherines Gdns
8 Shewell Cl
9 Spruce Cl
10 Sycamore Rd
11 Whitfield St

M6
1 Beckett Gv
2 Mountway

M7
1 King's Brow
2 Millwood
3 Rotherwood Cl
4 Sandfield Cl
5 Victoria Rd

M8
1 Derwent Cl
2 Glenmarsh Cl
3 Shalmarsh Cl
4 Welland Rd
5 Wilstan Av

Page 128

A1
1 Acuba Gv
2 Chamberlain St
3 Hampden Gv
4 Holly Gv
5 Kingsdown St
6 Leighton Rd
7 Olive Crs
8 Redmond St
9 Ripon St
10 Westbury St

B2
1 Alison Av
2 Beaconsfield Cl
3 Brougham Av
4 Cobden Ct
5 Cobden Pl
6 Gladstone Rd
7 Grenville Wy
8 Livingstone Rd
9 Lydbrook Cl
10 Orchard Ct
11 Rose Pl
12 Standard Pl
13 Stanley Ct
14 Strathlorne Cl
15 Wye Cl

B3
1 Aldersgate
2 Ashley St
3 Birchcliffe Rd
4 Byrne Av
5 Corinthian St
6 Doric St
7 Fairhaven Cl
8 Meadowfield Cl
9 Meadow Pk
10 Palmerston St
11 Rock Cl
12 The Sidings
13 Woburn Pl
14 Wycliffe St

C7
1 Apsley Gv
2 Wellesley Gv
3 Windy Bank

D5
1 Apsley Rd
2 Esher Rd
3 Field Cl
4 Kempton Rd
5 Thorburn Cl
6 Thorburn Crs

D6
1 Beaconsfield Rd
2 Mayfields South
3 Poolbank Rd
4 Woodhead St

D7
1 Causeway Cl
2 Elmbank Rd
3 Lancaster Cl
4 Lower Rd
5 Walker St
6 Willowbank Rd

D8
1 Cross St
2 Gardens Rd
3 Poets Cnr
4 Victoria St

E5
1 Pollitt Sq

E6
1 Ortega Cl

E7
1 The Anzacs

Page 129

H1
1 Anglesea Wy
2 Barclay St
3 Chatburn Wk
4 Chilhem Cl
5 Cleopas St
6 Greaves St
7 Hawkhurst Cl
8 Haylock Cl
9 Kirkburn Cl
10 Malwood St
11 Monro Cl
12 Netherby St
13 Royden St
14 Shelmore Dr
15 Whalley St
16 Woodruff St

H2
1 Armstrong Quay
2 Badminton St
3 Bowood St
4 The Bulrushes
5 Charlecote St
6 Herculaneum Ct
7 Orchid Gv
8 Sandbeck St

J1
1 Back Wellesley Rd
2 Bowring Cl
3 Bowring St
4 Bruce St
5 Dentwood St
6 Dingle Gv
7 Drysdale St
8 Drysdale Wk
9 Fair View Pl
10 Gredington St
11 Hawkstone St
12 Leonora St
13 Lockington Cl
14 Loxdale Cl
15 Mallins Cl
16 Menzies St
17 Miller Cl
18 Park Rd
19 Redburn Cl
20 St Lawrence Cl
21 Sundridge St
22 Wellesley Rd
23 Wilson St
24 Wyncroft St

J2
1 Dingle Brow
2 Emerald St
3 Hindlip St
4 Jasmine Ms
5 Monkswell St
6 Thistledown Cl
7 Thorntree Cl

L3
1 Battery Cl
2 Burgundy Cl
3 Hythedale Cl
4 Larkfield Cl
5 Larkfield Gv
6 Maybury Wy
7 Newmorn Ct
8 Oakbourne Cl
9 Oxford Cl
10 Rosebourne Cl
11 St Michael's Cl
12 Wrenfield Gv

Page 130

A3
1 Ashlar Gv
2 Bessbrook Rd
3 Rimmington Rd
4 Rowan Ct

C6
1 Beechwood Cl
2 Bennison Dr
3 Convent Cl
4 Dugdale Cl
5 Eslington St
6 Fletcher Dr
7 Lawrence Cl
8 Prior Farm Cl
9 Woodhey Rd

E7
1 Granville Rd
2 Island Pl
3 Jackson St
4 Mersey Vw
5 Milnthorpe St
6 Wilson Gv

E8
1 Leeming Cl
2 Lord St
3 Marlowe Cl
4 Mercer St
5 Shakespeare St
6 Thomas Cl
7 Woodger St

F2
1 Beech Ct

F3
1 Maryton Gra
2 Sycamore Pk

F5
1 Danefield Pl

F6
1 Stamfordham Pl

F7
1 Haxted Gdns

F8
1 Arthur St
2 Aston St

Page 131

J1
1 Parkwood Rd

J2
1 Woolton Park Cl

L2
1 Davids Wk
2 Halewood Pl
3 Knotty Ms

L3
1 Budworth Dr
2 Felsted Av
3 Halewood Wy
4 Kingham Cl
5 Warton Cl
6 Whitney Pl

L5
1 Dunmow Wy

L7
1 Braydon Cl

M3
1 Blackberry Gv
2 Edenhall Dr
3 Hazelwood Gv
4 Honeysuckle Cl
5 Magnolia Cl
6 Riding Fold

M4
1 Lancing Rd

M5
1 Pembrey Wy

Page 132

A3
1 Comfrey Gv
2 Okell Dr
3 Openfields Cl
4 Pipit Cl
5 Rogerson's Gn
6 Ruscar Cl

A5
1 Carlyon Wy
2 Cheriton Cl
3 Ravenfield Cl
4 Stainton Cl
5 Tarleton Cl

B5
1 Cambridge Dr
2 Catterick Cl
3 Fernwood Dr
4 Neasham Cl

D5
1 Rawlinson Crs

Page 133

L2
1 Aubourn Cl
2 Broxton Cl
3 Burnham Cl
4 Caxton Cl
5 Chatsworth Dr
6 Fenton Cl
7 Hambleton Cl
8 Madeline Mckenna Ct
9 Newland Cl
10 Warkworth Cl

L3
1 Rufford Cl

L4
1 Gaisgill Ct
2 Graham Cl
3 Kendal Rd
4 Sherwood Cl

L5
1 Kenneth Rd
2 Winchester Pl

Page 134

B2
1 Battersea Ct
2 Burton Cl
3 Giltbrook Cl
4 Grundy Cl
5 Whickham Cl

C6
1 Alexandra St
2 Alforde St
3 Bold St
4 Chapel St
5 Darlington Ct
6 Eleanor St
7 Ellis St
8 Emily St
9 Finlan Rd
10 Guest St
11 Lewis Crs
12 Luton St
13 Major Cross St
14 Market St
15 Millar Crs
16 Miners Wy
17 St Paul's Rd
18 Thomas St
19 Vicarage Rd
20 Victoria Rd
21 Violet St
22 Witt Rd

C8
1 Chidlow Cl
2 Constance Wy
3 Dock Rd
4 Queensway
5 Short St
6 White St
7 Wilkinson Cl

D2
1 Boxgrove Cl
2 Durham Rd
3 Griffin Ms

D3
1 Hawthorn Av
2 Larch Av
3 Lime Av
4 Mount Pleasant
5 Pine Av

D4
1 Bradley Wy
2 Cross St
3 Lower Appleton Rd
4 Maple Av
5 Mount St
6 Robert St
7 Routledge St
8 Saxon Ter
9 Westmorland Av

D5
1 Alfred Cl
2 Elliot St
3 Gerrard St
4 Grenfell St
5 Hibbert St
6 Liebig St
7 Lugsdale Rd
8 Midwood St
9 Rylands St
10 Salisbury St
11 Timperley St
12 Travis St

D6
1 Batherton Cl
2 Caroline St
3 Elizabeth Ct
4 Lacey Ct
5 Margaret Ct
6 Pool St
7 Sutton's La
8 Trinity Pl

E1
1 Claremont Av

E3
1 Doward St
2 Stanley Cl
3 Susan St

E4
1 Bell House Rd
2 Black Denton's Pl
3 Cliffe St
4 Edwin St
5 Esther St
6 Harris St
7 Henry St
8 Parr St
9 Richmond St
10 Sadler St
11 Taylor St

F2
1 Crow Wood Pl
2 Selwyn Cl

F3
1 Barnes Cl
2 Drummond Ct
3 Moore Cl

F4
1 East St
2 Edward St
3 Hargreaves Ct
4 Norland St
5 Sussex St
6 Walter St

Page 137

K1
1 Barbauld St
2 Bridge St
3 Friars Ga
4 Friars La
5 School St
6 Stanley St
7 Wilson Patten St

K5
1 Hill Cliffe Rd

K6
1 Cambridge Cl

L2
1 Causeway Av
2 Clelland St

M2
1 Beatrice St
2 Birch Gv
3 Cedar Gv
4 Florence St

Page 141

H2
1 Hawthorn Dr
2 Kentmere Dr
3 Stewart Cl

L5
1 Brimstage Cl
2 Speedwell Cl

M4
1 Northway

M5
1 Aspen Cl
2 Brimstage Gn
3 Cottesmore Dr

M6
1 Dovesmead Rd

Page 143

H2
1 Heath Dl
2 Kevelioc Cl
3 Mulveton Rd
4 Stanfield Dr

J1
1 Abbots Dr
2 Eversleigh Dr
3 Kirket Cl
4 Rolleston Dr

J3
1 Burdett Cl
2 Henley Cl
3 Hockenhull Cl
4 Langley Rd
5 Randle Cl
6 Sheldon Cl

Page 149

H2
1 Brackley St
2 Clarence St
3 Edith St
4 Egerton St
5 Greek St
6 Grove St
7 Handley St
8 Lord St
9 Speakman St

H3
1 Cavendish St
2 Hankey St
3 High St
4 Lowlands Rd
5 Rutland St
6 Shaw St
7 Waterloo Rd

H4
1 Burland Cl
2 Curzon St
3 Drayton Cl
4 The Elms
5 Havergal St
6 Lightburn St
7 Queen's Cl
8 Southlands Ms
9 Stapley Cl
10 Westfield Ms

H7
1 Ashton Cl
2 Company's Cl
3 Cresta Dr
4 Lambsickle Cl

J1
1 Beamont St
2 Bridge View Cl
3 Cholmondeley St
4 Hurst St
5 Parsonage Rd

J2
1 Alcock St
2 Bridgewater St
3 Canon St
4 Clarence Ter
5 Cooper St
6 Egerton St
7 Granville St
8 Loch St
9 Penketh's La
10 Princess St
11 Public Hall St
12 Wellington St

J3
1 Albert St
2 Arthur St
3 Back High St
4 Brook St
5 Devonshire Pl
6 Eaton St
7 Greenway Rd
8 High St
9 Nelson St
10 New St
11 Oakmere St
12 Queensway
13 Surrey St
14 Vine St
15 Walton St

L4
1 Bickley Cl
2 Lavender Cl

M3
1 Henley Ct
2 Needham Cl
3 Tenby Dr

M4
1 The Winnows

M5
1 Davenport Rw

M6
1 Cranage Cl

M7
1 Cantley Cl
2 Danby Cl
3 Handforth La
4 Hyde Cl
5 Whitchurch Wy

M8
1 Braithwaite Cl
2 Kendal Ri

Page 150

A7
1 Hobby Ct
2 Hunters Ct
3 Rothbury Cl
4 Seneschal Ct

A8
1 Bowland Cl
2 Brambling Cl
3 Mosedale Gv
4 Stonechat Cl
5 Whinfell Gv

D7
1 Allendale
2 Bodmin Cl
3 Mullion Cl
4 Wharfedale

D8
1 Bartlegate
2 Broome Ct
3 Clover Ct
4 Coney Gv
5 Goulders Ct
6 Kilncroft

E3
1 Priory Rd
2 Southwood Av
3 Townfield Rd

E4
1 Sandalwood

E5
1 Kings Meadow
2 Saddlers Ri
3 Stoney Holt

E6
1 Cloverfield

E7
1 Camborne Cl
2 Launceston Cl
3 Newbridge Cl
4 Penare Gorran Hvn
5 Tintagel Cl
6 Truro Cl

E8
1 Backford Cl
2 Calverly Cl
3 Granby Cl
4 Halsall Cl
5 Linwood Cl
6 Wellbrook Cl

F3
1 Adlington Rd
2 Ashbury Cl
3 Harvard Cl
4 Haywood Crs
5 Swinden Cl

F4
1 Camden Ct
2 Chorlton Cl
3 Culford Cl
4 Cooseberry La
5 Winton Gv

F5
1 Dorrington Cl
2 Heron Cl
3 Mellor Cl
4 Ossett Cl

F6
1 Barton Cl
2 Baxter Cl
3 Chiswick Cl
4 Hitchen's Cl
5 Humphrey's Cl
6 Micklegate
7 Neptune Cl
8 Sabre Cl
9 Sovereign Cl

F7
1 Bournemouth Cl
2 Navigation Cl
3 Quadrant Cl
4 Schooner Cl

Page 161

H1
1 Ashbrook Av
2 Aster Crs
3 Audlem Cl
4 Azalea Gv
5 Bluebell Ct
6 Larkspur Cl
7 Lobelia Gv
8 Magnolia Dr
9 Millington Cl
10 Ovington Cl
11 Peckforton Dr
12 Stonecrop Cl
13 Verbena Cl
14 Weaverside Av

Page 163

H2
1 Moston Wy
2 Overpool Gdns
3 Torridon Gv

H5
1 Badgers Cl
2 Bangor Cl
3 Bramley Cl
4 Gloucester Cl
5 Green Lawns Dr
6 Lambourne Cl
7 Larchdale Cl
8 Laxton Cl
9 St Georges Av
10 Salisbury Cl
11 Truro Cl
12 West Park Dr

K1
1 Chapel Ms

L1
1 Coronation Rd
2 Mcgarva Wy
3 Stanlaw Rd
4 Tarvin Cl

L5
1 Farne Cl